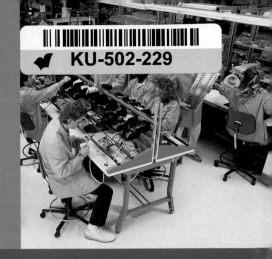

third edition

Economics for Business

John Sloman and Mark Sutcliffe

FT Prentice Hall
FINANCIAL TIMES

An imprint of **Pearson Education**
Harlow, England • London • New York • Boston • San Francisco • Toronto
Sydney • Tokyo • Singapore • Hong Kong • Seoul • Taipei • New Delhi
Cape Town • Madrid • Mexico City • Amsterdam • Munich • Paris • Milan

Pearson Education Limited
Edinburgh Gate
Harlow
Essex CM20 2JE
England

and Associated Companies throughout the world

Visit us on the World Wide Web at:
www.pearsoned.co.uk

First published by Prentice Hall 1998
Second edition published 2001
Third edition published 2004

© John Sloman and Mark Sutcliffe 1998
© Pearson Education 2001, 2004

ISBN 0–273–68335–7

British Library Cataloguing-in-Publication Data
A catalogue record for this book is available from the British Library

10 9 8 7 6 5 4 3 2 1
09 08 07 06 05 04

Typeset by 35 in 10.25/12pt Sabon
Printed and bound by Mateu Cromo, Spain

Brief contents

Detailed contents

Part D   Background to supply   164

Part E   Supply: short-run profit maximisation   208

Website resources

For students:

- Study material designed to help you improve your results
- Learning objectives for each chapter
- Multiple choice questions to help test your learning
- Up-to-date case studies with questions for self study
- Topical economic issues relating to material directly in the book
- Economics news articles with features on topical stories, with analysis and links to the book
- Hotlinks to over 200 relevant sites on the web

For lecturers:

- A secure, password-protected site with teaching material
- Complete, downloadable Instructor's Manual
- PowerPoint slides that can be downloaded and used as OHTs comprising:
  - Figures and tables from the book
  - Key models as full-colour animated slide shows
- Teaching and learning case studies discussing various aspects of economic principles
- Customisable lecture plans with integrated animated diagrams
- Workshops to accompany each chapter of the book
- Answers to workshops and question material

Also: This regularly maintained and updated site has a syllabus manager, search functions, and email results functions.

Preface

To the student

If you are studying economics on a business studies degree or diploma, then this book is written for you. Although we cover all the major principles of economics, the focus throughout is on the world of business. For this reason we also cover several topics that do not appear in traditional economics textbooks.

As well as making considerable use of business examples throughout the text, we have included many case studies (in boxes). These illustrate how economics can be used to understand particular business problems or aspects of the business environment. Many of these case studies cover issues that you are likely to read about in the newspapers. Some cover general business issues; others look at specific companies. There are also many additional case studies appearing on the book's website. These, along with references to various useful websites, are listed at the end of each Part of the book.

We hope that, in using this book, you will share some of our fascination for economics. It is a subject that is highly relevant to the world in which we live. And it is a world where many of our needs are served by business – whether as employers or as producers of the goods and services we buy. After graduating, you will probably take up employment in business. A thorough grounding in economic principles should prove invaluable in the business decisions you may well have to make.

Our aim throughout the book is to make this intriguing subject clear for you to understand and as relevant as possible to you as a student of business.

The style of writing is direct and straightforward, with short paragraphs to aid rapid comprehension. Definitions of all key terms are given in the margin, with defined terms appearing in **bold**. Also we have highlighted 37 'Key ideas', which are fundamental to 'thinking like an economist'. We refer back to these every time they recur in the book. This helps you to see how the subject ties together, and also helps you to develop a toolkit of concepts that can be used in a host of different contexts.

Summaries are given at the end of each chapter, with points numbered according to the section in which they appeared. These summaries should help you in reviewing the material you have covered and in revising for exams. Each chapter finishes with a series of questions. These can be used to check your understanding of the chapter and help you to see how its material can be applied to various business problems.

There are also questions interspersed throughout the text in 'Pause for thought' panels. These encourage you to reflect on what you are learning and to see how the various ideas and theories relate to different issues.

We hope you enjoy the book and come to appreciate the crucial role that economics plays in all our lives, and in particular in the practice of business.

Good luck and *bon appetit*.

To the tutor

The aim of this book is to provide a course in economic principles as they apply to the business environment. It is designed to be used by first-year undergraduates on business studies degrees and diplomas where economics is taught from the business perspective. It is also suitable for students studying economics on MBA, DMS and various professional courses.

Being essentially a book on economics, we cover all the major topics found in standard economics texts – indeed, much of the material in the principles sections is drawn directly from *Economics* (5th edition). But in addition there are several specialist business chapters and sections to build upon and enliven the subject for business studies students. These have been fully updated and revised for this new edition. The following are some examples of these additional topics:

- The business environment
- Business organisations
- Characteristics theory
- Marketing the product
- Business strategy (new chapter in this edition)
- Alternative aims of firms
- Growth strategy
- Strategic alliances
- The small-firm sector
- Pricing in practice
- Government and the firm, including policies towards research and technology development (R&TD) and policies towards training
- Government and the market, including environmental policy and transport policy
- Financial markets
- The multinational corporation
- Globalisation and business (new in this edition)
- Trading blocs
- Monetary union

The text is split into 32 chapters. Each chapter is kept relatively short to enable the material to be covered in a single lecture or class. Each chapter finishes with review questions, which can be used for seminars or discussion sessions.

The chapters are grouped into 11 Parts:

- Part A *Business and economics* (Chapters 1–3) establishes the place of business within the economy and the relevance of economics to business decision making.
- Part B *Business and markets* (Chapters 4 and 5) looks at the operation of markets. It covers supply and demand analysis and examines the importance of the concept of elasticity for business decisions.
- Part C *Background to demand* (Chapters 6–8) considers the consumer – how consumer behaviour can be predicted and how, via advertising and marketing, consumer demand can be influenced.

- Part D *Background to supply* (Chapters 9 and 10) focuses on business costs, revenue and profits.

- Part E *Supply: short-run profit maximisation* (Chapters 11 and 12) presents the traditional analysis of market structures and the implications that such structures have for business conduct and performance.

- Part F *Supply: alternative strategies* (Chapters 13–17) starts by looking at business strategy. It then considers various alternative theories of the firm. It also examines how business size can influence business actions, and how pricing strategies differ from one firm to another and how these strategies are influenced by the market conditions in which firms operate.

- Part G *The firm in the factor market* (Chapters 18 and 19) focuses on the market for labour and the market for capital. It examines what determines the factor proportions that firms use and how factor prices are determined.

- Part H *The relationship between government and business* (Chapters 20–22) establishes the theoretical rationale behind government intervention in the economy, and then assesses the relationship between the government and the individual firm and the government and the market.

- Part I *Business in the international environment* (Chapters 23–25) starts by examining the process of globalisation and the growth of the multinational business. It then turns to international trade and the benefits that accrue from it. It also examines the issue of protection and international moves to advance free trade. Finally it examines the expansion of regional trading agreements.

- Part J *The macroeconomic environment* (Chapters 26–29) considers the macroeconomic framework in which firms operate. We focus on the principal macroeconomic variables, investigate the role of money in the economy, and briefly outline the theoretical models underpinning the relationships between these variables.

- Part K *Macroeconomic policy* (Chapters 30–32) examines the mechanics of government intervention at a macro level as well as its impact on business and its potential benefits and drawbacks. Demand-side and supply-side policy and economic policy co-ordination between countries are all considered.

Special features

The book contains the following special features:

- A direct and straightforward written style, with short paragraphs to aid rapid comprehension. The aim all the time is to provide maximum clarity.

- (*New to this edition*) Attractive new full-colour design. The careful and consistent use of colour and shading makes the text more attractive to students and easier to use by giving clear signals as to the book's structure.

- (*New to this edition*) Key ideas highlighted and explained where they first appear. There are 37 of these ideas, which are fundamental to the study of economics. Students can see them recurring throughout the book, and an icon appears in the margin to refer back to the page where the idea first appears. Showing how ideas can be used in a variety of contexts helps students to 'think like an economist' and to relate the different parts of the subject together. All 37 Key ideas are defined in a special section at the end of the book.

- (*New to this edition*) 'Pause for thought' questions integrated throughout the text. These encourage students to reflect on what they have just read and make the learning process a more active one. Answers to these questions appear in the student section of the book's website.

- Double-page opening spreads for each of the 11 Parts of the book. These contain an introduction to the material covered and an article from the *Financial Times* on one of the topics.

- All technical terms are highlighted and clearly defined in the margin on the page on which they appear. This feature proved very popular in the first two editions and is especially useful for students when revising.

- A comprehensive index, including reference to all defined terms. This enables students to look up a definition as required and to see it used in context.

- Additional applied material to that found in the text can be found in the boxes within each chapter. All boxes include questions which relate the material back to the chapter in which the box is located. The extensive use of applied material makes learning much more interesting for students and helps to bring the subject alive. This is particularly important for business students who need to relate economic theory to their other subjects and to the world of business generally.

- Additional case studies appearing on the book's website are referred to at the end of each Part.

- Detailed summaries appear at the end of each chapter with the points numbered by the chapter section in which they are made. These allow students not only to check their comprehension of the chapter's contents, but also to get a clear overview of the material they have been studying.

- Each chapter concludes with a series of review questions to test students' understanding of the chapter's salient points. These questions can be used for seminars or as set work to be completed in the students' own time.

- (*New to this edition*) References at the end of each Part to a list of relevant websites, details of which can be found in the Web appendix at the end of the book. You can easily access any of these sites from the book's own website (at **www.booksites.net/sloman**). When you enter the site, click on 'Hotlinks'. You will find all the sites from the Web appendix listed. Click on the one you want and the 'hotlink' will take you straight to it.

Supplements

Website

Visit the book's website at

www.booksites.net/sloman

This has an extensive range of materials for students and tutors.

For students

- *Study material* designed to help you improve your results.

- *Answers* to all Pause for thought and Box questions, to allow you to check your understanding as you progress.
- *Economics news articles*, updated monthly: some 15 to 20 news items per month, with links to one or more newspaper articles per item. There are questions on each item and references to the relevant chapter(s) of the book.
- *Topical economic issues*, with analysis and links to key concepts and pages in the book.
- *Hotlinks* to over 200 useful websites listed in the book's Web appendix and referenced at the end of each Part of the text.
- Several additional *case studies* for each Part of the book and referenced at the end of each Part.
- *Self-test questions*, organised chapter by chapter.

For tutors

- A range of *teaching and learning case studies*, with the focus on improving student learning outcomes.
- All *figures and tables* from the book in PowerPoint®, in two versions, each animated and in full colour.
- Full colour OHTs of all figures and tables (on a clear background). Also suitable for black-and-white printing. Can be used for handouts.
- Customisable full-colour *lecture plans* in PowerPoint, with integrated animated diagrams and tables. Can also be used for handouts.
- *Key models* as full-colour animated PowerPoint® slide shows.
- *Answers* to end-of-chapter questions in a secure password protected area of the site.

CD-ROM (new edition)

The tutor's CD has been thoroughly revised to take account of the changes in the third edition. It is available free of charge from Pearson Education to tutors using the book as a course text. It contains the following:

- PowerPoint® slide shows in full colour for use with a data projector in lectures and classes. These can also be made available to students by loading them on to a local network. All PowerPoint® files are small enough to copy to a $3^1/_2$-inch disk (for portability) and are available in light on dark backgrounds, and dark on light background versions. The CD contains several types of these slide shows:
  - All figures from the book and most of the tables. Each figure is built up in a logical sequence, thereby allowing tutors to show them in lectures in an animated form.
  - A range of models. These show how the key models used in the book are developed. There are 30 of these models and each one builds up in around 20 to 50 screens.
  - Lecture plans. These are a series of bullet-point lecture plans. There is one for each chapter of the book. Each one can be easily edited, with points added, deleted or moved, so as to suit particular lectures. A consistent use of colour is made to show how the points tie together. The lecture plans are also available in Word®.

- Lecture plans with integrated diagrams. These lecture plans include animated diagrams and charts at the appropriate points.

■ PowerPoint slides for printing onto acetate for use with a conventional OHP. These are reverse image slides (i.e. dark lines on a clear background) designed to minimise printer ink. They can be printed in colour, or in black and white (and grey). These slides contain the figures, lecture plans and lecture plans with integrated diagrams referred to above.

■ Multiple-choice, short answer and true–false questions. This very large test bank is completely redesigned and contains many new questions. It is flexible and easy to use.

■ Case studies. These, also available on the book's website, can be reproduced and used for classroom exercises or for student assignments.

■ Answers. Full answers are given in Word files to all end-of-chapter, pause for thought, box and case study questions.

The CD also contains supplementary material from John's *Economics* (5th edition) and *Essentials of Economics* (3rd edition).

WinEcon and *BusEcon*

Most UK higher education institutions now have WinEcon on their network. This is a comprehensive computer-based learning programme for introductory economics, developed by the Economics Consortium (now known as the WinEcon Consortium) of the Teaching and Learning Technology Programme (TLTP). The Consortium has been developing a version of WinEcon for students studying economics on a business studies programme. This version, available in 2004, is called BusEcon and is particularly suitable for use with this book. Further details on the WinEcon and BusEcon software are available from the WinEcon Consortium. Please see their website for information on the software, release dates and the latest web-enabling features: http://www.winecon.com.

Acknowledgements

As with previous editions, we've had great support from the team at Pearson, including Catherine Yates, Stuart Hay and Karen McLaren. We'd like to thank all of them for their hard work and encouragement. Thanks too to the many users of the book who have given us feedback. We always value their comments. Please continue to send us your views.

Our two families, as usual, have been remarkably tolerant and supportive. Thanks especially to Alison and Sheila who seem to have perfected a subtle blend of encouragement, humour and patience.

John and Mark

Publisher's acknowledgements

We are grateful to the following for permission to reproduce copyright material:

National Statistics for Table 1.3 from *SME Database* 2003, Figure 26.11 and Tables 26.1 and 26.2 from *UK National Income and Expenditure 2002*, Department for the Environment, Food and Rural Affairs for Box 7.1 table from *Consumption of Selected Household Foods, 1942 to 2000*, Department of Trade and Industry for Tables 16.2 and 16.3 from *SME Statistics UK 2002*, Box 21.2 tables from *R&D Scorecard 2002*, The Institute of Manpower Studies for Figure 18.12 from *The Flexible Firm* (1984), HM Treasury for Box 31.1 figure from *Budget 2003, Economic and Fiscal Strategy Report*, Crown copyright material is reproduced with the permission of the Controller of Her Majesty's Stationery Office and the Queen's Printer for Scotland; The Guardian for Box 3.1 table from *Men Only, The Club for the Millionaire Executive* (Treanor, J., Finch, J. & Macalister, T., October 2002), © The Guardian; World Advertising Research Center for Tables 8.1, 8.2, 8.3, 8.4 and 8.5 from *Advertising Statistics Yearbook 2003*; Department of Trade and Industry for Box 9.3 figure from *UK Competitiveness: Moving to the Next Stage* (Porter, M.E. & Ketels, C.H.M., May 2003), p. 29, published by DTI and ESRC; The European Communities for Box 9.4 table from *The Single Market Review, Sub Series V, Volume 4* (1997), European Commission/Economics Advisory Group, Economics of Scale; The Free Press for Figure 13.1 from *Competitive Strategy: Techniques for Analysing Industries and Competitors* (Porter, M.E. 1998), copyright © 1980, 1998 by The Free Press, reprinted with the permission of The Free Press, a Division of Simon & Schuster Adult Publishing Group, all rights reserved; Palgrave Macmillan for Figure 15.1 from *Non-Price Decisions* (Koutsoyiannis, A. 1982); Routledge for Table 16.4 from *Understanding the Small-Business Section* (Storey, D.J. 1994); Bank of England for Box 17.2 tables from *Bank of England Quarterly Bulletin*, May 1996, Box 25.1 table from *Bank of England Inflation Report*, February 1998 and Box 30.4 figure from *The Use of Explicit Targets for Monetary Policy: Practical Experiences of 91 Economies in the 1990s* (August 1990), reprinted with permission of Publications Group, © Bank of England; Pearson Education, Inc. for Table 23.1 from *Total Global Strategy* (Yip, G. 1995), reprinted by permission of Pearson Education, Inc., Upper Saddle River, NJ; United Nations for Table 23.3 from *UNCTAD, FD/TNC* database and Box 23.1 table and figure from *World Investment Report* 2002; World Trade Organization for Figures 24.1 and 24.2 from *International Trade Statistics* 2002.

Ben & Jerry's Holdings, Inc. for an extract adapted from their web site, www.benjerry.com; Business Week for the headline 'The New Global Job Shift' published in *Business Week*, 3 February 2003, and extracts adapted from

'Samsung's Sashimi Theory of Success' published in *Business Week*, 11 June 2003 and 'The Samsung Way' published in *Business Week*, 16 June 2003; The Economist Newspaper Limited for extracts all published in *The Economist* adapted from 'Followers of Fashion', 23 December 1995, 'The Role of the Speculator', 3 February 1996, 'The Heyday of the Auction', 24 July 1999, 'Bridging Europe's Skills Gap', 31 March 2001, 'A Moving Story', 5 December 2002, and 'The Big Easy', 31 May 2003; The Independent Newspapers (UK) Limited for an extract adapted from 'A Price War Hotter Than a Vindaloo' by Jim White published in *The Independent*, 8 October 1993 © The Independent Newspapers (UK) Limited 1993; Department of Trade and Industry for an extract adapted from *R&D Scorecard 2002*, Crown copyright material is reproduced with the permission of the Controller of Her Majesty's Stationery Office and the Queen's Printer for Scotland; and News International Newspapers Limited for an extract adapted from 'Deflation Danger' by Dominic Rushe published in *The Sunday Times*, 11 May 2003 © Times Newspapers Limited 2003.

We are grateful to the Financial Times Limited for permission to reprint the following material:

'Casting off the chains', © *Financial Times*, 15 May 2003; 'Cocoa prices may be set to bubble again', © *Financial Times*, 21 June 2003; 'Sunny Delight tries to find a new dawn', © *Financial Times*, 27 June 2003; 'Smaller chips, bigger stakes: how new monster plants will transform the industry', © *Financial Times*, 11 June 2003; 'Morrison "could boost competition with Safeway"', © *Financial Times*, 24 June 2003; 'Brands brew a coffee coup', © *Financial Times*, 26 June 2003; 'Working poor continue to walk the line', © *Financial Times*, 26 June 2003; 'Ford's chief warns against industrial flight', © *Financial Times*, 24 June 2003; 'UN urges rich to restart trade talks', © *Financial Times*, 26 June 2003; 'Japan's economy remains in the doldrums', © *Financial Times*, 27 June 2003; 'Chancellor's plans "could destabilise" interest rates', © *Financial Times*, 25 June 2003; Box 18.3 quote © *Financial Times*, 22 February 2000; Box 20.3 quote from 'Body Shop's "Green Queen" steps aside', http://globalarchive.ft.com/globalarchive/articles.html?id=000918007369, © Financial Times.

Guided tour

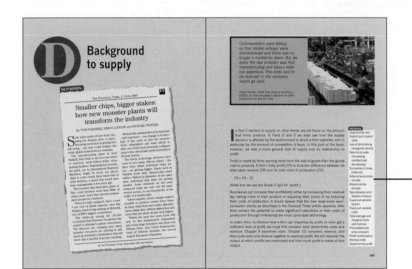

Parts. The book is divided into 11 Parts. Each Part introduction is spread over two pages and contains an introduction to the material covered and an article from the *Financial Times* about one of these topics.

Web material. At the end of each Part there are lists of additional case studies appearing on the book's Website and references to various other useful Web sites.

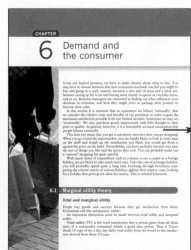

Chapter introductions. Most chapters have an introductory section, giving an overview of the topics to be covered in each chapter, and relate them to issues you are likely to hear about in the news or experience directly.

Definitions. All key terms are highlighted in the text where they first appear and are defined in the margin. This is very useful for revision and allows you to see the terms used in context.

Key ideas. These are highlighted and explained where they first appear. They are key elements in the economist's toolkit and whenever they recur later in the book, an icon appears in the margin. These help students to 'think like an economist'.

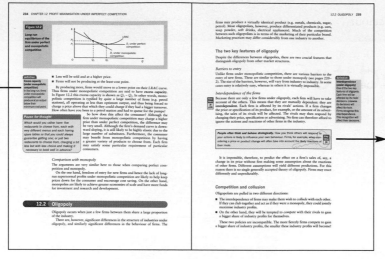

Boxes. These provide case studies to show how economics can be used to understand particular business problems or aspects of the business environment. Each box also has questions to relate the material back to the chapter.

Pause for thought questions. These help you reflect on what you have just read and to check on your understanding.

Full colour design.
A consistent use of colour is made in the diagrams which allows you to see at a glance how the diagram is constructed and the 'before' and 'after' positions when the diagram is used to illustrate the effects of a change in circumstances.

Chapter summaries.
Summaries at the end of each chapter allow you to check up on your understanding at frequent intervals and provide an important revision tool.

Review questions.
These can be used for self-testing, or for class exercises or debate.

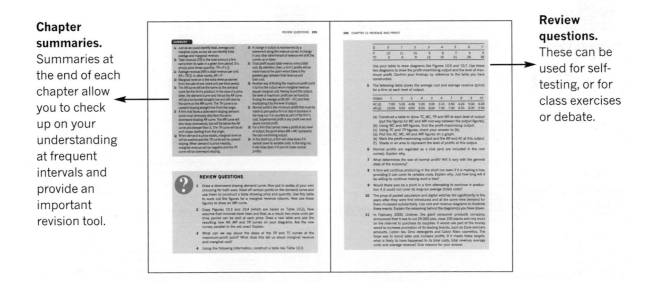

Guided tour of the student resources of the Companion Website

Multiple choice questions

Results graph for MCQs

Chapter-specific case studies

Topical issues, news articles, hotlinks

A Business and economics

THE FINANCIAL TIMES, 15 MAY 2003

Casting off the chains

By FIONA HARVEY

Remember when there was only one phone company, English people needed to negotiate a permit to work in France and supermarkets only sold groceries? Today, the utilities have almost all been broken up and opened to free market competition, it is much easier to work internationally and you are just as likely to get a loan from a supermarket or a motoring organisation as you are to get it from your bank.

Over the last few decades, deregulation has had an enormous impact on businesses, not just by helping them to be more flexible in their outlook, but also by forcing organisations to become more agile in response to increased competition, according to Gilbert Toppin, European operations officer at Deloitte Consulting. Beginning with utilities, successive waves of deregulation have rolled across industries as governments have espoused the idea of increasing commercial freedom in the market.

International mergers and acquisitions have also become more commonplace, even in industries that were formerly state monopolies. With the European postal market in the throes of deregulation, Deutsche Post recently took over the US courier company DHL, for instance.

Changes in regulations governing industry ownership and the break-up of utility companies have also had an important effect. Today, customers of gas companies may choose to get their electricity from the same utility. Scottish Power, for example, illustrated the new trend for cross-ownership when it took over Southern Water.

'There is a greater freedom in access to the customer now, which was not there before,' explains Mr Toppin. 'This is an opportunity, because it opens up new markets to companies, but also a threat because it means other people can easily come in and steal your customers.' Customers of supermarkets are no longer assumed to be simply after their weekly groceries; instead, they can be seen as consumers of all goods, leading supermarkets to offer them everything from electrical goods and clothes to financial products.

Under this new thinking, trusted brand names assume a far greater importance than the mere products that they sell. The approach of the Virgin Group, which seeks to sell the consumer everything from mobile phones to airline tickets and weddings, soft drinks and health club membership is a model of this view.

> *Economics is the new politics, and business is in the driving seat.*
>
> Noreena Hertz, *The Silent Takeover* (2001) p. 68

Businesses play a key role in all our lives. Whatever their size, and whatever the goods or services they provide, they depend on us as consumers to buy their products.

But just as businesses rely on us for their income, so equally many of us rely on firms for our income. The wages we earn depend on our employer's success, and that success in turn depends on us as suppliers of labour.

And it is not just as customers and workers that we are affected by business. The success of business in general affects the health of the whole economy and thus the lives of us all.

The extract opposite from the *Financial Times* describes some of the things that firms do to be more successful. It also explains how business organisation and performance is being determined by fundamental changes in the business environment. As markets become ever more deregulated, both business opportunities and potential threats become ever more pronounced.

In Part A of this book, we consider the relationship between business and economics.

In Chapter 1 we look at the structure of industry and its importance in determining firms' behaviour. We also look at a range of other factors that are likely to affect business decisions and how we can set about analysing the environment in which a firm operates in order to help it devise an appropriate business strategy.

Then in Chapter 2, we ask what is it that economists do and, in particular, how economists set about analysing the world of business and the things businesses do. In particular we focus on rational decision making – how to get the best outcome from limited resources.

Finally, in Chapter 3 we look at the different ways in which firms are organised: at their legal structure, at their internal organisation and at their goals.

key terms

The business environment
PEST analysis
Production
Firms
Industries
Industrial sectors
Standard Industrial Classification (SIC)
Industrial concentration
Structure – conduct – performance
Scarcity
Factors of production
Macroeconomics
Microeconomics
Opportunity cost
Marginal costs
Marginal benefits
Rational choices
Circular flow of income
Principal and agent
Business organisation
Price taker
Perfectly competitive market
Price mechanism
Demand
Supply

1 The business environment and business economics

What is business economics?

What is the role of *business economics*? What will you be studying in this book?

Clearly we will be studying *firms*: the environment in which they operate, the decisions they make, and the effects of these decisions – on themselves, on their customers, on their employees, on their business rivals and on the public at large.

But what particular aspects of business does the *economist* study? Firms are essentially concerned with using inputs to make output. Inputs cost money and output earns money. The difference between the revenue earned and the costs incurred constitutes the firm's profit. Firms will normally want to make as much profit as possible, or at the very least to avoid a decline in profits. In order to meet these and other objectives, managers will need to make choices: choices of what types of output to produce, how much to produce and at what price; choices of what techniques of production to use, how many workers to employ and of what type, what suppliers to use for raw materials, equipment, etc. In each case, when weighing up alternatives, managers will want to make the best choices. Business economists study these choices. They study economic decision making by firms.

The study of decision making can be broken down into three stages.

The external influences on the firm (the 'business environment'). Here we are referring to the various factors that affect the firm that are largely outside its direct control. Examples are the competition it faces, the prices it pays for raw materials, the state of the economy (e.g. whether growing or in recession) and the level of interest rates. Businesses will need to obtain a clear understanding of their environment before they can set about making the right decisions.

Internal decisions of the firm. Given a knowledge of these external factors, how do firms then decide on prices, output, inputs, marketing, investment, etc? Here the business economist can play a major role in helping firms achieve their business objectives.

The external effects of business decision making. When the firm has made its decisions and acted on them, how do the results affect the firm's rivals, its customers and the wider public? In other words, what is the impact of a firm's decision making on people *outside* the firm? Are firms' actions in the public interest, or is there a case for government intervention?

Key
Idea
1
p9

What do business economists do?

Our study of business will involve three types of activity:

- *Description.* For example, we will be describing the objectives of businesses (e.g. making profit or increasing market share), the types of market in which firms operate (e.g. competitive or non-competitive) and the constraints on decision making (e.g. the costs of production, the level of consumer demand and the state of the economy).

- *Analysis.* For example, we will analyse how a firm's costs and profits are likely to vary with the amount of output it produces and what would be the consequences of a change in consumer demand or a change in the price charged by rivals. We will also analyse the upswings and downswings in the economy: something that will have a crucial bearing on the profitability of many companies.

- *Recommendations.* Given the objectives of a firm, the business economist can help to show how those objectives can best be met. For example, if a firm wants to maximise its profits, the business economist can advise on what prices to charge, how much to invest, how much to advertise, etc. Of course, any such recommendations will only be as good as the data on which they are based. In an uncertain environment, recommendations will necessarily be more tentative.

In this chapter, as an introduction to the subject of business economics, we shall consider the place of the firm within its business environment, and assess how these external influences are likely to shape and determine its actions. In order to discuss the relationship between a business's actions and its environment, we first need to define what the business environment is.

1.1   The business environment

It is normal to identify four dimensions to the business environment: political/ legal, economic, social/cultural and technological.

Key
Idea
1
p9

Political/legal factors. Firms will be directly affected by the actions of government and other political events. These might be major events affecting the whole of the business community, such as the collapse of communism, the Iraq War or a change of government. Alternatively, they may be actions affecting just one part of the economy. For example, an anti-smoking campaign by the government will affect the tobacco industry. Similarly, businesses will be affected by the legal framework in which they operate. Examples include industrial relations legislation, product safety standards, regulations governing pricing in the privatised industries and laws preventing collusion between firms to keep prices up.

Economic factors. Economic factors can range from big to small, from local to national to international, from current to future; from the rising costs of raw materials to the market entry of a new rival, from the forthcoming Budget to the instability of international exchange rates, from the current availability of investment funds to the likely future cash flow from a new product. Business must constantly take such factors into account when devising and acting upon its business strategy.

It is normal to divide the economic environment in which the firm operates into two levels:

■ *The microeconomic environment.* This includes all the economic factors that are *specific* to a particular firm operating in its own particular market. Thus one firm may be operating in a highly competitive market, whereas another may not; one firm may be faced by rapidly changing consumer tastes (e.g. a designer clothing manufacturer), while another may be faced with a virtually constant consumer demand (e.g. a potato merchant); one firm may face rapidly rising costs, whereas another may find that costs are constant or falling.

■ *The macroeconomic environment.* This is the *national* and *international* economic situation in which business as a whole operates. Business in general will fare much better if the economy is growing than if it is in recession. In examining the macroeconomic environment, we will also be looking at the policies that governments adopt in their attempt to steer the economy, since these policies, by affecting things such as taxation, interest rates and exchange rates, will have a major impact on firms.

Social/cultural factors. This aspect of the business environment concerns social attitudes and values. These include attitudes towards working conditions and the length of the working day, equal opportunities for different groups of people (whether by ethnicity, gender, physical attributes, etc.), the nature and purity of products, the use and abuse of animals, and images portrayed in advertising. The social/cultural environment also includes social trends, such as an increase in the average age of the population, or changes in attitudes towards seeking paid employment while bringing up small children. In recent times, various ethical issues, especially concerning the protection of the environment, have had a big impact on the actions of business and the image that many firms seek to present.

Technological factors. Over the last twenty years the pace of technological change has quickened. This has had a huge impact not only on how firms produce products, but also on how their business is organised. The use of robots and other forms of computer-controlled production has changed the nature of work for many workers. It has also created a wide range of new opportunities for businesses, many of which are yet to be realised. The information-technology revolution is also enabling much more rapid communication and making it possible for many workers to do their job from home or while travelling.

The division of the factors affecting a firm into political, economic, social and technological is known as a **PEST analysis**, and is widely used by business enterprises to audit their environment and to help them establish a strategic approach to their business activities. It is nevertheless important to recognise that there is a great overlap and interaction among these four sets of factors. Laws and government policies reflect social attitudes; technological factors determine economic ones, such as costs and productivity; technological progress often reflects the desire of researchers to meet social needs; and so on.

As well as such interaction, we must also be aware of the fact that the business environment is constantly changing. Some of these changes are gradual, some are revolutionary.

---

definition

PEST analysis
Where the political, economic, social and technological factors shaping a business environment are assessed by a business so as to devise future business strategy.

Pause for thought

Under which heading of a PEST analysis would you locate training and education?

BOX 1.1

The biotechnology industry
Its business environment

There are few areas of business that cause such controversy as biotechnology. It has generated new medicines, created pest-resistant crops, developed eco-friendly industrial processes, and through genetic mapping, is providing incalculable advances in gene therapy. These developments, however, have raised profound ethical issues. Many areas of biotechnology are uncontentious, but genetic modification and cloning have met with considerable public hostility, colouring many people's views of biotechnology in general.

Biotechnology refers to the application of knowledge about living organisms and their components to make new products and develop new industrial processes. For many it is seen as the next wave in the development of the knowledge-based economy. According to EU estimates, by 2010 the biotechnology sector could well be worth some €2000 bn.

In global term, the US dominates this sector. In Europe, the UK is the region's leading biotechnology centre. It has some 300-specialist biotech companies, which is equivalent to a fifth of Europe's biotechnology sector, and is worth an estimated £1300 mn in revenue. It employs some 19 000 specialists, and a further 21 000 staff in all.

The industry is dominated by small and medium-sized businesses. Some 37 per cent of these are in biopharmaceuticals, 22 per cent in diagnostics, 15 per cent in agriculture and environmental products, and 25 per cent are biotech suppliers. As in the USA, biotech firms in the UK are geographically clustered, forming industry networks around key universities and research institutes. Such clusters can be found in Cambridge, Oxford and London. The link with universities and research institutes taps into the UK's strong science base.

In addition to such clustering, the biotech industry is well supported by the UK government and other charitable organisations such as the Wellcome Trust. Such support helps to fund what is a highly research-intensive sector. The UK government not only provides finance, but encourages firms to form collaborative agreements, and through such collaboration hopes to encourage better management and use of the results that research generates. It also offers help for biotechnology business start-ups, and guidance on identifying and gaining financial support.

The EU too provides a range of resources to support business within the biotech sector. The EUREKA programme attempts to help create pan-EU partnerships, and the EU Fifth Framework Programme provides financing for such collaborative ventures.

Such support by governments is seen as a crucial requirement for the creation of a successful biotechnology sector, as product development within the industry can take up to 12 years.

The majority of funding for the industry comes from 'venture capital' (investment by individuals and firms in new and possibly risky sectors). Even though the UK is Europe's largest venture capital market, such funding is highly volatile. Many of the biotech companies that are listed on the stock market, after significant share price rises in 1999 and 2000, then saw their share prices collapse, along with those of various hi-tech companies. With a depressed stock market, raising finance becomes much more difficult.

Question

From the brief outline above, identify the political, economic, social and technological dimensions shaping the biotechnology industry's business environment.

To be successful, a business will need to adapt to these changes and, wherever possible, take advantage of them. Ultimately, the better business managers understand the environment in which they operate, the more likely they are to be successful, either in exploiting ever changing opportunities or in avoiding potential disasters.

> **The behaviour and performance of firms is affected by the business environment.** The business environment includes economic, political/legal, social/cultural and technological factors.
>
> **Key Idea 1**

Although we shall be touching on political, social and technological factors, it is economic factors which will be our main focus of concern when examining the business environment.

The structure of industry   1.2

One of the most important and influential elements of the business environment is the *structure of industry*. How a firm performs depends on the state of its particular industry and the amount of competition it faces. A knowledge of the structure of an industry is therefore crucial if we are to understand business behaviour and its likely outcomes.

In this section we will consider how the production of different types of goods and services are classified and how firms are located into different industrial groups.

Classifying production

When analysing production it is common to distinguish three broad categories:

- **Primary production.** This refers to the production and extraction of natural resources such as minerals and sources of energy. It also includes output from agriculture.
- **Secondary production.** This refers to the output of the manufacturing and construction sectors of the economy.
- **Tertiary production.** This refers to the production of services, and includes a wide range of sectors such as finance, the leisure industry, retailing and transport.

Figures 1.1 and 1.2 show the share of output (or **gross domestic product (GDP)**) and employment of these three sectors in 1974 and 2002. They illustrate how the tertiary sector has expanded rapidly. In 2002, it contributed some 71 per cent to total output and employed approximately 80 per cent of all workers. By contrast, the share of output and employment of the secondary sector has declined. In 2002, it accounted for only some 23 per cent of output and 18 per cent of employment.

This trend is symptomatic of a process known as **deindustrialisation** – a decline in the share of the secondary sector in GDP. Many commentators argue that this process of deindustrialisation is inevitable and that the existence of a large and growing tertiary sector in the UK economy reflects its maturity.

The classification of production into primary, secondary and tertiary allows us to consider broad changes in the economy. However, if we require a more comprehensive analysis of the structure of industry and its changes over time, then such a general classification is of little value. What we need to do is to classify firms into particular industries. In the following section we identify the classification process used in the UK and the EU.

definition

Primary production
The production and extraction of natural resources, plus agriculture.

definition

Secondary production
The production from manufacturing and construction sectors of the economy.

definition

Tertiary production
The production from the service sector of the economy.

definition

Gross Domestic Product (GDP)
The value of output produced within the country over a twelve-month period.

definition

Deindustrialisation
The decline in the contribution to production of the manufacturing sector of the economy.

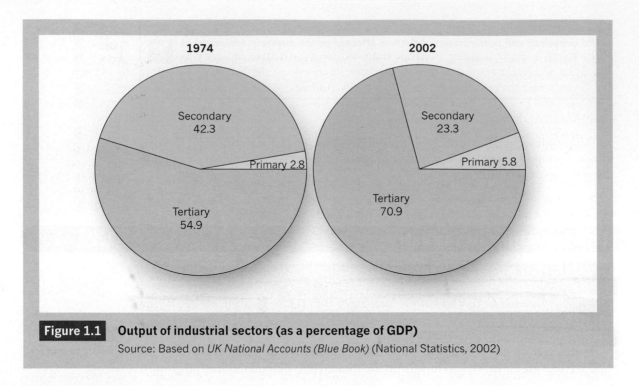

Figure 1.1 **Output of industrial sectors (as a percentage of GDP)**

Source: Based on *UK National Accounts (Blue Book)* (National Statistics, 2002)

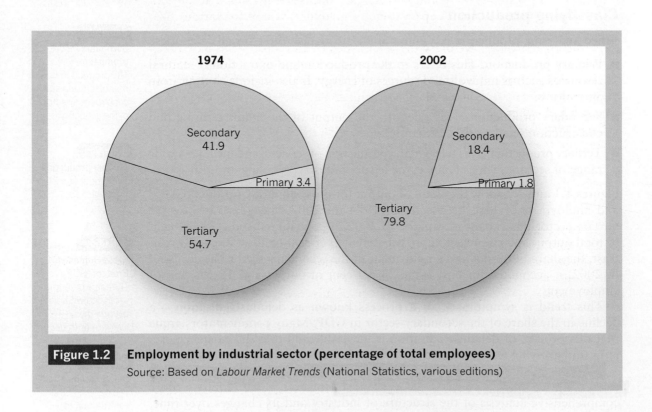

Figure 1.2 **Employment by industrial sector (percentage of total employees)**

Source: Based on *Labour Market Trends* (National Statistics, various editions)

Classifying firms into industries

An industry refers to a group of firms that produce a particular category of product. Thus we could refer to the electrical goods industry, the holiday industry, the aircraft industry or the insurance industry. Industries can then be grouped together into broad **industrial sectors**, such as manufacturing, or mining and quarrying, or construction, or transport.

Classifying firms into industrial groupings and subgroupings has a number of purposes. It helps us to analyse various trends in the economy and to identify areas of growth and areas of decline. It helps to identify parts of the economy with specific needs, such as training or transport infrastructure. Perhaps most importantly, it helps economists and business people to understand and predict the behaviour of firms that are in direct competition with each other. In such cases, however, it may be necessary to draw the boundaries of an industry quite narrowly.

To illustrate this, take the case of the vehicle industry. The vehicle industry produces cars, lorries, vans and coaches. The common characteristic of these vehicles is that they are self-propelled road transport vehicles. In other words, we could draw the boundaries of an industry in terms of the broad physical or technical characteristics of the products it produces. The problem with this type of categorisation, however, is that these products may not be substitutes in an *economic* sense. If I am thinking of buying a new vehicle to replace my car, I am hardly likely to consider buying a coach or a lorry! Lorries are not in competition with cars. If we are to group products together which are genuine competitors for each other, we will want to divide industries into more narrow categories. For example, we could classify cars into several groups according to size, price, function, engine capacity, etc.: e.g. luxury, saloon (of various size categories), estate (again of various size categories), seven seater and sports.

On the other hand, if we draw the boundaries of an industry too narrowly, we may end up ignoring the effects of competition from another closely related industry. For example, if we are to understand the pricing strategies of electricity supply companies in the household market, it might be better to focus on the whole domestic fuel industry.

Thus how narrowly or broadly we draw the boundaries of an industry depends on the purposes of our analysis.

Standard Industrial Classification

The formal system under which firms are grouped into industries is known as the **Standard Industrial Classification** (**SIC**). The SIC was first introduced in 1948. Its aim was to promote the collection by various government departments and non-governmental agencies of a uniform and comparable body of data on industry. Since 1948 the SIC has been periodically revised. Revisions to the SIC have been made in order to reflect changes in the UK's industrial structure, such as those resulting from the growth in new products and the new industries associated with them.

The most recent revision in 1992 was initiated as a response to the EU's desire to establish a new Europe-wide classification system. Such a revision was seen as a crucial requirement for the effective monitoring of business in the EU's 'internal market' (the system whereby there are not supposed to be any artificial barriers to trade between EU members).

SIC(92) is divided into seventeen sections (A–Q), each representing a production classification (see Table 1.1). Two of the sections (C and D) are in turn

---

> **definition**
> **Industry**
> A group of firms producing a particular product or service.

> **definition**
> **Industrial sector**
> A grouping of industries producing similar products or services.

> **definition**
> **Standard Industrial Classification (SIC)**
> The name given to the formal classification of firms into industries used by the government in order to collect data on business and industry trends.

Table 1.1	Standard Industrial Classification 1992

Section		Subsection	
A	Agriculture, hunting and forestry		
B	Fishing		
C	Mining and quarrying	CA	Mining and quarrying of energy producing materials
		CB	Mining and quarrying except energy producing materials
D	Manufacturing	DA	Manufacture of food products, beverages and tobacco
		DB	Manufacture of textiles and textile products
		DC	Manufacture of leather and leather products
		DD	Manufacture of wood and wood products
		DE	Manufacture of pulp, paper and paper products; publishing and printing
		DF	Manufacture of coke, refined petroleum products and nuclear fuel
		DG	Manufacture of chemicals, chemical products and man-made fibres
		DH	Manufacture of rubber and plastic products
		DI	Manufacture of other non-metallic mineral products
		DJ	Manufacture of basic metals and fabricated metal products
		DK	Manufacture of machinery and equipment not elsewhere classified
		DL	Manufacture of electrical and optical equipment
		DM	Manufacture of transport equipment
		DN	Manufacturing not elsewhere classified
E	Electricity, gas and water supply		
F	Construction		
G	Wholesale and retail trade, repair of motor vehicles and personal and household goods		
H	Hotels and restaurants		
I	Transport, storage and communication		
J	Financial intermediation		
K	Real estate, renting and business activities		
L	Public administration and defence; compulsory social security		
M	Education		
N	Health and social work		
O	Other community, social and personal service activities		
P	Private households with employed persons		
Q	Extra-territorial organisations and bodies		

Source: Based on *Standard Industrial Classification 1992* (CSO)

Table 1.2   The classification of the manufacture of cardboard boxes

Section D	Manufacturing (comprising divisions 15 to 37)
Subsection DE	Manufacture of pulp, paper and paper products; publishing and printing (comprising divisions 21 and 22)
Division 21	Manufacture of pulp, paper and paper products (comprising groups 21.1 and 21.2)
Group 21.2	Manufacture of articles of paper and paperboard (comprising classes 21.21 to 21.25)
Class 21.21	Manufacture of corrugated paper and paperboard and of containers of paper and paperboard (comprising subclasses 21.21/1 and 21.21/2)
Subclass 21.21/2	Manufacture of cartons, boxes, cases and other containers

Source: Based on *Standard Industrial Classification 1992* (CSO)

divided into subsections. Sections or subsections are then divided into divisions; divisions are divided into groups; groups are divided into classes; and some classes are further divided into subclasses. Table 1.2 gives an example of how a manufacturer of cardboard boxes would be classified according to this system.

In total, SIC(92) has 17 sections, 16 subsections, 60 divisions, 222 groups, 503 classes and 142 subclasses.

Changes in the structure of the UK economy

Given such a classification, how has UK industry changed over time? Figures 1.3 and 1.4 show the changes in output and employment of the various sectors identified by the SIC between various years from 1980 to 2002.

The figures reveal that only mining and quarrying (C) experienced a decline in output between 1985 and 1990 (reflecting the decline in the coal industry). However, the construction industry (F) declined after 1990, and manufacturing (D) remained largely stagnant. By contrast, the service sectors (G–O), and especially the finance and banking sector (J and K) and the transport, storage and communication sector (I), have grown very rapidly.

In respect to employment, a similar, although more dramatic, pattern emerges. Only the retail trade (G and H), finance and banking (J and K) and other services (L–O) have seen an increase in employment over the whole 22-year period. In all the other sectors, employment has fallen, and in mining and quarrying (C), electricity, gas and water supply (E) and manufacturing (D), the fall has been dramatic.

If we examine the subsections and divisions within the SIC, we can get a more detailed picture of how the structure of industry has changed. For example, we find that the process of deindustrialisation has not been experienced by all manufacturing industries. Certain divisions, such as instrument and electrical engineering, are in fact among the fastest growing in the whole UK economy. It is the more traditional manufacturing industries, such as metal manufacturing, which have experienced a substantial decline.

In respect to employment, there are again substantial variations between divisions. Thus whereas the financial services sector has seen a rapid growth in employment, there has been a decline in employment in parts of the retail banking sector (fewer counter staff are required in high street banks, given the growth in cash machines, direct debits, debit cards, etc.). And whereas there has been a

Figure 1.3

UK GDP by industry (1980 = 100)

Source: Based on *UK Economic Accounts (Blue Book)* (National Statistics, 2003)

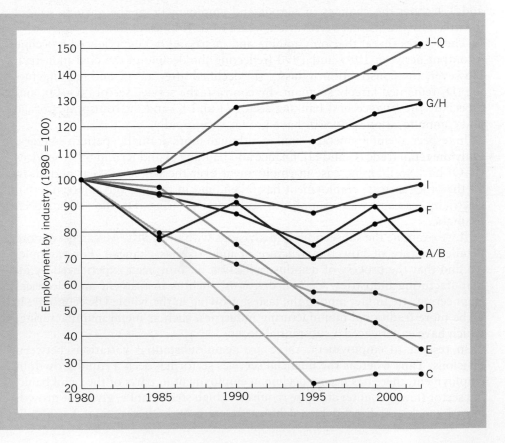

Figure 1.4

UK employment by industry (1980 = 100)

Source: Based on *Annual Abstract of Statistics* (National Statistics, 2003) decline in employment in primary industries (such as agriculture and mining) and traditional manufacturing industries (such as shipbuilding and metal manufacturing), there has been a growth in employment in some of the more 'high-tech' industries.

Analysing industrial concentration

The SIC also enables us to address wider issues such as changes in **industrial concentration**.

When we examine the size structure of UK industry, we find that some sectors are dominated by large business units (those employing 250 or more people), whereas in others it is small and medium-sized enterprises (SMEs) that dominate.

Table 1.3 shows that in the manufacturing sector (D) 49.2 per cent of all workers were employed by large firms in 2001, and such firms accounted for 63.6 per cent of the sector's turnover. The *number* of large manufacturing firms, however, was a mere 2325, compared with 290 425 SMEs. In some sectors, the

> **definition**
> **Industrial concentration**
> The degree to which an industry is dominated by large business enterprises.

Table 1.3 Number of enterprises, employment and turnover by industrial sector: 2001

Sector	Size of enterprise	Number of enterprises (and % of sector)	Employment (% of sector)	Turnover (% of sector)
All	SMEs[a]	3 739 565 (99.8)	55.4	51.4
	Large firms[b]	6 775 (0.2)	44.6	48.6
A, B	SMEs	181 115 (99.9)	97.5	97.5
	Large firms	25 (0.1)	2.5	2.5
C, E	SMEs	5 705 (98.4)	14.6	19.8
	Large firms	95 (1.6)	85.4	80.2
D	SMEs	290 425 (99.2)	50.8	36.4
	Large firms	2 325 (0.8)	49.2	63.6
F	SMEs	691 595 (99.9)	84.5	74.7
	Large firms	205 (0.1)	15.5	25.3
G	SMEs	540 655 (99.8)	50.1	52.8
	Large firms	1 000 (0.2)	49.9	47.2
H	SMEs	123 220 (99.8)	53.8	58.5
	Large firms	205 (0.2)	46.2	41.5
I	SMEs	235 110 (99.8)	39.1	38.1
	Large firms	455 (0.2)	60.9	61.9
J	SMEs	63 650 (99.5)	21.4	na
	Large firms	350 (0.5)	78.6	na
K	SMEs	866 470 (99.9)	70.2	71.9
	Large firms	1 015 (0.1)	29.8	28.1
M	SMEs	117 355 (99.9)	84.4	86.0
	Large firms	75 (0.1)	15.6	14.0
N	SMEs	232 470 (99.8)	42.0	36.8
	Large firms	565 (0.2)	58.0	63.2
O	SMEs	391 695 (99.9)	73.1	63.5
	Large firms	260 (0.1)	26.9	36.5

[a] Enterprises with fewer than 250 employees
[b] Enterprises with 250 or more employees
na Figures not available
Source: *SME database*, (National Statistics, 2003)

Pause for thought

Give some examples of things we might learn about the likely behaviour and performance of businesses in an industry by knowing something about the industrial concentration of that industry.

bulk of output is produced by small or medium-sized firms. This is especially true in the service sector, but also in agriculture, forestry and fishing, and in construction. In other sectors, production is highly concentrated in just a few firms. This is especially so in industries such as electricity, gas and water supply, and in the mining and quarrying sector. In most of these cases, production involves large-scale capital equipment and thus would not suit small firms.

We will be examining industrial structure and the scale of enterprises at several points in the book.

1.3 The determinants of business performance

Structure–conduct–performance

It should be apparent from our analysis thus far that business performance is strongly influenced by the market structure within which the firm operates. This is known as the *structure–conduct–performance paradigm.*

A business operating in a highly competitive market structure will conduct its activities differently from a business in a market with relatively few competitors. For example, the more competitive the market, the more aggressive the business may have to be in order to sell its product and remain competitive. The less competitive the market structure, the greater the chance that collusion between producers might be the preferred strategy, as this reduces the excesses and uncertainties that outright competition might produce.

Key
Idea
1
p9

Such conduct will in turn influence how well businesses perform. Performance can be measured by several different indicators, such as current profitability or profitability over the longer term, market share or growth in market share, and changes in share prices or share prices relative to those of other firms in the industry or to other firms in general, to name some of the most commonly used.

Throughout the book, we shall be seeing how market structure affects business conduct, and how business conduct affects business performance.

It would be wrong, however, to argue that business performance is totally shaped by external factors such as market structure. In fact, the internal aims and organisation of business may be very influential in determining success.

Internal aims and organisation

Economists have traditionally based their analysis of business activity on the assumption that its prime goal is the maximisation of profits. In the past, this was largely true. In the eighteenth and nineteenth centuries, enterprises were managed by the business owner: the true 'entrepreneur'. However, as businesses grew throughout the nineteenth century, and as the range of products became larger and production processes became more complex, so the managerial role became ever more specialist. Owners (the shareholders) and managers became increasingly distinct groups.

This distinction between owners and managers is crucial when we attempt to establish precisely what the objectives of business might be. Whose objectives are we referring to: those of the owner, or those of the manager who controls the

Key
Idea
6
p44

assets of the business enterprise? As we shall see in Chapters 3 and 14, the object-ives of managers and owners may well be at odds. Managers may pursue a range of objectives, and it could well be that these objectives conflict with each other. Thus a manager might like to maximise profits and also to maximise sales. The means to increase sales may be to cut prices, but that may have the effect of reducing profits. Thus managers may have to content themselves with merely achieving a *satisfactory* level of each goal.

Pause for thought

Other than profit and sales, what other objectives might managers have?

It is not only the aims of a business that affect its performance. Performance also depends on the following:

- Internal structure. The way in which the firm is organised (e.g. into depart-ments or specialised units) will affect its costs, its aggressiveness in the market, its willingness to innovate, etc.
- Information. The better informed a business is about its markets, about its costs of production, about alternative techniques and about alternative products it could make, the better will it be able to fulfil its goals.
- The competence of management. The performance of a business will depend on the skills, experience, motivation, dedication and sensitivity of its managers.
- The quality of the workforce. The more skilled and the better motivated is a company's workforce, the better will be its results.
- Systems. The functioning of any organisation will depend on the systems in place: information systems, systems for motivation (rewards, penalties, team spirit, etc.), technical systems (for sequencing production, for quality control, for setting specifications), distributional systems (transport, ordering and supply), financial systems (for accounting and auditing), and so on.

We shall be examining many of these features of internal organisation in sub-sequent chapters.

SUMMARY

1a Business economics is about the study of economic decisions made by business and the influences upon this. It is also concerned with the effects that this decision making has upon other businesses and the performance of the economy in general.

1b The business environment refers to the environment within which business decision making takes place. It is commonly divided into four dimensions: political, economic, social and technological.

1c The economic dimension of the business environment is divided into two: the microeconomic environment and the macroeconomic environment. The micro environment analyses factors specific to a particular firm in a particular market. The macro environment considers how national and international economic circumstances affect all business.

2a Production is divided into being primary, secondary or tertiary. Most recently in the UK the tertiary sector has grown and the secondary sector contracted.

2b Firms are classified into industries and industries into sectors. Such classification enables us to chart changes in industrial structure over time and to assess changing patterns of industrial concentration.

3 The performance of a business is determined by a wide range of both internal and external factors, such as business organisation, the aims of owners and managers, and market structure.

REVIEW QUESTIONS

1 Assume you are a UK car manufacturer and are seeking to devise a business strategy for the twenty-first century. Conduct a PEST analysis on the UK car industry and evaluate the various strategies that the business might pursue.

2 What is the Standard Industrial Classification (SIC)? In what ways might such a classification system be useful? Can you think of any limitations or problems such a system might have over time?

3 In Chapter 1 we have identified some of the major changes in the UK's industrial structure and concentration in recent times. What were these changes and what might they tell us about changes in the UK economy?

4 Outline the main determinants of business performance. Distinguish whether these are micro- or macroeconomic.

2 Economics and the world of business

2.1 What do economists study?

Tackling the problem of scarcity

We have looked at various aspects of the business environment and the influences on firms. We have also looked at some of the economic problems that businesses face. But what contribution can economists make to the analysis of these problems and to recommending solutions?

To answer this question we need to go one stage back and ask what it is that economists study in general. What is it that makes a problem an *economic* problem? The answer is that there is one central problem faced by all individuals and all societies. This is the problem of *scarcity*.

Scarcity is the excess of human wants over what can actually be produced. Because of scarcity, various choices have to be made between alternatives.

Key Idea 2

Of course, we do not all face the problem of scarcity to the same degree. A poor person unable to afford enough to eat or a decent place to live will hardly see it as a 'problem' that a rich person cannot afford a second Ferrari. But economists do not claim that we all face an *equal* problem of scarcity. The point is that people, both rich and poor, want more than they can have and this will cause them to behave in certain ways. Economics studies that behaviour.

Two of the key elements in satisfying wants are **consumption** and **production**. As far as consumption is concerned, economics studies how much the population spends; what the pattern of consumption is in the economy; and how much people buy of particular items. The business economist, in particular, studies consumer behaviour; how sensitive consumer demand is to changes in prices, advertising, fashion and other factors; and how the firm can seek to persuade the consumer to buy its products.

As far as production is concerned, economics studies how much the economy produces in total; what influences the rate of growth of production; and why the production of some goods increases and others falls. The business economist tends to focus on the role of the firm in this process: what determines the output

Key Idea 16 p169

> **definition**
>
> **Scarcity**
> The excess of human wants over what can actually be produced to fulfil these wants.

> **definition**
>
> **Consumption**
> The act of using goods and services to satisfy wants. This will normally involve purchasing the goods and services.

> **Pause for thought**
>
> *If we would all like more money, why does the government not print a lot more? Could it not thereby solve the problem of scarcity 'at a stroke'?*

> **definition**
>
> **Production**
> The transformation of inputs into outputs by firms in order to earn profit (or meet some other objective).

> **definition**
>
> **Factors of production (or resources)**
> The inputs into the production of goods and services: labour, land and raw materials, and capital.

> **definition**
>
> **Labour**
> All forms of human input, both physical and mental, into current production.

> **definition**
>
> **Land (and raw materials)**
> Inputs into production that are provided by nature: e.g. unimproved land and mineral deposits in the ground.

of individual businesses and the range of products they produce; what techniques firms use and why; and what determines their investment decisions and how many workers they employ.

The production of goods and services involves the use of inputs, or factors of production as they are often called. These are of three broad types:

- Human resources: **labour**. The labour force is limited both in number and in skills.
- Natural resources: **land and raw materials**. The world's land area is limited, as are its raw materials.
- Manufactured resources: **capital**. Capital consists of all those inputs that themselves have had to be produced in the first place. The world has a limited stock of capital: a limited supply of factories, machines, transportation and other equipment. The productivity of capital is limited by the state of technology.

We will be studying the use of these resources by firms for the production of goods and services: production to meet consumer demand – production which will thus help to reduce the problem of scarcity.

Demand and supply

We said that economics is concerned with consumption and production. Another way of looking at this is in terms of *demand* and *supply*. It is quite likely that you already knew that economics had something to do with demand and supply. In fact, demand and supply and the relationship between them lie at the very centre of economics. But what do we mean by the terms, and what is their relationship with the problem of scarcity?

Demand is related to wants. If goods and services were free, people would simply demand whatever they wanted. Such wants are virtually boundless: perhaps only limited by people's imagination. *Supply*, on the other hand, is limited. It is related to resources. The amount that firms can supply depends on the resources and technology available.

Given the problem of scarcity, given that human wants exceed what can actually be produced, *potential* demands will exceed *potential* supplies. Society therefore has to find some way of dealing with this problem. Somehow it has to try to match demand and supply. This applies at the level of the economy overall: *aggregate* demand will need to be balanced against *aggregate* supply. In other words, total spending in the economy must balance total production. It also applies at the level of individual goods and services. The demand and supply of cabbages must balance, as must the demand and supply of video recorders, cars, houses and haircuts.

But if potential demand exceeds potential supply, how are *actual* demand and supply to be made equal? Either demand has to be curtailed, or supply has to be increased, or a combination of the two. Economics studies this process. It studies how demand adjusts to available supplies, and how supply adjusts to consumer demands.

The business economist studies the role of firms in this process: how they respond to demand, or, indeed, try to create demand for their products; how they combine their inputs to achieve output in the most efficient way; how they decide the amount to produce and the price to charge their customers; and how

Key Idea 2 p19

they make their investment decisions. Not only this, the business economist also considers the wider environment in which firms operate and how they are affected by it: the effect of changes in the national and international economic climate, such as upswings and downswings in the economy, and changes in interest rates and exchange rates. In short, the business economist studies supply: how firms' output is affected by a range of influences, and how firms can best meet their objectives.

Dividing up the subject

Economics is traditionally divided into two main branches – *macroeconomics* and *microeconomics*, where 'macro' means big, and 'micro' means small.

Macroeconomics is concerned with the economy as a whole. It is thus concerned with **aggregate demand** and **aggregate supply**. By 'aggregate demand' we mean the total amount of spending in the economy, whether by consumers, by overseas customers for our exports, by the government, or by firms when they buy capital equipment or stock up on raw materials. By 'aggregate supply' we mean the total national output of goods and services.

Microeconomics is concerned with the individual parts of the economy. It is concerned with the demand and supply of *particular* goods and services and resources: cars, butter, clothes and haircuts; electricians, secretaries, blast furnaces, computers and coal.

Business economics, because it studies firms, is largely concerned with microeconomic issues. Nevertheless, given that businesses are affected by what is going on in the economy as a whole, it is still important for the business economist to study the macroeconomic environment and its effects on individual firms.

> **definition**
> **Capital**
> All inputs into production that have themselves been produced: e.g. factories, machines and tools.

> **definition**
> **Macroeconomics**
> The branch of economics that studies economic aggregates (grand totals): e.g. the overall level of prices, output and employment in the economy.

> **definition**
> **Aggregate demand**
> The total level of spending in the economy.

> **definition**
> **Aggregate supply**
> The total amount of output in the economy.

Business economics: the macroeconomic environment   2.2

Key Idea 2 p19

Because things are scarce, societies are concerned that their resources are being used as *fully as possible*, and that over time the national output should *grow*. Governments are keen to boast to their electorate how much the economy has grown since they have been in charge!

The achievement of growth and the full use of resources is not easy, however, as demonstrated by the periods of high unemployment and stagnation that have occurred from time to time throughout the world (for example, in the 1930s, the early 1980s, the early 1990s and the early 2000s). Furthermore, attempts by governments to stimulate growth and employment have often resulted in inflation and a large rise in imports. Even when societies do achieve growth, it can be short lived. Economies have often experienced cycles, where periods of growth alternate with periods of stagnation, such periods varying from a few months to a few years.

Macroeconomics, then, studies the determination of national output and its growth over time. It also studies the problems of stagnation, unemployment, inflation, the balance of international payments and cyclical instability, and the policies adopted by governments to deal with these problems.

> **definition**
> **Microeconomics**
> The branch of economics that studies individual units: e.g. households, firms and industries. It studies the interrelationships between these units in determining the pattern of production and distribution of goods and services.

Macroeconomic problems are closely related to the balance between aggregate demand and aggregate supply.

If aggregate demand is *too high* relative to aggregate supply, inflation and balance of payments deficits are likely to result.

- **Inflation** refers to a general rise in the level of prices throughout the economy. If aggregate demand rises substantially, firms are likely to respond by raising their prices. After all, if demand is high, they can probably still sell as much as before (if not more) even at the higher prices, and thus make more profits. If firms in general put up their prices, inflation results.

- **Balance of trade deficits** are the excess of imports over exports. If aggregate demand rises, people are likely to buy more imports. In other words, part of the extra expenditure will go on Japanese DVD players, German cars, French wine, etc. Also if inflation is high, home-produced goods will become uncompetitive with foreign goods. We are likely, therefore, to buy more foreign imports, and foreigners are likely to buy fewer of our exports.

If aggregate demand is *too low* relative to aggregate supply, unemployment and recession may well result.

- A **recession** is where output in the economy declines: in other words, growth becomes negative. A recession is associated with a low level of consumer spending. If people spend less, shops are likely to find themselves with unsold stocks. As a result they will buy less from the manufacturers, which in turn will cut down on production.

- **Unemployment** is likely to result from cutbacks in production. If firms are producing less, they will need a smaller labour force.

Macroeconomic *policy*, therefore, tends to focus on the balance of aggregate demand and aggregate supply. It can be **demand-side policy**, which seeks to influence the level of spending in the economy. This in turn will affect the level of production, prices and employment. Or it can be **supply-side policy**. This is designed to influence the level of production directly: for example, by trying to create more incentives for workers or business people.

Macroeconomic policy and its effects on business

Both demand-side and supply-side policy will affect the business environment. Take demand-side policy. If there is a recession, the government might try to boost the level of spending (aggregate demand) by cutting taxes, increasing government spending or reducing interest rates. If consumers respond by purchasing more, then this will clearly have an effect on businesses. But firms will want to be stocked up ready for an upsurge in consumer demand. Therefore, they will want to estimate the effect on their own particular market of a boost to aggregate demand. Studying the macroeconomic environment and the effects of government policy, therefore, is vital for firms when forecasting future demand for their product.

It is the same with supply-side policy. The government may introduce tax incentives for firms to invest, or for people to work harder; it may introduce new training schemes; it may build new motorways. These policies will affect firms' costs and hence the profitability of production. So, again, firms will want to predict how government policies are likely to affect them, so that they can plan accordingly.

definition
Rate of inflation The percentage increase in the level of prices over a twelve-month period.

definition
Balance of trade Exports of goods and services minus imports of goods and services. If exports exceed imports, there is a 'balance of trade surplus' (a positive figure). If imports exceed exports, there is a 'balance of trade deficit' (a negative figure).

definition
Recession A period where national output falls for a few months or more.

definition
Unemployment The number of people who are actively looking for work but are currently without a job. (Note that there is much debate as to who should officially be counted as unemployed.)

definition
Demand-side policy Government policy designed to alter the level of aggregate demand, and thereby the level of output, employment and prices.

definition
Supply-side policy Government policy that attempts to alter the level of aggregate supply directly.

Looking at macroeconomic data
Assessing different countries' macroeconomic performance

Rapid economic growth, low unemployment, low inflation and the avoidance of balance of trade deficits are the major macroeconomic policy objectives of most governments round the world. To help them achieve these objectives they employ economic advisers. But when we look at the performance of various economies, the success of government macroeconomic policies seems decidedly 'mixed'.

The table shows data for the USA, Japan, Germany and the UK from 1978 to 2003.

If the government does not have much success in managing the economy it could be for the following reasons:

■ Economists have incorrectly analysed the problems and hence have given the wrong advice.

■ Economists disagree and hence have given conflicting advice.

■ Economists have based their advice on inaccurate forecasts.

■ Governments have not heeded the advice of economists.

■ There is little else that governments could have done: the problems were insoluble.

Questions

1 Has the UK generally fared better or worse than the other three countries?

2 Was there a common pattern in the macroeconomic performance of each of the four countries over these 26 years?

Macroeconomic performance of four industrialised economies (average annual figures)

	Unemployment (% of workforce)				Inflation (%)				Economic growth (%)				Balance on current account[a] (% of national income)			
	USA	Japan	Germany	UK	USA	Japan	Germany	UK	USA	Japan	Germany	UK	USA	Japan	Germany	UK
1978–80	6.3	2.1	3.2	5.8	9.7	5.1	4.1	13.2	2.5	4.9	2.9	1.4	−0.2	−0.1	−0.3	0.6
1981–3	8.8	2.4	7.7	11.2	6.6	3.2	5.0	8.4	1.0	3.4	0.3	1.3	−0.5	0.9	0.4	1.8
1984–6	7.1	2.6	6.9	11.4	3.3	1.6	1.4	4.8	4.8	3.7	2.4	2.6	−3.2	3.6	2.9	0.3
1987–9	5.6	2.5	6.0	8.3	3.7	1.2	1.4	5.7	3.7	5.1	2.9	3.9	−2.8	2.8	4.4	−3.0
1990–2	6.6	2.1	4.5	8.7	4.2	2.7	3.4	6.4	1.5	3.3	4.3	−0.3	−0.7	2.2	0.5	−2.2
1993–5	6.2	2.8	8.0	9.4	2.8	0.6	3.0	2.5	3.2	0.8	1.0	3.2	−1.3	2.7	−0.9	−0.8
1996–8	4.9	3.6	9.2	7.0	2.3	0.9	1.1	3.0	4.1	1.4	1.4	3.0	−1.7	2.2	−0.2	−0.6
1999–2001	4.3	4.8	8.0	5.4	2.8	−0.6	1.3	2.1	2.7	1.1	1.8	2.5	−3.8	2.4	−0.6	−1.8
2000–3	5.9	5.6	8.6	5.1	2.3	−0.5	1.2	2.4	2.4	0.7	0.2	1.9	−5.1	2.9	2.7	−1.2

[a] The current account is the balance of trade plus net income flows and transfers of money to/from the country.
Source: various

The circular flow of income

One of the most useful diagrams for illustrating the macroeconomic environment and the relationships between producers and consumers is the *circular flow of income* diagram. This is illustrated in Figure 2.1.

The consumers of goods and services are labelled 'households'. Some members of households, of course, are also workers, and in some cases are the owners of other factors of production too, such as land. The producers of goods and services are labelled 'firms'.

Firms and households are in a twin 'demand and supply' relationship.

First, on the right-hand side of the diagram, households demand goods and services, and firms supply goods and services. In the process, exchange takes

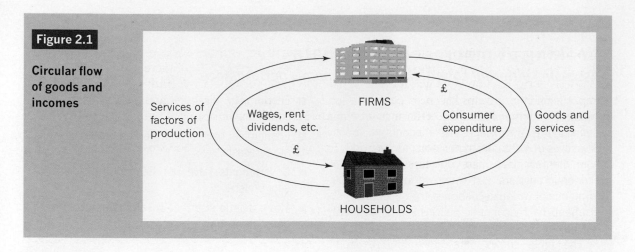

Figure 2.1

Circular flow of goods and incomes

definition

Barter economy
An economy where people exchange goods and services directly with one another without any payment of money. Workers would be paid with bundles of goods.

key terms

Market
The interaction between buyers and sellers.

place. In a money economy (as opposed to a **barter economy**), firms exchange goods and services for money. In other words, money flows from households to firms in the form of consumer expenditure, while goods and services flow the other way – from firms to households.

This coming together of buyers and sellers is known as a **market** – whether it be a street market, a shop, an auction, a mail-order system or whatever. Thus we talk about the market for apples, the market for oil, for cars, for houses, for televisions and so on.

Second, firms and households come together in the market for factors of production. This is illustrated on the left-hand side of the diagram. This time the demand and supply roles are reversed. Firms demand the use of factors of production owned by households – labour, land and capital. Households supply them. Thus the services of labour and other factors flow from households to firms, and in exchange firms pay households money – namely, wages, rent, dividends and interest. Just as we referred to particular goods markets, so we can also refer to particular factor markets – the market for bricklayers, for secretaries, for hairdressers, for land, etc.

There is thus a circular flow of incomes. Households earn incomes from firms and firms earn incomes from households. The money circulates. There is also a circular flow of goods and services, but in the opposite direction. Households supply factor services to firms, which then use them to supply goods and services to households.

Macroeconomics is concerned with the total size of the flow. If consumers choose to spend more, firms will earn more from the increased level of sales. They will probably respond by producing more or raising their prices, or some combination of the two. As a result, they will end up paying more out to workers in the form of wages, and to shareholders in the form of profits. Households will thus have gained additional income. This will then lead to an additional increase in consumer spending, and, therefore, a further boost to production. To summarise: increased spending generates additional income, which, in turn, generates additional spending, and so on as additional incomes flow round and round the circular flow of income.

The effect does not go on indefinitely, however. When households earn additional incomes, not all of it is spent: not all of it recirculates. Some of the additional income will be saved; some will be paid in taxes; and some will be spent on imports (and will not thus stimulate domestic production). The bigger these 'withdrawals', as they are called, the less will production carry on being stimulated.

It is important for firms to estimate the eventual effect of an initial rise in consumer demand (or a rise in government expenditure, for that matter). Will there be a boom in the economy, or will the rise in demand merely fizzle out? A study of macroeconomics helps business people to understand the effects of changes in aggregate demand, and the effects that such changes will have on their own particular business.

We examine the macroeconomic environment and the effects on business of macroeconomic policy in Chapters 27–33.

Business economics: microeconomic choices 2.3

Microeconomics and choice

Because resources are scarce, choices have to be made. There are three main categories of choice that must be made in any society:

- *What* goods and services are going to be produced and in what quantities, given that there are not enough resources to produce all the things that people desire? How many cars, how much wheat, how much insurance, how many rock concerts, etc. will be produced?

- *How* are things going to be produced, given that there is normally more than one way of producing things? What resources are going to be used and in what quantities? What techniques of production are going to be adopted? Will cars be produced by robots or by assembly-line workers? Will electricity be produced from coal, oil, gas, nuclear fission, renewable resources or a mixture of these?

- *For whom* are things going to be produced? In other words, how is the nation's income going to be distributed? After all, the higher your income, the more you can consume of the nation's output. What will be the wages of farm workers, printers, cleaners and accountants? How much will pensioners receive? How much profit will owners of private companies receive or will state-owned industries make?

All societies have to make these choices, whether they be made by individuals, by groups or by the government. These choices can be seen as *micro*economic choices, since they are concerned not with the *total* amount of national output, but with the *individual* goods and services that make it up: what they are, how they are made, and who gets the incomes to buy them.

Choice and opportunity cost

Choice involves sacrifice. The more food you choose to buy, the less money you will have to spend on other goods. The more food a nation produces, the fewer resources will there be for producing other goods. In other words, the production or consumption of one thing involves the sacrifice of alternatives. This sacrifice of alternatives in the production (or consumption) of a good is known as its **opportunity cost**.

definition

Opportunity cost
The cost of any activity measured in terms of the best alternative forgone.

BOX 2.2

The opportunity costs of studying economics
What are you sacrificing?

Key
Idea
3
p27

You may not have realised it, but you probably consider opportunity costs many times a day. The reason is that we are constantly making choices: what to buy, what to eat, what to wear, whether to go out, how much to study and so on. Each time we make a choice to do something, we are in effect rejecting doing some alternative. This alternative forgone is the opportunity cost of our action.

Sometimes the opportunity costs of our actions are the direct monetary costs we incur. Sometimes it is more complicated.

Take the opportunity costs of your choices as a student of economics.

Buying a textbook costing £34.95

This does involve a direct money payment. What you have to consider is the alternatives you could have bought with the £34.95. You then have to weigh up the benefit from the best alternative against the benefit of the textbook.

Question

What might prevent you from making the best decision?

Coming to classes

You may or may not be paying course fees. Even if you are, there is no extra (marginal) monetary cost in coming to classes once the fees have been paid. You will not get a refund by skipping classes!

So are the opportunity costs zero? No: by coming to classes you are *not* working in the library; you are *not* having an extra hour in bed; you are *not* sitting drinking coffee with friends, and so on. If you are making a rational decision to come to classes, then you will consider such possible alternatives.

Question

If there are several other things you could have done, is the opportunity cost the sum of all of them?

Revising for an economics exam

Again, the opportunity cost is the best alternative to which you could have put your time. This might be revising for some *other* exam. You will probably want to divide your time sensibly between your subjects. A *sensible* decision is not to revise economics on any given occasion if you will gain a greater benefit from revising for another subject. In such a case the (marginal) opportunity cost of revising economics exceeds the (marginal) benefit.

Choosing to study at university or college

What are the opportunity costs of being a student in higher education?

At first it might seem that the costs would include the following:

- Tuition fees.
- Books, stationery, etc.
- Accommodation expenses.
- Transport.
- Food, entertainment and other living expenses.

But adding these up does not give the opportunity cost. The opportunity cost is the sacrifice entailed by going to university or college rather than doing something else. Let us assume that the alternative is to take a job that has been offered. The correct list of opportunity costs of higher education would include:

- Books, stationery, etc.
- *Additional* accommodation and transport expenses over what would have been incurred by taking the job.
- Wages that would have been earned in the job *less* any student grant received.

Note that tuition fees are not included because it is assumed that these are paid by the student's local education authority.

Questions

1 *Why is the cost of food not included?*
2 *Make a list of the benefits of higher education.*
3 *Is the opportunity cost to the individual of attending higher education different from the opportunity costs to society as a whole?*

> The **opportunity cost** of something is what you give up to get it/do it. In other words, it is cost measured in terms of the best alternative forgone.
>
> **Key Idea 3**

If the workers on a farm can produce either 1000 tonnes of wheat or 2000 tonnes of barley, then the opportunity cost of producing 1 tonne of wheat is the 2 tonnes of barley forgone. The opportunity cost of buying a textbook is the new pair of jeans you also wanted that you have had to go without. The opportunity cost of working overtime is the leisure you have sacrificed.

Rational choices

Economists often refer to **rational choices**. This simply means the weighing-up of the *costs* and *benefits* of any activity, whether it be firms choosing what and how much to produce, workers choosing whether to take a particular job or to work extra hours, or consumers choosing what to buy.

Imagine you are doing your shopping in a supermarket and you want to buy some meat. Do you spend a lot of money and buy best steak, or do you buy cheap mince instead? To make a rational (i.e. sensible) decision, you will need to weigh up the costs and benefits of each alternative. Best steak may give you a lot of enjoyment, but it has a high opportunity cost: because it is expensive, you will need to sacrifice quite a lot of consumption of other goods if you decide to buy it. If you buy the mince, however, although you will not enjoy it so much, you will have more money left over to buy other things: it has a lower opportunity cost.

Thus rational decision making, as far as consumers are concerned, involves choosing those items that give you the best value for money: i.e. the *greatest benefit relative to cost.*

The same principles apply to firms when deciding what to produce. For example, should a car firm open up another production line? A rational decision will again involve weighing up the benefits and costs. The benefits are the revenues that the firm will earn from selling the extra cars. The costs will include the extra labour costs, raw material costs, costs of component parts, etc. It will be profitable to open up the new production line only if the revenues earned exceed the costs entailed: in other words, if it earns a profit.

> **definition**
> **Rational choices**
> Choices that involve weighing up the benefit of any activity against its opportunity cost.

> **Pause for thought**
> Assume that you are looking for a job and are offered two. One is more pleasant to do, but pays less. How would you make a rational choice between the two jobs?

> **Rational decision making involves weighing up the marginal benefit and marginal cost of any activity.** If the marginal benefit exceeds the marginal cost, it is rational to do the activity (or to do more of it). If the marginal cost exceeds the marginal benefit, it is rational not to do it (or to do less of it).
>
> **Key Idea 4**

In the more complex situation of deciding which model of car to produce, or how many of each model, the firm must weigh up the relative benefits and costs of each: i.e. it will want to produce the most profitable product mix.

Marginal costs and benefits

In economics we argue that rational choices involve weighing up **marginal costs** and **marginal benefits.** These are the costs and benefits of doing a little bit more or a little bit less of a specific activity. They can be contrasted with the *total* costs and benefits of the activity.

Take a familiar example. What time will you set the alarm clock to go off tomorrow morning? Let us say that you have to leave home at 8.30. Perhaps you will set the alarm for 7.00. That will give you plenty of time to get up and get ready, but it will mean a relatively short night's sleep. Perhaps then you will decide to set it for 7.30 or even 8.00. That will give you a longer night's sleep, but much more of a rush in the morning to get ready.

So how do you make a rational decision about when the alarm should go off? What you have to do is to weigh up the costs and benefits of *additional* sleep. Each extra minute in bed gives you more sleep (the marginal benefit), but gives you more of a rush when you get up (the marginal cost). The decision is therefore based on the costs and benefits of *extra* sleep, not on the *total* costs and benefits of a whole night's sleep.

This same principle applies to rational decisions made by consumers, workers and firms. For example, the car firm we were considering just now will weigh up the marginal costs and benefits of producing cars: in other words, it will compare the costs and revenue of producing *additional* cars. If additional cars add more to the firm's revenue than to its costs, it will be profitable to produce them.

Microeconomic choices and the firm

All economic decisions made by firms involve choices. The business economist studies these choices and their results.

We will look at the choices of how much to produce, what price to charge the customer, how many inputs to use, what type of inputs to use and in what combination, whether to expand the scale of the firm's operations, whether to invest in new plant, whether to engage in research and development, whether to merge with or take over another company, whether to diversify into other markets, whether to export. The right choices (in terms of best meeting the firm's objectives) will vary according to the type of market in which the firm operates, its predictions about future demand, its degree of power in the market, the actions and reactions of competitors, the degree and type of government intervention, the current tax regime, the availability of finance, and so on. In short, we will be studying the whole range of economic choices made by firms and in a number of different scenarios.

In all these cases, the owners of firms will want the best possible choices to be made: i.e. those choices that best meet the objectives of the firm. Making the best choices, as we have seen, will involve weighing up the marginal benefits against the marginal opportunity costs of each decision.

SUMMARY

1a The central economic problem is that of scarcity. Given that there is a limited supply of factors of production (labour, land and capital), it is impossible to provide everybody with everything they want. Potential demands exceed potential supplies.

1b The subject of economics is usually divided into two main branches: macroeconomics and microeconomics.

2a Macroeconomics deals with aggregates such as the overall levels of unemployment, output, growth and prices in the economy.

2b The macroeconomic environment will be an important determinant of a business's profitability.

3a Microeconomics deals with the activities of individual units within the economy: firms, industries, consumers, workers, etc. Because resources are scarce, people have to make choices. Society has to choose by some means or other *what* goods and services to produce, *how* to produce them and *for whom* to produce them. Microeconomics studies these choices.

3b Rational choices involve weighing up the marginal benefits of each activity against its marginal opportunity costs. If the marginal benefit exceeds the marginal cost, it is rational to choose to do more of that activity.

3c Businesses are constantly faced with choices: how much to produce, what inputs to use, what price to charge, how much to invest, etc. We will study these choices.

REVIEW QUESTIONS

1 Virtually every good is scarce in the sense we have defined it. There are, however, a few exceptions. Under *certain circumstances*, water and air are not scarce. When and where might this be true for (a) water and (b) air? Why is it important to define water and air very carefully before deciding whether they are scarce or abundant? Under circumstances where they are *not* scarce, would it be possible to charge for them?

2 Which of the following are macroeconomic issues, which are micro-economic ones and which could be either depending on the context?
   (a) Inflation.
   (b) Low wages in certain service industries.
   (c) The rate of exchange between the pound and the euro.
   (d) Why the price of cabbages fluctuates more than that of cars.
   (e) The rate of economic growth this year compared with last year.
   (f) The decline of traditional manufacturing industries.

3 Make a list of three things you did yesterday. What was the opportunity cost of each?

4 A washing machine manufacturer is considering whether to produce an extra batch of 1000 washing machines. How would it set about working out the marginal opportunity cost of so doing?

5 How would a firm use the principle of weighing up marginal costs and marginal benefits when deciding whether (a) to take on an additional worker; (b) to offer overtime to existing workers?

6 We identified three categories of withdrawal from the circular flow of income. What were they? There are also three categories of 'injection' of expenditure into the circular flow of income. What do you think they are?

APPENDIX

Some techniques of economic analysis

When students first come to economics, many are worried about the amount of mathematics they will encounter. Will it all be equations and graphs, and will there be lots of hard calculations to do and difficult theories to grasp?

As you will see if you glance through the pages of this book, there are many diagrams and tables and a few equations. But this does not mean that there are many mathematical techniques that you will have to master. In fact there are relatively few techniques, but they are ones which we use many times in many different contexts. You will find that, if you are new to the subject, you will very quickly become familiar with these techniques. If you are not new to the subject, perhaps you could reassure your colleagues who are!

Diagrams as pictures

In many cases, we use diagrams simply to provide a picture of a relationship. Just as a photograph in a newspaper can often provide a much more vivid picture of an event than any description in words, so too a diagram in economics can often picture a relationship with a vividness and clarity that could never be achieved by description alone.

For example, we may observe that as people's incomes rise, they spend a lot more on entertainment and only a little more on food. We can picture this relationship very nicely by the use of a simple graph.

In Figure 2.2, an individual's income is measured along the horizontal axis and the expenditure on food and entertainment is measured up the vertical axis. There are just two lines on this diagram: the one showing how the person's expenditure on entertainment rises as income rises, the other how the expenditure on food rises as income rises. Now we could use a diagram like this to plot actual data. But we may simply be using it as a sketch – as a picture. In this case we do not necessarily need to put figures on the two axes. We are simply showing the relative *shapes* of the two curves. These shapes tell us that the person's expenditure on entertainment rises more quickly than that on food, and that above a certain level of income the expenditure on entertainment becomes greater than that on food.

Figure 2.2

The effect of a rise in an individual's income on his/her expenditure on food and entertainment

Table 2.1   **Investment in the EU (15): percentage changes from previous year**

1980	1981	1982	1983	1984	1985	1986	1987	1988	1989	1990	1991
1.3	−4.4	−1.2	0.7	1.5	2.8	4.2	5.0	8.4	6.8	3.7	−0.5
1992	**1993**	**1994**	**1995**	**1996**	**1997**	**1998**	**1999**	**2000**	**2001**	**2002**	**2003**
−0.4	−5.7	2.8	2.9	1.8	3.1	6.5	5.1	4.7	0.0	−2.4	0.2

Source: Adapted from Statistical Annex of European Economy (EC, 2003)

If you were to describe in words all the information that this sketch graph depicts, you would need several lines of prose.

Figure 2.1 (the circular flow diagram) was an example of a sketch designed to give a simple, clear picture of a relationship: a picture stripped of all unnecessary detail.

Pause for thought

What else is the diagram telling us?

Representing real-life statistics

In many cases we will want to depict real-world data. We may want to show, for example, how the level of business investment has fluctuated over a given period of time, or we may want to depict the market shares of the different firms within a given industry. In the first case we will need to look at time-series data. In the second we will look at cross-section data.

Time-series data

Table 2.1 shows annual percentage changes in investment in the European Union between 1980 and 2003.

A table like this is a common way of representing **time-series data**. It has the advantage of giving the precise figures, and is thus a useful reference if we want to test any theory and see if it predicts accurately.

Notice that in this particular table the figures are given annually. Depending on the period of time over which we want to see the movement of a variable, it may be more appropriate to use a different interval of time. For example, if we wanted to see how investment had changed over the past 50 years, we might use intervals of five years or more. If, however, we wanted to see how investment had changed over the course of a year, we would probably use monthly figures.

Time-series data can also be shown graphically. In fact the data from a table can be plotted directly on to a graph. Figure 2.3 plots the data from Table 2.1. Each dot on the graph corresponds to one figure from the table. The dots are then joined up to form a single line.

Thus if you wanted to find the annual percentage change in investment in the EU at any time between 1980 and 2003, you would simply find the appropriate date on the horizontal axis, read vertically upward to the line you have drawn, then read across to find the annual rate of change in investment.

Although a graph like this cannot give you quite such an accurate measurement of each point as a table does, it gives a much more obvious picture of how the figures have moved over time and whether the changes are getting bigger (the curve getting steeper) or smaller (the curve getting shallower). We can also read off what the likely figure would be for some point *between* two observations.

definition

Time-series data information depicting how a variable (e.g. the price of eggs) changes over time.

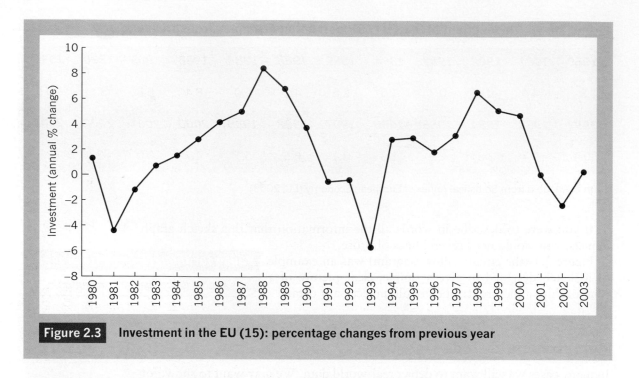

Figure 2.3 Investment in the EU (15): percentage changes from previous year

Table 2.2 National income in the EU (15): percentage changes from previous year (economic growth rates)

1980	1981	1982	1983	1984	1985	1986	1987	1988	1989	1990	1991
1.3	0.1	1.0	1.9	2.5	2.5	2.7	2.7	4.2	3.5	3.0	1.7

1992	1993	1994	1995	1996	1997	1998	1999	2000	2001	2002	2003
1.1	−0.3	2.8	2.4	1.6	2.5	2.9	2.8	3.5	1.6	1.1	1.3

Source: Adapted from Statistical Annex of European Economy (EC, 2003)

It is also possible to combine *two* sets of time-series data on one graph to show their relative movements over time. Table 2.2 shows annual percentage changes in EU national income (i.e. economic growth rates) for the same time period.

Figure 2.4 plots these data along with those from Table 2.1. This enables us to get a clear picture of how annual changes in investment and in national income moved in relation to each other over the period in question.

Cross-section data

Cross-section data show different observations made at the *same point in time*. For example, they could show the quantities of food and clothing purchased at various levels of household income, or the costs to a firm or industry of producing various quantities of a product.

Table 2.3 gives an example of cross-section data. It shows the percentage shares of the UK's largest brewers in 1985 and 2002. Cross-section data like these are often represented in the form of a chart. Figure 2.5 shows the data as a *bar chart*, and Figure 2.6 as a *pie chart*.

key terms

Cross-section data
Information showing how a variable (e.g. the consumption of eggs) differs between different groups or different individuals at a given time.

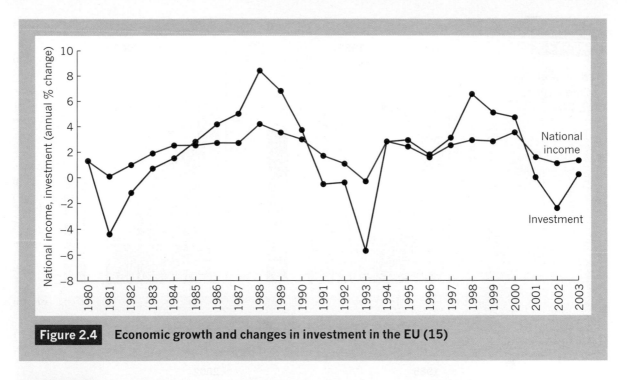

Figure 2.4 **Economic growth and changes in investment in the EU (15)**

Table 2.3 **UK market shares of the largest brewers**

1985 (%)		2002 (%)	
Bass	22	Scottish–Courage	27
Allied Lyons (Carlsberg)	13	Interbrew UK	20
Grand Met (Watneys)	12	Coors	18
Whitbread	11	Carlsberg-Tetley	12
Scottish and Newcastle	10	Diageo (Guinness)	7
Courage	9	Others	16
Others	23		
	100		100

Source: *Various newspaper articles*

It is possible to represent cross-section data at two or more different points in time, thereby presenting the figures as a time series. In Table 2.3, figures are given for just two years. With a more complete time series we could graph the movement of the market shares of each of the brewers over time.

Index numbers

Time-series data are often expressed in terms of **index numbers**. Consider the data in the top row of Table 2.4. It shows index numbers of manufacturing output in the UK from 1980 to 2002.

One year is selected as the **base year,** and this is given the value of 100. In our example this is 1995. The output for other years is then shown by their percentage variation from 100. For 1981 the index number is 75.9. This means that manufacturing output was 24.1 per cent lower in 1981 than in 1995. The index

definition

Index number
The value of a
variable expressed as
100 plus or minus its
percentage deviation
from a base year.

definition

**Base year (for index
numbers)**
The year whose index
number is set at 100.

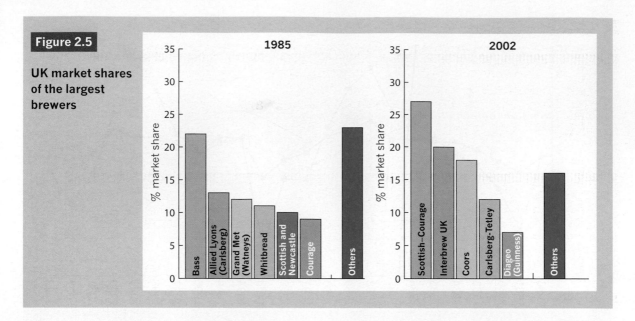

Figure 2.5

UK market shares of the largest brewers

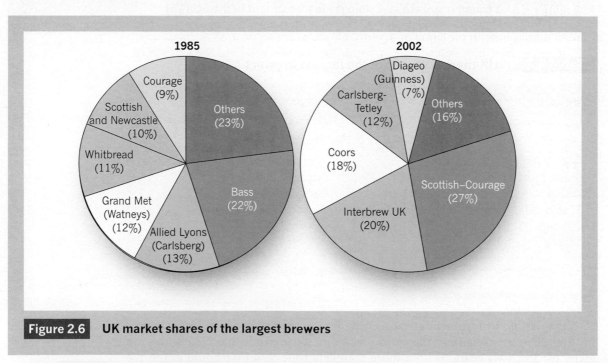

Figure 2.6   **UK market shares of the largest brewers**

number for 1998 is 102.8. This means that manufacturing output was 2.8 per cent higher than in 1995.

The use of index numbers allows us to see clearly any upward and downward movements, and to make an easy comparison of one year with another. For example, Table 2.4 shows quite clearly that manufacturing output fell from 1980 to 1982 and did not regain its 1980 level until after 1984.

Index numbers are very useful for comparing two or more time series of data. For example, suppose we wanted to compare the growth of manufacturing output

| Table 2.4 | UK manufacturing and service industry output: 1995 = 100 |

1980	1981	1982	1983	1984	1985	1986	1987	1988	1989	1990	1991
Output of manufacturing											
80.9	75.9	75.8	77.5	80.3	82.6	83.7	87.7	94.1	97.9	97.7	92.8
Output of services											
67.8	68.0	69.0	71.3	74.0	76.3	79.4	82.7	86.5	88.3	89.5	89.3

1992	1993	1994	1995	1996	1997	1998	1999	2000	2001	2002	
Output of manufacturing											
92.8	94.1	98.5	100.0	100.7	102.0	102.8	103.1	105.2	102.7	98.6	
Output of services											
89.7	92.5	96.8	100.0	103.6	108.1	112.9	116.6	120.8	124.9	128.3	

Source: Based on *Economic Trends* (ONS) various years

with that of the service industries. To do this we simply express both sets of figures as index numbers with the same base year. This is again illustrated in Table 2.4.

The figures show a quite different pattern for the two sectors. The growth of the service industries has been much more steady and more rapid.

Using index numbers to measure percentage changes

To find the annual percentage growth rate in any one year, we simply look at the percentage change in the index from the previous year. To work this out, we use the following formula:

$$\left(\frac{I_t - I_{t-1}}{I_{t-1}} \right) \times 100$$

where I_t is the index in the year in question and I_{t-1} is the index in the previous year.

Thus to find the growth rate in manufacturing output from 1987 to 1988, we first see how much the index has risen $I_t - I_{t-1}$. The answer is $94.1 - 87.7 = 6.4$. But this does *not* mean that the growth rate is 6.4 per cent. According to our formula, the growth rate is equal to:

$$\frac{94.1 - 87.7}{87.7} \times 100$$

$$= 6.4/87.7 \times 100$$

$$= 7.3\%$$

The price index

Perhaps the best known of all price indices is the **retail price index** (**RPI**) (in the USA known as the *consumer price index (CPI)*). It is an index of the prices of goods and services purchased by the average household. Movements in this index, therefore, show how the cost of living has changed. Annual percentage increases in the RPI are the commonest definition of the rate of inflation. Thus

definition

Retail price index (RPI)
An index of the prices of goods bought by a typical household.

Table 2.5 Constructing a weighted average index

Industry	Weight	Year 1 Index	Year 1 Index times weight	Year 2 Index	Year 2 Index times weight
A	0.7	100	70	90	63
B	0.2	100	20	110	22
C	0.1	100	10	130	13
Total	1.0		100		98

if the RPI went up from 100 to 110 over a twelve-month period, we would say that the rate of inflation was 10 per cent. If it went up from 150 to 162 over 12 months, the rate of inflation would be (162 − 150)/150 × 100 = 8 per cent.

The use of weighted averages

definition

Weighted average
The average of several items where each item is ascribed a weight according to its importance. The weights must add up to 1.

The RPI is a **weighted average** of the prices of many items. The index of manufacturing output that we looked at above was also a weighted average: an average of the output of many individual products.

To illustrate how a weighted average works, consider the case of a weighted average of the output of just three industries, A, B and C. Let us assume that in the base year (year 1) the output of A was £7 million, of B £2 million and of C £1 million, giving a total output of the three industries of £10 million. We now attach weights to the output of each industry to reflect its proportion of total output. Industry A is given a weight of 0.7 because it produces seven-tenths of total output. Industry B is given a weight of 0.2 and industry C of 0.1. We then simply multiply each industry's index by its weight and add up all these figures to give the overall industry index.

The index for each industry in year 1 (the base year) is 100. This means that the weighted average index is also 100. Table 2.5 shows what happens to output in year 2. Industry A's output falls by 10 per cent, giving it an index of 90 in year 2. Industry B's output rises by 10 per cent and industry C's output rises by 30 per cent, giving indices of 110 and 130, respectively. But as you can see from the table, despite the fact that two of the three industries have had a rise in output, the total industry index has *fallen* from 100 to 98. The reason is that industry A is so much larger than the other two that its decline in output outweighs their increase.

The retail prices index is a little more complicated. The reason is that it is calculated in two stages. First, products are grouped into categories such as food, clothing and services. A weighted average index is worked out for each group. Thus the index for food would be the weighted average of the indices for bread, potatoes, cooking oil, etc. Second, a weight is attached to each of the groups in order to work out an overall index.

definition

Functional relationships
The mathematical relationships showing how one variable is affected by one or more others.

Functional relationships

Business economists frequently examine how one economic variable affects another: how the purchases of cars are affected by their price; how consumer expenditure is affected by taxes, or by incomes; how the cost of producing washing machines is affected by the price of steel; how business investment is affected by changes in interest rates. These relationships are called functional relationships. We will need to express these relationships in a precise way. This can be done in the form of a table, as a graph or as an equation.

Simple linear functions

These are relationships which when plotted on a graph produce a straight line. Let us take an imaginary example of the relationship between total saving in the economy (S) and the level of national income (Y). This functional relationship can be written as:

$$S = f(Y)$$

This is simply shorthand for saying that saving is a function of (i.e. depends on) the level of national income.

If we want to know just *how much* will be saved at any given level of income, we will need to spell out this functional relationship. Let us do this in each of the three ways.

As a table. Table 2.6 gives a selection of values of Y and the corresponding level of S. It is easy to read off from the table the level of saving at one of the levels of national income listed. It is clearly more difficult to work out the level of saving if national income were £23.4 billion or £47.4 billion.

As a graph. Figure 2.7 plots the data from Table 2.6. Each of the dots corresponds to one of the points in the table. By joining the dots up into a single line we can easily read off the value for saving at some level of income other than those listed in the table. A graph also has the advantage of allowing us to see the relationship at a glance.

It is usual to plot the *independent variable* (i.e. the one that does not depend on the other) on the horizontal or *x*-axis, and the *dependent variable* on the vertical or *y*-axis. In our example, saving *depends* on national income. Thus saving is the dependent variable and national income is the independent variable.

Table 2.6   A saving function

National income (£bn per year)	Total saving (£bn per year)
0	0
10	2
20	4
30	6
40	8
50	10

Figure 2.7

A graph of the saving function: $S = 0.2Y$

As an equation. The data in the table can be expressed in the equation:

$$S = 0.2Y$$

This has the major advantage of being precise. We could work out *exactly* how much would be saved at any given level of national income.

This particular function starts at the origin of the graph (i.e. the bottom left-hand corner). This means that when the value of the independent variable is zero, so too is the value of the dependent variable. Frequently, however, this is not the case in functional relationships. For example, when people have a zero income, they will still have to live, and thus will draw from their past savings: they will have *negative* saving.

When a graph does not pass through the origin, its equation will have the form:

$$y = a + bx$$

where this time *y* stands for the dependent variable (not 'income') and *x* for the independent variable, and *a* and *b* will have numbers assigned in an actual equation. For example, the equation might be:

$$y = 4 + 2x$$

This would give Table 2.7 and Figure 2.8.

Table 2.7 $y = 4 + 2x$

x	y
0	4
1	6
2	8
3	10
4	12
5	14
⋮	⋮

Figure 2.8

$y = 4 + 2x$

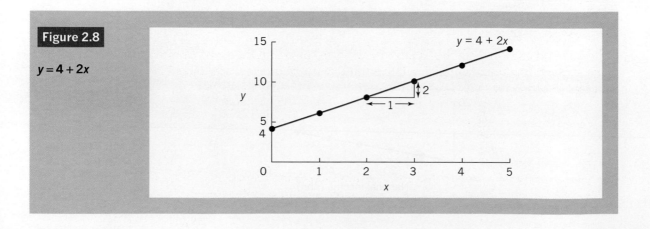

Table 2.8 $y = 4 + 10x - x^2$

x	y
0	4
1	13
2	20
3	25
4	28
5	29
6	28
⋮	⋮

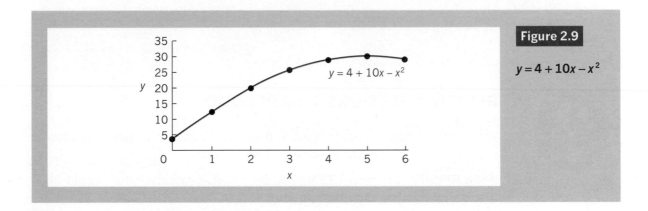

Figure 2.9

$y = 4 + 10x - x^2$

Notice two things about the relationship between the equation and the graph:

- The point where the line crosses the vertical axis (at a value of 4) is given by the constant (*a*) term. If the *a* term were negative, the line would cross the vertical axis *below* the horizontal axis.
- The slope of the line is given by the *b* term. The slope is 2/1: for every 1 unit increase in *x* there is a 2 unit increase in *y*.

Non-linear functions

These are functions where the equation involves a squared term (or other power terms). Such functions will give a curved line when plotted on a graph. As an example, consider the following equation:

$$y = 4 + 10x - x^2$$

Table 2.8 and Figure 2.9 are based on it.

As you can see, *y* rises at a decelerating rate and eventually begins to fall. This is because the negative x^2 term is becoming more and more influential as *x* rises, and eventually begins to outweigh the 10*x* term.

SUMMARY TO APPENDIX

1 Diagrams in economics can be used as pictures: to sketch a relationship so that its essentials can be perceived at a glance.

2 Tables, graphs and charts are also used to portray real-life data. These can be time-series data or cross-section data or both.

3 Presenting time-series data as index numbers gives a clear impression of trends and is a good way of comparing how two or more series (perhaps originally measured in different units) have changed over the same time period. A base year is chosen and the index for that year is set at 100. The percentage change in the value of a variable is given by the percentage change in the index. The formula is:

$$\left(\frac{I_t - I_{t-1}}{I_{t-1}}\right) \times 100$$

4 Several items can be included in one index by using a weighted value for each of the items. The weights must add up to 1 and each weight will reflect the relative importance of that particular item in the index.

5 Functional relationships can be expressed as an equation, a table or a graph. In the linear (straight-line) equation $y = a + bx$, the a term gives the vertical intercept (the point where the graph crosses the vertical axis) and the b term gives the slope. When there is a power term (e.g. $y = a + bx + cx^2$), the graph will be a curve.

REVIEW QUESTIONS TO APPENDIX

1 What are the relative advantages and disadvantages of presenting information in (a) a table; (b) a graph; (c) an equation?

2 If the RPI went up from 125 to 130 over twelve months, what would be the rate of inflation over that period?

3 On a diagram like Figure 2.8, draw the graphs for the following equations.

$y = -3 + 4x$

$y = 15 - 3x$

4 What shaped graph would you get from the following equations?

$y = -6 + 3x + 2x^2$

$y = 10 - 4x + x^2$

If you cannot work out the answer, construct a table like Table 2.8 and then plot the figures on a graph.

3 Business organisations

If you decide to grow strawberries in your garden or allotment, or if you decide to put up a set of shelves in your home, then you have made a production decision. Most production decisions, however, are not made by the individuals who will consume the product. Most production decisions are made by firms: whether by small one-person businesses or by giant multinational corporations, such as General Motors or Sony.

In this chapter we are going to investigate the firm: what is its role in the economy; what are the goals of firms; how do firms differ in respect to their legal status; and in what ways are they organised internally?

3.1 The nature of firms

Economists have traditionally paid little attention to the ways in which firms operate and to the different roles they might take. Firms were often seen merely as organisations for producing output and employing inputs in response to market forces. Virtually no attention was paid to just how firms were organised and how different forms of organisation would influence their behaviour. The firm was seen as a 'black box': inputs were fed in one end, they were used in the most efficient way, and output then emerged from the other end. But do firms have a more significant function to play in respect to resource allocation and production, and does their internal organisation affect their decisions? The answer to these questions is clearly yes.

Complex production

Very few goods or services are produced by one person alone. Most products require a complex production process that will involve many individuals. But how are these individuals to be organised in order to produce such goods and services? Two very different ways are:

- within markets via price signals;
- within firms via a hierarchy of managerial authority.

In the first of these two ways, each stage of production would involve establishing a distinct contract with each separate producer. Assume that you wanted to purchase a woollen jumper. You would need to enter a series of separate contracts: to have the jumper designed, to buy the wool, to get the wool spun, to get it dyed, to have the jumper knitted. There are many other stages in the production and distribution process that might also be considered. With each contract a price will have to be determined, and that price will reflect current market conditions. In most cases, such a form of economic organisation would prove to be highly inefficient and totally impractical. Consider the number of contracts that might be necessary if you wished to purchase a motor car!

With the second way of organising production, a single firm (or just a few firms) replaces the market. The co-ordination of the conversion of inputs into output takes place *within* the firm: not through the market mechanism, but by management issuing orders as to what to produce and the manner in which this is to take place. Hence the distinguishing feature of the firm is that the price mechanism plays little if any role in allocating resources within it.

The benefits of organising production within firms

The function of the firm is to bring together a series of production and distribution operations, doing away with the need for individuals to enter into narrowly specified contracts. If you want a woollen jumper, you go to a woollen jumper retailer.

The key advantage of organising production and distribution through firms, as opposed to the market, is that it involves lower **transaction costs**. Transaction costs are the costs of making economic arrangements about production, distribution and sales. The transaction costs associated with individual contracts made through the market are likely to be substantial for the following reasons:

■ The *uncertainty* in framing contracts. It is unlikely that decision makers will have perfect knowledge of the production process. Given, then, that such contracts are established on imperfect information, they are consequently subject to error.

■ The *complexity* of contracts. Many products require many stages of production. The more complex the product, the greater the number of contracts that would have to be made. The specifications within contracts may also become more complex, requiring high levels of understanding and knowledge of the production process. The more complex contracts become, the poorer is likely to be the quality of decision making, and the higher the costs of production.

■ *Monitoring* contracts. Entering into a contract with another person may require that you monitor whether the terms of the contract are fulfilled. This may incur a significant time cost for the individual, especially if a large number of contracts require monitoring.

■ *Enforcing* contracts. If one party breaks its contract, the legal expense of enforcing the contract or recouping any losses may be significant. Many individuals might find such costs prohibitive, and as a consequence be unable to pursue broken contracts through the legal system.

What is apparent is that, for most goods, the firm represents a superior way to organise production. The actions of management replace the price signals of the market and overcome many of the associated transaction costs.

Goals of the firm

Economists have traditionally assumed that firms will want to maximise profits. The 'traditional theory of the firm', as it is called, shows how much output firms should produce and at what price, in order to make as much profit as possible. But do firms necessarily want to maximise profits?

It is reasonable to assume that the *owners* of firms will want to maximise profits: this much most of the critics of the traditional theory accept. The question is, however, whether the owners make the decisions about how much to produce and at what price.

The divorce of ownership from control

As businesses steadily grew over the eighteenth and nineteenth centuries, many owner-managers were forced, however reluctantly, to devolve some responsibility for the running of the business to other individuals. These new managers brought with them technical skills and business expertise, a crucial prerequisite for a modern successful business enterprise. The managerial revolution that was to follow, in which business owners (shareholders) and managers became distinct groups, called into question what the precise goals of the business enterprise might now be. This debate was to be further fuelled by the development of the **joint-stock company**, in which the ownership of the enterprise was progressively dispersed over a large number of shareholders. The growth in the joint-stock company was a direct consequence of business owners looking to raise large amounts of investment capital in order to maintain or expand business activity.

This twin process of managerial expansion and widening share ownership led Berle and Means[1] to argue that the *ownership* of stocks and shares in an enterprise no longer meant *control* over its assets. They subsequently drew a distinction between 'nominal ownership', namely getting a return from investing in a business, and 'effective ownership', which is the ability to control and direct the assets of the business. The more dispersed nominal ownership becomes, the less and less likely it is that there will be effective ownership by shareholders. This issue will be considered in more detail in Chapter 14.

As you will discover in section 3.2, the modern company is *legally* separate from its owners. Hence the assets are legally owned by the business itself. Consequently, the group *in charge* of the business is that which controls the use of these assets: i.e. the group which determines the business's objectives and implements the necessary procedures to secure them. In most companies this group is the managers.

Berle and Means argued that, as a consequence of this transition from owner to manager control, conflicts are likely to develop between the goals of managers and those of the owners.

But what are the objectives of managers? Will they want to maximise profits, or will they have some other aim?

Managers may be assumed to want to maximise their *own* interests. This may well involve pursuits that conflict with profit maximisation. They may, for example, pursue higher salaries, greater power or prestige, greater sales, better working conditions or greater popularity with their subordinates. Different managers in the same firm may well pursue different aims.

Managers will still have to ensure that *sufficient* profits are made to keep shareholders happy, but that may be very different from *maximising* profits.

Alternative theories of the firm to those of profit maximisation, therefore, tend to assume that large firms are profit 'satisficers'. That is, managers strive hard for a minimum target level of profit, but are less interested in profits above this level.

---

[1] Adolf A. Berle and Gardiner C. Means, *The Modern Corporation and Private Property* (Macmillan, 1933).

Pause for thought

Make a list of six possible aims that a manager of a high street department store might have. Identify some conflicts that might arise between these aims.

Such theories fall into two categories: first, those theories that assume that firms attempt to maximise some other aim, provided that sufficient profits are achieved; and second, those theories that assume that firms pursue a number of potentially conflicting aims, of which sufficient profit is merely one. These alternative theories are examined more fully in Chapter 14.

> **The nature of institutions and organisations is likely to influence behaviour.** There are various forces influencing people's decisions in complex organisations. Assumptions that an organisation will follow one simple objective (e.g. short-run profit maximisation) is thus too simplistic in many cases.
>
> **Key Idea 5**

The principal–agent relationship

Can the owners of a firm ever be sure that their managers will pursue the business strategy most appropriate to achieving the owners' goals (which traditional economic theory tells us is the maximisation of profit)? This is an example of what is known as the **principal–agent problem**. One of the features of a complex modern economy is that people (principals) have to employ others (agents) to carry out their wishes. If you want to go on holiday, it is easier to go to a travel agent to sort out the arrangements than to do it all yourself. Likewise, if you want to buy a house, it is more convenient to go to an estate agent.

> **definition**
>
> **Principal–agent problem**
> One where people (principals), as a result of lack of knowledge, cannot ensure that their best interests are served by their agents.

The crucial advantage that agents have over their principals is specialist knowledge and information. This is frequently the basis upon which agents are employed. For example, owners employ managers for their specialist knowledge of a market or their understanding of business practice. But this situation of **asymmetric information** – that one party (the agent) knows more than the other (the principal) – means that it will be very difficult for the principal to judge in whose interest the agent is operating. Are the manager's own goals rather than the goals of the owner being pursued? It is the same in other walks of life. The estate agent trying to sell you a house may not tell you about the noisy neighbours or that the vendor is prepared to accept a much lower price. A second-hand car dealer may 'neglect' to tell you about the rust on the underside of the car, or that it had a history of unreliability.

> **definition**
>
> **Asymmetric information**
> A situation in which one party in an economic relationship knows more than another.

> **The principal–agent problem.** Where people (principals), as a result of a lack of knowledge, cannot ensure that their best interests are served by their agents. Agents may take advantage of this situation to the disadvantage of the principals.
>
> **Key Idea 6**

Principals may attempt to reconcile the fact that they have imperfect information, and are thus in an inherently weak position, in the following ways:

- *Monitoring* the performance of the agent. Shareholders could monitor the performance of their senior managers through attending annual general meetings. The managers could be questioned by shareholders and ultimately replaced if their performance is seen as unsatisfactory.

- Establishing a series of *incentives* to ensure that agents act in the principals' best interest. For example, managerial pay could be closely linked to business performance.

Within any firm there will exist a complex chain of principal–agent relationships – between workers and managers, between junior managers and senior managers, between senior managers and directors, and between directors and shareholders. All groups will hold some specialist knowledge which might be used to further their own distinct goals. Predictably, the development of effective monitoring and evaluation programmes and the creation of performance-related pay schemes have been two central themes in the development of business practices in recent years – a sign that the principal is looking to fight back.

Staying in business

Aiming for profits, sales, salaries, power, etc. will be useless if the firm does not survive! Trying to *maximise* any of the various objectives may be risky. For example, if a firm tries to maximise its market share by aggressive advertising or price cutting, it might invoke a strong response from its rivals. The resulting war may drive it out of business. Some of the managers may easily move to other jobs and may actually gain from the experience, but the majority are likely to lose. Concern with survival, therefore, may make firms cautious.

Not all firms, however, make survival the top priority. Some are adventurous and are prepared to take risks. Adventurous firms are most likely to be those dominated by a powerful and ambitious individual – an individual prepared to take gambles.

The more dispersed the decision-making power is in the firm, and the more worried managers are about their own survival, the more cautious are their policies likely to be: preferring 'tried and trusted' methods of production, preferring to stick with products that have proved to be popular, and preferring to expand slowly and steadily.

If a firm is too cautious, however, it may not after all survive. It may find that it loses markets to more aggressive competitors. Ultimately, therefore, if a firm is concerned to survive, it must be careful to balance caution against keeping up with competitors, ensuring that the customer is sufficiently satisfied and that costs are kept sufficiently low by efficient management and the introduction of new technology.

The efficient operation of the firm may be strongly influenced by its internal organisational structure. We will consider this in more detail in section 3.3, but first we must consider how the *legal* structure of the firm might influence its conduct within the market place.

The firm as a legal entity   3.2

The legal structure of the firm is likely to have a significant impact on its conduct, and subsequent performance, within the market place. There are several types of firm, each with a distinct legal status.

The sole proprietor

This is where the business is owned by just one person. Usually such businesses are small, with only a few employees. Retailing, building and farming are typical areas to find sole proprietorships. Such businesses are easy to set up and may

Managers and owners
High salaries and corporate goals

In 2001, the annual median salary plus bonuses for the chief executives of the top 100 UK companies was some £933 000. Average earnings in the UK in 2001 were only £24 376. What is more, executive pay increased by some 17 per cent in 2001 compared to only 3.4 per cent for average earnings. Remarkably, the rise in executive pay was at a time when the FTSE 100 stock exchange index lost nearly one third of its value. The table shows the remuneration of the ten top-paid company directors in the UK in 2001.

The earnings of senior executives in the USA are substantially higher still. A normal remuneration package for those at the top of large companies in the USA is more than $35 million per year. The average hourly remuneration rate for a chief executive in one of the top 100 US companies was $11 017, compared to just over $16 for the average worker.

The awards given to executive 'fat cats' have met with considerable protest in recent years. So how can such high pay awards to top executives be justified? The two main arguments put forward to justify such generosity are as follows:

- 'The best cost money.' Failure to offer high rewards may encourage the top executives within an industry to move elsewhere.
- 'High rewards motivate.' High rewards are likely to motivate not only top executives, but also those below them. Managers, especially those in the middle of the business hierarchy, will compete for promotion and seek to do well with such high rewards on offer.

In addition to using high salaries to motivate managers, shareholders, who ultimately determine the pay of top executives, have been keen to modify the manner in which top executives receive their rewards, in order to provide additional incentives.

Remuneration of the ten top-paid directors in the UK (2001)

Director	Company	Total remuneration
Ken Berry	EMI Group plc	£9 840 725
Bart Becht	Reckitt Benckiser	£9 062 100
Tony Ball	British Sky Broadcasting	£7 779 310
Jean-Pierre Garnier	GlaxoSmithKline	£7 044 843
Lord Browne	BP	£5 521 380
Martin Bandier	EMI	£4 950 550
Michael Benson	Amvescap	£4 517 000
Peter Clarke	Man	£4 239 609
Sir George Mathewson	Royal Bank of Scotland	£4 072 283
Paul Walsh	Diageo	£3 752 311

Source: *The Guardian* (5 October 2002)

require only a relatively small initial capital investment. They may well flourish if the owner is highly committed to the business, and they can be very flexible to changing market conditions. They suffer two main disadvantages, however:

- Limited scope for expansion. Finance is limited to what the owner can raise personally. Also there is a limit to the size of an organisation that one person can effectively control.
- Unlimited liability. The owner is personally liable for any losses that the business might make. This could result in the owner's house, car and other assets being seized to pay off any outstanding debts.

Increasingly there has been greater reliance on pay-outs of shares and share 'options', rather than on salaries and short-term bonuses. The justification for such a move is that giving rewards in the form of shares links the interests of managers, owners and investors. In such an environment, a rational 'reward-maximising' manager will always be seeking to enhance share value, and this will be linked to the company's success. As such, the need for monitoring managerial activity diminishes.

The drawback of simply giving shares (as opposed to share options) to top managers concerns how they might respond to *risk*. They might be 'risk averse' and seek to protect the value of their shares, preferring to avoid risky ventures that might jeopardise profits and cause share prices to fall. But in doing this, they will fail to embark on projects which could potentially be very profitable (albeit risky) and thereby fail to *add* value to investors' shares. Because of this, the giving of share *options* to top managers has become more prevalent.

Share options give top managers the right to buy shares at a set price. If the share value goes above this level, the manager makes the difference. If the share price falls below this level, the manager can exercise the option *not* to buy. In such circumstances, top managers are shielded from the risks of failure, but encouraged to do as well as possible.

All the above arguments imply that there should be a clear link between the remuneration top managers receive, whether as salary, bonuses or share options, and the performance of the business. However, a survey conducted by *Management Today* and William Mercer in July 1999[1] found that the correlation between reward and performance was far from clear, with many of the highest paid executives being in poorly performing companies. Although, as the article remarks:

It does not follow, simply because shares have fallen, that executives have performed badly. In some cases, it could have been a lot worse without their efforts.

Nevertheless, paying executives of failing companies huge sums of money has proved highly contentious. In 2002, there was considerable media attention focused on the granting of massive 'platinum parachutes' to senior executives. These are compensation packages paid to executives who are dismissed for poor performance. Such packages hardly act as an incentive for executives to perform well, although the promise of such compensation may attract them to the company in the first place.

In May 2002, after several such 'parachutes' had been unearthed by the press, the shareholders of GlaxoSmithKline, the UK's largest pharmaceutical company, voted down a plan to give chief executive Jean-Pierre Garnier a payoff of £22 million if he were dismissed.

Questions

1   *Explain how sky-high executive remuneration might illustrate the principal–agent problem.*

2   *In the UK, many of the highest-paid executives head former public utilities. Why might the giving of very high rewards to such individuals be a source of public concern?*

---

[1]   *Management Today* (July 1999)

The partnership

This is where two or more people own the business. In most partnerships there is a legal limit of 20 partners. Partnerships are common in the same fields as sole proprietorships. They are also common in the professions: solicitors, accountants, surveyors, etc. With more owners, there is more scope for expansion. More finance can be raised and the partners can each specialise in one aspect of the business.

Partners, however, still have unlimited liability. This problem could be very serious. The mistakes of one partner could jeopardise the personal assets of all the other partners.

Where large amounts of capital are required and/or when the risks of business failure are relatively high, partnerships are not an appropriate form of organisation. In such cases it is best to form a company (or 'joint-stock company' to give it its full title).

Companies

A company is legally separate from its owners. This means that it can enter into contracts and own property. Any debts are *its* debts, not the owners'.

Each owner has a share in the company. The size of their share holdings will vary from one shareholder to another and will depend on the amount they invest. Each shareholder will receive his or her share of the company's distributed profit. The payments to shareholders are called 'dividends'.

The owners have only *limited liability*. This means that, if the company goes bankrupt, the owners will lose the amount of money they have invested in the company, but no more. Their personal assets cannot be seized. This has the advantage of encouraging people to become shareholders, and indeed large companies may have thousands of shareholders – some with very small holdings and others, including institutional shareholders such as pension funds, with very large holdings. Without the protection of limited liability, many of these investors would never put their money into any company that involved even the slightest risk.

Shareholders often take no part in the running of the firm. They may elect a board of directors which decides broad issues of company policy. The board of directors in turn appoints managers who make the day-to-day decisions. There are two types of companies: public and private.

Public limited companies. Don't be confused by the title. A public limited company is still a private enterprise: it is not a nationalised industry. It is 'public' because it can offer new shares publicly: by issuing a prospectus, it can invite the public to subscribe to a new share issue. In addition, many public limited companies are quoted on the Stock Exchange. This means that existing shareholders can sell some or all of their shares on the Stock Exchange. The prices of these shares will be determined by demand and supply. A public limited company must hold an annual shareholders' meeting.

Private limited companies. Private limited companies cannot offer their shares publicly. Shares have to be sold privately. This makes it more difficult for private limited companies to raise finance, and consequently they tend to be smaller than public companies. They are, however, easier to set up than public companies.

Consortia of firms

It is common, especially in large civil engineering projects that involve very high risks, for many firms to work together as a consortium. The Channel Tunnel and Thames Barrier are products of this form of business organisation. Within the consortium one firm may act as the managing contractor, while the other members may provide specialist services. Alternatively, management may be more equally shared.

Co-operatives

These are of two types.

Consumer co-operatives. These, like the old high street Co-ops, are officially owned by the consumers. Consumers in fact play no part in the running of these co-ops. They are run by professional managers.

Producer co-operatives. These are firms that are owned by their workers, who share in the firm's profit according to some agreed formula. They are sometimes formed by people in the same trade coming together: for example, producers of handicraft goods. At other times they are formed by workers buying out their factory from the owners; this is most likely if it is due to close, with a resultant loss of jobs. Producer co-operatives, although still relatively few in number, have grown in recent years.

Public corporations

These are state-owned enterprises such as the BBC, the Bank of England and nationalised industries.

They have a legal identity separate from the government. The corporation is run by a board, but the members of the board are appointed by the relevant government minister. The boards have to act within various terms of reference laid down by Act of Parliament. Profits of public corporations that are not reinvested accrue to the Treasury. Since 1980 most public corporations have been 'privatised': that is, they have been sold directly to other firms in the private sector (such as Austin Rover to British Aerospace) or to the general public through a public issue of shares (such as British Gas).

The issue of privatisation is considered in Chapter 22.

The internal organisation of the firm   3.3

The internal operating structures of firms are frequently governed by their size. Small firms tend to be centrally managed, with decision making operating through a clear managerial hierarchy. In large firms, however, the organisational structure tends to be more complex, although technological change is forcing many organisations to reassess the most suitable organisational structure for their business.

Pause for thought

Before you read on, consider in what ways technology might influence the organisational structure of a business.

U-form

In small to medium-sized firms, the managers of the various departments – marketing, finance, production, etc. – are normally directly responsible to a chief executive, whose function is to co-ordinate their activities: relaying the firm's overall strategy to them and being responsible for interdepartmental communication. We call this type of structure **U (unitary) form** (see Figure 3.1).

When firms expand beyond a certain size, however, a U-form structure is likely to become inefficient. This inefficiency arises from difficulties in

definition

U-form business organisation
One in which the central organisation of the firm (the chief executive or a managerial team) is responsible both for the firm's day-to-day administration and for formulating its business strategy.

Figure 3.1

U-form business organisation

communication, co-ordination and control. It becomes too difficult to manage the whole organisation from the centre. The problem is that the chief executive suffers from **bounded rationality** – a limit on the rate at which information can be absorbed and processed. As the firm grows, more decisions are required. This leads to less time per decision and ultimately poorer decisions. The chief executive effectively loses control of the firm.

> *Good decision making requires good information.* Where information is poor, decisions and their outcomes may be poor.
>
> **Key Idea 7**

In attempting to regain control, it is likely that a further managerial layer will be inserted. The chain of command thus becomes lengthened as the chief executive must now co-ordinate and communicate via this intermediate managerial level. This leads to the following problems:

- Communication costs increase.
- Messages and decisions may be misinterpreted and distorted.
- The firm experiences a decline in organisational efficiency as various departmental managers, freed from central control, seek to maximise their personal departmental goals.

M-form

To overcome these organisational problems, the firm can adopt an **M (multi-divisional) form** of managerial structure (see Figure 3.2).

This suits medium to large firms. The firm is divided into a number of 'divisions'. Each division could be responsible for a particular product or group of products, or a particular market (e.g. a specific country). The day-to-day running and even certain long-term decisions of each division would be the responsibility of the divisional manager(s). This leads to the following benefits:

- Reduced length of information flows.
- The chief executive being able to concentrate on overall strategic planning.
- An enhanced level of control, with each division being run as a mini 'firm', competing with other divisions for the limited amount of company resources available.

Figure 3.2

M-form business organisation

The flat organisation

The shift towards the M-form organisational structure was primarily motivated by a desire to improve the process of decision making within the business. This involved adding layers of management. Recent technological innovations, especially in respect to computer systems such as E-mail and management information systems, have encouraged many organisations to think again about how to establish an efficient and effective organisational structure. The **flat organisation** is one that fully embraces the latest developments in information technology, and by so doing is able to reduce the need for a large group of middle managers. Senior managers, through these new information systems, can communicate easily and directly with those lower in the organisational structure. Middle managers are effectively bypassed.

The speed of information flows reduces the impact of bounded rationality on the decision-making process. Senior managers are able to re-establish and, in certain cases, widen their span of control over the business organisation.

In many respects the flat organisation represents a return to the U-form structure. It is yet to be seen whether we also have a return to the problems associated with this type of organisation.

> **definition**
>
> **Flat organisation**
> One in which technology enables senior managers to communicate directly with those lower in the organisational structure. Middle managers are bypassed.

Multinationals and business organisation

Further types of business organisation which we might identify are closely linked to the expansion and development of the multinational enterprise. Such organisational structures have developed as a response to these businesses attempting to control their business activities on a global scale. Three forms of multinational business organisation are identified below.

H-form. The H-form or **holding company** is in many respects a variation on the M-form structure. A holding company (or parent company) is one which owns a controlling interest in other subsidiary companies. These subsidiaries, in turn, may also have controlling interests in other companies.

H-form organisational structures can be highly complex. While the parent company has ultimate control over its various subsidiaries, it is likely that

> **definition**
>
> **Holding company**
> A business organisation in which the present company holds interests in a number of other companies or subsidiaries.

BOX 3.2

The changing nature of business
Knowledge rules

Companies in a fast-changing business environment need to be able to produce constant innovation, need to be constantly adapting, and be in a state of continual evolution, if they are to survive.

Weaving Complexity and Business: Engaging the Soul at Work
R. Lewin and B. Regine (Texere, New York, 2001)

Knowledge is fundamental to economic success in many industries, and for most firms, key knowledge resides in skilled members of the workforce. The result is a market in knowledge, with those having the knowledge being able to command high salaries and often being 'head hunted'. The 'knowledge economy' is affecting people from all walks of life, and fundamentally changing the nature, organisation and practice of business.

The traditional business corporation was based around five fundamental principles:

- Individual workers needed the business and the income it provided more than the business needed them. After all, employers could always find alternative workers. As such, the corporation was the dominant partner in the employment relationship.

- Employees who worked for the corporation tended to be full-time, and depended upon the work as their sole source of income.

- The corporation was integrated, with a single management structure overseeing all the various stages of production. This was seen as the most efficient way to organise productive activity.

- Suppliers, and especially manufacturers, had considerable power over the customer by controlling information about their product or service.

- Technology relevant to an industry was developed within the industry.

In more recent times, with the advent of the knowledge economy, the principles above have all but been turned on their head.

- The key factor of production in a knowledge economy is knowledge itself, and the workers that hold such knowledge. Without such workers, the corporation is unlikely to succeed. As such, the balance of power between the business and the worker in today's economy is far more equal.

- Even though the vast majority of employees still work full-time, the diversity in employment contracts, such as part-time and short-term contracts and consultancy, means that full-time work is not the only option. (We examine this in section 18.7.) The result is an increasing number of workers offering their services to business in non-conventional ways.

both tactical and strategic decision making is left to the individual companies within the organisation. Many multinationals are organised along the lines of an international holding company, where overseas subsidiaries pursue their own independent strategy. The Walt Disney Company (Holding Company) represents a good example of an H-form business organisation. Figure 3.3 shows the firm's organisational structure and the range of assets it owns.

Integrated international enterprise. The **integrated international enterprise** is an organisational structure where a company's international subsidiaries, rather than pursuing independent business strategies, co-ordinate and integrate their activities in pursuit of shared corporate aims and objectives. The co-ordination of such activities can be either at a regional level – for example, within the European market – or on a truly global scale. In such an organisation, the distinction between parent company and subsidiary is of less relevance than the identification of a clear corporate philosophy which dominates business goals and policy.

definition

Integrated international enterprise
One in which an international company pursues a single business strategy. It co-ordinates the business activities of its subsidiaries across different countries.

- As the domestic economy increasingly spills into the global economy, the complexity of the marketplace facing business means that few businesses have the expertise to provide an integrated product. With communication costs that are largely insignificant, businesses are likely to be more efficient and flexible if they outsource and de-integrate. Not only are businesses outsourcing various stages of production, but many are employing specialist companies to provide key areas of management, such as HRM (human resource management): hiring, firing, training, benefits, etc.

- Whereas in the past businesses controlled information, today access to information via sources such as the Internet means that power is shifting towards the consumer.

- Today, unlike in previous decades, technological developments are less specific to industries. Knowledge developments diffuse and cut across industry boundaries. What this means for business, in a knowledge-driven economy, is that they must look beyond their own industry if they are to develop and grow. We frequently see partnerships and joint ventures between businesses that cut across industry types and technology.

What is clear from the above is that the dynamics of the knowledge economy require a quite fundamental change in the nature of business. Organisationally it needs to be more flexible, helping it to respond to the ever-changing market conditions it faces. Successful companies draw upon their *core* competencies to achieve market advantage, and thus ultimately specialise in what they do best. Businesses must learn to work with others, either through outsourcing specialist tasks, or through more formal strategic partnerships.

Within this new business model the key assets are the specialist people in the organisation – its knowledge workers. How will businesses attract, retain and motivate the best? Will financial rewards be sufficient, or will workers seek more from their work and the organisation they work for?

With such issues facing the corporation we can expect to see a radical reinterpretation of what business looks like and how it is practised over the coming years.

Question

How is the development of the knowledge economy likely to affect the distribution of wage income? Will it become more equal or less equal?

Transnational association. A further form of multinational business organisation is the **transnational association**. Here the business headquarters holds little equity investment in its subsidiaries. These are largely owned and managed by local people. These subsidiaries receive from the headquarters managerial and technical assistance, in exchange for contractual agreements that output produced by the subsidiary is sold to the headquarters. Such output is most likely to take the form of product components rather than finished products. The headquarters then acts as an assembler, marketer or distributor of such output, or some combination of all three. The main advantage of organising international business in this way is that it reduces costs. This form of organisation is known as **global sourcing** and involves the international business using distinct production sites to produce large numbers of single components. With the transnational association, the headquarters still retains the decisive role in integrating business activity.

The organisational structures and issues surrounding multinational corporations will be investigated more fully in Chapter 25.

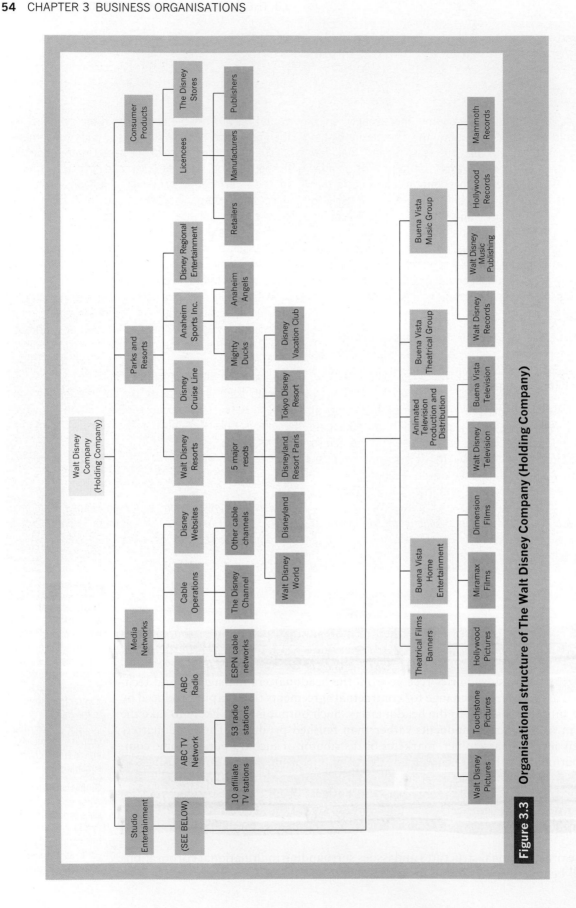

Figure 3.3 **Organisational structure of The Walt Disney Company (Holding Company)**

SUMMARY

1a The firm's role in the economy is to eliminate the need for making individual contracts through the market, and to provide a more efficient way to organise production.

1b Using the market to establish a contract is not costless. Transaction costs will mean that the market is normally less efficient than the firm as an allocator of resources.

1c The divorce of ownership from control implies that the objectives of owners and managers may diverge, and similarly the objectives of one manager from another. Hence the goals of firms may be diverse. What is more, as ownership becomes more dispersed, so the degree of control by owners diminishes yet further.

1d Managers might pursue maximisation goals other than profit, or look to achieve a wide range of targets in which profit acts as a constraint on other business aims.

1e The problem of managers not pursuing the same goals as the owners is an example of the *principal–agent problem*. Agents (in this case the managers) may not always carry out the wishes of their principals (in this case the owners). Because of asymmetric information, managers are able to pursue their own aims, just so long as they produce results that will satisfy the owners. The solution for owners is for there to be better means of monitoring the performance of managers, and incentives for the managers to behave in the owners' interests.

2a The legal status of the firm will influence both its actions and performance within the market place.

2b There are several types of legal organisation of firms: the sole proprietorship, the partnership, the private limited company, the public limited company, consortia of firms, co-operatives and public corporations. In the first two cases, the owners have unlimited liability: the owners are personally liable for any losses the business might make. With companies, however, shareholders' liability is limited to the amount they have invested. This reduced risk encourages people to invest in companies.

3a The relative success of a business organisation will be strongly influenced by its organisational structure. As a firm grows, its organisational structure will need to evolve in order to account for the business's growing complexity. This is particularly so if the business looks to expand overseas.

3b As firms grow, so they tend to move from a U-form to an M-form structure. In recent years, however, with the advance of information technology, many firms have adopted a flat organisation – a return to U-form.

3c Multinational companies often adopt relatively complex forms of organisation. These vary from a holding company (H-form) structure, to the integrated international enterprise, to transnational associations.

REVIEW QUESTIONS

1 What is meant by the term 'transaction costs'? Explain why the firm represents a more efficient way of organising economic life than relying on individual contracts.

2 Explain why the business objectives of owners and managers are likely to diverge. How might owners attempt to ensure that managers act in their interests and not in the managers' own interests?

3 Compare and contrast the relative strengths and weaknesses of the partnership and the public limited company.

4 Conduct an investigation into a recent large building project, such as the Channel Tunnel. Identify what firms were involved and the roles and responsibilities they had. Outline the advantages and disadvantages that such business consortia might have.

5 If a business is thinking of reorganisation, why and in what ways might new technology be an important factor in such considerations?

6 What problems are multinational corporations, as opposed to domestic firms, likely to have in respect to organising their business activity? What alternative organisational models might multinationals adopt? To what extent do they overcome the problems you have identified?

Additional Part A case studies on the *Economics for Business* website (www.booksites.net/sloman)

A.1 **The UK defence industry.** A PEST analysis of the changes in the defence industry in recent years.

A.2 **Scarcity and abundance.** If scarcity is the central economic problem, is anything truly abundant?

A.3 **Global economics.** This examines how macroeconomics and microeconomics apply at the global level and identifies some key issues.

A.4 **Buddhist economics.** A different perspective on economic problems and economic activity.

A.5 **Downsizing and business reorganisation.** Many companies in recent years have 'downsized' their operations and focused on their core competencies. This looks particularly at the case of IBM.

Websites relevant to Part A

Numbers and sections refer to websites listed in the Web appendix and hotlinked from this book's website at **www.booksites.net/sloman**

■ For a tutorial on finding the best economics websites see site C9 (*The Internet Economist*).

■ For news articles relevant to Part A, see the *Economics News Articles* link from the book's website.

■ For general economics news sources see websites in section A of the Web appendix at the end of the book, and particularly A1–9, 24, 38, 39. See also A38, 39 and 43 for links to newspapers worldwide; and A42 for links to economics news articles from newspapers worldwide.

■ For business news items, again see websites in section A of the Web appendix at the end of the book, and particularly A1–3, 20–26, 35, 36.

■ For sources of economic and business data, see sites in section B and particularly B1–4, 33, 34.

■ For general sites for students of economics for business, see sites in section C and particularly C1–7.

■ For sites giving links to relevant economics and business websites, organised by topic, see sites I4, 7, 8, 11, 12, 17, 18.

■ For details on companies, see sites B2 and A3.

Business and markets

THE FINANCIAL TIMES, 21 JUNE 2003

Cocoa prices may be set to bubble again

By KEVIN MORRISON

Cocoa prices have fallen more than 40 per cent since touching 16-year highs last October, prompting traders to take the view that prices are near their lower limit and are poised to bounce higher again.

The fall in price over the past eight months followed better than expected crops in Ghana, Nigeria and most importantly the Ivory Coast, which accounts for about 40 per cent of global production.

In London, the benchmark Euronext-Liffe cocoa price fell to £920 a tonne this week, its lowest price since January 2002 – down from its peak of £1620 reached on October 10, 2002. It recovered slightly to £940 a tonne yesterday.

'The price has fallen further than the market had expected,' said one London-based cocoa trader.

Late last summer investors piled into cocoa futures in anticipation that the civil war in the Ivory Coast would create crop shortages.

The London-based trading house Armajaro bought more than 5 per cent of last season's production, although some traders estimated the purchases to be much higher. However, it is understood Armajaro has since sold most of its cocoa stocks.

Ivory Coast production during the key October to April season was largely unaffected by the civil war following a failed coup last September. This week, the government of the west African nation raised its forecast for the October-to-September year to a near record 1.4m tonne harvest.

However, traders said Ivory Coast cocoa crop estimates can be difficult to rely on.

They also said that the high prices had given farmers a big incentive to pick the October to April crop and deliver it to a port for export.

'We don't know to what extent the war has affected supplies of fertilizers, and what other disruptions farmers are facing,' the trader said.

Despite the price declines, cocoa futures trading volumes are up. Euronext.liffe said cocoa volumes were up about 37 per cent to the end of May. This is on top of the 19 per cent increase last year.

Ian Dudden, director of commodity products at Euronext.liffe, said interest from managed funds has helped contribute to the higher volumes.

> *Businesses live and die by the market. It is a wonderful discipline, giving out its automatic signals as to where shortages lie, or unnecessary surpluses. It is, with its built-in incentives and penalties, a spur to innovation and improvement, but many do die in the process.*
>
> Charles Handy, *The Hungry Spirit* (1998) p. 17

Markets dominate economic life, from buying and selling raw materials, to supplying the final product to the customer. It would be difficult to imagine a world without markets. In fact we talk about economies today as 'market economies', with economic decisions made primarily by business, consumers and employees interacting with each other in a market environment.

As the article opposite illustrates, the determination of a market price is a complex business and often subject to great fluctuation. This is particularly so when you consider commodities, such as cocoa, which are highly dependent upon the weather and subject to considerable speculative buying and selling.

In Part B of this book we shall explore how the market system operates. In Chapter 4 we will consider those factors that influence both demand and supply, and how via their interaction we are able to derive a market price. We see how markets transmit information from consumers to producers and from producers to consumers. We see how prices act as an incentive – for example, if consumers want more mobile phones, how this increased demand leads to an increase in their price and hence to an incentive for firms to increase their production.

Changes in price affect the quantity demanded and supplied. But how much? How much will the demand for DVDs go up if the price of DVDs comes down? How much will the supply of new houses go up if the price of houses rises? In Chapter 5 we develop the concept of *elasticity* of demand and supply to examine this responsiveness. We also consider some of the issues the market raises for business, such as the effects on a business's revenue of a change in the price of the product, the impact of time on demand and supply and how businesses deal with the risk and uncertainty markets generate. We also look at speculation – people attempting to gain by anticipating price changes.

key terms
Price mechanism
Demand and demand curves
Income and substitution effects
Supply and supply curves
Equilibrium price and quantity
Shifts in demand and supply curves
Price elasticity of demand
Income elasticity of demand
Cross-price elasticity of demand
Price elasticity of supply
Speculation
Risk and uncertainty
Spot and futures markets

4 The working of competitive markets

4.1 Business in a competitive market

If a firm wants to increase its profits, should it raise its prices, or should it lower them? Should it increase its output, or should it reduce it? Should it modify its product, or should it keep the product unchanged? The answer to these and many other questions is that it depends on the market in which the firm operates. If the market is buoyant, it may well be a good idea for the firm to increase its output in anticipation of greater sales. It may also be a good idea to raise the price of its product in the belief that consumers will be willing to pay more. If, however, the market is declining, the firm may well decide to reduce output, or cut prices, or diversify across into an alternative product.

The firm is thus greatly affected by its market environment, an environment that is often outside the firm's control and subject to frequent changes. For many firms, prices are determined not by them, but by the market. Even where they do have some influence over prices, the influence is only slight. They may be able to put prices up a small amount, but if they raise them too much, they will find that they lose sales to their rivals.

The market dominates a firm's activities. The more competitive the market, the greater this domination becomes. In the extreme case, the firm may have no power at all to change its price: it is what we call a **price taker**. It has to accept the market price as given. If the firm attempts to raise the price above the market price, it will simply be unable to sell its product: it will lose all its sales to its competitors. Take the case of farmers selling wheat. They have to accept the price as dictated by the market. If individually they try to sell above the market price, no one will buy.

In competitive markets, consumers too are price takers. When we go into shops we have no control over prices. We have to accept the price as given. For example, when you get to the supermarket checkout, you cannot start haggling with the checkout operator over the price of a can of beans or a tub of margarine.

So how does a competitive market work? For simplicity we will examine the case of a **perfectly competitive market**. This is where both producers and consumers are too numerous to have any control over prices whatsoever: a situation where everyone is a price taker.

(Clearly, in other markets, firms will have some discretion over the prices they charge. For example, a manufacturing company such as Ford will have some discretion over the prices it charges for its Fiestas or Mondeos. In such cases the firm has some 'market power'. We will examine different degrees of market power in Chapters 11 and 12.)

Key
Idea
6
p44

definition

Price taker
A person or firm with no power to be able to influence the market price.

definition

Perfectly competitive market (preliminary definition)
A market in which all producers and consumers of the product are price takers. (There are other features of a perfectly competitive market; these are examined in Chapter 11.)

definition

Free market
One in which there is an absence of government intervention. Individual producers and consumers are free to make their own economic decisions.

definition

The price mechanism
The system in a market economy whereby changes in price in response to changes in demand and supply have the effect of making demand equal to supply.

The price mechanism

In a **free market** individuals are free to make their own economic decisions. Consumers are free to decide what to buy with their incomes: free to make demand decisions. Firms are free to choose what to sell and what production methods to use: free to make supply decisions. The resulting demand and supply decisions of consumers and firms are transmitted to each other through their effect on *prices*: through the **price mechanism**.

The price mechanism works as follows. Prices respond to *shortages* and *surpluses*. Shortages cause prices to rise. Surpluses cause prices to fall.

If consumers decide they want more of a good (or if producers decide to cut back supply), demand will exceed supply. The resulting *shortage* will cause *the price of the good to rise*. This will act as an incentive to producers to supply more, since production will now be more profitable. It will discourage consumers from buying so much. *Price will continue rising until the shortage has thereby been eliminated*.

If, on the other hand, consumers decide they want less of a good (or if producers decide to produce more), supply will exceed demand. The resulting *surplus* will cause *the price of the good to fall*. This will act as a disincentive to producers, who will supply less, since production will now be less profitable. It will encourage consumers to buy more. *Price will continue falling until the surplus has thereby been eliminated*.

The same analysis can be applied to labour (and other factor) markets, except that here the demand and supply roles are reversed. Firms are the demanders of labour. Households are the suppliers. If the demand for a particular type of labour exceeded its supply, the resulting shortage would drive up the wage rate (i.e. the price of labour), thus reducing firms' demand for that type of labour and encouraging more workers to take up that type of job. Wages would continue rising until demand equalled supply: until the shortage was eliminated.

Likewise if there were a surplus of a particular type of labour, the wage would fall until demand equalled supply.

The response of demand and supply to changes in price illustrates a very important feature of how economies work.

People respond to incentives. It is important, therefore, that incentives are appropriate and have the desired effect.

Key Idea 8

The effect of changes in demand and supply

How will the price mechanism respond to changes in consumer demand or producer supply? After all, the pattern of consumer demand changes over time. For example, people may decide they want more CDs and fewer cassettes. Likewise the pattern of supply also changes. For example, changes in technology may allow the mass production of microchips at lower cost, while the production of hand-built furniture becomes relatively expensive.

In all cases of changes in demand and supply, the resulting changes in *price* act as both *signals* and *incentives*.

A change in demand

A rise in demand is signalled by a rise in price. This then acts as an incentive for supply to rise. What in effect is happening is that the high price of these goods relative to their costs of production is signalling that consumers are willing to see resources diverted from other uses. Firms respond by doing just that. They divert resources from goods with lower prices relative to costs (and hence lower profits) to those goods that are more profitable.

A fall in demand is signalled by a fall in price. This then acts as an incentive for supply to fall. These goods are now less profitable to produce.

A change in supply

A rise in supply is signalled by a fall in price. This then acts as an incentive for demand to rise. A fall in supply is signalled by a rise in price. This then acts as an incentive for demand to fall.

Changes in demand or supply cause markets to adjust. Whenever such changes occur, the resulting 'disequilibrium' will bring an automatic change in prices, thereby restoring equilibrium (i.e. a balance of demand and supply).

The interdependence of markets

The interdependence of goods and factor markets

A rise in demand for a good will raise its price and profitability. Firms will respond by supplying more. But to do this they will require more inputs. Thus the demand for the inputs will rise, which, in turn, will raise the price of the inputs. The suppliers of inputs will respond to this incentive by supplying more. This can be summarised as follows:

Goods market

■ Demand for the good rises.
■ This creates a shortage.
■ This causes the price of the good to rise.
■ This eliminates the shortage by choking off some of the demand and encouraging firms to produce more.

Factor market

■ The increased supply of the good causes an increase in the demand for factors of production (i.e. inputs) used in making it.
■ This causes a shortage of those inputs.
■ This causes their prices to rise.

■ This eliminates their shortage by choking off some of the demand and encouraging the suppliers of inputs to supply more.

It can thus be seen that changes in goods markets will cause changes in factor markets. Figure 4.1 summarises this sequence of events. (It is common in economics to summarise an argument like this by using symbols.)

Figure 4.1

The price mechanism: the effect of a rise in demand

Goods market

$$D_g \uparrow \longrightarrow \text{shortage} \longrightarrow P_g \uparrow \nearrow S_g \uparrow \quad \text{until } D_g = S_g$$
$$(D_g > S_g) \qquad \searrow D_g \downarrow$$

Factor market

$$S_g \uparrow \longrightarrow D_i \uparrow \longrightarrow \text{shortage} \longrightarrow P_i \uparrow \nearrow S_i \uparrow \quad \text{until } D_i = S_i$$
$$(D_i > S_i) \qquad \searrow D_i \downarrow$$

(where D = demand, S = supply, P = price, g = the good, i = inputs, $\longrightarrow$ means 'leads to')

Interdependence exists in the other direction too: factor markets affect goods markets. For example, the discovery of raw materials will lower their price. This will lower the costs of production of firms using these raw materials and increase the supply of the finished goods. The resulting surplus will lower the price of the good, which, in turn, will encourage consumers to buy more.

The interdependence of different goods markets

A rise in the price of one good will encourage consumers to buy alternatives. This will drive up the price of alternatives. This in turn will encourage producers to supply more of the alternatives.

Key Idea
9
p63

Let us now turn to examine each side of the market – demand and supply – in more detail.

4.2 Demand

The relationship between demand and price

The headlines announce, 'Major crop failures in Brazil and East Africa: coffee prices soar.' Shortly afterwards you find that coffee prices have doubled in the shops. What do you do? Presumably you will cut back on the amount of coffee you drink. Perhaps you will reduce it from, say, six cups per day to two. Perhaps you will give up drinking coffee altogether.

This is simply an illustration of the general relationship between price and consumption: *when the price of a good rises, the quantity demanded will fall.* This relationship is known as the **law of demand.** There are two reasons for this law:

■ People will feel poorer. They will not be able to afford to buy so much of the good with their money. The purchasing power of their income (their *real income*) has fallen. This is called the **income effect** of a price rise.

■ The good will now be dearer relative to other goods. People will thus switch to alternative or 'substitute' goods. This is called the **substitution effect** of a price rise.

Table 4.1   The demand for potatoes (monthly)

	Price (pence per kg) (1)	Tracey's demand (kg) (2)	Darren's demand (kg) (3)	Total market demand (tonnes: 000s) (4)
A	20	28	16	700
B	40	15	11	500
C	60	5	9	350
D	80	1	7	200
E	100	0	6	100

Similarly, when the price of a good falls, the quantity demanded will rise. People can afford to buy more (the income effect), and they will switch away from consuming alternative goods (the substitution effect).

Therefore, returning to our example of the increase in the price of coffee, we will not be able to afford to buy as much as before, and we will probably drink more tea, cocoa, fruit juices or even water instead.

A word of warning: be careful about the meaning of the words **quantity demanded**. They refer to the amount consumers are willing and able to purchase at a given price over a given time period (for example, a week, or a month, or a year). They do *not* refer to what people would simply *like* to consume. You might like to own a luxury yacht, but your demand for luxury yachts will almost certainly be zero.

The demand curve

Consider the hypothetical data in Table 4.1. The table shows how many kilos of potatoes per month would be purchased at various prices.

Columns (2) and (3) show the **demand schedules** for two individuals, Tracey and Darren. Column (4), by contrast, shows the total **market demand schedule**. This is the total demand by all consumers. To obtain the market demand schedule for potatoes, we simply add up the quantities demanded at each price by *all* consumers: i.e. Tracey, Darren and everyone else who demands potatoes. Notice that we are talking about demand *over a period of time* (not at a *point* in time). Thus we would talk about daily demand or weekly demand or annual demand or whatever.

The demand schedule can be represented graphically as a **demand curve**. Figure 4.2 shows the market demand curve for potatoes corresponding to the schedule in Table 4.1. The price of potatoes is plotted on the vertical axis. The quantity demanded is plotted on the horizontal axis.

Point *E* shows that at a price of 100p per kilo, 100 000 tonnes of potatoes are demanded each month. When the price falls to 80p we move down the curve to point *D*. This shows that the quantity demanded has now risen to 200 000 tonnes per month. Similarly, if price falls to 60p, we move down the curve again to point *C*: 350 000 tonnes are now demanded. The five points on the graph (*A–E*) correspond to the figures in columns (1) and (4) of Table 4.1. The graph also enables us to read off the likely quantities demanded at prices other than those in the table.

definition

Substitution effect
The effect of a change in price on quantity demanded arising from the consumer switching to or from alternative (substitute) products.

definition

Quantity demanded
The amount of a good that a consumer is willing and able to buy at a given price over a given period of time.

definition

Demand schedule for an individual
A table showing the different quantities of a good that a person is willing and able to buy at various prices over a given period of time.

definition

Market demand schedule
A table showing the different total quantities of a good that consumers are willing and able to buy at various prices over a given period of time.

Figure 4.2

Market demand curve for potatoes (monthly)

---

definition

Demand curve
A graph showing the relationship between the price of a good and the quantity of the good demanded over a given time period. Price is measured on the vertical axis; quantity demanded is measured on the horizontal axis. A demand curve can be for an individual consumer or a group of consumers, or more usually for the whole market.

definition

Substitute goods
A pair of goods which are considered by consumers to be alternatives to each other. As the price of one goes up, the demand for the other rises.

definition

Complementary goods
A pair of goods consumed together. As the price of one goes up, the demand for both goods will fall.

A demand curve could also be drawn for an individual consumer. Like market demand curves, individuals' demand curves generally slope downward from left to right: they have negative slope.

Two points should be noted at this stage:

- In textbooks, demand curves (and other curves too) are only occasionally used to plot specific data. More frequently they are used to illustrate general theoretical arguments. In such cases the axes will simply be price and quantity, with the units unspecified.

- The term 'curve' is used even when the graph is a straight line! In fact, when using demand curves to illustrate arguments we frequently draw them as straight lines – it's easier.

Other determinants of demand

Price is not the only factor that determines how much of a good people will buy. Demand is also affected by the following.

Tastes. The more desirable people find the good, the more they will demand. Tastes are affected by advertising, by fashion, by observing other consumers, by considerations of health and by the experiences from consuming the good on previous occasions.

The number and price of substitute goods (i.e. competitive goods). The higher the price of **substitute goods**, the higher will be the demand for this good as people switch from the substitutes. For example, the demand for coffee will depend on the price of tea. If tea goes up in price, the demand for coffee will rise.

The number and price of complementary goods. **Complementary goods** are those that are consumed together: cars and petrol, shoes and polish, bread and butter. The higher the price of complementary goods, the fewer of them will be bought and hence the less the demand for this good. For example, the demand for compact discs will depend on the price of CD players. If the price of CD players goes up, so that fewer are bought, the demand for CDs will fall.

Income. As people's incomes rise, their demand for most goods will rise. Such goods are called **normal goods**. There are exceptions to this general rule, however. As people get richer, they spend less on **inferior goods**, such as cheap margarine, and switch to better quality goods.

Distribution of income. If, for example, national income were redistributed from the poor to the rich, the demand for luxury goods would rise. At the same time, as the poor got poorer, they might have to turn to buying inferior goods, whose demand would also rise.

Expectations of future price changes. If people think that prices are going to rise in the future, they are likely to buy more now before the price does go up.

Key Idea 12 p94

To illustrate these six determinants let us look at the demand for butter.

- Tastes: if it is heavily advertised, demand is likely to rise. If, on the other hand, there is a cholesterol scare, people may demand less for health reasons.

- Substitutes: if the price of margarine goes up, the demand for butter is likely to rise as people switch from one to the other.

- Complements: if the price of bread goes up, people will buy less bread and hence less butter to spread on it.

- Income: if people's incomes rise, they may well turn to consuming butter rather than margarine.

- Income distribution: if income is redistributed away from the poor, they may have to give up consuming butter and buy cheaper margarine instead, or simply buy less butter and be more economical with the amount they use.

- Expectations: if it is announced in the news that butter prices are expected to rise in the near future, people are likely to buy more now and stock up their freezers while current prices last.

> **definition**
> **Normal goods**
> Goods whose demand rises as people's incomes rise.

> **definition**
> **Inferior goods**
> Goods whose demand falls as people's incomes rise.

> **Pause for thought**
> Do all these six determinants of demand affect both an individual's demand and the market demand for a product?

Movements along and shifts in the demand curve

A demand curve is constructed on the assumption that 'other things remain equal' (*ceteris paribus*). In other words, it is assumed that none of the determinants of demand, other than price, changes. The effect of a change in price is then simply illustrated by a movement along the demand curve: for example, from point B to point D in Figure 4.2 when price rises from 40p to 80p per kilo.

What happens, then, when one of these other determinants does change? The answer is that we have to construct a whole new demand curve: the curve shifts. If a change in one of the other determinants causes demand to rise – say, income rises – the whole curve will shift to the right. This shows that at each price more will be demanded than before. Thus in Figure 4.3 at a price of P, a quantity of Q_0 was originally demanded. But now, after the increase in demand, Q_1 is demanded. (Note that D_1 is not necessarily parallel to D_0.)

If a change in a determinant other than price causes demand to fall, the whole curve will shift to the left.

To distinguish between shifts in and movements along demand curves, it is usual to distinguish between a change in *demand* and a change in the *quantity demanded*. A shift in demand is referred to as a **change in demand**, whereas a movement along the demand curve as a result of a change in price is referred to as a **change in the quantity demanded**.

> **definition**
> **Change in demand**
> The term used for a shift in the demand curve. It occurs when a determinant of demand *other* than price changes.

> **definition**
> **Change in the quantity demanded**
> The term used for a movement along the demand curve to a new point. It occurs when there is a change in price.

Figure 4.3

An increase in demand

4.3 Supply

Supply and price

Imagine you are a farmer deciding what to do with your land. Part of your land is in a fertile valley. Part is on a hillside where the soil is poor. Perhaps, then, you will consider growing vegetables in the valley and keeping sheep on the hillside.

Your decision will depend to a large extent on the price that various vegetables will fetch in the market, and likewise the price you can expect to get from sheep and wool. As far as the valley is concerned, you will plant the vegetables that give the best return. If, for example, the price of potatoes is high, you will probably use a lot of the valley for growing potatoes. If the price gets higher, you may well use the whole of the valley, perhaps being prepared to run the risk of potato disease. If the price is very high indeed, you may even consider growing potatoes on the hillside, even though the yield per acre is much lower there. In other words, the higher the price of a particular crop, the more you are likely to grow in preference to other crops.

This illustrates the general relationship between supply and price: *when the price of a good rises, the quantity supplied will also rise.* There are three reasons for this:

- As firms supply more, they are likely to find that, beyond a certain level of output, costs rise more and more rapidly.

  In the case of the farm we have just considered, once potatoes have to be grown on the hillside, the costs of producing them will increase. Also if the land has to be used more intensively, say by the use of more and more fertilisers, again the cost of producing extra potatoes is likely to rise quite rapidly. It is the same for manufacturers. Beyond a certain level of output, costs are likely to rise rapidly as workers have to be paid overtime and as machines approach their full capacity. If higher output involves higher costs of production, producers will need to get a higher price if they are to be persuaded to produce extra output.

■ The higher the price of the good, the more profitable it becomes to produce. Firms will thus be encouraged to produce more of it by switching from producing less profitable goods.

■ Given time, if the price of a good remains high, new producers will be encouraged to set up in production. Total market supply thus rises.

The first two determinants affect supply in the short run. The third affects supply in the long run. We distinguish between short-run and long-run supply later, in section 5.4.

The supply curve

The amount that producers would like to supply at various prices can be shown in a **supply schedule**. Table 4.2 shows a monthly supply schedule for potatoes, both for an individual farmer (farmer X) and for all farmers together (the whole market).

The supply schedule can be represented graphically as a **supply curve**. A supply curve may be an individual firm's supply curve or a market supply curve (i.e. that of the whole industry).

Figure 4.4 shows the *market* supply curve of potatoes. As with demand curves, price is plotted on the vertical axis and quantity on the horizontal axis. Each of the points *a–e* correspond to a figure in Table 4.2. Thus for example, a

definition

Supply schedule
A table showing the different quantities of a good that producers are willing and able to supply at various prices over a given time period. A supply schedule can be for an individual producer or group of producers, or for all producers (the market supply schedule).

definition

Supply curve
A graph showing the relationship between the price of a good and the quantity of the good supplied over a given period of time.

Table 4.2   The supply of potatoes (monthly)

	Price of potatoes (pence per kg)	Farmer X's supply (tonnes)	Total market supply (tonnes: 000s)
a	20	50	100
b	40	70	200
c	60	100	350
d	80	120	530
e	100	130	700

Figure 4.4

Market supply curve of potatoes (monthly)

price rise from 60p per kilogram to 80p per kilogram will cause a movement along the supply curve from point *c* to point *d*: total market supply will rise from 350 000 tonnes per month to 530 000 tonnes per month.

Not all supply curves will be upward sloping (positively sloped). Sometimes they will be vertical, or horizontal, or even downward sloping. This will depend largely on the time period over which firms' response to price changes is considered. This question is examined in the next chapter (page 91).

This question is examined in the next chapter (page 91).

> **Pause for thought**
>
> 1 How much would be supplied at a price of 70p per kilo?
> 2 Draw a supply curve for farmer X. Are the axes drawn to the same scale as in Figure 4.4?

Other determinants of supply

Like demand, supply is not determined simply by price. The other determinants of supply are as follows.

The costs of production. The higher the costs of production, the less profit will be made at any price. As costs rise, firms will cut back on production, probably switching to alternative products whose costs have not risen so much.

The main reasons for a change in costs are as follows:

- Change in input prices: costs of production will rise if wages, raw material prices, rents, interest rates or any other input prices rise.
- Change in technology: technological advances can fundamentally alter the costs of production. Consider, for example, how the microchip revolution has changed production methods and information handling in virtually every industry in the world.
- Organisational changes: various cost savings can be made in many firms by reorganising production.
- Government policy: costs will be lowered by government subsidies and raised by various taxes.

> **definition**
>
> **Substitutes in supply**
> These are two goods where an increased production of one means diverting resources away from producing the other.

The profitability of alternative products (substitutes in supply). If some alternative product (**a substitute in supply**) becomes more profitable to supply than before, producers are likely to switch from the first good to this alternative. Supply of the first good falls. Other goods are likely to become more profitable if:

- their price rises;
- their cost of production falls.

For example, if the price of carrots goes up, or the cost of producing carrots comes down, farmers may decide to produce more carrots. The supply of potatoes is therefore likely to fall.

> **definition**
>
> **Goods in joint supply**
> These are two goods where the production of more of one leads to the production of more of the other.

The profitability of goods in joint supply. Sometimes when one good is produced, another good is also produced at the same time. These are said to be **goods in joint supply**. An example is the refining of crude oil to produce petrol. Other grade fuels will be produced as well, such as diesel and paraffin. If more petrol is produced, due to a rise in demand, then the supply of these other fuels will rise too.

Nature, 'random shocks' and other unpredictable events. In this category we would include the weather and diseases affecting farm output, wars affecting the supply of imported raw materials, the breakdown of machinery, industrial disputes, earthquakes, floods and fire, etc.

The aims of producers. A profit-maximising firm will supply a different quantity from a firm that has a different aim, such as maximising sales.

Expectations of future price changes. If price is expected to rise, producers may temporarily reduce the amount they sell. Instead they are likely to build up their stocks and only release them on to the market when the price does rise. At the same time they may plan to produce more, by installing new machines, or taking on more labour, so that they can be ready to supply more when the price has risen.

To illustrate some of these determinants, let us consider the example of butter. What would cause the supply of butter to rise?

■ A reduction in the costs of producing butter. This could be caused, say, by a reduction in the price of nitrogen fertiliser. This would encourage farmers to use more fertiliser, which would increase grass yields, which in turn would increase milk yields per acre. Alternatively, new technology may allow more efficient churning of butter. Or again, the government may decide to give subsidies to farmers to produce more butter.

■ A reduction in the profitability of producing cream or cheese. If these products become less profitable, due say to a reduction in their price, due in turn to a reduction in consumer demand, more butter is likely to be produced instead.

■ An increase in the profitability of skimmed milk. If consumers buy more skimmed milk, then an increased supply of skimmed milk is likely to lead to an increase in the supply of butter and other cream products, since they are jointly produced with skimmed milk.

■ If weather conditions are favourable, grass yields and hence milk yields are likely to be high. This will increase the supply of butter and other milk products.

■ If butter producers expect butter prices to rise in the future, they may well decide to release less on to the market now and put more into frozen storage until the price does rise.

Movements along and shifts in the supply curve

The principle here is the same as with demand curves. The effect of a change in price is illustrated by a movement along the supply curve: for example, from point *d* to point *e* in Figure 4.4 when price rises from 80p to 100p. Quantity supplied rises from 530 000 to 700 000 tonnes.

If any other determinant of supply changes, the whole supply curve will shift. A rightward shift illustrates an increase in supply. A leftward shift illustrates a decrease in supply. Thus in Figure 4.5, if the original curve is S_0, the curve S_1 represents an increase in supply, whereas the curve S_2 represents a decrease in supply.

A movement along a supply curve is often referred to as a **change in the quantity supplied**, whereas a shift in the supply curve is simply referred to as a **change in supply**.

definition

Change in the quantity supplied
The term used for a movement along the supply curve to a new point. It occurs when there is a change in price.

definition

Change in supply
The term used for a shift in the supply curve. It occurs when a determinant other than price changes.

Figure 4.5

Shifts in the supply curve

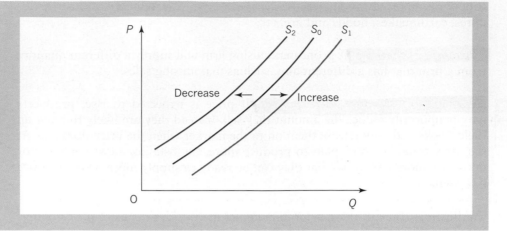

4.4 Price and output determination

Equilibrium price and output

We can now combine our analysis of demand and supply. This will show how the actual price of a product and the actual quantity bought and sold are determined in a free and competitive market.

Let us return to the example of the market demand and market supply of potatoes, and use the data from Tables 4.1 and 4.2. These figures are given again in Table 4.3.

What will be the price and output that actually prevail? If the price started at 20p per kilogram, demand would exceed supply by 600 000 tonnes ($A - a$). Consumers would be unable to obtain all they wanted and would thus be willing to pay a higher price. Producers, unable or unwilling to supply enough to meet the demand, will be only too happy to accept a higher price. The effect of the shortage, then, will be to drive up the price. The same would happen at a price of 40p per kilogram. There would still be a shortage; price would still rise. But as the price rises, the quantity demanded falls and the quantity supplied rises. The shortage is progressively eliminated.

What would happen if the price started at a much higher level: say at 100p per kilogram? In this case supply would exceed demand by 600 000 tonnes ($e - E$).

Table 4.3 **The market demand and supply of potatoes (monthly)**

Price of potatoes (pence per kg)	Total market demand (tonnes: 000s)	Total market supply (tonnes: 000s)
20	700 (A)	100 (a)
40	500 (B)	200 (b)
60	350 (C)	350 (c)
80	200 (D)	530 (d)
100	100 (E)	700 (e)

The effect of this surplus would be to drive the price down as farmers competed against each other to sell their excess supplies. The same would happen at a price of 80p per kilogram. There would still be a surplus; price would still fall.

In fact, only one price is sustainable. This is the price where demand equals supply: namely 60p per kilogram, where both demand and supply are 350 000 tonnes. When supply matches demand the market is said to **clear**. There is no shortage and no surplus.

This price, where demand equals supply, is called the **equilibrium price**. By **equilibrium** we mean a point of balance or a point of rest: in other words, a point towards which there is a tendency to move. The equilibrium price is the only price at which producers' and consumers' wishes are mutually reconciled: where the producers' plans to supply exactly match the consumers' plans to buy.

> *Equilibrium is the point where conflicting interests are balanced.* Only at this point is the amount that demanders are willing to purchase the same as the amount that suppliers are willing to supply. It is a point which will be automatically reached in a free market through the operation of the price mechanism.
>
> **Key Idea 10**

definition
Market clearing
A market clears when supply matches demand, leaving no shortage or surplus.

definition
Equilibrium price
The price where the quantity demanded equals the quantity supplied: the price where there is no shortage or surplus.

definition
Equilibrium
A position of balance. A position from which there is no inherent tendency to move away.

Demand and supply curves

The determination of equilibrium price and output can be shown using demand and supply curves. Equilibrium is where the two curves intersect.

Figure 4.6 shows the demand and supply curves of potatoes corresponding to the data in Table 4.3. Equilibrium price is P_e (60p) and equilibrium quantity is Q_e (350 000 tonnes).

At any price above 60p, there would be a surplus. Thus at 80p there is a surplus of 330 000 tonnes ($d - D$). More is supplied than consumers are willing and able to purchase at that price. Thus a price of 80p fails to clear the market. Price will fall to the equilibrium price of 60p. As it does so, there will be a movement along the demand curve from point D to point C, and a movement along the supply curve from point d to point c.

At any price below 60p, there would be a shortage. Thus at 40p there is a shortage of 300 000 tonnes ($B - b$). Price will rise to 60p. This will cause a

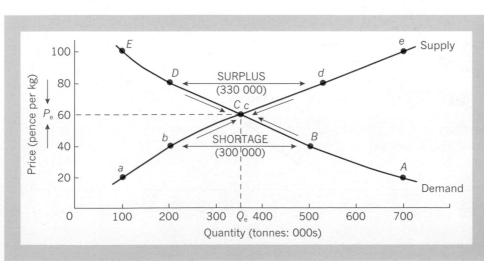

Figure 4.6

The determination of market equilibrium (potatoes: monthly)

BOX 4.1

UK house prices
The ups and downs of the housing market

If you are thinking of buying a house sometime in the future, then you may well follow the fortunes of the housing market with some trepidation. In the late 1980s there was a housing price explosion in the UK: in fact, between 1984 and 1989 house prices *doubled*. After several years of falling or gently rising house prices in the early and mid-1990s, there was another boom from 1996 to 2003, with house prices rising by 26 per cent per year at the peak (in the 12 months to January 2003). For many, owning a home of their own was becoming a mere dream.

House prices since the early 1980s

The diagram shows what happened to house prices in the period 1983 to 2003. There was rapid house price inflation up to 1989. It reached a peak in 1988, when average house prices rose by 23.3 per cent in that one year alone.

In their rush to buy a house before prices rose any further, many people in this period borrowed as much as they were able. Building societies and banks at that time had plenty of money to lend and were only too willing to do so. Many people, therefore, took out very large mortgages. In 1983 the average new mortgage was 2.08 times average annual earnings. By 1989 this figure had risen to 3.44.

After 1989 there followed a period of *falling* prices. From 1990 to 1995, house prices fell by 12.2 per cent. As a result of this, many people found themselves in a position of *negative equity*. This is the situation where the size of their mortgage is greater than the value of their house. In other words, if they sold their house, they would end up still owing money! For this reason many people found that they could not move house.

Then in 1996, house prices began to recover and for the next three years rose moderately – by around 5 per cent per annum. But then they started rising rapidly again, and by 2002, house price inflation had returned to rates similar to those in the 1980s. Was this good news or bad news? For those trapped in negative equity, it was good news. It was good news also for old people who wished to move into a retirement home and who had a house to sell. It was bad news, however, for the first-time buyer! As we shall see in many parts of this book, what is good news for one person is often bad news for another.

The determinants of house prices

House prices are determined by demand and supply. If demand rises (i.e. shifts to the right) or if supply falls (i.e. shifts to the left), the equilibrium price of houses will rise. Similarly, if demand falls or supply rises, the equilibrium price will fall.

So why did house prices rise so rapidly in the 1980s, only to fall in the early 1990s and then rise rapidly again in the late 1990s and early 2000s? The answer lies primarily in changes in the *demand* for

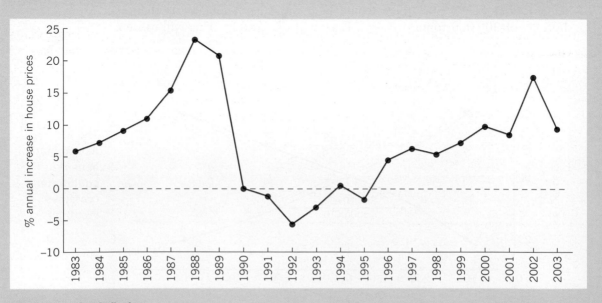

UK house price inflation

housing. Let us examine the various factors that affected the demand for houses.

Incomes (actual and anticipated). The second half of the 1980s was a period of rapidly rising incomes. The economy was experiencing an economic 'boom'. Many people wanted to spend their extra incomes on housing: either buying a house for the first time, or moving to a better one. What is more, many people thought that their incomes would continue to grow, and were thus prepared to stretch themselves financially in the short term by buying an expensive house, confident that their mortgage payments would become more and more affordable over time.

The early 1990s, by contrast, was a period of recession, with rising unemployment and much more slowly growing incomes. People had much less confidence about their ability to afford large mortgages.

The desire for home ownership. The prime minister in the 1980s, Mrs Thatcher, put great emphasis on the virtues of home ownership: her vision was one of a home-owning democracy. Certainly, the mood of the age was very much that it was desirable to own one's home. This fuelled the growth in demand.

The cost of mortgages. During the second half of the 1980s, mortgage interest rates were generally falling. This meant that people could afford larger mortgages, and thus afford to buy more expensive houses. In 1989, however, this trend was reversed. Mortgage interest rates were now rising. Many people found it difficult to maintain existing payments, let alone to take on a larger mortgage. From 1996 to 2003 mortgage rates were generally reduced again, once more fuelling the demand for houses.

The availability of mortgages. In the late 1980s, mortgages were readily available. Banks and building societies were prepared to accept smaller deposits on houses, and to grant mortgages of $3^1/_2$ times a person's annual income, compared with $2^1/_2$ times in the early 1980s. In the early 1990s, however, banks and building societies were more cautious about granting mortgages. They were aware that, with falling house prices, rising unemployment and the growing problem of negative equity, there was a growing danger that borrowers would default on payments. With the recovery of the economy in the mid-1990s, however, and with a growing number of mortgage

lenders, mortgages became more readily available and for greater amounts relative to people's income.

Speculation. In the 1980s, people generally believed that house prices would continue rising. This encouraged people to buy as soon as possible, and to take out the biggest mortgage possible, before prices went up any further. There was also an effect on supply. Those with houses to sell held back until the last possible moment in the hope of getting a higher price. The net effect was for a rightward shift in the demand curve for houses and a leftward shift in the supply curve. The effect of this speculation, therefore, was to help bring about the very effect that people were predicting (see section 5.4).

In the early 1990s, the opposite occurred. People thinking of buying houses held back, hoping to buy at a lower price. People with houses to sell tried to sell as quickly as possible before prices fell any further. Again the effect of this speculation was to aggravate the change in prices – this time a fall in prices.

Then, in the late 1990s, the return of rapidly rising prices encouraged people to buy more rapidly again, once more adding fuel to house price inflation. The speculation was compounded by worries about falling stock market prices. Many investors turned to buying property instead of shares.

What of the future?

By mid 2003, the boom in house prices seemed to be coming to an end. With growing economic uncertainty, people were becoming increasingly worried about taking on large mortgage debt. And with house price inflation slowing down, speculation could go into reverse. It seemed unlikely that there would be a house price crash, however, with interest rates only edging higher.

Questions

1 *Draw supply and demand diagrams to illustrate what was happening to house prices (a) in the second half of the 1980s and the late 1990s and early 2000s; (b) in the early 1990s.*

2 *Are there any factors on the supply side that contribute to changes in house prices? If so, what are they?*

3 *Find out what has happened to house prices over the past three years. Attempt an explanation of what has happened.*

BOX 4.2

The heyday of the auction
A revolution in the working of the price mechanism?

An example of supply and demand in action is the 'Internet auction'. This is similar to a regular auction, where people bid for items put up for sale, and the highest bidder wins. The price is that bid by the highest bidder. With an Internet auction, the bidding is online.

> The Internet provides a perfect medium for aggregating buyers and sellers from all around the world. If you are a collector of beanie babies, in the physical world you would have to spend a lot of time and effort to draw together all your fellow enthusiasts; online you can do it effortlessly. The second is that the Internet offers an excellent way of comparing prices and collecting information, for example on new products, or on recent bids. Once again, to replicate this offline would be costly and time-consuming.[1]

Economists have long recognised the virtues of auctions. In 1880, Léon Walras, a French economist, described the entire price mechanism as an auctioneer. The 'Walrasian auctioneer' would call out a price, see how many buyers and sellers there were and, if these did not balance, adjust the price until demand equalled supply.

But in practice, for most of human history, auctions have not played a starring role in the price-setting process. Mostly they have been limited to agricultural and other commodity markets, fine art and antiques, and – of increasing importance in recent decades – some types of financial securities.

Two other forms of price-setting have been dominant: one-to-one negotiation (haggling); and the non-negotiable menu of prices offered by seller to buyer. These two approaches are not bad: the price mechanism based on them obviously does a much better job of allocating scarce resources than do centrally planned systems that eschew prices altogether.

But each method has important flaws. When there is a menu, the most that people will reveal about their demand for a given product is whether or not they are willing to buy at the listed price. So unless the seller has, from other sources, an intimate knowledge of supply and demand conditions, the price he sets may have highly inefficient consequences. Moreover, menu prices can be 'sticky' – slow to adjust to changes in the balance of supply and demand.

One-to-one haggling has the advantages of interaction and dialogue, which improve the chances of reaching a mutually beneficial outcome. But it also carries a big risk: that the seller or buyer may not be negotiating with the best person (i.e. the one willing to pay the most, or sell for least).

Auctions can overcome these shortcomings by soliciting a wide range of bids from many people.

---

movement along the supply curve from point *b* to point *c* and along the demand curve from point *B* to point *C*.

Point *Cc* is the equilibrium: where demand equals supply.

Movement to a new equilibrium

The equilibrium price will remain unchanged only so long as the demand and supply curves remain unchanged. If either of the curves shifts, a new equilibrium will be formed.

A change in demand

If one of the determinants of demand changes (other than price), the whole demand curve will shift. This will lead to a movement *along* the *supply* curve to the new intersection point.

And the Internet, thanks to its cheap interconnection of millions of people, makes well-functioning auctions far easier. They are now possible for many goods and services that used to rely on haggling or menus. And even in markets where auctions have long been used to set prices, the Internet can make them much more sophisticated than ever before.

The largest online marketplace is eBay, which has tens of millions of users. Typically, on any day, more than 12 million items are listed across 18 000 categories. In 2002, the value of sales on eBay was $14.87 bn.

> The power of auction sites, says eBay's Pierre Omidyar, lies in their strong 'network effects': the more people that use them, the more useful they are. That also confers a potentially bigger first-mover advantage on auction sites than on electronic retailers – an advantage eBay is so bent on preserving that it has triggered antitrust inquiries into its efforts to stop rivals logging into its site for price and bidding data.[1]

Steve Kaplan, an economist at the University of Chicago, points out that online auctions have a big economic advantage over traditional online menu-priced sites, such as that pioneered by Amazon. Such sites cut out the cost of going to the shops, and make it cheaper to compare prices with other retailers. But Amazon's customers are no better off if it attracts more users. Whereas the more buyers and sellers turn up on eBay, the better their chances of getting a good deal, as the auction becomes deeper and more liquid.

...Needless to say, fixed prices are not going to disappear. Taking part in online auctions is time-consuming (and nerve-wracking). Economic theory suggests they are most useful in particular circumstances: when there is uncertainty about what is the right price. This could be for one of two reasons. Either the value of a product is a matter of private taste and opinion – such as a Van Gogh painting or a rare Spice Girls doll. Or the value is likely to be similar for everyone, but it is not obvious to the seller what it is – such as a rail-operating franchise or a radio-bandwidth licence.[2]

Questions

1 *What are the advantages of online auctions to (a) purchasers; (b) sellers?*

2 *In what ways do firms using traditional 'menu-based' pricing respond to an increase in demand for their product?*

---

[1] In the great web bazaar, *The Economist*, 24 February 2000
[2] The heyday of the auction, *The Economist*, 24 July 1999

For example, in Figure 4.7, if a rise in consumer incomes led to the demand curve shifting to D_2, there would be a shortage of $h - g$ at the original price P_{e_1}. This would cause price to rise to the new equilibrium P_{e_2}. As it did so there would be a movement along the supply curve from point g to point i, and along the new demand curve (D_2) from point h to point i. Equilibrium quantity would rise from Q_{e_1} to Q_{e_2}.

The effect of the shift in demand, therefore, has been a movement *along* the supply curve from the old equilibrium to the new: from point g to point i.

> **Pause for thought**
>
> *What would happen to price and quantity if the demand curve shifted to the left? Draw a diagram to illustrate your answer.*

A change in supply

Likewise, if one of the determinants of supply changes (other than price), the whole supply curve will shift. This will lead to a movement *along* the *demand* curve to the new intersection point.

Figure 4.7

The effect of a shift in the demand curve

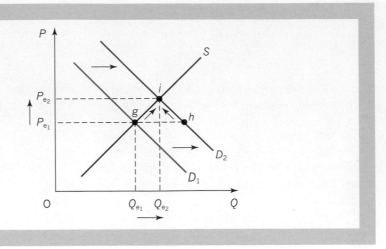

Figure 4.8

The effect of a shift in the supply curve

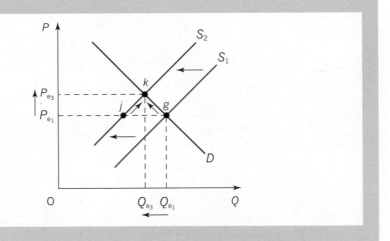

For example, in Figure 4.8, if costs of production rose, the supply curve would shift to the left: to S_2. There would be a shortage of $g - j$ at the old price of P_{e_1}. Price would rise from P_{e_1} to P_{e_3}. Quantity would fall from Q_{e_1} to Q_{e_3}. In other words, there would be a movement along the demand curve from point g to point k, and along the new supply curve (S_2) from point j to point k.

To summarise: a shift in one curve leads to a movement along the other curve to the new intersection point.

Sometimes a number of determinants might change. This may lead to a shift in *both* curves. When this happens, equilibrium simply moves from the point where the old curves intersected to the point where the new ones intersect.

Key Idea

10
p73

SUMMARY

1a A firm is greatly affected by its market environment. The more competitive the market, the less discretion the firm has in determining its price. In the extreme case of a perfect market, the price is entirely outside the firm's control. The price is determined by demand and supply in the market, and the firm has to accept this price: the firm is a price taker.

1b In a perfect market, price changes act as the mechanism whereby demand and supply are balanced. If there is a shortage, price will rise until the shortage is eliminated. If there is a surplus, price will fall until that is eliminated.

2a When the price of a good rises, the quantity demanded per period of time will fall. This is known as the 'law of demand'. It applies both to individuals' demand and to the whole market demand.

2b The law of demand is explained by the income and substitution effects of a price change.

2c The relationship between price and quantity demanded per period of time can be shown in a table (or 'schedule') or as a graph. On the graph, price is plotted on the vertical axis and quantity demanded per period of time on the horizontal axis. The resulting demand curve is downward sloping (negatively sloped).

2d Other determinants of demand include tastes, the number and price of substitute goods, the number and price of complementary goods, income, the distribution of income and expectations of future price changes.

2e If price changes, the effect is shown by a movement along the demand curve. We call this effect 'a change in the quantity demanded'.

2f If any other determinant of demand changes, the whole curve will shift. We call this effect 'a change in demand'. A rightward shift represents an increase in demand; a leftward shift represents a decrease in demand.

3a When the price of a good rises, the quantity supplied per period of time will usually also rise. This applies both to individual producers' supply and to the whole market supply.

3b There are two reasons in the short run why a higher price encourages producers to supply more: (a) they are now willing to incur higher costs per unit associated with producing more; (b) they will switch to producing this product and away from now less profitable ones. In the long run there is a third reason: new producers will be attracted into the market.

3c The relationship between price and quantity supplied per period of time can be shown in a table (or schedule) or as a graph. As with a demand curve, price is plotted on the vertical axis and quantity per period of time on the horizontal axis. The resulting supply curve is upward sloping (positively sloped).

3d Other determinants of supply include the costs of production, the profitability of alternative products, the profitability of goods in joint supply, random shocks and expectations of future price changes.

3e If price changes, the effect is shown by a movement along the supply curve. We call this effect 'a change in the quantity supplied'.

3f If any determinant *other* than price changes, the effect is shown by a shift in the whole supply curve. We call this effect 'a change in supply'. A rightward shift represents an increase in supply; a leftward shift represents a decrease in supply.

4a If the demand for a good exceeds the supply, there will be a shortage. This will lead to a rise in the price of the good.

4b If the supply of a good exceeds the demand, there will be a surplus. This will lead to a fall in the price.

4c Price will settle at the equilibrium. The equilibrium price is the one that clears the market: the price where demand equals supply. This is shown in a demand and supply diagram by the point where the two curves intersect.

4d If the demand or supply curves shift, this will lead either to a shortage or to a surplus. Price will therefore either rise or fall until a new equilibrium is reached at the position where the supply and demand curves *now* intersect.

REVIEW QUESTIONS

1 Using a diagram like Figure 4.1, summarise the effect of (a) a reduction in the demand for a good; (b) a reduction in the costs of production of a good.

2 Referring to Table 4.1, assume that there are 200 consumers in the market. Of these, 100 have schedules like Tracey's and 100 have schedules like Darren's. What would be the total market demand schedule for potatoes now?

3 Again referring to Table 4.1, draw Tracey's and Darren's demand curves for potatoes on one diagram. (Note that you will use the same vertical scale as in Figure 4.2, but you will need a quite different horizontal scale.) At what price is their demand the same? What explanations could there be for the quite different shapes of their two demand curves? (This question is explored in the next chapter.)

4 The price of pork rises and yet it is observed that the sales of pork increase. Does this mean that the demand curve for pork is upward sloping? Explain.

5 Refer to the list of determinants of supply (see pages 70–71). For what reasons might (a) the supply of potatoes fall; (b) the supply of leather rise?

6 This question is concerned with the supply of oil for central heating. In each case consider whether there is a movement along the supply curve (and in which direction) or a shift in it (and whether left or right): (a) new oil fields start up in production; (b) the demand for central heating rises; (c) the price of gas falls; (d) oil companies anticipate an upsurge in the demand for central-heating oil; (e) the demand for petrol rises; (f) new technology decreases the costs of oil refining; (g) all oil products become more expensive.

7 The price of cod is much higher today than it was 20 years ago. Using demand and supply diagrams, explain why this should be so.

8 The number of owners of compact disc players has grown rapidly and hence the demand for compact discs has also grown rapidly. Yet the price of CDs has fallen. Why? Use a supply and demand diagram to illustrate your answer.

9 What will happen to the equilibrium price and quantity of butter in each of the following cases? You should state whether demand or supply or both have shifted and in which direction: (a) a rise in the price of margarine; (b) a rise in the demand for yoghurt; (c) a rise in the price of bread; (d) a rise in the demand for bread; (e) an expected increase in the price of butter in the near future; (f) a tax on butter production; (g) the invention of a new, but expensive, process of removing all cholesterol from butter, plus the passing of a law which states that butter producers must use this process. In each case assume *ceteris paribus*.

10 If both demand and supply change, and if we know in which direction they have shifted but not by how much, why is it that we will be able to predict the direction in which *either* price or quantity will change, but not both? (Clue: consider the four possible combinations and sketch them if necessary: *D* left, *S* left; *D* right, *S* right; *D* left, *S* right; *D* right, *S* left.)

5 Business in a market environment

In Chapter 4 we examined how prices are determined in perfectly competitive markets: by the interaction of market demand and market supply. In such markets, although the *market* demand curve is downward sloping, the demand curve faced by the individual firm will be horizontal. This is illustrated in Figure 5.1.

The market price is P_m. The individual firm can sell as much as it likes at this market price: it is too small to have any influence on the market – it is a price taker. It will not force the price down by producing more because, in terms of the total market, this extra would be an infinitesimally small amount. If a farmer doubled the output of wheat sent to the market, it would be too small an increase to affect the world price of wheat!

In practice, however, many firms are not price takers; they have some discretion in choosing their price. Such firms will face a downward-sloping demand curve. If they raise their price, they will sell less; if they lower their price, they will sell more. But firms will want to know more than this. They will want to know just *how much* the quantity demanded will fall. In other words, they will want to know how *responsive* demand is to a rise in price. This responsiveness is measured using a concept called 'elasticity'.

> **Elasticity.** The responsiveness of one variable (e.g. demand) to a change in another (e.g. price). This concept is fundamental to understanding how markets work. The more elastic variables are, the more responsive is the market to changing circumstances.
>
> **Key Idea 11**

5.1 Price elasticity of demand

The responsiveness of quantity demanded to a change in price

The demand for an individual firm

For any firm considering changing its price, it is vital to know the likely effect on the quantity demanded. Take the case of two firms facing very different demand curves. These are shown in Figure 5.2.

Firm A can raise its price quite substantially – from £6 to £10 – and yet its level of sales only falls by a relatively small amount – from 100 units to 90 units. This firm will probably be quite keen to raise its price. After all, it could make

Figure 5.1

Market demand
curve for an
individual firm
under conditions
of perfect
competition

Figure 5.2

The demand for
an individual
firm's product

(a) Firm A   (b) Firm B

significantly more profits on each unit sold (assuming no rise in costs per unit), and yet only sell slightly fewer units.

Firm B, however, will think twice about raising its price. Even a relatively modest increase in price – from £6 to £7 – will lead to a substantial fall in sales from 100 units to 40 units. What is the point of making a bit more profit on those units it manages to sell, if in the process it ends up selling a lot fewer units? In such circumstances the firm may contemplate lowering its price.

The responsiveness of market demand

Economists too will want to know how responsive demand is to a change in price: except in this case it is the responsiveness of *market* demand that is being considered. This information is necessary to enable them to predict the effects of a shift in supply on the market price of a product.

Figure 5.3 shows the effect of a shift in supply with two quite different demand curves (D and D'). Assume that initially the supply curve is S_1, and that it intersects with both demand curves at point a, at a price of P_1 and a quantity of Q_1. Now supply shifts to S_2. What will happen to price and quantity? Economists will want to know! The answer is that it depends on the shape of the demand curve. In the case of demand curve D, there is a relatively large rise in price (to P_2) and a relatively small fall in quantity (to Q_2): equilibrium is at point b. In the case of demand curve D', however, there is only a relatively small rise in price (to P_3), but a relatively large fall in quantity (to Q_3): equilibrium is at point c.

**Key
Idea
9
p63**

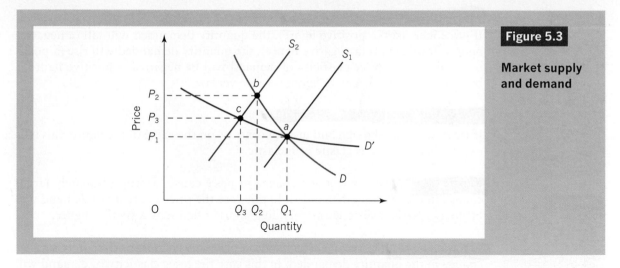

Figure 5.3

**Market supply
and demand**

Given the importance of knowing the responsiveness of demand to a change in price, we will need some way of measuring this responsiveness. *Elasticity* is the measure we use.

Defining price elasticity of demand

What we will want to compare is the size of the change in quantity demanded of a given product with the size of the change in price. Price elasticity of demand does just this. It is defined as follows:

$$P\epsilon_D = \frac{\text{Proportionate (or percentage) change in quantity demanded}}{\text{Proportionate (or percentage) change in price}}$$

> **definition**
>
> **Price elasticity of demand**
> A measure of the responsiveness of quantity demanded to a change in price.

If, for example, a 20 per cent rise in the price of a product causes a 10 per cent fall in the quantity demanded, the price elasticity of demand will be:

$$-10\%/20\% = -0.5$$

Three things should be noted at this stage about the figure that is calculated for elasticity.

The use of proportionate or percentage measures

Elasticity is measured in proportionate or percentage terms for the following reasons:

■ It allows comparison of changes in two qualitatively different things, which are thus measured in two different types of unit: i.e. it allows comparison of quantity changes (quantity demanded) with monetary changes (price).

■ It is the only sensible way of deciding *how big* a change in price or quantity is. Take a simple example. An item goes up in price by £1. Is this a big increase or a small increase? We can answer this only if we know what the original price was. If a can of beans goes up in price by £1, that is a huge price increase. If, however, the price of a house goes up by £1, that is a tiny price increase. In other words, it is the percentage or proportionate increase in price that we look at in deciding how big a price rise it is.

definition

Elastic
If demand is (price) elastic, then any change in price will cause the quantity demanded to change proportionately more. (Ignoring the negative sign) it will have a value greater than 1.

definition

Inelastic
If demand is (price) inelastic, then any change will cause the quantity demanded to change by a proportionately smaller amount. (Ignoring the negative sign) it will have a value less than 1.

definition

Unit elasticity
When the price elasticity of demand is unity, this is where quantity demanded changes by the same proportion as the price. Price elasticity is equal to –1.

The sign (positive or negative)

If price increases (a positive figure), the quantity demanded will fall (a negative figure). If price falls (a negative figure), the quantity demanded will rise (a positive figure). Thus price elasticity of demand will be negative: a positive figure is being divided by a negative figure (or vice versa).

The value (greater or less than 1)

If we now ignore the sign and just concentrate on the value of the figure, this tells us whether demand is **elastic** or **inelastic**.

Elastic ($\epsilon > 1$). This is where a change in price causes a proportionately larger change in the quantity demanded. In this case the price elasticity of demand will be greater than 1, since we are dividing a larger figure by a smaller figure.

Inelastic ($\epsilon < 1$). This is where a change in price causes a proportionately smaller change in the quantity demanded. In this case the price elasticity of demand will be less than 1, since we are dividing a smaller figure by a larger figure.

Unit elastic ($\epsilon = 1$). **Unit elasticity** is where the quantity demanded changes proportionately the same as price. This will give an elasticity equal to 1, since we are dividing a figure by itself.

The determinants of price elasticity of demand

The price elasticity of demand varies enormously from one product to another. But why do some products have a highly elastic demand, whereas others have a highly *in*elastic demand? What determines price elasticity of demand?

The number and closeness of substitute goods

This is the most important determinant. The more substitutes there are for a good, and the closer they are, the greater will be the price elasticity of demand. The reason is that people will be able to switch to the substitutes when the price of the good rises. The more numerous the substitutes and the closer they are, the more people will switch: in other words, the bigger will be the substitution effect of a price rise.

For example, the price elasticity of demand for a particular brand of a product will probably be fairly high, especially if there are many other, similar brands. If its price goes up, people can simply switch to another brand: there is a large substitution effect. By contrast the demand for a product in general will normally be pretty inelastic. If the price of food in general goes up, demand for food will fall only slightly. People will buy a little less, since they cannot now afford so much: this is the *income* effect of the price rise. But there is no alternative to food that can satisfy our hunger: there is therefore virtually no *substitution* effect.

The proportion of income spent on the good

The higher the proportion of our income we spend on a good, the more we will be forced to cut consumption when its price rises: the bigger will be the income effect and the more elastic will be the demand.

Thus salt has a very low price elasticity of demand. This is because we spend such a tiny fraction of our income on salt that we would find little difficulty in paying a relatively large percentage increase in its price: the income effect of a price rise would be very small. By contrast, there will be a much bigger income effect when a major item of expenditure rises in price. For example, if mortgage interest rates rise (the 'price' of loans for house purchase), people may have to cut down substantially on their demand for housing – being forced to buy somewhere much smaller and cheaper, or to live in rented accommodation.

> **Pause for thought**
>
> *Think of two products and estimate which is likely to have the higher price elasticity of demand. Explain your answer.*

The time period

When price rises, people may take a time to adjust their consumption patterns and find alternatives. The longer the time period after a price change, then, the more elastic is the demand likely to be.

The importance of price elasticity of demand to business decision making   5.2

A firm's sales revenue

Key Idea 7 p50

One of the most important applications of price elasticity of demand concerns its relationship with a firm's sales revenue. The **total sales revenue (TR)** of a firm is simply price times quantity:

> **definition**
>
> **Total (sales) revenue (TR)**
> The amount a firm earns from its sales of a product at a particular price. $TR = P \times Q$. Note that we are referring to *gross* revenue: that is, revenue before the deduction of taxes or any other costs.

$$TR = P \times Q$$

For example, 3000 units (Q) sold at £2 per unit (P) will earn the firm £6000 (TR). This is shown graphically in Figure 5.4 as the area of the shaded rectangle. But why? The area of a rectangle is simply its height multiplied by its length. But TR is simply price (the height of the shaded rectangle) multiplied by quantity (the length of the rectangle).

Key Idea 11 p81

Let us assume that a firm wants to increase its total revenue. What should it do? Should it raise its price or lower it? The answer depends on the price elasticity of demand.

Figure 5.4

Total revenue

Figure 5.5

Elastic demand between two points

Elastic demand and sales revenue

As price rises, so quantity demanded falls, and vice versa. When demand is elastic, quantity changes proportionately more than price. Thus the change in quantity has a bigger effect on total revenue than does the change in price. This can be summarised as follows:

P rises; *Q* falls proportionately more; therefore *TR* falls.

P falls; *Q* rises proportionately more; therefore *TR* rises.

In other words, total revenue changes in the same direction as *quantity*.

Pause for thought

If a firm faces an elastic demand curve, why will it not necessarily be in the firm's interests to produce more? (Clue: you will need to distinguish between revenue and profit. We will explore this relationship in the next chapter.)

This is illustrated in Figure 5.5. Demand is elastic between points *a* and *b*. A rise in price from £4 to £5 causes a proportionately larger fall in quantity demanded: from 20 to 10. Total revenue *falls* from £80 (the striped area) to £50 (the shaded area).

When demand is elastic, then, a rise in price will causes a fall in total revenue. If a firm wants to increase its revenue, it should *lower* its price.

Inelastic demand and sales revenue

When demand is inelastic, it is the other way around. Price changes proportionately more than quantity. Thus the change in price has a bigger effect on total revenue than does the change in quantity. To summarise the effects:

P rises; *Q* falls proportionately less; *TR* rises.

P falls; *Q* rises proportionately less; *TR* falls.

In other words, total revenue changes in the same direction as *price*.

This is illustrated in Figure 5.6. Demand is inelastic between points *a* and *c*. A rise in price from £4 to £8 causes a proportionately smaller fall in quantity demanded: from 20 to 15. Total revenue *rises* from £80 (the striped area) to £120 (the shaded area).

If a firm wants to increase its revenue in this case, therefore, it should *raise* its price.

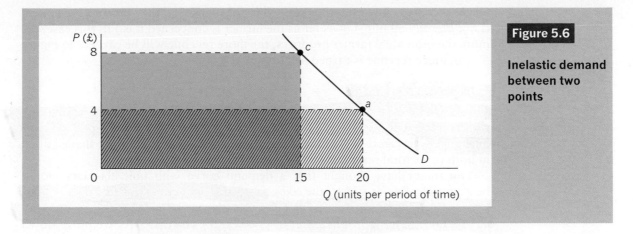

Figure 5.6

Inelastic demand between two points

Figure 5.7 (a) Totally inelastic demand ($P\epsilon_D = 0$); (b) Infinitely elastic demand ($P\epsilon_D = \infty$); (c) Unit elastic demand ($P\epsilon_D = -1$)

Special cases

Figure 5.7 shows three special cases: (a) a totally inelastic demand ($P\epsilon_D = 0$), (b) an infinitely elastic demand ($P\epsilon_D = \infty$) and (c) a unit elastic demand ($P\epsilon_D = -1$).

Totally inelastic demand

This is shown by a vertical straight line. No matter what happens to price, quantity demanded remains the same. It is obvious that the more the price is raised, the bigger will be the revenue. Thus in Figure 5.7(a), P_2 will earn a bigger revenue than P_1.

Infinitely elastic demand

This is shown by a horizontal straight line. At any price above P_1 demand is zero. But at P_1 (or any price below) demand is 'infinitely' large.

This seemingly unlikely demand curve is in fact relatively common. Many firms that are very small (like the small-scale grain farmer) are price takers. They have to accept the price as given by supply and demand in the *whole market*. If individual farmers were to try to sell above this price, they would sell nothing at all. At this price, however, they can sell to the market all they produce. (Demand is not *literally* infinite, but as far as the farmer is concerned it is.) In this case, the more the individual farmer produces, the more revenue will be earned. In Figure 5.7(b), more revenue is earned at Q_2 than at Q_1.

Unit elastic demand

This is where price and quantity change in exactly the same proportion. Any rise in price will be exactly offset by a fall in quantity, leaving total revenue unchanged. In Figure 5.7(c), the striped area is exactly equal to the shaded area: in both cases total revenue is £800.

You might have thought that a demand curve with unit elasticity would be a straight line at 45° to the axes. Instead it is a curve called a *rectangular hyperbola*. The reason for its shape is that the proportionate *rise* in quantity must equal the proportionate *fall* in price (and vice versa). As we move down the demand curve, in order for the *proportionate* (or percentage) change in both price and quantity to remain constant, there must be a bigger and bigger *absolute* rise in quantity and a smaller and smaller absolute fall in price. For example, a rise in quantity from 200 to 400 is the same proportionate change as a rise from 100 to 200, but its absolute size is double. A fall in price from £5 to £2.50 is the same percentage as a fall from £10 to £5, but its absolute size is only half.

> **Pause for thought**
>
> Two customers go to the fish counter at a supermarket to buy some cod. Neither looks at the price. Customer A orders 1 kilo of cod. Customer B orders £3 worth of cod. What is the price elasticity of demand of each of the two customers?

5.3   Other elasticities

Key Idea 11 p81

Firms are interested to know the responsiveness of demand not just to a change in price: they will also want to know the responsiveness of demand to changes in other determinants, such as consumers' incomes and the prices of substitute or complementary goods to theirs. They will want to know the **income elasticity of demand** – the responsiveness of demand to a change in consumers' incomes (Y); and the **cross-price elasticity of demand** – the responsiveness of demand for their good to a change in the price of another (whether a substitute or a complement).

> **definition**
>
> **Income elasticity of demand**
> The responsiveness of demand to a change in consumer incomes: the proportionate change in demand divided by the proportionate change in income.

> **definition**
>
> **Cross-price elasticity of demand**
> The responsiveness of demand for one good to a change in the price of another: the proportionate change in demand for one good divided by the proportionate change in price of the other.

Income elasticity of demand ($Y\epsilon_D$)

We define the income elasticity of demand for a good as follows:

$$Y\epsilon_D = \frac{\text{Proportionate (or percentage) change in quantity demanded}}{\text{Proportionate (or percentage) change in income}}$$

For example, if a 2 per cent rise in consumer incomes causes an 8 per cent rise in a product's demand, then its income elasticity of demand will be:

$$8\%/2\% = 4$$

The major determinant of income elasticity of demand is the degree of 'necessity' of the good.

In a developed country, the demand for luxury goods expands rapidly as people's incomes rise, whereas the demand for more basic goods, such as bread, rises only a little. Thus items such as cars and foreign holidays have a high income elasticity of demand, whereas items such as potatoes and bus journeys have a low income elasticity of demand.

The demand for some goods actually decreases as income rises. These are inferior goods such as cheap margarine. As people earn more, so they switch to butter or better quality margarine. Unlike normal goods, which have a positive income elasticity of demand, inferior goods have a negative income elasticity of demand (a rise in income leads to a *fall* in demand).

Income elasticity of demand and the firm

Income elasticity of demand is an important concept to firms considering the future size of the market for their product. If the product has a high income elasticity of demand, sales are likely to expand rapidly as national income rises, but may also fall significantly if the economy moves into recession.

Firms may also find that some parts of their market have a higher income elasticity of demand than others, and may thus choose to target their marketing campaigns on this group. For example, middle-income groups may have a higher income elasticity of demand for certain hi-fi products than lower-income groups (who are unlikely to be able to afford such products even if their incomes rise somewhat) or higher-income groups (who can probably afford them anyway, and thus would not buy much more if their incomes rose).

> **Pause for thought**
>
> Assume that you decide to spend a quarter of your income on clothes. What is (a) your income elasticity of demand; (b) your price elasticity of demand?

Cross-price elasticity of demand ($C\epsilon_{D_{ab}}$)

This is often known by its less cumbersome title of cross elasticity of demand. It is a measure of the responsiveness of demand for one product to a change in the price of another (either a substitute or a complement). It enables us to predict how much the demand curve for the first product will shift when the price of the second product changes. We define cross-price elasticity as follows:

$$C\epsilon_D = \frac{\text{Proportionate (or percentage) change in demand for good a}}{\text{Proportionate (or percentage) change in price of good b}}$$

If good b is a *substitute* for good a, a's demand will *rise* as b's price rises. For example, the demand for bicycles will rise as the price of public transport rises. In this case, cross elasticity will be a positive figure. If b is *complementary* to a, however, a's demand will *fall* as b's price rises and thus as the quantity of b demanded falls. For example, the demand for petrol falls as the price of cars rises. In this case, cross elasticity will be a negative figure.

Cross-price elasticity of demand and the firm

The major determinant of cross elasticity of demand is the closeness of the substitute or complement. The closer it is, the bigger will be the effect on the first good of a change in the price of the substitute or complement, and hence the greater will be the cross elasticity – either positive or negative.

Firms will wish to know the cross elasticity of demand for their product when considering the effect on the demand for their product of a change in the price of a rival's product (a substitute). If firm b cuts its price, will this make significant inroads into the sales of firm a? If so, firm a may feel forced to cut its prices too; if not, then firm a may keep its price unchanged. The cross-price elasticities of demand between a firm's product and those of each of its rivals are thus vital pieces of information for a firm when making its production, pricing and marketing plans.

Similarly, a firm will wish to know the cross-price elasticity of demand for its product with any complementary good. Car producers will wish to know the effect of petrol price increases on the sales of their cars.

Price elasticity of supply ($P\epsilon_S$)

Just as we can measure the responsiveness of demand to a change in one of the determinants of demand, so too we can measure the responsiveness of supply to a change in one of the determinants of supply. The **price elasticity of supply** refers to the responsiveness of supply to a change in price. We define it as follows:

definition

Price elasticity of supply
The responsiveness of quantity supplied to a change in price: the proportionate change in quantity supplied divided by the proportionate change in price.

$$P\epsilon_S = \frac{\text{Proportionate (or percentage) change in quantity supplied}}{\text{Proportionate (or percentage) change in price}}$$

Thus if a 15 per cent rise in the price of a product causes a 30 per cent rise in the quantity supplied, the price elasticity of supply will be:

30%/15% = 2

In Figure 5.8 curve S_2 is more elastic between any two prices than curve S_1. Thus, when price rises from P_1 to P_2 there is a larger increase in quantity supplied with S_2 (namely, Q_1 to Q_3) than there is with S_1 (namely, Q_1 to Q_2).

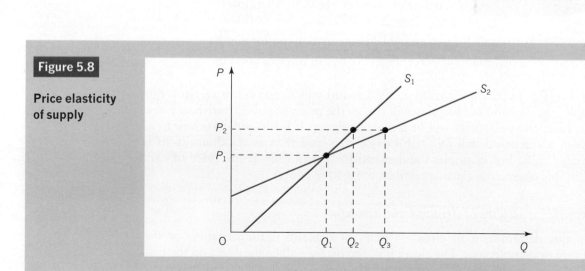

Figure 5.8

Price elasticity of supply

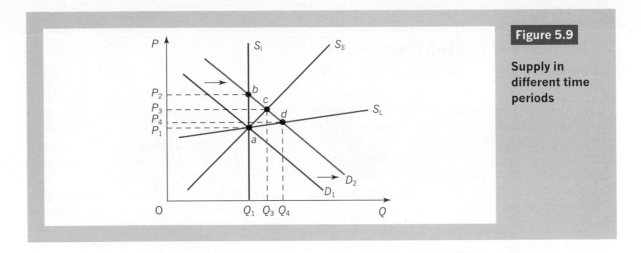

Figure 5.9

Supply in different time periods

Determinants of price elasticity of supply

The amount that costs rise as output rises. The less the additional costs of producing additional output, the more firms will be encouraged to produce for a given price rise: the more elastic will supply be.

Supply is thus likely to be elastic if firms have plenty of spare capacity, if they can readily get extra supplies of raw materials, if they can easily switch away from producing alternative products and if they can avoid having to introduce overtime working (at higher rates of pay). If all these conditions hold, costs will be little affected by a rise in output and supply will be relatively elastic. The less these conditions apply, the less elastic will supply be.

Time period (see Figure 5.9)

- Immediate time period. Firms are unlikely to be able to increase supply by much immediately. Supply is virtually fixed, or can vary only according to available stocks. Supply is highly inelastic. In the diagram S_I is drawn with $P\epsilon_S = 0$. If demand increases to D_2, supply will not be able to respond. Price will rise to P_2. Quantity will remain at Q_1. Equilibrium will move to point b.

- Short run. If a slightly longer time period is allowed to elapse, some inputs can be increased (e.g. raw materials), while others will remain fixed (e.g. heavy machinery). Supply can increase somewhat. This is illustrated by S_S. Equilibrium will move to point c with price falling again, to P_3, and quantity rising to Q_3.

- Long run. In the long run, there will be sufficient time for all inputs to be increased and for new firms to enter the industry. Supply, therefore, is likely to be highly elastic. This is illustrated by curve S_L. Long-run equilibrium will be at point d with price falling back even further, to P_4, and quantity rising all the way to Q_4. In some circumstances the supply curve may even slope downward. (See the section on economies of scale in Chapter 9, pages 179–80.)

BOX 5.1

The market for leather
A case study in demand and supply

Some markets are subject to considerable price fluctuations. The magnitude of these fluctuations depends on the amount by which demand and/or supply curves shift, and the price elasticity of demand and supply. The following extract, taken from an article in *The Independent* of 9 May 1994, considers price fluctuations in the market for sheepskin and cattle hides.

> Prices of sheepskin and cattle hides have soared in recent months as suppliers have struggled to meet demand. According to the British Leather Confederation, UK abattoir prices of sheepskin are now £7 to £7.50 compared with just under £1 in autumn 1990, Oxhides (steers and heifers) fetch £40 against a low of £17 to £18 in the first quarter of 1991, although traders and tanners believe the market has now peaked, at least for the moment.
>
> ... Normal laws of supply and demand do not apply as skins and hides are a by-product of the meat, wool and dairy industries. In the past 12 to 18 months, demand for leather goods has risen, yet the UK cattle kill was 9 per cent down in 1993 from the previous year and the lamb kill was 7 per cent down. Falling demand for red meat and a significant rise in the live export of UK lambs, particularly to France, are the main reasons.
>
> UK tanners have been left short of quality raw material and prices have risen steeply. However, consumers' resistance to higher prices of finished goods prevented increases being passed on and the tanners' margins have been squeezed.

There is little prospect of the by-product status of skins and hides changing. In the UK, the value of a cattle hide is only 7 to 10 per cent of the total carcass and the value of a sheepskin 10 to 15 per cent of the carcass. Farmers are more concerned about selling the meat.

Lack of a homogeneous raw material hampers the creation of an international market. Sheepskins are graded according to climate. Higher quality skins from temperate zones are further divided, with UK skins usually fetching a premium price over New Zealand domestics. South African Capes are considered high quality, but the supply is limited.

Questions

1 *Why had the supply of skins and hides fallen despite a rise in demand? Illustrate this using a demand and supply diagram.*

2 *According to the article, which of the following are likely to be relatively elastic and which relatively inelastic: (a) the price elasticity of supply of raw skins and hides; (b) the price elasticity of demand for raw skins and hides; (c) the price elasticity of demand for finished products made with skins and hides? Explain the reasoning behind your answers.*

3 *Given the answer to Q2, demonstrate with demand and supply curves why there had been a substantial rise in price of raw skins and hides which had nevertheless not been passed on in higher prices for finished goods made with skins and hides.*

4 *Why does the lack of a homogeneous raw material exacerbate the problem of price stability?*

5.4 The time dimension of market adjustment

The full adjustment of price, demand and supply to a situation of disequilibrium will not be instantaneous. It is necessary, therefore, to analyse the time path which supply takes in responding to changes in demand, and which demand takes in responding to changes in supply.

Key Idea
29
p409

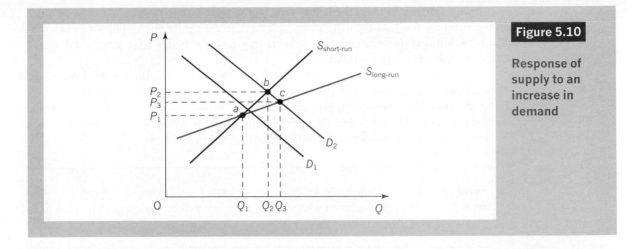

Figure 5.10

Response of supply to an increase in demand

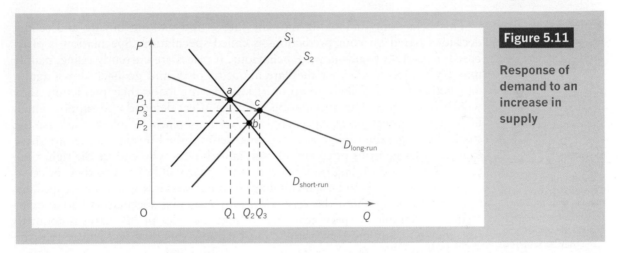

Figure 5.11

Response of demand to an increase in supply

Short-run and long-run adjustment

As we have already seen, elasticity varies with the time period under considera-tion. The reason is that producers and consumers take time to respond to a change in price. The longer the time period, the bigger the response, and thus the greater the elasticity of supply and demand.

This is illustrated in Figures 5.10 and 5.11. In both cases, as equilibrium moves from points a to b to c, there is a large short-run price change (P_1 to P_2) and a small short-run quantity change (Q_1 to Q_2), but a small long-run price change (P_1 to P_3) and a large long-run quantity change (Q_1 to Q_3).

Speculation

In a world of shifting demand and supply curves, prices do not stay the same. Sometimes they go up; sometimes they come down. If prices are likely to change in the foreseeable future, this will affect the behaviour of buyers and sellers *now*. If, for example, it is now December and you are thinking of buying a new winter coat, you might decide to wait until the January sales, and in the meantime make do with your old coat. If, on the other hand, when January comes you see a new summer dress in the sales, you might well buy it now and not wait until the summer for fear that the price will have gone up by then. Thus a belief that prices will go up will cause people to buy now; a belief that prices will come down will cause them to wait.

The reverse applies to sellers. If you are thinking of selling your house and prices are falling, you will want to sell it as quickly as possible. If, on the other hand, prices are rising sharply, you will wait as long as possible so as to get the highest price. Thus a belief that prices will come down will cause people to sell now; a belief that prices will go up will cause them to wait.

People's actions are influenced by their expectations. People respond not just to what is happening now (such as a change in price), but to what they anticipate will happen in the future.

Key Idea 12

---

definition

Speculation
This is where people make buying or selling decisions based on their anticipations of future prices.

This behaviour of looking into the future and making buying and selling decisions based on your predictions is called **speculation**. Speculation is often based on current trends in price behaviour. If prices are currently rising, people may try to decide whether they are about to peak and go back down again, or whether they are likely to go on rising. Having made their prediction, they will then act on it. This speculation will thus affect demand and supply, which in turn will affect price. Speculation is commonplace in many markets: the stock exchange, the foreign exchange market and the housing market are three examples. Large firms often employ specialist buyers who choose the right time to buy inputs, depending on what they anticipate will happen to their price.

definition

Self-fulfilling speculation
The actions of speculators tend to cause the very effect that they had anticipated.

Speculation tends to be **self-fulfilling**. In other words, the actions of speculators tend to bring about the very effect on prices that speculators had anticipated. For example, if speculators believe that the price of BP shares is about to rise, they will buy more BP shares. But by doing this they will ensure that the price *will* rise. The prophecy has become self-fulfilling.

Speculation can either help to reduce price fluctuations or aggravate them: it can be stabilising or destabilising.

definition

Stabilising speculation
This is where the actions of speculators tend to reduce price fluctuations.

Stabilising speculation

Speculation will tend to have a **stabilising** effect on price fluctuations when suppliers and/or demanders believe that a change in price is only *temporary*.

Key Idea 12 p94

Key Idea 9 p63

An initial fall in price. In Figure 5.12(a), demand has shifted from D_1 to D_2; equilibrium has moved from point *a* to point *b*, and price has fallen to P_2. How do people react to this fall in price?

Given that they believe this fall in price to be only temporary, suppliers *hold back*, expecting prices to rise again: supply shifts from S_1 to S_2. After all, why supply now when, by waiting, they could get a higher price?

Buyers *increase* their purchases, to take advantage of the temporary fall in price. Demand shifts from D_2 to D_3.

The equilibrium moves to point *c*, with price rising back towards P_1.

An initial rise in price. In Figure 5.12(b), demand has shifted from D_1 to D_2. Price has risen from P_1 to P_2.

Suppliers bring their goods to market now, before price falls again. Supply shifts from S_1 to S_2. Demanders, however, hold back until price falls. Demand

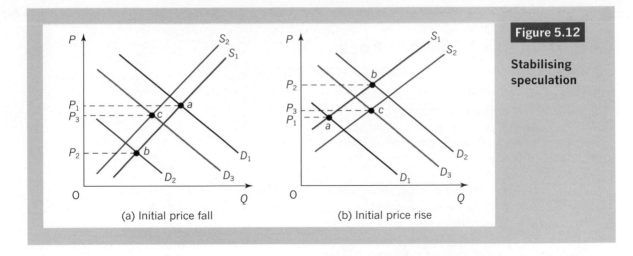

Figure 5.12

Stabilising speculation

(a) Initial price fall

(b) Initial price rise

shifts from D_2 to D_3. The equilibrium moves to point c, with price falling back towards P_1.

A good example of stabilising speculation is that which occurs in agricultural commodity markets. Take the case of wheat. When it is harvested in the autumn there will be a plentiful supply. If all this wheat were to be put on the market, the price would fall to a very low level. Later in the year, when most of the wheat would have been sold, the price would then rise to a very high level. This is all easily predictable.

So what do farmers do? The answer is that they speculate. When the wheat is harvested they know its price will tend to fall, and so instead of bringing it all to market they put a lot of it into store. The more price falls, the more they will put into store *anticipating that the price will later rise*. But this holding back of supplies prevents prices from falling. In other words, it stabilises prices.

Later in the year, when the price begins to rise, they will gradually release grain on to the market from the stores. The more the price rises, the more will they release on to the market *anticipating that the price will fall again by the time of the next harvest*. But this releasing of supplies will again stabilise prices by preventing them rising so much.

Key
Idea
12
p94

Destabilising speculation

Speculation will tend to have a **destabilising** effect on price fluctuations when suppliers and/or buyers believe that a change in price heralds similar changes to come.

definition

Destabilising speculation
This is where the actions of speculators tend to make price movements larger.

An initial fall in price. In Figure 5.13(a) demand has shifted from D_1 to D_2 and price has fallen from P_1 to P_2. This time, believing that the fall in price heralds further falls in price to come, suppliers sell now before the price does fall. Supply shifts from S_1 to S_2. And demanders wait: they wait until price does fall further. Demand shifts from D_2 to D_3.

Their actions ensure that the price does fall further: to P_3.

An initial rise in price. In Figure 5.13(b), a price rise from P_1 to P_2 is caused by a rise in demand from D_1 to D_2. Suppliers wait until the price rises further. Supply shifts from S_1 to S_2. Demanders buy now before any further rise in price. Demand shifts from D_2 to D_3. As a result the price continues to rise: to P_3.

Box 4.1 examined the housing market. In this market, speculation is frequently destabilising. Assume that people see house prices beginning to move

Adjusting to oil price shocks
Short-run and long-run demand and supply responses

Between December 1973 and June 1974, the Organisation of Petroleum Exporting Countries (OPEC) put up the price of oil from $3 to $12 per barrel. It was further raised to over $30 in 1979. In the 1980s the price fluctuated, but the trend was downward. Except for a sharp rise at the time of the Gulf War in 1990, the trend continued through most of the 1990s, at times falling as low as $11.

In the early 2000s, prices have generally been higher, fluctuating between $19 and $33 per barrel.

The price movements can be explained using simple demand and supply analysis.

The initial rise in price

OPEC raised the price from P_1 to P_2. To prevent surplus at that price, OPEC members restricted their output by agreed amounts. This had the effect of shifting the supply curve to S_2 (in diagram (a)), with Q_2 being produced. This reduction in output needed to be only relatively small because the short-run demand for oil was highly price inelastic: for most uses there are no substitutes in the short run.

Long-run effects on demand

The long-run demand for oil was more elastic. With high oil prices persisting, people tried to find ways of

(a) An initial restriction of supply

(b) Long-run demand response

Figure 5.13

Destabilising speculation

(a) Initial price fall

(b) Initial price rise

cutting back on consumption. People bought smaller cars. They converted to gas or solid-fuel central heating. Firms switched to other fuels. Less use was made of oil-fired power stations for electricity generation. Energy-saving schemes became widespread both in firms and in the home.

This had the effect of shifting the short-run demand curve from D_1 to D_2 in diagram (b). Price fell back from P_2 to P_3. This gave a long-run demand curve of D_L: the curve that joins points A and C.

The fall in demand was made bigger by a world recession in the early 1980s.

Long-run effects on supply

With oil production so much more profitable, there was an incentive for non-OPEC oil producers to produce oil. Prospecting went on all over the world and large oil fields were discovered and opened up in the North Sea, Alaska, Mexico, China and elsewhere. In addition, OPEC members were tempted to break their 'quotas' (their allotted output) and sell more oil.

The net effect was an increase in world oil supplies. In terms of the diagrams, the supply curve of oil started to shift to the right from the mid-1980s onwards, causing oil prices to fall through most of the period up to 1998.

Back to square one?

By the late 1990s, with the oil price as low as $10 per barrel, OPEC once more cut back supply. The story had come full circle. This cut-back is illustrated in diagram (a).

The trouble this time was that worldwide economic growth was picking up. Demand was shifting to the right. The result was a rise in oil prices to around $33, which then fell back again in 2001 as the world slipped into recession and the demand curve shifted to the left.

There were then some large price increases, first as a result of OPEC in late 2001 attempting once more to restrict supply (a leftward shift in supply), and then, before the Iraq war of 2003, because of worries about possible adverse effects on oil supplies (a rightward shift in demand as countries stocked up on oil).

Question

Give some examples of things that could make the demand for oil more elastic. What specific policies could the government take to make demand more elastic?

upward. This might be the result of increased demand brought about by a cut in mortgage interest rates or by growth in the economy. People may well believe that the rise in house prices signals a boom in the housing market: that prices will go on rising. Potential buyers will thus try to buy as soon as possible before prices rise any further. This increased demand (as in Figure 5.13(b)) will thus lead to even bigger price rises. This is precisely what happened in the UK housing market in 1999–2003 (see Box 4.1 on pages 74–5).

Conclusion

In some circumstances, then, the action of speculators can help keep price fluctuations to a minimum (stabilising speculation). This is most likely when markets are relatively stable in the first place, with only moderate underlying shifts in demand and supply.

In other circumstances, however, speculation can make price fluctuations much worse. This is most likely in times of uncertainty, when there are significant changes in the determinants of demand and supply. Given this uncertainty, people may see price changes as signifying some

Pause for thought

What are the advantages and disadvantages of speculation from the point of view of (a) the consumer; (b) firms?

trend. They then 'jump on the bandwagon' and do what the rest are doing, and further fuel the rise or fall in price.

5.5 Dealing with uncertainty

Risk and uncertainty

When price changes are likely to occur, buyers and sellers will try to anticipate them. Unfortunately, on many occasions no one can be certain just what these price changes will be. Take the case of stocks and shares. If you anticipate that the price of, say, BP shares is likely to go up substantially in the near future, you may well decide to buy some now and then sell them later after the price has risen. But you cannot be certain that they will go up in price: they may fall instead. If you buy the shares, therefore, you will be taking a gamble.

Key Idea 7 p50

Now gambles can be of two types. The first is where you know the odds. Let us take the simplest case of a gamble on the toss of a coin. Heads you win; tails you lose. You know that the odds of winning are precisely 50 per cent. If you bet on the toss of a coin, you are said to be operating under conditions of **risk**. *Risk is when the probability of an outcome is known.* Risk itself is a measure of the *variability* of an outcome. For example, if you bet £1 on the toss of a coin, such that heads you win £1 and tails you lose £1, then the variability is −£1 to +£1.

The second form of gamble is the more usual. This is where the odds are not known or are known only roughly. Gambling on the Stock Exchange is like this. You may have a good idea that a share will go up in price, but is it a 90 per cent chance, an 80 per cent chance or what? You are not certain. Gambling under these sorts of conditions is known as operating under **uncertainty**. *This is when the probability of an outcome is not known.*

You may well disapprove of gambling and want to dismiss people who engage in it as foolish or morally wrong. But 'gambling' is not just confined to horses, cards, roulette and the like. Risk and uncertainty pervade the whole of economic life and decisions are constantly having to be made whose outcome cannot be known for certain. Even the most morally upright person will still have to decide which career to go into, whether and when to buy a house, or even something as trivial as whether or not to take an umbrella when going out. Each of these decisions and thousands of others are made under conditions of uncertainty (or occasionally risk).

Key Idea 4 p27

> *People's actions are influenced by their attitudes towards risk.* Many decisions are taken under conditions of risk or uncertainty. Generally, the lower the probability of (or the more uncertain) the desired outcome of an action, the less likely will people be to undertake the action.
>
> Key Idea 13

We shall be examining how risk and uncertainty affect economic decisions at several points throughout the book. For example, in the next chapter we will see how it affects people's attitudes and actions as consumers, and how taking out insurance can help to reduce their uncertainty. At this point, however, let us focus on firms' attitudes when supplying goods.

definition

Risk
This is when an outcome may or may not occur, but where its probability of occurring is known.

definition

Uncertainty
This is when an outcome may or may not occur and where its probability of occurring is not known.

Stock holding as a way of reducing the problem of uncertainty. A simple way that suppliers can reduce risks is by holding stocks. Take the case of the wheat farmers we saw in the previous section. At the time when they are planting the wheat in the spring, they are uncertain as to what the price of wheat will be when they bring it to market. If they keep no stores of wheat, they will just have to accept whatever the market price happens to be at harvest time. If, however, they have storage facilities, they can put the wheat into store if the price is low and then wait until it goes up. Alternatively, if the price of wheat is high at harvest time, they can sell it straight away. In other words, they can wait until the price is right.

> **Pause for thought**
>
> The demand for pears is more price elastic than the demand for bread and yet the price of pears fluctuates more than that of bread. Why should this be so? If pears could be stored as long and as cheaply as flour, would this affect the relative price fluctuations? If so, how?

Purchasing information. One way of reducing uncertainty is to buy information. A firm could commission various forms of market research or purchase the information from specialist organisations. It is similar for consumers. You might take advice on shares from a stock broker, or buy a copy of a consumer magazine, such as *Which?*. The buying and selling of information in this way helps substantially to reduce uncertainty.

Better information can also, under certain circumstances, help to make any speculation more stabilising. With poor information, people are much more likely to be guided by rumour or fear, which could well make speculation destabilising as people 'jump on the bandwagon'. If people generally are better informed, however, this is likely to make prices go more directly to a long-run stable equilibrium.

Dealing in futures markets

Another way of reducing or even eliminating uncertainty is by dealing in **futures** or **forward markets**. Let us examine the activities first of sellers and then of buyers.

> **definition**
>
> **Futures or forward market**
> A market in which contracts are made to buy or sell at some future date at a price agreed today.

Sellers

Suppose you are a farmer and want to store grain to sell some time in the future, expecting to get a better price then than now. The trouble is that there is a chance that the price will go down. Given this uncertainty, you may be unwilling to take a gamble.

An answer to your problem is provided by the *commodity futures market*. This is a market where prices are agreed between sellers and buyers *today* for delivery at some specified date in the *future*.

For example, if it is 20 October today, you could be quoted a price *today* for delivery in six months' time (i.e. on 20 April). This is known as the six-month **future price**. Assume that the six-month future price is £60 per tonne. If you agree to this price and make a six-month forward contract, you are agreeing to sell a specified amount of wheat at £60 on 20 April. No matter what happens to the **spot price** (i.e. the current market price) in the meantime, your selling price has been agreed. The spot price could have fallen to £30 (or risen to £100) by April, but your selling price when 20 April arrives is fixed at £60. There is thus *no risk to you whatsoever of the price going down.* You will, of course, lose out if the spot price is *more* than £60 in April.

> **definition**
>
> **Future price**
> A price agreed today at which an item (e.g. commodities) will be exchanged at some set date in the future.

> **definition**
>
> **Spot price**
> The current market price.

BOX 5.3

The role of the speculator

...the greed of bond traders drives up interest rates, and so harms output and jobs. Stockmarkets punish companies that invest in their workers instead of boosting profits. The managers of pensions and mutual funds flood emerging markets with capital, then pull the plug on a whim. Even governments quail before the might of speculators. When they set their exchange rate at a vulnerable level, speculators sell the currency forcing them to devalue.[1]

This commonly held, yet largely unfair, view of the speculator emphasises all that might be bad in the speculators' business. In fact, speculators play a crucially important role in economic affairs, and it is this side of the speculators' actions that are largely ignored and taken for granted.

For example, take share prices. A firm's share price reflects the market estimation of the business's future prospects. A falling share price implies that the market's view of the firm is deteriorating, making it more expensive for the company to raise new finance in the stock market. The more expensive finance is for the business, the fewer investments it will make, which if the market is correct is desirable, as firms with better prospects will receive not only more but cheaper finance.

The criticism of this position is that speculators frequently get things wrong. They focus too much on the short term and on the current profitability of the business, ignoring long-run prospects and opportunities.

But is there any basis to this criticism? *The Economist* of 3 February 1996 thinks not.

Shares derive their worth from a firm's underlying assets. If the market in which these shares are traded 'undervalued' them, anyone who bought such a share would be getting a bargain: they would receive a windfall in the future when the firm's long-term investment paid off. It would then be easy for a few clever investors to exploit the market's shortsightedness. For example, if it were true, as it is sometimes said, that the market attaches too little value to corporate R&D, a few investors could make a bundle by buying shares in firms with large R&D budgets. In the process, of course, these firms' prices would rise until they were no longer undervalued.

If this sounds abstract, consider the concrete evidence that investors care about the long term. The shares of many bio-technology or software firms, some of which have never made a profit, continue to fetch dizzying prices in the stockmarket. Indeed, a common criticism of stockmarket speculators is that they push the prices of high-tech firms too high. In other words, they seem to care too much, not too little, about the long term.

By far the greatest criticism of speculators is the volatility they create by shifting prices up and down, apparently at a whim. But even this might be explained away as a virtue, as the speculators are simply responding to changing economic conditions, either at the level of the firm or within the economy generally. The speculators are adjusting their decisions in line with changing circumstances. In other words, they are being efficient, although this does not necessarily imply that their decisions are correct!

Question

How might it be beneficial for the economy if speculators were less efficient?

---

[1] *The Economist*, 3 February 1996

Buyers

Now suppose that you are a flour miller. In order to plan your expenditures, you would like to know the price you will have to pay for wheat, not just today, but also at various future dates. In other words, if you want to take delivery of wheat at some time in the future, you would like a price quoted *now*. You would like the risks removed of prices going *up*.

Let us assume that today (20 October) you want to *buy* the same amount of wheat on 20 April that a farmer wishes to sell on that same date. If you agree to the £60 future price, a future contract can be made with the farmer. You are then guaranteed that purchase price, no matter what happens to the spot price in the meantime. There is thus *no risk to you whatsoever of the price going up*. You will, of course, lose out if the spot price is *less* than £60 in April.

The determination of the future price

Prices in the futures market are determined in the same way as in other markets: by demand and supply. For example, the six-month wheat price or the three-month coffee price will be that which equates the demand for those futures with the supply. If the five-month sugar price is currently £200 per tonne and people expect by then, because of an anticipated good beet harvest, that the spot price for sugar will be £150 per tonne, there will be few who will want to buy the futures at £200 (and many who will want to sell). This excess of supply of futures over demand will push the price down.

Speculators

Many people operate in the futures market who never actually handle the commodities themselves. They are neither producers nor users of the commodities. They merely speculate. Such speculators may be individuals, but they are more likely to be financial institutions.

Let us take a simple example. Suppose that the six-month (April) coffee price is £1000 per tonne and that you, as a speculator, believe that the spot price of coffee is likely to rise above that level between now (October) and six months' time. You thus decide to buy 20 tonnes of April coffee futures now.

But you have no intention of taking delivery. After four months, let us say, true to your prediction, the spot price (February) has risen and as a result the April price (and other future prices) have risen too. You thus decide to *sell* 20 tonnes of April (two-month) coffee futures, whose price, let us say, is £1200. You are now 'covered'.

When April comes, what happens? You have agreed to buy 20 tonnes of coffee at £1000 per tonne and to sell 20 tonnes of coffee at £1200 per tonne. All you do is hand the futures contract to buy to the person to whom you agreed to sell. They sort out delivery between them and you make £200 per tonne profit.

If, however, your prediction had been wrong and the price had *fallen*, you would have made a loss. You would have been forced to sell coffee contracts at a lower price than you had bought them.

Speculators in the futures market thus incur risks, unlike the sellers and buyers of the commodities, for whom the futures market eliminates risk. Financial institutions offering futures contracts will charge for the service: for taking on the risks.

SUMMARY

1a Price elasticity of demand measures the responsiveness of demand to a change in price. It is defined as the proportionate (or percentage) change in quantity demanded divided by the proportionate (or percentage) change in price.

1b If quantity demanded changes proportionately more than price, the figure for elasticity will be greater than 1 (ignoring the sign): it is elastic. If the quantity demanded changes proportionately less than price, the figure for elasticity will be less than 1: it is inelastic. If they change by the same proportion, the elasticity has a value of 1: it is unit elastic.

1c Given that demand curves are downward sloping, price elasticity of demand will have a negative value.

1d Demand will be more elastic the greater the number and closeness of substitute goods, the higher the proportion of income spent on the good and the longer the time period that elapses after the change in price.

1e Demand curves normally have different elasticities along their length. We can thus normally refer only to the specific value for elasticity between two points on the curve or at a single point.

2a It is important for firms to know the price elasticity of demand for their product whenever they are considering a price change. The reason is that the effect of the price change on the firm's sales revenue will depend on the product's price elasticity.

2b When the demand for a firm's product is price elastic, a rise in price will lead to a reduction in consumer expenditure on the good and hence to a reduction in the total revenue of the firm.

2c When demand is price inelastic, however, a rise in price will lead to an increase in total revenue for the firm.

3a Income elasticity of demand measures the responsiveness of demand to a change in income. For normal goods it has a positive value. Demand will be more income elastic the more luxurious the good and the less rapidly demand is satisfied as consumption increases.

3b Cross-price elasticity of demand measures the responsiveness of demand for one good to a change in the price of another. For substitute goods the value will be positive; for complements it will be negative. The cross-price elasticity will be greater the closer the two goods are as substitutes or complements.

3c Price elasticity of supply measures the responsiveness of supply to a change in price. It has a positive value. Supply will be more elastic the less costs per unit rise as output rises and the longer the time period.

4a A complete understanding of markets must take into account the time dimension.

4b Given that producers and consumers take a time to respond fully to price changes, we can identify different equilibria after the elapse of different lengths of time. Generally, short-run supply and demand tend to be less price elastic than long-run supply and demand. As a result any shifts in demand or supply curves tend to have a relatively bigger effect on price in the short run and a relatively bigger effect on quantity in the long run.

4c If there is a time lag between the decision to supply and the supply coming on to the market, price oscillations are likely to occur. High prices cause producers to plan to supply more. This extra supply when it comes on to the market depresses market price. Producers respond by planning to produce less. When this reduced supply comes to market, market price will rise again. The path that these oscillations trace out on a demand and supply diagram is shaped like a cobweb. These cobwebs can be convergent or divergent depending on the shape of the demand and supply curves.

4d People often anticipate price changes and this will affect the amount they demand or supply. This speculation will tend to stabilise price fluctuations if people believe that the price changes are only temporary. However, speculation will tend to destabilise these fluctuations (i.e. make them more severe) if people believe that prices are likely to continue to move in the same direction as at present (at least for some time).

5a A lot of economic decision making is made under conditions of risk or uncertainty.

5b Risk is when the probability of an outcome occurring is known. Uncertainty is when the probability is not known.

5c One way of reducing risks is to hold stocks. If the price of a firm's product falls unexpectedly,

REVIEW QUESTIONS **103**

it can build up stocks rather than releasing its product on to the market. If the price later rises, it can then release stocks on to the market. Similarly with inputs: if their price falls unexpectedly, firms can build up their stocks, only to draw on them later if input prices rise.

5d A way of eliminating risk and uncertainty is to deal in the futures markets. When firms are planning to buy or sell at some point in the future, there is the danger that price could rise or fall unexpectedly in the meantime. By agreeing to buy or sell at some particular point in the future at a price agreed today (a 'future' price), this danger can be eliminated. The bank or other institution offering the price (the 'speculator') is taking on the risk, and will charge for this service.

REVIEW QUESTIONS

1 Why does price elasticity of demand have a negative value, whereas price elasticity of supply has a positive value?

2 Rank the following in ascending order of elasticity: jeans, black Levi jeans, black jeans, black Levi 501 jeans, trousers, outer garments, clothes.

3 How might a firm set about making the demand for its brand less elastic?

4 Will a general item of expenditure like food or clothing have a price elastic or inelastic demand?

5 Assuming that a firm faces an inelastic demand and wants to increase its total revenue, *how much* should it raise its price? Is there any limit?

6 Can you think of any examples of goods which have a totally inelastic demand (a) at *all* prices; (b) over a particular price range?

7 Which of these two pairs are likely to have the highest cross-price elasticity of demand: two brands of coffee, or coffee and tea?

8 Why are both the price elasticity of demand and the price elasticity of supply likely to be greater in the long run?

9 Redraw Figures 5.12 and 5.13, only this time assume that it was an initial shift in supply that caused price to change in the first place.

10 Give some examples of decisions you have taken recently that were made under conditions of uncertainty. With hindsight do you think you made the right decisions? Explain.

11 What methods can a firm use to reduce risk and uncertainty?

12 If speculators believed that the price of cocoa in six months was going to be *below* the six-month future price quoted today, how would they act?

Additional Part B case studies on the *Economics for Business* website (www.booksites.net/sloman)

B.1   **The interdependence of markets.** A case study of the operation of markets, examining the effects on a local economy of the discovery of a large coal deposit.

B.2   **Adam Smith (1723–1790).** Smith, the founder of modern economics, argued that markets act like an 'invisible hand' guiding production and consumption.

B.3   **The measurement of elasticity.** This examines how to work out the value for elasticity using the 'mid-point' method.

B.4   **Shall we put up our price?** Some examples of firms charging high prices in markets where demand is relatively inelastic.

B.5   **Any more fares?** Pricing on the buses: an illustration of the relationship between price and total revenue.

B.6   **Elasticities of demand for various foodstuffs.** An examination of the evidence about price and income elasticities of demand for food in the UK.

B.7   **Adjusting to oil price shocks.** A case study showing how demand and supply analysis can be used to examine the price changes in the oil market since 1973.

B.8   **Income elasticity of demand and the balance of payments.** This examines how a low income elasticity of demand for the exports of many developing countries can help to explain their chronic balance of payments problems.

B.9   **The cobweb.** An outline of the theory that explains price fluctuations in terms of time lags in supply.

B.10   **The role of the speculator.** This assesses whether the activities of speculators are beneficial or harmful to the rest of society.

B.11   **Rationing.** A case study in the use of rationing as an alternative to the price mechanism. In particular, it looks at the use of rationing in the UK during the Second World War.

B.12   **Rent control.** This shows how setting (low) maximum rents is likely to lead to a shortage of rented accommodation.

B.13   **Agriculture and minimum prices.** This shows how setting (high) minimum prices is likely to lead to surpluses.

B.14   **The fallacy of composition.** An illustration from agricultural markets of the fallacy of composition: 'what applies in one case will not necessarily apply when repeated in all cases'.

Websites relevant to Part B

Numbers and sections refer to websites listed in the Web appendix and hotlinked from this book's website at **www.booksites.net/sloman**

■ For news articles relevant to Part B, see the *Economics News Articles* link from the book's website.

■ For general news on markets see websites in section A, and particularly A2, 3, 4, 5, 8, 9, 18, 20–26, 35, 36. See also site A42 for links to economics news articles from newspapers worldwide.

■ For links to sites on markets, see the relevant sections of I4, 7, 11, 17.

■ For data on the housing market (Box 4.1), see sites B7, 8, 11.

■ For student resources relevant to Part B, see sites C1–7, 9, 10, 19; D3.

■ For sites favouring the free market, see C17 and E34.

C Background to demand

THE FINANCIAL TIMES, 27 JUNE 2003

Sunny Delight tries to find a new dawn

By CLAIRE MURPHY

It was a headline in *The Sun* in August 1999, mistakenly proclaiming that Sunny Delight was 'bigger than Coke', that set the drink on to the publicity rollercoaster.

Jerry Hogg, food and beverage market operations director for brand owner Procter & Gamble, recalls that his first reaction was to dash around the office holding the paper aloft with glee.

His second thought was to worry what might be coming next. This was prescient. In an effort to move the story on and prompted by food health lobby groups, the headlines turned sour. *The Daily Mail*'s 'Health row as sugary water sales reach £160m' was just one that started parents wondering whether buying Sunny Delight for their children was a good idea after all.

Jolted by negative headlines over sugar content, additives and a marketing strategy that looked as if the company was trying to dress the drink up as juice, sales plummeted. The brand is now worth £35.6m, according to Information Resources.

Two big contributors to the problem were P&G's legendary obsession with research and its traditionally closed culture. Even as waves of negative publicity were breaking around them, the marketing team refused to see it as more than a short-term nuisance.

'We underestimated the power of detractors like the Food Commission and their ability to influence non-consumers of the drink, who would in turn influence parents. The negative word of mouth eventually became too strong for buyers to resist,' says Mr Hogg.

The marketing team was puzzled that a two-year test market for Sunny Delight in Carlisle had failed to uncover these issues. 'All the nutritionists and other interested parties I spoke to in the test market area understood and accepted the brand,' says Gary Stephenson, P&G's principal scientist, external relations.

But the controlled environment of the test market failed to predict how UK consumers would be confused by this new category of drink – in between a juice and a squash – calling into question P&G's market research techniques.

Now though, P&G is mounting an all-out effort to arrest the decline by confronting the health issue head-on. Adverts on TV, radio and posters will push the message that the renamed Sunny D is a practical alternative to fizzy drinks for parents trying to make their children's diets a little healthier.

For years we thought ourselves as a production-orientated company, meaning we put all our emphasis on designing and manufacturing the product. But now we understand that the most important thing we do is market the product. We've come around to saying that Nike is a marketing-orientated company, and the product is our most important marketing tool.

Phil Knight, Nike CEO, in Naomi Klein
No Logo (2000) p. 22

If a business is to be successful, it must be able to predict the strength of demand for its products and be able to respond to any changes in consumer tastes. It will also want to know how its customers are likely to react to changes in its price or its competitors' prices, or to changes in income. In other words, it will want to know the price, cross-price and income elasticities of demand for its product. The better the firm's knowledge of its market, the better will it be able to plan its output to meet demand, and the more able will it be to choose its optimum price, product design, marketing campaigns, etc.

In Chapter 6 we will go behind the demand curve to gain a better under-standing of consumer behaviour. We will consider how economists analyse consumer satisfaction and how it varies with the amount consumed. We will then relate this to the shape of the demand curve.

Then, in Chapter 7, we will investigate how data on consumer behaviour can be collected and the problems that businesses face in analysing such information and using it to forecast changes in demand.

Chapter 8 explores how firms can expand and develop their markets by the use of various types of non-price competition. It looks at ways in which firms can differentiate their products from those of their rivals. It also considers how a business sets about deriving a marketing strategy, and assesses the role and implications of product advertising. In the case of Sunny D (see FT article opposite), its marketing strategy seems to be one of attempting to 're-educate' consumers as to the virtues of the product!

key terms

Marginal utility
Diminishing
  marginal utility
Consumer surplus
Rational consumer
Adverse selection
Moral hazard
Product
  characteristics
Indifference curves
Efficiency frontier
Market surveys
Market experiments
Demand function
Forecasting
Non-price
  competition
Product
  differentiation
Product marketing
Advertising

6 Demand and the consumer

Given our limited incomes, we have to make choices about what to buy. You may have to choose between that new economics textbook you feel you ought to buy and going to a rock concert, between a new pair of jeans and a meal out, between saving up for a car and having more money to spend on everyday items, and so on. Business managers are interested in finding out what influences your decisions to consume, and how they might price or package their product to increase their sales.

In this section it is assumed that as consumers we behave 'rationally': that we consider the relative costs and benefits of our purchases in order to gain the maximum satisfaction possible from our limited incomes. Sometimes we may act 'irrationally'. We may purchase goods impetuously with little thought to their price or quality. In general, however, it is a reasonably accurate assumption that people behave rationally.

This does not mean that you get a calculator out every time you go shopping! When you go round the supermarket, you are hardly likely to look at every item on the shelf and weigh up the satisfaction you think you would get from it against the price on the label. Nevertheless, you have probably learned over time the sort of things you like and the prices they cost. You can probably make out a 'rational' shopping list quite quickly.

With major items of expenditure such as a house, a car, a carpet or a foreign holiday, we are likely to take much more care. Take the case of a foreign holiday: you will probably spend quite a long time browsing through brochures comparing the relative merits of various holidays against their relative costs, looking for a holiday that gives good value for money. This is rational behaviour.

6.1 Marginal utility theory

Total and marginal utility

People buy goods and services because they get satisfaction from them. Economists call this satisfaction 'utility'.

An important distinction must be made between *total utility* and *marginal utility*.

Total utility (TU) is the total satisfaction that a person gains from all those units of a commodity consumed within a given time period. Thus if Tracey drank 10 cups of tea a day, her daily total utility from tea would be the satisfaction derived from those 10 cups.

definition

Total utility
The total satisfaction a consumer gets from the consumption of all the units of a good consumed within a given time period.

definition

Marginal utility
The extra satisfaction gained from consuming one extra unit of a good within a given time period.

definition

Principle of diminishing marginal utility
As more units of a good are consumed, additional units will provide less additional satisfaction than previous units.

Marginal utility (*MU*) is the additional satisfaction gained from consuming one *extra* unit within a give period of time. Thus we might refer to the marginal utility that Tracey gains from her third cup of tea of the day or her eleventh cup.

Diminishing marginal utility

Up to a point, the more of a commodity you consume, the greater will be your total utility. However, as you become more satisfied, each extra unit you consume will probably give you less additional utility than previous units. In other words, your marginal utility falls, the more you consume. This is known as the **principle of diminishing marginal utility**. For example, the second cup of tea in the morning gives you less additional satisfaction than the first cup. The third cup gives less satisfaction still.

> *The principle of diminishing marginal utility.* The more of a product a person consumes over a given period of time, the less will be the additional utility gained from one more unit.
>
> **Key Idea 14**

At some level of consumption, your total utility will be at a maximum. No extra satisfaction can be gained by the consumption of further units within that period of time. Thus marginal utility will be zero. Your desire for tea may be fully satisfied at twelve cups per day. A thirteenth cup will yield no extra utility. It may even give you displeasure (i.e. negative marginal utility).

Pause for thought

Are there any goods or services where consumers do not experience diminishing marginal utility?

The optimum level of consumption: the simplest case – one commodity

Just how much of a good should people consume if they are to make the best use of their limited income? To answer this question we must tackle the problem of how to measure utility. The problem is that utility is subjective. There is no way of knowing what another person's experiences are really like. Just how satisfying does Brian find his first cup of tea in the morning? How does his utility compare with Tracey's? We do not have utility meters that can answer these questions!

One solution to the problem is to measure utility with money. In this case, total utility becomes the value that people place on their consumption, and marginal utility becomes the amount of money that a person would be prepared to pay to obtain one more unit: in other words, what that extra unit is worth to that person. If Darren is prepared to pay 30p to obtain an extra packet of crisps, then that packet yields him 30p worth of utility: *MU* = 30p.

So how many packets should he consume if he is to act rationally? To answer this we need to introduce the concept of **consumer surplus**.

definition

Consumer surplus
The excess of what a person would have been prepared to pay for a good (i.e. the utility) over what that person actually pays.

Marginal consumer surplus

Marginal consumer surplus (*MCS*) is the difference between what you are willing to pay for one more unit of a good and what you are actually charged. If Darren was willing to pay 30p for another packet of crisps which in fact cost him only 25p, he would be getting a marginal consumer surplus of 5p.

$$MCS = MU - P$$

Total consumer surplus

Total consumer surplus (*TCS*) is the sum of all the marginal consumer surpluses you have obtained from all the units of a good you have consumed. It is the difference between the total utility from all the units and your expenditure on them. If Darren consumes 4 packets of crisps, and if he would have been prepared to spend £1.40 on them and only had to spend £1.00, then his total consumer surplus is 40p.

$$TCS = TU - TE$$

where *TE* is the total expenditure on a good: i.e. $P \times Q$.

(Note that total expenditure (*TE*) is a similar concept to total revenue (*TR*). They are both defined as $P \times Q$. But in the case of total expenditure, *Q* is the quantity *purchased* by the consumer(s) in question, whereas in the case of total revenue, *Q* is the quantity *sold* by the firm(s) in question.)

Rational consumer behaviour

> **Key Idea 4 p27**

Let us define **rational consumer behaviour** as the attempt to maximise (total) consumer surplus.

The process of maximising consumer surplus can be shown graphically. Let us take the case of Tina's annual purchases of petrol. Tina has her own car, but as an alternative she can use public transport or walk. To keep the analysis simple, let us assume that Tina's parents bought her the car and pay the licence duty, and that Tina does not have the option of selling the car. She does, however, have to buy the petrol. The current price is 80p per litre. Figure 6.1 shows her consumer surplus.

If she were to use just a few litres per year, she would use them for very important journeys for which no convenient alternative exists. For such trips she may

---

definition

Marginal consumer surplus
The excess of utility from the consumption of one more unit of a good (*MU*) over the price paid: $MCS = MU - P$.

definition

Total consumer surplus
The excess of a person's total utility from the consumption of a good (*TU*) over the amount that person spends on it (*TE*): $TCS = TU - TE$.

definition

Rational consumer behaviour
The attempt to maximise total consumer surplus.

Figure 6.1

Tina's consumer surplus from petrol

Figure 6.2

Consumer surplus

be prepared to pay up to 110p per litre. For the first few litres, then, she is getting a marginal utility of around 110p per litre, and hence a marginal consumer surplus of around 30p (i.e. 110p – 80p).

By the time her annual purchase is around 250 litres, she would only be prepared to pay around 100p for additional litres. The additional journeys, although still important, would be less vital. Perhaps these are journeys where she could have taken public transport, albeit at some inconvenience. Her marginal consumer surplus at 250 litres is 20p (i.e. 100p – 80p).

Gradually additional litres give less and less additional utility as fewer and fewer important journeys are undertaken. The 500th litre yields 91p worth of extra utility. Marginal consumer surplus is now 11p (i.e. 91p – 80p).

By the time she gets to the 900th litre, Tina's marginal utility has fallen to 80p. There is no additional consumer surplus to be gained. Her total consumer surplus is at a maximum. She thus buys 900 litres, where $P = MU$.

Her total consumer surplus is the sum of all the marginal consumer surpluses: the sum of all the 900 vertical lines between the price and the MU curve. This is represented by the total *area* between the dashed P line and the MU curve.

This analysis can be expressed in general terms. In Figure 6.2, if the price of a commodity is P_1, the consumer will consume Q_1. The person's total expenditure (TE) is P_1Q_1, shown by area 1. Total utility (TU) is the area under the marginal utility curve: i.e. areas 1 + 2. Total consumer surplus ($TU – TE$) is shown by area 2.

We can now state the general rule for maximising total consumer surplus. If $MU > P$ people should buy more. As they do so, however, MU will fall (diminishing marginal utility). People should stop buying more when MU has fallen to equal P. At that point total consumer surplus is maximised.

Marginal utility and the demand curve for a good

An individual's demand curve

Individual people's demand curves for any good will be the same as their marginal utility curve for that good, measured in money.

This is demonstrated in Figure 6.3, which shows the marginal utility curve for a particular person and a particular good. If the price of the good were P_1, the person would consume Q_1: where $MU = P$. Thus point a would be one point on that person's demand curve. If the price fell to P_2, consumption would rise to Q_2, since this is where $MU = P_2$. Thus point b is a second point on the demand curve.

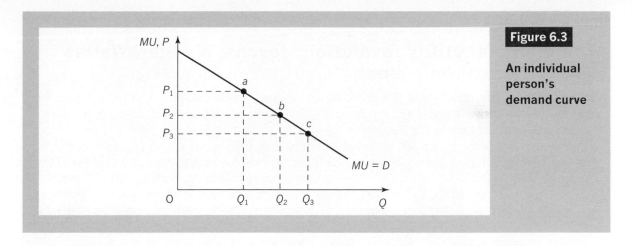

Figure 6.3

An individual person's demand curve

Likewise if price fell to P_3, Q_3 would be consumed. Point c is a third point on the demand curve.

Thus as long as individuals seek to maximise consumer surplus and hence consume where $P = MU$, their demand curve will be along the same line as their marginal utility curve.

The market demand curve

The market demand curve will simply be the (horizontal) sum of all individuals' demand curves and hence MU curves.

The shape of the demand curve. The price elasticity of demand will reflect the rate at which MU diminishes. If there are close substitutes for a good, it is likely to have an elastic demand, and its MU will diminish slowly as consumption increases. The reason is that increased consumption of this product will be accompanied by *decreased* consumption of the alternative product(s). Since total consumption of this product *plus* the alternatives has increased only slightly (if at all), the marginal utility will fall only slowly.

For example, the demand for a given brand of petrol is likely to have a fairly high price elasticity, since other brands are substitutes. If there is a cut in the price of Texaco petrol (assuming the prices of other brands stay constant), consumption of Texaco will increase a lot. The MU of Texaco petrol will fall slowly, since people consume less of other brands. Petrol consumption *in total* may be only slightly greater and hence the MU of petrol only slightly lower.

Shifts in the demand curve. How do *shifts* in demand relate to marginal utility? For example, how would the marginal utility of (and hence demand for) margarine be affected by a rise in the price of butter? The higher price of butter would cause less butter to be consumed. This would increase the marginal utility of margarine, since if people are using less butter, their desire for margarine is higher. The MU curve (and hence the demand curve) for margarine thus shifts to the right.

Weaknesses of the one-commodity version of marginal utility theory

A change in the consumption of one good will affect the marginal utility of substitute and complementary goods. It will also affect the amount of income left

The marginal utility revolution: Jevons, Menger, Walras
Solving the diamonds–water paradox

What determines the market value of a good? We already know the answer: demand and supply. So if we find out what determines the position of the demand and supply curves, we will at the same time be finding out what determines a good's market value.

This might seem obvious. Yet for years economists puzzled over just what determines a good's value.

Some economists like Karl Marx and David Ricardo concentrated on the supply side. For them, value depended on the amount of resources used in producing a good. This could be further reduced to the amount of *labour* time embodied in the good. Thus, according to the *labour theory of value*, the more labour that was directly involved in producing the good, or indirectly in producing the capital equipment used to make the good, the more valuable would the good be.

Other economists looked at the demand side. But here they came across a paradox.

Adam Smith in the 1760s gave the example of water and diamonds. 'How is it', he asked, 'that water which is so essential to human life, and thus has such a high "value-in-use", has such a low market value (or "value-in-exchange")? And how is it that diamonds which are relatively so trivial have such a high market value?' The answer to this paradox had to wait over a hundred years until the marginal utility revolution of the 1870s. William Stanley Jevons (1835–82) in England, Carl Menger (1840–1921) in Austria, and Leon Walras (1834–1910) in Switzerland all independently claimed that the source of the market value of a good was its *marginal* utility, not its *total* utility.

This was the solution to the diamonds–water paradox. Water, being so essential, has a high total utility: a high 'value in use'. But for most of us, given that we consume so much already, it has a very low marginal utility. Do you leave the cold tap running when you clean your teeth? If you do, it

shows just how trivial water is to you *at the margin*. Diamonds, on the other hand, although they have a much lower total utility, have a much higher marginal utility. There are so few diamonds in the world, and thus people have so few of them, that they are very valuable at the margin. If, however, a new technique were to be discovered of producing diamonds cheaply from coal, their market value would fall rapidly. As people had more of them, so their marginal utility would rapidly diminish.

Marginal utility still only gives the demand side of the story. The reason why the marginal utility of water is so low is that *supply* is so plentiful. Water is very expensive in Saudi Arabia! In other words, the full explanation of value must take into account both demand *and* supply.

Question

The diagram illustrates a person's MU curves of water and diamonds. Assume that diamonds are more expensive than water. Show how the MU of diamonds will be greater than the MU of water. Show also how the TU of diamonds will be less than the TU of water. (Remember: TU is the area under the MU curve.)

over to be spent on other goods. Thus a more satisfactory explanation of demand would involve an analysis of choices between goods, rather than looking at one good in isolation. We examine such choices in section 6.3.

Nevertheless, the assumptions of diminishing marginal utility and of the consumer making rational choices by considering whether it is 'worth' paying the price being charged are quite realistic assumptions about consumer behaviour. It is important for businesses to realise that the demand for their product tends to reflect consumers' perceptions of the *marginal* utility they expect to gain, rather than the *total* utility.

Demand under conditions of risk and uncertainty   6.2

The problem of imperfect information

So far we have assumed that when people buy goods and services, they know exactly what price they will pay and how much utility they will gain. In many cases this is a reasonable assumption. When you buy a bar of chocolate, you clearly do know how much you are paying for it and have a very good idea how much you will like it. But what about a video recorder, or a car, or a washing machine, or any other **consumer durable**? In each of these cases you are buying something that will last you a long time, and the further into the future you look, the less certain you will be of its costs and benefits to you.

> **definition**
>
> **Consumer durable**
> A consumer good that lasts a period of time, during which the consumer can continue gaining utility from it.

Take the case of a washing machine costing you £400. If you pay cash, your immediate outlay involves no uncertainty: it is £400. But washing machines can break down. In two years' time you could find yourself with a repair bill of £100. This cannot be predicted and yet it is a price you will have to pay, just like the original £400. In other words, when you buy the washing machine, you are uncertain as to the full 'price' it will entail over its lifetime.

If the costs of the washing machine are uncertain, so too are the benefits. You might have been attracted to buy it in the first place by the manufacturer's glossy brochure, or by the look of it, or by adverts on TV, in magazines, etc. When you have used it for a while, however, you will probably discover things you had not anticipated. The spin dryer does not get your clothes as dry as you had hoped; it is noisy; it leaks; the door sticks; and so on.

Buying consumer durables thus involves uncertainty. So too does the purchase of assets, whether a physical asset such as a house or financial assets such as shares. In the case of assets, the uncertainty is over their future *price*, which you cannot know for certain.

Attitudes towards risk and uncertainty

So how will uncertainty affect people's behaviour? The answer is that it depends on their attitudes towards taking a gamble. To examine these attitudes let us assume that a person does at least know the *odds* of the gamble. In other words, the person is operating under conditions of *risk* rather than *uncertainty*.

To illustrate different attitudes towards risk, consider the case of gambling that a particular number will come up on the throw of a dice. There is a one in six chance of this happening. Would you gamble? It depends on what odds you were offered and on your attitude to risk.

Odds can be of three types. They can be *favourable* odds. This is where on average you will gain. If, for example, you were offered odds of 10 to 1 on the throw of a dice, then for a £1 bet you would get nothing if you lost, but you would get £10 if your number came up. Since your number should come up on average one time in every six, on average you will gain. The longer you go on playing, the more money you are likely to win. If the odds were 6 to 1, they would be *fair* odds. On average you would break even. If, however, they were less than 6 to 1, they would be described as *unfavourable*. On average you would lose. There are three possible categories of attitude towards risk.

■ *Risk neutral*. This is where a person will take a gamble if the odds are favourable; not take a gamble if the odds are unfavourable; and be indifferent about taking a gamble if the odds are fair.

■ *Risk loving*. This is where a person is prepared to take a gamble even if the odds are unfavourable. The more risk loving a person is, the worse the odds he or she will be prepared to accept.

■ *Risk averse*. This is where a person may not be prepared to take a gamble even if the odds are favourable. The more risk averse the person is, the better would have to be the odds before he or she could be enticed to take a gamble. Few people are *totally risk averse* and thus totally unwilling to take a gamble. If I offered people a bet on the toss of a coin such that tails they pay me 10p and heads I pay them £100, few would refuse (unless on moral grounds).

Diminishing marginal utility of income and attitudes towards risk taking

Avid gamblers may be risk lovers. People who spend hours in the betting shop or at the race track may enjoy the risks, knowing that there is always the chance that they might win. On average, however, such people will lose. After all, the bookies have to take their cut and thus the odds are generally unfavourable.

Most people, however, for most of the time are risk averters. We prefer to avoid insecurity. But why? Is there a simple reason for this? Economists use marginal utility analysis to explain why.

They argue that the gain in utility to people from an extra £100 is less than the loss of utility from forgoing £100. Imagine your own position. You have probably adjusted your standard of living to your income (or are trying to!). If

Key Idea
14
p110

you unexpectedly gained £100, that would be very nice: you could buy some new clothes or have a weekend away. But if you lost £100, it could be very hard indeed. You might have very serious difficulties in making ends meet. Thus if you were offered the gamble of a 50:50 chance of winning or losing £100, you would probably decline the gamble.

> **Pause for thought**
>
> *Which gamble would you be more likely to accept, a 60:40 chance of gaining or losing £10 000, or a 40:60 chance of gaining or losing £1? Explain why.*

This risk-averting behaviour accords with the principle of *diminishing marginal utility*. Up to now in this chapter we have been focusing on the utility from the consumption of individual goods: Tracey and her cups of tea; Darren and his packets of crisps. In the case of each individual good, the more we consume, the less satisfaction we gain from each additional unit: the marginal utility falls. But the same principle applies if we look at our *total* consumption. The higher our level of total consumption, the less additional satisfaction will be gained from each additional £1 spent. What we are saying here is that there is a **diminishing marginal utility of income**. The more you earn, the lower will be the utility from each *extra* £1. If people on low incomes earn an extra £100, they will feel a lot better off: the marginal utility they will get from that income will be very high. If rich people earn an extra £100, however, their gain in utility will be less.

Why, then, does a diminishing marginal utility of income make us risk averters? The answer is illustrated in Figure 6.4, which shows the *total* utility you get from your income.

> **definition**
>
> **Diminishing marginal utility of income**
> Where each additional pound earned yields less additional utility.

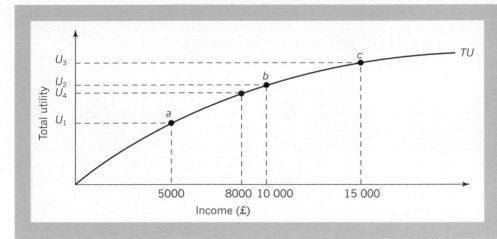

Figure 6.4

The total utility of income given diminishing marginal utility of income

The slope of this curve gives the *marginal* utility of your income. As the marginal utility of income diminishes, so the curve gets flatter. A rise in income from £5000 to £10 000 will cause a movement along the curve from point *a* to point *b*. Total utility rises from U_1 to U_2. A similar rise in income from £10 000 to £15 000, however, will lead to a move from point *b* to point *c*, and hence a *smaller* rise in total utility from U_2 to U_3.

Now assume that your income is £10 000 and you are offered a chance of gambling £5000 of it. You are offered the fair odds of a 50:50 chance of gaining an extra £5000 (i.e. doubling it) or losing it. Effectively, then, you have an equal chance of your income rising to £15 000 or falling to £5000.

At an income of £10 000, your total utility is U_2. If your gamble pays off and as a result your income rises to £15 000, your total utility will rise to U_3. If it does not pay off, you will be left with only £5000 and a utility of U_1. Given that you have a 50:50 chance of winning, your *average* expected utility will be midway between U_1 and U_3 (i.e. $\frac{(U_1 + U_3)}{2}$) = U_4. But this is the utility that would be gained from an income of £8000. Given that you would prefer U_2 to U_4 you will choose not to take the gamble.

Thus risk aversion is part of rational utility-maximising behaviour.

On most occasions we will not know the odds of taking a gamble. In other words, we will be operating under conditions of *uncertainty*. This could make us very cautious indeed. The more pessimistic we are, the more cautious we will be.

Insurance: a way of removing risks

Key Idea
13
p98

Insurance is the opposite of gambling. It takes the risk away. If, for example, you risk losing your job if you are injured, you can remove the risk of loss of income by taking out an appropriate insurance policy.

Given that people are risk averters, they will be prepared to pay the premiums even though they give them 'unfair odds'. The total premiums paid to insurance companies will be *more* than the amount the insurance companies pay out: that is, after all, how the companies make a profit.

But does this mean that the insurance companies are less risk averse than their customers? Why is it that the insurance companies are prepared to shoulder the risks that their customers were not? The answer is that the insurance company is able to **spread its risks**.

definition

Spreading risks (for an insurance company)
The more policies an insurance company issues and the more independent the risks of claims from these policies are, the more predictable will be the number of claims.

Problems for unwary insurance companies
'Adverse selection' and 'moral hazard'

Adverse selection

This is where the people taking out insurance are those who have the highest risk.

For example, suppose that a company offers medical insurance. It surveys the population and works out that the average person requires £200 of treatment per year. The company thus sets the premium at £250 (the extra £50 to cover its costs and provide a profit). But it is likely that the people most likely to take out the insurance are those most likely to fall sick: those who have been ill before, those whose families have a history of illness, those in jobs that are hazardous to health, etc. These people on average may require £500 of treatment per year. The insurance company would soon make a loss.

But cannot the company then simply raise premiums to £550 or £600? It can, but the problem is that it will thereby be depriving the person of *average* health of reasonably priced insurance.

The answer is for the company to discriminate more carefully between people. You may have to fill out a questionnaire so that the company can assess your own particular risk and set an appropriate premium. There may need to be legal penalties for people caught lying!

Question

What details does an insurance company require to know before it will insure a person to drive a car?

Moral hazard

This is where having insurance makes you less careful and thus increases your risk to the company. For example, if your bicycle is insured against theft, you may be less concerned to go through the hassle of chaining it up each time you leave it.

Again, if insurance companies work out risks by looking at the *total* number of bicycle thefts, these figures will understate the risks to the company because they will include thefts from *uninsured* people who are likely to be more careful.

Question

How will the following reduce moral hazard?

(a) *A no-claims bonus.*
(b) *Your having to pay the first so many pounds of any claim.*
(c) *Offering lower premiums to those less likely to claim (e.g. lower house contents premiums for those with burglar alarms).*

The problem of moral hazard occurs in many other walks of life. A good example is that of debt. If someone else is willing to pay your debts (e.g. your parents) it is likely to make you less careful in your spending! This argument has been used by some rich countries for not cancelling the debts of poor countries.

The spreading of risks

If there is a one in a hundred chance of your house burning down each year, although it is only a small chance it would be so disastrous that you are simply not prepared to take the risk. You thus take out house insurance and are prepared to pay a premium of *more than* 1 per cent (one in a hundred).

The insurance company, however, is not just insuring you. It is insuring many others at the same time. If your house burns down, there will be approximately 99 others that do not. The premiums the insurance company has collected will be more than enough to cover its payments. The more houses it insures, the smaller will be the variation in the proportion that actually burn down each year.

This is an application of the **law of large numbers**. What is unpredictable for an individual becomes highly predictable in the mass. The more people the insurance company insures, the more predictable is the total outcome.

What is more, the insurance company will be in a position to estimate just what the risks are. It can thus work out what premiums it must charge in order to make a profit. With individuals, however, the precise risk is rarely known. Do you know your chances of living to 70? Almost certainly you do not. But a life assurance company will know precisely the chances of a person of your age, sex and occupation living to 70! It will have the statistical data to show this. In other words, an insurance company will be able to convert your *uncertainty* into their *risk*.

The spreading of risks does not just require that there should be a large number of policies. It also requires that the risks should be **independent**. If any insurance company insured 1000 houses *all in the same neighbourhood*, and then there were a major fire in the area, the claims would be enormous. The risks of fire were not independent. The company would, in fact, have been taking a gamble on a single event. If, however, it provides fire insurance for houses scattered all over the country, the risks *are* independent.

Another way in which insurance companies can spread their risks is by **diversification**. The more types of insurance a company offers (car, house, life, health, etc.), the greater is likely to be the independence of the risks.

> **definition**
> **Independent risks**
> Where two risky events are unconnected. The occurrence of one will not affect the likelihood of the occurrence of the other.

> **definition**
> **Diversification**
> Where a firm expands into new types of business.

The characteristics approach to analysing consumer demand — 6.3

This section is optional. You may skip straight to the next chapter if you prefer.

As we concluded in the last section, to get a better understanding of consumer demand, we need to analyse how consumers choose *between* products. In other words, we must look at products, not in isolation, but in relation to other products. Any firm wanting to understand the basis on which consumers demand its products will want to know why they might choose *its* product rather than those of its rivals. A car manufacturer will want to know why consumers might choose one of its models rather than those of its competitors.

Such choices depend not only on price but on the characteristics of the products. If you were buying a car, in addition to its price you would consider features such as style, performance, comfort, reliability, durability, fuel economy, safety and various added features (such as air conditioning, stereo system, air bags, electric windows, etc.). Car manufacturers will thus design their cars to make them as attractive as possible to consumers, relative to the cost of manufacture. In fact, most firms will constantly try to find ways of improving their products to make them more appealing to consumers.

What we are saying here is that consumers derive utility from the various characteristics that a product possesses. To understand choices, then, we need to look at the attributes of different products and how these influence consumer choices between them. **Characteristics theory** (sometimes called 'attributes theory') was developed by the economist Kelvin Lancaster[1] in the mid-1960s to analyse such choices and to relate them to the demand for a product.

Characteristics theory is based on four key assumptions:

- All products possess various characteristics.
- Different brands possess them in different proportions.

> **Key Idea**
> **7**
> p50

> **Key Idea**
> **4**
> p27

> **definition**
> **Characteristics (or attributes) theory**
> The theory that demonstrates how consumer choice between different varieties of a product depends on the characteristics of these varieties, along with prices of the different varieties, the consumer's budget and the consumer's tastes.

---

[1] K. Lancaster, 'A New Approach to Consumer Theory', *Journal of Political Economy*, 74 (April 1966), pp. 132–57.

- The characteristics are measurable: they are 'objective'.
- The characteristics (along with price and consumers' incomes) determine consumer choice.

Identifying and plotting products' characteristics

Let us take a simple case of a product where consumers base their choice between brands on price and just two characteristics. For example, assume that consumers choose between different brands of breakfast cereal on the basis of taste and health-giving properties. To keep the analysis simple, let us assume that taste is related to the amount of sugar in the cereal and that health-giving properties are related to the amount of fibre.

Plotting the characteristics of different brands

The combinations of these two characteristics, sugar and fibre, can be measured on a diagram. In Figure 6.5, the quantity of sugar is measured on the horizontal axis and the quantity of fibre on the vertical axis. One brand, Healthbran, contains a lot of fibre, but only a little sugar. Another, Tastyflakes, contains a lot of sugar, but only a little fibre.

The ratio of the two attributes, fibre and sugar, in each of the two brands is given by the slope of the two rays out from the origin. Thus by consuming a certain amount of Healthbran, given by point h_1 on the Healthbran ray, the consumer is getting f_1 of fibre and s_1 of sugar. The consumption of more Healthbran is shown by a movement up the ray, say to h_2. At this point the consumer gets f_2 of fibre and s_2 of sugar. Notice that the ratio of fibre to sugar is the same in both cases. The ratio is given by f_1/s_1 ($= f_2/s_2$), which is simply the slope of the Healthbran ray.

The consumer of Tastyflakes can get relatively more sugar, but less fibre. Thus consumption at point t_1 gives s_3 of sugar, but only f_3 of fibre. The ratio of fibre to sugar for Tastyflakes is given by the slope of its ray, which is f_3/s_3.

Any number of rays can be put on the diagram, each one representing a particular brand. In each case, the ratio of fibre to sugar is given by the slope of the ray.

Figure 6.5

The characteristics of two brands of breakfast cereal

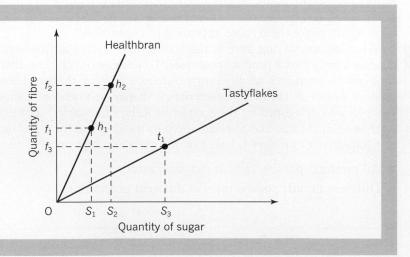

Changes in a product's characteristics. If a firm decides to change the mix of characteristics of a product, the slope of the ray will change. Thus if Healthbran were made sweeter, its ray would become shallower.

The budget constraint

The amount that a consumer buys of a brand will depend in part on the consumer's budget and on the price of the product. Assume that, given the current price of Healthbran, Jane's budget for breakfast cereals allows her to buy at h_1 per month: in other words, the amount of Healthbran that gives f_1 of fibre and s_1 of sugar. (This assumes that she only buys Healthbran and not some other brand too.)

A change in the budget. If she allocates more of her income to buying breakfast cereal, and sticks with Healthbran, she would move up the ray: say, to h_2. In other words, by buying more Healthbran, she would be buying more fibre and more sugar. Similarly, a reduction in expenditure on a product would be represented by a movement down its ray.

A change in price. If a product rises in price and the budget allocated to it remains the same, less will be purchased. There will be a movement down its ray.

The efficiency frontier

In practice, many consumers will buy a mixture of brands. Some days you may prefer one type of breakfast cereal, some days you may prefer another type. People get fed up with consuming too much of one brand or variety: they experience diminishing marginal utility from that particular mix of characteristics. You may allocate a certain amount of money for a summer holiday each year, but you may well want to go to a different place each year, since each place has a different mix of characteristics.

Assume that, given her current budget for breakfast cereals, the prices of Healthbran and Tastyflakes allow Jane to buy at either point *a* or point *b* in Figure 6.6. By switching completely from Healthbran to Tastyflakes, her consumption of fibre would go down from f_1 to f_2, and her consumption of sugar would go up from s_1 to s_2. She could, however, spend part of her budget on

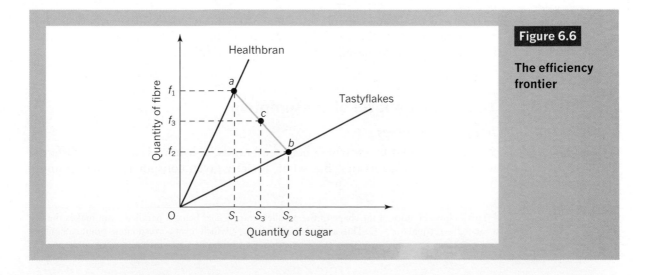

Figure 6.6

The efficiency frontier

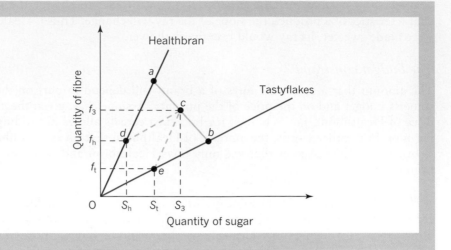

Figure 6.7

Consuming a mixture of two products

Healthbran and part on Tastyflakes. In fact, she could consume anywhere along the straight line joining points *a* and *b*. This line is known as the **efficiency frontier**. For example, by buying some of each brand, she could consume at point *c*, giving her f_3 of fibre and s_3 of sugar.

If she did consume at point *c*, how much of the two characteristics would she get from each of the two brands? This is shown in Figure 6.7 by drawing two lines from point *c*, each one parallel to one of the two rays. Consumption of the two brands takes place at points *d* and *e* respectively, giving her f_h units of fibre and s_h units of sugar from Healthbran, and f_t units of fibre and s_t units of sugar from Tastyflakes. The total amount of fibre and sugar from the two brands will be f_3 $(= f_h + f_t)$ and s_3 $(= s_h + s_t)$.[2]

It is easily possible to show an efficiency frontier between several brands, each with their own particular blend of characteristics. This is illustrated in Figure 6.8, which shows the case of four breakfast cereals, each with different combinations of fibre and sugar.

Any of the four points through which the efficiency frontier passes can change if the price of that brand changes. So if Oatybix went up in price, point *b* would move down the Oatybix ray, thereby altering the shape of the efficiency frontier.

If any of the brands changed their mix of characteristics, then the respective ray would pivot. If the consumer's budget changed, then the whole efficiency frontier would move parallel up or down all the rays.

The optimum level of consumption

Indifference curves

We have seen that by switching between brands, consumers can obtain different mixtures of characteristics. But what, for any given consumer, is the optimum

---

[2] This follows because of the shape of the parallelogram O*dce*. Being a parallelogram makes the distance $f_3 - f_h$ equal to $f_t - O$. Thus adding f_h and f_t gives f_3, which must correspond to point *c*. Similarly the distance $s_3 - s_t$ must equal $s_h - O$. Thus adding s_h and s_t gives s_3, which also must correspond to point *c*.

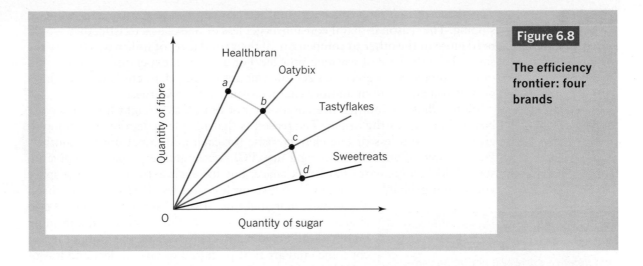

Figure 6.8

The efficiency frontier: four brands

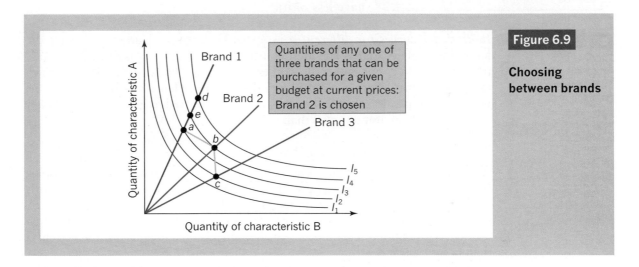

Figure 6.9

Choosing between brands

mixture? This can be shown by examining a consumer's preferences, and the way we do this is to construct **indifference curves**. This is illustrated in Figure 6.9, which shows five indifference curves, labelled I_1 to I_5.

An indifference curve shows all the different combinations of the two characteristics that yield an equal amount of satisfaction or utility. Thus any combination of characteristics along curve I_1 represents the same given level of utility. The consumer is, therefore, 'indifferent' between all points along curve I_1. Although the actual level of utility is not measured in the diagram, the further out the curve, the higher the level of utility. Thus all points on curve I_5 are preferred to all points along curve I_4, and all points along curve I_4 are preferred to all points along curve I_3, and so on. In fact, indifference curves are rather like contours on a map. Each contour represents all points on the ground that are a particular height above sea level. You can have as many contours as you like on the map, depending at what interval you draw them: 100 metre, 25 metre, 10 metre, or whatever. Similarly you could have as many indifference curves as you like on an *indifference map*. In Figure 6.9, we have drawn just five such curves, as that is all that is necessary to illustrate consumer choice.

definition

Indifference curve
A line showing all those combinations of two characteristics of a good between which a consumer is indifferent: i.e. those combinations that give a particular level of utility.

The shape of indifference curves. Indifference curves are drawn as downward sloping. The reason is that if consumers get less of one characteristic, they would need more of the other to compensate, if their total level of utility was to stay the same. Take the case of washing powder. For any given expenditure, you would only be prepared to give up a certain amount of one characteristic, say whiteness, if you got more of another characteristic, such as softness.

Notice that the indifference curves are not drawn as straight lines. They are bowed in towards the origin. The reason is that people generally are willing to give up less and less of one characteristic for each additional unit of another. For example, if you were buying a new PC, you might be prepared to give up some RAM to get extra hard disk space, but for each extra GB of disk space you would probably be prepared to give up less and less RAM. We call this a **diminishing marginal rate of substitution** between the two characteristics. The reason is that you get diminishing marginal utility from any characteristic the more of it you consume, and are thus prepared to give up less and less of another characteristic (whose marginal utility rises as you have less of it).

> **Key Idea**
> 14
> p110

Pause for thought

Can you think of any instances where the indifference curve will not be bowed in towards the origin?

Indifference curves for different consumers. Different consumers will have different indifference maps. The indifference map in Figure 6.9 is drawn for a particular consumer, say James. If another consumer, Henry, gets relatively more satisfaction from characteristic B than does James, Henry's indifference curves would be steeper. In other words, he would be prepared to give up more units of A to get a certain amount of B than would James.

The optimum combination of characteristics

We are now in a position to see how a 'rational' consumer would choose between brands. Figure 6.9 shows the rays for three brands of a product, with, at given prices, the efficiency frontier passing through points *a*, *b* and *c*. The consumer would choose to consume Brand 2, since point *b* is on a higher indifference curve than point *a* (Brand 1), which in turn is on a higher indifference curve than point *c* (Brand 3).

> **Key Idea**
> 4
> p27

Sometimes the consumer will choose to purchase a mixture of brands. This is shown in Figure 6.10, which takes the simple case of just two brands in the

Figure 6.10

Choosing a mixture of brands

market. By consuming at point *a* (i.e. a combination of point *b* on the Brand 1 ray and point *c* on the Brand 2 ray), the consumer is on a higher indifference curve than by consuming only Brand 1 (point *d*) or Brand 2 (point *e*).

Response to changes

We can now show how consumers would respond to changes in price, income, product characteristics and tastes.

Changes in price

Referring back to Figure 6.9, if the price of a brand changes, there is a shift in the efficiency frontier, so that it crosses the ray for that brand at a different point. For example, if the price of Brand 1 fell, there would be a movement of the efficiency frontier up the Brand 1 ray from point *a*. If the price fell far enough that the efficiency frontier now passed through point *d*, the consumer would switch from consuming just Brand 2 to just Brand 1. If the price fell less than this, so that the efficiency frontier passed through point *e*, then the consumer would buy a mixture of both brands. The optimum consumption point would lie on an indifference curve a little above I_4.

We can relate this analysis to the concept of cross-price elasticity of demand (see page 89). If two products are very close substitutes, they will have a high cross-price elasticity of demand. But what makes them close substitutes? The answer is that they are likely to have similar characteristics; their rays will have a similar slope. Even a slight rise in the price of one of them (i.e. a small movement along its ray) can lead the consumer to switch to the other. This will occur when the rays are close together: when they have a similar slope.

Changes in income

If there is a change in consumer incomes, so that people allocate a bigger budget to the product in question, then there will be a parallel movement outwards of the efficiency frontier. Whether this will involve consumers switching between brands depends on the shape of the indifference map.

Changes in the characteristics of a product (real or perceived)

If consumers believe that a brand now yields relatively more of characteristic B than A, the ray will become less steep. How far out will the efficiency point be on this new ray? This depends on the total perceived amount of the two characteristics that is obtained from the given budget spent on this brand.

To illustrate this, consider Figure 6.11. The firm producing Brand 1 changes its specifications, so that for a given budget a lot more characteristic B can be obtained and a little more characteristic A. The result is that the brand's ray shifts inwards and the efficiency frontier which originally connected points *a* and *b*, now connects points *c* and *b*. In this case the consumer represented by the indifference curves shown switches consumption from Brand 2 at point *b* to Brand 1 at point *c*.

If there is a proportionate increase in both characteristics (i.e. the brand has generally improved), the slope of the ray will not change. Instead, there will be a movement of the efficiency frontier outward along the ray. Graphically the effect is the same as a fall in the price of the product: more of both characteristics can be obtained for a given budget.

Figure 6.11

A change in the characteristics of Brand 1

Changes in tastes

If consumers' tastes change, their whole indifference map will change. If characteristic B now gives more utility relative to A than before, the curves will become steeper, and the consumer is likely to choose a product which yields relatively more of characteristic B (i.e. one with a relatively shallow ray).

Clearly firms will attempt to predict such changes in tastes and will try, through product design, advertising and marketing, to shift the ray for their brand in the desired direction (downwards in the above case). They will also try to persuade consumers that the product is generally better (i.e. has more of all characteristics) and thereby move outward the point where the efficiency frontier crosses the brand's ray.

Business and the characteristics approach

Characteristics analysis can help us understand the nature of consumer choice. When we go shopping and compare one product with another, it is the differences in the features of the various brands, along with price, that determine which products we end up buying. If firms, therefore, want to compete effectively with their rivals, it is not enough to compete solely in terms of price, it is important to focus on the specifications of their product and how these compare with those of their rivals' products.

Key Idea 7 p50

Characteristics analysis can help firms study the implications of changing their product's specifications (and of their rivals changing theirs). It also allows firms to analyse the effects of changes in their price, or their rivals' prices; the effects of changes in the budgets of various types of consumer; the effects of changes in consumer tastes; and the effects of repositioning themselves in the market.

Take the producer of Brand 1 in Figure 6.12. Clearly the firm would like to persuade consumers like the one illustrated to switch away from Brand 2 to Brand 1. It could do this by lowering its price. But a small reduction in price will have no effect on this consumer. Only when the price has fallen far enough for the efficiency frontier to rise nearly to point *d* will the consumer start switching; and only when the price has fallen further still, so that the efficiency

Figure 6.12

Options open to the firm producing Brand 1

frontier passes through a point a little above point d, will the consumer switch completely.

An alternative would be for the firm to reposition its product. It could introduce more of characteristic B into its product, thereby swinging the Brand 1 ray clockwise towards the Brand 2 ray. Clearly, it would have to be careful about its price too. The closer its brand became in quality to Brand 2, the more elastic would demand become, since Brand 1 would now be a closer substitute for Brand 2. In the extreme case of its ray becoming the same as that for Brand 2, its price would have to be low enough for the consumer to buy at or above point b. Depending on consumer tastes (and hence the shape of the indifference curves), it may choose to reposition its brand between the Brand 2 and Brand 3 rays. Again, a careful mix of product characteristics and price may enable it to capture a larger share of the market.

Another alternative would be for the firm to attempt to influence consumer tastes. In Figure 6.12, if it could persuade consumers to attach more value to characteristic A, the indifference curves would become shallower (i.e. less characteristic A would now be needed to give consumers a given level of utility). If the curves swung downwards enough, point a could be now on a higher indifference curve than point b. The consumer concerned would switch from Brand 2 to Brand 1. Clearly, the more consumers are influenced in this way, the more will sales of Brand 1 rise.

If a firm is thinking of launching a new product, again it will need to see how the characteristics of its product compare with those of the existing firms in the market. It will need to see where its ray would be compared with those of other firms, and whether the price it is thinking of charging would enable it to take sales off its rivals.

> **Pause for thought**
>
> *Before you read on, what do you think are the limitations of characteristics analysis?*

Limitations of characteristics analysis

Characteristics analysis, as we have seen, can help firms to understand their position in the market and the effects of changing their strategy. Nevertheless it cannot provide firms with a complete analysis of demand. There are four key limitations of the approach:

- It is sometimes difficult to identify and measure characteristics in a clear and unambiguous way. Take the look or design of a product, whether it be furniture, clothing, a painting or a car. What makes it visually appealing depends on the personal tastes of the consumer, and such tastes are virtually impossible to quantify.

- Most products have several characteristics. The analysis we have been examining, however, is limited to just two characteristics: one on each axis. It is possible, however, by using mathematical analysis to extend the number of characteristics. Nevertheless, the more characteristics that are included in the analysis, the more complex it becomes.

- Indifference curves, whilst being a good means of understanding consumer choice in theory, have practical limitations. To draw an indifference map for just one consumer would be very difficult, given that consumers often would find it hard having to imagine a series of combinations of characteristics between which they were indifferent. To draw indifference curves for millions of consumers would be virtually impossible. At best, therefore, they can provide a rough guide to consumer choice.

- Consumer tastes change. In what way consumer tastes will change, and how these changes will influence the shape of the indifference curves, is very difficult to predict.

Despite these problems, there are many useful insights that firms can gain from the analysis. Firms, through their market research, could gain considerable information about consumer attitudes towards their products' characteristics and thus the general shape, if not precise position, of indifference curves.

What is more, many markets divide into different **market segments** with consumers in each segment having similar tastes (and hence similar sets of indifference curves). For example, different models of car fall into different groups (such as medium-sized saloons, high-performance small cars, people carriers and small 'tall' cars), as do different types of restaurant and different types of holiday. Thus a tour operator will first identify the particular segment of the market it is aiming for (e.g. a young person's package holiday with the characteristics of guaranteed sunshine and plenty of nightlife) and then position itself in that particular market relative to its rival tour operators.

What is clear is that firms need good information about the demand for their products and to develop a careful marketing strategy. In Chapter 7 we look at how firms attempt to get information about demand, and in Chapter 8 we examine how firms set about developing, marketing and advertising their products.

definition

Market segment
A part of a market for a product where the demand is for a particular variety of that product.

SUMMARY

1a Economists call consumer satisfaction 'utility'. Marginal utility diminishes as consumption increases. This means that total utility will rise less and less rapidly as people consume more. At a certain point, total utility will reach a maximum, at which point marginal utility will be zero. Beyond this point, total utility will fall; marginal utility will be negative.

1b Consumers will attempt to maximise their total utility. They will do this by consuming more of a good as long as its marginal utility to them (measured in terms of the price they are prepared to pay for it) exceeds its price. They will stop buying additional amounts once *MU* has fallen to equal the price. At this point, the consumer's surplus will be maximised.

1c An individual's demand curve lies along the same line as the individual's marginal utility curve. The market demand curve is the sum of all individuals' marginal utility curves.

2a When people buy consumer durables they may be uncertain of their benefits and any additional repair and maintenance costs. When they buy financial assets they may be uncertain of what will happen to their price in the future. Buying under these conditions of imperfect knowledge is therefore a form of gambling. When we take such gambles, if we know the odds we are said to be operating under conditions of *risk*. If we do not know the odds we are said to be operating under conditions of *uncertainty*.

2b People can be divided into risk lovers, risk averters and those who are risk neutral. Because of the diminishing marginal utility of income it is rational for people to be risk averters (unless gambling is itself pleasurable).

2c Insurance is a way of eliminating risks for policy holders. Being risk averters, people are prepared to pay premiums in order to obtain insurance. Insurance companies, on the other hand, are prepared to take on these risks because they can spread them over a large number of policies. According to the law of large numbers, what is unpredictable for a single policy holder becomes highly predictable for a large number of them provided that their risks are independent of each other.

3a Consumers buy products for their characteristics. Characteristics can be plotted on a diagram and a ray drawn out from the origin for each product. The slope of the ray gives the amount of the characteristic measured on the vertical axis relative to the amount measured on the horizontal axis.

3b The amount purchased will depend on the consumer's budget. An efficiency frontier can be drawn showing the maximum quantity of various alternative brands (or combinations of them) that can be purchased for that budget.

3c An indifference map can be drawn on the same diagram. The map shows a series of indifference curves, each one measuring all the alternative combinations of two characteristics that give the consumer a given level of utility. The consumer is thus indifferent between all combinations along an indifference curve. Indifference curves further out to the right represent higher levels of utility and thus preferred combinations. Indifference curves are bowed in to the origin. This reflects a diminishing marginal rate of substitution between characteristics.

3d The optimum combination of characteristics is where the efficiency frontier is tangential to (i.e. just touches) the highest indifference curve. The 'rational' consumer will thus purchase at this point.

3e A change in a product's price, or a change in the consumer's budget, is represented by a movement along the product's ray. A change in the mix of characteristics of a product is represented by a swing in the ray (i.e. a change in its slope). A change in consumer tastes is represented by a shift in the indifference curves. They will become steeper if tastes shift towards the characteristic measured on the horizontal axis.

3f Although (a) some characteristics are difficult or impossible to measure, (b) only two characteristics can be measured on a simple two-dimensional diagram and (c) the position of indifference curves is difficult to identify in practice, characteristics theory gives useful insights into the process of consumer choice. It can help firms analyse the implications of changing their or their rivals' product's specifications, changes in consumer tastes and changes in their or their rivals' prices.

REVIEW QUESTIONS

1 Do you ever purchase things irrationally? If so, what are they and why is your behaviour irrational?

2 If you buy something in the shop on the corner when you know that the same item could have been bought more cheaply two miles up the road in the supermarket, is you behaviour irrational? Explain.

3 How would marginal utility and market demand be affected by a rise in the price of a complementary good?

4 Why do we get less consumer surplus from goods where our demand is relatively price elastic?

5 Explain why the price of a good is no reflection of the *total* value that consumers put on it.

6 Give some examples of risk taking or gambling where the odds are (a) unfavourable; (b) fair; (c) favourable.

7 If people are generally risk averse, why do so many people around the world take part in national lotteries?

8 Why are insurance companies unwilling to provide insurance against losses arising from war or 'civil insurrection'? Name some other events where it would be impossible to obtain insurance.

9 Make a list of characteristics of shoes. Which of these could be easily measured and which are more 'subjective'?

10 If two houses had identical characteristics, except that one was near a noisy airport and the other was in a quiet location, and if the market price of the first house was £80 000 and the second was £100 000, how would that help us to put a value on the characteristic of peace and quiet?

11 Assume that Rachel is attending university and likes to eat a meal at lunchtime. Assume that she has three options of where to eat: the university refectory, a nearby pub or a nearby restaurant. Apart from price, she takes into account the quality of the food and the pleasantness of the surroundings when choosing where to eat.

   Sketch her indifference map for the two characteristics, food quality and pleasantness of surroundings. Now, making your own assumptions about which locations provide which characteristics, the prices they charge and Rachel's weekly budget for lunches, sketch the rays for the three locations and draw a weekly efficiency frontier. Mark Rachel's optimum consumption point.

   Now illustrate the following (you might need to draw separate diagrams):

   (a) A rise in the price of meals at the local pub, but no change in the price of meals at the other two locations.
   (b) A shift in Rachel's tastes in favour of food quality relative to pleasantness of surroundings.
   (c) The refectory is refurbished and is now a much more attractive place to eat.

12 Why would consumption at a point inside the efficiency frontier not be 'rational'?

Demand and the firm

Given our analysis in Chapter 6, how might a business set about discovering the wants of consumers and hence the intensity of demand? The more effectively a business can identify such wants, the more likely it is to increase its sales and be successful. The clearer idea it can gain of the rate at which the typical consumer's utility will decline as consumption increases, the better estimate it can make of the product's price elasticity. Also the more it can assess the relative utility to the consumer of its product compared with those of its rivals, the more effectively will it be able to compete by differentiating its product from theirs. In this chapter we shall consider the alternative strategies open to business for collecting data on consumer behaviour, and how it can help business managers to estimate and forecast patterns of demand.

7.1 Estimating demand functions

If a business is to make sound strategic decisions, it must have a good understanding of its market. It must be able to predict things such as the impact of an advertising campaign, or the consequences of changing a brand's price or specifications. It must also be able to predict the likely growth (or decline) in consumer demand, both in the near future and over the longer term. The problem is that information on consumer behaviour can be costly and time consuming to acquire, and there is no guarantee as to its accuracy. As a result, business managers are frequently making strategic decisions with imperfect knowledge, never fully knowing whether the decision they have made is the 'best' one: i.e. the one which yields the most profit or sales, or best meets some other more specific strategic objective (such as driving a competitor from a segment of a market).

Key Idea
7
p50

But despite the fact that the information which a firm acquires is bound to be imperfect, it is still usually better than relying on hunches or 'instinct'. The firm having obtained information on consumer behaviour, there are two main uses to which it can be put:

- Estimating demand functions. Here the information is used to show the relationship between the quantity demanded and the various determinants of demand, such as price, consumers' incomes, advertising, the price of substitute and complementary goods, etc. Once this relationship (known as a *demand function*) has been established, it can be used to predict what would happen to demand if one of its determinants changed.

- Forecasting future demand. Here the information is used to project future sales potential. This can then be used as the basis for output and investment plans.
- In this section we concentrate on the first of these two uses. We examine methods for gathering data on consumer behaviour and then see how these data can be used to estimate a demand function.

Methods of collecting data on consumer behaviour

There are three general approaches to gathering information about consumers. These are: **observations of market behaviour**, **market surveys** and **market experiments**.

Market observations

The firm can gather data on how demand for its product has changed over time. Virtually all firms will have detailed information of their sales broken down by week, and/or month, and/or year. They will probably also have information on how sales have varied from one part of the market to another.

In addition, the firm will need to obtain data on how the various determinants of demand (such as price, advertising and the price of competitors' products) have themselves changed over time. Firms are likely to have much of this information already: for example, the amount spent on advertising and the prices of competitors' products. Other information might be relatively easy to obtain by paying an agency to do the research.

Having obtained this information, the firm can then use it to estimate how changes in the various determinants have affected demand in the past, and hence what effect they will be likely to have in the future (we examine this estimation process later in this section).

Even the most sophisticated analysis based on market observations, however, will suffer from one major drawback. Relationships that held in the past will not necessarily hold in the future. Consumers are human, and humans change their minds. Their perceptions of products change (something that the advertising industry relies on!) and their tastes change. It is for this reason that many firms turn to market surveys or market experiments to gain more information about the future.

Market surveys

It is not uncommon to be stopped in a city centre, or to have a knock at the door, and be asked whether you would kindly answer the questions of some market researcher. If the research interviewer misses you, then a postal questionnaire may well seek out the same type of information. A vast quantity of information can be collected in this way. It is a relatively quick and cheap method of data collection. Questions concerning all aspects of consumer behaviour might be asked, such as those relating to present and future patterns of expenditure, or how a buyer might respond to changing product specifications or price, both of the firm in question and of its rivals.

A key feature of the market survey is that it can be targeted at distinct consumer groups, thereby reflecting the specific information requirements of a business. For example, businesses selling luxury goods will be interested only in consumers falling within higher income brackets. Other samples might be drawn from a particular age group or gender, or from those with a particular lifestyle, such as eating habits.

The major drawback with this technique concerns the accuracy of the information acquired. Accurate information requires various conditions to be met.

A random sample. If the sample is not randomly selected, it may fail to represent a cross-section of the population being surveyed. As a result, it may be subject to various forms of research bias. For example, the sample might not contain the correct gender and racial balance. The information might then over-emphasise the views of a particular group (e.g. white men).

Clarity of the questions. It is important for the questions to be phrased in an unambiguous way, so as not to mislead the respondent.

Avoidance of leading questions. It is very easy for the respondent to be led into giving the answer the firm wants to hear. For example, when asking whether the person would buy a new product that the firm is thinking of launching, the questionnaire might make the product sound really desirable. The respondents might, as a result, say that they would buy the product, but later, when they see the product in the shops, they might realise that they do not want it.

Willingness of respondents. People might refuse to answer particular questions, possibly due to their personal nature. This may then lead to partial or distorted information.

Truthful response. It is very tempting for respondents who are 'keen to please' to give the answer that they think the questioner wants, or for other somewhat reluctant respondents to give 'mischievous' answers. In other words, people may lie!

Stability of demand. By the time the product is launched, or the changes to an existing product are made, time will have elapsed. The information may then be out of date. Consumer demand may have changed, as tastes and fashions have shifted, or as a result of the actions of competitors. The essence of the problem of market surveys is that they ask consumers what they are likely to do. People can and do change their mind.

As well as surveying consumers, businesses might survey other businesses, or panels of experts within a particular market. Both could yield potentially valuable information to the business.

Market experiments

Rather than asking consumers questions and getting them to *imagine* how they *would* behave, the market experiment involves observing consumer *behaviour* under simulated conditions. It can be used to observe consumer reactions to a new product or to changes in an existing product.

A simple experiment might involve consumers being asked to conduct a blind taste test for a new brand of toothpaste. The experimenter will ensure that the same amount of paste is applied to the brush, and that the subjects swill their mouths prior to tasting a further brand. Once the experiment is over, the 'consumers' are quizzed about their perceptions of the product.

More sophisticated experiments could be conducted. For example, a *laboratory shop* might be set up to simulate a real shopping experience. People could be given a certain amount of money to spend in the 'shop' and their reactions to changes in prices, packaging, display, etc. could be monitored.

The major drawback with such 'laboratories' is that consumers might behave differently because they are being observed. For example, they might spend more time comparing prices than they otherwise would, simply because they think that this is what a *good*, rational consumer should do. With real shopping, however, it might simply be habit, or something 'irrational' such as the colour of the packaging, that determines which product they select.

Another type of market experiment involves confining a marketing campaign to a particular town or region. The campaign could involve advertising, or giving out free samples, or discounting the price, or introducing an improved version of the product, but each confined to that particular locality. Sales in that area are then compared with sales in other areas in order to assess the effectiveness of the various campaigns.

> **Pause for thought**
>
> Before you read on, try to identify some other drawbacks in using market experiments to gather data on consumer behaviour.

Using the data to estimate demand functions

Once the business has undertaken its market analysis, what will it do with the information? How can it use its new knowledge to aid its decision making?

One way the information might be used is for the business to attempt to estimate the relationship between the quantity demanded and the various factors that influence demand. This would then enable the firm to predict how the demand for the product would be likely to change if one or more of the determinants of demand changed.

We can represent the relationship between the demand for a product and the determinants of demand in the form of an equation. This is called a **demand function**. It can be expressed in general terms or with specific values attached to the determinants.

> **definition**
>
> **Demand function**
> An equation showing the relationship between the demand for a product and its principal determinants.

General form of a demand function

In its general form the demand function is effectively a list of the various determinants of demand.

$$Q_d = f(P_g, T, P_{s_1}, P_{s_2} \ldots P_{s_n}, P_{c_1}, P_{c_2} \ldots P_{c_m}, Y, B, P_{g_{t+1}}^e)$$

This is merely saying in symbols that the quantity demanded (Q_d) is a 'function of' (f) – i.e. depends on – the price of the good itself (P_g), tastes (T), the price of substitute goods ($P_{s_1}, P_{s_2}, \ldots P_{s_n}$), the price of complementary goods ($P_{c_1}, P_{c_2}, \ldots P_{c_m}$), total consumer incomes (Y), the distribution of income (B), and the expected price of the good (P_g^e) at some future time ($t+1$). The equation is thus just a form of shorthand.

Note that this function could be extended by dividing determinants into subcategories. For example, income could be broken down by household type, age, gender or any other characteristic. Similarly, instead of having one term labelled 'tastes', we could identify various characteristics of the product or its marketing that determine tastes.

In this general form, there are no numerical values attached to each of the determinants. As such, the function has no predictive value for the firm.

Estimating demand equations

To make predictions, the firm must use its survey or experimental data to assign *values* to each of the determinants. These values show just how much demand

Figure 7.1

Consumption of electricity at different prices

will change if any one of the determinants changes (while the rest are held constant). For example, suppose that an electricity distributor reckons that there are three main determinants of demand (Q_d) for the electricity it supplies: its price (P), total consumer incomes (Y) and the price of gas (P_g). It will wish to assign values to the terms a, b, c and d (known as *coefficients*) in the following equation:

$$Q_d = a + bP + cY + dP_g$$

But how are the values of the coefficients to be estimated? This is done using a statistical technique called **regression analysis**. To conduct regression analysis, a number of observations must be used. For example, the electricity company could use its market observations (or the results from various surveys or experiments).

To show how these observations are used, let us consider the very simplest case: that of the effects of changes in just one determinant – for example, price. In this case the demand equation would simply be of the form $Q_d = a + bP$ (where the value of b would be negative).

The observations might be like those illustrated in Figure 7.1. The points show the amounts of electricity per time period actually consumed at different prices. We could, by eye, construct a demand curve through these points. Regression analysis is a technique that allows us to obtain the line of best fit. (We do not explain regression analysis in this book, but most business statistics texts cover the topic.)

Of course, in reality, there are many determinants of the demand for electricity. That is one reason why the observed points in Figure 7.1 do not all fall exactly along the line. Demand varies at each different price according to what is happening to the other determinants. The other major reason is if the observed points are based on different samples, where each sample is not identical in composition and tastes.

Regression analysis can also be used to determine more complex relationships: to derive the equation that best fits the data on changes in a number of variables. Unlike a curve on a diagram, which simply shows the relationship between two variables, an equation can show the relationship between several variables. Regression analysis can be used to find the 'best fit' equation from data on changes in a number of variables.

> **definition**
>
> **Regression analysis**
> A statistical technique which shows how one variable is related to one or more other variables.

The demand for lamb
A real-world demand function[1]

The following is an estimate of the UK's market demand curve for lamb. It has been estimated (using a computer regression package) from actual monthly data for the years 1966–99.

$$Q_d = 217.1 - 0.112P_L + 0.125P_B - 0.0198Y$$

where: Q_d is the quantity of lamb sold in grams per person per week;
P_L is the price of lamb (in pence per kg, at 1985 prices);
P_B is the price of beef (in pence per kg, at 1985 prices);
Y is annual personal disposable income per head (£, at 1995 prices).

From this, economists could forecast what would happen to the demand for lamb if any of three variables – the price of lamb, the price of beef or income – changed.

Question

From this equation, calculate what would happen to the demand for lamb if:

(a) the price of lamb went up by 10p per kg (at 1985 prices);

(b) the price of beef went up by 10p per kg (at 1985 prices);

(c) personal disposable income per head went up by £100 per annum (at 1995 prices).

There is a serious problem with estimated demand functions like these: they assume that *other* determinants of demand have not changed. In the case of this demand-for-lamb function, one of the other determinants *did* change. This was tastes – during the 1980s and 1990s there was a shift in demand away from lamb and other meats, partly for health reasons, and partly because of an expansion in the availability of and demand for vegetarian and low-meat alternatives.

Assuming that this shift in taste took place steadily over time, a new demand equation was estimated for the same years:

$$Q_d = 192.3 - 0.530P_L + 0.0738P_B + 0.0261Y - 7.352TIME$$

where the *TIME* term is as follows: 1966 = 1, 1967 = 2, 1968 = 3 … 1999 = 34.

Question

1 *How does the introduction of the TIME term affect the relationship between the demand for lamb and (a) the price of beef; (b) personal disposable income per head?*

2 *Is lamb a normal good or an inferior good?*

Then in the mid-1990s, there was the BSE scare and a temporary shift in demand to lamb from beef. The following table shows this shift.

Because of these large changes in demand, over just a few years, it is not possible to include their determinants in an equation in any meaningful way. But clearly, BSE did have a major effect and hence made the estimated equations less reliable for forecasting the demand for lamb.

Question

Use the second equation to estimate the demand for lamb in 1994, 1996 and 2000. In which of these three years was the estimation closest to the actual figure? Explain the divergences in the actual figures from the figures derived from the equation.

	Actual consumption of lamb	Actual consumption of beef	P_L	P_B	Y
1994	54	131	301.6	343.0	8266
1996	66	101	296.2	325.6	8607
2000	55	124	310.7	320.1	9604

Source: **www.defra.gov.uk/esg/Excel/allfood.xls**

[1] Thanks to Tony Flegg, John's 'office mate' at UWE for these calculations

For example, regression analysis could be applied to data showing the quantity of electricity consumed at various levels of price, consumer incomes and the price of gas. An equation similar to the following might be estimated:

$$Q_d = 2000 - 500P + 0.4Y + 200P_g$$

where Q_d is measured in millions of gigawatts per annum, P in pence per kilowatt hour, Y in £ millions and P_g in pence per kilowatt hour.

Thus if the price of electricity were 5p per kilowatt hour, consumer incomes were £20 billion and the price of gas were 2p per kilowatt hour, then the demand for electricity would be 7900 million gigawatts per annum. This is calculated as follows:

$$Q_d = 2000 - (500 \times 5) + (0.4 \times 20\,000) + (200 \times 2)$$
$$= 2000 - 2500 + 8000 + 400$$
$$= 7900$$

The branch of economics that applies statistical techniques to economic data is known as **econometrics**. The problem with using such techniques, however, is that they cannot produce equations and graphs that allow totally reliable predictions to be made. The data on which the equations are based are often incomplete or unreliable, and the underlying relationships on which they are based (often ones of human behaviour) may well change over time.

> **definition**
> **Econometrics**
> The branch of economics which applies statistical techniques to economic data.

Forecasting demand   7.2

Demand functions are useful in that they show what will happen to demand *if* one of the determinants changes. But businesses will want to know more than the answer to an 'If . . . then' question. They will want to know what will actually happen to the determinants and, more specifically, what will happen to demand itself. In other words, they will want *forecasts* of future demand. After all, if demand is going to increase, they may well want to invest *now* so that they have the extra capacity to meet the extra demand. But it will be a costly mistake to invest in extra capacity if demand is not going to increase.

We now, therefore, turn to examine some of the forecasting techniques used by business.

Simple time-series analysis

Simple time-series analysis involves directly projecting from past sales data into the future. Thus if it is observed that sales of a firm's product have been growing steadily by 3 per cent per annum for the last few years, the firm can use this to predict that sales will continue to grow at approximately the same rate in the future. Similarly, if it is observed that there are clear seasonal fluctuations in demand, as in the case of the demand for holidays or ice cream or winter coats, then again it can be assumed that fluctuations of a similar magnitude will continue into the future. In other words, using simple time-series analysis assumes that demand in the future will continue to behave in the same way as in the past.

Using simple time-series analysis in this way can be described as 'black box' forecasting. No *explanation* is offered as to *why* demand is behaving in this way:

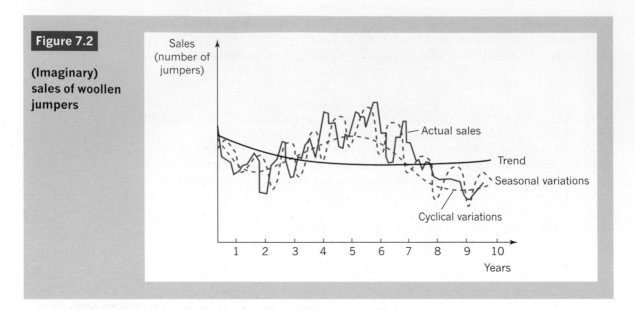

Figure 7.2

(Imaginary) sales of woollen jumpers

any underlying model of demand is 'hidden in a black box'. In a highly stable market environment, where the various factors affecting demand change very little or, if they do, change very steadily or regularly, such time-series analysis can supply reasonably accurate forecasts. The problem is that, without closer examination of the market, the firm cannot know whether changes in demand of the same magnitude as in the past will continue into the future. Just because demand has followed a clear pattern in the past, it does not inexorably follow that it will continue to exhibit the same pattern in the future. After all, the determinants of demand may well have changed. Successful forecasting, therefore, will usually involve a more sophisticated analysis of trends.

The decomposition of time paths

One way in which the analysis of past data can be made more sophisticated is to identify different elements in the time path of sales. Figure 7.2 illustrates one such time path: the (imaginary) sales of woollen jumpers by firm X. It is shown by the continuous red line, labelled 'Actual sales'.

Four different sets of factors normally determine the shape of a time path like this.

Trends. These are increases or decreases in demand over a number of years. In our example, there is a long-term decrease in demand for this firm's woollen jumpers up to year 7 and then a slight recovery in demand thereafter.

Trends may reflect factors such as changes in population structure, or technological innovation or longer-term changes in fashion. Thus if wool were to become more expensive over time compared with other fibres, or if there were a gradual shift in tastes away from woollen jumpers and towards acrylic or cotton jumpers, or towards sweatshirts, this could explain the long-term decline in demand up to year 7. A gradual shift in tastes back towards natural fibres, and to wool in particular, or a gradual reduction in the price of wool, could then explain the subsequent recovery in demand.

Alternatively, trends may reflect changes over time in the structure of an industry. For example, an industry might become more and more competitive with new firms joining. This would tend to reduce sales for existing firms (unless the market were expanding very rapidly).

Cyclical fluctuations. In practice, the level of actual sales will not follow the trend line precisely. One reason for this is the cyclical upswings and downswings in business activity in the economy as a whole. In some years incomes are rising rapidly and thus demand is buoyant. In other years, the economy will be in recession, with incomes falling. In these years, demand may well also fall. In our example, in boom years people may spend much more on clothes (including woollen jumpers), whereas in a recession, people may make do with their old clothes. The cyclical variations line thus rises above the trend line in boom years and falls below the trend line during a recession.

Seasonal fluctuations. The demand for many products also depends on the time of year. In the case of woollen jumpers, the peak demand is likely to be as winter approaches or just before Christmas. Thus the seasonal variations line is above the cyclical variations line in winter and below it in summer.

Short-term shifts in demand or supply. Finally, the actual sales line will also reflect various short-term shifts in demand or supply, causing it to diverge from the smooth seasonal variations line.

There are many reasons why the demand curve might shift. A competitor might increase its price, or there may be a sudden change in fashion, caused, say, by a pop group deciding to wear woollen jumpers for their new video: what was once seen as unfashionable by many people now suddenly becomes fashionable! Alternatively, there may be an unusually cold or hot, or wet or dry spell of weather.

Likewise there are various reasons for sudden shifts in supply conditions. For example, there may be a sheep disease which ruins the wool of infected sheep. As a result, the price of wool goes up, and sales of woollen jumpers falls.

These sudden shifts in demand or supply conditions are often referred to as 'random shocks' because they are usually unpredictable and temporarily move sales away from the trend. (Note that *long-term* shifts in demand and supply will be shown by a change in the trend line itself.)

Even with sophisticated time-series analysis, which breaks time paths into their constituent elements, there is still one major weakness: time-series analysis is merely a projection of the *past*. Most businesses will want to anticipate *changes* to sales trends – to forecast any deviations from the current time path. One method for doing this is *barometric forecasting*.

Barometric forecasting

Assume that you are a manager of a furniture business and are wondering whether to invest in new capital equipment. You would only want to do this if the demand for your product was likely to rise. You will probably, therefore, look for some indication of this. A good barometer of future demand for furniture would be the number of new houses being built. People will tend to buy new furniture some months after the building of their new house has commenced.

It is common for businesses to use **leading indicators** such as housing starts when attempting to predict the future. In fact some leading indicators, such as increased activity in the construction industry, rises in Stock Exchange prices, a depreciation of the rate of exchange and a rise in industrial confidence, are good indicators of a general upturn in the economy.

Barometric forecasting is a technique whereby forecasts of demand in industry A are based on an analysis of time-series data for industry (or sector, or indicator) B, where changes in B normally precede changes in the demand for A. If B rises by x per cent, it can be assumed (other things being equal) that the demand for A will change by y per cent.

Barometric forecasting is widely used to predict *cyclical* changes: the effects of the upswings and downswings in the economy. It is thus useful not only for individual firms, but also for governments, which need to plan their policies to counteract the effects of the business cycle: the unemployment associated with recessions, or the inflation associated with booms in the economy.

Barometric forecasting suffers from two major weaknesses. The first is that it only allows forecasting a few months ahead – as far ahead as is the time lag between the change in the leading indicator and the variable being forecasted. The second is that it can only give a general indication of changes in demand. It is simply another form of time-series analysis. Just because a relationship existed in the past between a leading indicator and the variable being forecasted, it cannot be assumed that exactly the same relationship will exist in the future.

Normally, then, firms use barometric forecasting merely to give them a rough guide as to likely changes in demand for their product: i.e. whether it is likely to expand or contract, and by 'a lot' or by 'a little'. Nevertheless information on leading indicators is readily available in government or trade statistics.

To get a more precise forecast, firms must turn to their demand function, and estimate the effects of predicted changes in the determinants of the demand for their product.

Using demand functions in forecasts

We have seen in section 7.1 how demand functions can be used to show the effects of changes in the determinants of demand. For example, in the following model:

$$Q_d = a + bP + cP_s + dY + eA$$

where the demand for the product (Q_d) is determined by its price (P), the price of a substitute product (P_s), consumer incomes (Y) and advertising (A), the parameters (b, c, d and e) show the effects on Q_d of changes in the determinants.

In order to forecast the demand for its product (the **dependent variable**), the firm will need to obtain values for P, P_s, Y and A (the **independent variables**). The firm itself chooses what price to charge and how much to advertise, and thus will decide the values of P and A. Forecasts of consumer incomes are readily available from the government's Office for National Statistics (ONS) or from private forecasting agencies. As far as P_s is concerned, here the firm will have to make an informed guess. Most firms will have a pretty good idea of the likely policies of their competitors.

Obviously, the accuracy of the forecasts will depend on the accuracy of the model as a description of the past relationship between demand and its determinants. Fortunately, this can be tested using various econometric techniques, and the reliability of the model can be determined. What is more, once the forecast is made, it can be compared with the actual outcome and the new data can be used to refine the model and improve its predictive power for next time.

The major strength of these econometric models is that they attempt to show how the many determinants affect demand. They also allow firms to feed in different assumptions to see how they will affect the outcome. Thus one forecast might be based on the assumption that the major competitor raises its price by x per cent, another that it raises its price by y per cent, and another that it leaves its price unchanged. The firm can then see how sensitive its sales will be to these possible changes. This is called **sensitivity analysis** and its use allows the firm to assess just how critical its assumptions are: would a rise in its rival's price by x per cent rather than y per cent make all the difference between a profit and a loss, or would it make little difference?

Econometric models can be highly complex, involving several equations and many variables. For example, there might be a separate variable for each of the prices and specifications of all the various products in competition with this one.

definition
Sensitivity analysis Assesses how sensitive an outcome is to different variables within an equation.

Problems with econometric forecasting

But despite the apparent sophistication of some of the econometric models used by firms or by forecasting agencies, the forecasts are often wrong.

One reason for this is that the variables specified in the model do not explain all the variation in the demand for the product. In order to take some account of these missing independent variables, it is normal to include an *error term* (r). But this error term will probably cover a number of unspecified determinants which are unlikely to move together over time. It does not therefore represent a stable or predictable 'determinant'. The larger the error term, the less confident we can be about using the equation to predict future demand.

Another reason for the inaccuracy of forecasts is that certain key determinants are difficult, if not impossible, to measure with any accuracy. This is a particular problem with subjective variables like taste and fashion. How can taste be modelled?

Perhaps the biggest weakness of using demand functions for forecasting is that the forecasts are themselves based on forecasts of what will happen to the various determinants. Take the cases of just two determinants: the specifications of competitors' products and consumer tastes. Just what changes will competitors make to their products? Just how will tastes change in the future? Consider the problems a clothing manufacturer might have in forecasting demand for a range of clothing! Income, advertising and the prices of the clothing will all be significant factors determining demand, but so too will be the range offered by other manufacturers and also people's perception of what is and what is not fashionable. But predicting changes in competitors' products and changes in fashion is notoriously difficult.

This is not to say that firms should give up in their attempt to forecast demand. Rather it suggests that they might need to conduct more sophisticated market research, and even then to accept that forecasts can only give an approximate indication of likely changes to demand.

SUMMARY

1a Businesses seek information on consumer behaviour so as to predict market trends and improve strategic decision making.

1b One source of data is the firm's own information on how its sales have varied in the past with changes in the various determinants of demand, such as consumer incomes and the prices of competitors' products.

1c Another source of data is market surveys. These can generate a large quantity of cheap information. Care should be taken, however, to ensure that the sample of consumers investigated reflects the target consumer group.

1d Market experiments involve investigating consumer behaviour within a controlled environment. This method is particularly useful when considering new products where information is scarce.

1e Armed with data drawn from one or more of these sources, the business manager can attempt to estimate consumer demand using various statistical techniques, such as regression analysis.

1f The estimation of the effects on demand of a change in a particular variable, such as price, depends upon the assumption that all other factors that influence demand remain constant.

However, factors that influence the demand for a product are constantly changing, hence there will always be the possibility of error when estimating the impact of change.

2a It is not enough to know what will happen to demand if a determinant changes. Businesses will want to forecast what will actually happen to demand. To do this they can use a variety of methods: time-series analysis, barometric forecasting and econometric modelling.

2b Time-series analysis bases future trends on past events. Time-series data can be decomposed into different elements: trends, seasonal fluctuations, cyclical fluctuations and random shocks.

2c Barometric forecasting involves making predictions based upon changes in key leading indicators.

2d If a firm has estimated its demand function (using econometric techniques), it can then feed into this model forecasts of changes in the various determinants of demand and use the model to predict the effect on demand. The two main problems with this approach are: the reliability of the demand function (although this can be tested using econometric techniques), and the reliability of forecasts of changes in the various determinants of demand.

REVIEW QUESTIONS

1 What are the relative strengths and weaknesses of using (a) market observations, (b) market surveys and (c) market experiments as means of gathering evidence on consumer demand?

2 You are working for a record company which is thinking of signing up some new bands. What market observations, market surveys and market experiments could you conduct to help you decide which bands to sign?

3 You are about to launch a new range of cosmetics, but you are still to decide upon the content and structure of your advertising campaign. Consider how market surveys and market experiments might be used to help you assess consumer perceptions of the product. What limitations might each of the research methods have in helping you gather data?

4 The following is an estimate of the UK's market demand curve for instant coffee. It has been derived (using a computer regression package) from actual data for the years 1973–85.

$$Q_c = 0.042 - 0.068P_c + 0.136P_T + 0.0067Y$$

where: Q_c is the quantity of instant coffee purchased in ounces per person per week;

P_c and P_T are respectively the 'real' prices of instant coffee and tea, calculated by dividing their market prices in pence per lb by the retail price index for all food (*RPI*) (1980 = 100);

Y is an index of real personal disposable income (1980 = 100): i.e. household income after tax.

The following table gives the prices of coffee and tea and real disposable income for three years (1973, 1985 and 1990).

Year	Market price of coffee (Mp_c) (pence per lb)	RPI of all food (1980 = 100)	Real price of coffee ($P_c = MP_c / RPI \times 100$)	Market price of tea (MP_T) (pence per lb)	Real price of tea ($P_T = MP_T / RPI \times 100$)	Index of real disposable income (Y) (1980 = 100)
1973	111.33	35.20		35.53		89.30
1985	511.65	131.40		184.39		106.10
1990	585.19	165.89		212.77		128.62

(a) Fill in the columns for the real price of coffee (P_c) and the real price of tea (P_T).

(b) Use the above equation to estimate the demand for instant coffee in 1973.

(c) Calculate the percentage growth in the market over the 13-year sample period (1973–85).

(d) The equation was used to forecast the demand for instant coffee in 1990. Purchases were estimated at 0.7543 ounces per person per week.
(i) Verify this from the equation.
(ii) The actual level of purchases is recorded as 0.48 ounces per week. Suggest reasons why the equation seriously over-estimates the level of demand for 1990.

5 Outline the alternative methods a business might use to forecast demand. How reliable do you think such methods are?

6 Imagine that you are an airline attempting to forecast demand for seats over the next two or three years. What, do you think, could be used as leading indicators?

8 Products, marketing and advertising

For most firms, selling their product is not simply a question of estimating demand and then choosing an appropriate price and level of production. In other words, they do not simply take their market as given. Instead they will seek to *influence* demand. They will do this by developing their product and differentiating it from those of their rivals, and then marketing it by advertising and other forms of product promotion.

Key Idea 1 p9

What firms are engaging in here is **non-price competition**. In such situations the job of the manager can be quite complex. It is likely to involve making a series of strategic decisions, not just concerning price, but also concerning each product's design and quality, its marketing and advertising, and the provision of various forms of after-sales service.

Central to non-price competition is **product differentiation**. Most firms' products differ in various ways from those of their rivals. Take the case of washing machines. Although all washing machines wash clothes, and as such are close substitutes for each other, there are many differences between brands. They differ not only in price, but also in their capacity, their styling, their range of programmes, their economy in the use of electricity, hot water and detergent, their reliability, their noise, their after-sales service, etc. Firms will attempt to design their product so that they can stress its advantages (real or imaginary) over the competitor brands. Just think of the specific features of particular models of car, hi-fi equipment or brands of cosmetic, and then consider the ways in which these features are stressed by advertisements. In fact, think of virtually any advertisement and consider how it stresses the features of that particular brand.

8.1 Product differentiation

Features of a product

A product has many dimensions, and a strategy to differentiate a product may focus on one or more of these dimensions.

- *Technical standards.* These relate to the product's level of technical sophistication: how advanced it is in relation to the current state of technology. This would be a very important product dimension if, for example, you were purchasing a PC.
- *Quality standards.* These relate to aspects such as the quality of the materials used in the product's construction and the care taken in assembly. These will

affect the product's durability and reliability. The purchase of consumer durables, such as televisions, hi-fi and toys, will be strongly influenced by quality standards.

■ *Design characteristics*. These relate to the product's direct appeal to the consumer in terms of appearance or operating features. Examples of design characteristics are colour, style and even packaging. The demand for fashion products such as clothing will be strongly influenced by design characteristics.

■ *Service characteristics*. This aspect is not directly concerned with the product itself, but with the support and back-up given to the customer after the product has been sold. Servicing, product maintenance and guarantees would be included under this heading. When purchasing a new car, the quality of after-sales service might strongly influence the choice you make.

Any given product will possess a 'bundle' of the above attributes. Within any product category, each brand is likely to have a different mix of technical and quality standards and design and service characteristics. Consumers will select the bundle of attributes they most prefer. The fact that these different dimensions exist means that producers can focus the marketing of their product on factors other than price – they can engage in 'non-price competition'.

> **definition**
> **Non-price competition**
> Competition in terms of product promotion (advertising, packaging, etc.) or product development.

> **definition**
> **Product differentiation**
> Where a firm's product is in some way distinct from its rivals' products.

Vertical and horizontal product differentiation

When firms are seeking to differentiate their product from those of their rivals, one important distinction they must consider is that between *vertical* and *horizontal* differentiation.

Vertical product differentiation. This is where products differ in quality, with some being perceived as superior and others as inferior. In general, the better the quality, the more expensive will the product be. Take the case of a DVD recorder. The cheaper (inferior) models will just have basic functions. As you move up the price range, so the models will have more and better functions, such as zoom, editing facilities, Dolby 5.1 and thumbnails.

Vertical product differentiation will usually be in terms of the quantity and quality of functions and/or the durability of the product (often a reflection of the quality of the materials used and the care spent in making the product). Thus a garment will normally be regarded as superior if it is better made and uses high-quality cloth. In general, the vertical quality differences between products will tend to reflect differences in production costs.

> **definition**
> **Vertical product differentiation**
> Where a firm's product differs from its rivals' products in respect to quality.

Horizontal product differentiation. This refers to differences between products that are not generally regarded as superior or inferior, but merely reflections of the different tastes of different consumers. One person may prefer black shoes and another brown. One may prefer milk chocolate, another plain. Within any product range there may be varieties which differ in respect to style, design, flavour, colour, etc. Such attributes are neither 'good' nor 'bad', simply different.

Horizontal differences within a range do not significantly alter the costs of production, and it is common for the different varieties to have the same price. A pot of red paint is likely to be the same price as a pot of blue (of the same brand). The point is that the products, although horizontally different, are of comparable quality.

> **definition**
> **Horizontal product differentiation**
> Where a firm's product differs from its rivals' products, although the products are seen to be of a similar quality.

Brands and own-brands
What's in a name?

The rise of supermarket own-brands since the early 1990s has been phenomenal. Their market penetration in the UK has been so great that, by 1995, 54.5 per cent of all sales in the major supermarket chains were of own-branded products. In 1992, just three years earlier, the figure had been a mere 27 per cent. What makes this rise even more striking is that it followed a period when branded products dominated the market and seemed to be growing in strength. During the 1980s, the profits of companies such as Kellogg's and Heinz were increasing by as much as 15 per cent a year.

As Alan Mitchell argued in *Marketing Week* (6 December 1996), the brand system seemed to be unassailable.

Brand manufacturers commanded economies of scale in both sourcing and production which enabled them to offer superior value to consumers. Mass advertising helped to drive the demand that, in turn, promoted mass production by keeping brands top of consumer awareness. National distribution created mass presence and availability, driving sales and reinforcing brands' share of mind.

And the healthy margins generated by the synergy between mass production, advertising and distribution, allowed manufacturers to invest in research and development and offer genuinely improved products. This in turn, created new reassurance of value for money and extra sales, thereby adding impetus to the virtuous circle.

However, towards the end of the 1980s, things started to go horribly wrong for branded products:

- The economic boom came to an end, and the UK went into recession, with the result that consumers became more price conscious.
- Supermarkets began to develop a more extensive range of own-label products.

As Alan Mitchell points out:

New technologies [were] allowing own-label manufacturers to produce smaller batch runs at lower costs: so the benefits of economies of scale [declined].

Own-label products also lay claim to cost advantages, both on marketing and distribution – a few dedicated trucks from factory to retailer regional distribution centre are nothing compared with the cost of a fleet serving every retailer, wholesaler, and convenience shop.

This means all the paraphernalia of advertising, distribution, and new product development that made the brand manufacturing model so powerful decades ago is unravelling, and becoming an enormous cost burden instead – a burden that adds up to 50 per cent on to the final consumer price and allows retailers to undercut brands while creaming off higher margins. The virtuous cycle goes into reverse, and becomes a vicious circle.

Pause for thought

Identify two other products that are vertically differentiated, two that are horizontally differentiated and two that are both.

In practice, most product ranges will have a mixture of horizontal and vertical differentiation. For example, some of the differences between different makes and models of motor car will be vertical (e.g. luxury or basic internal fittings, acceleration and fuel consumption); some will be horizontal (e.g. hatchback or saloon, colour and style).

Market segmentation

Different features of a product will appeal to different consumers. This applies both to vertically differentiated features and to horizontally differentiated ones. Where features are quite distinct, and where particular features or groups of features can be seen to appeal to a particular category of consumers, it might be

Such were the cost advantages of the own-label alternative that, for many products, the price discrepancy between brands and own-brands had become staggering, forcing brand manufacturers to make substantial price cuts. For example, the dairy producer Kraft was forced to slash prices on many of its cheese products, which in many cases were some 45 per cent more expensive than own-label alternatives.

The position of branded products has been further undermined. Technology has not only pushed down costs, but also raised the *quality* of products, making it easier for own-label producers to copy established brands, and in many cases to innovate themselves. Many own-brand retailers are now looking to move up market and compete with premium branded products.

> Supermarket ranges such as 'Be Good to Yourself' or 'Taste the Difference' are as recognised by consumers as any branded lines. The quality is as good if not better, and with dedicated marketing support from the likes of Jamie Oliver there is strong brand loyalty.[1]

What are brand manufacturers to do? One alternative adopted by many such firms is for themselves to make own-label products for the supermarkets. Such actions might be self-defeating, however, since they have reinforced the change in consumer perceptions of own-brands. Consumer surveys increasingly show that very little difference is perceived between branded products and own-brands. As a result, a product's price becomes far more significant in determining purchase. Established brand manufacturers are thus forced to cut costs in order to maintain profit margins on existing products.

There is another strategy, however, that they can pursue. This is to extend a brand to new products and use the brand image to promote them. Take the case of Virgin. The brand no longer applies just to record stores. It now embraces an airline, trains, finance, soft drinks, mobile phones, holidays, bridal wear, cinemas, radio, virtual car showrooms, online books, an online wine store, an Internet service provider, cosmetics, health clubs, balloon rides and gift 'experiences'.

Questions

1 *How has the improvement in the quality of own-brands affected the price elasticity of demand for branded products? What implications does this have for the pricing strategy of brand manufacturers?*

2 *Do the brand manufacturers have any actual or potential cost advantages over own-brand manufacturers?*

---

[1] *Marketing Week*, 17 April 2003

---

useful for producers to divide the market into segments. Taking the example of cars again, the market could be divided into luxury cars, large, medium and small family cars, sports cars, multi-terrain vehicles, six-seater people carriers, etc. Each type of car occupies a distinct market segment, and within each segment the individual models are likely to be both horizontally and vertically differentiated from competitor models.

When consumer tastes change over time, or where existing models do not cater for every taste, a firm may be able to identify a new segment of the market – a **market niche**. Having identified the appropriate market niche for its product, the marketing division within the firm will then set about targeting the relevant consumer group(s) and developing an appropriate strategy for promoting the product. In the next section we will explore more closely those factors which are likely to influence a business's marketing strategy.

definition

Market niche
A part of a market (or new market) that has not been filled by an existing brand or business.

8.2   Marketing the product

What is marketing?

There is no single accepted definition of marketing. It is generally agreed, how-ever, that marketing covers the following activities: establishing the strength of consumer demand in existing parts of the market, and potential demand in new niches; developing an attractive and distinct image for the product; informing potential consumers of various features of the product; fostering a desire by con-sumers for the product; and, in the light of all these, persuading consumers to buy the product.

Clearly, marketing must be seen within the overall goals of the firm. There would be little point in spending vast sums of money in promoting a product if it led to only a modest increase in sales and sales revenue.

Product/market strategy

Once the nature and strength of consumer demand (both current and potential) have been identified, the business will set about meeting and influencing this demand. In most cases it will be hoping to achieve a growth in sales. To do this, one of the first things the firm must decide is its *product/market strategy*. This will involve addressing two major questions:

Key Idea 20 p235

■ Should it focus on promoting its existing product, or should it develop new products?

■ Should it focus on gaining a bigger share of its existing market, or should it seek to break into new markets?

definition

Growth vector matrix
A means by which a business might assess its product/market strategy.

In 1957 Igor Ansoff illustrated these choices in what he called a **growth vector matrix**. This is illustrated in Figure 8.1.

The four boxes show the possible combinations of answers to the above questions: Box A – *market penetration* (existing product, existing market); Box B – *product development* (new product, existing market); Box C – *market development* (existing product, new market); Box D – *diversification* (new product, new market).

■ *Market penetration.* In the market penetration strategy, the business will seek not only to retain current customers, but to expand its customer base with

Figure 8.1

Growth vector components

Source: I. Ansoff, *Corporate Strategy* (McGraw-Hill, 1965); 'Strategies for diversification', *Harvard Business Review* (September–October 1957)

existing products in existing markets. Of the four strategies, this is generally the least risky: the business will be able to play to its product strengths and draw on its knowledge of the market. The business's marketing strategy will tend to focus upon aggressive product promotion and distribution. Such a strategy, however, is likely to lead to fierce competition from existing business rivals, especially if the overall market is not expanding and if the firm can therefore gain an increase in sales only by taking market share from its rivals.

- *Product development.* Product development strategies will involve introducing new models and designs in existing markets. This may involve either vertical differentiation (for example, the introduction of an upgraded model) or horizontal differentiation (the introduction of a new style).

- *Market development.* With a market development strategy the business will seek increased sales of current products by expanding into new markets. These may be in a different geographical location (for example, overseas), or new market segments. Alternatively, the strategy may involve finding new uses and applications for the product.

- *Diversification.* A diversification strategy will involve the business expanding into new markets with new products. Of all the strategies, this is the most risky given the unknown factors that the business is likely to face.

> **Pause for thought**
>
> *What unknown factors is the business likely to face following a diversification strategy?*

Once the product/market strategy has been decided upon, the business will then attempt to devise a suitable *marketing strategy*. This will involve looking at the marketing mix.

The marketing mix

In order to differentiate the firm's product from those of its rivals, there are four variables that can be adjusted. These are as follows:

- Product.
- Price.
- Place (distribution).
- Promotion.

The particular combination of these variables, known as 'the four Ps', represents the business's **marketing mix**, and it is around a manipulation of them that the business will devise its marketing strategy.

Figure 8.2 illustrates the various considerations that might be taken into account when looking at product, price, place and promotion.

> **definition**
>
> **Marketing mix**
> The mix of product, price, place (distribution) and promotion that will determine a business's marketing strategy.

- *Product considerations.* These involve issues such as quality and reliability, as well as branding, packaging and after-sales service.

- *Pricing considerations.* These involve not only the product's basic price in relation to those of competitors' products, but also opportunities for practising price discrimination (the practice of charging different prices in different parts of the market: Chapter 17), offering discounts to particular customers, and adjusting the terms of payment for the product.

- *Place considerations.* These focus on the product's distribution network, and involve issues such as where the business's retail outlets should be located, what warehouse facilities the business might require, and how the product should be transported to the market.

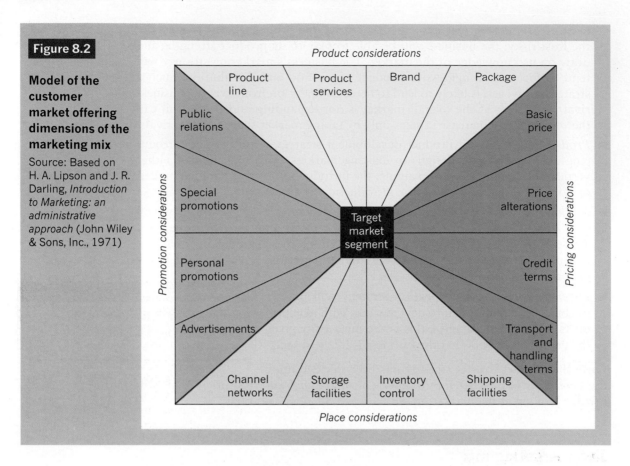

Figure 8.2

Model of the customer market offering dimensions of the marketing mix

Source: Based on H. A. Lipson and J. R. Darling, *Introduction to Marketing: an administrative approach* (John Wiley & Sons, Inc., 1971)

- *Promotion considerations.* These focus primarily upon the amount and type of advertising the business should use. In addition, promotion issues might also include selling techniques, special offers, trial discounts and various other public relations 'gimmicks'.

Every product is likely to have a distinct marketing *mix* of these four variables. Thus we cannot talk about an ideal value for one (e.g. the best price), without considering the other three. What is more, the most appropriate mix will vary from product to product and from market to market. If you wanted to sell a Rolls-Royce, you would be unlikely to sell any more by offering free promotional gifts or expanding the number of retail outlets. You might sell more Rolls-Royces, however, if you were to improve their specifications or offer more favourable methods of payment.

What the firm must seek to do is to estimate how sensitive demand is to the various aspects of marketing. The greater the sensitivity (elasticity) in each case, the more the firms should focus on that particular aspect. It must be careful, however, that changing one aspect of marketing does not conflict with another. For example, there would be little point in improving the product's quality, if at the same time promotional gimmicks were used which were associated in the minds of consumers with inferior, 'mass consumption' products.

Another consideration that must be taken into account is the stage in the product's life cycle (see section 17.6). The most appropriate marketing mix for a new and hence unfamiliar product, and one which may be facing little in the way of competition, may well be totally inappropriate for a product that is long established and may be struggling against competitors to maintain its market share.

Advertising 8.3

One of the most important aspects of marketing is advertising. The major aim of advertising is to sell more products, and business spends a vast quantity of money on advertising to achieve this goal. By advertising, the business will not only be informing the consumer of the product's existence and availability, but also deliberately attempting to persuade and entice the consumer to purchase the good. In doing so, it will tend to stress the specific and unique qualities of this firm's product over those of its rivals. This will be discussed in more detail below.

Advertising facts and figures

Advertising and the state of the economy

Advertising expenditure, like other business expenditure, is subject to the cyclical movement of the national economy. Indeed, advertising is particularly sensitive to the ups and downs in the economy. In times of rising demand and growing profitability of business, expenditure on advertising tends to rise substantially. Conversely, when economic growth slows, and product demand falls, advertising budgets will be cut. Thus between 1984 and 1989, when GDP in real terms (i.e. after accounting for inflation) increased by 22 per cent, advertising expenditure increased by 48 per cent in real terms. Similarly, in the long period of economic growth from 1992 to 2000, advertising expenditure in real terms grew faster, accounting for a higher and higher proportion of household expenditure (see Table 8.1).

Table 8.1 Total advertising expenditure (including direct mail)

	At current prices (£bn)	At constant (1995) prices (£bn)	As a percentage of	
			GDP	Household expenditure
1987	6.57	9.61	1.56	2.61
1988	7.61	10.62	1.63	2.68
1989	8.64	11.18	1.68	2.77
1990	8.93	10.55	1.60	2.64
1991	8.53	9.53	1.46	2.37
1992	8.86	9.54	1.45	2.33
1993	9.14	9.68	1.42	2.27
1994	10.14	10.48	1.49	2.40
1995	11.03	11.03	1.53	2.49
1996	12.08	11.79	1.58	2.55
1997	13.34	12.63	1.64	2.65
1998	14.42	13.19	1.68	2.69
1999	15.41	13.89	1.71	2.71
2000	16.99	14.87	1.79	2.81
2001	16.54	14.22	1.67	2.61
2002	16.73	14.16	1.60	2.52

Source: *Advertising Statistics Yearbook 2003* (NTC Publications Ltd)

| Table 8.2 | Total advertising expenditure excluding direct mail (% of total) |

	1938	*1948*	*1958*	*1968*	*1978*	*1988*	*1998*	*2002*
National newspapers	25.4	13.9	18.9	19.7	15.8	14.4	12.7	11.5
Regional newspapers	27.1	31.6	24.1	24.1	25.8	20.3	16.6	17.1
Consumer magazines	15.3	12.7	13.3	9.9	8.5	6.3	4.9	4.7
Business and professional	11.9	16.5	10.0	9.1	10.1	9.5	8.4	6.5
Directories	0.0	0.0	1.2	1.6	2.7	4.8	5.4	5.9
Press production costs	5.1	7.6	5.2	4.6	5.1	4.7	4.3	3.8
Total press	84.7	82.3	72.7	69.0	68.0	59.7	52.2	49.6
Television	0.0	0.0	19.3	25.6	25.8	27.9	28.0	25.8
Direct mail	0.0	0.0	0.0	0.0	0.0	7.0	11.6	14.2
Outdoor and transport	8.5	13.9	6.0	4.0	3.6	3.2	4.3	4.8
Radio	3.4	0.0	0.4	0.2	1.9	1.8	3.2	3.3
Cinema	3.4	3.8	1.6	1.2	0.7	0.4	0.7	1.1
Internet	0.0	0.0	0.0	0.0	0.0	0.0	0.1	1.2
Total	100.0	100.0	100.0	100.0	100.0	100.0	100.0	100.0

Source: *Advertising Statistics Yearbook 2003* (NTC Publications Ltd)

Conversely, in times of recession or very low economic growth, advertising budgets will be cut. Thus there was a 15 per cent fall in advertising expenditure in real terms between 1989 (the peak of the 1980s boom) and 1991 (a year of recession). Likewise there was a fall of 4.8 per cent between 2000 and 2002 (a period of relatively low economic growth).

Advertising media

When considering advertising expenditure by the main categories of media, we can see a long historical trend over which total press advertising has fallen from a high of 84.7 per cent in 1938 (although it reached a peak of nearly 90 per cent in 1953) to 49.6 per cent in 2002. By contrast, advertising on television (which only started in the UK in the mid-1950s) now accounts for over 25 per cent of total advertising expenditure and direct mail for over 14 per cent. Other types of advertising – posters, radio, cinema and the Internet – account for less than 11 per cent between them. Table 8.2 gives more details.

Product sectors

The distribution of advertising expenditure by product sectors shows that over 27 per cent of advertising expenditure is for consumables: i.e. food, drink, cosmetics, etc. A further 21 per cent is for consumer durables such as household appliances and equipment. Both these sectors tend to be dominated by just a few firms producing each type of product. This type of market is known as 'oligopoly', which is Greek for 'few sellers'. Oligopolists often compete heavily in terms of product differentiation and advertising. (Oligopoly is examined in Chapter 12.)

Details of the allocation of advertising expenditure between the different product sectors are given in Table 8.3.

If we take the 25 companies with the highest advertising expenditure, most are within the consumables and consumer durables sectors. The same applies to the 25 most advertised brands (see Table 8.4).

Table 8.3 Advertising expenditure by product sector (% of total advertising expenditure)

	1986	*1990*	*1994*	*1998*	*2002*
Retail	13.8	12.4	16.4	18.9	13.8
Industrial	8.7	7.4	7.8	8.9	12.8
Financial	10.2	10.5	10.2	8.3	10.6
Government	3.3	3.2	2.2	2.3	2.8
Services	8.5	10.8	10.4	11.1	11.4
Durables	20.5	19.6	19.4	21.4	24.1
Consumables	35.0	36.1	33.5	29.4	24.6
Total	100.0	100.0	100.0	100.0	100.0

Source: *Advertising Statistics Yearbook 2003* (NTC Publications Ltd)

Table 8.4 The top advertisers and advertising brands: 2002

(a) The top 25 advertisers

Rank 2001	Rank 2002	*Advertiser*	*Total spending on advertising (£000)*
2	1	Procter & Gamble	161 890
1	2	COI – Central Office of Information	119 523
3	3	British Telecom	96 644
4	4	Ford	94 911
10	5	L'Oréal Golden	70 845
6	6	Masterfoods	66 903
7	7	Renault	66 145
24	8	Toyota	65 459
8	9	Vauxhall Motors	63 358
5	10	Nestlé	62 987
9	11	DFS	59 393
13	12	Lever Fabergé Personal Care	59 646
18	13	Orange	55 686
23	14	Reckitt Benckiser	53 049
12	15	Sainsbury's	48 726
25	16	Boots	48 266
17	17	Volkswagen	45 372
14	18	Lever Fabergé Home Care	43 617
11	19	Peugeot	42 725
16	20	McDonald's	42 211
33	21	Diageo	41 901
39	22	Vodafone	41 841
19	23	Unilever Bestfoods	40 175
15	24	Kellogg's	39 413
21	25	Citroen	39 136

Table 8.4 *(continued)*

(b) The top 25 brands

Rank 2002	Brand	Total spending on advertising (£000)
1	McDonald's	41 973
2	PC World	32 195
3	Sainsbury's	31 512
4	TMobile network	30 556
5	DFS	26 285
6	B&Q	25 906
7	Toyota Corolla	23 983
8	DFS sofas/suites	22 340
9	Orange network	20 264
10	Ford Fiesta	19 308
11	AOL	19 191
12	Asda	19 156
13	Homebase	18 744
14	Boots	18 510
15	O_2 network	18 358
16	Argos	17 841
17	Vodafone network	17 822
18	BT Together	16 703
19	Vauxhall Vectra	16 504
20	Zzz small ads	16 401
21	Littlewoods – catalogue	16 121
22	BT Broadband	15 531
23	Peugeot 307	15 238
24	KFC	15 140
25	Ford Focus	14 574

Source: *Advertising Standards Yearbook 2003* (NTC Publications Ltd)

The advertising/sales ratio

definition

Advertising/ sales ratio
A ratio that reflects the intensity of advertising within a market.

If we wished to consider the intensity of advertising within a given product sector, we could construct an **advertising/sales ratio**. This relates the total expenditure on advertising for a particular product to the total value of product sales. A selection of products and their advertising/sales ratios can be seen in Table 8.5.

Dental fixatives have the highest advertising/sales ratio at 29.4 per cent. This tells us that 29.4 per cent of all earnings by firms producing dental fixatives go on advertising their product. At the other extreme, flour producers spend only 0.02 per cent of their sales revenue on advertising their product.

The wide variation in advertising intensity can be put down to two factors: market structure and product characteristics. As mentioned above, oligopolistic markets are likely to see high advertising outlays. But what types of product will be the most heavily advertised? There are three main categories here.

The first category is goods that represent a large outlay for consumers (e.g. furniture, electrical goods and other consumer durables). Consumers will not want to make a wrong decision: it would be an expensive mistake. They will thus tend to be cautious in their purchasing decision and will be likely to search for

Table 8.5 Advertising/sales ratios: 2002 (ranked by advertising/ sales ratio)

Product category	Advertising/sales ratio (%)
Denture fixatives	29.38
Bleaches and lavatory cleaners	25.51
Shampoos	20.17
Mouthwashes	14.37
Lawn fertilisers	12.15
Indigestion remedies	10.90
Vitamins and minerals	8.46
Potato crisps	8.24
Female fragrances	7.99
Toothpaste	6.73
Audio records and tapes	6.24
Margarine	5.12
Male fragrances	4.99
Instant coffee	4.27
Cameras	3.92
Ground coffee and coffee beans	2.63
Butter	2.32
Chocolate confectionery	2.59
Pet accessories	1.95
Ice cream	1.80
Bottled water	1.77
Alcopops	1.73
Tea	1.47
Contents insurance	1.41
Ready meals	1.06
Cheese	0.60
Buses	0.30
Milk and milk products	0.26
Fruit (total)	0.11
Cigarettes	0.07
Petrol and diesel	0.02
Flour	0.02

Source: *Advertising Statistics Yearbook 2003* (NTC Publications Ltd)

information before selecting a particular product. Advertisers will seek to provide information (but, of course, only information relating to their particular product).

The second category is new products which producers are attempting to establish on the market. The third category is goods, such as baby care products, which experience constant changes in their customer base.

Products with the lowest advertising/sales ratio will, by contrast, tend to be those goods whose specifications change very little, or where competition is minimal. For example, fish has a ratio of 0.10 per cent and bus travel 0.30 per cent.

Before we move on to consider the aims of advertising, we need to introduce one note of caution when considering the advertising/sales ratio. Many products

with low ratios, such as motor cars with a ratio of 1.19 per cent and tea with
1.47 per cent, are clearly products that are heavily advertised. What the advert-
ising/sales ratio does not reveal is the *absolute* amount spent on advertising.
Only 1.19 per cent of revenue from the sales of cars is spent on advertising. But
this commands significantly more advertising space and time than the 29.38 per
cent of revenue that is spent on denture fixatives. Thus in 2002, £657 million
was spent on advertising cars, compared with only £5 million on advertising
denture fixatives. A better way of measuring the intensity of advertising might
be to consider the air time or column centimetres in the press that a product or
sector buys.

The intended effects of advertising

We have argued that the main aim of advertising is to sell more of the product.
But when we are told that brand X will make us more beautiful, enrich our lives,
wash our clothes whiter, give us get-up-and-go, give us a new taste sensation or
make us the envy of our friends, just what are the advertisers up to? Are they
merely trying to persuade consumers to buy more?

In fact, there is a bit more to it than this. Advertisers are trying to do two
things:

■ Shift the product's demand curve to the right.
■ Make it less price elastic.

This is illustrated in Figure 8.3. D_1 shows the original demand curve with price
at P_1 and sales at Q_1. D_2 shows the curve after an advertising campaign. The
rightward shift allows an increased quantity (Q_2) to be sold at the original price.
If, at the same time, the demand is made less elastic, the firm can also raise its
price and still experience an increase in sales. Thus in the diagram, price can be
raised to P_2 and sales will be Q_3 – still substantially above Q_1. The total gain in
revenue is shown by the shaded area.

How can advertising bring about this new demand curve?

Shifting the demand curve to the right. This will occur if the advertising brings
the product to more people's attention and if it increases people's desire for the
product.

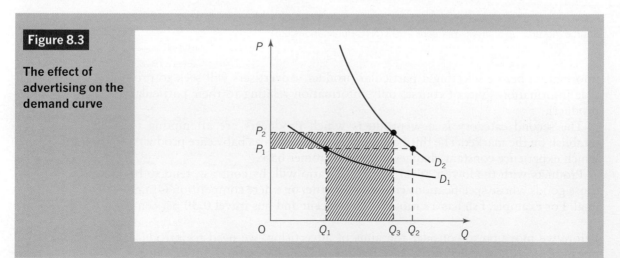

Figure 8.3

**The effect of
advertising on the
demand curve**

Making the demand curve less elastic. This will occur if the advertising creates greater brand loyalty. People must be led to believe (rightly or wrongly) that competitors' brands are inferior. This will allow the firm to raise its price above that of its rivals with no significant fall in sales. There will only be a small substitution effect of this price rise because consumers have been led to believe that there are no close substitutes.

The more successful an advertising campaign is, the more it will shift the demand curve to the right and the more it will reduce the price elasticity of demand.

Assessing the effects of advertising

The supporters of advertising claim that not only is it an important freedom for firms, but also it provides specific benefits for the consumer. By contrast, critics of advertising suggest that it can impose serious costs on the consumer and on society in general. In this section we will assess the basis of this difference.

> **Pause for thought**
>
> *Before considering the points listed below, see if you can identify the main arguments both for and against the use of advertising.*

The arguments put forward in favour of advertising include the following:

■ Advertising provides information to consumers on what products are available.

■ Advertising may be necessary in order to introduce new products. Without it, firms would find it difficult to break into markets in which there were established brands. In other words, it is a means of breaking down barriers to the entry of new firms and products.

■ It can aid product development by helping the firm emphasise the special features of its product.

■ It may encourage price competition, if prices feature significantly in the advertisement.

■ By increasing sales, it may allow the firm to gain economies of scale (see section 9.4), which in turn will help to keep prices down.

On the other side, the following arguments are put forward against advertising:

■ Advertising is designed to persuade people to buy the product. Consumers do not have perfect information and may thus be misled into purchasing goods whose qualities may be inferior to those goods which are not advertised.

■ Scarcity is defined as the excess of human wants over the means of fulfilling them. Advertising is used to *create* wants. It could thus be argued to increase scarcity.

■ It increases materialism.

■ Advertising costs money: it uses resources. These resources could be put to alternative uses in producing more goods.

■ If there are no reductions in costs to be gained from producing on a larger scale, the costs of advertising will tend to raise the price paid by the consumer. Even if the firm has potential economies of scale, it may be prevented from expanding its sales by retaliatory advertising from its rivals.

■ Advertising can create a barrier to the entry of new firms by promoting brand loyalty to *existing* firms' products. New firms may not be able to afford the large amount of advertising necessary to create a new brand image, whereas

BOX 8.2

Advertising and the long run
Promoting quality[1]

If brand communications are an investment, we should expect them to produce long-term benefits. Indeed, we need to do so, for it is rare for advertising to pay for itself through increased profits in the short term. Recognising this fact should focus our attention on the role of advertising (in particular) as a tool for building a brand over time. If our advertising and other brand communications are successful, we will not merely attain short-term sales targets, relatively cost-effectively, but we will also be creating a brand that has momentum and staying power.[2]

It is relatively straightforward to measure the short-term impact of an advertising campaign; a simple before and after assessment of sales will normally give a good indication of the advertising's effectiveness. But what about the medium and longer-term effects of an advertising campaign? How will sales and profits be affected over, say, a five-year period?

The typical impact of advertising on a product's sales is shown in Figure (a). Assume that there is an advertising campaign for the product between time t_1 and t_2. There is a direct effect on sales while the

advertising lasts and shortly afterwards. Sales rise from S_1 to S_2. After a while (beyond time t_3), the direct effect of the advertising begins to wear off, and wears off completely by time t_4. This is illustrated by the dashed line. But the higher level of sales declines much more slowly, given that many of the new customers continue to buy the product out of habit. Sales will eventually level off (at point t_5). It is likely, however, that sales will not return to the original level of S_1; there will be some new customers who will stick with the product over the long term. This long-term effect is shown by the increase in sales from S_1 to S_3.

But just what is this long-term effect? One way to explore the impact of advertising over the long run is to evaluate how advertising and profitability in general are linked.

In Figure (b) the argument is made that advertising shapes the key element of profitability, namely relative customer value. Customer value is determined by the product's perceived quality (and hence utility) relative to price. The more that advertising can enhance the perceived quality of a product, the more it will increase the product's profitability.

How this benefits the business over the longer term is best seen through examples.

(a)

(b)

Andrex has been using the 'puppy' to advertise its toilet tissues since 1972. It has, through this series of commercials, maintained a strong brand image and a perception of high quality. As a result, its share of the market is consistently at about 30 per cent. It has also been able to charge a price premium of around 30 per cent for its product. It is estimated that the past 10 years' worth of advertising has cost approximately £54 million but has led to extra sales worth at least £300 million.

PG Tips, launched in 1930, is another brand that leads its respective market. The UK tea market has been dominated by PG Tips since 1958, when it became market leader, a position it still holds today, with some 28 per cent of the 'traditional' tea market. The 'chimp' adverts, and since 2002, the Aardman T-Birds, have established a clear brand image, enabling PG Tips to hold its ground in a highly competitive market and charge a price premium. (Blind tests have revealed that consumers cannot distinguish between any of the leading tea brands!) Market analysis shows that PG Tips has a price elasticity of demand of –0.4 compared with its nearest rival, Tetley, which has an elasticity of –1.4. It is estimated that between 1980 and 2000 advertising

the PG Tips brand has cost £100 million but generated in the region of £2 billion in extra sales.

An alternative way to illustrate the impact of advertising on longer-term profitability is to assess how companies approach advertising in a recession. What happens when advertising expenditure is cut, and how quickly does profitability return once the recession is over and advertising expenditure once again begins to rise?

A study conducted in 1998 charted the profitability of 183 UK companies that all experienced recession in relation to their respective industries in the early 1990s. Of the 183 companies, 110 chose to cut their advertising expenditure, 53 chose to maintain it, and the remaining 20 increased it. The survey found that those which increased spending on advertising saw their profits suffer less than those which cut or maintained their advertising. They were nearly twice as profitable as the cutters and three times more profitable than those who maintained their advertising budgets.

The study also examined longer-term effects. It found that those which increased or maintained their advertising expenditure were the fastest to increase profits once the recession was over. Those that cut spending on advertising found that over the first two years of recovery their profits only increased by half the rate of those companies which had increased their advertising expenditure.

The message is that advertising should seek to promote a product's quality. This is the key to long-term sales and profits. What is also apparent is that successful brands have advertising campaigns which have been consistent over time. A brand image of quality is not created overnight, but once it is established it can endure and yield profits over the longer term.

Questions

1 *How are long-run profits and advertising linked?*
2 *Why does quality 'win out' in the end?*

[1] Adapted from *Admap* (July/August 1999)
[2] *Ibid.*, p. 17

existing firms can spread the cost of their advertising over their already large number of sales. In other words, there are economies of scale in advertising which act as a barrier to entry (see page 220).

This barrier is strengthened if existing firms sell many brands each (for example, in the washing powder industry many brands are produced by just two firms). This makes it even harder for new firms successfully to introduce a new brand, since the consumer already has so many to choose from.

The fewer the competitors, the less elastic will be the demand for each individual firm, and the higher will be the profit-maximising price (see Chapter 12).

■ People are constantly subjected to advertisements, whether on television, in magazines, on bill-boards, etc., and often find them annoying, tasteless or unsightly. Thus advertising imposes costs on society in general. These costs are external to the firm: that is, they do not cost the firm money, and hence are normally ignored by the firm.

The effects of advertising on competition, costs and prices are largely an empirical issue (an issue of *fact*), and clearly these effects will differ from one product to another. However, many of the arguments presented here involve judgements as to whether the effects are socially desirable or undesirable. Such judgements involve questions of taste and morality: things that are questions of opinion and cannot be resolved by a simple appeal to the facts.

SUMMARY

1a When firms seek to differentiate their product from those of their competitors, they can adjust one or more of four dimensions of the product: its technical standards, its quality, its design characteristics, and the level of customer service.

1b Products can be vertically and horizontally differentiated from one another. Vertical differentiation is where products are superior or inferior to others. Horizontal differentiation is where products differ, but are of a similar quality.

2a Marketing involves developing a product image and then persuading consumers to purchase it.

2b A business must choose an appropriate product/market strategy. Four such strategies can be identified: market penetration (focusing on existing product and market); product development (new product in existing market); market development (existing product in new markets); diversification (new products in new markets).

2c The marketing strategy of a product involves the manipulation of four key variables: product, price, place and promotion. Every product has a distinct marketing mix. The marketing mix is likely to change over the product's life cycle.

3a Advertising expenditure is cyclical, expanding and contracting with the upswings and downswings of the economy.

3b Most advertising expenditure goes on consumables and durable goods.

3c The advertising intensity within a given product sector can be estimated by considering the advertising/sales ratio. The advertising/sales ratio is likely to be higher the more oligopolistic the market, the more expensive the product, the newer the product, and the more the customer base for a product is subject to change.

3d The aims of advertising are to increase demand and make the product less price elastic.

3e Supporters of advertising claim that it: provides consumers with information; brings new products to consumers' attention; aids product development; encourages price competition; and generates economies of scale through increasing sales.

3f Critics of advertising claim that it: distorts consumption decisions; creates wants; pushes up prices; creates barriers to entry; and produces unwanted side effects, such as being unsightly.

REVIEW QUESTIONS

1 How might we account for the growth in non-price competition within the modern developed economy?

2 Distinguish between vertical and horizontal product differentiation. Give examples of goods that fall into each category.

3 Consider how the selection of the product/market strategy (market penetration, market development, product development and diversification) will influence the business's marketing mix. Identify which elements in the marketing mix would be most significant in developing a successful marketing strategy.

4 Why might the advertising/sales ratio be a poor guide to the degree of exposure of the consumer to advertisements for a particular category of product?

5 Imagine that 'Sunshine' sunflower margarine, a well-known brand, is advertised with the slogan, 'It helps you live longer' (the implication being that butter and margarines high in saturates shorten your life). What do you think would happen to the demand curve for a supermarket's *own* brand of sunflower margarine? Consider both the direction of shift and the effect on elasticity. Will the elasticity differ markedly at different prices? How will this affect the pricing policy and sales of the supermarket's own brand? Could the supermarket respond other than by adjusting the price of its margarine?

6 On balance, does advertising benefit (a) the consumer; (b) society in general?

Additional Part C case studies on the *Economics for Business* website (www.booksites.net/sloman)

C.1 **Bentham and the philosophy of utilitarianism.** This looks at the historical and philosophical underpinning of the ideas of utility maximisation.

C.2 **Choices within the household.** Is what is best for the individual best for the family?

C.3 **Taking account of time.** The importance of the time dimension in consumption decisions.

C.4 **The demand for butter.** An examination of a real-world demand function.

Websites relevant to Part C

Numbers and sections refer to websites listed in the Web appendix and hotlinked from this book's website at **www.booksites.net/sloman**

■ For news articles relevant to Part C, see the *Economics News Articles* link from the book's website.

■ For general news on demand, consumers and marketing see websites in section A, and particularly A2, 3, 4, 8, 9, 11, 12, 23, 25, 36. See also site A41 for links to economics news articles on particular search topics (e.g. advertising).

■ For data, information and sites on products and marketing, see sites B2, 10, 11, 13, 17.

■ For student resources relevant to Part C, see sites C1–7, 19.

■ For data on advertising, see site E37.

■ For links to sites on various aspects of advertising and marketing, see section *Industry and Commerce > Consumer Protection > Advertising* in sites I7 and 11.

D Background to supply

THE FINANCIAL TIMES, 11 JUNE 2003

Smaller chips, bigger stakes: how new monster plants will transform the industry

By TOM FOREMSKI, SIMON LONDON and RICHARD WATERS

Sixty miles north of New York City, along the Hudson river, a manufacturing revolution is getting into full swing – one that could reshape the entire global semiconductor business.

The manufacturing plant in East Fishkill, New York, is one of a new breed of outsized, multi-billion-dollar chip-making facilities. Beginning last autumn, the plant, run by International Business Machines, began to churn out silicon chips at a rate nearly three times that of older facilities, a speed that would have been unimaginable a few years ago.

This monster chip fabrication plant, or Fab, could produce more than $8bn of chips a year, more than several medium-sized producers combined.

'When it's fully equipped, that's a new 5 per cent of global capacity,' says Ray Burgess, head of chip strategy at Motorola, one of IBM's biggest competitors.

The shake-up among the 20-odd companies that dominate the global chip market is starting to gather momentum. Old alliances are changing and many industry executives are starting to talk about an inevitable consolidation that will leave only a handful of groups standing.

Behind this upheaval lies a fundamental – and expensive – sea change in technology. It has come at just the moment when chipmakers can least afford it, after one of the most traumatic collapses seen in the chronically cyclical industry's 40-year history.

The latest technology advances have come in two areas. Silicon wafers – the discs from which individual chips are cut – are getting bigger. Plants such as Fishkill work with dinner-plate-sized wafers, 300mm in diameter. At the same time, individual chip sizes are getting smaller. Some elements on the most advanced chips are now only 90 nanometres across, or one-thousandth of the width of a human hair.

Taken together, these changes make it possible to produce nearly three times as many chips from each wafer. Manufacturers using older, 200mm wafers face unit costs that are about 40 per cent higher.

'Within the next few years there will only be five independent chipmakers plus some large foundries with their own 300mm Fabs,' says Ulrich Schumacher, head of Infineon Systems, the second largest European chipmaker.

Commentators were telling us that model railways were old-fashioned and there was no longer a market for them. But we knew the real problem was that manufacturing and labour were too expensive. The costs had to be reduced or the company would go bust.

Frank Martin, Chief Executive of Hornby's (2001) on the company's decision to shift production to the Far East

key terms
Opportunity cost
Explicit and implicit costs
Law of diminishing (marginal) returns
Returns to scale (increasing, constant and decreasing)
Economies of scale (internal)
External economies of scale
Diseconomies of scale
Specialisation and division of labour
Fixed and variable factors
Fixed and variable costs
Total average and marginal costs and revenue
Price takers and price choosers
Profit maximisation
Normal profit
Supernormal profit

In Part C we turn to supply. In other words, we will focus on the amount that firms produce. In Parts D and E we shall see how the supply decision is affected by the environment in which a firm operates, and in particular by the amount of competition it faces. In this part of the book, however, we take a more general look at supply and its relationship to profit.

Profit is made by firms earning more from the sale of goods than the goods cost to produce. A firm's total profit ($T\Pi$) is thus the difference between its total sales revenue (*TR*) and its total costs of production (*TC*):

$$T\Pi = TR - TC$$

(Note that we use the Greek Π (pi) for 'profit'.)

Businesses can increase their profitability either by increasing their revenue (by selling more of their product or adjusting their price) or by reducing their costs of production. It would appear that the new large-scale semi-conductor plants, as described in the *Financial Times* article opposite, offer their owners the potential to make significant reductions in their costs of production through embracing the most up-to-date technology.

In order, then, to discover how a firm can maximise its profit, or even get a sufficient level of profit, we must first consider what determines costs and revenue. Chapter 9 examines costs. Chapter 10 considers revenue, and then puts costs and revenue together to examine profit. We will discover the output at which profits are maximised and how much profit is made at that output.

9 Costs of production

9.1 The meaning of costs

Opportunity cost

When measuring costs, economists always use the concept of opportunity cost. As we saw in Chapter 2, opportunity cost is the cost of any activity measured in terms of the sacrifice made in doing it: in other words, the cost measured in terms of the opportunities forgone. If a car manufacturer can produce 10 small saloon cars with the same amount of inputs as it takes to produce 6 large saloon cars, then the opportunity cost of producing 1 small car is 0.6 of a large car. If a taxi and car hire firm uses its cars as taxis, then the opportunity cost includes not only the cost of employing taxi drivers and buying fuel, but also the sacrifice of rental income from hiring its vehicles out.

Key
Idea
3
p27

Measuring a firm's opportunity costs

Just how do we measure a firm's opportunity cost? First we must discover what factors of production it has used. Then we must measure the sacrifice involved in using them. To do this it is necessary to put factors into two categories.

Factors not owned by the firm: explicit costs

The opportunity cost of those factors not already owned by the firm is simply the price that the firm has to pay for them. Thus if the firm uses £100 worth of electricity, the opportunity cost is £100. The firm has sacrificed £100 which could have been spent on something else.

These costs are called **explicit costs** because they involve direct payment of money by firms.

Factors already owned by the firm: implicit costs

When the firm already owns factors (e.g. machinery) it does not as a rule have to pay out money to use them. Their opportunity costs are thus **implicit costs**. They are equal to what the factors *could* earn for the firm in some alternative use, either within the firm or hired out to some other firm.

Here are some examples of implicit costs:

- A firm owns some buildings. The opportunity cost of using them is the rent it could have received by letting them out to another firm.

BOX 9.1

The fallacy of using historic costs
Or there's no point crying over spilt milk

'What's done is done.'

'Write it off to experience.'

'You might as well make the best of a bad job.'

These familiar sayings are all everyday examples of a simple fact of life: once something has happened, you cannot change the past. You have to take things as they are *now*.

If you fall over and break your leg, there is little point in saying, 'If only I hadn't done that I could have gone on that skiing holiday; I could have taken part in that race; I could have done so many other things (sigh).' Wishing things were different won't change history. You have to manage as well as you can *with* your broken leg.

It is the same for a firm. Once it has purchased some inputs, it is no good then wishing it hadn't. It has to accept that it has now got them, and make the best decisions about what to do with them.

Take a simple example. The local convenience store in early December decides to buy 100 Christmas trees for £10 each. At the time of purchase this represents an opportunity cost of £10 each, since the £10 could have been spent on something else. The shopkeeper estimates that there is enough local demand to sell all 100 trees at £20 each, thereby making a reasonable profit (even after allowing for handling costs).

But the estimate turns out to be wrong. On 23 December there are still 50 trees unsold. What should be done? At this stage the £10 that was paid for the trees is irrelevant. It is a historic cost. It cannot be recouped: the trees cannot be sold back to the wholesaler!

In fact the opportunity cost is now zero. It might even be negative if the shopkeeper has to pay to dispose of any unsold trees. It might, therefore, be worth selling the trees at £10, £5 or even £1. Last thing on Christmas Eve it might even be worth giving away any unsold trees.

Question

Why is the correct price to charge (for the unsold trees) the one at which the price elasticity of demand equals –1? (Assume no disposal costs.)

Key Idea
3
p27

Pause for thought

Assume that a farmer decides to grow wheat on land that could be used for growing barley. Barley sells for £100 per tonne. Wheat sells for £150 per tonne. Seed, fertiliser, labour and other costs of growing crops are £80 per tonne for both wheat and barley. What are the farmer's costs and profit per tonne of growing wheat?

- A firm draws £100 000 from the bank out of its savings in order to invest in new plant and equipment. The opportunity cost of this investment is not just the £100 000 (an explicit cost), but also the interest it thereby forgoes (an implicit cost).

- The owner of the firm could have earned £15 000 per annum by working for someone else. This £15 000 is the opportunity cost of the owner's time.

If there is no alternative use for a factor of production, as in the case of a machine designed to produce a specific product, and if it has no scrap value, the opportunity cost of using it is *zero*. In such a case, if the output from the machine is worth more than the cost of all the *other* inputs involved, the firm might as well use the machine rather than let it stand idle.

What the firm paid for the machine – its **historic cost** – is irrelevant. Not using the machine will not bring that money back. It has been spent. These are sometimes referred to as 'sunk costs'.

definition

Opportunity cost
Cost measured in terms of the next best alternative forgone.

definition

Explicit costs
The payments to outside suppliers of inputs.

> **The 'bygones' principle** states that sunk (fixed) costs should be ignored when deciding whether to produce or sell more or less of a product. Only variable costs should be taken into account.

Key Idea
15

Likewise, the **replacement cost** is irrelevant. That should be taken into account only when the firm is considering replacing the machine.

Production in the short run   9.2

The cost of producing any level of output will depend on the amount of inputs used and the price that the firm must pay for them. Let us first focus on the quantity of inputs used.

> ***Output depends on the amount of resources and how they are used.*** Different amounts and combinations of inputs will lead to different amounts of output. If output is to be produced efficiently, then inputs should be combined in the optimum proportions.
>
> **Key Idea 16**

Short-run and long-run changes in production

If a firm wants to increase production, it will take time to acquire a greater quantity of certain inputs. For example, a manufacturer can use more electricity by turning on switches, but it might take a long time to obtain and install more machines, and longer still to build a second or third factory.

If, then, the firm wants to increase output in a hurry, it will only be able to increase the quantity of certain inputs. It can use more raw materials, more fuel, more tools and possibly more labour (by hiring extra workers or offering overtime to its existing workforce). But it will have to make do with its existing buildings and most of its machinery.

The distinction we are making here is between **fixed factors** and **variable factors**. A *fixed* factor is an input that cannot be increased within a given time period (e.g. buildings). A *variable* factor is one that can.

The distinction between fixed and variable factors allows us to distinguish between the **short run** and the **long run**.

The short run is a time period during which at least one factor of production is fixed. In the short run, then, output can be increased only by using more variable factors. For example, if a shipping line wanted to carry more passengers in response to a rise in demand, it could accommodate more passengers on existing sailings if there was space. It could increase the number of sailings with its existing fleet, by hiring more crew and using more fuel. But in the short run it could not buy more ships: there would not be time for them to be built.

The long run is a time period long enough for all inputs to be varied. Given long enough, the shipping company can have a new ship built.

The actual length of the short run will differ from firm to firm. It is not a fixed period of time. Thus if it takes a farmer a year to obtain new land, buildings and equipment, the short run is any time period up to a year and the long run is any time period longer than a year. But if it takes a shipping company three years to obtain an extra ship, the short run is any period up to three years and the long run is any period longer than three years.

For this and the next section we will concentrate on *short-run* production and costs. We will look at the long run in sections 9.4 and 9.5.

---

definition

Implicit costs
Costs which do not involve a direct payment of money to a third party, but which nevertheless involve a sacrifice of some alternative.

definition

Historic costs
The original amount the firm paid for factors it now owns.

definition

Replacement costs
What the firm would have to pay to replace factors it currently owns.

definition

Fixed factor
An input that cannot be increased in supply within a given time period.

definition

Variable factor
An input that *can* be increased in supply within a given time period.

definition

Short run
The period of time over which at least one factor is fixed.

Pause for thought

How will the length of the short run for the shipping company depend on the state of the ship building industry?

definition

Long run
The period of time long enough for *all* factors to be varied.

Production in the short run: the law of diminishing returns

Production in the short run is subject to *diminishing returns*. You may well have heard of 'the law of diminishing returns': it is one of the most famous of all 'laws' of economics. To illustrate how this law underlies short-run production, let us take the simplest possible case where there are just two factors: one fixed and one variable.

Take the case of a farm. Assume the fixed factor is land and the variable factor is labour. Since the land is fixed in supply, output per period of time can be increased only by increasing the number of workers employed. But imagine what would happen as more and more workers crowded on to a fixed area of land. The land cannot go on yielding more and more output indefinitely. After a point the additions to output from each extra worker will begin to diminish.

We can now state the **law of diminishing (marginal) returns**.

definition

Law of diminishing (marginal) returns
When one or more factors are held fixed, there will come a point beyond which the extra output from additional units of the variable factor will diminish.

The law of diminishing marginal returns. When increasing amounts of a variable factor are used with a given amount of a fixed factor, there will come a point when each extra unit of the variable factor will produce less extra output than the previous unit.

Key Idea 17

A good example of the law of diminishing returns is given in Case 9.1 on the book's website (**www.booksites.net/sloman**). The case looks at diminishing returns to the application of nitrogen fertiliser on farmland.

The short-run production function: total product

definition

Total physical product
The total output of a product per period of time that is obtained from a given amount of inputs.

Let us now see how the law of diminishing returns affects total output or **total physical product** (*TPP*).

The relationship between inputs and output is shown in a **production function**. In the simple case of the farm with only two factors – namely, a fixed supply of land ($\bar{L}n$) and a variable supply of farm workers (Lb) – the production function would be:

Key Idea 16 p169

$$TPP = f(\bar{L}n, Lb)$$

definition

Production function
The mathematical relationship between the output of a good and the inputs used to produce it. It shows how output will be affected by changes in the quantity of one or more of the inputs.

This states that total physical product (i.e. the output of the farm) over a given period of time is a function of (i.e. depends on) the quantity of land and labour employed.

The production function can also be expressed in the form of a table or a graph. Table 9.1 and Figure 9.1 show a hypothetical production function for a farm producing wheat. The first two columns of Table 9.1 and the top diagram in Figure 9.1 show how wheat output per year varies as extra workers are employed on a fixed amount of land.

With nobody working on the land, output will be zero (point *a*). As the first farm workers are taken on, wheat output initially rises more and more rapidly. The assumption behind this is that with only one or two workers efficiency is low, since the workers are spread too thinly. With more workers, however, they can work together – each, perhaps, doing some specialist job – and thus they can use the land more efficiently. In the top diagram of Figure 9.1, output rises more and more rapidly up to the employment of the third worker (point *b*).

Table 9.1	Wheat production per year from a particular farm (tonnes)			
	Number of workers (Lb)	TPP	APP (= TPP/Lb)	MPP (= ΔTPP/ΔLb)
a	0	0	–	
				3
	1	3	3	
				7
b	2	10	5	
				14
	3	24	8	
				12
c	4	36	9	
				4
	5	40	8	
				2
d	6	42	7	
				0
	7	42	6	
				–2
	8	40	5	

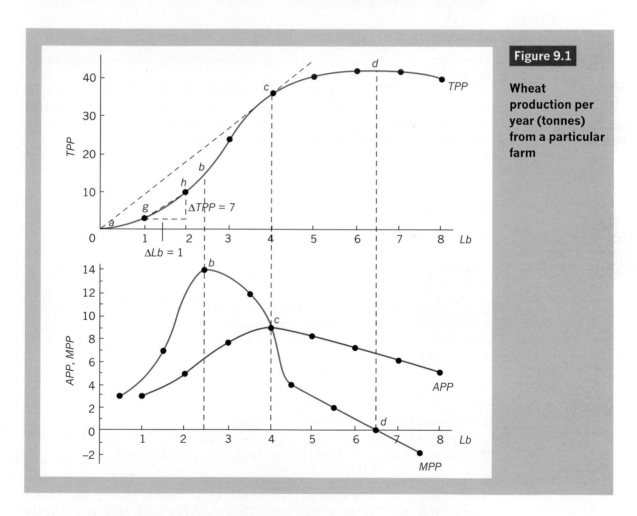

Figure 9.1

Wheat production per year (tonnes) from a particular farm

After point *b*, however, diminishing marginal returns set in: output rises less and less rapidly, and the *TPP* curve correspondingly becomes less steeply sloped.

When point *d* is reached, wheat output is at a maximum: the land is yielding as much as it can. Any more workers employed after that are likely to get in each other's way. Thus beyond point *d*, output is likely to fall again: eight workers produce less than seven workers.

The short-run production function: average and marginal product

In addition to total physical product, two other important concepts are illustrated by a production function: namely, **average physical product** (*APP*) and **marginal physical product** (*MPP*).

Average physical product

This is output (*TPP*) per unit of the variable factor (*Qv*). In the case of the farm, it is the output of wheat per worker.

$$APP = TPP/Qv$$

Thus in Table 9.1, the average physical product of labour when four workers are employed is $36/4 = 9$ tonnes.

Marginal physical product

This is the *extra* output (ΔTPP) produced by employing *one more* unit of the variable factor.

Thus in Table 9.1 the marginal physical product of the fourth worker is 12 tonnes. The reason is that, by employing the fourth worker, wheat output has risen from 24 tonnes to 36 tonnes: a rise of 12 tonnes.

In symbols, marginal physical product is given by:

$$MPP = \Delta TPP/\Delta Qv$$

Thus in our example:

$$MPP = 12/1 = 12$$

The reason why we divide the increase in output (ΔTPP) by the increase in the quantity of the variable factor (ΔQv) is that some variable factors can be increased only in multiple units. For example, if we wanted to know the *MPP* of fertiliser and we found out how much extra wheat was produced by using an extra 20 kg bag, we would have to divide this output by 20 (ΔQv) to find the *MPP* of *one* more kilogram.

Note that in Table 9.1 the figures for *MPP* are entered in the spaces between the other figures. The reason is that *MPP* can be seen as the *difference* in output *between* one level of input and another. Thus in the table the difference in output between five and six workers is 2 tonnes.

The figures for *APP* and *MPP* are plotted in the lower diagram of Figure 9.1. We can draw a number of conclusions from these two diagrams.

- The *MPP* between two points is equal to the slope of the *TPP* curve between those two points. For example, when the number of workers increases from 1 to 2 ($\Delta Lb = 1$), *TPP* rises from 3 to 10 tonnes ($\Delta TPP = 7$). *MPP* is thus 7: the slope of the line between points *g* and *h*.

- *MPP* rises at first: the slope of the *TPP* curve gets steeper.

- *MPP* reaches a maximum at point *b*. At that point the slope of the *TPP* curve is at its steepest.

- After point *b*, diminishing returns set in. *MPP* falls. *TPP* becomes less steep.

Key Idea 17 p170

- *APP* rises at first. It continues rising as long as the addition to output from the last worker (*MPP*) is greater than the average output (*APP*): the *MPP* pulls the *APP* up. This continues beyond point *b*. Even though *MPP* is now falling, the *APP* goes on rising as long as the *MPP* is still above the *APP*. Thus *APP* goes on rising to point *c*.

- Beyond point *c*, *MPP* is below *APP*. New workers add less to output than the average. This pulls the average down: *APP* falls.

- As long as *MPP* is greater than zero, *TPP* will go on rising: new workers add to total output.

- At point *d*, *TPP* is at a maximum (its slope is zero). An additional worker will add nothing to output: *MPP* is zero.

- Beyond point *d*, *TPP* falls. *MPP* is negative.

> **Pause for thought**
>
> *What is the significance of the slope of the line ac in the top part of Figure 9.1?*

Costs in the short run   9.3

Having looked at the background to costs in the short run, we now turn to examine short-run costs themselves. We will be examining how costs change as a firm changes the amount it produces. Obviously, if it is to decide how much to produce, it will need to know just what the level of costs will be at each level of output.

Costs and inputs

A firm's costs of production will depend on the factors of production it uses. The more factors it uses, the greater will its costs be. More precisely, this relationship depends on two elements.

> *The productivity of the factors.* The greater their physical productivity, the smaller will be the quantity of them that is needed to produce a given level of output, and hence the lower will be the cost of that output. In other words, there is a direct link between *TPP*, *APP* and *MPP* and the costs of production.

> *The price of the factors.* The higher their price, the higher will be the costs of production.

In the short run, some factors are fixed in supply. Their total costs, therefore, are fixed, in the sense that they do not vary with output. Rent on land is a **fixed cost**. It is the same whether the firm produces a lot or a little.

The cost of variable factors, however, does vary with output. The cost of raw materials is a **variable cost**. The more that is produced, the more raw materials are used and therefore the higher is their total cost.

Total cost

The **total cost** (**TC**) of production is the sum of the *total variable costs* (*TVC*) and the *total fixed costs* (*TFC*) of production.

$$TC = TVC + TFC$$

> **definition**
> **Fixed costs**
> Total costs that do not vary with the amount of output produced.

> **definition**
> **Variable costs**
> Total costs that do vary with the amount of output produced.

> **definition**
> **Total cost (*TC*)**
> The sum of total fixed costs (*TFC*) and total variable costs (*TVC*): *TC* = *TFC* + *TVC*.

Table 9.2	**Total costs for firm X**		
Output *(Q)*	*TFC* *(£)*	*TVC* *(£)*	*TC* *(£)*
0	12	0	12
1	12	10	22
2	12	16	28
3	12	21	33
4	12	28	40
5	12	40	52
6	12	60	72
7	12	91	103
.	.	.	.

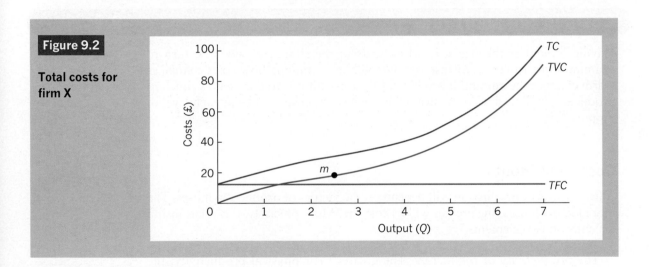

Figure 9.2

Total costs for firm X

Consider Table 9.2 and Figure 9.2. They show the total costs for an imaginary firm for producing different levels of output (*Q*). Let us examine each of the three cost curves in turn.

Total fixed cost (TFC)

In our example, total fixed cost is assumed to be £12. Since this does not vary with output, it is shown by a horizontal straight line.

Total variable cost (TVC)

With a zero output, no variable factors will be used. Thus *TVC* = 0. The *TVC* curve, therefore, starts from the origin.

The shape of the *TVC* curve follows from the law of diminishing returns. Initially, *before* diminishing returns set in, *TVC* rises less and less rapidly as more variable factors are added. For example, in the case of a factory with a fixed supply of machinery, initially as more workers are taken on the workers can do increasingly specialist tasks and make a fuller use of the capital equipment. This corresponds to the portion of the *TPP* curve that rises more rapidly (up to point *b* in the top diagram of Figure 9.1).

Key Idea
17
p170

As output is increased beyond point *m* in Figure 9.2, diminishing returns set in. Given that extra workers (the extra variable factors) are producing less and less extra output, the extra units of output they do produce will be costing more and more in terms of wage costs. Thus *TVC* rises more and more rapidly. The *TVC* curve gets steeper. This corresponds to the portion of the *TPP* curve that rises less rapidly (between points *b* and *d* in Figure 9.1).

Total cost (TC)

Since *TC* = *TVC* + *TFC*, the *TC* curve is simply the *TVC* curve shifted vertically upwards by £12.

Average and marginal cost

Average cost (*AC*) is cost per unit of production.

$$AC = TC/Q$$

Thus if it costs a firm £2000 to produce 100 units of a product, the average cost would be £20 for each unit (£2000/100).

Like total cost, average cost can be divided into the two components, fixed and variable. In other words, average cost equals **average fixed cost** (*AFC* = *TFC*/*Q*) plus **average variable cost** (*AVC* = *TVC*/*Q*).

$$AC = AFC + AVC$$

Marginal cost (*MC*) is the *extra* cost of producing *one more unit*: that is, the rise in total cost per one unit rise in output.

$$MC = \frac{\Delta TC}{\Delta Q}$$

where Δ means 'a rise in'.

For example, assume that a firm is currently producing 1 000 000 boxes of matches a month. It now increases output by 1000 boxes, (another batch): ΔQ = 1000. As a result its total costs rise by £30: ΔTC = £30. What is the cost of producing *one* more box of matches? It is:

$$MC = \frac{\Delta TC}{\Delta Q} = \frac{£30}{1000} = 3p$$

(Note that all marginal costs are variable, since, by definition, there can be no extra fixed costs as output rises.)

Given the *TFC*, *TVC* and *TC* for each output, it is possible to derive the *AFC*, *AVC*, *AC* and *MC* for each output using the above definitions. For example, using the data of Table 9.2, Table 9.3 can be constructed.

What will be the shapes of the *MC*, *AFC*, *AVC* and *AC* curves? These follow from the nature of the *MPP* and *APP* curves that we looked at in section 9.2.

definition

Average (total) cost (*AC*)
Total cost (fixed plus variable) per unit of output: $AC = TC/Q = AFC + AVC$.

definition

Average fixed cost (*AFC*)
Total fixed cost per unit of output: $AFC = TFC/Q$.

definition

Average variable cost (*AVC*)
Total variable cost per unit of output: $AVC = TVC/Q$.

definition

Marginal cost (*MC*)
The cost of producing one more unit of output: $MC = \Delta TC/\Delta Q$.

Table 9.3   Costs

Output (Q) (units)	TFC (£)	AFC (TFC/Q) (£)	TVC (£)	AVC (TVC/Q) (£)	TC (TFC + TVC) (£)	AC (TC/Q) (£)	MC (ΔTC/ΔQ) (£)
0	12	–	0	–	12	–	
							10
1	12	12.6	10	10	22	22	
							6
2	12	6	16	8	28	14	
							5
3	12	4	21	7	33	11	
							7
4	12	3	28	7	40	10	
							12
5	12	2.4	40	8	52	10.4	
							20
6	12	2	60	10	72	12	
							31
7	12	1.7	91	13	103	14.7	

Figure 9.3

Average and marginal costs

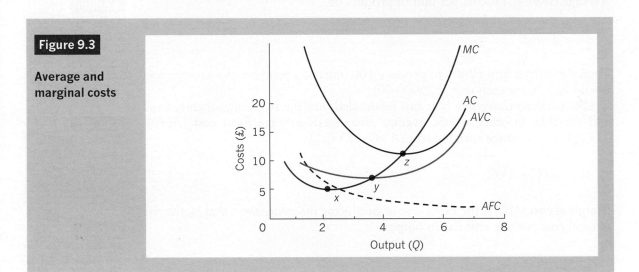

Marginal cost (MC)

The shape of the *MC* curve follows directly from the law of diminishing returns. Initially, in Figure 9.3, as more of the variable factor is used, extra units of output cost less than previous units. *MC* falls. This corresponds to the portion of the *TVC* curve in Figure 9.2 to the left of point *m*.

Beyond a certain level of output, diminishing returns set in. This is shown as point *x* in Figure 9.3 and corresponds to point *m* in Figure 9.2. Thereafter *MC* rises. Additional units of output cost more and more to produce, since they require ever increasing amounts of the variable factor.

Average fixed cost (AFC)

This falls continuously as output rises, since *total* fixed costs are being spread over a greater and greater output.

Average variable cost (AVC)

The shape of the *AVC* curve depends on the shape of the *APP* curve. As the average product of workers rises, the average labour cost per unit of output (the *AVC*) falls: up to point *y* in Figure 9.3. Thereafter, as *APP* falls, *AVC* must rise.

Short-run cost curves in practice
When fixed factors are divisible

Are short-run cost curves always the shape depicted in this chapter? The answer is no. Sometimes, rather than being U-shaped, the *AVC* and *MC* curves are flat bottomed, like the curves in the diagram. Indeed, they may be constant (and equal to each other) over a *substantial* range of output.

The reason for this is that sometimes fixed factors may not have to be in full use all the time. Take the case of a firm with 100 identical machines, each one requiring one person to operate it. Although the firm cannot use *more* than the 100 machines, it could use fewer: in other words, some of the machines could be left idle. Assume, for example, that instead of using 100 machines, the firm uses only 90. It would need only 90 operatives and 90 per cent of the raw materials. Similarly, if it used only 20 machines, its total variable costs (labour and raw materials) would be only 20 per cent. What we are saying here is that *average* variable cost remains constant – and over a very large range of output: using anything from 1 machine to 100 machines.

The reason for the constant *AVC* (and *MC*) is that by varying the amount of fixed capital used, the *proportions* used of capital, labour and raw materials can be kept the same and hence the average and marginal productivity of labour and raw materials will remain constant.

Only when all machines are in use (at Q_1) will *AVC* start to rise if output is further expanded. Machines may then have to work beyond their optimal speed, using more raw materials per unit of output (diminishing returns to raw materials), or workers may have to work longer shifts with higher (overtime) pay.

Output (*Q*)

Questions

1 *Assume that a firm has 5 identical machines, each operating independently. Assume that with all 5 machines operating normally, 100 units of output are produced each day. Below what level of output will AVC and MC rise?*

2 *Manufacturing firms like the one we have been describing will have other fixed costs (such as rent and managerial overheads). Does the existence of these affect the argument that the AVC curve will be flat bottomed?*

Average (total) cost (AC)

This is simply the vertical sum of the *AFC* and *AVC* curves. Note that, as *AFC* gets less, the gap between *AVC* and *AC* narrows.

The relationship between average cost and marginal cost

This is simply another illustration of the relationship that applies between *all* averages and marginals.

As long as new units of output cost less than the average, their production must pull the average cost down. That is, if *MC* is less than *AC*, *AC* must be falling. Likewise, if new units cost more than the average, their production must drive the average up. That is, if *MC* is greater than *AC*, *AC* must be rising. Therefore, the *MC* crosses the *AC* at its minimum point (point *z* in Figure 9.3).

Pause for thought

Before you read on, can you explain why the marginal cost curve will always cut the average cost curve at its lowest point.

Since all marginal costs are variable, the same relationship holds between *MC* and *AVC*.

9.4 Production in the long run

In the long run *all* factors of production are variable. There is time for the firm to build a new factory (maybe in a different part of the country), to install new machines, to use different techniques of production, and in general to combine its inputs in whatever proportion and in whatever quantities it chooses.

In the long run, then, a firm will have to make a number of decisions: about the scale of its operations, the location of its operations and the techniques of production it will use. These decisions will affect the costs of production. It is important, therefore, to get them right.

The scale of production

If a firm were to double all of its inputs – something it could do in the long run – would it double its output? Or would output more than double or less than double? We can distinguish three possible situations.

- *Constant returns to scale*. This is where a given percentage increase in inputs will lead to the same percentage increase in output.
- *Increasing returns to scale*. This is where a given percentage increase in inputs will lead to a larger percentage increase in output.
- *Decreasing returns to scale*. This is where a given percentage increase in inputs will lead to a smaller percentage increase in output.

Notice the terminology here. The words 'to scale' mean that *all* inputs increase by the same proportion. Decreasing returns to *scale* are therefore quite different from *diminishing* marginal returns (where only the *variable* factor increases). The differences between marginal returns to a variable factor and returns to scale are illustrated in Table 9.4.

In the short run, input 1 is assumed to be fixed in supply (at 3 units). Output can be increased only by using more of the variable factor (input 2). In the long run, however, both input 1 and input 2 are variable.

In the short-run situation, diminishing returns can be seen from the fact that output increases at a decreasing rate (25 to 45 to 60 to 70 to 75) as input 2 is

| Table 9.4 | Short-run and long-run increases in output |

Short run			Long run		
Input 1	*Input 2*	*Output*	*Input 1*	*Input 2*	*Output*
3	1	25	1	1	15
3	2	45	2	2	35
3	3	60	3	3	60
3	4	70	4	4	90
3	5	75	5	5	125

increased. In the long-run situation, the table illustrates increasing returns to scale. Output increases at an *increasing* rate (15 to 35 to 60 to 90 to 125) as both inputs are increased.

Economies of scale

The concept of increasing returns to scale is closely linked to that of **economies of scale**. A firm experiences economies of scale if costs per unit of output fall as the scale of production increases. Clearly, if a firm is getting increasing returns to scale from its factors of production, then as it produces more, it will be using smaller and smaller amounts of factors per unit of output. Other things being equal, this means that it will be producing at a lower unit cost.

There are a number of reasons why firms are likely to experience economies of scale. Some are due to increasing returns to scale; some are not.

Specialisation and division of labour. In large-scale plants, workers can do more simple repetitive jobs. With this **specialisation and division of labour**, less training is needed; workers can become highly efficient in their particular job, especially with long production runs; there is less time lost in workers switching from one operation to another; supervision is easier. Workers and managers can be employed who have specific skills in specific areas.

Indivisibilities. Some inputs are of a minimum size. They are indivisible. The most obvious example is machinery. Take the case of a combine harvester. A small-scale farmer could not make full use of one. They only become economical to use, therefore, on farms above a certain size. The problem of **indivisibilities** is made worse when different machines, each of which is part of the production process, are of a different size. For example, if there are two types of machine, one producing 6 units a day, the other packaging 4 units a day, a minimum of 12 units per day will have to be produced, involving two production machines and three packaging machines, if all machines are to be fully utilised.

The 'container principle'. Any capital equipment that contains things (blast furnaces, oil tankers, pipes, vats, etc.) will tend to cost less per unit of output, the larger its size. The reason has to do with the relationship between a container's volume and its surface area. A container's cost will depend largely on the materials used to build it and hence roughly on its *surface area*. Its output will depend largely on its *volume*. Large containers have a bigger volume relative to surface area than do small containers. For example, a container with a bottom, top and four sides, with each side measuring 1 metre, has a volume of 1 cubic metre and a surface area of 6 square metres (6 surfaces of 1 square metre each). If each side were now to be doubled in length to 2 metres, the volume would be 8 cubic metres and the surface area 24 square metres (6 surfaces of 4 square metres each). Thus an eightfold increase in capacity has been gained at only a fourfold increase in the container's surface area, and hence an approximate fourfold increase in cost.

Greater efficiency of large machines. Large machines may be more efficient, in the sense that more output can be gained for a given amount of inputs. For example, only one worker may be required to operate a machine whether it be large or small. Also, a large machine may make more efficient use of raw materials.

Key Idea 16 p169

definition
Economies of scale
When increasing the scale of production leads to a lower cost per unit of output.

definition
Specialisation and division of labour
Where production is broken down into a number of simpler, more specialised tasks, thus allowing workers to acquire a high degree of efficiency.

definition
Indivisibilities
The impossibility of dividing a factor into smaller units.

By-products. With production on a large scale, there may be sufficient waste products to enable them to make some by-product.

Multistage production. A large factory may be able to take a product through several stages in its manufacture. This saves time and cost moving the semi-finished product from one firm or factory to another. For example, a large cardboard-manufacturing firm may be able to convert trees or waste paper into cardboard and then into cardboard boxes in a continuous sequence.

All the above are examples of **plant economies of scale**. They are due to an individual factory or workplace or machine being large. There are other economies of scale that are associated with the firm being large – perhaps with many factories.

Organisational. With a large firm, individual plants can specialise in particular functions. There can also be centralised administration of the firms. Often, after a merger between two firms, savings can be made by **rationalising** their activities in this way.

Spreading overheads. Some expenditures are economic only when the *firm* is large, such as research and development: only a large firm can afford to set up a research laboratory. This is another example of indivisibilities, only this time at the level of the firm rather than the plant. The greater the firm's output, the more these **overhead costs** are spread.

Financial economies. Large firms may be able to obtain finance at lower interest rates than small firms. They may be able to obtain certain inputs cheaper by buying in bulk.

Economies of scope. Often a firm is large because it produces a range of products. This can result in each individual product being produced more cheaply than if it was produced in a single-product firm. The reason for these **economies of scope** is that various overhead costs and financial and organisational economies can be shared between the products. For example, a firm that produces a whole range of CD players, cassette recorders, amplifiers and tuners can benefit from shared marketing and distribution costs and the bulk purchase of electronic components.

Diseconomies of scale

When firms get beyond a certain size, costs per unit of output may start to increase. There are several reasons for such **diseconomies of scale**:

- Management problems of co-ordination may increase as the firm becomes larger and more complex, and as lines of communication get longer. There may be a lack of personal involvement by management.
- Workers may feel 'alienated' if their jobs are boring and repetitive, and if they feel an insignificantly small part of a large organisation. Poor motivation may lead to shoddy work.
- Industrial relations may deteriorate as a result of these factors and also as a result of the more complex interrelationships between different categories of worker.
- Production-line processes and the complex interdependencies of mass production can lead to great disruption if there are hold-ups in any one part of the firm.

---

definition

Plant economies of scale
Economies of scale that arise because of the large size of the factory.

definition

Rationalisation
The reorganising of production (often after a merger) so as to cut out waste and duplication and generally to reduce costs.

definition

Overheads
Costs arising from the general running of an organisation, and only indirectly related to the level of output.

definition

Economies of scope
When increasing the range of products produced by a firm reduces the cost of producing each one.

definition

Diseconomies of scale
Where costs per unit of output increase as the scale of production increases.

Whether firms experience economies or diseconomies of scale will depend on the conditions applying in each individual firm.

Location

In the long run, a firm can move to a different location. The location will affect the cost of production, since locations differ in terms of the availability and cost of raw materials, suitable land and power supply, the qualifications, skills and experience of the labour force, wage rates, transport and communications networks, the cost of local services, and banking and financial facilities. In short, locations differ in terms of the availability, suitability and cost of the factors of production.

Transport costs will be an important influence on a firm's location. Ideally, a firm will wish to be as near as possible to both its raw materials and the market for its finished product. When market and raw materials are in different locations, the firm will minimise its transport costs by locating somewhere between the two. In general, if the raw materials are more expensive to transport than the finished product, the firm should locate as near as possible to the raw materials. This will normally apply to firms whose raw materials are heavier or more bulky than the finished product. Thus heavy industry, which uses large quantities of coal and various ores, tends to be concentrated near the coal fields or near the ports. If, on the other hand, the finished product is more expensive to transport (e.g. bread or beer), the firm will probably be located as near as possible to its market.

When raw materials or markets are in many different locations, transport costs will be minimised at the 'centre of gravity'. This location will be nearer to those raw materials and markets whose transport costs are greater per mile.

The size of the whole industry

As an *industry* grows in size, this can lead to **external economies of scale** for its member firms. This is where a firm, whatever its own individual size, benefits from the *whole industry* being large. For example, the firm may benefit from having access to specialist raw material or component suppliers, labour with specific skills, firms that specialise in marketing the finished product, and banks and other financial institutions with experience of the industry's requirements. What we are referring to here is the **industry's infrastructure**: the facilities, support services, skills and experience that can be shared by its members.

The member firms of a particular industry might experience **external diseconomies of scale**. For example, as an industry grows larger, this may create a growing shortage of specific raw materials or skilled labour. This will push up their prices, and hence the firms' costs.

The optimum combination of factors

In the long run, all factors can be varied. The firm can thus choose what techniques of production to use: what design of factory to build, what types

definition
External economies of scale
Where a firm's costs per unit of output decrease as the size of the whole *industry* grows.

definition
Industry's infrastructure
The network of supply agents, communications, skills, training facilities, distribution channels, specialised financial services, etc. that support a particular industry.

Pause for thought
Would you expect external economies of scale to be associated with the concentration of an industry in a particular region? Explain.

definition
External diseconomies of scale
Where a firm's costs per unit of output increase as the size of the whole industry increases.

BOX 9.3

UK competitiveness: moving to the next stage
The importance of location

In October 2002, a jointly funded project by the Economic and Social Research Council and the Department of Trade and Industry, appointed Professor Michael Porter and Christian Ketels of Harvard Business School to conduct a review of the UK's competitiveness and identify how it might be improved. In May 2003 the report was published. The authors declared that since 1980 the UK had done remarkably well in halting its economic decline on world markets, and had in fact matched and even bettered its main rivals in many industrial sectors. However, they were quick to sound a note of caution.

> The UK currently faces a transition to a new phase of economic development. The old approach to economic development is reaching the limits of its effectiveness, and government, companies, and other institutions need to rethink their policy priorities. This rethinking is not a sign of the past strategy's failure; it is a necessary part of graduating to the new stage.[1]

Porter's view is that economic development is achieved through a series of stages. The factor-driven stage identifies factors of production as the basis of competitive advantage: you have an advantage in those industries where you have a plentiful supply of the relevant factors of production. The investment-driven stage of development focuses upon efficiency and productivity as the key to competitive success. The third stage, into which Porter believes the UK is shifting, is innovation-driven. Here competitive advantage is achieved through the production of innovative products and services.

> We find that the competitiveness agenda facing UK leaders in government and business reflects the challenges of moving from a location competing on relatively low costs of doing business to a location competing on unique value and innovation.[2]

The importance of industrial clusters

One of the key characteristics of a successful innovation-led development strategy is the existence of industrial clusters.

> Clusters are geographically proximate groups of interconnected companies, suppliers, service providers, and associated institutions in a particular field, linked by commonalties and complementarities.[3]

Porter suggests that clusters are vital for competitiveness in three crucial respects:

- Clusters improve productivity. The close proximity of suppliers and other service providers enhances flexibility.
- Clusters aid innovation. Interaction among business within a cluster stimulates new ideas and aids their dissemination.
- Clusters contribute to new business formation. Clusters are self-reinforcing, in so far as specialist factors such as dedicated venture capital, and labour skills, help reduce costs and lower the risks of new business start-up.

Given that national economies tend to specialise in certain industrial clusters, we can identify where clusters occur and their importance, by considering their share of national output and export earnings. Export earnings in particular are a good indicator as to how globally competitive a cluster might be.

The UK's industrial clusters were seen by Porter as being relatively weak, and in fact many traditional clusters, such as steel and car manufacturing, had thinned to the point where they now lacked critical mass and failed to benefit from the clustering effect. Where the UK had strengths were in the areas of services, such as financial services and media, defence, products for personal use, health care and telecommunications.

of machine to buy, how to organise the factory, and whether to use highly automated processes or more labour-intensive techniques. It must be very careful in making these decisions. Once it has built its factory and installed the machinery, these then become fixed factors of production, maybe for many years: the subsequent 'short-run' time period may in practice last a very long time!

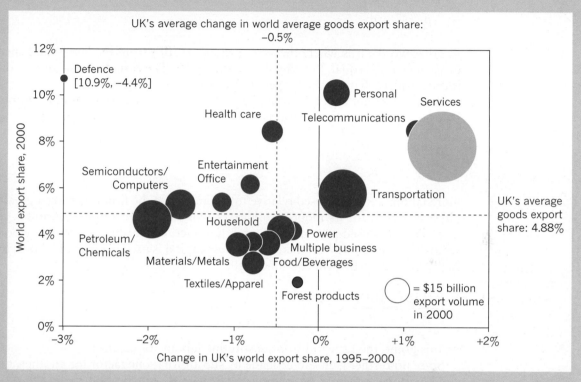

UK's export performance by broad sector

Source: Michael E. Porter and Christian H. M. Ketels, *UK Competitiveness: moving to the next stage (DTI and ESRC, May 2003), page 29*

Lesser clusters in entertainment, semiconductors and computers, transportation and office products could also be identified.

Porter and Katels conclude that, to improve its competitiveness, the UK must not only support what clusters it has but endeavour to up-grade and contribute to their development.

The UK needs to mount a sustained programme of cluster development to create a more conducive environment for productivity growth and innovation through the collective action of companies and other institutions.... It will be essential to mobilise businesses and business institutions that

are willing and able to engage in the upgrading of their clusters.[4]

Question

What policies or initiatives might a 'programme of cluster development' involve? Distinguish between policies that government and business might initiate.

[1] Michael E. Porter and Christian H. M. Ketels, *UK Competitiveness: moving to the next stage* (DTI and ESRC, May 2003), page 5
[2] *Ibid.*, page 5
[3] *Ibid.*, page 27
[4] *Ibid.*, page 46

For any given scale, how should the firm decide what technique to use? How should it decide the optimum 'mix' of factors of production?

The profit-maximising firm will obviously want to use the least costly combination of factors to produce any given output. It will therefore substitute factors, one for another, if by so doing it can reduce the cost of a given output. What, then, is the optimum combination of factors?

The simple two-factor case

Take first the simplest case where a firm uses just two factors: labour (L) and capital (K). The least-cost combination of the two will be where:

$$\frac{MPP_L}{P_L} = \frac{MPP_K}{P_K}$$

In other words, it is where the extra product (MPP) from the last pound spent on each factor is equal. But why should this be so? The easiest way to answer this is to consider what would happen if they were not equal.

If they were not equal, it would be possible to reduce cost per unit of output, by using a different combination of labour and capital. For example, if:

$$\frac{MPP_L}{P_L} > \frac{MPP_K}{P_K}$$

more labour should be used relative to capital, since the firm is getting a greater physical return for its money from extra workers than from extra capital. As more labour is used per unit of capital, however, diminishing returns to labour set in. Thus MPP_L will fall. Likewise, as less capital is used per unit of labour, the MPP_K will rise. This will continue until:

$$\frac{MPP_L}{P_L} = \frac{MPP_K}{P_K}$$

At this point, the firm will stop substituting labour for capital.

Since no further gain can be made by substituting one factor for another, this combination of factors or 'choice of techniques' can be said to be the most efficient. It is the least-cost way of combining factors for any given output. Efficiency in this sense of using the optimum factor proportions is known as **technical** or **productive efficiency**.

The multifactor case

Where a firm uses many different factors, the least-cost combination of factors will be where:

$$\frac{MPP_a}{P_a} = \frac{MPP_b}{P_b} = \frac{MPP_c}{P_c} \ldots = \frac{MPP_n}{P_n}$$

where a . . . n are different factors of production.

The reasons are the same as in the two-factor case. If any inequality exists between the MPP/P ratios, a firm will be able to reduce its costs by using more of those factors with a high MPP/P ratio and less of those with a low MPP/P ratio until the ratios all become equal.

A major problem for a firm in choosing the least-cost technique is in predicting future factor price changes.

If the price of a factor were to change, the MPP/P ratios would cease to be equal. The firm, to minimise costs, would then like to alter its factor combinations until the MPP/P ratios once more become equal. The trouble is that, once it has committed itself to a particular technique, it may be several years before it can switch to an alternative one. Thus if a firm invests in labour-intensive methods of production and is then faced with an unexpected wage rise, it may regret not having chosen a more capital-intensive technique.

Postscript: decision making in different time periods

We have distinguished between the short run and the long run. Let us introduce two more time periods to complete the picture. The complete list then reads as follows.

Very short run (immediate run). All factors are fixed. Output is fixed. The supply curve is vertical. On a day-to-day basis, a firm may not be able to vary output at all. For example, a flower seller, once the day's flowers have been purchased from the wholesaler, cannot alter the amount of flowers available for sale on that day. In the very short run, all that may remain for a producer to do is to sell an already-produced good.

Short run. At least one factor is fixed in supply. More can be produced, but the firm will come up against the law of diminishing returns as it tries to do so.

Long run. All factors are variable. The firm may experience constant, increasing or decreasing returns to scale. But although all factors can be increased or decreased, they are of a fixed *quality*.

Very long run. All factors are variable, *and* their quality and hence productivity can change. Labour productivity can increase as a result of education, training, experience and social factors. The productivity of capital can increase as a result of new inventions (new discoveries) and innovation (putting inventions into practice).

Improvements in factor quality will increase the output they produce: *TPP*, *APP* and *MPP* will rise. These curves will shift vertically upward.

Just how long the 'very long run' is will vary from firm to firm. It will depend on how long it takes to develop new techniques, new skills or new work practices.

It is important to realise that decisions *for* all four time periods can be made *at* the same time. Firms do not make short-run decisions *in* the short run and long-run decisions *in* the long run. They can make both short-run and long-run decisions today. For example, assume that a firm experiences an increase in consumer demand and anticipates that it will continue into the foreseeable future. It thus wants to increase output. Consequently, it makes the following four decisions *today*:

- *(Very short run)* It accepts that for a few days it will not be able to increase output. It informs its customers that they will have to wait. It may temporarily raise prices to choke off some of the demand.

- *(Short run)* It negotiates with labour to introduce overtime working as soon as possible, to tide it over the next few weeks. It orders extra raw materials from its suppliers. It launches a recruitment drive for new labour so as to avoid paying overtime longer than is necessary.

- *(Long run)* It starts proceedings to build a new factory. The first step may be to discuss requirements with a firm of consultants.

> **Pause for thought**
>
> 1 What will the long-run market supply curve for a product look like? How will the shape of the long-run curve depend on returns to scale?
> 2 Why would it be difficult to construct a very-long run supply curve?

■ *(Very long run)* It institutes a programme of research and development and/or training in an attempt to increase productivity.

Although we distinguish these four time periods, it is the middle two we are primarily concerned with. The reason for this is that there is very little that the firm can do in the *very* short run. And in the *very* long run, although the firm will obviously want to increase the productivity of its inputs, it will not be in a position to make precise calculations of how to do it. It will not know precisely what inventions will be made, or just what will be the results of its own research and development.

9.5 Costs in the long run

When it comes to making long-run production decisions, the firm has much more flexibility. It does not have to operate with plant and equipment of a fixed size. It can expand the whole scale of its operations. All its inputs are variable, and thus the law of diminishing returns does not apply. The firm may experience economies of scale or diseconomies of scale, or its average costs may stay constant as it expands the scale of its operations.

Since there are no fixed factors in the long run, there are no long-run fixed costs. For example, the firm may rent more land in order to expand its operations. Its rent bill therefore goes up as it expands its output.

All costs, then, in the long run are variable costs.

definition

Long-run average cost (*LRAC*) curve
A curve that shows how average cost varies with output on the assumption that *all* factors are variable. (It is assumed that the least-cost method of production will be chosen for each output.)

Long-run average costs

Although it is possible to draw long-run total, marginal and average cost curves, we will concentrate on **long-run average cost (*LRAC*) curves**. These curves can take various shapes.

If the firm experiences economies of scale, its *LRAC* curve will fall as the scale of production increases (diagram (a) in Figure 9.4). This, after all, is how we define economies of scale: namely, a reduction in average costs as the scale of production increases. If diseconomies of scale predominate, the *LRAC* curve will rise (diagram (b)). Alternatively, if the firm experiences neither economies nor diseconomies of scale, the *LRAC* curve will be horizontal (diagram (c)).

Figure 9.4

Alternative long-run average cost curves
(a) Economies of scale
(b) Diseconomies of scale
(c) Constant costs

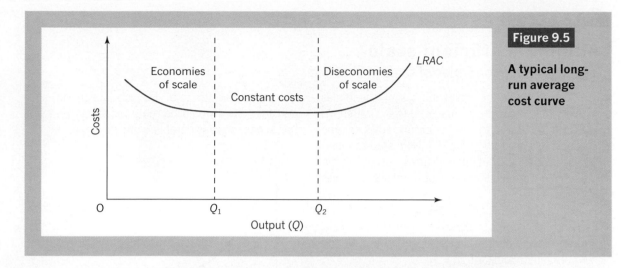

Figure 9.5

A typical long-run average cost curve

It is often assumed that, as a firm expands, it will initially experience economies of scale and thus face a downward-sloping *LRAC* curve. After a point, however, all such economies will have been achieved and thus the curve will flatten out. Then (possibly after a period of constant *LRAC*), the firm will get so large that it will start experiencing diseconomies of scale and thus a rising *LRAC*. At this stage, production and financial economies begin to be offset by the managerial problems of running a giant organisation.

The effect of this is to give a L-shaped or saucer shaped curve, as in Figure 9.5.

Assumptions behind the long-run average cost curve

We make three key assumptions when constructing long-run average cost curves.

Factor prices are given. At each output, a firm will be faced with a given set of factor prices. If factor prices *change*, therefore, both short- and long-run cost curves will shift. Thus an increase in wages would shift the curves upwards.

However, factor prices might be different at *different* levels of output. For example, one of the economies of scale that many firms enjoy is the ability to obtain bulk discount on raw materials and other supplies. In such cases the curve does *not* shift. The different factor prices are merely experienced at different points along the curve, and are reflected in the shape of the curve. Factor prices are still given for any particular level of output.

The state of technology and factor quality are given. These are assumed to change only in the *very* long run. If a firm gains economies of scale, it is because it is being able to exploit *existing* technologies and make better use of the existing availability of factors of production.

Firms choose the least-cost combination of factors for each output. The assumption here is that firms operate efficiently: that they choose the cheapest possible way of producing any level of output. In other words, at every point along the LRAC curve the firm will adhere to the cost-minimising formula:

$$\frac{MPP_a}{P_a} = \frac{MPP_b}{P_b} = \frac{MPP_c}{P_c} \ldots = \frac{MPP_n}{P_n}$$

where a . . . n are the various factors that the firm uses.

BOX 9.4

Minimum efficient scale
The extent of economies of scale in practice

Two of the most important studies of economies of scale have been those made by C. F. Pratten[1] in the late 1980s and by a group advising the European Commission[2] in 1997. Both studies found strong evidence that many firms, especially in manufacturing, experienced substantial economies of scale.

In a few cases long-run average costs fell continuously as output increased. For most firms, however, they fell up to a certain level of output and then remained constant.

The extent of economies of scale can be measured by looking at a firm's *minimum efficient scale* (*MES*). The *MES* is the size beyond which no significant additional economies of scale can be achieved: in other words, the point where the *LRAC* curve flattens off. In Pratten's studies he defined this level as the minimum scale above which any possible doubling in scale would reduce average costs by less than 5 per cent (i.e. virtually the bottom of the *LRAC* curve). In the diagram *MES* is shown at point *a*.

The *MES* can be expressed in terms either of an individual factory or of the whole firm. Where it refers to the minimum efficient scale of an individual factory, the *MES* is known as the *minimum efficient plant size* (*MEPS*).

The *MES* can then be expressed as a percentage of the total size of the market or of total domestic production. Table (a), based on the Pratten study, shows *MES* for plants and firms in various industries. The first column shows *MES* as a percentage of total UK production. The second column shows *MES* as a percentage of total EU production. Table (b), based on the 1997 study, shows *MES* for various plants as a percentage of total EU production.

Expressing *MES* as a percentage of total output gives an indication of how competitive the industry could be. In some industries (such as footwear and carpets), economies of scale were exhausted (i.e. *MES* was reached) with plants or firms that were still small relative to total UK production and even

smaller relative to total EU production. In such industries there would be room for many firms and thus scope for considerable competition.

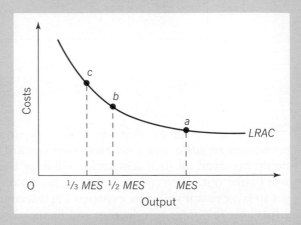

In other industries, however, even if a single plant or firm were large enough to produce the whole output of the industry in the UK, it would still not be large enough to experience the full potential economies of scale: the *MES* is greater than 100 per cent. Examples from Table (a) include factories producing cellulose fibres, and car manufacturers. In such industries there is no possibility of competition. In fact, as long as the *MES* exceeds 50 per cent there will not be room for more than one firm large enough to gain full economies of scale. In this case the industry is said to be a *natural monopoly*. As we shall see in the next few chapters, when competition is lacking consumers may suffer by firms charging prices considerably above costs.

A second way of measuring the extent of economies of scale is to see how much costs would increase if production were reduced to a certain fraction of *MES*. The normal fractions used are ½ or ⅓ *MES*. This is illustrated in the diagram. Point *b* corresponds to ½ *MES*; point *c* to ⅓ *MES*. The greater the percentage by which *LRAC* at point *b*

Table (a)

Product	MES as % of production		% additional cost
	UK	EU	at $\frac{1}{2}$ MES
Individual plants			
Cellulose fibres	125	16	3
Rolled aluminium semi-manufactures	114	15	15
Refrigerators	85	11	4
Steel	72	10	6
Electric motors	60	6	15
TV sets	40	9	9
Cigarettes	24	6	1.4
Ball-bearings	20	2	6
Beer	12	3	7
Nylon	4	1	12
Bricks	1	0.2	25
Tufted carpets	0.3	0.04	10
Shoes	0.3	0.03	1
Firms			
Cars	200	20	9
Lorries	104	21	7.5
Mainframe computers	>100	n.a.	5
Aircraft	100	n.a.	5
Tractors	98	19	6

Sources: C. F. Pratten (1988); M. Emerson, *The Economics of 1992* (Oxford University Press, 1988)

or *c* is higher than at point *a*, the greater will be the economies of scale to be gained by producing at *MES* rather than at $\frac{1}{2}$ *MES* or $\frac{1}{3}$ *MES*. For example, in the table there are greater economies of scale to be gained from moving from $\frac{1}{2}$ *MES* to *MES* in the production of electric motors than in cigarettes.

The main purpose of the studies was to determine whether the single EU market is big enough to allow both economies of scale and competition. The tables suggest that in all cases, other things being equal,

Table (b)

Plants	MES as % of total EU production
Aerospace	12.19
Tractors and agricultural machinery	6.57
Electric lighting	3.76
Steel tubes	2.42
Shipbuilding	1.63
Rubber	1.06
Radio and TV	0.69
Footwear	0.08
Carpets	0.03

Source: see footnote 2 below

the EU market is large enough for firms to gain the full economies of scale *and* for there to be enough firms for the market to be competitive.

The second study also found that 47 of the 53 manufacturing sectors analysed had scope for further exploitation of economies of scale.

Questions

1 *Why might a firm operating with one plant achieve MEPS and yet not be large enough to achieve MES? (Clue: are all economies of scale achieved at plant level?)*

2 *Why might a firm producing bricks have an MES which is only 0.2 per cent of total EU production and yet face little effective competition from other EU countries?*

---

[1] C. F. Pratten, 'A survey of the economies of scale', in *Research on the 'Costs of Non-Europe'*, vol. 2 (Office for Official Publications of the European Communities, 1988)

[2] European Commission/Economists Advisory Group Ltd, 'Economies of Scale', *The Single Market Review, Subseries V, Volume 4*. Office for official publications of the European Communities, Luxembourg, 1997

Figure 9.6

Constructing long-run average cost curves from short-run average cost curves

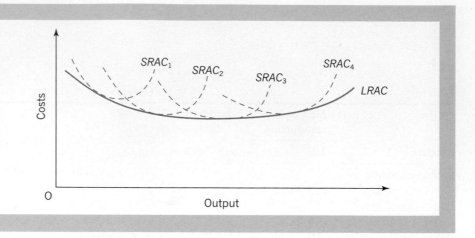

If the firm did not choose the optimum factor combination, it would be producing at a point above the LRAC curve.

The relationship between long-run and short-run average cost curves

Take the case of a firm which has just one factory and faces a short-run average cost curve illustrated by $SRAC_1$ in Figure 9.6.

In the long run, it can build more factories. If it thereby experiences economies of scale (due, say, to savings on administration), each successive factory will allow it to produce with a new lower $SRAC$ curve. Thus with two factories it will face curve $SRAC_2$; with three factories curve $SRAC_3$, and so on. Each $SRAC$ curve corresponds to a particular amount of the factor that is fixed in the short run: in this case, the factory. (There are many more $SRAC$ curves that could be drawn between the ones shown, since factories of different sizes could be built or existing ones could be expanded.)

From this succession of short-run average cost curves we can construct a long-run average cost curve. This is known as the **envelope curve**, since it envelops the short-run curves.

definition

Envelope curve
A long-run average cost curve drawn as the tangency points of a series of short-run average cost curves.

Pause for thought

Will the envelope curve be tangential to the bottom of each of the short-run average cost curves? Explain why it should or should not be.

Long-run cost curves in practice

Firms do experience economies of scale. Some experience continuously falling $LRAC$ curves, as in Figure 9.4(a). Others experience economies of scale up to a certain output and thereafter constant returns to scale.

Evidence is inconclusive on the question of diseconomies of scale. There is little evidence to suggest the existence of *technical* diseconomies, but the possibility of diseconomies due to managerial and industrial relations problems cannot be ruled out.

BOX 9.5

Followers of fashion

For many products, style is a key component to their success. Two such products are clothing and cars. Both markets exhibit 'fashion price cycles'. In recent times, however, whereas seasonal price variations for clothes have become more pronounced, those for cars have diminished. The extract below, taken from *The Economist* of 23 December 1995, explores the factors affecting the price of fashion products, and in particular looks at the role of costs.

> According to standard economic theory, Giorgio Armani, a world-famous Italian fashion designer, runs a simple business. His company combines inputs of labour (seamstresses), capital (dyeing and weaving machines) and raw materials (cloth) to make clothes with the best possible trade-off between cost and quality. He then calculates what the demand is for his designs, and estimates how many units he can make without marginal costs exceeding marginal revenues. He sells these at the market-clearing price, and earns just enough profit to compensate him for his investment of time and money.
>
> The flaw of this stylised view is that it ignores the most important thing that designers such as Mr Armani sell: fashion itself.

The article observes that the prices of fashion-sensitive goods, such as clothing and cars, follow well-established 'fashion cycles'. At the beginning of the season, prices are set at a high level. Then, as the season progresses, prices gradually fall, only to rise again as new styles are introduced for the next season.

> The main reason for this is uncertainty. When producers introduce a new line they do not know how successful it will be. To avoid selling it for less than is necessary, they initially set a high price, then lower it for lines that do not sell well. A good way to measure the importance of fashion, therefore, is to look at the variation in seasonal prices.
>
> Over the past few decades, seasonal price variations for women's clothing have become more pronounced. However, prices in the American car market, which also tend to follow a 'fashion' cycle, have displayed the opposite trend.

Clothing prices, relative to the average

The explanation for these differences, claims the article, is to be found in changes in technology in the two industries.

> Advances in the textile industry, such as the development of sophisticated electronic weaving, have made it cheaper for designers to revamp their lines each season. But in the car industry, it has become more costly to make radical style changes each year. Although new technology has made it easier to change the size and shape of a car's body, the costs of doing so as a share of the total production costs have actually risen.

Questions

1 *If consumers are aware that unsuccessful lines of clothing will fall in price as the season progresses, why do they buy when prices are set high at the start of the season? What does this tell us about the shape of the demand curve for a given fashion product (a) at the start, and (b) at the end of the season?*

2 *What has happened to fixed costs as a proportion of total costs in the production of cars? How has this affected car design strategy?*

3 *How might we account for the changing magnitudes of the fashion price cycles of clothing and cars? What role do fixed costs play in the explanation?*

SUMMARY

1a When measuring costs of production, we should be careful to use the concept of opportunity cost.

1b In the case of factors not owned by the firm, the opportunity cost is simply the explicit cost of purchasing or hiring them. It is the price paid for them.

1c In the case of factors already owned by the firm, it is the implicit cost of what the factor could have earned for the firm in its next best alternative use.

2a A production function shows the relationship between the amount of inputs used and the amount of output produced from them (per period of time).

2b In the short run it is assumed that one or more factors (inputs) are fixed in supply. The actual length of the short run will vary from industry to industry.

2c Production in the short run is subject to diminishing returns. As greater quantities of the variable factor(s) are used, so each additional unit of the variable factor will add less to output than previous units: total physical product will rise less and less rapidly.

2d As long as marginal physical product is above average physical product, average physical product will rise. Once *MPP* has fallen below *APP*, however, *APP* will fall.

3a With some factors fixed in supply in the short run, their total costs will be fixed with respect to output. In the case of variable factors, their total cost will increase as more output is produced and hence as more of them are used.

3b Total cost can be divided into total fixed and total variable cost. Total variable cost will tend to increase less rapidly at first as more is produced, but then, when diminishing returns set in, it will increase more and more rapidly.

3c Marginal cost is the cost of producing one more unit of output. It will probably fall at first (corresponding to the part of the *TVC* curve where the slope is getting shallower), but will start to rise as soon as diminishing returns set in.

3d Average cost, like total cost, can be divided into fixed and variable costs. Average fixed cost will decline as more output is produced. The reason is that the total fixed cost is being spread over a greater and greater number of units of output.

Average variable cost will tend to decline at first, but once the marginal cost has risen above it, it must then rise.

4a In the long run, a firm is able to vary the quantity it uses of all factors of production. There are no fixed factors.

4b If it increases all factors by the same proportion, it may experience constant, increasing or decreasing returns to scale.

4c Economies of scale occur when costs per unit of output fall as the scale of production increases. This can be due to a number of factors, some of which are directly caused by increasing (physical) returns to scale. These include the benefits of specialisation and division of labour, the use of larger and more efficient machines, and the ability to have a more integrated system of production. Other economies of scale arise from the financial and administrative benefits of large-scale organisations.

4d Long-run costs are also influenced by a firm's location. The firm will have to balance the need to be as near as possible both to the supply of its raw materials and to its market. The optimum balance will depend on the relative costs of transporting the inputs and the finished product.

4e To minimise costs per unit of output, a firm should choose that combination of factors which gives an equal marginal product for each factor relative to its price: i.e. $MPP_a/P_a = MPP_b/P_b = MPP_c/P_c$, etc. (where a, b and c are different factors). If the MPP/P ratio for any factor is greater than that for another, more of the first should be used relative to the second.

4f Four distinct time periods can be distinguished. In addition to the short- and long-run periods, we can also distinguish the very-short- and very-long-run periods. The very short run is when all factors are fixed. The very long run is where not only the quantity of factors but also their quality is variable (as a result of changing technology, etc.).

5a In the long run, all factors are variable. There are thus no long-run fixed costs.

5b When constructing long-run cost curves, it is assumed that factor prices are given, that the state of technology is given and that firms will choose the least-cost combination of factors for each given output.

SUMMARY

5c The *LRAC* curve can be downward sloping, upward sloping or horizontal, depending in turn on whether there are economies of scale, diseconomies of scale or neither. Typically, *LRAC* curves are drawn as <-shaped (sometimes with a flat bottom), or as saucer-shaped curved. As output expands, initially there are economies of scale. When these are exhausted, the curve will become flat. When the firm becomes very large, it may begin to experience diseconomies of

scale. If this happens, the *LRAC* curve will begin to slope upward again.

5d The long-run marginal cost curve will be below the *LRAC* curve when *LRAC* is falling, above it when *LRAC* is rising and equal to it when *LRAC* is neither rising nor falling.

5e An envelope curve can be drawn which shows the relationship between short-run and long-run average cost curves. The *LRAC* curve envelops the short-run *AC* curves: it is tangential to them.

REVIEW QUESTIONS

1 Are all explicit costs variable costs? Are all variable costs explicit costs?

2 Up to roughly how long is the short run in the following cases?

   (a) A mobile disco firm;
   (b) Electricity power generation;
   (c) A small grocery retailing business;
   (d) 'Superstore Hypermarkets plc'.

   In each case, specify your assumptions.

3 Given that there is a fixed supply of land in the world, what implications can you draw from Figure 9.1 about the effects of an increase in world population for food output per head?

4 The following are some costs incurred by a shoe manufacturer. Decide whether each one is a fixed cost or a variable cost or has some element of both.

   (a) The cost of leather;
   (b) The fee paid to an advertising agency;
   (c) Wear and tear on machinery;
   (d) Business rates on the factory;
   (e) Electricity for heating and lighting;
   (f) Electricity for running the machines;
   (g) Basic minimum wages agreed with the union;
   (h) Overtime pay;
   (i) Depreciation of machines as a result purely of their age (irrespective of their condition).

5 Assume that you are required to draw a *TVC* curve corresponding to Figure 9.1. What will happen to this *TVC* curve beyond point *d*?

6 Why is the minimum point of the *AVC* curve at a lower level of output than the minimum point of the *AC* curve?

7 Which economies of scale are due to increasing returns to scale and which are due to other factors?

8 What economies of scale is a large department store likely to experience?

9 Why are many firms likely to experience economies of scale up to a certain size and then diseconomies of scale after some point beyond that?

10 Why are bread and beer more expensive to transport per mile than the raw materials used in their manufacture?

11 Name some industries where external economies of scale are gained. What are the specific external economies in each case?

12 How is the opening up of trade and investment between eastern and western Europe likely to affect the location of industries within Europe that have (a) substantial economies of scale; (b) little or no economies of scale?

13 If factor X costs twice as much as factor Y ($P_X/P_Y = 2$), what can be said about the relationship between the *MPP*s of the two factors if the optimum combination of factors is used?

14 Could the long run and the very long run ever be the same length of time?

15 Examine Figure 9.4. What would (a) the firm's long-run total cost curve, and (b) its long-run marginal cost curve look like in each of these three cases?

16 Under what circumstances is a firm likely to experience a flat-bottomed *LRAC* curve?

10 Revenue and profit

In this chapter we will identify the output and price at which a firm will maximise its profits, and how much profit will be made at that level. Remember that we defined a firm's total profit ($T\Pi$) as its total revenue minus its total costs of production.

$$T\Pi = TR - TC$$

In the previous chapter we have looked at costs in some detail. We must now turn to the revenue side of the equation. As with costs, we distinguish between three revenue concepts: total revenue (TR), average revenue (AR) and marginal revenue (MR).

10.1 Revenue

Total, average and marginal revenue

Total revenue (TR)

Total revenue is the firm's total earnings per period of time from the sale of a particular amount of output (Q).

For example, if a firm sells 1000 units (Q) per month at a price of £5 each (P), then its monthly total revenue will be £5000: in other words, £5 × 1000 ($P \times Q$). Thus:

$$TR = P \times Q$$

Average revenue (AR)

Average revenue is the amount the firm earns per unit sold. Thus:

$$AR = TR/Q$$

So if the firm earns £5000 (TR) from selling 1000 units (Q), it will earn £5 per unit. But this is simply the price! Thus:

$$AR = P$$

(The only exception to this is when the firm is selling its products at different prices to different consumers. In this case AR is simply the (weighted) average price.)

definition

Total revenue
A firm's total
earnings from a
specified level of
sales within a
specified period:
$TR = P \times Q$.

definition

Average revenue
Total revenue per
unit of output. When
all output is sold
at the same price,
average revenue will
be the same as price:
$AR = TR/Q = P$.

definition

Marginal revenue
The extra revenue
gained by selling
one or more unit
per time period:
$MR = \Delta TR/\Delta Q$.

definition

Price taker
A firm that is too
small to be able
to influence the
market price.

Marginal revenue (MR)

Marginal revenue is the extra total revenue gained by selling one more unit (per time period). So if a firm sells an extra 20 units this month compared with what it expected to sell, and in the process earns an extra £100, then it is getting an extra £5 for each extra unit sold: $MR = £5$. Thus:

$$MR = \Delta TR/\Delta Q$$

We now need to see how each of these three revenue concepts (*TR*, *AR* and *MR*) varies with output. We can show this relationship graphically in the same way as we did with costs.

The relationship will depend on the market conditions under which a firm operates. A firm which is too small to be able to affect market price will have different-looking revenue curves from a firm which is able to choose the price it charges. Let us examine each of these two situations in turn.

Revenue curves when price is not affected by the firm's output

Average revenue

If a firm is very small relative to the whole market, it is likely to be a **price taker**. That is, it has to accept the price given by the intersection of demand and supply in the whole market. But, being so small, it can sell as much as it is capable of producing at that price. This is illustrated in Figure 10.1.

Diagram (a) shows market demand and supply. Equilibrium price is £5. Diagram (b) looks at the demand for an individual firm which is tiny relative to the whole market. (Look at the difference in the scale of the horizontal axes in the two diagrams.)

Being so small, any change in the firm's output will be too insignificant to affect the market price. The firm thus faces a horizontal demand 'curve' at this price. It can sell 200 units, 600 units, 1200 units or whatever without affecting this £5 price.

Average revenue is thus constant at £5. The firm's average revenue curve must therefore lie along exactly the same line as its demand curve.

Figure 10.1

Deriving a firm's *AR* and *MR*: price-taking firm

(a) The market

(b) The firm

Table 10.1   Deriving total revenue

Quantity (units)	Price ≡ AR = MR(£)	TR (£)
0	5	0
200	5	1000
400	5	2000
600	5	3000
800	5	4000
1000	5	5000
1200	5	6000
.	.	.

Figure 10.2

Total revenue curve for a price-taking firm

Marginal revenue

In the case of a horizontal demand curve, the marginal revenue curve will be the same as the average revenue curve, since selling one more unit at a constant price (*AR*) merely adds that amount to total revenue. If an extra unit is sold at a constant price of £5, an extra £5 is earned.

Total revenue

Table 10.1 shows the effect on total revenue of different levels of sales with a constant price of £5 per unit.

As price is constant, total revenue will rise at a constant rate as more is sold. The *TR* 'curve' will therefore be a straight line through the origin, as in Figure 10.2.

> **Pause for thought**
>
> *What would happen to the TR curve if the market price rose to £10? Try drawing it.*

Revenue curves when price varies with output

The three curves (*TR*, *AR* and *MR*) will look quite different when price does vary with the firm's output.

If a firm has a relatively large share of the market, it will face a downward-sloping demand curve. This means that if it is to sell more, it must lower the price. But it could also choose to raise its price. If it does so, however, it will have to accept a fall in sales.

Table 10.2	Revenues for a firm facing a downward-sloping demand curve		

Q (units)	P = AR (£)	TR (£)	MR (£)
1	8	8	
2	7	14	6
3	6	18	4
4	5	20	2
5	4	20	0
6	3	18	−2
7	2	14	−4
.	.	.	.

Average revenue

Remember that average revenue equals price. If, therefore, the price has to be reduced to sell more output, average revenue will fall as output increases.

Table 10.2 gives an example of a firm facing a downward-sloping demand curve. The demand curve (which shows how much is sold at each price) is given by the first two columns.

Note that, as in the case of a price-taking firm, the demand curve and the AR curve lie along exactly the same line. The reason for this is simple: AR = P, and thus the curve relating price to quantity (the demand curve) must be the same as that relating average revenue to quantity (the AR curve).

Marginal revenue

When a firm faces a downward-sloping demand curve, marginal revenue will be less than average revenue, and may even be negative. But why?

If a firm is to sell more per time period, it must lower its price (assuming it does not advertise). This will mean lowering the price not just for the extra units it hopes to sell, but also for those units it would have sold had it not lowered the price.

Thus the marginal revenue is the price at which it sells the last unit, *minus* the loss in revenue it has incurred by reducing the price on those units it could otherwise have sold at the higher price. This can be illustrated with Table 10.2.

Assume that price is currently £7. Two units are thus sold. The firm now wishes to sell an extra unit. It lowers the price to £6. It thus gains £6 from the sale of the third unit, but loses £2 by having to reduce the price by £1 on the two units it could otherwise have sold at £7. Its net gain is therefore £6 − £2 = £4. This is the marginal revenue: it is the extra revenue gained by the firm from selling one more unit. Try using this method to check out the remaining figures for MR in Table 10.2. (Note that in the table the figures for MR are entered in the spaces between the figures for the other three columns.)

There is a simple relationship between marginal revenue and *price elasticity of demand*. Remember from Chapter 5 (see p. 86) that if demand is price elastic, a *decrease* in price will lead to a proportionately larger increase in the quantity demanded and hence an *increase* in revenue. Marginal revenue will thus be positive. If, however, demand is inelastic, a decrease in price will lead to a proportionately smaller increase in sales. In this case the price reduction will more than offset the increase in sales and as a result revenue will fall. Marginal revenue will be negative.

Key Idea 11 p81

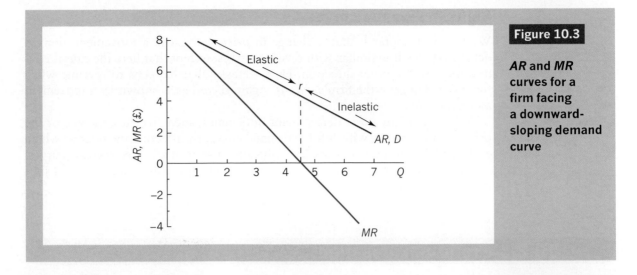

Figure 10.3

AR and *MR* curves for a firm facing a downward-sloping demand curve

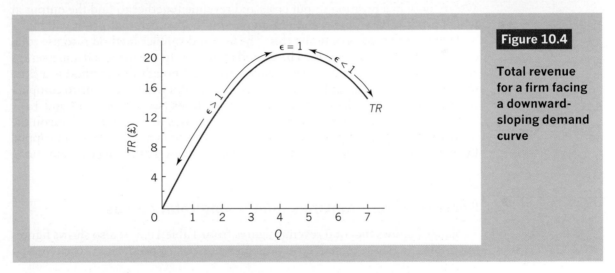

Figure 10.4

Total revenue for a firm facing a downward-sloping demand curve

If, then, marginal revenue is a positive figure (i.e. if sales per time period are 4 units or less in Figure 10.3), the demand curve will be elastic at that point, since a rise in quantity sold (as a result of a reduction in price) would lead to a rise in total revenue. If, on the other hand, marginal revenue is negative (i.e. at a level of sales of 5 or more units in Figure 10.3), the demand curve will be inelastic at that point, since a rise in quantity sold would lead to a *fall* in total revenue.

Thus the demand (*AR*) curve of Figure 10.3 is elastic to the left of point *r* and inelastic to the right.

Total revenue

Total revenue equals price times quantity. This is illustrated in Table 10.2. The *TR* column from Table 10.2 is plotted in Figure 10.4.

Unlike in the case of a price-taking firm, the *TR* curve is not a straight line. It is a curve that rises at first and then falls. But why? As long as marginal revenue is positive (and hence demand is price elastic), a rise in output will raise total revenue. However, once marginal revenue becomes negative (and hence demand is inelastic), total revenue will fall. The peak of the *TR* curve will be where *MR* = 0. At this point, the price elasticity of demand will be equal to –1.

Shifts in revenue curves

We saw in Chapter 4 that a change in *price* will cause a movement along a demand curve. It is similar with revenue curves, except that here the causal connection is in the other direction. Here we ask what happens to revenue when there is a change in the firm's *output*. Again the effect is shown by a movement along the curves.

A change in any *other* determinant of demand, such as tastes, income or the price of other goods, will shift the demand curve. By affecting the price at which each level of output can be sold, it will cause a shift in all three revenue curves. An increase in revenue is shown by a vertical shift upwards; a decrease by a shift downwards.

10.2   Profit maximisation

We are now in a position to put costs and revenue together to find the output at which profit is maximised, and also to find out how much that profit will be.

There are two ways of doing this. The first and simpler method is to use total cost and total revenue curves. The second method is to use marginal and average cost and marginal and average revenue curves. Although this method is a little more complicated (but only a little!), it is more useful when we come to compare profit maximising under different market conditions (see Chapters 11 and 12).

We will look at each method in turn. In both cases we will concentrate on the short run: namely, that period in which one or more factors are fixed in supply. In both cases we take the case of a firm facing a downward-sloping demand curve.

Short-run profit maximisation: using total curves

Table 10.3 shows the total revenue figures from Table 10.2. It also shows figures for total cost. These figures have been chosen so as to produce a *TC* curve of a typical shape.

Total profit (*TΠ*) is found by subtracting *TC* from *TR*. Check this out by examining the table. Where *TΠ* is negative, the firm is making a loss. Total profit is maximised at an output of 3 units: namely, where there is the greatest gap between total revenue and total costs. At this output, total profit is £4 (£18 – £14).

Table 10.3

Q (units)	TR (£)	TC (£)	TΠ (£)
0	0	6	–6
1	8	10	–2
2	14	12	2
3	18	14	4
4	20	18	2
5	20	25	–5
6	18	36	–18
7	14	56	–42
.	.	.	.

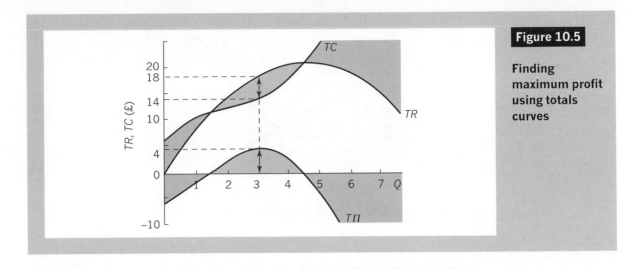

Figure 10.5

Finding maximum profit using totals curves

Table 10.4

Q (units)	P = AR (£)	TR (£)	MR (£)	TC (£)	AC (£)	MC (£)	TΠ (£)	AΠ (£)
0	9	0		6	–		–6	–
			8			4		
1	8	8		10	10		–2	–2
			6			2		
2	7	14		12	6		2	1
			4			2		
3	6	18		14	4⅔		4	1⅓
			2			4		
4	5	20		18	4½		2	½
			0			7		
5	4	20		25	5		–5	–1
			–2			11		
6	3	18		36	6		–18	–3
			–4			20		
7	2	14		56	8		–42	–6
.	.	.	.	.	.	.	.	.

The *TR*, *TC* and *TΠ* curves are plotted in Figure 10.5. The size of the maximum profit is shown by the arrows.

definition

Profit-maximising rule Profit is maximised where marginal revenue equals marginal cost.

Short-run profit maximisation: using average and marginal curves

Table 10.4 is based on the figures in Table 10.3.

Finding the maximum profit that a firm can make is a two-stage process. The first stage is to find the profit-maximising output. To do this we use the *MC* and *MR* curves. The second stage is to find out just how much profit is at this output. To do this we use the *AR* and *AC* curves.

Pause for thought

Why are the figures for MR and MC entered in the spaces between the lines in Table 10.4?

Stage 1: Using marginal curves to arrive at the profit-maximising output

There is a very simple **profit-maximising rule**: if profits are to be maximised, *MR must equal MC*. From Table 10.4 it can be seen that *MR* = *MC* at an output of 3. This is shown as point *e* in Figure 10.6.

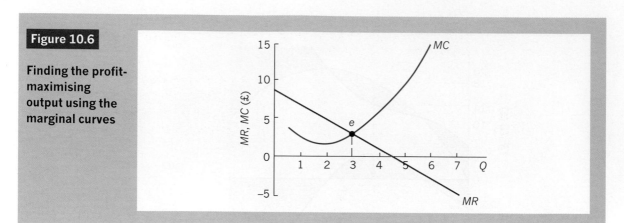

Figure 10.6

Finding the profit-maximising output using the marginal curves

But why are profits maximised when *MR* = *MC*? The simplest way of answering this is to see what the position would be if *MR* did not equal *MC*.

Referring to Figure 10.6, at a level of output below 3, *MR* exceeds *MC*. This means that by producing more units there will be a bigger addition to revenue (*MR*) than to cost (*MC*). Total profit will *increase*. As long as MR exceeds MC, *profit can be increased by increasing production.*

At a level of output above 3, *MC* exceeds *MR*. All levels of output above 3 thus add more to cost than to revenue and hence *reduce* profit. As long as MC exceeds MR, *profit can be increased by cutting back on production.*

Profits are thus maximised where *MC* = *MR*: at an output of 3. This can be confirmed by reference to the *TΠ* column in Table 10.4.

Students worry sometimes about the argument that profits are maximised when *MR* = *MC*. Surely, they say, if the last unit is making no profit, how can profit be at a *maximum*? The answer is very simple. If you cannot *add* anything more to a total, the total must be at the maximum. Take the simple analogy of going up a hill. When you cannot go any higher, you must be at the top.

Stage 2: Using average curves to measure the size of the profit

Once the profit-maximising output has been discovered, we now use the average curves to measure the *amount* of profit at the maximum. Both marginal and average curves corresponding to the data in Table 10.4 are plotted in Figure 10.7.

Key Idea 4 p27

Figure 10.7

Measuring the maximum profit using average curves

First, average profit ($A\Pi$) is found. This is simply $AR - AC$. At the profit-maximising output of 3, this gives a figure for $A\Pi$ of £6 − £4²/₃ = £1¹/₃. Then total profit is obtained by multiplying average profit by output:

$$T\Pi = A\Pi \times Q$$

This is shown as the shaded area. It equals £1¹/₃ × 3 = £4. This can again be confirmed by reference to the $T\Pi$ column in Table 10.4.

Pause for thought

What will be the effect on a firm's profit maximising output of a rise in fixed costs?

Some qualifications

Long-run profit maximisation

Assuming that the AR and MR curves are the same in the long run as in the short run, long-run profits will be maximised at the output where MR equals the *long-run MC*. The reasoning is the same as with the short-run case.

The meaning of 'profit'

One element of cost is the opportunity cost to the owners of the firm incurred by being in business. This is the minimum return that the owners must make on their capital in order to prevent them from eventually deciding to close down and perhaps move into some alternative business. It is a *cost* since, just as with wages, rent, etc., it has to be covered if the firm is to continue producing. This opportunity cost to the owners is sometimes known as **normal profit**, and is included in the cost curves.

What determines this normal rate of profit? It has two components. First, someone setting up in business invests capital in it. There is thus an opportunity cost. This is the interest that could have been earned by lending it in some risk-less form (e.g. by putting it in a savings account in a bank). Nobody would set up a business unless they expected to earn at least this rate of profit. Running a business is far from riskless, however, and hence a second element is a return to compensate for risk. Thus:

Normal profit (%) = rate of interest on a riskless loan + a risk premium

The risk premium varies according to the line of business. In those with fairly predictable patterns, such as food retailing, it is relatively low. Where outcomes are very uncertain, such as mineral exploration or the manufacture of fashion garments, it is relatively high.

Thus if owners of a business earn normal profit, they will (just) be content to remain in that industry. If they earn more than normal profit, they will also (obviously) prefer to stay in this business. If they earn less than normal profit, then after a time they will consider leaving and using their capital for some other purpose.

Given that normal profits are included in costs, any profit that is shown diagrammatically (e.g. the shaded area in Figure 10.7) must therefore be over and above normal profit. It is known by several alternative names: **supernormal profit**, **pure profit**, **economic profit**, **abnormal profit**, **producer's surplus** or sometimes simply **profit**. They all mean the same thing: the excess of profit over normal profit.

Key Idea 3 p27

definition

Normal profit
The opportunity cost of being in business. It consists of the interest that could be earned on a riskless asset, plus a return for risk taking in this particular industry. It is counted as a cost of production.

definition

Supernormal profit
(also known as **pure profit, economic profit, abnormal profit, producer's surplus** or simply **profit**) The excess of total profit above normal profit.

definition

Short-run shut-down point
This is where the AR curve is tangential to the AVC curve. The firm can only just cover its variable costs. Any fall in revenue below this level will cause a profit-maximising firm to shut down immediately.

Figure 10.8

Loss-minimising
output

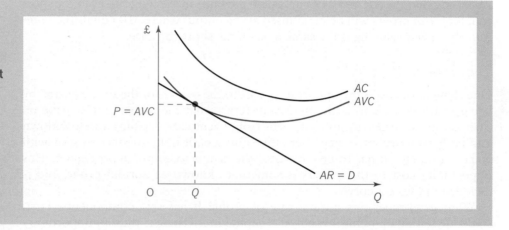

Figure 10.9

The short-run
shut-down point

definition
Long-run shut-down point
This is where the *AR* curve is tangential to the *LRAC* curve. The firm can just make normal profits. Any fall in revenue below this level will cause a profit-maximising firm to shut down once all costs have become variable.

Pause for thought

Why might it make sense for a firm which cannot sell its output at a profit to continue in production for the time being?

Loss minimising

It may be that there is no output at which the firm can make a profit. Such a situation is illustrated in Figure 10.8: the *AC* curve is above the *AR* curve at all levels of output.

In this case, the output where *MR* = *MC* will be the loss-minimising output. The amount of loss at the point where *MR* = *MC* is shown by the shaded area in Figure 10.8.

Whether or not to produce at all

The short run. Fixed costs have to be paid even if the firm is producing nothing at all. Rent has to be paid, business rates have to be paid, etc. Providing, therefore, that the firm is more than covering its *variable* costs, it can go some way to paying off these fixed costs and therefore will continue to produce.

It will shut down if it cannot cover its variable costs: that is, if the *AVC* curve is above, or the *AR* curve is below, that illustrated in Figure 10.9. This situation is known as the **short-run shut-down point**.

Key Idea 15 p168

The long run. All costs are variable in the long run. If, therefore, the firm cannot cover its long-run average costs (which include normal profit), it will close down. The **long-run shut-down point** will be where the *AR* curve is tangential to the *LRAC* curve.

SUMMARY

1a Just as we could identify total, average and marginal costs, so too we can identify total, average and marginal revenue.

1b Total revenue (TR) is the total amount a firm earns from its sales in a given time period. It is simply price times quantity: $TR = P \times Q$.

1c Average revenue (AR) is total revenue per unit: $AR = TR/Q$. In other words, $AR = P$.

1d Marginal revenue is the extra revenue earned from the sale of one more unit per time period.

1e The AR curve will be the same as the demand curve for the firm's product. In the case of a price taker, the demand curve and hence the AR curve will be a horizontal straight line and will also be the same as the MR curve. The TR curve is an upward-sloping straight line from the origin.

1f A firm that faces a downward-sloping demand curve must obviously also face the same downward-sloping AR curve. The MR curve will also slope downwards, but will be below the AR curve and steeper than it. The TR curve will be an arch shape starting from the origin.

1g When demand is price elastic, marginal revenue will be positive and the TR curve will be upward sloping. When demand is price inelastic, marginal revenue will be negative and the TR curve will be downward sloping.

1h A change in output is represented by a movement along the revenue curves. A change in any other determinant of revenue will shift the curves up or down.

2a Total profit equals total revenue minus total cost. By definition, then, a firm's profits will be maximised at the point where there is the greatest gap between total revenue and total cost.

2b Another way of finding the maximum-profit point is to find the output where marginal revenue equals marginal cost. Having found this output, the level of maximum profit can be found by finding the average profit ($AR - AC$) and then multiplying it by the level of output.

2c Normal profit is the minimum profit that must be made to persuade a firm to stay in business in the long run. It is counted as part of the firm's cost. Supernormal profit is any profit over and above normal profit.

2d For a firm that cannot make a profit at any level of output, the point where $MR = MC$ represents the loss-minimising output.

2e In the short run, a firm will close down if it cannot cover its variable costs. In the long run, it will close down if it cannot make normal profits.

REVIEW QUESTIONS

1 Draw a downward-sloping demand curve. Now put in scales of your own choosing for both axes. Read off various points on the demand curve and use them to construct a table showing price and quantity. Use this table to work out the figures for a marginal revenue column. Now use these figures to draw an MR curve.

2 Copy Figures 10.3 and 10.4 (which are based on Table 10.2). Now assume that incomes have risen and that, as a result, two more units per time period can be sold at each price. Draw a new table and plot the resulting new AR, MR and TR curves on your diagrams. Are the new curves parallel to the old ones? Explain.

3 What can we say about the slope of the TR and TC curves at the maximum-profit point? What does this tell us about marginal revenue and marginal cost?

4 Using the following information, construct a table like Table 10.3.

Q	0	1	2	3	4	5	6	7
P	12	11	10	9	8	7	6	5
TC	2	6	9	12	16	21	28	38

Use your table to draw diagrams like Figures 10.5 and 10.7. Use these two diagrams to show the profit-maximising output and the level of maximum profit. Confirm your findings by reference to the table you have constructed.

5 The following table shows the average cost and average revenue (price) for a firm at each level of output.

Output	1	2	3	4	5	6	7	8	9	10
AC (£)	7.00	5.00	4.00	3.30	3.00	3.10	3.50	4.20	5.00	6.00
AR (£)	10.00	9.50	9.00	8.50	8.00	7.50	7.00	6.50	6.00	5.50

(a) Construct a table to show *TC*, *MC*, *TR* and *MR* at each level of output (put the figures for *MC* and *MR* mid-way between the output figures).
(b) Using *MC* and *MR* figures, find the profit-maximising output.
(c) Using *TC* and *TR* figures, check your answer to (b).
(d) Plot the *AC*, *MC*, *AR* and *MR* figures on a graph.
(e) Mark the profit-maximising output and the *AR* and *AC* at this output.
(f) Shade in an area to represent the level of profits at this output.

6 Normal profits are regarded as a cost (and are included in the cost curves). Explain why.

7 What determines the size of normal profit? Will it vary with the general state of the economy?

8 A firm will continue producing in the short run even if it is making a loss, providing it can cover its variable costs. Explain why. Just how long will it be willing to continue making such a loss?

9 Would there ever be a point in a firm attempting to continue in production if it could not cover its *long-run* average (total) costs?

10 The price of pocket calculators and digital watches fell significantly in the years after they were first introduced and at the same time demand for them increased substantially. Use cost and revenue diagrams to illustrate these events. Explain the reasoning behind the diagram(s) you have drawn.

11 In February 2000, Unilever, the giant consumer products company, announced that it was to cut 25 000 jobs, close 100 plants and rely more on the internet to purchase its supplies. It would use part of the money saved to increase promotion of its leading brands, such as Dove skincare products, Lipton tea, Omo detergents and Calvin Klein cosmetics. The hope was to boost sales and increase profits. If it meets these targets, what is likely to have happened to its total costs, total revenue, average costs and average revenue? Give reasons for your answer.

Additional Part D case studies on the *Economics for Business* website (www.booksites.net /sloman)

D.1 **Malthus and the dismal science of economics.** A gloomy warning, made over 200 years ago by Robert Malthus, that diminishing returns to labour would lead to famine for much of the world's population.

D.2 **Division of labour in a pin factory.** This is the famous example of division of labour given by Adam Smith in his *Wealth of Nations* (1776).

D.3 **Diminishing returns to nitrogen fertiliser.** This case study provides a good illustration of diminishing returns in practice by showing the effects on grass yields of the application of increasing amounts of nitrogen fertiliser.

D.4 **Diminishing returns in the bread shop.** An illustration of the law of diminishing returns.

D.5 **The relationship between averages and marginals.** An examination of the rules showing how an average curve relates to a marginal curve.

D.6 **Deriving cost curves from total physical product information.** This shows how total, average and marginal costs can be derived from a total product information and the price of inputs.

Websites relevant to Part D

Numbers and sections refer to websites listed in the Web appendix and hotlinked from this book's website at **www.booksites.net/sloman**

- For news articles relevant to Part D, see the *Economics News Articles* link from the book's website.
- For student resources relevant to Part D, see sites C1–7, 9, 10, 14, 19, 20.
- For a case study examining costs, see site D2.
- For sites that look at companies, their scale of operation and market share, see B2; E4, 10; G7, 8.
- For links to sites on various aspects of production and costs, see section *Microeconomics > Production* in sites I7 and 11.

Supply: short-run profit maximisation

FT

THE FINANCIAL TIMES, 24 JUNE 2003

Morrison 'could boost competition with Safeway'

By FRIEDERIKE VON TIESENHAUSEN and SUSANNA VOYLE

The UK Competition Commission on Tuesday singled out Wm Morrison as the only bidder among the four supermarket operators vying for Safeway that could promote competition nationwide, boosting the chances of the family-owned company.

'A Morrison/Safeway merger could be pro-competitive in creating a powerful fourth national player to offer competition to Asda, Sainsbury and Tesco,' the Commission said in a lengthy remedies statement.

John Kershaw, retail analyst at ING in Liverpool, said: 'We have always held the view that Morrison is the best-placed bidder, though they probably would have to look at disposing some stores locally', he added.

The Commission echoed this view on Tuesday saying it might force the potential buyer of Safeway to divest stores in local areas where competition would be reduced before allowing a takeover.

Competition lawyers agreed that the watchdog's latest issue clearly lent in favour of Morrison, 'It does not look good for the "Big Three",' said Alistair Gorrie of Coudert Brothers, an independent lawyer.

'There is a whole number of issues which point against them and the Commission has expressedly distinguished on the issue of national competition and recognised that it could create a fourth force.'

In another move, the Commission said that it was only looking at the competitive situation in groceries and would turn a blind eye on concentration in other goods such as fashion or electronics.

This, according to Mr Gorrie, would play into the hands of Asda as the out-of-town retailer had been pushed higher up the supermarket league tables by its strong non-food offerings. Taking clothes and electronics out of the consideration meant that Wal-Mart's adjusted market share would decrease.

The regulator also highlighted that it would not take into account internet shopping and petrol stations owned by supermarkets. However, it warned that it could look into the broader petrol retail market if the main players were to hike their petrol prices after a merger.

> *In some industries, low marginal costs and network effects will result in increasing returns to scale, and thus the emergence of monopolies. But because the Internet will in general reduce barriers to entry, making markets more contestable, competition and efficiency are still likely to increase across the economy as a whole.*
>
> *The Economist*, 30 March 2000

As we saw in Chapter 10, a firm's profits are maximised where its marginal cost equals its marginal revenue. But we will want to know more than this.

■ What determines the *amount* of profit that a firm will make? Will profits be large, or just enough for the firm to survive, or so low that it will be forced out of business?

■ Will the firm produce a high level of output or a low level?

■ Will it be producing efficiently?

■ Will the price charged to the consumer be high or low?

■ And, more generally, will the consumer benefit from the decisions that a firm makes?

The answers to all these questions depend on the amount of *competition* that a firm faces. A firm in a highly competitive environment will behave quite differently than a firm facing little or no competition. Quite clearly, in the *Financial Times* article opposite, maintaining the level of competition within the grocery retail market, was seen as the key factor shaping the UK Competition Commission's decision to favour Morrison's bid for Safeway over that of the bigger and more established rivals, Asda, Sainsbury and Tesco.

In Part D we will look at *different types of market structure*: from highly competitive markets at one end of the spectrum ('perfect competition'), to ones with no competition at all at the other ('monopoly'). We will also look at the intermediate cases of 'imperfect competition': monopolistic competition (where there are quite a lot of firms competing against each other) and oligopoly (where there are just a few).

key terms

Market structures
Perfect competition
Monopoly
Natural monopoly
Competition for corporate control
Barriers to entry
Contestable markets
Sunk costs
Monopolistic competition
Product differentiation
Oligopoly
Interdependence
Collusive and non-collusive oligopoly
Open and tacit collusion
Price leadership
Benchmark pricing
Game theory
Dominant and non-dominant strategy games
Prisoners' dilemma
Nash equilibrium
Credible threat
First mover advantage
Decision tree
Countervailing power

CHAPTER

11 Profit maximisation under perfect competition and monopoly

11.1 Alternative market structures

It is traditional to divide industries into categories according to the degree of competition that exists between the firms within the industry. There are four such categories.

At one extreme is **perfect competition**, where there are very many firms competing. Each firm is so small relative to the whole industry that it has no power to influence price. It is a price taker. At the other extreme is **monopoly**, where there is just one firm in the industry, and hence no competition from *within* the industry. In the middle comes **monopolistic competition**, which involves quite a lot of firms competing and where there is freedom for new firms to enter the industry, and **oligopoly**, where there are only a few firms and where entry of new firms is restricted.

To distinguish more precisely between these four categories, the following must be considered:

■ How freely can firms enter the industry: is entry free or restricted? If it is restricted, just how great are the barriers to the entry of new firms?

■ The nature of the product. Do all firms produce an identical product, or do firms produce their own particular brand or model or variety?

■ The degree of control the firm has over price. Is the firm a price taker or can it choose its price, and if it can, how will changing its price affect its profits? What we are talking about here is the nature of the demand curve it faces. How elastic is it? If it puts up its price, will it lose (a) all its sales (a horizontal demand curve), or (b) a large proportion of its sales (a relatively elastic demand curve), or (c) just a small proportion of its sales (a relatively inelastic demand curve)?

Key Idea
11
p81

> *Market power benefits the powerful at the expense of others.* When firms have market power over prices, they can use this to raise prices and profits above the perfectly competitive level. Other things being equal, the firm will gain at the expense of the consumer. Similarly, if consumers or workers have market power they can use this to their own benefit.

Key Idea
18

Table 11.1 shows the differences between the four categories.

The market structure under which a firm operates will determine its behaviour. Firms under perfect competition behave quite differently from firms that are monopolists, which behave differently again from firms under oligopoly or monopolistic competition.

Table 11.1   Features of the four market structures

Type of market	Number of firms	Freedom of entry	Nature of product	Examples	Implication for demand curve for firm
Perfect competition	Very many	Unrestricted	Homogeneous (undifferentiated)	Cabbages, carrots (these approximate to perfect competition)	Horizontal. The firm is a price taker
Monopolistic competition	Many/ several	Unrestricted	Differentiated	Builders, restaurants	Downward sloping, but relatively elastic. The firm has some control over price
Oligopoly	Few	Restricted	1. Undifferentiated or 2. Differentiated	1. Cement 2. Cars, electrical appliances	Downward sloping, relatively inelastic but depends on reactions of rivals to a price change
Monopoly	One	Restricted or completely blocked	Unique	Local water company, many prescription drugs	Downward sloping, more inelastic than oligopoly. Firm has considerable control over price

Pause for thought

Give one more example in each of the four market categories in Table 11.1.

This behaviour (or 'conduct') will in turn affect the firm's performance: its prices, profits, efficiency, etc. In many cases it will also affect other firms' performance: *their* prices, profits, efficiency, etc. The collective conduct of all the firms in the industry will affect the whole industry's performance.

Economists thus see a causal chain running from market structure to the performance of that industry.

Structure → Conduct → Performance

First, we look at the two extreme market structures: perfect competition and monopoly. Then we turn to look at the two intermediate cases of monopolistic competition and oligopoly (Chapter 12).

These two intermediate cases are sometimes referred to collectively as **imperfect competition**. The vast majority of firms in the real world operate under imperfect competition. It is still worth studying the two extreme cases, however, because they provide a framework within which to understand the real world. Some industries tend more to the competitive extreme, and thus their performance corresponds to some extent to perfect competition. Other industries tend more to the other extreme: for example, when there is one dominant firm and a few much smaller firms. In such cases, their performance corresponds more to monopoly.

Perfect competition   11.2

The theory of perfect competition illustrates an extreme form of capitalism. In it firms are entirely subject to market forces. They have no power whatsoever to affect the price of the product. The price they face is that determined by the interaction of demand and supply in the whole *market*.

Assumptions

The model of perfect competition is built on four assumptions:

- Firms are *price takers*. There are so many firms in the industry that each one produces an insignificantly small proportion of total industry supply, and therefore has *no power whatsoever* to affect the price of the product. It faces a horizontal demand 'curve' at the market price: the price determined by the interaction of demand and supply in the whole market.
- There is complete *freedom of entry* into the industry for new firms Existing firms are unable to stop new firms setting up in business. Setting up a business takes time, however. Freedom of entry therefore applies in the long run.
- All firms produce an *identical product*. (The product is 'homogeneous'.) There is therefore no branding or advertising.
- Producers and consumers have *perfect knowledge* of the market. That is, producers are fully aware of prices, costs and market opportunities. Consumers are fully aware of price, quality and availability of the product.

These assumptions are very strict. Few, if any, industries in the real world meet these conditions. Certain agricultural markets perhaps are closest to perfect competition. The market for fresh vegetables is an example.

The short run and the long run

Before we can examine what price, output and profits will be, we must first distinguish between the short run and the long run as they apply to perfect competition.

In the **short run**, the number of firms is fixed. Depending on its costs and revenue, a firm might be making large profits, small profits, no profits or a loss; and in the short run it may continue to do so.

In the **long run**, however, the level of profits will affect entry into and exit from the industry. If profits are high, new firms will be attracted into the industry, whereas if losses are being made, firms will leave.

This leads us to the distinction we made in Chapter 10: that between *normal* and *supernormal* profits. Let us examine them in the context of perfect competition.

Normal profit. This is the level of profit that is just enough to persuade firms to stay in the industry in the long run, but not high enough to attract new firms. If less than normal profits are made, firms will leave the industry in the long run.

Supernormal profit. This is any profit above normal profit. If supernormal profits are made, new firms will be attracted into the industry in the long run.

---

definition

Monopolistic competition
A market structure where, like perfect competition, there are many firms and freedom of entry into the industry, but where each firm produces a differentiated product and thus has some control over its price.

definition

Oligopoly
A market structure where there are few enough firms to enable barriers to be erected against the entry of new firms.

definition

Imperfect competition
The collective name for monopolistic competition and oligopoly.

definition

The short run under perfect competition
The period during which there is too little time for new firms to enter the industry.

definition

The long run under perfect competition
The period of time which is long enough for new firms to enter the industry.

BOX 11.1

Concentration ratios
Measuring the degree of competition

We can get some indication of how competitive a market is by observing the number of firms: the more the firms, the more competitive the market would seem to be. However, this does not tell us anything about how *concentrated* the market might be. There may be *many* firms (suggesting a situation of perfect competition or monopolistic competition), but the largest two firms might produce 95 per cent of total output. This would make these two firms more like oligopolists.

Thus even though a large number of producers may make the market *seem* highly competitive, this could be deceiving. Another approach, therefore, to measuring the degree of competition is to focus on the level of concentration of firms.

The simplest measure of industrial concentration involves adding together the market share of the largest so many firms: e.g. the largest three or the largest five. This would give what is known as the '3-firm' or '5-firm concentration ratio'.

The table shows the 5-firm concentration ratios of selected industries in the UK. As you can see, there is an enormous variation in the degree of concentration from one industry to another.

One of the main reasons for this is differences in the percentage of total industry output at which economies of scale are exhausted. If this occurs at a low level of output, there will be room for several firms in the industry which are all benefiting from the maximum economies of scale.

The degree of concentration will also depend on the barriers to entry of other firms into the industry

(see pages 220–2) and on various factors such as transport costs and historical accident. It will also depend on how varied the products are within any one industrial category. For example, in categories as large as frozen foods there is room for many firms, each producing a specialised range of products. Within each sub-category, e.g. frozen Indian meals, there may be relatively few firms producing (see table).

So is the degree of concentration a good guide to the degree of competitiveness of the industry? The answer is that it is *some* guide, but on its own it can be misleading. In particular it ignores the degree of competition from abroad, and from other areas within the country. Thus the five largest book publishers in the UK may produce 37.6 per cent of the UK's books, but these manufacturers face considerable competition from books published overseas that are imported into the country.

Questions

1 *What are the advantages and disadvantages of using a 5-firm concentration ratio rather than a 10-firm, 3-firm or even a 1-firm ratio?*

2 *Why are some industries like bread baking and brewing relatively concentrated, in that a few firms produce a large proportion of total output (see web case E9), and yet there are also many small producers?*

Concentration ratios in selected UK industries (2001)

Industry	5-firm ratio	Industry	5-firm ratio
Chilled Indian ready meals	89.3	Bottled water (still)	58.0
Frozen Indian ready meals	75.0	Bottled water (sparkling)	35.0
Record companies	73.9	Frozen foods	34.4
Batteries	70.9		
Skin care products	64.4		3-firm ratio
Jeans retail	39.0	Chocolate manufactures	76.0
Book publishing	37.6	Breakfast cereals	69.0

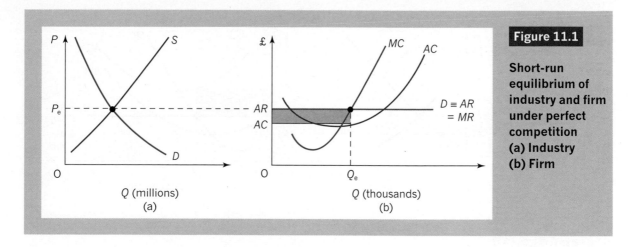

Figure 11.1

Short-run equilibrium of industry and firm under perfect competition
(a) Industry
(b) Firm

The short-run equilibrium of the firm

The determination of price, output and profit in the short run under perfect competition can best be shown in a diagram.

Figure 11.1 shows a short-run equilibrium for both industry and a firm under perfect competition. Both parts of the diagram have the same scale for the vertical axis. The horizontal axes have totally different scales, however. For example, if the horizontal axis for the firm were measured in, say, thousands of units, the horizontal axis for the whole industry might be measured in millions or tens of millions of units, depending on the number of firms in the industry.

Let us examine the determination of price, output and profit in turn.

Price

The price is determined in the industry by the intersection of demand and supply. The firm faces a horizontal demand (or average revenue) 'curve' at this price. It can sell all it can produce at the market price (P_e), but nothing at a price above P_e.

Output

The firm will maximise profit where marginal cost equals marginal revenue ($MR = MC$), at an output of Q_e. Note that, since the price is not affected by the firm's output, marginal revenue will equal price (see page 197 and Figure 10.1).

Profit

If the average cost (AC) curve (which includes normal profit) dips below the average revenue (AR) 'curve', the firm will earn supernormal profit. Supernormal profit per unit at Q_e is the vertical difference between AR and AC at Q_e. Total supernormal profit is the shaded rectangle in Figure 11.1 (i.e. profit per unit times quantity sold).

What happens if the firm cannot make a profit at *any* level of output? This situation would occur if the AC curve were above the AR curve at all points. This is illustrated in Figure 11.2 where the market price is P_1. In this case, the point where $MC = MR$ represents the *loss-minimising* point (where loss is defined as anything less than normal profit). This amount of the loss is represented by the shaded rectangle.

As we saw in Chapter 10, whether the firm is prepared to continue making a loss in the short run or whether it will close down immediately depends on

Figure 11.2

Loss minimising under perfect competition

(a)

(b)

Figure 11.3

Long-run equilibrium under perfect competition (a) Industry (b) Firm

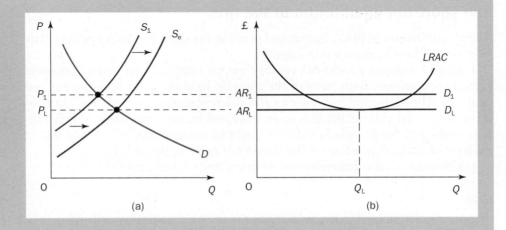

(a)

(b)

whether it can cover its *variable* costs. Provided price is above average variable cost (AVC), the firm will continue producing in the short run: it can pay its variable costs and go some way to paying its fixed costs. It will shut down in the short run only if the market price falls below P_2 in Figure 11.2.

The long-run equilibrium of the firm

In the long run, if typical firms are making supernormal profits, new firms will be attracted into the industry. Likewise, if existing firms can make supernormal profits by increasing the scale of their operations, they will do so, since all factors of production are variable in the long run.

The effect of the entry of new firms and/or the expansion of existing firms is to increase industry supply. This is illustrated in Figure 11.3.

The industry supply curve shifts to the right. This in turn leads to a fall in price. Supply will go on increasing, and price falling, until firms are making only normal profits. This will be when price has fallen to the point where the demand 'curve' for the firm just touches the bottom of its long-run average cost curve. Q_L is thus the long-run equilibrium output of the firm, with P_L the long-run equilibrium price.

Key Idea
9
p63

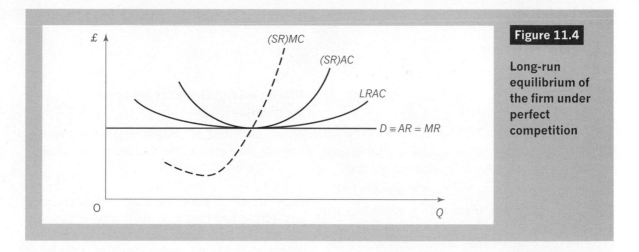

Figure 11.4

Long-run equilibrium of the firm under perfect competition

Key Idea 10 p73

Since the *LRAC* curve is tangential to all possible short-run *AC* curves (see section 9.5), the full long-run equilibrium will be as shown in Figure 11.4 where:

$$LRAC = AC = MC = MR = AR$$

Pause for thought

Before you read on, can you explain why perfect competition and substantial economies of scale are likely to be incompatible?

The incompatibility of perfect competition and substantial economies of scale

Why is perfect competition so rare in the real world – if it even exists at all? One important reason for this has to do with economies of scale.

In many industries, firms may have to be quite large if they are to experience the full potential economies of scale. But perfect competition requires there to be *many* firms. Firms must therefore be small under perfect competition: too small in most cases for economies of scale.

Once a firm expands sufficiently to achieve economies of scale, it will usually gain market power. It will be able to undercut the prices of smaller firms, which will thus be driven out of business. Perfect competition is destroyed.

Perfect competition could only exist in any industry, therefore, if there were no (or virtually no) economies of scale.

Does the firm benefit from operating under perfect competition?

Under perfect competition the firm faces a constant battle for survival. If it becomes less efficient than other firms, it will make less than normal profits and be driven out of business. If it becomes more efficient, it will earn supernormal profits. But these supernormal profits will not last for long. Soon other firms, in order to survive themselves, will be forced to copy the more efficient methods of the new firm.

Economic efficiency is achieved when each good is produced at the minimum cost and where consumers get maximum benefit from their income.

Key Idea 19

BOX 11.2

E-commerce
A modern form of perfect competition?

Anyone who fails to become an e-business will become an ex-business.

(Phil Lawler, managing director of Hewlett-Packard)

In 5 years' time, all companies will be Internet companies, or they won't be companies at all.

(Andy Grove, Chairman of Intel)[1]

The massive growth in companies selling over the Internet has raised many questions. Will all companies become Internet companies? Is this the beginning of the end of shops as we know them? Will we all be caught up in a web, where big companies swallow up little ones, and where we, as consumers, end up with no power at all?

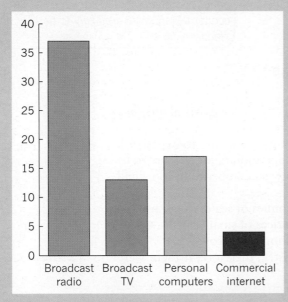

Years to achieve 50 million users

Source: US Commerce Department

In practice, e-commerce could have large benefits for consumers. These include not only the obvious benefits of being able to do your shopping from your own home, but also of having a wider choice of products and at more reasonable prices. But why should prices be more reasonable? The answer is that e-commerce has the potential to make markets more competitive: in fact, in many cases, pretty close to *perfectly* competitive.

Moving markets back towards perfect competition?

To see the extent to which e-commerce is making markets more competitive, let's look at the assumptions of perfect competition.

Large number of firms. The growth of e-commerce has led to many new firms starting up in business. It's not just large firms like Amazon.com that are providing increased competition for established firms, but the thousands of small online companies that are being established every day. Many of these firms are selling directly to us as consumers. This is known as 'B2C' e-commerce (business-to-consumers). But many more are selling to other firms ('B2B'). More and more companies, from the biggest to the smallest, are transferring their purchasing to the web and are keen to get value for money.

The reach of the web is global. This means that firms, whether conventional or web-based, are having to keep an eye on the prices and products of competitors in the rest of the world, not just in the local neighbourhood. Firms' demand curves are thus becoming very price elastic. This is especially so for goods that are cheap to transport, or for services such as insurance and banking.

Perfect knowledge. If you go shopping to buy a new household item and want to get the best deal, then it can take you some time going from shop to shop comparing prices. If, however, you go online to buy the same item, you can very rapidly compare prices. Search engines can quickly locate a list of alternative suppliers. Alternatively you can use an online shopping mall, such as ShoppingTrolley.net or Kelkoo. Better still, you can use a 'shopping bot', such as DealTime.com, mySimon.com or BottomDollar.com. These websites automatically inform you of the best available prices. And improved information is not confined to prices. 'Shopping agents', such as Frictionless.com give additional information on quality and service.

The competition through increased information over the Internet extends beyond e-commerce: it spills over to shops. As people increasingly compare prices in shops with prices online, so shops are having to be more and more competitive with their online counterparts.

Freedom of entry. Internet companies often have lower start-up costs than their conventional rivals. Their premises are generally much smaller, with no 'shop-front' costs and lower levels of stock holding. Marketing costs can also be relatively low, especially given the ease with which companies can be located with search engines and shopping bots. Internet companies are often smaller and more specialist, relying on Internet 'outsourcing' (buying parts, equipment and other supplies through the Internet), rather than making everything themselves. They are also more likely to use delivery firms rather than having their own transport fleet.

All this makes it relatively cheap for new firms to set up and begin trading over the Internet. Also, if the set-up costs are relatively low, there is less to lose if the company fails. This makes it more tempting for small firms to 'have a go'. It is also relatively easy for large firms to 'diversify' across into new businesses, especially if they are already trading on the Internet.

Identical products. With the use of shopping agents, customers can compare the prices of different firms for supplying identical products. This makes price competition very intense.

Not only do these factors make markets more price competitive, they also bring other benefits. Costs are driven down, as firms economise on stock holding, rely more on outsourcing and develop more efficient relationships with suppliers. The competition also encourages innovation, which improves quality and the range of products.

Is there a limit to e-commerce?

In 20 years, will we be doing all our shopping on the net? Will the only shopping malls be virtual ones? Although e-commerce is revolutionising some markets, it is unlikely that things will go anything like that far.

For a start, going out shopping is itself an enjoyable experience. Many people like wandering round the shops, meeting friends, seeing what takes their fancy, trying on clothes, browsing through CDs and so on. 'Retail therapy' for many is an important means of 'de-stressing'. Also, with 'real shopping' you can see the goods and assess how much you like them. Then, of course, if you buy something, you can take it home with you straight away, rather than waiting for it to be delivered.

With online shopping, you have to rely on the web. Access may be slow and frustrating. 'Surfing' may instead become 'wading'. Then if you do buy something, you may not know how long you will have to wait for it to be delivered, or whether it will even arrive!

The Internet may reduce the costs of producing some items, but not all. With heavy or bulky items, or items where special deliveries have to be made, the extra distribution costs may outweigh cost savings elsewhere.

Finally there is the role of big companies. They do not like to see their powerful position in the market threatened and are likely to try to dominate Internet sales, thereby reducing the market's competitiveness. Amazon.com may have gained a foothold in the market, but large established booksellers are retaliating. Waterstones and Blackwells are now heavily promoting their Internet sales. Amazon.com may survive, but it will be difficult for new general booksellers to break into the market. As in any market, large powerful firms will try to erect barriers to the entry of new firms. The movement towards perfect competition is likely to be strongly resisted!

Questions

1 *Why may the Internet work better for replacement buys than for new purchases?*

2 *Give three examples of products that are particularly suitable for selling over the Internet and three that are not. Explain your answer.*

---

[1] Quotes from 'The net imperative', *The Economist*, (26 June 1999)

It is the same with the development of new products. If a firm is able to produce a new product that is popular with consumers, it will be able to gain a temporary advantage over its rivals. But again, any supernormal profits will last only as long as it takes other firms to respond. Soon the increase in supply of the new product will drive the price down and eliminate these supernormal profits. Similarly, the firm must be quick to copy new products developed by its rivals. If it does not, it will soon make a loss and be driven out of the market.

Thus being in perfect competition is a constant battle for survival. It might benefit the consumer, but most firms in such an environment would love to be able to gain some market power: power to be able to restrict competition and to retain supernormal profits into the long run.

The extreme case of market power is that of monopoly: a firm that faces no competition – at least not from *within* its industry. Monopoly is the subject of the next section.

11.3 Monopoly

What is a monopoly?

This may seem a strange question because the answer seems obvious. A monopoly exists when there is only one firm in the industry.

But whether an industry can be classed as a monopoly is not always clear. It depends how narrowly the industry is defined. For example, a textile company may have a monopoly on certain types of fabric, but it does not have a monopoly on fabrics in general. The consumer can buy fabrics other than those supplied by the company. A rail company may have a monopoly over rail services between two cities, but it does not have a monopoly over public transport between these two cities. People can travel by coach or air. They could also use private transport.

To some extent, the boundaries of an industry are arbitrary. What is more important for a firm is the amount of monopoly *power* it has, and that depends on the closeness of substitutes produced by rival industries. The Post Office has a monopoly over the delivery of letters, but it faces competition in communications from telephone, faxes and e-mail.

Barriers to entry

For a firm to maintain its monopoly position, there must be barriers to the entry of new firms. Barriers also exist under oligopoly, but in the case of monopoly they must be high enough to block the entry of new firms. Barriers can take various forms.

Economies of scale. If the monopolist's costs go on falling significantly up to the output that satisfies the whole market, the industry may not be able to support more than one producer. This case is known as **natural monopoly**. It is particularly likely if the market is small. For example, two bus companies might find it unprofitable to serve the same routes, each running with perhaps only half-full buses, whereas one company with a monopoly of the routes could make a profit. Electricity transmission via a national grid is another example of a natural monopoly.

Even if a market could support more than one firm, a new entrant is unlikely to be able to start up on a very large scale. Thus the monopolist which is already experiencing economies of scale can charge a price below the cost of the new entrant and drive it out of business. If, however, the new entrant is a firm already established in another industry, it may be able to survive this competition.

Economies of scope. A firm that produces a range of products is also likely to experience a lower average cost of production. For example, a large pharmaceutical company producing a range of drugs and toiletries can use shared research, marketing, storage and transport facilities across its range of products. These lower costs make it difficult for a new single-product entrant to the market, since the large firm will be able to undercut its price and drive it out of the market.

Product differentiation and brand loyalty. If a firm produces a clearly differentiated product, where the consumer associates the product with the brand, it will be very difficult for a new firm to break into that market. Rank Xerox invented, and patented, the plain paper photocopier. After this legal monopoly (see below) ran out, people still associated photocopiers with Rank Xerox. It is still not unusual to hear someone say that they are going to 'Xerox the article' or, for that matter, 'Hoover their carpet'. Other examples of strong brand image include Guinness, Kelloggs Cornflakes, Coca-Cola, Nescafé and Sellotape. This barrier can occur even though the market is potentially big enough for two firms, each gaining all the available economies of scale. In other words, the problem for the new firm is not in being able to produce at low enough costs, but in being able to produce a product sufficiently attractive to consumers who are loyal to the familiar brand.

Lower costs for an established firm. An established monopoly is likely to have developed specialised production and marketing skills. It is more likely to be aware of the most efficient techniques and the most reliable and/or cheapest suppliers. It is likely to have access to cheaper finance. It is thus operating on a lower cost curve. New firms would therefore find it hard to compete and would be likely to lose any price war.

> **Pause for thought**
>
> Illustrate the situation described above using AC curves for both a new entrant and an established firm.

Ownership of, or control over, key factors of production. If a firm governs the supply of vital inputs (say, by owning the sole supplier of some component part), it can deny access to these inputs to potential rivals. On a world scale, the de Beers company has a monopoly in fine diamonds because all diamond producers market their diamonds through de Beers.

Ownership of, or control over, wholesale or retail outlets. Similarly, if a firm controls the outlets through which the product must be sold, it can prevent potential rivals from gaining access to consumers. For example, Birds Eye Walls used to supply freezers free to shops on the condition that they stocked only Wall's ice cream in them.

Legal protection. The firm's monopoly position may be protected by patents on essential processes, by copyright, by various forms of licensing (allowing, say, only one firm to operate in a particular area) and by tariffs (i.e. customs duties) and other trade restrictions to keep out foreign competitors. Examples of monopolies protected by patents include most new medicines developed by pharmaceutical companies (e.g. anti-AIDS drugs), Microsoft's Windows operating systems and agro-chemical companies, such as Monsanto, with various genetically modified plant varieties and pesticides.

Mergers and takeovers. The monopolist can put in a takeover bid for any new entrant. The sheer threat of takeovers may discourage new entrants.

Aggressive tactics. An established monopolist can probably sustain losses for longer than a new entrant. Thus it could start a price war, mount massive advertising campaigns, offer attractive after-sales service, introduce new brands to compete with new entrants, and so on.

Intimidation. The monopolist may resort to various forms of harassment, legal or illegal, to drive a new entrant out of business.

Equilibrium price and output

Since there is, by definition, only one firm in the industry, the firm's demand curve is also the industry demand curve.

Compared with other market structures, demand under monopoly will be relatively inelastic at each price. The monopolist can raise its price and consumers have no alternative firm to turn to within the industry. They either pay the higher price, or go without the good altogether.

Unlike the firm under perfect competition, the monopoly firm is thus a 'price maker'. It can choose what price to charge. Nevertheless, it is still constrained by its demand curve. A rise in price will reduce the quantity demanded.

As with firms in other market structures, a monopolist will maximise profit where $MR = MC$. In Figure 11.5 profit is maximised at Q_m. The supernormal profit obtained is shown by the shaded area.

These profits will tend to be larger, the less elastic is the demand curve (and hence the steeper is the MR curve), and thus the bigger is the gap between MR and price (AR). The actual elasticity will depend on whether reasonably close substitutes are available in *other* industries. The demand for a rail service will be much less elastic (and the potential for profit greater) if there is no bus service to the same destination.

Since there are barriers to the entry of new firms, a monopolist's supernormal profits will not be competed away in the long run. The only difference, therefore, between short-run and long-run equilibrium is that in the long run the firm will produce where $MR = long$-$run MC$.

Key Idea
11
p81

Key Idea
4
p27

Key Idea
18
p211

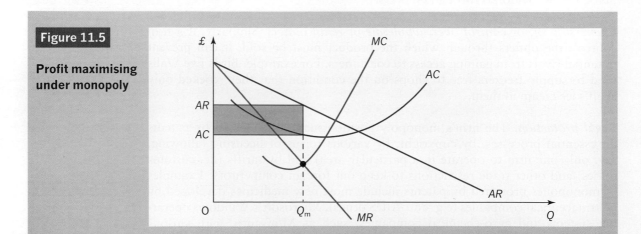

Figure 11.5

Profit maximising under monopoly

Comparing monopoly with perfect competition

Because it faces a different type of market environment, the monopolist will produce a quite different output and at a quite different price from a perfectly competitive industry.

Let us compare the two.

The monopolist will produce a lower output at a higher price in the short run. Figure 11.6 compares the profit-maximising position for an industry under monopoly with that under perfect competition. Note that we are comparing the monopoly with the whole *industry* under perfect competition. That way we can assume, for the sake of comparison, that they both face the same demand curve. We also assume for the moment that they both face the same cost curves.

The monopolist will produce Q_1 at a price of P_1. This is where $MC = MR$.

If the same industry were under perfect competition, however, it would produce at Q_2 and P_2 – a higher output and a lower price. But why? The reason for this is that for each of the firms in the industry – and it is at this level that the decisions are made – marginal revenue is the same as price. Remember that the *firm* under perfect competition faces a perfectly elastic demand (*AR*) curve, which also equals *MR* (see Figure 11.1). Thus producing where $MC = MR$ also means producing where $MC = P$. When *all* firms under perfect competition do this, price and quantity in the *industry* will be given by P_2 and Q_2 in Figure 11.6.

The monopolist may also produce a lower output at a higher price in the long run. Under perfect competition, freedom of entry eliminates supernormal profit and forces firms to produce at the bottom of their *LRAC* curve. The effect, therefore, is to keep long-run prices down. Under monopoly, however, barriers to entry allow profits to remain supernormal in the long run. The monopolist is not forced to operate at the bottom of the *AC* curve. Thus, other things being equal, long-run prices will tend to be higher, and hence output lower, under monopoly.

> **Pause for thought**
>
> If the shares in a monopoly (such as a water company) were very widely distributed among the population, would the shareholders necessarily want the firm to use its monopoly power to make larger profits?

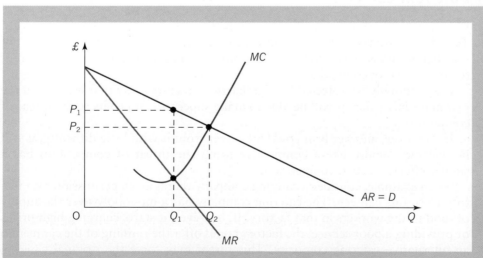

Figure 11.6

Equilibrium of the industry under perfect competition and monopoly: with the same *MC* curve

Costs under monopoly. The sheer survival of a firm in the long run under perfect competition requires that it uses the most efficient known technique, and develops new techniques wherever possible. The monopolist, however, sheltered by barriers to entry, can still make large profits even if it is not using the most efficient technique. It has less incentive, therefore, to be efficient.

On the other hand, the monopoly may be able to achieve substantial economies of scale due to larger plant, centralised administration and the avoidance of unnecessary duplication (e.g. a monopoly water company would eliminate the need for several sets of rival water mains under each street). If this results in an *MC* curve substantially below that of the same industry under perfect competition, the monopoly may even produce a *higher* output at a *lower* price.

Another reason why a monopolist may operate with lower costs is that it can use part of its supernormal profits for research and development and investment. It may not have the same *incentive* to become efficient as the perfectly competitive firm which is fighting for survival, but it may have a much greater *ability* to become efficient than has the small firm with limited funds.

> Key
> Idea
> 8
> p62

Although a monopoly faces no competition in the goods market, it may face an alternative form of competition in financial markets. A monopoly, with potentially low costs, which is currently run inefficiently, is likely to be subject to a takeover bid from another company. This **competition for corporate control** may thus force the monopoly to be efficient in order to prevent being taken over.

> definition
>
> **Competition for corporate control**
> The competition for the control of companies through takeovers.

Innovation and new products. The promise of supernormal profits, protected perhaps by patents, may encourage the development of new (monopoly) industries producing new products. It is this chance of making monopoly profits that encourages many people to take the risks of going into business.

11.4 Potential competition or potential monopoly? The theory of contestable markets

Potential competition

In recent years, economists have developed the theory of contestable markets. This theory argues that what is crucial in determining price and output is not whether an industry is *actually* a monopoly or competitive, but whether there is the real *threat* of competition.

> Key
> Idea
> 20
> p235

If a monopoly is protected by high barriers to entry – say that it owns all the raw materials – then it will be able to make supernormal profits with no fear of competition.

If, however, another firm *could* take over from it with little difficulty, it will behave much more like a competitive firm. The threat of competition has a similar effect to actual competition.

As an example, consider a catering company that is given permission by a factory to run its canteen. The catering company has a monopoly over the supply of food to the workers in that factory. If, however, it starts charging high prices or providing a poor service, the factory could offer the running of the canteen to an alternative catering company. This threat may force the original catering company to charge 'reasonable' prices and offer a good service.

Perfectly contestable markets

A market is perfectly contestable when the costs of entry and exit by potential rivals are zero, and when such entry can be made very rapidly. In such cases, the moment the possibility of earning supernormal profits occurs, new firms will enter, thus driving profits down to a normal level. The sheer threat of this happening, so the theory goes, will ensure that the firm already in the market will (a) keep its prices down, so that it just makes normal profits, and (b) produce as efficiently as possible, taking advantage of any economies of scale and any new technology. If the existing firm did not do this, entry would take place and potential competition would become actual competition.

definition

Perfectly contestable market
A market where there is free and costless entry and exit.

Contestable markets and natural monopolies

So why in such cases are the markets not *actually* perfectly competitive? Why do they remain monopolies?

The most likely reason has to do with economies of scale and the size of the market. To operate on a minimum efficient scale, the firm may have to be so large relative to the market that there is only room for one such firm in the industry. If a new firm does come into the market, then one or other of the two firms will not survive the competition. The market is simply not big enough for both of them.

If, however, there are no entry or exit costs, new firms will be perfectly willing to enter even though there is only room for one firm, provided they believe that they are more efficient than the existing firm. The existing firm, knowing this, will be forced to produce as efficiently as possible and with only normal profit.

The importance of costless exit

Setting up in a new business usually involves large expenditures on plant and machinery. Once this money has been spent, it becomes fixed costs. If these fixed costs are no higher than those of the existing firm, then the new firm could win the battle. But, of course, there is always the risk that it might lose.

But does losing the battle really matter? Can the firm not simply move to another market?

Key Idea
15
p168

It does matter if there are substantial costs of exit. This will be the case if the capital equipment cannot be transferred to other uses. In this case these fixed costs are known as **sunk costs**. The losing firm is left with capital equipment it cannot use. The firm may therefore be put off entering in the first place. The market is not perfectly contestable, and the established firm can make supernormal profit.

If, however, the capital equipment can be transferred, the exit costs will be zero (or at least very low), and new firms will be more willing to take the risks of entry. For example, a rival coach company may open up a service on a route previously operated by only one company, and where there is still only room for one operator. If the new firm loses the resulting battle, it can still use the coaches it has purchased. It simply uses them for a different route. The cost of the coaches is not a sunk cost.

Costless exit, therefore, encourages firms to enter an industry, knowing that, if unsuccessful, they can always transfer their capital elsewhere.

The lower the exit costs, the more contestable the market. This implies that firms already established in other similar markets may provide more effective

definition

Sunk costs
Costs that cannot be recouped (e.g. by transferring assets to other uses).

BOX 11.3

Windows cleaning
Microsoft, the Internet and the US Justice Department

On 18 May 1998, the US government initiated its biggest competition case for 20 years: it sued Microsoft, the world's largest software company. It accused Microsoft of abusing its market power and seeking to crush its rivals.

The case against Microsoft had been building for many years, but it was with the release of *Windows 98* that the US government decided to act. Windows, owned by Microsoft, is the operating system installed on more than 90 per cent of the world's personal computers. With *Windows 98,* Microsoft integrated its own Internet browser, *Internet Explorer*, into the Windows system. But it is in this area of Internet browsers that Microsoft faces stiff competition from Netscape Communications, which at the time controlled over 60 per cent of the market. US anti-trust officials argued that the integration of Microsoft's Internet browser with its operating system would stifle competition in Internet software. In other words, by controlling the operating software, Microsoft could force its Internet browser on to consumers and computer manufacturers.

The US Justice Department alleged that Microsoft had committed the following anti-competitive actions:

■ Back in May 1995, Microsoft attempted to collude with Netscape Communications to divide the Internet browser market. Netscape Communications refused.

■ Microsoft had forced personal computer manufacturers to install *Internet Explorer* in order to obtain a *Windows 95* operating licence.

■ Microsoft insisted that PC manufacturers conformed to a Microsoft front screen for Windows. This included specified icons, one of which was Microsoft's *Internet Explorer*.

■ It had set up reciprocal advertising arrangements with America's largest Internet service providers, such as America Online. Here Microsoft would promote America Online via Windows. In return, America Online would not promote Netscape's browsers.

In the face of these alleged abuses of its monopoly position, the US Justice Department argued that Microsoft should be required to do the following:

■ Remove the integrated browser from its *Windows 98* package, or include access to rival products.

■ End its practice of forcing PC manufacturers to install its Internet browser in order to gain a Windows licence.

■ Allow PC manufacturers to determine the opening screen when using the Windows system.

■ End agreements with Internet service providers that solely promoted Microsoft products.

Microsoft, in its defence, argued that the integration of its own browser into the Windows system was a natural part of the process of product innovation and development. Microsoft officials claimed that accusations of unfair trading practices were not founded: it was simply attempting to improve the quality of its product. If Microsoft was to do nothing with its Windows product, it would, over time, lose its dominant market position, and be replaced by a more innovative and superior product manufactured by a rival software producer. Bill Gates, the founder of Microsoft, reiterated this point. He argued:

> This suit is all about Microsoft's right to innovate on behalf of consumers, the right to integrate new technologies into the operating system as they develop.[1]

In this respect, Microsoft could be seen to be operating in the consumer's interest. The argument is that, in an environment where technology is changing rapidly, Microsoft's control over standards gives the user a measure of stability, knowing that any new products and applications will be compatible with existing ones. In other words, new software can be incorporated into existing systems.

Network effects

The key issue in respect to Microsoft then, was not so much the browser war, but far more fundamentally to do with the operating system, and how Microsoft used its ownership of this system to extend its leverage into other related high-technology markets.

An operating system attracts software developed around that operating system, thereby discouraging new competition since any alternative faces not only the challenge of creating a better operating system but competing against a whole array of already existing software applications. Businesses train employees in one technology and are reluctant to abandon that investment in training, while the existence of a pool of people trained in that technology encourages other businesses to adopt that technology. And as desktop software has to be able to work with client–server networks and an array of other technologies, it becomes nearly impossible to abandon an established set of technology standards that tie those different parts together. These so-called 'network effects' give an incredible anti-competitive edge to companies like Microsoft that control so many different parts of the network.[2]

Network effects arise when consumers of a product benefit from it being used by *other* consumers. The more people that use it, the greater the benefit to each individual user. The problem for the consumer in such a scenario is that these network effects can lead to the establishment of a monopoly producer and hence to higher prices. There is also the problem of whether the best product is being produced by the monopolist. In such an instance, the consumer may be 'locked in' to using an inferior product or technology with limited opportunity (if any) to change.

Microsoft had been able to use consumer lock-in to drive competitors from the market. Where choice did exist, for example in Internet browsers, Microsoft was using its operating system dominance to rectify its inferior market position.

Court findings

A verdict was reached on 7 June 2000, when Federal Judge Thomas Penfield Jackson ruled that Microsoft be split in two to prevent it operating as a monopoly. One company would produce and market the *Windows* operating system; the other would produce and market the applications software, such as *Microsoft Office* and the web browser, *Internet Explorer*.

Microsoft appealed against the judgment to the US Federal Appeals Court, and in June 2001 it overturned the ruling and referred the case to a different judge for reconsideration. Judge Colleen Kollar-Kotelly urged both sides (Microsoft and the US Justice Department) to try to reach a settlement and in November 2001 they did just that. They agreed that Microsoft would provide technical information about *Windows* to other companies to enable them to write software that would compete with Microsoft's own software. Also Microsoft would not be allowed to retaliate against computer manufacturers that installed rival products or removed icons for Microsoft applications.

Nine states, however, refused to sign up to the agreement and a further year went past before Judge Kollar-Kotelly gave her final ruling. Whilst she agreed with many of Judge Jackson's original findings, she did not require that Microsoft be split into two companies. Instead, she upheld the November 2001 agreement.

Questions

1 *In what respects might Microsoft's behaviour be deemed to have been: (a) against the public interest; (b) in the public interest?*

2 *Being locked-in to a product or technology is only a problem if such a product can be clearly shown to be inferior to an alternative. What difficulties might there be in establishing such a case?*

---

[1] *Financial Times*, 21/5/98
[2] N. Newman, From MS Word to MS World: How Microsoft is Building a Global Monopoly (1997), www.netaction.org/msoft/world

competition against monopolists, since they can simply transfer capital from one market to another. For example, studies of airlines in the USA show that entry to a particular route may be much easier for an established airline, which can simply transfer planes from one route to another.

Assessment of the theory

Simple monopoly theory merely focuses on the existing structure of the industry and makes no allowance for potential competition. The theory of contestable markets, however, goes much further and examines the *size* of entry barriers and exit costs. The bigger these are, the less contestable the market and therefore the greater the monopoly power of the existing firm. Various attempts have been made to measure monopoly power in this way.

One criticism of the theory, however, is that it does not take sufficient account of the possible reactions of the established firm. There may be no cost barriers to entry or exit (i.e. a perfectly contestable market), but the established firm may let it be known that any firm that dares to enter will face all-out war! This may act as a deterrent to entry. In the meantime, the established firm may charge high prices and make supernormal profits.

If a monopoly operates in a perfectly contestable market, it might bring the 'best of both worlds' for the consumer. Not only will it be able to achieve low costs through economies of scale, but also the potential competition will keep profits and hence prices down.

> **Pause for thought**
>
> *Think of two examples of highly contestable monopolies (or oligopolies). How well is the consumer's interest served?*

SUMMARY

1a There are four alternative market structures under which firms operate. In ascending order of firms' market power, they are: perfect competition, monopolistic competition, oligopoly and monopoly.

1b The market structure under which a firm operates will affect its conduct and its performance.

2a The assumptions of perfect competition are: a very large number of firms, complete freedom of entry, a homogeneous product and perfect knowledge of the good and its market by both producers and consumers.

2b In the short run, there is not time for new firms to enter the market, and thus supernormal profits can persist. In the long run, however, any supernormal profits will be competed away by the entry of new firms.

2c The short-run equilibrium for the firm will be where the price, as determined by demand and supply in the market, is equal to marginal cost. At this output the firm will be maximising profit.

2d The long-run equilibrium will be where the market price is just equal to firms' long-run average cost.

2e There are no substantial economies of scale to be gained in a perfectly competitive industry. If there were, the industry would cease to be perfectly competitive as the large, low-cost firms drove the small high-cost ones out of business.

3a A monopoly is where there is only one firm in an industry. In practice, it is difficult to determine where a monopoly exists because it depends on how narrowly an industry is defined.

3b Barriers to the entry of new firms will normally be necessary to protect a monopoly from competition. Such barriers include economies of scale (making the firm a natural monopoly or at least giving it a cost advantage over new (small) competitors), control over supplies of inputs or over outlets, patents or copyright, and tactics to eliminate competition (such as takeovers or aggressive advertising).

3c Profits for the monopolist (as for other firms) will be maximised where $MC = MR$.

3d If demand and cost curves are the same in a monopoly and a perfectly competitive industry, the monopoly will produce a lower output and at a higher price than the perfectly competitive industry.

SUMMARY

3e On the other hand, any economies of scale will in part be passed on to consumers in lower prices, and the monopolist's high profits may be used for research and development and investment, which in turn may lead to better products at possibly lower prices.

4a Potential competition may be as important as actual competition in determining a firm's price and output strategy.

4b The threat of this competition is greater, the lower are the entry and exit costs to and from the industry. If the entry and exit costs are zero, the market is said to be *perfectly* contestable. Under such circumstances, an existing monopolist will be forced to keep its profits down to the normal level if it is to resist entry of new firms. Exit costs will be lower, the lower are the sunk costs of the firm.

4c The theory of contestable markets provides a more realistic analysis of firms' behaviour than theories based simply on the *existing* number of firms in the industry.

REVIEW QUESTIONS

1   Why do economists treat normal profit as a cost of production? What determines (a) the level and (b) the rate of normal profit for a particular firm?

2   Why is perfect competition so rare?

3   Why does the market for fresh vegetables approximate to perfect competition, whereas that for frozen or tinned ones does not?

4   Illustrate on a diagram similar to Figure 11.3 what would happen in the long-run if price were initially below P_L.

5   As an illustration of the difficulty in identifying monopolies, try to decide which of the following are monopolies: a train operating company; your local evening newspaper; British Gas; the village post office; the Royal Mail; Interflora; the London Underground; ice creams in the cinema; Guinness; food on trains; TippEx; the board game 'Monopoly'.

6   Try this brain teaser. A monopoly would be expected to face an inelastic demand. After all, there are no direct substitutes. And yet, if it produces where $MR = MC$, MR must be positive, demand must therefore be *elastic*. Therefore the monopolist must face an elastic demand! Can you solve this conundrum?

7   For what reasons would you expect a monopoly to charge (a) a higher price, and (b) a lower price than if the industry were operating under perfect competition?

8   In which of the following industries are exit costs likely to be low: (a) steel production; (b) market gardening; (c) nuclear power generation; (d) specialist financial advisory services; (e) production of fashion dolls; (f) production of a new drug; (g) contract catering; (h) mobile discos; (i) car ferry operators? Are these exit costs dependent on how narrowly the industry is defined?

9   Think of three examples of monopolies (local or national) and consider how contestable their markets are.

12 Profit maximisation under imperfect competition

Very few markets in practice can be classified as perfectly competitive or as a pure monopoly. The vast majority of firms do compete with other firms, often quite aggressively, and yet they are not price takers: they do have some degree of market power. Most markets, therefore, lie between the two extremes of monopoly and perfect competition, in the realm of 'imperfect competition'. As we saw in section 11.1, there are two types of imperfect competition: namely, monopolistic competition and oligopoly.

12.1 Monopolistic competition

Monopolistic competition is nearer to the competitive end of the spectrum. It can best be understood as a situation where there are a lot of firms competing, but where each firm does nevertheless have some degree of market power (hence the term 'monopolistic' competition): each firm has some discretion as to what price to charge for its products.

Assumptions of monopolistic competition

- There is *quite a large number of firms*. As a result, each firm has only a small share of the market and, therefore, its actions are unlikely to affect its rivals to any great extent. What this means is that each firm in making its decisions does not have to worry about how its rivals will react. It assumes that what its rivals choose to do will *not* be influenced by what it does.

    This is known as the assumption of **independence**. (As we shall see later, this is not the case under oligopoly. There we assume that firms believe that their decisions *do* affect their rivals, and that their rivals' decisions will affect them. Under oligopoly we assume that firms are *inter*dependent.)

- There is *freedom of entry* of new firms into the industry. If any firm wants to set up in business in this market, it is free to do so.

In these two respects, therefore, monopolistic competition is like perfect competition.

- Unlike perfect competition, however, each firm produces a product or provides a service that is in some way different from its rivals. As a result, it can raise its price without losing all its customers. Thus its demand curve is downward sloping, albeit relatively elastic given the large number of competitors to whom customers can turn. This is known as the assumption of **product differentiation**.

Petrol stations, restaurants, hairdressers and builders are all examples of monopolistic competition.

A typical feature of monopolistic competition is that, although there are many firms in the industry, there is only one firm in a particular location. This applies particularly in retailing. There may be many newsagents in a town, but only one in a particular street. In a sense, therefore, it has a local monopoly. People may be prepared to pay higher prices there to avoid having to go elsewhere.

Equilibrium of the firm

Short run

As with other market structures, profits are maximised at the output where $MC = MR$. The diagram will be the same as for the monopolist, except that the AR and MR curves will be more elastic. This is illustrated in Figure 12.1(a). As with perfect competition, it is possible for the monopolistically competitive firm to make supernormal profit in the short run. This is shown as the shaded area.

Just how much profit the firm will make in the short run depends on the strength of demand: the position and elasticity of the demand curve. The further to the right the demand curve is relative to the average cost curve, and the less elastic the demand curve is, the greater will be the firm's short-run profit. Thus a firm facing little competition and whose product is considerably differentiated from its rivals may be able to earn considerable short-run profits.

Long run

If typical firms are earning supernormal profit, new firms will enter the industry in the long run. As new firms enter, they will take some of the customers away from established firms. The demand for the established firms' products will therefore fall. Their demand (AR) curve will shift to the left, and will continue doing so as long as supernormal profits remain and thus new firms continue entering.

> **definition**
> **Independence (of firms in a market)**
> When the decisions of one firm in a market will not have any significant effect on the demand curves of its rivals.

> **definition**
> **Product differentiation**
> When one firm's product is sufficiently different from its rivals' to allow it to raise the price of the product without customers all switching to the rivals' products. A situation where a firm faces a downward-sloping demand curve.

> **Pause for thought**
>
> *Which of these two items is a petrol station more likely to sell at a discount: (a) oil; (b) sweets? Why?*

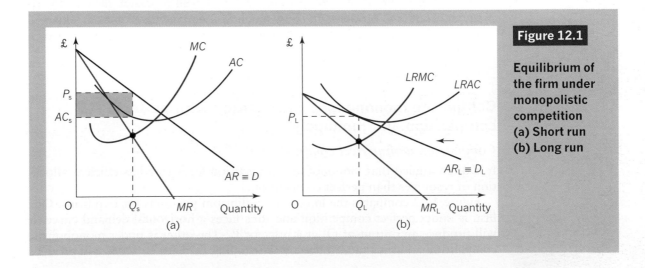

Figure 12.1

Equilibrium of the firm under monopolistic competition (a) Short run (b) Long run

Long-run equilibrium will be reached when only normal profits remain: when there is no further incentive for new firms to enter. This is illustrated in Figure 12.1(b). The firm's demand curve settles at D_L, where it is tangential to (i.e. just touches) the firm's $LRAC$ curve. Output will be Q_L: where $AR_L = LRAC$. (At any other output, $LRAC$ is greater than AR and thus less than normal profit would be made.)

Limitations of the model

There are various problems in applying the model of monopolistic competition to the real world:

■ Information may be imperfect. Firms will not enter an industry if they are unaware of the supernormal profits currently being made, or if they under-estimate the demand for the particular product they are considering selling.

■ Firms are likely to differ from each other, not only in the product they produce or the service they offer, but also in their size and in their cost structure. What is more, entry may not be *completely* unrestricted. Two petrol stations could not set up in exactly the same place – on a busy crossroads, say. Thus although the typical or 'representative' firm may only earn normal profit in the long run, other firms may be able to earn long-run supernormal profit. They may have some cost advantage or produce a product that is impossible to duplicate perfectly.

■ Existing firms may make supernormal profits, but if a new firm entered, this might reduce everyone's profits below the normal level. Thus a new firm will not enter and supernormal profits will persist into the long run. An example would be a small town with two chemist shops. They may both make more than enough profit to persuade them to stay in business. But if a third set up (say midway between the other two), there would not be enough total sales to allow them all to earn even normal profit. This is a problem of *indivisibilities*. Given the overheads of a chemist shop, it is not possible to set up one small enough to take away just enough customers to leave the other two with normal profits.

■ One of the biggest problems with the simple model outlined above is that it concentrates on price and output decisions. In practice, the profit-maximising firm under monopolistic competition will also need to decide the exact variety of product to produce, and how much to spend on advertising it. This will lead the firm to take part in non-price competition (which we examined in Chapter 8).

Comparing monopolistic competition with perfect competition and monopoly

Comparison with perfect competition

It is often argued that monopolistic competition leads to a less efficient allocation of resources than perfect competition.

Figure 12.2 compares the long-run equilibrium positions for two firms. One firm is under perfect competition and thus faces a horizontal demand curve. It will produce an output of Q_1 at a price of P_1. The other is under monopolistic competition and thus faces a downward-sloping demand curve. It will produce

BOX 12.1

Curry wars
Competition hotter than a vindaloo

The growth in the popularity of Indian food in the 1980s and 1990s has led to the proliferation of restaurants and take-away outlets. The close geographic proximity of many such businesses on a well-known street in Bristol led to what became known as the 'Curry War'.

The restaurants had appeared to exist alongside one another quite happily, providing a range of Indian food. In line with the assumptions of monopolistic competition, the restaurants competed in terms of non-price factors such as comfort, advertising and opening hours. Business boomed.

Then with the recession of the early 1990s a price war suddenly erupted. Take-away prices were slashed at first by 20 and 30 per cent, and eventually by 50 per cent at the war's peak. Similar price cuts for dining-in meals were soon to follow. As the war grew more intense, many restaurants saw their profits fall. This was particularly true for those restaurants which tried to resist cutting their prices.

Due to the geographical proximity and cultural links of these businesses, the cut-throat nature of such competition was eventually averted. The local traders' association formed what amounted to a curry cartel. Minimum prices were fixed for curries and prices rose once again.

But as prices in Bristol were rising, prices in other towns were plummeting. On 8 October 1993 *The Independent* reported on a new curry war in Hampstead.

Mr Khan looked around the Fleet Tandoori, packed, on a Tuesday night, with lager-swilling curry-shovellers, and expressed himself delighted with his night's work.

'We are doing this for the hard-pressed consumer,' he said. 'We are the consumer's friend. At our prices the consumer can eat at the Fleet for dinner every night for less than the cost of breakfast.'

It may seem unlikely, but if you want a cheap curry to warm you up this autumn, forget Brick Lane, Bradford or the Balti houses of Birmingham. Head instead for Hampstead, the plushest of London districts, where you can indulge in Bombay duck, onion bhaji and vindaloo and still have enough change from a fiver for a packet of extra strong mints...

...The opening skirmishes came in September, when the Light of Kashmir restaurant, operating in Hampstead since 1962, started a 'Sunday Madness' promotion, halving, at a stroke, its prices.

...Within a fortnight, the restaurant had extended its half-price offer to Saturdays and thence to every night of the week...Two doors down on Fleet Road's parade of shops, on the other side of a Mexican restaurant that offers an 'eat-all-you-like buffet' for just £4.99, is the Fleet Tandoori. A week after the Light started its Seven-Day Madness, a sign appeared outside the Fleet advertising meals at half price.

...What has upset Mr Khan...is that all the curry men of Fleet Road are friends and neighbours from way back...Over the years they have shared staff, poached each other's chefs, cartelled their prices. But the recession put an end to this camaraderie.

Questions

1 What impact do you think curry wars have on other types of take-away and restaurant meals in the same geographic area? What is the relevance of the concepts of price and cross-price elasticities of demand to these effects?

2 Why are curry wars likely to last only a limited period of time?

3 Collusion between restaurants suggests that they are operating under oligopoly, not monopolistic competition. Do you agree?

the lower output of Q_2 at the higher price of P_2. A crucial assumption here is that a firm would have the *same* long-run average cost (*LRAC*) curve in both cases. Given this assumption, we can make the following two predictions about monopolistic competition:

Figure 12.2

Long-run equilibrium of the firm under perfect and monopolistic competition

- Less will be sold and at a higher price.
- Firms will not be producing at the least-cost point.

By producing more, firms would move to a lower point on their *LRAC* curve. Thus firms under monopolistic competition are said to have **excess capacity**. In Figure 12.2 this excess capacity is shown as $Q_1 - Q_2$. In other words, monopolistic competition is typified by quite a large number of firms (e.g. petrol stations), all operating at less than optimum output, and thus being forced to charge a price above that which they could charge if they had a bigger turnover. How often have you been to a petrol station and had to queue for the pumps?

So how does this affect the consumer? Although the firm under monopolistic competition may charge a higher price than under perfect competition, the difference may be very small. Although the firm's demand curve is downward sloping, it is still likely to be highly elastic due to the large number of substitutes. Furthermore, the consumer may benefit from monopolistic competition by having a greater variety of products to choose from. Each firm may satisfy some particular requirement of particular consumers.

> **Pause for thought**
>
> *Which would you rather have: five restaurants to choose from, each with very different menus and each having spare tables so that you could always guarantee getting one; or just two restaurants to choose from, charging a bit less but with less choice and making it necessary to book well in advance?*

Comparison with monopoly

The arguments are very similar here to those when comparing perfect competition and monopoly.

On the one hand, freedom of entry for new firms and hence the lack of long-run supernormal profits under monopolistic competition are likely to help keep prices down for the consumer and encourage cost saving. On the other hand, monopolies are likely to achieve greater economies of scale and have more funds for investment and research and development.

12.2 Oligopoly

Oligopoly occurs when just a few firms between them share a large proportion of the industry.

There are, however, significant differences in the structure of industries under oligopoly, and similarly significant differences in the behaviour of firms. The firms may produce a virtually identical product (e.g. metals, chemicals, sugar, petrol). Most oligopolists, however, produce differentiated products (e.g. cars, soap powder, soft drinks, electrical appliances). Much of the competition between such oligopolists is in terms of the marketing of their particular brand. Marketing practices may differ considerably from one industry to another.

The two key features of oligopoly

Despite the differences between oligopolies, there are two crucial features that distinguish oligopoly from other market structures.

Barriers to entry

Unlike firms under monopolistic competition, there are various barriers to the entry of new firms. These are similar to those under monopoly (see pages 220–2). The size of the barriers, however, will vary from industry to industry. In some cases entry is relatively easy, whereas in others it is virtually impossible.

Interdependence of the firms

Because there are only a few firms under oligopoly, each firm will have to take account of the others. This means that they are mutually dependent: they are **interdependent**. Each firm is affected by its rivals' actions. If a firm changes the price or specification of its product, for example, or the amount of its advertising, the sales of its rivals will be affected. The rivals may then respond by changing their price, specification or advertising. No firm can therefore afford to ignore the actions and reactions of other firms in the industry.

> *People often think and behave strategically.* How you think others will respond to your actions is likely to influence your own behaviour. Firms, for example, when considering a price or product change will often take into account the likely reactions of their rivals.
>
> **Key Idea 20**

It is impossible, therefore, to predict the effect on a firm's sales of, say, a change in its price without first making some assumption about the reactions of other firms. Different assumptions will yield different predictions. For this reason there is no single generally accepted theory of oligopoly. Firms may react differently and unpredictably.

Competition and collusion

Oligopolists are pulled in two different directions:

■ The interdependence of firms may make them wish to *collude* with each other. If they can club together and act as if they were a monopoly, they could jointly maximise industry profits.

■ On the other hand, they will be tempted to *compete* with their rivals to gain a bigger share of industry profits for themselves.

These two policies are incompatible. The more fiercely firms compete to gain a bigger share of industry profits, the smaller these industry profits will become!

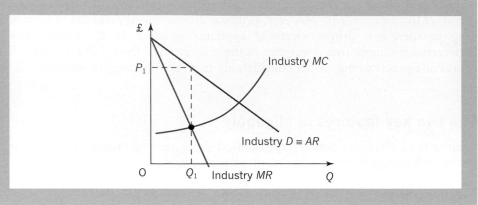

Figure 12.3

Profit-maximising cartel

For example, price competition drives down the average industry price, while competition through advertising raises industry costs. Either way, industry profits fall.

Sometimes firms will collude. Sometimes they will not. The following sections examine first **collusive oligopoly** (both open and tacit), and then **non-collusive oligopoly**.

Equilibrium of industry under collusive oligopoly

When firms under oligopoly engage in collusion, they may agree on prices, market share, advertising expenditure, etc. Such collusion reduces the uncertainty they face. It reduces the fear of engaging in competitive price cutting or retaliatory advertising, both of which could reduce total industry profits.

A formal collusive agreement is called a **cartel**. The cartel will maximise profits if it acts like a monopoly: if the members behave as if they were a single firm. This is illustrated in Figure 12.3.

The total market demand curve is shown with the corresponding market MR curve. The cartel's MC curve is the *horizontal* sum of the MC curves of its members (since we are adding the *output* of each of the cartel members at each level of marginal cost). Profits are maximised at Q_1 where $MC = MR$. The cartel must therefore set a price of P_1 (at which Q_1 will be demanded).

Having agreed on the cartel price, the members may then compete against each other using *non-price competition*, to gain as big a share of resulting sales (Q_1) as they can.

Alternatively, the cartel members may somehow agree to divide the market between them. Each member would be given a **quota**. The sum of all the quotas must add up to Q_1. If the quotas exceeded Q_1, either there would be output unsold if price remained fixed at P_1, or the price would fall.

But if quotas are to be set by the cartel, how will it decide the level of each individual member's quota? The most likely method is for the cartel to divide the market between the members according to their current market share. That is the solution most likely to be accepted as 'fair'.

Pause for thought

If this 'fair' solution were adopted, what effect would it have on the industry MC curve in Figure 12.3?

In many countries cartels are illegal, being seen by the government as a means of driving up prices and profits and thereby as being against the public interest. Government policy towards cartels is examined in Chapter 21.

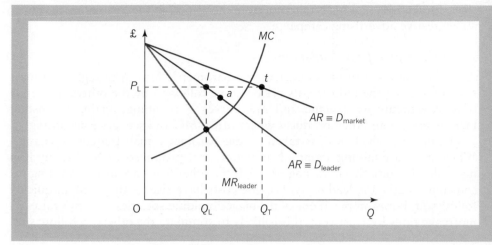

Figure 12.4

A price leader aiming to maximise profits for a given market share

Where open collusion is illegal, firms may simply break the law, or get round it. Alternatively, firms may stay within the law, but still *tacitly* collude by watching each other's prices and keeping theirs similar. Firms may tacitly 'agree' to avoid price wars or aggressive advertising campaigns.

Tacit collusion

One form of **tacit collusion** is where firms keep to the price that is set by an established leader. The leader may be the largest firm: the firm which dominates the industry. This is known as **dominant firm price leadership**. Alternatively, the price leader may simply be the one that has proved to be the most reliable one to follow: the one that is the best barometer of market conditions. This is known as **barometric firm price leadership**. Let us examine each of these two types of price leadership in turn.

Dominant firm price leadership

How does the leader set the price? This depends on the assumptions it makes about its rivals' reactions to its price changes. If it assumes that rivals will simply follow it by making exactly the same percentage price changes up or down, then a simple model can be constructed. This is illustrated in Figure 12.4. The leader assumes that it will maintain a constant market share (say 50 per cent).

The leader will maximise profits where its marginal revenue is equal to its marginal cost. It knows its current position on its demand curve (say, point *a*). It then estimates how responsive its demand will be to industry-wide price changes and thus constructs its demand and *MR* curves on that basis. It then chooses to produce Q_L at a price of P_L: at point *l* on its demand curve (where $MC = MR$). Other firms then follow that price. Total market demand will be Q_T, with followers supplying that portion of the market not supplied by the leader: namely, $Q_T - Q_L$.

There is one problem with this model. That is the assumption that the followers will want to maintain a constant market share. It is possible that, if the leader raises its price, the followers may want to supply more, given that the new price (= *MR* for a price-taking follower) may well be above their marginal cost. On the other hand, the followers may decide merely to maintain their market

definition

Quota (set by a cartel)
The output that a given member of a cartel is allowed to produce (production quota) or sell (sales quota).

definition

Tacit collusion
When oligopolists take care not to engage in price cutting, excessive advertising or other forms of competition. There may be unwritten 'rules' of collusive behaviour such as price leadership.

definition

Dominant firm price leadership
When firms (the followers) choose the same price as that set by a dominant firm in the industry (the leader).

definition

Barometric firm price leadership
Where the price leader is the one whose prices are believed to reflect market conditions in the most satisfactory way.

share for fear of invoking retaliation from the leader, in the form of price cuts or an aggressive advertising campaign.

Barometric firm price leadership

A similar exercise can be conducted by a barometric firm. Although the firm is not dominating the industry, its price will be followed by the others. It merely tries to estimate its demand and MR curves – assuming, again, a constant market share – and then produces where $MR = MC$ and sets price accordingly.

In practice, which firm is taken as the barometer may frequently change. Whether we are talking about oil companies, car producers or banks, any firm may take the initiative in raising prices. If the other firms are merely waiting for someone to take the lead – say, because costs have risen – they will all quickly follow suit. For example, if one of the bigger building societies or banks raises its mortgage rates by 1 per cent, this is likely to stimulate the others to follow suit.

Other forms of tacit collusion

An alternative to having an established leader is for there to be an established set of simple 'rules of thumb' that everyone follows.

Pause for thought

If a firm has a typical shaped average cost curve and sets prices 10 per cent above average cost, what will its supply curve look like?

One such example is **average cost pricing**. Here producers, instead of equating MC and MR, simply add a certain percentage for profit on top of average costs. Thus, if average costs rise by 10 per cent, prices will automatically be raised by 10 per cent. This is a particularly useful rule of thumb in times of inflation, when all firms will be experiencing similar cost increases.

definition

Average cost pricing
Where a firm sets its price by adding a certain percentage for (average) profit on top of average cost.

Another rule of thumb is to have certain **price benchmarks**. Thus clothes may sell for £9.95, £14.95 or £39.95 (but not £12.31 or £36.42). If costs rise, then firms simply raise their price to the next benchmark, knowing that other firms will do the same. Average cost pricing, benchmark pricing and other pricing strategies are considered in more detail in Chapter 17.

Rules of thumb can also be applied to advertising (e.g. you do not criticise other firms' products, only praise your own); or to the design of the product (e.g. lighting manufacturers tacitly agreeing not to bring out an everlasting light bulb).

definition

Price benchmark
This is a price which is typically used. Firms, when raising prices, will usually raise it from one benchmark to another.

Factors favouring collusion

Collusion between firms, whether formal or tacit, is more likely when firms can clearly identify with each other or some leader and when they trust each other not to break agreements. It will be easier for firms to collude if the following conditions apply:

- There are only very few firms, all well known to each other.
- They are open with each other about costs and production methods.
- They have similar production methods and average costs, and are thus likely to want to change prices at the same time and by the same percentage.
- They produce similar products and can thus more easily reach agreements on price.
- There is a dominant firm.

- There are significant barriers to entry and thus there is little fear of disruption by new firms.

- The market is stable. If industry demand or production costs fluctuate wildly, it will be difficult to make agreements, partly due to difficulties in predicting and partly because agreements may frequently have to be amended. There is a particular problem in a declining market where firms may be tempted to undercut each other's price in order to maintain their sales.

- There are no government measures to curb collusion.

Non-collusive oligopoly: the breakdown of collusion

In some oligopolies, there may be only a few (if any) factors favouring collusion. In such cases, the likelihood of price competition is greater.

Even if there is collusion, there will always be the temptation for individual oligopolists to 'cheat', by cutting prices or by selling more than their allotted quota. The danger, of course, is that this would invite retaliation from the other members of the cartel, with a resulting price war. Price would then fall and the cartel could well break up in disarray.

When considering whether to break a collusive agreement, even if only a tacit one, a firm will ask: (1) 'How much can we get away with without inviting retaliation?' and (2) 'If a price war does result, will we be the winners? Will we succeed in driving some or all of our rivals out of business and yet survive ourselves, and thereby gain greater market power?'

The position of rival firms, therefore, is rather like that of generals of opposing armies or the players in a game. It is a question of choosing the appropriate *strategy*: the strategy that will best succeed in outwitting your opponents. The strategy that a firm adopts will, of course, be concerned not just with price, but also with advertising and product development.

The firm's choice of strategy will depend on (a) how it thinks its rivals will react to any price changes or other changes it makes; (b) its willingness to take a gamble. Economists have developed **game theory**, which examines the best strategy that a firm can adopt for each assumption about its rivals' behaviour.

Non-collusive oligopoly: game theory

Simple dominant strategy games

The simplest case is where there are just two firms with identical costs, products and demand. They are both considering which of two alternative prices to charge. Table 12.1 shows typical profits they could each make.

Let us assume that at present both firms (X and Y) are charging a price of £2 and that they are each making a profit of £10 million, giving a total industry profit of £20 million. This is shown in the top left-hand box (A).

Now assume they are both (independently) considering reducing their price to £1.80. In making this decision, they will need to take into account what their rival might do, and how this will affect them. Let us consider X's position. In our simple example there are just two things that its rival, firm Y, might do. Either Y could cut its price to £1.80, or it could leave its price at £2. What should X do?

One alternative is to go for the *cautious* approach and think of the worst thing that its rival could do. If X kept its price at £2, the worst thing for X would be if its rival Y cut its price. This is shown by box C: X's profit falls to £5 million.

definition

Game theory (or the theory of games) The study of alternative strategies that oligopolists may choose to adopt, depending on their assumptions about their rivals' behaviour.

Table 12.1	Profits for firms A and B at different prices

Table showing X's price (£2 and £1.80) across columns and Y's price (£2 and £1.80) down rows:

- Box A (X £2, Y £2): £10 m each
- Box B (X £1.80, Y £2): £5 m for Y, £12 m for X
- Box C (X £2, Y £1.80): £12 m for Y, £5 m for X
- Box D (X £1.80, Y £1.80): £8 m each

If, however, X cut its price to £1.80, the worst outcome would again be for Y to cut its price, but this time X's profit only falls to £8 million. In this case, then, if X is cautious, it will *cut its price to £1.80*. Note that Y will argue along similar lines, and if it is cautious, it too will cut its price to £1.80. This policy of adopting the safer strategy is known as **maximin**. Following a maximin strategy, the firm will opt for the alternative that will *max*imise its *min*imum possible profit.

An alternative strategy is to go for the *optimistic* approach and assume that your rivals react in the way most favourable to you. Here the firm will go for the strategy that yields the highest possible profit. In X's case this will be again to cut price, only this time on the optimistic assumption that firm Y will leave its price unchanged. If firm X is correct in its assumption, it will move to box B and achieve the maximum possible profit of £12 million. This strategy of going for the maximum possible profit is known as **maximax**. Note that again the same argument applies to Y. Its maximax strategy will be to cut price and hopefully end up in box C.

Given that in this 'game' *both* approaches, maximin and maximax, lead to the *same* strategy (namely, cutting price), this is known as a **dominant strategy game**. The result is that the firms will end up in box D, earning a lower profit (£8 million each) than if they had charged the higher price (£10 million each in box A).

The equilibrium outcome of a game where there is no collusion between the players (box D in this game) is known as a **Nash equilibrium**, after John Nash, a US mathematician (and subject of the film *A Beautiful Mind*) who introduced the concept in 1951.

In our example, collusion rather than a price war would have benefited both firms. Yet, even if they did collude, both would be tempted to cheat and cut prices. This is known as the **prisoners' dilemma** (see Box 12.2 opposite).

More complex games with no dominant strategy

More complex 'games' can be devised with more than two firms, many alternative prices, differentiated products and various forms of non-price competition (e.g. advertising). In such cases, the cautious (maximin) strategy may suggest a different policy (e.g. do nothing) from the high-risk (maximax) strategy (e.g. cut prices substantially).

In many situations, firms will have a number of different options open to them and a number of possible reactions by rivals. In such cases, the choice facing firms may be many. They may opt for a compromise strategy between maximax

BOX 12.2

The prisoners' dilemma

Game theory is relevant not just to economics. A famous non-economic example is the prisoners' dilemma.

Nigel and Amanda have been arrested for a joint crime of serious fraud. Each is interviewed separately and given the following alternatives:

■ First, if they say nothing, the court has enough evidence to sentence both to a year's imprisonment.

■ Second, if either Nigel or Amanda *alone* confesses, he or she is likely to get only a three-month sentence but the partner could get up to ten years.

■ Third, if both confess, they are likely to get three years each.

	Amanda's alternatives	
	Not confess	Confess
Not confess Nigel's alternatives Confess	**A** Each gets 1 year	**B** Nigel gets 10 years Amanda gets 3 months
	C Nigel gets 3 months Amanda gets 10 years	**D** Each gets 3 years

What should Nigel and Amanda do?

Let us consider Nigel's dilemma. Should he confess in order to get the short sentence (the maximax strategy)? This is better than the year he would get for not confessing. There is, however, an even better reason for confessing. Suppose Nigel doesn't confess but, unknown to him, Amanda does confess. Then Nigel ends up with the long sentence. Better than this is to confess and to get no more than three years: this is the safest (maximin) strategy.

Amanda is in the same dilemma. The result is simple. When both prisoners act selfishly by confessing, they both end up in position D with relatively long prison terms. Only when they collude will they end up in position A with relatively short prison terms, the best combined solution.

Of course the police know this and will do their best to prevent any collusion. They will keep Nigel and Amanda in separate cells and try to persuade each of them that the other is bound to confess.

Thus the choice of strategy depends on:

■ Nigel's and Amanda's risk attitudes: i.e. are they 'risk lovers' or 'risk averse'?

■ Nigel's and Amanda's estimates of how likely the other is to own up.

Questions

1 *Why is this a dominant strategy game?*

2 *How would Nigel's choice of strategy be affected if he had instead been involved in a joint crime with Jeremy, Pauline, Diana and Dave, and they had all been caught?*

Let us now look at two real-world examples of the prisoners' dilemma.

Standing at concerts

When people go to some public event, such as a concert or a match, they often stand in order to get a better view. But once people start standing, everyone is likely to do so: after all, if they stayed sitting, they would not see at all. In this Nash equilibrium, most people are worse off, since, except for tall people, their view is likely to be worse and they lose the comfort of sitting down.

Too much advertising

Why do firms spend so much on advertising? If they are aggressive, they do so to get ahead of their rivals (the maximax approach). If they are cautious, they do so in case their rivals increase their advertising (the maximin approach). Although in both cases it may be in the individual firm's best interests to increase advertising, the resulting Nash equilibrium is likely to be one of excessive advertising: the total spent on advertising (by all firms) is not recouped in additional sales.

Question

Give one or two other examples (economic or non-economic) of the prisoners' dilemma.

and maximin. This could be a strategy that is more risky than the maximin one, but with the chance of a higher profit; but not as risky as the maximax one, but where the maximum profit possible is not so high.

The importance of threats and promises

In many situations, an oligopolist will make a threat or promise that it will act in a certain way. As long as the threat or promise is **credible** (i.e. its competitors believe it), the firm can gain and it will influence its rivals' behaviour.

Take the simple situation where a large oil company, such as Esso, states that it will match the price charged by any competitor within a given radius. Assume that competitors believe this 'price promise' but also that Esso will not try to *undercut* their price. In the simple situation where there is only one other filling station in the area, what price should it charge? Clearly it should charge the price which would maximise its profits, assuming that Esso will charge the *same* price. In the absence of other filling stations in the area, this is likely to be a relatively high price.

Now assume that there are several filling stations in the area. What should the company do now? Its best bet is probably to charge the same price as Esso and hope that no other company charges a lower price and forces Esso to cut its price. Assuming that Esso's threat is credible, other companies are likely to reason in a similar way.

The importance of timing

Most decisions by oligopolists are made by one firm at a time rather than simultaneously by all firms. Sometimes a firm will take the initiative. At other times it will respond to decisions taken by other firms.

Take the case of a new generation of large passenger aircraft which can fly further without refuelling. Assume that there is a market for a 500-seater version of this type of aircraft and a 400-seater version, but that the market for each sized aircraft is not big enough for the two manufacturers, Boeing and Airbus, to share it profitably. Let us also assume that the 400-seater market would give an annual profit of £50 million to a single manufacturer and the 500-seater would give an annual profit of £30 million, but that if both manufacturers produced the same version, they would each make an annual loss of £10 million.

Assume that Boeing announces that it is building the 400-seater plane. What should Airbus do? The choice is illustrated in Figure 12.5. This diagram is called a **decision tree** and shows the sequence of events. The small square at the left of the diagram is Boeing's decision point (point A). If it had decided to build the 500-seater plane, we would move up the top branch. Airbus would now have to make a decision (point B_1). If it too built the 500-seater plane, we would move to outcome 1: a loss of £10 million for both manufacturers. Clearly, with Boeing building a 500-seater plane, Airbus would choose the 400-seater plane: we would move to outcome 2, with Boeing making a profit of £30 million and Airbus a profit £50 million. Airbus would be very pleased!

Boeing's best strategy at point A, however, would be to build the 400-seater plane. We would then move to Airbus's decision point B_2. In this case, it is in Airbus's interests to build the 500-seater plane. Its profit would be only £30 million (outcome 3), but this is better than a £10 million loss if it too built the 400-seater plane (outcome 4). With Boeing deciding first, the Nash equilibrium will thus be outcome 3.

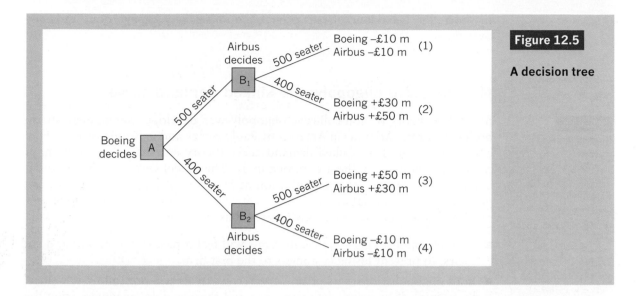

Figure 12.5

A decision tree

There is clearly a **first-mover advantage** here. Once Boeing has decided to build the more profitable version of the plane, Airbus is forced to build the less profitable one. Naturally, Airbus would like to build the more profitable one and be the first mover. Which company succeeds in going first depends on how advanced they are in their research and development and in their production capacity.

More complex decision trees. The aircraft example is the simplest version of a decision tree, with just two companies and each one making only one key decision. In many business situations, much more complex trees could be constructed. The 'game' would be more like one of chess, with many moves and several options on each move. If there were more than two companies, the decision tree would be more complex still.

Pause for thought

Give an example of decisions that two firms could make in sequence, each one affecting the other's next decision.

The usefulness of game theory

The advantage of the game-theory approach is that the firm does not need to know which response its rivals will make. It does, however, need to be able to measure the effect of each possible response. This will be virtually impossible to do when there are many firms competing and many different responses that could be made. The approach is only useful, therefore, in relatively simple cases, and even here the estimates of profit from each outcome may amount to no more than a rough guess.

It is thus difficult for an economist to predict with any accuracy what price, output and level of advertising the firm will choose. This problem is compounded by the difficulty of predicting the type of strategy – safe, high risk, compromise – that the firm will adopt.

In some cases, firms may compete hard for a time (in price or non-price terms) and then realise that maybe no one is winning. Firms may then jointly raise prices and reduce advertising. Later, after a period of tacit collusion, competition may break out again. This may be sparked off by the entry of a new firm, by the development of a new product design, by a change in market demand, or simply by one or more firms no longer being able to resist the temptation to 'cheat'.

In short, the behaviour of particular oligopolists may change quite radically over time.

Non-collusive oligopoly: the kinked demand curve

In 1939 a theory of non-collusive oligopoly was developed simultaneously on both sides of the Atlantic: in America by Paul Sweezy and in Britain by R. L. Hall and C. J. Hitch. This **kinked demand curve** theory has since become perhaps the most famous of all theories of oligopoly. The model seeks to explain how it is that, even when there is no collusion at all between oligopolists, prices can nevertheless remain stable.

The theory is based on two asymmetrical assumptions:

■ If an oligopolist cuts its price, its rivals will feel forced to follow suit and cut theirs, to prevent losing customers to the first firm.

■ If an oligopolist raises its price, however, its rivals will *not* follow suit since, by keeping their prices the same, they will thereby gain customers from the first firm.

On these assumptions, each oligopolist will face a demand curve that is *kinked* at the current price and output (see Figure 12.6). A rise in price will lead to a large fall in sales as customers switch to the now lower-priced rivals. The firm will thus be reluctant to raise its price. Demand is relatively elastic above the kink. On the other hand, a fall in price will bring only a modest increase in sales, since rivals lower their prices too and therefore customers do not switch. The firm will thus also be reluctant to reduce its price. Demand is relatively inelastic below the kink. Thus oligopolists will be reluctant to change prices at all.

Despite its simple demonstration of the real-world phenomenon of price stability, the model does have two major limitations.

■ Price stability may be due to *other* factors. Firms may not want to change prices too frequently, as it will involve modifying price lists, working out new revenue predictions and revaluing stocks of finished goods, and it may also upset customers. Price stability, therefore, is not proof of the accuracy of the model.

Key Idea 11 p81

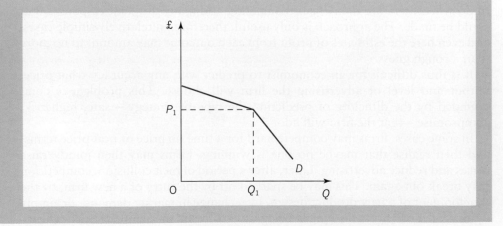

Figure 12.6

Kinked demand curve for a firm under oligopoly

- Although the model can help to explain price stability, it does not explain how prices are set in the first place. To do this, some other model would be required (see Chapter 17 for an analysis of pricing in practice). This is a serious limitation in times of inflation, when oligopolists, like other firms, will raise prices in response to higher costs and higher demand.

Oligopoly and the consumer

When oligopolists act collusively and jointly maximise industry profits, they are in effect acting together as a monopoly. In such cases, prices may be very high. This is clearly not in the best interests of consumers.

Furthermore, in two respects, oligopoly may be more disadvantageous than monopoly:

- Depending on the size of the individual oligopolists, there may be less scope for economies of scale to mitigate the effects of market power.
- Oligopolists are likely to engage in much more extensive advertising than a monopolist.

These problems will be less severe, however, if oligopolists do not collude, if there is some degree of price competition and if barriers to entry are weak.

Moreover, the power of oligopolists in certain markets may to some extent be offset if they sell their product to other powerful firms. Thus oligopolistic producers of baked beans or soap powder sell a large proportion of their output to giant supermarket chains, which can use their market power to keep down the price at which they purchase these products. This phenomenon is known as **countervailing power**.

In some respects, oligopoly may be more beneficial to the consumer than other market structures:

- Oligopolists, like monopolists, can use part of their supernormal profit for research and development. Unlike monopolists, however, oligopolists will have a considerable *incentive* to do so. If the product design is improved, this may allow the firm to capture a larger share of the market, and it may be some time before rivals can respond with a similarly improved product. If, in addition, costs are reduced by technological improvement, the resulting higher profits will enable the firm better to withstand a price war should one break out.
- Non-price competition through product differentiation may result in greater choice for the consumer. Take the case of stereo equipment. Non-price competition has led to a huge range of different products of many different specifications, each meeting the specific requirements of different consumers.

It is difficult to draw any general conclusions, since oligopolies differ so much in their performance.

Oligopoly and contestable markets

The theory of contestable markets has been applied to oligopoly as well as to monopoly, and similar conclusions are drawn.

BOX 12.3

Rip-off Britain

Evidence of oligopolistic collusion?

In recent years there have been repeated allegations that British consumers are paying much higher prices than their European counterparts on a wide range of goods. The car industry, the large supermarket chains and the banks have all been charged with 'ripping-off' the consumer. Such has been the level of concern, that all three industries have been referred to the Competition Commission (see section 20.1).

Car industry

The clearest evidence of anti-competitive pricing behaviour in the UK car industry came with the admission by Volvo in July 1999 that it had entered secret agreements to keep British car prices high. This appeared to be just the tip of an iceberg, with car manufacturers fixing prices through the system of selective and exclusive distribution (SED). In other words, manufacturers would only supply through 'official' dealers who would sell at the list price (or at small agreed 'discounts').

When we consider the difference in price between identical models in Britain and mainland Europe the discrepancies are huge. The Competition Commission report, published in April 2000, found that car buyers in Britain were paying on average some 10 to 12 per cent more than those in France, Germany and Italy for the same models. For 58 of the 71 models analysed by the Commission, the UK price was at least 20 per cent higher than in the cheapest country. The Commission concluded that British car buyers were paying around 10 per cent too much for new cars, or some £1100 for an average car.

The price discrepancies between Britain and Europe were maintained by car manufacturers blocking cheaper European cars coming into the UK. Manufacturers have been accused of adopting a number of anti-competitive practices. These include threatening mainland European car dealers with losing their dealership if they sell to British buyers, and delaying the delivery date of right-hand drive models to mainland European dealers in the hope that British buyers will change their minds and go back to a British dealership.

Supermarkets

The Competition Commission enquiry into supermarkets, which began in April 1999, followed a nine-month investigation by the Office of Fair Trading into the major supermarket chains' business activities. The OFT identified three major areas of concern: the use of barriers to entry, the lack of effective price competition, and the relationship between the large supermarket chains and their suppliers.

The main issue concerns the major supermarket chains' huge buying and selling power. They have been able to drive costs down by forcing suppliers to offer discounts. Many suppliers, such as growers, have found their profit margins cut to the bone. However, these cost savings have not been passed on from supplier to shopper. The supermarket chains have adopted a system of 'shadow pricing', a form of tacit collusion whereby they all observe each other's prices and ensure that they remain at similar levels: often similarly high levels rather than similarly low levels! This has limited the extent of true price competition, and the resulting high prices have seen profits grow as costs have been driven ever downwards.

Since the OFT referral, the £6.7 billion take-over of Asda by Wal-Mart, the world's largest retailer, with a reputation of being a ruthless price cutter, promised to change the whole issue of pricing in the supermarket sector. Of the supermarket chains,

The lower the entry and exit costs for new firms, the more difficult it will be for oligopolists to collude and make supernormal profits. If oligopolists do form a cartel (whether legal or illegal), this will be difficult to maintain if it very soon faces competition from new entrants. What a cartel has to do in such a situation is to erect entry barriers, thereby making the 'contest' more difficult. For example, the cartel could form a common research laboratory, denied to outsiders. It might attempt to control the distribution of the finished product by buying up wholesale or retail outlets. Or it might simply let it be known to potential entrants that they will face all-out price, advertising and

Asda has always been one of the cheapest. With the Wal-Mart take-over, the drive to cut prices gained fresh momentum. Asda planned to slash prices on hundreds of products, with most seeing some price reduction.

Tesco in response, striving to maintain its position as the UK's number one supermarket retailer, launched its own price-cutting campaign. It was determined not to get left behind in the price-cutting war.

Despite these apparent price wars, the Competition Commission was still concerned that competition was being restricted. It sought to answer a number of questions. Is price competition limited to a relatively small number of frequently purchased items, and at stores which face the most local competition? Are cost reductions 'being rapidly and fully passed through to consumers'? Is 'the pattern of prices and margins across different types of product, including branded and own label products, related to costs to the extent that would be expected in a fully competitive market? This would include products persistently sold at a loss, which may benefit consumers in the short term but which may distort competition and consumer choice, and may adversely affect the supply or availability of such products in the longer term.'[1]

One solution suggested by the Competition Commission would be to force supermarkets to publish their prices on the Internet, thereby allowing consumers or consumers' organisations to make easy comparisons of the prices charged by different supermarkets.

Banks

According to a Treasury report, chaired by Don Cruickshank,[2] UK banks are making excessive profits of some £3 billion to £5 billion per year, with bank customers paying up to £400 a year too much in charges and interest rates. The report found that current accounts were the least competitive product. They pay little or no interest to customers in credit and charge exorbitant amounts if you go overdrawn. But it was not just current accounts: mortgages, savings accounts, credit cards and personal loans were all identified as often being poor products.

Banks have tight control over cheque clearing, money transmission systems and cash machines. This makes it difficult for new competitors to enter the market. For example, a new bank without an extensive network of cash machines would find it difficult to attract customers, given the hefty charges for using other banks' machines. In addition, bank customers are often unwilling to consider changing accounts, fearing that this will involve a lot of time and expense.

Small businesses were found to be facing even more excessive charges. The government thus asked the Competition Commission to inquire into this particular aspect of the provision of banking services.

Questions

1 *Identify the main barriers to entry in the supermarket and banking sectors.*

2 *In what forms of tacit collusion are firms in the three industries likely to engage?*

---

[1] 'Supply of Groceries from Multiple Stores Monopoly Inquiry: Annex 2 To Issues Letter' (Competition Commission, 2000)
[2] 'Competition in UK Banking: a Report to the Chancellor of the Exchequer' (TSO, 2000)

---

product competition from all the members if they should dare to set up in competition.

The industry is thus likely to behave competitively if entry and exit costs are low, with all the benefits and costs to the consumer of such competition – even if the new firms do not actually enter. However, if entry and/or exit costs are high, the degree of competition will simply depend on the relations between existing members of the industry.

> **Pause for thought**
>
> *Which of the following markets do you think are contestable: (a) credit cards; (b) brewing; (c) petrol retailing; (d) insurance services; (e) compact discs?*

SUMMARY

1a Monopolistic competition occurs where there is free entry to the industry and quite a large number of firms operating independently of each other, but where each firm has some market power as a result of producing differentiated products or services.

1b In the short run, firms can make supernormal profits. In the long run, however, freedom of entry will drive profits down to the normal level. The long-run equilibrium of the firm is where the (downward-sloping) demand curve is tangential to the long-run average cost curve.

1c The long-run equilibrium is one of excess capacity. Given that the demand curve is downward sloping, its tangency point with the *LRAC* curve will not be at the bottom of the *LRAC* curve. Increased production would thus be possible at *lower* average cost.

1d In practice, supernormal profits may persist into the long run: firms have imperfect information; entry may not be completely unrestricted; there may be a problem of indivisibilities; firms may use non-price competition to maintain an advantage over their rivals.

1e Monopolistically competitive firms, because of excess capacity, may have higher costs, and thus higher prices, than perfectly competitive firms, but consumers may gain from a greater diversity of products.

1f Monopolistically competitive firms may have less economies of scale than monopolies and conduct less research and development, but the competition may keep prices lower than under monopoly. Whether there will be more or less choice for the consumer is debatable.

2a An oligopoly is where there are just a few firms in the industry with barriers to the entry of new firms. Firms recognise their mutual dependence.

2b Oligopolists will want to maximise their joint profits. This will tend to make them collude to keep prices high. On the other hand, they will want the biggest share of industry profits for themselves. This will tend to make them compete.

2c Whether they compete or collude depends on the conditions in the industry. They are more likely to collude if there are few of them; if they are open with each other; if they have similar products and cost structures; if there is a dominant firm; if there are significant entry barriers; if the market is stable; and if there is no government legislation to prevent collusion.

2d Collusion can be open or tacit.

2e A formal collusive agreement is called a 'cartel'. A cartel aims to act as a monopoly. It can set price and leave the members to compete for market share, or it can assign quotas. There is always a temptation for cartel members to 'cheat' by undercutting the cartel price if they think they can get away with it and not trigger a price war.

2f Tacit collusion can take the form of price leadership. This is where firms follow the price set by either a dominant firm in the industry or one seen as a reliable 'barometer' of market conditions. Alternatively, tacit collusion can simply involve following various rules of thumb such as average cost pricing and benchmark pricing.

2g Non-collusive oligopolists will have to work out a price strategy. This will depend on their attitudes towards risk and on the assumptions they make about the behaviour of their rivals.

2h Game theory examines various strategies that firms can adopt when the outcome of each is not certain. They can adopt a low-risk 'maximin' strategy of choosing the policy that has the least-bad worst outcome, or a high-risk 'maximax' strategy of choosing the policy with the best possible outcome, or some compromise. Either way, a 'Nash' equilibrium is likely to be reached which is not in the best interests of the firms collectively. It will entail a lower level of profit than if they had colluded.

2i Because firms are likely to face a kinked demand curve, they are likely to keep their prices stable unless there is a large shift in costs or demand.

2j Whether consumers benefit from oligopoly depends on the particular oligopoly and how competitive it is; whether there is any countervailing power; whether the firms engage in extensive advertising and of what type; whether product differentiation results in a wide range of choice for the consumer; how much of the profits are ploughed back into research and development; and how contestable the market is. Since these conditions vary substantially from oligopoly to oligopoly, it is impossible to state just how well or how badly oligopoly in general serves the consumer's interest.

REVIEW QUESTIONS

1 Think of ten different products or services and estimate roughly how many firms there are in the market. You will need to decide whether 'the market' is a local one, a national one or an international one. In what ways do the firms compete in each of the cases you have identified?

2 Imagine there are two types of potential customer for jam sold by a small food shop. One is the person who has just run out and wants some now. The other is the person who looks in the cupboard, sees that the pot of jam is less than half full and thinks, 'I will soon need some more.' How will the price elasticity of demand differ between these two customers?

3 Why may a food shop charge higher prices than supermarkets for 'essential items' and yet very similar prices for delicatessen items?

4 How will the position and shape of a firm's short-run demand curve depend on the prices that rivals charge?

5 Assuming that a firm under monopolistic competition can make supernormal profits in the short run, will there be any difference in the long-run and short-run elasticity of demand? Explain.

6 Firms under monopolistic competition generally have spare capacity. Does this imply that if, say, half of the petrol stations were closed down, the consumer would benefit? Explain.

7 Will competition between oligopolists always reduce total industry profits?

8 In which of the following industries is collusion likely to occur: bricks, beer, margarine, cement, crisps, washing powder, blank audio or video cassettes, carpets?

9 Draw a diagram like Figure 12.4. Illustrate what would happen if there were a rise in market demand.

10 Devise a box diagram like that in Table 12.1, only this time assume that there are three firms, each considering the two strategies of keeping price the same or reducing it by a set amount. Is the game still a 'dominant strategy game'?

11 What are the limitations of game theory in predicting oligopoly behaviour?

12 Which of the following are examples of effective countervailing power?
   (a) A power station buying coal from a large local coal mine.
   (b) A large factory hiring a photocopier from Rank Xerox.
   (c) Marks and Spencer buying clothes from a garment manufacturer.
   (d) A small village store (but the only one for miles around) buying food from a wholesaler.

   Is it the size of the purchasing firm that is important in determining its power to keep down the prices charged by its suppliers?

Additional Part E case studies on the *Economics for Business* website (www.booksites.net/sloman)

E.1 **Is perfect best?** An examination of the meaning of the word 'perfect' in perfect competition.

E.2 **B2B electronic marketplaces.** This case study examines the growth of firms trading with each other over the Internet (business to business or 'B2B') and considers the effects on competition.

E.3 **Measuring monopoly power.** An examination of how the degree of monopoly power possessed by a firm can be measured.

E.4 **X-inefficiency.** A type of inefficiency suffered by many large firms, resulting in a wasteful use of resources.

E.5 **Competition in the pipeline.** An examination of attempts to introduce competition into the gas industry in the UK.

E.6 **Airline deregulation in the USA and Europe.** Whether the deregulation of various routes has led to more competition and lower prices.

E.7 **The motor vehicle repair and servicing industry.** A case study of monopolistic competition.

E.8 **Bakeries: oligopoly or monopolistic competition.** A case study on the bread industry, showing that small-scale local bakeries can exist alongside giant national bakeries.

E.9 **Oligopoly in the brewing industry.** A case study showing how the UK brewing industry is becoming more concentrated.

E.10 **OPEC.** A case study examining OPEC's influence over oil prices from the early 1970s to the current day.

Websites relevant to Part E

Numbers and sections refer to websites listed in the Web appendix and hotlinked from this book's website at **www.booksites.net/sloman**

- For news articles relevant to Part E, see the *Economics News Articles* link from the book's website.

- For general news on companies and markets see websites in section A, and particularly A1, 2, 3, 4, 5, 8, 9, 18, 23, 24, 25, 26, 35, 36. See also A38, 39 and 43 for links to newspapers world wide; and A42 for links to economics news articles from newspapers worldwide.

- For sites that look at competition and market power, see B2; E4, 10, 18; G7, 8. See also links in I7, 11, 14 and 17. In particular see the following links in sites I7: *Microeconomics > Competition and Monopoly*.

- For a site on game theory, see A40 including its home page. See also D4; C20; I17 and 4 (in the EconDirectory section).

Supply: alternative strategies

THE FT REPORTS...

THE FINANCIAL TIMES, 26 JUNE 2003

Brands brew a coffee coup

By ASTRID WENDLANDT

The British, once regarded as a nation of tea drinkers, are having a passionate affair with coffee, a report confirms today.

The number of cups of coffee drunk in branded coffee bar chains has risen 60 per cent over the past two years with customers developing a preference for larger cups, according to the research by Allegra Strategies, a consulting and research company.

The growth comes in spite of cappuccino prices in leading coffee bars rising by 3.7 per cent between March 2002 and May of this year, now averaging £1.69 for a 12-ounce cup.

Allegra predicts the coffee shop market will grow at a compound annual rate of 5.1 per cent from May 2003 to December 2005. By then, Allegra is forecasting turnover from branded coffee chains, including Starbucks, Costa Coffee and Caffè Nero, to exceed £1 bn.

It expects the number of branded coffee-focused bars to rise from 1460 to 1900 by the end of 2005. The chains will focus their expansion outside London where rents are cheaper.

The report says that the fundamental drivers of profitability are the right location, increasing sales with food offerings and keeping a tight lid on rental costs.

The report reveals that 67.8 per cent of coffee bar customers will occasionally also purchase something to eat but 49 per cent consider the food to be expensive.

Jeffrey Young, managing director of Allegra, said Coffee Republic's idea of trialling a New York-style sandwich deli at its Baker Street outlet was 'clever', but 'needs to be proven'.

The market may still be growing but it is also becoming increasingly crowded, the report finds.

Allegra points out that coffee bars are facing fresh competition from outlets in supermarket chains and convenience stores, such as Sainsbury's Local and Marks & Spencer.

Gerry Ford, chief executive and chairman of Caffè Nero, said: 'These competitors can take sales from coffee bars but the person who will have a coffee while shopping at M&S is generally different from the one who will go to a coffee bar chain.'

The report confirms Starbucks' lead in the UK, with 350 outlets and a 24 per cent market share. The US group increased its market share by 3.7 per cent last year.

For years, young people have been inspired by celebrities like pop stars and footballers. I want to see entrepreneurs become more admired and respected for their contribution to society.

Nigel Griffiths, UK Small Business Minister (January 2003), on the launch of a new online mentoring scheme for young people with award-winning business owners

Many small companies, especially those facing fierce competition, may be forced to pursue profit as their overriding goal, merely to survive. The maximum profit they can make may be only just enough for them to stay in business in the long term (i.e. normal profit).

With large companies, however, where mere survival is not the overriding concern, the pursuit of short-run profit is likely to be only one of many business objectives. The modern business enterprise is often a complex organisation, with many different departments and divisions. What is more, the ownership and control of the firm are often in totally different hands: i.e. shareholders and managers. With many competing interests there are often several objectives being pursued simultaneously.

In Part F we will consider what these alternative objectives might be and the strategies that businesses might adopt in their pursuit.

We start, in Chapter 13, by introducing you to the world of business strategy. We show how crucial the degree of competition is in shaping not only business success but the strategic approaches open to business.

In Chapter 14 we will outline various alternative theories of the firm – alternative, that is, to the traditional theory of short-run profit maximisation. Then, in Chapter 15, we will focus on one particular theory: that of growth maximisation.

Chapter 16 looks at the small-firm sector, and compares the objectives and behaviour of small firms with those of their bigger rivals.

Finally, in Chapter 17, we will look at alternative pricing strategies and how they vary with market structure and the different aims that firms might pursue.

key terms

Porter's five forces
Strategic management
Value chain
Core competence
Profit satisficing
Managerial utility
Behavioural theories of the firm
Organisational slack
Takeover constraint
Horizontal and vertical integration
Diversification
Merger
Enterprise
Strategic alliance
SME
Cost-based pricing
Price discrimination
Transfer pricing
Product life cycle

CHAPTER

13 An introduction to business strategy

Ben & Jerry's is dedicated to the creation & demonstration of a new corporate concept of linked prosperity. Our mission consists of three interrelated parts.

- Product: To make, distribute and sell the finest quality all natural ice cream and related products in a wide variety of innovative flavors made from Vermont dairy products.
- Economic: To operate the Company on a sound financial basis of profitable growth, increasing value for our shareholders, and creating career opportunities and financial rewards for our employees.
- Social: To operate the Company in a way that actively recognizes the central role that business plays in the structure of society by initiating innovative ways to improve the quality of life of a broad community – local, national, and international.

Underlying the mission of Ben & Jerry's is the determination to seek new & creative ways of addressing all three parts, while holding a deep respect for individuals inside and outside the Company and for the communities of which they are a part.

© Ben & Jerry's Homemade, Inc.

Being a successful business means what? According to their mission statement, for Ben & Jerry's it means producing a high quality product, being ice-cream innovators, returning a profit, presiding over business growth and enhancing shareholder value. They also claim that a successful business rests upon a 'deep respect for individuals' and the communities within which they live. What strategy or strategies will Ben & Jerry's need to adopt in order to achieve these goals?

Ben & Jerry's was formed in 1978 by Ben Cohen and Jerry Greenfield. In 2000, it was taken over by Unilever, the Anglo-Dutch multinational, but still maintains its identity and its mission. Since its early years Ben & Jerry's has managed to increase sales year on year and, with the exception of 1994, the company has returned a consistent profit. However, as the mission statement suggests, the founders of Ben & Jerry's were in search of more than profits from their business activities. With a clear philosophy of social responsibility, the business strategy has been one in which the search for profit has been regulated by a wider set of social and environmental goals.

13.1 What is strategy?

Defining strategy

Football teams use strategy to help them win on the playing field. Generals employ strategy on the battlefield in order to outwit their opponents. Students are taught strategy in order to help them pass exams. Businesses use strategy in an attempt to be more competitive than their rivals. Sometimes strategies are successful: football teams and generals leave the field victorious, students pass exams and businesses outperform their competitors. But new opponents, new subjects and new market conditions may require new strategies. Different football teams, like armies, have differing strengths and weaknesses, and distinct strategies may be required to overcome them. Likewise business must respond to changes in its environment, adapting to circumstances, exploiting its opportunities and minimising threats to its vulnerabilities.

Key Idea 20 p235

Sometimes strategies fail. Football teams and generals are defeated, and students do not pass their exams. If lucky they might have the opportunity to play, fight or retake their exam on another day to make up for their mistakes. Likewise a business will hope it gets the opportunity to change strategy in an attempt to regain its competitive position.

Clearly the term 'strategy' can mean different things depending upon how it is used. In an attempt to capture the diversity of the term, Henry Mintzberg (1987) suggests that we need to look at the 'five Ps' of strategy. A strategy can be:

- a **plan**
- a **ploy**
- a **pattern** of behaviour
- a **position** with respect to others
- a **perspective**

A *plan*

This represents the most common use of the term strategy. It involves, as Mintzberg states' a 'consciously intended course of action to deal with a situation'. Plans most commonly operate over a given period of time, in which the business outlines where it would like to be at a given point in the future. This might be in terms of its market share or its level of profitability, or some other combination of criteria upon which business progress or success might be evaluated. As such, plans tend to focus on long-term issues facing the business rather than operational details.

A *ploy*

In contrast to the long-term nature of the plan, strategy as a ploy is generally short term in its application. It often focuses on a specific manoeuvre by business in order to outwit or counteract the behaviour of rivals. Aggressive pricing policy and the use of special offers by supermarkets is a frequently adopted ploy to gain, or more commonly protect, market share. Such strategy has limited objectives and is liable to frequent changes.

A *pattern of behaviour*

Rather than a consciously planned framework of action, business strategy may in fact emerge naturally from a consistent response to events: e.g. introducing a new product variety each year. Such consistent action forms a pattern of behaviour, which takes on a strategic form. Such strategies tend to evolve as circumstances change. There is no clear long-term objective; unlike plan and ploy, here strategy just happens.

A position with respect to others

Here strategy is determined by the position of the business in its market. For example, a firm may attempt to gain or defend market share. Thus a car company such as BMW may set out to defend its position as a manufacturer of high quality motorcars by focusing on design and performance in its product development and advertising campaigns. Conversely, Asda Wal-Mart might focus on defending and developing its claim to have some of the lowest prices in grocery retailing.

A perspective

In this respect strategy is based upon establishing a common way of perceiving the world, primarily within the organisation itself. This will not only impact upon employee behaviour but fundamentally shape and influence how the business operates. Businesses with strong ethical and environmental objectives, such as Ben & Jerry's, would see a shared perspective as an important part of their business strategy. Employees are encouraged to take on board the company's philosophy. This, it is hoped, will not only contribute to the business's success through motivation and commitment, but also encourage employees to feel good about what they do.

Mintzberg notes in his analysis of the term 'strategy' that businesses might adopt any number of approaches to strategic behaviour. Pursuing strategy as a plan, for example, does not preclude using strategy as a ploy or as a position in respect to others. Businesses may interpret strategy in a number of ways simultaneously. What these different understandings of strategy do is to enable us to analyse different aspects of business behaviour and organisation.

Strategic management

For most of the time most managers have as their primary function the managing of the routine day-to-day activities of the business, such as dealing with personnel issues, checking budgets and looking for ways to enhance efficiency. In other words, they are involved in the detailed operational activities of the business.

Some managers, however, especially those high up in the business organisation, such as the managing director, will be busy in a different way, thinking about big, potentially complex issues, which affect the whole company. For example, they might be analysing the behaviour of competitors, or evaluating the company's share price or considering ways to expand the business. In other words, these managers are involved in the strategic long-term activities of the business.

Both types of management are equally important in the management process, as each contributes in its own way to the business's overall success. However, what is clear is that strategic and operational management are quite distinct managerial functions.

BOX 13.1

Sashimi theory
Business the Samsung way

The following extracts are taken from two articles from *BusinessWeek*. They sketch an outline of some of the strategic initiatives undertaken by one of the most successful consumer electronic firms of recent times, Samsung.

Samsung's recent success is quite an achievement, given the massive financial problems it faced following the Asian financial crisis in the late 1990s. Since that time it has managed not only to shake off its debts and post significant improvements in profits, but to reposition itself upmarket within the consumer electronics industry.

How has Samsung achieved this? What have been the keys to its success? The following extracts are from *Samsung's 'Sashimi Theory' of Success* (11 June 2003).

Yun Jong Yong has a vivid way of describing his survival strategy in today's hypercompetitive consumer-electronics market, where today's hot-selling novelty can become a cheap commodity within months. The vice-chairman and CEO of Samsung Electronics calls it the 'sashimi theory'. When prime fish is first caught, it's very expensive at a top-notch Japanese restaurant. If some of the fish is left over, it sells the next day for half the price at a second-tier restaurant. By the third day, it goes for one-fourth the price. 'After that,' Yun says, 'it's dried fish.'

So the secret to success in consumer electronics is getting the most advanced products onto retail shelves ahead of the competition. That way, you can charge premium prices – until the rest of the pack catches up and the product is no longer fresh. 'In our business, there's money to be made if you can reduce the lead time to customers,' Yun says. 'If I can reduce that time by one week, it makes a big difference. If you're two months late to the market, the game is finished.'

Few electronics companies are doing a better job than Samsung at keeping their products from turning into yesterday's sashimi. Samsung has been consistently hitting global markets with cutting-edge cell phones, widescreen TVs, memory chips, and video cameras ahead of its main rivals, enabling it to charge some of the highest prices in the industry.

It's a dramatic change for a company that just six years ago was in perilous financial shape and whose brand was mainly associated with low-end TVs and air conditioners.

...Yun took aggressive measures to clean up Samsung's finances. He laid off 24 000 employees – about 30% of Samsung Electronics' payroll – and sold off $2 billion worth of corporate assets. In another break from tradition, Yun ordered Samsung's consumer-appliance factories shut for several months.

...Samsung had always been obsessed with boosting production and sales volume. After the Asia crisis, it took careful stock of where all the output went and discovered it had four months' worth of inventory of TVs, computers, and other products sitting in offshore warehouses. The value of the excess inventory was more than $2 billion.

...[A major step was] reducing inventory cycles. At one point in 1996, prices of DRAMs – which then accounted for 60% of Samsung's exports – were dropping by 1% every week, or by 50% each year. The longer the chips sat in inventory, the lower the price they fetched on the market. By dramatically shrinking the period between which an electronics product is made and the time it's sold, therefore, Samsung was able to reap higher average prices.

...Another key to the turnaround was Samsung's decision to recreate itself as an up-market brand. Not only would it spend heavily on more sophisticated marketing and focus on producing high-end phones and appliances but Yun also declared that Samsung would completely abandon low-end products, even if that meant passing up easy opportunities for big sales.

The following extracts are from *The Samsung Way* (16 June 2003).

A few measures of Samsung's progress: it has become the biggest maker of digital mobile phones using code division multiple access (CDMA) technology – and while it still lags no. 2 Motorola Inc. in handsets sold, it has just passed it in overall global revenues. A year ago, you'd have been hard pressed to find a Samsung high-definition TV in the US. Now, Samsung is the best-selling brand in TVs priced at $3000 and above – a mantle long held by Sony and Mitsubishi Corp. In the new market for digital music players, Samsung's three-year-old Yepp is behind only the Rio of Japan's D&M Holdings Inc. and Apple Computer Inc.'s iPod. Samsung has blown past Micron Technology, Infineon Technologies, and Hynix Semiconductor in dynamic random-access memory (DRAM) chips – used in all PCs – and is gaining on Intel in the market for flash memory, used in digital cameras, music players, and handsets. In 2002, with most of techdom reeling, Samsung earned $5.9 billion on sales of $33.8 billion.

... Rather than outsource manufacturing, the company sinks billions into huge new factories. Instead of bearing down on a few 'core competencies', Samsung remains diversified and vertically integrated – Samsung chips and displays go into its own digital products.

... Yet the industrial history of the past two decades suggests that this model does not work in the long run. The hazard – as many Japanese, US, and European companies learned in the 1980s and '90s – is that Samsung must keep investing heavily in R&D and new factories across numerous product lines. Samsung has sunk $19 billion over five years into new chip facilities. Rivals can buy similar technologies from other vendors without tying up capital or making long-term commitments. What's more, the life cycle of much hardware is brutally short and subject to relentless commoditization. The average price of a TV set has dropped 30% in five years; a DVD player goes for less than a quarter. The Chinese keep driving prices ever lower, leveraging supercheap wages and engineering talent. Meanwhile, the Japanese are building their own Chinese factories to lower costs. No wonder Samsung exited the low-margin market for TV sets 27 inches and under.

Faced with these perils, Samsung needs a constant stream of well-timed hits to stay on top.

... Samsung's strategy to win is pretty basic, but it's executing it with ferocious drive over a remarkably broad conglomerate.

... Samsung managers who have worked for big competitors say they go through far fewer layers of bureaucracy to win approval for new products, budgets, and marketing plans, speeding up their ability to seize opportunities.

... Second, Samsung often forces its own units to compete with outsiders to get the best solution. In the liquid-crystal-display business, Samsung buys half of its color filters from Sumitomo Chemical Co. of Japan and sources the other half internally, pitting the two teams against each other.

... The next step is to customize as much as possible. Even in memory chips, the ultimate commodity, Samsung commands prices that are 17% above the industry average. A key reason is that 60% of its memory devices are custom-made for products like Dell servers, Microsoft Xbox game consoles, and even Nokia's cell phones.

The final ingredient is speed. Samsung says it takes an average of five months to go from new product concept to rollout, compared to 14 months six years ago.

This year alone, Samsung will launch 95 new products in the US, including 42 new TVs. Motorola plans to introduce a dozen new cell-phone models, says Technology Business Research Inc. analyst Chris Foster. Samsung will launch 20. Nokia also is a whiz at snapping out new models. But most are based on two or three platforms, or basic designs. The 130 models Samsung will introduce globally this year are based on 78 platforms. Whereas Motorola completely changes its product line every 12 to 18 months, Foster says, Samsung refreshes its lineup every nine months. Samsung has already introduced the first voice-activated phones, handsets with MP3 players, and digital camera phones that send photos over global system for mobile (GSM) communications networks.

Questions

1 *Identify the main features of Samsung's recent business strategy.*

2 *Given Mintzberg's 5 P's, which would you say fit(s) Samsung's approach to strategy most closely and why?*

Strategic management comprises three main components.

- *Strategic analysis* is concerned with examining those factors, both present and future, which are likely to affect the business's performance. These could include internal factors such as the development of business skills and knowledge, and external factors, such as the competitive environment and changes in technology. It also involves considering how the business's vision and mission might influence its future direction.

- *Strategic choice*, by contrast, is primarily concerned with the formulation and evaluation of alternative courses of action that might be adopted in order to achieve the business's strategic objectives. What strategic choices are available? How suitable are such strategies, given constraints such as time, cost and the business's values?

- *Strategic implementation* is concerned with how strategic choices might be put into effect. In other words, it considers how a strategy might be translated into action. Who is responsible for its implementation? How is its success or otherwise to be monitored?

In the following sections of this chapter we are going to consider these three dimensions of strategic management and the issues they raise for the conduct of business. Before we do so, it is worth considering what strategic management means for different business types. How might businesses differ in respect to their analysis, choice and implementation of strategy?

Big business/small business

The strategic requirements of a small local computer assembler and Microsoft are clearly going to be massively different. A small business, operating in a niche market, providing a limited range of products or services, would certainly not require the complex strategic assessment of a large business operating in many markets and providing a whole range of products. Not only would the strategy for a small business be generally simpler, it would probably be easier to formulate, given that the managers of small businesses are often the owners and generally the principal creators of the businesses strategy.

Manufacturing business/service provider business

Although in many respects the strategic commitments of both a manufacturer and a service-sector business might be similar, in some crucial respects the focus of strategy will differ. Manufacturers will tend to focus a large part of their strategy effort on product issues (technology, design, inputs, etc.), whereas service providers will tend to focus on strategic issues related to the customer, especially in the area of retailing.

Domestic business/multinational business

The crucial difference in strategic thinking between a domestic business and a multinational business concerns the geographic spread of the multinational corporation. The multinational will need to focus its strategy not only in global terms but possibly within the context of each international market within which it operates. Depending upon the diversity of these markets, this may require a quite distinct strategic approach within each. Similarly, a business serving a national market will have more complex strategic issues to consider than one serving a local market.

Private-sector business/public-sector business

Quite clearly the strategic considerations of the National Health Service will in many respects be quite different from, say, Rolls Royce, but how different will they be from those of BUPA, the private-sector medical care provider? Increasingly public-sector organisations, like their private-sector counterparts, are having to adopt a more business-orientated approach to service provision. Stakeholders may be different and profit may not be the principal motivation of business activity, but efficiency, targets and accountability are increasingly becoming public-sector as well as private-sector organisational goals.

For-profit organisations/not-for-profit organisations

Not-for-profit business such as charities are essentially based upon a mission underpinned by principles of value. In shaping their strategic goals such values will be paramount in shaping the direction and focus of strategic behaviour.

Strategic analysis   13.2

In this section we examine the factors that determine a firm's strategic choices. Take the case of Ben & Jerry's. Clearly their proclaimed ethical stance will limit potential strategic avenues; also the nature of their supply chain is likely to affect not only the quality of the product but the ability of the company to develop and grow.

Strategic choices also depend on the business environment. How much competition does the firm face and what forms does it take? What other external factors, such as laws and regulations, technological changes and changes in consumer tastes, are likely to affect the firm's decisions?

The business environment

In Chapter 1 we considered the various dimensions of the business environment and how they shape and influenced business activity. We divided the business environment into four distinct sets of factors: political, economic, social and technological. Such factors comprise what we call a PEST analysis. In this section we will take our analysis of the business environment forward and consider more closely those factors that are likely to influence the competitive advantage of the organisation.

The Five Forces Model of competition

Developed by Professor Michael Porter of Harvard Business School in 1980, the Five Forces Model sets out to identify those factors which are likely to affect an organisation's competitiveness (see Figure 13.1). This then helps a firm choose an appropriate strategy to enhance its competitive opportunities and to protect itself from competitive threats. The five forces that Porter identifies are:

- the bargaining power of suppliers;
- the bargaining power of buyers;
- the threat of potential new entrants;
- the threat of substitutes;
- the extent of competitive rivalry.

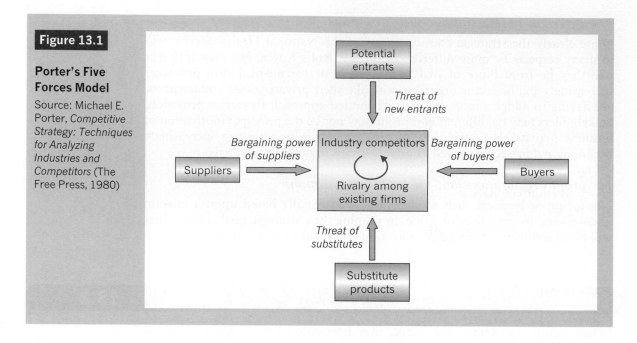

Figure 13.1

Porter's Five Forces Model

Source: Michael E. Porter, *Competitive Strategy: Techniques for Analyzing Industries and Competitors* (The Free Press, 1980)

The bargaining power of suppliers. Most business organisations depend upon suppliers to some extent, whether to provide raw materials or simply stationery. Indeed, many businesses have extensive supply or 'value chain' networks (as we shall discuss in section 13.3). Such suppliers can have a significant and powerful effect on a business when:

Key Idea 18 p211

- there are relatively few suppliers in the market, reducing the ability of the firm to switch from one supply source to another;
- there are no alternatives to the supplies they offer;
- the prices of suppliers form a large part of the firm's total costs;
- a supplier's customers are small and fragmented and as such have little power over the supplying business.

Car dealers often find that car manufacturers can exert considerable pressure over them in terms of pricing, display and after-sales service.

The bargaining power of buyers. The bargaining power of companies that purchase a firm's products will be greater when:

- these purchasing companies are large and there are relatively few of them;
- there are many other firms competing for their custom, and hence a firm that produces an undifferentiated product is likely to be more prone to 'buyer power' than one that produces a unique or differentiated product;
- the costs for the purchasing companies of switching to other suppliers are low;
- purchasing companies are able to backward integrate and effectively displace the supplying firm.

The UK grocery-retailing sector is dominated by a small number of large supermarket chains such as Tesco, Sainsbury and Asda Wal Mart. These exert massive levels of buyer power over farmers and food processors. Not only do such supermarkets dominate the market, but they can normally find many alternative supply sources, both domestic and international, at relatively little switching cost. Also, all the supermarkets sell own-brand labels, either produced themselves or through agreement with existing manufacturers, and these are often sold at prices considerably below those of equivalent branded products (see Box 8.1 on page 146).

The threat of potential new entrants. The ability of new entrants to enter the marketplace depends largely upon the existence and effectiveness of various barriers to entry. These barriers to entry were described fully in section 11.3 (pages 220–2), but are listed here as a reminder.

■ Economies of scale and scope

■ Product differentiation

■ Capital requirements

■ Lower costs of established firm

■ Ownership of/control over key factors of production

■ Ownership of/control over wholesale or retail outlets

■ Legal protection

■ Aggressive tactics and retaliation

Barriers to entry tend to be very industry, product and market specific. Nevertheless two useful generalisations can be made. First, companies with products that have a strong brand identity will often attempt to use this form of product differentiation to restrict competition; second, manufacturers will tend to rely on economies of scale and low costs as a basis for restricting competitive pressure.

The threat of substitutes. The availability of substitutes can be a major threat to a business and its profitability. Issues that businesses need to consider in relation to the availability of substitute products are:

■ the ability and cost to customers of switching to the substitute;

■ the threat of competitors bringing out a more advanced or up-to-date product;

■ the impact that substitute products are likely to have on pricing policy.

The market for video recorders and videotape is a good example of one that has been greatly affected by the arrival of a substitute in the form of DVD players and recorders. As DVD players have fallen in price, the prices of video players and videotapes have plummeted. Early switching costs, such as those of obtaining DVDs, are slowly being overcome as DVD recorders have entered the market. Clearly video recorders and tape are facing imminent obsolescence.

The extent of competitive rivalry. The previous two chapters focused on market structure and were primarily concerned with how businesses respond to differing levels of competition. Clearly the degree of competition a firm faces is a crucial element in shaping its strategic analysis. Competitive rivalry will be enhanced when there is the potential for new firms to enter the market, when there is a real threat from substitute products and when buyers and suppliers have some element of influence over the firm's performance. In addition to this, competitive rivalry is likely to be enhanced in the following circumstances:

■ Competitors are of equal size.

■ Markets are growing slowly. This makes it difficult to acquire additional sales without taking market share from rivals.

Hybrid strategy
Stuck in the middle?

Michael Porter, in his analysis of alternative business strategies, suggested that it could be disastrous for a business to be 'stuck in the middle', having no clear strategic direction. Attempting both to differentiate its product and to offer lower prices would be a serious strategic error. According to Porter, consumers would be confused, as the business would have no clear market identity to which they could relate. His advice was to pick one strategy and stick with it exclusively.

But is a single generic strategy always the best choice? Is a mixed strategy always inappropriate? Consumers often demand a range of product characteristics that cover not only issues such quality and reliability, but also price and convenience. As such, businesses are often forced to adopt a strategic position that attempts to capture both difference and low prices simultaneously.

Hybrid theories that focus on a combination of strategy are greatly influenced by the market within which business is operating. Grocery retailing in the UK offers a clear example of hybrid strategy. The various supermarket chains not only look to differentiate themselves from their rivals in terms of the look and feel of their stores, customer service, and loyalty schemes such as Sainsbury's Nectar card and Tesco's Clubcard, but also compete fiercely over price.

Then there is the range of their products. At the 'bottom' end of the range, with their own-branded 'basic' products, the supermarkets compete primarily in terms of price. But with more up-market products, they compete in terms of the variety of lines stocked and their quality.

Questions

1 *Choose three supermarket chains and identify the strategy or strategies they adopt.*

2 *Do you feel the classification of business strategy options into cost leadership, differentiation and focus is adequate to describe the strategic approaches businesses might adopt?*

- There are high fixed costs, which require the firm gaining a large market share to break even.
- Productive capacity in an industry increases in large increments, often resulting in over production in the short term. This adds to competitive pressure by putting downward pressure on prices.
- Product differentiation is difficult to achieve; hence product switching by consumers is a real threat.
- There exist high exit costs. When a business invests in non-transferable fixed assets, such as highly specialist capital equipment, it may be reluctant to leave a market. It may thus compete fiercely to maintain its market position. On the other have, as we have seen in the section on contestable markets (page 225), high exit costs may deter firms from entering a market in the first place and thus make the market less contestable.
- There exists the possibility for merger and acquisition. This competition for corporate control may have considerable influence on the firm's strategy.

Limitations of the Five Forces Model

One of the great values of the Five Forces Model is that it creates a structured framework for a business to analyse the strategic issues that it faces. However, it does have a number of weaknesses.

First, the Five Forces Model presents a largely static view of the business environment, whereas in reality it is likely to be constantly changing.

Second, the model starts from the premise that the business environment is a competitive threat to the business organisation, which, if the business is to be successful, needs to be manipulated in particular ways. Often, however, success might be achievable not via competition but rather through co-operation and collaboration. For example, a business might set up close links with one of its major buyers; or businesses in an industry might establish links either to build barriers or share costs via some form of collaborative research and development. In such instances, the business environment of the Five Forces Model might be viewed as a collaborative opportunity rather than a competitive threat. The section on strategic alliances in Chapter 15 (section 15.7) will offer a fuller evaluation of collaborative business agreements.

Finally, critics of the model argue that it fails to take sufficient account of the microenvironment of the organisation and its human resources. For example, factors such as country culture and management skills might have a decisive impact on a firm's choice of strategy and its successful implementation.

Value chain analysis and sustainable competitive advantage

As with the Five Forces Model, value chain analysis was developed by Michael Porter, and as such the two concepts are closely related. A **value chain** shows how value is added to a product as it moves through each stage of production: from the raw material stage to its purchase by the final consumer. Value chain analysis is concerned with evaluating how each of the various operations within and around an organisation, such as handling inputs, manufacturing the product and marketing it, contributes to the competitive position of the business. Ultimately it is these value-creating activities which shape a firm's strategic capabilities. A firm's value chain can be split into two separate sets of activities: primary and support (see Figure 13.2).

definition

Value chain
The stages or activities that help to create product value.

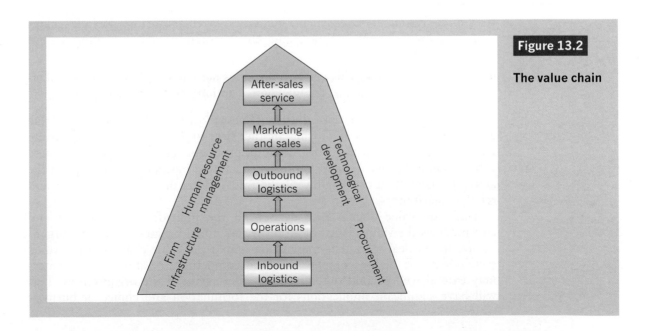

Figure 13.2

The value chain

Primary activities

Primary activities are those directly concerned with the production, distribution and sales of the firm's product. Such primary activities can be grouped into five categories:

- *Inbound logistics*. Here we are concerned with the handling of inputs, storage and distribution of such inputs throughout the business.
- *Operations*. These activities involve the conversion of inputs into the final product or service. Operations might include manufacturing, packaging and assembly.
- *Outbound logistics*. These are concerned with transferring the final product to the consumer. Such activities would include warehousing and transport.
- *Marketing and sales*. This section of the value chain is concerned with bringing the product to the consumer's attention and would involve product advertising and promotion.
- *Service*. This can include activities such as installation and repair, as well as customer requirements such as training.

A business might attempt to add value to its activities by improving its performance in one or more of the above categories. For example, it might attempt to lower production costs or be more efficient in outbound logistics.

Support activities

Such primary activities are underpinned by support activities. These are activities that do not add value directly to any particular stage within the value chain. They do, however, provide support to such a chain and ensure that its various stages are undertaken effectively. Support activities include:

- *Procurement*. This involves the acquisition of inputs by the firm.
- *Technological development*. This includes activities within the business that support new product and process developments, such as the use of research departments.
- *Human resource management*. Activities in this category include things such as recruitment, training, and the negotiation and determination of wage rates.
- *Firm infrastructure*. This category includes activities such as financial planning and control systems, quality control and information management.

As well as creating value directly themselves, most firms buy in certain value chain activities, such as employing another firm to do its advertising, or using an external delivery firm to distribute its products. The outsourcing of these activities might prove to be far more beneficial to a business than providing the activities itself. You can employ the best advertisers or the most efficient and reliable distributors.

Thus the value system extends beyond the individual organisation and encompasses the value chains of all those individual businesses that the organisation might deal with. The implication is that the value chain and the value system may be highly complex, and the competitive position of a business may extend well beyond the immediate value chain of the organisation. This will have significant implications for the formulation and choice of business strategy.

Vision and mission

So far in our assessment of those factors that are likely to influence a firm's choice of strategy, we have focused on both the external influences of the business environment, and the internal implications of value chain analysis. In addition to such external and internal conditions, we need to consider how a firm's vision and mission might affect its strategic behaviour.

At the beginning of this chapter, we referred to the mission statement of Ben & Jerry's in which the company clearly expresses a purpose for its business: a purpose that goes far beyond simply making a profit. Such wider social, environmental and ethical considerations are increasingly shaping business thinking, as expectations regarding corporate responsibility grow. It is now widely expected that a business must look beyond 'the bottom line' (i.e. profitability) and take account of the interests of a wide group of stakeholders, such as employees, customers, creditors and the local community, and not just the owners of the business. It would be a risky business strategy indeed that pursued profit without taking into account the social, environmental and ethical implications that this might entail. As such, the formulation of strategy must take into account the purpose of the organisation and the values and objectives that such a purpose involves. Organisational purpose is most often found in a business's mission statement, which is in turn shaped by a number of distinct influences (see Figure 13.3).

Corporate governance

Corporate governance refers to the way in which a business is run and the structure of decision taking. It also includes the monitoring and supervising, and in some cases regulation, of executive decisions. The way a business is run depends on the purposes of the business and in *whose interests* it is run.

Stakeholders

Stakeholders differ in power and influence, but ultimately they might all shape the purpose of the organisation in certain respects. Given the wide number of stakeholders, many conflicts of interest can arise.

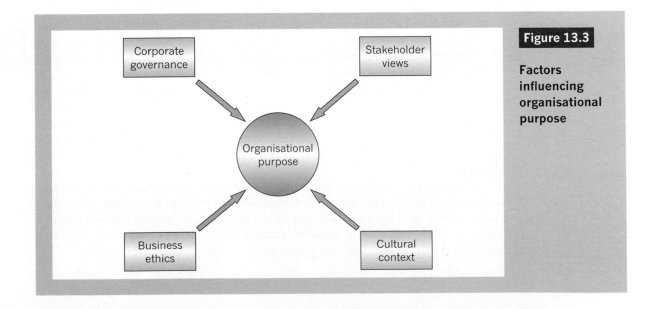

Figure 13.3

Factors influencing organisational purpose

Business ethics

A business's ethical position, might, as in the case of Ben & Jerry's, be driven by the values of its founders. Alternatively, ethics might be determined and shaped by wider cultural values and standards regarding what is and what is not acceptable behaviour. As previously remarked, business today would find it very difficult to pursue a strategy that failed to exhibit a degree of social responsibility. A number of recent high profile cases such as those regarding Nike, Reebok and Royal Dutch Shell, in which ethical standards were sacrificed in the pursuit of profit, has had a significant impact on their reputation and standing in both the business community and society in general. All three companies are trying to clean up their image and present a more socially responsible approach to business. They recognise that ethically sound behaviour is good for business and the bottom line.

Cultural context

How does the cultural context of the organisation influence its objectives? Not only will national culture be significant here, but also the subculture of managers will be significant. Wider questions are also raised given the growth in multinational business activity, and the cross-cultural nature of such organisations. Recognising such differing cultural contexts might be crucial in shaping business success within such increasingly global markets.

> **Pause for thought**
>
> *Give some examples of cultural differences between countries or regions which might influence business strategy.*

With the background to strategic analysis defined, we can now shift our focus to consider strategic choice and implementation. What strategies are potentially open to businesses and how do they choose the right ones and set about implementing them?

13.3   Strategic choice

Theories of strategic choice fall into two main categories: market based and resources based.

Market-based theories argue that strategic choices are ultimately determined by the competitive environment that the business faces. As such, understanding this competitive environment and identifying appropriate ways to deal with it will determine whether you are successful or not.

Key Idea
1
p9

Resource-based theory also looks at the firm's competitive position, but focuses on its internal situation. It considers how strategic decision making is affected by the ownership, control and use of an organisation's resources. It is seen that such resources ultimately deliver profits and it is through a manipulation of such resources that a business can maintain and enhance its competitive position.

Clearly market- and resource-based explanations of strategic choice overlap and interact, and in practice, most businesses will attempt to evaluate *both* their resource base and the threats posed by competitors. However, the two types of explanation do address the issue of strategic choice from quite distinct starting points and this, as we shall see, affects the strategic solutions they offer.

Environment or market-based strategy

As with many other areas in this field, our analysis of market-based theory starts with the observations of Michael Porter. As an extension of his Five Forces Model of competition, Porter argued that there are three fundamental (or 'generic') strategies that a business might adopt:

■ Cost leadership
■ Differentiation
■ Focus

In order to identify which of these was the most appropriate strategy, a business would need to establish two things: (a) the basis of its competitive advantage – whether it lies in lower costs or differentiation; (b) the nature of the target market – is it broad or a distinct market niche?

Cost leadership

As the title implies, a business that is a low-cost leader is able to manufacture and deliver its product more cheaply than its rivals, thereby gaining competitive advantage. The strategic emphasis here is on driving out inefficiency at every stage of the value chain. 'No-frills' budget airlines, such as easyJet and Ryanair, are classic examples of companies that pursue a cost-leadership strategy.

A strategy based upon cost leadership may require a fundamentally different use of resources or organisational structure if the firm is to stay ahead of its rivals. Wal-Mart's hub and spoke distribution system would be an example in point. Here the company distributes its products to shops from regional depots in order to minimise transport costs.

In addition, firms which base their operations on low costs in order to achieve low prices (although that may not necessarily be the aim of low costs), are unlikely to have a high level of brand loyalty. In other words, if customer choice is going to be driven largely by price, demand is likely to be relatively price elastic. Other virtues of the product that might tie in buyers, such as quality or after-sales service, are largely absent from such firms' strategic goals.

Differentiation

A differentiation strategy aims to emphasise and promote the uniqueness of the firm's product. As such, high rather than low prices are often attached to such products. Product characteristics such as quality, design and reliability are the basis of the firm's competitive advantage. Hence a strategy that adds to such differences and creates value for the customer needs to be identified.

Such a strategy might result in higher costs, especially in the short term, as the firm pursues constant product development through innovation, design and research. However, with the ability to charge premium prices, revenues may increase more than costs: in other words, the firm may achieve higher profits. Games console manufacturers, such as Sony with its Playstation and Microsoft with its X Box, are a good example. Even though they are in fierce competition with each other, both manufacturers focus their strategy on trying to differentiate their products from their rival's. This differentiation is in terms of features and performance, not price. Processor speed, online capabilities, software support and product image are all characteristics used in the competitive battle.

Differentiation strategies are not, however, risk free. Pricing differentiated products can be problematic. At what point does the price premium for the product deter potential buyers, such that the differentiated nature of the product is insufficient to outweigh such price considerations? The fact that tastes and fashion change could also have a significant impact upon the sales of a differentiated product. Laura Ashley clothing was a case in point. In an attempt to differentiate itself from other high street clothing rivals, Laura Ashley promoted a strategy producing rather exclusive good quality clothing for women, that was very feminine and rooted in a country lifestyle. During the early 1980s Laura Ashley's profits grew as its differentiated product attracted a large following. But the fickle nature of fashion had turned by the early 1990s and Laura Ashley's fashion products were seen as dated and stuffy. Its differentiated product and brand image had become somewhat of a liability – something which the company has worked hard to change ever since.

Focus strategy

Rather than considering a whole market as a potential for sales, a focus strategy involves identifying market niches and designing and promoting products for such niches. Such a strategy may or may not be applicable to other niches. As such, a business might pursue any number of different strategies simultaneously for different market niches. In such cases a business that does not hold a competitive advantage in a market in general, may be able to identify distinct market segments in which it might exploit some advantage it might have over its rivals, whether in terms of costs, or product difference. Ben & Jerry's ice cream would be a case in point. The mass low cost ice cream market is served by a number of large multinational food manufacturers and processors, but the existence of niche high quality ice cream markets offers opportunities for companies like Ben & Jerry's and Hagen Daaz. By focusing on such consumers they are able to sell and market their product at premium prices.

Niche markets, however profitable, are by their nature small and as such limited in their growth potential. Hence firms that focus upon niche market opportunities are likely to have limited growth prospects. There is also the possibility that niches shift or over time disappear. This would require business to be flexible in setting out their strategic position.

Sometimes a focus strategy may be combined with a cost-leadership strategy to develop a niche market into a mass market. Amazon.com, the online bookseller, was until relatively recently, a business that had a clear cost focus strategy. With low overheads it was able to sell books at knockdown prices to online customers (its niche market segment) and over time, thanks to lower costs, lower prices and the spread of the Internet, this has become a mass market.

Resource-based strategy

Resource-based strategy, as already mentioned, focuses on exploiting a firm's internal organisation and production processes in order to develop its competitive advantage. It is the firm's *distinctiveness* that sets it apart from its competitors. If a business does not have a distinctive feature then it needs to set about creating one.

Core competencies

definition
Core competence
The key skills of a business that underpin its competitive advantage.

Core competencies are those skills, knowledge and technologies that underpin the organisation's competitive advantage. These competencies are likely to differ from one business to another, reflecting the uniqueness of each individual organisation, and ultimately determining its potential for success. Given these differences, how does a firm select an appropriate strategy?

When a firm has unique competencies, its strategy should seek to exploit these, whether in the design of the product or in its methods of production. In many cases, however, firms do not have any competencies that give them a distinctive competitive advantage, even though they may still be profitable. In such instances, strategy often focuses upon either developing such resources or more effectively using the resources the firm already has.

What defines a core competence?

A core competence must satisfy the following four capabilities to serve as a source of competitive advantage for the business. It must be:

- *Valuable*: a competence that helps the firm deal with threats or contributes to business opportunities.
- *Rare*: a competence or resource that is not possessed by competitors.
- *Costly to imitate*: a competence or resource that other firms find difficult to develop and copy.
- *Non-substitutable*: a competence or resource for which there is no alternative.

Clearly then, whether we adopt a market-based view of strategic choice or a resource-based view will have significant implications for how a firm can develop and exploit competitive advantage.

> **Pause for thought**
>
> *Referring back to Box 13.1, what core competencies does Samsung have? Remember, you must justify a core competence in terms of all four listed criteria.*

Before we consider issues of how to implement strategy, there is one dimension of the business environment that we need to consider and that is the impact of globalisation on the world economy in general and business activity in particular. Few businesses have been left untouched by the phenomenon. So how has globalisation affected strategic analysis and strategic choice?

Business strategy in a global economy   13.4

In many respects a firm's global strategy is simply an extension of its strategy within its own domestic market. However, opening up to global markets can present many new business opportunities: access to new markets, new customers, new supply sources, new ideas and skills. In addition to such opportunities, the global marketplace can also present competitive threats, as new market entrants from abroad arrive with lower costs, innovative products and marketing, or some other core competency which the domestic firm finds difficult to match. In this section we explore the strategic implications for business in facing up to the global economic system.

Why go global?

The following are reasons why a business may wish to expand beyond its domestic market.

Market size

International markets can potentially offer a business massive new opportunities for growth and expansion. Such markets would be particularly attractive to a business where domestic growth opportunities are limited as a result of either the maturity of the market or shifting consumer taste. Businesses that conduct extensive research and development (R&D) would also be attracted to larger markets as potential returns can be used to offset the firm's R&D investment costs and risk.

Increased profitability

Expanding beyond the domestic economy offers a number of opportunities for increasing profits.

Location economies. The internationalisation of a firm's value chain would enable it to place each value-creating activity in the most appropriate or effective geographic location. So if production costs are lower in one country it could locate production there. If another country has the specialist skills to offer superior product design and research facilities, then these functions could be located there. Nike, the US training shoe and sportswear manufacturer, under- takes all its manufacturing at production sites in south-east Asia. However, product innovation and research, along with marketing and promotion, are all undertaken in the USA. As businesses relocate many dimensions of their value chain, the structure and organisation of the business takes on a web-like appearance, with its various opera- tions being spread throughout the world.

> **Pause for thought**
>
> *Identify some of the potential strengths and weaknesses of businesses having their value chains located in a variety of different countries.*

Scope for significant cost reductions. It is widely observed that over the life cycle of a product a firm's average costs fall. This is partly the result of economies of scale as the firm gets bigger and plants can specialise in particular functions. Clearly, these cost reductions can be greater by expanding globally.

Cost reductions over time are also the result of what is known as 'learning by doing'. This is where skills and productivity improve with experience. Such learning effects apply not only to workers in production, sales, distribution, etc., but also to managers, who learn to develop more efficient forms of organisation. When a firm expands globally, there may be more scope for learning by doing. For example, if a firm employs low-cost labour in developing countries, initially the lower cost per worker will to some extent be offset by lower productivity. As learning by doing takes place, and productivity increases, so initial small cost advantages may become much more substantial.

Using core competencies. A firm may be able to exploit its core competencies in competing effectively in global markets. The firm might look to expanding first in those countries where it has a clear competitive advantage over already estab- lished companies. Wal-Mart's logistic expertise is one example of a business that might exploit such an advantage in particular overseas markets.

Learning from experience in diverse markets. Successful businesses will learn from their global operations, copying or amending production techniques, organ- isation, marketing, etc. from one country to another as appropriate. In other words, they can draw lessons from experiences in one country for use in another.

Spreading risk (diversification)

Clearly one of the main reasons a business might have for going global is to spread risk, avoiding being overly reliant on any specific market or geographic

Key Idea
13
p98

region. As such, falling profitability in one region of the global economy might be effectively offset by improved or more favourable economic conditions elsewhere. A large number of German and Japanese businesses have diversified globally in order to reduce their reliance on domestic markets, which in recent years have been growing very slowly and, in the case of Japan, has been suffering from a significant squeeze on prices. For example, Toyota and Honda, the two largest Japanese car manufacturers, both showed record profits for 2002 despite the depressed state of the Japanese economy. They were able to do this by focusing on production in foreign markets – in particular the USA, where three-quarters of the cars sold by Honda and Toyota are also manufactured.

Keeping up with rivals

Increasingly it seems that the globalisation of business is like a game of competitive leapfrog, with businesses having to look overseas in order to maintain their competitive position in respect to their rivals. A fiercely competitive global environment, in which small cost differences or design improvements can mean the difference between business success and failure, ensures that strategic thinking within a global context is high on the business agenda.

It would seem at this point we need to raise a few notes of caution regarding the adoption of a global strategy. It is clearly not without its potential pitfalls. Within any global strategy there exists a high degree of both economic and political risk. Investing in developing economies or emerging markets, such as China, is likely to be much riskier than investing in developed market economies. However, it is often within emerging markets that the greatest returns are achieved. It is essentially this trade-off between potential returns and risk that a firm needs to consider in its strategic decisions.

A global business will need a strategy for effectively embracing foreign cultures and traditions into its working practices, and for devising an efficient system for global logistics. Some businesses may be more suited to deal with such global issues than others.

The global strategy trade-off

A firm's drive to reduce costs and enhance profitability by embracing a global strategy, is tempered by one critical consideration – the need to meet the demands of customers in foreign markets. To minimise costs, a firm may seek to standardise its product and its operations throughout the world. However, to meet foreign buyers' needs and respond to local market conditions, a firm may be required to differentiate both its product and its operations, such as marketing. In such cases, customisation will *add* to costs and generate a degree of duplication within the business. If a business is required to respond to local market conditions in many different markets, it might be faced with significantly higher costs. But if it fails to take into account the uniqueness of the market in which it wishes to sell, it may lose market share.

The trade-off between the cost reduction and local responsiveness can be a key strategic consideration for a firm to take into account when selling or producing overseas. As a general rule we will tend to find that cost pressures will be greatest in those markets where price is the principal competitive weapon. Where product differentiation is high, and attributes such as quality or some other non-price factor predominates within the competitive process, local responsiveness will tend to shape business thinking. In other words cost considerations will tend to be secondary.

13.5 Strategy: evaluation and implementation

Evaluation

In deciding what strategy to pursue, global or otherwise, the business will need to evaluate the alternatives open to it. How feasible are they? Are they acceptable strategic goals given the business's mission and vision and other stakeholder demands? How will the strategy contribute to the business's competitive position?

If the choice of strategy is deliberate or prescriptive, i.e. planned in advance, then evaluation tools such as investment appraisal and cost–benefit analysis (CBA) might be used to help identify the best strategy (see section 19.3). Most strategies, however, tend to be emergent: in other words, they evolve over time as conditions change and as the success or otherwise of the firm's decisions become apparent. The result is that techniques such as investment appraisal have limited value, given the incomplete information available at the time an appraisal is conducted.

Key
Idea

7
p50

Implementation

When a business considers implementing a strategy this often involves an assessment of three areas:

- resourcing;
- business culture and structure;
- managing change.

Resourcing

All businesses will need to evaluate the resource implications of their strategic choices. What resources will be required? Where might such resources be drawn from within the organisation? What new resources will need to be brought into the organisation? From where will the finance for such resources come? Predictably, the more adventurous the strategy, the greater the impact on resources it is likely to have.

Business culture and structure

Similarly, the more radical the strategic shift, the greater the impact this is likely to have on a business's culture and structure. Is the organisation of the business flexible enough to adapt to the new strategic demands placed upon it? This might be particularly relevant if the strategic shift in the business is towards a greater focus on the global marketplace.

Managing change

Managing change can be both difficult and time consuming. With change often comes uncertainty for employees, especially if the changes are not understood or managers are not trusted. The more the uncertainty, the more difficult managing change becomes. In addition to barriers to change from employees, there may be organisational barriers. Entrenched power structures and control systems may be quite unsuitable for the new strategy. There may need to be fundamental organisational restructuring before the new strategy can be implemented.

In this chapter we have introduced you to the basic principles underpinning the determination, choice and evaluation of business strategy. This is a massive subject area, and we can but hope to cover a small fraction of the material here. However, from what we have covered you can see how the market environment in which a business operates has a significant impact on its strategic behaviour – and it is such behaviour that ultimately determines its success.

As we have seen, one key factor in determining a business's choice of strategy is its vision and mission – in other words, its aims. In traditional microeconomic theory the firm is assumed to aim for maximum profit. In the next chapter we turn to 'alternative theories of the firm'. These examine the effects of pursuing aims other than simple profit maximisation, especially on prices and output.

SUMMARY

1a Strategy can be understood in many ways. It can be a plan, a ploy, a pattern of behaviour, a position in respect to others, a perspective, or any combination of them.

1b Strategic management differs from operational management (the day-to-day running of the business) as it focuses on issues which affect the whole business, usually over the long-term.

1c Strategic management is composed of three components: strategic analysis (factors affecting business performance), strategic choice (the formulation and evaluation of alternative sources of action), and strategic implementation (how strategic choices are put into effect).

1d Different strategic issues will face different types of businesses, depending on whether they are large or small, manufacturing or service providers, domestic or multinational, private sector or public sector, and whether they are for-profit or not-for-profit organisations.

2a The Five Forces Model of competition identifies those factors that are most likely to influence the competitive environment of a business. The five forces are: the bargaining power of suppliers, the bargaining power of buyers, the threat of potential new entrants, the threat of substitutes, and the extent of competitive rivalry.

2b The weakness of the Five Forces Model is that it is not only a static view of the business environment, but that it does not see the business environment as a collaborative opportunity but merely a competitive threat. Critics also argue that it underplays the impact of country culture and management skills on strategic choice and implementation.

2c A business value chain shapes its strategic capabilities. The value chain can be split into primary and support activities. Primary activities are those that directly create value, such as operations and marketing and sales. Support activities are those that underpin value creation in other areas, such as procurement and human resource management.

2d A business's vision and mission is shaped by a number of considerations: in whose interest the business is run, the influence of different stakeholder groups, the prevailing ethical expectations of society or the business owners, and the cultural context of the environment in which the organisation operates.

3a Strategic choices are determined either by the competitive nature of the environment within which the organisation operates, or by the internal resources controlled by the business. Strategic choice often involves a consideration of both internal and external factors.

3b Environment- or market-based strategies are of three types: cost-leadership strategy, where competitiveness is achieved by lower costs; differentiation strategy, where the business promotes the uniqueness of its product; focus strategy, where competitiveness is achieved by identifying market niches and tailoring products for different groups of consumers.

3c The resource-based view of strategy involves identifying core competencies as the key to a business's competitive advantage. A core competence will be valuable, rare, costly to imitate and non-substitutable.

4a A firm might go global in order to increase market size, increase profitability, spread risk and keep up with rivals.

4b When a firm does go global it must weigh up the potential benefits against ensuring they meet the local markets needs. There is a trade-off between cost reduction and local responsiveness.

5a The impact of a chosen strategy is difficult to evaluate, as the strategy often evolves over time as conditions change.

5b When implementing a strategy, a business must consider the following: the resource implications of the strategic choice, how the strategic choice might fit (or not fit) into existing business culture and structure, and the difficulties in managing the change resulting from the new strategic direction of the business.

REVIEW QUESTIONS

1 What do you understand by the term 'business strategy'?

2 Explain why different types of business will see strategic management in different ways? Give examples.

3 Outline the Five Forces Model of competition. Identify both the strengths and weaknesses of analysing industry in this manner.

4 Distinguish between a business's primary and support activities in its value chain. Why might a business be inclined to outsource its support activities? Can you see any weaknesses in doing this?

5 Explain what is meant by a business's vision and mission? What implications might different missions have for its strategic decision making?

6 Distinguish between a market-based and a resource-based view of strategic choice.

7 What do you understand by the term 'core competence' when applied to a business?

8 How might going global affect a business's strategic decision making?

9 'Going global, thinking local'. Explain this phrase, and identify the potential conflicts for a business in behaving in this way.

10 Why is the choice of business strategy and its potential for success difficult to evaluate?

11 When implementing a business strategy what issues does it raise for a firm?

14 Alternative theories of the firm

14.1 Problems with traditional theory

The traditional profit-maximising theories of the firm have been criticised for being unrealistic. The criticisms are mainly of two sorts: (a) that firms wish to maximise profits, but for some reason or other are unable to do so; or (b) that firms have aims other than profit maximisation. Let us examine each in turn.

Difficulties in maximising profit

One criticism of traditional theory sometimes put forward is that firms do not use *MR* and *MC* concepts. This may be true, but firms could still arrive at maximum profit by trial and error adjustments of price, or by finding the output where *TR* and *TC* are furthest apart. Provided they end up maximising profits, they will be equating *MC* and *MR*, even if they do not know it! In this case, traditional models will still be useful in predicting price and output.

Lack of information

The main difficulty in trying to maximise profits is a lack of information.

Firms may well use accountants' cost concepts not based on opportunity cost (see section 9.1). If it is thereby impossible to measure true profit, a firm will not be able to maximise profit except by chance.

More importantly, firms are unlikely to know precisely (or even approximately) their demand curves and hence their *MR* curves. Even though (presumably) they will know how much they are selling at the moment, this only gives them one point on their demand curve and no point at all on their *MR* curve. In order to make even an informed guess about marginal revenue, they must have some idea of how responsive demand will be to a change in price. But how are they to estimate this price elasticity? Market research may help. But even this is frequently very unreliable.

Key Idea 7 p50

The biggest problem in estimating the firm's demand curve is in estimating the actions and reactions of *other* firms and their effects. Collusion between oligopolists or price leadership would help, but there will still be a considerable area of uncertainty, especially if the firm faces competition from abroad or from other industries.

Game theory may help a firm decide its price and output strategy: it may choose to sacrifice the chance of getting the absolute maximum profit (the high-risk, maximax option), and instead go for the safe strategy of getting probably

Key Idea 20 p235

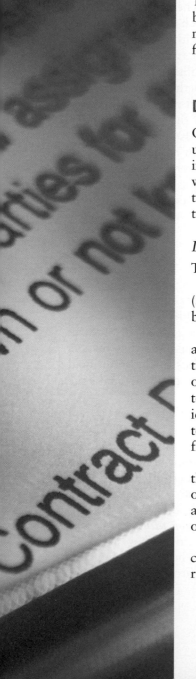

Pause for thought

What cost concepts are there other than those based on opportunity cost? Would the use of these concepts be likely to lead to an output greater or less than the profit-maximising one?

at least reasonable profits (maximin). But even this assumes that it knows the consequences for its profits of each of the possible reactions of its rivals. In reality, it will not even have this information to any degree of certainty, because it simply will not be able to predict just how consumers will respond to each of its rivals' alternative reactions.

Time period

Finally, there is the problem in deciding the *time period* over which the firm should be seeking to maximise profits. Firms operate in a changing environment. Demand curves shift; supply curves shift. Some of these shifts occur as a result of factors outside the firm's control, such as changes in competitors' prices and products, or changes in technology. Some, however, change as a direct result of a firm's policies, such as an advertising campaign, the development of a new improved product, or the installation of new equipment. The firm is not, therefore, faced with static cost and revenue curves from which it can read off its profit-maximising price and output. Instead it is faced with a changing (and often highly unpredictable) set of curves. If it chooses a price and an output that maximise profits this year, it may as a result jeopardise profits in the future.

Take a simple example. The firm may be considering whether to invest in new expensive equipment. If it does, its costs will rise in the short run and thus short-run profits will fall. On the other hand, if the quality of the product thereby increases, demand is likely to increase over the longer run. Also variable costs are likely to decrease if the new equipment is more efficient. In other words, long-run profit is likely to increase, but probably by a highly uncertain amount.

Given these extreme problems in deciding profit-maximising price and output, firms may adopt simple rules of thumb for pricing. These are examined in Chapter 17.

Alternative aims

An even more fundamental attack on the traditional theory of the firm is that firms do not even *aim* to maximise profits (even if they could).

The traditional theory of the firm assumes that it is the *owners* of the firm that make price and output decisions. It is reasonable to assume that owners *will* want to maximise profits: this much most of the critics of the traditional theory accept. The question is, however, whether the owners do in fact make the decisions.

In Chapter 3 we saw that in public limited companies there is generally a separation of ownership and control. The shareholders are the owners and presumably will want the firm to maximise profits so as to increase their dividends and the value of their shares. Shareholders elect directors. Directors in turn employ professional managers, who are often given considerable discretion in making decisions. But what are the objectives of managers? Will *they* want to maximise profits, or will they have some other aim?

Managers may be assumed to want to *maximise their own utility*. This may well involve pursuits that conflict with profit maximisation. They may, for example, pursue higher salaries, greater power or prestige, better working conditions, greater sales, etc. Different managers in the same firm may well pursue different aims.

Managers will still have to ensure that *sufficient* profits are made to keep shareholders happy, but that may be very different from *maximising* profits.

Alternative theories of the firm to those of profit maximisation, therefore, tend to assume that large firms are **profit satisficers**. That is, managers strive hard for a minimum target level of profit, but are less interested in profits above this level.

Such theories fall into two categories: first those theories that assume that firms attempt to maximise some other aim, provided that sufficient profits are achieved (these are examined in section 14.2); and second, those theories that assume that firms pursue a number of potentially conflicting aims, of which sufficient profit is merely one (these theories are examined in section 14.3).

> **definition**
>
> **Profit satisficing**
> Where decision makers in a firm aim for a target level of profit rather than the absolute maximum level.

Alternative maximising theories   14.2

Long-run profit maximisation

The traditional theory of the firm is based on the assumption of *short-run* profit maximisation. Many actions of firms may be seen to conflict with this aim and yet could be consistent with the aim of **long-run profit maximisation**. For example, policies to increase the size of the firm or the firm's share of the market may involve heavy advertising or low prices to the detriment of short-run profits. But if this results in the firm becoming larger, with a larger share of the market, the resulting economic power may enable the firm to make larger profits in the long run.

At first sight, a theory of long-run profit maximisation would seem to be a realistic alternative to the traditional short-run profit-maximisation theory. In practice, however, the theory is not a very useful predictor of firms' behaviour and is very difficult to test.

A claim by managers that they were attempting to maximise long-run profits could be an excuse for virtually any policy. When challenged as to why the firm had, say, undertaken expensive research, or high-cost investment, or engaged in a damaging price war, the managers could reply, 'Ah, yes, but in the long run it will pay off.' This is very difficult to refute (until it is too late!).

Even if long-run profit maximisation *is* the prime aim, the means of achieving it are extremely complex. The firm will need a plan of action for prices, output, investment, etc., stretching from now into the future. But today's prices and marketing decisions affect tomorrow's demand. Therefore, future demand curves cannot be taken as given. Similarly, today's investment decisions will affect tomorrow's costs. Therefore, future cost curves cannot be taken as given. These shifts in demand and cost curves will be very difficult to estimate with any precision. Quite apart from this, the actions of competitors, suppliers, unions and so on are difficult to predict. Thus the picture of firms making precise calculations of long-run profit-maximising prices and outputs is a false one.

It may be useful, however, simply to observe that firms, when making current price, output and investment decisions, try to judge the approximate effect on new entrants, consumer demand, future costs, etc., and try to avoid decisions that would appear to conflict with long-run profits. Often this will simply involve avoiding making decisions (e.g. cutting price) that may stimulate an unfavourable reaction from rivals (e.g. rivals cutting their price).

> **definition**
>
> **Long-run profit maximisation**
> An alternative theory which assumes that managers aim to shift cost and revenue curves so as to maximise profits over some longer time period.

In search of long-run profits
The video games war

Traditional economic theory argues that firms will seek to maximise their short-run profits, and therefore adopt a range of strategies to achieve this goal. There are, however, plenty of examples from the world of business to suggest that firms often take a longer-term perspective. One example, is the long-running video games war between Sony, Nintendo and, most recently, Microsoft.

The industry is dominated by Sony and its Playstation 2. By the end of 2002 it had sold over 50 million units since its launch in March 2000. In joint second place, and launched at about the same time are Microsoft's Xbox and Nintendo's Game Cube. Since 2001 they have both sold about 10 million consoles.

The market for game consoles is an interesting one, as it appears to have its own cycle that is quite distinct from the broader economic cycle of the economy. Console purchases are strongly linked to new console developments, which occur every few years. In addition

Each gaming boom is bigger than the last. Children who have grown up with games keep on playing, which expands the market.... It also increases the player's average age: according to the Interactive Digital Software Association, the average American gamer is 28. Older players tend to have more disposable income to spend on games than do teenagers.[1]

This would explain why sales of gaming hardware and software continue to expand. In 2002 it reached an all-time high in the UK of £2.1m, an 8 per cent increase on the previous year. Product development has also been influenced by this trend towards older gamers. Mature-rated games now account for 13 per cent of the American market, up 6 per cent on 2001.

Even given the market's staggering growth, it has proved to be fiercely competitive. The launch price of Microsoft's XBox in March 2002 was £299. Just one year later it was £129.99 – a fall of 56 per cent. However, even with such aggressive price-cutting, XBox's market share has remained largely unaffected.

Question

Why has Microsoft's pricing strategy for its XBox proved to be so ineffective? Could, in fact, the reduction in price be detrimental to the XBox?

Managerial utility maximisation

definition

Managerial utility maximisation
An alternative theory which assumes that managers are motivated by self-interest. They will adopt whatever policies are perceived to maximise their own utility.

One of the most influential of the alternative theories of the firm has been that developed by O.E. Williamson[1] in the 1960s. Williamson argued that, provided satisfactory levels of profit are achieved, managers often have the discretion to choose what policies to pursue. In other words, they are free to pursue their own interests. And what are the managers' interests? To maximise their own utility, argued Williamson.

Williamson identified a number of factors that affect a manager's utility. The four main ones were salary, job security, dominance (including status, power and prestige) and professional excellence.

Of these only salary is *directly* measurable. The rest have to be measured indirectly. One way of doing this is to examine managers' expenditure on various items, and in particular on *staff*, on *perks* (such as a company car and a plush office) and on *discretionary investment*. The greater the level of expenditure by managers on these items, the greater is likely to be their status, power, prestige, professional excellence and job security, and hence utility.

---

[1] *The Economics of Discretionary Behaviour* (Prentice Hall, 1964), p. 3.

In an attempt to capture new markets and lead the field in gaming technology innovation, the three main protagonists are locked in battles not only to produce new and improved consoles, but also to develop online gaming and mobile gaming – two major growth areas.

The growth in online gaming is heavily dependent on the development and spread of broadband Internet connections. Both Microsoft and Sony have invested heavily in developing an online gaming capability. Microsoft in particular intends to develop its XBox Live online service, into a 'digital entertainment centre', through which to distribute a range of entertainment content, including films and music.

Mobile gaming, a gaming niche dominated by Nintendo and its Gameboy, is also facing new competitive pressure. Sony is set to enter the market in 2004 with its own mobile gaming handset. Nokia, the mobile phone manufacturer, entered the market in October 2003 with its Ngage hybrid phone, which has gaming capability.

Until the next generation of consoles appear in 2005/6, these two market areas are likely to be the source of most competition between the gaming industry's major players. All three companies – Sony, Microsoft and Nintendo – know that, to be successful in the gaming industry, you must look to the long term and constantly seek to innovate.

It would be a poor business strategy not to look to the future in this ever changing market, and so long as competition remains, and products need replacing over a period of time, then long-run profits are likely to be the goal rather than the maximisation of profits over the short run.[2]

Questions

1 *How does the maximisation of long-run profits conflict with the maximisation of short-run profits?*

2 *What factors might favour collusion in the video games market? What factors might make collusion unlikely?*

---

[1] 'Strong players', *The Economist*, 12 December 2002
[2] *Financial Times*, 1–2 March 1997

Having identified the factors that influence a manager's utility, Williamson developed several models in which managers seek to maximise their utility. He used these models to predict managerial behaviour under various conditions and argued that they performed better than traditional profit-maximising theory.

One important conclusion was that average costs are likely to be higher when managers have the discretion to pursue their own utility. For example, perks and unnecessarily high staffing levels add to costs. On the other hand, the resulting 'slack' allows managers to rein in these costs in times of low demand (see page 285). This enables them to maintain their profit levels. To support these claims he conducted a number of case studies. These did indeed show that staff and perks were cut during recessions and expanded during booms, and that new managers were frequently able to cut staff without influencing the productivity of firms.

Sales revenue maximisation (short run)

Perhaps the most famous of all alternative theories of the firm is that developed by William Baumol in the late 1950s. This is the theory of **sales revenue maximisation.** Unlike the theories of long-run profit maximisation and managerial

> **definition**
>
> **Sales revenue maximisation**
> An alternative theory of the firm which assumes that managers aim to maximise the firm's short-run total revenue.

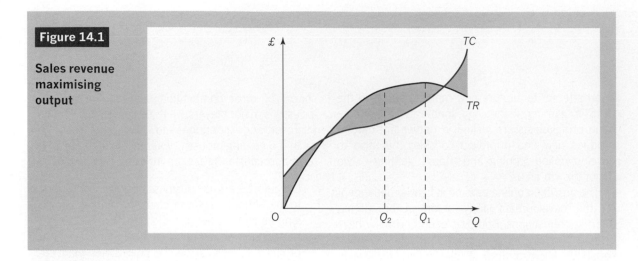

Figure 14.1

Sales revenue
maximising
output

utility maximisation, it is easy to identify the price and output that meet this aim – at least in the short run.

So why should managers want to maximise their firm's sales revenue? The answer is that the success of managers, and especially sales managers, may be judged according to the level of the firm's sales. Sales figures are an obvious barometer of the firm's health. Managers' salaries, power and prestige may depend directly on sales revenue. The firm's sales representatives may be paid commission on their sales. Thus sales revenue maximisation may be a more dominant aim in the firm than profit maximisation, particularly if it has a dominant sales department.

Sales revenue will be maximised at the top of the TR curve at output Q_1 in Figure 14.1. Profits, by contrast, would be maximised at Q_2. Thus, for given total revenue and total cost curves, sales revenue maximisation will tend to lead to a higher output and a lower price than profit maximisation.

The firm will still have to make sufficient profits, however, to keep the shareholders happy. Thus firms can be seen to be operating with a profit constraint. They are *profit satisficers*.

The effect of this profit constraint is illustrated in Figure 14.2. The diagram shows a total profit curve. (This is found by simply taking the difference between TR and TC at each output.) Assume that the minimum acceptable profit is Π (whatever the output). Any output greater than Q_3 will give a profit less than Π. Thus the sales revenue maximiser who is also a profit satisficer will produce Q_3 not Q_1. Note, however, that this output is still greater than the profit-maximising output Q_2.

If the firm could maximise sales revenue and still make more than the minimum acceptable profit, it would probably spend this surplus profit on advertising to increase revenue further. This would have the effect of shifting the TR curve upward and also the TC curve (since advertising costs money).

Sales revenue maximisation will tend to involve more advertising than profit maximisation. Ideally the profit-maximising firm will advertise up to the point where the marginal revenue of advertising equals the marginal cost of advertising (assuming diminishing returns to advertising). The firm aiming to maximise sales revenue will go beyond this, since further advertising, although costing more than it earns the firm, will still add to total revenue. The firm will continue advertising until surplus profits above the minimum have been used up.

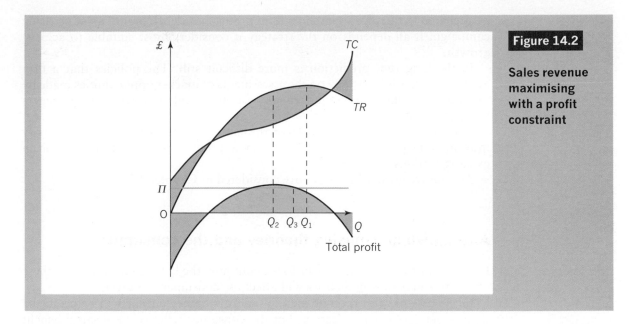

Figure 14.2

Sales revenue maximising with a profit constraint

Growth maximisation

Rather than aiming to maximise *short-run* revenue, managers may take a longer-term perspective and aim for **growth maximisation** in the size of the firm. They may gain utility directly from being part of a rapidly growing 'dynamic' organisation; promotion prospects are greater in an expanding organisation, since new posts tend to be created; large firms may pay higher salaries; managers may obtain greater power in a large firm.

Growth is probably best measured in terms of a growth in sales revenue, since sales revenue (or 'turnover') is the simplest way of measuring the size of a business. An alternative would be to measure the capital value of a firm, but this will depend on the ups and downs of the stock market and is thus a rather unreliable method.

If a firm is to maximise growth, it needs to be clear about the time period over which it is setting itself this objective. For example, maximum growth over the next two or three years might be obtained by running factories to absolute maximum capacity, cramming in as many machines and workers as possible, and backing this up with massive advertising campaigns and price cuts. Such policies, however, may not be sustainable in the longer run. The firm may simply not be able to finance them. A longer-term perspective (say, 5–10 years) may therefore require the firm to 'pace' itself, and perhaps to direct resources away from current production and sales into the development of new products that have a potentially high and growing long-term demand.

Equilibrium for a growth-maximising firm

What will a growth-maximising firm's price and output be? Unfortunately, there is no simple formula for predicting this.

In the short run, the firm may choose the profit-maximising price and output – so as to provide the greatest funds for investment. On the other hand, it may be prepared to sacrifice some short-term profits in order to mount an advertising campaign. It all depends on the strategy it considers most suitable to achieve growth.

In the long run, prediction is more difficult still. The policies that a firm adopts will depend crucially on the assessments of market opportunities made by managers. But this involves judgement, not fine calculation. Different managers will judge a situation differently.

One prediction can be made. Growth-maximising firms are likely to diversify into different products, especially as they approach the limits to expansion in existing markets.

Alternative growth strategies are considered in Chapter 15.

Alternative maximising theories and the consumer

It is difficult to draw firm conclusions about how the behaviour of firms in these alternative maximising theories will affect the consumer's interest.

In the case of sales revenue maximisation, a higher output will be produced than under profit maximisation, but the consumer will not necessarily benefit from lower prices, since more will be spent on advertising – costs that will be passed on to the consumer.

In the case of growth and long-run profit maximisation, there are many possible policies that a firm could pursue. To the extent that a concern for the long run encourages firms to look to improved products, new products and new techniques, the consumer may benefit from such a concern. To the extent, however, that growth encourages a greater level of industrial concentration through merger, so the consumer may lose from the resulting greater level of monopoly power.

As with the traditional theory of the firm, the degree of competition that a firm faces is a crucial factor in determining just how responsive it will be to the wishes of the consumer.

Pause for thought

How will competition between growth-maximising firms benefit the consumer?

Key Idea 18 p211

14.3 Multiple aims

Satisficing and the setting of targets

Firms may have more than one aim. For example, they may try to achieve increased sales revenue *and* increased profit. The problem with this is that, if two aims conflict, it will not be possible to maximise both of them. For example, sales revenue will probably be maximised at a different price and output from that at which profits are maximised. Where firms have two or more aims, a compromise may be for targets to be set for individual aims which are low enough to achieve simultaneously, and yet which are sufficient to satisfy the interested parties.

Such target setting is also likely when the maximum value of a particular aim is unknown. If, for example, the maximum achievable profit is unknown, the firm may well set a target for profit which it feels is both satisfactory and achievable.

Behavioural theories of the firm: the setting of targets

A major advance in alternative theories of the firm has been the development of **behavioural theories**.[2] Rather than setting up a model to show how various objectives could in theory be achieved, behavioural theories of the firm are based on observations of how firms *actually* behave.

Large firms are often complex institutions with several departments (sales, production, design, purchasing, personnel, finance, etc.). Each department is likely to have its own specific set of aims and objectives, which may possibly come into conflict with those of other departments. These aims in turn will be constrained by the interests of shareholders, workers, customers and creditors (collectively known as **stakeholders**), who will need to be kept sufficiently happy.

Behavioural theories do not lay down rules of how to *achieve* these aims, but rather examine what these aims are, the motivations underlying them, the conflicts that can arise between aims, and how these conflicts are resolved.

It is assumed that targets will be set for production, sales, profit, stock holding, etc. If, in practice, target levels are not achieved, a 'search' procedure will be started to find what went wrong and how to rectify it. If the problem cannot be rectified, managers will probably adjust the target downwards. If, on the other hand, targets are easily achieved, managers may adjust them upwards. Thus the targets to which managers aspire depend to a large extent on the success in achieving *previous* targets. Targets are also influenced by expectations of demand and costs, by the achievements of competitors and by expectations of competitors' future behaviour. For example, if it is expected that the economy is likely to move into recession, sales and profit targets may be adjusted downwards.

If targets conflict, the conflict will be settled by a bargaining process between managers. The outcome of the bargaining, however, will depend on the power and ability of the individual managers concerned. Thus a similar set of conflicting targets may be resolved differently in different firms.

definition

Behavioural theories of the firm
Theories that attempt to predict the actions of firms by studying the behaviour of various groups of people within the firm and their interactions under conditions of potentially conflicting interests.

definition

Stakeholders (in a company)
People who are affected by a company's activities and/or performance (customers, employees, owners, creditors, people living in the neighbourhood, etc.). They may or may not be in a position to take decisions, or influence decision taking, in the firm.

Behavioural theories of the firm: organisational slack

Since changing targets often involves search procedures and bargaining processes and is therefore time consuming, and since many managers prefer to avoid conflict, targets tend to be changed fairly infrequently. Business conditions, however, often change rapidly. To avoid the need to change targets, therefore, managers will tend to be fairly conservative in their aspirations. This leads to the phenomenon known as **organisational slack**.

When the firm does better than planned, it will allow slack to develop. This slack can then be taken up if the firm does worse than planned. For example, if the firm produces more than it planned, it will build up stocks of finished goods and draw on them if production subsequently falls. It would not, in the meantime, increase its sales target or reduce its production target. If it did, and production then fell below target, the production department might not be able to supply the sales department with its full requirement.

Thus keeping targets fairly low and allowing slack to develop allows all targets to be met with minimum conflict.

definition

Organisational slack
When managers allow spare capacity to exist, thereby enabling them to respond more easily to changed circumstances.

---

[2] See in particular: R. M. Cyert and J. G. March, *A Behavioural Theory of the Firm* (Prentice Hall, 1963).

BOX 14.2

Stakeholder power?
Who governs the firm?

The concept of the 'stakeholder economy' became fashionable in the late 1990s. Rather than the economy being governed by big business, and rather than businesses being governed in the interests of shareholders (many of whom are big institutions, such as insurance companies and pension funds), the economy should serve the interests of everyone. But what does this mean for the governance of firms?

The stakeholders of a firm include customers, employees (from senior managers to the lowest-paid workers), shareholders, suppliers, lenders and the local and national communities.

The supporters of a stakeholding economy argue that *all* these interest groups ought to have a say in the decisions of the firm. Trades unions or workers' councils ought to be included in decisions affecting the workforce, or indeed all company decisions. They could be represented on decision-making bodies and perhaps have seats on the board of directors. Alternatively, the workforce might be given the power to elect managers.

Banks or other institutions lending to firms ought to be included in investment decisions. In Germany, where banks finance a large proportion of investment, banks are represented on the boards of most large companies.

Local communities ought to have a say in any projects (such as new buildings or the discharge of effluent) that affect the local environment. Customers ought to have more say in the quality of products being produced, for example by being given legal protection against the production of shoddy or unsafe goods. Where interest groups cannot be directly represented in decision making, then companies ought to be regulated by the government in order to protect the interests of the various groups. For example, if farmers and other suppliers to supermarkets are paid very low prices, then the purchasing behaviour of the supermarkets could be regulated by some government agency.

But is this vision of a stakeholder economy likely to become reality? Trends in the international economy suggest that the opposite might be occurring. The growth of multinational corporations, with their ability to move finance and production to wherever it is most profitable, has weakened the power of employees, local interest groups and even national governments.

Employees in one part of the multinational may have little in the way of common interests with employees in another. In fact, they may vie with each other, for example over which plant should be expanded or closed down. What is more, many firms are employing a larger and larger proportion of casual, part-time, temporary or agency workers. With these new 'flexible labour markets' such employees have far less say in the company than permanent members of staff: they are 'outsiders' to decision making within the firm (see section 18.7).

Also, the widespread introduction of share incentive schemes for managers (whereby managers are rewarded with shares), has increasingly made profits their driving goal. Finally, the policies of opening up markets and deregulation, policies that were adopted by many governments round the world up to the mid-1990s, has again weakened the power of many stakeholders.

Question

Are customers' interests best served by profit-maximising firms, answerable primarily to shareholders, or by firms where various stakeholder groups are represented in decision taking?

Organisational slack, however, adds to a firm's costs. If firms are operating in a competitive environment, they may be forced to cut slack in order to survive. In the 1970s, many Japanese firms succeeded in cutting slack by using **just-in-time** methods of production. These involve keeping stocks to a minimum and ensuring that inputs are delivered as required. Clearly, this requires that production is tightly controlled and that suppliers are reliable. Many firms today have successfully cut their warehouse costs by using such methods. These methods are examined in section 18.7.

Multiple goals: some predictions of behaviour

Conservatism

Some firms may be wary of unnecessary change. Change is risky. They may prefer to stick with tried and tested practices. 'If it works, stick with it.' This could apply to pricing policies, marketing techniques, product design and range, internal organisation of the firm, etc.

If something does not work, however, managers will probably change it, but again they may be conservative and only try a cautious change: perhaps imitating successful competitors.

This safe, satisficing approach makes prediction of any given firm's behaviour relatively easy. You simply examine its past behaviour. Making generalisations about all such cautious firms, however, is more difficult. Different firms are likely to have established different rules of behaviour depending on their own particular experiences of their market.

Comparison with other firms

Managers may judge their success by comparing their firm's performance with that of rival firms. For example, growing market share may be seen as a more important indicator of 'success' than simple growth in sales. Similarly, they may compare their profits, their product design, their technology or their industrial relations with those of rivals. To many managers it is *relative* performance that matters, rather than absolute performance.

What predictions can be made if this is how managers behave? The answer is that it depends on the nature of competition in the industry. The more profitable, innovative and efficient are the competitors, the more profitable, innovative and efficient will managers try to make their particular firm.

The further ahead of their rivals that firms try to stay, the more likely it is that there will be a 'snowballing' effect: each firm trying to outdo the other.

> **definition**
>
> **Just-in-time methods**
> Where a firm purchases supplies and produces both components and finished products as they are required. This minimises stock holding and its associated costs.

> **Pause for thought**
>
> *Will this type of behaviour tend to lead to profit maximisation?*

Satisficing and the consumer's interest

Firms with multiple goals will be satisficers. The greater the number of goals of the different managers, the greater is the chance of conflict and the more likely it is that organisational slack will develop. Satisficing firms are therefore likely to be less responsive to changes in consumer demand and changes in costs than profit-maximising firms. They may thus be less efficient.

On the other hand, such firms may be less eager to exploit their economic power by charging high prices, or to use aggressive advertising, or to pay low wages.

The extent to which satisficing firms do act in the public interest will, as in the case of other types of firm, depend to a large extent on the amount and type of competition they face, and their attitudes towards this competition. Firms that compare their performance with that of their rivals are more likely to be responsive to consumer wishes than firms that prefer to stick to well-established practices. On the other hand, they may be more concerned to 'manipulate' consumer tastes than the more traditional firm.

SUMMARY

1a There are two major types of criticism of the traditional profit-maximising theory: (a) firms may not have the information to maximise profits; (b) they may not even want to maximise profits.

1b Lack of information on demand and costs and on the actions and reactions of rivals, and a lack of use of opportunity cost concepts may mean that firms adopt simple 'rules of thumb' for pricing.

1c In large companies there is likely to be a divorce between ownership and control. The shareholders (the owners) may want maximum profits, but it is the managers who make the decisions, and managers are likely to aim to maximise their own utility rather than that of the shareholders. This leads to profit 'satisficing'. This is where managers aim to achieve sufficient profits to keep shareholders happy, but this is a secondary aim to one or more alternative aims.

1d Some alternative theories assume that there is a single alternative aim that firms seek to maximise. Others assume that managers have a series of (possibly conflicting) aims.

2a Rather than seeking to maximise short-run profits, a firm may take a longer-term perspective. It is very difficult, however, to predict the behaviour of a long-run profit-maximising firm, since (a) different managers are likely to make different judgements about how to achieve maximum profits, and (b) demand and cost curves may shift unpredictably both in response to the firm's own policies and as a result of external factors.

2b Managers may seek to maximise their own utility, which, in turn, will depend on factors such as salary, job security, power within the organisation and the achievement of professional excellence. Given, however, that managerial utility depends on a range of variables, it is difficult to use the theory to make general predictions of firms' behaviour.

2c Managers may gain utility from maximising sales revenue. However, they will still have to ensure that a satisfactory level of profit is achieved. The output of a firm which seeks to maximise sales revenue will be higher than that for a profit-maximising firm. Its level of advertising will also tend to be higher. Whether price will be higher or lower depends on the relative effects on demand and cost of the additional advertising.

2d Many managers aim for maximum growth of their organisation, believing that this will help their salaries, power, prestige, etc.

2e As with long-run profit-maximising theories, it is difficult to predict the price and output strategies of a growth-maximising firm. Much depends on the judgements of particular managers about growth opportunities.

3a In large firms, decisions are taken by, or influenced by, a number of different people, including various managers, shareholders, workers, customers, suppliers and creditors. If these different people have different aims, then a conflict between them is likely to arise. A firm cannot maximise more than one of these conflicting aims. The alternative is to seek to achieve a satisfactory target level of a number of aims.

3b Behavioural theories of the firm examine how managers and other interest groups actually behave, rather than merely identifying various equilibrium positions for output, price, investment, etc.

3c If targets were easily achieved last year, they are likely to be made more ambitious next year. If they were not achieved, a search procedure will be conducted to identify how to rectify the problem. This may mean adjusting targets downwards, in which case there will be some form of bargaining process between managers.

3d Life is made easier for managers if conflict can be avoided. This will be possible if slack is allowed to develop in various parts of the firm. If targets are not being met, the slack can then be taken up without requiring adjustments in other targets.

3e Satisficing firms may be less innovative, less aggressive and less willing to initiate change. If they do change, it is more likely to be in response to changes made by their competitors. Managers may judge their performance by comparing it with that of rivals.

3f Satisficing firms may be less aggressive in exploiting a position of market power. On the other hand, they may suffer from greater inefficiency.

REVIEW QUESTIONS

1   In the traditional theory of the firm, decision makers are often assumed to have perfect knowledge and to be able to act, therefore, with complete certainty. It is now widely accepted that in practice firms will be certain about very few things. Of the following: (a) production costs; (b) demand; (c) elasticity; (d) supply; (e) consumer tastes; (f) technology; (g) government policy, which might they be certain of? Which might they be uncertain of?

2   Make a list of six aims that a manager of a high street department store might have. Identify some conflicts that might arise between these aims.

3   When are increased profits in a manager's personal interest?

4   Draw a diagram with *MC* and *MR* curves. Mark the output (a) at which profits are maximised; (b) at which sales revenue is maximised.

5   Since advertising increases a firm's costs, will prices necessarily be lower with sales revenue maximisation than with profit maximisation?

6   We have seen that a firm aiming to maximise sales revenue will tend to produce more than a profit-maximising firm. This conclusion certainly applies under monopoly and oligopoly. Will it also apply under (a) perfect competition and (b) monopolistic competition, where in both cases there is freedom of entry?

7   A frequent complaint of junior and some senior managers is that they are frequently faced with new targets from above, and that this makes their life difficult. If their complaint is true, does this conflict with the hypothesis that managers will try to build in slack?

8   What evidence about firms' behaviour could be used to refute the argument that firms will tend to build in organisational slack and as a result be inherently conservative?

15 Growth strategy

Whether businesses wish to grow or not, many are forced to. The dynamic competitive process of the market drives producers on to expand in order to remain in the marketplace. If a business fails to grow, this may benefit its more aggressive rivals. They may secure a greater share of the market, leaving the first firm with reduced profits. Thus business growth is often vital if a firm is to survive.

The goal of business growth is closely linked to the key objectives of managers. As mentioned in Chapter 14, managerial status, prestige, promotion and salary might be more directly related to such a goal rather than that of profit maximisation. Business growth might also be essential if the business is successfully to manage change and deal with many of the inherent uncertainties of the business environment.

In this chapter we shall consider the various growth strategies open to firms and assess their respective advantages and disadvantages. First, however, we shall need to look at the relationship between a firm's growth and its profitability, and also at those factors which are likely to constrain the growth of the business.

15.1 Growth and profitability

In using traditional theories of the firm, economists often assume that there is a limit to the expansion of the firm: that there is a level of output beyond which profits will start to fall. The justification for this view can be found on both the supply side and the demand side.

On the supply side, it is assumed that if a firm grows beyond a certain size, it will experience rising long-run average costs. In other words, the long-run average cost curve is assumed to be U-shaped, possibly with a horizontal section at the bottom (see page 187). This argument is often based on the assumption that it is *managerial* diseconomies of scale which start driving costs up once a firm has expanded beyond a certain point: there are no more plant economies to be achieved (the firm has passed its **minimum efficient scale (MES)** – see Box 9.4); instead, the firm is faced with a more complex form of organisation, with longer lines of management, more difficult labour relations and a greater possibility of lack of effort going unnoticed.

On the demand side it is assumed that the firm faces a downward-sloping demand curve (and hence marginal revenue curve) for its product. Although this demand curve can be shifted by advertising and other forms of product promotion, finite demand naturally places a constraint on the expansion of the firm.

These two assumptions can be challenged, however. On the supply side, with a multidivisional form of organisation and systems in place for monitoring performance, it is quite possible to avoid diseconomies of scale.

As far as demand is concerned, although the demand (or at least its rate of growth) for any one product may be limited, the firm could diversify into new markets.

It is thus incorrect to say that there is a limit to the size of a business. An individual business may be able to go on expanding its capacity or diversifying its interests indefinitely. There does, however, exist an upper limit on the firm's *rate* of growth – the *speed* at which it can expand its capacity or diversify. The reason behind this constraint is that growth is determined by the profitability of the business. The growth rate/profitability relationship can operate in two ways:

- Growth depends upon profitability. The more profitable the firm, the more likely it is to be able to raise finance for investment.

- Growth affects profitability. In the short run, growth above a certain rate may *reduce* profitability. Some of the finance for the investment necessary to achieve growth may have to come from the firm's sales revenue. A firm wishing to expand its operations in an existing market will require greater advertising and marketing; and a firm seeking to diversify may have to spend considerable sums on market research and employing managers with specialist knowledge and skills. In both cases, investment is likely to be needed in new plant and machinery. In other words, the firm may have to sacrifice some of its short-run profits for the long-run gains that greater growth might yield.

  But what about long-run profits? Will growth increase or decrease these? The answer depends on the nature of the growth. If growth leads to expansion into new markets in which demand is growing, or to increased market power, or to increased economies of scale, then growth may well increase long-run profits – not only total profits, but the rate of profit on capital, or the ratio of profits to revenue. If, however, growth leads to diseconomies of scale, or to investment in risky projects, then growth may well be at the expense of long-run profitability.

To summarise: greater profitability may lead to higher growth, but higher growth, at least in the short run, may be at the expense of profits.

> **definition**
> **Minimum efficient scale (MES)**
> The size of the individual factory or of the whole firm, beyond which no significant additional economies of scale can be gained. For an individual factory the MES is known as the *minimum efficient plant size* (MEPS).

Constraints on growth   15.2

However much a firm may want to grow, it might simply not be possible. There are several factors that can restrict the ability of a business to expand.

> **Pause for thought**
>
> *Before you read on, what constraints on its growth do you feel a business might experience?*

Financial conditions. Financial conditions determine the ability of a firm to fund its growth. Growth can be financed in three distinct ways: from internal funds, from borrowing or from the issue of new shares.

The largest source of finance for investment in the UK is **internal funds** (i.e. ploughed-back profit). The principal limitation in achieving growth via this means is that such funds are linked to business profitability, and this in turn is subject to the cyclical nature of economic activity – to the booms and slumps that the economy experiences. Profitability tends to fall in a recession along

> **definition**
> **Internal funds**
> Funds used for business expansion that come from ploughed-back profit.

with the level of sales. In such times it is often difficult for a firm to afford new investment.

The *borrowing* of finance to fund expansion may be constrained by a wide range of factors, from the availability of finance in the banking sector, to the creditworthiness of the business.

The *issuing of new shares* to fund growth depends not only on confidence within the stock market in general, but on the stock market's assessment of the potential performance of the individual firm in particular. It should be noted that finance from this source is not open to all firms. For most small and medium-sized enterprises (i.e. those not listed on the Stock Exchange), raising finance through issuing new shares must be done privately, and normally this source of finance is very limited.

We will examine the financing of investment in more detail in sections 19.4 and 19.5.

Shareholder confidence. Whichever way growth is financed – internal funds, borrowing or new share issues – the likely outcome in the short run is a reduction in the firm's share dividend. If the firm *retains* too much *profit*, there will be less to pay out in dividends. Similarly, if the firm *borrows* too much, the interest payments that it incurs are likely to make it difficult to maintain the level of dividends to shareholders. Finally, if it attempts to raise capital by a *new issue of shares*, the distributed profits will have to be divided between a larger number of shares. Whichever way it finances investment, therefore, the more it invests, the more the dividends on shares in the short run will probably fall. Unless shareholders are confident that *long*-run profits and hence dividends will rise again, thus causing the share price to remain high in the long run, they may well sell their shares. This will cause share prices to fall. If they fall too far, the firm runs the risk of being taken over and certain managers risk losing their jobs.

This **takeover constraint**, therefore, requires that the growth-maximising firm distribute sufficient profits to avoid being taken over. Hence the rate of business growth is influenced by shareholder demands and expectations and the fear of takeover.

The converse to this situation is also true. If a business fails to grow fast enough, it may be that a potential buyer sees the firm as a valuable acquisition, whose resources might be put to more profitable use over the longer term. Hence businesses must avoid being overcautious and paying high share dividends, but, as a result, failing to invest and failing to exploit their true potential.

The likelihood of takeover depends in large part on the stock market's assessment of the firm's potential: how is the firm's investment strategy perceived to affect its future performance and profitability? The views of the stock market are reflected in the **valuation ratio** of the firm. This is the ratio of the stock market value of the firm's shares (the number of issued shares times the current share price) to the book value of the firm's assets. A low ratio means that the real assets of the business are effectively undervalued: that they can be purchased at a low market price. The business is thus likely to be more attractive to potential bidders. Conversely, firms with a high valuation ratio are seen as overvalued and are unlikely to be the target of takeover bids.

In the long run, a rapidly growing firm may find its profits increasing, especially if it can achieve economies of scale and a bigger share of the market. These profits can then be used to finance further growth. The firm will still not have unlimited finance, however, and therefore will still be faced by the takeover constraint if it attempts to grow too rapidly.

---

definition

Takeover constraint
The effect that the fear of being taken over has on a firm's willingness to undertake projects that reduce distributed profits.

definition

Valuation ratio
The ratio of stock market value to book value. The stock market value is an assessment of the firm's past and anticipated future performance. The book value is a calculation of the current value of the firm's assets.

Demand conditions. Our analysis of business growth has shown that finance for growth is largely dependent upon the business's profitability. The more profit it makes, the more it can draw on internal funds; the more likely financial institutions will be to lend; and the more readily will new share issues be purchased by the market. The profitability of a business is in turn dependent upon market demand and demand growth. If the firm is operating in an expanding market, profits are likely to grow and finance will be relatively easy to obtain.

If, on the other hand, the firm's existing market becomes saturated, it will find that profits and sales are unlikely to rise unless it diversifies into related or non-related markets. One means of overcoming this demand constraint is to expand overseas, either by attempting to increase export sales or by locating new production facilities in foreign markets.

Managerial conditions. The growth of a firm is usually a planned process, and as such must be managed. But the management team might lack entrepreneurial vision, or various organisational skills.

Equally, as with other resources within the business, the management team might grow, or alternatively its composition might change in order to reflect the new needs of the growing business. However, new managers take time to be incorporated into, and become part of, an effective management team. They must undergo a period of training and become integrated into their new firm, as well as join a team of managers accustomed to working together. The rate of growth of business is thus constrained by this process of managerial expansion.

In the sections below we will explore the alternative growth strategies open to businesses and the various advantages and limitations that such strategies present.

> **definition**
> **Internal expansion**
> Where a business adds to its productive capacity by adding to existing or by building new plant.

> **definition**
> **External expansion**
> Where business growth is achieved by merging with or taking over businesses within a market or industry.

> **definition**
> **Product differentiation**
> In the context of growth strategies, this is where a business upgrades existing products or services so as to make them different from those of rival firms.

Alternative growth strategies   15.3

In pursuit of growth, a firm will seek to increase its markets: whether at home or internationally. In either case the firm will need to increase its capacity. This may be achieved by one or both of the following:

- **Internal expansion.** This is where a business looks to expand its productive capacity by adding to existing plant or by building new plant.
- **External expansion.** This is where a business grows by merging with other firms or by taking them over.

Whether the business embarks upon internal or external expansion, a number of alternative growth paths are open to the business. Figure 15.1 shows these various routes.

Internal expansion

In order to achieve additional sales, the business must seek new demand in order to justify investment in additional capacity. There are three main ways of doing this:

- The firm can expand or **differentiate its product** within existing markets, by, for example, updating or restyling its product, or improving its technical characteristics.

> **definition**
> **Vertical integration**
> A business growth strategy that involves expanding within an existing market, but at a different stage of production. Vertical integration can be 'forward', such as moving into distribution or retail, or 'backward', such as expanding into extracting raw materials or producing components.

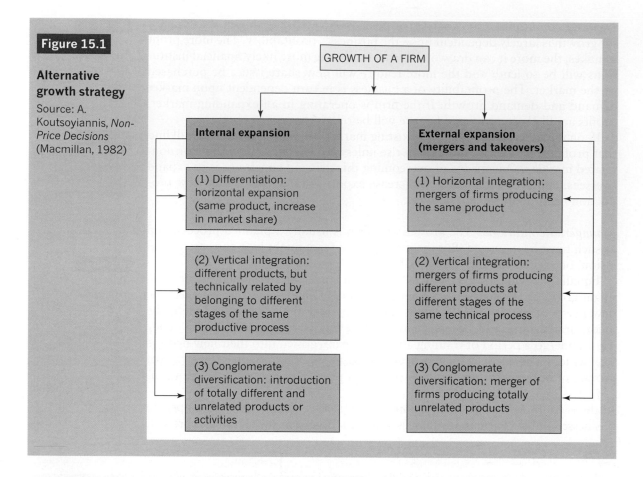

Figure 15.1

Alternative growth strategy

Source: A. Koutsoyiannis, *Non-Price Decisions* (Macmillan, 1982)

GROWTH OF A FIRM

Internal expansion

(1) Differentiation: horizontal expansion (same product, increase in market share)

(2) Vertical integration: different products, but technically related by belonging to different stages of the same productive process

(3) Conglomerate diversification: introduction of totally different and unrelated products or activities

External expansion (mergers and takeovers)

(1) Horizontal integration: mergers of firms producing the same product

(2) Vertical integration: mergers of firms producing different products at different stages of the same technical process

(3) Conglomerate diversification: merger of firms producing totally unrelated products

definition

Diversification
A business growth strategy in which a business expands into new markets outside of its current interests.

definition

Horizontal merger
Where two firms in the same industry at the same stage of the production process merge.

definition

Vertical merger
Where two firms in the same industry at different stages in the production process merge.

- Alternatively, the business might seek to expand via **vertical integration**. This involves the firm expanding within the same product market, but at a different stage of production. For example, a car manufacturer might wish to produce its own components ('backward vertical integration') or distribute and sell its own car models ('forward vertical integration').

- As a third option, the business might seek to expand outside of its current product range, and move into new markets. This is known as a process of **diversification**.

External expansion (growth through mergers and takeovers)

Similar growth paths can be pursued via external expansion. However, in this case the business does not create the productive facilities itself, but purchases existing production. As Figure 15.1 identifies, we can distinguish three types of merger: horizontal, vertical and conglomerate.

- A **horizontal merger** is where two firms at the same stage of production within an industry merge.

- A **vertical merger,** is where businesses at different stages of production within the same industry merge. As such we might identify backward and forward vertical mergers for any given firm involved in the merger.

- A **conglomerate merger** is where firms in totally unrelated industries merge.

A further dimension of business growth that we should note at this point is that all of the above-mentioned growth paths can be achieved by the business looking beyond its national markets. In other words, the business might decide to become multinational and invest in expansion overseas. This raises a further set of issues, problems and advantages that a business might face. These will be discussed in Chapter 23 when we consider multinational business.

We have already considered business expansion through product differentiation in Chapter 8. In this chapter, therefore, we will focus on the other possibilities facing the firm: internal expansion via vertical integration or diversification, and external expansion via merger or takeover (whether horizontal, vertical or conglomerate). We will also investigate the increasing tendency for business to enter into strategic alliances with other businesses as an alternative to all of the above.

definition

Conglomerate merger
Where two firms in different industries merge.

Growth through vertical integration 15.4

Vertical integration, as we have seen, can be of two types: backward or forward. Backward integration (or, as it is sometimes known, 'upstream' integration) involves the business expanding into earlier stages of the production process, such as the extraction or refinement of raw materials or the manufacture of intermediate inputs: for example, various components required for the product's final assembly.

Forward integration (or, as it is sometimes known, 'downstream' integration) involves the business expanding into later stages of production, or into distribution or retailing. Such expansion might involve the business co-ordinating its own haulage and managing its own retail network.

The level or extent of vertical integration within a business is surprisingly difficult to measure. The reason lies in the difficulty of defining exactly what constitutes a 'stage' of production: just how far could the productive process be divided up, such that the individual stages could realistically be undertaken by separate firms? Where does one stage finish and another start? This is a very difficult judgement to make.

One way of assessing the level of vertical integration within a business is to distinguish between its *primary production* operation and its *auxiliary* operations. Auxiliary operations are those stages of production which either supply inputs or contribute to the downstream output of the primary production operation. Once a business's primary production operation is identified, the extent of vertical integration should become more apparent. If we wish to measure the degree of vertical integration, one widely used method is to estimate the ratio of the level of employment in auxiliary production to the total level of employment within the business. The higher this figure, the greater the degree of vertical integration.

A classic example of a vertically integrated firm is a steel manufacturer. Excluding distribution we might argue that there are seven distinct stages of production. These involve: the mining of the ore; the preparation of the ore for use; the smelting of the ore to produce pig iron; the refining of the pig iron to produce steel; the production of semi-finished steel products (the rolling stage); the production of finished steel components, such as pipes; and finally the last stage, fabrication, which involves the manufacture of steel products. If we were to include aspects of distribution and retailing, the stages in steel production would be considerable. We can also see that the steel producer's primary production operation – refining (and possibly smelting) – is in fact a very small part of the overall manufacture of steel products.

Pause for thought

See if you can identify two other companies that are vertically integrated.

Why vertical integration?

We can identify a number of reasons why a business might wish to expand via vertical integration.

Greater efficiency

When vertical integration results in a fall in a business's long-run average costs, it is effectively experiencing various economies of scale. We can identify four categories under which vertical integration might lead to cost savings.

Key
Idea
19
p217

- *Production economies.* These occur when a business, through integration, lowers its costs by performing *complementary* stages of production within a single business unit. The classic example of this is the steel manufacturer combining the furnacing and milling stages of production, saving the costs that would have been required to reheat the iron had such operations been undertaken by independent businesses. Clearly, for most firms, the performing of more than one stage on a single site is likely to reduce transport costs, as semi-finished products no longer have to be moved from one plant to another.

- *Co-ordination economies.* Such economies arise from the internal structure of the business and its ability to transfer intermediate products between its various divisions. The business is able to avoid purchasing and selling expenses, including those related to the marketing and advertising of the product(s).

- *Managerial economies.* Even though each production stage or division might have its own management or administrative team, economies can be gained from having a single source of supervision.

- *Financial economies.* A vertically integrated business may gain various financial economies. Given the link between vertical integration and business size, such companies may be more able to negotiate favourable deals from key suppliers and secure lower borrowing rates of interest from the financial markets.

For a more detailed analysis of economies of scale, you should refer back to Chapter 9.

Reduced uncertainty

A business that is not vertically integrated may find itself subject to various uncertainties in the market place. Examples include: uncertainty over future price movements, supply reliability or access to markets.

Backward vertical integration will enable the business to control its supply chain. Without such integration the firm may feel very vulnerable, especially if there are only a few suppliers within the market. In such cases the suppliers would be able to exert considerable control over price. Alternatively, suppliers may be unreliable.

Forward vertical integration creates greater certainty in so far as it gives the business guaranteed access to distribution and retailing on its own terms. As with supply, forward markets might be dominated by large monopsonists (monopoly buyers) which are able not only to dictate price, but also to threaten market foreclosure (being shut out from a market). Forward vertical integration can remove the possibility of such events occurring.

Monopoly power

Forward or backward vertical integration may allow the business to acquire a greater monopoly/monopsony position in the market. Depending upon the type of vertical integration, the business might be able to set prices both for final products and for factor inputs.

Barriers to entry

Vertical integration may give the firm greater power in the market by enabling it to erect entry barriers to potential competitors. For example, a firm that undertakes backward vertical integration and acquires a key input resource can effectively close the market to potential new entrants, either by simply refusing to supply a competitor, or by charging a very high price for the factor such that new firms face an absolute cost disadvantage.

A further barrier to entry might arise from an increase in the minimum efficient size of the business. As the firm becomes more integrated, it is likely to experience greater economies of scale (i.e. long-run average costs that go on falling below their previous minimum level). New entrants are then forced to come into the market at the level of integration that existing firms are operating under. Failure to do so will mean that new entrants will be operating at an instant cost disadvantage, and hence will be less competitive.

Problems with vertical integration

The major problem with vertical integration as a form of expansion is that the security it gives the business may reduce its ability to respond to changing market demands. A business that integrates, either backward or forward, ties itself to particular supply sources or particular retail outlets. If, by contrast, it were free to choose between suppliers, inputs might be obtained at a lower price than the firm could achieve by supplying itself. Equally, the ability to shift between retail outlets would allow the firm to locate in the best market positions. This may not be possible if it is tied to its own retail network.

As with all business strategy, one course of action may well preclude the pursuit of an alternative. The decision of the business to expand its operations via vertical integration means that resources will be diverted to this goal. The potential advantages from other growth strategies, such as the spreading of risk through diversification, are lost. This is not a problem of vertical integration as such, but it represents the opportunity costs of selecting this strategy to the *exclusion* of others.

Tapered vertical integration

How can a firm gain the benefits of vertical integration but avoid the costs? One alternative means of expansion is **tapered vertical integration**. This is where a business begins producing some of an input itself, while still buying some from another firm (often through subcontracting). This growth strategy is different from a situation where you are relying totally on subcontractors to provide supply (which we will explore in section 15.7). For example, Coca-Cola and Pepsi are large vertically integrated enterprises. They have, as part of their operations, wholly-owned bottling subsidiaries. However, in certain markets they subcontract to independent bottlers both to produce and to market their product.

The advantages of both making and buying an input are:

- The firm, by making an input or providing a service in-house, will have information concerning the costs and profitability of such an operation. Such

definition

Tapered vertical integration
Where a firm is partially integrated with an earlier stage of production: where it produces *some* of an input itself and buys some from another firm.

BOX 15.1

Enron
A cautionary tale of business growth

Not many companies come bigger than Enron, and none bigger has ever filed for bankruptcy, as Enron did on 1 December 2001.

Enron seemed to have everything going for it, being the largest energy trader in the USA with 25 per cent of the market. In 2000, Enron earned $100 billion in revenue and turned a profit of $1 billion. But by the time it filed for bankruptcy, the seventh largest company in the USA had seen its market value collapse from $80 billion to less than $400 million. Its shares fell from a high of $89.50 in the previous year to a meagre 26 cents. How did it all go so wrong so quickly?

Enron was created in 1986, following the merger of two gas pipeline companies, Houston Natural Gas and InterNorth. As US energy and utility markets were deregulated, Enron diversified rapidly into alternative sources of energy supply such as electricity, and established interests in areas such as water. This diversification in Enron's interests was not restricted to the US market. Enron embarked upon a global growth strategy, which involved it in acquiring interests in utilities throughout the world.

As Enron grew, it also shifted its business focus. It gradually reduced its role in gas and oil production,

its traditional core business activities, and moved into the new world of online energy trading. This appeared to have been a wise move, as by November 1999 it had traded more than $1 trillion of electricity and gas online. Enron was, at this time, the largest business on the Internet. So what went wrong?

The weakness in Enron's growth strategy lay in both the speed of its expansion and, most crucially, in how its growth was financed. On declaring bankruptcy in December 2001, the scale of Enron's debts were revealed to be both massive and global. Creditors were estimated to be owed some $18.7 billion (see table).

Clearly, Enron had financed an overwhelming part of its growth through borrowing. As a source of finance for business growth, this only becomes a problem if revenue begins to fall and you are unable to meet the payments on the money owed. Given the public picture presented by Enron, and its apparent success, revenue and profits seemed to be guaranteed. The business was a clear winner. Such a picture would certainly have helped Enron to attract significant amounts of capital to fund its expansion plans.

However, everything was not as it seemed. Enron's financial position was precarious. In October

information helps in the negotiation of contracts with independent producers. In addition, the firm will be able to use the threat of producing more itself to ensure that independent suppliers do not exploit their supply position, which they might be able to do if they held a monopolistic position within the supply chain. The firm is not totally at the mercy of an independent third party over which it has no control.

■ The firm does not require the same level of capital outlay that would be required if it were to rely solely on an input or service produced by itself. As such it is able to externalise some of the costs and risks of its business operations.

The major drawback with this growth strategy is that shared production might fail to generate economies of scale, and is hence less efficient than might otherwise be the case. In other words, if Coca-Cola bottled all its own cola, then it might achieve significantly greater economies of scale then by sharing bottling with other firms. None might be large enough to achieve the efficiency gains that a single production site might generate.

Other significant costs with subcontracting are largely borne by the firm doing the subcontracted work, not by the contractor. Many small and medium-sized enterprises (SMEs), which might see doing subcontracted work for a large firm as a means of expanding their business and hence of growing themselves, find

Who is owed money by Enron	$ millions
JP Morgan	900
Citigroup	800
Credit Lyonnais	250
Bank of Tokyo-Mitsubishi	248
Chubb Corp	220
Canadian Imperial Bank	215
Sumitomo Mitsui Banking Corp	210
Abbey National	164
National Australia Bank	104
Duke Energy Corp	100
Royal Bank of Scotland	855 (estimated)
Barclays Bank	428 (estimated)
Aegon	300 (estimated)

2001, Enron announced unexpected losses, which led it to reduce capital by $1.2 billion. A series of bad investments overseas were held to be the main reason for this decision. The announcement of losses was swiftly followed by the revelation that Enron was to be investigated by the US Securities and Exchange Commission for financial irregularities. It was subsequently revealed that through some accounting loophole Enron had been overstating its earnings since 1997 to the value of some $600 million. Predictably many of Enron's trading partners had by this stage begun to lose confidence in the business and started to pull out of deals.

At this point Dynegy, one of Enron's smaller rivals, agreed to buy the company for $9 billion in stock. However, as more losses were disclosed, and the need to get regulatory approval for the acquisition was established, Dynegy pulled out of the deal. Shareholder confidence had by this point totally collapsed and Enron's credit rating plummeted.

Enron's rise and fall reveals a tale of unsustainable growth and expansion that was bought on debt. It reveals not only the folly of such a strategy, but the need to have a strong system of financial regulation to ensure that a business's true financial position is reflected in its balance sheet.

Questions

1 *Why might a business favour borrowing, as a means of financing growth, over other sources of finance?*

2 *What are the strengths and weaknesses of diversification as a business growth strategy?*

that the relationship between them and the large firm is often a highly unequal one. SMEs find that they not only bear some of the large firm's risk, but are easily expendable. Such vulnerability intensifies, the greater the proportion of the SME's production that is done for a particular customer. When a high level of reliance occurs, the SME finds that its business is, in essence, vertically integrated with its customer, but without the benefits that such a position should confer.

Growth through diversification 15.5

Diversification is the process whereby a firm shifts from being a single-product to a multiproduct producer. Such products need not cover similar activities. We can in fact identify four directions in which diversification might be undertaken:

- Using the existing technological base and market area.
- Using the existing technological base and new market area.
- Using a new technological base and existing market area.
- Using a new technological base and new market area.

Categorising the strategies in this way would suggest that the direction of diversification is largely dependent upon both the nature of technology and the market opportunities open to the firm. But the ability to capitalise on these features depends on the experience, skills and market knowledge of the managers of the business. In general, diversification is likely to occur in areas where the business can use and adapt existing technology and knowledge to its advantage.

A good example of a highly diversified company is Virgin. As we saw in Box 8.1 (page 147), Virgin's interests include planes, trains, cars, finance, music, mobile phones, holidays, wine, cinemas, radio, cosmetics and publishing.

Why diversification?

There are three principal factors which might encourage a business to diversify.

- *Stability*. So long as a business produces a single product in a single market, it is vulnerable to changes in that market's conditions. If a farmer produces nothing but potatoes, and the potato harvest fails, the farmer is ruined. If however, the farmer produces a whole range of vegetable products, or even diversifies into livestock, then he or she is less subject to the forces of nature and the unpredictability of the market. Diversification therefore enables the business to *spread risk*.

    Key Idea 13 p98

- *Maintaining profitability*. Businesses might also be encouraged to diversify if they wish to protect existing profit levels. It may be that the market in which a business is currently located is saturated and that current profitability is perceived to be at a maximum. Alternatively, the business might be in a market where demand is stagnant or declining. In such cases the business is likely to see a greater return on its investment by diversifying into new product ranges located in dynamic expanding markets.

- *Growth*. If the current market is saturated, stagnant or in decline, diversification might be the only avenue open to the business if it wishes to maintain a high growth performance. In other words, it is not only the level of profits that may be limited in the current market, but also the growth of sales.

---

definition

Merger
The outcome of a mutual agreement made by two firms to combine their business activities.

15.6 Growth through merger

A merger is a situation in which, as a result of mutual agreement, two firms decide to bring together their business operations. A **merger** is distinct from a takeover in so far as a **takeover** involves one firm bidding for another's shares (often against the will of the directors of the target firm). One firm thereby acquires another.

The distinction between merger and takeover is an important one. For example, an important difference is that, in order to acquire a firm, a business will require finance, whereas a merger might simply involve two firms swapping their existing shares for shares in the newly created merged company. A further difference might concern managerial relations between the two businesses. A merger implies that managers, through negotiation, have reached an agreement acceptable to both sides, whereas a takeover involves one group of managers, working in opposition to another group, looking to fend off the aggressor. The acquired firm usually finds its management team dismissed following such action!

---

definition

Takeover
Where one business acquires another. A takeover may not necessarily involve mutual agreement between the two parties. In such cases, the takeover might be viewed as 'hostile'.

In order to avoid confusion at this stage, we will use the term 'merger' to refer to *both* mergers ('mutual agreements') and takeovers ('acquisitions'), although where necessary we will draw a distinction between the two.

Why merge?

Why do firms want to merge with or take over others? Is it purely that they want to grow: are mergers simply evidence of the hypothesis that firms are growth maximisers? Or are there other motives that influence the predatory drive?

Merger for growth. Mergers provide a much quicker means to growth than does internal expansion. Not only does the firm acquire new capacity, but also it acquires additional consumer demand. Building up this level of consumer demand by internal expansion might have taken a considerable length of time.

The telecommunications, media and technology (TMT) sector has seen many mergers in recent times where companies in different market segments have come together. The acquisition by America Online (AOL), the Internet group, of Time Warner brought together a firm strong in media distribution with a media content provider. The two businesses were clearly complementary and allowed AOL to grow and expand its range of media-based interests.

Merger for economies of scale. Once the merger has taken place, the constituent parts can be reorganised through a process of 'rationalisation'. The result can be a reduction in costs. For example, only one head office will now be needed. On the marketing side, the two parts of the newly merged company may now share distribution and retail channels, benefiting from each other's knowledge and operation in distinct market segments or geographical locations.

The merger of Airbus Industries' partners, Aerospatiale-Matra of France, DaimlerChrysler Aerospace of Germany and Construcciones Aeronauticas of Spain, is estimated to save, through rationalisation, hundreds of millions of pounds annually. The newly created firm European Aeronautics Space and Defence Company (EADS) owns 80 per cent of Airbus, while BAE Systems of the UK owns the remaining 20 per cent. The rationalisation process was seen by many as necessary if Airbus was effectively to challenge its main rival Boeing of the USA.

In fact, the evidence on costs suggests that most mergers result in few if any cost savings: either potential economies of scale are not exploited due to a lack of rationalisation, or diseconomies result from the disruptions of reorganisation. New managers installed by the parent company are often seen as unsympathetic, and morale may go down.

Merger for monopoly power. Here the motive is to reduce competition and thereby gain greater market power and larger profits. With less competition, the firm will face a less elastic demand and be able to charge a higher percentage above marginal cost. What is more, the new more powerful company will be in a stronger position to regulate entry into the market by erecting effective entry barriers, thereby enhancing its monopoly position yet further.

> **Pause for thought**
>
> *Which of the three types of merger (horizontal, vertical and conglomerate) are most likely to lead to (a) reductions in average costs; (b) increased market power?*

Merger for increased market valuation. A merger can benefit shareholders of *both* firms if it leads to an increase in the stock market valuation of the merged firm. If both sets of shareholders believe that they will make a capital gain on their shares, then they are more likely to give the go-ahead for the merger.

BOX 15.2

Merger activity

A European perspective

Mergers[1] within Europe have been predominantly horizontal rather than vertical or conglomerate. This has led to an increase in concentration within a wide range of manufacturing and service-sector industries in a number of European countries, especially in the UK, France, Germany, Holland and Sweden. Research suggests that such merger activity has led to few gains in efficiency and only minimal improvements in competitiveness.

Main motives for mergers and joint ventures in the EU: 1988/9–1991/2	
Strengthening of market position	648
Expansion	419
Restructuring (including rationalisation and synergy)	158
Complementarity	72
Diversification	55
Co-operation	13
Research and development	3
Other	73
Total cases specifying reasons	1441

Source: *Reports on Competition Policy* (Commission of the European Communities, various years)

Pre-single market (1993)

The table shows the main motives given for industrial mergers and acquisitions in the EU between 1988/9 and 1991/2. Clearly the desire to gain greater market power and market share was the driving force behind mergers in the EU.

For most of the 1980s, the majority of mergers occurring in Europe were within national boundaries. But as inter-EU trade grew and as Europe was increasingly seen by business as a 'single market', so an increasing proportion of mergers were 'cross-border'. The proportion of total EU mergers that were between companies in different member states grew from 8.3 per cent in 1987/8 to 20.5 per cent in 1992/3.

An important factor explaining the increase in inter-EU mergers was the process of dismantling barriers to trade to create a true 'common market' by 1993 (see section 26.3). Firms took the opportunity to establish a European network and restructure their operations as well as to expand productive capacity.

A notable feature of European merger activity was the large size of many of the firms involved. The larger the firms, the more likely they are to be involved in cross-border mergers rather than purely domestic ones. The implication of these trends is that markets are becoming increasingly concentrated.

Since 1993

When the single market came into being in January 1993, many commentators predicted that there would be a new wave of merger activity as companies, faced with new competition, would be forced to rationalise, or would take the opportunity to expand their operations in other EU countries.

As it turned out, the recession gripping Europe caused merger activity initially to decline (see the diagram). The main determinant of merger activity in the short run remains the overall state of the economy. When an economy moves into recession, so merger activity also declines.

After 1994 the growth in mergers in the EU resumed. There were several explanations for this:

■ A recovery in growth throughout the EU.

■ A growing process of 'globalisation'. With the dismantling of trade barriers around the world and increasing financial deregulation, so international competition has increased. Companies have felt the need to become bigger in order to compete more effectively.

■ Falling interest rates, making investment in the stock-market more attractive than saving in a bank.

■ A deepening of the single market, making Europe-wide operation by companies easier.

■ An increasing conviction that there would be a successful move to a single currency, making it easier for companies to operate on an EU-wide basis.

As 1999 approached, and with it the arrival of the euro, so merger activity reached fever pitch, stimulated also by the strong growth experienced throughout the EU (see diagram). Then, with the worldwide economic slowdown in 2001, there was a fall in all types of merger in the EU: between companies in a single EU country, in two or more EU countries and in an EU and a non-EU country.

Recent years have seen some very large mergers. These have included a €29.4 billion marriage of pharmaceutical companies Zeneca of the UK and

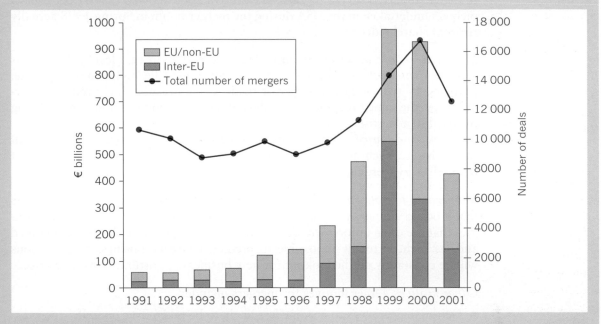

Mergers and acquisitions involving an EU company

Source: *European Economy*, Supplement A, No. 12, December 2001 (European Commission): based on Table 1 and Graphs 7 and 10

Astra of Sweden in 1998, a €205 billion takeover of telecoms giant Mannesmann of Germany by Vodafone of the UK in 1999 and a €50.8 billion takeover of Orange of the UK by France Telecom in 2000.

Other sectors in which merger activity has been rife are financial services and the privatised utilities sector. In the UK, in particular, most of the privatised water and electricity companies have been taken over, with buyers attracted by the sector's monopoly profits. French and US buyers have been prominent.

Many of the deals in the EU are 'hostile'. In other words, the company being taken over does not want to be. The deals are often concluded after prolonged boardroom battles, with bosses of the acquiring company seeking opportunities to build empires, and bosses of the target company attempting all sorts of manoeuvres to avoid being taken over. This may involve them seeking deals with alternative, more 'friendly' companies. Generally companies are increasingly using the services of investment banks to help them in the process of making or warding off deals.

Despite the growing number of horizontal mergers, there has also been a tendency for companies to become more focused, by selling off parts of their business which are not seen as 'core activities'. For

example, not long after its takeover of Wellcome, Glaxo decided to concentrate on the production of *prescription* drugs, and as a consequence to sell its share of Warner Wellcome, which produced non-prescription drugs. Another example was Volvo. After unsuccessfully attempting to merge with Renault in 1993, it subsequently divested itself of several companies that it owned in a variety of industries, ranging from banking and finance to food, matches and pharmaceuticals.

This trend of horizontal mergers and conglomerate and vertical de-mergers has allowed companies to increase their market power in those specific sectors where they have expertise. Consumers may gain from lower costs, but the motives of the companies are largely to gain increased market power – something of dubious benefit to consumers.

Question

Are the motives for merger likely to be different in a recession from in a period of rapid economic growth?

---

[1] When we refer to 'mergers' this also includes acquisitions (i.e. takeovers)

In practice, however, there is little evidence to show that mergers lead to a capital gain. One possible reason for this is the lack of reduction in costs referred to above. In fact, a survey by *BusinessWeek* in 2002 showed that 61 per cent of mergers undertaken in the USA during the merger boom in Spring 1998 actually *reduced* shareholder value.

Merger to reduce uncertainty. Firms face uncertainty at two levels. The first is in their own markets. The behaviour of rivals may be highly unpredictable. Mergers, by reducing the number of rivals, can correspondingly reduce uncertainty. At the same time, they can reduce the *costs* of competition (e.g. reducing the need to advertise).

The second source of uncertainty is the economic environment. In a period of rapid change, such as often accompanies a boom, firms may seek to protect themselves by merging with others.

Merger due to opportunity. A widely held theory concerning merger activity is that it occurs simply as a consequence of opportunities that may arise: opportunities that are often unforeseen. Therefore business mergers are largely unplanned and, as such, virtually impossible to predict. Dynamic business organisations will be constantly on the lookout for new business opportunities as they arise.

Other motives. Other motives for mergers include:

■ Getting bigger so as to become less likely to be taken over oneself.
■ Merging with another firm so as to defend it from an unwanted predator (the 'White Knight' strategy).
■ Asset stripping. This is where a firm takes over another and then breaks it up, selling off the profitable bits and probably closing down the remainder.
■ Empire building. This is where owners or managers favour takeovers because of the power or prestige of owning or controlling several (preferably well-known) companies.
■ Geographical expansion. The motive here is to broaden the geographical base of the company by merging with a firm in a different part of the country or the world.

Mergers will generally have the effect of increasing the market power of those firms involved. This could lead to less choice and higher prices for the consumer. For this reason, mergers have become the target for government competition policy. Such policy is the subject of Chapter 21.

15.7 Growth through strategic alliance

The term **strategic alliance** is used to cover a wide range of alternative collaborative arrangements. These might involve businesses working together on a project, or sharing information, or even sharing productive resources.

Such working relationships might be long term. An example is Airbus Industries, a consortium of European aircraft manufacturers, which was created in the late 1960s. Alternatively, the collaboration between businesses might be just for a single project. An example here is the company set up to build the Channel Tunnel, Trans Manche Link.

Such agreements also vary in respect to their formality. At one extreme, the alliance might entail creating a new jointly-owned enterprise, such as the merger of the mobile phone businesses of Ericsson and Sony. At the other extreme, the working agreement might be totally informal, with businesses remaining largely

definition

Strategic alliance Where two firms work together, formally or informally, to achieve a mutually desirable goal.

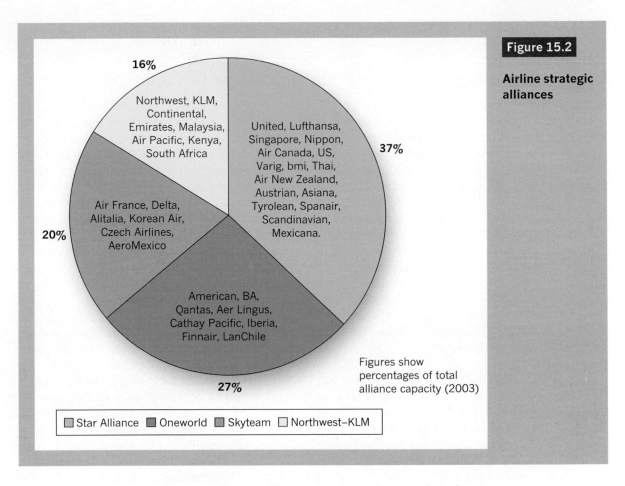

Figure 15.2

Airline strategic alliances

16%

Northwest, KLM, Continental, Emirates, Malaysia, Air Pacific, Kenya, South Africa

United, Lufthansa, Singapore, Nippon, Air Canada, US, Varig, bmi, Thai, Air New Zealand, Austrian, Asiana, Tyrolean, Spanair, Scandinavian, Mexicana.

37%

Air France, Delta, Alitalia, Korean Air, Czech Airlines, AeroMexico

20%

American, BA, Qantas, Aer Lingus, Cathay Pacific, Iberia, Finnair, LanChile

27%

Figures show percentages of total alliance capacity (2003)

☐ Star Alliance ☐ Oneworld ☐ Skyteam ☐ Northwest–KLM

independent of one another. In addition, alliances vary in respect to their focus. Some agreements might focus upon very specific stages in the supply chain. An example here is the decision by three of the world's largest steel manufacturers, NKK, Kawasaki and ThyssenKrupp, to share information on the technology for producing car panels. Other agreements might be more free ranging and flexible. An example here would be two car manufacturers looking to develop a new type of car.

One of the best known sets of alliances in recent years has been in the airline industry. The four main alliances are shown in Figure 15.2. In addition there are many bilateral arrangements between airlines over specific routes.

Types of alliance

There are many types of alliance between businesses.

Joint ventures. A **joint venture** is where two or more firms decide to create, and jointly own, a new independent organisation. The creation of Cellnet (now O₂) by BT and Securicor is an example of such a strategy.

Consortia. In recent years, many consortia have been created. Camelot, the company that runs the UK National Lottery, and Trans Manche Link, the company that built the Channel Tunnel, are two examples. A **consortium** is usually created for very specific projects, such as a large civil engineering work. As such they have a very focused objective and once the project is completed the consortium is usually dissolved. A consortium, however, like joint ventures,

definition

Joint venture
Where two or more firms set up and jointly own a new independent firm.

definition

Consortium
Where two or more firms work together on a specific project and create a separate company to run the project.

BOX 15.3

Logistics
Outsourcing the supply-chain

One area of business in which companies are outsourcing a significant amount of their activity is in logistics. Logistics refers to 'the management of the flow of materials through an organisation, from raw materials to finished goods'. With the advent of new technology and the use of the Internet, logistics have become far more complex. Figures suggest that up to 10 per cent of a firm's costs can be taken up in organising supply-chain issues. It is thus important for firms to deploy logistics effectively so as to improve business efficiency and profitability.

In an attempt to cut stocks (inventories) and manage their supply chain more effectively, many companies are looking to logistics specialists to provide expert help. The following extract from *The Economist* examines the issues.

So what exactly can smart logistics do for companies? One example is TPG's contract with Ford to service its Toronto factory. This plant produces 1500 Windstar minivans a day. To keep it running virtually round the clock, TPG has to organise 800 deliveries a day from 300 different parts makers. Its software must be tied into Ford's computerised production system. Loads have to arrive at 12 different points along the assembly lines without ever being more than 10 minutes late. Parts must be loaded into trucks in a pre-arranged sequence to speed unloading at the assembly line. To make all this run like clockwork takes a team of ten computer-wielding operations planners and 200 unskilled workers, who make up the loads in the right sequence at a warehouse down the road. The vehicles involved are mostly owner-operated, but under contract to TPG. It is a seven-year contract, and TPG has to lower its price by 2% a year.

Another example is an arrangement between Maxtor, a maker of computer disk-drives, and Exel, the world's leading firm for pure logistics. Exel, formed from a merger of a shipping line and a road haulier, now owns no ships or trucks, focusing instead on logistics contracts. The Maxtor deal requires it to shift drives from factories in Asia to companies such as Dell, Compaq and HP in Asia and America, all within 48 hours. As John Allan, Exel's chief executive, says, 'there is no inventory'.

For Mr Allan, the difference between pure logistics companies, such as Exel and TPG, and traditional freight firms is that 'we analyse and optimise the supply-chain for the company and

involves the creation of a new business to co-ordinate the activities of the partners and to oversee work on the project.

Franchising. A less formal strategic alliance is where a business agrees to **franchise** its operations to third parties. McDonald's and Coca-Cola are good examples of businesses that use a franchise network. In such a relationship the franchisee is responsible for manufacturing and/or selling, and the franchiser retains responsibility for branding and marketing.

Licensing. **Licensing** is where the owner of a patented product allows another company to produce it for a fee. Such a strategy is often seen in high-technology markets. For example, companies like Edios and Square, who create and manufacture games for the Playstation, have been given licences by Sony.

Subcontracting. Like licensing and franchising, **subcontracting** is a less formal source of strategic alliance, where companies maintain their independence. When a business subcontracts, it employs an independent business to manufacture or supply some service rather conduct the activity itself. Car manufacturers are major subcontractors. Given the multitude and complexity of components that are required to manufacture a car, the use of subcontractors to supply specialist items, such as brakes and lights, seems a logical way to organise the business. In

definition
Franchise
A formal agreement whereby a company uses another company to produce or sell some or all of its product.

definition
Licensing
Where the owner of a patented product allows another firm to produce it for a fee.

so create value'. He sees his role as orchestrating the supply chain. The rest of the industry are under his baton. One of Exel's biggest contracts is with Ford, for which it organises supplies for seven factories around Europe.

The more they get into orchestrating the flow of inbound goods, the sequencing of parts delivery and the management of supplier parks for vehicle assemblers, the closer these companies come to managing actual production. Along the supply chain, the different freight companies now increasingly do packaging, labelling and some manufacturing, especially in consumer electronics. TPG's TNT Logistics operation even does light assembly-work for DaimlerChrysler in America.

Some industry analysts reckon that in consumer electronics, the growth of such contract manufacturing, often organised through logistics companies, will lead to over a third of electronics manufacturing being outsourced by 2005. Some forecasters think that the share could then double again. Technology is partly driving this growth. According to a report by Accenture, advances such as the use of radio-frequency identification and the Internet could significantly improve supply-chain management. Transponders on

product packages can communicate with devices in factories or warehouses, leaving a trail of where things are at any given time. All this makes it easier for manufacturers or their logistics contractors to track their products across the whole supply-chain. Accenture claims it is the biggest advance in supply management since the arrival of the bar-code.

Given these technological advances, and as logistics firms reach ever deeper into clients' core businesses, traditional manufacturing, whether of cars or personal computers, could start to disappear. The logistics operators may then organise everything but product development, design and marketing. Then they will be even more vital to the success of such companies as Nokia and ICI.[1]

Questions

1 What advantages are companies that outsource their logistics likely to gain from doing so?
2 Why is the process of globalisation likely to enhance the role of the logistic firm?

[1] 'A moving story', The Economist (5 December 2002)

Japan, for example, it has been found that the ten largest car manufacturers obtain as much as 75 per cent of their components from independent suppliers.

Networks. **Networks** are less formal than any of the above alliances. A network is where two or more businesses work collaboratively but without any formal relationship binding one to the other. Such a form of collaboration is highly prevalent in Japan. Rather than a formal contract regulating the behaviour of the partners to the agreement, their relationship is based upon an understanding of trust and loyalty.

Why form strategic alliances?

There are many reasons why firms may decide to set up a strategic alliance. Often these reasons are specific to a particular time or set of circumstances.

New markets. As a business expands, possibly internationally, it may well be advantageous to join with an existing player in the market. Such a business would have local knowledge and an established network of suppliers and distributors. Similar arguments apply if a business is seeking to diversify. Rather than developing the prerequisite skills, knowledge and networks necessary to

definition
Subcontracting
Where a firm employs another firm to produce part of its output or some of its input(s).

definition
Network
An informal arrangement between businesses to work together towards some common goal.

succeed, the process might be curtailed by establishing an alliance with a firm already operating in the market.

Risk sharing. Many business ventures might just be too risky for a solitary firm. Creating some form of strategic alliance spreads risk and creates opportunity. The Channel Tunnel and the consortium of firms that built it is one such example. The construction of the Channel Tunnel was a massive undertaking and far too risky for any single firm to embark upon. With the creation of a consortium, risk was spread, and the various consortium members were able to specialise in their areas of expertise.

Key Idea
13
p98

Capital pooling. Projects that might have prohibitively high start-up costs, or running costs, may become feasible if firms co-operate and pool their capital. In addition, an alliance of firms, with their combined assets and credibility, may find it easier to generate finance, whether from investors in the stock market or from the banking sector.

The past 20 years have seen a flourishing of strategic alliances. They have become a key growth strategy for business both domestically and internationally. They are seen as a way of expanding business operations quickly without the difficulties associated with the more aggressive approach of acquisition or the more lengthy process of merger.

> **Pause for thought**
>
> What are the difficulties associated with acquisitions and mergers?

One sector in which the formation of strategic alliances is rife is that of logistics. Box 15.3 shows some of the recent developments in this area and assesses the implications for business and the economy.

SUMMARY

1a Business growth and business profitability are likely to be inversely related in the short run. A growing firm will bear certain additional costs, such as higher advertising and marketing bills.

1b In the long run, the relationship could be positive. A growing firm may take advantage of new market opportunities and may achieve greater economies of scale and increased market power. On the other hand, a rapidly growing firm may embark on various risky projects or projects with a low rate of return.

2a Constraints on business growth include (i) financial conditions, (ii) shareholder confidence, (iii) the level and growth of market demand and (iv) managerial conditions.

2b (i) financial conditions determine the business's ability to raise finance. (ii) Shareholder confidence is likely to be jeopardised if a firm ploughs back too much profit into investment and distributes too little to shareholders. (iii) A firm is unlikely to be able to grow unless it faces a growing demand: either in its existing market, or by diversifying into new markets. (iv) The knowledge, skills and dynamism of the management team will be an important determinant of the firm's growth.

3a A business can expand either internally, or externally by merging with other firms.

3b Using either of these routes, there are three potential growth strategies open to business: product differentiation, vertical integration and diversification.

4a Vertical integration involves remaining in the same market, but expanding into a different stage of production.

4b Vertical integration can reduce a firm's costs through various economies of scale. It can also help to reduce uncertainty, as the vertically integrated business can hopefully secure supply routes and/or retail outlets. This strategy can also enhance the business's market power by enabling it to erect various barriers to entry.

4c A vertically integrated business will trade off the security of such a strategy with the reduced ability to respond to change and to exploit the advantages that the market might present.

4d Through a process of tapered vertical integration, many firms make part of a given input themselves and subcontract the production of the remainder to one or more other firms. By making a certain amount of an input itself, the firm is less reliant on suppliers, but does not require as much capital equipment as if it produced all the input itself.

5a The nature and direction of diversification depends upon the skills and abilities of managers, and the type of technology employed.

5b Diversification offers the business a growth strategy that not only frees it from the limitations of a particular market, but also enables it to spread its risks, and seek profit in potentially fast-growing markets.

6a There are three types of merger: horizontal, vertical and conglomerate. The type of merger adopted will be determined by the aims of

business: that is, whether to increase market power, improve business security or spread risks.

6b There is a wide range of motives for merger. Some have more statistical backing than others.

7a One means of achieving growth is through the formation of strategic alliances with other firms. They are a means whereby business operations can be expanded relatively quickly and at relatively low cost.

7b Types of strategic alliance include: joint ventures, consortia, franchising, licensing, subcontracting and networks.

7c Advantages of strategic alliances include easier access to new markets, risk sharing and capital pooling.

REVIEW QUESTIONS

1 Explain the relationship between a business's rate of growth and its profitability.

2 'Business managers must constantly tread a fine line between investing in business growth and paying shareholders an "adequate" dividend on their holdings.' Explain why this is such a crucial consideration.

3 Distinguish between internal and external growth strategy. Identify a range of factors which might determine whether an internal or external strategy is pursued.

4 What is meant by the term 'vertical integration'? Why might business wish to pursue such a growth strategy?

5 A firm can grow by merging with or taking over another firm. Such mergers or takeovers can be of three types: horizontal, vertical or conglomerate. Which of the following is an example of which type of merger (takeover)?

(a) A soft drinks manufacturer merges with a pharmaceutical company.
(b) A car manufacturer merges with a car distribution company.
(c) A large supermarket chain takes over a number of independent grocers.

6 To what extent will consumers gain or lose from the three different types of merger identified above?

7 Assume that an independent film company, which has up to now specialised in producing documentaries for a particular television broadcasting company, wishes to expand. Identify some possible horizontal, vertical and other closely related fields. What types of strategic alliances might it seek to form and with what types of company? What possible drawbacks might there be for it in such alliances?

CHAPTER

16   The small-firm sector

How often do you hear of small business making it big? Not very often, and yet many of the world's major corporations began life as small businesses. From acorns have grown oak trees! But small and large businesses are usually organised and run quite differently and face very different problems.

Key Idea
5
p44

In this chapter we consider the place of small firms in the economy: their strengths and weaknesses, their ability to grow and the factors that limit expansion. We also consider the small-business policies of governments, both in the UK and in the European Union.

16.1   Defining the small-firm sector

Unfortunately, there is no single agreed definition of a 'small' firm. In fact, a firm considered to be small in one sector of business, such as manufacturing, may be considerably different in size from one in, say, the road haulage business. Nevertheless, the most widely used definition is that adopted by the EU for its statistical data. Three categories of SME (small and medium enterprise) are distinguished. These are shown in Table 16.1.

This subdivision of small firms into three categories allows us to distinguish features of enterprises that vary with the degree of smallness (e.g. practices of hiring and firing, pricing and investment strategies, competition and collusion, innovation). It also enables us to show changes over time in the size and composition of the small-firm sector. However, we might still question the adequacy

Table 16.1   EU SME definitions

Criterion	Micro	Small	Medium
Maximum number of employees	9	49	249
Maximum annual turnover	–	€7 million	€40 million
Maximum annual balance sheet total	–	€5 million	€27 million
Maximum % owned by one, or jointly by several, enterprise(s) not satisfying the same criteria	–	25%	25%

Note: To qualify as an SME, both the employee and the independence criteria must be satisfied and either the turnover or the balance sheet total criteria

Table 16.2	Number of UK business, employment and turnover by number of employees (2002)

Size (number of employees)	Businesses (number)	Employment (000s)	Turnover[1] (£m ex VAT)	Businesses (%)	Employment (%)	Turnover (%)
0–9 (Micro) ⎫ (Small)	3 596 860	6 673	482 984	94.7	29.4	22.0
10–49 ⎬	167 020	3 237	330 487	4.4	14.3	15.0
50–249 (Medium)	27 260	2 688	330 435	0.7	11.9	15.0
250+ (Large)	6 585	10 075	1 056 016	0.2	44.4	48.0
All	3 797 725	22 674	2 199 923	100.0	100.0	100.0
All with employee(s)	1 167 530	19 737	2 045 001	31.8	89.4	93.2

[1] Excluding finance sector (Sector J)
Source: SME Statistics UK 2002, (DTI, 2003)

of such a definition, given the diversity that can be found in business activity, organisational structure and patterns of ownership within the small-firm sector.

The small-firm sector in the UK

In the UK, firms are divided into four categories by number of employees: micro (0–9 employees), small (0–49 employees) (includes micro), medium (50–249 employees), large (250 or more employees). The Department of Trade and Industry publishes an annual SME dataset, which is available in the National Statistics site (**www.statistics.gov.uk**). Table 16.2 is taken from the 2002 dataset.

The most significant feature of the data is that micro businesses (between 0 and 9 employees) accounted for 94.7 per cent of all businesses and provided 29.4 per cent of all employment. The table also shows that there were 3 763 880 micro and small businesses out of a total of 3 797 725 businesses: i.e. 99.1 per cent. Micro and small businesses also accounted for 43.7 per cent of employment and 37 per cent of turnover. From such information we can see that the small-firm sector clearly represents a very important part of the UK's industrial structure.

There are significant variations between sectors in the percentage of SMEs, whether by number of firms, employment or turnover. This is illustrated in Table 16.3.

Service providers (categories G to O in Table 16.3) contribute the overwhelming number of micro and small firms within the economy, accounting for 68.1 per cent of all micro and 68.2 per cent of all small firms.

Changes over time

How has the small-firm sector changed over time? The problems associated with definition and data collection make time-series analysis of the small-firm sector very difficult and prone to various inconsistencies. However, it is possible to identify certain trends. The percentage of small firms fell from the early part of the twentieth century, but from the mid-1960s began to rise again.

> **Pause for thought**
>
> What inconsistencies might there be in time series data on the small firm sector?

What is the explanation for this rise in small businesses in recent years? A wide range of factors have been advanced to explain this phenomenon, and include the following.

Table 16.3 SME share of UK businesses, employment and turnover by industrial sector (2002)

Industrial sector	Businesses		Employment		Turnover	
	Total number	SME percentage share	Total employment (000s)	SME percentage share	Total turnover (£ millions)	SME percentage share
All industries	3 797 725	99.8	22 674	55.6	2 199 923	52.0
A, B Agriculture, forestry and fishing	175 290	100.0	442	100.0	26 802	100.0
D Manufacturing	298 425	99.3	3 834	52.8	442 776	38.5
F Construction	733 610	100.0	1 778	82.6	166 202	68.5
G Wholesale, retail and repairs	527 185	99.8	4 701	48.9	754 325	52.8
H Hotels and restaurants	131 190	99.8	1 574	55.2	55 692	56.1
I Transport, storage and communication	240 800	99.8	1 717	38.2	187 721	36.4
J Financial intermediation	63 290	99.5	1 096	21.0	–	–
K Real estate, business activities	882 440	99.9	3 614	69.4	313 905	72.9
N Health and social work	224 205	99.8	2 200	42.6	75 521	37.2
O Other social/ personal services	418 340	99.9	1 246	73.5	81 628	65.5

Note: Figures not available for Mining and quarrying (C), Electricity, gas and water supply (E) and Education (M)
Source: SME Statistics UK 2002, (DTI, 2003)

- *The growth in the service sector of the economy.* Many services are, by their nature, small in scale and/or specialist. For example, many small businesses have developed in the area of computer support and back-up.

- *The growth in niche markets.* Rising consumer affluence creates a growing demand for specialist products and services. Key examples might be in textiles and in other fashion/craft-based markets. Such goods and services are likely to be supplied by small firms, in which economies of scale and hence price considerations are of less relevance.

- *New working practices which require greater labour force flexibility.* Forms of employment such as **subcontracting** have become more pronounced, as businesses attempt to achieve certain cost and flexibility advantages over their rivals. This often forces individuals either to set up their own companies to provide such services, or to become self-employed.

- *A higher level of unemployment in the 1980s and early 1990s.* The higher the level of unemployment, the more people turned to self-employment as an alternative to trying to find work with an employer. With the fall in unemployment in the late 1990s and early 2000s, so the rise in self-employment has ceased.

- *The role of government.* Government attitudes and policy initiatives shifted in favour of small business creation during the 1980s. The development of an **enterprise culture**, in which individuals were to be given the opportunity, and various financial incentives, to start their own businesses, was one of the principal aims of the Conservative government over the 1980s and 1990s, and the Labour government since 1997. In section 16.3 we shall consider government policy initiatives in more detail.

The growth in small businesses in the UK has been pronounced since the early 1970s. But has a similar trend been apparent in other developed economies?

International comparisons

We have already seen the difficulties associated with the poor quality of data and the problems in defining the small-firm sector. These problems are particularly severe when it comes to making international comparisons. Best estimates suggest that the pattern in the UK is *not* generally repeated elsewhere. In most countries, both within Europe (e.g. Germany and France) and outside Europe (e.g. the USA and Japan), there has been no clear trend towards a growing small-firm sector, and in some cases the proportion of small businesses has declined. Italy is the only country, apart from the UK, where there has been a definite growth in the small-firm sector.

In the rest of this chapter we shall put the definitional and statistical problems regarding the small-firm sector to one side, and focus on the role that SMEs play within the economy and at what determines their success or failure.

The survival, growth and failure of small businesses   16.2

Evidence suggests that a small business stands a significantly higher chance of failure than a large business, and yet many small businesses survive and some grow. What characteristics distinguish a successful small business from one that is likely to fail? The following section looks at this issue.

Competitive advantage and the small-firm sector

The following have been found to be the key competitive advantages that small firms might hold.

> **Pause for thought**
>
> Before you read on, try to identify what competitive advantages a small business might have over larger rivals.

- *Flexibility*. Small firms are more able to respond to changes in market conditions and to meet customer requirements effectively. For example, they may be able to develop or adapt products for specific needs. Small firms may also be able to make decisions quickly, avoiding the bureaucratic and formal decision-making processes that typify many larger companies.
- *Quality of service*. Small firms are more able to deal with customers in a personal manner and offer a more effective after-sales service.
- *Production efficiency and low overhead costs*. Small firms can avoid some of the diseconomies of scale that beset large companies. A small firm can benefit from: management that avoids waste; good labour relations; the employment of a skilled and motivated workforce; lower accommodation costs.

BOX 16.1

The Dyson Dual Cyclone vacuum cleaner
A small business redefining the Hoover

In 1995, Dyson Appliances recorded turnover of £55 million. Just one year later, with sales of 30 000 vacuum cleaners and a turnover of £8 million a month, Dyson Appliances was outperforming the market's major players, Hoover and Electrolux.

The tale of the Dyson Dual Cyclone vacuum cleaner records the successful and dramatic rise of James Dyson. As a budding entrepreneur, in the early 1980s he invented a revolutionary bagless vacuum cleaner, which worked, in effect, by creating a mini cyclone, whereby a high-speed air vortex pushed dust particles to the side of a collector. Without a bag, the suction power of the cleaner would not diminish over time, unlike conventional vacuums. When he initially developed this product (there were 5000 prototypes before a marketable product was finalised), neither Electrolux nor Hoover was interested – largely because of the profits they made from selling bags!

After an early and unsuccessful attempt to launch the project, Dyson managed to secure a deal with a Japanese company to produce and sell his product in Japan, where his vacuum retailed for a staggering £1200. At this price, it was unlikely to yield the mass sales Dyson hoped for, even given the superiority of the product. Thus Dyson set out to manufacture the product himself.

Finding it difficult to raise capital and find backers, Dyson reinvested his profits from the Japanese sales, and managed to raise the £4.5 million required to design and patent his product, to establish a network of subcontractor suppliers, and to create an assembly plant in the UK. With his vacuum cleaner priced at £200, Dyson hoped to enter the market at an affordable price.

Today, Dyson's vacuum cleaner has 50 per cent of the UK market and accounts for one-fifth of all vacuum cleaner sales across Western Europe.

Not content to sit on his success, James Dyson, at the end of 1999, launched his robot cleaner, a £5 million project which he hopes will have the same impact on the cleaner market as his bagless vacuum. He is hoping that by 2005 worldwide sales from the robot vacuum will be in the region of £2 billion, a substantial increase over the £400 million that the company currently earns.

The Dyson Dual Cyclone vacuum cleaner is a classic example of how a small business with a revolutionary product can have a massive impact on a market, and within a short period of time become established as a market leader.

In recognition of his contribution to innovation, the Trade and Industry Secretary, Patricia Hewitt, in 2003 named James Dyson as her 'innovation tsar'. The Dyson story has not, however, been all good news for the UK. In 2002, Dyson shifted production from its Malmesbury plant in the UK to Malaysia, with the loss of 800 UK jobs.

Questions

1 *What conditions existed to enable James Dyson's small business to do so well in such a short period of time?*

2 *In retrospect, were Electrolux and Hoover correct not to produce the new type of vacuum cleaner? Should they do so now?*

■ *Product development.* As we have seen, many small businesses operate in niche markets, offering specialist goods or services. The distinctiveness of such products gives the small firm a crucial advantage over its larger rivals. A successful small business strategy, therefore, would be to produce products that are clearly differentiated from those of large firms in the market, thereby avoiding head-on competition – competition which the small firm would probably not be able to survive.

■ *Innovation.* Small businesses, especially those located in high-technology markets, are frequently product or process innovators. Such businesses, usually through entrepreneurial vision, manage successfully to match such innovations to changing market needs. Many small businesses are, in this respect, path breakers or market leaders.

Small businesses do, however, suffer from a number of significant limitations.

Problems facing small businesses

The following points have been found to hinder the success of small firms.

- *Selling and marketing*. Small firms face many problems in selling and marketing their products, especially overseas. Small firms are perceived by their customers to be less stable and reliable than their larger rivals. This lack of credibility is likely to hinder their ability to trade. This is a particular problem for 'new' small firms which have not had long enough to establish a sound reputation.
- *Funding R&D*. Given the specialist nature of many small firms, their long-run survival may depend upon developing new products and processes in order to keep pace with changing market needs. Such developments may require significant R&D investment. However, the ability of small firms to attract finance is limited, as many of them have virtually no collateral and they are frequently perceived by banks as a highly risky investment.
- *Management skills*. A crucial element in ensuring that small businesses not only survive but grow is the quality of management. If key management skills, such as being able to market a product effectively, are limited, then this will limit the success of the business.
- *Economies of scale*. Small firms will have fewer opportunities and scope to gain economies of scale, and hence their costs are likely to be somewhat higher than their larger rivals. This will obviously limit their ability to compete on price.

The question often arises whether it is possible to distinguish between those small businesses which are likely to grow and prosper and those that are likely to fail. In the section below we will consider not only how businesses grow, but whether there is a key to success.

How do small businesses grow?

It is commonly assumed that all businesses wish to grow. But is it true? Do small businesses want to become big businesses? It may well be that the owners of a small firm have no aspirations to expand the operations of their enterprise. They might earn sufficient profits and experience a level of job satisfaction that would in no way be enhanced with a bigger business operation. In fact the negative aspects of big business – formalised management structure, less customer contact and a fear of failure – might reduce the owner's level of satisfaction.

If growth is a small business objective, what are the chances of success? Evidence from both the UK and the USA suggests that for every 100 firms established, after a ten-year period only 40 will survive; but they are more likely to survive if they have grown.

Hypergrowth companies
The secrets of exceptional business performance?

Of all the beasts in the corporate jungle, the most fascinating is the one that emerges from nowhere, grows at a phenomenal rate and, before too long, is challenging some of the bigger animals. Hypergrowth companies are known in America as fast-growth tigers, in Britain as baby sharks.[1]

On rare occasions companies appear in the market place that grow at a phenomenal rate. What special ingredients do such businesses have which enable them to perform so well?

Coopers and Lybrand, in a study of hypergrowth businesses, defined them as 'firms which have achieved an increase in both turnover and employment of 100 per cent over the last three years'.

They applied this criterion to 501 medium-sized enterprises. They found that 26 companies fell into the hypergrowth category. The 26 companies were found to have the following features:

- They tended to be young. Half were under 10 years old.
- 70 per cent of them were privately owned, with turnover ranging from £13 million to £50 million a year.
- The majority of them served a single market or supplied a single product or service.
- The niche markets in which they tended to be located were under-exploited by bigger businesses or in many cases completely ignored.
- Most of them were located in service industries, such as transport, professional services and finance.

As well as sharing the above features, hypergrowth companies were also found to follow very similar business strategies. These included the following:

- Improving the speed at which new products and services got to the market.
- Maintaining tight control over stocks.
- Fostering a close relationship with main suppliers and customers.
- Ensuring that the best use of new technology was made in all aspects of business.
- Recruiting managers from outside the main market of the business, so as to ensure expertise in other core business activities: for example, marketing and retailing.
- Adopting employee incentive schemes, which included share ownership programmes.

The process of growth

Small businesses are frequently perceived to grow in five stages. These are shown in Table 16.4.

In the initial stage, *inception*, the entrepreneur plays the key role in managing the enterprise with little if any formalised management structure. In the next two stages we see the firm establish itself (the *survival* stage) and then *begin to grow*. The entrepreneur devolves management responsibility to non-owner managers. Such non-owner managers are able to add certain skills to the business which might enhance its chances of growth and success. The fourth and fifth phases, *expansion* and *maturity*, see the firm become more bureaucratic and rationalised; power within the organisation becomes more dispersed.

This picture of the growth of small businesses is *descriptive* rather than explanatory. To *explain* why a small firm grows we need to examine a number of factors. It is useful to group them under three headings – the entrepreneur, the firm and strategy.

The entrepreneur

Factors in this section relate predominantly to the attributes and experience of the individual entrepreneur. They include the following.

■ Keeping company borrowing low, with growth funded, as far as possible, from the reinvestment of profits.

The main challenge for hypergrowth companies is whether they maintain their dramatic growth over the longer term. There are essentially two competing views regarding the long-term sustainability of hypergrowth.

The first is that 'baby sharks' create a virtuous circle, where fast growth fuels itself. Profits and performance, if managed correctly, create the necessary conditions to maintain hypergrowth. Essentially, high growth leads to high profits, which lead to high investment, which, in turn, can lead to high growth.

The alternative view is that hypergrowth businesses are hypergrowth by successfully exploiting a particular market or opportunity: a 'niche market'. Once the niche attracts the attention of rival firms, the ability to maintain hypergrowth diminishes. Hypergrowth is ultimately only short term.

What does seem apparent from recent investigations is that the main threat to hypergrowth businesses comes from their relationship with larger companies in the market place. Findings show that hypergrowth companies tend, on balance, to have more large company customers and suppliers than other medium-sized enterprises. As the *Management Today* article states:

> The danger for hypergrowth middle-sized businesses is that they will be squeezed when they begin to become a serious threat. Either that or they get taken over by one of their bigger customers, suppliers or competitors and lose the edge that made them special in the first place.

Questions

1 *In what respects do hypergrowth companies share the same characteristics as enterprises in the small business sector?*

2 *Why is there potentially greater opportunity for small businesses, rather than medium or large enterprises, to become hypergrowth companies?*

3 *It is apparent from the evidence that medium-sized businesses might find it difficult to maintain hypergrowth. Explain why. What additional problems, if any, might a small business face if it attempts to maintain hypergrowth in the long term?*

[1] *Management Today*, February 1996

Table 16.4   **Management role and style in the five stages of small business growth**

Stage	Top management role	Management style	Organisation structure
1 Inception	Direct supervision	Entrepreneurial, individualistic	Unstructured
2 Survival	Supervised supervision	Entrepreneurial, administrative	Simple
3 Growth	Delegation/ co-ordination	Entrepreneurial, co-ordinate	Functional, centralised
4 Expansion	Decentralisation	Professional, administrative	Functional, decentralised
5 Maturity	Decentralisation	Watchdog	Decentralised functional/product

Source: D. J. Storey, *Understanding the Small-Business Sector* (Routledge, 1994)

■ *Entrepreneurial motivation and a desire to succeed*. Motivation, drive and determination are clearly important attributes for a successful entrepreneur. On their own, however, they are unlikely to be sufficient. If motivation is not complemented with things such as good business knowledge and decision making, then a business is likely to fail irrespective of its owner's motives.

■ *Educational attainment*. Although educational attainment does not necessarily generate business success (indeed, it is often claimed that running a business is not an 'intellectual' activity), the level of education of an entrepreneur is positively related to the rate of growth of the firm.

■ *Prior management experience and business knowledge*. Previous experience by the owner in the same or a related industry is likely to offer a small firm a far greater chance of survival and growth. 'Learning by doing' will enable the new business owner to avoid past mistakes or to take advantage of missed previous opportunities.

The firm

The following are the key characteristics of a small business that determine its rate of growth.

■ *The age of the business*. New businesses grow faster than mature businesses.

■ *The sector of the economy in which the business is operating*. A firm is more likely to experience growth if it is operating in a growing market. Examples include the financial services sector during the 1980s, and specialist high-technology sectors today.

■ *Legal forms*. Limited companies have been found to grow faster than sole proprietorships or partnerships. Evidence suggests that limited companies tend to have greater market credibility with both banks and customers.

■ *Location*. Small firms tend to be highly dependent for their performance on a localised market. Being in the right place is thus a key determinant of a small business's growth.

Strategy

Various strategies adopted by the small firm will affect its rate of growth. Strategies that are likely to lead to fast growth include the following.

Key Idea
20
p000

■ *Workforce and management training*. Training is a form of investment. It adds to the firm's stock of human capital, and thereby increases the quantity, and possibly also the quality, of output per head. This, in turn, is likely to increase the long-term growth of the firm.

■ *The use of external finance*. Taking on additional partners, or, more significantly, taking on shareholders, will increase the finance available to firms and therefore allow a more rapid expansion.

■ *Product innovation*. Firms that introduce new products have been found on the whole to grow faster than those that do not.

■ *Export markets*. Even though small firms tend to export relatively little, export markets can frequently offer additional opportunities for growth. This is especially important when the firm faces stiff competition in the domestic market.

■ *The use of professional managers.* The devolving of power to non-owning managers is identified as a major characteristic of fast-growth small firms. Such managers, as previously mentioned, widen the skills and knowledge base of the organisation, and shift the reliance of the business away from the entrepreneur, whose skills might be limited to specific areas.

What the above factors suggest is that, if a small business is to be successful and subsequently grow, then it must consider its business strategy – the organisation of the business, and the utilisation of individuals' abilities and experience. It is a combination of these factors which is likely to generate success, and only those businesses that co-ordinate such characteristics are likely to grow. Conversely, those businesses that fail to embrace these key characteristics are likely to fall by the wayside.

A potentially crucial factor in aiding success is the contribution and role of public policy. In the next section we shall consider the attitude of the UK government to small business and the policy initiatives it has introduced. We will also assess how such initiatives differ from, complement or duplicate those provided by the EU.

Government assistance and the small firm — 16.3

When the UK Labour government was elected in 1997, it stated that its principal economic objective was to develop a strategy that would enable the country to achieve its full economic potential. A key element of the strategy was the encouragement and promotion of entrepreneurial talent; and one way of achieving this was by supporting small and medium-sized enterprises.

SME policy in the UK

UK governments in recent years have recognised the importance of small firms to the economy and have introduced various forms of advisory services and tax concessions. In particular, it has tried to encourage the establishment of new small firms. In the UK, the level of small business start-ups is about three businesses per 100 adults. In the USA, it is over seven businesses per 100 adults.

> **Pause for thought**
>
> *Why might the government wish to distinguish SME start-up policies from SME growth and performance policies?*

Tax concessions

Small firms pay a 19 per cent rate of corporation tax compared with 30 per cent for larger companies. In 2003/4, companies with profits up to £10 000 are exempt from corporation tax. Above that, the rate rises gradually to reach 19 per cent for companies with profits between £50 000 and £300 000. Above that, it again rises gradually to reach 30 per cent for companies with profits over £1.5 million. Also, tax credits are available to small companies for spending on research and development.

Under the Enterprise Investment Scheme, people investing by buying shares in small companies not quoted on the Stock Exchange are granted income tax relief of 20 per cent on investments of up to £150 000 per tax year.

Grants

The Enterprise Grants scheme provides help for small firms in assisted areas. They are one-off grants for projects that would not otherwise go ahead. The Grant for Research and Development are 'grants to help individuals and small and medium-sized businesses to research and develop technologically innovative products and processes'. Amounts available depend on the size of the business: up to £20 000 is available for businesses with fewer than 10 employees, £75 000 for those with fewer than 50 employees and £200 000 for those with fewer than 250 employees.

The £30 million Phoenix Fund was created to help those wishing to set up a business in an area of high unemployment. As well as offering finance, the fund is also looking to recruit 1000 volunteer business mentors to offer help and advice in starting-up and running a small business. It is also backing a pro-gramme of Entrepreneurial Scholarships, where entrepreneurs from deprived areas will be given the opportunity to develop management and business skills to help them set up and survive in business on their own.

Loans

Under the Small Firms Loan Guarantee Scheme, the government guarantees commercial loans by banks to small businesses against default. The guarantee is for 75 per cent of loans from two to ten years of up to £100 000. This therefore encourages banks to lend to businesses they might otherwise regard as too risky. In return for the guarantee, the borrower has to pay a premium of 2 per cent to the Small Business Service (see below). Firms with turnover of up to £3 million, or £5 million in the case of manufacturers, are eligible for the guarantee.

Small firms can also get government loans of up to seven years for paying for training for their employees. Firms can borrow from £500 to £125 000.

Investment in small firms by other companies

In an attempt to draw in private venture capital funds, a programme of 'Corporate Venturing' has been introduced. Corporate Venturing involves investment by larger companies in new or expanding small business. In order to encourage such relations, the investor will be able to claim corporation tax relief at 20 per cent on all investments in the smaller firm.

The creation of the National Business Angels Network is a similar initiative. Here private individuals, or 'angels', wishing to invest in growing businesses are brought together with companies that require investment.

Advice

One of the most significant measures has been the creation of the Small Business Service (SBS). The SBS is designed to give small firms, or those thinking of setting up a small firm, easy access to advice and support. (Prior to the SBS, the large diversity of initiatives and regulations applying to small business meant that there was no clear point of reference for anyone seeking advice or guidance.) In addition to this, the SBS is designed to ensure that the interests and problems of small business are taken into account when the government formulates its economic policy.

Business Links are government-funded agencies providing specialist advice in the fields of management skills, exporting, marketing, design, etc.

Reductions in 'red tape'

Small firms are subject to fewer planning and other bureaucratic controls than large companies.

Small-firm policy in the EU

The need for an EU policy for SMEs was first recognised in the Colonna report on industrial policy back in 1970. However, it was not until 1985 that the European Council gave top priority to SME policy.

Limited assistance was available for SMEs within the EU between 1970 and 1985. A division within DG-3[1] (the part of the European Commission dealing with industrial policy) was set up to work with the Business Co-operation Centre, which helped SMEs to establish co-operative ventures with other firms, and also provided limited subsidies for certain trade activities.

Further assistance might have been gained from other divisions. DG-1 (External Relations) gave SMEs priority budget allocations that promoted international business. DG-16 (Regional Development) provided a wide range of grants for business creation projects in depressed regions. DG-5 (Employment, Social Affairs and Education) encouraged local employment initiatives, with small business being seen as a prime source of job creation.

Such initiatives as these, however, were not co-ordinated, but instead were pursued as largely separate strategies. However, in 1983, the 'European Year of the SME and Craft Industry', the European Parliament focused its attention on the needs of SMEs and the crucial requirement of a co-ordinated and independent policy. As a result, an SME task force was established in June 1986. This task force had two functions:

■ To co-ordinate the various policies towards SMEs within the different EU divisions.

■ To develop a general programme to aid SMEs which did not substitute or interfere with national actions within the EU, but rather operated in a complementary way.

The EU's *SME Action Programme* was set out in 1986. Its thirteen points fell into two categories. The first seven points considered regulatory and administrative issues; the final six points considered ways to help the creation and development of SMEs. The thirteen points of the Action Programme are outlined in Table 16.5.

The most significant moves towards a fully integrated SME policy occurred in 1993 when, as part of the EU's enterprise policy, SME initiatives were given an independent budget of ECU112.2 bn (where 1 ECU = €1) for the period 1993 to 1996. In conjunction with this, it was stated that the impact of community policies on SMEs was to be more tightly monitored, co-ordinated and scrutinised.

In January 2000 this goal came a step closer with the formation of an Enterprise DG, following a merger of the DGs for SMEs and for industry and innovation. The aim of the Enterprise DG is to promote entrepreneurship and innovation within the EU.

The major sources of financial support for SMEs are the Structural Fund and the European Investment Bank (EIB). The Structural Fund provides finance to help correct regional imbalance within the EU. Some €16 billion from the EU's Structural Funds is being allocated to SME-targeted projects for the period 2002–6. The EIB finances primarily large-scale projects (typically of at least €25 million). Smaller projects are normally supported indirectly through EIB loans to

---

[1] DG stands for 'Directorate General'. There are 36 DGs in the European Commission, each headed by a director-general, who reports to one of 20 Commissioners. DGs are no longer known by number but by name: e.g. Economic and Financial Affairs, Social affairs, Consumer Protection, Enterprise.

Table 16.5   **EU SME Action Programme**

Regulatory and administrative matters	Initiatives to encourage the establishment and development of SMEs
1 Promoting the spirit of enterprise 2 Improving the administrative environment 3 Monitoring the completion of the internal market 4 Adapting company law 5 Adapting competition law 6 Improving the tax environment	7 Improving the social environment of SMEs 8 Training 9 Information 10 Exports 11 Encouraging new firms and innovation 12 Co-operation between firms and regions 13 Provision of capital

banks, which then distribute the money to the projects. The EIB also indirectly finances SMEs through loans to selected venture capital operators, which then invest in the SMEs.

A wide range of policy initiatives have also been adopted in order to encourage SMEs to participate in the EU's technology programme. In the 6th Framework Programme (2002–6), SMEs have been allocated nearly €2.2 billion to support research and innovation efforts.

In addition to providing funding, the EU's policy is to act as a networking facility, setting up partnerships and disseminating information. The Innovation Relay Centre Network was set up to advise small business on technology and innovation, and to assist in developing links to partners or to potential buyers of technologies developed by SMEs.

The EU's commitment to SMEs has clearly grown in recent years. The EU provides not only extensive finance, but also advice, training and channels for communication to other enterprises.

The EU has recognised the valuable role that SMEs play within the economy, not only as employers and contributors to output, but in respect to their ability to innovate and initiate technological change – vital components in a successful and thriving regional economy.

SUMMARY

1a The small-firm sector is difficult to define. Different criteria might be used. However, the level of employment tends to be the most widely used.

1b The difficulties in defining what a small firm is mean that measuring the size of the small-firm sector is also difficult and subject to a degree of error. However, it appears that in the UK the small-firm sector has been growing since the mid-1960s. This is the result of a variety of influences including: industrial structure, working practices, the level of unemployment, the role of government and consumer affluence.

1c The growth in the small-firm sector in the UK is not mirrored elsewhere in the major industrial nations other than in Italy.

2a Small firms survive because they provide or hold distinct advantages over their larger rivals. Such advantages include: greater flexibility, greater quality of service, production efficiency, low overhead costs and product innovation.

2b Small businesses are prone to high rates of failure, however. This is due to problems of credibility, finance and limited management skills.

2c Of those small businesses that manage to survive, a small fraction will grow. The growth of business tends to proceed through a series of stages, in which the organisation and management of the firm evolves, becoming less and less dependent upon the owner-manager.

2d Those small businesses that do grow are likely to have distinct characteristics relating to individual abilities, business organisation and business strategy. Combinations of variables from these three categories will tend to favour growth of the SME.

3a Government policy aimed at the small firm within the UK is particularly concerned with business start-ups, although we can also identify initiatives that look to stimulate growth and improve performance.

3b Small business policy within the EU seeks to complement national programmes. It provides a wide range of grants, projects and information for SMEs. A large emphasis is placed upon the development and transmission of technological innovations within the SME sector.

REVIEW QUESTIONS

1 Why is it so difficult to define the small-firm sector? What problems does this create?

2 'Small businesses are crucial to the vitality of the economy.' Explain.

3 Compare and contrast the competitive advantages held by both small and big business.

4 It is often argued that the success of a small business depends upon a number of conditions. Such conditions can be placed under the general headings of: the entrepreneur, the firm and the strategy. How are conditions under each of these headings likely to contribute to small business success?

5 Compare and contrast UK and EU approaches to SME policy.

CHAPTER

17 Pricing strategy

How are prices determined in practice? Is there such a thing as an 'equilibrium price' for a product that will be charged to all customers and by all firms in the industry? In most cases the answer is no.

Take the case of the price of a rail ticket. On asking, 'What's the train fare to London?', you are likely to receive any of the following replies: Do you want an 'Apex' ticket (one booked in advance)? Do you want single or return? How old are you? Do you have a railcard (family, young person's, student, senior citizen's)? Do you want a day return, a 'saver', a 'super saver' or an open return? Will you be travelling back on a Friday? Will you be travelling out before 10 a.m.? Will you be leaving London between 4 p.m. and 6 p.m.? Do you want to reserve a seat? Do you want to take advantage of our special low-priced winter Saturday fare?

How you respond to the above questions will determine the price you pay, a price that can vary several hundred per cent from the lowest to the highest. And it is not just train fares that vary in this way: air fares and holidays are other examples. Selling the same product to different groups of consumers at different prices is known as **price discrimination**. (We shall examine price discrimination in detail later in this chapter.) But prices for a product do not just vary according to the customer. They vary according to a number of other factors as well.

- The life cycle of the product. When a firm launches a product, it may charge a very different price from when the product has become established in the market, or, later, when it is beginning to be replaced by more up-to-date products.

- The aims of the firm. Is the firm aiming to maximise profits, or is it seeking to maximise sales or growth, or does it have a series of aims? Which aim or aims that it pursues will determine the price it charges?

- The competition that the firm faces. Firms operating under monopoly or collusive oligopoly are likely to charge very different prices from firms operating in highly competitive markets.

- Information on costs and demand. Firms in the real world may have very scant information about the elasticity of demand for their product and for the products of their competitors, and how demand is likely to change. It is the same with information on costs: firms may have only a rough idea of how costs are likely to change over time. The picture of a firm choosing its price by a careful calculation of marginal cost and marginal revenue may be far from reality.

Key Idea 7 p50

In this chapter we will explore the pricing strategies of business. We will identify different pricing models, show how a firm's pricing policy is likely to change over a product's life cycle, and how and under what circumstances businesses might practise price discrimination. We will also consider a number of other pricing issues, such as those linked to a multiproduct business and the use of a practice known as 'transfer pricing'.

> **definition**
>
> **Price discrimination**
> Where a firm sells the same product at different prices.

Pricing and market structure   17.1

The firm's power over prices

In a free and competitive market we know that the quantity bought and sold, and the actual price of the product, are determined by the forces of supply and demand. If demand is in excess of supply, the consequent market shortage will cause the price level to rise. Equally, if supply is in excess of demand, the resulting market surplus will cause the market price to fall. At some point we have an equilibrium or market-clearing price, to which the market will naturally move. In such an environment, the firm cannot have a 'pricing strategy': the price is set for it by the market. It is a price taker.

But, even if a firm were able to identify the market demand and supply schedules, which is not at all certain given the problem of acquiring accurate market information, the market equilibrium price is likely to be short lived as market conditions change and demand and supply shift. This would be particularly the case for those goods or services that are fashionable and subject to changing consumer preferences, or where production technology is undergoing a period of innovation, influencing both the cost structure of the product and the potential output decisions open to the business. The best business could hope for, given the uncertainty of demand and supply, is to be flexible enough to continue making a profit when market conditions shift.

When a firm has a degree of market power, however, it will have some discretion over the price it can charge for its product. The smaller the number of competitors, and the more distinct its product is from those of its rivals, the more inelastic will the firm's demand become and the greater will be its control over price.

We saw in Chapter 12 that, in oligopolistic markets, firms are dependent on each other: what one firm does, in terms of pricing, product design, product promotion, etc., will affect its rivals. The degree of interdependence, and the extent to which firms acknowledge it, will affect the degree to which they either compete or collude. This, in turn, will affect their pricing strategy. The result is that prices may be very difficult to predict in advance and bear little resemblance to those that would have been determined through the operation of free-market forces. At one time there may be an all-out price war, with firms madly trying to undercut each other in order to grab market share, or even drive their rivals out of business. At other times, prices may be very high, with the oligopolists colluding with each other to achieve maximum industry profits. In such cases the price may be even higher than if the industry were an unregulated monopoly, because there might still be considerable *non*-price competition, which would add to costs and hence to the profit-maximising price.

It is clear from this that, under oligopoly, pricing is likely to be highly strategic. One of the key strategic issues is the effect of prices on potential new entrants, and here it is not only the oligopolist, but also the monopolist that

BOX 17.1

Easy pricing

The following extract, taken from an article in *The Economist* of 29 May 2003, describes the radical approach to pricing adopted by Stelios Haji-Ioannou, the chairman and founder of the Easy group of businesses. Although the approach is far from revolutionary, Easy's entry to markets such as air flights, car rental and Internet cafés, has had a major impact on competition and the pricing behaviour of rivals.

It is perhaps fitting that microeconomics should have one of its most interesting ideas tested in Milton Keynes, a smallish town north of London which combines (by accident) the names of two of the last century's greatest economists. The 600-odd people who went to the opening showing of easyCinema there last Friday were doubtless more interested in seeing a film cheaply (prices started at 20p) than in being guinea-pigs for the theory of marginal pricing.

But it is this that fires the imagination of Stelios Haji-Ioannou, multi-millionaire, self-publicist and founder of easyCinema, easyJet, a budget airline, easyCar, a car-rental outfit, easyInternetcafé and others. As demand goes up, he argues, so should prices. So people who buy early, or choose slack times of day, get better deals. For example, charges at his Internet cafés rise as the seats fill up. The more people that hire

his cars, the greater the cost to the remaining customers. The first seats sold on easyJet flights are cheap, the last few the most expensive.

Although many businesses practise such 'yield management', none does it as radically as Mr Haji-Ioannou. Worked correctly, it should mean that he makes a lot more money than conventional fixed-price operators when his services are popular. Other businesses simply turn away customers when, say, the cinema showing or the flight is full. They may even lose money at peak times when they buy in extra capacity to provide customers with the service they want at the promised price.

Mr Haji-Ioannou's model, by contrast, milks the demand curve for every penny he can get. He can pocket the extra that the impatient and spendthrift are willing to pay to have just what they want when they want it.

The other leg of his strategy is ruthlessness with costs. Extras, such as meals, flexibility or convenience are stripped out. People pay for the basic service and nothing more. EasyCinema customers, for example, have no tickets: they print out a bar-coded entry pass from their computer. As with his other businesses, all booking is online. EasyCar offers one kind of car at each location; these are spartan outfits – one-person huts in the

Pause for thought

Would prices generally be lower or higher if a business was aiming to maximise long-run growth rather than short-run profits?

must think strategically. If the firm sets its prices too high, will new firms take the risk of entering the market? If so, should the firm keep its price down and thereby deliberately limit the size of its profits so as not to attract new entrants?

Limit pricing

definition

Limit pricing
Where a business keeps prices low, restricting its profits, so as to deter new rivals entering the market.

This policy of **limit pricing** is illustrated in Figure 17.1. Two *AC* curves are drawn: one for the existing firm and one for a potential entrant. The existing firm, being experienced and with a capital base and established supply channels, is shown having a lower *AC* curve. The new entrant, if it is to compete successfully with the existing firm, must charge the same price or a lower one. Thus provided the existing firm does not raise price above P_L, the other firm, unable to make supernormal profit, will not be attracted into the industry.

P_L may well be below the existing firm's short-run profit-maximising price, but it may prefer to limit its price to P_L to protect its long-run profits from damage by competition.

corner of a car park. Customers must bring their car back within a one-hour slot, clean and ready for the next user, or pay a penalty. EasyJet offers short-haul flights only, from minor airports, with no food or drink. Service, in short, is as commoditised as possible.

That allows gimmicky low-cost offerings. The 20p starting price for his cinema was a one-off, but Mr Haji-Ioannou reckons that he breaks even if he sells half the seats in each screening for £1.50–£2.00 – about a third of what other cinemas charge.

The biggest effect of this approach is not on his own customers, but on those of the many competing companies that have cut prices and empowered customers as a result. Online booking at British Airways, for example, now gives the customer a lot more choice about time and price. His Internet cafés have driven down prices sharply.

The six main distributors who control 90% of the films shown in Britain prefer to keep seats empty rather than flog them cheaply; they dislike easyCinema's cut-price offerings. The result is that, for now at least, his cinema can only show second-rate or second-run films. Until he cracks this cartel, Mr Haji-Ioannou's story, for all the admirable ideas behind it, will still be the stuff of

an interesting documentary film rather than the box-office blockbuster it could be.

Questions

1 Explain the theory of marginal pricing as practised at easyCinema.

2 Examine the above demand curve for an easyJet flight. Assume that the plane holds 100 passengers. Does the area marked represent the revenue that a full flight would earn easyJet? Explain.

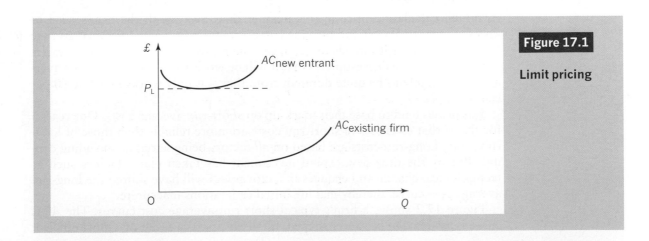

Figure 17.1

Limit pricing

17.2 Alternative pricing strategies

What is the typical procedure by which firms set prices? Do they construct marginal cost and marginal revenue curves (or equations) and find the output where they are equal? Do they then use an average revenue curve (or equation) to work out the price at that output?

To do this requires a detailed knowledge of costs and revenues that few firms possess. To work out *marginal* revenue, the firm requires information not just on current price and sales. It must know what will happen to demand if price *changes*. In other words, it must know the price elasticity of demand for its product. Similarly, to work out *marginal* cost, the firm must know how costs will *change* as output changes. In reality this is highly unlikely. The business environment is in a constant state of change and uncertainty. The costs of production and the potential revenues from sales will be difficult to predict, shaped as they are by many complex and interrelated variables (changes in tastes, advertising, technological innovation, etc.). Under oligopoly in particular, it is virtually impossible to identify a demand curve for the firm's product. Demand for one firm's product will depend on what its rivals do: and that can never be predicted with any certainty. As a consequence, managers' 'knowledge' of future demand and costs will take the form of estimates (or even 'guesstimates'). Trying to equate marginal costs and marginal revenue, therefore, is likely to be a highly unreliable means of achieving maximum profits (if, indeed, that were the aim).

If, then, the marginalist principle of traditional theory is not followed by most businesses, what alternative pricing strategy can be adopted? In practice, firms look for rules of pricing that are relatively simple to apply.

Cost-based pricing

definition

Mark-up pricing
A pricing strategy adopted by business in which a profit mark-up is added to average costs.

One alternative to marginalist pricing is **average cost** or **mark-up pricing**. In this case, producers derive a price by simply adding a certain percentage (mark-up) for profit on top of average costs (average fixed costs plus average variable costs).

$$P = AFC + AVC + \text{Profit mark-up}$$

The size of the profit mark-up will depend on the firm's aims: whether it is aiming for high or even maximum profits, or merely a target based on previous profit.

Choosing the level of output

Although calculating price in this manner does away with the firm's need to know its marginal cost and revenue curves, it still requires the firm to estimate how much output it intends to produce. The reason is that average cost varies with output. If the firm estimates that it will be working to full capacity, its average cost is likely to be quite different from that if it only works at 80 or 60 per cent of capacity.

Businesses tend to base their mark-up on *short-run* average costs. One reason for this is that estimates of short-run costs are more reliable than those of long-run costs. Long-run costs are based on *all* factors being variable, including capital. But by the time new capital investment has taken place, factors such as technological change and changes in factor prices will have shifted the long-run average cost curve, thereby making initial estimations inaccurate.

Figure 17.2 shows a firm's typical short-run average cost curves. The *AVC* curve is assumed to be saucer shaped. It falls at first as a result of a more efficient

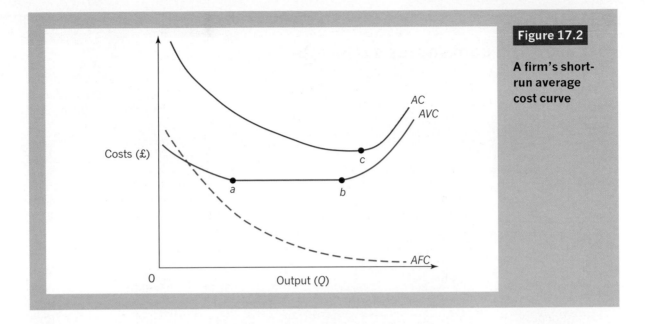

Figure 17.2

A firm's short-run average cost curve

deployment of resources; then is probably flat, or virtually so, over a range of output; then rises as a result of diminishing marginal returns and possibly the need to pay overtime. The flat range of the average variable cost curve reflects the **reserve capacity** held by the business. This is spare capacity that the business can draw upon, if needed, to respond to changes in the market. For example, demand for the product may be subject to seasonal variation. The point is that many businesses can accommodate such changes with very little change in their average variable costs.

> **definition**
> **Reserve capacity**
> A range of output over which business costs will tend to remain relatively constant.

Most firms that use average-cost pricing will base their price on this horizontal section of the AVC curve (between points a and b in Figure 17.2). This section represents the firm's *normal* range of output. This normal range of output is that within which the plant has been designed to operate, and the business expects to be producing.

Average fixed costs will carry on falling as more is produced: overheads are spread over a greater output. This is illustrated in Figure 17.2. The result is that average (total) cost (AC) will continue falling over the range of output where AVC is constant, with minimum AC being reached at point c – beyond the flat section of the AVC curve. In practice, many firms do not regard average fixed costs in this way. Instead, they focus on average variable costs and then just add an element for overheads (AFC). This element is probably calculated at the normal level of output (i.e. somewhere in the flat section of the AVC curve), and then assumed to be *constant* as output changes. Although this is clearly wrong, changes in output from the normal level may be sufficiently small as to cause only an insignificantly small change in AFC. Thus AC at point c may be only very slightly below AC at the normal level of output.

Choosing the mark-up

The level of profit mark-up on top of average cost will be influenced by a range of possible considerations, such as fairness and the response of rivals (this will be discussed in more detail below). However, the most significant consideration is likely to be the implications of price for the level of market demand.

BOX 17.2

How do UK companies set prices?

In 1995 the Bank of England conducted a survey of price-setting behaviour in 654 UK companies.[1] Among other things, the survey sought to establish what factors influenced companies' pricing decisions. The results are given in Table (a).

Companies were asked to rank alternative methods of pricing of their main product...The most popular response was that prices were set with respect to market conditions. The top preference[2] for almost 40 per cent of respondents was that prices were set at the highest level that the market could bear. An additional 25 per cent of respondents stated that they set prices in relation to their competitors – this was the second choice most popular among companies.

...The survey also confirmed the importance of company-specific factors. The first preference of about 20 per cent of respondents was that price was made up of a direct cost per unit plus a variable percentage mark-up...A further 17 per cent of companies, particularly retailing companies, stated that they priced on the basis of costs plus a fixed percentage mark-up.

Cost plus mark-ups tended to be more important for small companies, which cannot afford expensive market research.

The survey also sought to establish those factors which could cause prices to change – either up or down.

The survey asked companies to rank those factors most likely to push prices up or down. It found that there were substantial differences between the factors that influenced price increases and those that influenced price decreases. First, many more companies said that cost rises were likely to push prices up than said that cost reductions were likely to push prices down. Second, a rise in demand seemed less

(a) How are prices determined?

	1st	%	2nd	%	3rd	%
Market level	257	39	140	21	78	12
Competitors' prices	161	25	229	35	100	15
Direct cost plus variable mark-up	131	20	115	18	88	14
Direct cost plus fixed mark-up	108	17	49	8	42	6
Customer set	33	5	52	8	47	7
Regulatory agency	11	2	3	1	5	1

Source: *Bank of England Quarterly Bulletin*, May 1996

If a firm could estimate its demand curve, it could then set its output and profit mark-up at levels to avoid a shortage or surplus. Thus in Figure 17.3 it could choose a lower output (Q_1) with a higher mark-up (*fg*), or a higher output (Q_2) with a lower mark-up (*hj*). If a firm could not estimate its demand curve, then it could adjust its mark-up and output over time by a process of trial and error, according to its success in meeting profit and sales aims.

The equilibrium price and output?

Is it possible to identify an equilibrium price and output for the firm which sets its prices by adding a mark-up to average cost? To answer this, we need to identify a supply curve for the firm.

If a firm is aiming for a particular profit *per unit* of output and does not adjust this target, the firm's supply curve will be as in Figure 17.4(a). It is derived by adding the mark-up to the *AC* curve. If, however, a firm is aiming for a

Key Idea
10
p73

(b) Factors leading to a rise or fall in price

Rise	Number[a]	%	Fall	Number[a]	%
Increase in material costs	421	64	Decrease in material costs	186	28
Rival price rise	105	16	Rival price fall	235	36
Rise in demand	101	15	Fall in demand	146	22
Prices never rise	26	4	Prices never fall	75	12
Increase in interest rates	18	3	Decrease in interest rates	8	1
Higher market share	14	2	Lower market share	69	11
Fall in productivity	5	1	Rise in productivity	22	3

[a] Numbers citing a scenario as most important
Note: Top preferences only
Source: *Bank of England Quarterly Bulletin*, May 1996

likely to lead to a price increase than a fall in demand was to lead to a price cut.

...The importance of strategic interaction with competitors suggests that when contemplating a price cut, companies need to consider the chance of sparking off a price war...The finding that companies were much more likely to match rival price falls than they are to follow rival price rises appears to support the importance of strategic behaviour.

Questions

1 *Which of the following is more likely to be consistent with the aim of maximising profits: pricing on the basis of (a) cost per unit plus a variable percentage mark-up; (b) cost per unit plus a fixed percentage mark-up?*

2 *Explain the differences between the importance attached to the different factors leading to price increases and those leading to price reductions.*

3 *Is the strategic behaviour referred to in the second quote consistent with the kinked demand curve theory (see pages 244–5)?*

4 *Why might we require a more detailed analysis of firm size and the different industrial sectors within the survey in order to evaluate the price-setting data presented above?*

[1] Simon Hall, Mark Walsh and Tony Yates, 'How do UK companies set prices?', *Bank of England Quarterly Bulletin*, May 1996
[2] Companies were able to show more than one response as their top preference. This means the total percentage of companies expressing first preferences for all of the explanations of price determination exceeds 100%

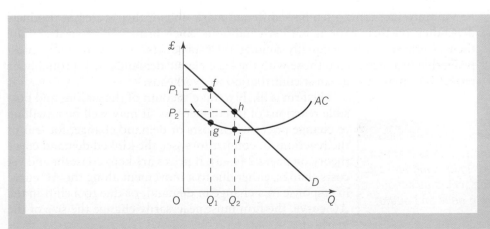

Figure 17.3

Choosing the output and profit mark-up

Figure 17.4

A firm's supply curve (a) For a given profit per unit (b) For a given total profit

particular level of *total* profit, and does not adjust this target, the firm's supply curve will be as in Figure 17.4(b). The greater the output, the less the profit per unit needs to be (and hence the less the mark-up) to give a particular level of total profit.

In either case, price and quantity can be derived from the intersection of demand and supply. Price and output will change if the demand or cost (and hence supply) curve shifts.

However, if the firm adjusts its profit target in the light of its experience or predictions, the mark-up will change. Under such circumstances, it may not be possible to derive a supply curve.

One problem here is that prices have to be set in advance of the firm knowing just how much it will sell and therefore how much it will need to produce. In practice, firms will usually base their assumptions about next year's sales on this year's figures, add a certain percentage to allow for growth in demand and then finally adjust this up or down if they decide to change the mark-up.

Variations in the mark-up

In most firms, the mark-up is not rigid. In expanding markets, or markets where firms have monopoly/oligopoly power, the size of the mark-up is likely to be greater. In contracting markets, or under conditions of rising costs and constant demand, a firm may well be forced to accept lower profits and thus reduce the mark-up.

Multiproduct firms often have different mark-ups for their different products depending on their various market conditions. Such firms will often distribute their overhead costs unequally among their products. The potentially most profitable products, often those with the least elastic demands, will probably be required to make the greatest contribution to overheads.

The firm is likely to take account of the actions and possible reactions of its competitors. It may well be unwilling to change prices when costs or demand change, for fear of the reactions of competitors (see the kinked demand curve theory on pages 244–5). If prices are kept constant and yet costs change, either due to a movement along the *AC* curve in response to a change in demand, or due to a shift in the *AC* curve, the firm must necessarily change the size of the mark-up.

Pause for thought

If the firm adjusts the size of its mark-up according to changes in demand and the actions of competitors, could its actions approximate to setting price and output where MC = MR?

All this suggests that, whereas the mark-up may well be based on a target profit, firms are often prepared to change their target and hence their mark-up.

Price discrimination   **17.3**

Up to now we have assumed that a firm will sell its output at a single price. Sometimes, however, firms may practise price discrimination. There are three major varieties of price discrimination:

- **First-degree price discrimination** is where the firm charges each consumer the maximum price he or she is prepared to pay for each unit. For example, stallholders in a bazaar will attempt to do this when bartering with their customers.

Pause for thought

Is the pricing system adopted by the 'easy' group of companies a form of first-degree price discrimination (see Box 17.1 on page 326)?

- **Second-degree price discrimination** is where the firm charges customers different prices according to how much they purchase. It may charge a high price for the first so many units, a lower price for the next so many units, a lower price again for the next, and so on. For example, electricity companies in some countries charge a high price for the first so many kilowatts. This is the amount of electricity that would typically be used for lighting and running appliances: in other words, the uses for which there is no substitute fuel. Additional kilowatts are charged at a much lower rate. This is electricity that is typically used for heating and cooking, where there are alternative fuels.

- **Third-degree price discrimination** is where consumers are grouped into two or more independent markets and a separate price is charged in each market. Examples include different-priced seats on buses for adults and children, and different prices charged for the same product in different countries. Third-degree price discrimination is much more common than first- or second-degree discrimination.

Conditions necessary for price discrimination to operate

As we shall see, a firm will be able to increase its profits if it can engage in price discrimination. But under what circumstances will it be able to charge discriminatory prices? There are three conditions that must be met:

- The firm must be able to set its price. Thus price discrimination will be impossible under perfect competition, where firms are price takers.
- The markets must be separate. Consumers in the low-priced market must not be able to resell the product in the high-priced market. For example, children must not be able to resell a half-priced child's cinema ticket for use by an adult.
- Demand elasticity must differ in each market. The firm will charge the higher price in the market where demand is less elastic, and thus less sensitive to a price rise.

definition

First-degree price discrimination
Where a firm charges each consumer for each unit the maximum price which that consumer is willing to pay for that unit.

definition

Second-degree price discrimination
Where a firm charges a consumer so much for the first so many units purchased, a different price for the next so many units purchased, and so on.

definition

Third-degree price discrimination
Where a firm divides consumers into different groups and charges a different price to consumers in different groups, but the same price to all the consumers within a group.

Key Idea
11
p81

Figure 17.5

Third-degree price discrimination

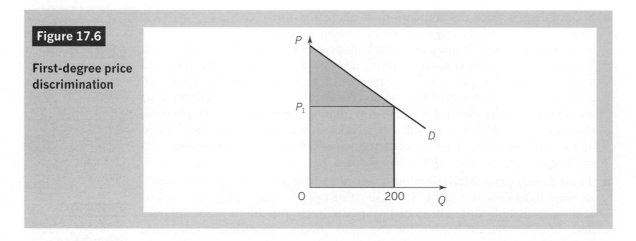

Figure 17.6

First-degree price discrimination

Advantages to the firm

Price discrimination will allow the firm to earn a higher revenue from any given level of sales. Let us first examine the case of third-degree price discrimination.

Figure 17.5 represents a firm's demand curve. If it is to sell 200 units without price discrimination, it must charge a price of P_1. The total revenue it earns is shown by the grey area. If, however, it can practise third-degree price discrimination by selling 150 of those 200 units at the higher price of P_2, it will gain the blue area in addition to the grey area in Figure 17.5.

In the case of first-degree price discrimination, the firm can earn even more revenue. If every unit is sold at the maximum price that each consumer is prepared to pay, the price for each unit can be found from the point on the demand curve above that quantity. Thus in Figure 17.6, the revenue from selling 200 units will be the grey area plus the blue area.

Another advantage to the firm of price discrimination is that it may be able to use it to drive competitors out of business. If a firm has a monopoly in one market (e.g. the home market), it may be able to charge a high price due to relatively inelastic demand, and thus make high profits. If it is under oligopoly in another market (e.g. the export market), it may use the high profits in the first market to subsidise a very low price in the oligopolistic market, thus forcing its competitors out of business.

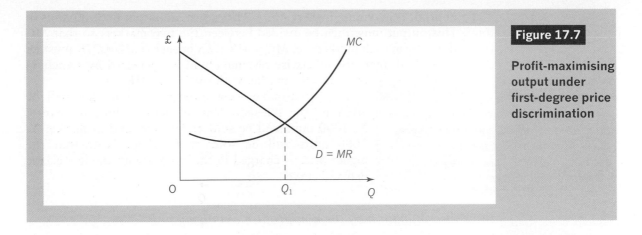

Figure 17.7

Profit-maximising output under first-degree price discrimination

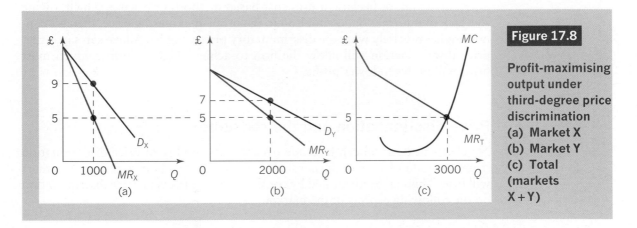

Figure 17.8

Profit-maximising output under third-degree price discrimination
(a) Market X
(b) Market Y
(c) Total (markets X+Y)

Profit-maximising prices and output

Assuming that the firm wishes to maximise profits, what discriminatory prices should it charge and how much should it produce? Let us first consider the case of first-degree price discrimination.

First-degree price discrimination

Since an increase in sales does not involve lowering the price for any unit save the *extra* one sold, the extra revenue gained from the last unit (MR) will be its price. Thus profit is maximised at Q_1 in Figure 17.7, where $MC = MR$ (= P of the *last* unit).

Third-degree price discrimination

Assume that a firm sells an identical product in two separate markets X and Y with demand and MR curves as shown in Figure 17.8.

Diagram (*c*) shows the MC and MR curves for the firm as a whole. This MR curve is found by adding the amounts sold in the two markets at each level of MR (in other words, the horizontal addition of the two MR curves). Thus, for example, with output of 1000 units in market X and 2000 in market Y, making 3000 in total, revenue would increase by £5 if one extra unit were sold, whether in market X or Y.

Total profit is maximised where $MC = MR$: i.e. at an output of 3000 units in total. This output must then be divided between the two markets so that MC is equal to MR in each market: i.e. $MC = MR = £5$ in each market. MR must be the same in both markets, otherwise revenue could be increased by switching output to the market with the higher MR.

The profit-maximising price in each market will be given by the relevant demand curve. Thus, in market X, 1000 units will be sold at £9 each, and in market Y, 2000 units will be sold at £7 each. Note that the higher price is charged in the market with the less elastic demand curve.

> **Pause for thought**
>
> *How would profit-maximising output and price be determined under third-degree price discrimination if there were three separate markets? Draw a diagram to illustrate your answer.*

Price discrimination by the non-profit-maximising firm

If a firm does not set a profit-maximising price, either because it has some alternative aim, or because it uses cost-based methods of pricing, which, owing to a lack of information, do not lead to the profit-maximising price, then we cannot predict precisely what the discriminatory prices will be. All we can say is that price discrimination will allow the firm to achieve higher profits, which most firms will prefer to lower profits.

Price discrimination and the consumer

No clear-cut decision can be made over the desirability of price discrimination from the point of view of the consumer. Some people will benefit from it; others will lose. This can be illustrated by considering the effects of price discrimination on the following aspects of the market.

Distribution

Those paying the higher price will probably feel that price discrimination is unfair to them. On the other hand, those charged the lower price may thereby be able to obtain a good or service that they could otherwise not afford: e.g. concessionary bus fares for old-aged pensioners. Price discrimination is likely to increase output and make the good or service available to more people.

Key Idea
26
p402

Competition

As explained above, a firm may use price discrimination to drive competitors out of business. This is known as **predatory pricing**. On the other hand, it might use its profits from its high-priced market to break into another market and withstand a possible price war. Competition is thereby increased.

> **definition**
>
> **Predatory pricing**
> Where a firm sets its average price below average cost in order to drive competitors out of business.

Profits

Price discrimination raises a firm's profits. This could be seen to be against the interests of the consumer, especially if the average price of the product is raised. On the other hand, the higher profits may be reinvested and lead to lower costs in the future.

Multiple product pricing 17.4

Thus far in our analysis of pricing strategy, we have been concerned only with a single product produced by a single firm. However, many businesses produce a range of products. Such products might be totally distinct and sold in different markets, or the firm might offer a range of models in the same market that differ in design and performance. For example, a vacuum cleaner manufacturer might also produce other household appliances such as irons, as well as offering a range of vacuums with different suction abilities and design features.

Each of these products and product ranges will require its own distinct price, and probably a longer-term pricing strategy. However, multiproduct pricing raises a wider set of issues due to the interrelated nature of demand and production.

Interrelated demand

Many of the large supermarkets or DIY stores are in fierce competition for business. It is quite normal to see them offering 'bargain buys', whose prices are cut dramatically in order to attract customers to the store. Often their price is even below average cost. Such cases are known as **loss leaders**. The hope is that customers will purchase not just the loss leader, but additional amounts of other products with full profit mark-ups, thereby bringing a net gain in profits.

This strategy is known as **full-range pricing** and involves the business assessing the prices of all its products together, and deciding from this how it might improve its profit performance. One of the most important considerations is the price elasticity of demand for the loss leader. The more elastic it is, the more customers will tend to be attracted into the store by the bargain. The business will also consider additional factors such as advertising the loss leaders and their positioning in the store, so as to attract customers to see other items at full price that they had not intended to buy.

Other demand interrelations that might influence the pricing policy of a business are where a business produces either complementary or substitute products. If a business produces complementary products, then increased sales of one product, such as British Telecom telephones, will raise the revenue gained from the other, such as the use of the telephone network. Alternatively, if the products produced by a business are substitutes, such as those of a breakfast cereal manufacturer like Kellogg's, then the increased sales of one product within its range may well detract from the revenue gained from the others. Businesses like BT and Kellogg's should therefore determine the prices of all their substitute and complementary products jointly so as to assess the total revenue implications. Here it is vital for the firm to have estimates of the cross-price elasticities of demand for their products (see section 5.3).

Interrelated production

The production of **by-products** is the most common form of interrelated production. A by-product is a good or service that is produced as a consequence of producing another good or service. For example, whey is a by-product of cheese. By-products have their own distinct market demand. However, the by-product

Key Idea
11
p81

definition
Loss leader
A product whose price is cut by the business in order to attract custom.

definition
Full-range pricing
A pricing strategy in which a business, seeking to improve its profit performance, assesses the pricing of its goods as a whole rather than individually.

definition
By-product
A good or service that is produced as a consequence of producing another good or service.

is only produced following demand for the main production good: it may well not be profitable to produce as a separate product.

To consider whether the by-product is profitable to sell, it is important to allocate the correct costs to its production. The raw materials and much of the other inputs to produce it can be considered to have a zero cost, since they have already been paid in producing the main product. But packaging, marketing and distributing the by-product clearly involve costs that have to be allocated directly to it, and the price it sells for must more than cover these costs.

It is not as simple as this, however, since the pricing of the by-product, and the subsequent revenue gained from its sale, might significantly influence the pricing of the main production good. Given that the two products share joint costs, a business must carefully consider how to allocate costs between them and what pricing policy it is going to pursue.

If it is aiming to maximise profits, it should add the marginal costs from both products to get an *MC* curve for the 'combined' product. Similarly, it should add the marginal revenues from both products at each output to get an *MR* curve for the combined product. It should then choose the combined output where the combined *MC* equals the combined *MR*. It should read off the price at this output for each of the two products from their separate demand curves.

> **Key Idea**
> **4**
> p27

In practice, many firms simply decide on the viability of selling by-products *after* a decision has been made on producing the main product. If the specific costs associated with the by-product can be more than covered, then the firm will go ahead and sell it.

17.5 Transfer pricing

The growth of modern business, both national and international, has meant that its organisation has become ever more complex. In an attempt to reduce the diseconomies that stem from co-ordinating such large business enterprises, the setting of price and output levels is frequently decentralised to individual divisions or profit centres. Such divisions or profit centres are assumed to operate in a semi-independent way, aiming to maximise their individual performance and, in so doing, benefit the business as a whole.

However, the decentralisation of pricing and output decision making can become problematic. This is particularly the case when the various divisions within the firm represent distinct stages in the production process. In these instances, certain divisions may well produce intermediate products that they will sell to other divisions within the business. There then arises the difficulty of how such intermediate products should be priced. This is known as the problem of **transfer pricing**.

> **definition**
> **Transfer pricing**
> The pricing system used within a business organisation to transfer intermediate products between the business's various divisions.

One implication of this is that a division which is seeking to maximise its own profits when selling to another division will attempt to exploit its 'monopoly' position and increase the transfer price. As it does so, the purchasing division, unless it, in turn, can pass on the higher cost, will see its profits fall. Indeed, if it could, the purchasing division would seek to drive down the purchase price as low as possible.

This conflict between divisions may not necessarily be in the interests of the business as a whole. The solution to this problem is for divisions to base their pricing of intermediate products on marginal costs. The marginal cost of the final product produced by the business will then be a 'true' marginal cost. If the business is seeking to maximise overall profits, it can then compare this final marginal cost with marginal revenue in order to decide on the level of total output. The lesson is that, for maximum company profits, individual divisions should seek to be efficient and produce with the lowest possible marginal costs, but not seek to attempt to maximise their own division's profits.

Key
Idea
19
p217

Pricing and the product life cycle   17.6

New products are launched and then become established. Later they may be replaced by more up-to-date products. Many products go through such a 'life cycle'. Four stages can be identified in a typical life cycle (see Figure 17.9):

1 Being launched.
2 A rapid growth in sales.
3 Maturity: a levelling off in sales.
4 Decline: sales begin to fall as the market becomes saturated, or as the product becomes out of date.

Black and white televisions, twin-tub washing machines and gramophone records have all reached stage 4. Colour televisions, automatic washing machines and audio cassettes have reached stage 3. Writable CDs, herbal teas, home security systems and DVD players are probably still in stage 2. DVD recorders, picture messaging phones and CD ROM home entertainment systems are probably still in stage 1.

At each stage, the firm is likely to be faced with quite different market conditions: not only in terms of consumer demand, but also in terms of competition from rivals. What does this mean for pricing strategy?

The launch stage

In this stage the firm will probably have a monopoly (unless there is a simultaneous launch by rivals).

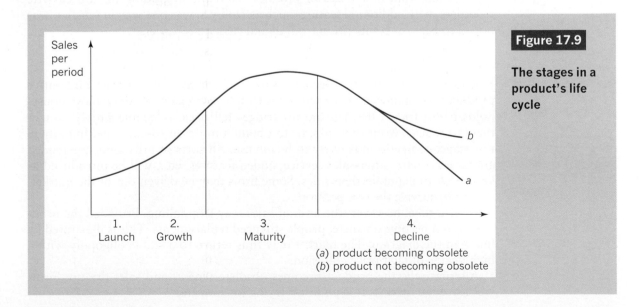

Figure 17.9

The stages in a product's life cycle

Given the lack of substitutes, the firm may be able to charge very high prices and make large profits. This will be especially true if it is a radically new product – like the ballpoint pen, the home computer and the mobile phone were. Such products are likely to have a rapidly expanding and price-inelastic demand.

The danger of a high-price policy is that the resulting high profits may tempt competitors to break into the industry, even if barriers are quite high. As an alternative, then, the firm may go for maximum 'market penetration': keeping the price low to get as many sales and as much brand loyalty as possible, before rivals can become established.

Which policy the firm adopts will depend on its assessment of its current price elasticity of demand and the likelihood of an early entry by rivals.

The growth stage

Unless entry barriers are very high, the rapid growth in sales will attract new firms. The industry becomes oligopolistic.

Despite the growth in the number of firms, sales are expanding so rapidly that all firms can increase their sales. Some price competition may emerge, but it is unlikely to be intense at this stage. New entrants may choose to compete in terms of minor product differences, while following the price lead set by the original firm.

The maturity stage

Now that the market has grown large, there are many firms competing. New firms – or, more likely, firms diversifying into this market – will be entering to get 'a piece of the action'. At the same time, the growth in sales is slowing down.

Competition is now likely to be more intense and collusion may well begin to break down. Pricing policy may become more aggressive as businesses attempt to hold on to their market share. Price wars may break out, only to be followed later by a 'truce' and a degree of price collusion.

It is in this stage particularly that firms may invest considerably in product innovation in order to 'breathe new life' into old products, especially if there is competition from new types of product. Thus the upgrading of hi-fi cassette recorders, with additional features such as Dolby S, was one way in which it was hoped to beat off competition from digital cassette recorders.

The decline stage

Eventually, as the market becomes saturated, or as new superior alternative products are launched, sales will start to fall. For example, once most house-holds had a fridge, the demand for fridges fell back as people simply bought them to replace worn-out ones, or to obtain a more up-to-date one. Initially in this stage, competition is likely to be intense. All sorts of price offers, extended guarantees, better after-sales service, added features, etc., will be introduced as firms seek to maintain their sales. Some firms may be driven out of the market, unable to survive the competition.

After a time, however, the level of sales may stop falling. Provided the product has not become obsolete, people still need replacements. This is illustrated by line *b* in the diagram. The market may thus return to a stable oligopoly with a high degree of tacit price collusion.

Alternatively, the product becomes obsolete (line *a*) and sales dry up. Firms will leave the market. It is pointless trying to compete.

SUMMARY

1a Prices are determined by a wide range of factors, principal among which are demand and supply, market structure and the aims of managers.

1b Firms with market power will not always attempt to maximise short-run profits, even if maximum profit is the aim. They may well limit prices so as to forestall the entry of new firms.

2a Traditional economic theory assumes that businesses will set prices corresponding to the output where the marginal costs of production are equal to marginal revenue. They will do so in pursuit of maximum profits.

2b The difficulties that a business faces in deriving its marginal cost and revenue curves suggest that this is unlikely to be a widely practised pricing strategy.

2c Cost-based pricing involves the business adding a profit mark-up to its average costs of production. The profit mark-up set by the business is likely to alter depending upon market conditions, such as the level of consumer demand and the degree of market competition.

3a Many businesses practise price discrimination, in an attempt to maximise profits from the sale of a product. There are different levels of price discrimination that a business might practise.

3b For a business to practise price discrimination it must be able to set prices, separate markets so as to prevent resale from the cheap to the expensive market, and identify distinct demand elasticities in each market.

3c Whether price discrimination is in the consumer's interest or not is uncertain. Some individuals will gain and some will lose.

4 Businesses that produce many products need to consider the demand and production interrelations between them when setting prices.

5a The organisation of a business as a series of divisions, each pursuing an independent strategy, has implications for pricing policy, especially when products are sold within a business enterprise.

5b The optimum transfer price between divisions from the point of view of the whole organisation is likely to be equal to marginal cost.

6a Products will be priced differently depending upon where they are in the product's life cycle.

6b New products can be priced cheaply so as to gain market share, or priced expensively to recoup cost. Later on in the product's life cycle, prices will have to reflect the degree of competition, which may become intense as the market stabilises or even declines.

REVIEW QUESTIONS

1 Explain why a business will find it difficult to set prices following the *MC = MR* rule of traditional economic theory.

2 'Basing prices on average cost is no less problematical than using marginal cost and marginal revenue.' Assess this statement.

3 Outline the main factors that might influence the size of the profit mark-up set by a business.

4 If a cinema could sell all its seats to adults in the evenings at the end of the week, but only a few on Mondays and Tuesdays, what price discrimination policy would you recommend to the cinema in order for it to maximise its weekly revenue?

5 What is the role of a loss leader and what lessons might a business learn when pricing a range of products? Are there any supermarket products that would *not* be suitable to sell as loss leaders?

6 How will a business's pricing strategy differ at each stage of its product's life cycle? First assume that the business has a monopoly position at the launch stage; then assume that it faces a high degree of competition right from the outset.

Additional Part F case studies on the *Economics for Business* website (www.booksites.net/sloman)

F.1 What do you maximise? An examination of 'rational' behaviour from an individual's point of view – including individual managers.

F.2 When is a theory not a theory? A light-hearted examination of the difficulties of formulating theories from evidence.

F.3 Business divorce. A case study of the demergers of ICI and Hanson.

F.4 The global information economy and strategic alliances. A case study illustrating the scope for alliances within the information economy.

F.5 Peak load pricing. An example of price discrimination: charging more when it costs more to produce.

F.6 Price discrimination in the cinema. An illustration of why it might be in a cinema's interests to offer concessionary prices at off-peak times, but not at peak times.

Websites relevant to Part F

Numbers and sections refer to websites listed in the Web appendix and hotlinked from this book's website at **www.booksites.net/sloman**

- For news articles relevant to Part F, see the *Economics News Articles* link from the book's website.

- For general news relevant to alternative strategies see websites in section A, and particularly A2, 3, 8, 9, 23, 24, 25, 26, 35, 36. See also A38, 39 and 43 for links to newspapers worldwide; and A42 for links to economics news articles on particular search topics from newspapers worldwide.

- For student resources relevant to Part F, see sites C1–7, 9, 10, 19.

- For information on mergers, see sites E4, 10, 18, 20.

- For data on SMEs, see the SME database in B3 or E10.

- For information on pricing, see site E10 and the sites of the regulators of the privatised industries: E16, 19, 21, 22, 25.

- Sites I7 and 11 in the Business section contain links to *Business > Management > Organisational Management*.

The firm in the factor market

THE FT REPORTS...

THE FINANCIAL TIMES, 26 JUNE 2003

Working poor continue to walk the line

By RICHARD DONKIN

How much do we need to earn just to get by in today's society? In the US the figure for a family of four, including both parents, ranges from $27 000 a year in rural areas to $52 000 in one of the big cities, according to estimates produced at a London-based symposium this week.

Eileen Appelbaum, the Rutgers University professor who outlined the figures at a Future of Work symposium organised by the Economic and Social Research Council, said the national median was about $33 500. Yet in 2001 some 34m Americans – about 24 per cent of the labour force – were earning less than $8.70 an hour ($17 400 a year), a figure she described as close to the poverty line for a family of four.

People rarely mention the poverty line these days. Reports of earnings tend to be dominated by the seven-figure salaries awarded to the bosses of big businesses. So the revelation that so many Americans can be classified as 'working poor' is a reminder of the broadening inequalities in the world's richest nation.

Prof. Appelbaum's work on low-paid Americans is an indictment of US corporate sector short-termism and the way that deregulation and cost-cutting, principally of wage bills, has been tolerated and sometimes encouraged by successive US administrations.

[Her] work and other recent economic studies suggest that it is time for the US and the UK to re-examine their 25-year infatuation with free market economics. At the same time, governments must rethink their interventionist policies.

A Financial Times survey this week revealed that UK government regional investment grants were failing to stimulate employment on anything approaching the scale originally envisaged.

In the same week, a study published by the Centre for Economic Performance highlighted differences in the relative pay of skilled workers in different regions of the UK. This noted that the relative wages for skilled workers were a third lower in the South East, which has the highest living costs in the UK, than in Wales or Scotland, thereby questioning policies that steer skill-intensive industries towards regions with high levels of unskilled labour. The study found that companies needed to pay more for their skilled labour in regions where there was a scarcity of qualified workers.

Each of these studies illustrates the complexity of labour markets. Nevertheless there seems to be a broad consensus among academics on the relationship between education and skills training, economic performance and earnings potential.

> *UK companies are operating with lower levels of capital intensity than their competitors in Europe and the United States. Business investment has increased to the level of other advanced economies over the past decade, but that has not been enough to close the gap in terms of capital intensity.*
>
> Michael Porter and Christian Ketels on UK competitiveness (May 2003)

So far we have considered the role of the firm as a supplier of goods and services. In other words, we have looked at the operation of firms in the goods market. But to produce goods and services involves using factors of production: labour, capital and raw materials. In Part F, therefore, we turn to examine the behaviour of firms in factor markets and, in particular, the market for labour and the market for capital.

In factor markets, the supply and demand roles are reversed. The firm is *demanding* factors of production in order to *produce* goods and services. This demand for factors is thus a *derived* demand: one that is derived from consumers' demand for the firm's products. Households, on the other hand, in order to earn the money to buy goods and services, are *supplying* labour.

Chapter 18 focuses upon labour and the determination of wage rates. It also shows how the existence of power, whether of employers or trade unions, affects the wage rate and the level of employment in a given labour market. In addition to the issue of wage determination, we will consider the problem of low pay and discrimination, and the implications for the labour market of growing levels of flexibility in employment practices.

In Chapter 19 we will consider the employment of capital by firms and look at the relationship between the business and investment. We will consider how businesses appraise the profitability of investment. We will also examine the various sources of finance for investment. The chapter finishes by examining the stock market. We ask whether it is an efficient means of allocating capital.

key terms

Derived demand
Wage taker
Wage setter
Marginal revenue product
Monopsony
Bilateral monopoly
Trade union
Collective bargaining
Efficiency wages
Minimum wage rates
Discrimination
The flexible firm
Core and peripheral workers
Insiders and outsiders
Capital
Capital services
Investment
Discounting
Net present value
Financial intermediaries
Maturity transformation
Risk transformation
Retail and wholesale banking
Efficient capital markets
Weak, semi-strong and strong efficiency
Random walk

18 Labour markets, wages and industrial relations

In this chapter we will consider how labour markets operate. In particular, we will focus on the determination of wage rates in different types of market: ones where employers are wage takers, ones where they can choose the wage rate, and ones where wage rates are determined by a process of collective bargaining.

We start by examining some of the key trends in the structure of the labour market.

18.1 The UK labour market

The labour market has undergone great change in recent years. Advances in technology, changes in the pattern of output, a need to be competitive in international markets and various social changes have all contributed to changes in work practices and in the structure and composition of the workforce.

Major changes in the UK include the following:

- A shift from agricultural and manufacturing to service-sector employment. Figure 18.1 reveals that employment in agriculture has been falling over a long historical period. The fall in manufacturing employment, however, has been more recent, starting in the 1960s and gathering pace through the 1970s, 1980s and 1990s. By contrast, employment in the service industries has grown steadily since 1946. In fact since 1979, it has expanded by over 5 million jobs.

- A rise in part-time employment, and a fall in full-time employment (see Figure 18.2). In 1971 one in six workers was part time; by 2003 this had risen to one worker in four. In the EU as a whole, the figure is one in six. The fall in the proportion of full-time employees closely mirrors the decline in manufacturing, where jobs were more likely to be on a full-time basis. At the same time, the growth in part-time work reflects the growth in the service sector, where many jobs are part time. Since 1979 part-time employment has risen by over 2.2 million.

- A rise in female participation rates. Women now constitute approximately half of the paid labour force. The rise in participation rates is strongly associated with the growth in the service sector and the creation of part-time positions. Nearly half of all female workers, about 6.3 million, are in part-time work.

- A rise in the proportion of workers employed on fixed-term contracts, or on a temporary or casual basis. Many firms nowadays prefer to employ only their core workers/managers on a permanent ('continuing') basis. They feel

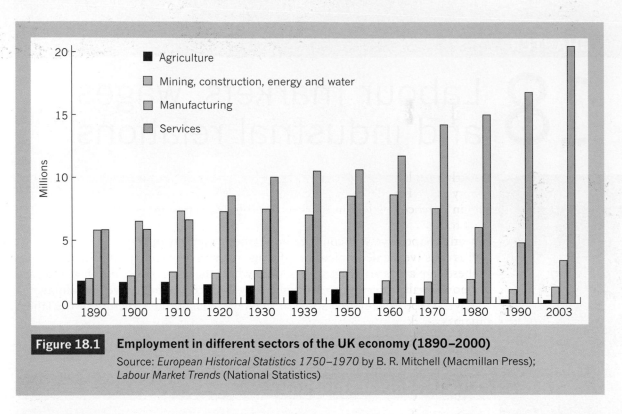

Figure 18.1 **Employment in different sectors of the UK economy (1890–2000)**

Source: *European Historical Statistics 1750–1970* by B. R. Mitchell (Macmillan Press);
Labour Market Trends (National Statistics)

Figure 18.2

Full-time and part-time employment in the UK

Source: Based on *Labour Market Trends* (National Statistics) various editions

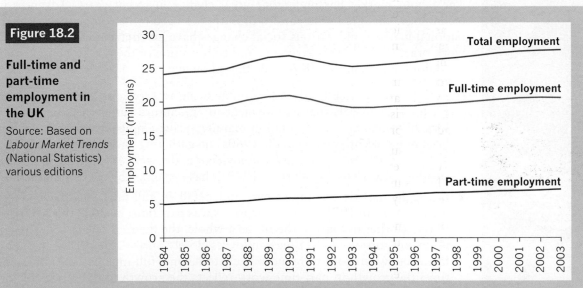

definition

Downsizing
Where a business reorganises and reduces its size, especially in respect to levels of employment, in order to cut costs.

that it gives them more flexibility to respond to changing market conditions to have the remainder of their workers employed on a short-term basis and, perhaps, to make use of agency staff or to contract out work.

■ **Downsizing.** It has become very fashionable in recent years for companies to try to 'trim' the numbers of their employees in order to reduce costs. There is now, however, a growing consensus that the process may have gone too far. The cost of reducing its workforce may be that a company loses revenue: if it cuts back on people employed to market its products, develop new products or ensure that quality is maintained, then it is likely to lose market share. It might reduce unit costs, but total profits could nevertheless fall, not rise.

Market-determined wage rates and employment   18.2

Perfect labour markets

When looking at the market for labour, it is useful to make a similar distinction to that made in the theory of the firm: the distinction between perfect and imperfect markets. Although in practice few labour markets are totally perfect, many do at least approximate to it.

The assumptions of perfect labour markets are similar to those of perfect goods markets. The main one is that everyone is a **wage taker**. In other words, neither employers nor employees have any economic power to affect wage rates. This situation is not uncommon. Small employers are likely to have to pay the 'going wage rate' to their employees, especially where the employee is of a clear category, such as an electrician, a bar worker, a secretary or a porter. As far as employees are concerned, being a wage taker means not being a member of a union and therefore not being able to use collective bargaining to push up the wage rate.

The other assumptions of a perfect labour market are as follows:

definition

Wage taker
The wage rate is determined by market forces.

■ Freedom of entry. There are no restrictions on the movement of labour. For example, workers are free to move to alternative jobs or to areas of the country where wage rates are higher. There are no barriers erected by, say, unions, professional associations or the government. Of course, it takes time for workers to change jobs and maybe to retrain. This assumption therefore applies only in the long run.

■ Perfect knowledge. Workers are fully aware of what jobs are available at what wage rates and with what conditions of employment. Likewise employers know what labour is available and how productive that labour is.

■ Homogeneous labour. It is usually assumed that, in perfect markets, workers of a given category are identical in terms of productivity. For example, it would be assumed that all bricklayers are equally skilled and motivated.

> **Pause for thought**
>
> *Which of these assumptions do you think would be correct in each of the following cases? (a) Supermarket checkout operators. (b) Agricultural workers. (c) Crane operators. (d) Business studies teachers. (e) Call centre workers.*

Key Idea 10 p73

Wage rates and employment under perfect competition are determined by the interaction of the market demand and supply of labour. This is illustrated in Figure 18.3(b).

Generally it would be expected that the supply and demand curves slope the same way as in goods markets. The higher the wage paid for a certain type of job, the more workers will want to do that job. This gives an upward-sloping supply curve of labour. On the other hand, the higher the wage that employers have to pay, the less labour they will want to employ. Either they will simply produce less output, or they will substitute other factors of production, like machinery, for labour. Thus the demand curve for labour slopes downwards.

Figure 18.3(a) shows how an individual employer has to accept this wage. The supply of labour to that employer is infinitely elastic. In other words, at the market wage W_m, there is no limit to the number of workers available to that employer (but no workers at all will be available below it: they will all be working elsewhere). At the market wage W_m, the employer will employ Q_1 hours of labour.

BOX 18.1

'Telecommuters'
The electronic cottage

One of the causes of inequality of wages has been the geographical immobility of labour. Within countries this manifests itself in different rates of pay between different regions: often, those regions furthest from the capital city pay the lowest rates.

It also applies between countries. Poorer countries pay lower wages because there is not the mobility of labour between countries to counteract it.

Nevertheless within countries people are often prepared to commute long distances in order to earn the higher pay that large cities have to offer. Witness the army of people who travel into London each day from many miles away, getting up early, arriving back late and paying huge sums of money for travelling.

One important development in recent years, however, is helping to reverse this trend. The increasing sophistication of information technology, with direct computer linking, the Internet, fax machines and mobile phones, has meant that many people can work at home. The number of these 'telecommuters' has grown steadily since the information technology revolution of the early 1980s.

It has been found that where 'telecommuting networks' have been established, gains in productivity levels have been significant, when compared with comparable office workers. Most studies indicate rises in productivity of over 35 per cent. With fewer interruptions and less chatting with fellow workers, less working time is lost. Add to this the stress-free environment, free from the strain of commuting, and the individual worker's performance is enhanced.

With further savings in time, in the renting and maintenance of offices (often in high-cost inner city locations) and in heating and lighting costs, the economic arguments in favour of telecommuting seem very persuasive.

Then there are the broader gains to society. Telecommuting opens up the labour market to a wider group of workers who might find it difficult to leave the home-groups such as single parents and the disabled. Also, concerns that managers lose control over their employees, and that the quality of work falls, appear unfounded. In fact the reverse seems to have occurred: the quality of work in many cases has improved.

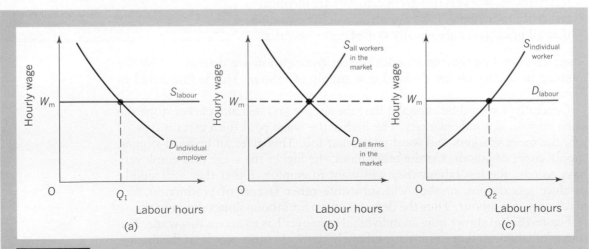

Figure 18.3 A perfectly competitive labour market (a) Individual employer (b) Whole market (c) Individual worker – marginal disutility of work

But do such employees feel isolated? For many people, work is an important part of their social environment, providing them with an opportunity to meet others and to work as a team. For those who are unable to leave the home, however, telecommuting may be the *only* means of earning a living: the choice of travelling to work may simply not be open to them.

Ironically, it appears that whereas the industrial revolution destroyed cottage industries and people's ability to work from home, information technology is doing the reverse, and may in the end contribute to the destruction of the office – at least of large central offices. Small local offices, however, may flourish as the developments in technology (such as video conferencing) mean that people do not have to travel long distances for meetings.

These technological developments have been the equivalent of an increase in labour mobility. Work can be taken to the workers rather than the workers coming to the work. The effect will be to reduce the premium that needs to be paid to workers in commercial centres, such as the City of London.

There is no reason, of course, why telecommuters cannot work in different countries. Increasingly companies in developed countries are employing low-wage workers in the developing world to do data processing, telesales and various types of 'back-office' work.

However, telecommuters can be exploited. According to the Low Pay Commission, in 2002 up to a quarter of all homeworkers in the UK were paid below £3.60 per hour, and of these nine out of ten were female. Manual homeworkers were particularly affected with up to 75 per cent paid below £3.60. The problem with homeworking is its largely hidden nature, which makes it difficult to ensure that minimum wages are paid. Maybe, along with the flexibility, some of the less desirable elements of cottage industry are also returning!

Questions

1 *What effects are such developments likely to have on (a) trade union membership; (b) trade union power?*

2 *How is a growth in telecommuting likely to affect relative house prices between capital cities and the regions?*

Figure 18.3(c) shows how an individual worker also has to accept this wage. In this case it is the demand curve for that worker that is infinitely elastic. In other words, there is as much work as the worker cares to do at this wage (but none at all above it).

We now turn to look at the supply and demand for labour in more detail.

The supply of labour

We can look at the supply of labour at three levels. The supply of hours by an individual worker (Figure 18.3(c)), the supply of workers to an individual employer (Figure 18.3(a)) and the total market supply of a given category of labour (Figure 18.3(b)). Let us examine each in turn.

The supply of hours by an individual worker

Work involves two major costs (or 'disutilities') to the worker:

■ When people work they sacrifice leisure.

■ The work itself may be unpleasant.

Each extra hour worked will involve additional disutility. This **marginal disutility of work** (*MDU*) will tend to *increase* as people work more hours. There are two

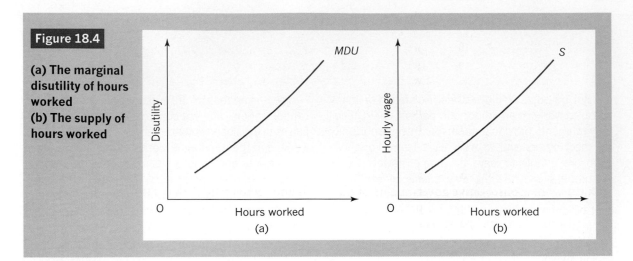

Figure 18.4

(a) The marginal disutility of hours worked
(b) The supply of hours worked

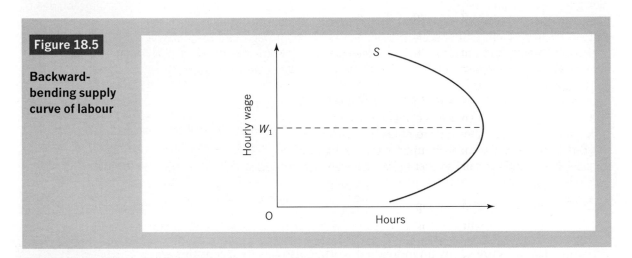

Figure 18.5

Backward-bending supply curve of labour

Substitution effect of a rise in wages
Workers will tend to substitute income for leisure as leisure now has a higher opportunity cost. This effect leads to *more* hours being worked as wages rise.

Income effect of a rise in wages
Workers get a higher income for a given number of hours worked and may thus feel they need to work fewer hours as wages rise.

reasons for this. First, the less the leisure they have left, the greater the disutility they experience in sacrificing a further hour of leisure. Second, the unpleasantness they experience in doing the job will tend to increase due to boredom or tiredness.

This increasing marginal disutility (see Figure 18.4(a)) will tend to give an upward-sloping supply curve of hours by an individual worker (see Figure 18.4(b)). The reason is that, in order to persuade people to work more hours, a higher hourly wage must be paid to compensate for the higher marginal disutility incurred. This helps explain why overtime rates are higher than standard rates.

Under certain circumstances, however, the supply of hours curve might bend backwards (see Figure 18.5). The reason is that, when wage rates go up, there will be two opposing forces operating on the individual's labour supply.

On the one hand, with higher wage rates people will tend to work more hours, since leisure would now involve a greater sacrifice of income and hence consumption. They substitute income for leisure. This is called the **substitution effect** of the increase in wage rates.

On the other hand, people may feel that with higher wage rates they can afford to work less and have more leisure. This is called the **income effect**.

The relative magnitude of these two effects determines the slope of the individual's supply curve. It is normally assumed that the substitution effect outweighs the income effect, especially at lower wage rates. A rise in wage rates acts as an incentive: it encourages a person to work more hours. It is possible, however, that the income effect will outweigh the substitution effect. Particularly at very high wage rates people say, 'There's not so much point now in doing overtime. I can afford to spend more time at home.'

If the wage rate becomes high enough for the income effect to dominate, the supply curve will begin to slope backward. This occurs above a wage rate of W_1 in Figure 18.5.

These considerations are particularly important for a government considering tax cuts. The Conservative governments of the 1980s and 1990s argued that cuts in income taxes are like giving people a pay rise, and thus provide an incentive for people to work harder. This analysis is only correct, however, if the substitution effect dominates. If the income effect dominates, people will work less after the tax cut.

The supply of labour to an individual employer

Under perfect competition, the supply of labour to a particular firm will be perfectly elastic, as in Figure 18.3(a). The firm is a 'wage taker' and thus has no power to influence wages.

The market supply of a given type of labour

This will typically be upward sloping. The higher the wage rate offered in a particular type of job, the more people will want to do that job.

The *position* of the market supply curve of labour will depend on the number of people willing and able to do the job at each given wage rate. This depends on three things:

- The number of qualified people.
- The non-wage benefits or costs of the job, such as the pleasantness or otherwise of the working environment, job satisfaction or dissatisfaction, status, power, the degree of job security, holidays, perks and other fringe benefits.
- The wages and non-wage benefits in alternative jobs.

> **Pause for thought**
>
> *Which way will the supply curve shift if the wage rates in alternative jobs rise?*

A change in the wage rate will cause a movement along the supply curve. A change in any of these other three determinants will shift the whole curve.

The elasticity of the market supply of labour

Key Idea 11 p81

How *responsive* will the supply of labour be to a change in the wage rate? If the market wage rate goes up, will a lot more labour become available or only a little? This responsiveness (elasticity) depends on (a) the difficulties and costs of changing jobs and (b) the time period.

Another way of looking at the elasticity of supply of labour is in terms of the **mobility of labour**: the willingness and ability of labour to move to another job, whether in a different location (geographical mobility) or in a different industry (occupational mobility). The mobility of labour (and hence the elasticity of supply of labour) will be higher when there are alternative jobs in the same location, when alternative jobs require similar skills and when people have good information about these jobs. It is also much higher in the long run, when people have the time to acquire new skills and when the education system has had time to adapt to the changing demands of industry.

> **definition**
>
> **Mobility of labour** The ease with which labour can either shift between jobs (occupational mobility) or move to other parts of the country in search of work (geographical mobility).

The demand for labour: the marginal productivity theory

The traditional 'neoclassical' theory of the firm assumes that firms aim to maximise profits. The same assumption is made in the neoclassical theory of labour demand. This theory is generally known as the **marginal productivity theory**.

The profit-maximising approach

How many workers will a profit-maximising firm want to employ? The firm will answer this question by weighing up the costs of employing extra labour against the benefits. It will use exactly the same principles as in deciding how much output to produce.

In the goods market, the firm will maximise profits where the marginal cost of an extra unit of *goods* produced equals the marginal revenue from selling it: $MC = MR$.

In the labour market, the firm will maximise profits where the marginal cost of employing an extra *worker* equals the marginal revenue that the worker's output earns for the firm: MC of labour $= MR$ of labour. The reasoning is simple. If an extra worker adds more to a firm's revenue than to its costs, the firm's profits will increase. It will be worth employing that worker. But as more workers are employed, diminishing returns to labour will set in (see page 170). Each extra worker will produce less than the previous one, and thus earn less revenue for the firm. Eventually the marginal revenue from extra workers will fall to the level of their marginal cost. At that point the firm will stop employing extra workers. There are no additional profits to be gained. Profits are at a maximum.

Measuring the marginal cost and revenue of labour

Marginal cost of labour (MC_L). This is the extra cost of employing one more worker. Under perfect competition the firm is too small to affect the market wage. It faces a horizontal supply curve (see Figure 18.3(a)). In other words, it can employ as many workers as it chooses at the market wage rate. Thus the additional cost of employing one more person will simply be the wage rate: $MC_L = W$.

Marginal revenue of labour (MRP_L). The marginal revenue that the firm gains from employing one more worker is called the **marginal revenue product of labour** (MRP_L). The MRP_L is found by multiplying two elements – the *marginal physical product* of labour (MPP_L) and the marginal revenue gained by selling one more unit of output (MR).

$$MRP_L = MPP_L \times MR$$

The MPP_L is the extra output produced by the last worker. Thus if the last worker produces 100 tonnes of output per week (MPP_L), and if the firm earns an extra £2 for each additional tonne sold (MR), then the worker's MRP is £200. This extra worker is adding £200 to the firm's revenue.

The profit-maximising level of employment for a firm

The MPP_L curve was illustrated in Figure 9.1 (see page 171). As more workers are employed, there will come a point when diminishing returns set in (point *b*). The MPP_L curve thus slopes down after this point. The MRP_L curve will be of a

Figure 18.6

The profit-maximising level of employment

Figure 18.7

Deriving the firm's demand curve for labour

similar shape to the MPP_L curve, since it is merely being multiplied by a constant figure, MR. (Under perfect competition, $MR = P$ and does not vary with output). The MRP_L curve is illustrated in Figure 18.6, along with the MC_L 'curve'.

Pause for thought

Why is the MC_L curve horizontal?

Profits will be maximised at an employment level of Q_e, where MC_L (i.e. W) $= MRP_L$. Why? At levels of employment below Q_e, MRP_L exceeds MC_L. The firm will increase profits by employing more labour. At levels of employment above Q_e, MC_L exceeds MRP_L. In this case the firm will increase profits by reducing employment.

Derivation of the firm's demand curve for labour

No matter what the wage rate, the quantity of labour demanded will be found from the intersection of W and MRP_L (see Figure 18.7). At a wage rate of W_1, Q_1 labour is demanded (point a); at W_1, Q_2 is demanded (point b); at W_3, Q_3 is demanded (point c).

Thus the MRP_L curve shows the quantity of labour employed at each wage rate. But this is just what the demand curve for labour shows. Thus the MRP_L curve is the demand curve for labour.

There are three determinants of the demand for labour:

■ The wage rate. This determines the position *on* the demand curve. (Strictly speaking, we would refer here to the wage determining the 'quantity demanded' rather than the 'demand'.)

definition

Derived demand
The demand for a factor of production depends on the demand for the good which uses it.

■ The productivity of labour (MPP_L). This determines the position *of* the demand curve.

■ The demand for the good. The higher the market demand for the good, the higher will be its market price, and hence the higher will be the MR, and thus the MRP_L. This too determines the position of the demand curve. It shows how the demand for labour (and other factors) is a **derived demand**: i.e. one derived from the demand for the good. For example, the higher the demand for houses, and hence the higher their price, the higher will be the demand for bricklayers.

Pause for thought

If the productivity of a group of workers rises by 10 per cent, will the wage rate they are paid also rise by 10 per cent? Explain why or why not.

A change in the wage rate is represented by a movement *along* the demand curve for labour. A change in the productivity of labour or in the demand for the good *shifts* the curve.

The elasticity of demand for labour

Key Idea
11
p81

The elasticity of demand for labour (with respect to changes in the wage rate) will be greater:

■ The greater the price elasticity of demand for the good. A fall in W will lead to higher employment and more output. This will drive P down. If the market demand for the good is elastic, this fall in P will lead to a lot more being sold and hence a lot more people being employed.

■ The easier it is to substitute labour for other factors of production and vice versa. If labour can be readily substituted for other factors, then a reduction in W will lead to a large increase in labour used to replace these other factors.

■ The greater the wage cost as a proportion of total costs. If wages are a large proportion of total costs and the wage rate falls, total costs will fall significantly; therefore production will increase significantly, and so will the demand for labour.

■ The longer the time period. Given sufficient time, firms can respond to a fall in wage rates by reorganising their production processes to make use of the now relatively cheap labour.

Wages and profits under perfect competition

The wage rate (W) is determined by the interaction of demand and supply in the labour market. This will be equal to the value of the output that the last person produces (MRP_L).

Profits to the individual firm will arise from the fact that the MRP_L curve slopes downward (diminishing returns). Thus the last worker adds less to the revenue of firms than previous workers already employed.

If *all* workers in the firm receive a wage equal to the MRP of the *last* worker, everyone but the last worker will receive a wage less than their MRP. This excess of MRP_L over W of previous workers provides a surplus to the firm over its wages bill (see Figure 18.8). Part of this will be required for paying non-wage costs; part will be the profits for the firm.

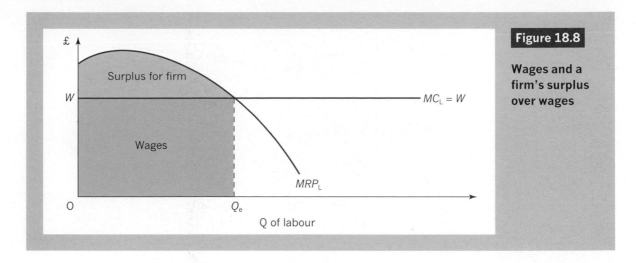

Figure 18.8

Wages and a firm's surplus over wages

Perfect competition between firms will ensure that profits are kept down to *normal* profits. If the surplus over wages is such that *supernormal* profits are made, new firms will enter the industry. The price of the good (and hence MRP_L) will fall, and the wage will be bid up, until only normal profits remain.

Firms with power in the labour market   18.3

In the real world, many firms have the power to influence wage rates: they are not wage takers. This is one of the major types of labour market 'imperfection'.

When a firm is the only employer of a particular type of labour, this situation is called a **monopsony**. The Post Office is a monopsony employer of postal workers. Another example is when a factory is the only employer of certain types of labour in that district. It therefore has local monopsony power. When there are just a few employers, this is called **oligopsony**.

Monopsonists (and oligopsonists too) are 'wage setters' not 'wage takers'. Thus a large employer in a small town may have considerable power to resist wage increases or even to force wage rates down.

Such firms face an upward-sloping supply curve of labour. This is illustrated in Figure 18.9. If the firm wants to take on more labour, it will have to pay a higher wage rate to attract workers away from other industries. But conversely, by employing less labour it can get away with paying a lower wage rate.

The supply curve shows the wage that must be paid to attract a given quantity of labour. The wage it pays is the *average cost* to the firm of employing labour (AC_L): i.e. the cost per worker. The supply curve is also therefore the AC_L curve.

The *marginal* cost of employing one more worker (MC_L) will be above the wage (AC_L): see Figure 18.9. The reason is that the wage rate has to be raised to attract extra workers. The MC_L will thus be the new higher wage paid to the new employee *plus* the small rise in the total wages bill for existing employees: after all, they will be paid the higher wage too.

The profit-maximising employment of labour would be at Q_1, where $MC_L = MRP_L$. The wage (found from the AC_L curve) would thus be W_1.

If this had been a perfectly competitive labour market, employment would have been at the higher level Q_2, with the wage rate at the higher level W_2, where

definition

Monopsony
A market with a single buyer or employer.

definition

Oligopsony
A market with just a few buyers or employers.

Key
Idea
18
p211

Key
Idea
4
p27

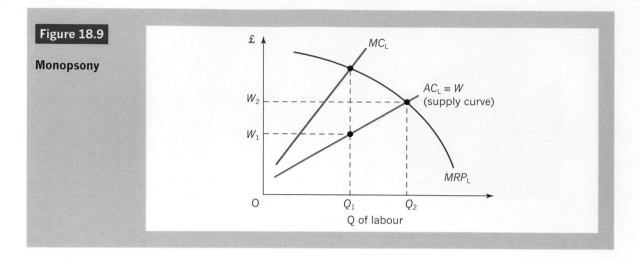

Figure 18.9

Monopsony

$W = MRP_L$. What in effect the monopsonist is doing, therefore, is forcing the wage rate down by restricting the number of workers employed.

18.4   The role of trade unions

How can unions influence the determination of wages, and what might be the consequences of their actions?

The extent to which unions will succeed in pushing up wage rates depends on their power and militancy. It also depends on the power of firms to resist and on their ability to pay higher wages. In particular, the scope for unions to gain a better deal for their members depends on the sort of market in which the employers are producing.

Key Idea 18 p211

Unions facing competitive employers

If the employers are producing under perfect or monopolistic competition, unions can raise wages only at the expense of employment. Firms are only earning normal profit. Thus if unions force up wages, the marginal firms will go bankrupt and leave the industry. Fewer workers will be employed. The fall in output will lead to higher prices. This will enable the remaining firms to pay a higher wage rate.

Figure 18.10 illustrates these effects. If unions force the wage rate up from W_1 to W_2, employment will fall from Q_1 to Q_2. There will be a surplus of people ($Q_3 - Q_2$) wishing to work in this industry for whom no jobs are available.

The union is in a doubly weak position. Not only will jobs be lost as a result of forcing up the wage rate, but also there is a danger that these unemployed people could undercut the union wage, unless the union can prevent firms employing non-unionised labour.

In a competitive market, then, the union is faced with the choice between wages and jobs. Its actions will depend on its objectives.

Pause for thought

Which of the following unions find themselves in a weak bargaining position for the reasons given?

(a) *The seafarers' part of the rail and maritime union RMT.*
(b) *The shopworkers' union (USDAW).*
(c) *The National Union of Mineworkers.*
(d) *The farmworkers' union (part of the Transport and General Workers' Union).*

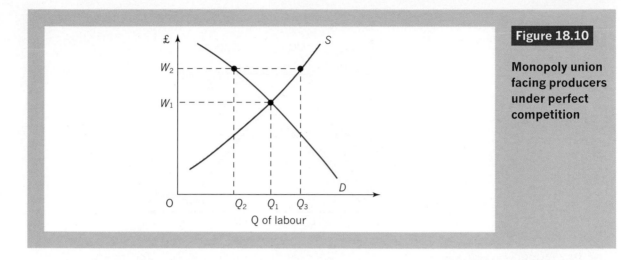

Figure 18.10

Monopoly union facing producers under perfect competition

Wages can be increased without a reduction in the level of employment only if, as part of the bargain, the productivity of labour is increased. This is called a **productivity deal**. The *MRP* curve, and hence the demand curve in Figure 18.10, shifts to the right.

Bilateral monopoly

What happens when a union monopoly faces a monopsony employer? What will the wage rate be? What will the level of employment be? Unfortunately, economic theory cannot give a precise answer to these questions. There is no 'equilibrium' level as such. Ultimately, the wage rate and level of employment will depend on the relative bargaining strengths and skills of unions and management.

Strange as it may seem, unions may be in a stronger position to make substantial gains for their members when they are facing a powerful employer. There is often considerable scope for them to increase wage rates *without* this leading to a reduction in employment, or even for them to increase both the wage rate *and* employment. Figure 18.11 shows how this can be so.

Assume first that there is no union. The monopsonist will maximise profits by employing Q_1 workers at a wage rate of W_1 (Q_1 is where $MRP_L = MC_L$).

What happens when a union is introduced into this situation? Wages will now be set by negotiation between unions and management. Once the wage rate has been agreed, the employer can no longer drive the wage rate down by employing fewer workers. If it tried to pay less than the agreed wage, it could well be faced by a strike, and thus have a zero supply of labour!

Similarly, if the employer decided to take on *more* workers, it would not have to *increase* the wage rate as long as the negotiated wage were above the free-market wage: as long as the wage rate were above that given by the supply curve S_1.

The effect of this is to give a new supply curve that is horizontal up to the point where it meets the original supply curve. For example, let us assume that the union succeeds in negotiating a wage rate of W_2 in Figure 18.11. The supply curve will be horizontal at this level to the left of point x. To the right of this point it will follow the original supply curve S_1, since to acquire more than Q_3 workers the employer would have to raise the wage rate above W_2.

If the supply curve is horizontal to the left of point x at a level of W_2, so too will be the MC_L curve. The reason is simply that the extra cost to the employer

Figure 18.11

Bilateral monopoly

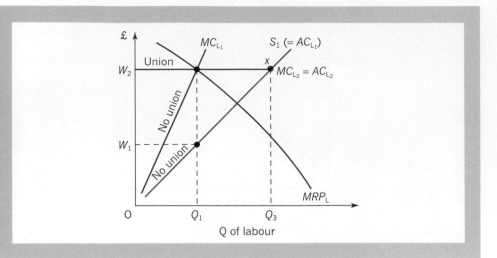

of taking on an extra worker (up to Q_3) is merely the negotiated wage rate: no rise has to be given to existing employees. If MC_L is equal to the wage, the profit-maximising employment ($MC_L = MRP_L$) will now be where $W = MRP_L$. At a negotiated wage rate of W_2, the firm will therefore choose to employ Q_1 workers.

What this means is that the union can push the wage right up from W_1 to W_2 and the firm will still *want* to employ Q_1. In other words, a wage rise can be obtained *without* a reduction in employment.

The union could go further still. By threatening industrial action, it may be able to push the wage rate above W_2 and still insist that Q_1 workers are employed (i.e. no redundancies). The firm may be prepared to see profits drop right down to normal level rather than face a strike and risk losses. The absolute upper limit to the wage rate will be that at which the firm is forced to close down.

The actual wage rate under bilateral monopoly is usually determined through a process of negotiation or 'collective bargaining'. The outcome of this bargaining will depend on a wide range of factors, which vary substantially from one industry or firm to another.

Collective bargaining

Sometimes when unions and management negotiate, *both* sides can gain from the resulting agreement. For example, the introduction of new technology may allow higher wages, improved working conditions and higher profits. Usually, however, one side's gain is the other's loss. Higher wages mean lower profits. Either way, both sides will want to gain the maximum for themselves.

The outcome of the negotiations will depend on the relative bargaining strengths of both sides. In bargaining there are various threats or promises that either side can make. For these to be effective, of course, the other side must believe that they will be carried out.

Union *threats* might include strike action, **picketing**, **working to rule** or refusing to co-operate with management, for example in the introduction of new technology. Alternatively, in return for higher wages or better working conditions, unions might *offer* no strike agreements (or an informal promise not to take industrial action), increased productivity, reductions in the workforce or long-term deals over pay.

In turn, employers might threaten employees with plant closure, **lock-outs**, redundancies or the employment of non-union labour. Or they might offer, in return for lower wage increases, various 'perks' such as productivity bonuses, profit-sharing schemes, better working conditions, more overtime, better holidays or security of employment.

Strikes, lock-outs and other forms of industrial action impose costs on both unions and firms. Unions lose pay. Firms lose revenue. It is usually in both sides' interests, therefore, to settle by negotiation. Nevertheless to gain the maximum advantage, each side must persuade the other that it will carry out its threats if pushed.

The approach described so far has essentially been one of confrontation. The alternative is for both sides to concentrate on increasing the total net income of the firm by co-operating on ways to increase efficiency or the quality of the product. This approach is more likely when unions and management have built up an atmosphere of trust over time.

The role of government

The government can influence the outcome of collective bargaining in a number of ways. One is to try to set an example. It may take a tough line in resisting wage demands by public-sector workers, hoping thereby to persuade employers in the private sector to do likewise.

Alternatively, it could set up arbitration or conciliation machinery. For example, in the UK, the Advisory Conciliation and Arbitration Service (ACAS) conciliates in over 1000 disputes each year. It also provides, on request by both sides, an arbitration service, where its findings will be binding.

Another approach is to use legislation. The government could pass laws that restrict the behaviour of employers or unions. It could pass laws that set a minimum wage rate (see pages 364–7), or prevent discrimination against workers on various grounds. Similarly, it could pass laws that curtail the power of unions. The Conservative governments between 1979 and 1997 put considerable emphasis on reducing the power of trade unions and making labour markets more 'flexible'. Several Acts of Parliament were passed during these years and included the following measures:

- Employees were given the right to join any union, or not to join a union at all. This effectively ended **closed-shop** agreements.

- Secret postal ballots of the union membership were made mandatory for the operation of a political fund, the election of senior union officials, and strikes and other official industrial action.

- Political strikes, sympathy action and action against other non-unionised companies were made illegal.

- Lawful action would be confined to that against workers' own direct employers, even to their own particular place of work. All **secondary action** was made unlawful.

- It was made unlawful for employers to penalise workers for choosing to join or refusing to join a trade union. It was also made unlawful for employers to deny employment on the grounds that an applicant does not belong to a union.

The effect of these measures was considerably to weaken the power of trade unions in the UK.

definition
Lock-outs
Union members are temporarily laid off until they are prepared to agree to the firm's conditions.

definition
Closed shop
Where a firm agrees to employ only members of a recognised union.

definition
Secondary action
Industrial action taken against a firm not directly involved in the dispute.

18.5 The efficiency wage hypothesis

We have seen that a union may be able to force an employer to pay a wage above the market-clearing rate. But it may well be in an employers' interests to do so, even in non-unionised sectors.

One explanation for this phenomenon is the **efficiency wage hypothesis**. This states that the productivity of workers rises as the wage rate rises. As a result, employers are frequently prepared to offer wage rates above the market-clearing level, attempting to balance increased wage costs against gains in productivity. But why may higher wage rates lead to higher productivity? Several explanations have been advanced.

Key Idea 19 p217

Less 'shirking'. In many jobs it is difficult to monitor the effort that individuals put into their work. Workers may thus get away with shirking or careless behaviour. The business could attempt to reduce shirking by imposing a series of sanctions, the most serious of which would be dismissal. The greater the wage rate currently received, the greater will be the cost to the individual of dismissal, and the less likely it is that workers will shirk. The business will benefit not only from the additional output, but also from a reduction in the costs of having to monitor workers' performance. As a consequence the **efficiency wage rate** for the business will lie above the market-determined wage rate.

Reduced labour turnover. If workers receive on-the-job training or retraining, then to lose a worker once the training has been completed is a significant cost to the business. Labour turnover, and hence its associated costs, can be reduced by paying a wage above the market-clearing rate. By paying such a wage, the business is seeking a degree of loyalty from its employees.

Self-selection. A high wage rate will tend to attract the most productive workers. It therefore acts as a form of selection device, reducing the costs to the business of employing workers of lower quality.

Morale. A simple reason for offering wage rates above the market-clearing level is to motivate the workforce – to create the feeling that the firm is a 'good' employer that cares about its employees. As a consequence, workers might be more industrious and more willing to accept the introduction of new technology (with the reorganisation that it involves).

The paying of efficiency wages above the market-clearing wage will depend upon the type of work involved. Workers who occupy skilled positions, especially where the business has invested time in their training (thus making them costly to replace) are likely to receive efficiency wages considerably above the market wage. By contrast, workers in unskilled positions, where shirking can be easily monitored, little training takes place and workers can be easily replaced, are unlikely to command an 'efficiency wage premium'. In such situations, rather than keeping wage rates high, the business will probably try to pay as little as possible.

Low pay and discrimination   18.6

Low pay

Identifying workers as being low paid clearly involves making certain value judgements about what constitutes 'low'.

One way is to consider pay relative to living standards. The problem here, though, is that pay is only one of the determinants of living standards. Pay of a certain level may give a reasonable living standard for a single person, especially if he or she has property, such as a house and furniture. The same pay may result in dire poverty for a large household with several dependants on that one income, and considerable outgoings.

It is more usual, therefore, to define low pay relative to average rates of pay. Low pay will be anything below a certain percentage of the average wage rate. The larger the percentage selected, the bigger the low-paid sector will become.

The Council of Europe defines low pay as anything below two-thirds of the mean wage level. It refers to this as the 'decency threshold'. If a minimum hourly wage were to be based on this, then in the UK it would be set at just under £8, and would raise wages for about 36 per cent of full-time workers. Other studies have identified the low-pay threshold at two-thirds of *median* hourly earnings of *male* workers.[1] A minimum hourly wage set at this level would be just under £7 and would raise wage rates for about 20 per cent of male workers and about 30 per cent of female workers.

In practice, as we shall see below, the UK defines low pay as being below the minimum wage, which in October 2003 was set at £4.50 per hour for those aged 22 and over and £3.80 per hour for those aged 18–21. Some 2.5 per cent of jobs are paid at the minimum rate, with another 2 per cent paid at less than 10p above the minimum wage.

Another approach to the analysis of low pay is to see how the wage rates of the lowest paid workers have changed over time compared to the average worker. Evidence from various *New Earnings Surveys* indicates that inequality in pay has widened. The lowest 10 per cent of wage earners have seen hourly wage rates fall from 70 per cent of the median wage in 1979 to 57 per cent in 2002. By contrast, hourly wage rates of the top 10 per cent have risen from 167 to 213 per cent of the median over the same period.

Low pay tends to be concentrated in certain sectors. Catering, retail trades and textile manufacturing are classic examples. Nearly 30 per cent of bar staff and more than 20 per cent of hairdressers and waiters/waitresses are paid less than 10p above the minimum wage. Low pay also occurs disproportionately between women and men. In 2002, women were three times as likely as men to be paid under £5 per hour.

The growth in low pay

Key
Idea
26
p402

A number of factors have contributed to the progressive rise in the size of the low-paid sector and the widening disparity between high and low income earners since 1979.

---

[1] The mean hourly wage is the arithmetical average: i.e. the total level of gross wage payments divided by the total number of hours worked by the population (over a specified time period). The median hourly wage is found by ranking the working population from lowest to highest paid, and then finding the hourly pay of the middle person in the ranking.

Unemployment due to recession. Very high rates of unemployment in the early 1980s and early 1990s shifted the balance of power from workers to employers. Employers have been able to force many wage rates downwards, especially of unskilled and semi-skilled workers.

Unemployment due to technological change. Changes in technology have led industry to shift its demand for labour away from unskilled to skilled workers. As might be expected, wage rates for skilled workers have generally risen (except for those with older, now irrelevant skills), while relative employment rates of the unskilled have worsened. In 2002, the unemployment rate among unskilled workers was 8.4 per cent, compared with an overall unemployment rate of 5.1 per cent and rates of 3.8 per cent for skilled workers and 1.7 per cent for professional occupations.

Growth in part-time employment. Changes in the structure of the UK economy – in particular, the growth of the service sector and the growing proportion of women seeking work – have led to an increase in part-time work. Many service-sector jobs suit such employment patterns, especially since demand often varies substantially during the course of the week. In principle, the part-time nature of employment should make little difference to earnings. However, many part-time workers do not receive the same rights, privileges and hourly pay as their full-time equivalents. On the other hand, the work rate of part-time workers is often higher given that, with fewer hours worked, they are often less tired or bored.

Changes in labour laws. The drive to establish a flexible labour market (discussed in section 18.7) encouraged the Conservative governments of the 1980s and 1990s to reform labour market legislation (see page 361). The most significant change with respect to the issue of low pay was the abolition of the Wages Councils in 1993. The Wages Councils were set up in 1945 and at the height of their powers, set minimum wages for about 4.25 million workers, or about 20 per cent of the working population. Their powers had already been eroded in the 1986 Wages Act, but with their abolition, one of the few safe-guards for workers in the poorest-paid sectors of the economy was removed.

But just what are the costs and benefits of minimum wages? We examine this issue in the next section.

Minimum wages

Before April 1999 there was no statutory minimum wage in the UK. The principle of a minimum or fair wage was based around a voluntary tradition in which, other than in the most poorly paid sectors of the economy, earnings and wages were determined through the process of collective bargaining.

The abolition of the Wages Councils in 1993 had been, according to their critics, a necessary step in creating a flexible labour market, which helped improve the employment prospects of the lowest-paid workers within the economy. To re-establish a national minimum wage rate would simply reverse such benefits and cause unemployment and poverty to rise. The supporters of a national minimum wage, including the Labour government, argued that its introduction would not only help to reduce poverty among the low paid, but would also have little or no adverse effects on unemployment. Some went further. They argued that it would actually *increase* employment.

In order to assess the background to this debate, we need to revisit our earlier analysis of the demand and supply of labour.

Minimum wages in a competitive labour market

In a competitive labour market, workers will be hired up to the point where the marginal revenue product of labour (MRP_L), i.e. the demand for labour, is equal to the marginal cost of labour (MC_L), which gives the supply curve. Referring back to Figure 18.10 on page 359, the free-market equilibrium wage is W_1 and the level of employment is Q_1. A national minimum wage, set at W_2, will reduce the level of employment to Q_2 and increase the supply of labour to Q_3, thereby creating unemployment of the amount $Q_3 - Q_2$.

The level of unemployment created as a result of the national minimum wage will be determined not only by the level of the minimum wage, but also by the elasticity of labour demand and supply. The more elastic the demand and supply of labour, the bigger the unemployment effect will be. Evidence suggests that the demand for low-skilled workers is likely to be relatively wage sensitive. The most likely reason for this is that many of the goods or services produced by low-paid workers are very price sensitive, the firms frequently operating in very competitive markets. It would seem at first sight, therefore, that any increase in wage rates is likely to force up prices and thereby reduce output and employment.

It is important to be careful in using this argument, however. What is relevant is not so much the price elasticity of demand for *individual* firms' products, but rather for the products of the low-paid sector as a whole. If one firm alone raised its prices, it might well lose a considerable number of sales. But with minimum wage legislation applying to *all* firms, if all the firms in an industry or sector put up their prices, demand for any one firm would fall much less. Here the problem of consumers switching away from a firm's products, and hence of that firm being forced to reduce its workforce, would mainly occur (a) if there were cheaper competitor products from abroad, where the new minimum wage legislation would not apply, or (b) if other firms produced the products with more capital-intensive techniques, involving fewer workers to whom the minimum wage legislation applied.

Minimum wages and monopsony employers

In an imperfect labour market where the employer has some influence over rates of pay, the impact of the national minimum wage on levels of employment is even less clear cut.

The situation can be illustrated by referring back to Figure 18.11 on page 360. A monopsonistic employer will employ Q_1 workers: where the MC_L is equal to MRP_L. At this point the firm is maximising its return from the labour it employs. The MC_L curve lies above the supply of labour curve (AC_L), since the additional cost of employing one more unit of labour involves paying all existing employees the new wage. The wage rate paid by the monopsonist will be W_1.

If the minimum wage is set above W_1, but below W_2, the level of employment within the firm is likely to grow! Why should this be so? The reason is that the minimum wage cannot be bid down by the monopsonist cutting back on its workforce. The minimum wage rate is thus both the new AC_L and also the new MC_L: the additional cost of employing one more worker (up to Q_3) is simply the minimum wage rate. The $MC_L = AC_L$ line is thus a horizontal straight line up to the original supply curve ($S_1 = AC_1$). The level of employment that maximises the monopsonist's profits will be found from the intersection of this new $MC_L = AC_L$ line with the MRP_L curve. With a wage rate between W_1 and W_2 this intersection

BOX 18.2

The UK national minimum wage
The answer to low pay?

Despite the adoption of national minimum wage rates in most of the developed world, the Conservative government in the UK (1979–97), following its philosophy of free-market economics, resisted introducing such a policy. But the number of low-paid workers was increasing. There were many people working as cleaners, kitchen hands, garment workers, security guards and shop assistants, who were receiving pittance rates of pay, sometimes less than £2 per hour.

The incoming Labour government in 1997 was committed to introducing a minimum wage, which it did in April 1999 at a rate of £3.60 per hour. There was a lower 'development rate' of £3.00 for those between 18 and 21. The government had sought advice from the Low Pay Commission, which argued that a £3.60 rate would 'offer real benefits to the low paid, while avoiding unnecessary risks to business and jobs'. The minimum wage has been raised in October each year: to £3.70 in 2000, £4.10 in 2001, £4.20 in 2002, £4.50 in 2003 and £4.85 in 2004, with equivalent rises in the development rate (£4.10 in 2004).

Some 1.3 million workers benefit from the minimum wage and there have been virtually no adverse effects on unemployment. The main beneficiaries have been women, the majority of whom work part time and many of whom are lone parents, and people from ethnic minorities. Even the Conservative party, previously staunch opponents of a minimum wage, has dropped its opposition.

Questions

1 *If an increase in wage rates for the low paid led to their being more motivated, how would this affect the marginal revenue product and the demand for such workers? What implications does your answer have for the effect on employment in such cases?*

2 *If minimum wages encourage employers to substitute machines for workers, will this necessarily lead to higher long-term unemployment in (a) that industry and (b) the economy in general?*

will be to the right of Q_1: i.e. the imposition of a minimum wage rate will *increase* the level of employment.

Clearly, if the minimum wage rate were very high, then, other things being equal, the level of employment would fall. This would occur in Figure 18.11 if the minimum wage rate were above W_2. But even this argument is not clear cut, given that (a) a higher wage rate may increase labour productivity by improving worker motivation and (b) other firms, with which the firm might compete in the product market, will also be faced with paying the higher minimum wage rate. The resulting rise in prices is likely to shift the MRP_L curve to the right.

On the other hand, to the extent that the imposition of a minimum wage rate reduces a firm's profits, this may lead it to cut down on investment, which may threaten long-term employment prospects.

Evidence on the effect of minimum wages

Which of the views concerning the effects of a national minimum wage are we to believe? Evidence from the USA and other countries suggests that modest increases in the minimum wage have had a neutral effect upon employment. It has been found that there exists a 'range of indeterminacy' over which wage rates can fluctuate with little impact upon levels of employment. Even above this 'range', research findings have suggested that, whereas some employers might reduce the quantity of labour they employ, others might respond to their higher wage bill, and hence higher costs, by improving productive efficiency.

Table 18.1 Average gross hourly earnings, excluding the effects of overtime, for full-time UK employees, aged 18 and over, 1970–2002 (pence per hour)

	1970	1974	1978	1982	1986	1988	1990
Men	67	105	200	355	482	573	689
Women	42	71	148	262	358	429	528
Differential	25	34	52	93	124	144	161
Women's earnings as a % of men's	63.1	67.4	73.9	73.9	74.3	75.0	76.6

	1992	1994	1996	1998	2000	2002
Men	810	865	939	1026	1126	1259
Women	638	688	750	822	913	1022
Differential	172	177	189	204	213	237
Women's earnings as a % of men's	78.8	79.5	79.9	80.1	81.1	81.2

Source: Based on *New Earnings Survey* (National Statistics, various years)

Since the introduction of the minimum wage in the UK in 1999 (see Box 18.2), there is little evidence to suggest that employers have responded by employing fewer workers. In fact, unemployment rates have fallen. This, however, can be explained by a buoyant economy and increasing labour market flexibility (see section 18.7). Whether there would continue to be little effect if the minimum wage were to rise substantially (e.g. from £4.50 to the Council of Europe 'decency threshold' of around £8) is another matter! The issue, then, seems to be how *high* can the minimum wage be set before unemployment begins to rise.

Gender and the labour market

One of the key characteristics shown in Table 18.1 is that female gross hourly earnings relative to male gross hourly earnings increased substantially during the early 1970s. Having peaked at around 74 per cent in the late 1970s, they remained at about that level for the next ten years. They then rose again to just above 81 per cent by the early 2000s.

Pause for thought

If we were to look at weekly rather than hourly pay and included the effects of overtime, what do you think would happen to the pay differentials in Table 18.1?

Key Idea 26 p402

The inequality between male and female earnings can in part be explained by the fact that men and women are occupationally segregated. Seeing that women predominate in poorly paid occupations, the difference in earnings is somewhat to be expected. But if you consider Table 18.2, you can see that quite substantial earning differentials persist *within* particular occupations.

So why has this inequality persisted? There are a number of possible reasons:

■ The marginal productivity of labour in typically female occupations may be lower than in typically male occupations. This may in part be due to simple questions of physical strength. More often, however, it is due to the fact that women tend to work in more labour-intensive occupations. If there is less capital equipment per female worker than there is per male worker, then the marginal product of a woman is likely to be less than that of a man.

Table 18.2 Average gross hourly earnings, excluding the effects of overtime, for selected occupations, full-time UK employees on adult rates, 2002

Occupation	Men (£ per hour)	Women (£ per hour)	Women's earnings as a % of men's
Nurses	12.13	11.89	98.0
Bar staff	5.40	5.07	93.9
Social workers	12.38	11.58	93.5
Police officers (sergeant and below)	14.74	13.30	90.2
Secondary school teachers	19.32	17.37	89.9
Laboratory technicians	10.64	9.46	88.9
Legal professionals	26.77	22.78	85.1
Sales assistants	6.69	5.67	84.8
Personnel managers	20.26	17.07	84.3
Chefs/cooks	7.34	6.13	83.5
Medical practitioners	29.39	23.76	80.8
Computer operators	10.01	7.58	75.7
Assemblers and lineworkers	8.46	6.35	75.1
All occupations	12.59	10.22	81.2
Average gross weekly pay	513.80	383.40	74.6
Average weekly hours worked (incl. overtime)	40.9	37.5	
Average weekly overtime (hours)	2.4	0.7	

Source: Adapted from *New Earnings Survey* (National Statistics, 2002)

■ Many women take career breaks to have children. For this reason, employers are sometimes more willing to invest money in training men (thereby increasing their marginal productivity), and more willing to promote men.

■ Women tend to be less geographically mobile than men. If social norms are such that the man's job is seen as somehow more 'important' than the woman's, then a couple will often move if that is necessary for the man to get promotion. The woman, however, will have to settle for whatever job she can get in the same locality as her partner.

■ A smaller proportion of women workers are members of unions than men. Even when they are members of unions, they are often in jobs where unions are weak (e.g. clothing industry workers, shop assistants and secretaries).

■ Part-time workers (mainly women) have less bargaining power, less influence and less chance of obtaining promotion.

■ Custom and practice. Despite equal pay legislation, many jobs done wholly or mainly by women continue to be low paid, irrespective of questions of productivity.

■ Prejudice. Some employers may prefer to give senior posts to men on grounds purely of sexual prejudice. This is very difficult to legislate against when the employer can simply claim that the 'better' person was given the job.

Which of the above reasons could be counted as economically 'irrational' (i.e. paying different wage rates to women and men for other than purely economic reasons)? Certainly the last two would qualify. Paying different wage rates on these grounds would *not* be in the profit interests of the employer.

Some of the others, however, are more difficult to classify. The causes of inequality in wage rates may be traced back beyond the workplace: perhaps to the educational system, or to a culture which discourages women from being so aggressive in seeking promotion or in 'self-advertisement', or to the legal right to maternity but not paternity leave. Even if it is a manifestation of profit-maximising behaviour by employers that women in some circumstances are paid less than their male counterparts, the reason *why* it is more profitable for employers to pay men more than women may indeed reflect discrimination elsewhere or at some other point in time.

The flexible firm and the market for labour   18.7

The past 25 years have seen sweeping changes in the ways that firms organise their workforce. Three world recessions combined with rapid changes in technology have led many firms to question the wisdom of appointing workers on a permanent basis to specific jobs. Instead, they want to have the greatest flexibility possible to respond to new situations. If demand falls, they want to be able to 'shed' labour without facing large redundancy costs. If demand rises, they want rapid access to additional labour supplies. If technology changes, say with the introduction of new computerised processes, they want to have the flexibility to move workers around, or to take on new workers in some areas and lose workers in others.

Key Idea
5
p44

What many firms seek, therefore, is flexibility in employing and allocating labour. What countries are experiencing is an increasingly flexible labour market, as workers and employment agencies respond to the new 'flexible firm'.

There are three main types of flexibility in the use of labour:

- **Functional flexibility.** This is where an employer is able to transfer labour between different tasks within the production process. It contrasts with traditional forms of organisation where people were employed to do a specific job, and then stuck to it. A functionally flexible labour force will tend to be multi-skilled and relatively highly trained.

- **Numerical flexibility.** This is where the firm is able to adjust the size and composition of its workforce according to changing market conditions. To achieve this, the firm is likely to employ a large proportion of its labour on a part-time or casual basis, or even subcontract out specialist requirements, rather than employing such labour skills itself.

- **Financial flexibility.** This is where the firm has flexibility in its wage costs. In large part it is a result of functional and numerical flexibility. Financial flexibility can be achieved by rewarding individual effort and productivity rather than paying a given rate for a particular job. Such rates of pay are increasingly negotiated at the local level rather than being nationally set. The result is not only a widening of pay differentials between skilled and unskilled workers, but also growing differentials in pay between workers within the same industry but in different parts of the country.

Figure 18.12 shows how these three forms of flexibility are reflected in the organisation of a **flexible firm,** an organisation quite different from that of the traditional firm. The most significant difference is that the labour force is

definition
Functional flexibility
Where employers can switch workers from job to job as requirements change.

definition
Numerical flexibility
Where employers can change the size of their workforce as their labour requirements change.

definition
Financial flexibility
Where employers can vary their wage costs by changing the composition of their workforce or the terms on which workers are employed.

definition
Flexible firm
A firm that has the flexibility to respond to changing market conditions by changing the composition of its workforce.

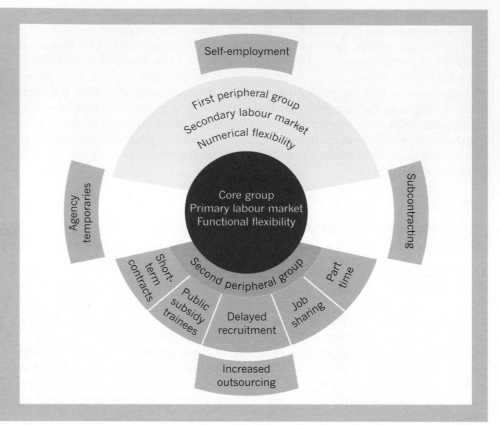

Figure 18.12

The flexible firm

Source: Institute of Manpower Studies (1984)

definition

Primary labour market
The market for permanent full-time core workers.

definition

Secondary labour market
The market for peripheral workers, usually employed on a temporary or part-time basis, or a less secure 'permanent' basis.

segmented. The core group, drawn from the **primary labour market,** will be composed of *functionally* flexible workers, who have relatively secure employment and are generally on full-time permanent contracts. Such workers will be relatively well paid and receive wages reflecting their scarce skills.

The periphery, drawn from the **secondary labour market,** is more fragmented than the core, and can be subdivided into a first and a second peripheral group. The first peripheral group is composed of workers with a lower level of skill than those in the core, skills that tend to be general rather than firm specific. Thus workers in the first peripheral group can usually be drawn from the external labour market. Such workers may be employed on full-time contracts, but they will generally face less secure employment than those workers in the core.

The business gains a greater level of numerical flexibility by drawing labour from the second peripheral group. Here workers are employed on a variety of short-term, part-time contracts, often through a recruitment agency. Some of these workers may be working from home, or online from another country, such as India, where wage rates are much lower. Workers in the second peripheral group have little job security.

As well as supplementing the level of labour in the first peripheral group, the second periphery can also provide high-level specialist skills that supplement the core. In this instance the business can subcontract or hire self-employed labour, minimising its commitment to such workers. The business thereby gains both functional and numerical flexibility simultaneously.

Pause for thought

How is the advent of flexible firms likely to alter the gender balance of employment and unemployment?

BOX 18.3

The Internet and labour mobility
Online flexibility

A firm may be wish to be flexible, but is the *labour market* sufficiently flexible to meet the firm's needs?

It is all well and good a firm looking to expand employment in a prosperous period, but how will it find the individuals it needs, whether they be self-employed, subcontracted or added to the core labour group? This question becomes far more critical, the more highly skilled (and hence scarce) are the workers that the firm requires. Generally, it is the core/skilled workers that flexible firms find most difficulty in recruiting.

The article below, taken from the *Financial Times* of 22 February 2000, considers the impact the Internet is having on the labour market and in particular its impact on labour mobility.

The cinematic cliché of a character searching for a new job is firmly established. The hero pounds the streets, looking in employment agencies' windows; he pores over the classified sections of newspapers, circling likely vacancies in red pen; finally, wearily, he picks up the phone and starts calling.

But modern jobseekers familiar with the Internet can cut out all of this and simply sit in a cafe waiting for a message on their mobile phone. As the labour market increasingly goes on-line, some experts say the speed of information transfer could radically change the traditional process of matching jobseekers – including the unemployed – to work. Paul Rapacioli is head of Reed Online, the Internet branch of the recruitment agency Reed. He says that although fewer than a quarter of Reed's vacancies are filled through on-line recruitment, the cost savings mean that Internet business is extremely profitable and expanding fast. "People have been talking about labour market flexibility and mobility for years, but until recently the reality has been that a London-based worker prepared to work in Manchester has had to go up there and scout around." Now, he says, the Internet can search the pool of jobs on offer across the country, identify suitable matches and automatically e-mail them to jobseekers, or send text messages to their mobile phones.

Economists say the behaviour of the whole labour market could be revolutionised by such developments. Professor Richard Layard, a leading labour market expert and government adviser at the London School of Economics, says the Internet could help bring a long-awaited improvement in the matching process between the unemployed and available jobs. Although unemployment has fallen over the past 10 years, the number of vacancies – and the average length of time they take to be filled – has risen, indicating the lack of a radical improvement in job-matching efficiency.

Question

Using the article, explain how a flexible firm's flexibility would be enhanced by on-line recruitment.

The Japanese model

The application of new flexible working patterns is becoming more prevalent in businesses in the UK and elsewhere in Europe and North America. In Japan, flexibility has been part of the business way of life for many years and was crucial in shaping the country's economic success in the 1970s and 1980s. In fact we now talk of a Japanese model of business organisation, which many of its competitors seek to emulate.

The model is based around four principles:

- Total quality management (TQM). This involves all employees working towards continuously improving all aspects of quality, both of the finished product and of methods of production.

- Elimination of waste. According to the 'just-in-time' (JIT) principle, businesses should take delivery of just sufficient quantities of raw materials and parts, at the right time and place. Stocks are kept to a minimum and hence the whole system of production runs with little, if any, slack. For example, supermarkets today have smaller storerooms relative to the total shopping area than they did in the past, and take more frequent deliveries.

- A belief in the superiority of team work in the core group. Collective effort is a vital element in Japanese working practices. Team work is seen not only to enhance individual performance, but also to involve the individual in the running of the business and thus to create a sense of commitment.

- Functional and numerical flexibility. Both are seen as vital components in maintaining high levels of productivity.

The principles of this model are now widely accepted as being important in creating and maintaining a competitive business in a competitive marketplace.

Within the EU, the UK has been one of the most successful in cutting unemployment and creating jobs. Much of this has been attributed to increased labour market flexibility. As a result, other EU countries, such as Italy and Germany, are seeking to emulate many of the measures the UK has adopted.

SUMMARY

1 Major changes in the UK labour market over recent years include: the movement towards service-sector employment; the rise in part-time working; the growth in female employment levels; a rise in the proportion of temporary, short-term contract and casual employment; and downsizing.

2a Wages in a competitive labour market are determined by the interaction of demand and supply. The individual's supply of labour will be determined by the substitution and income effects from a given increase in the wage rate. At low wage levels, it is likely that individuals will substitute work for leisure. At high wage levels, it is possible that individuals will work less and consume more leisure time, giving a backward-bending supply curve of labour by the individual.

2b The elasticity of labour supply will largely depend upon the geographical and occupational mobility of labour. The more readily labour can transfer between jobs and regions, the more elastic the supply.

2c The demand for labour is traditionally assumed to be based upon labour's productivity. Marginal productivity theory assumes that the employer will demand labour up to the point where the cost of employing one additional worker (MC_L) is equal to the revenue earned from the output of that worker (MRP_L). The firm's demand curve for labour is its MRP_L curve.

2d The elasticity of demand for labour is determined by: the price elasticity of demand for the good that labour produces; the substitutability of labour for other factors; the proportion of wages to total costs; and time.

3 In an imperfect labour market, where a business has monopoly power in employing labour, it is known as a monopsonist. Such a firm will employ workers to the point where the $MRP_L = MC_L$. Since the wage is below the MC_L, the monopsonist, other things being equal, will employ fewer workers at a lower wage than would be employed in a perfectly competitive labour market.

4a If a union has monopoly power, its power to raise wages will be limited if the employer operates under perfect or monopolistic competition in the goods market. A rise in wage rates will force the employer to cut back on employment, unless there is a corresponding rise in productivity.

4b In a situation of bilateral monopoly (where a monopoly union faces a monopsony employer), the union may have considerable scope to raise wages above the monopsony level, without the employer wishing to reduce the level of employment. There is no unique equilibrium wage. The wage will depend on the outcome of a process of collective bargaining between union and management.

5 The efficiency wage hypothesis states that business might hold wages above the market-clearing wage rate so as to: reduce shirking; reduce labour turnover; improve the quality of labour recruited; and stimulate worker morale.

SUMMARY

The level of efficiency wage will be determined largely by the type of job the worker does, and the level and scarcity of skill they possess.

6a Low pay is difficult to define. There is no accepted definition. The widening disparity in wages between high and low income earners is due to: unemployment resulting from recession; unemployment resulting from a shift in technology; the growth in part-time employment; and changes in labour market legislation.

6b A statutory minimum wage is one way of tackling the problem of low pay. It is argued, however, that in a perfect labour market, where employers are forced to accept the wage as determined by the market place, any attempt to impose a minimum wage above this level will create unemployment. In an imperfect labour market, where an employer has some monopsonistic power, the impact of a minimum wage is uncertain. The impact will depend largely upon how much workers are currently paid below their *MRP* and whether a higher wage encourages them to work more productively.

6c Differences between male and female earnings between occupations can in part be explained by differences in the types of work that men and women do; they are occupationally segregated. Differences within occupations are less easily accounted for. It would seem that some measure of discrimination is being practised.

7a Changes in technology have had a massive impact upon the process of production and the experience of work. Labour markets and business organisations have become more flexible as a consequence. There are three major forms of flexibility: functional, numerical and financial. The flexible firm will incorporate these different forms of flexibility into its business operations. It will organise production around a core workforce, to which it will supplement workers and skills drawn from a periphery. Peripheral workers will tend to hold general skills rather than firm-specific skills, and be employed on part-time and temporary contracts.

7b The application of the flexible firm model is closely mirrored in the practices of Japanese business. Commitments to improve quality, reduce waste, build team work and introduce flexible labour markets are seen as key components in the success of Japanese business organisation.

REVIEW QUESTIONS

1 If a firm faces a shortage of workers with very specific skills, it may decide to undertake the necessary training itself. If on the other hand it faces a shortage of unskilled workers it may well offer a small wage increase in order to obtain the extra labour. In the first case it is responding to an increase in demand for labour by attempting to shift the supply curve. In the second case it is merely allowing a movement along the supply curve. Use a demand and supply diagram to illustrate each case. Given that elasticity of supply is different in each case, do you think that these are the best policies for the firm to follow?

2 The wage rate a firm has to pay and the output it can produce varies with the number of workers as follows (all figures are hourly):

Number of workers	1	2	3	4	5	6	7	8
Wage rate (AC_L) (£)	3	4	5	6	7	8	9	10
Total output (TPP_L)	10	22	32	40	46	50	52	52

Assume that output sells at £2 per unit.

(a) Copy the table and add additional rows for TC_L, MC_L, TRP_L and MRP_L. Put the figures for MC_L and MRP_L in the spaces between the columns.
(b) How many workers will the firm employ in order to maximise profits?
(c) What will be its hourly wage bill at this level of employment?
(d) How much hourly revenue will it earn at this level of employment?
(e) Assuming that the firm faces other (fixed) costs of £30 per hour, how much hourly profit will it make?
(f) Assume that the workers now form a union and that the firm agrees to pay the negotiated wage rate to all employees. What is the maximum to which the hourly wage rate could rise without causing the firm to try to reduce employment below that in (b) above? (See Figure 18.11.)
(g) What would be the firm's hourly profit now?

3 If, unlike a perfectly competitive employer, a monopsonist has to pay a higher wage to attract more workers, why, other things being equal, will a monopsonist pay a lower wage than a perfectly competitive employer?

4 The following are figures for a monopsonist employer:

Number of workers (1)	Wage rate (£) (2)	Total cost of labour (£) (3)	Marginal cost of labour (£) (4)	Marginal revenue product (£) (5)
1	100	100		230
			110	
2	105	210		240
			120	
3	110	230		240
4	115			230
5	120			210
6	125			190
7	130			170
8	135			150
9	140			130
10	145			

Fill in the missing figures for columns (3) and (4). How many workers should the firm employ if it wishes to maximise profits?

5 To what extent could a trade union succeed in gaining a pay increase from an employer with no loss in employment?

6 Do any of the following contradict marginal productivity theory: wage scales related to length of service (incremental scales), nationally negotiated wage rates, discrimination, firms taking the lead from other firms in determining this year's pay increase?

7 What is the efficiency wage hypothesis? Explain what employers might gain from paying wages above the market-clearing level.

8 'Minimum wages will cause unemployment.' Is this so?

9 How might we explain why men earn more than women?

10 Identify the potential costs and benefits of the flexible firm to (a) employers and (b) employees.

19 Investment and the employment of capital

19.1 The pricing of capital and capital services

Capital includes all manufactured products that are used to produce goods and services. Thus capital includes such diverse items as a blast furnace, a bus, a cinema projector, a computer, a factory building and a screwdriver.

The capital goods described above are physical assets and are known as *physical* capital. The word 'capital' is also used to refer to various *paper* assets, such as shares and bonds. These are the means by which firms raise finance to purchase physical capital, and are known as *financial* capital. Being merely paper assets, however, they do not count as factors of production. Nevertheless, financial markets have an important role in determining the level of investment in physical capital, and we shall be examining these markets in the final two sections of this chapter.

Factor prices versus the price of factor services

A feature of most manufactured factors of production is that they last a period of time. A machine may last 10 years; a factory may last 20 years or more. This leads to an important distinction: that between the income that the owner will get from *selling* the factor and that which the owner will get from *using* it or *hiring* it out.

- The income from selling the factor is the factor's *price*. It is a once-and-for-all payment. Thus a factory might sell for £1 million, a machine for £20 000 or a computer disk for £1.

- The income gained from using a factor is its *return*, and the income gained from hiring a factor out is its *rental*. This income therefore represents the value or price of the factor's *services*, expressed per period of time. Thus a firm might have to pay a rental of £1000 per year for a photocopier.

Obviously the price of capital will be linked to the value of its services: to its return. A highly productive machine will sell for a higher price than one producing a lower output and hence yielding a lower return.

The discussion of the rewards to capital leads to a very important distinction: that between stocks and flows.

A **stock** is a quantity of something held. You may have £1000 in a savings account. A factory may contain 100 machines. These are both stocks: they are quantities held at a given point in time. A **flow** is an increase or decrease in quantity over a specified time period. You may save £10 per month. The factory may invest in another 20 machines next year.

definition

Stock
The quantity of something held.

definition

Flow
An increase or decrease in quantity over a specified period.

Stocks and flows. A stock is a quantity of something at a given point in time. A flow is an increase or decrease in something over a specified period of time. This is an important distinction and a common cause of confusion.

Key Idea 21

Pause for thought

Which of the following are stocks and which are flows?

(a) *Unemployment.*
(b) *Redundancies.*
(c) *Profits.*
(d) *A firm's stock market valuation.*
(e) *The value of property after a period of inflation.*

Wages, rental and interest are all rewards to *flows*. Wages are the amount paid not to purchase a person (as a slave!), but for the services of that person's labour for a week. Rental is the amount paid per period of time to use the services of machinery or equipment, not to buy it outright. Likewise interest is the reward paid to people per year for the use of their money.

An important example of stocks and flows arises with capital and investment. If a firm has 100 machines, that is a stock of capital. It may choose to build up its stock by investing. Investment is a flow concept. The firm may choose to invest in 10 new machines each year. This may not add 10 to the stock of machines, however, as some may be wearing out (a negative flow).

The profit-maximising employment of capital

definition

Marginal cost of capital
The cost of one additional unit of capital.

On the demand side, the same rules apply for capital as for labour, if a firm wishes to maximise profits. Namely, it should demand additional capital (K) up to the point where the **marginal cost of capital** equals its **marginal revenue product**: $MC_K = MRP_K$. This same rule applies whether the firm is buying the capital outright, or merely hiring it.

Key Idea 4 p27

Figure 19.1 illustrates the two cases of perfect competition and monopsony. In both diagrams the *MRP* curve slopes downwards. This is just another illustration of the law of diminishing returns, but this time applied to capital. If a firm

Key Idea 17 p170

Figure 19.1 **(a) Perfectly competitive factor market (b) Firm with monopsony power in factor market**

increases the amount of capital while *holding other factors constant*, diminishing returns to capital will occur. Diminishing returns will equally apply whether the firm is buying the extra capital or hiring it.

In diagram (a) the firm is a price taker. The capital price is given at P_{K_1}. Profits are maximised at Q_{K_1} where $MRP_K = P_K$ (since $P_K = MC_K$).

In diagram (b) the firm has monopsony power. The price it pays for capital will vary, therefore, with the amount it uses. The firm will again buy or hire capital to the point where $MRP_K = MC_K$. In this case, it will mean using Q_{K_2} at a price of P_{K_2}.

What is the difference when applying these principles between buying capital and hiring it? Although the $MRP_K = MC_K$ rule remains the same, there are differences. As far as buying capital is concerned, MC_K is the extra outlay for the firm in *purchasing* one more unit of capital – say, a machine – and MRP_K is all the revenue produced by that machine over its *whole life* (but measured in terms of what this is worth when purchased: see section 19.3). In the case of hiring the machine, MC_K is the extra outlay for the firm in rental *per period of time*, while MRP_K is the extra revenue earned from it *per period of time*.

The demand for and supply of capital services 19.2

In this section we will consider the *hiring* of capital equipment for a given period of time.

Demand for capital services

The analysis is virtually identical to that of the demand for labour. As with labour we can distinguish between an individual firm's demand for capital services (K) and the whole market demand for capital services.

Individual firm's demand

Take the case of a small painting and decorating firm that requires some scaffolding in order to complete a job. It could use ladders, but the job would take longer to complete. It goes along to a company that hires out scaffolding and is quoted a daily rate.

If it hires the scaffolding for one day, it can perhaps shorten the job by two or three days. If it hires it for a second day, it can perhaps save another one or two days. Hiring it for additional days may save extra still. But diminishing returns are occurring: the longer the scaffolding is up, the less intensively it will be used, and the less additional time it will save. Perhaps for some of the time it will be used when ladders could have been used equally easily.

The time saved allows the firm to take on extra work. Thus each extra day the scaffolding is hired gives the firm extra revenue. This is the scaffolding's marginal revenue product of capital (MRP_K). Diminishing returns to the scaffolding means that the MRP_K curve has the normal downward-sloping shape (see Figure 19.1).

Market demand

The market demand for capital services depends on the demand by individual firms. The higher the MRP_K for individual firms, the greater will be the market demand.

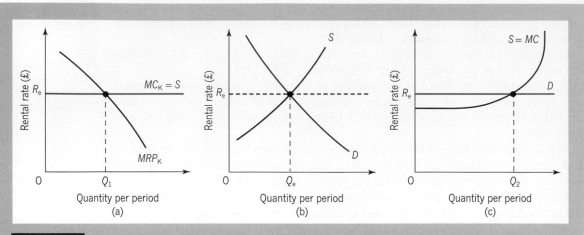

Figure 19.2 Long-run equilibrium rental rate for the services of a particular type of capital (a) Individual user of capital services (b) Market for capital services (c) Individual supplier of capital services

Supply of capital services

It is necessary to distinguish (a) the supply *to* a single firm, (b) the supply *by* a single firm and (c) the market supply.

Supply to a single firm

This is illustrated in Figure 19.2(a). The small firm renting capital equipment is probably a price taker. If so, it faces a horizontal supply curve at the going rental rate (R_e). This is the firm's AC_K and MC_K curve. If, however, it has monopsony power, it will face an upward-sloping supply curve as in Figure 19.1(b).

Supply by a single firm

This is illustrated in Figure 19.2(c). Again, the firm is likely to be a price taker. It has to accept the going rental rate (R_e) established in the market. If it tries to charge more, then customers are likely to turn to rival suppliers. This means that individual suppliers under such conditions will face an infinitely elastic *demand* curve.

But what will the individual supplier's *supply* curve look like? It will be the firm's *MC* curve, where the *MC* is the extra cost of supplying one more unit of capital equipment for rent over a given time period. But why is the *MC* curve the supply curve? The reason is that profits are maximised under perfect competition where marginal cost equals price (see page 215), where price in this case is the rental rate. So whatever the rental rate (R) is, the firm will supply that quantity where $R = MC$: in other words, the *MC* curve will show the amount supplied at that level of R and hence must be the supply curve.

The problem with working out the marginal cost of renting out capital equipment is that the piece of equipment probably cost a lot to buy in the first place, but lasts a long time. How are these large costs to be apportioned to each new rental? The answer is that it depends on the time period under consideration.

The short run. In the short run the hire company is not buying any new equipment: it is simply hiring out its existing equipment. In the case of our scaffolding firm, the marginal costs of doing this will include the following:

- Depreciation. Scaffolding has second-hand value. Each time the scaffolding is hired out it deteriorates, and thus its second-hand value falls. This loss in value is called 'depreciation'.

- Maintenance and handling. When equipment is hired out, it can get damaged and thus incur repair costs. The equipment might need servicing. Also, hiring out equipment involves labour time (e.g. in the office) and possibly transport costs.

These marginal costs are likely to rise relatively slowly. In other words, for each extra day a piece of equipment is hired out, the company will incur the same or only slightly higher additional costs. This gives a relatively flat supply curve of capital services in Figure 19.2(c) up to the hire company's maximum capacity. Once the scaffolding firm is hiring out all its scaffolding, the supply curve becomes vertical.

> **Pause for thought**
>
> *Assume now that the firm has monopoly power in hiring out equipment, and thus faces a downward-sloping demand curve. Draw in two such demand curves on a diagram like Figure 19.2(c), one crossing the MC curve in the horizontal section, and one in the vertical section. How much will the firm supply in each case and at what price? (You will need to draw in MR curves too.) Is the MC curve still the supply curve?*

The long run. In the long run, the hire company will consider purchasing additional equipment. It can therefore supply as much as it likes in the long run. The supply curve will be relatively elastic, or if it is a price taker itself (i.e. if the scaffolding firm simply buys scaffolding at the market price), the supply curve will be horizontal. This long-run supply curve will be vertically higher than the short-run curve, since the long-run *MC* includes the cost of purchasing each additional piece of equipment.

Market supply

This is illustrated in Figure 19.2(b). The market supply curve of capital services is the sum of the quantities supplied by all the individual firms. It can be either the total supply of a particular type of capital (e.g. scaffolding) or, more narrowly, the supply of a particular type of capital to a certain industry (e.g. the catering industry or the car industry).

In the short run, market supply of a particular type of capital equipment will be relatively inelastic, given that it takes time to manufacture new equipment and that stocks of equipment currently held by manufacturers are likely to be relatively small. Moreover, hire companies may be unwilling to purchase (expensive) new equipment immediately there is a rise in demand: after all, the upsurge in demand may turn out to be short lived.

In the long run, the supply curve will be more elastic because extra capital equipment can be produced. The hire companies will also be more willing to purchase additional equipment if the rental rates continue to be at a higher level.

Determination of the price of capital services

Key Idea 10 p73

As Figure 19.2(b) shows, in a perfect market the market rental rate for capital services will be determined by the interaction of market demand and supply.

If there is monopsony power on the part of the users of hired capital, this will have the effect of depressing the rental rate below the MRP_K (see Figure 19.1(b)). If, on the other hand, there is monopoly power on the part of hire companies, the analysis is similar to that of monopoly in the goods market (see Figure 11.5 on page 222). The firm, by reducing the supply of capital for hire, can drive up the rental rate. It will maximise profit where the marginal revenue from hiring out the equipment is equal to the marginal cost of so doing: at a rental rate (price) *above* the marginal cost.

19.3 Investment appraisal

The alternative to hiring capital is to buy it outright. This section examines the demand and supply of capital for purchase.

The demand for capital: investment

How many computers will an engineering firm want to buy? Should a steelworks install another blast furnace? Should a removal firm buy another furniture lorry? Should it buy another warehouse? These are all **investment** decisions. Investment is the purchasing of additional capital.

The demand for capital, or 'investment demand', by a profit-maximising firm is based on exactly the same principles as the demand for labour or the demand for capital services. The firm must weigh up the marginal revenue product of that investment (i.e. the money it will earn for the firm) against its marginal cost.

However, the benefits of the investment occur not all at once, but over a number of years. The reason is that capital is durable. It goes on producing goods, and hence yielding revenue for the firm, for a considerable period of time. Calculating these benefits, therefore, involves taking account of their *timing*.

There are two ways of approaching the problem. The first involves calculating the monetary benefits over the life of the investment and comparing them with the monetary costs. This is called the **present value approach**. The second is called the **rate of return approach**. It involves calculating these benefits as a *percentage* of the costs of the investment. This 'rate of return' on the investment is then compared with the rate of interest that the firm would have to pay to borrow the money in order to make the investment.

In both cases the firm is comparing the marginal benefits with the marginal costs of the investment.

Present value approach

To work out the benefit of an investment (its *MRP*), the firm must estimate all the future earnings it will bring and then convert them to a *present value*. Let us take a simple example.

Assume that a firm is considering buying a machine. It will produce £1000 per year (net of operating costs) for four years and then wear out and sell for £1000 as scrap. What is the benefit of this machine to the firm? At first sight the answer would seem to be £5000. This, after all, is the total income earned from the machine. Unfortunately, it is not as simple as this. The reason is that money earned in the future is less beneficial to the firm than having the same amount of money today: after all, if the firm has the money today, it can earn interest on it by putting it in the bank or reinvesting it in some other project. (Note that this has nothing to do with inflation. In the case we are considering, we are assuming constant prices.)

To illustrate this, assume that you have £100 today and can earn 10 per cent interest by putting it in a bank. In one year's time that £100 will have grown to £110, in two years' time to £121, in three years' time to £133.10 and so on. This process is known as **compounding**.

From this it follows that, if someone offered to give you £121 in two years' time, that would be no better than giving you £100 today, since, with interest, £100 would grow to £121 in two years. What we say, then, is that with a 10 per cent interest rate, £121 in two years' time has a *present value* of £100.

The procedure of reducing future values back to a present value is known as **discounting**.

> **The principle of discounting.** People generally prefer to have benefits today than in the future. Thus future benefits have to be reduced (discounted) to give them a present value.
>
> **Key Idea 22**

When we do discounting, the rate which we use is called the **rate of discount**: in this case 10 per cent. The formula for discounting is given by:

$$PV = \sum \frac{X_t}{(1+r)^t}$$

where PV is the present value
X_t is the earnings from the investment in year t.
r is the rate of discount (expressed as a decimal: i.e. 10 per cent $= 0.1$).
$\sum$ is the sum of each of the years' discounted earnings.

So what is the present value of the investment in the machine that produced £1000 for four years and then is sold as scrap for £1000 at the end of the four years? According to the formula it is:

$$= \frac{\overset{\text{Year 1}}{£1000}}{1.1} + \frac{\overset{\text{Year 2}}{£1000}}{(1.1)^2} + \frac{\overset{\text{Year 3}}{£1000}}{(1.1)^3} + \frac{\overset{\text{Year 4}}{£2000}}{(1.1)^4}$$

$$= £909 + £826 + £751 + £1366$$

$$= £3852$$

Thus the present value of the investment (i.e. its *MRP*) is £3852, *not* £5000 as it might seem at first sight. In other words, if the firm had £3852 today and deposited it in a bank at a 10 per cent interest rate, the firm would earn exactly the same as it would by investing in the machine.

So is the investment worthwhile? It is now simply a question of comparing the £3852 benefit with the cost of buying the machine. If the machine costs less than £3852, it will be worth buying. If it costs more, the firm would be better off keeping its money in the bank and earning the 10 per cent rate of interest.

The difference between the present value of the benefits (PV_b) of the investment and its cost (C) is known as the **net present value** (NPV).

$$NPV = PV_b - C$$

If the *NPV* is positive, the investment is worthwhile.

> **Pause for thought**
>
> *What is the present value of a machine that lasts three years, earns £100 in year 1, £200 in year 2, and £200 in year 3, and then has a scrap value of £100? Assume that the rate of discount is 5 per cent. If the machine costs £500, is the investment worthwhile? Would it be worthwhile if the rate of discount were 10 per cent?*

BOX 19.1

Investing in roads
The assessment of costs and benefits

In the UK, the Department of Transport uses the following procedure to evaluate new road schemes, a procedure very similar to that used in many countries.

Estimating demand

The first thing to be done is to estimate likely future traffic flows. These are based on the government's National Road Traffic Forecast. This makes two predictions: a 'low-growth case', based on the assumption of low economic growth and high fuel prices, and a 'high-growth case', based on the assumption of high economic growth and low fuel prices. The actual growth in traffic, therefore, is likely to lie between the two.

Identifying possible schemes

Various road construction and improvement schemes are constantly under examination by the government, especially in parts of the network where traffic growth is predicted to be high and where congestion is likely to occur. In each case forecasts are then made of the likely use of the new roads and the diversion of traffic away from existing parts of the network. Again, two forecasts are made in each case: a 'low-growth' and a 'high-growth' one.

The use of cost–benefit analysis

The costs and benefits of each scheme are assigned monetary values and are compared with those of merely maintaining the existing network. The government uses a computer program known as COBA to assist it in the calculations.

Estimating the benefits of a scheme (relative to the existing network)

Three types of benefit are included in the analysis:

- Time saved. This is broken down into two categories: working time and non-working time (including travelling to and from work). The evaluation of working time is based on average national wage rates, while that of non-working time is based on surveys and the examination of traveller behaviour (the aim being to assess the value placed by the traveller on time saved). This results in non-working time per minute being given a value of approximately a quarter of that given to working time.

- Reductions in vehicle operating costs. These include: fuel, oil, tyres, maintenance and depreciation from usage. There will be savings if the scheme reduces the distance of journeys or allows a more economical speed to be maintained.

Rate of return approach

The alternative approach when estimating whether an investment is worthwhile is to calculate the investment's *rate of return*. This rate of return is known as the firm's **marginal efficiency of capital** (MEC) or **internal rate of return** (IRR).

We use the same formula as for calculating present value:

$$PV = \sum \frac{X_t}{(1 + r)^t}$$

and then calculate what value of r would make the PV equal to the cost of investment: in other words, the rate of discount that would make the investment just break even. Say this worked out at 20 per cent. What we would be saying is that the investment will just cover its costs if the current rate of interest (rate of discount) is 20 per cent. In other words, this investment is equivalent to receiving 20 per cent interest: it has a 20 per cent rate of return.

So should the investment go ahead? Yes, if the actual rate of interest (i) is less than 20 per cent. The firm is better off investing its money in this

■ Reductions in accidents. There are two types of benefit here: (a) the reduction in casualties (divided into three categories – fatal, serious non-fatal, and slight); and (b) the reduction in monetary costs, such as vehicle repair or replacement, medical costs and police, fire service and ambulance costs.

The reductions in monetary costs are relatively easy to estimate. The benefits from the reduction in casualties are more difficult. The current method of evaluating them is based on the amount people are prepared to pay to reduce the risks of accidents. This clearly has the drawback that people are often unaware of the risks of accidents or of the extent of the resulting pain and suffering.

In 2001, the following figures were used to value each accident prevented: fatal, £1194 240: serious non-fatal, £134 190; slight, £10 350. The human cost element for each type was valued at £783 000, £108 800 and £7970 respectively.

Estimating the costs of the scheme (relative to the existing network)

There are two main categories of cost: construction costs and additional road maintenance costs. If the new scheme results in a saving in road maintenance compared with merely retaining the existing network, then the maintenance costs will be negative.

The analysis

The costs and benefits of the scheme are assessed for the period of construction and for a standard life (in the UK this is 30 years). The costs and benefits are discounted back to a present value. The rate of discount used in the UK is 6 per cent. If the discounted benefits exceed the discounted costs, there is a positive net present value, and the scheme is regarded as justified on economic grounds. If there is more than one scheme, then their net present values will be compared so as to identify the preferable scheme.

It is only at this final stage that environmental considerations are taken into account. In other words, they are not included in the calculation of costs and benefits, but may have some influence in determining the choice between schemes. Clearly, if a socially efficient allocation of road space is to be determined, such externalities need to be included in the cost and benefit calculations.

Question

Are there any other drawbacks of using a willingness to pay principle to evaluate human costs?

---

project than keeping its money in the bank. If $IRR > i$, the investment should go ahead.

This is just one more application of the general rule that if $MRP_K > MC_K$ then more capital should be used: only in this case MRP_K is expressed as a rate of return (IRR), and the MC_K is expressed as a rate of interest (i).

The risks of investment

One of the problems with investment is that the future is uncertain. The return on an investment will depend on the value of the goods it produces. But this will depend on the goods market. For example, the return on investment in the car industry will depend on the demand and price of cars. But future markets cannot be predicted with accuracy: they depend on consumer tastes, the actions of rivals and the whole state of the economy. Investment is thus risky.

How is this risk accounted for when calculating the benefits of an investment? The answer is to use a higher rate of discount. The higher the risk, the bigger the premium that must be added to the rate.

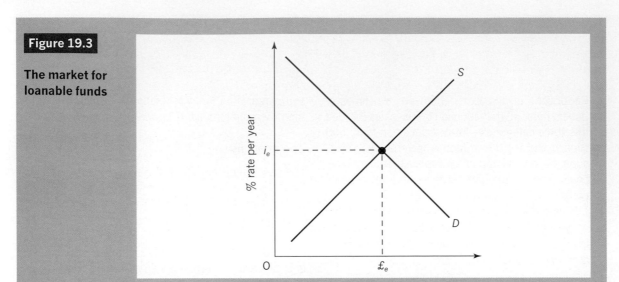

Figure 19.3

The market for loanable funds

The supply of capital

It is important to distinguish between the supply of *physical* capital and the supply of *finance* to be used by firms for the purchase of capital.

Supply of physical capital. The principles here are just the same as those in the goods market. It does not matter whether a firm is supplying lorries (capital) or cars (a consumer good): it will still produce up to the point where $MC = MR$ if it wishes to maximise profits.

Supply of finance. When firms borrow to invest, this creates a demand for finance (or 'loanable funds'). The supply of loanable funds comes from the deposits that individuals and firms make in financial institutions. These deposits are savings, and represent the resources released when people refrain from consumption. In other words, the less people consume, the more loanable funds there will be available to finance investment.

Among other things, the level of savings depends on the rate of interest that depositors receive. The higher the rate of interest, the more people will be encouraged to save. This is illustrated by an upward-sloping supply curve of loanable funds, as shown in Figure 19.3.

Savings also depend on the level of people's incomes, their expectations of future price changes, and their general level of 'thriftiness' (their willingness to forgo present consumption in order to be able to have more in the future). A change in any of these other determinants will shift the supply curve.

Determination of the rate of interest

What determines the rate of interest: the rate that is used for working out the present value of investment? The answer lies in the demand and supply of loanable funds (see Figure 19.3).

The supply curve is the total supply of savings, which in the long run can be used to build up the capital stock.

Key Idea 10 p73

The demand curve includes the demand by households for credit and the demand by firms for funds to finance their investment. This demand curve slopes downward for two reasons. First, households will borrow more at lower rates of interest. It effectively makes goods cheaper for them to buy. Second, it reflects the falling rate of return on investment as investment increases. This is simply due to diminishing returns to investment. As rates of interest fall, it will now become profitable for firms to invest in projects that have a lower rate of return: the quantity of loanable funds demanded thus rises.

Equilibrium will be achieved where demand equals supply at an interest rate of i_e and a quantity of loanable funds $£_e$.

How will this market adjust to a change in demand or supply? Assume that there is a rise in demand for capital equipment, due, say, to an improvement in technology which increases the productivity of capital. There is thus an increase in demand for loanable funds. The demand curve shifts to the right in Figure 19.3. The equilibrium rate of interest will rise and this will encourage more savings. The end result is that more money will be spent on capital equipment.

Calculating the costs of capital

When calculating the net present value or internal rate of return of an investment, it is clearly important for the firm to estimate the cost of the investment. The cost does not just include the cost of the equipment that the firm buys: it also includes the costs of raising the finance to pay for the investment.

A firm can finance investment from three major sources:

■ Retaining profits.
■ Borrowing from the banking sector – either domestic or overseas.
■ Issuing new shares (equities) or debentures (fixed-interest loan stock).

It is quite common for a firm to raise finance for a particular project from a mixture of all three sources. The problem is that each source of finance will have a different cost. What is needed, then, for each project is a weighted average of the interest rate (or equivalent) charged or implied by each component of finance.

For investment financed by retained profits, the opportunity cost depends on what would have been done with the profits as the next best alternative. It might be the interest forgone by not putting the money into a bank or other financial institution, or by not purchasing assets. If the next best alternative was to distribute the profits to shareholders, then the opportunity cost would be the cost associated with the increased risks of the firm's share price falling, and the consequent risks of a takeover by another company. (Share prices would fall if shareholders, disillusioned with the reduced dividends, sold their shares.)

For a bank loan, or for debentures, the cost is simply the rate of interest paid on the loan. The only estimation problem here is that of forecasting future rates of interest on loans where the rate of interest is variable.

For equity finance, the cost is the rate of return that must be paid to shareholders to persuade them not to sell their shares. This will depend on the rate of return on shares elsewhere. The greater the return on shares generally, the higher must be the dividends paid by any given firm in order to persuade its shareholders not to switch into other companies' shares.

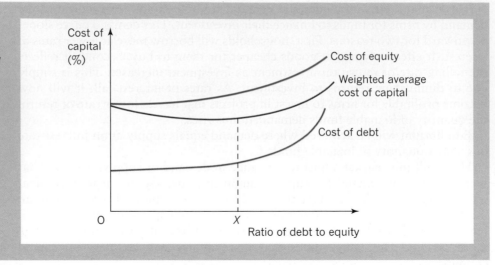

Figure 19.4

The debt/equity ratio

Leverage and the cost of capital

The cost of capital will increase as the risks for those supplying finance to the company increase: they will need a higher rate of return to warrant incurring the higher risks. One of the most important determinants of the risk to suppliers of finance is the company's leverage. **Leverage** is a measure of the extent to which the company relies on debt finance (i.e. loans) as opposed to equity finance.

There are two common measures of leverage. The first is the **gearing ratio**. This is the ratio of debt finance (debentures and borrowing from banks) to total finance. The other is the **debt/equity ratio**. This is the ratio of debt finance to equity finance.

The higher the company's leverage, the higher will be the risks to creditors and hence the higher will be the interest charged (see Figure 19.4). But why should this be so? The reason is that interest on loans (bank loans and debentures) has to be paid, irrespective of the company's profits. If there is a downturn in the company's profits, then, if it has 'low gearing' (i.e. a low debt/equity ratio), it can simply cut its dividends and as a result will find it relatively easy to make its interest payments. If, however, it is 'highly geared', it may find it impossible to pay all the interest due, even by cutting dividends, in which case it will be forced into receivership.

Given that a highly geared company poses greater risks to creditors, they will demand a higher interest rate to compensate. Similarly with shareholders: given that dividends are likely to fluctuate more with a highly geared company, shareholders will require a higher average dividend over the years. In other words, investors in a highly geared company – whether banks, debenture holders or shareholders – will demand a higher **risk premium**. As gearing increases, so the risk premium, and hence the average cost of capital, will rise at an accelerating rate (see Figure 19.4).

Key Idea
13
p98

19.4 Financing investment

It is often claimed that the UK has 'fair weather' bankers: that is, bankers who are prepared to lend when things are going well, but less inclined to lend when times are hard. They are accused of taking a short-term perspective in their lending practices and of being over-eager to charge high rates of interest on loans, thereby discouraging investment. But the problem for business does not end there. Dealers on the stock market are also accused of focusing their speculative behaviour on short-run returns, thereby generating volatility in share prices and creating business caution, as firms seek ways of maintaining shareholder confidence in their stock (usually through paying high dividends).

In this section we will consider the sources from which business might draw finance, and the roles played by the various UK financial institutions. We will assess the extent to which 'short-termism' is an endemic problem in the capital market.

Sources of business finance

As mentioned in section 19.3 above, the firm can finance growth by borrowing, by retaining profits or by a new issue of shares.

As we noted in Chapter 15, the largest source of finance for investment in the UK is firms' own internal funds (i.e. ploughed-back profit). Given that business profitability depends in large part on the general state of the economy, internal funds as a source of business finance are likely to show considerable cyclical variation. When profits are squeezed in a recession, this source of investment will decline – but so also will the *demand* for investment: after all, what is the point in investing if your market is declining?

Other sources of finance, which include borrowing and the issue of shares and debentures, are known as 'external funds'. These are then categorised as short-term, medium-term or long-term sources of finance.

- Short-term finance is usually in the form of a short-term bank loan or overdraft facility, and is used by firms as a form of working capital to aid them in their day-to-day business operations. Another way of borrowing for a short period of time is for a firm to issue *commercial bills of exchange* (see below, page 391).

- Medium-term finance, again provided largely by banks, is usually in the form of a loan with set repayment targets. It is common for such loans to be made at a fixed rate of interest, with repayments being designed to fit in with the business's expected cash flow. Bank lending tends to be the most volatile source of business finance, and has been particularly sensitive to the state of the economy. While part of the reason is the lower demand for loans during a recession, part of the reason is the caution of banks in granting loans if prospects for the economy are poor.

- Long-term finance, especially in the UK, tends to be acquired through the stock and bond markets. The proportion of business financing from this source clearly depends on the state of the stock market. In the late 1990s, with a buoyant stock market, the proportion of funds obtained through share issue increased. Then with a decline in stock market prices from 2000 to 2003, this proportion fell.

  Despite the traditional reliance on the stock market for long-term sources of finance, there has been a growing involvement of banks in recent years. Banks have become more willing to provide finance for business start-ups and for diversification. Nevertheless, there is a concern that banks are still relatively cautious. This results in a problem of short-termism, with bankers often demanding a quick return on their money or charging high interest rates, and being less concerned to finance long-term inventment.

BOX 19.2

Financing innovation

A flourishing domestic economy is, in no small part, the result of firms successfully innovating and responding to the changing conditions and technologies within the market place. Through such adaptation and innovation the economy prospers, stimulating growth, income and employment. Conversely, an economy that fails to innovate and respond to change is likely to be set upon the rocky road to stagnation and decline.

Given the stark contrast in these alternative realities, not only is the development of new ideas and their diffusion throughout the economy crucial to its vitality, but it is essential that the financial system supports such innovation, and does so in the most efficient way. It must ensure not only that finance is available, but that it goes to those projects with the greatest potential.

Unfortunately, the projects with the greatest potential may involve considerable risk and uncertainty. Because of this, the private sector may be unwilling to fund their development. It may also be unwilling to finance various forms of research, where the outcomes are uncertain: something that is inevitable in much basic research.

As a result of this reluctance by the private sector, innovation funding has traditionally operated at three levels:

■ Level one: government financing of 'upstream' or basic research, where outcomes are likely to yield few if any financial returns.

■ Level two: self-financed business R&D (i.e. financed out of ploughed-back profit), where the profitability of such R&D activity is difficult to assess, especially by those outside of the business, and thus where banks and other financial institutions would be reluctant to provide finance.

■ Level three: external financing using accepted financial assessment criteria for risk and uncertainty.

In this traditional model, the state's role in financing innovation and investment does not end at the level of basic research. It will also compensate for market failures at later stages of the innovation-financing process. For example, it may adopt measures to improve the self-financing capacity of firms (e.g. tax relief), or measures to facilitate easier access to external finance (e.g. interest rate subsidies), or measures to extend and protect the ownership of intellectual property rights (e.g. tightening up and/or extending patent or copyright legislation).

There is much to suggest, however, that this traditional model is changing, and, along with it, the perceived role of the state in the process of conducting, funding and supporting the innovation process. The most significant of these changes can be found in the liberalisation of global finance.

Three of the major effects of financial liberalisation on innovation financing are as follows:

■ Channels of finance have diversified, widening the range of potential investment sources.

■ Financial innovations have increased the ability of potential innovators to locate and negotiate favourable financial deals.

■ Government regulations over capital market activities have diminished.

The implications of these changes have been to increase the efficiency and flexibility of the financial system. This has resulted in a reduction in international differences in the costs of capital for any businesses having access to global financing. Projects with high earning potential, but high risk, have been able to raise finance from a wider range of sources, national and international.

Although such financial globalisation has not removed the need for state support, it appears that financial changes are certainly diminishing its significance as a supporter of innovation finance.

Questions

1 *What market failures could account for a less than optimal amount of innovation in the absence of government support?*

2 *If financial markets were perfectly competitive and could price risk accurately, would there be any case at all for government support of innovation?*

Another source of finance is that from outside the country. Part of this is direct investment by externally based companies in the domestic economy. Part is finance from foreign financial institutions. In either case, a major determinant of the amount of finance from this source is the current state of the economy and predictions of its future state. One of the major considerations here is anticipated changes in the exchange rate (see Chapter 27). If the exchange rate is expected to rise, this will increase the value of any given profit in terms of foreign currency. As would be expected, this source of finance is particularly volatile.

Comparison of the UK with other European countries

In other European countries, notably Germany and France, the attitude towards business funding is quite different from that in the UK. In these countries, banks provide a significant amount of *long-term*, fixed interest rate finance. While this tends to increase companies' gearing ratios and thus increases the risk of bankruptcy, it does provide a much more stable source of finance and creates an environment where banks are much more committed to the long-run health of companies. For this reason the net effect may be to *reduce* the risks associated with financing investment.

The role of the financial sector

Before we look at the financial institutions operating within the UK, and assess their differing financial roles, it should be noted that they all have the common function of providing a link between those who wish to lend and those who wish to borrow. In other words, they act as the mechanism whereby the supply of funds is matched to the demand for funds.

As **financial intermediaries**, these institutions provide four important services.

Expert advice

Financial intermediaries can advise their customers on financial matters: on the best way of investing their funds and on alternative ways of obtaining finance. This should help to encourage the flow of savings and the efficient use of them.

As far as businesses are concerned, banks often play a central role in advising on investment and on possible mergers and acquisitions. With the opening up of the financial sector after the deregulation of 1986 (the 'Big Bang'), and especially with the influx of American and Japanese banks, there is now much more active competition between banks in terms of the advisory services that they offer to businesses.

Expertise in channelling funds

Financial intermediaries have the specialist knowledge to be able to channel funds to those areas that yield the highest return. This too encourages the flow of saving as it gives savers the confidence that their savings will earn a good rate of interest. Financial intermediaries help to ensure that investment projects that are potentially profitable, at least in the short run, are able to obtain finance. They thereby help to increase allocative efficiency.

Maturity transformation

Many people and firms want to borrow money for long periods of time, and yet many depositors want to be able to withdraw their deposits on demand or at short notice. If people had to rely on borrowing directly from other people, there

definition

Financial intermediaries
The general name for financial institutions (banks, building societies, etc.) which act as a means of channelling funds from depositors to borrowers.

would be a problem: the lenders would not be prepared to lend for a long enough period. If you had £100 000 of savings, would you be prepared to lend it to a friend to buy a house if the friend was going to take 25 years to pay it back? Even if there was no risk whatsoever of your friend defaulting, most people would be totally unwilling to tie up their savings for so long. This is where a bank or building society comes in. It borrows money from a vast number of small savers, who are able to withdraw their money on demand or at short notice. It then lends the money to house purchasers for a long period of time by granting mortgages (typically these are paid back over 20 to 30 years).

This process whereby financial intermediaries lend for longer periods of time than they borrow is known as **maturity transformation**. They are able to do this because with a large number of depositors it is highly unlikely that they would all want to withdraw their deposits at the same time. On any one day, although some people will be withdrawing money, others will be making new deposits.

There is still the problem, however, that long-term loans by banks, especially to industry, often carry greater risks. With banking tradition, especially in the UK, being to err on the side of caution, this can limit the extent to which maturity transformation takes place, and can result in a less than optimum amount of investment finance, when viewed from a long-term perspective.

Risk transformation

You may be unwilling to lend money directly to another person in case they do not pay up. You are unwilling to take the risk. Financial intermediaries, however, by lending to large numbers of people, are willing to risk the odd case of default. They can absorb the loss because of the interest they earn on all the other loans. This spreading of risk is known as **risk transformation**. What is more, financial intermediaries may have the expertise to be able to assess just how risky a loan is. Again, however, banks in the UK have been accused of being too cautious, and too unwilling to lend to industry for long-term investment, given the risks associated with such loans.

In addition to channelling funds from depositors to borrowers, certain financial institutions have another important function. This is to provide a means of transmitting payments. Thus by the use of debit cards, credit cards, cheques, standing orders, etc., money can be transferred from one person or institution to another without having to rely on cash.

> **definition**
> **Maturity transformation**
> The transformation of deposits into loans of a longer maturity.

> **definition**
> **Risk transformation**
> The process whereby banks can spread the risks of lending by having a large number of borrowers.

> **Pause for thought**
> *Which of the above are examples of economies of scale?*

Financial institutions in the UK

The different types of financial intermediary can be grouped according to the types of deposit taking and lending in which they specialise.

Retail banks

These include the familiar high street banks such as Barclays and HSBC. They specialise in providing branch banking facilities to members of the general public, but, as we have seen, they also lend to business, albeit often on a short-term basis. They operate current (cheque-book) accounts, on most of which overdraft facilities can be arranged, and deposit accounts, which, by offering a higher interest rate but no cheque book, are designed to encourage savers. They also provide personal loan facilities and financial advice to their customers. Unlike most other financial institutions, they are involved in operating the *payments* system – the transmission of money through cheques, standing orders, direct debits, etc.

Since the deregulation of the mid-1980s, retail banks have diversified their business, and each one now provides a range of financial services, often through one or more of its subsidiaries. These services include insurance, share dealing, pensions, mortgages and estate agency.

Retail banks are now increasingly moving into the wholesale banking market (see below).

The retail banking sector has been joined in recent years by many former building societies, the first of which was the Abbey National in 1989. Building societies are institutions which specialise in granting loans (mortgages) for house purchase, and which compete for the savings of the general public through a network of high street branches. Building societies have 'mutual' status. This means that people who save with them (their 'members') are, in effect, their owners. Given that there are no shareholders claiming a dividend, the interest paid to savers can, in principle, be higher. By changing their status to a bank, however, and thereby becoming public limited companies with shareholders, the institutions gain increased freedom to diversify their activities.

Investment banks

Investment banks, often known as wholesale banks, specialise in receiving large deposits from and making large loans to industry and other financial institutions: these are known as **wholesale deposits and loans**. These may be for short periods of time to account for the non-matching of the firm's payments and receipts from its business. They may be for longer periods of time, for various investment purposes. These wholesale deposits and loans are very large sums of money. Banks thus compete against each other for them and negotiate individual terms with the firm to suit the firm's particular requirements. The rates of interest negotiated will reflect the current market rates of interest and the terms of the particular loan/deposit. Very large loans to firms are often divided ('syndicated') between several banks.

Merchant banks. One category of investment bank is the merchant banks. Examples include Morgan Stanley, Rothschild, SG Hambros and Goldman Sachs. They often act as 'brokers', arranging loans for companies from a number of different sources. They also offer financial advice to industry and provide assistance to firms in raising new capital through the issue of new shares.

Their traditional business was in 'accepting' **commercial bills of exchange**. Commercial bills of exchange are issued by companies and are a means whereby they can raise money for a short period of time (typically three months). Bills are, in effect, an IOU, with the company that issues them promising to pay the holder a specified sum on a particular date. Since bills do not pay interest, they are sold below their face value in order to enable the purchaser to earn a return. There are financial markets (the 'money market') where these bills can be sold by their holders if they need to get their money back before the due date. This is where the merchant banks come in. They can help to make these bills more marketable by 'accepting' them. This means that the merchant bank will make payment to the holder if the firm issuing the bill fails to do so.

The merchant banks have been particularly affected by the financial deregulation of recent years, with much of their business being threatened by competition from retail banks, overseas banks and other financial institutions. In response to this competition, merchant banks have attempted to diversify their business, and there have been many mergers between merchant banks and other financial institutions.

definition

Wholesale deposits and loans
Large-scale deposits and loans made by and to firms at negotiated interest rates.

definition

Commercial bill
A certificate issued by a firm promising to repay a stated amount on a certain date, typically three months from the issue of the bill. Bills pay no interest as such, but are sold at a discount and redeemed at their face value, thereby earning a rate of discount for the purchaser.

Overseas banks. Investment banks also include many overseas banks, especially Japanese and American. They have expanded their business in the UK enormously in recent years, especially since the abolition of foreign exchange controls in 1979. Their major specialism is the finance of international trade and capital movements, and they deal extensively in the foreign exchange market. Most of their deposits are in foreign currencies.

Finance houses. These specialise in providing hire-purchase finance for the purchase of consumer durables such as cars and electrical goods. This is normally arranged through the retailer, which will offer credit to its customers. Finance houses also lease out capital equipment to firms – something that the retail banks are increasingly doing too. Their main source of funds is the banks, but they also receive deposits from the general public. Several finance houses are subsidiaries of commercial banks.

Conclusions

The trend in banking and finance since the early 1980s has been away from the narrow specialisation of the past and towards the offering of a wider and wider range of services. Inevitably, as this trend continues, so the services offered by the various institutions will increasingly overlap.

19.5 The stock market

In this section, we will look at the role of the stock market and consider the advantages and limitations of raising finance through it. We will also consider whether the stock market is efficient.

The role of the Stock Exchange

The London Stock Exchange operates as both a primary and secondary market in capital.

As a **primary market** it is where public limited companies (see page 48) can raise finance by issuing new shares, whether to new shareholders or to existing ones. To raise finance on the Stock Exchange a business must be 'listed'. The Listing Agreement involves directors agreeing to abide by a strict set of rules governing behaviour and levels of reporting to shareholders. Companies must have at least three years' trading experience and make at least 25 per cent of its shares available to the public. In May 2003, there were 1637 UK and 401 international companies on the Official List. During 2002 £17.3 billion's worth of new capital was raised by selling equity (ordinary shares) and fixed-interest securities on the London Stock Exchange.

As well as those on the Official List, there are some 700 companies on what is known as the Alternative Investment Market (AIM). Companies listed here tend to be young but with growth potential, and do not have to meet the strict criteria or pay such high costs as companies on the Official List.

As a **secondary market**, the Stock Exchange operates as a market where investors can sell existing shares to one another. In 2002, on an average day's trading, £7.2 billion's worth of trading in UK equities and £11.0 billion's worth of trading in international equities took place.

definition

Primary market in capital
Where shares are sold by the issuer of the shares (i.e. the firm) and where, therefore, finance is channelled directly from the purchasers (i.e. the shareholders) to the firm.

definition

Secondary market in capital
Where shareholders sell shares to others. This is thus a market in 'second-hand' shares.

The advantages and disadvantages of using the stock market to raise capital

As a market for raising capital the stock market has a number of advantages:

- It brings together those that wish to invest and those that seek investment. It thus represents a way that savings can be mobilised to create output, and does so in a relatively low-cost way.
- Firms that are listed on the stock exchange are subject to strict regulations. This is likely to stimulate investor confidence, making it easier for business to raise finance.
- The process of merger and acquisition is facilitated by having a share system. It enables business more effectively to pursue this as a growth strategy.

The main weaknesses of the stock market for raising capital are:

- The cost to a business of getting listed can be immense, not only in a financial sense, but also in being open to public scrutiny. Directors' and senior managers' decisions will often be driven by how the market is likely to react, rather by what they perceive to be in the business's best interests. They always have to think about the reactions of those large shareholders in the City that control a large proportion of their shares.
- It is often claimed that the stock market suffers from **short-termism**. Investors on the Stock Exchange are more concerned with a company's short-term performance and it share value. In responding to this, the business might neglect its long-term performance and potential.

Is the stock market efficient?

One of the arguments made in favour of the stock market is that it acts as an arena within which share values can be accurately or efficiently priced. If new information comes on to the market concerning a business and its performance, this will be quickly and rationally transferred into the business's share value. This is known as the **efficient market hypothesis**. So for example, if an investment analyst found that, in terms of its actual and expected dividends, a particular share was under-priced and thus represented a 'bargain', the analyst would advise investors to buy. As people then bought the shares, their price would rise, pushing their value up to their full worth. So by attempting to gain from inefficiently priced securities, investors will encourage the market to become more efficient.

> **definition**
> **Short-termism**
> Where firms and investors take decisions based on the likely short-term performance of a company, rather than on its long-term prospects. Firms may thus sacrifice long-term profits and growth for the sake of quick return.

> **definition**
> **Efficient (capital) market hypothesis**
> The hypothesis that new information about a company's current or future performance will be quickly and accurately reflected in its share price.

Efficient capital markets. Capital markets are efficient when the prices of shares accurately reflect information about companies' current and expected future performance.

Key Idea 23

So how efficient is the stock market in pricing securities? Is information rationally and quickly conveyed into the share's price? Or are investors able to prosper from the stock market's inefficiencies?

We can identify three levels of efficiency.

definition

Weak efficiency (of share markets)
Where share dealing prevents cyclical movements in shares.

definition

Semi-strong efficiency (of share markets)
Where share prices adjust quickly, fully and accurately to publicly available information.

definition

Strong efficiency (of share markets)
Where share prices adjust quickly, fully and accurately to all available information, both public and that available only to insiders.

definition

Random walk
Where fluctuations in the value of a share away from its 'correct' value are random: i.e. have no systematic pattern. When charted over time, these share price movements would appear like a 'random walk': like the path of someone staggering along drunk!

Weak form of efficiency. Share prices often move in cycles which do not reflect the underlying performance of the firm. If information is imperfect, those with a better understanding of such cycles gain from buying shares at the trough and selling them at the peak of the cycles. They are taking advantage of the market's inefficiency.

The technical analysis used by investment analysts to track share cycles is a complex science, but more and more analysts are using the techniques. As they do so and knowledge becomes more perfect, so the market will become more efficient and the cycles will tend to disappear. But why?

As more people buy a company's shares as the price falls towards its trough, so this extra demand will prevent the price falling so far. Similarly, as people sell as the price rises towards its peak, so this extra supply will prevent the price rising so far. This is an example of stabilising speculation (see page 94). As more and more people react in this way, so the cycle all but disappears. When this happens, **weak efficiency** has been achieved.

The semi-strong form of efficiency. **Semi-strong efficiency** is when share prices adjust fully to publicly available information. In practice, not all investors will interpret such information correctly: their knowledge is imperfect. But as investors become more and more sophisticated, and as more and more advice is available to shareholders (through stock brokers, newspapers, published accounts, etc.), and as many shares are purchased by professional fund managers, so the interpretation of public information becomes more and more perfect and the market becomes more and more efficient in the semi-strong sense.

If the market were efficient in the semi-strong sense, then no gain could be made from studying a company's performance and prospects, as any such information would *already* be included in the current share price. In selecting shares, you would do just as well by pinning the financial pages of a newspaper on the wall, throwing darts at them, and buying the shares the darts hit!

The strong form of efficiency. If the stock market showed the **strong form of efficiency**, then share prices would fully reflect *all* available information – whether public or not. For this to be so, all 'inside' information would have to be reflected in the share price the moment the information is available.

If the market is *not* efficient at this level, then people who have access to privileged information will be able to make large returns from their investments by acting on such information. For example, directors of a company would know if the company was soon to announce better than expected profits. In the meantime, they could gain by buying shares in the company, knowing that the share price would rise when the information about the profits became public. Gains made from such 'insider dealing' are illegal. However, proving whether individuals are engaging in it is very difficult. Nevertheless, there are people in prison for insider dealing: so it does happen!

Given the penalties for insider dealing and the amount of private information that firms possess, it is unlikely that all such information will be reflected in share prices. Thus the strong form of stock market efficiency is unlikely to hold.

If stock markets were fully efficient, the expected returns from every share would be the same. The return is referred to as the **yield**: this is measured as the dividends paid on the share as a percentage of the share's market price. For example, if you hold shares whose market price is £1 per share and you receive an annual dividend of 3p per share, then the yield on the shares is 3 per cent. But why should the expected returns on shares be the same? If any share was expected to yield a higher-than-average return, people would buy it; its price would rise and its yield would correspondingly fall.

It would only be unanticipated information, therefore, that would cause share prices to deviate from that which reflected expected average yields. Such information must, by its nature, be random, and as such would cause share prices to deviate randomly from their expected price, or follow what we call a **random walk**. Evidence suggests that share prices do tend to follow random patterns.

definition

Yield on a share
The dividend received per share expressed as a percentage of the current market price of the share.

SUMMARY

1a We need to distinguish between factor prices and factor services. A factor's price is income from its sale, whereas a factor's service is the income from its use.

1b The profit-maximising employment of capital will be at the point where the marginal cost of capital equals the marginal revenue product.

2a The demand for capital services will be equal to MRP_K. As a result of diminishing returns, this will decline as more capital is used.

2b The supply of capital services to a firm will be horizontal or upward sloping, depending on whether the firm is perfectly competitive or has monopsony power.

2c The supply curve of capital services *by* a firm in the short run will be relatively elastic up to capacity supply. In the long run, the supply curve will be very elastic, but at a higher rental rate than in the short run, given that the cost of purchasing the equipment must be taken into account in the rental rate.

2d The market supply of capital services is likely to be highly inelastic in the short run, given that capital equipment tends to have very specific uses and cannot normally be transferred from one use to another. In the long run it will be more elastic.

2e The price of capital services will be determined by the interaction of demand and supply.

3a The demand for capital for purchase will depend on the return it earns for the firm. To calculate the return, all future earnings from the investment have to be reduced to present value by discounting at a market rate of interest. If the present value exceeds the cost of the investment, the investment is worthwhile. Alternatively, a rate of return from the investment (IRR) can be calculated and then this can be compared with the return that the firm could have earned by investing elsewhere.

3b The supply of finance for investment depends on the supply of loanable funds, which in turn depends, in large part, on the rate of interest.

3c The rate of interest will be determined by the demand and supply of loanable funds.

3d The costs of capital supplied to the firm will rise the more it is in debt, and hence the more risky the investment becomes.

4a Business finance can come from internal and external sources. Sources external to the firm include borrowing and the issue of shares.

4b The role of the financial sector is to act as a financial intermediary between those who wish to borrow and those who wish to lend.

4c UK financial institutions specialise in different types of deposit taking and lending.

5a The stock market operates as both a primary and secondary market in capital. As a primary market it channels finance to companies as people purchase new shares. It is also a market for existing shares.

5b It helps to stimulate growth and investment by bringing together companies and people who want to invest in them. By regulating firms and by keeping transaction costs of investment low, it helps to ensure that investment is efficient.

5c It does impose costs on firms, however. It is expensive for firms to be listed and the public exposure may make them too keen to 'please' the market. It can also foster short-termism.

5d The stock market is relatively efficient. It achieves weak efficiency by reducing cyclical movements in share prices. It achieves semi-strong efficiency by allowing share prices to respond quickly and fully to publicly available information. Whether it achieves strong efficiency by adjusting quickly and fully to *all* information (both public or insider), however, is more doubtful.

REVIEW QUESTIONS

1 Draw the MRP_K, AC_K and MC_K curves for a firm which has monopsony power when hiring capital equipment. Mark the amount of capital equipment it will choose to hire and show what hire charge it will pay.

2 Using a diagram like Figure 19.2, demonstrate what will happen under perfect competition (in the short run) when there is an increase in the productivity of a particular type of capital. Consider the effects on the demand, price (rental rate) and quantity supplied of the services of this type of capital. In what way will the long-run effect differ from the short-run one that you have illustrated?

3 Suppose an investment costs £12 000 and yields £5000 per year for three years. At the end of the three years, the equipment has no value. Work out whether the investment will be profitable if the rate of discount is:

(a) 5%   (b) 10%   (c) 20%.

4 If a project's costs occur throughout the life of the project, how will this affect the appraisal of whether the project is profitable?

5 What factors would cause a rise in the market rate of interest?

6 What is meant by the two terms 'gearing ratio' and 'debt/equity ratio'? What is their significance?

7 Explain the various roles that financial intermediaries play within the finance sector.

8 In what circumstances is the stock market likely to be 'efficient' in the various senses of the term?

Additional Part G case studies on the *Economics for Business* website (www.booksites.net/sloman)

G.1 **Stocks and flows.** This examines one of the most important distinctions in economics and one which we shall come across on several occasions.

G.2 **Poverty in the past.** Extreme poverty in Victorian England.

G.3 **The rise and decline of the labour movement.** A brief history of trade unions in the UK.

G.4 **How useful is marginal productivity theory?** How accurately does the theory describe employment decisions by firms?

G.5 **Profit sharing.** An examination of the case for and against profit sharing as a means of rewarding workers.

G.6 **How can we define poverty?** This examines different definitions of poverty and, in particular, distinguishes between absolute and relative measures of poverty.

G.7 **How to reverse the UK's increased inequality.** Recommendations of the Rowntree Foundation.

G.8 **Calculating net present value.** A numerical example using discounting techniques to show how net present value is calculated.

G.9 **Catastrophic risk.** This examines the difficulties in assigning a monetary value to the remote chance of a catastrophe happening (such as an explosion at a nuclear power station).

Websites relevant to Part G

Numbers and sections refer to websites listed in the Web appendix and hotlinked from this book's website at **www.booksites.net/sloman**

■ For news articles relevant to Part G, see the *Economics News Articles* link from the book's website.

■ For general news on labour and capital markets see websites in section A, and particularly A1–5, 7, 8, 21–26, 35, 36. See also A42 for links to economics news articles from newspapers worldwide.

■ For data on labour markets, see links in B1 or 2, especially to *Labour Market Trends* on the National Statistics site. Also see B9 and links in B19. Also see the labour topic in B33 and the *resources > statistics* links in H3.

■ For information on international labour standards and employment rights, see site H3.

■ Sites I7 and 11 contain links to *Labour economics*, *Labour force and markets* and *Labour unions* in the *Microeconomics* section and to *Distribution of income and wealth* in the *Macroeconomics* section. Site I4 has links in the *Directory* section to *Labor* and *Labor Economics*. Site I17 in the *Labor Economics* section has links to various topics, such as *Labor Unions*, *Minimum Wage*, *Poverty* and *Work*.

■ Links to the TUC and Confederation of British Industry sites can be found at E32 and 33.

■ For information on poverty and inequality, see sites B18; E9, 13.

■ For information on taxes, benefits and the redistribution of income, see E9, 30, 36; G5, 13. See also *The Virtual Economy* at D1.

■ For information on stock markets, see sites F18 and A3.

■ Sites I7 and 11 contain links to *Financial Economics*.

■ For student resources relevant to Part G, see sites C1–7, 9, 10, 19; D3.

The relationship between government and business

THE FT REPORTS...

THE FINANCIAL TIMES, 24 JUNE 2003

Ford's chief warns against industrial flight

By PETER MARSH

Britain faces 'stagnation and decay' if it does not do more to curtail industrial flight to lower cost countries, Sir Nick Scheele, chief operating officer of the Ford Motor Company, will say in a speech in Birmingham tonight.

Manufacturing in the UK should not be protected from competition, nor should companies be stopped from relocating, but the government should do more to foster well-paid, technologically challenging jobs in manufacturing, Mr Scheele will tell the Royal Society for the Encouragement of Arts, Manufactures and Commerce.

He will add: 'Where we go astray is when such industries [as manufacturing] leave developed economies such as ours and are not replaced by others of greater technological sophistication. Industrial flight, when industries depart and are not replaced by others, is not a sign of progress. It is a sign of stagnation and decay.'

Sir Nick will speak against the background of a bleak outlook for manufacturing, with many companies relocating because of the high rate of the pound, the weak economic climate, and competitive rivalry from businesses in low cost regions such as China.

However, he will add that manufacturing in the UK still supports 4m employees, and 2.4m in service jobs, while manufactured goods account for 86 per cent of the country's exports.

The chief operating officer of the world's second biggest carmaker, which employs 40 000 in the UK, will state he is not advocating a government blueprint for manufacturing along the lines of similar actions in the 1980s.

'But clearly, given the potential impact of various government actions on industry's competitive position . . . we need common objectives and a reasoned approach.'

Sir Nick will advocate a strong level of manufacturing in an advanced economy is an overwhelming national asset.

He will also maintain that government policies, in areas such as education, planning and fostering of innovation, should be based on ensuring a 'diverse economy' that 'helps create jobs for the widest variety of people' and so inevitably do more to help manufacturers.

Companies that do relocate to take advantage of cheaper labour costs may not always be acting in their own best interests, he will say.

As a result, companies remaining in UK manufacturing should step up their efforts to maintain high quality so that they can charge higher prices for their products and thereby retain a competitive advantage even in the context of Britain's relatively high costs.

> *Improving productivity is the Government's key economic objective for this Parliament. Higher productivity generates prosperity, increases wages and profits, and permits investment in modern high quality public services.*
>
> Patricia Hewitt, UK Secretary of State for Trade and Industry (2002)

Despite the fact that most countries today can be classified as 'market economies', governments nevertheless intervene substantially in the activities of business in order to protect the interests of consumers, workers or the environment.

Firms might collude to fix prices, use misleading advertising, create pollution, produce unsafe products, or use unacceptable employment practices. In such cases, government is expected to intervene to correct for the failings of the market system: for example, by outlawing collusion, by establishing advertising standards, by taxing or otherwise penalising polluting firms, by imposing safety standards on firms' behaviour and products, or by protecting employment rights.

For Sir Nick Scheele, the chief operating officer for Ford Motor Company, the role of government is even more fundamental (see FT article opposite). Intervention is a necessary requirement in order to safeguard against the inevitable long-term decline of the national economy.

In Part H, we explore the relationship between business and government. In Chapter 20 we will consider how markets might fail to achieve ideal outcomes, and what government can do to correct such problems. We will also consider how far firms should go in adopting a more socially responsible position.

In Chapter 21 we will focus upon the relationship between the government and the individual firm, and consider three policy areas: monopolies and oligopolies, research and technology, and training.

In Chapter 22, we will broaden our analysis and look at government policy aimed at the level of the market, and its impact upon all firms. Here we will consider environmental policy, transport policy and the issue of privatisation and regulation.

key terms

Social efficiency
Equity
Market failure
Externalities
Private and social costs and benefits
Deadweight welfare loss
Public goods
Free-rider problem
Merit goods
Government intervention
Laissez-faire
Social responsibility
Competition policy
Restrictive practices
Technology policy
Training policy
Environmental policy
Green taxes
Tradable permits
Cost–benefit analysis
Road pricing
Transport policy
Privatisation
Regulation
Deregulation
Franchising

20 Reasons for government intervention in the market

20.1 Markets and the role of government

Government intervention and social objectives

In order to decide the optimum amount of government intervention, it is first necessary to identify the various social goals that intervention is designed to meet. Two of the major objectives of government intervention identified by economists are **social efficiency** and **equity**.

Social efficiency. If the marginal benefits to society – or 'marginal social benefits' (*MSB*) – of producing any given good or service exceed the marginal costs to society or 'marginal social costs' (*MSC*) – then it is said to be socially efficient to produce more. For example, if people's gains from having additional motorways exceed *all* the additional costs to society (both financial and non-financial) then it is socially efficient to construct more motorways.

If, however, the marginal social costs of producing any good or service exceed the marginal social benefits, then it is socially efficient to produce less.

It follows that if the marginal social benefits of any activity are equal to the marginal social costs, then the current level is the optimum. To summarise: for social efficiency in the production of any good or service:

$MSB > MSC \rightarrow$ produce more

$MSC > MSB \rightarrow$ produce less

$MSB = MSC \rightarrow$ keep production at its current level

Similar rules apply to consumption. For example, if the marginal social benefits of consuming more of any good or service exceed the marginal social costs, then society would benefit from more of the good being consumed.

Social efficiency is an example of 'allocative efficiency': in other words, the best allocation of resources between alternative uses.

> *Allocative efficiency in any activity is achieved where any reallocation would lead to a decline in net benefit.* It is achieved where marginal benefit equals marginal cost. Private efficiency is achieved where marginal private benefit equals marginal private cost ($MB = MC$). Social efficiency is achieved where marginal social benefit equals marginal social cost ($MSB = MSC$).
>
> **Key Idea 24**

> **definition**
> **Social efficiency**
> Production and consumption at the point where $MSB = MSC$.

> **definition**
> **Equity**
> The fair distribution of a society's resources.

In the real world, the market rarely leads to social efficiency: the marginal social benefits of most goods and services do not equal the marginal social costs. In this chapter we examine why the free market fails to lead to social efficiency and what the government can do to rectify the situation. We also examine why the government itself may fail to achieve social efficiency.

> ***Markets generally fail to achieve social efficiency.*** There are various types of market failure. Market failures provide one of the major justifications for government intervention in the economy.
> **Key Idea 25**

Equity. Most people would argue that the free market fails to lead to a *fair* distribution of resources, if it results in some people living in great affluence while others live in dire poverty. Clearly what constitutes 'fairness' is a highly contentious issue: those on the political right generally have a quite different view from those on the political left. Nevertheless, most people would argue that the government does have some duty in redistributing incomes from the rich to the poor through the tax and benefit system, and perhaps in providing various forms of legal protection for the poor (such as a minimum wage rate).

> ***Equity*** is where income is distributed in a way that is considered to be fair or just. Note that an equitable distribution is not the same as a totally equal distribution and that different people have different views on what is equitable.
> **Key Idea 26**

Although out prime concern in this chapter is the question of social efficiency, we will be touching on questions of distribution too.

20.2 Types of market failure

Externalities

> **definition**
> **Externalities**
> Costs or benefits of production or consumption experienced by society but not by the producers or consumers themselves. Sometimes referred to as 'spillover' or 'third-party' costs or benefits.

The market will not lead to social efficiency if the actions of producers or consumers affect people *other than themselves*. These effects on other people are known as **externalities**: they are the side-effects, or 'third-party' effects, of production or consumption. Externalities can be either desirable or undesirable. Whenever other people are affected beneficially, there are said to be **external benefits**. Whenever other people are affected adversely, there are said to be **external costs**.

> ***Externalities are spillover costs or benefits.*** Where these exist, even an otherwise perfect market will fail to achieve social efficiency.
> **Key Idea 27**

Thus the full cost to society (the **social cost**) of the production of any good or service is the private cost faced by firms plus any externalities of production (positive or negative). Likewise the full benefit to society (the **social benefit**) from

Figure 20.1

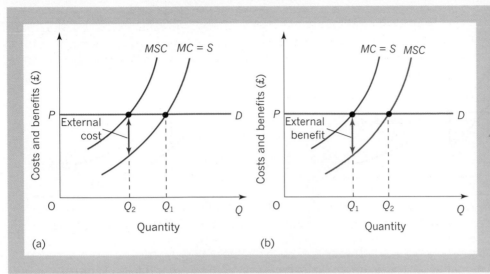

Externalities in production (a) External costs from production (b) External benefits from production

the consumption of any good is the private benefit enjoyed by consumers plus any externalities of consumption (positive or negative).

There are four major types of externality.

External costs of production (MSC > MC)

When a chemical firm dumps waste in a river or pollutes the air, the community bears costs additional to those borne by the firm. The marginal *social* cost (*MSC*) of chemical production exceeds the marginal private cost (*MC*). Diagrammatically, the *MSC* curve is above the *MC* curve. This is shown in Figure 20.1(a), which assumes that the firm in other respects is operating in a perfect market, and is therefore a price taker (i.e. faces a horizontal demand curve).

The firm maximises profits at Q_1: the output where marginal cost equals price (see section 11.2). The price is what people buying the good are prepared to pay for one more unit (if it wasn't they wouldn't buy it) and therefore reflects their marginal benefit. We assume no externalities from consumption, and therefore the marginal benefit to consumers is the same as the marginal *social* benefit (*MSB*).

The socially optimum output would be Q_2, where P (i.e. *MSB*) = *MSC*. The firm, however, produces Q_1, which is more than the optimum. Thus external costs lead to overproduction from society's point of view.

The problem of external costs arises in a free-market economy because no one has legal ownership of the air or rivers and no one, therefore, can prevent or charge for their use as a dump for waste. Such a 'market' is missing. Control must, therefore, be left to the government or local authorities.

Other examples include extensive farming that destroys hedgerows and wildlife, acid rain caused by smoke from coal-fired power stations, and nuclear waste from nuclear power stations.

External benefits of production (MSC < MC)

Imagine a bus company that spends money training its bus drivers. Each year some drivers leave to work for coach and haulage companies. These companies' costs are reduced as they do not have to train such drivers. Society has benefited from their training (including the bus drivers themselves, who have acquired marketable skills), even though the bus company has not. The marginal *social*

definition
External benefits
Benefits from production (or consumption) experienced by people *other* than the producer (or consumer).

definition
External costs
Costs of production (or consumption) borne by people *other* than the producer (or consumer).

definition
Social cost
Private cost plus externalities in production.

definition
Social benefit
Private benefit plus externalities in consumption.

Figure 20.2 **Externalities in consumption (a) External cost from consumption (b) External benefits from consumption**

cost of the bus service, therefore, is less than the marginal *private* cost to the company.

In Figure 20.1(b), the *MSC* curve is *below* the *MC* curve. The level of output (i.e. number of passenger miles) provided by the bus company is Q_1, where $P = MC$, a *lower* level than the social optimum, Q_2, where $P = MSC$.

Another example of external benefits in production is that of research and development. If other firms have access to the results of the research, then clearly the benefits extend beyond the firm which finances it. Since the firm only receives the private benefits, it will conduct a less than optimal amount of research. Similarly, a forestry company planting new woodlands will not take into account the beneficial effect on the atmosphere.

External costs of consumption (MSB < MB)

When people use their cars, other people suffer from their exhaust, the added congestion, the noise, etc. These 'negative externalities' make the marginal social benefit of using cars less than the marginal private benefit (i.e. marginal utility to the car user).

Figure 20.2(a) shows the marginal utility and price to a motorist (i.e. the consumer) of using a car. The optimal distance travelled for this motorist will be Q_1 miles: i.e. where $MU = P$ (where price is the cost of petrol, oil, wear and tear, etc. per mile). The *social* optimum, however, would be less than this, namely Q_2, where $MSB = P$.

Other examples of negative externalities of consumption include noisy radios in public places, the smoke from cigarettes, and litter.

External benefits of consumption (MSB > MB)

When people travel by train rather than by car, other people benefit by there being less congestion and exhaust and fewer accidents on the roads. Thus the marginal social benefit of rail travel is *greater* than the marginal private benefit (i.e. the marginal utility to the rail passenger). There are external benefits from rail travel. In Figure 20.2(b), the *MSB* curve is *above* the private *MB* curve. The socially optimal level of consumption (Q_2) is thus above the actual level

Key Idea 14 p110

of consumption (Q_1). In other words, when there are 'positive externalities' in consumption, the actual level of consumption will be too low from society's point of view.

Other examples of positive externalities of consumption include deodorants, vaccinations and attractive gardens in front of people's houses.

To summarise: whenever there are external benefits, there will be too little produced or consumed. Whenever there are external costs, there will be too much produced or consumed. The market will not equate *MSB* and *MSC*.

The above arguments have been developed in the context of perfect competition with prices given to the producer or consumer by the market. Externalities also occur in all other types of market.

Public goods

There is a category of goods where the positive externalities are so great that the free market, whether perfect or imperfect, may not produce at all. They are called **public goods**. Examples include lighthouses, pavements, flood control dams, public drainage, public services such as the police and even government itself.

Public goods have two important characteristics: *non-rivalry* and *non-excludability*:

■ If I consume a bar of chocolate, it cannot then be consumed by someone else. If, however, I enjoy the benefits of street lighting, it does not prevent you or anyone else doing the same. There is thus what we call **non-rivalry** in the consumption of such goods. These goods tend to have large external benefits relative to private benefits. This makes them socially desirable, but privately unprofitable. No one person on their own would pay to have a pavement built along his or her street. The private benefit would be too small relative to the cost. And yet the social benefit to all the other people using the pavement may far outweigh the cost.

■ If I spend money erecting a flood control dam to protect my house, my neighbours will also be protected by the dam. I cannot prevent them enjoying the benefits of my expenditure. This feature of **non-excludability** means that they would get the benefits free, and would therefore have no incentive to pay themselves. This is known as the **free-rider problem**.

definition
Public good
A good or service which has the features of non-rivalry and non-excludability and as a result would not be provided by the free market.

definition
Non-rivalry
Where the consumption of a good or service by one person will not prevent others from enjoying it.

The free-rider problem. People are often unwilling to pay for things if they can make use of things other people have bought. This problem can lead to people not purchasing things which would be to the benefit of them and other members of society to have. **Key Idea 28**

definition
Non-excludability
Where it is not possible to provide a good or service to one person without it thereby being available for others to enjoy.

When goods have these two features, the free market will simply not provide them. Thus these public goods can only be provided by the government or by the government subsidising private firms. (Note that not all goods and services produced by the public sector come into the category of public goods and services: thus education and health are publicly provided, but they *can* be, and indeed are, privately provided.)

Figure 20.3

The monopolist producing less than the socially efficient level of output

Free-rider problem
When it is not possible to exclude other people from consuming a good that someone has bought.

Market power

Whenever markets are imperfect, whether as pure monopoly or monopsony or whether as some form of imperfect competition, the market will fail to equate MSB and MSC, even if there are no externalities.

Take the case of monopoly. A monopoly will produce less than the socially efficient output. This is illustrated in Figure 20.3. A monopoly faces a downward-sloping demand curve, and therefore marginal revenue is below average revenue (= P = MSB). Profits are maximised at an output of Q_1, where marginal revenue equals marginal cost (see Figure 11.6 on page 223). If there are no externalities, the socially efficient output will be at the higher level of Q_2, where $MSB = MSC$.

Deadweight loss under monopoly

One way of analysing the welfare loss that occurs under monopoly is to use the concepts of *consumer* and *producer surplus*. The two concepts are illustrated in Figure 20.4. The diagram shows an industry which is initially under perfect competition and then becomes a monopoly (but faces the same revenue and cost curves).

Figure 20.4

Deadweight loss from monopoly

Consumer surplus. As we saw on page 111, **consumer surplus** from a good is the difference between the total utility received by consumers and their total expenditure on the good. Under *perfect competition* the industry will produce an output of Q_{pc} at a price of P_{pc}, where $MC(=S) = P(=AR)$: i.e. at point *a*. Consumers' total utility is given by the area under the demand (MU) curve (the sum of all the areas 1–7). Consumers' total expenditure is $P_{pc} \times Q_{pc}$ (areas 4 + 5 + 6 + 7). Consumers' surplus is thus the area between the price and the demand curve (areas 1 + 2 + 3).

Producer surplus. **Producer surplus** is similar to profit. It is the difference between total revenue and total variable cost. (It will be more than profit if there are any fixed costs.) Total revenue is $P_{pc} \times Q_{pc}$ (areas 4 + 5 + 6 + 7). Total cost is the area under the MC curve (areas 6 + 7). The reason for this is that each point on the marginal cost curve shows what the last unit costs to produce. The area under the MC curve thus gives all the marginal costs starting from an output of zero to the current output: i.e. it gives total costs. Producer surplus is thus the area between the price and the MC curve (areas 4 + 5).

Total (private) surplus. Total consumer plus producer surplus is therefore the area between the demand and MC curves. This is shown by the total shaded area (areas 1 + 2 + 3 + 4 + 5).

The effect of monopoly on total surplus

What happens when the industry is under *monopoly*? The firm will produce where $MC = MR$, at an output of Q_m and a price of P_m (at point *b* on the demand curve). Total revenue is $P_m \times Q_m$ (areas 2 + 4 + 6). Total cost is the area under the MC curve (area 6). Thus the producer surplus is areas 2 + 4. This is clearly a *larger* surplus than under perfect competition (since area 2 is larger than area 5): monopoly profits are larger than profits under perfect competition.

Consumer surplus, however, will be much smaller. With consumption at Q_m, total utility is given by areas 1 + 2 + 4 + 6, whereas consumer expenditure is given by areas 2 + 4 + 6. Consumer surplus, then, is simply area 1. (Note that area 2 has been transformed from consumer surplus to producer surplus.)

Total surplus under monopoly is therefore areas 1 + 2 + 4: a smaller surplus than under perfect competition. 'Monopolisation' of the industry has resulted in a loss of total surplus of areas 3 + 5. The producer's gain has been more than offset by the consumers' loss. This loss of surplus is known as **deadweight welfare loss** of monopoly.

Ignorance and uncertainty

Perfect competition assumes that consumers, firms and factor suppliers have perfect knowledge of costs and benefits. In the real world there is often a great deal of ignorance and uncertainty. Thus people are unable to equate marginal benefit with marginal cost.

Consumers purchase many goods only once or a few times in a lifetime. Cars, washing machines, televisions and other consumer durables fall into this category. Consumers may not be aware of the quality of such goods until they have purchased them, by which time it is too late. Advertising may contribute to people's ignorance by misleading them as to the benefits of a good.

Firms are often ignorant of market opportunities, prices, costs, the productivity of workers (especially white-collar workers), the activity of rivals, etc.

Key
Idea

27
p000

BOX 20.1

Can the market provide adequate protection for the environment?

In recent years people have become acutely aware of the damage being done to the environment by pollution. But if the tipping of chemicals and sewage into the rivers and seas and the spewing of toxic gases into the atmosphere cause so much damage, why does it continue? If we all suffer from these activities, both consumers and producers alike, then why will a pure market system not deal with the problem? After all, a market should respond to people's interests.

The reason is that the costs of pollution are largely *external* costs. They are borne by society at large and only very slightly (if at all) by the polluter. If, for example, 10 000 people suffer from the smoke from a factory (including the factory owner) then that owner will only bear approximately 1/10 000 of the suffering. That personal cost may be quite insignificant when the owner is deciding whether the factory is profitable. And if the owner lives far away, the personal cost of the pollution will be zero.

Thus the *social* costs of polluting activities exceed the *private* costs. If people behave selfishly and only take into account the effect their actions have on themselves, there will be an *overproduction* of polluting activities.

Thus it is argued that governments must intervene to prevent or regulate pollution, or alternatively to tax the polluting activities or subsidise measures to reduce the pollution.

But if people are purely selfish, why do they buy 'green' products? Why do they buy, for example, 'ozone-friendly' aerosols? After all, the amount of damage done to the ozone layer from their own personal use of 'non-friendly' aerosols would be absolutely minute. The answer is that many people have a social conscience. They *do* sometimes take into account the effect their actions have on other people. They are not totally selfish. They like to do their own little bit, however small, towards protecting the environment.

Nevertheless to rely on people's consciences may be a very unsatisfactory method of controlling pollution. In a market environment where people are all the time being encouraged to consume more and more goods and where materialism is the religion of the age, there would have to be a massive shift towards 'green thinking' if the market were to be a sufficient answer to the problem of pollution.

Certain types of environmental problem may get high priority in the media, like acid rain, the greenhouse effect, damage to the ozone layer and brain damage to children from leaded petrol. However, the sheer range of polluting activities makes reliance on people's awareness of the problems and their social consciences far too arbitrary.

Question

The following table gives the costs and benefits of an imaginary firm operating under perfect competition whose activities create a certain amount of pollution. (It is assumed that the costs of this pollution to society can be accurately measured.)

(a) What is the profit-maximising level of output for this firm?

(b) What is the socially efficient level of output?

(c) Why might the marginal pollution costs increase in the way illustrated in this example?

Output (units)	Price per unit (MSB) (£)	Marginal (private) costs to the firm (MC) (£)	Marginal external (pollution) costs (MEC) (£)	Marginal social costs (MSC = MC + MEC) (£)
1	100	30	20	50
2	100	30	22	52
3	100	35	25	60
4	100	45	30	75
5	100	60	40	100
6	100	78	55	133
7	100	100	77	177
8	100	130	110	240

Many economic decisions are based on expected future conditions. Since the future can never be known for certain, many decisions will be taken that in retrospect will be seen to have been wrong.

Immobility of factors and time-lags in response

Even under conditions of perfect competition, factors may be very slow to respond to changes in demand or supply. Labour, for example, may be highly immobile both occupationally and geographically. This can lead to large price changes and hence to large supernormal profits and high wages for those in the sectors of rising demand or falling costs. The long run may be a very long time coming!

In the meantime, there will be further changes in the conditions of demand and supply. Thus the economy is in a constant state of disequilibrium and the long run never comes. As firms and consumers respond to market signals and move towards equilibrium, so the equilibrium position moves and the social optimum is never achieved.

> ***The problem of time lags.*** Many economic actions can take a long time to take effect. This can cause problems of instability and an inability of the economy to achieve social efficiency.
>
> **Key Idea 29**

Whenever monopoly/monopsony power exists, the problem is made worse as firms or unions put up barriers to the entry of new firms or factors of production.

Protecting people's interests

The government may feel that people need protecting from poor economic decisions that they make on their *own* behalf. It may feel that in a free market people will consume too many harmful things. Thus if the government wants to discourage smoking and drinking, it can put taxes on tobacco and alcohol. In more extreme cases it could make various activities illegal: activities such as prostitution, certain types of gambling, and the sale and consumption of drugs.

On the other hand, the government may feel that people consume too little of things that are good for them: things such as education, health care and sports facilities. Such goods are known as **merit goods**. The government could either provide them free or subsidise their production.

> **definition**
>
> **Merit goods**
> Goods which the government feels that people will underconsume and which therefore ought to be subsidised or provided free.

Government intervention in the market   20.3

Faced with all the problems of the free market, what is a government to do?

There are several policy instruments that the government can use. At one extreme, it can totally replace the market by providing goods and services itself. At the other extreme, it can merely seek to persuade producers, consumers or workers to act differently. Between the two extremes the government has a number of instruments it can use to change the way markets operate. These include taxes, subsidies, laws and regulatory bodies. In this section we examine these different forms of government intervention.

Government intervention may be able to rectify various failings of the market. Government intervention in the market can be used to achieve various economic objectives which may not be best achieved by the market. Governments, however, are not perfect, and their actions may bring adverse as well as beneficial consequences.

Key Idea 30

Taxes and subsidies

When there are imperfections in the market, social efficiency will not be achieved. Marginal social benefit (*MSB*) will not equal marginal social cost (*MSC*). A different level of output would be more desirable.

Key Idea 25 p402

Taxes and subsidies can be used to correct these imperfections. Essentially the approach is to tax those goods or activities where the market produces too much, and subsidise those where the market produces too little.

Taxes and subsidies to correct externalities. The rule here is simple: the government should impose a tax equal to the marginal external cost (or grant a subsidy equal to the marginal external benefit).

Key Idea 27 p402

Assume, for example, that a chemical works emits smoke from a chimney and thus pollutes the atmosphere. This creates external costs for the people who breathe in the smoke. The marginal social cost of producing the chemicals thus exceeds the marginal private cost to the firm: $MSC > MC$.

This is illustrated in Figure 20.5. For simplicity, it is assumed that the firm is a price taker. It produces Q_1 where $P = MC$ (its profit-maximising output), but in doing so takes no account of the external pollution costs it imposes on society. If the government imposes a tax on production equal to the marginal pollution cost, it will effectively 'internalise' the externality. The firm will have to pay an amount equal to the external cost it creates. It will therefore now maximise profits at Q_2, which is the socially optimum output where $MSB = MSC$.

Taxes and subsidies to correct for monopoly. If the problem of monopoly that the government wishes to tackle is that of *excessive profits*, it can impose a lump-sum tax on the monopolist: that is, a tax of a fixed absolute amount irrespective of how much the monopolist produces, or the price it charges. Since a lump-sum tax is an additional *fixed* cost to the firm, and hence will not affect the firm's

Figure 20.5

Using taxes to correct a distortion: the first-best world

marginal cost, it will not reduce the amount that the monopolist produces (which *would* be the case with a per-unit tax). The 'windfall tax' imposed in 1997 by the UK Labour government on the profits of various privatised utilities is an example of such a tax.

If the government is concerned that the monopolist produces *less* than the socially efficient output, it could give the monopolist a per-unit *subsidy* (which would encourage the monopolist to produce more). But would this not *increase* the monopolist's profit? The answer to this is to impose a harsh lump-sum tax in addition to the subsidy. The tax would not undo the subsidy's benefit of encouraging the monopolist producing more, but it could be used to reduce the monopolist's profits below the original (i.e. pre-subsidy) level.

Advantages of taxes and subsidies

Many economists favour the tax/subsidy solution to market imperfections (especially the problem of externalities) because it still allows the market to operate. It forces firms to take on board the full social costs and benefits of their actions. It also has the flexibility of being adjustable according to the magnitude of the problem. For example, the bigger the external costs of a firm's actions, the bigger the tax can be.

Key Idea 8 p62

What is more, by taxing firms for polluting, say, they are encouraged to find cleaner ways of producing. The tax thus acts as an incentive over the longer run to reduce pollution: the more a firm can reduce its pollution, the more taxes it can save.

Likewise, when *good* practices are subsidised, firms are given the incentive to adopt more good practices.

Disadvantages of taxes and subsidies

Infeasible to use different tax and subsidy rates. Each firm produces different levels and types of externality and operates under different degrees of imperfect competition. It would be expensive and administratively very difficult, if not impossible, to charge every offending firm its own particular tax rate (or grant every relevant firm its own particular rate of subsidy).

Lack of knowledge. Even if a government did decide to charge a tax equal to each offending firm's marginal external costs, it would still have the problem of measuring that cost. The damage from pollution is often extremely difficult to assess. It is also difficult to apportion blame. For example, the damage to lakes and forests from acid rain has been a major concern since the beginning of the 1980s. But just how serious is that damage? What is its current monetary cost? How long lasting is the damage? What will be the position in twenty years? Just what and who are to blame? These are questions that cannot be answered precisely. It is thus impossible to fix the 'correct' pollution tax on, say, a particular coal-fired power station.

Key Idea 7 p50

> **Pause for thought**
>
> *Why is it easier to use taxes and subsidies to tackle the problem of car exhaust pollution than to tackle the problem of peak-time traffic congestion in cities?*

Despite these problems, it is nevertheless possible to charge firms by the amount of a particular emission. For example, firms could be charged for chimney smoke by so many parts per million of a given pollutant. Although it is difficult to 'fine-tune' such a system so that the charge reflects the precise number of people affected by the pollutant and by how much, it does go some way to internalising the externality.

BOX 20.2

Deadweight loss from taxes on goods and services
The excess burden of taxes

Taxation can be used to correct market failures, but taxes can have adverse effects themselves. One such effect is the deadweight loss that results when taxes are imposed on goods and services.

The diagram shows the demand and supply of a particular good. Equilibrium is initially at a price of P_1 and a level of sales of Q_1, (i.e. where $D = S$). Now an excise tax is imposed on the good. The supply curve shifts upwards by the amount of the tax, to $S + $ tax. Equilibrium price rises to P_2 and equilibrium quantity falls to Q_2. Producers receive an after-tax price of $P_2 - $ tax.

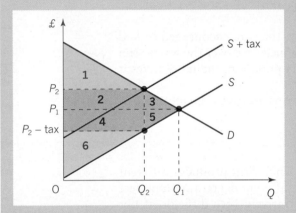

Deadweight loss from an indirect tax

Consumer surplus falls from areas $1 + 2 + 3$, to area 1 (the upper grey area). Producer surplus falls from areas $4 + 5 + 6$ to area 6 (the lower grey area). Does this mean, therefore, that total surplus falls by areas $2 + 3 + 4 + 5$? The answer is no, because there is a gain to the government from the tax revenue (and hence a gain to the population from the resulting government expenditure). The revenue from the tax is known as the **government surplus**. It is given by areas $2 + 4$ (the blue area).

But, even after including government surplus, there is still a fall in total surplus of areas $3 + 5$ (the pink area). This is the deadweight loss of the tax. It is sometimes known as the **excess burden** of the tax.

Does this loss of total surplus from taxation imply that taxes on goods are always a 'bad thing'? The answer is no. This conclusion would only follow in a 'first-best' world where there were no market failures: where competition was perfect, where there were no externalities and where income distribution was optimum. In such a world, the loss of surplus from imposing a tax on a good would represent a reduction in welfare.

In the real world of imperfect markets and inequality, taxes can do more good than harm. As we have shown in this section, they can help to correct for externalities. They can also be used as a means of redistributing incomes. Nevertheless, the excess burden of taxes is something that ideally ought to be considered when weighing up the desirability of imposing taxes on goods and services, or of increasing their rate.

Question

How far can an economist contribute to this highly political debate over the desirability of an excise tax?

Changes in property rights

One cause of market failure is the limited nature of property rights. If someone dumps a load of rubble in your garden, the law should protect you. It is *your* garden, *your* property, and you can thus insist that it is removed. If, however, someone dumps a load of rubble in his or her *own* garden, which is next door to yours, what can you do? You can still see it from your window. It is still an eyesore. But you have no property rights over the next-door garden.

Property rights define who owns property, to what uses it can be put, the rights other people have over it and how it may be transferred. By *extending* these rights, individuals may be able to prevent other people imposing costs on them, or charge them for doing so.

Key Idea
27
p402

The trouble is that in many instances this type of solution is totally impractical. It is impractical when *many* people are *slightly* inconvenienced, especially if there are many culprits imposing the costs. For example, if I were disturbed by noisy lorries outside my home, it would not be practical to negotiate with every haulage company involved. What if I wanted to ban the lorries from the street, but my next-door neighbour wanted to charge them 10p per journey? Who gets their way?

The extension of private property rights becomes a more practical solution where the culprits are few in number, are easily identifiable and impose clearly defined costs. Thus a noise abatement act could be passed which allowed me to prevent my neighbours playing noisy radios, having noisy parties or otherwise disturbing the peace in my home. The onus would be on me to report them. Or if I chose, I could agree not to report them if they paid me adequate compensation.

But even in cases where only a few people are involved, there may still be the problem of litigation. I may have to incur the time and expense of taking people to court. Justice may not be free, and there is thus a conflict with equity. The rich can afford 'better' justice. They can employ top lawyers. Thus even if I have a right to sue a large company for dumping toxic waste near me, I may not have the legal muscle to win.

Finally, there is the broader question of *equity*. The extension of private property rights may favour the rich (who tend to have more property) at the expense of the poor. Ramblers may get great pleasure from strolling across a great country estate, along public rights of way. This may annoy the owner. If the owner's property rights were now extended to exclude the ramblers, is this a social gain?

Of course, equity consideration can also be dealt with by altering property rights, but in a different way. *Public* property like parks, open spaces, libraries and historic buildings could be extended. Also the property of the rich could be redistributed to the poor. Here it is less a question of the rights that ownership confers, and more a question of altering the ownership itself.

> **Pause for thought**
>
> *Would it be a good idea to extend countries' territorial waters in order to bring key open seas fishing grounds within countries' territory? Could it help to solve the problem of over fishing?*

Laws prohibiting or regulating undesirable structures or behaviour

Laws are frequently used to correct market imperfections. Laws can be of three main types: those that prohibit or regulate behaviour that imposes external costs, those that prevent firms providing false or misleading information, and those that prevent or regulate monopolies and oligopolies (see Chapter 21).

Advantages of legal restrictions

- They are usually simple and clear to understand and are often relatively easy to administer. For example, various polluting activities could be banned or restricted.

- When the danger is very great, it might be much safer to ban various practices altogether (e.g. the use of various toxic chemicals) rather than to rely on taxes or on individuals attempting to assert their property rights through the civil courts.

- When a decision needs to be taken quickly, it might be possible to invoke emergency action. For example, in a city like Athens it has been found to be simpler to ban or restrict the use of private cars during a chemical smog emergency than to tax their use.
- Because consumers suffer from imperfect information, consumer protection laws can make it illegal for firms to sell shoddy or unsafe goods, or to make false or misleading claims about their products.

Disadvantages of legal restrictions

The main problem is that legal restrictions tend to be a rather blunt weapon. If, for example, a firm were required to reduce the effluent of a toxic chemical to 20 tonnes per week, there would be no incentive for the firm to reduce it further. With a tax on the effluent, however, the more the firm reduced the effluent, the less tax it would pay. Thus with a system of taxes there is a *continuing* incentive to cut pollution, to improve safety, or whatever.

Regulatory bodies

Rather than using the blunt weapon of general legislation to ban or restrict various activities, a more 'subtle' approach can be adopted. This involves the use of various regulatory bodies. Having identified possible cases where action might be required (e.g. potential cases of pollution, misleading information or the abuse of monopoly power), the regulatory body would probably conduct an investigation and then prepare a report containing its findings and recommendations. It might also have the power to enforce its decisions. In the UK there are regulatory bodies for each of the major privatised utilities (see section 22.3). Another example is the Office of Fair Trading (OFT), which investigates and reports on suspected cases of anti-competitive practices. The OFT can order such firms to cease or modify these practices. Alternatively it can refer them to the Competition Commission (CC), which then conducts an investigation, and makes a ruling (see section 21.1).

The advantage of this approach is that suspected cases of abuse can be dealt with on a case-by-case basis. All the various circumstances surrounding a particular case can be taken into account, with the result that the most appropriate solution can be adopted.

Pause for thought

What other forms of intervention are likely to be necessary to back up the work of regulatory bodies?

The problems with this approach are (a) that investigations may be expensive and time consuming, (b) that only a few cases may be examined and (c) that the offending firms may make various promises of good behaviour which may not in fact be carried out owing to a lack of follow-up by the regulatory body.

Price controls

Price controls can be used either to raise prices above, or to reduce them below, the free-market level.

Prices could be raised above the market equilibrium to support the incomes of certain suppliers. For example, until recently, under the Common Agricultural Policy of the European Union, high prices for food were set so as to raise farmers' incomes above the free-market level.

Prices could be lowered in order to protect consumers' interests. For example, the government, or another body, may prevent a monopoly or oligopoly from charging excessive prices. This is one of the major roles of the regulatory bodies for the privatised utilities. Here the industry is not allowed to raise its prices by more than a certain amount below the rate of inflation.

Provision of information

When ignorance is a reason for market failure, the direct provision of information by the government or one of its agencies may help to correct that failure. An example is the information on jobs provided by job centres to those looking for work. They thus help the labour market to work better and increase the elasticity of supply of labour. Another example is the provision of consumer information: for example, on the effects of smoking, or of eating certain foodstuffs. Another is the provision of government statistics on prices, costs, employment, sales trends, etc. This enables firms to plan with greater certainty.

The direct provision of goods and services

In the case of public goods and services, such as streets, pavements, seaside illumination and national defence, the market may completely fail to provide. In this case the government must take over the role of provision. Central government, local government or some other public agency could provide these goods and services directly. Alternatively, they could pay private firms to do so. The public would pay through central and local taxation.

The government could also provide goods and services directly which are *not* public goods. Examples include health and education. There are four reasons why such things are provided free or at well below cost.

Social justice. Society may feel that these things should not be provided according to ability to pay. Rather they should be provided as of right: an equal right based on need.

Large positive externalities. People other than the consumer may benefit substantially. If a person decides to get treatment for an infectious disease, other people benefit by not being infected. A free health service thus helps to combat the spread of disease.

Dependants. If education were not free, and if the quality of education depended on the amount spent, and if parents could choose how much or little to buy, then the quality of children's education would depend not just on their parents' income, but also on how much they cared. A government may choose to provide such things free in order to protect children from 'bad' parents. A similar argument is used for providing free prescriptions and dental treatment for all children.

Ignorance. Consumers may not realise how much they will benefit. If they have to pay, they may choose (unwisely) to go without. Providing health care free may persuade people to consult their doctors for what they perceive to be a minor complaint, which is then diagnosed to be the first symptom of something serious.

20.4   The case for *laissez-faire*

Government intervention in the market can itself lead to problems. The case for non-intervention (*laissez-faire*) or very limited intervention is not that the market is the *perfect* means of achieving given social goals, but rather that the problems created by intervention are greater than the problems overcome by that intervention.

Drawbacks of government intervention

Shortages and surpluses. If the government intervenes by fixing prices at levels other than the equilibrium, this will create either shortages or surpluses.

If the price is fixed *below* the equilibrium, there will be a shortage. For example, if the rent of council houses is fixed below the equilibrium in order to provide cheap housing for poor people, demand will exceed supply. In the case of such shortages the government will have to adopt a system of waiting lists, or rationing, or giving certain people preferential treatment. Alternatively it will have to allow allocation to be on a first-come, first-served basis or allow queues to develop. Black markets are likely to develop.

If the price is fixed *above* the equilibrium price, there will be a surplus. For example, if the price of food is fixed above the equilibrium in order to support farmers' incomes, supply will exceed demand. Either government will have to purchase such surpluses and then perhaps store them, throw them away or sell them cheaply in another market, or it will have to ration suppliers by allowing them to produce only a certain quota, or allow them to sell to whom they can.

Poor information. The government may not know the full costs and benefits of its policies. It may genuinely wish to pursue the interests of consumers or any other group and yet may be unaware of people's wishes or misinterpret their behaviour.

Bureaucracy and inefficiency. Government intervention involves administrative costs. The more wide reaching and detailed the intervention, the greater the number of people and material resources that will be involved. These resources may be used wastefully.

Lack of market incentives. If government intervention removes market forces or cushions their effect (by the use of subsidies, welfare provisions, guaranteed prices or wages, etc.), it may remove certain useful incentives. Subsidies may allow inefficient firms to survive. Welfare payments may discourage effort. The market may be imperfect, but it does tend to encourage efficiency by allowing the efficient to receive greater rewards.

Shifts in government policy. The economic efficiency of industry may suffer if government intervention changes too frequently. It makes it difficult for firms to plan if they cannot predict tax rates, subsidies, price and wage controls, etc.

Lack of freedom for the individual. Government intervention involves a loss of freedom for individuals to make economic choices. The argument is not just that the pursuit of individual gain is seen to lead to the social good, but that it is desirable in itself that individuals should be as free as possible to pursue their own interests with the minimum of government interference: that minimum being largely confined to the maintenance of laws consistent with the protection of life, liberty and property.

Advantages of the free market

Although markets in the real world are not perfect, even imperfect markets can be argued to have positive advantages over government provision or even government regulation. These might include the following.

Automatic adjustments. Government intervention requires administration. A free-market economy, on the other hand, leads to the automatic, albeit imperfect, adjustment to demand and supply changes.

Dynamic advantages of capitalism. The chances of making high monopoly/oligopoly profits will encourage capitalists to invest in new products and new techniques. Prices may be high initially, but consumers will gain from the extra choice of products. Furthermore, if profits are high, new firms will sooner or later break into the market and competition will ensue.

> **Pause for thought**
>
> *Are there any features of free-market capitalism that would* discourage *innovation?*

A *high degree of competition even under monopoly/oligopoly*. Even though an industry at first sight may seem to be highly monopolistic, competitive forces may still work as a result of the following:

- A fear that excessively high profits might encourage firms to attempt to break into the industry (assuming that the market is contestable).
- Competition from closely related industries (e.g. coach services for rail services, or electricity for gas).
- The threat of foreign competition.
- Countervailing powers. Large powerful producers often sell to large powerful buyers. For example, the power of detergent manufacturers to drive up the price of washing powder is countered by the power of supermarket chains to drive down the price at which they purchase it. Thus power is to some extent neutralised.
- The competition for corporate control (see page 224).

Firms and social responsibility   20.5

It is often assumed that firms are simply concerned to maximise profits: that they are not concerned with broader issues of **social responsibility**. What this assumption means is that firms are only concerned with the interests of shareholders (or managers) and are not concerned for the well-being of the community at large.

It is then argued, however, that competitive forces could result in society *benefiting* from the self-interested behaviour of firms: i.e. that profit maximisation

definition

Social responsibility
Where a firm takes into account the interests and concerns of a community rather than just its shareholders.

will lead to social efficiency under conditions of perfect competition and the absence of externalities. But, as we have seen, in the real world markets are not perfect and there are often considerable externalities. In such cases, a lack of social responsibility on the part of firms can have profoundly adverse effects on society. Indeed, many forms of market failure can be attributed directly to business practices that could not be classified as 'socially responsible': advertising campaigns that seek to misinform, or in some way deceive the consumer; monopoly producers exploiting their monopoly position through charging excessively high prices; the conscious decision to ignore water and air pollution limits, knowing that the chances of being caught are slim.

So should businesses be simply concerned with profit, or should they take broader social issues into account? If they do behave in an anti-social way, is the only answer to rely on government intervention, or are there any social pressures that can be brought to bear to persuade businesses to modify their behaviour?

Two views of social responsibility

The classical view. According to this view, business managers are responsible only to their shareholders, and as such should be concerned solely with profit maximisation. If managers in their business decisions take into account a wider set of social responsibilities, not only will they tend to undermine the market mechanism, but they will be making social policy decisions in fields where they may have little skill or expertise. If being socially responsible ultimately reduces profits, then the shareholder loses and managers have failed to discharge their duty. By diluting their purpose in pursuit of *social* goals, businesses extend their influence over society as a whole, which cannot be good given the lack of public accountability to which business leaders are subject.

The socioeconomic view. This view argues that the role of modern business has changed, and that society expects business to adhere to certain moral and social responsibilities. Modern businesses are seen as more than economic institutions, as they are actively involved in society's social, political and legal environments. As such, all businesses are responsible not only to their shareholders but to all **stakeholders**. Stakeholders are all those affected by the business's operations: not only shareholders, but workers, customers, suppliers, creditors and people living in the neighbourhood. Given the far-reaching environmental effects of many businesses, stakeholding might extend to the whole of society.

definition

Stakeholder
An individual affected by the operations of a business.

In this view of corporate social responsibility, it is not just a moral argument that managers should take into account broader social and environmental issues, but also a financial one. It is argued that a business will maximise profits over the *long term* only if its various social responsibilities are taken into account. If a business is seen as ignoring the interests of the wider community and failing to protect society's welfare, then this will be 'bad for business': the firm's reputation and image will suffer.

definition

Environmental scanning
Where a business surveys social and political trends in order to take account of changes in its decision-making process.

In many top corporations, **environmental scanning** is now an integral part of the planning process. This involves the business surveying changing social and political trends in order to remain in tune with consumer concerns. For example, the general public's growing concern over 'green' issues has significantly influenced many businesses' product development programmes and R & D strategies (see Box 20.3). The more successful a business is in being able to associate the

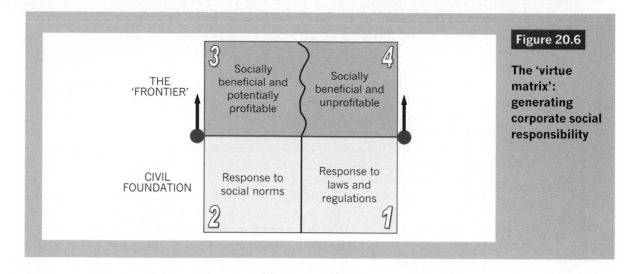

Figure 20.6

The 'virtue matrix': generating corporate social responsibility

image of 'environmentally friendly' to a particular product or brand, the more likely it is to enhance its sales or establish a measure of brand loyalty, and thereby to strengthen its competitive position.

Many businesses today thus feel that it is not enough to be seen merely *complying* with laws on the environment, product standards or workplace conditions: i.e. just to be doing the legal minimum. There is now a growing philosophy of 'compliance plus', with many businesses competing against each other in terms of their social image.

But does social responsibility not impose costs on firms, which might more than offset any increase in revenue from increased sales? In fact, the opposite can occur. Socially responsible business can reduce the need for government regulation, and the subsequent costs and restrictions that such intervention places upon managerial decision making. Many industries prefer to be self-regulating, not just to avoid government interference and restrictions, but because they can achieve any given social goal at lower costs: after all, a firm is likely to be better placed than government to know how given standards can be met in its own specific case. It is nevertheless the case that there are still many firms that care little about the environment. For them, self-regulation might be preferred because it makes it easier for them to avoid their social responsibilities!

The virtue matrix: generating corporate social responsibility

In an article in the *Harvard Business Review*,[1] Roger L. Martin developed a framework for analysing corporate social responsibility and the factors that influence it. The framework is the 'virtue matrix' and an adaptation of it is illustrated in Figure 20.6.

The matrix is divided into four cells, each of which shows types of action taken by a firm that have social effects.

---

[1] Roger L. Martin 'The Virtue Matrix: Calculating the Return on Corporate Responsibility', *Harvard Business Review*, March 2002.

The civil foundation

The bottom two cells are in what is termed the 'civil foundation'. They refer to socially responsible actions that society expects firms to take and firms will normally do so.

Cell 1 refers to actions in response to laws and regulations. For example, firms may control the emissions of toxic waste because they are obliged to do so by law. Similarly, they may provide a clean and safe environment for their workers because of health and safety legislation.

Cell 2 refers to the types of behaviour expected of firms by society and where firms would come in for criticism, or even condemnation, if they did not abide by these social norms. For example, employers may operate flexible working hours or set up nursery facilities to help workers with small children; manufacturers may landscape the surroundings to their factories or build factories of a pleasant design so as to make them more attractive to local residents and visitors. They are not obliged to take such actions by law, but feel that it is expected of them.

A key point about actions in the civil foundation is that they are likely to be consistent with the aim of profit maximisation or maximising shareholder value. In other words, shareholders' and society's interests are likely to coincide. This is obvious in the case of abiding by the law. Except in cases where breaking the law can go undetected, firms must abide by the law if they are to avoid prosecution with all the risks to profits that this entails. But abiding by social norms (cell 2) is also likely to contribute towards profit. The extra costs associated with such actions will probably be recouped from extra sales associated with achieving a good public image or extra productivity from a contented workforce.

The frontier

The top two cells represent 'the frontier'. These refer to activities that are not directly in the interests of shareholders, but have a moral or social motivation.

Cell 3 represents those actions that are not immediately profitable, but could possibly become so in the future because of positive reactions from consumers, employees, competitors or government. To quote from Martin 'When Prudential allowed people with AIDS to tap the death benefits in their life assurance policies to pay for medical expenses, the move generated so much goodwill that competing insurers soon offered [such] settlements as well. Very quickly, corporate behavior that had seemed radical became business as usual throughout the insurance industry'.[2] Generally activities in cell 3 are risky and the willingness of firms to engage in them depends on their attitudes towards risk.

Cell 4 represents the most radical departure from shareholders' interests. Here managers take action that benefits society but at the *expense* of profit. As we saw in Chapter 14, managers are not always ruthless profit maximisers. They can be motivated by a range of objectives. One of these is 'to do the right thing' by employees, customers or society generally. For example, improving working conditions for employees is seen not just as a way of improving productivity, but as a moral duty towards the workforce. Likewise managers may control toxic emissions beyond the legal minimum requirement because of their genuine concern for the environment.

---

[2] *Ibid.* page 8.

The development of corporate social responsibility over time

Various competitive pressures are likely to increase corporate social responsibility over time. First, the boundary between the civil foundation and the frontier is likely to move upwards as activities that start in the frontier and then are copied by competitor firms become the norm. The norms of corporate behaviour in Victorian Britain would seem totally unacceptable in Britain today. The long hours, child labour, appalling working conditions, lack of redress for grievances, the filthy conditions of the workplace, the smoke and other pollution pouring from factories are not only illegal nowadays, but are totally alien to the norms of society.

Although the boundary tends to move upwards, this is not necessarily the case. Martin gives the example of Russia in the immediate post-communist period, where a collapse of the old order and the development of 'cowboy' capitalism led to a decline in standards and the non-enforcement of many regulations governing things such as working conditions and child labour. Many developing countries have a very much lower boundary, which is constantly in danger of being pushed lower by ruthless forces of globalisation and non-representative governments conniving in the process.

Another factor leading to the development of corporate social responsibility is the movement of activities from cell 4 to cell 3. Activities that start as socially desirable but unprofitable, tend to become profitable as consumers come to expect firms to behave in socially responsible ways and punish firms that do not by boycotting their products. Thus companies such as Nestlé, McDonald's and Nike have been very concerned to 'clean up' their corporate image because of adverse publicity. Of course, part of the reaction of companies to social pressure may be simply to improve their public relations, but part may be a genuine improvement in their behaviour.

Globalisation and corporate social responsibility

As the world economy becomes ever more intertwined, many companies in rich countries, with a relatively deep civil foundation, are outsourcing much of their production to developing countries, which have a relatively shallow and less secure civil foundation. This can have the effect of either levelling up or levelling down. Nike and Gap, which produce much of their footwear and clothing in south-east Asia, have been accused of operating sweatshops in these countries, with low wages and poor working conditions – a case of levelling down to the civil foundation of these developing countries. Nike and Gap reply that, compared with other factories in these countries, pay and conditions are better – a case of levelling up.

Economic performance and social responsibility

If corporate social responsibility has grown as a business objective, has this in any way impinged upon business performance? Studies, empirical and otherwise, suggest that rather than detracting from business performance and harming shareholder value, in fact the opposite appears to be the case. Corporate social responsibility appears to offer a positive contribution to business performance, especially over the longer term.

The following factors have been identified as some of the positive economic benefits that firms have gained from adopting a more socially responsible position.

Improved economic performance

A large number of studies have attempted to identify and evaluate the economic returns from social responsibility. Factors that have been considered include business growth rates, stock prices and sales and revenue. A survey by Roman, Hayibor and Agle[3] evaluated the findings of 52 studies that considered the link between business ethics and enhanced profits. They concluded that 33 studies showed a positive link, 14 suggested neutral effects or were inconclusive, and the remaining 5 suggested that there was a negative relationship.

Although this evidence would on balance favour an argument that corporate social responsibility is good business practice, the whole area of linking ethics and responsibility to profit is a contentious one. When considering ethics and social responsibility, what are we including within this definition? Is the business merely complying with a business code, either developed within the business or by a third party. Such codes essentially state what is not acceptable business behaviour, such as taking bribes or pursuing anti-competitive behaviour. Such codes can be seen as lying in the civil foundation. Or does the understanding of an 'ethical business' go further and entail positive social actions, ranging from giving money to good causes, to contributing to particular programmes in which the business has competency. For example, a pharmaceutical company might develop a drug that might benefit the populations of the world's poorest countries, with no possibility of profit. Such actions lie in the frontier.

So at what level do we identify an ethical business, and to what degree might this level of responsibility influence profitability?

The concept of profitability is also contentious, most crucially so in respect to the time frame over which the assessment takes place. Linking long-run profitability with an ethical or socially responsible programme is fraught with difficulties. How are all the other factors that influence business performance over the longer term accounted for? How do you attribute a given percentage or contribution to profit to the adoption of a more socially responsible business position? Can it ever be this precise, or are we merely left with intimating that a link exists, and is this good enough?

Enhancing the brand

Related to profitability is the issue as to how far corporate social responsibility enhances brand image and the firm's reputation. Not only would this strengthen consumer loyalty but also aid the firm in raising finance and attracting trading partners. Several studies have identified that the social image of the firm is becoming increasingly important in consumer buying decisions. A 1997 study by Walker Research found that, given two products with similar quality and price criteria, 76 per cent of those surveyed stated they would purchase the product produced by the company most associated with good causes. Surveys suggest that environmental responsibility and active participation in the community are the social factors most likely to influence consumer purchasing behaviour.

Firms may be further encouraged to develop the social image of their brand with the increasing number of awards given to recognise and promote corporate social responsibility. 'Most admired companies' lists, such as those presented by

---

[3] Ronald M. Roman, Sefa Hayibor and Bradley R. Agle 'The Relationship Between Social and Financial Performance', *Business and Society*, Vol. 38, No. 1, March 1999, (University of Pittsburgh).

Management Today in the UK and *Fortune* in America, are based on criteria such as reputation for ethics and honesty, use of corporate assets, and community and environmental responsibility. The public relations and marketing potential that can be gained from such awards help firms to strengthen further their socially responsible image.

Attracting and retaining employees

It increasingly appears to be the case that companies with clear ethical and social positions find it easier, not only to recruit, but to hold on to their employees. In a number of surveys of graduate employment intentions, students have claimed that they would be prepared to take a lower salary in order to work for a business with high ethical standards and a commitment to socially responsible business practices.

A survey conducted in June 2000[4] found that when employees were asked to rank the reason for admiring certain companies, 24 per cent identified respect for their employees, and a further 21 per cent identified environmental responsibility. The survey concluded that the reputation of the employer was crucial in the recruitment and retention of staff. The survey also found that 64 per cent of business leaders 'agreed strongly' that corporate responsibility will affect their own decisions.

Access to capital

Investment in ethically screened investment funds has grown rapidly in recent years. This has been driven not only by the demands of shareholders for ethical funds, but also by a realisation from investors generally that socially responsible business has the potential to be hugely profitable.

A survey in 1999 by the Ethical Investment Research Service[5] revealed that 77 per cent of members of pension schemes wanted their pension funds to adhere to some form of socially responsible investment, so long as it did not impinge upon their returns.

The likelihood of returns being lower in ethically screened funds has been questioned by the findings of a report in 2001.[6] This concluded that, in respect to environmental responsibility in particular, those companies that exhibit superior environmental performance over their peers achieve better financial performance on the stock market. It is suggested that the reason for this is that environmental performance is a good indicator of general management quality, which is the main determinant of stock price.

Social responsibility appears not only to bring a range of benefits to business and society, but also to be generally profitable. It is likely to enhance business performance, strengthen brand image, reduce employee turnover and increase access to stock market funds. Box 20.3 gives an example of a company that has built its reputation of being socially and environmentally responsible – The Body Shop.

---

[4] *The Responsible Century?* The Prince of Wales Business Leaders Forum, Burson-Marsteller (2000).

[5] 'The EIRS Guide for Pension Fund Trustees' *The Ethical Investor 1999* (Ethical Investment Research Service).

[6] *Screening of Screening Companies* (MISTRA, The Foundation for Strategic Environmental Research, 2001).

BOX 20.3

The Body Shop
Embodying social responsibility

The Body Shop shot to fame in the 1980s. It stood for environmental awareness and an ethical approach to business. But its success had as much to do with what it sold as what it stood for. It sold natural cosmetics, Raspberry Ripple Bathing Bubbles and Camomile Shampoo, products that were immensely popular with consumers.

Its profits increased from a little over £1 million in 1985 to £24.0 million in 2003 (although it had been as high as £38.0 million in 1998). Sales, meanwhile, grew even more dramatically, from £4.9 million to £697.1 million over the same period.

What makes this success so remarkable is that The Body Shop does virtually no advertising. Its promotion has largely stemmed from the activities and environmental campaigning of its founder Anita Roddick, and the company's uncompromising claims that it sells only 'green' products and conducts its business operations with high ethical standards. It actively supports green causes such as saving whales and protecting rainforests, and it refuses to allow its products to be tested on animals. Perhaps most surprising in the world of big business has been its high-profile initiative 'trade not aid', whereby it claimed to pay 'fair' prices for its ingredients, especially those supplied from people in developing countries, who were open to exploitation by large companies.

The growth strategy of The Body Shop, since its founding in 1976, has focused upon developing a distinctive and highly innovative product range, and at the same time identifying such products with major social issues of the day such as the environment and animal rights.

In the 1990s, sales growth was less rapid and in 2000 Roddick announced that she was planning to leave the company. The day after the announcement, the following article appeared in *The Financial Times*.

... At the beginning it was a green fairy tale, the company's commitment to fair trade and the environment and its stance on animal testing was a combination that caught the imagination in the newly affluent 1980s. For over a decade sales and profits continued to grow, on average by 50 per cent a year. Franchises sprung up like mushrooms and following its flotation in 1984 the share price rose from just 5p to a high of 370p in 1992.

With a new shop opening every two and a half days it seemed as if nothing could go wrong for the Roddicks, that is, until they hit America. In 1988 they launched into the US market. Initially the venture was successful. The once successful franchising of the company soon began to disintegrate. 'We just got everything wrong', said Ms Roddick, who was criticised for conducting no market research, paying scant attention to marketing and giving little thought to where the shops appeared.

By 1998 the company's earnings had collapsed by 90 per cent and the share price fell to under 117p.

In the City there was a certain amount of *schadenfreude*. Many investors were not impressed with Roddick's cuddly hippie attitude to business and analysts criticised the company for developing new products too quickly.

They were also unimpressed with Ms Roddick's off-hand attitude to finances, especially her comments that finance 'bored the pants off her' and her frequent denouncements of the 'pin-striped dinosaurs in Throgmorton Street'.

When she was forced to step down as chief executive in 1998, following shareholder pressure for 'positive and demonstrable change', she compared the experience to handing over a child to complete strangers.

The day-to-day running of Body Shop was handed over to Patrick Gournay, a former vice president at Groupe Danone and Ms Roddick became joint co-chairman with husband Gordon.

In 2002, Anita Roddick's time at The Body Shop came to an end when she and her husband stepped down as co-chairmen of the company.

Questions

1 *What assumptions has The Body Shop made about the 'rational consumer'?*

2 *How would you describe the aims of The Body Shop?*

SUMMARY

1 Government intervention in the market sets out to attain two goals: social efficiency and equity. Social efficiency is achieved at the point where the marginal benefits to society for either production or consumption are equal to the marginal costs of either production or consumption. Issues of equity are difficult to judge due to the subjective assessment of what is, and what is not, a fair distribution of resources.

2a Externalities are spillover costs or benefits. Whenever there are external costs, the market will (other things being equal) lead to a level of production and consumption above the socially efficient level. Whenever there are external benefits, the market will (other things being equal) lead to a level of production and consumption below the socially efficient level.

2b Public goods will be underprovided by the market. The problem is that they have large external benefits relative to private benefits, and without government intervention it would not be possible to prevent people having a 'free ride' and thereby escaping contributing to their cost of production.

2c Monopoly power will (other things being equal) lead to a level of output below the socially efficient level. It will lead to a deadweight welfare loss: a loss of consumer plus producer surplus.

2d Ignorance and uncertainty may prevent people from consuming or producing at the levels they would otherwise choose. Information may sometimes be provided (at a price) by the market, but it may be imperfect; in some cases it may not be available at all.

2e Markets may respond sluggishly to changes in demand and supply. The time lags in adjustment can lead to a permanent state of disequilibrium and to problems of instability.

2f In a free market there may be inadequate provision for dependants and an inadequate output of merit goods.

3a Taxes and subsidies are one means of correcting market distortions. Externalities can be corrected by imposing tax rates equal to the size of the marginal external cost, and granting rates of subsidy equal to marginal external benefits.

3b Taxes and subsidies can also be used to affect monopoly price, output and profit. Subsidies can be used to persuade a monopolist to increase output to the competitive level. Lump-sum taxes can be used to reduce monopoly profits without affecting price or output.

3c Taxes and subsidies have the advantages of 'internalising' externalities and of providing incentives to reduce external costs. On the other hand, they may be impractical to use when different rates are required for each case, or when it is impossible to know the full effects of the activities that the taxes or subsidies are being used to correct.

3d An extension of property rights may allow individuals to prevent others from imposing costs on them. This is not practical, however, when many people are affected to a small degree, or where several people are affected but differ in their attitudes towards what they want doing about the 'problem'.

3e Laws can be used to regulate activities that impose external costs, to regulate monopolies and oligopolies, and to provide consumer protection. Legal controls are often simpler and easier to operate than taxes, and are safer when the danger is potentially great. However, they tend to be rather a blunt weapon.

3f Regulatory bodies can be set up to monitor and control activities that are against the public interest (e.g. anti-competitive behaviour of oligopolists). They can conduct investigations of specific cases, but these may be expensive and time consuming, and may not be acted on by the authorities.

3g The government may provide information in cases where the private sector fails to provide an adequate level. It may also provide goods and services directly. These could be either public goods or other goods where the government feels that provision by the market is inadequate. The government could also influence production in publicly owned industries.

4a Government intervention in the market may lead to shortages or surpluses; it may be based on poor information; it may be costly in terms of administration; it may stifle incentives; it may be disruptive if government policies change too frequently; it may not represent the majority of voters' interests if the government is elected by a minority, or if voters did not fully understand the issues at election time, or if the policies were not in the government's manifesto; it may remove certain liberties.

SUMMARY

4b By contrast, a free market leads to automatic adjustments to changes in economic conditions; the prospect of monopoly/ oligopoly profits may stimulate risk taking and hence research and development and innovation, and this advantage may outweigh any problems of resource misallocation; there may still be a high degree of actual or potential competition under monopoly and oligopoly.

5a There are two views of social responsibility. The first states that it should be of no concern to business, which would do best for society by serving the interests of its shareholders. Social policy should be left to politicians. The alternative view is that business needs to consider the impact of its actions upon society, and to take changing social and political considerations into account when making decisions. This is good business.

5b The virtue matrix is a means of illustrating the drivers of corporate social responsibility. Firms will take socially responsible actions if they are required to by law or if social norms dictate. These pressures on firms represent the 'civil foundation'. Some firms will take corporate social responsibility further and thus move into the 'frontier'. Here they may do things that are socially beneficial and may only possibly lead to higher profits, or may even clearly reduce profits. As firms become more socially responsible over time and as social pressures on business increase, so the civil foundation is likely to grow.

5c Evidence suggests that economic performance is likely to be enhanced as the corporate responsibility of firms grows.

REVIEW QUESTIONS

1 Assume that a firm discharges waste into a river. As a result, the marginal social costs (MSC) are greater than the firm's marginal (private) costs (MC). The following table shows how MC, MSC, AR and MR vary with output.

Output	1	2	3	4	5	6	7	8
MC(£)	23	21	23	25	27	30	35	42
MSC(£)	35	34	38	42	46	52	60	72
TR(£)	60	102	138	168	195	219	238	252
AR(£)	60	51	46	42	39	36.5	34	31.5
MR(£)	60	42	36	30	27	24	19	14

(a) How much will the firm produce if it seeks to maximise profits?

(b) What is the socially efficient level of output (assuming no externalities on the demand side)?

(c) How much is the marginal external cost at this level of output?

(d) What size tax would be necessary for the firm to reduce its output to the socially efficient level?

(e) Why is the tax less than the marginal externality?

(f) Why might it be equitable to impose a lump-sum tax on this firm?

(g) Why will a lump-sum tax not affect the firm's output (assuming that in the long-run the firm can still make at least normal profit)?

2 Distinguish between publicly provided goods, public goods and merit goods.

3   Name some goods or services provided by the government or local authorities that are not public goods.

4   Some roads could be regarded as a public good, but some could be provided by the market. Which types of road could be provided by the market? Why? Would it be a good idea?

5   Assume that you wanted the information given in (a)–(h) below. In which cases could you (i) buy perfect information; (ii) buy imperfect information; (iii) be able to obtain information without paying for it; (iv) not be able to obtain information?

   (a) Which washing machine is the most reliable?
   (b) Which of two jobs that are vacant is the most satisfying?
   (c) Which builder will repair my roof most cheaply?
   (d) Which builder will make the best job of repairing my roof?
   (e) Which builder is best value for money?
   (f) How big a mortgage would it be wise for me to take out?
   (g) What course of higher education should I follow?
   (h) What brand of washing powder washes whiter?

   In which cases are there non-monetary costs to you of finding out the information? How can you know whether the information you acquire is accurate or not?

6   Make a list of pieces of information a firm might want to know and consider whether it could buy the information and how reliable that information might be.

7   Why might it be better to ban certain activities that cause environmental damage rather than to tax them?

8   Consider the advantages and disadvantages of extending property rights so that everyone would have the right to prevent people imposing any costs on them whatsoever (or charging them to do so).

9   How suitable are legal restrictions in the following cases?

   (a) Ensuring adequate vehicle safety (e.g. that tyres have sufficient tread or that the vehicle is roadworthy).
   (b) Reducing traffic congestion.
   (c) Preventing the use of monopoly power.
   (d) Ensuring that mergers are in the public interest.
   (e) Ensuring that firms charge a price equal to marginal cost.

10 Evaluate the following statement: 'Despite the weaknesses of a free market, the replacing of the market by the government generally makes the problem worse.'

11 In what ways might business be socially responsible?

12 What economic costs and benefits might a business experience if it decided to adopt a more socially responsible position? How might such costs and benefits change over the longer term?

Government and the firm

In this chapter we shall consider the relationship between government and the individual firm. This relationship is not simply one of regulation and control, but can involve the active intervention of government in attempting to improve the economic performance of business. We shall consider government attitudes and policy towards enhancing research and technology development, and training, as well as the more punitive area of business regulation through the use of monopolies and mergers legislation.

Key
Idea
30
p410

21.1 Competition policy

Key
Idea
18
p211

Competition, monopoly and the public interest

Most markets in the real world are imperfect, with firms having varying degrees of market power. But will this power be against the public interest? This question has been addressed by successive governments in framing legislation to deal with monopolies and oligopolies.

It might be thought that market power is always 'a bad thing', certainly as far as the consumer is concerned. After all, it enables firms to make supernormal profit, thereby 'exploiting' the consumer. The greater the firm's power, the higher will prices be relative to the costs of production. Also, a lack of competition removes the incentive to become more efficient.

But market power is not necessarily a bad thing. Firms may not fully exploit their position of power – perhaps for fear that very high profits would eventually lead to other firms overcoming entry barriers, or perhaps because they are not aggressive profit maximisers. Even if they do make large supernormal profits, they may still charge a lower price than more competitive sectors of the industry because of their economies of scale. Finally, they may use their profits for research and development and for capital investment. The consumer might then benefit from improved products at lower prices.

Competition policy could seek to ban various structures or activities. For example, it could ban mergers leading to market share of more than a certain amount, or it could ban price-fixing arrangements between oligopolists. However, most countries prefer to adopt a more flexible approach and examine each case on its merits. Such an approach does not presume that the mere possession of power is against the public interest, but rather that certain uses of that power may be.

There are three possible targets of competition policy:

■ The abuse of the existing power of monopolies and oligopolies: monopoly policy.
■ The growth of power through mergers and acquisitions: merger policy.
■ Oligopolistic collusion: restrictive practices policy.

Competition policy in the European Union

EU competition legislation is contained in Articles 81 and 82 of the Treaty of Amsterdam and, since 1990, in additional regulations covering mergers.

Article 81 is concerned with restrictive practices and Article 82 with monopolies and mergers. The Articles are largely confined to firms trading between EU members and thus do not cover monopolies or oligopolies operating solely within a member country. The policy is implemented by the European Commission. If any firm appears to be breaking the provisions of either of the Articles, the Commission can refer it to the European Court of Justice.

EU restrictive practices policy

Article 81 covers *agreements* between firms, *joint decisions*, and concerted *practices* which prevent, restrict or distort competition. In other words it covers all types of oligopolistic collusion that are against the interests of consumers.

Article 81 is not designed to prevent oligopolistic *structures* (i.e. the simple existence of co-operation between firms), but rather collusive *behaviour*. No matter what form collusion takes, if the European Commission finds that firms are committing anti-competitive *practices*, they will be banned from doing so and possibly fined (up to 10 per cent of annual turnover), although firms do have the right of appeal to the European Court of Justice.

Practices considered anti-competitive include firms colluding to do any of the following:

■ Fix prices (i.e. above competitive levels).
■ Limit production, markets, technical development or investment.
■ Share out markets or sources of supply.
■ Charge discriminatory prices or operate discriminatory trading conditions, such as to benefit the colluding parties and disadvantage others.
■ Make other firms who sign contracts with any of the colluding firms accept unfavourable obligations which, by their nature, have no connection with the subject of such contracts.

In recent years the Commission has adopted a tough stance and has fined many firms.

EU monopoly policy

Article 82 relates to the abuse of market power and has also been extended to cover mergers. As with Article 81, it is the *behaviour* of firms that is the target of the legislation. The following are cited as examples of abuse of market power. As you can see, they are very similar to those in Article 81.

■ Charging unfairly high prices to consumers, or paying unfairly low prices to suppliers.

- Limiting production, markets or technical developments to the detriment of consumers.

- Using price discrimination or other discriminatory practices to the detriment of certain parties.

- Making other firms who sign contracts with it accept unfavourable obligations which, by their nature, have no connection with the subject of such contracts.

Under Article 82, such practices can be banned and firms can be fined where they are found to have abused a dominant position. A firm does not have to have some specified minimum market share before Article 82 can be invoked. Instead, if firms are able to conduct anti-competitive practices, it is simply assumed that they must be in a position of market power. This approach is sensible, given the difficulties of identifying the boundaries of a market, either in terms of geography or in terms of type of product.

EU merger policy

The 1990 merger control measures tightened up the legislation in Article 82. They cover mergers where combined worldwide annual sales exceed €5 billion; where EU sales of at least two of the companies exceed €250 million; and where at least one of the companies conducts no more than two-thirds of its EU-wide business in a single member state. (Less than 4 per cent of mergers involving European companies meet these conditions.)

All relevant mergers must be notified to the European Commission within one week of their announcement. The merger will then normally be suspended for three weeks. Within one month of the notification, the Commission, on the basis of preliminary investigations (Phase 1), must decide whether to conduct a formal investigation (Phase 2) or to let the merger proceed.

The 1990 measures have made the process of EU merger control very rapid and administratively inexpensive. The measures are also quite tough, if limited in scope (being confined to companies operating in more than one member country). Nevertheless several criticisms have been made of the system.

- The decisions of the Commission are often based on limited and poorly presented analysis and are inconsistent between different cases.

- The Commission, in being willing to show flexibility, can easily be persuaded by firms, and the conditions imposed on them are often very lax and rely on the firms' co-operation.

- Not enough emphasis is placed on possible cost reductions from mergers. The stress is almost exclusively on questions of competition.

- In the first 13 years of the merger control measures, 2187 mergers were notified, but only 124 proceeded to Phase 2. In many cases (too many, claim critics) the Commission accepted the undertakings of firms. By 2003, only 18 mergers had been prohibited.

There is considerable disagreement in the EU between those who want to encourage competition *within* the EU and those who want to see European companies being world leaders. For them, the ability to compete in *world* markets normally requires that companies are large, which may well imply having monopoly power within the EU.

> **Pause for thought**
>
> To what extent is Article 82 consistent with both these points of view?

In December 2001, the European Commission launched a Green Paper on reform of the merger regulations. The main objectives were to simplify the

Table 21.1 UK competition legislation

Year	Act	Provisions
1948	Monopolies and Restrictive Practices Act	Set up Monopolies and Restrictive Practices Commission (MRC) to investigate suspected cases of abuse by a firm or group of firms of a dominant market position.
1956, 1968, 1976	Restrictive Trade Practices Act	Set up Restrictive Practices Court (RPC). All restrictive practices had to be registered. These would then have to be justified to the RPC. MRC renamed Monopolies Commission.
1964, 1976	Resale Prices Acts	Resale price maintenance banned unless firm could demonstrate to the RPC that it was in the public interest.
1965	Monopolies and Mergers Act	Role of Monopolies Commission now extended to examine mergers that would lead to a dominant market position.
1973	Fair Trading Act	Office of Fair Trading established. Its Director-General (DGFT) is responsible for referrals to the RPC or the renamed Monopolies and Mergers Commission (MMC).
1980	Competition Act	Various types of anti-competitive practice were specified. OFT would investigate alleged cases of such practices and possibly refer to MMC.
1989	Companies Act	Simplified and speeded-up mergers investigation procedures.
1998	Competition Act	Brought UK legislation in line with EU legislation. Chapter I prohibition applies to restrictive practices. Chapter II prohibition applies to the abuse of a dominant position. MMC replaced by Competition Commission (CC).
2002	Enterprise Act	Made OFT and CC independent of government. Made various cartel agreements a criminal offence. Mergers investigated by OFT and referred, if necessary, to CC for ruling.

merger control process; to allow more time for consideration of mergers where the issues are complex; to avoid cases where mergers were considered by both EU and national authorities; to tighten up the scrutiny of companies' assurances about competition; to introduce the possibility of 'dawn raids' on businesses planning to merge; to focus on the effects of mergers on competition rather than market share; and to invite a debate on whether the effects on competition should be the only test of whether a merger should be allowed to proceed.

UK competition policy

There have been substantial changes to UK competition policy since the first legislation was introduced in 1948 (see Table 21.1). The current approach is based on the 1998 Competition Act and the 2002 Enterprise Act.

The Competition Act brought UK policy in line with EU policy, detailed above. The Act has two key sets (or 'chapters') of prohibitions. Chapter I prohibits various restrictive practices, and mirrors Article 81. Chapter II prohibits various abuses of monopoly power, and mirrors Article 82.

The Enterprise Act strengthened the Competition Act and introduced new measures for the control of mergers.

Under the two Acts, the body charged with ensuring that the prohibitions are carried out is the Office of Fair Trading (OFT). The OFT can investigate any firms suspected of engaging in one or more of the prohibited practices. Its officers have the power to enter and search premises and can require the production and explanation of documents. Where the OFT decides that an infringement of one of the prohibitions has occurred, it can direct the offending firms to modify their behaviour or cease their practices altogether. Companies in breach of a prohibition are liable to fines of up to 10 per cent of their annual UK turnover. Third parties adversely affected by such breaches can seek compensation through the courts.

The Competition Act also set up a Competition Commission (CC) to which the OFT can refer cases for further investigation. The CC is charged with determining whether the structure of an industry or the practices of firms within it are detrimental to competition.

The Enterprise Act made the OFT and CC independent of government. It also set up a Markets and Policy Initiatives Division (MPI) of the OFT. This carries out investigations into particular markets suspected of not working in the best interests of consumers. The MPI's investigations could lead to the OFT enforcing its findings if anti-competitive practices were taking place (see below). Alternatively, the MPI could refer the case to the CC or make proposals to the government for changes in the law.

If a case is referred to the Competition Commission, it will carry out an investigation to establish whether competition is adversely affected. If it finds that it is, it will decide on the appropriate remedies, such as prohibiting various practices.

Firms affected by an OFT or CC ruling have the right of appeal to the Competition Appeal Tribunal (CAT), which can uphold or quash the original decision. The CAT is entirely independent of the CC and OFT.

UK restrictive practices policy

Under the Chapter I prohibition of the 1998 Act, any agreement or collusive activity that prevents, restricts or distorts competition was made illegal. The *form* of any agreement was irrelevant. It is the *effects* of oligopolistic collusion that were the object of the legislation. To contravene the Chapter I prohibition, the effects on competition had to be appreciable. It was assumed under the Act that the effects of any agreement would not normally be appreciable if the firms' combined share was less than 25 per cent of the relevant market.

The 2002 Enterprise Act tightened up the law by making it a *criminal* offence to engage in cartel agreements (i.e. horizontal, rather than vertical agreements between firms), irrespective of whether there are appreciable effects on competition. Convicted offenders may receive a prison sentence of up to five years and/or an unlimited fine. Prosecutions may be brought by the Serious Fraud Office or the OFT. The Act strengthened the OFT's power to enter premises, seize documents and to require people to answer questions or provide information.

But what practices constitute 'cartel agreements'? These involve one or more of the following: price fixing, limiting supply, sharing out markets, limiting supply or bid-rigging. In more detail these include:

■ Horizontal price-fixing agreements. These are agreements between competitors to set one or more of the following: fixed prices, minimum prices, the amount or percentage by which prices may be increased, or a range outside which prices may not move. The object is to restrict price competition and thus to keep prices higher than they would otherwise be.

■ Agreements to share out markets. These may be by geographical area, type or size of customer, or nature of outlet. By limiting or even eliminating competition within each part of the market, such agreements can be an effective means of keeping prices high (or quality low).

■ Agreements to limit production. This may involve output quotas or a looser agreement not to increase output wherever this would drive down prices.

■ Agreements to limit or co-ordinate investment. By restraining capacity, this will help firms to keep output down and prices up.

■ **Collusive tendering**. This is where two or more firms put in a tender for a contract at secretly agreed (high) prices. A well-known case throughout most of the 1980s and 1990s was that of firms supplying ready-mixed concrete agreeing on prices they would tender to local authorities (see Box 21.1).

■ Agreements between purchasers. These could be to reduce prices paid to suppliers. For example, large supermarkets could collude to keep prices low to farmers. An alternative form of agreement would be to deal with certain suppliers only.

■ Agreements to boycott suppliers or distributors who deal with competitors to the colluding firms.

In the case of other types of agreement, the OFT has the discretion to decide, on a case-by-case basis, whether or not competition is appreciably restricted, and whether, therefore, they should be terminated or the firms should be exempted. Such cases include the following:

■ Vertical price-fixing agreements. These are price agreements between purchasing firms and their suppliers. An example of this is **resale price maintenance**. This is where a manufacturer or distributor sets the price for retailers to charge. It may well distribute a price list to retailers (e.g. a car manufacturer may distribute a price list to car showrooms). Resale price maintenance is a way of preventing competition between retailers driving down retail prices and ultimately the price they pay to the manufacturer. Both manufacturers and retailers, therefore, are likely to gain from resale price maintenance.

■ Agreements to exchange information that could have the effect of reducing competition. For example, if producers exchange information on their price intentions, it is a way of allowing price leadership, a form of tacit collusion, to continue.

UK monopoly policy

Under the Chapter II prohibition of the 1998 Competition Act, it is illegal for a dominant firm to exercise its market power in such a way as to reduce competition. Any suspected case is investigated by the OFT. If the OFT then decides that a breach of the prohibition has taken place, it can levy a fine of up to 10 per cent of annual UK turnover.

The OFT uses a two-stage process in deciding whether an abuse has taken place. The first stage is to establish whether a firm has a position of dominance. If it has, the second is to establish whether it is abusing that dominant position.

What constitutes market dominance? According to the OFT, a firm has market dominance if it is able to behave independently of competitive pressures, and can, as a result, charge higher prices than if it faced effective competition. In deciding which firms have dominance, the OFT uses two criteria.

The first is the firm's market share. Although there is no minimum share specified in the Act, the OFT considers that firms will normally need to have at least a 40 per cent share of the market (national or local, whichever is appropriate), if they are to have a position of dominance, although this figure will vary from industry to industry.

The second criterion is the contestability of the market in which the firm is operating (see section 11.4). The higher the barriers to the entry of new firms, the less contestable will be the market, and the more dominant a firm is likely to be for any given current market share. In looking at barriers, the OFT classifies them into three types:

- Absolute advantages. The dominant firm may have patents, copyright or ownership of key factors or outlets.
- Strategic advantages. The dominant firm has advantages from already being in the market. For example, new firms are likely to incur sunk costs (costs that occur on entry, but cannot be recovered on exit: e.g. specialised plant and equipment with little or no second-hand value).
- Expansionary behaviour. The dominant firm may deter entrants through its reputation for aggressive behaviour, such as charging predatory prices (see below), or doing deals with retailers to sell only its products.

If the firm *is* deemed to be dominant, the OFT then decides whether the firm's practices constitute an abuse of its position. As with restrictive practices, Chapter II follows EU legislation. It specifies the same four types of market abuse as does Article 82 (see above). Within these four categories, the OFT identifies the following practices as being overtly anti-competitive:

- Charging excessively high prices. These are prices above those the firm would charge if it faced effective competition. One sign of excessively high prices is abnormally high rates of profit.
- Price discrimination. This is only regarded as an abuse to the extent that the higher prices are excessive or the lower prices are used to exclude competitors.
- Predatory pricing. This is where prices are set at loss-making levels, so as to drive competitors out of business (see page 336). The test is to look at the dominant firm's price in relation to its average costs. If its price is below average variable cost, predation would be assumed. If its price is above average variable cost, but below average total cost, then the Director General would need to establish whether the reason was to eliminate a competitor.

Key Idea
20
p235

- **Vertical restraints**. This is where a supplying firm imposes conditions on a purchasing firm (or vice versa). Examples include:
  - resale price maintenance. This comes under Chapter II rather than Chapter I, if there is no *agreement* between supplier and purchaser, but rather the *imposition* of conditions on the one by the other.
  - manufacturers imposing rules on retailers about displaying the product or the provision of after-sales service.
  - selective distribution: where manufacturers refuse to supply certain outlets (e.g. perfume manufacturers refusing to supply discount chains, such as Superdrug).
  - exclusive purchasing: where a retailer is only prepared to buy from a particular supplier.
  - tie-in-sales: where a firm controlling the supply of a first product insists that its customers buy a second product from it rather than from its rivals.

- Refusal to supply. A firm may refuse to supply competitors with key inputs, or it may be used as a vertical restraint to limit the number of outlets selling its products.

The simple *existence* of any of these practices may not constitute an abuse. The OFT has to decide whether their *effect* is to restrict competition.

If the case is not straightforward, the OFT can refer it to the Competition Commission (CC). The CC will then carry out a detailed investigation to establish whether competition is restricted or distorted. If it is, the CC will rule what actions must be taken to remedy the situation.

UK merger policy

Merger policy is covered by the 2002 Enterprise Act. It seeks to prevent mergers that are likely to result in a substantial lessening of competition.

A merger or takeover will be investigated by the OFT if the target company has a turnover of £70 million or more, or if the merger results in the new company having a market share of 25 per cent or more. The OFT conducts a preliminary investigation to see whether competition is likely to be threatened. If it is, and if there are unlikely to be any substantial compensating benefits to consumers, the OFT refers the case to the Competition Commission.

If reference is made to the CC, it conducts a detailed investigation to establish whether the merger is likely to lead to a significant reduction in competition. If so, it can prohibit the merger. Alternatively, it can require the merged firm to behave in certain ways in order to protect consumers' interests. In such cases, the OFT then monitors the firm to ensure that it is abiding by the CC's conditions. CC investigations must normally be completed within 24 weeks.

The 2002 Act tightened up merger legislation. In the past, the OFT did not have to refer mergers to the CC that potentially threatened competition. What is more, the Secretary of State (a government minister), not the CC, had the final say on whether a merger should be permitted. The vast majority (over 97 per cent) of mergers in the past were not referred to the CC (or its predecessor, the Monopolies and Mergers Commission (MMC)). Even those that were referred were either abandoned or, after the MMC investigation, blocked by the minister.

This suggests that the policy had not been tough enough, with many mergers not being referred which should have been. Indeed, studies had shown that mergers were generally *not* in the public interest. Significant benefits from cost reduction and research had not occurred, and yet mergers had contributed to a growing degree of market concentration in the UK. The 2002 Act sought to rectify this problem.

Assessment of EU and UK competition policy

With UK competition legislation having been brought in line with EU legislation it is possible to consider the two together.

It is generally agreed by commentators that the policy is correct to concentrate on anti-competitive *practices* and their *effects* rather than simply on the existence of agreements or on the size of a firm's market share. After all, economic power is only a problem when it is abused. When, by contrast, it enables firms to achieve economies of scale, or more finance for investment, the result can be to the benefit of consumers. In other words, the assumption that structure determines conduct and performance (see pages 16 and 212) is not necessarily true, and certainly it is not necessarily true that market power is always bad and competitive industries are always good.

Secondly, most commentators favour the system of certain practices being *prohibited*, with fines applicable to the first offence. This acts as an important deterrent to anti-competitive behaviour.

Taking your vitamins – at a price
The global vitamin cartel

In a report on worldwide cartels published in 2000, the OECD found that;

> Actions against price fixing and other such 'hard core' cartels have halted billions of dollars in secret overcharges to individual consumers and business purchasers. The lesson of these successful cases is that such cartels are much more prevalent and harmful to the global economy than previously believed.'[1]

The report cited the following cases:

- A global citric acid cartel, which raised prices by over 30 per cent and collected $1.5 billion in overcharges.

- A graphite electrode cartel, which raised prices by over 50 per cent and made monopoly profits from worldwide sales estimated at some $7 billion over a five-year period.

- A global lysine cartel, which doubled world prices. Over the time of the cartel $1.4 billion worth of sales were affected leading to estimated overcharges of $140 million.

In the United States, it is estimated that recently exposed cartels have affected over $10 billion worth of commerce, with overcharges in the US market alone standing at $1 billion. Globally the impact would be many billions of dollars. It has also been estimated in the United States that the average gain from price fixing is about 10 per cent of the selling price. However, when taking into account the waste and inefficiency generated by such cartels, the cost to society may be as high as 20 per cent.

The case of vitamins

In November 2001, the EU announced that it would be imposing fines on companies colluding in a worldwide vitamin cartel. This cartel was shown to be one of the most sophisticated and well organised so far discovered. Mario Monti, the EU Competition Commissioner, referred to the cartel as the 'most damaging' the Commission had ever had to investigate. Not only was the cartel extensive, covering 12 different vitamins, but as Monti remarked:

> It is particularly unacceptable that this illegal behaviour concerned substances which are vital elements for nutrition and essential for normal growth and maintenance of life.[2]

Vitamins are added both to animal foodstuffs and human food products, such as cereals. They are used in cosmetics and form an important part of skin and health care products. The Competition Commission estimated that in the EU, in 1998, the market covered by vitamin products was worth over €800 million.

Similar conclusions have been reached in the USA, where the application of competition law has undergone changes in recent years. In the past, the focus was on the structure of an industry. Under the Sherman Act of 1890, oligopolistic collusion in the 'restraint of trade' was made illegal, as was any attempt to establish a monopoly. Although, under the Clayton Act of 1914, various potentially anti-competitive practices (such as price discrimination) were only illegal when they substantially lessened competition, the application of these two 'anti-trust' laws was largely directed to breaking up large firms. Today, the approach is to focus on efficiency, rather than on market share; and on the effects on consumers of any collusion or co-operation between firms, rather than on the simple collusion itself.

A problem with any policy to deal with collusion is the difficulty in rooting it out. When firms do all their deals 'behind closed doors' and are careful not to keep records or give clues, then collusion can be very hard to spot. The cases that have come to light, such as that of collusive tendering between firms supplying ready-mixed concrete, may be just the tip of an iceberg.

The EU investigation revealed that a series of 12 global vitamin cartels had been established, the earliest in 1989, the most recent in 1993. Thirteen companies were involved in these cartels, however only Hoffman La-Roche, the world's largest vitamin producer, was present in all of them. BASF was present in 10 out of the 12. In each of the cartels, prices were fixed for different vitamin products; companies had allocated sales quotas; and they agreed upon and implemented price increases. In addition, they set up a system to monitor and enforce the agreements, which involved regular meetings between the cartel members. These meetings detailed the cartel's operations, which involved the exchange of sales values, volumes of sales and pricing information. As the EU report into the cartel remarks: 'The arrangements were part of a strategic plan conceived at the highest levels to control the world market in vitamins by illegal means'.[3]

Given the severity of the collusion and the long length of time over which the cartel had been operating, the EU imposed record fines on the cartel members, totalling €855.2 million. Because Swiss firm Hoffman La-Roche was not only present in all 12 cartels, but was also seen as one of the prime instigators of these cartels, it received the heaviest fine, totalling some €462 million. Such fines might have been far larger had not the conspirators aided the EU's investigation. As a result of doing so, they received a reduction in their fines of 50 per cent.

As well as facing financial penalties in the EU, the global vitamin cartel has been prosecuted in the United States, Canada and Australia. In the USA, fines have totalled over $1 billion, and two Hoffman La-Roche executives, as well as paying individual fines, have received prison sentences for their parts in the cartel's activities.

In the face of such abuses of market power, the OECD is attempting to toughen anti-competitive legislation in its members' countries. It is also, given the global scale of such cartels, seeking to co-ordinate the activities of different countries' investigations into such cartels. The problem is clearly a global one, which requires a global solution to be truly effective.

Question

Why might global cartels be harder to identify and eradicate than cartels solely located within the domestic economy? What problems does this raise for competition policy?

---

[1] *Hard Core Cartels*, (OECD, 2000).
[2] *Commission imposes fines on vitamin cartels*, (EU Press Release, 21/11/2001).
[3] *Ibid.*

Policies towards research and technology development (R&TD)   21.2

The impact of technology not only on the practice of business, but on the economy in general is vividly illustrated by the development and use of the Internet. In 1997, worldwide some 40 million people and 25 000 firms used the Internet. By early 2003, there were 620 million users. By 2005 the figure is forecast to be 1 billion. The commercial possibilities of the Internet range from the selling of information and services, to global forms of catalogue shopping where you can browse through a business's product range (or surf the net) and use your credit card number to pay. The Internet is just one example of how technology and technological change are shaping the whole structure and organisation of business (see Chapter 3 on the flat organisation), the experience of work for the worker, and the productivity of business and hence the competitive performance of national economies.

If a business fails to embrace new technology, its productivity and profitability will almost certainly lag behind those businesses that do. It is the same for countries. Unless they embrace new technology, the productivity gap between them and those that do is likely to widen. Once such a gap has been opened, it will prove very difficult to close. Those countries ahead in the technological race will tend to get further ahead as the dynamic forces of technology enhance their competitiveness, improve their profits, and provide yet greater potential for technological advance. How then might countries set about preventing such technological gaps opening, or, once they have become established, set about closing them?

Technology policy refers to a series of government initiatives to affect the process of technological change and its rate of adoption. The nature of the policy will depend on which stage of the introduction of new technology it is designed to affect. Three stages can be identified:

- *Invention.* In this initial stage, research leads to new ideas and new products. Sometimes the ideas arise from general research; sometimes the research is directed towards a particular goal, such as the development of a new type of car engine or computer chip.
- *Innovation.* In this stage, the new ideas are put into practice. A firm will introduce the new technology, and will hopefully gain a commercial advantage from so doing.
- *Diffusion.* In the final stage, the new products and processes are copied, and possibly adapted, by competitor firms. The effects of the new technology thus spread throughout the economy, affecting general productivity levels and competitiveness.

Technology policy can be focused on any or all of these stages of technological change.

definition
Technology policy
Involves government initiatives to affect the process and rate of technological change.

Technological change and market failure

Why is a technology policy needed in the first place? The following reasons can be advanced to explain why the market system might fail to provide those factors vital to initiate technological change.

R&TD free riders. If an individual business can benefit from the results of *other* businesses conducting R&TD, with all its associated costs and risks, then it is less likely to conduct R&TD itself. It will simply 'free ride' on such activity. As a consequence, it would be in the interest of the firm conducting R&TD to keep its findings secret or under some kind of property right, such as a patent, so as to gain as much competitive advantage as possible from its investment.

Although it is desirable to encourage firms to conduct R&TD, and for this purpose it may be necessary to have a strict patent system in force, it is also desirable that there is the maximum *social* benefit from such R&TD. This would occur only if such findings were widely disseminated. It is thus important that technology policy finds the optimum balance between the two objectives of (a) encouraging individual firms to conduct research and (b) disseminating the results.

Monopolistic and oligopolistic market structures. The more a market is dominated by a few large producers, the less incentive they will have to conduct R&TD

and innovate as a means of reducing costs. The problem is most acute under monopoly. Nevertheless, despite a lower incentive to innovate, the higher profits of firms with monopoly power will at least put them in a position of being more able to afford to conduct research.

Duplication. Not only is it likely that there is too little R&TD being conducted, there is also the danger that resources may be wasted in duplicating research. The more firms there are conducting R&TD, the greater the likelihood of some form of duplication. Given the scarcity of R&TD resources, any duplication would be a highly inefficient way to organise production.

Risk and uncertainty. Because the payoffs from R&TD activity are so uncertain, there will tend to be a natural caution on the part of both the business conducting R&TD and (if different) the financier. Only R&TD activity which has a clear market potential, or is of low risk, is likely to be considered. It has been found that financial markets in particular will tend to adopt risk-averting strategy and fail to provide an adequate pool of long-term funds. This is another manifestation of the 'short-termism' we considered in section 19.4.

Forms of intervention

Attempts to correct the above market failures and develop a technology policy might include the use of the following.

> **Pause for thought**
>
> Before you read on, can you identify the main forms of intervention the government might use in order to encourage and support R&TD.

The patent system. The strengthening of legal rights over the development of new products will encourage businesses to conduct R&TD, as they will be able to reap greater rewards from successful R&TD investment.

Public provision. In an attempt to overcome the free-rider problem and the inefficiency of R&TD duplication, government might provide R&TD itself, either through its own research institutions or via funding to university and other research councils. This is of particular importance in the case of basic research, where the potential outcomes are far less certain than those of applied research.

R&TD subsidies. If the government provided subsidies to businesses conducting R&TD activity, it not only would reduce the cost and hence the risk for business, but could ensure that the outcome from the R&TD activity is more rapidly diffused throughout the economy than might otherwise be expected. This would help improve general levels of technological innovation.

Co-operative R&TD. Given that the benefits of technological developments are of widespread use, the government could encourage co-operative R&TD. The government could take various roles here, from being actively involved in the R&TD process, to acting as a facilitator, bringing private-sector businesses together. The key advantages of this policy are that it will not only reduce the potential for duplication, but also encourage the pooling of scarce R&TD resources.

Diffusion policies. Such policies tend to be of two types: the provision of information concerning new technology, and the use of subsidies to encourage businesses to adopt new technology.

Other policies. A wide range of other policies, primarily adopted for other purposes, might also influence R&TD. These might include: education and training policy; competition policy; national defence policies and initiatives; and policies on standards and compatibility.

Technology policy in the UK and EU

The UK's poor technological performance since 1945 can be attributed to many factors, from a lack of entrepreneurial vision on the part of business, to the excessive short-termism of the UK's financial institutions. Equally there appears to have been a failure on the part of government to initiate suitable strategies to overcome such problems.

In the UK, the current attitude towards technology policy is one in which the role of government is kept to a minimum, and support is given only when 'a worthwhile and viable project is at risk through the failure of the market mechanism'. Actively interventionist strategies, such as the use of R&TD subsidies, are kept to a minimum, and the emphasis of policy is to encourage greater collaboration between companies within the private sector.

This strategy does not appear to have been very successful. Since 1990, UK gross expenditure on research and development (GERD) as a percentage of GDP has been lower than that of its main economic rivals (see Figure 21.1).

In contrast to the UK's approach to R&TD, the EU is more interventionist, and attempts to provide a unified strategy of R&TD subsidies and collaborative R&TD research programmes. EU initiatives range from general programmes such as the European Strategic Programme for Research in Information Technology (ESPRIT), to specific research fields such as that of medicine and health (BIOMED) and communications technology and services (ACTS), to name but two from a wide range of such initiatives. The main source of funding is from the Research and Technology Programme, which currently operates in a

Figure 21.1

Gross expenditure on R&D as a percentage of GDP

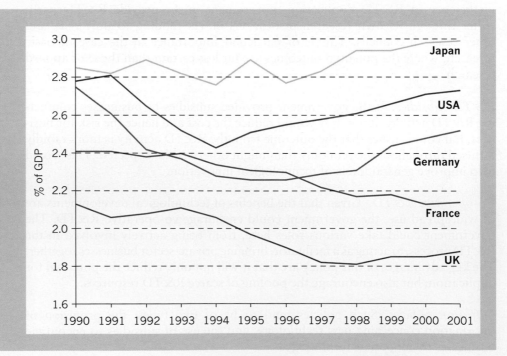

four-year framework. The sixth programme, which runs from 2003–6 has a budget of €17.5 billion, some 3.9 per cent of the EU's total budget.

The EU has in recent years attempted to encourage greater levels of inter-European collaboration on research and technology projects. The European Research Co-ordination Agency (EUREKA) was set up in 1985 (although not formally an EU programme it receives EU backing and funds) and includes all members of the EU and those of EFTA. The European Scientific and Technical Co-operation programme (COST) has a wider membership than EUREKA and extends to businesses in central and eastern Europe. The role of both schemes is to co-ordinate the activities of private business, providing, in most cases, only limited funds. The approach here, therefore, is similar to that adopted in the UK.

Even given the active participation of the EU in funding and encouraging R&TD, there is still some doubt as to whether the various programmes receive adequate finance: whether, if European countries are to remain competitive with their main economic rivals (the USA, Japan and other south-east Asian countries), yet more might be required.

Policies towards training   21.3

It is generally recognised by economists and politicians alike that improvements in training and education can yield significant supply-side gains. Indeed, the UK's failure to invest as much in training as many of its major competitors is seen as a key explanation for the country's poor economic performance since the early 1970s. In the UK over 55 per cent of workers are classified as low skilled. This compares with only 20 per cent in Germany.

Training and economic performance

Training and economic performance are linked in three main ways.

Labour productivity. In various studies comparing the productivity of UK and German industry, education and training was seen as the principal reason for the productivity gap between the two countries. In 1999, 20 per cent of the productivity difference between Germany and the UK was attributed to the superior skills of German workers.

Innovation and change. A key factor in shaping a firm's willingness to introduce new products or processes will be the adaptability and skills of its workforce. If the firm has to spend a lot of money on retraining, or on attracting skilled workers away from other firms, the costs may prove prohibitive.

Costs of production. A shortage of skilled workers will quickly create labour bottlenecks and cause production costs to increase. This will stifle economic growth.

Training policy

If training is left to the employer, the benefits will become an externality if the workers leave to work elsewhere. Society has benefited from the training, but the

The R&D Scoreboard

For many years it has been suggested that the UK's poor international competitive record has been in no small part due to its failure to invest in research and development. The UK's R&D intensity – that is, the ratio of R&D spending to sales – has been considerably lower than that of its main economic rivals.

Each year the Department of Trade and Industry publishes the R&D Scoreboard. This gives details of the R&D expenditures of the top R&D spending companies in the UK and worldwide. It also investigates emerging trends and patterns in R&D spending. The 2002 Scoreboard is composed of the 600 leading R&D spending UK companies and the 600 leading international R&D spenders. Of the world's leading 600 companies 36 UK companies make the list.

The following is taken from the 2002 R&D Scoreboard.[1]

Regional analysis

The total R&D for the 600 UK companies in the 2002 Scoreboard is £16bn compared to £206bn for the 600 international companies. The totals have increased over the last year by 5% and 4% respectively. The 36 UK companies in the international 600 have increased their total R&D by only 1% over the last year...

The breakdown of total R&D by world region is given in Table (a).

European R&D intensity is significantly lower than that of the US or Japan and the UK is low compared to the rest of Europe. Note the very high intensity of the Americas at 5.1% (US also 5.1%). The UK figure is based on the 36 larger UK companies included in the international 600. In Table (b), this UK (36) R&D intensity is compared to that of the other major European nations and to the average for the 600 UK companies in the UK Scoreboard.

It can be seen from Table (b) that the overall UK R&D intensity is lower than that of France, Germany or Switzerland whether calculated using the top 36 UK companies or all 600 in the UK Scoreboard.

The UK is unique in having an unusually large proportion of its R&D in pharmaceuticals (37% overall) and an unusually large percentage of overall sales from oil and gas (32% of the 600 and 50% of the 36). Both UK sectors are dominated by two very large companies. These two special factors tend to cancel and Table (b) shows that the UK 600 R&D intensity excluding the pharmaceutical and oil and gas sectors is 2.1%.

Table (a) R&D investment and intensity by region

	Europe	Americas	RoW	Total
Number of companies	170 (UK 36)	287 (US 275)	143 (Japan 132)	600
R&D investment (£bn)	63.9 (UK 10.7)	98.0 (US 94.6)	44.6 (Japan 42.5)	206.5
R&D intensity (%)	3.6 (UK 2.5)	5.1 (US 5.1)	4.1 (Japan 4.3)	4.3

Table (b) R&D intensities in European countries

R&D Intensity	UK (600)	UK (36)*	France (31)*	Germany (40)*	Switzerland (17)*
All Sectors %	2.2	2.5	3.1	4.1	5.7
All Sectors except Pharmaceuticals and oils %	2.1	2.9	2.9	3.9	3.0
Pharmaceuticals %	14.6	14.3	15.3	12.8	13.5
Total R&D (£bn)	16	10.7	12.7	20.1	5.8

* The figure in brackets is the number of companies in the International 600.

Table (c) R&D by sector

Sector	Proportion of total R&D		R&D Intensity		
	International %	UK %	International %	UK %	Ratio UK/Inter.
IT Hardware	25.1	8.2	9.4	7.1	0.8
Automotive	16.5	6.4	4.0	4.8	1.2
Pharmaceuticals and biotechnology	16.3	36.7	13.0	14.6	1.1
Electronic and electrical	10.4	4.5	5.3	2.6	0.5
Software and IT services	6.7	5.1	10.2	5.8	0.6
Chemicals	4.9	3.8	4.2	2.2	0.5
Aerospace and defence	3.9	9.8	4.3	6.5	1.5
Engineering	3.0	2.6	2.6	1.5	0.6
Telecomms	2.2	3.0	1.9	1.0	0.5
Health	2.0	1.9	4.9	6.5	1.3
Food processors	0.8	5.1	1.7	1.5	0.9
Oil and gas	1.4	3.8	0.4	0.3	0.8
Others	6.8	9.1	–	–	–

This can be compared with 4.4% for the US top 1000 companies. However, if the top 36 UK companies are compared with the top companies in France, Germany and Switzerland, the gap is smaller and, excluding pharmaceuticals and oils, the UK is level pegging with France and Switzerland although still well behind Germany.

As far as the UK 600 is concerned, it is interesting that the overall UK Scoreboard R&D intensity has been steadily rising from 1.8% in 1998 to 1.9% in 1999, 2.1% in 2000 and 2001 to 2.2% in 2002. The R&D intensity for the US 1000 company Scoreboard is 4.3% (both 2000 and 2001).

While R&D intensity is important, the total amount of R&D is also significant. The top 36 UK companies account for two-thirds of the R&D of the top 600 UK companies. For those European companies in the international 600, the UK 36 with £10.7bn of R&D represents only just over 50% of the £20.1bn total for the 40 German companies and 84% of the £12.7bn total for the 31 French companies. Switzerland, with a population of only seven million, has 17 companies in the international 600 with nearly £6bn R&D....

Industrial sector mix

[30 industrial sectors] are represented in the UK Scoreboard and 26 in the international Scoreboard.... [Table (c) identifies the top sectors for the UK and internationally].

[Two of the] main conclusions that can be drawn from Table (c) are:

■ UK R&D is dominated by pharmaceuticals and biotechnology and aerospace and defence which together account for over 46% of the total compared to 20% internationally.

■ International R&D on the other hand is dominated by IT hardware, automotive and pharmaceuticals which together account for 58% of the total. IT hardware and automotive comprise 42% of the total compared to 15% for the UK....

Table (d) shows the dominance of the USA in all high R&D sectors except electronics and electrical where Japan is a clear leader. Europe (represented by the three largest countries) is well behind the US in all sectors and also behind Japan in all sectors but software and IT services

Continued

Table (d) Number of companies by country in the five high R&D sectors

Sector	USA	Japan	UK	Germany	France
IT Hardware	83	15	2	0	3
Pharmaceuticals and biotechnology	26	15	5	5	2
Electronics and electrical	13	23	1	2	2
Software and IT services	53 + 2*	0 + 2*	4 + 1*	1	1 + 2*
Health	15	1	2	4	0
Totals	192	56	15	12	10

* Electronic leisure companies classified under leisure are included in software for the purposes of this table

and health. The UK has the largest number of companies in Europe in these five sectors of the international 600.

Questions

1 What are the economic costs and benefits of R&D spending to the national economy? Distinguish between the short and long run.

2 R&D is only one indicator, albeit an important one, of innovation potential. What other factors are likely to affect innovation?

3 What is the economic case for and against government intervention in the field of R&D?

[1] www.innovation.gov.uk/projects/rd_scoreboard/analysis/analysis.htm

firm has not. The free market, therefore, will provide a less than optimal amount of training. The more mobile the labour force, and the more 'transferable' the skills acquired from training, the more likely it is that workers will leave, and the less willing will firms be to invest in training.

In the UK, there is a high level of labour turnover. What is more, wage differentials between skilled and unskilled workers are narrower than in many other countries, and so there is less incentive for workers to train.

How can increased training be achieved? There are three broad approaches:

■ Workers could be encouraged to stay with their employer so that employers would be more willing to invest in training. Externalities would be reduced.

■ The government could provide subsidies for training. Alternatively, the government or some other agency could provide education and training directly.

■ Firms could co-operate to prevent 'poaching' and set up industry-wide training programmes, perhaps in partnership with the government and unions.

Training policy in various countries

As far as the first approach is concerned, most countries have seen a movement towards *greater* labour mobility. The rise in the 'flexible firm' has involved the employment of fewer permanent workers and more part-time and temporary workers. Some countries, such as Japan and Germany, however, have a generally lower rate of labour turnover than most. In Japan, in particular, it is common for workers to stay with one employer throughout their career. There the relationship between employer and employee extends well beyond a simple short-term economic arrangement. Workers give loyalty and commitment to their employer, which in return virtually guarantees long-term employment and provides various fringe benefits (such as housing, child care, holiday schemes and health care). It is not surprising that Japanese firms invest highly in training.

In the USA, labour turnover is very high and yet there is little in the way of industry-wide training. Instead, by having a high percentage of young people in further and higher education, the US government hopes that sufficient numbers and quality of workers are available for industry. Approximately 45 per cent of the US population enters higher education with 33 per cent of the population graduating, and only just over 0.2 per cent of GDP is spent on training.

In Germany the proportion entering higher education is considerably lower (some 28 per cent, with just over 19 per cent of the population graduating), but expenditure on training accounts for nearly 1.6 per cent of GDP. Most young people who do not enter higher education embark on some form of apprenticeship. They attend school for part of the week, and receive work-based training for the rest. The state, unions and employers' associations work closely in determining training provision, and they have developed a set of vocational qualifications based around the apprenticeship system. Given that virtually all firms are involved in training, the 'free-rider' problem of firms poaching labour without themselves paying for training is virtually eliminated. The result is that the German workforce is highly skilled. Many of the skills, however, are highly specific. This is a problem when the demand for particular skills declines.

In the UK, the former Conservative government's attitude toward training was initially influenced by its free-market approach to supply-side policy. Training was to be left largely to employers. However, with growing worries over the UK's 'productivity gap', the government set up Training and Enterprise Councils (TECs) in 1988. The TECs identified regional skills needs, organised training and financed work-based training schemes.

> **Pause for thought**
>
> What advantages and drawbacks are there in leaving training provision to employers? Clue: think about how training provision might be influenced by the business cycle (the cycle of booms and recessions in the economy).

The TECs were replaced in 2001 by the Learning and Skills Council (LSC). This has a budget of some £6 billion and is responsible for planning and funding sixth forms, further education colleges, work-based training for young people aged 16 to 24 ('Modern Apprenticeships'), adult and community learning, the provision of information, advice and guidance for adults and developing links between education and business. Through its 'Connexions service', it offers training and employment advice and support for young people between the ages of 13 and 19.

In 1991 the National Vocational Qualification (NVQ) was launched. Students work for an employer and receive on-the-job training. They also attend college on an occasional basis. The NVQ is awarded when they have achieved sufficient experience. In addition, the government launched General National Vocational Qualifications (GNVQs). These further-education qualifications were aimed to bridge the gap between education and work, by ensuring that education was more work relevant.

The GNVQ system was modelled on that in France, where a clear vocational educational route is seen as the key to reducing skills shortages. At the age of fourteen, French students can choose to pursue academic or vocational education routes. The vocational route provides high-level, broad-based skills (unlike in Germany, where skills tend to be more job specific).

Another approach adopted by the Labour government in the UK has been to encourage 'lifelong learning'. Measures include:

■ A University of Industry, which through its 'Learndirect' brand offers online courses in a range of business, technical and IT subjects.

BOX 21.3

Bridging Europe's skills gap

It seems a strange irony that, with unemployment running at between 8 and 9 per cent within the European Union, the European economy is suffering from an acute labour shortage. In certain sectors, business leaders are claiming that shortages are so severe that business growth and performance are being seriously affected. In the following extract taken from *The Economist* of 29 March 2001, the economic and social consequences of Europe's labour shortage are considered.

All over the continent, there are shortages of qualified workers. Romano Prodi, president of the European Commission, identified a growing skills gap as a priority facing the European Council when it met in Stockholm on March 23rd. The EU, he argued, urgently needs to ease restrictions on labour mobility, particularly in the technology sector, which faces a shortage of up to 1.7 m qualified workers by 2003.

Mr Prodi is far from being the only worried observer of Europe's labour market. Just before the summit, TMP Worldwide, a recruitment agency, surveyed 350 European managers. Almost half of them said that the skills shortage was having severe adverse effects on their business. Four-fifths thought that their problems would worsen over the next year, and that red tape was making it too difficult to hire foreign workers.

The issues over immigrant labour are complex. In the past, most immigrants were temporary workers who entered countries such as France or Spain to do low-paid seasonal work in agriculture. This form of legal migration continues, albeit in gentle decline. But there is a new category: skilled, well-paid workers who fill gaps that locals cannot.

Most obviously, Europe has too few qualified computer engineers, which has sent wages spiralling in that business and caused governments to intervene. Germany, for example, attracted much criticism last August when it announced a special immigration programme for 30 000 computer engineers from India. But that stirred strong complaints from trade unions and became a political issue after opponents branded it discriminatory. As a result, the scheme has been scaled back; by the end of January, fewer than 5000 workers had signed on. Most have come from Eastern Europe, not from India.

Unglamorous industries such as construction and metalworking also face growing staff shortages. In Denmark, for example, around 9000 skilled bricklayers and masons will retire by the end of this decade, but only half that number will finish their apprenticeships and be available to replace them. France lacks workers in activities that range from agriculture to hotel-keeping.

Europe's problem has been caused partly by prosperity. Healthy economies, particularly those such as Ireland's, with fast-growing high-technology industries, have outstripped the local markets' ability to furnish qualified workers. Unqualified workers, by contrast, should be relatively easy to find, given that unemployment in the EU stands at 8.1%, twice as high as in America. But, as people have grown richer, they have become less willing to take manual jobs that are seen as undesirable and undignified, and often pay only the minimum wage. In France, the introduction of a 35-hour working week means that more workers are needed to produce the same economic output, which is aggravating labour shortages.

There are also some structural reasons behind Europe's problems over skilled labour. In many countries, education and training have struggled to adapt to the needs of a changing economy. For example, Germany's demanding and lengthy training courses mean that only a limited number of qualified workers emerge each year. Demand for more flexible courses is growing, but progress has been slow.

- Some 700 information and communication technology (ICT) learning centres, which provide basic IT, literacy and numeracy skills.
- *Work-based Learning for Adults* in England and Wales and *Training for Work* in Scotland: two schemes to provide work-based training for people aged 25 and over who have been out of work for six months or more, with grants paid to employers.

In general, Europeans remain less willing than Americans to move – even within countries, let alone across borders. In Italy, for example, there is persistent high unemployment in the south and a labour squeeze in the north, but southern workers are reluctant to relocate. This has encouraged companies in the prosperous north to fill the gap with immigrants.

Several countries, notably France, remain deeply suspicious of immigration, even when it is clear that it would benefit local companies and not threaten communities. 'With more than 2 m unemployed in France, it is political dynamite to suggest that immigration is the answer to labour shortages,' says a leading commentator. That explains why Medef, France's employers' federation, has no official position on whether immigrant workers should be encouraged.

Jean-Paul Vermes, author of a recent report by the Paris Chamber of Commerce on the recruitment crisis in France, notes that many politicians conflate legal and illegal immigration, producing alarmist statistics about the number of jobs going to foreigners. In fact, he points out, France admits on average only around 20 000 legal immigrant workers each year, one of the smallest totals in Europe. His report made a series of recommendations, including revamping technical and professional training systems, and allowing skilled retirees to re-enter the workforce without losing their pension rights.

Shipping in foreigners

In the short term, however, many companies have no choice but to look around Europe, or farther afield, to find staff. A case in point is Alstom Marine, the shipbuilding arm of France's leading engineering and construction group. In the past three years, it has tripled its business at St Nazaire on the Atlantic coast. By landing a string of contracts for cruise ships, Alstom has put into reverse the long-term decline of France's maritime industry.

French subcontractors have, however, been unable to recruit qualified workers locally, and as much as 70% of each boat is now built by non-French contractors. Welders skilled enough to work on aluminium come from Poland and Sweden, recruited by French companies that can legally employ foreigners provided they pay them above a minimum salary. High-quality electrical engineering and fitting-out work is done by Italians and Swedes. Of Alstom's 13 000 workers at St Nazaire, 5% are non-French. That proportion is expected to rise next year.

Similar stories can be found wherever companies or regions are growing strongly. And as demand for workers increases, companies are putting pressure on governments to become more flexible in their approach to immigration.

A recent report on migration by the OECD noted that there has been a decisive shift towards more temporary migration, particularly related to work. 'All over Europe there are examples of specific exemptions to tough immigration laws being allowed for professions where there are shortages,' says Jean-Pierre Garson, author of the report. He says that Britain has the most innovative approach. For example, it has been prepared to drop eligibility criteria and replace them with fast-track work permits for workers in areas that suffer the worst shortages. Companies such as Alstom will be hoping that this pragmatism spreads. Without it, their ability to grow will be severely hampered.

Questions

1 *What solutions does the article offer to help solve the EU's skills shortage?*

2 *What are the possible social/political implications of such solutions?*

Another measure, launched in England in 2001, was the introduction of two-year foundation degrees. These are offered by universities or higher education colleges. They are designed in conjunction with employers to meet various skill shortages. They are taken at the university or an associated college, normally on a part-time basis and often with work-based study with local employers.

Critics of the UK strategy have argued that employers still face the threat of having newly trained labour poached; that the regional activities of the LSC fail to account for national, long-term training issues; and that NVQs often provide too narrow a form of training. Most importantly, the funding devoted to training is still low compared with most other industrialised countries. They claim that the UK system has the worst features of both the US and the German systems: too little training and too specific training.

SUMMARY

1a Competition policy in most countries recognises that monopolies, mergers and restrictive practices can bring both costs and benefits to the consumer. Generally, though, restrictive practices tend to be more damaging to consumers' interests than simple monopoly power or mergers.

1b European Union legislation applies to firms trading between EU countries. Article 81 applies to restrictive practices. Article 82 applies to dominant firms. There are also separate merger control provisions.

1c UK legislation is largely covered by the 1998 Competition Act and 2002 Enterprise Act. The Chapter I prohibition of the 1998 Act applies to restrictive practices and is similar to Article 81. The Chapter II prohibition applies to dominant firms and is similar to Article 82. The 2002 Act made certain cartel agreements a criminal offence and required mergers over a certain size to be investigated by the Office of Fair Trading with possible reference to the Competition Commission. Both the OFT and CC were made independent of government.

1d The focus of both EU and UK legislation is on anti-competitive practices rather than on the simple existence of agreements between firms or market dominance. Practices that are found after investigation to be detrimental to competition are prohibited and heavy fines can be imposed, even for a first offence.

2a The importance of technology in determining national economic success is growing. There is now a need for government to formulate a technology policy to ensure that the national economy has every chance to remain competitive.

2b Technological change, when left to the market, is unlikely to proceed rapidly enough or to a socially desirable level. Reasons for this include R&TD free riders, monopolistic market structures, duplication of R&TD activities, and risk and uncertainty.

2c Government technology policy might involve intervention at different levels of the technology process (invention, innovation and diffusion). Such intervention might involve extending ownership rights over new products, providing R&TD directly or using subsidies to encourage third parties. Government might also act in an advisory/co-ordinating capacity.

2d Technology policy in the UK has tended to emphasise the market as the principal provider of technological change. Where possible, government's role has been kept to a minimum. Within the EU, policy has been more interventionist and a wide range of initiatives have been launched to encourage greater levels of R&TD.

3a A well-trained workforce contributes to economic performance by enhancing productivity, encouraging and enabling change, and, in respect to supplying scarce skills to the workplace, helps to reduce wage costs.

3b Training policy in the UK has largely been the responsibility of industry. The result has been a less than optimum amount of training. In other countries, such as Germany, the state plays a far greater role in training provision. Since 1979 training and education policy in the UK has become increasingly vocational.

REVIEW QUESTIONS

1   Try to formulate a definition of the public interest.

2   What are the advantages and disadvantages of the current system of controlling restrictive practices?

3   What problems are likely to arise in identifying which firms' practices are anti-competitive? Should the OFT take firms' assurances into account when deciding whether to grant an exemption?

4   If anti-monopoly legislation is effective enough, is there ever any need to prevent mergers from going ahead?

5   If two or more firms were charging similar prices, what types of evidence would you look for to prove that this was collusion rather than mere coincidence?

6   Should governments or regulators always attempt to eliminate the supernormal profits of monopolists/oligopolists?

7   We can distinguish three clear stages in the development and application of technology: invention, innovation and diffusion. How might forms of technology policy intervention change at each stage of this process?

8   Governments and educationalists generally regard it as desirable that trainees acquire transferable skills. Why may many employers disagree?

9   There are externalities (benefits) when employers provide training. What externalities are there from the undergoing of training by the individual? Do they imply that individuals will choose to receive more or less than the socially optimal amount of training?

22 Government and the market

In the previous chapter we considered examples of the relationship between the government and the individual firm. In this chapter we turn to examine government policy at the level of the whole market. Although such policies are generally directed at a whole industry or sector, they nevertheless still affect individual businesses, and indeed the effects may well vary from one firm to another.

22.1 Environmental policy

Growing concerns over acid rain, the depletion of the ozone layer, industrial and domestic waste, traffic fumes and other forms of pollution have made the protection of the environment a major political and economic issue. The subject of environmental deterioration lies clearly within the realm of economics, since it is a direct consequence of production and consumption decisions. So how can economic analysis help us to understand the nature of the problem and contribute to the designing of an effective environmental policy?

The environment and production

In Chapter 20 we considered how pollution could be classified as a 'negative externality' of production or consumption. In the case of production, this means that the marginal social costs (*MSC*) are greater than the marginal private costs (*MC*) to the polluter. The failure of the market system to equate *MSC* and marginal social benefit (*MSB*) is due to the lack of property rights of those suffering the pollution. The fact that no charge is levied on the producer for use of the air or rivers means that the environment is effectively a free good, and as such is overused.

Key Idea 27 p402

Key Idea 25 p402

In order to ensure that the environment is taken sufficiently into account by both firms and consumers, the government must intervene. It must devise an appropriate **environmental policy**. Such a policy will involve measures to ensure that at least a specified minimum level of environmental quality is achieved. Ideally, however, the policy would ensure that all externalities are fully 'internalised'. This means that firms and consumers are forced to pay the *full* costs of production or consumption: i.e. their marginal private costs *plus* any external costs.

Problems with policy intervention

definition

Environmental policy
Initiatives by government to ensure a specified minimum level of environmental quality.

Valuing the environment

The principal difficulty facing government in constructing its environmental policy is that of *valuing* the environment and hence of estimating the costs of its pollution. If policy is based upon the principle that the polluter pays, then an accurate assessment of pollution costs is vital if the policy is to establish a socially efficient level of production.

Three common methods used for valuing environmental damage are: the financial costs to *other* users; revealed preferences; and 'contingent valuation' (or stated preference).

The financial costs to other users. In this method, environmental costs are calculated by considering the financial costs imposed on other businesses or individuals by polluting activities. For example, if firm A feeds chemical waste into a local stream, then firm B, which is downstream and requires a clean water supply, may have to introduce a water purification process. The expense of this to firm B can be seen as an external cost of firm A.

The main problem with this method is that not all external costs entail a direct financial cost for the sufferers. Many external costs may therefore be overlooked.

Revealed preferences. If the direct financial costs of pollution are difficult to identify, let alone calculate, then an alternative approach to valuing the environment might be to consider how individuals or businesses change their *behaviour* in response to environmental changes. Such changes in behaviour frequently carry a financial cost, which makes calculation easier. For example, the building of a new superstore on a greenfield site overlooked by your house might cause you to move. Moving house entails a financial cost, including the loss in value of your property resulting from the opening of the store. Clearly, in such a case, by choosing to move you would be regarding the cost of moving to be less than the cost to you of the deterioration in your environment.

Contingency valuation. In this method, people likely to be affected are asked to evaluate the effect on them of any proposed change to their environment. In the case of the superstore, local residents might be asked how much they would be willing to pay in order for the development not to take place, or alternatively, how much they would need to be compensated if it were to take place.

The principal concern with this method is how reliable the answers are to the questionnaires. There are two major problems:

- Ignorance. People will not know just how much they will suffer *until* the project goes ahead.
- Dishonesty. People will tend to exaggerate the compensation they would need. After all, if compensation is actually going to be paid, people will want to get as much as possible. But even if it is not, the more people exaggerate the costs to them, the more likely it is that they can get the project stopped.

These problems can be lessened if people are questioned who have already experienced a similar project elsewhere. They are more knowledgeable and have less to gain from being dishonest.

Research on contingency valuation has focused heavily on the questioning process and how monetary values of costs and benefits might be accurately established. Of all the methods, contingency valuation has grown most in popularity over recent years, despite its limitations.

Other problems

As well as the problems of value, other aspects of environmental damage make policy making particularly difficult. These include the following:

■ Spatial issues. The place where pollution is produced and the places where it is deposited may be geographically very far apart. Pollution crosses borders (e.g. acid rain) or can be global (e.g. greenhouse gases). In both cases, national policies might be of little value, especially if you are a receiver of others' pollution! In such circumstances, international agreements would be needed, and these can be very difficult to reach.

■ Temporal issues. Environmental problems such as acid rain and the depletion of the ozone layer have been occurring over many decades. Thus the full effect of pollution on the environment may be identifiable only in the long term. As a consequence, policy initiatives are required to be forward looking and pro-active, if the cumulative effects of pollution are to be avoided. Most policy tends to be *reactive*, however, dealing only with problems as they arise. In such cases, damage to the environment may have already been done.

■ Irreversibility issues. Much environmental damage might be irreversible: once a species is extinct, for example, it cannot be reintroduced.

Environmental policy options

Environmental policy can take many forms. However, it is useful to put the different types of policy into three broad categories: market based, non-market based, and mixed. The most important market-based solution is to use taxes and subsidies. Non-market-based solutions usually involve imposing regulations and controls. The most important mixed system is that of tradable permits. Let us examine each of these three categories in turn.

Key Idea
30
p410

Market-based environmental policy: taxation

Market-based solutions attempt to internalise the costs of the externality, and ensure that the polluter pays. The most common market-based approach to environmental policy is to impose indirect taxes on specific types of polluting activity, such as the use of carbon-based fuels. To achieve a socially efficient output, the rate of tax should be equal to the marginal external cost (see Figure 20.5 on page 410).

Taxes have the advantage of relating the size of the penalty to the amount of pollution. This means that there is continuous pressure to cut down on production or consumption of polluting products or activities in order to save tax.

One approach is to modify *existing* taxes. In most developed countries there are now higher taxes on leaded than unleaded petrol, and lower taxes on low-emission cars. Tax regimes can also be modified which currently *encourage* environmental degradation. For example, lower taxes on diesel could be abolished (given the higher pollution from diesel engines), as could tax relief for commuting expenses. Tax benefits which encourage the use of fertilisers and pesticides in farming, or the felling of trees or hedgerows, could also be abolished.

Increasingly, however, countries are introducing *new* 'green' taxes in order to discourage pollution as goods are produced, consumed or disposed of. Table 22.1 shows the wide range of green taxes and charges used around the world and Figure 22.1 shows green tax revenues as a percentage of GDP in

Table 22.1 Types of environmental taxes and charges

Motor fuels
Leaded/unleaded
Diesel (quality differential)
Carbon/energy taxation
Sulphur tax

Other energy products
Carbon/energy tax
Sulphur tax or charge
NO_2 charge
Methane charge

Agricultural inputs
Fertilisers
Pesticides
Manure

Vehicle-related taxation
Sales tax depends on car size
Road tax depends on car size

Other goods
Batteries
Plastic carrier bags
Glass containers
Drink cans
Tyres
CFCs/halons
Disposable razors/cameras
Lubricant oil charge
Oil pollutant charge
Solvents

Waste disposal
Municipal waste charges
Waste-disposal charges
Hazardous waste charges
Landfill tax or charges
Duties on waste water

Air transport
Noise charges
Aviation fuels

Water
Water charges
Sewage charges
Water effluent charges
Manure charges

Direct tax provisions
Tax relief on green investment
Taxation on free company cars
Employer-paid commuting
  expenses taxable
Employer-paid parking
  expenses taxable
Commuter use of public
  transport tax deductible

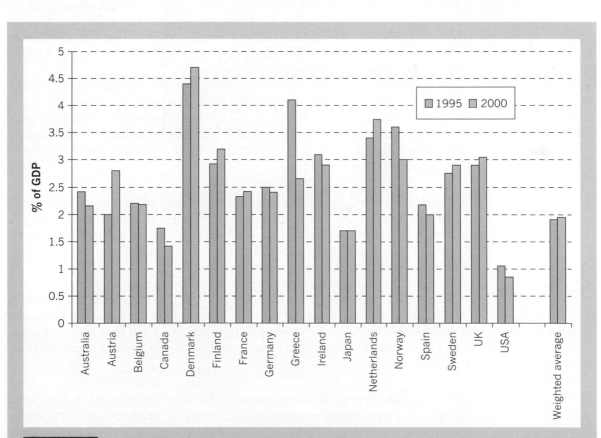

Figure 22.1 Green tax revenues as a percentage of GDP

Source: Based on figures in *Environmentally related taxes database* (OECD, 2003) various countries. As you can see, they are higher than average in Scandinavian countries, reflecting the strength of their environmental concerns. They are lowest in the USA. By far the largest green tax revenues come from fuel taxes. Fuel taxes are relatively high in the UK and so, therefore, are green tax revenues.

There are various problems with using the tax weapon in the fight against pollution.

Conflicts with revenue objectives. The more successful a tax is in reducing consumption, the less revenue it will earn for the government. (This is a problem that governments have experienced for years in the use of taxes on tobacco.) In Denmark, where energy used in households has been taxed at higher rates than in most other countries, energy consumption fell by 25 per cent between 1973 and 1989. In Sweden, a sulphur tax reduced the sulphur content of fuel oils by 40 per cent between 1990 and 1992. Clearly, reduced consumption reduces the tax revenue.

But the revenue will still be more than if no tax had been imposed! Provided green taxes are imposed on a wide range of products and at high enough rates, their revenue-earning potential can be considerable. After all, the aim is not to reduce the consumption of energy and many other potentially polluting activities to zero. If it were, it would be simplest just to ban the activity.

Redistributive effects. The poor spend a higher proportion of their income on domestic fuel than the rich. A 'carbon tax' on such fuel will, therefore, have the effect of redistributing incomes away from the poor. The poor also spend a larger proportion of their income on food than do the rich. Taxes on agriculture, designed to reduce intensive use of fertilisers and pesticides, will again tend to hit the poor proportionately more than the rich.

However, not all green taxes are regressive. The rich spend a higher proportion of their income on motoring than the poor. Thus petrol and other motoring taxes could have a progressive effect. Also, other taxes, such as those on packaging, batteries and disposable items, are likely to be neutral in their impact, since their prime purpose is to encourage people to switch to non-polluting alternatives.

Problems with international trade. If a country imposes pollution taxes on its industries, its products will become less competitive in world trade. To compensate for this, the industries may need to be given tax rebates for exports. Also taxes would need to be imposed on imports of competitors' products from countries where there is no equivalent green tax.

Evidence on the adverse effect of environmental taxes on a country's exports is inconclusive, however. Over the long term, in countries with high environmental taxes (or other tough environmental measures), firms will be stimulated to invest in low-pollution processes and products. This will later give such countries a competitive advantage if *other* countries then impose tougher environmental standards.

Effects on employment. Reduced output in the industries affected by green taxes will lead to a reduction in employment. If, however, the effect was to encourage investment in new cleaner technology, employment might not fall. Furthermore, employment opportunities could be generated elsewhere if the extra revenues from the green taxes were spent on alternative products, such as buses and trains rather than cars.

Non-market-based environmental policy: command-and-control systems (laws and regulations)

The traditional way of tackling pollution has been to set maximum permitted levels of emission or resource use, or minimum acceptable levels of environmental quality, and then to fine firms contravening these limits. Measures of this type are known as **command-and-control (CAC) systems**. Clearly, there have to be inspectors to monitor the amount of pollution, and the fines have to be large enough to deter firms from exceeding the limit.

Virtually all countries have environmental regulations of one sort or another. For example, the EU has over 200 items of legislation covering areas such as air and water pollution, noise, the marketing and use of dangerous chemicals, waste management, the environmental impacts of new projects (such as power stations, roads and quarries), recycling, depletion of the ozone layer and global warming.

Typically there are three approaches to devising CAC systems.[1]

■ **Technology-based standards** The focus could be on the amount of pollution generated, irrespective of its environmental impact. As technology for reducing pollutants improves, so tougher standards could be imposed, based on the 'best available technology' (as long as the cost was not excessive). Thus car manufacturers could be required to ensure that new car engines meet lower CO_2 emission levels as the technology enabled them to do so.

■ **Ambient-based standards**. Here the focus is on the environmental impact. For example, standards could be set for air or water purity. Depending on the location and the number of polluters in that area, a given standard would be achieved with different levels of discharge. If the object is a cleaner environment, then this approach is more efficient than technology-based standards.

■ **Social-impact standards**. Here the focus is on the effect on people. Thus tougher standards would be imposed in densely populated areas. Whether this approach is more efficient than that of ambient-based standards depends on the approach to sustainability. If the objective is to achieve social efficiency, then human-impact standards are preferable. If the objective is to protect the environment for its own sake (a 'deeper green' approach), then ambient standards would be preferable.

Assessing CAC systems. Given the uncertainty over the environmental impacts of pollutants, especially over the longer term, it is often better to play safe and set tough emissions or ambient standards. These could always be relaxed at a later stage if the effects turn out not to be so damaging, but it might be too late to reverse damage if the effects turn out to be more serious. Taxes may be a more sophisticated means of reaching a socially efficient output, but CAC methods are usually more straightforward to devise, easier to understand by firms and easier to implement. Also, setting standards is more in accordance with the pro-environment ethic of many environmental pressure groups, such as Greenpeace and Friends of the Earth. Using taxes, by contrast, focuses on the effects on people rather than the environment itself.

Where command-and-control systems are weak is that they fail to offer business any incentive to do better than the legally specified level. By contrast, with a pollution tax, the lower the pollution level, the less tax there will be to pay. There is thus a continuing incentive for businesses progressively to cut pollution levels and introduce cleaner technology.

> **definition**
> **Command-and-control (CAC) systems**
> The use of laws or regulations backed up by inspections and penalties (such as fines) for non-compliance.

> **definition**
> **Technology-based standards**
> Pollution control that requires firms' emissions to reflect the levels that could be achieved from using the best available pollution control technology.

> **definition**
> **Ambient-based standards**
> Pollution control that requires firms to meet minimum standards for the environment (e.g. air or water quality).

> **definition**
> **Social-impact standards**
> Pollution control that focuses on the effects on people (e.g. on health or happiness).

---

[1] See R. K. Turner, D. Pearce and I. Bateman, *Environmental Economics* (Harvester Wheatsheaf, 1994), page 198.

BOX 22.1

Selling the environment
The market-led solution of the Kyoto Protocol

In its *Climate Change 2001* report, the United Nations Intergovernmental Panel on Climate Change stated that even if every factory was to close immediately, carbon dioxide (CO_2) levels would continue to rise and reach 450 parts per million by 2050. This compares with the current figure of 366 parts per million. To do nothing, the report estimates, would result in CO_2 levels reaching 550 parts per million – double the level that existed prior to the industrial revolution. World temperature will, by this time, have increased by 1.4 degrees centigrade and the global climate will have changed beyond belief. The panel paints an apocalyptic picture of biblical-scale floods and unpredictable weather, with all countries and continents affected.

Given that no one is likely to be spared from this nightmare vision of the future, one would expect a degree of unanimity between all countries and corporations. Global warming does not respect or discriminate between national or commercial boundaries. It should be clearly in the interest of all that this global problem is resolved to the best of our ability. But how? It is this question that has brought recent environmental talks to the point of collapse.

The Kyoto Protocol

The 1997 Kyoto Protocol established a set of legally binding agreements to reduce greenhouse gases by an average of 5.2 per cent (based on 1990 levels) by the year 2012. Although scientists and environmentalists decried the 5.2 per cent as pitiful, the agreement was something of a landmark. It was not only a recognition that something needed to be done to control the growth in CO_2 emissions, but also a global agreement – something which is at the best of times difficult to negotiate. How was the agreement to work?

The agreement, although not originally envisaged in this way, involves the climate being turned into a market, where the right to pollute can be bought and sold through a system of emission credits. These credits can be earned by reducing emission levels below those agreed or by creating conditions which help to minimise the impact of CO_2 on global warming, for example by the planting of a forest. The Kyoto Protocol is composed of three distinct market-based solutions:

- emissions trading;
- joint implementation;
- Clean Development Mechanism (CDM).

Emissions trading. The 39 countries signed-up to the Kyoto protocol will, by 2008, be allowed to trade amongst themselves rights to pollute. If a country reduces emissions below its agreed limit it will be able to sell the additional reduction as a credit. So if a country is finding it difficult to cut CO_2 emissions, it will be able to buy these carbon credits within some kind of marketplace.

Joint implementation. Here a country will be able to earn credits, in effect reducing its need to cut carbon dioxide elsewhere, by setting up special projects with business aimed at reducing emissions. For example, the planting of forests, which reduce CO_2 in the atmosphere and thereby act as a 'carbon sink', would attract a carbon dioxide credit.

Clean Development Mechanism. This is similar to the joint implementation process above; only in this case the agreement to earn credit is between one industrial government or corporation and one Southern country. So a Northern industrial country or corporation might find it less expensive to invest in emission reductions projects abroad rather than at home. Supporters of this solution argue that it leads not only to a reduction in CO_2 but also to a transfer of clean technology from the North to the South. For example,

> A typical CDM project could be the Dutch government financing a factory producing energy-efficient light bulbs in Russia, or BP Amoco installing solar panels in Zimbabwe.[1]

The use of such strategies enables companies to buy the right to pollute. But is this a problem? If total emissions are falling in line with any agreement, irrespective of by whom or geography, what is wrong with such a market-driven solution?

Critics argue that, as in other environmental cases, the market is not the whole solution. They suggest that the Kyoto Protocol as it currently stands would:

- have little or no impact upon emissions;
- lead to greater inequality between North and South;
- have negative social and environmental impacts.

Assessing the Kyoto Protocol

Emission levels are likely to remain unchanged for a number of reasons.

Business will, rather than cutting carbon dioxide production, attempt to earn credits elsewhere, i.e. by investing in carbon sinks or by buying credits offered for sale on the open market, many of which, initially, will not be earned from bettering carbon dioxide targets. For example Russia has CO_2 emissions 45 per cent below its 1990 level and as such has a massive emission credit. However, such credit is not the result of Russian environmental policy but rather the consequence of the collapse and closure of Russian industry! The EU has consistently argued that, to ensure some real gains are made, no more than 50 per cent of the emissions reduction should be achieved through these market-based mechanisms.

The USA, by contrast, sought an unlimited use of the market-based mechanisms to meet CO_2 emissions targets. It has been suggested that, if there were an unlimited use of carbon sinks in the Kyoto agreement, Northern countries would be able to emit 12.5 per cent more carbon dioxide than is permitted within the treaty.

Critics also argue that Southern countries, in need of hard currency, will sell their emission credits cheaply and simply receive investment for emission-credit-generating projects, potentially restraining development and creating problems in place of global warming.

Once again, on this point, the EU and USA had very different positions. The EU has argued that CDM should be limited to sound technologies, e.g. renewable energy. The USA insisted that it should include all technologies that impact upon CO_2 emissions.

George W. Bush and the Kyoto Protocol

The differences in position on the operation of the Kyoto Protocol between the USA and Europe ceased to be an issue in early 2001 when George Bush announced that the USA was withdrawing from the agreement. The EU has insisted that it is pressing ahead with the agreed reductions in CO_2 emissions and hoped other nations will follow suit.

Then in November 2001 at the climate summit in Marrakesh, 165 nations agreed to the Kyoto Protocol, despite the absence of the USA. There would be an enforcement system with international observers if countries failed to met their targets.

So did the Bush administration take any measures to cut greenhouse gases? In its 'clear skies and global climate change initiative', launched in February 2002, the USA stated its aim was to cut the growth in greenhouse gas emissions relative to the growth in the economy. There would be tax incentives to encourage renewable energy schemes and fuel efficiency schemes, but corporations would not be obliged to meet any CO_2 targets. But the effect would still be one of a *growth* in greenhouse gases. By 2012, US CO_2 emissions would be some 25 per cent above 1990 levels: not the 7 per cent below that the Clinton administration had agreed at Kyoto in 1997.

Question

Explain who are likely to be the 'winners' and 'losers' as a result of recent talks on carbon dioxide emissions. Use the concepts of game theory to illustrate your argument.

---

[1] *Greenhouse Market Mania* (Corporate Europe Observatory, November 2000)

Tradable permits

A policy measure that has grown in popularity in recent years is that of **tradable permits**. This is a combination of command-and-control and market-based systems. A maximum permitted level of emission is set for a given pollutant for a given factory, and the firm is given a permit to emit up to this amount. If it emits less than this amount, it is given a credit for the difference, which it can then use in another of its factories, or sell to another firm, to enable it to go that amount *over* its permitted level. Thus the overall level of emissions is set by CAC methods, whereas their distribution is determined by the market.

Take the example of firms A and B, which are currently producing 12 units of a pollutant each. Now assume that a standard is set permitting them to produce only 10 units each. If firm A managed to reduce the pollutant to 8 units, it would be given a credit for 2 units. It could then sell this to firm B, enabling B to continue emitting 12 units. The effect would still be a total reduction of 4 units between the two firms. However, by allowing them to trade in pollution permits, pollution reduction can be concentrated in the firms where it can be achieved at lowest cost. In our example, if it cost firm B more to reduce its pollution than firm A, then the permits could be sold from A to B at a price that was profitable to both (i.e. at a price above the cost of emission reduction to A, but below the cost of emission reduction to B). Given the resulting reduced cost of pollution control, it might be politically easier to impose tougher standards (i.e. impose lower permitted levels of emission).

> **Pause for thought**
>
> To what extent will the introduction of tradable permits lead to a lower level of total pollution (as opposed to its redistribution)?

The principle of tradable permits can be used as the basis of international agreements on pollution reduction. Each country could be required to achieve a certain percentage reduction in a pollutant (e.g. CO_2 or SO_2), but any country exceeding its reduction could sell its right to these emissions to other (presumably richer) countries (see Box 22.1).

A similar principle can be used for using natural resources. Thus fish quotas could be assigned to fishing boats or fleets or countries. Any parts of these quotas not used could then be sold.

Assessing the system of tradable permits. The main advantage of tradable permits is that they combine the simplicity of CAC methods with the benefits of achieving pollution reduction in the most efficient way. The government can simply set the total amount of permitted discharge according to the ability of the environment to absorb the pollutants; and it can do this without any knowledge of the specific costs and benefits of individual firms. This is the main benefit of CAC methods over taxes and charges. Then it can let the market in tradable permits allocate the reduction in pollution to where it can be achieved at least cost (the same effect as with taxes).

How are the permitted levels to be decided? The way that seems to be the most acceptable is to base them on firms' *current* levels, with any subsequent reduction in total permitted pollution being achieved by requiring firms to reduce their emissions by the *same* percentage. This approach is known as **grandfathering**. The main problem with this approach is that it could be seen as unfair by those firms that are already using cleaner technology. Why should they be required to make the same reductions as firms using dirty technology?

There are other more general problems with tradable permits. One is the possibility that trade will lead to pollution being concentrated in certain geographical areas. Another is that it may reduce the pressure on dirtier factories (or countries) to cut their emissions. An example of this problem is the approach of the USA at international climate conferences, such as that at Buenos Aires in 1998. The USA has advocated an international tradable permits system to allow it to buy up other countries' rights to pollute, and thereby avoiding having to cut pollution itself.

Pause for thought

What determines the size of the administrative costs of a system of tradable permits? For what reasons might green taxes be cheaper to administer than a system of tradable permits?

Environmental policy in the UK and EU

In the UK, current policy is embodied in the 1990 Environmental Protection Act. The Act was an attempt to establish an integrated pollution control strategy. This has been the approach in other European countries. In Holland, for example, the first National Environmental Plan was put in place in 1989. Its aim was to establish a series of targets for improving environmental quality. Such goals and targets were then incorporated into government policies and initiatives throughout the economy.

National strategies in European countries to tackle pollution and improve the environment are being increasingly determined by decisions within the EU. It is hoped that eventually there will be a Europe-wide pollution strategy with its own regulatory and enforcement body. In its environmental strategy document, *Environment 2010: Our Future, Our Choice*, the European Commission has identified four major areas for action: climate change, health and the environment, nature and bio-diversity and natural resource management.

Transport policy   22.2

Traffic congestion is a problem that faces all countries, especially in the large cities and at certain peak times: a problem that has grown at an alarming rate as our lives have become increasingly dominated by the motor car. Sitting in a traffic jam is both time wasting and frustrating. It adds considerably to the costs and stress of modern living.

And it is not only the motorist that suffers. Congested streets make life less pleasant for the pedestrian, and increased traffic leads to increased accidents. What is more, the inexorable growth of traffic has led to significant problems of pollution. Traffic is noisy and car fumes are unpleasant and lead to substantial environmental damage. It is true that the move to unleaded petrol has reduced the problem of lead pollution, but the growing emissions of carbon dioxide and nitrogen dioxide have aggravated the problem of global warming and acid rain.

Between 1970 and 2000 road traffic in Great Britain rose by 133 per cent, whereas the length of public roads rose by only 21 per cent (albeit some roads were widened). Most passenger and freight transport is by road. In 2000, 92 per cent of passenger kilometres and 64 per cent of freight tonnage in Great Britain were by road, whereas rail accounted for a mere 6 per cent of passenger traffic and 7 per cent of freight tonnage. Of road passenger kilometres, over 92 per cent was by car in 2000, and, as Table 22.2 shows, this proportion has been growing. Motoring costs now amount to over 15 per cent of household expenditure.

But should the government do anything about the problem? Is traffic congestion a price worth paying for the benefits we gain from using cars? Or are there things that can be done to ease the problem without greatly inconveniencing the traveller? And if something is to be done, should the government seek to extend

Table 22.2		Passenger transport in Great Britain: percentage of passenger kilometres by road		
Year	**Cars**	**Motor cycles**	**Buses and coaches**	**Bicycles**
1960	57.6	4.6	32.8	5.0
1970	81.4	1.1	16.4	1.1
1980	85.0	1.8	11.5	1.1
1990	91.2	0.9	7.1	0.8
2000	92.0	0.7	6.7	0.6

Source: *Annual Abstract of Statistics* (National Statistics, various years)

the role of the market (e.g. by encouraging the building of private toll roads) or merely to amend market forces (e.g. by subsidising public transport) or should it seek to replace the market (e.g. by banning cars in certain areas)?

The existing system of allocating road space

The allocation of road space depends on both demand and supply. Demand is by individuals who base their decisions on largely private considerations. Supply, by contrast, is usually by the central government or local authorities. Let us examine each in turn.

Demand for road space (by car users)

The demand for road space can be seen largely as a *derived* demand. What people want is not the car journey for its own sake, but to get to their destination. The greater the benefit they gain at their destination, the greater the benefit they gain from using their car to get there.

The demand for road space, like the demand for other goods and services, has a number of determinants. If congestion is to be reduced, it is important to know how responsive demand is to a change in any of these: it is important to consider the various elasticities of demand.

Price. This is the *marginal cost* to the motorist of a journey. It includes petrol, oil, maintenance, depreciation and any toll charges.

The price elasticity of demand for motoring tends to be relatively low. There can be a substantial rise in the price of petrol, for example, and there will be only a modest fall in traffic. After the 1973/4 oil crisis, the price of petrol doubled, but traffic in London fell by only 4 per cent.

The low price elasticity of demand suggests that any schemes to tackle traffic congestion that merely involve raising the costs of motoring will have only limited success.

Income. The demand for road space also depends on people's income. As incomes rise, so car ownership and hence car usage increase substantially. Demand is elastic with respect to income. Figure 22.2 shows the increase in car ownership in various countries.

Price of substitutes. If bus and train fares came down, people might switch from travelling by car. The cross-price elasticity is likely to be relatively low, however,

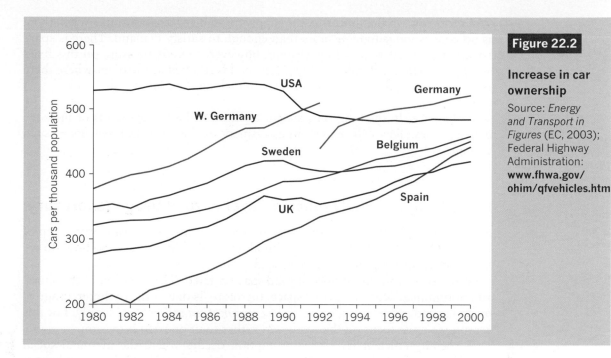

Figure 22.2

Increase in car ownership

Source: *Energy and Transport in Figures* (EC, 2003); Federal Highway Administration: **www.fhwa.gov/ohim/qfvehicles.htm**

given that most people regard these alternatives as a poor substitute for travelling in their own car. Cars are seen as more comfortable and convenient.

Price of complements. Demand for road space will depend on the price of cars. The higher the price of cars, the fewer people will own cars and thus the fewer will be the cars on the road.

Demand will also depend on the price of complementary services, such as parking. A rise in car parking charges will reduce the demand for car journeys. But here again the cross elasticity is likely to be relatively low. In most cases, the motorist will either pay the higher charge or park elsewhere, such as in side streets.

> **Pause for thought**
>
> *Go through each of the determinants we have identified so far and show how the respective elasticity of demand makes the problem of traffic congestion difficult to tackle.*

Tastes/utility. Another factor explaining the preference of many people for travelling by car is the pleasure they gain from it compared with alternative modes of transport. Car ownership is regarded by many people as highly desirable, and once accustomed to travelling in their own car, most people are highly reluctant to give it up.

One important feature of the demand for road space is that it fluctuates. There will be periods of peak demand, such as during the rush hour or at holiday weekends. At such times, roads can get totally jammed. At other times, however, the same roads may be virtually empty. The problem is that supply cannot fluctuate to match demand. Empty road space available in the middle of the night cannot be 'stored' and then transferred as additional space during periods of peak demand!

Supply of road space

The supply of road space can be examined in two contexts: the short run and the long run.

The short run. In the short run, the supply of road space is constant. When there is no congestion, supply is more than enough to satisfy demand. There is spare road capacity. At times of congestion, however, there is pressure on this fixed supply. Maximum supply for any given road is reached at the point where there is the maximum flow of vehicles per minute along the road.

The long run. In the long run, the authorities can build new roads or improve existing ones. This will require an assessment of the costs and benefits of such schemes.

Identifying a socially efficient level of road usage (short run)

The existing system of *government* provision of roads and *private* ownership of cars is unlikely to lead to an optimum allocation of road space. So how do we set about identifying just what the social optimum is?

In the short run, the supply of road space is fixed. The question of the short-run optimum allocation of road space, therefore, is one of the optimum usage of existing road space. It is a question of *consumption* rather than supply. For this reason we must focus on the road user, rather than on road provision.

A socially efficient level of consumption occurs where the marginal social benefit of consumption equals its marginal social cost ($MSB = MSC$). So what are the marginal social benefits and costs of using a car?

Key Idea
24
p401

Marginal social benefit of road usage

Marginal social benefit equals marginal private benefit plus externalities.

Marginal private benefit is the direct benefit to the car user and is reflected in the demand for car journeys, the determinants of which we examined above. For example, the benefit from using your car depends on its relative comfort and convenience compared with alternative modes of transport.

External benefits are few. The one major exception occurs when drivers give lifts to other people.

Marginal social cost of road usage

Marginal social cost equals marginal private cost plus externalities.

Marginal private costs to the motorist were identified when we looked at demand. They include the costs of petrol, wear and tear, and tolls. They also include the time costs of travel.

There may also be substantial external costs. These include the following.

Key Idea
27
p402

Congestion costs: time. When a person uses a car on a congested road, it will add to the congestion. This will therefore slow down the traffic even more and increase the journey time of *other* car users.

Congestion costs: monetary. Congestion increases fuel consumption, and the stopping and starting increases the costs of wear and tear. So when a motorist adds to congestion, there will be additional monetary costs imposed on other motorists.

Environmental costs. When motorists use a road, they reduce the quality of the environment for others. Cars emit fumes and create noise. This is bad enough for pedestrians and other car users, but can be particularly distressing for people

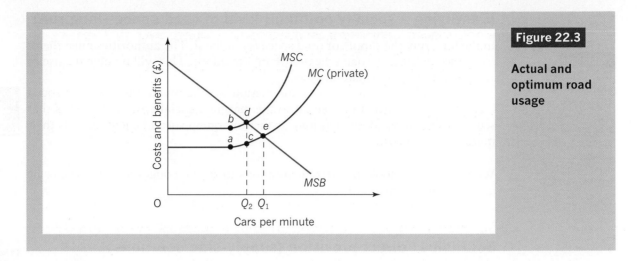

Figure 22.3

Actual and optimum road usage

living along the road. Driving can cause accidents, a problem that increases as drivers become more impatient as a result of delays.

The socially efficient level of road usage

The optimum level of road use is where the marginal social benefit is equal to the marginal social cost. In Figure 22.3 costs and benefits are shown on the vertical axis and are measured in money terms. Thus any non-monetary costs or benefits (such as time costs) must be given a monetary value. The horizontal axis measures road usage in terms of cars per minute passing a specified point on the road.

For simplicity it is assumed that there are no external benefits from car use and that therefore marginal private and marginal social benefits are the same. The MSB curve is shown as downward sloping. The reason for this is that different road users put a different value on this particular journey. If the marginal (private) cost of making the journey were high, only those for whom the journey had a high marginal benefit would travel along the road. If the marginal cost of making the journey fell, more people would make the journey: people would choose to make the journey at the point at which the marginal cost of using their car had fallen to the level of their marginal benefit. Thus the greater the number of cars, the lower the marginal benefit.

The marginal (private) cost curve (MC) is likely to be constant up to the level of traffic flow at which congestion begins to occur. This is shown as point a in Figure 22.3. Beyond this point, marginal cost is likely to rise as time costs increase and as fuel consumption rises.

The marginal *social* cost curve (MSC) is drawn above the marginal private cost curve. The vertical difference between the two represents the external costs. Up to point b, external costs are simply the environmental costs. Beyond point b, there are also external congestion costs, since additional road users slow down the journey of *other* road users. These external costs get progressively greater as the level of traffic increases.

The actual level of traffic flow will be at Q_1, where marginal private costs and benefits are equal (point e). The socially efficient level of traffic flow, however, will be at the lower level of Q_2, where marginal social costs and benefits are equal (point d). In other words, the existing system of allocating road space is likely to lead to an excessive level of road usage.

Identifying a socially optimum level of road space (long run)

In the long run, the supply of road space is not fixed. The authorities must therefore assess what new road schemes (if any) to adopt. This will involve the use of some form of **cost–benefit analysis**.

The socially efficient level of construction will be where the marginal social benefit from construction is equal to the marginal social cost. This means that schemes should be adopted as long as their marginal social benefit exceeds their marginal social cost.

We now turn to look at different solutions to traffic congestion. These can be grouped into three broad types.

Solution 1: direct provision (supply-side solutions)

The road solution

One obvious solution to traffic congestion is to build more roads. At first sight this may seem an optimum strategy, provided the costs and benefits of road-building schemes are carefully assessed and only those schemes are adopted where the benefits exceed the costs.

However, there are serious problems with this approach.

The objective of equity. The first problem concerns that of *equity*. After all, social efficiency is not the only possible economic objective. For example, when an urban motorway is built, those living beside it will suffer from noise and fumes. Motorway users gain, but the local residents lose. The question is whether this is fair.

The more the government tries to appeal to the car user by building more and better roads, the fewer will be the people who use public transport, and thus the more will public transport decline. Those without cars lose, and these tend to be from the most vulnerable groups – the poor, the elderly, children and the disabled.

Congestion may not be solved. Increasing the amount of road space may encourage more people to use cars. Apart from the adverse effects of this on the profitability of public transport, it may mean that the problem of congestion persists. The government's forecasts have often underestimated the growth in traffic on new or improved roads.

Thus new roads may simply generate extra traffic, with little overall effect on congestion.

The environmental impact of new roads. New roads lead to loss of agricultural land, the destruction of many natural habitats, noise, the splitting of communities and disruption to local residents. To the extent that they encourage a growth in traffic, they add to atmospheric pollution and a depletion of oil reserves.

Government or local authority provision of public transport

An alternative supply-side solution is to increase the provision of public transport. If, for example, a local authority ran a local bus service and decided to invest in additional buses, open up new routes and operate a low-fare policy, these services might encourage people to switch from using their cars.

Solution 2: regulation and legislation

An alternative strategy is to restrict car use by various forms of regulation and legislation.

Restricting car access

One approach involves reducing car access to areas that are subject to high levels of congestion. The following three measures are widely used:

- Bus and cycle lanes.
- No entry to side streets.
- Pedestrian-only areas.

However, there is a serious problem with these measures. They tend not to solve the problem of congestion, but merely to divert it. Bus lanes tend to make the car lanes more congested; no entry to side streets tends to make the main roads more congested; and pedestrian-only areas often make the roads round these areas more congested.

Parking restrictions

An alternative to restricting road access is to restrict parking. If cars are not allowed to park along congested streets, this will improve the traffic flow. Also, if parking is difficult, this will discourage people from using their cars to come into city centres.

The problems with this solution include the following:

- Possibly *increased* congestion as people drive round and round looking for parking spaces.
- Illegal parking.
- Parking down side streets, causing a nuisance for local residents.

Solution 3: changing market signals

The solution favoured by many economists is to use the price mechanism. As we have seen, one of the causes of traffic congestion is that road users do not pay the full marginal social costs of using the roads. If they could be forced to do so, a social optimum usage of road space could be achieved.

So how can these external costs be charged to the motorist? There are several possible ways.

Extending existing taxes

Three major types of tax are levied on the motorist: fuel tax, taxes on new cars and car licences. Could increasing these taxes lead to the optimum level of road use being achieved?

Increasing the rates of new car tax and car licences may have some effect on reducing the total level of car ownership, but will probably have little effect on car use. The problem is that these taxes do not increase the marginal cost of car use. They are fixed costs. Once you have paid these taxes, there is no extra to pay for each extra journey you make. They do not discourage you from using your car.

Unlike the other two, fuel taxes are a marginal cost of car use. The more you use your car, the more fuel you use and the more fuel tax you pay. They are

BOX 22.2

Road pricing in Singapore
Part of an integrated transport policy

It takes only one hour to drive from one end of Singapore to the other. Yet the average Singaporean driver travels an estimated 18 600 km per year, more than the average US driver, and over 50 per cent more than the average Japanese driver. In Singapore in 2003 there were a little over 400 000 cars, giving a vehicle density of 225 motor vehicles per kilometre of road. This compares with a vehicle density in the USA of only 27 motor vehicles per kilometre. It is hardly surprising that traffic congestion has become a major focus of public debate, particularly as the demand for cars is set to increase as consumer affluence grows.

In contrast to its neighbours, many of which are suffering more acute urban traffic congestion problems, Singapore has an integrated transport policy. This includes the following:

■ Restricting the number of new car licences, and allowing their price to rise to the corresponding equilibrium. This makes cars in Singapore among the most expensive in the world.

■ A 111-kilometre long mass rail transit (MRT) system with subsidised fares. Trains are comfortable, clean and frequent. Stations are air-conditioned.

■ A programme of building new estates near MRT stations.

■ Cheap, frequent buses, serving all parts of the island.

But it is in respect to road usage that the Singaporean authorities have been most innovative.

The first innovation came in 1975. The city centre was made a restricted zone. Motorists who wished to enter this zone had to buy a ticket (an 'area licence') at any one of 33 entry points. Police were stationed at these entry points to check that cars had paid and displayed.

Then in 1990 a quota system for new cars was established. The government decides the total number of cars the country should have, and issues just enough licences each month to maintain that total. These licences (or 'Certificates of Entitlement') are for 10 years and are offered at auction. Their market price varies from around £10 000 to £30 000.

A problem with the licences is that they are a once-and-for-all payment, which does not vary with the amount people use their car. In other words, their marginal cost (for additional miles driven) is zero. Many people feel that, having paid such a high

also mildly related to the level of congestion, since fuel consumption tends to increase as congestion increases. Nevertheless, they are not ideal. The problem is that all motorists would pay an increase in fuel tax, even those travelling on uncongested roads. There is also a political problem. Most motorists regard fuel taxes as too high and would resent paying higher rates. The blockade of fuel terminals in the UK and many other countries in late 2000 in protest against high fuel prices demonstrated the strength of feeling on this issue.

Pause for thought

Would a tax on car tyres be a good way of restricting car usage?

Road pricing

Charging people for using roads is a direct means of achieving an efficient use of road space. The higher the congestion, the higher should be the charge.

The scheme most favoured by many economists and traffic planners is that of electronic road pricing. It is the scheme that can most directly relate the price charged to the motorist to the specific level of marginal social cost. It involves having sensors attached to cars, perhaps in the numberplate. When the car passes a recording device in the road, a charge is registered to that car on a central computer. The car owner then receives a bill at periodic intervals, in much the

Key Idea
24
p401

price for their licence, they ought to use their car as much as possible in order to get value for money!

With traffic congestion steadily worsening, it was recognised that something more had to be done. Either the Area Licensing Scheme had to be widened, or some other form of charging had to be adopted. The decision was taken to introduce electronic road pricing (ERP). This alternative would not only save on police labour costs, but enable charge rates to be varied according to levels of congestion, times of the day, and locality. What, then would be the optimum charge? If the objective is to reduce traffic from Q_1 to Q_2 in Figure 22.3, then a charge of $d - c$ should be levied.

Since 1998 all vehicles in Singapore have been fitted with an in-vehicle unit (IU). Every journey made requires the driver to insert a smart card into the IU. On specified roads, overhead gantries read the IU and deduct the appropriate charge from the card. The charge varies with the time of day. If a car does not have sufficient funds on its smart card, the car's details are relayed to a control centre and a fine is imposed. The system has the benefit of operating on three-lane highways and does not require traffic to slow down. What is more, it is very

flexible, with the possibility of adjusting the road price (i.e. the charge) to keep traffic at the desired level. The ERP system operates on Mondays to Fridays from 7.30am to 7.00pm in the central area and from 7.30am to 9.30am on the expressways and outer ring roads.

The system was expensive to set up, however. Cheaper schemes have been adopted elsewhere, such as Norway and parts of the USA. These operate by funnelling traffic into a single lane in order to register the car, but these have the disadvantage of slowing the traffic down.

One message is clear from the Singapore solution. Road pricing alone is not enough. Unless there are fast, comfortable and affordable public transport alternatives, the demand for cars will be highly price inelastic. People have to get to work!

Question

Explain how, by varying the charge debited from the smart card according to the time of day or level of congestion, a socially optimal level of road use can be achieved.

same way as a telephone bill. The charge rate can easily be varied electronically according to the level of congestion (and pollution too). The rates could be in bands and the current bands displayed by the roadside so that motorists knew what they were being charged.

An alternative scheme involves having a device fitted to your car that deactivates the car unless a 'smart card' (like a telephone or photocopying card) is inserted. The cards have to be purchased and contain a certain number of units. The device deducts units from the card when the average speed of your car over a specified distance falls below a certain level, or when more than a certain number of stops are made within a specified distance. (Either would be the result of congestion.) Alternatively, beacons or overhead gantries could deduct units from the smart cards at times of congestion.

The most sophisticated scheme, still under development, involves equipping all cars with a receiver. Their position is located by satellites, which then send this information to a dashboard unit, which deducts charges according to location, distance travelled, time of day and type of vehicle. The charges can operate either through smart cards or central computerised billing.

Various road-pricing schemes have been advocated for many cities around the world and pilot schemes are now in operation in several of them. Some cities, such as London and Singapore (see Box 22.2) are already using road pricing.

Congestion charging in London. In London, car drivers must pay £5 per day to enter the inner London area (or 'congestion zone') any time between 7.00am and 6.30pm, Monday to Friday. Payment can be made by various means, including post, Internet, telephone, mobile phone SMS text message and various shops and petrol stations. Payment can be in advance or up to 10.00pm on the day of travel, or up to midnight for an extra £5. Cars entering the congestion zone have their number plate recorded by camera and a computer check then leads to a fine of £80 being sent to those who have not paid.

The London congestion charging system has reduced traffic in the zone by about 20 per cent and has significantly increased the rate of traffic flow. The charge is not a marginal one, however, in the sense that it does not vary with the degree of congestion or the amount of time spent or distance travelled by a motorist within the zone. Nevertheless, its simplicity makes it easy to understand and relatively cheap to operate.

Subsidising alternative means of transport

An alternative to charging for the use of cars is to subsidise the price of alternatives, such as buses and trains. But cheaper fares alone may not be enough. The government may also have to invest directly in or subsidise an *improved* public transport service: more frequent services, more routes, more comfortable buses and trains.

Subsidising public transport need not be seen as an alternative to road pricing: it can be seen as complementary. If road pricing is to persuade people not to travel by car, the alternatives must be attractive. Unless public transport can be made to be seen by the traveller as a close substitute for cars, the elasticity of demand for car use is likely to remain low.

Subsidising public transport can also be justified on grounds of equity. It benefits poorer members of society who cannot afford to travel by car.

It is unlikely that any one policy can provide the complete solution. Certain or mixes of policies are better suited to some situations than others. It is important for governments to learn from experiences both within their own country and in others, in order to find the optimum solution to each specific problem.

22.3 Privatisation and regulation

One solution to market failure, advocated by some on the political left, is nationalisation. If industries are not being run in the public interest by the private sector, then bring them into public ownership. This way, so the argument goes, the market failures can be corrected. Problems of monopoly power, externalities, inequality, etc. can be dealt with directly if these industries are run with the public interest, rather than private gain, at heart. In the late 1940s and early 1950s the Labour government of the time nationalised many of the key transport, communications and power industries, such as the railways, freight transport, airlines, coal, gas, electricity and steel.

The political right is against nationalisation. The failures of the market (which, they claim, are often relatively small) are best dealt with by encouraging more competition, and by generally improving the market. Public ownership, they argue, far from serving the public interest, actually creates more problems than it solves. **Nationalised industries**, they claim, are bureaucratic, inefficient, unresponsive to consumer wishes and often a burden on the taxpayer.

definition

Nationalised industries
State-owned industries that produce goods or services that are sold in the market.

The Thatcher and Major governments thus engaged in extensive programmes of 'privatisation', returning most of the nationalised industries in the UK to the private sector. Other countries have followed similar programmes of privatisation in what has become a worldwide phenomenon. Privatisation has been seen as a means of revitalising ailing industries and as a golden opportunity to raise revenues to ease budgetary problems.

The arguments for and against privatisation

The following are the major arguments that have been used for and against privatisation.

Arguments for privatisation

Market forces. The first argument is that privatisation will expose these industries to market forces, from which will flow the benefits of greater efficiency, greater growth and greater responsiveness to the wishes of the consumer.

If privatisation involved splitting an industry into competing companies, this greater competition in the goods market would force the companies to keep their costs as low as possible in order to stay in business.

Privatised companies do not have direct access to government finance. To finance investment they must now go to the market: they must issue shares or borrow from banks or other financial institutions. In doing so, they will be competing for funds with other companies, and thus must be seen as capable of using these funds profitably.

Market discipline will also be enforced by shareholders. Shareholders want a good return on their shares and will thus put pressure on the privatised company to perform well. If the company does not make sufficient profits, shareholders will sell their shares. The share price will fall, and the company will be in danger of being taken over.

Reduced government interference. In nationalised industries, managers may frequently be required to adjust their targets for political reasons. At one time they may have to keep prices low as part of a government drive against inflation. At another they may have to raise their prices substantially in order to raise extra revenue for the government and help finance tax cuts. Privatisation frees the company from these constraints and allows it to make more rational economic decisions and plan future investments with greater certainty.

Financing tax cuts. The privatisation issue of shares directly earns money for the government and thus reduces the amount it needs to borrow. Effectively, then, the government can use the proceeds of privatisation to finance tax cuts.

Arguments against privatisation

Natural monopolies. The market forces argument for privatisation largely breaks down if a public monopoly is simply replaced by a private monopoly, as in the case of the water companies, which each have a monopoly in their own area. Critics of privatisation argue that at least a public-sector monopoly is not out to maximise profits and thereby exploit the consumer.

The public interest. Will the questions of externalities and social justice not be ignored after privatisation? Critics of privatisation argue that only the most

The right track to reform?
Reorganising the railways in the UK

Over the past 35 years, freight transported by road in Europe has risen by just under 300 per cent, whereas freight transported by rail has fallen by 8 per cent. While there has been a modest growth in passenger traffic on the railways, it is tiny compared with the growth in journeys by private car. Today more than 70 per cent of all passengers and freight use road transport. The result is that European railways generally operate at a loss, except for a few high-speed routes.

But why has rail transport performed so poorly? Losses on freight are partly the result of the decline in heavy manufacturing industries. A large proportion of freight trains carried coal, iron ore, steel and chemicals. In addition there is the competition from long-distance road haulage, made more competitive with the growth of the motorway network and the flexibility of delivering directly to the ultimate destination.

In the case of passenger services, railways have not managed to match the flexibility of car transport, made increasingly available with the growth in car ownership. Then there is the problem that many road costs are not marginal costs to the motorist. This gives road transport a cost advantage to the traveller. Finally, railways have often been forced to keep unprofitable routes open to meet public-service obligations.

Such has been the strain placed upon public finances that European governments in recent years have been looking for ways of reforming their railways. The most radical approach has been adopted in the UK, which involved dividing up the rail system and privatising its various parts.

The privatised rail system in the UK

The UK Conservative government in 1993 stated that the aim of rail privatisation was to 'improve the quality of rail services for the travelling public and for freight customers'. The 1993 Railways Act detailed the privatisation programme. The management of rail infrastructure, such as track, signalling and stations, was to be separated from the responsibility for running trains. There would be 25 passenger train operating companies (TOCs), each having a franchise lasting between seven and fifteen years. These companies would have few assets, being forced to rent track and lease stations from the infrastructure owner (Railtrack), and to lease trains and rolling stock from three new rolling-stock companies. There would be three freight companies, which would also pay Railtrack for the use of track and signalling. In practice, the 25 franchises are operated by just 11 companies (with one, National Express, having nine of the franchises).

Railtrack would be responsible for maintaining and improving the rail infrastructure, but rather than providing this itself, it would be required to purchase the necessary services from private contractors.

To oversee the new rail network, two new posts were created. The first was a rail franchising director, who would be responsible for specifying the length and cost of franchises, as well as for outlining passenger service requirements, including minimum train frequency, stations served and weekend provision. The second post created was that of the rail regulator, who would be responsible both for promoting competition and for protecting consumer interests, which might include specifying maximum permitted fares.

Although the individual train operators generally have a monopoly over a given route, many see themselves directly competing with coaches and private cars. Several have begun replacing or refurbishing rolling stock and running additional services.

Despite these apparent benefits, considerable costs have been associated with this privatisation programme. Huge subsidies had to be paid in order to make various parts of the system saleable. The size of the subsidies was determined by the competitive bidding process for the franchises. Total subsidies in the ten years following privatisation have amounted to over £15 billion, boosted in recent

glaring examples of externalities and injustice can be taken into account, given that the whole ethos of a private company is different from that of a nationalised one: private profit is the goal rather than public service. Externalities, they argue, are extremely widespread and need to be taken into account by the industry itself

Key Idea 27 p402

years by the need to spend large sums on improving the state of the track.

Critics have argued that, apart from being costly, the new system has created a bureaucratic system. There is a fragmentation of responsibility, with highly complex transactions between the individual companies adding to costs.

The government set out new proposals in 2000 for the future of the rail network, as the first set of seven-year franchises drew to an end. The intention was to reintroduce a degree of regional monopoly control back over the rail system. By reducing the number of rail franchises from 25 to 14 (and possibly the number of operators from 11 to 8), it was suggested that the role of the regulator in monitoring and enforcing performance and fare criteria would become less complex and easier to manage. The rail franchising regulator was replaced by a new Strategic Rail Authority (SRA), with wider powers and a remit that covered overseeing the integration of the rail network.

In addition, to encourage business to invest long term, new franchise licences would be for 20 years. The original seven-year franchises were argued by many to offer little or no incentive for a rail company to invest or plan long term, when after seven years it might potentially lose its franchise.

Has the model been adopted elsewhere?

Other countries, such as Japan and Germany, have rejected the UK model in favour of maintaining a vertically integrated rail network, where rail infrastructure and train services are managed by the same company. It is suggested that a single management would be far more capable of successfully co-ordinating infrastructure and train service activities than two.

Nevertheless, some aspects of the UK model have been adopted under EC Directive 91/440, which allows European train operators access to the rail networks of other companies. This means that several companies (say, from different EU countries) can offer competing services on the same international route.

Recent developments in the UK

Since the Hatfield rail disaster in October 2000, when lives were lost as a result of a faulty rail, the UK rail network has been in a virtual state of crisis. Trains are unreliable; fares have been rising by more than the rate of inflation; services are being reduced; and passenger complaints rise. There seem to be few, if any, benefits from privatisation.

In fact, part of the industry was 'semi' re-nationalised, when Railtrack, the privatised track owner, was placed into receivership in 2002. It was replaced by Network Rail, which is a not-for-profit company, wholly dependent upon the UK Treasury for any shortfall in its funds. Any profits are re-invested in the rail infrastructure. Six of the train operating companies are operating under short-term management contracts, and seven have been given government subsidies totalling some £100 million to prevent them going bust.

In June 2003 the SRA decided to withdraw the operating licence of the French company Connex South Eastern. Not only was one in every five of its trains running late but, following the receipt of £58 million of public money, the company had failed to turn around its failing financial position. In fact, Connex was asking for a further £200 million in state aid.

Many critics are now suggesting running the privatised rail network is becoming increasingly difficult, and Connex's failure may be the signal that more public money than expected may yet be required to keep the network afloat.

Question

Why are subsidies more likely to be needed for commuter and regional services than for medium-to-long-distance passenger services?

and not just by an occasionally intervening government. A railway or an underground line, for example, may considerably ease congestion on the roads, thus benefiting road as well as rail users. Other industries may cause substantial external costs. Nuclear power stations may produce nuclear waste that is costly

Pause for thought

To what extent can the problems with privatisation be seen as arguments in favour of nationalisation?

to dispose of safely, and/or provides hazards for future generations. Coal-fired power stations may pollute the atmosphere and cause acid rain.

In assessing these arguments, a lot depends on the toughness of government legislation and the attitudes and powers of regulatory agencies after privatisation.

Regulation

Identifying the short-run optimum price and output

Privatised industries, if left free to operate in the market, will have monopoly power; they will create externalities; and they will be unlikely to take into account questions of fairness. An answer to these problems is for the government or some independent agency to regulate their behaviour so that they produce at the socially optimum price and output. This has been the approach adopted for the major privatisations in the UK.

Key Idea 24 p401

Regulation in practice

To some extent the behaviour of privatised industries may be governed by general monopoly and restrictive practice legislation. For example, in the UK, privatised firms can be investigated by the Office of Fair Trading and if necessary referred to the Competition Commission.

Key Idea 30 p410

In addition to this, there is a separate regulatory office to oversee the structure and behaviour of each of the privatised utilities. These regulators are as follows: the Office for Gas and Electricity Markets (Ofgem), the Office for Telecommunications (Oftel), replaced by the Office of Communications (Ofcom) at the end of 2003, the Office of the Rail Regulator (ORR) and the Office of Water Services (Ofwat). The regulators set terms under which the industries have to operate. For example, Ofgem requires the pipeline division of British Gas (TransCo) to allow other gas producers to use its pipelines, and for the same charge as that made to British Gas' supply division (now part of a separate company, Centrica). The terms set by the regulator can be reviewed by negotiation between the regulator and the industry. If agreement cannot be reached, the Competition Commission acts as an appeal court and its decision is binding.

The regulator for each industry also set limits to the prices that certain parts of the industry can charge. These parts are those where there is little or no competition: for example, the charge made to electricity companies by the National Grid Company for transmitting electricity.

The price-setting formulae are essentially of the 'RPI minus X' variety. What this means is that the industries can raise their prices by the rate of increase in the retail price index (i.e. by the rate of inflation) *minus* a certain percentage (X) to take account of expected increases in efficiency. Thus if the rate of inflation were 6 per cent, and if the regulator considered that the industry (or firm) could be expected to reduce its costs by 2 per cent (X = 2%), then price rises would be capped at 4 per cent. The *RPI – X* system is thus an example of **price-cap regulation**. The idea of this system of regulation is that it forces the industry to pass cost savings on to the consumer.

definition

Price-cap regulation
Where the regulator puts a ceiling on the amount by which a firm can raise its price.

Pause for thought

If an industry regulator adopts an RPI – X formula for price regulation, is it desirable that the value of X should be adjusted as soon as cost conditions change?

Assessing the system of regulation in the UK

The system that has evolved in the UK has various advantages over that employed in the USA and elsewhere (where regulation often focuses on the level of *profits*).

■ It is a *discretionary* system, with the regulator able to judge individual examples of the behaviour of the industry on their own merits. The regulator has a detailed knowledge of the industry which would not be available to government ministers or other bodies such as the Office of Fair Trading. The regulator could thus be argued to be the best person to decide on whether the industry is acting in the public interest.

■ The system is *flexible*, since it allows for the licence and price formula to be changed as circumstances change.

■ The '*RPI* minus *X*' formula provides an *incentive* for the privatised firms to be as efficient as possible. If they can lower their costs by more than *X*, they will, in theory, be able to make larger profits and keep them. If on the other hand, they do not succeed in reducing costs sufficiently, they will make a loss. There is thus a continuing pressure on them to cut costs.

There are, however, some inherent problems with the way in which regulation operates in the UK:

■ The '*RPI* minus *X*' formula was designed to provide an incentive for the firms to cut costs. But if *X* is too low, the firm might make excessive profits. Frequently, regulators have underestimated the scope for cost reductions resulting from new technology and reorganisation, and have thus initially set *X* too low. As a result, instead of *X* remaining constant for a number of years, as intended, new higher values for *X* have been set after only one or two years. Alternatively, one-off price cuts have been ordered, as happened when the water companies were required by Ofwat to cut prices by an average of 10 per cent in 2000. In either case, the incentive for the industry to cut costs is reduced. What is the point of being more efficient if the regulator is merely going to insist on a higher value for *X* and thus take away the extra profits?

■ Regulation is becoming increasingly complex. This makes it difficult for the industries to plan and may lead to a growth of 'short-termism'. One of the claimed advantages of privatisation was to give greater independence to the industries from short-term government interference, and allow them to plan for the longer term. In practice, one type of interference may have been replaced by another.

■ As regulation becomes more detailed and complex and as the regulator becomes more and more involved in the detailed running of the industry, so managers and regulators will become increasingly involved in game of strategy: each trying to outwit the other. Information will become distorted and time and energy will be wasted in playing this game of cat and mouse.

■ There may also be the danger of **regulatory capture**. As regulators become more and more involved in their industry and get to know the senior managers at a personal level, so they are increasingly likely to see the managers' point of view and become less and less tough. Commentators do not believe that this has happened yet: the regulators are generally independently minded. But it is a danger for the future.

definition

Regulatory capture
Where the regulator is persuaded to operate in the industry's interests rather than those of the consumer.

■ Alternatively, regulators could be captured by government. Instead of being totally independent, there to serve the interests of the consumer, they might bend to pressures from the government to do things which might help the government win the next election.

Increasing competition in the privatised industries

Where natural monopoly exists (see page 220), competition is impossible in a free market. Of course, the industry *could* be broken up by the government, with firms prohibited from owning more than a certain percentage of the industry. But this would lead to higher costs of production. Firms would be operating further back up a downward-sloping long-run average cost curve.

But many parts of the privatised industries are not natural monopolies. Generally it is only the *grid* that is a natural monopoly. In the case of gas and water, it is the pipelines. It would be wasteful to duplicate these. In the case of electricity, it is the power lines: the national grid and the local power lines. In the case of the railways, it is the track. *Other* parts of these industries, however, have generally been opened up to competition (with the exception of water). Thus there are now many producers and sellers of electricity and gas. This is possible because they are given access, by law, to the national and local electricity grids and gas pipelines. The telecommunications market too has become more competitive with the growth of mobile phones and lines supplied by cable operators.

To help the opening up of competition, regulators have sometimes restricted the behaviour of the established firms (like BT or British Gas), to prevent them using their dominance in the market as a barrier to entry of new firms. For example, British Gas since 1995 has had to limit its share of the industrial gas market to 40 per cent.

As competition has been introduced into these industries, so price-cap regulation has been progressively abandoned. The intention is ultimately to confine price regulation to the operation of the grids: the parts that are natural monopolies.

Even for the parts where there is a natural monopoly, they could be made *contestable* monopolies. One way of doing this is by granting operators a licence for a specific period of time. This is known as **franchising**. This has been the approach used for the railways (see Box 22.3). Once a company has been granted a franchise, it has the monopoly of passenger rail services over specific routes. But the awarding of the franchise can be highly competitive, with rival companies putting in competitive bids, in terms of both price (or, in the case of railways, the level of government subsidy required) and the quality of service. Another approach is to give all companies equal access to the relevant grid (such as the electricity grid, gas pipelines and the rail network).

But despite attempts to introduce competition into the privatised industries, they are still dominated by giant companies. Even if they are no longer strictly monopolies, they still have considerable market power and the scope for price leadership or other forms of oligopolistic collusion is great. Thus although regulation through the price formula has been progressively abandoned as elements of competition have been introduced, the regulators have retained a role similar to that of the OFT: they can intervene to prevent cases of collusion and the abuse of monopoly power. The companies, however, do have the right of appeal to the Competition Commission.

---

definition

Franchising
Where a firm is granted the licence to operate a given part of an industry for a specified length of time.

SUMMARY

1a Pollution is a negative externality, and due to the lack of property rights over the environment, it will be treated as a free good and hence over-used. Environmental policy attempts to ensure that the full costs of production or consumption are paid for by those who produce and consume.

1b The environment is difficult to value, so it is difficult to estimate the costs of environmental pollution. This is a major problem in being able to devise an efficient environmental policy.

1c Environmental policy can be either market based or non-market based, or a mixture of the two. Market-based solutions focus upon the use of taxes and subsidies to correct market signals. Non-market-based solutions involve the use of regulations and controls over polluting activities.

1d The problem with using taxes and subsidies is in identifying the appropriate rates, since these will vary according to the environmental impact.

1e Command-and-control systems, such as making certain practices illegal or putting limits on discharges, are a less sophisticated alternative to taxes or subsidies. However, they may be preferable when the environmental costs of certain actions are unknown and it is wise to play safe.

1f Tradable permits are a mix of command-and-control and market-based systems. Firms are given permits to emit a certain level of pollution and then these can be traded. A firm that can relatively cheaply reduce its pollution below its permitted level can sell this credit to another firm which finds it more costly to do so. The system is an efficient and administratively cheap way of limiting pollution to a designated level. It can, however, lead to pollution being concentrated in certain areas and can reduce the pressure on firms to find cleaner methods of production.

2a The allocation of road space depends on demand and supply. Demand is derived from the demand by travellers to get to their destination. Demand depends on the price to motorists of using their cars, incomes, the cost of alternative means of transport, the price of cars and complementary services (such as parking), and the comfort and convenience of car transport. The price and cross-price elasticities of demand for car usage tend to be low: many people are unwilling to switch to alternative modes of transport. The income elasticity, on the other hand, is high. The demand for cars and car usage grows rapidly as incomes grow.

2b With road space fixed (at least in the short term), allocation depends on the private decisions of motorists. The problem is that motorists create two types of external cost: pollution costs and congestion costs. Thus $MSC > MC$. Because of these externalities, the actual use of road space (where $MB = MC$) is likely to be greater than the optimum (where $MSB = MSC$).

2c There are various types of solution to traffic congestion. These include direct provision by the government or local authorities (of additional road space or better public transport); regulation and legislation (such as restricting car access – by the use of bus and cycle lanes, no entry to side streets and pedestrian-only areas – and various forms of parking restrictions); changing market signals (by the use of taxes, by road pricing, and by subsidising alternative means of transport).

2d Problems associated with building additional roads include the decline of public transport, attracting additional traffic on to the roads and environmental costs.

2e The main problem with restricting car access is that it tends merely to divert congestion elsewhere. The main problem with parking restrictions is that they may actually increase congestion.

2f Increasing taxes is effective in reducing congestion only if it increases the *marginal* cost of motoring. Even when it does, as in the case of additional fuel tax, the additional cost is only indirectly related to congestion costs, since it applies to all motorists and not just those causing congestion.

2g Road pricing is the preferred solution of many economists. By the use of electronic devices, motorists can be charged whenever they add to congestion. This should encourage less essential road users to travel at off-peak times or to use alternative modes of transport, while those who gain a high utility from car transport can still use their cars, but at a price. Variable tolls and supplementary licences are alternative forms of congestion pricing, but are generally less effective than the use of electronic road pricing.

SUMMARY

2h If road pricing is to be effective, there must be attractive substitutes available. A comprehensive policy, therefore, should include subsidising efficient public transport. The revenues required for this could be obtained from road pricing.

3a From around 1983 the Conservative government in the UK embarked on a large programme of privatisation. The justification was partly ideological and partly to do with the perceived economic failures of the nationalised industries and their better prospects under private ownership.

3b The economic arguments for privatisation include: greater competition, not only in the goods market but in the market for finance and for corporate control; reduced government interference; and raising revenue to finance tax cuts.

3c The economic arguments against privatisation are largely the market failure arguments that were used to justify nationalisation. In reply the advocates of privatisation argue that these problems can be overcome through appropriate regulation and increasing the amount of competition.

3d Regulation in the UK has involved setting up regulatory offices for the major privatised utilities. These generally operate informally, using negotiation and bargaining to persuade the industries to behave in the public interest. As far as prices are concerned, the industries are required to abide by an '*RPI* minus *X*' formula. This forces them to pass potential cost reductions on to the consumer. At the same time they are allowed to retain any additional profits gained from cost reductions greater than *X*. This provides them with an incentive to achieve even greater increases in efficiency. The regulator can seek a revision of the industry's licence or price formula. If the firm does not agree, an appeal can be made to the Competition Commission whose decision is binding.

3e Many parts of the privatised industries are not natural monopolies. In these parts, competition may be a more effective means of pursuing the public interest. Various attempts have been made to make the privatised industries more competitive, often at the instigation of the regulator. Nevertheless, considerable market power remains in the hands of many privatised firms, and thus the need for regulation will continue.

REVIEW QUESTIONS

1   Why is it so difficult to value the environment? What are the implications of this for government policy on the environment?

2   Is it a good idea to use the revenues from green taxes to subsidise green alternatives (e.g. using petrol taxes for subsidising rail transport)?

3   Compare the relative merits of increased road fuel taxes, electronic road pricing and tolls as means of reducing urban traffic congestion. Why is the price inelasticity of demand for private car transport a problem here, whichever of the three policies is adopted? What could be done to increase the price elasticity of demand?

4   How would you set about measuring the external costs of road transport?

5   Consider the argument that whether an industry is in the public sector or private sector has far less bearing on its performance than the degree of competition it faces.

6   To what extent do the various goals of privatisation conflict?

7   Is it desirable after an industry has been privatised for profitable parts of the industry to cross-subsidise unprofitable parts if they are of public benefit (e.g. profitable railway lines cross-subsidising unprofitable ones)?

8   Should regulators of utilities that have been privatised into several separate companies permit (a) horizontal mergers (within the industry); (b) vertical mergers; (c) mergers with firms in other related industries (e.g. gas and electricity suppliers)?

Additional Part H case studies on the *Economics for Business* website (www.booksites.net/sloman)

H.1 **The police as a public service.** The extent to which policing can be classified as a public good.

H.2 **Should health care provision be left to the market?** An examination of the market failures that would occur if health care provision were left to the free market.

H.3 **Corporate social responsibility.** An examination of social responsibility as a goal of firms and its effect on business performance.

H.4 **Public choice theory.** This examines how economists have attempted to extend their analysis of markets to the field of political decision making.

H.5 **Cartels set in concrete, steel and cardboard.** This examines some of the best-known Europe-wide cartels of recent years.

H.6 **Productivity performance and the UK economy.** A detailed examination of how the UK's productivity compares with that in other countries.

H.7 **Technology and economic change.** How to get the benefits from technological advance.

H.8 **The economics of non-renewable resources.** An examination of how the price of non-renewable resources rises as stocks become depleted, and of how the current price reflects this.

H.9 **A deeper shade of green.** This looks at different perspectives on how we should treat the environment.

H.10 **Perverse subsidies.** An examination of the use of subsidies around the world that are harmful to the environment.

H.11 **Can the market provide adequate protection for the environment?** This explains why markets generally fail to take into account environmental externalities.

H.12 **Environmental auditing.** Are businesses becoming greener? A growing number of firms are subjecting themselves to an 'environmental audit' to judge just how 'green' they are.

H.13 **Restricting car access to Athens.** A case study that examines how the Greeks have attempted to reduce local atmospheric pollution from road traffic.

H.14 **Selling power to the people.** Attempts to introduce competition into the UK electricity industry.

Websites relevant to Part H

Numbers and sections refer to websites listed in the Web appendix and hotlinked from this book's website at **www.booksites.net/sloman**

■ For news articles relevant to Part H, see the *Economics News Articles* link from the book's website.

■ For general news on market failures and government intervention see websites in section A, and particularly A1–5, 18, 19, 24, 31. See also links to newspapers in A38, 39 and 43; and see A42 for links to economics news articles from newspapers worldwide.

■ Sites I7 and 11 contain links to *Competition and monopoly, Policy and regulation* and *Transport* in the *Microeconomics* section; they also have an *Industry and commerce* section. Site I4 has links to *Environmental* and *Environmental Economics* in the *EconDirectory* section. Site I17 has several sections of links in the *Issues in Society* section.

■ Sites I7 and 11 also contain links to sites related to corporate social responsibility: see *Industry and Commerce > Fair Trade > Corporate Social Responsibility*.

■ For information on taxes and subsidies, see E30, 36; G13. For use of green taxes, see H5; G11; E2, 14, 30.

■ For information on health and the economics of health care (web case H.2: see above), see E8; H9. See also links in I8 and 17.

■ For sites favouring the free market, see C17; D34. See also C18 for the development of ideas on the market and government intervention.

■ For information on training, see E5; G14; H3.

■ For the economics of the environment, see links in I4, 7, 11, 17. For policy on the environment and transport, see E2, 7, 11, 14, 29; G10, 11. See also H11.

■ UK and EU departments relevant to competition policy can be found at sites E10; G7, 8.

■ UK regulatory bodies can be found at sites E4, 11, 15, 16, 18, 19, 21, 22, 25, 29.

■ For student resources relevant to this chapter, see sites C1–7, 9, 10, 19.

Business in the international environment

THE FINANCIAL TIMES, 26 JUNE 2003

UN urges rich to restart trade talks

By FRANCES WILLIAMS

The United Nations called yesterday on the rich world to kickstart stalled global trade negotiations by unilaterally scrapping agricultural export subsidies and ending dumping of farm products on developing country markets.

The UN's latest world economic survey says governments should see the Doha round of World Trade Organisation talks not as a traditional trade negotiation but as a way of promoting development and stimulating lacklustre growth in the world economy.

It says huge agricultural subsidies, which undermine the livelihoods of millions of poor farmers, directly contradict pledges made by the industrialised countries over the past two years to support a new development partnership with developing nations.

'Developed countries should therefore begin to reduce agricultural subsidies without delay and make time-bound commitments to eliminating them without a *quid pro quo* in other Doha negotiations,' the survey says.

Ending the $300bn-plus (€260bn, £180bn) paid out each year in farm subsidies worldwide would boost developing countries' annual income by $150bn–$400bn within five years, according to World Bank estimates. However, last year's US farm bill added billions to its subsidy programmes while the European Union, the world's biggest subsidiser, is racked by divisions over reform of its protectionist common agricultural policy.

The UN also calls for a prompt solution in the WTO to ease poor countries' access to cheap medicines, and urges other advanced nations to emulate the EU's 'everything but arms' programme in extending duty- and quota-free access to least developed countries.

UN economists expect world trade to rise by 4 per cent this year in volume terms, against 2 per cent last year, while output growth is forecast to rise only slightly to 2.25 per cent in 2003 from 2 per cent in 2002. Overcapacity stemming from excessive investment in the 1990s continues to damp business investment necessary to sustain recovery, the UN says.

Progress in the Doha round, due to conclude by December next year, and more debt relief and aid for poorer nations would help put global recovery on a broader base, the survey says, voicing concerns about the impact of a depreciating dollar. www.un.org/publications

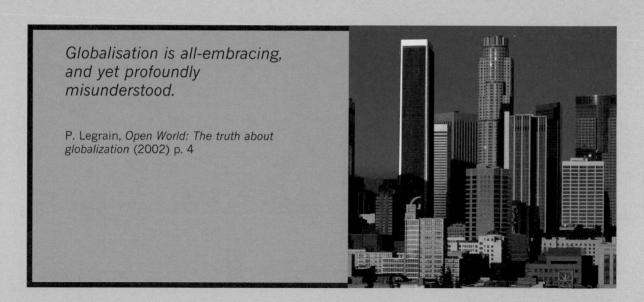

With falling barriers to international trade, with improved communications and with an increasingly global financial system, so nations have found that their economies have become ever more intimately linked. Economic events in one part of the world, such as changes in interest rates or a downturn in economic growth, will have a myriad of knock-on effects for the international community at large – from the international investor, to the foreign exchange dealer, to the domestic policy maker, to the business which exports or imports, or which has subsidiaries abroad.

In Part H we explore the international environment and its impact on business. Chapter 23 considers the issue of globalisation and the rise and spread of multinational enterprises within the world economy. It not only looks at why certain businesses become multinational, but evaluates their impact upon host nations, within both the developed and the developing worlds.

In Chapter 24 we focus on international trade. We consider why trading is advantageous and why, nevertheless, certain countries feel the need to restrict trade.

Finally, in Chapter 25, we examine one of the most significant trends in international trade over the past 50 years – namely, the rise of the trade bloc. We outline the advantages and disadvantages of regional trading. We also look briefly at trading blocs in North America and South-East Asia and the Pacific. Then, as an extended case study, we consider the position of the European Union and the effects of the creation of a single European market on both businesses and consumers.

key terms

Comparative advantage
The gains from trade
Terms of trade
Protectionism
Tariffs
Quotas
Infant and senile industries
World Trade Organisation (WTO)
Multinational corporation
Trade bloc
Preferential trading
Free trade areas, customs unions and common markets
Trade creation and diversion
North America Free Trade Association (NAFTA)
Asian-Pacific Economic Co-operation forum (APEC)
European Union (EU)
Single European market

23 Globalisation and multinational business

23.1 Globalisation: setting the scene

According to an article in *Business Week*, entitled 'The New Global Job Shift',[1] a new wave in the globalisation process is underway which will radically reshape the world economy. In the past many multinational companies had located much of their manufacturing in developing countries. Under this new wave, they are increasingly locating service and 'knowledge-based' jobs there too. Such jobs range from telesales to dataprocessing to research and development.

Some of these jobs require high levels of skills and training, once seen as the preserve of the rich economies and the source of their competitive advantage in international trade. No longer would this seem to be the case. With digitisation, the Internet and high-speed data networks, business is able to tap into talent no matter where it is located in the global economy. Countries such as India and China, as well as many others, produce a massive number of well-trained and well-educated engineers and IT specialists every year. Such workers are predictably cheap to employ compared to their US, European and Japanese counterparts. Brian Valentine, a senior Microsoft executive, remarked that labour costs in developing countries were around 50 to 60 per cent of those for similar jobs in the USA.

The outcomes of this exodus of jobs are beginning to show. Employment in Silicon Valley, the US IT industrial cluster and driving force behind US technological innovation, fell by 20 per cent from 2001 to 2003. Wages are also being forced down. A senior software engineer received a salary of $130 000 in 2000; in 2003 the equivalent job commanded a salary of around $100 000. Admittedly the US economy was suffering a slowdown during this period, but the fall in jobs and wages was more than the fall in output and would seem an inevitable consequence of such trends.

But it is not all bad news for the developed economies, especially if you are a knowledge industry buyer. Lower costs and service prices are likely to result in significant improvements in both profits and efficiency. For developing economies, such as India and China, it is hard to see a downside with this new wave of globalisation. Not only are foreign companies investing in high value-added, knowledge-rich production, most of which is subsequently exported, they are paying relatively high salaries which will have significant economic benefits throughout the economy. With companies such as Microsoft announcing significant increases in its R&D outsourcing in China, the trends towards transferring knowledge jobs from developed to developing markets looks set not only to continue but to intensify.

---

[1] *Business Week*, 3 February 2003.

This exodus of jobs from developed to developing countries is a good example of the process of globalisation. In this chapter we are going to explore what globalisation is, how it is evolving, the impacts it is likely to have on different groups of people throughout the world and the motivations behind the increasing 'multinationalisation' of business.

Defining globalisation

At the time of writing (mid-2003), the world is trying to deal with an outbreak of Severe Acute Respiratory Syndrome or SARS virus. This virus has spread throughout the global economy with China, Toronto and Singapore being particularly hard hit, but cases have also been reported in New Zealand, the UK and many other countries. Beyond the human cost, the economic impact has been dramatic. Stock markets, especially in Asia have slumped, and tourists and business travellers have stayed away from the worst affected areas. Singapore estimates that SARS may cost it up to $US41.5 billion this year alone. The spread of the virus throughout the world, in which geographic boundaries offer little protection, reflects very much what globalisation is all about. As Phillipe Legrain suggests, globalisation is 'shorthand for how our lives are becoming increasingly intertwined with those of distant people and places around the world – economically, politically and culturally.'[2]

Economically we are bound through trade, investment, production and finance; politically through organisations, formal and informal, such as the United Nations, the World Trade Organisation (WTO) and non-governmental organisations such as Greenpeace. Through such organisations we attempt to establish frameworks and rules to govern almost every aspect of our lives. Culturally we are subject to the same advertising and branding; we migrate; we go on holiday; we share ideas, fashions and music; we compete in global sporting events, such as the Olympics; and increasingly we communicate globally through the Internet.

Globalisation is then the process of developing these links. Supporters and critics of globalisation alike tend to agree that globalisation is nothing new. There has always been a degree of economic, political and cultural interdependence. What makes globalisation an issue today is the speed at which interdependence is growing. This is partly the result of unprecedented technological change, particularly in respect to transport and communication, and partly the result of a political drive to remove barriers between countries and embrace foreign influences.

Business, caught within this process of globalisation, will invariably seek to take advantage of what it has to offer, which is essentially a borderless world or one that is increasingly so. As we saw in Chapter 13, a global economy enables a business to locate the different dimensions of its value chain wherever its likely to get the best deal, whether this is lower costs or better quality or both. Globalisation encourages this process of relocation and the framing of business strategy within a global context.

What is driving globalisation?

Within any global system certain industries and markets are likely to be more prone to the forces of globalisation than others. This becomes apparent when you attempt to identify the conditions influencing the globalisation process. These

---

[2] P. Legrain *Open World* (2002).

globalisation drivers can be categorised in a number of ways. Yip (1995) suggests that the globalisation potential of an industry, that is its ability to set global strategy and compete in a global marketplace, can be analysed under four headings:

- Market drivers
- Cost drivers
- Government drivers
- Competitive drivers.

These are shown in Table 23.1.

Table 23.1   **The drivers of globalisation**

Market drivers
Per capita income converging among industrialized nations
Convergence of lifestyles and tastes
Organizations beginning to behave as global customers
Increasing travel creating global consumers
Growth of global and regional channels
Establishment of world brands
Push to develop global advertising

Cost drivers
Continuing push for economies of scale
Accelerating technological innovation
Advances in transportation
Emergence of newly industrialized countries with productive capability and low
   labour costs
Increasing cost of product development relative to market life

Government drivers
Reduction of tariff barriers
Reduction of non-tariff barriers
Creation of blocs
Decline in role of governments as producers and customers
Privatisation in previously state-dominated economies
Shift to open market economies from closed communist systems in eastern
   Europe
Increasing participation of China and India in the global economy

Competitive drivers
Continuing increases in the level of world trade
Increased ownership of corporations by foreign acquirors
Rise of new competitors intent upon becoming global competitors
Growth of global networks making countries interdependent in particular
   industries
More companies becoming globally centered rather than nationally centered
Increased formation of global strategic alliances

Other drivers
Revolution in information and communication
Globalisation of financial markets
Improvements in business travel

Source: George Yip, *Total Global Strategy* (Prentice Hall, 1995)

Market drivers. Market drivers focus on the extent to which markets throughout the world are becoming similar. The more similar consumers are in respect to income and taste the more significant globalisation market drivers will become.

Cost drivers. Cost drivers present the business with the potential to reorganise its operations globally and reduce costs as a consequence. Global economies of scale, and transport and distribution issues will be significant.

Government drivers. Governments often play a key role in driving the process of globalisation, especially when they are positively welcoming to trade and inward investment.

Global political agreements, such as those made at the WTO covering world trade and related issues, not only directly affect the operation of markets, but also help establish global rules and protocols.

Competition drivers. As competitiveness builds, whether in the domestic market or overseas, businesses will be forced to consider how to maintain their competitive position. This often involves embracing a global business strategy, which invariably contributes towards globalisation. Global business networks and cross-border strategic alliances are key reflections of this growing competitive global process.

What is clear is that globalisation is driven forward by a wide variety of conditions. Such conditions will vary from industry to industry, reflecting why certain industries are more global than others.

Globalisation: the good and the bad

Even though supporters and critics of globalisation are in agreement that globalisation is nothing new, and that it is primarily driven by technological change and shifting political attitudes, they are far from agreeing about the consequences of globalisation and whether these are beneficial or harmful.

The supporters

Supporters of globalisation argue that it has massive potential to benefit the entire global economy. With freer trade and greater competition, countries and businesses within them are encouraged to think, plan and act globally. Technology spreads faster; countries specialise in particular products and processes and thereby exploit their core competitive advantages.

Both rich and poor, it is argued, benefit from such a process. Politically, globalisation brings us closer together. Political ties help stabilise relationships and offer the opportunity for countries to discuss their differences. However imperfect the current global political system might be, the alternative of independent nations is seen as potentially far worse. The globalisation of culture is also seen as beneficial, as a world of experience is opened, whether in respect to our holiday destinations, or the food we eat, or the music we listen to or the movies we watch.

Supporters of globalisation recognise that not all countries benefit equally from globalisation: those that have wealth will, as always, possess more opportunity to benefit from the globalisation process, whether from lower prices, global political agreements or cultural experience. However, long term, supporters of globalisation see it as ultimately being for the benefit of all – rich and poor alike.

The critics

Critics of globalisation argue that it contributes to growing inequality and further impoverishes poor nations. As an economic philosophy, globalisation allows multinational corporations (MNCs), based largely in the USA, Europe and Japan, to exploit their dominant position in foreign markets. Without effective competition in these markets such companies are able to pursue profit with few constraints.

By 'exploiting' low-wage labour, companies are able to compete more effectively on world markets. As competitive pressures intensify and companies seek to cut costs further, this can put downward pressure on such wages.

In political terms, critics of globalisation see the world being dominated by big business. Multinationals put pressure on their home governments to promote their interests in their dealings with other countries, thereby heightening the domination of rich countries over the poor.

Critics are no less damning of the cultural aspects of globalisation. They see the world dominated by multinational brands, western fashion, music and TV. Rather than globalisation fostering a mix of cultural expression, critics suggest that cultural differences are being replaced by the dominant (Western) culture of the day.

The above views represent the extremes, and to a greater or lesser degree both have elements of truth within them. The impact of globalisation on different groups is not even, and never will be. However, to suggest that big business rules, is also an unrealistic exaggeration. Clearly big business is influential, but it is a question of degree. Influence will invariably fluctuate over time, between events, and between and within countries.

At present the momentum within the global economy is for barriers to come down. This is having profound effects on both multinational business and the peoples of the world.

In the following sections we consider why it is that businesses decide to go multinational, and evaluate what impact they have on their host countries. Before we do this we shall first offer a definition of multinational business and assess the importance of multinational investment within the global economy.

What is a multinational corporation? 23.2

There are some 65 000 **multinational corporations** (MNCs) worldwide. Between them they control a total of 85 000 foreign subsidiaries. In 2001, the global stock of foreign direct investment (FDI) was nearly $7 trillion. Foreign affiliates accounted for approximately 11 per cent of world GDP, up from 7 per cent in 1990.

Even given their obvious gigantic size and overwhelming importance within the global economy, MNCs defy simple definition. At the most basic level, an MNC is a business that either owns or controls foreign subsidiaries in more than one country.

It is this ownership or control of productive assets in other countries which makes the MNC distinct from an enterprise that does business overseas by simply exporting goods or services. However, merely to define an MNC as a company with overseas subsidiaries fails to reflect the immense diversity of multinationals.

> **definition**
>
> **Multinational corporations**
> Businesses that either own or control foreign subsidiaries in more than one country.

Table 23.2 Comparison of the 10 largest multinational corporations (by gross revenue) and selected countries (by GDP): 2002

MNC rank	Country or company (headquarters)	GDP ($bn) or gross revenue ($bn)
	USA	10 869.1
1	Wal-Mart Stores	219.8
	Indonesia	212.9
	Denmark	205.1
2	Exxon Mobil	191.6
3	General Motors	177.3
4	BP	174.2
	Greece	165.2
	China: Hong Kong	165.1
5	Ford Motor	162.4
	Finland	158.2
	Ireland	150.2
6	Enron	138.7
7	DaimlerChrysler	136.9
8	Royal Dutch/Shell Group	135.2
	Thailand	132.4
	Iran	127.8
9	General Electric	125.9
	Argentina	121.8
10	Toyota Motor	120.8
	Malaysia	102.7
	Chile	65.9
	Luxembourg	23.8
	Kenya	12.9
	Albania	5.3

Sources: companies: *Fortune Global 500* (**www.fortune.com/fortune/global500/**); countries: World Economic Outlook *database, IMF, 2000* (**www.imf.org/external/pubs/ft/weo/2003/01/data/ngdpd_a.csv**)

Diversity among MNCs

Size. Many, if not most, of the world's largest firms – IBM, Shell, General Motors, etc. – are multinationals. Indeed, the turnover of some of them exceeds the national income of many smaller countries (see Table 23.2). And yet there are also thousands of very small, often specialist multinationals, which are a mere fraction of the size of the giants.

The nature of business. MNCs cover the entire spectrum of business activity, from manufacturing to extraction, agricultural production, chemicals, processing, service provision and finance. There is no 'typical' line of activity of a multinational.

Overseas business relative to total business. MNCs differ in respect to how extensive their overseas operations are relative to their total business. Nearly 50 per cent of IBM's sales and profits come from its activities outside the USA. The foreign operations of other MNCs represent only a small fraction of their total business.

Production locations. Some MNCs are truly 'global', with production located in a wide variety of countries and regions. Other MNCs, by contrast, only locate in one other region, or in a very narrow range of countries.

There are, however, a number of potentially constraining factors on the location of multinational businesses. For example, businesses concerned with the extraction of raw materials will locate as nature dictates! Businesses that provide services will tend to locate in the rich markets of developed regions of the world economy, where the demand for services is high. Others locate according to the factor intensity of the stage of production. Thus a labour-intensive stage might be located in a developing country where wage rates are relatively low, while another stage which requires a high level of automation might be located in an industrially advanced country.

Ownership patterns. As businesses expand overseas, they are faced with a number of options. They can decide to go it alone and create wholly owned subsidiaries. Alternatively, they might share ownership and hence some of the risk, by establishing joint ventures. In such cases the MNC might have a majority or minority stake in the overseas enterprise.

In certain countries, where MNC investment is regulated, many governments insist on owning or controlling a share in the new enterprise. Whether governments insist on domestic companies (or themselves) having a majority or minority stake varies from country to country. It also depends on the nature of the business and its perceived national importance. For example, until recently the Indian government insisted on having a majority stake in all multinational business ventures in the high-technology sector of the Indian economy.

Organisational structure. In Chapter 3 we discussed the variety of organisational forms that MNCs might adopt – from the model where the headquarters, or parent company, is dominant and the overseas subsidiary subservient, to that where international subsidiaries operate as self-standing organisations, bound together only in so far as they strive towards a set of global objectives.

The above characteristics of MNCs reveal that they represent a wide and very diverse group of enterprises. Beyond sharing the common link of having production activities in more than one country, MNCs differ widely in the nature and forms of their overseas business, and in the relationship between the parent and its subsidiaries.

> **Pause for thought**
>
> Given the diverse nature of multinational business, how useful is the definition given on page 487 for describing a multinational corporation?

Trends in multinational investment 23.3

Since the mid-1980s multinational businesses have been downsizing. They have been shrinking the size of their headquarters, removing layers of bureaucracy, and reorganising their global operations into smaller autonomous profit centres. Gone is the philosophy that big companies will inevitably do better than small ones. In fact, it now appears that multinationals are seeking to create a hybrid form of business organisation, which combines the advantages of size (i.e. economies of scale) with the responsiveness and market knowledge of smaller firms.

The key for the modern multinational is flexibility, and to be at one and the same time both global and local.

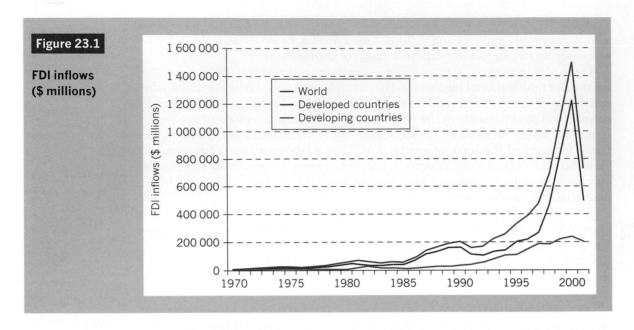

Figure 23.1

FDI inflows ($ millions)

The size of multinational investment

We can estimate the size of multinational investment by looking at figures for foreign direct investment (FDI). FDI represents the finance used either to purchase the assets for setting up a new subsidiary abroad (or expanding an existing one), or to acquire an existing business operation through either merger or acquisition.

In 2001, FDI flows declined sharply as the world's major industrial economies stagnated and stock markets experienced a sharp downturn in activity. World FDI inflows and outflows in 2001 stood at $735 billion and $621 billion respectively, a drop of 51 per cent and 55 per cent on the year previous. This was the most significant fall in both FDI inflows and outflows for over three decades. FDI in the two years prior to 2001 had risen steeply, primarily due to extensive cross-border merger and acquisition activity.

Figure 23.1 shows FDI inflows in dollars and Figure 23.2 shows FDI as a percentage of host countries' investment or 'gross fixed capital formation' (GFCF). As you can see, with the exception of 2001, both have risen dramatically in recent years.

In the world's developed economies, FDI inflows fell from $1 trillion in 2000 to $503 billion in 2001, a 50 per cent fall. In developing economies, inflows fell far less dramatically, from $238 billion to $205 billion, a 14 per cent decline. Since 1986 the trend for FDI inflows has been towards developing economies. In 2001, developing economies received 28 per cent of the world's FDI inflows, with a further 4 per cent going to Central and Eastern European economies (see Table 23.3). The five largest host countries in the developing world received 62 per cent of all FDI inflows to developing economies. FDI is highly concentrated – so much so that the world's 49 poorest countries received only 2 per cent of the total FDI to developing countries, and only 0.5 per cent of world FDI.

As previously mentioned, the global stock of FDI was valued in 2001 at nearly $7 trillion, and the 850 000 foreign affiliates accounted for an estimated 11 per cent of world GDP.

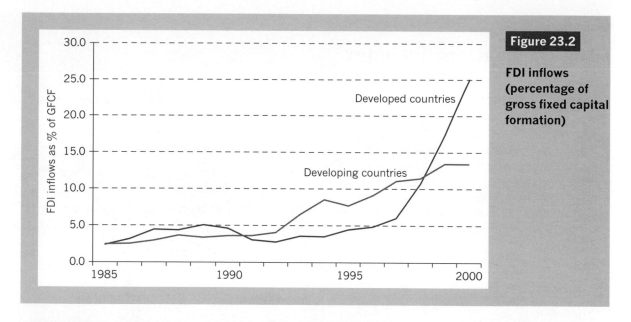

Figure 23.2

FDI inflows (percentage of gross fixed capital formation)

Table 23.3 **Distribution of world FDI inflows, 1986–2001**

Region	1986–1990	1991–1992	1993–1998	1999–2000ᵃ	2001
Developed countries	82.4	66.5	61.2	80.0	68.4
Western Europe	38.4	46.0	33.7	51.9	45.7
European Union	36.2	45.3	32.1	50.2	43.9
Japan	0.2	1.2	0.3	0.8	0.8
United States	34.6	12.7	21.7	22.6	16.9
Developing countries	17.5	31.2	35.3	17.9	27.9
Africa	1.8	2.2	1.8	0.8	2.3
Latin America and the Caribbean	5.0	11.7	12.3	7.9	11.6
Asia and the Pacific	10.6	17.4	21.2	9.2	13.9
Central and Eastern Europe	0.1	2.2	3.5	2.0	3.7
Memorandum					
Least developed countries	0.4	1.1	0.6	0.4	0.5

ᵃ Years characterized by exceptionally high cross-border M&A activity.
Note: The years with a yellow background are FDI trough periods, while non-shaded years are FDI growth periods.
Source: UNCTAD, FDI/TNC database

Countries that have a large foreign multinational sector, such as the UK, are significantly affected by the actions of foreign companies and their decisions about where to locate and invest. It is estimated that foreign affiliates world-wide employ some 54 million workers. In the UK it is estimated that, in 1997, 18 per cent of manufacturing employment, 34 per cent of all manufacturing sales, 6 per cent of value added and 32.5 per cent of all R&D expenditure came from foreign affiliates.

Before we consider the potential costs and benefits resulting from having a large multinational sector within the economy, we will first investigate what business can hope to gain from 'going multinational'.

BOX 23.1

The transnationality index

As part of the UNCTAD annual World Investment Report, attempts have been made to measure the 'transnationality' of both host countries and multinational businesses. Transnationality refers to the significance of foreign activities as part of either the performance of a country or business as a whole. The index offers both the opportunity to evaluate the degree of globalisation, as well as being able to identify the most globally orientated countries and business.

The transnationality index for host countries

The transnationality index for a country is based on the average of four variables:

- FDI inflows as a percentage of gross fixed capital formation (investment)
- FDI inward stock as a percentage of GDP
- Value added by foreign affiliates as a percentage of GDP

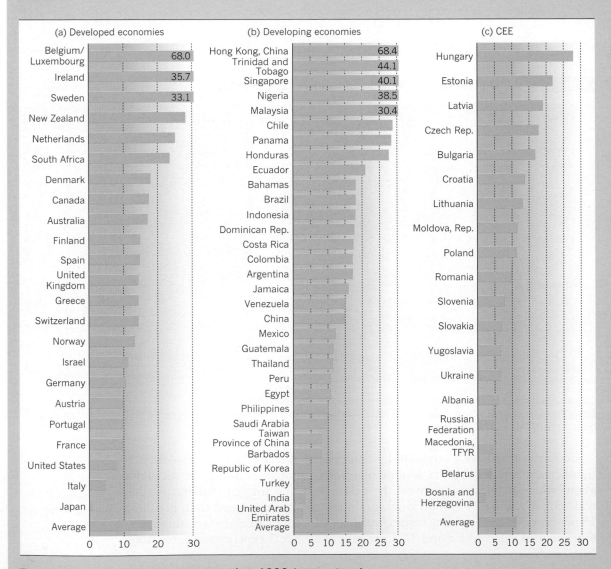

Transnationality index of host economies, 1999 (percentage)

Source: *World Investment Report 2002*, page 21 (UNCTAD)

The world's top 10 MNCs in terms of transnationality

Ranking in 2000		Ranking in 1999					
Foreign assets	TNI	Foreign assets	TNI	Corporation	Home country	Industry	TNI (Per cent)
39	1	86	34	Rio Tinto	United Kingdom	Mining and quarrying	98.2
49	2	56	1	Thomson	Canada	Media	95.3
24	3	21	3	ABB	Switzerland	Machinery and equipment	94.9
18	4	11	2	Nestlé	Switzerland	Food and beverages	94.7
31	5	35	7	British American Tobacco	United Kingdom	Tobacco	94.4
91	6	79	4	Electrolux	Sweden	Electrical and electronic equipment	93.2
86	7	–	–	Interbrew	Belgium	Food and beverages	90.2
26	8	–	–	Anglo American	United Kingdom	Mining and quarrying	88.4
52	9	90	20	Astrazeneca	United Kingdom	Pharmaceuticals	86.9
25	10	33	35	Philips Electronics	Netherlands	Electrical and electronic equipment	85.7

Source: *World Investment Report 2002*, Table IV.8, page 97 (UNCTAD)

■ Employment by foreign affiliates as a percentage of total employment.

In 1999 the average transnationality index for the 74 countries for which it was calculated was 16.9 per cent. For developed countries the index average was 18.0 per cent, and for developing economies 19.5 per cent. Central and Eastern European countries had the lowest index, standing at 11.2 per cent. The world's most transnational host economy is Hong Kong, followed by Belgium and Luxembourg, Trinidad and Tobago, and Singapore (see chart).

The transnationality index for business

The transnationality index for multinational business is composed of the average of three ratios:

■ Foreign assets to total assets
■ Foreign sales to total sales
■ Foreign employment to total employment.

Between 1991 and 2000 the average transnationality index for the world's 100 largest multinational companies rose from 51 to 56 per cent, implying a growing level of transnationality. In recent times it has been sales and employment that have driven the index upwards, while the ratio of foreign assets to total assets has in fact fallen. In 2000, 25 of the top 100 MNCs had an index value of 75 per cent or higher. The top 10 companies ranked by transnationality are given in the table.

Questions

1 *The leading nations in the transnationality index are all small. Is there a relationship between their size and the fact that they are at the top of the index?*

2 *Looking at the table can you offer any explanation to explain why no American and Japanese companies appear on this list?*

3 *How adequate do you feel such indices are in identifying how open or global an economy or business is? Should other indicators be considered as well? If so what?*

23.4 Why do businesses go multinational?

There are many reasons why companies choose to go multinational. These depend on the nature of their business and their corporate strategy. Before identifying the various motives for producing overseas rather than merely exporting to such countries, it is necessary to distinguish different categories of multinational.

- A **horizontally integrated multinational**. This type of multinational seeks to produce essentially the same product in different countries (but perhaps with some variations in product specification to suit the needs of the local market). The primary objective of this strategy is to achieve growth by expanding into new markets.

- A **vertically integrated multinational**. In this case, the multinational undertakes the various stages of production in different countries for a core business. Thus in some countries it will go backwards into the business's supply chain to the components or raw materials stages, and in others it will go forwards into the product's assembly or distribution. Oil companies such as Shell and Exxon (Esso) are good examples of vertically integrated multinationals, undertaking in a global operation the extraction of crude oil, controlling its transportation, refining it and producing by-products, and controlling the retail sale of petrol and other oil products. The principal motive behind such a growth strategy is to be able to exert greater control over costs and reduce the uncertainty of the business environment.

- A **conglomerate multinational**. Such multinationals produce a range of different products in different countries. By this process of diversification, conglomerate multinationals look to spread risks, and maximise returns through the careful buying of overseas assets. Unilever is a good example of a conglomerate multinational. It operates worldwide from 103 sites in various food, home care and personal care markets. Its brands include Walls and Ben & Jerry's ice cream; Birds Eye and Findus frozen foods; Slimfast diet foods; Knorr soups; Lawry's spices; Bertorelli pasta sauces; Hellman's mayonnaise; Lipton tea; Flora, Blue Band, Rama and Pro-activ margarines; Signal toothpaste; Domestos; Cif; Omo; Comfort; Organics and SunSilk shampoos; Vaseline, Dove and Lux soaps; Ponds skin care products; Impulse, Calvin Klein, Fabergé and Elizabeth Arden fragrances and deodorants.

We can see from the above classification that a clear distinction can be made between MNCs that are using their multinational base primarily as a means of reducing costs (vertically integrated multinationals) and those that are using it to achieve growth (horizontal and conglomerate multinationals). Let us now consider how, by going multinational, such goals might be achieved.

Reductions in costs

Nations, like individuals, are not equally endowed with factors of production. Some nations are rich in labour, some in capital, some in raw materials. In other words, individual nations might have specific advantages over others. Because such factors of production are largely immobile, especially between nations, businesses respond by becoming multinational: that is, they locate where the necessary factors of production they require can be found. In the case of a business that wishes to extract raw materials, it has little choice but to do this. But why might a business wish to move for labour? Here it is not simply a question of the *availability* of labour: rather it is a question of the relative *cost* of labour.

For example, it might locate an assembly plant in a developing country (i.e. a country with relatively low labour costs), if that plant uses large amounts of labour relative to the value added to the product at that stage. Thus foreign countries, with different cost conditions, are able to provide business with a more competitive environment within which to produce its products.

Cost differences between countries are ruthlessly exploited by Nike, the American sportswear manufacturer. Nike has organised itself globally such that it can respond rapidly to changing cost conditions in its international subsidiaries. Its product development operations are carried out in the USA, but all of its production operations are subcontracted out to over 40 overseas locations, mostly in south and south-east Asia. If wage rates, and hence costs, rise in one host country, then production is simply transferred to a more profitable subsidiary. So long as Nike headquarters has adequate information regarding the cost conditions of its subsidiaries, management decision-making concerning the location of production simply follows the operation of market forces.

Key Idea
16
p169

The location of multinational operations does not simply depend on factor *prices*: it also depends on factor *quality*. For example, a country might have a highly skilled or highly industrious workforce, and it is this, rather than simple wage rates, that attracts multinational investment. The issue here is still largely one of costs. Highly skilled workers might cost more to employ *per hour*, but if their productivity is higher, they might well cost less to employ *per unit of output*. It is also the case, however, that highly skilled workers might produce a better quality product, and thus increase the firm's sales.

If a country has both lower-priced factors and high-quality factors, it will be very attractive to multinational investors. In recent years, the UK government has sought to attract multinational investment through its lower labour costs and more flexible employment conditions than those of its European rivals, while still having a relatively highly trained labour force compared with those in developing countries, although, as the opening example to this chapter illustrates, such advantages are disappearing rapidly.

> **Pause for thought**
>
> Before reading on, try to identify other ways in which locating production overseas might help reduce costs.

Locating production in a foreign country can also reduce costs in other ways. For example, a business locating production overseas would be able to reduce transport costs if those overseas plants served local or regional markets, or used local raw materials. One of the biggest cost advantages concerns the avoidance of tariffs (customs duties). If a country imposes tariffs on imports, then, by locating *within* that country (i.e. behind the 'tariff wall'), the MNC gains a competitive advantage over its rivals which are attempting to import their products from outside the country, and which are thus having to pay the tariff.

Costs might also be reduced as a consequence of the host government's attitude towards MNC investment. In an attempt to attract inward investment, a government might offer the MNC a whole range of financial and cost-reducing incentives, many of which help reduce the fixed (or 'sunk') costs of the investment, thereby reducing the investment's risk. The granting of favourable tax differentials and depreciation allowances, and the provision of premises are all widely used government strategies to attract foreign business. A recent case in the UK saw a potential investor offered financial incentives valued at £37 000 per employee to locate production in an area of Wales!

In highly competitive global markets, even small cost savings might mean the difference between success and failure. Thus MNCs will be constantly searching for ways of minimising costs and locating production where the greatest advantage might be gained.

Growth strategy

Once markets within the domestic economy have become saturated, and opportunities for growth diminish, dynamic firms may seek new markets and hence new opportunities by expanding production overseas. As we saw in Chapter 15, businesses can look to expand in one of two ways: through either internal or external expansion. MNCs are no exception to this rule. They can expand overseas, either by creating a new production facility from scratch (such as Nissan in the north-east of England), or by merging with or taking over existing foreign producers (such as the acquisition of Asda by Wal-Mart).

Expanding by becoming multinational enables the business to spread its risks (it is no longer tied to the specific market conditions of one particular country), and in addition it enables the business to exploit any specific advantages or core competencies it might have over its foreign rivals in their home markets. Such advantages might include the following:

■ The ownership of superior technology. Such ownership will not only enhance the productivity levels of the MNC, but probably also contribute to the production of superior-quality products.

■ Entrepreneurial and managerial skills. With the arrival of Japanese multinationals in the UK, it became instantly apparent that Japanese managers conducted business in a very different way from their British counterparts. The most fundamental difference concerned working practices. Japanese MNCs quickly established themselves as among the most efficient and productive businesses in the UK (see section 18.7 on the flexible firm).

■ Research and development capacity. Like big business generally, MNCs are likely to invest heavily in R&D in an attempt to maintain their global competitiveness. The global scale of their operations allows them to spread the costs of this R&D over a large output (i.e. the R&D has a low average fixed cost). MNCs, therefore, are often world leaders in process innovation and product development.

The product life cycle and the multinational company

By shifting production overseas at a particular point in the product's life cycle, the business is able to reduce costs and maintain competitiveness. The product life cycle hypothesis was discussed at length in Chapter 17. However, it is worth reviewing its elements here in order to identify how an MNC, by altering the geographical production of a good, might extend its profitability.

A product's life cycle can be split into four phases: launch, growth, maturity and decline.

The launch phase. This will tend to see the new product produced in the economy where the product is developed. It will be exported to the rest of the world. At this stage of the product's life cycle, the novelty of the product and the monopoly position of the producer enable the business to charge high prices and make high profits.

The growth phase. As the market begins to grow, other producers will seek to copy or imitate the new product. Prices begin to fall. In order to maintain competitiveness, the business will look to reduce costs, and at this stage might consider shifting production overseas to lower-cost production centres.

Maturity. At the early stage of maturity, the business is still looking to sell its product in the markets of the developed economies. Thus it may still be happy to locate some of its plants in such economies. As the original market becomes increasingly saturated, however, the MNC will seek to expand into markets overseas which are at an earlier stage of development. Part of this expansion will be by the MNC simply exporting to these economies, but increasingly it will involve relocating its production there too.

Maturity and decline. By the time the original markets are fully mature and moving into decline, the only way to extend the product's life is to cut costs and sell the product in the markets of developing countries. The location of production may shift once again, this time to even lower-cost countries. By this stage, the country in which the product was developed will almost certainly be a net importer (if there is a market left for the product), but it may well be importing the product from a subsidiary of the same company that produced it within that country in the first place!

Thus we can see that the ability to transfer production to different locations reduces costs and enables profits to be made from a product that could have become unprofitable if its production had continued from its original production base.

Problems facing multinationals

In the vast majority of cases, businesses go multinational for sound business and economic reasons, which we have outlined above. However, multinational corporations may face a number of problems resulting from their geographical expansion:

■ Language barriers. The problem of language is less of a difficulty in the developed economies of the world than it is in the developing markets of, for example, Africa or Latin America. The more that the MNC employs expatriate rather than local staff, the greater the problem will be.

■ Selling and marketing in foreign markets. Strategies that work at home might fail overseas, given wide social and cultural differences. Many US multinationals, such as McDonald's and Coca-Cola, are frequently accused of imposing American values in the design and promotion of their products, irrespective of the country and its culture. This can lead to resentment and hostility in the host country, which may ultimately backfire on the MNC.

■ Attitudes of host governments. Governments will often try to get the best possible deal for their country from multinationals. This could result in governments insisting on part ownership in the subsidiary (either by themselves or by domestic firms), or tight rules and regulations governing the MNC's behaviour, or harsh tax regimes. In response, the MNC can always threaten to locate elsewhere.

■ Communication and co-ordination between subsidiaries. Diseconomies of scale may result from an expanding global business. Lines of communication become longer and more complex. These problems are likely to be greater, the greater is the attempted level of control exerted by the parent company: in other words, the more the parent company attempts to conduct business as though the subsidiaries were regional branches. Multinational organisational structures where international subsidiaries operate largely independently of the parent state will tend to minimise such problems.

BOX 23.2

The UK and the changing face of FDI

In 2000 global flows of FDI reached record levels, and even though the UK's share in this year fell, FDI money flowing into the country jumped by over 44 per cent to a record £78.5 billion. In the past two years FDI has been falling in absolute terms, a trend that has been happening throughout the world economy. The UK's share of European FDI has fallen from 20.6 per cent in 1997 to 18.7 per cent in 2001. Analysts expect this trend to continue as business shifts ever-larger volumes of manufacturing production to low cost sites such as China.

By the end of 2002 the number of new FDI projects planned for the UK was down 12 per cent, and more worryingly the number of jobs tied to these projects was 52 per cent down. So not only are there fewer FDI projects but they are smaller and less likely to create significant employment opportunities.

Not only is the UK finding it increasingly hard to attract FDI, but like its international rivals, British business is increasingly looking to invest overseas in order to maintain its global competitiveness. According to Deloite Research, it is estimated that western financial institutions will ship over 2 million jobs to India alone over the next five years. Given the UK's prominent role in this sector, and its close ties with the Indian subcontinent, this translates into the loss of 200 000 British jobs.

If such trends continue the net FDI position of the UK looks increasingly precarious and not the source of job creation and prosperity that it once was.

Question

What do you think the UK government might do to either minimise FDI outflows, or attract a greater volume of FDI inflow?

23.5 The advantages of MNC investment for the host state

As mentioned previously, host governments are always on the look-out to attract foreign direct investment, and are prepared to put up considerable finance and make significant concessions to attract overseas business. So what benefits do MNCs bring to the economy?

Employment

If MNC investment is in new plant (as opposed to merely taking over an existing company) this will generate employment. Most countries attempt to entice MNCs to depressed regions where investment is low and unemployment is high. Often these will be regions where a major industry has closed (e.g. the coal mining regions of South Wales). The employment that MNCs create is both direct, in the form of people employed in the new production facility, and indirect, through the impact that the MNC has on the local economy. This might be the consequence of establishing a new supply network, or simply the result of the increase in local incomes and expenditure, and hence the stimulus to local business.

When Lucky Goldstar (LG) invested £1.7 billion in South Wales in 1995, it created 6100 jobs directly in its new production facilities. It was estimated that a further 8400 jobs were created within the local economy as a result of that investment. Such additional jobs were generated primarily by component suppliers and the development of a distribution network.

It is possible, however, that jobs created in one region of a country by a new MNC venture, with its superior technology and working practices, might cause a business to fold elsewhere, thus leading to increased unemployment in that region.

The balance of payments

A country's balance of payments is likely to improve on a number of counts as a result of inward MNC investment. First, the investment will represent a direct flow of capital into the country. Second, and perhaps more important (especially in the long term), MNC investment is likely to result in both **import substitution** and export promotion. Import substitution will occur as products, previously purchased as imports, are now produced domestically. Export promotion will be enhanced as many multinationals use their new production facilities as export platforms. For example, many Japanese MNCs invest in the UK in order to gain access to the European Union.

definition

Import substitution
The replacement of imports by domestically produced goods or services.

The beneficial effect on the balance of payments, however, will be offset to the extent that profits earned from the investment are repatriated to the parent country, and to the extent that the exports of the MNC displace the exports of domestic producers.

In the UK it is estimated that around half of all output produced by overseas-owned manufacturers is exported, and that the net effect of inward investment represents a positive contribution to the UK balance of payments of about £1 billion a year.

Technology transfer

Technology transfer refers to the benefits gained by domestic producers from the technology imported by the MNC. Such benefits can occur in a number of ways. The most common is where domestic producers copy the production technology and working practices of the MNC. This is referred to as the 'demonstration effect' and has occurred widely in the UK as British businesses have attempted to emulate many of the practices brought into the country by Japanese multinationals.

definition

Technology transfer
Where a host state benefits from the new technology that an MNC brings with its investment.

In addition to copying best practice, technology might also be transferred through the training of workers. When workers move jobs from the MNC to other firms in the industry, or to other industrial sectors, they take their newly acquired technical knowledge and skills with them.

Taxation

MNCs, like domestic producers, are required to pay tax and therefore contribute to public finances. Given the highly profitable nature of many MNCs, the level of tax revenue raised from this source could be highly significant.

The disadvantages of MNC investment for the host state   23.6

Thus far we have focused on the positive effects resulting from multinational investment. However, multinational investment may not always be beneficial in either the short or the long term.

Uncertainty. MNCs are often 'footloose', meaning that they can simply close down their operations in foreign countries and move. This is especially likely with older plants which would need updating if the MNC were to remain, or with plants that can be easily sold without too much loss. The ability to close down its business operations and shift production, while being a distinct economic advantage to the MNC, is a prime concern facing the host nation. If a country has a large foreign multinational sector within the economy, it will become very vulnerable to such footloose activity, and face great uncertainty in the long term. It may thus be forced to offer the multinational 'perks' (e.g. grants, special tax relief or specific facilities) in order to persuade it to remain. These perks are clearly costly to the taxpayer.

Control. The fact that an MNC can shift production locations not only gives it economic flexibility, but enables it to exert various controls over its host. This is particularly so in many developing countries, where MNCs are not only major employers but in many cases the principal wealth creators. Thus attempts by the host state, for example, to improve worker safety or impose pollution controls may be against what the MNC sees as its own best interests. It might thus oppose such measures or even threaten to withdraw from the country if such measures are not modified or dropped. The host nation is in a very weak position.

Transfer pricing. MNCs, like domestic producers, are always attempting to reduce their tax liabilities. One unique way that an MNC can do this is through a process known as *transfer pricing* (see page 338). This enables the MNC to reduce its profits in countries with high rates of profit tax, and increase them in countries with low rates of profit tax. This can be achieved by simply manipulating its internal pricing structure. For example, take a vertically integrated MNC where subsidiary A in one country supplies components to subsidiary B in another. The price at which the components are transferred between the two subsidiaries (the 'transfer price') will ultimately determine the costs and hence the levels of profit made in each country. Assume that in the country where subsidiary A is located, the level of corporation tax is half that of the country where subsidiary B is located. If components are transferred from A to B at very high prices, then B's costs will rise and its profitability will fall. Conversely, A's profitability will rise. The MNC clearly benefits as more profit is taxed at the lower rather than the higher rate. Had it been the other way around, with subsidiary B facing the lower rate of tax, then the components would be transferred at a low price. This would increase subsidiary B's profits and reduce A's.

The practice of transfer pricing has reached such a level in the USA that, according to recent estimates, the federal government is losing over $100 million per day in tax revenue. The extent of this tax evasion was revealed when it was found that a US-based multinational subsidiary purchased toothbrushes from an affiliate for a price of $18 each!

The environment. Many MNCs are accused of simply investing in countries to gain access to natural resources, which are subsequently extracted or used in a way that is not sensitive to the environment. Host nations, especially developing countries, that are keen for investment are frequently prepared to allow MNCs to do this. They often put more store on the short-run gains from the MNC's presence than on the long-run depletion of precious natural resources or damage to the environment. Governments, like many businesses, often have a very short-run focus: they are concerned more with their political survival (whether through the ballot box or through military force) than with the long-term interests of their people.

Multinational corporations and developing economies

23.7

Many of the benefits and costs of MNC investment that we have considered so far are most acutely felt in developing countries. The poorest countries of the world are most in need of investment and yet are most vulnerable to exploitation by multinationals and have the least power to resist it. There tends, therefore, to be a love–hate relationship between the peoples of the developing world and the giant corporations that are seen to be increasingly dominating their lives: from the spread of agribusiness into the countryside through the ownership and control of plantations, to international mining corporations despoiling vast tracts of land; from industrial giants dominating manufacturing, to international banks controlling the flow of finance; from international tour operators and hotels bringing the socially disruptive effects of affluent tourists from North America, Japan, Europe and Australasia, to the products of the rich industrialised countries fashioning consumer tastes and eroding traditional culture.

Although MNCs employ only a small proportion of the total labour force in developing countries, they have a powerful effect on these countries' economies, often dominating the import and export sectors. They also often exert considerable power and influence over political leaders and their policies and over civil servants, and are frequently accused of 'meddling' in politics.

It is easy to see the harmful social, environmental and economic effects of multinationals on developing countries, and yet governments in these countries are so eager to attract overseas investment that they are frequently prepared to offer considerable perks to MNCs and to turn a blind eye to many of their excesses.

Does MNC investment aid development?

Whether investment by multinationals in developing countries is seen to be a net benefit or a net cost to these countries depends on what are perceived to be their development goals. If maximising the growth in national income is the goal, then MNC investment has probably made a positive contribution. If, however, the objectives of development are seen as more wide reaching, and include goals such as greater equality, the relief of poverty, a growth in the provision of basic needs (such as food, health care, housing and sanitation) and a general growth in the freedom and sense of well-being of the mass of the population, then the net effect of multinational investment could be argued to be anti-developmental.

Advantages to the host country

In order for countries to achieve economic growth, there must be investment. In general, the higher the rate of investment, the higher will be the rate of economic growth. The need for economic growth tends to be more pressing in developing countries than in advanced countries. One obvious reason is their lower level of income. If they are ever to aspire to the living standards of the rich North, then income per head will have to grow at a considerably faster rate than in rich countries and for many years. Another reason is the higher rates of population growth in developing countries – often some 2 per cent higher than in the rich countries. This means that for income per head to grow at merely the *same* rate as in rich countries, developing countries will have to achieve growth rates 2 per cent higher.

Investment requires finance. But developing countries are generally acutely short of funds: FDI can help to make up the shortfall. Specifically, there are key 'gaps' that FDI can help to fill.

The savings gap. A country's rate of economic growth (*g*) depends crucially on two factors:

■ The amount of extra capital that is required to produce an extra unit of output per year: i.e. the marginal capital/output ratio (*k*). The greater the marginal capital/output ratio, the lower will be the output per year that results from a given amount of investment.

■ The proportion of national income that a country saves (*s*). The higher this proportion, the greater the amount of investment that can be financed.

There is a simple formula that relates the rate of economic growth to these two factors. It is known as the **Harrod–Domar model** (after the two economists, Sir Roy Harrod and Evsey Domar, who independently developed the model). The formula is:

$$g = s/k$$

Thus if a developing country saved 10 per cent of its national income (*s* = 10%), and if £4 of additional capital were required to produce £1 of extra output per annum (*k* = 4), then the rate of economic growth would be 10%/4 = 2.5 per cent.

If that developing country wanted to achieve a rate of economic growth of 5 per cent, then it would require a rate of saving of 20 per cent (5% = 20%/4). There would thus be a shortfall of savings: a **savings gap**. Most, if not all, developing countries perceive themselves as having a savings gap. Not only do they require relatively high rates of economic growth in order to keep ahead of population growth and to break out of poverty, but they tend to have relatively low rates of saving. Poor people cannot afford to save much out of their income.

This is where FDI comes in. It can help to fill the savings gap by directly financing the investment required to achieve the target rate of growth.

The foreign exchange gap. There are many items, especially various raw materials and machinery, that many developing countries do not produce themselves and yet which are vital if they are to develop. Such items have to be imported. But this requires foreign exchange, and most developing countries suffer from a chronic shortage of foreign exchange. Their demand for imports grows rapidly: they have a high income elasticity of demand for imports – for both capital goods and consumer goods. Yet their exports tend to grow relatively slowly. Reasons include: the development of synthetic substitutes for the raw material exports of developing countries (e.g. plastics for rubber and metal) and the relatively low income elasticity of demand for primary products (the demand for things such as tea, coffee, sugar cane and rice tends to grow relatively slowly).

FDI can help to alleviate the shortage of foreign exchange: it can help to close the **foreign exchange gap**. Not only will the MNC bring in capital which might otherwise have had to be purchased with scarce foreign exchange, but any resulting exports by the MNC will increase the country's future foreign exchange earnings.

Public finance gap. Governments in developing countries find it difficult to raise enough tax revenues to finance all the projects they would like to. MNC profits provide an additional source of tax revenue.

definition

Harrod–Domar model
A model that relates a country's rate of economic growth to the proportion of national income saved and the ratio of capital to output.

definition

Savings gap
The shortfall in savings to achieve a given rate of economic growth.

definition

Foreign exchange gap
The shortfall in foreign exchange that a country needs to purchase necessary imports such as raw materials and machinery.

Skills and technology gaps. MNCs bring management expertise and often provide training programmes for local labour. The capital that flows into the developing countries with MNC investment often embodies the latest technology, access to which the developing country would otherwise be denied.

Disadvantages to the host country

Whereas there is the potential for MNCs to make a significant contribution to closing the above gaps, in practice they close them only slightly, or even make them bigger! The following are the main problems:

- They may use their power in the markets of host countries to drive domestic producers out of business, thereby lowering domestic profits and domestic investment.

- They may buy few, if any, of their components from domestic firms, but import them instead: perhaps from one of their subsidiaries.

- The bulk of their profits may simply be repatriated to shareholders in the rich countries, with little, if any, reinvested in the developing country. This, plus the previous point, will tend to make the foreign exchange gap worse.

- Their practice of transfer pricing may give little scope for the host government to raise tax revenue from them. Governments of developing countries are effectively put in competition with each other, each trying to undercut the others' tax rates in order to persuade the MNC to price its intermediate products in such a way as to make its profits in their country.

- Similarly, governments of developing countries compete with each other to offer the most favourable terms to MNCs (e.g. government grants, government contracts, tax concessions and rent-free sites). The more favourable the terms, the less the gain for developing countries as a whole.

- The technology and skills brought in by the multinationals may be fiercely guarded by the MNC. What is more, the dominance of the domestic market by MNCs may lead to the demise of domestic firms and indigenous technology, thereby worsening the skill and technology base of the country.

In addition to these problems, MNCs can alter the whole course of development in ways that many would argue are undesirable. By locating in cities, they tend to attract floods of migrants from the countryside looking for work, but of whom only a small fraction will find employment in these industries. The rest swell the ranks of the urban unemployed, often dwelling in squatter settlements on the outskirts of cities and living in appalling conditions.

More fundamentally, they are accused of distorting the whole pattern of development and of worsening the gap between the rich and poor. Their technology is capital intensive (compared with indigenous technology). The result is too few job opportunities. Those who are employed, however, receive relatively high wages, and are able to buy their products. These are the products consumed in affluent countries – from cars, to luxury foodstuffs, to household appliances – products that the MNCs often advertise heavily, and where they have considerable monopoly/oligopoly power. The resulting 'coca-colanisation', as it has been called, creates wants for the mass of people, but wants that they have no means of satisfying.

> **Pause for thought**
>
> *What problems is a developing country likely to experience if it adopts a policy of restricting, or even preventing, access to its markets by multinational business?*

BOX 23.3

Grocers go global

Carrefour in its Chinese stores, alongside the fish department, has a fresh snake counter. Wal-Mart boasts that in its Chinese stores you can find local delicacies such as whole roasted pigs and live frogs. Are fresh snakes and live frogs what's needed to succeed in China? It would seem so. Global companies thinking local, customising themselves to each market is increasingly seen as the key to success in Asia and elsewhere around the world.

The expansion of European and American grocer retailers into global markets has been underway for a number of years. Driven by stagnant markets at home with limited growth opportunities, the major players in Europe, such as Carrefour and Casino from France, Tesco in the UK, Ahold from Holland and Metro from Germany, have been looking to expand their overseas operations – but with mixed success.

In recent times, Asia has been the market's growth sector. Tesco entered the Thai market in 1998. Tesco Lotus, the company's regional subsidiary, is now the country's number-one retailer, with 26 stores. Carrefour and the US-based Wal-Mart have plans to open hundreds of new outlets within the region over the next few years.

Given the distinctive nature of markets within Asia, business must learn to adapt to local conditions. Joint ventures and local knowledge are seen as the key ingredients to success. Even the most closed markets, such as those of Japan, are not immune from the global grocers' onslaught. Wal-Mart has recently acquired a large stake in the ailing 400-store food and clothing chain Seiyu. Tesco has let it be known that it is seeking a suitable partner to move into China.

Facing up to the big boys

With the rapid expansion of hypermarkets throughout Asia, the retail landscape is undergoing revolutionary change. With a wide range of products all under one roof, from groceries to pharmaceuticals to white goods, and at cut-rate prices, local neighbourhood stores stand little chance in the competitive battle. 'Mom and pop operations have no economies of scale.' As well as local retailers, local suppliers are also facing a squeeze on profits, as hypermarkets demand lower prices and use their buying power as leverage.

Such has been the dramatic impact these stores have had upon the retail and grocery sector, that a number of Asian economies, such as Malaysia and Thailand, have introduced restrictions on the building of new outlets. China has restricted licensing to foreign companies, such as Carrefour, wishing to locate in Beijing, as well as offering tax incentives and other subsidies to encourage domestic retailers to gain ground in the market.

What can developing countries do?

Can developing countries gain the benefits of FDI while avoiding the effects of growing inequality and inappropriate products and technologies? If a developing country is large and is seen as an important market for the multinational, if it would be costly for the multinational to relocate and if the government is well informed about the multinational's costs, then the country's bargaining position will be relatively strong. It may be able to get away with relatively high taxes on the MNC's profits and tight regulation of its behaviour (e.g. its employment practices and its care for the environment). If, however, the country is economically weak and the MNC is footloose, then the deal it can negotiate is unlikely to be very favourable.

The bargaining position of developing countries would be enhanced if they could act jointly in imposing conditions on multinational investment and behaviour. Such agreement is unlikely, however, given the diverse nature of developing countries' governments and economies, and the pro free market, deregulated world of the early 2000s.

SUMMARY

1a The process of globalisation can have profound effects on economies. One current feature of globalisation is the relocating of various service and knowledge-based jobs from developed to developing countries.

1b There are various drivers of globalisation, including market, cost, government and competitive drivers.

1c Supporters of globalisation point to its potential to lead to faster growth and greater efficiency through trade, competition and investment. It also has the potential to draw the world closer together politically.

1d Critics of globalisation argue that it contributes to growing inequality and further impoverishes poor nations. It also erodes national cultures and can have adverse environmental consequences.

2 There is great diversity among multinationals in respect to size, nature of business, size of overseas operations, location, ownership and organisational structure.

3 Foreign direct investment (FDI) tends to fluctuate with the ups and downs of the world economy. Thus in 2001, a year of global economic slowdown, worldwide FDI fell. Over the years, however, FDI has grown substantially, and has accounted for a larger and larger proportion of total investment.

4a Why businesses go multinational depends largely upon the nature of their business and their corporate strategy. However, we can draw a clear line between businesses which seek to reduce costs by becoming multinational, and those which become multinational in order to achieve growth.

4b An influential theory on MNC development is the product life cycle hypothesis. In this theory, a business will shift production around the world seeking to reduce costs and extend a given product's life. The phases of a product's life will

be conducted in different countries. As the product nears maturity and competition grows, reducing costs to maintain competitiveness will force business to locate production in low-cost markets, such as developing economies.

4c Although becoming an MNC is largely advantageous to the business, it can experience problems with language barriers, selling and marketing in foreign markets, attitudes of the host state and the communication and co-ordination of global business activities.

5 Host states find multinational investment advantageous in respect to employment creation, contributions to the balance of payments, the transfer of technology and the contribution to taxation.

6 Host states find multinational investment disadvantageous in so far as it creates uncertainty; foreign business can control or manipulate the country or regions within it; tax payments can be avoided by transfer pricing; and MNCs might misuse the environment.

7a The benefits of MNCs to developing countries depend upon the developing countries' development goals.

7b MNCs bring with them investment, which is crucial to economic growth. They also provide the host state with foreign exchange, which might be crucial in helping purchase vital imports.

7c MNCs might prove to be disadvantageous to developing economies if they drive domestic producers out of business, source production completely from other countries, repatriate profits, practise transfer pricing to avoid tax, force host states to offer favourable tax deals or subsidies for further expansion, and guard technology to prevent its transfer to domestic producers.

REVIEW QUESTIONS

1 What are the advantages and disadvantages to an economy, like that of the UK, of having a large multinational sector?

2 How might the structure of a multinational differ depending upon whether its objective of being multinational is to reduce costs or to grow?

3 If reducing costs is so important for many multinationals, why is it that many locate production not in low-cost developing economies, but in economies within the developed world?

4 Explain the link between the life cycle of a product and multinational business.

5 Assess the advantages and disadvantages facing a host state when receiving MNC investment.

6 Debate the following:

'Multinational investment can be nothing but good for developing economies seeking to grow and prosper.'

24 International trade

Without international trade we would all be much poorer. There would be some items like pineapples, coffee, cotton clothes, foreign holidays and uranium that we would simply have to go without. Then there would be other items like wine and spacecraft that we could produce only very inefficiently.

Key Idea 2 p19

International trade has the potential to benefit *all* participating countries. This chapter explains why.

Totally free trade, however, may bring problems to countries or to groups of people within those countries. Many people argue strongly for restrictions on trade. Textile workers see their jobs threatened by cheap imported cloth. Car manufacturers worry about falling sales as customers switch to Japanese models or other east Asian ones. This chapter, therefore, also examines the arguments for restricting trade. Are people justified in fearing international competition, or are they merely trying to protect some vested interest at the expense of everyone else?

24.1 Trading patterns

Since 1947, world trade has consistently grown faster than world output. In 2003, world merchandise exports were worth over $6 trillion. In real terms, that represents a 21-fold increase since 1950, compared with a 7-fold increase in world real GDP. In 1950, only 8 per cent of countries' output of goods and services was sold abroad; today the figure is 26 per cent. As can be seen in Figure 24.1, the growth in world trade has, on average, consistently outstripped the growth in world production.

The geography of international trade

The major industrial economies dominate world trade (see Figure 24.2). Some 70 per cent of all merchandise trade is conducted by the developed economies. The EU countries with approximately 41 per cent of exports (by value) and 40 per cent of imports (by value) are the most important trading region. The most important individual country in respect to trade is the USA, followed by Germany and Japan. The USA sells some 12 per cent of world exports and consumes approximately 18 per cent of world imports. Germany sells about 9 per cent of world exports and consumes about 8 per cent of world imports. The concentration of world trade is further highlighted by the fact that the top eight nations account for over 50 per cent of all world trade.

Figure 24.1

Growth in world real GDP and world merchandise exports (volume)

Source: *Trade Statistics*, WTO (**www.wto.org**)

Figure 24.2

Share of world merchandise exports, by value (2001)

Note: includes intra-EU trade.
Source: *International Trade Statistics 2002*, WTO (**www.wto.org**)

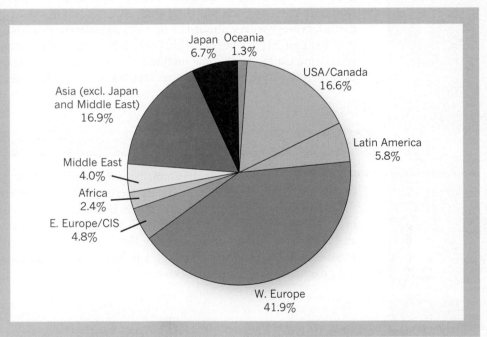

On a regional basis, Europe exhibits the highest level of intra-regional trading, selling nearly 70 per cent of its exports to other European countries. Other areas such as Latin America and Africa trade very little with themselves and rely heavily on North America merchandise and Europe to sell their products. Some 60 per cent of Latin American merchandise exports go to North America, whereas over 50 per cent of Africa's merchandise exports go to Europe.

Figure 24.3 shows the *growth* of exports and imports by region. China has achieved the most spectacular growth rate in exports (14 per cent annual average from 1990–2001). Although Latin American growth in exports (8 per cent over

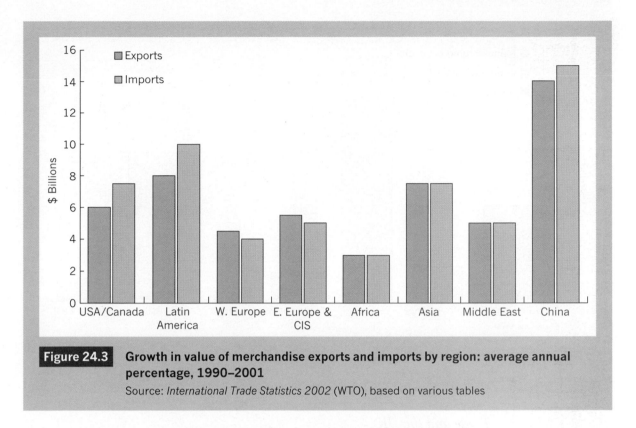

Figure 24.3 **Growth in value of merchandise exports and imports by region: average annual percentage, 1990–2001**

Source: *International Trade Statistics 2002* (WTO), based on various tables

the same period) has also been high by international standards, the region's growth in imports (10 per cent) has been much higher. Asian growth in exports has also been high, with the six Asian 'Tigers' (Singapore, Hong Kong, Malaysia, South Korea, Taiwan and Thailand) achieving an average of 7 per cent. In contrast, African countries only managed a 3 per cent growth in exports and imports. Middle Eastern countries experienced virtually no growth in export earnings during the 1990s, thanks to the generally falling price of oil. This changed in 1999–2001 as world oil prices surged. In 2000 alone, Middle Eastern export earnings rose by 42 per cent.

The composition of international trade

Trade in goods

By far the largest category of traded goods is that of manufactured products (see Figure 24.4). In 2001 manufactured products accounted for 74.8 per cent of all merchandise exports and 60.0 per cent of *total* exports (which include services). Agricultural products accounted for 9.1 per cent of merchandise exports and mining products 13.2 per cent.

Trade in services

Services in 2001 accounted for about 20 per cent of total trade. As with trade in manufactured products, trade in services is concentrated in the hands of the largest industrial nations. The USA is by far the largest exporter with some 18 per cent of all service exports, followed by the UK (7.4 per cent) and France (5.5 per cent). The largest importer of services is the USA with 13.0 per cent of the total, followed by Germany (9.2 per cent) and Japan (7.4 per cent).

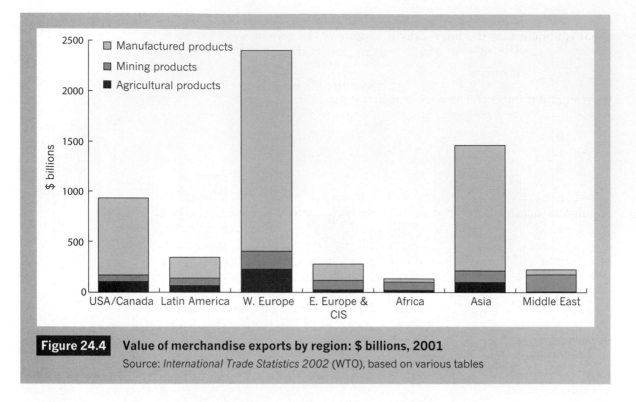

Figure 24.4 **Value of merchandise exports by region: $ billions, 2001**

Source: *International Trade Statistics 2002* (WTO), based on various tables

Trade and the UK

In 2001 the UK sold 4.4 per cent of world exports of goods and services and consumed 5.2 per cent of world imports.

In 2002, 55.2 per cent of the UK's exports of goods went to countries in the eurozone, 62.2 per cent to Western Europe as a whole, 17.3 per cent to North America and 14.6 per cent to developing countries.

UK imports, like UK exports, are strongly tied to Europe. In 2002, 50.6 per cent of the imports of goods came from eurozone countries, 59.4 per cent from Western Europe as a whole, 13.4 per cent from North America and 19.6 per cent from developing countries.

24.2 The advantages of trade

Specialisation as the basis for trade

Why do countries trade with each other and what do they gain out of it? The reasons for international trade are really only an extension of the reasons for trade *within* a nation. Rather than people trying to be self-sufficient and do everything for themselves, it makes sense to specialise.

Firms specialise in producing certain types of goods. This allows them to gain economies of scale and to exploit their entrepreneurial and management skills and the skills of their labour force. It also allows them to benefit from their particular location and from the ownership of any particular capital equipment or other assets they might possess. With the revenues that firms earn, they buy in the inputs they need from other firms and the labour they require. Firms thus trade with each other.

Countries also specialise. They produce more than they need of certain goods. What is not consumed domestically is exported. The revenues earned from the exports are used to import goods which are not produced in sufficient amounts at home.

But which goods should a country specialise in? What should it export and what should it import? The answer is that it should specialise in those goods in which it has a *comparative advantage*. Let us examine what this means.

The law of comparative advantage

Countries have different endowments of factors of production. They differ in population density, labour skills, climate, raw materials, capital equipment, etc. These differences tend to persist because factors are relatively immobile between countries. Obviously land and climate are totally immobile, but even with labour and capital there tend to be more restrictions (physical, social, cultural or legal) on their international movement than on their movement within countries. Thus the ability to supply goods differs between countries.

What this means is that the relative costs of producing goods will vary from country to country. For example, one country may be able to produce 1 fridge for the same cost as 6 tonnes of wheat or 3 compact disc players, whereas another country may be able to produce 1 fridge for the same cost as only 3 tonnes of wheat but 4 CD players. It is these differences in relative costs that form the basis of trade.

At this stage we need to distinguish between *absolute advantage* and *comparative advantage*.

Absolute advantage

When one country can produce a good with less resources than another country, it is said to have an **absolute advantage** in that good. If France can produce wine with less resources than the UK, and the UK can produce gin with less resources than France, then France has an absolute advantage in wine and the UK an absolute advantage in gin. Production of both wine and gin will be maximised by each country specialising and then trading with the other country. Both will gain.

Comparative advantage

The above seems obvious, but trade between two countries can still be beneficial even if one country could produce *all* goods with less resources than the other, providing the *relative* efficiency with which goods can be produced differs between the two countries.

Take the case of a developed country that is absolutely more efficient than a less developed country at producing both wheat and cloth. Assume that with a given amount of resources (labour, land and capital) the alternatives shown in Table 24.1 can be produced in each country.

Despite the developed country having an absolute advantage in both wheat and cloth, the less developed country (LDC) has a *comparative* **advantage** in wheat, and the developed country has a *comparative* advantage in cloth. This is because wheat is relatively cheaper in the LDC: only 1 metre of cloth has to be sacrificed to produce 2 kilos of wheat, whereas 8 metres of cloth would have to be sacrificed in the developed country to produce 4 kilos of wheat. In other words, the opportunity cost of wheat is 4 times higher in the developed country (8/4 compared with 1/2).

Key Idea

3
p27

Table 24.1 Production possibilities for two countries

		Kilos of wheat		Metres of cloth
Less developed country	Either	2	or	1
Developed country	Either	4	or	8

On the other hand, cloth is relatively cheaper in the developed country. Here the opportunity cost of producing 8 metres of cloth is only 4 kilos of wheat, whereas in the LDC 1 metre of cloth costs 2 kilos of wheat. Thus the opportunity cost of cloth is 4 times higher in the LDC (2/1 compared with 4/8).

To summarise: countries have a comparative advantage in those goods that can be produced at a lower opportunity cost than in other countries.

If countries are to gain from trade, they should export those goods in which they have a comparative advantage and import those goods in which they have a comparative disadvantage. Given this, we can state a **law of comparative advantage**.

The law of comparative advantage. Provided opportunity costs of various goods differ in two countries, both of them can gain from mutual trade if they specialise in producing (and exporting) those goods that have relatively low opportunity costs compared with the other country.

Key Idea 31

But why do they gain if they specialise according to this law? And just what will that gain be? We will consider these questions next.

The gains from trade based on comparative advantage

Before trade, unless markets are very imperfect, the prices of the two goods are likely to reflect their opportunity costs. For example, in Table 24.1, since the less developed country can produce 2 kilos of wheat for 1 metre of cloth, the *price* of 2 kilos of wheat will roughly equal 1 metre of cloth.

Key Idea 3 p27

Assume, then, that the pre-trade exchange ratios of wheat for cloth are as follows:

LDC   : 2 wheat for 1 cloth
Developed country : 1 wheat for 2 cloth (i.e. 4 for 8)

Both countries will now gain from trade, provided the exchange ratio is somewhere between 2:1 and 1:2. Assume, for the sake of argument, that it is 1:1. In other words, 1 wheat trades internationally for 1 cloth. How will each country gain?

The LDC gains by exporting wheat and importing cloth. At an exchange ratio of 1:1, it now only has to give up 1 kilo of wheat to obtain a metre of cloth, whereas before trade it had to give up 2 kilos of wheat.

The developed country gains by exporting cloth and importing wheat. Again at an exchange ratio of 1:1, it now only has to give up 1 metre of cloth to obtain a kilo of wheat, whereas before it had to give up 2 metres of cloth.

Thus both countries have gained from trade.

The actual exchange ratios will depend on the relative prices of wheat and cloth after trade takes place. These prices will depend on total demand for and supply of the two goods. It may be that the trade exchange ratio is nearer to the pre-trade exchange ratio of one country than the other. Thus the gains to the two countries need not be equal.

> **Pause for thought**
>
> *Show how each country could gain from trade if the LDC could produce (before trade) 3 wheat for 1 cloth and the developed country could produce (before trade) 2 wheat for 5 cloth, and if the exchange ratio (with trade) was 1 wheat for 2 cloth. Would they both still gain if the exchange ratio was (a) 1 wheat for 1 cloth; (b) 1 wheat for 3 cloth?*

The limits to specialisation and trade

Does the law of comparative advantage suggest that countries will completely specialise in just a few products? In practice, countries are likely to experience *increasing* opportunity costs. The reason for this is that, as a country increasingly specialises in one good, it will have to use resources that are less and less suited to its production and which were more suited to other goods. Thus ever-increasing amounts of the other goods will have to be sacrificed. For example, as a country specialises more and more in grain production, it will have to use land that is less and less suited to growing grain.

These increasing costs as a country becomes more and more specialised will lead to the disappearance of its comparative cost advantage. When this happens, there will be no point in further specialisation. Thus whereas a country like Germany has a comparative advantage in capital-intensive manufactures, it does not produce only manufactures. It would make no sense not to use its fertile lands to produce food or its forests to produce timber. The opportunity costs of diverting all agricultural labour to industry would be very high.

Other reasons for gains from trade

Decreasing costs. Even if there are no initial comparative cost differences between two countries, it will still benefit both to specialise in industries where economies of scale can be gained, and then to trade. Once the economies of scale begin to appear, comparative cost differences will also appear, and thus the countries will have gained a comparative advantage in these industries.

This reason for trade is particularly relevant for small countries where the domestic market is not large enough to support large-scale industries. Thus exports form a much higher percentage of GDP in small countries such as Singapore than in large countries such as the USA.

Differences in demand. Even with no comparative cost differences and no potential economies of scale, trade can benefit both countries if demand conditions differ.

If people in country A like beef more than lamb, and people in country B like lamb more than beef, then rather than A using resources better suited for lamb to produce beef, and B using resources better suited for producing beef to produce lamb, it will benefit both to produce beef *and* lamb and to export the one they like less in return for the one they like more.

Increased competition. If a country trades, the competition from imports may stimulate greater efficiency at home. This extra competition may prevent domestic monopolies/oligopolies from charging high prices. It may stimulate greater research and development and the more rapid adoption of new technology. It may lead to a greater variety of products being made available to consumers.

Trade as an 'engine of growth'. In a growing world economy, the demand for a country's exports is likely to grow over time, especially when these exports have a high income elasticity of demand. This will provide a stimulus to growth in the exporting country.

Non-economic advantages. There may be political, social and cultural advantages to be gained by fostering trading links between countries.

The terms of trade

What price will our exports fetch abroad? What will we have to pay for imports? The answer to these questions is given by the **terms of trade**. The terms of trade are defined as:

$$\frac{\text{The average price of exports}}{\text{The average price of imports}}$$

expressed as an index, where prices are measured against a base year in which the terms of trade are assumed to be 100. Thus if the average price of exports relative to the average price of imports have risen by 20 per cent since the base year, the terms of trade will now be 120.

If the terms of trade rise (export prices rising relative to import prices), they are said to have 'improved', since fewer exports now have to be sold to purchase any given quantity of imports. Changes in the terms of trade are caused by changes in the demand and supply of imports and exports and by changes in the exchange rate.

24.3 Arguments for restricting trade

We have seen how trade can bring benefits to all countries. But when we look around the world, we often see countries erecting barriers to trade. Their politicians know that trade involves costs as well as benefits.

In looking at the costs and benefits of trade, the choice is not the stark one of whether to have free trade or no trade at all. Although countries may sometimes contemplate having completely free trade, typically countries limit their trade. However, they certainly do not ban it altogether.

Before we look at the arguments for restricting trade, we must first see what types of restriction governments can employ.

Methods of restricting trade

Tariffs (customs duties). These are taxes on imports and are usually **ad valorem**: i.e. a percentage of the price of the import. Tariffs used to restrict imports are most effective if demand is elastic (e.g. when there are close domestically produced substitutes). Tariffs can also be used as a means of raising revenue. Here they will be more effective if demand is inelastic. They can also be used to raise the price of imported goods to prevent 'unfair' competition for domestic producers.

Quotas. These are limits on the quantity of a good that can be imported. Quotas can be imposed by the government, or negotiated with other countries which agree 'voluntarily' to restrict the amount of exports to the first country.

Exchange controls. These include limits on the amount of foreign exchange made available to importers (financial quotas), or to citizens travelling abroad, or for investment. Alternatively, they can be in the form of charges for the purchase of foreign currencies.

Import licensing. The imposition of exchange controls or quotas will often involve importers obtaining licences so that the government can better enforce its restrictions.

Embargoes. This is where the government completely bans certain imports (e.g. drugs) or exports to certain countries (e.g. to enemies during war).

Export taxes. These can be used to increase the price of exports when the country has monopoly power in their supply.

Subsidies. These can be given to domestic producers to prevent competition from otherwise lower-priced imports. They can also be applied to exports in a process known as **dumping**. The goods are 'dumped' at artificially low prices in the foreign market.

> **definition**
> **Dumping**
> Where exports are sold at prices below marginal cost – often as a result of government subsidy.

Administrative barriers. Regulations may be designed to exclude imports. For example, all lagers that do not meet certain rigid purity standards could be banned. The Germans effectively excluded foreign brands by such measures. Other administrative barriers include taxes which favour locally produced products or ingredients.

Procurement policies. This is where governments favour domestic producers when purchasing equipment (e.g. defence equipment).

Arguments in favour of restricting trade

Arguments having some general validity

The infant industry argument. Some industries in a country may be in their infancy but have a potential comparative advantage. This is particularly likely in developing countries. Such industries are too small yet to have gained economies of scale; their workers are inexperienced; there is a lack of back-up facilities – communications networks, specialist research and development, specialist suppliers, etc. – and they may have only limited access to finance for expansion. Without protection, these **infant industries** will not survive competition from abroad.

Protection from foreign competition, however, will allow them to expand and become more efficient. Once they have achieved a comparative advantage, the protection can then be removed to enable them to compete internationally.

> **definition**
> **Infant industry**
> An industry which has a potential comparative advantage, but which is as yet too underdeveloped to be able to realise this potential.

Similar to the infant industry argument is the *senile industry* argument. This is where industries with a potential comparative advantage have been allowed to run down and can no longer compete effectively. They may have considerable potential, but be simply unable to make enough profit to afford the necessary investment without some temporary protection from foreign competition. This argument has been used to justify the use of special protection for the automobile and steel industries in the USA.

To reduce reliance on goods with little dynamic potential. Many developing countries have traditionally exported primaries: foodstuffs and raw materials. The world demand for these, however, is fairly income inelastic, and thus grows relatively slowly. In such cases, free trade is not an engine of growth. Instead, if it encourages countries' economies to become locked into a pattern of primary production, it may prevent them from expanding in sectors like manufacturing which have a higher income elasticity of demand. There may thus be a valid argument for protecting or promoting manufacturing industry.

To prevent 'dumping' and other unfair trade practices. A country may engage in dumping by subsidising its exports. Alternatively, firms may practise price discrimination by selling at a higher price in home markets and a lower price in foreign markets in order to increase their profits. Either way, prices may no longer reflect comparative costs. Thus the world would benefit from tariffs being imposed by importers to counteract the subsidy.

It can also be argued that there is a case for retaliating against countries which impose restrictions on your exports. In the *short* run, both countries are likely to be made worse off by a contraction in trade. But if the retaliation persuades the other country to remove its restrictions, it may have a longer-term benefit. In some cases, the mere threat of retaliation may be enough to get another country to remove its protection.

To prevent the establishment of a foreign-based monopoly. Competition from abroad could drive domestic producers out of business. The foreign company, now having a monopoly of the market, could charge high prices with a resulting misallocation of resources. The problem could be tackled either by restricting imports or by subsidising the domestic producer(s).

Key Idea 18 p211

All the above arguments suggest that governments should adopt a 'strategic' approach to trade. **Strategic trade theory** argues that protecting certain industries allows a net gain in the *long* run from increased competition in the market (see Box 24.1).

To spread the risks of fluctuating markets. A highly specialised economy – Zambia with copper, Cuba with sugar – will be highly susceptible to world market fluctuations. Greater diversity and greater self-sufficiency, although maybe leading to less efficiency, can reduce these risks.

To reduce the influence of trade on consumer tastes. The assumption of fixed consumer tastes dictating the pattern of production through trade is false. Multinational companies through their advertising and other forms of sales promotion may influence consumer tastes. Thus some restriction on trade may be justified in order to reduce this 'producer sovereignty'.

To prevent the importation of harmful goods. A country may want to ban or severely curtail the importation of things such as drugs, pornographic literature and live animals.

BOX 24.1

Strategic trade theory
The case of Airbus

Supporters of *strategic trade theory* hold that comparative advantage need not be the result of luck or circumstance, but may in fact be created by government. By diverting resources into selective industries, usually high tech and high skilled, a comparative advantage can be created through intervention.

An example of such intervention was the European aircraft industry, and in particular the creation of the European Airbus Consortium.

The European Airbus Consortium was established in the late 1960s, its four members being Aérospatiale (France), British Aerospace (now BAE Systems) (UK), CASA (Spain) and DASA (Germany). The setting up of this consortium was seen as essential for the future of the European aircraft industry for three reasons:

■ To share high R&D costs.
■ To generate economies of scale.
■ To compete successfully with the market's major players in the USA – Boeing and McDonnell Douglas (which have since merged).

The consortium, although privately owned, was sponsored by government and received state aid, especially in its early years when the company failed to make a profit. In more recent times Airbus has become very successful, capturing a larger and larger share of the world commercial aircraft market. By 2002, its share of the large civil aircraft market had risen to 57 per cent. As a consequence, it should come as no surprise to find that the Americans, and Boeing in particular, have brought accusations that Airbus is founded upon unfair trading practices and ought not to receive the level of governmental support that it does (see Box 25.2).

In 1999/2000, there were three major developments. The first was the merger of Aerospatiale-Matra, Dasa (DaimlerChrysler Aerospace) and Casa to form the giant European Aeronautic Defence and Space Company (EADS). The second was the creation of an Airbus Integrated Company (from EADS and BAE Systems) as a single entity to replace the looser Airbus Consortium. Then towards the end of 2000, it was announced that enough orders had been secured for the planned new 550+ seater A3XX for production to go ahead. This new jumbo will be a serious competitor to the long-established Boeing 747.

So does the experience of Airbus support the arguments of the strategic trade theorists? Essentially three kinds of benefit were expected to flow from Airbus and its presence in the aircraft market: lower prices, economic spillovers and profits.

■ Without Airbus the civil aircraft market would have been monopolised by two American firms, Boeing and McDonnell Douglas (and possibly one, if the 1997 merger had still gone ahead). Therefore the presence of Airbus would be expected to promote competition and thereby keep prices down. Studies in the 1980s and 1990s tended to support this view, suggesting that consumers have made significant gains from lower prices. One survey estimated that without Airbus commercial aircraft prices would have been 3.5 per cent higher than they currently are, and without both Airbus *and* McDonnell Douglas they would have been 15 per cent higher.

■ Economic spillovers from the Airbus Consortium, such as skills and technology developments, might be expected to benefit other industries. Findings are inconclusive on this point. It is clear, however, that although aggregate R&D in the whole aircraft industry has risen, so has the level of R&D duplication.

■ Airbus's presence in the market is estimated to have reduced Boeing's profits by as much as $100 billion, and McDonnell Douglas's by two-thirds. Airbus's turnover in 2002 was €19.4 billion.

On balance it appears that Airbus has had many positive effects and that the strategic trade theory that has underpinned state aid, in this instance, has led to a successful outcome. A competitive advantage has been created, and it looks as though it will be maintained into the future, and probably without state aid!

Questions

1 *In what other industries could the setting up of a consortium, backed by government aid, be justified as a means of exploiting a potential comparative advantage?*

2 *Is it only in industries that could be characterised as world oligopolies that strategic trade theory is relevant?*

To take account of externalities. Free trade will tend to reflect private costs. Both imports and exports, however, can involve externalities. The mining of many minerals for export may adversely affect the health of miners; the production of chemicals for export may involve pollution; the importation of juggernaut lorries may lead to structural damage to houses.

Key Idea 27 p402

Arguments having some validity for specific groups or countries

The arguments considered so far are of general validity: restricting trade for such reasons could be of net benefit to the world. There are other arguments, however, that are used by individual governments for restricting trade, where their country will gain, but at the expense of other countries, such that there will be a net loss to the world. Such arguments include the following.

The exploitation of monopoly power. If a country, or a group of countries, has monopsony power in the purchase of imports (i.e. they are individually or collectively a very large economy, such as the USA or the EU), then they could gain by restricting imports so as to drive down their price. Similarly, if countries have monopoly power in the sale of some export (e.g. OPEC countries with oil), then they could gain by forcing up the price.

Key Idea 18 p211

To protect declining industries. The human costs of sudden industrial closures can be very high. In such circumstances, temporary protection may be warranted to allow the industry to decline more slowly, thus avoiding excessive structural unemployment. Such policies will be at the expense of the consumer, who will be denied access to cheaper foreign imports.

'Non-economic' arguments for restricting trade. A country may be prepared to forgo the direct economic advantages of free trade in order to achieve objectives that are often described as 'non-economic':

- It may wish to maintain a degree of self-sufficiency in case trade is cut off in times of war. This may apply particularly to the production of food and armaments.
- It may decide not to trade with certain countries with which it disagrees politically.
- It may wish to preserve traditional ways of life. Rural communities or communities built round old traditional industries may be destroyed by foreign competition.
- It may prefer to retain as diverse a society as possible, rather than one too narrowly based on certain industries.

Pursuing such objectives, however, will involve costs. Preserving a traditional way of life, for example, may mean that consumers are denied access to cheaper goods from abroad. Society must therefore weigh up the benefits against the costs of such policies.

Problems with protection

Protection will tend to push up prices and restrict the choice of goods available. But apart from these direct costs to the consumer, there are several other problems. Some are a direct effect of the protection, others follow from the reactions of other nations.

Protection as 'second-best'. Many of the arguments for protection amount merely to arguments for some type of government intervention in the economy. Protection, however, may not be the best way of dealing with the problem, since protection may have undesirable side-effects. There may be a more direct form of intervention that has no side-effects. In such a case, protection will be no more than a *second-best* solution.

For example, using tariffs to protect old inefficient industries from foreign competition may help prevent unemployment in those parts of the economy, but the consumer will suffer from higher prices. A better solution would be to subsidise retraining and investment in those areas of the country in *new efficient* industries – industries with a comparative advantage. In this way, unemployment is avoided, but the consumer does not suffer.

World multiplier effects. If the UK imposes tariffs or other restrictions, imports will be reduced. But these imports are other countries' exports. A reduction in their exports will reduce the level of injections into the 'rest-of-the-world' economy, and thus lead to a multiplied fall in rest-of-the-world income. This in turn will lead to a reduction in demand for UK exports. This, therefore, tends to undo the benefits of the tariffs.

Retaliation. If the USA imposes restrictions on, say, imports from the EU, then the EU may impose restrictions on imports from the USA. Any gain to US firms competing with EU imports is offset by a loss to US exporters. What is more, US consumers suffer, since the benefits from comparative advantage have been lost.

The increased use of tariffs and other restrictions can lead to a trade war, with each country cutting back on imports from other countries. In the end, everyone loses.

Protection may allow firms to remain inefficient. By removing or reducing foreign competition, tariffs etc. may reduce firms' incentive to reduce costs. Thus if protection is being given to an infant industry, the government must ensure that the lack of competition does not prevent it 'growing up'. Protection should not be excessive and should be removed as soon as possible.

Bureaucracy. If a government is to avoid giving excessive protection to firms, it should examine each case carefully. This can lead to large administrative costs.

> **Pause for thought**
>
> (a) Protection to allow the exploitation of monopoly/monopsony power can be seen as a 'first-best' policy for the country concerned. Similarly, the use of tariffs to counteract externalities directly involved in the trade process (e.g. the environmental costs of an oil tanker disaster) could be seen to be a first-best policy. Explain why.
>
> (b) Most of the other arguments for tariffs or other forms of protection that we have considered can be really be seen as arguments for intervention, with protection being no more than a second-best form of intervention. Go through each of the arguments and consider what would be a 'first-best' form of intervention.

World attitudes towards trade and protection   24.4

Pre-Second World War growth in protectionism

After the Wall Street crash of 1929, the world plunged into the Great Depression. Countries found their exports falling dramatically and many suffered severe balance of payments difficulties. The response of many countries was to restrict imports by the use of tariffs and quotas. Of course, this reduced other countries' exports, which encouraged them to resort to even greater protectionism.

BOX 24.2

Steel barriers
Looking after the US steel industry

With the worldwide economic slowdown in 2001, the US steel industry was making heavy losses. In March 2002, George W. Bush announced that the US steel industry was to receive protection from imported steel. Tariffs were to rise from 8 per cent on steel wire, to 30 per cent on steel plate. The decision was met with dismay throughout the world. The Americans were accused of putting domestic politics ahead of the country's international legal commitments. As Pascal Lamy, the EU trade commissioner, remarked:

> When the US is caught between domestic pressure and respecting its international commitments, the former prevails. The world steel market is not the wild west, where people do as they like. There are rules to guarantee the multilateral system.[1]

The EU, along with China, Korea, Japan and other steel producing nations decided to challenge the US decision in the WTO and demanded compensation for their resulting lost earnings in the USA.

But it was not just the loss of sales in the USA that concerned the EU (which are, in fact, very small). More importantly, it was the likelihood that steel from the rest of the world, otherwise destined for the US market, would be diverted to the EU. Such a surge in steel imports would not only threaten EU producers with enhanced competition, but would drive down steel prices. This would make profitability even harder to maintain. It was estimated at the time that as much as 16 million tonnes of cheap steel, which would otherwise have gone to the USA, would head for the EU. A worst-case scenario predicted that as many as 18 000 jobs might be at risk in the EU, 5000 of which would be in the UK. The EU estimated that the USA's action could cost it over €2 billion a year in lost sales.

The US position

As a supporter of free trade, how could the USA justify its actions? The first justification, ironically, was that they were designed to support free trade. The support for the steel industry, and possibly textiles in the near future, was seen as a way of gaining political support within the USA. This was necessary to push forward with the more general free-trade agenda resulting from the WTO Doha trade talks (see Box 24.3).

Second, the steel tariffs were justified as an overdue response to a worldwide industry that was

The net effect of the Depression and the rise in protectionism was a dramatic fall in world trade. The volume of world trade in manufactures fell by more than a third in the three years following the Wall Street crash. Clearly there was a net economic loss to the world from this decline in trade.

Post-Second World War reduction in protectionism and the role of GATT

After the Second World War there was a general desire to reduce trade restrictions, so that all countries could gain the maximum benefits from trade. There was no desire to return to the beggar-my-neighbour policies of the 1930s.

In 1947, 23 countries got together and signed the General Agreement on Tariffs and Trade (GATT). By 2003, there were 146 members of its successor organisation, the World Trade Organisation (WTO), which was formed in 1995. Between them, the members of the WTO account for over 93 per cent of world trade. The aims of GATT, and now the WTO, have been to liberalise trade. Periodically, member countries have met to negotiate reductions in tariffs heavily distorted by subsidies and unfair practices. The USA argued that it was often the victim of these practices, and that the impositions of tariffs on steel products was simply a mechanism for tilting the industry back in its favour.

Response to the US actions

Critics of the American action argued that the US steel industry has, for many years, been an industry in decline. It suffers from prolonged under-investment and the use of outdated technology. It has a fragmented and inefficient industrial structure, with strong and powerful union representation. The result is that steel is expensive to produce. The price of sheet steel in the USA averages $475 a tonne; in South Korea it is $350 a tonne, and in Kazakhstan it is a mere $175.

In the light of this, the USA was accused of blatant protectionism. It was attempting to look after a failing industry and, in the process, was totally disregarding the WTO and the global trade system as a whole.

In response, the EU sought to safeguard its markets from unwanted steel previously destined for the US. It initiated its own rise in tariffs of between 14.9 and 26 per cent on a wide range of steel imports. In addition, it drew up a list of 316 products exported from the USA to the EU which would face an increase in duties, unless the US compensated EU steel producers for lost earnings. These products ranged from textiles and clothing to citrus juices and even toothbrushes.

Many commentators suggested that the US actions and the worldwide response to them could seriously threaten future agreements on trade liberalisation. For example, Digby Jones, the CBI director-general, stated that:

> It is going to be extremely difficult to get the developing world to work towards meaningful free trade when the greatest economy on earth has basically said it doesn't want to play.[2]

Questions

1 *Can the US action to protect its steel industry be justified on economic grounds?*

2 *What alternative economic strategy might the US government have adopted to improve the competitiveness of steel producers?*

---

[1] *Financial Times* 7 March 2002
[2] *The Sunday Times,* 10 March 2002

and other trade restrictions. There have been nine 'rounds' of such negotiations since 1947. The four major ones were the Kennedy Round (1964–7), the Tokyo Round (1973–9) and the Uruguay Round (1986–93) and, beginning in 2001, the Doha round (the 'Doha Development Agenda'). On completion of the Uruguay round, the average tariff on manufactured products was 4 per cent and falling. In 1947 the figure was nearly 40 per cent.

The re-emergence of protectionist sentiments in the 1980s

The balance of payments problems that many countries experienced after the oil crisis of 1973 and the recession of the early 1980s led many politicians round the world to call for trade restrictions. Although a tariff war was averted, there was a gradual increase in non-tariff barriers, such as subsidies on domestic products, the prohibition of imports that did not meet precise safety or other specifications, administrative delays in customs clearance, limits on investment by foreign companies, and governments favouring domestic firms when purchasing supplies.

The Doha development agenda
A new direction for the WTO?

Globalisation, based on the free play of comparative advantage, economies of scale and innovation, has produced a genuinely radical force, in the true sense of the word. It essentially amplifies and reinforces the strengths, but also the weaknesses, of market capitalism: its efficiency, its instability, and its inequality. If we want globalisation not only to be efficiency-boosting but also fair, we need more international rules and stronger multilateral institutions.[1]

In November 1999, the members of the World Trade Organisation met in Seattle in the USA. What ensued became known as the 'battle of Seattle' (see web case I.3). Anti-globalisation protesters fought with police; the world's developing economies fell out with the world's developed economies; and the very future of the WTO was called into question. The WTO was accused of being a free trader's charter, in which the objective of free trade was allowed to ride rough-shod over anything that might stand in its way. Whatever the issue – the environment, the plight of developing countries, the dominance of trade by multinationals – free trade was king.

At Seattle, both the protesters and developing countries argued that things had gone far enough. The WTO must redefine its role, they argued, to respect *all* stakeholders. More radical voices called for the organisation to be scraped. As Pascal Lamy, the EU Trade Commissioner, made clear in the quote above, rules had to be strengthened, and the WTO had to ensure that the gains from trade were more fair and sustainable.

The rebuilding process of the WTO began in Doha, Qatar in November 2001. The meeting between the then 142 members of the WTO concluded with the decision to launch a new round of WTO trade talks, to be called the 'Doha Development Agenda'. The talks are designed to increase the liberalisation of trade. However, such a goal is to be tempered by a policy of strengthening assistance to developing economies.

The Doha Development Agenda moves the WTO into a new era: one which allows the organisation to play a fuller role in the pursuit of economic growth, employment and poverty reduction, in global governance, and in the promotion of sustainable development, while

---

Voluntary restraint arrangements (VRAs) or voluntary export restraints (VERs)
A form of agreed or voluntary quota between the exporting country and the country receiving the exports.

Quotas were increasingly used, especially against Japanese imports. In most cases these were 'voluntary' agreements. Japan, on a number of occasions, agreed to restrict the number of cars it exported to various European countries. Similar restrictions applied to Japanese televisions and videos. Over 200 **voluntary restraint arrangements (VRAs)** (also known as **voluntary export restraints (VERs)**) were in force around the world in the early 1990s.

The problem of increasing non-tariff barriers were recognised in the Uruguay Round of GATT negotiations, and agreements were sought to dismantle many of them.

The Uruguay Round

The Uruguay Round was much more comprehensive than previous rounds. Unlike the others, it included negotiations on tariff reductions in agricultural products and in services (as well as in industrial products), and reductions in non-tariff barriers. Despite fears that an agreement would never be reached, negotiations were completed in December 1993 and a deal was signed in April 1994. This involved a programme of phasing in substantial reductions in tariffs and other restrictions up to the year 2002. These included:

maintaining its key function of increasing and improving the conditions for world-wide trade and investment.[2]

The talks are due to start in January 2005, and will last for 3 years.

At Doha it was agreed that the new trade talks would address questions such as:

- Sustainable development and the environment. In the past, international trade agreements always seemed to take precedence over international environmental agreements, even though they are legally equivalent. In the new Doha round, this relationship is to be clarified. The hope is to achieve greater coherence between various areas of international policy making.

- Trade and development. The Doha Round will attempt to address a number of issues of concern to developing countries as they become more integrated into the world's trading system. For example, it will seek to extend special provisions to developing economies to improve their access to markets in developed countries. It will also attempt to strengthen the current special treatment that developing countries receive, such as

the ability to maintain higher rates of tariff protection.

Other areas identified for discussion include: greater liberalisation of agriculture; rules to govern foreign direct investment; the co-ordination of countries' competition policies; the use and abuse of patents on medicines and the needs of developing countries.

The proof of the pudding is in the eating. Only time will show whether the rhetoric of the Doha Development Agenda is transformed into fundamental improvements for the world's poorest countries, and whether the outcome will reduce the fears of those who feel that the global economy is increasingly beyond their influence.

Question

Outline the advantages and drawbacks of adopting a free trade strategy for developing economies. How might the Doha Development Agenda go some way to reducing these drawbacks?

---

[1] *Global Policy without Democracy*, (speech by Pascal Lamy, EU Trade Commissioner, given in 2001)

[2] EU summary of Doha Ministerial Conference (**http://trade-info.cec.eu.int/europa/2001newround/compas.htm**)

- Tariffs on industrial products cut by an average of 38 per cent (more than the original target) and eliminated entirely on certain products.
- Prohibition of export subsidies and voluntary export restraints (VERs).
- Non-tariff measures to be converted to tariffs.
- The Multifibre Agreement, which protected industrialised countries against imports of textiles from developing countries, to be phased out over ten years.
- Tariffs on agricultural products reduced by 36 per cent over six years in industrialised countries and ten years in developing countries.
- An agreement by the EU to cut subsidised farm exports by 21 per cent in volume and by 36 per cent in value within six years. Over the same period, support for domestic farmers would be cut by 20 per cent.
- Protection of intellectual property rights strengthened (including patents, copyrights and trademarks).
- Adoption of rules limiting the power of countries to restrict the provision of services (e.g. banking and insurance) by foreign companies, and to restrict multinational investment (e.g. by forcing them to use a proportion of local inputs). Existing measures to be phased out within seven years.

■ Adoption of voluntary codes limiting anti-dumping measures and the practice of government procurement favouring domestic suppliers.

But despite these successes, the cuts in agricultural protection were less than was originally hoped for. Although it was agreed to replace food import quotas into the EU and other industrialised countries by tariff equivalents, the degree of protection remains high, and the industrialised world continues to export food to many developing countries which have a comparative advantage in food production!

The World Trade Organisation

The Uruguay Round deal also led to the setting up of the World Trade Organisation (WTO) in 1995 as the successor to the GATT. The WTO adopted and strengthened most of the GATT rules governing trade. These include the following:

■ Non-discrimination. Under the 'most favoured nations clause', any trade concession that a country makes to one member must be granted to *all* signatories.

■ Reciprocity. Any nation benefiting from a tariff reduction made by another country must reciprocate by making similar tariff reductions itself.

■ The general prohibition of quotas.

■ Fair competition. If unfair barriers are erected against a particular country, the WTO can sanction retaliatory action by that country. The country is not allowed, however, to take such action without permission.

■ Binding tariffs. Countries cannot raise existing tariffs without negotiating with their trading partners.

Unlike the GATT, the WTO has the power to impose sanctions on countries breaking trade agreements. If there are disputes between member nations, these will be settled by the WTO, although there is provision for appeals, and the parties can agree to go to arbitration. However, countries then found to be in the wrong must abide by the ruling or face sanctions.

The greater power of the WTO has persuaded many countries to bring their disputes to it. In the first 9 years of its existence it had dealt with over 300 disputes (compared with 300 by GATT over the whole of its 48 years). The WTO has also carried on from the Uruguay Round and has completed several new international agreements, for example to lower trade barriers in telecommunications and information technology.

SUMMARY

1a World trade has grown, for many years, significantly faster than the growth in world output.

1b World trade is highly concentrated in the developed world and in particular between the top six trading nations.

1c The composition of world trade is largely dominated by manufacturing products, although trade in services has expanded over recent years.

2a Countries can gain from trade if they specialise in producing those goods in which they have a comparative advantage: i.e. those goods that can be produced at relatively low opportunity costs. This is merely an extension of the argument that gains can be made from the specialisation and division of labour.

2b If two countries trade, then, provided that the trade price ratio of exports and imports is between the pre-trade price ratios of these goods in the two countries, both countries can gain.

2c With increasing opportunity costs there will be a limit to specialisation and trade. As a country increasingly specialises, its (marginal) comparative advantage will eventually disappear.

2d The terms of trade give the price of exports relative to the price of imports expressed as an index, where the base year is 100.

2e Gains from trade also arise from decreasing costs (economies of scale), differences in demand between countries, increased competition from trade and the transmission of growth from one country to another. There may also be non-economic advantages from trade.

3a Countries use various methods to restrict trade, including tariffs, quotas, exchange controls, import licensing, export taxes, and legal and administrative barriers. Countries may also promote their own industries by subsidies.

3b Reasons for restricting trade that have some validity in a world context include the infant industry argument, the problems of relying on exporting goods whose market is growing slowly or even declining, dumping and other unfair trade practices, the danger of the establishment of a foreign-based monopoly, the need to spread the risks of fluctuating export prices, and the problems that free trade may adversely affect consumer tastes, may allow the importation of harmful goods and may not take account of externalities.

3c Often, however, the arguments for restricting trade are in the context of one country benefiting even though other countries may lose more. Countries may intervene in trade in order to exploit their monopoly/monopsony power or to protect declining industries.

3d Finally, a country may have other objectives in restricting trade, such as remaining self-sufficient in certain strategic products, not trading with certain countries of which it disapproves, protecting traditional ways of life or simply retaining a non-specialised economy.

3e Arguments for restricting trade, however, are often fallacious. In general, trade brings benefits to countries, and protection to achieve one objective may be at a very high opportunity cost. Even if government intervention to protect certain parts of the economy is desirable, restricting trade is unlikely to be a first-best solution to the problem, since it involves side-effect costs. What is more, restricting trade may have adverse world multiplier effects; it may encourage retaliation; it may allow inefficient firms to remain inefficient; it may involve considerable bureaucracy and possibly even corruption.

4 Most countries of the world are members of the WTO and in theory are in favour of moves towards freer trade. The Uruguay Round brought significant reductions in trade restrictions, both tariff and non-tariff. Nevertheless, countries have been very unwilling to abandon restrictions if they believe that they can gain from them, even though they might be at the expense of other countries.

REVIEW QUESTIONS

1   What is likely to be the impact of rising levels of intra-regional trade for the world economy?

2   Imagine that two countries, Richland and Poorland, can produce just two goods, computers and coal. Assume that for a given amount of land and capital, the output of these two products requires the following constant amounts of labour:

	Richland	Poorland
1 computer	2	4
100 tonnes of coal	4	5

Assume that each country has 20 million workers.

(a) Draw the production possibility curves for the two countries (on two separate diagrams).

(b) If there is no trade, and in each country 12 million workers produce computers and 8 million workers produce coal, how many computers and tonnes of coal will each country produce? What will be the total production of each product?

(c) What is the opportunity cost of a computer in (i) Richland; (ii) Poorland?

(d) What is the opportunity cost of 100 tonnes of coal in (i) Richland: (ii) Poorland?

(e) Which country has a comparative advantage in which product?

(f) Assuming that price equals marginal cost, which of the following would represent possible exchange ratios?
(i) 1 computer for 40 tonnes of coal; (ii) 2 computers for 140 tonnes of coal; (iii) 1 computer for 100 tonnes of coal; (iv) 1 computer for 60 tonnes of coal; (v) 4 computers for 360 tonnes of coal.

(g) Assume that trade now takes place and that 1 computer exchanges for 65 tonnes of coal. Both countries specialise completely in the product in which they have a comparative advantage. How much does each country produce of its respective product?

(h) The country producing computers sells 6 million domestically. How many does it export to the other country?

(i) How much coal does the other country consume?

3   Why doesn't the USA specialise as much as General Motors or Texaco? Why doesn't the UK specialise as much as ICI? Is the answer to these questions similar to the answer to the questions, 'Why doesn't the USA specialise as much as Luxembourg?', and 'Why doesn't ICI or Unilever specialise as much as the local florist?'

4   To what extent are the arguments for countries specialising and then trading with each other the same as those for individuals specialising in doing the jobs to which they are relatively well suited?

5   The following are four items that are traded internationally: wheat; computers; textiles; insurance. In which one of the four is each of the following most likely to have a comparative advantage? India; the UK; Canada; Japan. Give reasons for your answer.

6   Go through each of the arguments for restricting trade (both those of general validity and those having some validity for specific countries) and provide a counter-argument for not restricting trade.

7   If countries are so keen to reduce the barriers to trade, why do many countries frequently attempt to erect barriers?

8   Debate the following:
    'All arguments for restricting trade boil down to special pleading for particular interest groups. Ultimately there will be a net social cost from any trade restrictions.'

9   If rich countries stand to gain substantially from freer trade, why have they been so reluctant to reduce the levels of protection of agriculture?

10 Make out a case for restricting trade between the UK and Japan. Are there any arguments here that could not equally apply to a case for restricting trade between Scotland and England or between Liverpool or Manchester?

25 Trading blocs

The world economy seems to have been increasingly forming into a series of trade blocs, based upon regional groupings of countries: a European region centred on the European Union, an Asian region on Japan, and a North American region on the United States. Although such trade blocs clearly encourage trade between their members (intra-regional trade has been growing significantly faster than trade between regions), many countries outside these blocs complain that they benefit the members at the expense of the rest of the world. For many developing economies, in need of access to the most prosperous nations in the world, this represents a significant check on their ability to grow and develop.

In this chapter we shall first consider why groups of countries might wish to establish trade blocs, and what they seek to gain beyond the benefits that result from free and open trade. We will then look at the world's trade blocs as they currently stand, paying particular attention to the European Union, which is by far the most advanced in respect to establishing a high level of regional integration.

25.1 Preferential trading

Types of preferential trading arrangement

If a group of countries wish to become more open and trade more freely with each other, but do not want the vulnerability of facing unbridled global competition, they might attempt to remove trade restrictions between themselves, but maintain them with the rest of the world.

There are three possible forms that such trading arrangements might take.

Free trade areas

A **free trade area** is where member countries remove tariffs and quotas between themselves, but retain whatever restrictions *each member chooses* with non-member countries. Some provision will have to be made to prevent imports from outside coming into the area via the country with the lowest external tariff.

Customs unions

A **customs union** is like a free trade area, but in addition members must adopt *common* external tariffs and quotas with non-member countries.

Common markets

A **common market** is where member countries operate as a *single* market. Like a customs union there are no tariffs and quotas between member countries and there are common external tariffs and quotas. But a common market goes further than this. A full common market includes the following features: a common system of taxation, and common laws and regulations governing production, employment and trade. It also includes the free movement of labour and capital. It might also include features such as a single currency or fixed exchange rates between members, and the pursuit of a common macroeconomic policy.

The direct effects of a customs union: trade creation and trade diversion

By joining a customs union (or free trade area), a country will find that its trade patterns change. Two such changes can be distinguished: trade creation and trade diversion.

Trade creation

Trade creation is where consumption shifts from a high-cost producer to a low-cost producer. The removal of trade barriers allows greater specialisation according to comparative advantage. Instead of consumers having to pay high prices for domestically produced goods in which the country has a comparative disadvantage, the goods can now be obtained more cheaply from other members of the customs union. In return, the country can export to them goods in which it has a comparative advantage.

Trade diversion

Trade diversion is where consumption shifts from a lower-cost producer outside the customs union to a higher-cost producer within the union.

Assume that the most efficient producer of good y in the world is New Zealand – outside the EU. Assume that before membership of the EU, the UK paid a similar tariff on good y from any country, and thus imported the product from New Zealand rather than from the EU.

After joining the EU, however, the removal of the tariff made the EU product cheaper, since the tariff remained on the New Zealand product. Consumption thus switched to a higher-cost producer. There was thus a net loss in world efficiency. As far as the UK was concerned, consumers still gained, since they were paying a lower price than before. However, there was a loss to producers (from the reduction in protection, and hence reduced prices and profits) and to the government (from reduced tariff revenue). These losses may have been smaller or larger than the gain to consumers: in other words, there may have still been a net gain to the UK, but there could have been a net loss, depending on the circumstances.

Longer-term effects of a customs union

Over the longer term, there may be other gains and losses from being a member of a customs union.

definition

Free trade area
A group of countries with no trade barriers between themselves.

definition

Customs union
A free trade area with common external tariffs and quotas.

definition

Common market
A customs union where the member countries act as a single market with free movement of labour and capital, common taxes and common trade laws.

definition

Trade creation
Where a customs union leads to greater specialisation according to comparative advantage and thus a shift in production from higher-cost to lower-cost sources.

definition

Trade diversion
Where a customs union diverts consumption from goods produced at a lower cost outside the union to goods produced at a higher cost (but tariff free) within the union.

Pause for thought

Is joining a customs union more likely to lead to trade creation or trade diversion in each of the following cases? (a) The union has a very high external tariff. (b) Costs differences are very great between the country and members of the union.

Longer-term advantages

- Increased market size may allow a country's firms to exploit *(internal) economies of scale*. This argument is more important for small countries, which therefore have more to gain from an enlargement of their markets.

- *External economies of scale*. Increased trade may lead to improvements in the infrastructure of the members of the customs union (better roads, railways, financial services, etc.). This in turn could then bring bigger long-term benefits from trade between members, and from external trade too, by making the transport and handling of imports and exports cheaper.

- The bargaining power of the whole customs union with the rest of the world may allow member countries to gain *better terms of trade*. This, of course, will necessarily involve a degree of political co-operation between the members.

- *Increased competition* between member countries may stimulate efficiency, encourage investment and reduce monopoly power. Of course, a similar advantage could be gained by the simple removal of tariffs with any competing country.

- Integration may encourage a *more rapid spread of technology*.

Longer-term disadvantages

- Resources may flow from the country to more efficient members of the customs union, or to the geographical centre of the union (so as to minimise transport costs). This can be a major problem for a *common market* (where there is free movement of labour and capital). The country could become a depressed 'region' of the community.

- If integration encourages greater co-operation between firms in member countries, it may also encourage *greater oligopolistic collusion*, thus keeping prices higher to the consumer. It may also encourage mergers and takeovers, which would increase monopoly power.

- *Diseconomies of scale*. If the union leads to the development of very large companies, they may become bureaucratic and inefficient.

- *The costs of administering* the customs union may be high. This problem is likely to worsen the more intervention there is in the affairs of individual members.

25.2 Preferential trading in practice

Preferential trading has the greatest potential to benefit countries whose domestic market is too small, taken on its own, to enable them to benefit from economies of scale, and where they face substantial barriers to their exports. Most developing countries fall into this category and as a result many have attempted to form preferential trading arrangements.

Examples in Latin America and the Caribbean include the Latin American Integration Association (LAIA), the Andean Community, the Central American Common Market (CACM) and the Caribbean Community (CARICOM). A Southern Common Market (MerCoSur) was formed in 1991, consisting of Argentina, Brazil, Paraguay and Uruguay. It has a common external tariff and most of its internal trade is free of tariffs.

In 1993, the six ASEAN nations (Brunei, Indonesia, Malaysia, the Philippines, Singapore and Thailand) agreed to work towards an ASEAN Free Trade Area (AFTA). ASEAN (the Association of South-East Asian Nations) now has ten members (the new ones being Laos, Myanmar, Vietnam and Cambodia) and is dedicated to increased economic co-operation within the region. What progress has been made in achieving AFTA? By 2002 the original six members had reduced internal tariffs to a maximum of 5 per cent on most products. Plans are to eliminate all tariffs between these six by 2010 and for the remaining countries by 2015.

In Africa the Economic Community of West African States (ECOWAS)[1] has been attempting to create a common market between its sixteen members and plans to move to the adoption of a single currency for most of its members in July 2005.

The most significant and advanced trade blocs, however, are to be found not in the developing world but in the developed, notably in Europe and North America.

North America Free Trade Association (NAFTA)

Along with the EU, NAFTA is one of the two most powerful trading blocs in the world. It was formed in 1993 and consists of the USA, Canada and Mexico. These three countries have agreed to abolish tariffs between themselves in the hope that increased trade and co-operation will follow. Tariffs between the USA and Canada were phased out by 1999 and those between Mexico and the other two countries will be phased out by 2009. New non-tariff restrictions will not be permitted either, but many existing ones can remain in force, thus preventing the development of true free trade between the members. Indeed, some industries, such as textiles and agriculture, will continue to have major non-tariff restrictions.

NAFTA members hope that, with a market similar in size to the EU (a combined GDP of $12.5 trillion and a population of over 420 million), they will be able to rival the EU's economic power in world trade. Other countries may join in the future, so NAFTA may eventually develop into a Western Hemisphere free trade association.

NAFTA is, however, at most only a free trade area and not a common market. Unlike the EU, it does not seek to harmonise laws and regulations, except in very specific areas such as environmental management and labour standards. Member countries are permitted total legal independence, subject to the one proviso that they must treat firms of other member countries equally with their own firms. Nevertheless, NAFTA has encouraged a growth in trade between its members, most of which is trade creation rather than trade diversion.

Of the three countries in NAFTA, Mexico potentially has the most to gain from the agreement. With easier access to US and Canadian markets, and the added attractiveness it now has to foreign investors, especially US multinationals looking to reduce labour costs, the Mexican economy could reap huge benefits.

Although it is still early days, Mexico seems to have done well from the NAFTA agreement. It has become a thriving export economy and attracts sufficient foreign direct investment to finance its total current account deficit. Many EU and south-east Asian businesses are using the Mexican economy to gain access to the USA, although strong demand within Mexico itself is fast making it a valuable market in its own right.

[1] www.ecowas.net.

BOX 25.1

Crisis in south-east Asia
Birth of a contagion

Stanley Fischer, the First Deputy Managing Director of the International Monetary Fund, refers to Asia's economic success up to 1997 as 'a remarkable historical achievement', where growth and trade performance reached unprecedented levels. The statistics of the region speak for themselves.

- The annual growth rate of GDP in the ASEAN-5 countries (Indonesia, Malaysia, the Philippines, Singapore and Thailand) averaged 8 per cent in the decade up to 1997.

- In the 30 years up to 1997, per capita income levels increased tenfold in Korea, fivefold in Thailand, and fourfold in Malaysia. For nations like Hong Kong and Singapore, per capita income is now well in line with that of many industrial countries.

- It is estimated that only 2 out of 10 people in east Asia are now being paid less than $1 per day, compared with 6 out of 10 in 1975 (at today's prices).

- Prior to the recent crisis, Asia attracted over half of all capital inflows going to developing countries, approximately $100 billion in 1996.

- Asian economies have managed, over the decade up to 1997, to double their share of world exports to almost one-fifth of the world's total.

- Further, such economic success has been achieved within the context of stable inflation, high levels of domestic saving (on average a third of GDP) and sound fiscal management, with some countries, such as Thailand and Indonesia, managing to run significant budget surpluses (1.6 and 1.4 per cent of GDP respectively in 1997).

As well as the directly benefiting the citizens of these countries, the development of the south-east Asian economies has contributed to the economic well-being of the global economy. They have become major consumers of foreign goods: for example, the region purchased 19 per cent of all US exports in 1996. In addition, rising levels of consumption have helped to reduce the scale of downturns in economic activity experienced in the world's developed economies. The south-east Asian economies have also provided attractive investment opportunities to foreign investors, helping to support the remarkable growth of the world's financial markets.

Causes of the crisis

Given this remarkable success how did it go so horribly wrong so quickly?

The crisis broke in Thailand in the summer of 1997. Up to this point, Thailand had been experiencing strong economic growth, averaging about 10 per cent per annum since the mid-1980s. With sound public accounts, the economy presented itself as an attractive investment opportunity for foreign investors. And just as foreign investors were keen to lend, so domestic borrowers were keen to borrow, especially from overseas.

The Thai government operated a pegged exchange rate against the US dollar, and, given the stability of the Thai baht, foreign funds were readily used to meet investment demand. Little attention was paid by domestic borrowers to the extensive foreign exchange risk that they were placing themselves in. What was this risk? Should the baht ever be devalued, interest payments (in dollars) would cost more in local currency.

Things began to go wrong as growth in the Thai economy began to slow and its balance of payments deficit widened. A series of speculative attacks against the Thai baht led the Thai government to unpeg the currency from the dollar. The baht collapsed. The effect then quickly spread to other currencies within the region. This spread or 'contagion' was the result partly of other nations attempting to maintain their competitiveness against the baht, and partly of speculators realising that other economies within the region – Indonesia and Korea, in particular – shared problems very similar to those of Thailand: weak financial markets and a heavily indebted corporate sector.

The region's currencies, interest rates and economic growth have become more synchronised. When Thailand devalued, its neighbours in the Association of south-east Asian Nations (ASEAN) were confronted with intense speculative pressures. Investors identified a regional pattern of slowing export growth, rising current-account deficits and weak banking systems. Market participants realised that concerns about relative competitiveness would cause these currencies to move in tandem since the so-called ASEAN four – Thailand, Malaysia, Indonesia and the Philippines – compete in broadly the same export markets.[1]

As currencies came under pressure from international speculators, those that had borrowed heavily from overseas began to see their debt service costs rise (with weaker currencies, more local currency was needed to pay interest denominated in dollars). With such large foreign debts, they sought desperately to find ways of reducing payments on their external liabilities. However, their actions merely put further pressure on their currencies, intensifying the speculative wave and plunging the region's economies into deeper financial chaos.

The following have been identified as the major contributing factors in the south-east Asian crisis:

■ Governments in the region had failed to deal with overheating pressures, growing balance of payments deficits and property and stock-market bubbles.

■ Pegged exchange rates were pegged for too long. This gave a false sense of stability and encouraged excessive external borrowing by the corporate sector, with a correspondingly excessive risk from exchange rate devaluation.

■ The liberalisation of financial markets in south-east Asia was not accompanied by an increase in regulation and supervision. The result was that banks made excessively risky loans and were inadequately monitored. As Joseph Stiglitz, Senior Vice-President of the World Bank remarked:

In the last decade Thailand has reduced reserve requirements, eased the rules governing non-bank financial institutions, expanded the scope of permissible capital market activities, and increased access to off-shore borrowing. Beginning somewhat earlier, Korea eliminated many interest rate controls, removed restrictions on corporate debt financing and cross-border flows, and permitted intensified competition in financial services. While the advantages of these changes were lauded, the necessary increase in safeguards was not adequately emphasised.[2]

As well as domestic problems, international factors also may have contributed to south-east Asia's problems. For example, weak growth in Japan and Europe, with resulting low domestic interest rates, encouraged investors to search for higher yields overseas, especially in south-east Asia. Lenders, like borrowers, failed to appreciate the risk of their loans and became overexposed in the region.

Consequences for the south-east Asian economies

Joseph Stiglitz expressed the magnitude of the economic collapse for the south-east Asia region when he stated:

> ... capital outflows, and the accompanying depreciating currencies and falling asset prices, exacerbated the strains on private-sector balance sheets. The vicious circle has become even more vicious as financial problems have led to restricted credit, undermining the real economy, and slowing growth. Given the region's financial fragility, the economic downturn may well feed on itself – worsening bankruptcies and weakening confidence. Finally, the economic crisis has fostered political and social instability in some countries, further deepening the crisis.[3]

By early 1998, all leading forecasters expected output in south-east Asia to fall, and had revised their predictions for 1998 to reflect this. The table shows revisions to IMF forecasts. However, there still remained uncertainty as to how great the impact on output would be.

The fall in output reflected both the lower level of consumer and investor confidence and the tighter fiscal and monetary conditions many of the countries were having to embrace in order to: (a) instil greater confidence in their financial systems; (b) meet the conditions imposed by the IMF for financial assistance.

Global effects

But it would be wrong to see the problem as just south-east Asia's: the consequences of the region's collapse were truly global. With weak demand in these countries, the consumption of imports also

Continued

Revisions to IMF forecasts for 1998 (% points)	
	Difference between IMF December 1997 and May 1998 forecasts
G7	−0.3
USA	+0.2
Germany	−0.4
France	−0.3
Italy	−0.1
Japan	−1.8
UK	−0.4
Asian newly industrialised economies	−2.5

Source: *Bank of England Inflation Report* (February 1998)

declined, thereby reducing the sales of foreign suppliers. In addition, such companies faced enhanced competition in their own domestic economies as south-east Asian producers focused on increasing the sales of their exports, which, given the depressed exchange rate values, had become super-competitive. Of course, the more successful the south-east Asian countries were in expanding their exports, the more this helped to alleviate the effects of their recession.

Speculative pressures on currencies in Brazil, Argentina, Mexico, Greece, Russia and the Ukraine were all argued to have been the consequence of the south-east Asian currency collapse. All were forced to increase interest rates to protect their exchange rates.

The most significant form of long-term contagion is likely to stem from the reduction in foreign capital flows, especially in bank lending. Not only will Asian businesses be affected but businesses around the world are likely to find it harder to acquire foreign capital, as lenders become more cautious and risk averse.

Policy response

In the wake of the collapse, Thailand, Indonesia and South Korea all sought financial assistance from the IMF. A loan of $3.9 billion was agreed for Thailand, $9.9 billion for Indonesia, and a staggering $20.9 billion for South Korea. The purpose of these loans was to help establish a measure of economic stability. As with all IMF financial help, such loans came with various conditions concerning the fiscal and monetary approaches that the countries had to adopt and the financial restructuring that had to be undertaken.

Questions

1 *Why did the 'contagion' spread to countries outside south-east Asia?*

2 *What policy measures could the south-east Asian countries have adopted before the crisis to prevent it occurring?*

---

[1] *Financial Times* (13/10/97)
[2] J. Stiglitz, *The role of International Financial Institutions in the Current Global Economy* (1998), **www.worldbank.org**
[3] *Ibid*

Despite the largely positive effects of NAFTA, the Mexican economy nevertheless faces a number of real and potential threats from the agreement. For example, as trade barriers fall, Mexican companies are being faced with competition from bigger and more efficient US and Canadian rivals.

The Asia-Pacific Economic Co-operation forum (APEC)

The most significant move towards establishing a more widespread regional economic organisation in east Asia appeared with the creation of the Asia-Pacific Economic Co-operation forum. APEC links the economies of the Pacific rim, including Asian, Australasian and North and South American countries (19 countries, plus Hong Kong and Taiwan). These countries account for some 62 per cent of the world's total output and 47 per cent of world trade. At the 1994 meeting of APEC leaders, it was resolved to create a free trade area across the Pacific by 2010 for the developed industrial countries, and by 2020 for the rest.

Unlike the EU and NAFTA, APEC is likely to remain solely a free trade area and not to develop into a customs union, let alone a common market. Within the region there exists a wide disparity in GDP per capita, ranging from Japan at over $34 000 to Vietnam at a mere $400. Such disparities create a wide range of national interests and goals. Countries are unlikely to share common economic problems or concerns. In addition, political differences and conflicts within the region are widespread, reducing the likelihood that any organisational agreement beyond a simple economic one would succeed. However, the economic benefits from free trade and the resulting closer regional ties could be immense.

By far the most developed trading bloc is that of the EU. In the remainder of this chapter we will consider the development of the EU and its implications for business.

The European Union 25.3

The European Economic Community (EEC) was formed by the signing of the Treaty of Rome in 1957 and came into operation on 1 January 1958.

The original six member countries of the EEC (Belgium, France, Italy, Luxembourg, Netherlands and West Germany) had already made a move towards integration with the formation of the European Coal and Steel Community in 1952. This had removed all restrictions on trade in coal, steel and iron ore between the six countries. The aim had been to gain economies of scale and allow more effective competition with the USA and other foreign producers.

The EEC extended this principle and aimed eventually to be a full common market with completely free trade between members in all products, and with completely free movement of labour, enterprise and capital. By uniting many of the countries of western Europe, it was hoped too that the conflicts of the two world wars would never be repeated, and that acting together the countries of the EEC could be an effective political and economic force in a world dominated by political giants such as the USA and the USSR, and economic giants such as the USA (and later Japan).

All internal tariffs between the six members had been abolished and common external tariffs established by 1968. But this still only made the EEC a *customs union*, since a number of restrictions on internal trade remained (legal, administrative, fiscal, etc.). Nevertheless the aim was eventually to create a full common market.

In 1973 the UK, Denmark and Ireland became members. Greece joined in 1981, Spain and Portugal in 1986, and Sweden, Austria and Finland in 1995. May 2004 marks the latest expansion, with 10 new members joining. These are Cyprus, the Czech Republic, Estonia, Hungary, Latvia, Lithuania, Malta, Poland, Slovakia and Slovenia.

From customs union to common market

The European Union (as it is now known) is clearly a customs union. It has common external tariffs and no internal tariffs. But is it also a common market? For years there have been certain common economic policies.

The Common Agricultural Policy (CAP). The Union sets common high prices for farm products. This involves charging variable import duties to bring foreign food imports up to EU prices and intervention to buy up surpluses of food produced within the EU at these above-equilibrium prices.

Regional policy. EU regional policy provides grants to firms and local authorities in depressed regions of the Union.

Monopoly and restrictive practice policy. EU policy here has applied primarily to companies operating in more than one member state (see section 21.1). For example, Article 81 of the Treaty of Amsterdam prohibits agreements between firms (e.g. over pricing or sharing out markets) which adversely affect competition in trade between member states.

Harmonisation of taxation. VAT is the standard form of indirect tax throughout the EU. However, there are substantial differences in VAT rates between member states, as there are with other tax rates.

Social policy. Articles 117–28 refer to social policy, and include calls for collaboration between member states on laws relating to employment, health and safety at work and collective bargaining rights, and equal pay for women and men for doing the same work.

In 1989 the European Commission presented a *social charter* to the EU heads of state. This spelt out a series of worker and social rights that should apply in all member states. These rights were grouped under twelve headings covering areas such as the guarantee of decent levels of income for both the employed and the non-employed, freedom of movement of labour between EU countries, freedom to belong to a trade union and equal treatment of women and men in the labour market. The social charter was only a recommendation and each element had to be approved separately by the European Council of Ministers.

The social chapter of the Maastricht Treaty (1991) attempted to move the Community forward in implementing the details of the social charter in areas such as maximum working hours, minimum working conditions, health and safety protection, the provision of information to and consultation with workers, and equal opportunities.

The UK Conservative government refused to sign this part of the Maastricht Treaty. It maintained that such measures would increase costs of production and would, therefore, make EU goods less competitive in world trade and would increase unemployment. Critics of the UK position argued that the refusal to adopt minimum working conditions (and also a minimum wage rate) would make the UK the 'cheap labour sweat-shop' of Europe. One of the first acts of the incoming Labour government in 1997 was to sign up to the social chapter.

Pause for thought

Does the adoption of laws enforcing improved working conditions necessarily lead to higher costs per unit of output?

Despite these various common policies, in other respects the Community of the 1970s and 1980s was far from a true common market: there were all sorts of non-tariff barriers, such as high taxes on wine by non-wine-producing countries, special regulations designed to favour domestic producers, governments giving contracts to domestic producers (e.g. for defence equipment), and so on.

The Single European Act of 1986, however, sought to remove these barriers and to form a genuine common market by the end of 1992. One of the most crucial aspects of the Act was its acceptance of the principle of **mutual**

BOX 25.2

Beyond bananas
EU/US trade disputes

Trade relations between the EU and US seem to be at an all-time low. The World Trade Organisation (WTO), set up to manage trade and prevent such disputes arising, appears helpless in resolving the issues and restoring order.

The current round of bad blood between the EU and US started over bananas.

Bananas

The EU/US 'banana war', which has now come to a conclusion, began in 1993 when the EU adopted a tariff and quota system that favoured banana producers in African, Caribbean and Pacific (ACP) countries, mostly ex-European colonies. Predictably, Latin American banana producers, owned by large American multinationals like Chiquita and Dole, took exception to this move. Latin American producers, with huge economies of scale, were able to produce bananas at considerably lower cost than producers in the ACP countries. But, faced with significant tariffs on entry into the EU market, their bananas became more expensive. Championed by the USA, the Latin American producers won the case at the WTO for removing the agreement.

The EU, however, failed to comply, arguing that the preferential access to EU markets for ACP producers was part of a general development strategy, known as the 'Lomé Convention', to support developing economies. Without preferential access, it was argued, ACP banana producers could simply not compete on world markets. As a European Commission document highlighted, 'The destruction of the Caribbean banana industry would provoke severe economic hardship and political instability in a region already struggling against deprivation.'

As the EU refused to comply with the WTO ruling, the USA imposed $191 million worth of tariffs on EU exports in March 1999. After a series of battles over the issue at the WTO, the EU finally agreed to reform its banana protocol and remove all preferential quotas to ACP banana producers by 2006.

Hormone-treated beef

If the banana dispute could be resolved, many equally contentious issues could be found to take its place. The dispute between the EU and USA over hormone-treated beef has been going on for a staggering 15 years. The EU, despite being subject to sanctions of $117 million, refuses to import any animal products, live or processed, that have received growth hormones. The ban was made on grounds of public health, and this remains the crux of the dispute. The EU argues that it has not been proven that hormone-treated beef is safe. In reply, the Americans argue that the EU has not provided evidence that it is otherwise.

Genetically modified (GM) foods

A more recent trade dispute, again in the field of public health, concerns the development of GM food. GM strains of maize and soya have been available in the USA for many years, but the export of such products, whether as seed or food, is banned from the EU. The US position is that EU consumers should be free to choose whether they have GM food or not. This, not surprisingly, is rejected by the EU on the basis that GM foods might contaminate the entire food supply once introduced. In July 2000, the EU decided to continue with its GM food ban indefinitely.

Airbus

The most recent branch of the current EU/US trade dispute concerns the Airbus Consortium and EU industrial policy (an area which has been a bone of contention for the USA for many years). The current issue concerns the new superjumbo, the A3XX. The Americans are very unhappy with the loans and subsidies being provided by EU members to companies within the Airbus Consortium to develop the aircraft. The American complaint is that such subsidies are breaking the WTO subsidy code and, as such, are unfair. Estimated at $4 billion, the subsidies will cover a third of the aircraft's development costs. The issue is yet to be brought before the WTO, but it is highly likely to be so, given the current trading climate between the EU and the USA.

Question

Why does the WTO appear to be so ineffective in resolving the disputes between the EU and USA?

recognition. This is the principle whereby if a firm or individual is permitted to do something under the rules and regulations of *one* EU country, it must thereby also be permitted to do it in all other EU countries. This means that firms and individuals can choose the country's rules that are least constraining. It also means that individual governments can no longer devise special rules and regulations that keep out competitors from other EU countries.

The benefits and costs of the single market

It is difficult to quantify the benefits and costs of the single market, given that many occur over a long period. Also it is difficult to know to what extent the changes taking place are the direct result of the single market. Nevertheless it is possible to identify the *types* of benefit and cost that have resulted. The benefits have included the following:

Trade creation. Costs and prices have fallen as a result of a greater exploitation of comparative advantage. Member countries can now specialise further in those goods and services that they can produce at a comparatively low opportunity cost.

Key
Idea
31
p512

Reduction in the direct costs of barriers. This category includes administrative costs, border delays and technical regulations. Their abolition or harmonisation has led to substantial cost savings.

Economies of scale. With industries based on a Europe-wide scale, many firms and their plants can be large enough to gain the full potential economies of scale. Yet the whole European market is large enough for there still to be adequate competition. Such gains vary from industry to industry depending on the minimum efficient scale of a plant or firm.

Greater competition. More effective competition from other EU countries has (a) squeezed profit margins and thus brought prices more in line with costs, and (b) encouraged more efficient use of resources and thus reduced costs. In the long run, greater competition can stimulate greater innovation, the greater flow of technical information and the rationalisation of production.

Despite, these gains, the single market has not received universal welcome within the EU. Its critics argue that, in a Europe of oligopolies, unequal ownership of resources, rapidly changing technologies and industrial practices, and factor immobility, the removal of internal barriers to trade has merely exaggerated the problems of inequality and economic power. More specifically, the following criticisms are made.

Radical economic change is costly. Substantial economic change is necessary to achieve the full economies of scale and efficiency gains from a single European market. These changes necessarily involve redundancies – from bankruptcies, takeovers, rationalisation and the introduction of new technology. The severity of this 'structural' and 'technological' unemployment (see section 26.3) depends on (a) the pace of economic change and (b) the mobility of labour – both occupational and geographical. Clearly, the more integrated markets become across the EU, the less the costs of future economic change will be.

Adverse regional effects. Firms are likely to locate as near as possible to the 'centre of gravity' of their markets and sources of supply. If, before barriers are removed, a firm's prime market is the UK, it might well locate in the Midlands or the north of England. If, however, with barriers now removed, its market has become Europe as a whole, it may choose to locate in the south of England or in France, Germany or the Benelux countries instead. The creation of a single European market thus tends to attract capital and jobs away from the edges of the Union to its geographical centre.

In an ideal market situation, areas like Cornwall, the south of Italy and Portugal should attract resources from other parts of the Union. Being relatively depressed areas, wage rates and land prices are lower. The resulting lower industrial costs should encourage firms to move there. In practice, however, as capital and labour (and especially young and skilled workers) leave the extremities of the Union, so these regions are likely to become more depressed. If, as a result, their infrastructure is neglected, they then become even less attractive to new investment.

The development of monopoly/oligopoly power. The free movement of capital can encourage the development of giant 'Euro-firms' with substantial economic power. Indeed, recent years have seen some very large European mergers (see Box 15.2). This can lead to higher, not lower prices and less choice for the consumer. It all depends on just how effective competition is, and how effective EU competition policy is in preventing monopolistic and collusive practices.

Trade diversion. Just as trade creation has been a potential advantage of completing the internal market, so trade diversion has been a possibility too. This is more likely if *external* barriers remain high (or are even increased) and internal barriers are *completely* abolished.

Perhaps the biggest objection raised against the single European market is a political one: the loss of national sovereignty. Governments find it much more difficult to intervene at a microeconomic level in their own economies.

Recent developments

By the mid-1990s it was becoming clear from the evidence that the single market was bringing substantial benefits.

■ The elimination of border controls for goods had reduced costs and shortened delivery times and resulted in a larger choice of suppliers.

■ The simplification of VAT arrangements had reduced costs.

■ Substantial trade creation had taken place.

■ Increased competition between firms had led to lower costs, lower prices and a wider range of products available to consumers. This was particularly so in newly liberalised service sectors such as transport, financial services, telecommunications and broadcasting.

■ Mergers and other forms of industrial restructuring had resulted in economies of scale and lower prices.

The economic evidence was backed up by the perceptions of business. Firms from across the range of industries felt that the single market project had removed a series of obstacles to trade within the EU and had increased market opportunities.

Nevertheless, the internal market was still not 'complete'. In other words, various barriers to trade between member states still remained. Thus, in June 1997, an Action Plan was adopted by the European Council. Its aim was to ensure that all barriers were dismantled by the launch of the euro in January 1999.

The Action Plan was largely, but not totally successful. In 1997, individual member countries had on average failed to transpose into their national law 35 per cent of over 1300 measures identified as being necessary to complete the internal market. By 1999, this 'transposition deficit' was less than 10 per cent. By 2002, the figure was just 1.8 per cent, although it had risen again to 2.4 per cent by May 2003.

Despite this success, national governments have continued to introduce *new* technical standards, several of which have had the effect of erecting new barriers to trade. Also, infringements of single market rules by governments have not always been dealt with. The net result is that, although trade is much freer today than in the early 1990s, especially given the transparency of pricing with the euro, there still do exist various barriers, especially to the free movement of goods.

Every six months, the EU publishes an 'Internal Market Scoreboard' to show progress towards the total abandonment of any forms of internal trade restrictions. In addition to giving each country's implementation deficit, the Scoreboard identifies the number of infringements of the internal market that have taken place. The hope is that the 'naming and shaming' of countries will encourage them to make more rapid progress towards totally free trade within the EU.

The future

In future years, with the euro being used by at least 12 of the member states, trade within the EU is likely to continue to grow as a proportion of GDP. We examine the benefits and costs of the single currency and the whole process of economic and monetary union in the EU in section 32.3.

A major issue is the question of the impact of the ten new members of the Union. This puts new pressures on the EU and calls upon its budget. The larger the EU becomes, the more difficult will be political union and full monetary union, and the more likely it is that the European Union will remain primarily a single market.

> **Pause for thought**
>
> Why may the new members of the EU have the most to gain from the single market, but also the most to lose?

SUMMARY

1a Countries may make a partial movement towards free trade by the adoption of a preferential trading system. This involves free trade between the members, but restrictions on trade with the rest of the world. Such a system can be either a simple free trade area, or a customs union (where there are common restrictions with the rest of the world), or a common market (where in addition there is free movement of capital and labour, and common taxes and trade laws).

1b A preferential trading area can lead to trade creation where production shifts to low-cost producers within the area, or to trade diversion where trade shifts away from lower-cost producers outside the area to higher-cost producers within the area.

1c Preferential trading may bring dynamic advantages of increased external economies of scale, improved terms of trade from increased bargaining power with the rest of the world, increased efficiency from greater competition between member countries, and a more rapid spread of technology. On the other hand, it can lead to increased regional problems for members, greater oligopolistic collusion and various diseconomies of scale. There may also be large costs of administering the system.

SUMMARY

2 There have been several attempts around the world to form preferential trading systems. The two most powerful are the European Union and the North America Free Trade Association (NAFTA).

3a The European Union is a customs union in that it has common external tariffs and no internal ones. But virtually from the outset it has also had elements of a common market, particularly in the areas of agricultural policy, regional policy, monopoly and restrictive practice policy, and to some extent in the areas of tax harmonisation, transport policy and social policy.

3b The Single European Act of 1986 sought to sweep away any remaining restrictions and to establish a genuine free market within the EU: to establish a full common market. Benefits from completing the internal market have included trade creation, cost savings from no longer having to administer barriers, economies of scale for firms now able to operate on a Europe-wide scale, and greater competition leading to reduced costs and prices, greater flows of technical information and more innovation.

3c The actual costs and benefits of EU membership to the various countries vary with their particular economic circumstances – for example, the extent to which they gain from trade creation, or lose from adverse regional multiplier effects – and with their contributions to and receipts from the EU budget.

3d These cost and benefits in the future will depend on just how completely the barriers to trade are abolished, on the extent of monetary union and on the effects of the enlargement of the Union.

REVIEW QUESTIONS

1 What factors will determine whether a country's joining a customs union will lead to trade creation or trade diversion?

2 Assume that a group of countries forms a customs union. Is trade diversion in the union more likely or less likely in the following cases?

(a) Producers in the union gain monopoly power in world trade.
(b) Modern developments in technology and communications reduce the differences in production costs associated with different locations.
(c) The development of an internal market within the union produces substantial economies of scale in many industries.

3 Are NAFTA and APEC likely to develop along the same lines as the EU? Explain your answer.

4 Why is it difficult to estimate the magnitude of the benefits of completing the internal market of the EU?

5 Look through the costs and benefits that we identified from the single European market. Do the same costs and benefits arise from a substantially enlarged EU?

6 To what extent do non-EU countries gain or lose from the existence of the EU?

7 If there have been clear benefits from the single market programme, why do individual member governments still try to erect barriers, such as new technical standards?

Additional Part I case studies on the *Economics for Business* website (www.booksites.net/sloman)

I.1 **Investing in Wales.** The factors influencing the investment in Wales by the Korean multinational, Lucky Goldstar (LG).

I.2 **The Maharaja Mac.** An examination of activities of McDonald's in India.

I.3 **Ethical business.** An examination of the likelihood of success of companies which trade fairly with developing countries.

I.4 **Fallacious arguments for restricting trade.** Some of the more common mistaken arguments for protection.

I.5 **Free trade and the environment.** Do whales, the rainforests and the atmosphere gain from free trade?

I.6 **The Uruguay Round.** An examination of the negotiations that led to substantial cuts in trade barriers.

I.7 **The Battle of Seattle.** This looks at the protests against the WTO at Seattle in November 1999 and considers the arguments for and against the free trade policies of the WTO.

I.8 **The World Trade Organisation.** This looks at the various opportunities and threats posed by this major international organisation.

I.9 **High oil prices.** What is their effect on the world economy?

I.10 **A miracle gone wrong.** Lessons from east Asia.

I.11 **Assessing NAFTA.** Who are the winners and losers from NAFTA?

I.12 **The social dimension of the EU.** The principles of the Social Charter.

I.13 **The Internal Market Scoreboard.** Keeping a tally on progress to a true single market.

Websites relevant to Part I

Numbers and sections refer to websites listed in the Web appendix and hotlinked from this book's website at **www.booksites.net/sloman**

- For news articles relevant to Part I, see the *Economics News Articles* link from the book's website.

- For general news on business in the international environment, see websites in section A, and particularly A1–5, 7–9, 24, 25, 31. See also links to newspapers worldwide in A38, 39 and 43, and the news search feature in Google at A41. See also links to economics news in A42.

- For articles on various aspects of trade and developing countries, see A27, 28; I9.

- For international data on imports and exports, see site H16 > *Resources > Trade statistics*. See also *World Economic Outlook* in H4 and trade data in B23. See also the trade topic in I14.

- For details of individual countries' structure of imports and exports, see B32.

- For UK data, see B1, *1. National Statistics* > the fourth link > *Compendia and Reference* > *Annual Abstract* > *External trade and investment*. See also B3 and 34. For EU data, see G1 > *The Statistical Annex* > *Foreign trade and current balance*.

- For discussion papers on trade, see H4 and 7.

- For trade disputes see H16.

- For various pressure groups critical of the effects of free trade and globalisation, see H12–14.

- For information on various preferential trading arrangements, see H20–22.

- For EU sites, see G1, 3, 7–14, 16–18.

- For information on trade and developing countries, see H4, 7, 9, 10, 16, 17. See also links to development sites in I9.

- Sites I7 and 11 contain links to various topics in *International Economics* (*International trade, International agreements, Economic co-operation* and *EU Economics*) and to *Trade and trade policy* in *Economic Development*. Site I4 has links to *International economics, Development economics* and *Economic development*. Site I17 has links to *International economics, Trade policy* and *Development economics*.

- For student resources relevant to this chapter, see sites C1–7, 9, 10, 19.

The macroeconomic environment

THE FINANCIAL TIMES, 27 JUNE 2003

Japan's economy remains in the doldrums

By MARIKO SANCHANTA

Economic data released on Friday showed that the Japanese economy remains locked in a low to no-growth pattern, with unemployment hovering near post-war highs and consumer spending continuing to fall amid a decline in wages.

The April core consumer price index (CPI), a key gauge of deflation in Japan, remained unchanged at negative 0.4 per cent, year-on-year. Economists said deflationary pressures were likely to worsen amid the current trend of declining wages.

'Going forward, we see little possibility of a sustained rise in consumption and upward push on prices amid the downward trend in wages,' said Mamoru Yamazaki, chief economist at Barclays Capital in Tokyo. 'To the contrary, we expect retailers to continue lowering prices as they see consumers pinching pennies.'

Against this backdrop, May consumer spending fell 1.8 per cent, year-on-year, as households pared expenditures amid salary reductions and continuing high unemployment rates.

The May unemployment rate remained unchanged at 5.4 per cent, just shy of a post-war high of 5.5 per cent last reached in January. The percentage of 15–24 year-olds who were unemployed reached 11.1 per cent, a rise of 30 000 from a year ago, almost double the unemployment rate of any other age bracket.

The increasing number of youths out of work reflects the increasingly stringent hiring practises of firms, which are cutting back on taking on new graduates amid cost-cutting and restructuring measures. It also reflects a social shift, as high school and college graduates increasingly shun the Japanese tradition of lifetime employment at a single company in favour of part-time jobs or pursuing creative interests.

The one bright spot amid the dreary data were May industrial production figures, which showed output growth of 2.5 per cent, month-on-month, about 1 percentage point better than market expectations. Economists pointed out that over the past six to nine months, Japanese industrial production has been stable, whereas US output has been weakening.

Richard Jerram, economist at ING in Tokyo, said: 'Japanese industrial production has been able to achieve marginal growth despite soft exports, which implies that some area of domestic demand is improving.'

> *Financial markets are supposed to swing like a pendulum: They may fluctuate wildly in response to exogenous shocks, but eventually they are supposed to come to rest at an equilibrium point that is supposed to reflect the fundamentals (of the economy). Instead financial markets behaved more like a wrecking ball, swinging from country to country, knocking over the weakest and transforming the fundamentals.*
>
> George Soros, *Open Society: Reforming Global Capitalism* (2000) p. 209, referring to the south-east Asian financial crisis of 1997–9

The success of an individual business depends not only on its own particular market and its own particular decisions. It also depends on the whole *macroeconomic* environment in which it operates, as can be seen in the article opposite.

If the economy is booming, then individual businesses are likely to be more profitable than if the economy is in recession. If the exchange rate rises (or falls), this will have an impact on the competitiveness of businesses trading overseas, and on the costs and profitability of business in general. Similarly, business profitability will be affected by interest rates, the general level of prices and wages and the level of unemployment.

It is thus important for managers to understand the forces that affect the performance of the economy. In the remaining chapters of the book, we will examine these macroeconomic forces and their effects on the business sector.

In Chapter 26 we identify the main macroeconomic objectives that governments pursue and examine how these objectives are related. In particular, we look at the objectives of economic growth, low unemployment and low inflation.

Chapter 27 looks at macroeconomic issues arising from a country's economic relationships with the rest of the world. In particular, it looks at the balance of payments and the role of exchange rates in influencing economic performance.

Chapter 28 looks at the role of money in the economy and considers the operation of the UK's financial system.

Finally, in Chapter 29 we examine various theories about how the economy operates and the implications for business. We look at the relationship between inflation and unemployment and examine the possible causes of the business cycle. We also see the important role played by the expectations of both business and consumers.

CHAPTER

26 The macroeconomic environment of business

Government macroeconomic policy aims primarily to achieve two goals:

- To ensure that the key macroeconomic variables (such as economic growth and inflation) are at acceptable levels.
- To create a *stable* economic environment in which the economy can flourish: i.e. to minimise fluctuations in economic activity.

In this chapter we shall identify what the main macroeconomic variables are and how they are related. We shall also have a preliminary look at how the government can influence these variables in order to create a more favourable environment for business. Government macroeconomic policy will be discussed in more detail in Part K.

Key Idea 30 p410

26.1 Macroeconomic objectives

There are several macroeconomic variables that governments seek to control, but these can be grouped under four main headings.

Economic growth. Governments try to achieve high rates of **economic growth** over the long term: in other words, growth that is sustained over the years and is not just a temporary phenomenon. To this end, governments also try to achieve *stable* growth, avoiding both recessions and excessive short-term growth that cannot be sustained (albeit, governments are sometimes happy to give the economy an excessive boost as an election draws near!).

Key Idea 2 p19

Economies suffer from inherent instability. As a result, economic growth and other macroeconomic indicators tend to fluctuate.

Key Idea 32

Unemployment. Governments also aim to ensure that unemployment is as low as possible, not only for the sake of the unemployed themselves, but also because it represents a waste of human resources and because unemployment benefits are a drain on government revenues.

Inflation. By **inflation** we mean a general rise in prices throughout the economy. Government policy here is to keep inflation both low and stable. One of the most

Rate of economic growth
The percentage increase in output over a twelve-month period.

Rate of inflation
The percentage increase in prices over a twelve-month period.

Balance of payments account
A record of the country's transactions with the rest of the world. It shows the country's payments to or deposits in other countries (debits) and its receipts or deposits from other countries (credits). It also shows the balance between these debits and credits under various headings.

important reasons for this is that it will aid the process of economic decision making. For example, businesses will be able to set prices and wage rates, and make investment decisions, with far more confidence. Today we are used to inflation rates of around 2 or 3 per cent, but it was not long ago that inflation in most developed countries was in double figures. In 1991, UK inflation reached 11 per cent; in 1975 it had reached 24 per cent!

The balance of payments. Governments aim to provide an environment in which exports can grow without an excessive growth in imports. They also aim to make the economy attractive to inward investment. In other words, they seek to create a climate in which the country's earnings of foreign currency at least match, or preferably exceed, the country's demand for foreign currency: they seek to achieve a favourable **balance of payments**.

In order to achieve these goals, the government may seek to control several 'intermediate' variables. These include interest rates, the supply of money, taxes, government expenditure and exchange rates. For example, the achievement of a favourable balance of payments depends, in part, on whether changes in **exchange rates** allow the country's goods and services to remain price competitive on international markets. A lower exchange rate (i.e. fewer dollars, yen, euros, etc. to the pound) will make UK goods cheaper to overseas buyers, and thus help to boost UK exports. The government may thus seek to manipulate exchange rates to make them 'more favourable'.

In later chapters we will be looking at the various types of macroeconomic policy that governments can adopt. First we will look at the four macroeconomic objectives and identify their main determinants. In this chapter we will examine economic growth, unemployment and inflation. In Chapter 27 we will focus on the balance of payments and its relation to the exchange rate.

26.2 Economic growth

The distinction between actual and potential growth

Exchange rate
The rate at which one national currency exchanges for another. The rate is expressed as the amount of one currency that is necessary to purchase one unit of another currency (e.g. DM2.50 = £1).

Actual growth
The percentage annual increase in national output actually produced.

Before examining the causes of economic growth, it is essential to distinguish between *actual* and *potential* economic growth.

Actual growth is the percentage annual increase in national output or 'GDP' (gross domestic product): in other words the rate of growth in actual output produced. When statistics on GDP growth rates are published, it is actual growth they are referring to. (We examine the measurement of GDP in the appendix to this chapter.)

Potential growth is the speed at which the economy *could* grow. It is the percentage annual increase in the economy's *capacity* to produce: the rate of growth in **potential output**. Potential output represents a ceiling on a country's output and hence will limit the living standards that can be achieved by its residents.

Living standards are limited by a country's ability to produce. Potential national output depends on the country's resources, technology and productivity.

Key Idea
33

Two of the major factors contributing to potential economic growth are:

- An increase in resources – natural resources, labour or capital.
- An increase in the efficiency with which these resources are used, through advances in technology, improved labour skills or improved organisation.

If the potential growth rate exceeds the actual growth rate, there will be an increase in spare capacity and an increase in unemployment: there will be a growing gap between potential and actual output. To close this gap, the actual growth rate would temporarily have to exceed the potential growth rate. In the long run, however, the actual growth rate will be limited to the potential growth rate.

There are thus two major issues concerned with economic growth: the short-run issue of ensuring that actual growth is such as to keep actual output as close as possible to potential output; and the long-run issue of what determines the rate of potential economic growth.

> **definition**
> **Potential growth**
> The percentage annual increase in the capacity of the economy to produce.

> **definition**
> **Potential output**
> The output that could be produced in the economy if there were a full employment of resources (including labour).

Economic growth and the business cycle

Although growth in potential output varies to some extent over the years – depending on the rate of advance of technology, the level of investment and the discovery of new raw materials – it nevertheless tends to be much more steady than the growth in actual output.

Actual growth tends to fluctuate. In some years there is a high rate of economic growth: the country experiences a boom. In other years, economic growth is low or even negative: the country experiences a recession. This cycle of booms and recessions is known as the **business cycle** or **trade cycle**.

There are four 'phases' of the business cycle. They are illustrated in Figure 26.1.

1 *The upturn.* In this phase, a stagnant economy begins to recover and growth in actual output resumes.
2 *The expansion.* During this phase, there is rapid economic growth: the economy is booming. A fuller use is made of resources and the gap between actual and potential output narrows.
3 *The peaking out.* During this phase, growth slows down or even ceases.
4 *The slowdown, recession or slump.* During this phase, there is little or no growth or even a decline in output. Increasing slack develops in the economy.

> Key Idea 32 p547

> **definition**
> **Business cycle or trade cycle**
> The periodic fluctuations of national output round its long-term trend.

Figure 26.1

The business cycle

BOX 26.1

Output gaps
An alternative measure of excess or deficient demand

If the economy grows, how fast and for how long can it grow before it runs into inflationary problems? What level of growth might be sustainable over the longer term?

To answer this question, economists have developed the concept of 'output gaps'[1] The output gap is the difference between actual output and *sustainable* output. **Sustainable output**[2] is the level

of output corresponding to stable inflation. If output is below this level (the gap is negative) there will be a deficiency of demand and hence demand-deficient unemployment, but a fall in inflation. If output is above this level (the gap is positive) there will be excess demand and a rise in inflation. Generally output will be below this level in a recession and above it in a boom. In other

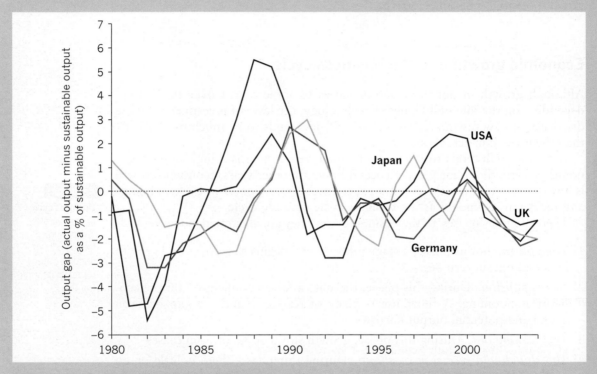

Output gaps in selected countries: 1980–2004

Source: *Datastream*

Long-term output trend. A line can be drawn showing the trend of national output over time (i.e. ignoring the cyclical fluctuations around the trend). This is shown as the dashed line in Figure 26.1. If the average level of potential output that is unutilised stays constant from one cycle to another, then the trend line will have the same slope as the potential output line. In other words, the trend rate of growth will be the same as the potential rate of growth. If, however, the level of unutilised potential changes form one cycle to another, then the trend line will have a different slope from the potential output line. For

---

Pause for thought

If the average percentage (as opposed to the average level) of potential output that was unutilised remained constant, would the trend line have the same slope as the potential output line?

words, output gaps follow the course of the business cycle.

The chart shows output gaps for four countries from 1980 to 2004. As you can see, there was a large positive output gap in the UK in the late 1980s. This corresponded to a rapid rise in output and inflation and a fall in unemployment. You will also see that there was a negative output gap for all countries in 2002 and 2003. This corresponded to a slowdown in the world economy and rising unemployment, but low inflation or, in the case of Japan, actually falling prices.

Over the *long* term, the rate of economic growth will be approximately the same as the rate of growth of sustainable output. In other words, over the years, the average output gap will tend towards zero.

But how do we measure the output gap? There are two possible methods.

Measuring trend growth. The simplest way of calculating the output gap is by measuring the trend growth rate of the economy (i.e. the average growth rate over the course of the business cycle: see Figure 26.1 on page 549) and then seeing how much actual output differs from trend output. The assumption here is that the sustainable level of output grows steadily. This is, in fact, a major weakness of this method. Technological innovations tend to come in waves, generating surges in an economy's sustainable output. Rates of innovation, in turn, depend upon how flexible the economy is in adapting to such new technologies and how much investment takes place in equipment using this technology and in training labour in the necessary skills.

Business surveys. An alternative way to measure the output gap is to ask businesses directly. The CBI Industrial Trends Survey asks manufacturers, 'Is your present level of output below capacity?' The British Chambers of Commerce Survey asks similar questions of service-sector providers. However, such survey-based evidence can only provide a broad guide to rates of capacity utilisation and whether there is deficient or excess demand. Survey evidence tends to focus on specific sectors, which might, or might not, be indicative of the capacity position of the economy as a whole. So firms might be running above normal capacity (e.g. by overtime working) in one sector of the economy, while firms in another sector might have plenty of spare capacity to continue expansion. Thus survey evidence may give an incomplete picture of overall capacity utilisation in the economy.

Question

Under what circumstances would sustainable output (i.e. a zero output gap) move further away from the potential output ceiling shown in Figure 26.1?

---

[1] See Giorno *et al.*, 'Potential output, output gaps and structural budget balances', *OECD Economic Studies*, No. 24, 1995:1

[2] The level of sustainable output is sometimes referred to as the level of 'potential output'. This, however, is confusing, as the term *potential output* is used elsewhere (including this book) to refer to full-capacity output. Such a level of output, however, would not normally be sustainable over the longer term because of the upward pressure on inflation caused by various bottlenecks in the economy. Thus sustainable output is *below* the level of potential output in the sense that we are using the term 'potential output' (e.g. as in Figure 26.1.)

---

example, if unemployment and unused industrial capacity *rise* from one peak to another, or from one trough to another, then the trend line will move further away from the potential output line (i.e. it will be less steep).

definition

Sustainable output
The level of national output corresponding to no excess of deficiency of aggregate demand.

The business cycle in practice

The business cycle illustrated in Figure 26.1 is a 'stylised' cycle. It is nice and smooth and regular. Drawing it this way allows us to make a clear distinction between each of the four phases. In practice, however, business cycles are highly irregular. They are irregular in two ways.

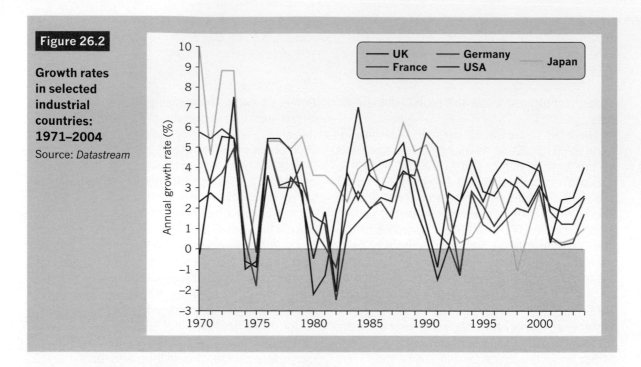

Figure 26.2

Growth rates in selected industrial countries: 1971–2004

Source: *Datastream*

The length of the phases. Some booms are short lived, lasting only a few months or so. Others are much longer, lasting perhaps three or four years. Likewise some recessions are short, while others are long.

The magnitude of the phases. Sometimes in phase 2 there is a very high rate of economic growth, perhaps 5 per cent per annum or more. On other occasions in phase 2 growth is much gentler. Sometimes in phase 4 there is a recession, with an actual decline in output (e.g. in the early 1980s and early 1990s). On other occasions, phase 4 is merely a 'pause', with growth simply slowing down.

Nevertheless, despite the irregularity of the fluctuations, cycles are still clearly discernible, especially if we plot *growth* on the vertical axis rather than the *level* of output. This is done in Figure 26.2, which shows the business cycles in selected industrial countries from 1971 to 2004.

Causes of fluctuations in actual growth

The major determinants of variations in the rate of actual growth in the *short run* are variations in the growth of aggregate demand.

Aggregate demand (*AD*) is the total spending on goods and services made within the country. This spending consists of four elements: consumer spending (*C*), investment expenditure by firms (*I*), government spending (*G*) and the expenditure by foreign residents on the country's goods and services (i.e. their purchases of its exports and their new investments in the country) (*X*). From these four must be subtracted any expenditure that goes on imports (*M*), since this is expenditure that 'leaks' abroad and is not spent on domestic goods and services. Thus:

$$AD = C + I + G + X - M$$

A rapid rise in aggregate demand will create shortages. This will tend to stimulate firms to increase output, thereby reducing slack in the economy. Likewise, a reduction in aggregate demand will leave firms with increased stocks of unsold goods. They will therefore tend to reduce output.

Aggregate demand and actual output therefore fluctuate together in the short run. A boom is associated with a rapid rise in aggregate demand: the faster the rise in aggregate demand, the higher the short-run rate of actual growth. A recession, by contrast, is associated with a reduction in aggregate demand.

A rapid rise in aggregate demand, however, is not enough to ensure a continuing high level of growth over a *number* of years. Without an expansion of potential output too, rises in actual output must eventually come to an end. Once spare capacity has been used up, once there is full employment of labour and other resources, the rate of growth of actual output will be restricted to the rate of growth of potential output. This is illustrated in Figure 26.1. As long as actual output is below potential output, the actual output curve can slope upward more steeply than the potential output curve. But once the gap between the two curves has been closed, the actual output curve can only slope as steeply as the potential output curve: the two curves cannot cross – actual output cannot be above potential output.

In the long run, therefore, there are two determinants of actual growth:

■ The growth in aggregate demand. This determines whether potential output will be realised.

■ The growth in potential output.

Causes of potential growth

There are two main determinants of potential output: (a) the amount of resources available and (b) their productivity.

Increases in the quantity of resources

Capital. The nation's output depends on its stock of capital (K). An increase in this stock will increase output. If we ignore the problem of machines wearing out or becoming obsolete and needing replacing, then the stock of capital will increase by the amount of investment. The rise in output that results will depend on the productivity of capital.

As we saw in section 23.7 (page 502), the rate of growth depends on the marginal capital/output ratio (k). This is the amount of extra capital (ΔK) divided by the amount of extra annual output that it produces (ΔY). The lower the value of k, the higher is the productivity of capital (i.e. the less extra capital you need to produce extra output). The rate of growth in potential output also depends on the proportion of national income that is invested (i), which, assuming that all saving is invested, will equal the proportion of national income that is saved (s). The formula for growth becomes:

$$g = i/k \text{ (or } g = s/k)$$

Thus if 20 per cent of national income went in new investment ($i = 20\%$), and if each £1 of new investment yielded 25p of extra income per year ($k = 4$), then the growth rate would be 5 per cent. A simple example will demonstrate this. If national income is £100 billion, then £20 billion will be invested ($i = 20\%$). This will lead to extra annual output of £5 billion ($k = 4$). Thus national income grows to £105 billion: a growth of 5 per cent.

But what determines the rate of investment? There are a number of determinants. These include the confidence of business people about the future demand for their products, the profitability of business, the tax regime, the rate of growth in the economy and the rate of interest.

Over the long term, if investment is to increase, then *saving* must increase in order to finance that investment. Put another way, people must be prepared to forgo a certain amount of consumption in order to allow resources to be diverted into producing more capital goods: factories, machines, etc.

Note that if investment is to increase, there may also need to be a steady increase in *aggregate demand*. In other words, if firms are to be encouraged to increase their capacity by installing new machines or building new factories, they may need first to see the *demand* for their products growing. Here a growth in *potential* output is the result of a growth in aggregate demand and hence *actual* output.

Labour. If there is an increase in the working population, there will be an increase in potential output. This increase in working population may result from a larger 'participation rate': a larger proportion of the total population in work or seeking work. For example, if a greater proportion of women with children decide to join the labour market, the working population will rise.

Alternatively, a rise in the working population may be the result of an increase in total population. There is a problem here. If a rise in total population does not result in a greater *proportion* of the population working, output *per head of the population* may not rise at all. In practice, many developed countries are faced with a growing proportion of their population above retirement age, and thus a potential *fall* in output per head of the population.

Land and raw materials. Land is virtually fixed in quantity. Land reclamation schemes and the opening up of marginal land can only add tiny amounts to national output. Even if new raw materials are discovered (e.g. oil), this will only result in *short-term* growth: i.e. while the rate of extraction is building up. Once the rate of extraction is at a maximum, economic growth will cease. Output will simply remain at the new higher level, until eventually the raw materials will begin to run out. Output will then fall back again.

The problem of diminishing returns. If a single factor of production increases in supply while others remain fixed, diminishing returns will set in. For example, if the quantity of capital increases with no increase in other factors of production, then diminishing returns to capital will set in. The rate of return on capital will fall. Unless *all* factors of production increase, therefore, the rate of growth is likely to slow down.

The solution to the problem of diminishing returns is for there to be an increase in the *productivity* of resources.

Increases in the productivity of resources

Technological improvements can increase the marginal productivity of capital. Much of the investment in new machines is not just in extra machines, but in superior machines producing a higher rate of return. Consider the microchip revolution of recent years. Modern computers can do the work of many people and have replaced many machines which were cumbersome and expensive to build. Improved methods of transport have reduced the costs of moving goods and materials. Improved communications (such as fax machines and the Internet) have reduced the costs of transmitting information.

As a result of technical progress, the productivity of capital has tended to increase over time. Similarly, as a result of new skills, improved education and training, and better health, the productivity of labour has also tended to increase over time.

Policies to achieve growth

How can governments increase a country's growth rate? Policies differ in two ways.

First, they may focus on the demand side or the supply side of the economy. In other words, they may attempt to create sufficient *aggregate demand* to ensure that firms wish to invest and that potential output is realised. Or alternatively, they may seek to increase *aggregate supply* by concentrating on measures to increase potential output: measures to encourage research and development, innovation and training.

Second, they may be market-orientated or interventionist policies. Many economists and politicians, especially those on the political right, believe that the best environment for encouraging economic growth is one where private enterprise is allowed to flourish: where entrepreneurs are able to reap substantial rewards from investment in new techniques and new products. Such economists therefore advocate policies designed to free up the market. Others, however, argue that a free market will be subject to considerable cyclical fluctuations. The resulting uncertainty will discourage investment. Such economists, therefore, tend to advocate intervention by the government to reduce these fluctuations.

definition

Number unemployed (economist's definition)
Those of working age who are without work, but who are available for work at current wage rates.

Unemployment 26.3

The meaning of unemployment

Unemployment can be expressed either as a number (e.g. 1.5 million) or as a percentage (e.g. 5 per cent). But just who should be included in the statistics? Should it be everyone without a job? The answer is clearly no, since we would not want to include children and pensioners. We would probably also want to exclude those who were not looking for work, such as parents choosing to stay at home to look after children.

The most usual definition that economists use for the **number unemployed** is: *those of working age who are without work, but who are available for work at current wage rates*. If the figure is to be expressed as a percentage, then it is a percentage of the total **labour force**. The labour force is defined as: *those in employment plus those unemployed*. Thus if 22.5 million people were employed and 2.5 million people were unemployed, the **unemployment rate** would be:

$$\frac{2.5}{22.5 + 2.5} \times 100 = 10 \text{ per cent}$$

definition

Labour force
The number employed plus the number unemployed.

definition

Unemployment rate
The number unemployed expressed as a percentage of the labour force.

definition

Claimant unemployment
Those in receipt of unemployment-related benefits.

Official measures of unemployment

Two common measures of unemployment are used in official statistics. The first is **claimant unemployment**. This is simply a measure of all those in receipt of unemployment-related benefits. In the UK, claimants receive the 'job-seeker's allowance'.

The second measure is the **standardised unemployment rate**. Since 1998, this has been the main measure used by the UK government. It is the measure used by the International Labour Organisation (ILO) and the Organisation for Economic Co-operation and Development (OECD), two international organisations that publish unemployment statistics for many countries.

In this measure, the unemployed are defined as people of working age who are without work, available to start work within two weeks and *actively seeking employment* or waiting to take up an appointment. The figures are compiled from the results of national labour force surveys. In the UK the labour force survey is conducted quarterly.

But is the standardised unemployment rate likely to be higher or lower than the claimant unemployment rate? The standardised rate is likely to be higher to the extent that it includes people seeking work who are nevertheless not entitled to claim benefits, but lower to the extent that it excludes those who are claiming benefits and yet who are not actively seeking work. Clearly, the tougher the benefit regulations, the lower the claimant rate will be relative to the standardised rate.

> **definition**
>
> **Standardised unemployment rate**
> The measure of the unemployment rate used by the ILO and OECD. The unemployed are defined as people of working age who are without work, available for work and actively seeking employment.

The costs of unemployment

The most obvious cost of unemployment is to the *unemployed themselves*. There is the direct financial cost of the loss in their earnings, measured as the difference between their previous wage and their unemployment benefit. Then there are the personal costs of being unemployed. The longer people are unemployed, the more dispirited they may become. Their self-esteem is likely to fall, and they are more likely to succumb to stress-related illness.

Then there are the costs to the *family and friends* of the unemployed. Personal relations can become strained, and there may be an increase in domestic violence and the number of families splitting up.

Then there are the *broader costs to the economy*. Unemployment benefits are a cost borne by taxpayers. There may also have to be extra public spending on benefit offices, social services, health care and the police. What is more, unemployment represents a loss of output. In other words, actual output is below potential output. Apart from the lack of income to the unemployed themselves, this under-utilisation of resources leads to less incomes for other people too:

■ Firms lose the profits that could have been made, had there been full employment.

■ The government loses tax revenues, since the unemployed pay no income tax and national insurance, and, given that the unemployed spend less, they pay less VAT and excise duties.

■ Other workers lose any additional wages they could have earned from higher national output.

The costs of unemployment are to some extent offset by benefits. If workers voluntarily quit their job to look for a better one, then they must reckon that the benefits of a better job more than compensate for their temporary loss of income. From the nation's point of view, a workforce that is prepared to quit jobs and spend a short time unemployed will be a more adaptable, more mobile workforce – one that is responsive to changing economic circumstances. Such a

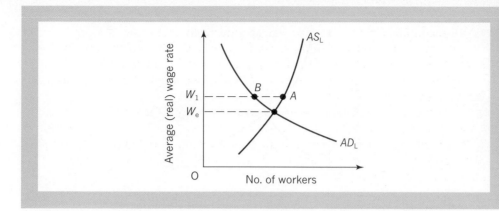

Figure 26.3

Disequilibrium unemployment

workforce will lead to greater allocative efficiency in the short run and more rapid economic growth over the longer run.

Long-term involuntary unemployment is quite another matter. The costs clearly outweigh any benefits, both for the individuals concerned and for the economy as a whole. A demotivated, deskilled pool of long-term unemployed is a serious economic and social problem.

Unemployment and the labour market

We now turn to the causes of unemployment. These causes fall into two broad categories: *equilibrium* unemployment and *disequilibrium* unemployment. To make clear the distinction between the two, it is necessary to look at how the labour market works.

Figure 26.3 shows the **aggregate demand for labour** and the **aggregate supply of labour**: that is, the total demand and supply of labour in the whole economy. The *real* average wage rate is plotted on the vertical axis. This is the average wage rate expressed in terms of its purchasing power: in other words, after taking inflation into account.

The aggregate supply of labour curve (AS_L) shows the number of workers *willing to accept jobs* at each wage rate. This curve is relatively inelastic, since the size of the workforce at any one time cannot change significantly. Nevertheless it is not totally inelastic because (a) a higher wage rate will encourage some people to enter the labour market (e.g. parents raising children) and (b) the unemployed will be more willing to accept job offers rather than continuing to search for a better-paid job.

The aggregate demand for labour curve (AD_L) slopes downward. The higher the wage rate, the more will firms attempt to economise on labour and to substitute other factors of production for labour.

The labour market is in equilibrium at a wage of W_e in Figure 26.3, where the demand for labour equals the supply. If the wage were above W_e, the labour market would be in a state of disequilibrium. At a wage rate of W_1, there is an excess supply of labour of $A - B$. This is called **disequilibrium unemployment**.

For disequilibrium unemployment to occur, two conditions must hold:

- The aggregate supply of labour must exceed the aggregate demand.

- There must be a 'stickiness' in wages. In other words, the wage rate must not immediately fall to W_e.

Key
Idea
10
p73

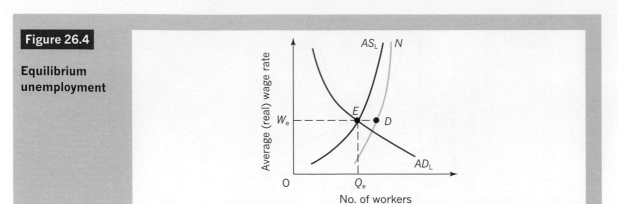

Figure 26.4

Equilibrium
unemployment

Even when the labour market *is* in equilibrium, however, not everyone looking for work will be employed. Some people will hold out, hoping to find a better job. The curve N in Figure 26.4 shows the total number in the labour force. The horizontal difference between it and the aggregate supply of labour curve (AS_L) represents the excess of people looking for work over those actually willing to accept jobs. Q_e represents the equilibrium level of employment and the distance $D - E$ represents the **equilibrium level of unemployment**. This is sometimes known as the *natural level of unemployment*.

Types of disequilibrium unemployment

There are three possible causes of disequilibrium unemployment.

Real-wage unemployment

This is where trade unions use their monopoly power to drive wages above the market-clearing level. In Figure 26.3, the wage rate is driven up above W_e. Excessive real wage rates were blamed by the Thatcher and Major governments for the high unemployment of the 1980s and early 1990s. The possibility of higher real-wage unemployment was also one of the reasons for their rejection of a national minimum wage.

The solution to real-wage unemployment would seem to be a reduction in real wage rates. However, it may be very difficult to prevent unions pushing up wages. Even if the government did succeed in reducing the average real wage rate, there would then be a problem of reduced consumer expenditure and hence a reduced demand for labour, with the result that unemployment might not fall at all.

Pause for thought

If this analysis is correct, namely that a reduction in wages will reduce the aggregate demand for goods, what assumption must we make about the relative proportions of wages and profits that are spent (given that a reduction in real wage rates will lead to a corresponding increase in rates of profit)? Is this a realistic assumption?

Demand-deficient or cyclical unemployment

Demand-deficient unemployment is associated with economic recessions. As the economy moves into recession, consumer demand falls. Firms find that they are unable to sell their current level of output. For a time they may be prepared to build up stocks of unsold goods, but sooner or later they will start to cut back on production and cut back on the amount of labour they employ. In Figure 26.3

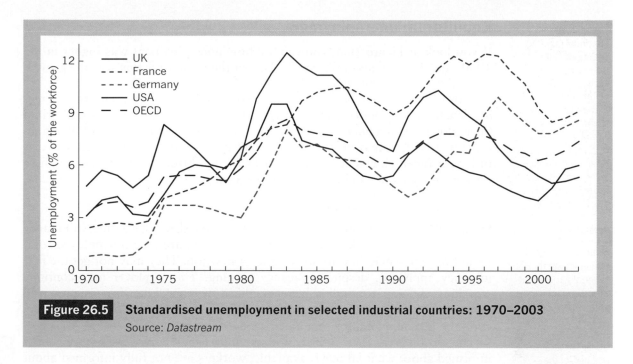

Figure 26.5 | **Standardised unemployment in selected industrial countries: 1970–2003**
Source: *Datastream*

the AD_L curve shifts to the left. The deeper the recession becomes and the longer it lasts, the higher will demand-deficient unemployment become.

As the economy recovers and begins to grow again, so demand-deficient unemployment will start to fall. Because demand-deficient unemployment fluctuates with the business cycle, it is sometimes referred to as 'cyclical unemployment'. Figure 26.5 shows the fluctuations in unemployment in various industrial countries and for the OECD[1] as a whole. If you compare this figure with Figure 26.2, you can see how unemployment tends to rise in recessions and fall in booms.

Demand-deficient unemployment can also exist in the longer term if the economy is constantly run at below full capacity and labour markets continue not to be in equilibrium. Even at the peak of the trade cycle, actual output may be considerably below potential output.

Growth in the labour supply

If labour supply rises with no corresponding increase in the demand for labour, the equilibrium real wage rate will fall. If the real wage rate is 'sticky' downward, unemployment will occur. This tends not to be such a serious cause of unemployment as demand deficiency, since the supply of labour changes relatively slowly. Nevertheless there is a problem of providing jobs for school leavers each year with the sudden influx of new workers on to the labour market.

There is also a potential problem over the longer term if social trends lead more women with children to seek employment. In practice, however, with the rapid growth of part-time employment and the lower average wage rate paid to women, this has not been a major cause of excess labour supply.

> **definition**
>
> **Demand-deficient or cyclical unemployment** Disequilibrium unemployment caused by a fall in aggregate demand with no corresponding fall in the real wage rate.

---

[1] The Organisation for Economic Co-operation and Development: the 29 major industrialised countries including the Czech Republic, Hungary, Poland, Korea, Mexico and Turkey.

definition
Frictional (search) unemployment Unemployment that occurs as a result of imperfect information in the labour market. It often takes time for workers to find jobs (even though there are vacancies) and in the meantime they are unemployed.

definition
Structural unemployment Unemployment that arises from changes in the pattern of demand or supply in the economy. People made redundant in one part of the economy cannot immediately take up jobs in other parts (even though there are vacancies).

definition
Technological unemployment Structural unemployment that occurs as a result of the introduction of labour-saving technology.

definition
Regional unemployment Structural unemployment occurring in specific regions of the country.

definition
Seasonal unemployment Unemployment associated with industries or regions where the demand for labour is lower at certain times of the year.

Equilibrium unemployment

If you look at Figure 26.5, you can see how unemployment was higher in the 1980s and 1990s than in the 1970s. Part of the reason for this was the growth in equilibrium unemployment.

Although there may be overall *macro*economic equilibrium, with the *aggregate* demand for labour equal to the *aggregate* supply, and thus no disequilibrium unemployment, at a *micro*economic level supply and demand may not match. In other words, there may be vacancies in some parts of the economy, but an excess of labour (unemployment) in others. This is equilibrium unemployment. There are various types of equilibrium unemployment.

Frictional (search) unemployment

Frictional unemployment occurs when people leave their jobs, either voluntarily or because they are sacked or made redundant, and are then unemployed for a period of time while they are looking for a new job. They may not get the first job they apply for, despite a vacancy existing. The employer may continue searching, hoping to find a better-qualified person. Likewise, unemployed people may choose not to take the first job they are offered. Instead they may continue searching, hoping that a better one will turn up.

The problem is that information is imperfect. Employers are not fully informed about what labour is available; workers are not fully informed about what jobs are available and what they entail. Both employers and workers, therefore, have to search: employers search for the right labour and workers search for the right jobs.

Key Idea
7
p50

Structural unemployment

Structural unemployment is where the structure of the economy changes. Employment in some industries may expand while in others it contracts. There are two main reasons for this.

A change in the pattern of demand. Some industries experience declining demand. This may be due to a change in consumer tastes. Certain goods may go out of fashion. Or it may be due to competition from other industries. For example, consumer demand may shift away from coal and to other fuels. This will lead to structural unemployment in mining areas.

A change in the methods of production (technological unemployment). New techniques of production often allow the same level of output to be produced with fewer workers. This is known as 'labour-saving technical progress'. Unless output expands sufficiently to absorb the surplus labour, people will be made redundant. This creates **technological unemployment**. An example is the job losses in the banking industry caused by the increase in the number of cash machines and by the development of telephone and Internet banking.

Structural unemployment often occurs in particular regions of the country. When it does, it is referred to as **regional unemployment**. This is most likely to occur when particular industries are concentrated in particular areas. For example, the decline in the South Wales coal mining industry led to high unemployment in the Welsh valleys.

Seasonal unemployment

Seasonal unemployment occurs when the demand for certain types of labour fluctuates with the seasons of the year. This problem is particularly severe in holiday areas such as Cornwall, where unemployment can reach very high levels in the winter months.

Inflation

The rate of inflation measures the annual percentage increase in prices. The most usual measure is that of *retail* prices. The government publishes an index of consumer prices each month, and the rate of inflation is the percentage increase in that index over the previous twelve months. Figure 26.6 shows the rates of inflation for the USA, Japan, the UK, the EU and the OECD. As you can see, inflation was particularly severe between 1973 and 1983, and relatively low in the mid-1980s and in recent years.

It is also possible to give the rates of inflation for other prices. For example, indices are published for commodity prices, food prices, house prices, import prices, prices after taking taxes into account and so on. Their respective rates of inflation are simply their annual percentage increase. Likewise it is possible to give the rate of inflation of wage rates ('wage inflation').

When there is inflation, we have to be careful in assessing how much national output, consumption, wages, etc. are increasing. Take the case of GDP. GDP in year 2 may seem higher than in year 1, but this may be partly (or even wholly) the result of higher prices. Thus GDP in money terms may have risen by 5 per cent, but if inflation is 3 per cent, **real growth in GDP** will be only 2 per cent. In other words, the volume of output will be only 2 per cent higher.

definition

Real growth values
Values of the rate of growth of GDP or any other variable after taking inflation into account. The real value of the growth in a variable equals its growth in money (or 'nominal') value minus the rate of inflation.

> *The distinction between nominal and real figures.* Nominal figures are those using current prices, interest rates, etc. Real figures are figures corrected for inflation.
>
> **Key Idea 34**

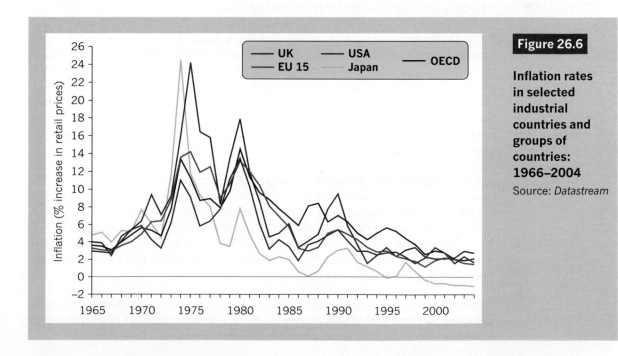

Figure 26.6

Inflation rates in selected industrial countries and groups of countries: 1966–2004

Source: *Datastream*

Before we proceed, a word of caution: be careful not to confuse a rise or fall in *inflation* with a rise or fall in *prices*. A rise in inflation means a *faster* increase in prices. A fall in inflation means a *slower* increase in prices (but still an increase as long as inflation is positive).

The costs of inflation

A lack of growth is obviously a problem if people want higher living standards. Unemployment is obviously a problem, both for the unemployed themselves and also for society, which suffers a loss in output and has to support the unemployed. But why is inflation a problem? If firms are faced with rising costs, does it really matter if they can simply pass them on in higher prices? Similarly for workers, if their wages keep up with prices, there will not be a cut in their living standards.

If people could correctly anticipate the rate of inflation and fully adjust prices and incomes to take account of it, then the costs of inflation would indeed be relatively small. For us as consumers, they would simply be the relatively minor inconvenience of having to adjust our notions of what a 'fair' price is for each item when we go shopping. For firms, they would again be the relatively minor costs of having to change price labels, or prices in catalogues or on menus, or to adjust slot machines. These are known as **menu costs**.

In reality, people frequently make mistakes when predicting the rate of inflation and are not able to adapt fully to it. This leads to the following problems, which are likely to be more serious the higher the rate of inflation becomes and the more the rate fluctuates.

Redistribution. Inflation redistributes income away from those on fixed incomes and those in a weak bargaining position, to those who can use their economic power to gain large pay, rent or profit increases. It redistributes wealth to those with assets (e.g. property) that rise in value particularly rapidly during periods of inflation, and away from those with savings that pay rates of interest below the rate of inflation and hence whose value is eroded by inflation. Pensioners may be particularly badly hit by rapid inflation.

Uncertainty and lack of investment. Inflation tends to cause uncertainty in the business community, especially when the rate of inflation fluctuates. (Generally, the higher the rate of inflation, the more it fluctuates.) If it is difficult for firms to predict their costs and revenues, they may be discouraged from investing. This will reduce the rate of economic growth. On the other hand, as will be explained below, policies to reduce the rate of inflation may themselves reduce the rate of economic growth, especially in the short run. This may then provide the government with a policy dilemma.

Balance of payments. Inflation is likely to worsen the balance of payments. If a country suffers from relatively high inflation, its exports will become less competitive in world markets. At the same time, imports will become relatively cheaper than home-produced goods. Thus exports will fall and imports will rise. As a result the balance of payments will deteriorate and/or the exchange rate will fall, or interest rates will have to rise. Each of these effects can cause problems. This is examined in more detail in the next chapter.

Resources. Extra resources are likely to be used to cope with the effects of inflation. Accountants and other financial experts may have to be employed by companies to help them cope with the uncertainties caused by inflation.

BOX 26.2

Is inflation dead?
No, just kept under control

'What's the big fuss about inflation?' That might seem to be a justified question today. After all, inflation rates in developed countries are typically around 2–3 per cent (see Figure 26.6), and that is hardly a cause for concern.

Indeed, having some inflation, provided that it is relatively modest, could even be seen to be an advantage. This is because wages and prices are often 'sticky' downwards: unions are not prepared to accept wage cuts; firms are often unwilling to cut prices. Having a modest amount of inflation allows relative prices and wages in different parts of the economy to be adjusted up *and* down, in line with changes in demand and supply. Where demand has risen (or supply fallen) prices and wages can rise. Where demand has fallen (or supply risen) prices and wages can be held steady. There will be an overall rise in prices and wages in the economy (a modest inflation) and yet *relative* prices and wages will have adjusted.

So why be concerned about inflation, given that it is so low and, at such levels, can be useful? The reason *why* it is so low is that it has been made the main target of macroeconomic policy in many countries. For example, in the UK, the Bank of England tries to keep inflation at 2 per cent. Similarly, in the 12 EU countries using the euro,

the European Central Bank tries to keep inflation at or below 2 per cent. In both cases interest rates are adjusted up or down to keep inflation on target. If inflation is predicted to go above its target level, interest rates are raised. The resulting higher cost of borrowing dampens consumer expenditure and investment by firms. The resulting lower aggregate demand leads to a fall in demand-pull inflation.

If controlling inflation was *not* the main target of macroeconomic policy, then it could well rise, causing the problems we have been considering in this section. It is true that inflation is not a problem at present, but only because keeping it low has been given such a high priority.

But has targeting inflation meant giving a lower priority to raising growth and reducing unemployment? Could we have higher growth and lower unemployment if we were prepared to accept a higher rate of inflation? Or is low inflation a means to achieving these other goals? We shall consider these questions in the following chapters.

Question

How is the policy of targeting inflation likely to affect the expected rate of inflation?

The costs of inflation may be relatively mild if inflation is kept to single figures. They can be very serious, however, if inflation gets out of hand. If inflation develops into 'hyperinflation', with prices rising perhaps by several hundred or even thousand per cent per year, the whole basis of the market economy will be undermined. Firms constantly raise prices in an attempt to cover their rocketing costs. Workers demand huge pay increases in an attempt to stay ahead of the rocketing cost of living. Thus prices and wages chase each other in an ever-rising inflationary spiral. People will no longer want to save money. Instead they will spend it as quickly as possible before its value falls any further. People may even resort to barter in an attempt to avoid using money altogether.

Pause for thought

Do you personally gain or lose from inflation? Why?

Aggregate demand and supply and the level of prices

Key Idea 10 p73

The level of prices in the economy is determined by the interaction of aggregate demand and aggregate supply. The analysis is similar to that of demand and supply in individual markets, but there are some crucial differences. Figure 26.7 shows aggregate demand and supply curves. Let us examine each in turn.

Figure 26.7

Aggregate
demand and
aggregate supply

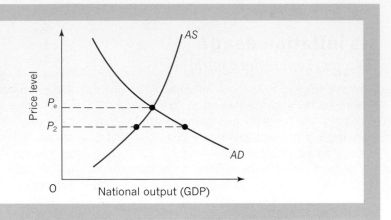

Aggregate demand curve

Remember what we said about aggregate demand earlier in the chapter. It is the total level of spending on the country's products: that is, by consumers, by the government, by firms on investment, and by people residing abroad. The aggregate demand curve shows how much national output (GDP) will be demanded at each level of prices. But why does the *AD* curve slope downwards: why do people demand fewer products as prices rise? There are three main reasons:

- If prices rise, people will be encouraged to buy fewer of the country's products and more imports instead (which are now relatively cheaper); also the country will sell fewer exports. Thus aggregate demand will be lower.
- As prices rise, people will need more money to pay for their purchases. With a given supply of money in the economy, this will have the effect of driving up interest rates (we will explore this in Chapter 28). The effect of higher interest rates will be to discourage borrowing and encourage saving. Both will have the effect of reducing spending and hence reducing aggregate demand.
- If prices rise, the value of people's savings will be eroded. They may thus save more (and spend less) to compensate.

Aggregate supply curve

The aggregate supply curve slopes upwards – at least in the short run. In other words, the higher the level of prices, the more will be produced. The reason is simple: provided that factor prices (and, in particular, wage rates) do not rise as rapidly as product prices, firms' profitability at each level of output will be higher than before. This will encourage them to produce more.

Equilibrium

The equilibrium price level will be where aggregate demand equals aggregate supply. To demonstrate this, consider what would happen if aggregate demand exceeded aggregate supply: for example, at P_2 in Figure 26.7. The resulting shortages throughout the economy would drive up prices. This would cause a movement up along both the *AD* and *AS* curves until *AD* = *AS* (at P_e).

Shifts in the AD or AS curves

If there is a change in the price level there will be a movement *along* the *AD* and *AS* curves. If any other determinant of *AD* or *AS* changes, the respective curve will shift. The analysis here is very similar to shifts and movements along demand and supply curves in individual markets (see pages 68 and 72).

The aggregate demand curve will shift if there is a change in any of its components – consumption, investment, government expenditure or exports minus imports. Thus if the government decides to spend more, or if consumers spend more as a result of lower taxes, or if business confidence increases so that firms decide to invest more, the *AD* curve will shift to the right.

Similarly, the aggregate supply curve will shift to the right if there is a rise in labour productivity or in the stock of capital: in other words, if there is a rise in potential output.

Pause for thought

Give some examples of events that could shift (a) the AD *curve to the left; (b) the* AS *curve to the left.*

Causes of inflation

Demand-pull inflation

Demand-pull inflation is caused by continuing rises in aggregate demand. In Figure 26.7, the *AD* curve shifts to the right, and continues doing so. Firms will respond to the rise in aggregate demand partly by raising prices and partly by increasing output (there is a move up along the *AS* curve). Just how much they raise prices depends on how much their costs rise as a result of increasing output. This in turn depends upon how close actual output is to potential output. The less slack there is in the economy, the more will firms respond to a rise in demand by raising their prices (the steeper will be the *AS* curve).

Demand-pull inflation is typically associated with a booming economy. Many economists therefore argue that it is the counterpart of demand-deficient unemployment. When the economy is in recession, demand-deficient unemployment will be high, but demand-pull inflation will be low. When, on the other hand, the economy is near the peak of the business cycle, demand-pull inflation will be high, but demand-deficient unemployment will be low.

Cost-push inflation

Cost-push inflation is associated with continuing rises in costs and hence continuing leftward (upward) shifts in the *AS* curve. If firms face a rise in costs, they will respond partly by raising prices and passing the costs on to the consumer, and partly by cutting back on production (there is a movement back along the *AD* curve).

Just how much firms raise prices and cut back on production depends on the shape of the aggregate demand curve. The less elastic the *AD* curve, the less sales will fall as a result of any price rise, and hence the more will firms be able to pass on the rise in their costs to consumers as higher prices.

The rise in costs may originate from a number of different sources. As a result we can distinguish various types of cost-push inflation.

- *Wage-push inflation.* This is where trades union push up wages independently of the demand for labour.
- *Profit-push inflation.* This is where firms use their monopoly power to make bigger profits by pushing up prices independently of consumer demand.
- *Import-price-push inflation.* This is where import prices rise independently of the level of aggregate demand. An example is when OPEC quadrupled the price of oil in 1973/4.

definition

Demand-pull inflation
Inflation caused by persistent rises in aggregate demand.

definition

Cost-push inflation
Inflation caused by persistent rises in costs of production (independently of demand).

In all these cases, inflation occurs because one or more groups are exercising economic power. The problem is likely to get worse, therefore, if there is an increasing concentration of economic power over time (for example, if firms or unions get bigger and bigger, and more monopolistic) or if groups become more militant.

Demand-pull and cost-push inflation can occur together, since wage and price rises can be caused both by increases in aggregate demand and by independent causes pushing up costs. Even when an inflationary process *starts* as either demand-pull or cost-push, it is often difficult to separate the two. An initial cost-push inflation may encourage the government to expand aggregate demand to offset rises in unemployment. Alternatively, an initial demand-pull inflation may strengthen the power of certain groups, who then use this power to drive up costs. Either way, the result is likely to be continuing rightward shifts in the *AD* curve and leftward shifts in the *AS* curve. Prices will carry on rising.

Structural (demand-shift) inflation

When the *pattern* of demand (or supply) changes in the economy, certain industries will experience increased demand and others decreased demand. If prices and wages are inflexible downwards in the contracting industries, and prices and wages rise in the expanding industries, the overall price and wage level will rise. The problem will be made worse, the less elastic is supply to these shifts.

Thus a more rapid structural change in the economy can lead to both increased structural unemployment and increased structural inflation. An example of this problem was the so called north–south divide in the UK during the second half of the 1980s. The north experienced high structural unemployment as old industries declined, while the south experienced excess demand. This led to, among other things, rapid house price inflation and rapid increases in incomes for various groups of workers and firms. With many prices and wages being set *nationally*, the inflation in the south then 'spilt over' into the north.

Expectations and inflation

Workers and firms take account of the *expected* rate of inflation when making decisions.

Imagine that a union and an employer are negotiating a wage increase. Let us assume that both sides expect a rate of inflation of 5 per cent. The union will be happy to receive a wage rise somewhat above 5 per cent. That way the members would be getting a *real* rise in incomes. The employers will be happy to pay a wage rise somewhat below 5 per cent. After all, they can put their price up by 5 per cent, knowing that their rivals will do approximately the same. The actual wage rise that the two sides agree on will thus be somewhere around 5 per cent.

Now let us assume that the expected rate of inflation is 10 per cent. Both sides will now negotiate around this benchmark, with the outcome being somewhere round about 10 per cent.

Thus the higher the expected rate of inflation, the higher will be the level of pay settlements and price rises, and hence the higher will be the resulting actual rate of inflation.

In recent years the importance of expectations in explaining the actual rate of inflation has been increasingly recognised by economists. We examine this in Chapter 29.

BOX 26.3

Deflation danger
Running out of steam?

Deflation is stalking the global economy. No longer is it solely a problem for the Japanese whose economy has been in deflation for the past 10 years. The US Federal Reserve and the European Central Bank have sounded warnings that deflation is a real and present danger, set to engulf the global economic system. The following article, extracted from *The Sunday Times* of 11 May 2003, assesses the extent of the deflationary threat, its potential economic effects and the reasons behind its growth.

Consumers have had a good run in America. Twenty years ago a Burger King Whopper cost $1.40. Today the same burger costs 99c. Ten years ago Delta Airlines charged $388 for a flight from New York to San Francisco; this weekend flights are available for $302. Five years ago the average new car cost $25 000; now it is $24 500.

The same is true for clothes, computers, holidays and television sets. As wages have risen, prices seem to have fallen across the board. But you can have too much of a good thing.

Last week, America's central bankers warned that falling prices could harm the US economy. The Federal Reserve even went as far as to raise the spectre of deflation – an economic malaise that has paralysed the Japanese economy for a decade and was last seen in America during the Great Depression of the 1930s.

Not all prices are falling – house prices remain high, insurance costs are rising and so are medical bills. But the Fed's move signalled a profound change in attitude.

The European Central bank (ECB) followed suit with a subtle yet significant shift in policy. The ECB now says its aim is to keep inflation 'close to 2%'; in the past its aim was for inflation to hover between 0% and 2%.

Consumers normally welcome falling prices, but in a deflating economy such falls can create a damaging downward spiral. Profits fall as companies are unable to offset costs by raising prices. Companies then cut staff to save money. Job losses lead to falling sales.

Declining sales also make it harder for companies and people to meet their debts, leading to further declines in sales and a rise in bankruptcies. Falling prices also lead people to defer purchases in the belief that prices will come down further.

Such a spiral of decline had held back the Japanese economy since the 1990s. Most economists see the threat of deflation as a remote possibility in America, but it is a possibility that they are starting to take seriously....

Since December, the key Consumer Price Index – which excludes volatile food and energy items – has declined to 1.7%, the lowest level since the mid-1960s. Most economists expect the index to decline further this year.

Stephen Roach, Morgan Stanley's chief economist, has consistently warned of the dangers of deflation. 'The hope is that if we take this threat dead seriously, it won't happen,' he says.

Roach says there are three factors pushing America towards deflation.

■ The business cycle. Recessions by their very nature are deflationary. A weak recovery like the one we are experiencing does not favour price increases.

■ The bubble. The economy is till struggling to find its feet after over-indulging during the boom of the late 1990s. 'Too much supply was put into the market. The legacy is still there,' says Roach.

■ Globalisation. 'It's not a bad thing but it is deflationary. Low-cost countries are brought into the equation, and not just in goods but in services too.' The increasing transfer of call centres to countries like India is an example of this.

'The net result is that the unthinkable has become possible. I believe it is perfectly appropriate for policymakers to view deflation as the single greatest risk in shaping their economies,' he says.

Questions

1 *Describe the impact of deflation on the practice of business.*

2 *What long-term economic benefits might deflation generate for business and the economy in general?*

26.5 The business cycle and macroeconomic objectives

In the short term (up to about two years), the four objectives of faster growth in output, lower unemployment, lower inflation and the avoidance of balance of payments deficits are all related. They all depend on aggregate demand and vary with the course of the business cycle. This is illustrated in Figure 26.8.

Key Idea
32
p547

In the expansionary phase of the business cycle (phase 2), aggregate demand grows rapidly. The gap between actual and potential output will narrow. There will be relatively rapid growth in output, and (demand-deficient) unemployment will fall. Thus two of the problems are getting better. On the other hand, the other two problems will be getting worse. The growing shortages lead to higher (demand-pull) inflation and a deteriorating balance of payments as the extra demand 'sucks in' more imports and as higher prices make domestic goods less competitive internationally.

At the peak of the cycle (phase 3), unemployment is probably at its lowest and output at its highest (for the time being). But growth has already ceased or at least slowed down. Inflation and balance of payments problems are probably acute.

As the economy moves into phase 4 (let us assume that this is an actual recession with falling output), the reverse will happen to that of phase 2. Falling aggregate demand will make growth negative and demand-deficient unemployment higher, but inflation is likely to slow down and the balance of payments will improve. These two improvements may take some time to occur, however.

Governments are thus faced with a dilemma. If they reflate the economy, they will make two of the objectives better (growth and unemployment), but the other two worse (inflation and balance of payments). If they deflate the economy, it is the other way round: inflation and the balance of payments will improve, but unemployment will rise and growth, or even output, will fall.

Key Idea
35
p568

Societies face trade-offs between economic objectives. For example, the goal of faster growth may conflict with that of greater equality; the goal of lower unemployment may conflict with that of lower inflation (at least in the short run). This is an example of opportunity cost: the cost of achieving more of one objective may be achieving less of another. The existence of trade-offs means that policy makers must make choices.

Key Idea
35

Figure 26.8

The business cycle and the four macroeconomic objectives

The circular flow of income   26.6

Another way of understanding the relationship between the four objectives is to use a simple model of the economy. This is the circular flow of income, which is shown in Figure 26.9. In the diagram, the economy is divided into two major groups: *firms* and *households*. Each group has two roles. Firms are producers of goods and services; they are also the employers of labour and other factors of production. Households (which is the word we use for individuals) are the consumers of goods and services; they are also the suppliers of labour and various other factors of production. In the diagram there is an inner flow and various outer flows of income between these two groups.

Before we look at the various parts of the diagram, a word of warning. Do not confuse *money* and *income*. Money is a stock concept. At any given time, there is a certain quantity of money in the economy (e.g. £1 billion). But that does not tell us the level of national *income*. Income is a flow concept (as is expenditure). It is measured as so much *per period of time*. The relationship between money and income depends on how rapidly the money *circulates*: its 'velocity of circulation'. (We will examine this concept in detail later on.) If there is £1 billion of money in the economy and each £1 on average is paid out as income five times per year, then annual national income will be £5 billion.

The inner flow, withdrawals and injections

The inner flow

Firms pay money to households in the form of wages and salaries, dividends on shares, interest and rent. These payments are in return for the services of the factors of production – labour, capital and land – that are supplied by households. Thus on the left-hand side of the diagram money flows directly from firms to households as 'factor payments'.

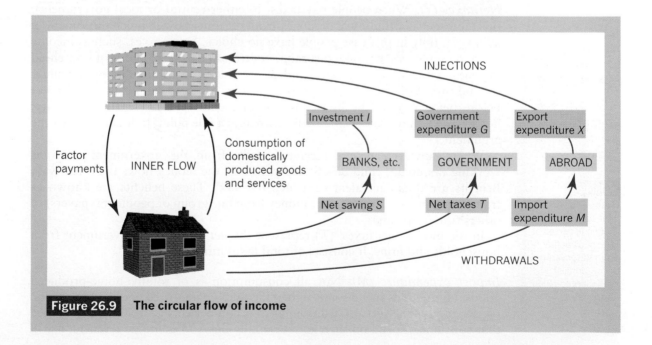

Figure 26.9   **The circular flow of income**

definition

The consumption of domestically produced goods and services (C_d)
The direct flow of money payments from households to firms.

Households, in turn, pay money to domestic firms when they **consume domestically produced goods and services (C_d)**. This is shown on the right-hand side of the inner flow. There is thus a circular flow of payments from firms to households to firms and so on.

If households spend *all* their incomes on buying domestic goods and services, and if firms pay out *all* this income they receive as factor payments to domestic households, and if the velocity of circulation does not change, the flow will continue at the same level indefinitely. The money just goes round and round at the same speed and incomes remain unchanged.

Pause for thought

Would this argument still hold if prices rose?

In the real world, of course, it is not as simple as this. Not all income gets passed on round the inner flow; some is *withdrawn*. At the same time, incomes are injected into the flow from outside. Let us examine these withdrawals and injections.

Withdrawals

Only part of the incomes received by households will be spent on the goods and services of domestic firms. The remainder will be withdrawn from the inner flow. Likewise, only part of the incomes generated by firms will be paid to domestic households. The remainder of this will also be withdrawn. There are three forms of **withdrawals (W)** (or 'leakages' as they are sometimes called).

definition

Withdrawals (W) (or leakages)
Incomes of households or firms that are not passed on round the inner flow. Withdrawals equal net saving (S) plus net taxes (T) plus import expenditure (M):
$W = S + T + M$.

Net saving (S). Saving is income that households choose not to spend but to put aside for the future. Savings are normally deposited in financial institutions such as banks and building societies. This is shown in the bottom right of the diagram. Money flows from households to 'banks, etc'. What we are seeking to measure here, however, is the net flow from households to the banking sector. We therefore have to subtract from saving any borrowing or drawing on past savings by households in order to get the *net* saving flow. Of course, if household borrowing exceeded saving, the net flow would be in the other direction: it would be negative.

Net taxes (T). When people pay taxes (to either central or local government), this represents a withdrawal of money from the inner flow in much the same way as saving: only in this case people have no choice. Some taxes, such as income tax and employees' national insurance contributions, are paid out of household incomes. Others, such as VAT and excise duties, are paid out of consumer expenditure. Others, such as corporation tax, are paid out of firms' incomes before being received by households as dividends on shares. (For simplicity, however, we show taxes being withdrawn at just one point. It does not affect the argument.)

When, however, people receive *benefits* from the government, such as working tax credit, child benefit and pensions, the money flows the other way. Benefits are thus equivalent to a 'negative tax'. These benefits are known as **transfer payments**. They transfer money from one group of people (taxpayers) to others (the recipients).

In the model, 'net taxes' (T) represent the *net* flow to the government from households and firms. It consists of total taxes minus benefits.

definition

Transfer payments
Moneys transferred from one person or group to another (e.g. from the government to individuals) without production taking place.

Import expenditure (M). Not all consumption is of totally home-produced goods. Households spend some of their incomes on imported goods and services, or on goods and services using imported components. Although the money that consumers spend on such goods initially flows to domestic retailers, it will eventually find its way abroad, either when the retailers or wholesalers themselves import them, or when domestic manufacturers purchase imported inputs to make their products. This expenditure on imports constitutes the third withdrawal from the inner flow. This money flows abroad.

Total withdrawals are simply the sum of net saving, net taxes and the expenditure on imports:

$$W = S + T + M$$

Injections

Only part of the demand for firms' output arises from consumers' expenditure. The remainder comes from other sources outside the inner flow. These additional components of aggregate demand are known as **injections** (*J*). There are three types of injection.

definition

Injections (J)
Expenditure on the production of domestic firms coming from outside the inner flow of the circular flow of income. Injections equal investment (*I*) plus government expenditure (G) plus expenditure on exports (*X*).

Investment (I). This is the money that firms spend which they obtain from various financial institutions – either past savings or loans, or through a new issue of shares. They may invest in plant and equipment or may simply spend the money on building up stocks of inputs, semi-finished or finished goods.

Government expenditure (G). When the government spends money on goods and services produced by firms, this counts as an injection. Examples of such government expenditure are spending on roads, hospitals and schools. (Note that government expenditure in this model does not include state benefits. These transfer payments, as we saw above, are the equivalent of negative taxes and have the effect of reducing the *T* component of withdrawals.)

Export expenditure (X). Money flows into the circular flow from abroad when residents abroad buy our exports of goods and services.

Total injections are thus the sum of investment, government expenditure and exports:

$$J = I + G + X$$

The relationship between withdrawals and injections

There are indirect links between saving and investment, taxation and government expenditure, and imports and exports, via financial institutions, the government (central and local) and foreign countries respectively. If a greater proportion of income is saved, there will be more available for banks and other financial institutions to lend out. If tax receipts are higher, the government may be more keen to increase its expenditure. Finally, if imports increase, incomes of people abroad will increase, which will enable them to purchase more of our exports.

These links, however, do not guarantee that $S = I$ or $G = T$ or $M = X$. For a period of time, financial institutions can lend out (*I*) more or less than they receive from depositors (*S*); governments can spend (*G*) more or less than they receive in taxes (*T*); and exports (*X*) can exceed imports (*M*) or vice versa.

A major point here is that the decisions to save and invest are made by different people, and thus they plan to save and invest different amounts. Likewise the demand for imports may not equal the demand for exports. As far as the government is concerned, it may choose not to make $T = G$. It may choose not to spend all its tax revenues: to run a 'budget surplus' $(T > G)$; or it may choose to spend more than it receives in taxes: to run a 'budget deficit' $(G > T)$, by borrowing or printing money to make up the difference.

Thus planned injections (J) may not equal planned withdrawals (W).

The circular flow of income and the four macroeconomic objectives

If planned injections are not equal to planned withdrawals, what will be the consequences? If injections exceed withdrawals, the level of expenditure will rise. The extra aggregate demand will generate extra incomes. In other words, *actual* national income will rise. If this rise in actual income exceeds any rise there may have been in potential income, there will be the following effects upon the four macroeconomic objectives:

■ There will be economic growth. The greater the initial excess of injections over withdrawals, the bigger will be the rise in national income.

■ Unemployment will fall as firms take on more workers in order to meet the extra demand for output.

■ Inflation will tend to rise. The more the gap is closed between actual and potential income, the more difficult will firms find it to meet extra demand, and the more likely they will be to raise prices.

■ The balance of payments will tend to deteriorate. The higher demand sucks more imports into the country, and higher domestic inflation makes exports less competitive and imports relatively cheaper compared with home-produced goods. Thus imports will tend to rise and exports will tend to fall.

Pause for thought

What will be the effect on each of the four objectives if planned injections are less than planned withdrawals?

Changes in injections and withdrawals thus have a crucial effect on the whole macroeconomic environment in which businesses operate. We will examine some of these effects in more detail in the following chapters.

SUMMARY

1 The four main macroeconomic goals that are generally of most concern to governments are economic growth, reducing unemployment, reducing inflation, and avoiding balance of payments and exchange rate problems.

2a Actual growth must be distinguished from potential growth. The actual growth rate is the percentage annual increase in the output that is actually produced, whereas potential growth is the percentage annual increase in the capacity of the economy to produce (whether or not it is actually produced).

2b Actual growth will fluctuate with the course of the business cycle. The cycle can be broken down

into four phases: the upturn, the expansion, the peaking-out, and the slowdown or recession. In practice the length and magnitude of these phases will vary: the cycle is thus irregular.

2c Actual growth is determined by potential growth and by the level of aggregate demand. If actual output is below potential output, actual growth can temporarily exceed potential growth, if aggregate demand is rising sufficiently. In the long term, however, actual output can only grow as fast as potential output will permit.

2d Potential growth is determined by the rate of increase in the *quantity* of resources: capital, labour, land and raw materials; and by the *productivity* of resources. The productivity of capital can be increased by technological improvements and the more efficient use of the capital stock; the productivity of labour can be increased by better education, training, motivation and organisation.

3a The two most common measures of unemployment are claimant unemployment (those claiming unemployment-related benefits) and ILO/OECD standardised unemployment (those available for work and actively seeking work or waiting to take up an appointment).

3b The costs of unemployment include the financial and other personal costs to the unemployed person, the costs to relatives and friends, and the costs to society at large in terms of lost tax revenues, lost profits and lost wages to other workers, and in terms of social disruption.

3c Unemployment can be divided into disequilibrium and equilibrium unemployment.

3d Disequilibrium unemployment occurs when the average real wage rate is above the level that will equate the aggregate demand and supply of labour. It can be caused by unions or government pushing up wages (real-wage unemployment), by a fall in aggregate demand but a downward 'stickiness' in real wages (demand-deficient unemployment), or by an increase in the supply of labour.

3e Equilibrium unemployment occurs when there are people unable or unwilling to fill job vacancies. This may be due to poor information in the labour market and hence a time lag before people find suitable jobs (frictional unemployment), to a changing pattern of demand or supply in the economy and hence a mismatching of labour with jobs (structural unemployment – specific types being technological and regional unemployment), or to seasonal fluctuations in the demand for labour.

4a Inflation redistributes incomes from the economically weak to the economically powerful; it causes uncertainty in the business community and as a result reduces investment; it tends to lead to balance of payments problems and/or a fall in the exchange rate; it leads to resources being used to offset its effects. The costs of inflation can be very great indeed in the case of hyperinflation.

4b Equilibrium in the economy occurs when aggregate demand equals aggregate supply.

Inflation can occur if there is a rightward shift in the aggregate demand curve or an upward (leftward) shift in the aggregate supply curve.

4c Demand-pull inflation occurs as a result of increases in aggregate demand. This can be due to monetary or non-monetary causes.

4d Cost-push inflation occurs when there are increases in the costs of production independent of rises in aggregate demand. Cost-push inflation can be of a number of different varieties: wage-push, profit-push or import-price-push.

4e Cost-push and demand-pull inflation can interact to form spiralling inflation.

4f Inflation can also be caused by shifts in the pattern of demand in the economy, with prices rising in sectors of increasing demand but being reluctant to fall in sectors of declining demand.

4g Expectations play a crucial role in determining the level of inflation. The higher people expect inflation to be, the higher it will be.

5 In the short run, the four macroeconomic objectives are related to aggregate demand and the business cycle. In the expansion phase, growth is high and unemployment is falling, but inflation is rising and the current account of the balance of payments is moving into deficit. In the recession, the reverse is the case.

6a The circular flow of income model depicts the flows of money round the economy. The inner flow shows the direct flows between firms and households. Money flows from firms to households in the form of factor payments, and back again as consumer expenditure on domestically produced goods and services.

6b Not all income gets passed on directly round the inner flow. Some is withdrawn in the form of saving, some is paid in taxes, and some goes abroad as expenditure on imports.

6c Likewise not all expenditure on domestic firms is by domestic consumers. Some is injected from outside the inner flow in the form of investment expenditure, government expenditure and expenditure on the country's exports.

6d Planned injections and withdrawals are unlikely to be the same. If injections exceed withdrawals, national income will rise, unemployment will tend to fall, inflation will tend to rise and the current account of the balance of payments will tend to deteriorate. The reverse will happen if withdrawals exceed injections.

REVIEW QUESTIONS

1 The following table shows index numbers for real GDP (national output) for various countries (1995 = 100).

	1995	1996	1997	1998	1999	2000	2001	2002	2003
USA	100.0	103.6	108.1	112.8	117.1	121.6	121.9	124.9	126.9
Japan	100.0	103.5	105.4	104.2	104.4	107.3	107.8	108.1	108.3
Germany	100.0	100.8	102.2	104.3	106.3	109.6	110.3	110.6	110.7
France	100.0	101.1	103.0	106.6	110.0	114.6	116.7	118.1	119.2
UK	100.0	102.6	106.1	109.3	111.9	115.4	117.7	119.6	121.0

Sources: Various

Using the formula $G = (Y_t - Y_{t-1})/Y_{t-1} \times 100$ (where G is the rate of growth, Y is the index number of output, t is any given year and $t - 1$ is the previous year):

(a) Work out the growth rate for each country for each year from 1996 to 2003.
(b) Plot the figures on a graph. Describe the pattern that emerges.

2 Will the rate of actual growth have any effect on the rate of potential growth?

3 Figure 26.1 shows a decline in actual output in recessions. Redraw the diagram, only this time show a mere slowing down of growth in phase 4.

4 At what point of the business cycle is the country now? What do you predict will happen to growth over the next two years? On what basis do you make your prediction?

5 For what possible reasons may one country experience a persistently faster rate of economic growth than another?

6 Would it be desirable to have zero unemployment?

7 What major structural changes have taken place in the UK economy in the past 10 years that have contributed to structural unemployment?

8 What would be the benefits and costs of increasing the rate of unemployment benefit?

9 Do any groups of people gain from inflation?

10 If everyone's incomes rose in line with inflation, would it matter if inflation were 100 per cent or even 1000 per cent per annum?

11 Imagine that you had to determine whether a particular period of inflation was demand pull, or cost push, or a combination of the two. What information would you require in order to conduct your analysis?

12 In terms of the UK circular flow of income, are the following net injections, net withdrawals or neither? If there is uncertainty, explain your assumptions.

(a) Firms are forced to take a cut in profits in order to give a pay rise.
(b) Firms spend money on research.
(c) The government increases personal tax allowances.
(d) The general public invests more money in building societies.
(e) UK investors earn higher dividends on overseas investments.
(f) The government purchases US military aircraft.
(g) People draw on their savings to finance holidays abroad.
(h) People draw on their savings to finance holidays in the UK.
(i) The government runs a budget deficit (spends more than it receives in tax revenues) and finances it by borrowing from the general public.

APPENDIX

Measuring national income and output

Three routes: one destination

To assess how fast the economy has grown, we must have a means of *measuring* the value of the nation's output. The measure we use is called *gross domestic product* (GDP).

GDP can be calculated in three different ways, which should all result in the same figure. These three methods are illustrated in the simplified circular flow of income shown in Figure 26.10.

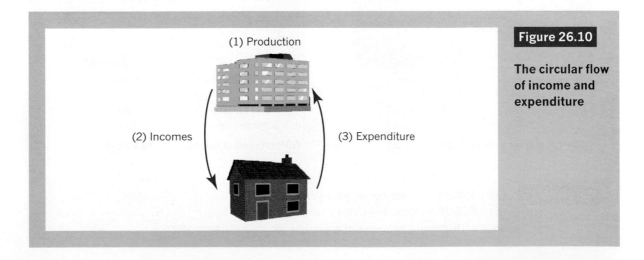

Figure 26.10

The circular flow of income and expenditure

The product method

This first method of measuring GDP is to add up the value of all the goods and services produced in the country, industry by industry. In other words, we focus on firms and add up all their production. This method is known as the *product method*.

In the national accounts these figures are grouped together into broad categories such as manufacturing, construction and distribution. The figures for the UK economy for 2001 are shown in Figure 26.11(a).

(a)	Percentage of GVA
Agriculture, forestry and fishing £8 241 m	0.9
Mining, energy and water supply £41 378 m	4.7
Manufacturing £153 132 m	17.5
Construction £47 327 m	5.4
Wholesale and retail trade; repairs £106 766 m	12.2
Hotels and restaurants £29 359 m	3.4
Transport and communication £70 252 m	8.0
Banking, finance, insurance, etc. £6 667 m	0.8
Letting of property £209 839 m	24.0
Public administration and defence £42 096 m	4.8
Education, health and social work £114 069 m	13.0
Other services £45 101 m	5.2
Gross value added (GVA) at basic prices £874 227 m	100.0
plus Taxes on products £120 499 m *less* Subsidies on products £6 712 m	
GDP (at market prices) £988 014 m	

(b)	Percentage of GVA
Compensation of employees (wages and salaries) £556 371 m	63.6
Operating surplus (gross profit, rent and interest of firms government and other institutions) £238 625 m	27.3
Mixed incomes £60 073 m	6.4
Tax less subsidies on production (other than those on products) plus statistical discrepancy £19 158 m	2.2
Gross value added (GVA) at basic prices £874 227 m	
plus Taxes on products £120 499 m *less* Subsidies on products £6 712 m	
GDP (at market prices) £988 014 m	

Figure 26.11 (a) UK GDP product-based measure: 2001
(b) UK GDP by category of income: 2001

Source: *UK National Income and Expenditure* (National Statistics 2002)

When we add up the output of various firms, we must be careful to avoid *double counting*. For example, if a manufacturer sells a television to a retailer for £200 and the retailer sells it to the consumer for £300, how much has this television contributed to GDP? The answer is *not* £500. We do not add the £200 received by the manufacturer to the £300 received by the retailer: that would be double counting. Instead we either just count the final value (£300) or the value added at each stage (£200 by the manufacturer + £100 by the retailer).

The sum of all the values added by all the various industries in the economy is known as **gross value added (GVA) at basic prices**.

How do we get from GVA to GDP? The answer has to do with taxes and subsidies on products. Taxes paid on goods and services (such as VAT and duties on petrol and alcohol) and any subsidies on products are *excluded* from gross value added (GVA), since they are not part of the value added in production. Nevertheless the way GDP is measured throughout the EU is at *market prices*: i.e. at the prices actually paid at each stage of production. Thus **GDP at market prices** (sometimes referred to simply as GDP) is GVA *plus* taxes on products *minus* subsidies on products.

The income method

The second approach is to focus on the incomes generated from the production of goods and services. A moment's reflection will show that this must be the same as the sum of all values added at each stage of production. Value added is simply the difference between a firm's revenue from sales and the costs of its purchases from other firms. This difference is made up of wages and salaries, rent, interest and profit. In other words, it consists of the incomes earned by those involved in the production process.

Since GVA is the sum of all values added, it must also be the sum of all incomes generated: the sum of all wages and salaries, rent, interest and profit.

Figure 26.11(b) shows how these incomes are grouped together in the official statistics. As you can see, the total is the same as that in Figure 26.11(a), even though the components are quite different.

Note that we do not include *transfer payments* such as social security benefits and pensions. Since these are not payments for the production of goods and services, they are excluded from GVA. Conversely, part of people's gross income is paid in income taxes. Since it is this *gross* (pre-tax) income that arises from the production of goods and services, we count wages, profits, interest and rent *before* the deduction of income taxes.

As with the product approach, if we are working out GVA, we measure incomes before the payment of taxes on products or the receipt of subsidies on products, since it is these pre-tax-and-subsidy incomes that arise from the value added by production. When working out GDP, however, we add in these taxes and subtract these subsidies to arrive at a *market price* valuation.

> **Pause for thought**
>
> If a retailer buys a product from a wholesaler for £80 and sells it to a consumer for £100, then the £20 of value that has been added will go partly in wages, partly in rent and partly in profits. Thus £20 of income has been generated at the retail stage. But the good actually contributes a total of £100 to GDP. Where, then, is the remaining £80 worth of income recorded?

The expenditure method

The final approach to calculating GDP is to add up all expenditure on final output (which will be at market prices). This will include the following:

Table 26.1	UK GDP at market prices by category of expenditure: 2001		
		£ million	**% of GDP**
Consumption expenditure of households and NPISH (*C*)		655 265	66.3
Government final consumption (*G*)		190 663	19.3
Gross capital formation (*I*)		164 048	16.6
Exports of goods and services (*X*)		268 451	27.2
Imports of goods and services (*M*)		–290 912	–29.5
Statistical discrepancy		499	0.1
GDP at market prices		988 014	100.0

Source: *UK National Income and Expenditure*, National Statistics © Crown Copyright 2002

- Consumer expenditure (*C*). This includes all expenditure on goods and services by households and by non-profit institutions serving households (NPISH) (e.g. clubs and societies).
- Government expenditure (*G*). This includes central and local government expenditure on final goods and services. Note that it includes non-marketed services (such as health and education), but excludes transfer payments, such as pensions and social security payments.
- Investment expenditure (*I*). This includes investment in capital, such as buildings and machinery. It also includes the value of any increase (+) or decrease (–) in inventories, whether of raw materials, semi-finished goods or finished goods.
- Exports of goods and services (*X*).
- Imports of goods and services (*M*). These have to be *subtracted* from the total in order to leave just the expenditure on *domestic* product. In other words, we subtract the part of consumer expenditure, government expenditure and investment that goes on imports. We also subtract the imported component (e.g. raw materials) from exports.

$$GDP \text{ (at market prices)} = C + G + I + X - M$$

Table 26.1 shows the calculation of UK GDP by the expenditure approach.

From GDP to National income

Gross national income

Some of the incomes earned in the country will go abroad. These include wages, interest, profit and rent earned in this country by foreign residents and remitted abroad, and taxes on production paid to foreign governments and institutions (e.g. the EU). On the other hand, some of the incomes earned by domestic residents will come from abroad. Again, these can be in the form of wages, interest, profit or rent, or in the form of subsidies received from governments or institutions abroad. Gross *domestic* product, however, is concerned with those incomes generated *within* the country, irrespective of ownership. If, then, we are to take 'net income from abroad' into account (i.e. these inflows minus outflows), we need a new measure. This is **gross national income (GNY)**.[2] It is defined as follows:

GNY at market prices = GDP at market prices + net income from abroad

definition

Gross national income (GNY)
GDP plus net income from abroad.

---

[2] In the official statistics, this is referred to as *GNI*. We use Y to stand for income, however, to avoid confusion with investment.

Table 26.2	UK GDP, GNY and NNY at market prices: 2001

	£ million
Gross domestic product (GDP)	**988 014**
Plus net income from abroad	5 756
Gross national income (GNY)	**993 770**
Less capital consumption (depreciation)	–111 275
Net national income (NNY)	**882 495**

Source: *UK National Income and Expenditure,* National Statistics © Crown Copyright 2002

Thus GDP focuses on the value of domestic production, whereas GNY focuses on the value of incomes earned by domestic residents.

Net national income
The measures we have used so far ignore the fact that each year some of the country's capital equipment will wear out or become obsolete: in other words, they ignore capital **depreciation**. If we subtract an allowance for depreciation (or 'capital consumption') we get **net national income (NNY)**:

NNY at market prices = GNY at market prices – Depreciation

Table 26.2 shows GDP, GNY and NNY figures for the UK.

Households' disposable income

Finally, we come to a term called **households' disposable** income. It measures the income people have available for spending (or saving): i.e. after any deductions for income tax, national insurance, etc. have been made. It is the best measure to use if want to see how changes in household income affect consumption.

How do we get from GNY at market prices to households' disposable income? We start with the incomes that firms receive[3] from production (plus income from abroad) and then deduct that part of their income that is *not* distributed to households. This means that we must deduct taxes that firms pay – taxes on goods and services (such as VAT), taxes on profits (such as corporation tax) and any other taxes – and add in any subsidies they receive. We must then subtract allowances for depreciation and any undistributed profits. This gives us the gross income that households receive from firms in the form of wages, salaries, rent, interest and distributed profits.

To get from this what is available for households to spend we must subtract the money households pay in income taxes and national insurance contributions, but add all benefits to households such as pensions and child benefit.

Households' disposable income = GNY at market prices – Taxes paid by firms + Subsidies received by firms – Depreciation – Undistributed profits – Personal taxes + Benefits

---

[3] We also include income from any public-sector production of goods or services (e.g. health and education) and production by non-profit institutions serving households.

SUMMARY TO APPENDIX

1 National income is usually expressed in terms of gross domestic product. This is simply the value of domestic production over the course of the year. It can be measured by the product, expenditure or income methods.

2 The product method measures the values added in all parts of the economy.

3 The income method measures all the incomes generated from domestic production: wages and salaries, rent and profit.

4 The expenditure method adds up all the categories of expenditure: consumer expenditure, government expenditure, investment and exports. We then have to deduct the element of each that goes on imports in order to arrive at expenditure on *domestic* products. Thus $GDP = C + G + I + X - M$.

5 GDP at *market prices* measures what consumers pay for output (including taxes and subsidies on what they buy). Gross value added (GVA) measures what factors of production actually receive. GVA, therefore, is GDP at market prices minus taxes on products plus subsidies on products.

6 Gross *national* income (GNY) takes account of incomes earned from abroad (+) and incomes earned by people abroad from this country (–). Thus GNY = GDP plus net income from abroad.

7 Net national income (NNY) takes account of the depreciation of capital. Thus NNY = GNY – depreciation.

8 Households' disposable income is a measure of household income after the deduction of income taxes and the addition of benefits.

REVIEW QUESTIONS TO APPENDIX

1 Should we include the sale of used items in the GDP statistics? For example, if you sell your car to a garage for £2000 and it then sells it to someone else for £2500, has this added £2500 to GDP, or nothing at all, or merely the value that the garage adds to the car, i.e. £500?

2 What items are excluded from national income statistics which would be important to take account of if we were to get a true indication of a country's standard of living?

27 The balance of payments and exchange rates

In Part I we examined the role of international trade for a country and for business, and saw how trade has grown rapidly since 1945. The world economy has become progressively more interlinked, with multinational corporations dominating a large proportion of international business. In this chapter we return to look at international trade and the financial flows associated with it. In particular, we shall examine the relationship between the domestic economy and the international trading environment. This will involve considering both the balance of payments and the exchange rate.

We will first explain what is meant by the balance of payments. In doing so, we will see just how the various monetary transactions between the domestic economy and the rest of the world are recorded.

Then we will examine how rates of exchange are determined, and how they are related to the balance of payments. Then we will see what causes exchange rate fluctuations, and what will happen if the government intervenes in the foreign exchange market to prevent these fluctuations. Finally, we will consider how exchange rates have been managed in practice.

27.1 The balance of payments account

A country's balance of payments account records all the flows of money between residents of that country and the rest of the world. *Receipts* of money from abroad are regarded as *credits* and are entered in the accounts with a positive sign. *Outflows* of money from the country are regarded as *debits* and are entered with a negative sign.

There are three main parts of the balance of payments account: the *current account*, the *capital account* and the *financial account*. Each part is then subdivided. We shall look at each part in turn, and take the UK as an example. Table 27.1 gives a summary of the UK balance of payments for the years 1989 and 2002.

The current account

The **current account** records payments for imports and exports of goods and services, plus incomes flowing into and out of the country, plus net transfers of money into and out of the country. It is normally divided into four subdivisions.

Table 27.1 UK balance of payments (£m)

	1989	2002
Current account		
1 Trade in goods	+92 611	+186 170
(a) Exports of goods		
(b) Imports of goods	−117 335	−221 352
Balance on trade in goods	−24 724	−35 182
2 Trade in services		
(a) Exports of services	+29 272	+83 467
(b) Imports of services	−25 355	−69 308
Balance on trade in services	+3 917	+14 159
Balance on trade in goods and services	−20 807	−21 023
3 Net income flows (wages and investment income)	−64	+20 646
4 Net current transfers (government and private)	−2 620	−9 247
Current account balance	**−23 491**	**−9 624**
Capital account		
5 Net capital transfers, etc:	+270	+1 096
Capital account balance	**+270**	**+1 096**
Financial account		
6 Investment (direct and portfolio)		
(a) Net investment in UK from abroad	+36 789	+80 039
(b) Net UK investment abroad	−60 336	+4 141
Balance of direct and portfolio investment	−23 547	+84 180
7 Other financial flows (mainly short-term)		
(a) Net deposits in UK from abroad and borrowing from abroad by UK residents	+72 629	+53 751
(b) Net deposits abroad by UK residents and UK lending to overseas residents	−35 498	−131 202
Balance of other financial flows	+37 131	−77 451
8 Reserves (drawing on + adding to −)	+5 440	+459
Financial account balance	**+19 024**	**+7 188**
Total of all three accounts	−4 197	−1 340
9 Net errors and omissions	+4 197	+1 340
	0	**0**

Sources: *Economic Trends Annual Supplement* (ONS); *Financial Statistics* (ONS)

The trade in goods account. This records imports and exports of physical goods (previously known as 'visibles'). Exports result in an inflow of money and are therefore a credit item. Imports result in an outflow of money and are therefore a debit item. The balance of these is called the **balance on trade in goods** or **balance of visible trade** or **merchandise balance**. A *surplus* is when exports exceed imports. A *deficit* is when imports exceed exports.

The trade in services account. This records imports and exports of services (such as transport, tourism and insurance). Thus the purchase of a foreign holiday would be a debit since it represents an outflow of money, whereas the purchase by an overseas resident of a UK insurance policy would be a credit to the UK services account. The balance of these is called the **services balance**.

The balance of both the goods and services accounts together is known as the **balance on trade in goods and services** or simply the **balance of trade**.

Income flows. These consist of wages, interest and profits flowing into and out of the country. For example, dividends earned by a foreign resident from shares in a UK company would be an outflow of money (a debit item).

Current transfers of money. These include government contributions to and receipts from the EU and international organisations, and international transfers of money by private individuals and firms. Transfers out of the country are debits. Transfers into the country (e.g. money sent from Greece to a Greek student studying in the UK) would be a credit item.

The **current account balance** is the overall balance of all the above four sub-divisions. A *current account surplus* is where credits exceed debits. A *current account deficit* is where debits exceed credits. Figure 27.1 shows the current account balances of the UK, the USA and Japan as a proportion of their GDP (national output).

> **definition**
>
> **Current account of the balance of payments**
> The record of a country's imports and exports of goods and services, plus incomes and transfers of money to and from abroad.

> **definition**
>
> **Balance on trade in goods** or **balance of visible trade** or **merchandise balance**
> Exports of goods minus imports of goods.

> **definition**
>
> **Services balance**
> Exports of services minus imports of services.

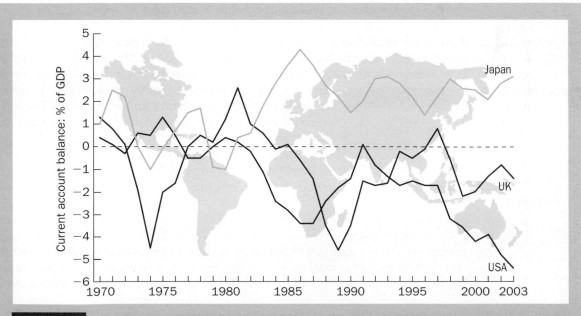

Figure 27.1 **Current account balance as a percentage of GDP in selected countries: 1970–2003**
Source: *Datastream*

The capital account

The **capital account** records the flows of funds, into the country (credits) and out of the country (debits), associated with the acquisition or disposal of fixed assets (e.g. land), the transfer of funds by migrants, and the payment of grants by the government for overseas projects and the receipt of EU money for capital projects (e.g. from the Agricultural Guidance Fund).

The financial account[1]

The *financial account* of the balance of payments records cross-border changes in the holding of shares, property, bank deposits and loans, government securities, etc. In other words, unlike the current account which is concerned with money incomes, the financial account is concerned with the purchase and sale of assets.

Investment (direct and portfolio). This account covers primarily long-term investment.

■ Direct investment. If a foreign company invests money from abroad in one of its branches or associated companies in the UK, this represents an inflow of money when the investment is made and is thus a credit item. (Any subsequent profit from this investment that flows abroad will be recorded as an *investment income outflow* on the current account.) Investment abroad by UK companies represents an outflow of money when the investment is made. It is thus a debit item. (Note that what we are talking about here is the acquisition or sale of assets: e.g. a factory or farm, or the takeover of a whole firm, not the imports or exports of equipment.)

■ Portfolio investment. This is changes in the holding of paper assets, such as company shares. Thus if a UK resident buys shares in an overseas company, this is an outflow of funds and is hence a debit item.

Other financial flows. These consist primarily of various types of short-term monetary movement between the UK and the rest of the world. Deposits by overseas residents in banks in the UK and loans to the UK from abroad are credit items, since they represent an inflow of money. Deposits by UK residents in overseas banks and loans by UK banks to overseas residents are debit items. They represent an outflow of money.

Short-term monetary flows are common between international financial centres to take advantage of differences in countries' interest rates and changes in exchange rates.

Flows to and from the reserves. The UK, like all other countries, holds reserves of gold and foreign currencies. From time to time the Bank of England (acting as the government's agent) will sell some of these reserves to purchase sterling on the foreign exchange market. It does this normally as a means of supporting the rate of exchange (as we shall see below). Drawing on reserves represents a *credit*

Pause for thought

Where would interest payments on short-term foreign deposits in UK banks be entered on the balance of payments account?

---

[1] Prior to October 1998, this account was called the 'capital account'. The account that is *now* called the capital account used to be included in the transfers section of the current account. This potentially confusing change of names was adopted in order to bring the UK accounts in line with the system used by the International Monetary Fund (IMF), the EU and most individual countries.

Key Idea 21 p376 item in the balance of payments accounts: money drawn from the reserves represents an *inflow* to the balance of payments (albeit an outflow from the reserves account). The reserves can thus be used to support a deficit elsewhere in the balance of payments.

Conversely, if there is a surplus elsewhere in the balance of payments, the Bank of England can use it to build up the reserves. Building up the reserves counts as a debit item in the balance of payments, since it represents an outflow from it (to the reserves).

When all the components of the balance of payments account are taken together, the balance of payments should exactly balance: credits should equal debits. As we shall see below, if they were not equal, the rate of exchange would have to adjust until they were, or the government would have to intervene to make them equal.

When the statistics are compiled, however, a number of errors are likely to occur. As a result there will not be a balance. To 'correct' for this, a **net errors and omissions item** is included in the accounts. This ensures that there will be an exact balance. The main reason for the errors is that the statistics are obtained from a number of sources, and there are often delays before items are recorded and sometimes omissions too.

> **definition**
>
> **Net errors and omissions**
> A statistical adjustment to ensure that the two sides of the balance of payments account balance. It is necessary because of errors in compiling the statistics.

The exchange rate   27.2

An exchange rate is the rate at which one currency trades for another on the foreign exchange market.

If you want to go abroad, you will need to exchange your pounds into euros, dollars, Swiss francs or whatever. To do this you will go to a bank. The bank will quote you that day's exchange rates: for example, €1.45 to the pound, or $1.60 to the pound. It is similar for firms. If an importer wants to buy, say, some machinery from Japan, it will require yen to pay the Japanese supplier. It will thus ask the foreign exchange section of a bank to quote it a rate of exchange of the pound into yen. Similarly, if you want to buy some foreign stocks and shares, or if companies based in the UK want to invest abroad, sterling will have to be exchanged into the appropriate foreign currency.

Likewise, if Americans want to come on holiday to the UK or to buy UK assets, or American firms want to import UK goods or to invest in the UK, they will require sterling. They will be quoted an exchange rate for the pound in the USA: say, £1 = $1.64. This means that they will have to pay $1.64 to obtain £1 worth of UK goods or assets.

Exchange rates are quoted between each of the major currencies of the world. These exchange rates are constantly changing. Minute by minute, dealers in the foreign exchange dealing rooms of the banks are adjusting the rates of exchange. They charge commission when they exchange currencies. It is therefore important for them to ensure that they are not left with a large amount of any currency unsold. What they need to do is to balance the supply and demand of each currency: to balance the amount they purchase to the amount they sell. To do this they will need to adjust the price of each currency, namely the exchange rate, in line with changes in supply and demand.

One of the problems in assessing what is happening to a particular currency is that its rate of exchange may rise against some currencies (weak currencies) and fall against others (strong currencies). In order to gain an overall picture of

> **definition**
>
> **Exchange rate index**
> A weighted average exchange rate expressed as an index, where the value of the index is 100 in a given base year. The weights of the different currencies in the index add up to 1.

Table 27.2 Sterling exchange rates: 1980–2003

	US dollar	Japanese yen	French franc	German mark	Italian lira	Euro	Sterling exchange rate index (1990 = 100)
1980	2.33	526	9.83	4.23	1992		124.4
1981	2.03	445	10.94	4.56	2287		127.9
1982	1.75	435	11.48	4.24	2364		123.2
1983	1.52	360	11.55	3.87	2302		115.6
1984	1.34	317	11.63	3.79	2339		111.4
1985	1.30	307	11.55	3.78	2453		111.3
1986	1.47	247	10.16	3.18	2186		101.4
1987	1.64	236	9.84	2.94	2123		99.4
1988	1.78	228	10.60	3.12	2315		105.4
1989	1.64	226	10.45	3.08	2247	(1.45)	102.3
1990	1.79	258	9.69	2.88	2133	(1.40)	100.0
1991	1.77	238	9.95	2.92	2187	(1.43)	100.7
1992	1.77	224	9.32	2.75	2163	(1.36)	96.9
1993	1.50	167	8.51	2.48	2360	(1.28)	89.0
1994	1.53	156	8.49	2.48	2467	(1.29)	89.2
1995	1.58	148	7.87	2.26	2571	(1.22)	84.8
1996	1.56	170	7.99	2.35	2408	(1.25)	86.3
1997	1.64	198	9.56	2.84	2789	(1.45)	100.5
1998	1.66	217	9.77	2.91	2876	(1.48)	103.9
1999	1.62	184	(9.96)	(2.97)	(2941)	1.52	103.8
2000	1.52	163	(10.77)	(3.21)	(3180)	1.64	107.5
2001	1.44	175	(10.55)	(3.15)	(3115)	1.61	105.5
2002	1.50	188	–	–	–	1.59	106.0
2003Q2	1.62	192	–	–	–	1.43	99.1

Note: Prior to 1999, a 'synthetic' euro has been used, based on the exchange rates with the countries which have adopted the euro. From 1999–2001, exchange rates into the French franc, German mark and Italian lira are based on the fixed exchange rates of these 'residual' currencies with the euro.
Source: *Datastream*

Pause for thought

How did the pound 'fare' compared with the dollar, the (former) lira and the yen from 1980 to 2001? What conclusions can be drawn about the relative movements of these three currencies?

its fluctuations, it is best to look at a weighted average exchange rate against all other currencies. This is known as the **exchange rate index**. The weight given to each currency in the index depends on the proportion of transactions done with that country. Table 27.2 shows exchange rates between the pound and various currencies and the sterling exchange rate index from 1980 to 2003.

The determination of the rate of exchange in a free market

In a free foreign exchange market, the rate of exchange is determined by demand and supply. Thus the sterling exchange rate is determined by the demand and supply of pounds. This is illustrated in Figure 27.2.

For simplicity, assume that there are just two countries: the UK and the USA. When UK importers wish to buy goods from the USA, or when UK residents wish to invest in the USA, they will *supply* pounds on the foreign exchange

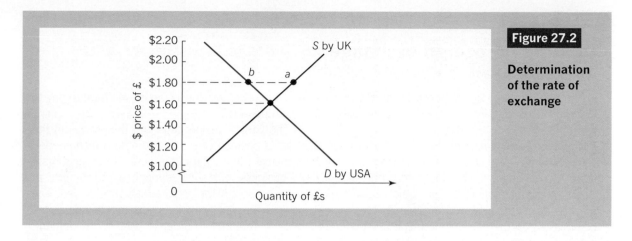

Figure 27.2

Determination of the rate of exchange

market in order to obtain dollars. In other words, they will go to banks or other foreign exchange dealers to buy dollars in exchange for pounds. The higher the exchange rate, the more dollars they will obtain for their pounds. This will effectively make American goods cheaper to buy, and investment more profitable. Thus the *higher* the exchange rate, the *more* pounds will be supplied. The supply curve of pounds therefore typically slopes upwards.

When US residents wish to purchase UK goods or to invest in the UK, they will require pounds. They *demand* pounds by selling dollars on the foreign exchange market. In other words, they will go to banks or other foreign exchange dealers to buy pounds in exchange for dollars. The lower the dollar price of the pound (the exchange rate), the cheaper it will be for them to obtain UK goods and assets, and hence the more pounds they are likely to demand. The demand curve for pounds, therefore, typically slopes downwards.

The equilibrium exchange rate will be where the demand for pounds equals the supply. In Figure 27.2 this will be at an exchange rate of £1 = $1.60. But what is the mechanism that equates demand and supply?

If the current exchange rate were above the equilibrium, the supply of pounds being offered to the banks would exceed the demand. For example, in Figure 27.2 if the exchange rate were $1.80, there would be an excess supply of pounds of *a* − *b*. Banks would not have enough dollars to exchange for all these pounds. But the banks make money by *exchanging* currency, not by holding on to it. They would thus lower the exchange rate in order to encourage a greater demand for pounds and reduce the excessive supply. They would continue lowering the rate until demand equalled supply.

Similarly, if the rate were below the equilibrium, say at $1.40, there would be a shortage of pounds. The banks would find themselves with too few pounds to meet all the demand. At the same time, they would have an excess supply of dollars. The banks would thus raise the exchange rate until demand equalled supply.

In practice, the process of reaching equilibrium is extremely rapid. The foreign exchange dealers in the banks are continually adjusting the rate as new customers make new demands for currencies. What is more, the banks have to watch closely what each other is doing. They are constantly in competition with each other and thus have to keep their rates in line. The dealers receive minute-by-minute updates on their computer screens of the rates being offered round the world.

Key Idea 10 p73

BOX 27.1

Dealing in foreign exchange
A daily juggling act

Imagine that a large car importer in the UK wants to import 5000 cars from Japan costing ¥15 billion. What does it do?

It will probably contact a number of banks' foreign exchange dealing rooms in London and ask them for exchange rate quotes. It thus puts all the banks in competition with each other. Each bank will want to get the business and thereby obtain the commission on the deal. To do this it must offer a higher rate than the other banks, since the higher the ¥/£ exchange rate, the more yen the firm will get for its money. (For an importer a rate of, say, ¥200 to £1 is better than a rate of, say, ¥180.)

Now it is highly unlikely that any of the banks will have a spare ¥15 billion. But a bank cannot say to the importer 'Sorry, you will have to wait before we can agree to sell them to you.' Instead the bank will offer a deal and then, if the firm agrees, the bank will have to set about obtaining the ¥15 billion. To do this it must offer Japanese who are *supplying* yen to obtain pounds at a sufficiently *low* ¥/£ exchange rate. (The lower the ¥/£ exchange

rate, the fewer yen the Japanese will have to pay to obtain pounds.)

The banks' dealers thus find themselves in the delicate position of wanting to offer a *high* enough exchange rate to the car importer in order to gain its business, but a *low* enough exchange rate in order to obtain the required amount of yen. The dealers are thus constantly having to adjust the rates of exchange in order to balance the demand and supply of each currency.

In general, the more of any foreign currency that dealers are asked to supply (by being offered sterling), the lower will be the exchange rate they will offer. In other words, a higher supply of sterling pushes down the foreign currency price of sterling.

Question

Assume that an American firm wants to import Scotch whisky from the UK. Describe how foreign exchange dealers will respond.

Figure 27.3

Floating exchange rates: movement to a new equilibrium

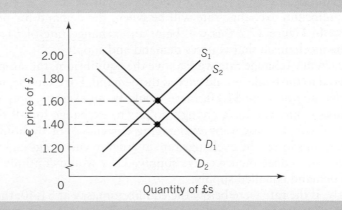

Shifts in the currency demand and supply curves

Key Idea 9 p63

Any shift in the demand or supply curves will cause the exchange rate to change. This is illustrated in Figure 27.3, which this time shows the euro/sterling exchange rate. If the demand and supply curves shift from D_1 and S_1 to D_2 and S_2 respectively, the exchange rate will fall from €1.60 to €1.40. A fall in the exchange rate is called a **depreciation**. A rise in the exchange rate is called an **appreciation**.

But why should the demand and supply curves shift? The following are the major possible causes of a depreciation:

definition

Depreciation
A fall in the free-market exchange rate of the domestic currency with foreign currencies.

BOX 27.2

Euro on the up
Is it all bad news for business in the eurozone?

As we shall see in Box 27.3, the euro depreciated substantially against the dollar and other currencies after its launch in January 1999, but then appreciated substantially – by 37 per cent against the dollar from June 2001 to June 2003.

These movements have been less to do with what is going on in Europe as to what is happening in America. With the 1990s seeing high growth rates, massive improvements in productivity and high corporate profitability, investment predictably flooded into the United States, sending the dollar soaring and the euro tumbling to a low of 83 cents in the Autumn of 2000 – a fall of 35 per cent from its launch value of $1.18 in January 1999.

Then over the course of 2001, with US growth stagnating, US interest rates were cut substantially (see figure in Box 27.3). In addition, massive debts on the US current account, and a budget deficit nearing 4 per cent of GDP, made foreign investors reluctant to invest in the American economy. In fact, investors were pulling out of the USA. One estimate suggests that European investors alone sold $70 billion of US assets during 2002. The result of all this was a massive depreciation of the dollar.

So is a strong euro bad for European business? With over 20 per cent of the eurozone's GDP determined by export sales, and a large part of those exports going to America, the dollar/euro exchange rate will invariably be significant. The question is how significant? The concern was that, with slow growth in the eurozone, the rise in the euro and the resulting fall in exports would slow growth rates even further. With the German economy on the brink of recession, the euro's rise might be simply too much for the German economy to bear. The investment bank Morgan Stanley, estimated that for every 10 per cent rise in the value of the euro against the dollar, European corporate profits fall by 3 per cent.

And it was not just the fact that the euro was strong. What also worried European business was the *speed* at which the euro strengthened against the dollar. The question was whether they could adjust quickly enough to accommodate the rise.

However, the impact of the euro's rise on eurozone business was tempered by a number of other factors:

- Companies are increasingly using sophisticated management and operational systems, in which value creation is spread throughout a global value chain. Often procurement systems are priced in dollars.

- Firms hedge their currency risks. BMW, for example, uses forward markets to hedge its entire overseas profits.

- Many European companies (again BMW is an example) have located some of their production facilities in the USA and use them to help meet demand in the American market. This helps to insulate them from the effects of the rise in the value of the euro.

Businesses in the eurozone seem initially to have accommodated the euro's rapid rise. However, if the value of the euro continues to strengthen on world markets, the achievement of even slow eurozone growth might prove increasingly difficult to maintain.

Questions

1 *What long-term advantage might there be in having a high exchange rate?*

2 *Given the scenario of the rising euro, would eurozone businesses be encouraged to relocate outside of the eurozone area?*

3 *Find out what has happened to the euro/dollar exchange rate in recent months. Have the problems facing the USA and EU changed?*

- *A fall in domestic interest rates.* UK rates would now be less competitive for savers and other depositors. More UK residents would be likely to deposit their money abroad (the supply of sterling would rise), and fewer people abroad would deposit their money in the UK (the demand for sterling would fall).

■ *Higher inflation in the domestic economy than abroad.* UK exports will become less competitive. The demand for sterling will fall. At the same time, imports will become relatively cheaper for UK consumers. The supply of sterling will rise.

■ *A rise in domestic incomes relative to incomes abroad.* If UK incomes rise, the demand for imports, and hence the supply of sterling, will rise. If incomes in other countries fall, the demand for UK exports, and hence the demand for sterling will fall.

■ *Relative investment prospects improving abroad.* If investment prospects become brighter abroad than in the UK, perhaps because of better incentives abroad, or because of worries about an impending recession in the UK, again the demand for sterling will fall and the supply of sterling will rise.

Pause for thought
Go through each of the above reasons for shifts in the demand for and supply of sterling and consider what would cause an appreciation of the pound.

■ *Speculation that the exchange rate will fall.* If businesses involved in importing and exporting, and also banks and other foreign exchange dealers, think that the exchange rate is about to fall, they will sell pounds *now* before the rate does fall. The supply of sterling will thus rise.

Key
Idea
12
p94

27.3 Exchange rates and the balance of payments

Exchange rates and the balance of payments: no government or central bank intervention

In a free foreign exchange market, the balance of payments will *automatically* balance. But why?

The credit side of the balance of payments constitutes the demand for sterling. For example, when people abroad buy UK exports or assets they will demand sterling in order to pay for them. The debit side constitutes the supply of sterling. For example, when UK residents buy foreign goods or assets, the importers of them will require foreign currency to pay for them. They will thus supply pounds. A **floating exchange rate** will ensure that the demand for pounds is equal to the supply. It will thus also ensure that the credits on the balance of payments are equal to the debits: that the balance of payments balances.

Key
Idea
10
p73

This does not mean that each part of the balance of payments account will separately balance, but simply that any current account deficit must be matched by a capital plus financial account surplus and vice versa.

For example, suppose initially that each part of the balance of payments did separately balance. Then let us assume that interest rates rise. This will encourage larger short-term financial inflows as people abroad are attracted to deposit money in the UK: the demand for sterling would shift to the right (e.g. from D_2 to D_1 in Figure 27.3). It will also cause smaller short-term financial outflows as UK residents keep more of their money in the country: the supply of sterling shifts to the left (e.g. from S_2 to S_1 in Figure 27.3). The financial account will go into surplus. The exchange rate will appreciate.

As the exchange rate rises, this will cause imports to be cheaper and exports to be more expensive. The current account will move into deficit. There is a movement up along the new demand and supply curves until a new equilibrium is reached. At this point, any financial account surplus is matched by an equal current (plus capital) account deficit.

Exchange rates and the balance of payments: with government or central bank intervention

The government may be unwilling to let the country's currency float freely. Frequent shifts in the demand and supply curves would cause frequent changes in the exchange rate. This, in turn, might cause uncertainty for businesses, which might curtail their trade and investment.

The government may thus intervene in the foreign exchange market. But what can it do? The answer to this will depend on its objectives. It may simply want to reduce the day-to-day fluctuations in the exchange rate, or it may want to prevent longer-term, more fundamental shifts in the rate.

Reducing short-term fluctuations

Assume that the government believes that an exchange rate of €1.60 to the pound is approximately the long-term equilibrium rate. Short-term leftward shifts in the demand for sterling and rightward shifts in the supply, however, are causing the exchange rate to fall below this level (see Figure 27.3). What can the government do to keep the rate at €1.60?

Using reserves. The Bank of England can sell gold and foreign currencies from the reserves to buy pounds. This will shift the demand for sterling back to the right.

Borrowing from abroad. The government can negotiate a foreign currency loan from other countries or from an international agency such as the International Monetary Fund. It can then use these moneys to buy pounds on the foreign exchange market, thus again shifting the demand for sterling back to the right.

Raising interest rates. If the government raises interest rates, it will encourage people to deposit money in the UK and encourage UK residents to keep their money in the country. The demand for sterling will increase and the supply of sterling will decrease.

Maintaining a fixed rate of exchange over the longer term

Governments may choose to maintain a fixed rate over a number of months or even years. The following are possible methods it can use to achieve this (we are assuming that there are downward pressures on the exchange rate: e.g. as a result of higher aggregate demand and higher inflation.)

Deflation. This is where the government deliberately curtails aggregate demand by either *fiscal policy* or *monetary policy* or both.

Deflationary fiscal policy will involve raising taxes and/or reducing government expenditure. Deflationary monetary policy will involve reducing the supply of money and raising interest rates. Note that in this case we are not just talking about the temporary raising of interest rates to prevent a short-term outflow of money from the country, but the use of higher interest rates to reduce borrowing and hence dampen aggregate demand.

A reduction in aggregate demand will work in two ways:

- It will reduce the level of consumer spending. This will directly cut imports since there will be reduced spending on Japanese videos, German cars, Spanish holidays and so on. The supply of sterling coming on to the foreign exchange market thus decreases.

■ It will reduce the rate of inflation. This will make UK goods more competitive abroad, thus increasing the demand for sterling. It will also cut back on imports as UK consumers switch to the now more competitive home-produced goods. The supply of sterling falls.

Supply-side policies. This is where the government attempts to increase the long-term competitiveness of UK goods by encouraging reductions in the costs of production and/or improvements in the quality of UK goods. For example, the government may attempt to improve the quantity and quality of training and research and development.

> **Pause for thought**
>
> What problems might arise if the government were to adopt this third method of maintaining a fixed exchange rate?

Controls on imports and or foreign exchange dealing. This is where the government restricts the outflow of money, either by restricting people's access to foreign exchange, or by the use of tariffs (customs duties) and quotas.

27.4 Fixed versus floating exchange rates

Are exchange rates best left free to fluctuate and be determined purely by market forces, or should the government or central bank intervene to fix exchange rates, either rigidly or within bands?

Advantages of fixed exchange rates

Surveys reveal that most business people prefer relatively rigid exchange rates: if not totally fixed, then at least pegged for periods of time. The following arguments are used to justify this preference.

Certainty. With fixed exchange rates, international trade and investment become much less risky, since profits are not affected by movements in the exchange rate.

Assume a firm correctly forecasts that its product will sell in the USA for $1.50. It costs 80p to produce. If the rate of exchange is fixed at £1 = $1.50, each unit will earn £1 and hence make a 20p profit. If, however, the rate of exchange were not fixed, exchange fluctuations could wipe out this profit. If, say, the rate appreciated to £1 = $2, and if units continued to sell for $1.50, they would now earn only 75p each, and hence make a 5p loss.

Little or no speculation. Provided the rate is *absolutely* fixed – and people believe that it will remain so – there is no point in speculating. For example, between 1999 and 2001, when the old currencies of the eurozone countries were still used, but were totally fixed to the euro, there was no speculation that the German mark, say, would change in value against the French franc or the Dutch guilder.

Prevents governments pursuing 'irresponsible' macroeconomic policies. If a government deliberately and excessively expands aggregate demand – perhaps in an attempt to gain short-term popularity with the electorate – the resulting balance of payments deficit will force it to constrain demand again (unless it resorts to import controls).

Governments cannot allow their economies to have a persistently higher inflation rate than competitor countries without running into balance of payments crises, and hence a depletion of reserves. Fixed rates thus force governments (in the absence of trade restrictions) to keep the rate of inflation roughly to world levels.

Disadvantages of fixed exchange rates

Exchange rate policy may conflict with the interests of domestic business and the economy as a whole. A balance of payments deficit can occur even if there is no excess demand. For example, there can be a fall in the demand for the country's exports as a result of an external shock or because of increased foreign competition. If protectionism is to be avoided, and if supply-side policies work only over the long run, the government (or central bank) will be forced to raise interest rates. This is likely to have two adverse effects on the domestic economy:

- Higher interest rates may discourage business investment. This in turn will lower firms' profits in the long term and reduce the country's long-term rate of economic growth. The country's capacity to produce will be restricted and businesses are likely to fall behind in the competitive race with their international rivals to develop new products and improve existing ones.

- Higher interest rates will have a deflationary effect on the economy by making borrowing more expensive and thereby cutting back on both consumer demand and investment. This can result in a recession with rising unemployment. It will, however, improve the balance of payments. There will be an improvement not only on the financial account, as money flows into the country to take advantage of the higher rates of interest, but also on the current account. The recession will lead to reduced demand for imports, and lower inflation is likely to make exports more competitive and imports relatively more expensive.

The problem is that, with fixed exchange rates, domestic policy is entirely constrained by the balance of payments. Any attempt to cure unemployment by cutting interest rates will simply lead to a balance of payments deficit and thus force governments to raise interest rates again.

Competitive deflations leading to world depression. If deficit countries deflated, but surplus countries *reflated*, there would be no overall world deflation or reflation. Countries may be quite happy, however, to run a balance of payments surplus and build up reserves. Countries may thus competitively deflate – all trying to achieve a balance of payments surplus. But this is beggar-my-neighbour policy. Not all countries can have a surplus. Overall the world must be in balance. The result of these policies is to lead to general world deflation and a restriction in growth.

Problems of international liquidity. If trade is to expand, there must be an expansion in the supply of currencies acceptable for world trade (dollars, euros, pounds, gold, etc.): there must be adequate **international liquidity**. Countries' reserves of these currencies must grow if they are to be sufficient to maintain a fixed rate at times of balance of payments disequilibrium. Conversely, there must not be excessive international liquidity. Otherwise the extra demand that would result would lead to world inflation. It is important under fixed exchange rates, therefore, to avoid too much or too little international liquidity. The problem is whether there is adequate control of international liquidity. The supply of dollars, for example, depends largely on US policy, which may be dominated by

definition

International liquidity
The supply of currencies in the world acceptable for financing international trade and investment.

its internal economic situation rather than by a concern for the well-being of the international community.

Inability to adjust to shocks. With sticky prices and wage rates, there is no swift mechanism for dealing with sudden balance of payments crises – like that caused by a sudden increase in oil prices. In the short run, countries will need huge reserves or loan facilities to support their currencies. There may be insufficient international liquidity to permit this. In the longer run, countries may be forced into a depression, by having to deflate. The alternative may be to resort to protectionism, or to abandon the fixed rate and **devalue**.

Speculation. If speculators believe that a fixed rate simply cannot be maintained, speculation is likely to be massive. If, for example, there is a large balance of payments deficit, speculative selling will worsen the deficit, and may itself force a devaluation.

Advantages of a free-floating exchange rate

The advantages and disadvantages of free-floating rates are to a large extent the opposite of fixed rates.

Automatic correction. The government simply lets the exchange rate move freely to the equilibrium. In this way, balance of payments disequilibria are automatically and instantaneously corrected without the need for specific government policies.

No problem of international liquidity and reserves. Since there is no central bank intervention in the foreign exchange market, there is no need to hold reserves. A currency is automatically convertible at the current market exchange rate.

Insulation from external economic events. A country is not tied to a possibly unacceptably high world inflation rate, as it could be under a fixed exchange rate. It is also to some extent protected against world economic fluctuations and shocks.

Governments are free to choose their domestic policy. Under a floating rate the government can choose whatever level of domestic demand it considers appropriate, and simply leave exchange rate movements to take care of any balance of payments effect. Similarly, the central bank can choose whatever rate of interest is necessary to meet domestic objectives, such as achieving a target rate of inflation. The exchange rate will simply adjust to the new rate of interest – a rise in interest rates causing an appreciation, a fall causing a depreciation. This freedom for the government and central bank is a major advantage, especially when the effectiveness of deflation under fixed exchange rates is reduced by downward wage and price rigidity, and when competitive deflation between countries may end up causing a world recession.

Disadvantages of a free-floating exchange rate

Despite these advantages there are still a number of serious problems with free-floating exchange rates.

Unstable exchange rates. The less elastic are the demand and supply curves for the currency in Figure 27.3, the greater the change in exchange rate that will be necessary to restore equilibrium following a shift in either demand or supply. In the long run, in a competitive world with domestic substitutes for imports and foreign substitutes for exports, demand and supply curves are relatively elastic. Nevertheless, in the short run, given that many firms have contracts with specific overseas suppliers or distributors, the demands for imports and exports are less elastic.

Speculation. In an uncertain world, where there are few restrictions on currency speculation, where the fortunes and policies of governments can change rapidly, and where large amounts of short-term deposits are internationally 'footloose', speculation can be highly destabilising in the short run. If people think that the exchange rate will fall, then they will sell the currency, and this will cause the exchange rate to fall even further, perhaps overshooting the eventual equilibrium.

> **Pause for thought**
>
> *If speculators on average gain from their speculation, who loses?*

Uncertainty for traders and investors. The uncertainty caused by currency fluctuations can discourage international trade and investment. To some extent this problem can be overcome by using the **forward exchange market**. Here traders agree with a bank *today* the rate of exchange for some point in the *future* (say, six months' time). This allows traders to plan future purchases of imports or sales of exports at a known rate of exchange. Of course, banks charge for this service, since they are taking on the risks themselves of adverse exchange rate fluctuations.

definition

Forward exchange market Where contracts are made today for the price at which a currency will be exchanged at some specified future date.

But dealing in the futures market only takes care of short-run uncertainty. Banks will not be prepared to take on the risks of offering forward contracts for several years hence. Thus firms simply have to live with the uncertainty over exchange rates in future years. This will discourage long-term investment. For example, the possibility of exchange rate appreciation may well discourage firms from investing abroad, since a higher exchange rate will mean that foreign exchange earnings will be worth less in the domestic currency.

Figure 27.4 shows the fluctuations in the dollar/pound exchange rate and the exchange rate index from 1976 to 2003. As you can see, there have been large changes in exchange rates. Such changes not only make it difficult for exporters. Importers too will be hesitant about making long-term deals. For example, a UK manufacturing firm signing a contract to buy US components in 1980, when $2.40 worth of components could be purchased for £1, would find it a struggle to make a profit some four years later when only just over $1.00 worth of US components could be purchased for £1!

Lack of discipline on the domestic economy. Governments may pursue irresponsibly inflationary policies (e.g. for short-term political gain). This will have adverse effects over the longer term as the government will at some point have to deflate the economy again, with a resulting fall in output and rise in unemployment.

definition

Adjustable peg A system whereby exchange rates are fixed for a period of time, but may be devalued (or revalued) if a deficit (or surplus) becomes substantial.

Exchange rates in practice

Most countries today have a relatively free exchange rate. Nevertheless, the problems of instability that this can bring are well recognised, and thus many countries seek to regulate or manage their exchange rate.

BOX 27.3

Currency turmoil
Unleashing the power of speculation

For periods of time, world currency markets can be quite peaceful, with only modest changes in exchange rates. But with the ability to move vast sums of money very rapidly from one part of the world to another and from one currency to another, speculators can suddenly turn this relatively peaceful world into one of extreme turmoil. In this box we examine three periods over just eight years when such turmoil occurred.

1995

The problem started towards the end of 1994 with an economic crisis in Mexico. To help its neighbour, the USA quickly arranged a $20 billion aid package. But speculators saw trouble for the dollar. A decline in US sales to Mexico was likely to damage the USA's export recovery. On top of this, market analysts were predicting that US interest rates, which had previously been rising, would now fall as US economic growth slowed. In contrast, interest rates in Germany looked set to rise, as the German authorities faced growing inflationary pressures. Faced by all this, many investors moved out of dollars and into the more stable German mark.

By March the dollar had reached post-war lows against the German mark and the Japanese yen. The fall in value against the yen represented a 32 per cent depreciation since 1992.

In Europe, the knock-on effect of the strong mark was felt in some measure by all the currencies, especially those within the ERM (see section 32.3). The Spanish peseta, under pressure prior to the mark's rise, was devalued by 7 per cent, and the Portuguese escudo by 3.5 per cent. Both the French and Swedish governments, with their currencies reaching record lows against the mark, were forced to put up interest rates to prevent further depreciation.

The high yen and mark proved to be equally problematic for Japan and Germany, which found their competitive positions significantly eroded: exports were falling and domestic firms found it very difficult to compete with cheap imports.

The US Federal Reserve seemed unconcerned about the falling dollar and took no steps to support it. This expression of total indifference led speculators to believe that the dollar's fall was not yet over, encouraging yet further selling of dollar balances.

1997

In the summer of 1997, the Thai baht collapsed. It had been pegged to the US dollar and, with strong economic growth, this had encouraged large-scale inward investment. But with a slowing economy in 1997 and a widening trade deficit investors began to question whether the pegged rate could be maintained. There was massive speculative selling of the currency, and hence the collapse.

The massive depreciation of the baht acted as a catalyst, plunging the whole of south-east Asia into financial turmoil. The shock waves, as one currency after another came under speculative attack, spread outwards from the region. Brazil, Argentina, Mexico, Russia and the Ukraine all saw their currencies come under speculative pressure. All were forced to raise interest rates in an attempt to prevent further depreciation of their exchange rates.

As short-term financial flows increase and currency markets become freer, as the growth in information technology and the process of globalisation make the world's financial markets more integrated, and as fear and rumour seem increasingly able to spread like a bush fire around the world's financial capitals, so the greater is the potential for financial volatility and economic crisis.

1999–2003

On 1 January 1999, the euro was launched and exchanged for $1.16. By October 2000 the euro had fallen to $0.85. What was the cause of this 27 per cent depreciation? The main cause was the growing fear that inflationary pressures were increasing in the USA and that, therefore, the Federal Reserve bank would have to raise interest rates. At the same time, the eurozone economy was growing only slowly and inflation was well below the 2 per cent ceiling set by the ECB. There was thus pressure on the ECB to cut interest rates.

The speculators were not wrong. As the diagram shows, US interest rates rose, and ECB interest rates

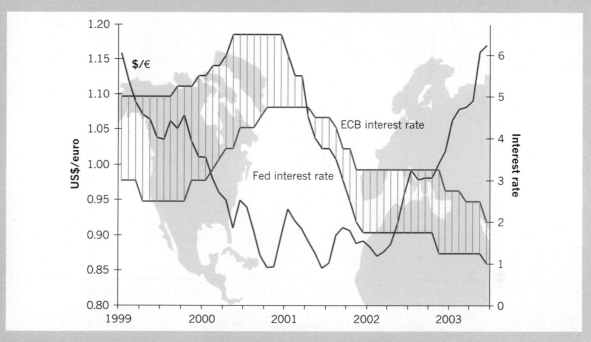

Fluctuations between the euro and the dollar

initially fell, and when eventually they did rise (in October 1999), the gap between US and ECB interest rates soon widened again.

In addition to the differences in interest rates, a lack of confidence in the recovery of the eurozone economy and a continuing confidence in the US economy encouraged investment to flow to the US. This inflow of finance (and lack of inflow to the eurozone) further pushed up the dollar relative to the euro.

The low value of the euro meant a high value of the pound relative to the euro. This made it very difficult for UK companies exporting to eurozone countries and also for those competing with imports from the eurozone (which had been made cheaper by the fall in the euro).

In October 2000, with the euro trading at around 85¢, the ECB plus the US Federal Reserve Bank (America's central bank), the Bank of England and the Japanese central bank all intervened on the foreign exchange market to buy euros. This arrested the fall, and helped to restore confidence in the currency. People were more willing to hold euros, knowing that central banks would support it.

The position completely changed in 2001. With the US economy slowing rapidly and fears of an impending recession, the Federal Reserve Bank reduced interest rates 11 times during the year: from 6.5 per cent at the beginning of the year to 1.75 per cent at the end. Although the ECB also cut interest rates, the cuts were relatively modest: from 4.75 at the beginning of the year to 3.25 at the end. With eurozone interest rates now considerably above US rates, the euro began to rise. This rise was substantial throughout 2002 and into 2003, so that by June 2003 the exchange rate had risen to $1.17: a 37 per cent appreciation since June 2001.

These massive currency fluctuations are a major disincentive to US and eurozone companies thinking of trading with each other or investing in each other's country/region.

Question

If in 1995 the Japanese yen was already above its long-term equilibrium exchange rate, and was therefore likely to depreciate some time in the future, why did speculators still continue to buy yen? Similarly, why did people sell euros in 1999/2000?

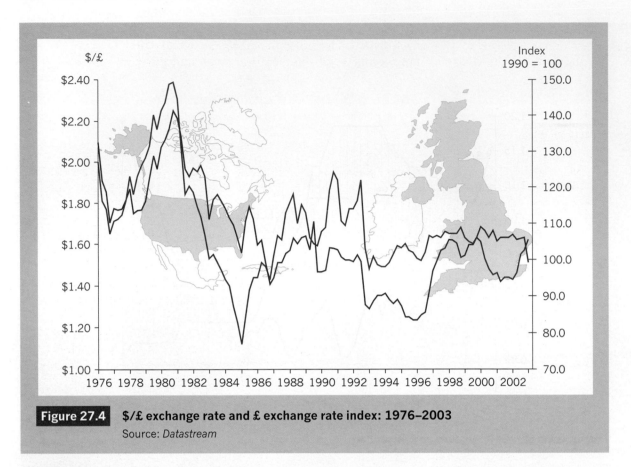

| Figure 27.4 | **$/£ exchange rate and £ exchange rate index: 1976–2003** |

Source: *Datastream*

There have been many attempts to regulate exchange rates since 1945. By far the most successful was the Bretton Woods system, which was adopted worldwide from the end of World War II until 1971. This was a form of **adjustable peg** exchange rate, where countries pegged (i.e. fixed) their exchange rate to the US dollar, but could re-peg it at a lower or higher level ('devalue' or 'revalue' their exchange rate) if there was a persistent and substantial balance of payments deficit or surplus.

With growing world inflation and instability from the mid-1960s, it became more and more difficult to maintain fixed exchange rates, and the growing likelihood of devaluations and revaluations fuelled speculation. The system was abandoned in the early 1970s. What followed was a period of exchange rate management known as **managed flexibility**. Under this system, exchange rates were not pegged but allowed to float. However, central banks intervened from time to time to prevent excessive exchange rate fluctuations. This system largely continues to this day.

However, on a regional basis, especially within Europe, there were attempts to create greater exchange rate stability. The European system, which began in 1979, involved establishing exchange rate bands: upper and lower limits within which exchange rates were allowed to fluctuate. The name given to the EU system was the **exchange rate mechanism (ERM)**. The hope was that this would eventually lead to a single European currency. With a single currency there can be no exchange rate fluctuations between the member states, any more than there can be fluctuations between the Californian and New York dollar, or between the English, Scottish and Welsh pound.

The single currency, the euro, finally came into being in January 1999 (although notes and coins were not introduced until January 2002). We examine the euro and its effects on the economies of the member states, and those outside too, in section 32.3.

SUMMARY

1a The balance of payments account records all payments to and receipts from foreign countries. The current account records payments for imports and exports, plus incomes and transfers of money to and from abroad. The capital account records all transfers of capital to and from abroad. The financial account records inflows and outflows of money for investment and as deposits in banks and other financial institutions. It also includes dealings in the country's foreign exchange reserves.

1b The whole account must balance, but surpluses or deficits can be recorded on any specific part of the account. Thus the current account could be in deficit but it would have to be matched by an equal and opposite capital plus financial account surplus.

2a The rate of exchange is the rate at which one currency exchanges for another. Rates of exchange are determined by demand and supply in the foreign exchange market. Demand for the domestic currency consists of all the credit items in the balance of payments account. Supply consists of all the debit items.

2b The exchange rate will depreciate (fall) if the demand for the domestic currency falls or the supply increases. These shifts can be caused by a fall in domestic interest rates, higher inflation in the domestic economy than abroad, a rise in domestic incomes relative to incomes abroad, relative investment prospects improving abroad, or the belief by speculators that the exchange rate will fall. The opposite in each case would cause an appreciation (rise).

3a The government can attempt to prevent the rate of exchange from falling by central bank purchases of the domestic currency in the foreign exchange market, either by selling foreign currency reserves or by using foreign loans. Alternatively, the central bank can raise interest rates. The reverse actions can be taken if the government wants to prevent the rate from rising.

3b In the longer term it can prevent the rate from falling by pursuing deflationary policies, protectionist policies, or supply-side policies to increase the competitiveness of the country's exports.

4a Fixed exchange rates bring the advantage of certainty for the business community, which encourages trade and foreign investment. They also help to prevent governments from pursuing irresponsible macroeconomic policies.

4b Fixed exchange rates bring the disadvantages of conflicting policy goals, the tendency to lead to competitive deflation, the problems of ensuring adequate international liquidity to enable intervention, and the restrictions that fixed rates place upon countries when attempting to respond to system shocks.

4c The advantages of free-floating exchange rates are that they automatically correct balance of payments disequilibria; they eliminate the need for reserves; and they give governments a greater independence to pursue their chosen domestic policy.

4d On the other hand, a completely free exchange rate can be highly unstable, especially when the elasticities of demand for imports and exports are low; also speculation may be destabilising. This may discourage firms from trading and investing abroad. What is more, a flexible exchange rate, by removing the balance of payments constraint on domestic policy, may encourage governments to pursue irresponsible domestic policies for short-term political gain.

4e There have been various attempts to manage exchange rates, without them being totally fixed. One example was the Bretton Woods system: a system of pegged exchange rates, but where devaluations or revaluations were allowed from time to time. Another was the ERM, which was the forerunner to the euro. Member countries' currencies were allowed to fluctuate against each other within a band.

REVIEW QUESTIONS

1 The following are the items in the UK's 2001 balance of payments:

	£ billions
Exports of goods	191.2
Imports of goods	224.3
Exports of services	77.1
Imports of services	65.4
Net income flows	+11.2
Net current transfers	−7.2
Net capital transfers	+1.4
Net investment in UK from abroad (direct and portfolio)	75.5
Net UK investment abroad (direct and portfolio)	116.7
Other financial inflows	219.1
Other financial outflows	161.1
Reserves	+3.1

Calculate the following: (a) the balance on trade in goods; (b) the balance on trade (in goods and services); (c) the balance of payments on current account; (d) the financial account balance; (e) the total current plus capital plus financial account balance; (f) net errors and omissions.

2 Assume that there is a free-floating exchange rate. Will the following cause the exchange rate to appreciate or depreciate? In each case you should consider whether there is a shift in the demand or supply curves of sterling (or both) and which way the curve(s) shift(s).

(a) More video recorders are imported from Japan.
Demand curve *shifts left/shifts right/does not shift*
Supply curve *shifts left/shifts right/does not shift*
Exchange rate *appreciates/depreciates*

(b) Non-UK residents increase their purchases of UK government securities.
Demand curve *shifts left/shifts right/does not shift*
Supply curve *shifts left/shifts right/does not shift*
Exchange rate *appreciates/depreciates*

(c) UK interest rates fall relative to those abroad.
Demand curve *shifts left/shifts right/does not shift*
Supply curve *shifts left/shifts right/does not shift*
Exchange rate *appreciates/depreciates*

(d) The UK experiences a higher rate of inflation than other countries.
Demand curve *shifts left/shifts right/does not shift*
Supply curve *shifts left/shifts right/does not shift*
Exchange rate *appreciates/depreciates*

(e) The result of a further enlargement of the EU is for investment in the UK by the rest of the EU to increase by a greater amount than UK investment in other EU countries.

Demand curve *shifts left/shifts right/does not shift*
Supply curve *shifts left/shifts right/does not shift*
Exchange rate *appreciates/depreciates*

(f) Speculators believe that the rate of exchange will fall.

Demand curve *shifts left/shifts right/does not shift*
Supply curve *shifts left/shifts right/does not shift*
Exchange rate *appreciates/depreciates*

3 Explain how the current account of the balance of payments is likely to vary with the course of the business cycle.

4 Is it a 'bad thing' to have a deficit on the direct investment part of the financial account?

5 Why may credits on a country's short-term financial account create problems for the its economy in the future?

6 What is the relationship between the balance of payments and the rate of exchange?

7 Consider the argument that in the modern world of large-scale short-term international financial movements, the ability of individual countries to affect their exchange rate is very limited.

8 To what extent can dealing in forward exchange markets remove the problems of a free-floating exchange rate?

9 What adverse effects on the domestic economy may follow from (a) a depreciation of the exchange rate and (b) an appreciation of the exchange rate?

10 What will be the effects on the domestic economy under free-floating exchange rates if there is a rapid expansion in world economic activity? What will determine the size of these effects?

28 Money and interest rates

In this chapter we are going to look at the special role that money plays in the economy. The demand and supply of money between them determine the rate of interest, and this has a crucial impact on business. Money and interest rates also have a major effect on the performance of the whole economy, and in particular on the level of national output and prices.

First we define what is meant by money, and examine its functions. Then we look at the operation of the financial sector of the economy and its role in determining the supply of money. We then turn to look at the demand for money, and finally put supply and demand together to show how interest rates are determined.

The control of the financial sector, and the money supply and interest rates in particular, will be considered in more detail in Chapter 30, when we examine monetary policy as one of the means whereby the government or central bank can attempt to manage the economy.

28.1 The meaning and functions of money

Before going any further we must define precisely what we mean by 'money' – not as easy a task as it sounds. Money is more than just notes and coin. In fact the main component of a country's money supply is not cash, but deposits in banks and other financial institutions. Only a very small proportion of these deposits are kept by the banks in their safes or tills in the form of cash. The bulk of the deposits appear merely as bookkeeping entries in the banks' accounts.

This may sound very worrying. Will a bank have enough cash to meet its customers' demands? The answer is yes. Only a small fraction of a bank's total deposits will be withdrawn at any one time, and banks always make sure that they have the ability to meet their customers' demands. The chances of banks running out of cash are practically nil. What is more, the bulk of all but very small transactions are not conducted in cash at all. With the use of cheques, and the growing use of credit cards and debit cards, most money is simply transferred from the purchaser's to the seller's bank account without the need for first withdrawing it in cash.

What items should be included in the definition of money? To answer this we need to identify the *functions* of money.

The functions of money

The main purpose of money is for buying and selling goods, services and assets: i.e. as a **medium of exchange**. It also has three other important functions. Let us examine each in turn.

A medium of exchange

In a subsistence economy where individuals make their own clothes, grow their own food, provide their own entertainments, etc., people do not need money. If people want to exchange any goods, they will do so by barter. In other words, they will do swaps with other people.

The complexities of a modern developed economy, however, make barter totally impractical for most purposes. Someone else may have something you want, but there is no guarantee that they will want what you have to offer them in return. What is more, under a system of capitalism where people are employed by others to do a specialist task, it would be totally impractical for people to be paid in food, clothes, cars, electrical goods, etc. What is necessary is a medium of exchange which is generally acceptable as a means of payment for goods and services, and as a means of payment for labour and other factor services. 'Money' is any such medium.

To be a suitable physical means of exchange, money must be light enough to carry around, come in a number of denominations, large and small, and not be easy to forge. Alternatively, money must be in a form that enables it to be transferred *indirectly* through some acceptable mechanism. For example, money in the form of bookkeeping entries in bank accounts can be transferred from one account to another by the use of such mechanisms as cheques, debit cards, standing orders and direct debits.

A means of storing wealth

Individuals and businesses need a means whereby income earned *today* can be used to purchase goods and services in the *future*. People need to be able to store their wealth: they want a means of saving. Money is one such medium in which to hold wealth. It can be saved.

A means of evaluation

Money allows the value of goods, services and assets to be compared. The value of goods is expressed in terms of prices, and prices are expressed in money terms. Money also allows dissimilar things, such as a person's wealth or a company's assets, to be added up. Similarly, a country's GDP is expressed in money terms. Money thus serves as a 'unit of account'.

A means of establishing the value of future claims and payments

People often want to agree *today* the price of some *future* payment. For example, workers and managers will want to agree the wage rate for the coming year. Firms will want to sign contracts with their suppliers, specifying the price of raw materials and other supplies. The use of money prices is the most convenient means of measuring future claims.

What should count as money?

What items, then, should be included in the definition of money? Unfortunately, there is no sharp borderline between money and non-money.

Cash (notes and coin) obviously counts as money. It readily meets all the functions of money. Goods (fridges, cars and cabbages) do not count as money. But what about various financial assets such as bank and building society accounts, stocks and shares? Do they count as money? The answer is: it depends on how narrowly money is defined.

Pause for thought

Why are debit and credit cards not counted as money?

Countries thus use several different measures of money supply. All include cash, but they vary according to what additional items are included. To understand their significance and the ways in which money supply can be controlled, it is first necessary to look at the various types of account in which money can be held and at the various financial institutions involved.

28.2 The financial system in the UK

In order to understand the role of the financial sector in determining the supply of money, it is important to distinguish different types of financial institution. Each type has a distinct part to play in determining the size of the money supply.

The key role of banks in the monetary system

By far the largest element of money supply is bank deposits. It is not surprising then that banks play an absolutely crucial role in the monetary system.

The most important of the banks in the UK for functioning of the economy and for the implementation of monetary policy are the *retail banks*. These are the familiar high street banks, such as Barclays, Lloyds TSB, HSBC, National Westminster, Co-operative Bank and Royal Bank of Scotland, and ex-building societies such as the Abbey National and the Alliance and Leicester. The other major category of banks is the *wholesale* banks (investment banks). These deal primarily with business and are concerned with large-scale deposits and loans at negotiated rates of interest. (See section 19.4 for a more detailed account of their activities.)

Banks are in the business of deposit taking and lending. To understand this, we must distinguish between banks' liabilities and assets. The total liabilities and assets for the UK banks are set out in a balance sheet in Table 28.1.

Liabilities

Customers' deposits in banks (and other depositing-taking institutions such as building societies) are **liabilities** to these institutions. This means simply that the customers have the claim on these deposits and thus the institutions are liable to meet the claims.

There are four major types of deposit: sight deposits, time deposits, certificates of deposit and 'repos'.

Sight deposits. **Sight deposits** are any deposits that can be withdrawn on demand by the depositor without penalty. In the past, sight accounts did not pay interest. Today, however, there are some sight accounts that do.

The most familiar form of sight deposits are current accounts at banks. Depositors are normally issued with cheque books and/or debit cards (e.g. Switch or Connect) which enable them to spend the money directly without first having to go to the bank and draw the money out in cash. In the case of debit cards, the person's account is electronically debited when the purchase is made and the

definition

Liabilities
All legal claims for payment that outsiders have on an institution.

definition

Sight deposits
Deposits that can be withdrawn on demand without penalty.

Table 28.1   **Balance sheet of UK banks: February 2003**

Sterling liabilities	£bn	%	Sterling assets	£bn	%
Sight deposits		(36.2)	Notes and coin	7.2	(0.4)
UK banks, etc.	105.1		Balances with Bank of England	1.7	(0.1)
UK public sector	4.6				
UK private sector	459.7		Market loans		(22.9)
Non-residents	59.3		UK banks	236.1	
Time deposits		(34.8)	CDs, etc.	77.5	
UK banks, etc.	142.4		Non-residents	88.1	
UK public sector	9.1		Bills of exchange		(1.7)
UK private sector	299.6		Treasury	12.3	
Non-residents	153.0		UK Bank bills	6.8	
Certificates of deposit	157.7	(9.1)	Other	11.0	
Sale and repurchase agreements (repos)	104.2	(6.0)	Reverse repos	92.0	(5.2)
Other	242.9	(13.9)	Investments	128.6	(7.3)
			Advances	1034.8	(59.0)
			Miscellaneous	58.8	(3.4)
Total sterling liabilities	**1737.6**	**(100.0)**	**Total sterling assets**	**1754.9**	**(100.0)**
Liabilities in other currencies	2133.4		Assets in other currencies	2116.1	
Total liabilities	3871.0		Total assets	3871.0	

card is 'swiped' across the machine. This process is known as EFTPOS (electronic funds transfer at point of sale).

An important feature of current accounts is that banks often allow customers to be overdrawn. That is, they can draw on their account and make payments to other people in excess of the amount of money they have deposited.

Time deposits. **Time deposits** require notice of withdrawal. However, they normally pay a higher rate of interest than sight accounts. With some types of account, a depositor can withdraw a certain amount of money on demand, but will have to pay a penalty of so many days' interest. They are not cheque-book or debit-card accounts. The most familiar forms of time deposits are the deposit and savings accounts in banks and the various savings accounts in building societies. No overdraft facilities exist with time deposits.

Sale and repurchase agreements ('repos'). If banks have a temporary shortage of funds, they can sell some of their financial assets to other banks or to the Bank of England (see below), and later repurchase them on some agreed date, often about a fortnight later. These **sale and repurchase agreements (repos)** are in effect a form of loan, the bank borrowing for a period of time using some of its financial assets as the security for the loan. The most usual assets to use in this way are government bonds, normally called 'gilt-edged securities' or simply 'gilts' (see below). Sale and repurchase agreements involving gilts are known as *gilt repos*. As we shall see, gilt repos play a vital role in the operation of monetary policy.

Certificates of deposit. CDs are certificates issued by banks to customers (usually firms) for large deposits of a fixed term (e.g. £100 000 for 18 months). They can be sold by one customer to another, and are thus relatively liquid to the depositor but illiquid to the bank. The use of CDs has grown rapidly in recent years. Their use by firms has meant that, at a wholesale level, sight accounts have become *less* popular.

Assets

Banks' financial **assets** are its claims on others. There are three main categories of assets.

Cash and operational balances in the central bank (Bank of England in the UK, European Central Bank (ECB) in the eurozone). Banks need to hold a certain amount of their assets as cash. This is largely to meet the day-to-day demands by customers for cash. They also keep 'operational balances' in the central bank. These are like the banks' own current accounts and are used for clearing purposes. They can be withdrawn in cash on demand and are thus also totally liquid. In the UK banks are also required to deposit a small fraction of their assets as 'cash ratio deposits' with the Bank of England.

Cash and balances in the Bank of England, however, earn no interest for banks. The vast majority of banks' assets are therefore in the form of various types of loan – to individuals and firms, to other financial institutions and to the government. These are 'assets' because they represent claims that the banks have on other people. Loans can be grouped into two types: short and long term.

Short-term loans. These are in the form of *market loans*, *bills of exchange* or *reverse repos*. The market for these various types of loan is known as the **money market**.

- **Market loans** are made primarily to other banks or financial institutions. They consist of (a) money lent 'at call' (i.e. reclaimable on demand or at 24 hours' notice), (b) money lent 'at short notice' (i.e. money lent for a few days) and (c) CDs (i.e. certificates of deposit made in other banks or building societies).
- **Bills of exchange** are loans either to companies (guaranteed by another bank and hence called 'bank bills') or to the government (Treasury bills). As explained in section 19.4, these are, in effect, an IOU, with the company issuing them (in the case of bank bills) or the Bank of England (in the case of Treasury bills) promising to pay the holder a specified sum on a particular date (typically three months' later). Since bills do not pay interest, they are sold below their face value (at a 'discount') but redeemed on maturity at face value. This enables the purchaser, in this case the bank, to earn a return.
- **Reverse repos.** When a sale and repurchase agreement is made, the financial institution *purchasing* the assets (e.g. gilts) is, in effect, giving a short-term loan. The other party agrees to buy back the assets (i.e. pay back the loan) on a set date. The assets temporarily held by the bank making the loan are known as 'reverse repos'.

Longer-term loans. These consist primarily of loans to customers, both personal customers and businesses. These loans, also known as *advances*, are of three main types: fixed-term (repayable in instalments over a set number of years, typically six months to five years), overdrafts (often for an unspecified term) and mortgages (typically for 25 years).

---

definition

Certificates of deposit
Certificates issued by banks for fixed-term interest-bearing deposits. They can be resold by the owner to another party.

definition

Assets
Possessions, or claims held on others.

definition

Money market
The market for short-term loans and deposits.

definition

Market loans
Loans made to other financial institutions.

definition

Bill of exchange
A certificate promising to repay a stated amount on a certain date, typically three months from the issue of the bill. Bills pay no interest as such, but are sold at a discount and redeemed at face value, thereby earning a rate of discount for the purchaser.

definition

Reverse repos
When gilts or other assets are *purchased* under a sale and repurchase agreement. They become an asset of the purchaser.

Key Idea 22 p381

Are the days of cash numbered?
EFTPOS versus ATMs

Banking is becoming increasingly automated, with computer debiting and crediting of accounts replacing the moving around of pieces of paper. What was once done by a bank clerk is often now done by computer.

One possible outcome of this replacement of labour by computers is the gradual elimination of cash from the economy – or so some commentators have claimed.

The most dramatic example of computerisation in recent years has been EFTPOS (electronic funds transfer at the point of sale). This is where you pay for goods in the shops by means of a card – either a credit card (like Access or Visa) or a debit card (like Switch or Connect). The card is simply 'swiped' across a machine at the till which may then require you to enter your PIN (personal identification number). The details of the transaction (the amount, the retailer and your card number) are then transmitted down the line to the EFTPOS UK processing centre. If necessary, the information is then directed down the line to the card issuer for authorisation. If the card is valid and the transaction acceptable, then within seconds the machine will issue a slip for you to sign and the purchase is complete. Subsequently your account will be automatically debited and the retailer's account automatically credited.

The advantage of this system is that it does away with the processing by hand of pieces of paper. In particular it does away with the need for (a) credit-card slips when used in conjunction with credit cards and (b) cheques. Both cheques and credit-card slips have to be physically moved around and then read and processed by *people*. If this EFTPOS system were to become widely used for *small* transactions, it could well reduce the need for cash. But

reducing the need for cash is not the prime purpose of EFTPOS. Its prime purpose is to do away with cheques and credit-card slips.

So are we moving towards a cashless society? Probably not. Cash is still the simplest and most efficient way of paying for a host of items, from your bus ticket to a newspaper to a packet of mints. What is more, another technical innovation is moving us in the direction of using *more* cash, not less! This is the cash machine – or *ATM* (automated teller machine), to give it its official title. The spread of cash machines to virtually every bank and building society branch and to many larger stores and supermarkets has been rapid in recent years. The sheer simplicity of obtaining cash at all hours from these machines, not only from your current account but also on your credit card, is obviously a huge encouragement to the use of cash.

So are we using more cash or less cash? The evidence suggests that, until recent years, there was a gradual decline in cash in circulation as a proportion of GDP. It fell from just over 5 per cent of GDP in 1980 to just over 3 per cent in the mid-1990s. Since then it has risen slightly. By 2002 the figure was $3\frac{1}{2}$ per cent.

But although the effects of EFTPOS and ATMs may be quite different in terms of the use of cash, they both have the same advantage to banks: they reduce the need for bank staff and thereby reduce costs.

Question

Under what circumstances are cheques more efficient than cash and vice versa? Would you get the same answer from everyone involved in transactions: individuals, firms and banks?

Banks also make *investments*. These are partly in government bonds ('gilts'), which are effectively loans to the government. The government sells bonds, which then pay a fixed sum each year in interest until the maturity date (perhaps 20 years in the future), when the loan will be repaid at face value by the government. Once issued, bonds can then be bought and sold on the Stock Exchange. Banks are normally only prepared to buy bonds that have less than five years to maturity. Banks also invest in various subsidiary financial institutions and in building societies.

Liquidity and profitability

As we have seen, banks keep a range of liabilities and assets. The balance of items in this range is influenced by two important considerations: profitability and liquidity.

Profitability. Profits are made by lending money out at a higher rate of interest than that paid to depositors.

definition

Liquidity
The ease with which an asset can be converted into cash without loss.

Liquidity. The **liquidity** of an asset is the ease with which it can be converted into cash without loss. Cash itself, by definition, is perfectly liquid.

Some assets, such as money lent at call to other financial institutions, are highly liquid. Although not actually cash, these assets can be converted into cash on demand with no financial penalty. Other assets, however, are much less liquid. Personal loans to the general public or mortgages for house purchase can only be redeemed by the bank as each instalment is paid. Other advances for fixed periods are only repaid at the end of that period.

Banks must always be able to meet the demands of their customers for withdrawals of money. To do this, they must hold sufficient cash or other assets that can be readily turned into cash. In other words, banks must maintain sufficient liquidity.

Profitability is the major aim of banks and most other financial institutions. However, the aims of profitability and liquidity tend to conflict. In general, the more liquid an asset, the less profitable it is, and vice versa. Personal and business loans to customers are profitable to banks, but highly illiquid. Cash is totally liquid, but earns no profit. Thus financial institutions like to hold a range of assets with varying degrees of liquidity and profitability.

Pause for thought

Why might a bank choose to reduce the proportion of liquid assets that it holds?

definition

Liquidity ratio
The proportion of a bank's total assets held in liquid form.

The ratio of an institution's liquid assets to total assets is known as its **liquidity ratio**. For example, if a bank had £100 million of assets, of which £10 million were liquid and £90 million were illiquid, the bank would have a 10 per cent liquidity ratio. If a financial institution's liquidity ratio is too high, it will make too little profit. If the ratio is too low, there will be the risk that customers' demands will not be able to be met: this would cause a crisis of confidence and possible closure. Institutions thus have to make a judgement as to what liquidity ratio is best – one that is neither too high nor too low.

The central bank

The Bank of England is the UK's central bank. The European Central Bank (ECB) is the central bank for the countries using the euro. The Federal Reserve Bank of America (the Fed) is the USA's central bank. All countries have a central bank and they fulfil two vital roles in the economy.

The first is to oversee the whole monetary system and ensure that banks and other financial institutions operate as stably and as efficiently as possible.

The second is to act as the government's agent, both as its banker and in carrying out monetary policy. The Bank of England traditionally worked in very close liaison with the Treasury and there used to be regular meetings between the Governor of the Bank of England and the Chancellor of the Exchequer. Although the Bank may have disagreed with Treasury policy, it always carried it out. With the election of the Labour government in 1997, however, the Bank of

BOX 28.2

Changes in the banking industry
Is bigger better?

There are considerable economies of scale in banking. These have resulted in a wave of mergers and takeovers. The process has been hastened by increasing deregulation in the banking industry, which has permitted banks to take on a whole range of functions.

The economies arise in the process known as 'financial intermediation'. This involves providing a link between those who want to deposit money and those who want to borrow it. It involves matching the supply of funds to the demand for them.

If there were many small banks, much of their business would be in dealing with each other: in balancing inflows and outflows of funds between them. Even with computers, this would be a costly process and involve the banks having to maintain substantial reserves in case outflows exceeded inflows. With fewer bigger banks, however, an increased proportion of the flow of funds would be between their *own* customers and thus would not involve dealing with other banks. Thus reserves could be smaller as a percentage of total assets.

Also, as banks get bigger and the number of customers increases, so *net* withdrawals (positive or negative) diminish as a proportion of total deposits held. This, again, means that banks need to hold a smaller proportion of reserves: they can operate with a lower liquidity ratio. This increases bank's profitability, since cash reserves earn banks no money, and money at call earns a low rate.

Banks also benefit from economies of scope (see page 180). This means that they gain economies by diversifying into different but related activities. Thus traditional retail banks, such as Barclays and NatWest, have diversified into wholesale banking, stockbroking, discounting bills, insurance, foreign exchange dealing and a whole range of financial services to the corporate sector. This diversification not only reduces average costs, since customers can receive more than one service from the same premises or through the same Internet site or telephone service, but it also reduces risk. If one part of the business became less profitable, this could be offset by increased profits from another.

Today it makes more sense to talk of retail or wholesale banking *activity*, rather than retail or wholesale banks. After all, the same banks are involved in both types of activity – and many more.

Questions

1 *Are there any circumstances where diversification could lead to increased risks?*

2 *To what extent are the lower costs associated with Internet banking attributable to economies of scale?*

England was given independence to decide the course of monetary policy. In particular, this meant that the Bank of England and not the government would now decide interest rates.

Another example of an independent central bank is the European Central Bank (ECB). The ECB operates monetary policy for the countries using the euro and it alone, not the member governments, determines common interest rates for these countries. Similarly, the Federal Reserve Bank of America (the US central bank) is independent of both President and Congress, and its chairman is generally regarded as having great power in determining the country's economic policy. Although the degree of independence of central banks from government varies considerably around the world, there has nevertheless been a general trend to make central banks more independent.

If the UK adopts the euro, there will be a much reduced role for the Bank of England. At present, however, within its two broad roles, it has a number of different functions. Although we shall consider the case of the Bank of England, the same principles apply to other central banks.

It issues notes

The Bank of England is the sole issuer of banknotes in England and Wales (in Scotland and Northern Ireland retail banks issue banknotes). The amount of banknotes issued by the Bank of England depends largely on the demand for notes from the general public. If people draw more cash from their bank accounts, the banks will have to draw more cash from their balances in the Bank of England.

It acts as a bank

To the government. It keeps the two major government accounts: 'The Exchequer' and the 'National Loans Fund'. Taxation and government spending pass through the Exchequer. Government borrowing and lending pass through the National Loans Fund. The government tends to keep its deposits in the Bank of England to a minimum. If the deposits begin to build up (from taxation), the government will probably spend them on paying back government debt. If, on the other hand, the government runs short of money, it will simply borrow more.

To the banks. As we have seen, banks hold operational balances in the Bank of England. These are used for clearing purposes between the banks and to provide them with a source of liquidity.

To overseas central banks. These are deposits of sterling held by overseas authorities as part of their official reserves and/or for purposes of intervening in the foreign exchange market in order to influence the exchange rate of their currency.

It provides liquidity, as necessary, to banks

It ensures that there is always an adequate supply of liquidity to meet the legitimate demands of depositors in banks. As we shall see below, it does this through the discount and gilt repo markets.

It operates the country's monetary and exchange rate policy

Monetary policy. The Bank of England's Monetary Policy Committee (MPC) sets interest rates (the rate on gilt repos) at its monthly meetings. This nine-member committee consists of four experts appointed by the Chancellor of the Exchequer and four senior members of the Bank of England, plus the Governor in the chair. By careful management of the issue and repurchasing of government bonds and Treasury bills, the Bank of England then keeps interest rates at the level decided by the MPC. It also, in the process, influences the size of the money supply. This is explained in Chapter 30.

> **definition**
>
> **Exchange equalisation account**
> The gold and foreign exchange reserves account in the Bank of England.

Exchange rate policy. The Bank of England manages the country's gold and foreign currency reserves. This is done through the **exchange equalisation account**. As we saw in Chapter 27, by buying and selling foreign currencies on the foreign exchange market, the Bank of England can affect the exchange rate.

The role of the London money market

It is through the London money market that the Bank of England exercises its control of the economy. The market deals in short-term lending and borrowing. It is normally divided into the 'discount and repo' markets and the 'parallel' or 'complementary' markets.

The discount and repo markets

The markets for bills of exchange (the discount market) and for repos play a crucial role in ensuring that banks have sufficient liquidity to meet all their needs.

Assume that bank customers start drawing out more cash. As a result, banks find themselves short of liquid assets. What can they do? The answer is that they borrow from the Bank of England. There are two ways in which this can be done.

The first is to enter a repo agreement, whereby the Bank of England buys gilts from the banks (thereby supplying them with money) on the condition that the banks buy the gilts back at a fixed price and on a fixed date, typically two weeks later. The repurchase price will be above the sale price. The difference is the equivalent of the interest that the banks are being charged for having what amounts to a loan from the Bank of England. The repurchase price (and hence the 'repo rate') is set by the Bank of England to reflect the rate chosen by the MPC (see section 30.3).

The second method is to sell Treasury bills back to the Bank of England before they have reached maturity (i.e. before the three months are up). This process is known as **rediscounting**. The Bank of England will pay a price below the face value, thus effectively charging interest to the banks. Again, the price is set so that the 'rediscount rate' reflects the interest rate set by the MPC.

In being prepared to rediscount bills or provide money through gilt repos, the Bank of England is thus the ultimate guarantor of sufficient liquidity in the monetary system and is known as **lender of last resort**.

The need for banks to acquire liquidity in this way is not uncommon: the 'last resort' occurs on most days! It is generally a deliberate policy of the Bank of England to create a shortage of liquidity in the economy to force banks to obtain liquidity from it. But why should the Bank of England do this? It does it as a means of controlling interest rates. If the banks are forced to obtain liquidity from the Bank of England, they will be borrowing at the Bank of England's *chosen rate* (i.e. the repo rate). The banks will then have to gear their other rates to it, and other institutions will gear their rates to those of the banks.

The way in which the Bank of England creates a shortage of liquidity and the way in which it forces through changes in interest rates are examined in section 30.3.

definition
Rediscounting bills of exchange Buying bills before they reach maturity.

definition
Lender of last resort The role of the Bank of England as the guarantor of sufficient liquidity in the monetary system.

The parallel money markets

The parallel money markets include the following:

- The inter-bank market (wholesale loans from one bank to another from one day to up to several months).
- The market for certificates of deposit.
- The inter-companies deposit market (short-term loans from one company to another arranged through the market).
- The foreign currencies market (dealings in foreign currencies deposited short term in London).
- The finance house market (short-term borrowing to finance hire purchase).
- The building society market (wholesale borrowing by the building societies).
- The commercial paper market (borrowing in sterling by companies, banks and other financial institutions by the issue of short-term (less than one year) 'promissory notes'. These, like bills of exchange, are sold at a discount and redeemed at their face value, but in the interim can be traded on the market at any time.)

The parallel markets have grown in size and importance in recent years. The main reasons for this are (a) the opening-up of markets to international dealing, given the abolition of exchange controls in 1979, (b) the deregulation of banking and money-market dealing and (c) the volatility of interest rates and exchange rates, and thus the desire of banks to keep funds in a form that can be readily switched from one form of deposit to another, or from one currency to another. The main areas of growth have been in inter-bank deposits, certificates of deposit and the foreign currency markets.

Although the Bank of England does not deal directly in the parallel markets and does not provide 'last resort' lending facilities, it nevertheless closely monitors the various money-market rates of interest and, if necessary, seeks to influence them, through its dealings in the repo and discount markets.

28.3 The supply of money

If money supply is to be monitored and possibly controlled, it is obviously necessary to measure it. But what should be included in the measure? Here we need to distinguish between the *monetary base* and *broad money*.

The **monetary base** (or 'high-powered money') consists of cash (notes and coin) in circulation outside the central bank. Thus, in the eurozone, the monetary base is given by cash (euros) in circulation outside the ECB.

In the UK, it is sometimes referred to as the 'narrow monetary base' to distinguish it from the **wide monetary base**, which also includes banks' balances with the central bank. In the UK, the wide monetary base in known as *M0*.

But the monetary base gives us a very poor indication of the effective money supply, since it excludes the most important source of liquidity for spending: namely, bank deposits. The problem is which deposits to include. We need to answer three questions:

- Should we include just sight deposits, or time deposits as well?
- Should we include just retail deposits, or wholesale deposits as well?
- Should we include just bank deposits, or building society (savings institution) deposits as well?

In the past there has been a whole range of measures, each including different combinations of these accounts. However, financial deregulation, the abolition of foreign exchange controls and the development of computer technology have led to huge changes in the financial sector throughout the world. This has led to a blurring of the distinctions between different types of account. It has also made it very easy to switch deposits from one type of account to another. For these reasons, the most usual measure that countries use for money supply is **broad money**, which in most cases includes both time and sight deposits, retail and wholesale deposits, and bank and building society (savings institutions) deposits.

In the UK this measure of broad money is known as *M4*. In most other European countries and the USA it is known as *M3*. There are, however, minor differences between countries in what is included. (Official UK and eurozone measures of money supply are given in Box 28.3.)

As we have seen, bank deposits of one form or another constitute by far the largest component of (broad) money supply. To understand how money supply expands and contracts, and how it can be controlled, it is thus necessary to understand what determines the size of bank deposits. Banks can themselves

definition

Monetary base
Notes and coin outside the central bank.

definition

Wide monetary base (M0)
Notes and coin outside the central bank plus banks' operational deposits with the central bank.

definition

Broad money
Cash in circulation plus retail and wholesale bank and building society deposits.

Table 28.2   Banks' original balance sheet

Liabilities	£bn	Assets	£bn
Deposits	100	Balances with the central bank	10
		Advances	90
Total	100	Total	100

Table 28.3   The initial effect of an additional deposit of £10 billion

Liabilities	£bn	Assets	£bn
Deposits (old)	100	Balances with the central bank (old)	10
Deposits (new)	10	Balances with the central bank (new)	10
		Advances	90
Total	110	Total	110

expand the amount of bank deposits, and hence the money supply, by a process known as 'credit creation'.

The creation of credit

To illustrate this process in its simplest form, assume that banks have just one type of liability – deposits – and two types of asset – balances with the central bank (to achieve liquidity) and advances to customers (to earn profit).

Banks want to achieve profitability while maintaining sufficient liquidity. Assume that they believe that sufficient liquidity will be achieved if 10 per cent of their assets are held as balances with the central bank. The remaining 90 per cent will then be in advances to customers. In other words, the banks operate a 10 per cent liquidity ratio.

Assume initially that the combined balance sheet of the banks is as shown in Table 28.2. Total deposits are £100 billion, of which £10 billion (10 per cent) are kept in balances with the central bank. The remaining £90 billion (90 per cent) are lent to customers.

Now assume that the government spends more money – £10 billion, say, on roads or education. It pays for this with cheques drawn on its account with the central bank. The people receiving the cheques deposit them in their banks. Banks return these cheques to the central bank and their balances correspondingly increase by £10 billion. The combined banks' balance sheet now is shown in Table 28.3.

But this is not the end of the story. Banks now have surplus liquidity. With their balances in the central bank having increased to £20 billion, they now have a liquidity ratio of 20/110, or 18.2 per cent. If they are to return to a 10 per cent liquidity ratio, they need only retain £11 billion as balances at the central bank (£11 billion/£110 billion = 10 per cent). The remaining £9 billion they can lend to customers.

Key
Idea
21
p376

BOX 28.3

UK monetary aggregates
How long is a piece of string?

UK measures

In the recent past, measures of 'money supply' in the UK have included M0, non-interest-bearing M1, M1, M2, M3, M3H, M3c, M4, M4c, M5. This confusing array of measures reflected the many different types of deposit that might be considered to be part of money.

Today, there are just three official measures: M0, M4 and M3 (eurozone measure). M0 is referred to as the 'wide monetary base' and M4 is referred to as 'broad money' or simply as 'the money supply'. The definitions of the two UK aggregates are:

M0: Cash in circulation with the public and cash held by banks and building societies, plus banks' operational balances with the Bank of England.

M4: Cash in circulation with the public (but not cash in banks and building societies), plus private-sector retail sterling deposits in banks and building societies, plus private-sector wholesale sterling deposits in banks and building societies, plus sterling certificates of deposit.

Table (a) gives the figures for all these aggregates for the end of February 2003.

Question

Why is cash in banks and building societies included in M0 but not in M4?

(a) UK monetary aggregates, end February 2003

		£ million
	Cash outside Bank of England	36 861
+	Banks' operational deposits with Bank of England	91
=	**M0**	**36 952**
	Cash outside banks (i.e. in circulation with the public and non-bank firms)	30 630
+	Private-sector retail bank and building society deposits	676 969
=	Retail deposits and cash in M4 (previously known as M2)	**707 599**
+	Private-sector wholesale bank and building society deposits + CDs	295 996
=	**M4**	**1 003 595**

Assume now that customers spend this £9 billion in shops and the shopkeepers deposit the cheques in their bank accounts. When the cheques are cleared, the balances in the central bank of the customers' banks will duly be debited by £9 billion, but the balances in the central bank of the shopkeepers' banks will be credited by £9 billion: leaving *overall balances in the central bank unaltered*. There is still a surplus of £9 billion over what is required to maintain the 10 per cent liquidity ratio. The new deposits of £9 in the shopkeepers' banks, backed by balances in the central bank, can thus be used as the basis for *further* loans. Ten per cent (i.e. £0.9 billion) must be kept back in the central bank, but the remaining 90 per cent (i.e. £8.1 billion) can be lent out again. When the money is spent and the cheques are cleared, this £8.1 billion will still remain as surplus balances in the central bank and can therefore be used as the basis for yet more loans. Again, 10 per cent must be retained and the remaining 90 per cent can be lent out. This process goes on and on until eventually the position is as shown in Table 28.4.

(b) UK Money supply using ECB measures: end February 2003

	£ million
Currency in circulation	31 351
+ Overnight deposits	513 292
= **M1**	**544 643**
+ Deposits with agreed maturity up to 2 years	81 696
+ Deposits redeemable up to 3 month's notice	296 518
= **M2**	**922 857**
+ Repos	88 978
+ Money market funds and paper	57 496
+ Debt securities with residual maturity up to 2 years	0
+ **M3**	**1 069 331**

Source: *Monetary and Financial Statistics* (Bank of England)

Eurozone measures

The ECB uses three measures of the money supply. They are all different from those used by the Bank of England. The narrowest definition (M1) includes overnight deposits (i.e. call money) as well as cash, and is thus much broader than the UK's M0 measure. The broadest eurozone measure (M3) is again broader than the UK's broadest measure (M4), since the eurozone measure includes various other moderately liquid assets. The definitions of the three eurozone aggregates are:

M1: Cash in circulation with the public, plus overnight deposits.

M2: M1, plus deposits with agreed maturity up to 2 years, plus deposits redeemable up to 3 month's notice.

M3: M2, plus repos, plus money market funds and paper, plus debt securities with residual maturity up to 2 years.

Question

What are the benefits of including these additional items in the broad measure of money supply?

Table 28.4 **The full effect of an additional deposit of £10 billion**

Liabilities	£bn	Assets	£bn
Deposits (old)	100	Balances with the central bank (old)	10
Deposits (new: initial)	10	Balances with the central bank (new)	10
(new: subsequent)	90	Advances (old)	90
		Advances (new)	90
Total	200	Total	200

The initial increase in balances with the central bank of £10 billion has allowed banks to create new advances (and hence deposits) of £90 billion, making a total increase in money supply of £100 billion.

This effect is known as the **bank (or deposits) multiplier.** In this simple example with a liquidity ratio of $1/10$ (i.e. 10 per cent), the deposits multiplier is 10. An initial increase in deposits of £10 billion allowed total deposits to rise by £100 billion. In this simple world, therefore, the deposits multiplier is the inverse of the liquidity ratio (L).

$$\text{Deposits multiplier} = 1/L$$

The creation of credit: the real world

In practice, the creation of credit is not as simple as this. There are three major complications.

Banks' liquidity ratio may vary

Banks may choose a different liquidity ratio. At certain times, banks may decide that it is prudent to hold a bigger proportion of liquid assets. If Christmas or the summer holidays are approaching and people are likely to make bigger cash withdrawals, banks may decide to hold more liquid assets. They may also do so if they anticipate that their liquid assets may soon be squeezed by government monetary policy.

On the other hand, there may be an upsurge in consumer demand for credit. Banks may be very keen to grant additional loans and thus make more profits, even though they have acquired no additional assets. They may simply go ahead and expand credit, and accept a lower liquidity ratio.

Customers may not want to take up the credit on offer. Banks may wish to make additional loans, but customers may not want to borrow. There may be insufficient demand. But will the banks not then lower their interest rates, thus encouraging people to borrow? Possibly, but if they lower the rate they charge to borrowers, they must also lower the rate they pay to depositors. But then depositors may switch to other institutions such as building societies.

Banks may not operate a simple liquidity ratio

The fact that banks hold a number of fairly liquid assets, such as money at call, bills of exchange and certificates of deposit, makes it difficult to identify a simple liquidity ratio. If the banks use extra cash to buy such liquid assets, can they then use these assets as the basis for creating credit? It is largely up to banks' judgements on their overall liquidity position.

Some of the extra cash may be withdrawn from the banks

If extra cash comes into the banking system, and as a result extra deposits are created, part of them may be held by the public as cash *outside* the banks. In other words, some of the extra cash leaks out of the banking system. This will result in an overall multiplier effect that is smaller than the full deposits multiplier.

What causes money supply to rise?

The money supply might rise as a consequence of the following.

Banks choose to hold a lower liquidity ratio

If banks collectively choose to hold a lower liquidity ratio, they will have surplus liquidity. The banks have tended to choose a lower liquidity ratio over time because of the increasing use of direct debits, cheques and debit-card and credit-card transactions. Surplus liquidity can be used to expand advances, which will lead to a multiplied rise in the money supply.

An important trend in recent years has been the growth in *inter-bank lending*. These wholesale loans are often short term and are thus a liquid asset to the bank making them. Short-term loans to other banks and CDs are now the two largest elements in banks' liquid assets. Being liquid, these assets may be used by a bank as the basis for expanding loans and thereby starting a chain of credit creation. But although these assets are liquid to an *individual* bank, they do not add to the liquidity of the banking system *as a whole*. Thus by using them as the basis for credit creation, the banking system is operating with a lower *overall* liquidity ratio.

An inflow of funds from abroad

Sometimes the Bank of England will choose to build up the foreign currency reserves. To do this it will buy foreign currencies on the foreign exchange market using sterling. When the recipients of this extra sterling deposit it in UK banks, or spend it on UK exports and the exporters deposit in UK banks, credit will be created on the basis of it, leading to a multiplied increase in money supply.

A public-sector deficit: a PSNCR

The public-sector net cash requirement (PSNCR) is the difference between public-sector expenditure and public-sector receipts. To meet this deficit the government has to borrow money by selling interest-bearing securities (Treasury bills and gilts). In general, the bigger the PSNCR, the greater will be the growth in the money supply. Just how the money supply will be affected, however, depends on who buys the securities.

Such securities could be sold to the Bank of England. In this case the Bank of England credits the government's account to the value of the securities it has purchased. When the government spends the money, it pays with cheques drawn on its account with the Bank of England. When the recipients of these cheques pay them into their bank accounts, the banks will present the cheques to the Bank of England and their balances at the Bank will be duly credited. These additional balances will then become the basis for credit creation. There will be a multiplied expansion of the money supply.

Similarly, if the government borrows through additional Treasury bills, and if these are purchased by the banking sector, there will be a multiplied expansion of the money supply. The reason is that, although banks' balances at the Bank of England will go down when the banks purchase the bills, they will go up again when the government spends the money. In addition, the banks will now have additional liquid assets (bills), which can be used as the basis for credit creation.

If, however, the government securities are purchased by the 'non-bank private sector' (i.e. the general public and non-bank firms), then the money supply will remain unchanged. When the public buy the bonds or bills, they will draw money from their banks. When the government spends the money, it will be redeposited in banks. There is no increase in money supply. It is just a case of existing money changing hands.

The government could attempt to minimise the boost to money supply by financing the PSNCR through the sale of bonds.

Figure 28.1

(a) The supply-of-money curve: exogenous money supply
(b) The supply-of-money curve: endogenous money supply

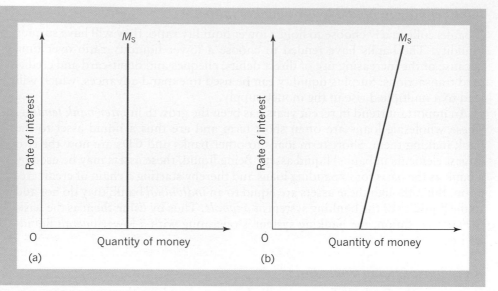

Pause for thought

Identify the various factors that could cause a fall in the money supply.

We can now summarise the components of any increase in money supply (M4). $\Delta M4 = (1)$ PSNCR less any purchases of public-sector debt by the *non*-bank private sector, plus (2) increased lending by banks, plus (3) net inflows of funds from abroad.

---

definition

Exogenous money supply
Money supply that does not depend on the demand for money but is set by the authorities (i.e. the central bank or the government).

definition

Endogenous money supply
Money supply that is determined (at least in part) by the demand for money.

The relationship between money supply and the rate of interest

Simple monetary theory often assumes that the supply of money is totally independent of interest rates. The money supply is **exogenous**. This is illustrated in Figure 28.1(a). The supply of money is assumed to be determined by the government or central bank ('the authorities'): what the authorities choose it to be, or what they allow it to be by their choice of the level and method of financing the PSNCR.

Some economists, however, argue that money supply is **endogenous**, with higher interest rates leading to increases in the supply of money. This is illustrated in Figure 28.1(b). The argument is that the supply of money is responding to the demand for money. If people start borrowing more money, the resulting shortage of money in the banks will drive up interest rates. But if banks have surplus liquidity or are prepared to operate with a lower liquidity ratio, they will create extra credit in response to the increased demand and higher interest rates: money supply has expanded.

28.4 The demand for money

The demand for money refers to the desire to *hold* money: to keep your wealth in the form of money, rather than spending it on goods and services or using it to purchase financial assets such as bonds or shares. It is usual to distinguish three reasons why people want to hold their assets in the form of money.

The transactions motive. Since money is a medium of exchange, it is required for conducting transactions. But since people only receive money at intervals (e.g. weekly or monthly) and not continuously, they require to hold balances of money in cash or in current accounts.

The precautionary motive. Unforeseen circumstances can arise, such as a car breakdown. Thus individuals often hold some additional money as a precaution. Firms too keep precautionary balances because of uncertainties about the timing of their receipts and payments. If a large customer is late in making payment, a firm may be unable to pay its suppliers unless it has spare liquidity.

The assets or speculative motive. Money is not just a medium of exchange, it is also a means of storing wealth (see page 603). Keeping some or all of your wealth as money in a bank account has the advantage of carrying no risk. It earns a relatively small, but safe rate of return. Some assets, such as company shares or bonds, may earn you more on average, but there is a chance that their price will fall. In other words, they are risky.

What determines the size of the demand for money?

What would cause the demand for money to rise? We now turn to examine the various determinants of the size of the demand for money (M_D). In particular we will look at the role of the rate of interest. First, however, let us identify the other determinants of the demand for money.

Money national income. The more money people earn, the greater will be their expenditure and hence the greater the transactions demand for money. A rise in money ('nominal') incomes in a country can be caused either by a rise in real GDP (i.e. real output) or by a rise in prices, or some combination of the two.

The frequency with which people are paid. The less frequently people are paid, the greater the level of money balances that will be required to tide them over until the next payment.

Financial innovations. The increased use of credit cards, debit cards and cash machines, plus the advent of interest-paying current accounts, have resulted in changes in the demand for money. The use of credit cards reduces both the transactions and precautionary demands. Paying once a month for goods requires less money on average than paying separately for each item purchased. Moreover, the possession of a credit card reduces or even eliminates the need to hold precautionary balances for many people. On the other hand, the increased availability of cash machines, the convenience of debit cards and the ability to earn interest on current accounts have all encouraged people to hold more money in bank accounts. The net effect has been an increase in the demand for money.

Speculation about future returns on assets. The assets motive for holding money depends on peoples' expectations. If they believe that share prices are about to fall on the stock market, they will sell shares and hold larger balances of money in the meantime. The assets demand, therefore, can be quite high when the price of securities is considered certain to fall. Some clever (or lucky)

individuals anticipated the 2000–2003 stock market decline. They sold shares and 'went liquid'.

Generally, the more risky such alternatives to money become, the more will people want to hold their assets as money balances in a bank or building society.

People also speculate about changes in the exchange rate. If businesses believe that the exchange rate is about to appreciate (rise), they will hold greater balances of domestic currency in the meantime, hoping to buy foreign currencies with them when the rate has risen (since they will then get more foreign currency for their money).

The rate of interest. In terms of the operation of money markets, this is the most important determinant. It is related to the opportunity cost of holding money. The opportunity cost is the interest forgone by not holding higher interest-bearing assets, such as shares, bills or bonds. With most bank accounts today paying interest, this opportunity cost is less than in the past and thus the demand for money for assets purposes has increased.

But what is the relationship between money demand and the rate of interest? Generally, if rates of interest rise, they will rise more on shares, bills and bonds than on bank accounts. The demand for money will thus fall. The demand for money is thus inversely related to the rate of interest.

The demand-for-money curve

Key Idea
13
p98

Pause for thought

Which way is the demand-for-money curve likely to shift in each of the following cases? (a) Prices rise, but real incomes stay the same. (b) Interest rates abroad rise relative to domestic interest rates. (c) People anticipate that share prices are likely to fall in the near future.

The demand-for-money curve with respect to interest rates is is shown in Figure 28.2. It is downward sloping, showing that lower interest rates will encourage people to hold additional money balances (mainly for speculative purposes).

A change in interest rates is shown by a movement along the demand-for-money curve. A change in any other determinant of the demand for money (such as national income or expectations about exchange rate movements) will cause the whole curve to shift: a rightward shift represents an increase in demand; a leftward shift represents a decrease.

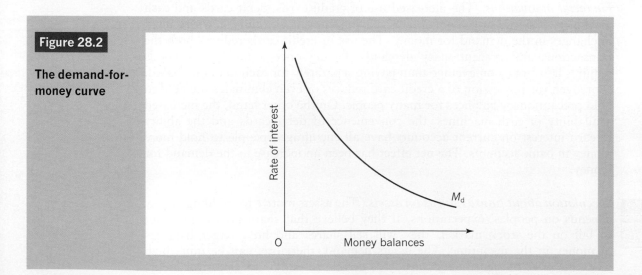

Figure 28.2

The demand-for-money curve

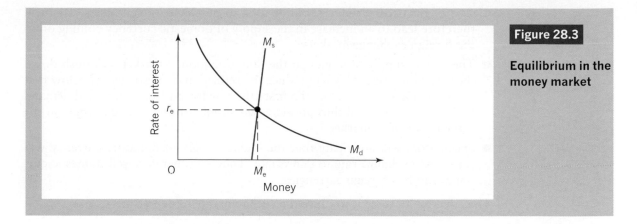

Figure 28.3

Equilibrium in the money market

Equilibrium

28.5

Equilibrium in the money market

Equilibrium in the money market occurs when the demand for money (M_d) is equal to the supply of money (M_s). This equilibrium is achieved through changes in the rate of interest.

In Figure 28.3 the equilibrium rate of interest is r_e and the equilibrium quantity of money is M_e. If the rate of interest were above r_e, people would have money balances surplus to their needs. They would use these to buy shares, bonds and other assets. This would drive up the price of these assets. But the price of assets is inversely related to interest rates. The higher the price of an asset (such as a government bond), the less will any given interest payment be as a percentage of its price (e.g. £10 as a percentage of £100 is 10 per cent, but as a percentage of £200 is only 5 per cent). Thus a higher price of assets will correspond to lower interest rates.

As the rate of interest fell, so there would be a contraction of the money supply (a movement down along the M_s curve) and an increase in the demand for money balances, especially speculative balances (a movement down along the M_d curve). The interest rate would go on falling until it reached r_e. Equilibrium would then be achieved.

Similarly, if the rate of interest were below r_e, people would have insufficient money balances. They would sell securities, thus lowering their prices and raising the rate of interest until it reached r_e.

A shift in either the M_s or the M_d curve will lead to a new equilibrium quantity of money and rate of interest at the new intersection of the curves. For example, a rise in the supply of money will cause the rate of interest to fall, whereas a rise in the demand for money will cause the rate of interest to rise.

Equilibrium in the foreign exchange market

Changes in the money supply will not only affect interest rates, they will also have an effect on exchange rates. Assume, for example, that the money supply increases. This has three direct effects:

■ *Part* of the excess balances will be used to purchase foreign assets. This will therefore lead to an increase in the supply of domestic currency coming on to the foreign exchange markets.

■ The excess supply of money in the domestic money market will push down the rate of interest. This will reduce the return on domestic assets below that on foreign assets. This, like the first effect, will lead to an increased demand for foreign assets and thus an increased supply of domestic currency on the foreign exchange market.

■ Speculators will anticipate that the higher supply of domestic currency will cause the exchange rate to depreciate. They will therefore sell domestic currency and buy foreign currencies.

The effect of all three is to cause the exchange rate to depreciate.

The full effect of changes in the money supply

The effect of changes in the money supply on interest rates and exchange rates will in turn affect the level of activity in the economy. Assume that there is a rise in UK money supply. The sequence of events is as follows:

■ A rise in money supply will lead to a fall in the rate of interest: this is necessary to restore equilibrium in the money market.

■ The fall in the rate of interest will lead to a rise in investment and other forms of borrowing. (Since borrowing money will be cheaper, investment will cost less.)

■ The fall in the domestic rate of interest and the resulting outflow of money from the country, plus the increased demand for foreign assets resulting from the increased money supply, will cause the exchange rate to depreciate.

■ The fall in the exchange rate will mean that people abroad have to pay less for a pound. This will make UK exports cheaper and hence more will be sold. People in the UK will get less foreign currency for a pound. This will make imports more expensive and hence less will be purchased.

Pause for thought

What determines the amount that real output rises as a result of a rise in the money supply?

■ The rise in investment and exports will mean increased injections into the circular flow of income (see section 26.6), and the fall in imports will mean reduced withdrawals from it. The effect will be a rise in aggregate demand and a resulting rise in national income and output, and possibly a rise in inflation too.

Just how much will aggregate demand, national income and inflation change as a result of changes in the money supply? We will examine this in the next chapter. Then in Chapter 30 we will examine how the government can attempt to *control* the level of aggregate demand: both by changing the money supply and interest rates ('monetary policy') and by changing taxation and/or government expenditure ('fiscal policy').

SUMMARY

1 Money's main function is as a medium of exchange. In addition it is a means of storing wealth, a means of evaluation and a means of establishing the value of future claims and payments.

2a Banks aim to make profits, but they must also maintain sufficient liquidity. Liquid assets, however, tend to be unprofitable and profitable assets tend to be illiquid. Banks therefore hold a range of assets of varying degrees of profitability and liquidity.

2b Banks' liabilities include both sight and time deposits. They also include certificates of deposit and repos. Their assets include in descending order of liquidity: notes and coin, balances with the Bank of England, market loans, bills of exchange, investments (government bonds and inter-bank investments) and advances to customers (the biggest item, including overdrafts, personal loans and mortgages).

2c The Bank of England is the UK's central bank. It issues notes; it acts as banker to the government, to the banks, to various overseas central banks and to certain private customers; it manages the government's borrowing programme; it provides liquidity to the banking sector; it operates the country's monetary and exchange rate policy.

2d The money market is the market in short-term deposits and loans. It consists of the discount and repo markets and the parallel money markets. The Bank of England operates in the discount and repo markets. By buying (rediscounting) bills and through gilt repos, it provides liquidity to the banks at its chosen rate of interest.

2e The parallel money markets consist of various markets in short-term finance between various financial institutions.

3a Money supply can be defined in a number of different ways, depending on what items are included. A useful distinction is between narrow money and broad money. Narrow money includes just cash, and possibly banks' balances at the central bank. Broad money also includes deposits in banks and possibly various other short-term deposits in the money market. In the UK, M4 is the preferred measure of broad money. In the eurozone it is M3.

3b Bank deposits are a major proportion of money supply (except M0). The expansion of bank deposits is the major element in the expansion of the money supply.

3c Bank deposits expand through a process of credit creation. If banks' liquid assets increase, they can be used as a base for increasing loans. When the loans are redeposited in banks, they form the base for yet more loans, and thus takes place a process of multiple credit expansion. The ratio of the increase of deposits to an expansion of banks' liquidity base is called the 'bank multiplier'. It is the inverse of the liquidity ratio.

3d In practice it is difficult to predict the precise amount by which money supply will expand if there is an increase in cash. The reasons are that banks may choose to hold a different liquidity ratio; customers may not take up all the credit on offer; there may be no simple liquidity ratio given the range of near money assets; and some of the extra cash may leak away into extra cash holdings by the public.

3e Money supply will rise if (a) banks choose to hold a lower liquidity ratio and thus create more credit for an existing amount of liquidity; (b) there is a total currency flow surplus; (c) the government runs a PSNCR and finances it by borrowing from the banking sector or from abroad.

3f Simple monetary theory assumes that the supply of money is independent of interest rates. In practice, a rise in interest rates will often lead to an increase in money supply. But conversely if the government raises interest rates, the supply of money may fall in response to a lower demand for money.

4a The three motives for holding money are the transactions, precautionary and assets (or speculative) motives.

4b The demand for money will be higher, (a) the higher the level of money national income (i.e. the higher the level of real national income and the higher the price level), (b) the less frequently people are paid, (c) the greater the advantages of holding money in bank accounts, such as access to cash machines and the use of debit cards, (d) the more risky alternative assets become and the more likely they are to fall in value, and the more likely the exchange rate is to rise, and (e) the lower the opportunity cost of holding money in terms of interest forgone on alternative assets.

4c The demand for money curve with respect to interest rates is downward sloping.

5 Equilibrium in the money market is where the supply of money is equal to the demand. Equilibrium is achieved through changes in the interest rate and the exchange rate.

REVIEW QUESTIONS

1 Imagine that the banking system receives additional deposits of £100 million and that all the individual banks wish to retain their current liquidity ratio of 20 per cent.

   (a) How much will banks choose to lend out initially?
   (b) What will happen to banks' liabilities when the money that is lent out is spent and the recipients of it deposit it in their bank accounts?
   (c) How much of these latest deposits will be lent out by the banks?
   (d) By how much will total deposits (liabilities) eventually have risen, assuming that none of the additional liquidity is held outside the banking sector?
   (e) How much of these are matched by (i) liquid assets; (ii) illiquid assets?
   (f) What is the size of the bank multiplier?
   (g) If one half of any additional liquidity is held outside the banking sector, by how much less will deposits have risen compared with (d) above?

2 What is meant by the terms *narrow money* and *broad money*? Does broad money fulfil all the functions of money?

3 Why do banks hold a range of assets of varying degrees of liquidity and profitability?

4 Define the term 'liquidity ratio'. How will changes in the liquidity ratio affect the process of credit creation? Why might a bank's liquidity ratio vary over time?

5 Why might the relationship between the demand for money and the rate of interest be an unstable one?

6 What effects will the following have on the equilibrium rate of interest? (You should consider which way the demand and/or supply curves of money shift.)

   (a) Banks find that they have a higher liquidity ratio than they need.
   (b) A rise in incomes.
   (c) A growing belief that interest rates will rise from their current level.

29 Business activity, employment and inflation

In this chapter we examine what determines the level of business activity and why it fluctuates. We also look at the effects of business activity on employment and inflation.

We start, in section 29.1, by looking at the determinants of GDP and, in particular, the role of aggregate demand. After all, the higher the level of aggregate demand, the more will business produce in response to that demand.

In the first section we ignore the role of money and interest rates. In section 29.2, however, we show that changes in money and interest rates can have important, but possibly uncertain, effects on aggregate demand and business activity.

In section 29.3, we turn to the problems of unemployment and inflation and the relationship between the two. An important influence on both of them is what people *expect* to happen. Generally, if people are optimistic and believe that the economy will grow and unemployment will fall, this will happen. Similarly, if people expect inflation to stay low, it will do. In other words, people's expectations tend to be self-fulfilling.

We then examine, in section 29.4, why GDP and business activity fluctuate. In other words, we examine possible causes of the business cycle.

Finally, in section 29.5 we summarise some of the key points of the chapter.

29.1 The determination of business activity

How much will business as a whole produce? How many people will be employed? The analysis of output and employment, at least in the short run (one or two years), can be explained most simply in terms of the circular flow of income diagram. Figure 29.1 shows a simplified version of the circular flow with injections entering at just one point, and likewise withdrawals leaving at just one point (this simplification does not affect the argument).

If injections (J) do not equal withdrawals (W), a state of disequilibrium exists. What will bring them back into equilibrium is a change in national income (GDP) and employment.

Start with a state of equilibrium, where injections equal withdrawals. If there is now a rise in injections – say, firms decide to invest more – aggregate demand ($C_d + J$) will be higher. Firms will respond to this increased demand by using more labour and other resources and thus paying out more incomes (Y) to households. Household consumption will rise and so firms will sell more.

Figure 29.1

The circular flow of income

$$J = I + G + X$$

$$C_d$$

$$W = S + T + M$$

Firms will respond by producing more, and thus using more labour and other resources. Household incomes will rise again. Consumption and hence production will rise again, and so on. There will thus be a multiplied rise in incomes and employment. This is known as the **multiplier effect**.

The principle of cumulative causation. An initial event can cause an ultimate effect which is much larger.

Key Idea 36

The process, however, does not go on for ever. Each time household incomes rise, households save more, pay more taxes and buy more imports. In other words, withdrawals rise. When withdrawals have risen to match the increase in injections, equilibrium will be restored and national income (GDP) and employment will stop rising. The process can be summarised as follows:

$$J > W \rightarrow Y\uparrow \rightarrow W\uparrow \text{ until } J = W$$

Similarly, an initial fall in injections (or rise in withdrawals) will lead to a multiplied fall in GDP and employment:

$$J < W \rightarrow Y\downarrow \rightarrow W\downarrow \text{ until } J = W$$

Thus equilibrium in the circular flow of income can be at *any* level of GDP and employment.

Key Idea 10 p73

Identifying the equilibrium level of GDP

Equilibrium can be shown on a 'Keynesian 45° line diagram'. This is named after the great economist, John Maynard Keynes (1883–1946). Keynes argued that GDP is determined by aggregate demand. A rise in aggregate demand will cause GDP to rise; a fall in aggregate demand will cause GDP to fall.

Equilibrium GDP can be at any level of capacity. If aggregate demand is buoyant, equilibrium GDP can be where businesses are operating at full capacity with full employment. If aggregate demand is low, however, equilibrium GDP can be at well below full capacity with high unemployment (i.e. a recession). Keynes

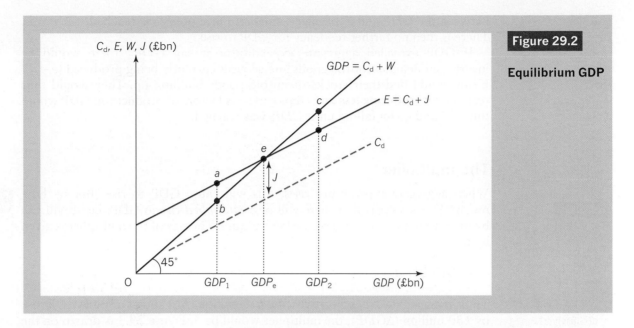

Figure 29.2

Equilibrium GDP

argued that it is important, therefore, for governments to manage the level of aggregate demand to avoid recessions.

The 45° line diagram plots various elements of the circular flow of income, such as consumption, withdrawals, injections and aggregate demand, against GDP (national income).

In Figure 29.2 two continuous lines are shown. The 45° line out from the origin plots $C_d + W$ against GDP. It is a 45° line because by definition GDP = C_d + W. To understand this, consider what can happen to the income earned from GDP: either it must be spent on domestically produced goods (C_d) or it must be withdrawn from the circular flow – there is nothing else that can happen to it. Thus if GDP were £100 billion, then $C_d + W$ must also be £100 billion. If you draw a line such that whatever value is plotted on the horizontal axis (GDP) is also plotted on the vertical axis ($C_d + W$), the line will be at 45° (assuming that the axes are drawn to the same scale).

The other continuous line plots aggregate demand. In this diagram it is known as the *aggregate expenditure line* (E). It consists of $C_d + J$: in other words, the total spending on domestic firms.

To show how this line is constructed, consider the dashed line. This shows C_d. It is flatter than the 45° line. The reason is that for any given rise in GDP and hence people's incomes, only *part* will be spent on domestic product, while the remainder will be withdrawn: i.e. C_d rises less quickly than GDP. The E line consists of $C_d + J$. But we have assumed that J is constant with respect to changes in GDP. Thus the E line is simply the C_d line shifted upward by the amount of J.

If aggregate expenditure exceeded GDP, at say GDP_1, there would be excess demand in the economy (of $a - b$). In other words, people would be buying more than was currently being produced. Firms would thus find their stocks dwindling and would therefore increase their level of production. In doing so, they would employ more factors of production. GDP would thus rise. As it did so, C_d and hence E would rise. There would be a movement up along the E line. But because not all the extra incomes earned from the rise in GDP would be consumed (i.e. some would be withdrawn), expenditure would rise less quickly than income: the E line is flatter than the *GDP* line. As income rises towards GDP_e, the gap between the *GDP* and *E* lines gets smaller. Once point *e* is reached, *GDP* = *E*. There is then no further tendency for GDP to rise.

If GDP exceeded aggregate expenditure, at say GDP_2, there would be insufficient demand for the goods and services currently being produced (*c* – *d*). Firms would find their stocks of unsold goods building up. They would thus respond by producing less and employing less factors of production. GDP would thus fall and go on falling until GDP_e was reached.

The multiplier

When aggregate expenditure rises, this will cause GDP to rise. But by how much? The answer is that there will be a *multiplied* rise in GDP: i.e. it will rise by more than the rise in aggregate expenditure. The size of the **multiplier** is given by the letter *k*, where:

$$k = \Delta GDP / \Delta E$$

Thus, if aggregate expenditure rose by £10 million (ΔE) and as a result GDP rose by £30 million (ΔGDP), the multiplier would be 3. Figure 29.3 is drawn on the assumption that the multiplier is 3.

Assume in Figure 29.3 that aggregate expenditure rises by £20 billion, from E_1 to E_2. This could be caused by a rise in injections, or by a fall in withdrawals (and hence a rise in consumption of domestically produced goods) or by some combination of the two. Equilibrium GDP rises by £60 billion, from £100 billion to £160 billion (where the E_2 line crosses the *GDP* line).

What determines the size of the multiplier? The answer is that it depends on the 'marginal propensity to consume domestically produced goods' (mpc_d). The mpc_d is the proportion of any rise in GDP that gets spent on domestically produced goods (in other words the proportion that is not withdrawn).

$$mpc_d = \Delta C_d / \Delta GDP$$

definition

The multiplier
The number of times a rise in GDP (ΔGDP) is bigger than the initial rise in aggregate expenditure (ΔE) that caused it. Using the letter *k* to stand for the multiplier, the multiplier is defined as

$$k = \Delta GDP / \Delta E$$

Figure 29.3

The multiplier: a rise in aggregate expenditure

In Figure 29.3, $mpc_d = \Delta C_d / \Delta GDP = £40bn/£60bn = {}^2/_3$ (i.e. the slope of the C_d line). The higher the mpc_d the greater the proportion of income generated from GDP that re-circulates around the circular flow of income and thus generates extra output.

Pause for thought

Think of two reasons why a country might have a steep E line, and hence a high value for the multiplier.

The **multiplier formula** is given by:

$$k = \frac{1}{1 - mpc_d}$$

definition

Multiplier formula
The formula for the multiplier is $k = 1/(1 - mpc_d)$.

In our example, with $mpc_d = {}^2/_3$

$$k = \frac{1}{1 - {}^2/_3} = \frac{1}{{}^1/_3} = 3$$

If the mpc_d were ${}^3/_4$, the multiplier would be 4. Thus the higher the mpc_d, the higher the multiplier.

The relationship between money and GDP   29.2

In this section we examine how changes in the money supply affect GDP. One of the simplest ways of understanding this relationship is in terms of the 'equation of exchange'.

The equation of exchange

The **equation of exchange** shows the relationship between money, aggregate demand and GDP. This identity may be expressed as follows:

$$MV = PY$$

definition

The equation of exchange
$MV = PQ$. The total level of spending on GDP (MV) equals the total value of goods and services produced (PQ) that go to make up GDP.

M is the supply of money in the economy. V is its **velocity of circulation**. This is the average number of times per year that money is spent on buying goods and services that have been produced in the economy that year (GDP). P is the level of prices, expressed as an index, where the index is 1 in a chosen base year (e.g. 1990). Thus if prices today are double those in the base year, P would be 2. Y is *real* national income (real GDP): in other words, the quantity of national output produced in that year measured in base-year prices.

Key Idea
34
p561

definition

Velocity of circulation
The number of times annually that money on average is spent on goods and services that make up GDP.

PY is thus *nominal* national income: i.e. GDP measured at current prices. For example, if GDP at base-year prices is £40 billion and the price index is 2, then GDP at current prices is £80 billion.

MV is the total spending on national output. For example, if money supply is £20 billion, and money, as it passes from one person to another, is spent on average four times a year on national output, then total spending (MV) would be £80 billion a year. But this too *must* equal GDP at current prices. The reason is that what is spent on output (by consumers, by firms on investment, by the government or by people abroad on exports) must equal the value of goods produced (PY).

The equation of exchange (or 'quantity equation') is true by definition. MV is *necessarily* equal to PY because of the way the terms are defined.

But what does a change in money supply (M) do to the individual terms within the equation? For example, what effect does a rise in money supply have on prices (P) and on real GDP (Y)?

In the extreme case we could assume that V and Y are not affected at all by changes in money supply. In this case any change in money supply will be entirely reflected in changes in P. This is the prediction of one of the oldest theories in economics: the **quantity theory of money**. This theory dates back to Roman times and states that increases in the supply of money will simply lead to higher prices. An implication of this theory is that if you want to control inflation, it is important to control the money supply. This was the central argument of a group of economists called 'monetarists' whose views were very influential in the 1970s and 1980s when inflation throughout much of the world was very high.

Returning to the quantity equation, the effect of money supply on prices will depend on what happens to V and Y. Let us examine each in turn.

The velocity of circulation (V)

In the short run V tends to vary inversely with M (as one rises, the other falls). An increase in money supply will not necessarily have much effect on spending; instead, people may simply increase their holdings of money balances as the means of holding some of their assets (i.e. for speculative purposes), with a corresponding decline in the speed with which money circulates (V). How much of these extra speculative balances people hold will depend on their expectations of changes in interest rates, prices and exchange rates. Since expectations are difficult to predict, the amount by which V will fall is also difficult to predict:

$$M\uparrow \rightarrow V\downarrow (?) \rightarrow MV?$$

It is thus likely that control of the money supply will be an unreliable means of controlling aggregate demand – at least in the short run. A good example of this is what happened in Japan for much of the period since the early 1990s. Japan has been stuck in a prolonged recession. In an attempt to boost consumer spending and thus stimulate firms to produce more, the Bank of Japan has increased money supply on a number of occasions. But Japanese consumers have been unwilling to increase their expenditure, preferring instead to hold on to the extra money, particularly since prices have been falling and waiting, therefore, will mean that people can buy goods cheaper later.

Real GDP (Y)

Many economists argue that aggregate supply (GDP) is relatively responsive in the short run to increases in aggregate demand, provided there is slack in the economy. Similarly, reductions in aggregate demand are likely to lead to reductions in GDP. Many also argue, however, that aggregate supply is inelastic in the long run. They see GDP being determined largely or wholly independently of aggregate demand. In the long run, therefore, any rise in MV will be mainly or totally reflected in a rise in prices (P).

In the long run, according to this view, the stock of money therefore determines the price level, and the rate of increase in money supply determines the rate of inflation. It is thus important to ensure that money supply is kept under control if inflation is to be avoided.

We examine monetary policy in section 30.3.

Monetary transmission mechanisms

The short run

As we saw in the last chapter, changes in money supply affect aggregate demand through the following mechanism:

1 A rise in money supply will lead to a fall in the rate of interest.

2 (a) The fall in the rate of interest will lead to a rise in investment and other forms of borrowing.

   (b) The fall in the domestic rate of interest and the resulting outflow of money from the country, plus the increased demand for foreign assets resulting from the increased money supply, will cause the exchange rate to depreciate.

3 The fall in the exchange rate will cause an increased demand for exports and a decreased demand for imports.

4 The rise in investment and exports, and the fall in imports will mean a rise in aggregate demand and a resulting rise in GDP and output, and possibly a rise in inflation too.

However, stages 1–3 are unreliable, and often weak.

Problems with stage 1: the money–interest link

The demand for money for assets purposes can be large and highly responsive to interest rates (relative to those on alternative assets). Indeed large sums of money move around the money market as firms and financial institutions respond to and anticipate changes in interest rates. Thus, with an increase in money supply, only a relatively *small* fall in interest rates on bonds and other assets may be necessary to persuade people to hold all the extra money in bank accounts, thereby greatly slowing down the average speed at which money circulates. The fall in V may virtually offset the rise in M.

A more serious criticism is that the demand for money is *unstable*. People hold speculative balances of money when they anticipate that the prices of other assets, such as shares, bonds and bills will fall (and hence the rate of return or interest on these assets will rise). Many factors could affect such expectations, such as changes in foreign interest rates, changes in exchange rates, statements of government intentions on economic policy, good or bad industrial news, or newly published figures on inflation or money supply. With an unstable demand for money it is difficult to predict the effect on interest rates of a change in money supply.

Problems with stage 2(a): the interest rate–investment link

The problem here is that investment may be insensitive to changes in interest rates. Businesses are more likely to be influenced in their decision to invest by predictions of the future buoyancy of markets. Interest rates do have some effect on businesses, investment decisions, but the effect is unpredictable, depending on the confidence of investors. Where interest rates are likely to have a stronger effect on spending is via mortgages. If interest rates go up, and mortgage rates follow suit, people will suddenly be faced with higher monthly repayments and will therefore have to cut down their expenditure on goods and services.

Problems with stage 2(b): the interest rate–exchange rate link

Just how much people will switch out of the domestic currency depends on *how much* they think the exchange rate will depreciate. The effect may be quite strong, especially given the large amount of speculative money ('hot money') moving from country to country. But these expectations are highly unpredictable, and thus the effect on exchange rates is likely to be unpredictable too.

Problems with stage 3: the exchange rate–trade link

Given time, the demand by consumers abroad for UK exports and demand in the UK for imports may be quite elastic. In the short run, however, the effect may be rather limited. But here again, the size of the effect is uncertain and *could* be quite large. It depends on people's expectations of exchange rate movements. If people think that the exchange rate will fall further, importers will buy *now* before the rate does fall and they have to pay more for the imports. Exporters, on the other hand, will hold back as long as possible before shipping their exports: if the rate does fall, they will earn more sterling per dollar's worth of exports. These actions will tend to push the exchange rate down. But such speculation is very difficult to predict as it depends on often highly volatile expectations.

To summarise: the effects of a change in the money supply *might* be quite strong, but their precise magnitude is usually highly unpredictable.

The long run

In the long run, there will be a stronger link between money supply and aggregate demand. If money supply increases over the longer term, people will have more money than they require to hold. They will spend this surplus. Much of this spending will go on goods and services, thereby directly increasing aggregate demand.

The theoretical underpinning for this is given by the *theory of portfolio balance*. People have a number of ways of holding their wealth. They can hold it as money, or as financial assets such as bills, bonds or shares, or as physical assets such as houses, cars and televisions. In other words, people hold a whole portfolio of assets of varying degrees of liquidity – from cash to central heating.

If money supply expands, people will find themselves holding more money than they require: their portfolios are unnecessarily liquid. Some of this money will be used to purchase financial assets and some, possibly after a period of time, to purchase *goods and services*. As more assets are purchased, this will drive up their price. This will effectively reduce their 'yield'. For bonds and other *financial* assets, this means a reduction in their rate of interest. For goods and services, this means a reduction in their marginal utility/price ratio: a higher level of consumption will reduce their marginal utility and drive up their price. The process will stop when a balance has been restored in people's portfolios. In the meantime, there will have been extra consumption and hence an increase in aggregate demand.

29.3 Unemployment and inflation

We turn now to examine the relationship between aggregate demand and both inflation and unemployment. You might find it useful first to revise sections 26.3 to 26.5.

Unemployment and inflation in the simple Keynesian model

'Full-employment' GDP

In the simple 'Keynesian' theory that we outlined in section 29.1, it is assumed that there is a maximum level of GDP that can be obtained at any one time. If equilibrium GDP is at this level, there will be no deficiency of aggregate demand and hence no disequilibrium unemployment. This level of GDP is referred to as the **full-employment level of GDP** (GDP_F). (In practice, there would still be some unemployment at this level because of the existence of equilibrium unemployment – structural, frictional and seasonal.)

The deflationary gap

If the equilibrium level of GDP (GDP_e) is below the full-employment level (GDP_F), there will be excess capacity in the economy and hence demand-deficient unemployment. This situation is illustrated in Figure 29.4(a). If GDP is to be raised from GDP_e to GDP_F, aggregate expenditure (E) will have to be raised, either by increasing injections or by reducing withdrawals, so as to close the gap $a - b$. This gap is known as the **deflationary gap**.

Note that the size of the deflationary gap is *less* than the amount by which GDP_e falls short of GDP_F. This is another illustration of the multiplier. If aggregate expenditure is raised by $a - b$, GDP will rise by $GDP_F - GDP_e$. The multiplier is thus given by:

$$\frac{GDP_F - GDP_e}{a - b}$$

The inflationary gap

If, at the full-employment level of GDP, aggregate expenditure *exceeds* GDP, there will be a problem of excess demand. GDP_e will be above GDP_F. The problem is that GDP_F represents a real ceiling to output. In the short run, GDP *cannot* expand beyond this point. GDP_e cannot be reached. The result will be demand-pull inflation.

This situation is illustrated in Figure 29.4(b). If aggregate expenditure is reduced (by reducing injections or raising withdrawals) so as to close the gap $c - d$ (known as the **inflationary gap**), then the excess demand will be eliminated, and GDP_e will equal GDP_F. This can be done by a deliberate government policy of deflation. This could be either a deflationary *fiscal* policy of lowering government expenditure or raising taxes, or a deflationary *monetary* policy of reducing the amount of money in the economy and/or deliberately raising interest rates.

> **definition**
> **Full-employment level of GDP**
> The level of GDP at which there is no deficiency of demand.

> **definition**
> **Deflationary gap**
> The shortfall of aggregate expenditure below GDP at the full-employment level of GDP.

> **definition**
> **Inflationary gap**
> The excess of aggregate expenditure over GDP at the full-employment level of GDP.

> **Pause for thought**
>
> Assume that full-employment GDP is £500 billion and that current GDP is £450 billion. Assume also that the mpc_d is ⁴/₅. (a) Is there an inflationary or deflationary gap? (b) What is the size of this gap?

Many economists thus advocate an active policy of 'demand management': raising aggregate demand (for example, by raising government expenditure or lowering taxes) to close a deflationary gap, and reducing aggregate demand to close an inflationary gap. We explore these 'demand-side' policies in the next chapter).

Unemployment and inflation at the same time

The simple analysis of deflationary and inflationary gaps implies that the aggregate supply curve looks like AS_1 in Figure 29.5. (See pages 563–5 to remind

Figure 29.4

(a) Deflationary gap
(b) Inflationary gap

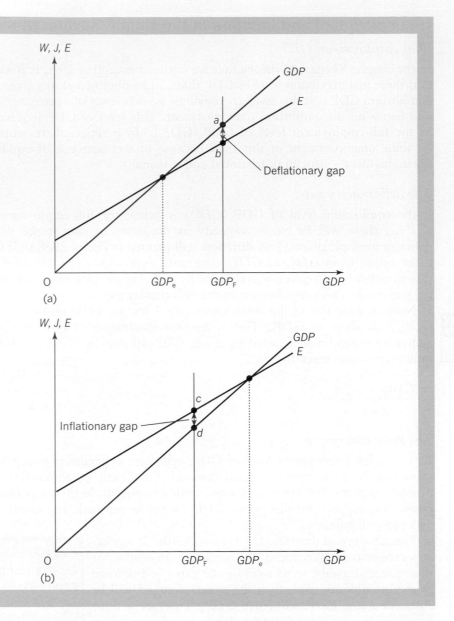

(a)

(b)

Figure 29.5

Unemployment and inflation

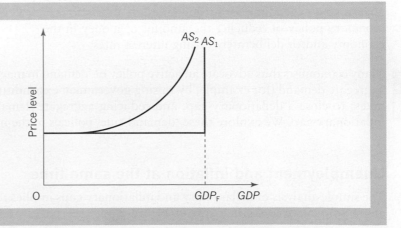

yourself about aggregate demand and supply analysis.) Up to GDP_F, output and employment can rise with no rise in prices at all. The deflationary gap is being closed. At GDP_F no further rises in output are possible. Any further rise in aggregate demand is entirely reflected in higher prices. An inflationary gap opens. In other words, this implies that either inflation *or* unemployment can occur, but not both simultaneously.

We can make two important qualifications to this analysis to explain the occurrence of both unemployment *and* inflation at the same time.

First, there are *other* types of inflation and unemployment not caused by an excess or deficiency of aggregate demand: for example, cost-push and expectations-generated inflation; frictional and structural unemployment.

Thus, even if a government could manipulate GDP so as to get GDP_e and GDP_F to coincide, this would not eliminate all inflation and unemployment – only demand-pull inflation and demand-deficient unemployment. For this reason governments may choose to use a whole package of policies, each tailored to the specific type of problem.

Second, not all firms operate with the same degree of slack. This may be due to different policies of firms over how much spare capacity to maintain and how many stocks to carry. It may be due to shifts in consumer demand away from some firms and towards others.

The implication of this is that a rise in aggregate demand can lead to *both* a reduction in unemployment *and* a rise in prices: some firms respond to the rise in demand by taking up slack and hence increasing output; other firms, having little or no slack, respond by raising prices; others do both. Similarly, labour markets have different degrees of slack and therefore the rise in demand will lead to various mixes of higher wages and lower unemployment.

Thus the AS curve will look like AS_2 in Figure 29.5.

The Phillips curve

The relationship between inflation and unemployment was examined by A. W. Phillips in 1958. He showed the statistical relationship between wage inflation and unemployment in the UK from 1861 to 1957. With wage inflation ($\dot{W}$) on the vertical axis and the unemployment rate (U) on the horizontal axis, a scatter of points was obtained. Each point represented the observation for a particular year. The curve that best fitted the scatter has become known as the **Phillips curve**. It is illustrated in Figure 29.6 and shows an inverse relationship between inflation and unemployment.

Given that wage increases over the period were approximately 2 per cent above price increases (made possible by increases in labour productivity), a similar-shaped, but lower curve could be plotted showing the relationship between *price* inflation and unemployment.

The curve was often used to illustrate the effects of changes in aggregate demand. When aggregate demand rose (relative to potential output), inflation rose and unemployment fell: there was an upward movement along the curve. When aggregate demand fell, there was a downward movement along the curve.

The Phillips curve was bowed in to the origin. The usual explanation for this is that as aggregate demand expanded, at first there would be plenty of surplus labour, which could be employed to meet the extra demand without the need to raise wage rates very much. But as labour became increasingly scarce, firms would find that they had to offer increasingly higher wage rates to obtain the

definition

Phillips curve
A curve showing the relationship between (price) inflation and unemployment. The original Phillips curve plotted *wage* inflation against unemployment for the years 1861–1957.

Figure 29.6

The Phillips curve

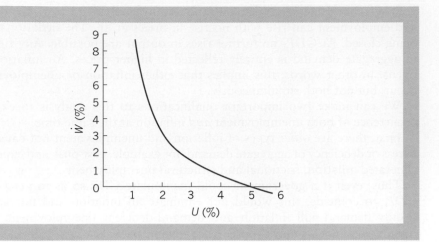

labour they required, and the position of trade unions would be increasingly strengthened.

The *position* of the Phillips curve depended on *non*-demand factors causing inflation and unemployment: frictional and structural unemployment; and cost-push, structural and expectations-generated inflation. If any of these non-demand factors changed so as to raise inflation or unemployment, the curve would shift outward to the right. The relative stability of the curve, over the 100 years or so observed by Phillips, suggested that these non-demand factors had changed little.

The Phillips curve seemed to present governments with a simple policy choice. They could trade off inflation against unemployment. Lower unemployment could be bought at the cost of higher inflation, and vice versa. Unfortunately, the experience since the late 1960s has suggested that no such simple relationship exists beyond the short run. Both inflation and unemployment were generally worse in the 1970s, 1980s and early to mid-1990s than in the 1950s and 1960s, but have both improved in recent years. What is more, with central banks around the world making the targeting of a particular rate of inflation their number one priority, inflation seems to have become largely de-coupled from unemployment. (We explore inflation targeting in the next chapter.)

Key Idea
35
p568

To explain this apparent breakdown of the Phillips curve, various theories of inflation and unemployment were developed in the 1960s and 1970s that incorporated expectations into the analysis. What was developed was an 'expectations-augmented' version of the Phillips curve.

The effect of expectations

definition

Expectations-augmented Phillips curve
A (short-run) Phillips curve whose position depends on the expected rate of inflation.

In its simplest form, the **expectations-augmented Phillips curve** is given by the following:

Key Idea
12
p94

$$\dot{P} = f(1/U) + \dot{P}^{\text{e}}$$

What this states is that inflation ($\dot{P}$) depends on two things:

■ The inverse of unemployment ($1/U$). This is simply the normal Phillips curve relationship. The higher the rate of (demand-deficient) unemployment, the lower the rate of inflation.

■ The expected rate of inflation ($\dot{P}^e$). The higher the rate of inflation that people expect, the higher will be the level of wage demands and the more willing will firms be to raise prices. Thus the higher will be the actual rate of inflation and thus the vertically higher will be the whole Phillips curve.

Let us assume for simplicity that the rate of inflation people expect this year ($\dot{P}^e_t$) (where t represents the current time period: i.e. this year) is the same rate that inflation actually was last year ($\dot{P}_{t-1}$).

$$\dot{P}^e_t = \dot{P}_{t-1}$$

Thus if unemployment is such as to push up prices by 4 per cent ($f(1/U) = 4\%$) and if last year's inflation was 6 per cent, then inflation this year will be 4 per cent + 6 per cent = 10 per cent.

The accelerationist theory of inflation

Let us trace the course of inflation and expectations over a number of years in an imaginary economy. To keep the analysis simple, assume there is no growth in the economy.

Year 1. Assume that at the outset, in year 1, there is no inflation at all; that none is expected; that $AD = AS$; and that equilibrium unemployment is 8 per cent. The economy will be at point *a* in Figure 29.7 and Table 29.1.

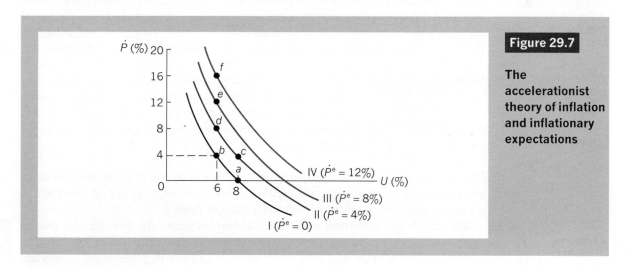

Figure 29.7

The accelerationist theory of inflation and inflationary expectations

Table 29.1 The accelerationist theory of inflation and inflationary expectations

Year	Point on graph	$\dot{P}$	=	$f(1/U)$	+	$\dot{P}^e$
1	a	0	=	0	+	0
2	b	4	=	4	+	0
3	c	4	=	0	+	4
4	d	8	=	4	+	4
5	e	12	=	4	+	8
6	f	16	=	4	+	12

Year 2. Now assume that the government expands aggregate demand in order to reduce unemployment. Unemployment falls to 6 per cent. The economy moves to point *b* along curve I. Inflation has risen to 4 per cent, but people, basing their expectations of inflation on year 1, still expect zero inflation. There is therefore no shift as yet in the Phillips curve. Curve I corresponds to an expected rate of inflation of zero.

Year 3. People now revise their expectations of inflation to the level of year 2. The Phillips curve shifts up by 4 percentage points to position II. If nominal aggregate demand (i.e. demand purely in money terms, irrespective of the level of prices) continues to rise at the same rate, the whole of the increase will now be absorbed in higher prices. *Real* aggregate demand will fall back to its previous level and the economy will move to point *c*. Unemployment will return to 8 per cent. There is no *demand-pull* inflation now, ($f(1/U) = 0$), but inflation is still 4 per cent due to expectations, ($\dot{P}^e = 4\%$).

Year 4. Assume now that the government expands *real* aggregate demand again so as to reduce unemployment once more to 6 per cent. This time it must expand nominal aggregate demand *more* than it did in year 2, because this time, as well as reducing unemployment, it also has to validate the 4 per cent expected inflation. The economy moves to point *d* along curve II. Inflation is now 8 per cent.

Year 5. Expected inflation is now 8 per cent (the level of actual inflation in year 4). The Phillips curve shifts up to position III. If at the same time the government tries to keep unemployment at 6 per cent, it must expand nominal aggregate demand 4 per cent faster in order to validate the 8 per cent expected inflation. The economy moves to point *e* along curve III. Inflation is now 12 per cent.

Year 6. To keep unemployment at 6 per cent, the government must continue to increase nominal aggregate demand by 4 per cent more than the previous year. As the expected inflation rate goes on rising, the Phillips curve will go on shifting up each year.

Thus in order to keep unemployment below the initial equilibrium rate, inflation must go on *accelerating* each year. For this reason, this theory of the Phillips curve is sometimes known as the **accelerationist theory**.

The more the government reduces unemployment, the greater the rise in inflation that year, and the more the rise in expectations the following year and each subsequent year; and hence the more rapidly will price rises accelerate. Thus the true longer-term trade-off is between unemployment and the rate of increase in inflation.

The long-run Phillips curve and the natural rate of unemployment

As long as there are demand-pull pressures ($f(1/U) > 0$), inflation will accelerate as the expected rate of inflation ($\dot{P}^e$) rises. In the long run, therefore, the Phillips curve will be vertical at the rate of unemployment where *real* aggregate demand equals *real* aggregate supply. This is the *equilibrium* rate of unemployment. It is also known as the **natural rate** or the **non-accelerating-inflation rate of unemployment (NAIRU)**. In Figure 29.7 the equilibrium rate of unemployment is 8 per cent.

The implication for government policy is that expansionary monetary and fiscal policy can only reduce unemployment below the equilibrium rate in the

BOX 29.1

The political business cycle
The art of looping the loop

Imagine that a politically naïve government has been fulfilling election promises to cure unemployment, cut taxes and increase welfare spending. In the figure this is shown by a move from points *a* to *b* to *c*.

To its dismay, by the time the next election comes, inflation is accelerating and unemployment is rising again. The economy is moving from point *d* to *e* to *f*. You would hardly be surprised to learn that it loses the election!

But now suppose a much more politically adroit government is elected. What does it do? The answer is that it does politically unpopular things at first, so that before the next election it can do nice things and curry favour with the electorate.

The first thing it does is to have a tough Budget and to raise interest rates. 'We are having to clear up the economic mess left by the last government.' It thus engineers a recession and begins to squeeze down inflationary expectations. The economy moves from point *f* to *g* to *h*.

But people have very short memories (despite opposition attempts to remind them). After a couple of years of misery, the government announces that the economy has 'begun to turn the corner'. Things are looking up. Inflation has fallen and unemployment has stopped rising. The economy has moved from point *h* to *i* to *j*.

'Thanks to prudent management of the economy', claims the Chancellor, 'I am now in a position to reduce taxes and to allow modest increases in government expenditure.' Unemployment falls rapidly; the economy grows rapidly; the economy moves from point *j* to *a* to *b*.

Clockwise Phillips loops

The government's popularity soars; the pre-election 'give-away' Budget is swallowed by the electorate who trustingly believe that similar ones will follow if the government is returned to office. The government wins the election

Then comes the nasty medicine again. But who will be blamed this time?

Questions

1 *Why might a government sometimes 'get it wrong' and find itself at the wrong part of the Phillips loop at the time of an election?*

2 *Which electoral system would most favour a government being re-elected: the US fixed-term system with presidents being elected every four years, or the UK system where the government can choose to hold an election any time within five years of the last one?*

short run. In the long run, the effect will be purely inflationary. On the other hand, a policy of restraining the growth in the money supply will *not* in the long run lead to higher unemployment: it will simply lead to lower inflation at the equilibrium rate of unemployment. The implication is that governments should make it a priority to control money supply and thereby nominal aggregate demand and inflation.

Rational expectations

One group, known as 'New classical' economists, go further than the theory described above. They argue that even the short-run Phillips curve is vertical:

that there is *no* trade-off between unemployment and inflation, even in the short run. They base their arguments on two key assumptions:

- Prices and wage rates are flexible and thus markets clear very rapidly. This means that there will be no disequilibrium unemployment, even in the short run. All unemployment will be equilibrium unemployment – or 'voluntary unemployment' as new classical economists prefer to call it.
- Expectations are 'rational', but are based on imperfect information.

In the accelerationist theory, expectations are based on *past* information and thus take time to catch up with changes in aggregate demand. Thus for a short time a rise in nominal aggregate demand will raise output and reduce unemployment below the equilibrium rate, while prices and wages are still relatively low.

The new classical analysis is based on **rational expectations**. Rational expectations are not based on past rates of inflation. Instead they are based on the current state of the economy and the current policies being pursued by the government. Workers and firms look at the information available to them – at the various forecasts that are published, at various economic indicators and the assessments of them by various commentators, at government pronouncements, and so on. From this information they predict the rate of inflation as well as they can. It is in this sense that the expectations are 'rational': people use their reason to assess the future on the basis of current information.

But forecasters frequently get it wrong, and so do economic commentators! And the government does not always do what it says it will. Thus workers and firms will be basing expectations on *imperfect information*. The crucial point about the rational expectations theory, however, is that these errors in prediction are *random*. People's predictions of inflation are just as likely to be too high as too low.

If the government raises aggregate demand in an attempt to reduce unemployment, people will anticipate that this will lead to higher prices and wages, and that there will be *no* effect on output and employment. If their expectations of higher inflation are correct, this will thus *fully* absorb the increase in nominal aggregate demand such that there will have been no increase in *real* aggregate demand at all. Firms will not produce any more output or employ any more people: after all, why should they? If they anticipate that people will spend 10 per cent more money but that prices will rise by 10 per cent, their *volume* of sales will remain the same.

Output and employment will only rise, therefore, if people make an error in their predictions (i.e. if they under-predict the rate of inflation and interpret an increase in money spent as an increase in *real* demand). But they are as likely to *over*predict the rate of inflation, in which case output and employment will fall! Thus there is no systematic trade-off between inflation and unemployment, even in the short run.

definition

Rational expectations
Expectations based on the *current* situation. These expectations are based on the information people have to hand. While this information may be imperfect and therefore people will make errors, these errors will be random.

Pause for thought

For what reasons would a new classical economist support the policy of the Bank of England publishing its inflation forecasts and the minutes of the deliberations of the Monetary Policy Committee?

Expectations of output and employment

Many economists, especially those who would describe themselves as 'Keynesian', criticise the approach of focusing exclusively on price expectations. Expectations, they argue, influence *output* and *employment* decisions, not just pricing decisions.

Unless the economy is at full employment or very close to it, an expansion of demand *will* lead to an increase in output and employment, even in the long run after expectations have fully adjusted. If there is a gradual but sustained expansion of aggregate demand, firms, seeing the economy expanding and seeing their orders growing, will start to invest more and make longer-term plans for expanding their labour force. Business and consumers will generally *expect* a higher level of output, and this optimism will cause that higher level of output to be produced. In other words, expectations will affect output and employment as well as prices.

Graphically, the increased output and employment from the recovery in investment will shift the Phillips curve to the left, offsetting (partially, wholly or more than wholly) the upward shift from higher inflationary expectations.

The lesson here for governments is that a sustained, but moderate, increase in aggregate demand can lead to a sustained growth in aggregate supply. What should be avoided is an excessive and unsustainable expansion of aggregate demand, as occurred in the late 1980s. This will lead to a boom, only to be followed by a 'bust' and a consequent recession.

Changes in equilibrium unemployment

How is it that both inflation *and* unemployment were generally worse in the 1970s, 1980s and early 1990s than in the 1950s, 1960s, late 1990s and early 2000s? One explanation lies in changes in equilibrium unemployment.

Structural unemployment. Most economists include growth in equilibrium unemployment as part of the explanation of a rightward shift in the Phillips curve in the 1970s and 1980s. In particular, they highlight the considerable structural rigidities in the economy in a period of rapid industrial change. The changes included the following:

- Dramatic changes in technology. The microchip revolution, for example, has led to many traditional jobs becoming obsolete.
- Competition from abroad. The introduction of new products from abroad, often of superior quality to domestic goods, or produced at lower costs, has led to the decline of many older industries: e.g. the textile industry.
- Shifts in demand away from the products of older labour-intensive industries to new capital-intensive products.

The free market seemed unable to cope with these changes without a large rise in structural/technological unemployment. Labour was not sufficiently mobile – either geographically or occupationally – to move to industries where there are labour shortages or into jobs where there are skill shortages. A particular problem here was the lack of investment in education and training, with the result that the labour force was not sufficiently flexible to respond to changes in demand for labour.

Hysteresis. If a recession causes a rise in unemployment which is not then fully reversed when the economy recovers, then there is a problem of **hysteresis**. This term, used in physics, refers to the lagging or persistence of an effect, even when the initial cause has been removed. In our context it refers to the persistence of unemployment even when the initial demand deficiency no longer exists.

> **definition**
> **Hysteresis**
> The persistence of an effect even when the initial cause has ceased to operate. In economics it refers to the persistence of unemployment even when the demand deficiency that caused it no longer exists.

The recessions of the early 1980s and early 1990s created a growing number of people who were both deskilled and demotivated. Many in their forties and fifties who had lost their jobs were seen as too old by prospective employers. Many young people, unable to obtain jobs, became resigned to 'life on social security' or to doing no more than casual work. What is more, many firms, in an attempt to cut costs, cut down on training programmes. In these circumstances, a rise in aggregate demand would not simply have enabled the long-term unemployed to be employed again.

Recessions also cause a lack of investment. The reduction in their capital stock meant that many firms could not respond to a recovery in demand by making significant increases in output and taking on many more workers. Instead, as the economy pulled out of the recessions of both the early 1980s and early 1990s, firms tended to raise prices. Unemployment thus only fell modestly and yet inflation rose substantially.

The effect was a rightward shift in the Phillips curve: a rise in the equilibrium rate of unemployment. In such circumstances, argue Keynesians, the government should embark on a radical programme of retraining.

If the economy achieves sustained expansion, with no recession, as occurred after 1992, then gradually these effects can be reversed. In other words, the hysteresis is not permanent. As firms increase their investment, the capital stock will expand; firms will engage in more training; the long-term unemployed will fall. The Phillips curve will shift back to the left again and the equilibrium rate of unemployment will fall.

The persistence of demand-deficient unemployment

If there is demand-deficient unemployment, why will there not be a long-run fall in real wage rates so as eliminate the surplus labour (see Figure 26.3 on page 557)? There are two major explanations for the persistence of real wage rates above equilibrium.

Efficiency wages. The argument here is that wage rates fulfil two functions. The first is the traditional one of balancing the demand and supply of labour. The other is to motivate workers. If real wage rates are reduced when there is a surplus of labour (demand-deficient unemployment), then those workers already in employment may become dispirited and work less hard. If, on the other hand, firms keep wage rates up, then by maintaining a well-motivated workforce, by cutting down on labour turnover and by finding it easier to attract well-qualified labour, firms may find that their costs are reduced: a higher real wage is thus more profitable for them. The maximum-profit real wage rate (the **efficiency wage rate**) is likely to be above the market-clearing real wage rate (see section 18.5 on page 382). Demand-deficient unemployment is likely to persist.

Insider power. If those still in employment (the insiders) are members of unions while those out of work are not (the outsiders), or if the insiders have special skills or knowledge that give them bargaining power with employers while the outsiders have no influence, then there is no mechanism whereby the surplus labour – the outsiders – can drive down the real wage and eliminate the demand-deficient unemployment.

These two features help to explain why real wage rates did not fall during the recessions of the early 1980s and early 1990s.

definition

Efficiency wage rate
The profit-maximising wage rate for the firm after taking into account the effects of wage rates on worker motivation, turnover and recruitment.

Key
Idea
18
p211

Business cycles

Business cycles and aggregate demand

Many economists, particularly Keynesian, blame fluctuations in output and employment on fluctuations in aggregate demand. Theirs is therefore a 'demand-side' explanation of the business cycle. In the upturn (phase 1), aggregate demand starts to rise (see Figure 26.1 on page 549). It rises rapidly in the expansionary phase (phase 2). It then slows down and may start to fall in the peaking-out phase (phase 3). It then falls or remains relatively stagnant in the recession (phase 4).

Instability of investment: the accelerator

One of the major factors contributing to the ups and downs of the business cycle is the instability of investment.

In a recession, investment in new plant and equipment can all but disappear. After all, what is the point of investing in additional capacity if you cannot even sell what you are currently producing? When an economy begins to recover from a recession, however, and confidence returns, investment can rise very rapidly. In percentage terms the rise in investment may be *several times that of the rise in income*. When the growth of the economy slows down, however, investment can fall dramatically.

The point is that investment depends not so much on the *level* of GDP and consumer demand, as on their *rate of change*. The reason is that investment (except for replacement investment) is to provide *additional* capacity, and thus depends on how much demand has risen, not on its level. But growth rates change by much more than the level of output. For example, if economic growth is 1 per cent in 2004 and 2 per cent in 2005, then in 2005 output has gone up by 2 per cent, but growth has gone up by 100 per cent! (i.e. it has doubled). Thus changes in investment tend to be much more dramatic than changes in GDP. This is known as the **accelerator theory**.

These fluctuations in investment, being injections into the circular flow, will then have a multiplied effect on GDP and will thus magnify the upswings and downswings of the business cycle.

> **definition**
>
> **Accelerator theory**
> The *level* of investment depends on the *rate of change* of national income, and the result tends to be subject to substantial fluctuations.

> **Pause for thought**
>
> Under what circumstances would you expect a rise in GDP to cause a large accelerator effect?

Fluctuations in stocks

Firms hold stocks of finished goods. These stocks tend to fluctuate with the course of the business cycle, and these fluctuations in stocks themselves contribute to fluctuations in output.

Imagine an economy that is recovering from a recession. At first, firms may be cautious about increasing production. Doing so may involve taking on more labour or making additional investment. Firms may not want to make these commitments if the recovery could soon peter out. They may therefore run down their stocks rather than increase output. Initially, the recovery from recession will be slow.

If the recovery continues, however, firms will start to gain more confidence and will increase their production. Also they will find that their stocks have got rather low and will need building up. This gives a further boost to production, and for a time the growth in output will exceed the growth in demand. This extra growth in output will then, via the multiplier, lead to a further increase in demand.

BOX 29.2

Business expectations and their effect on investment
Recent European experience

Investment is highly volatile. It is subject to far more violent swings than GDP. This can be seen in Figure (a) which shows EU growth in GDP and growth in investment from 1985 to 2003. The maximum annual growth in GDP was 4.2 per cent and the maximum fall was 0.4 per cent. By contrast, the maximum annual growth in investment was 9.5 per cent and the maximum fall was 8.8 per cent. The differences were even greater for individual EU countries.

These figures are consistent with the accelerator theory, which argues that the *level* of investment depends on the *rate of change* of national income. A relatively small percentage change in national income can give a much bigger percentage change in investment.

Another factor affecting investment is the degree of business optimism. While this is partly determined by current rates of economic growth, there are many other factors that can affect the business climate. These include world political events (such as a war or a US election), national and international macro-economic policies and shocks to the world economy (such as oil price changes). Of course, to the extent that these other factors affect confidence, which in turn affects investment, so they will affect economic growth.

In the boom years of the late 1980s, business optimism was widespread throughout Europe. Investment was correspondingly high, and with it there was a high rate of economic growth.

Surveys of European business expectations in the early 1990s, however, told a very different story. Pessimism was rife. Europe was in the grip of a recession. Growth slowed right down and output

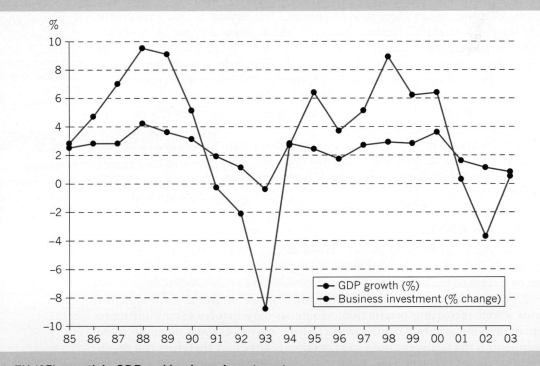

(a) EU (15) growth in GDP and business investment

Source: *European Economy, Statistical Annex* (European Commission, 2003)

(b) EU (15) Industry confidence indicator

Source: *Business and Consumer surveys* (European Commission)

actually fell in 1993. Along with this decline in growth and deteriorating levels of business and consumer confidence, there was a significant fall in investment.

The industrial confidence indicator for the EU as a whole is plotted in Figure (b). The indicator shows the percentage excess of confident over pessimistic replies to business questionnaires: a negative figure means that there was a higher percentage of pessimistic responses. You can see that the indicator was strongly negative in 1993. After 1993, pessimism began to decrease, and by the last quarter of 1994 the EU industrial confidence indicator became positive.

Between 1995 and 2000, the industrial confidence indicator swung between positive and negative values. These swings were similar in direction to those in the rate of economic growth. For example, both the rate of growth and the confidence indicator rose in 1997/8 and 2000 and fell in 1996.

Then, in 2001, with the world economy slowing down and the September 11 attack on the World Trade Center in New York, industrial confidence plummeted, and so did investment. As global uncertainties persisted and with impending and then actual war against Iraq, the confidence indicator remained low through 2002 and into 2003.

Questions

1 *How is the existence of surveys of business confidence likely to affect firms' expectations and actions?*

2 *Why, if the growth in output slows down (but is still positive), is investment likely to fall (i.e. the growth in investment be negative)? If you look at Figure (a) you will see that this happened in 1991 and 1992, and in 2001 and 2002. (See the section on the accelerator on page 643.)*

Once stocks have been built up again, the growth in output will slow down to match the growth in demand. This slowing down in output will, via the accelerator and multiplier, contribute to the ending of the expansionary phase of the business cycle.

As the economy slows down, firms may for a time be prepared to carry on producing and build up stocks. The increase in stocks thus cushions the effect of falling demand on output and employment.

If the recession continues, firms will be unwilling to go on building up stocks. But as firms attempt to reduce their stocks back to the desired level, production will fall *below* the level of sales, despite the fact that sales themselves are lower. This could therefore lead to a dramatic fall in output and, via the multiplier, to an even bigger fall in sales.

Eventually, once stocks have been run down to the minimum, production will have to rise again to match the level of sales. This will contribute to a recovery and the whole cycle will start again.

Aggregate demand and the course of the business cycle

Why do booms and recessions last for several months or even years, and why do they eventually come to an end? Let us examine each in turn.

Why do booms and recessions persist for a period of time?

Time lags. It takes time for changes in injections and withdrawals to be fully reflected in changes in GDP, output and employment. The multiplier process takes time. Moreover, consumers, firms and government may not all respond immediately to new situations. Their responses are spread out over a period of time.

'Bandwagon' effects. Once the economy starts expanding, expectations become buoyant. People think ahead and adjust their expenditure behaviour: they consume and invest more *now*. Likewise in a recession, a mood of pessimism may set in. The effect is cumulative.

The multiplier and accelerator interact: they feed on each other. A rise in GDP causes a rise in investment (the accelerator). This, being an injection into the circular flow, causes a multiplied rise in income. This then causes a further accelerator effect, a further multiplier effect, and so on.

Key Idea 36 p626

Why do booms and recessions come to an end? What determines the turning points?

Ceilings and floors. Actual output can go on growing more rapidly than potential output only as long as there is slack in the economy. As full employment is approached and as more and more firms reach full capacity, so a ceiling to output is reached.

At the other extreme, there is a basic minimum level of consumption that people tend to maintain. During a recession, people may not buy much in the way of luxury and durable goods, but they will continue to buy food and other basic goods. There is thus a floor to consumption.

The industries supplying these basic goods will need to maintain their level of replacement investment. Also there will always be some minimum investment demand as firms, in order to survive competition, need to install the latest equipment. There is thus a floor to investment too.

Echo effects. Durable consumer goods and capital equipment may last several years, but eventually they will need replacing. The replacement of goods and capital purchased in a previous boom may help to bring a recession to an end.

The accelerator. For investment to continue rising, consumer demand must rise at a *faster and faster* rate. If this does not happen, investment will fall back and the boom will break.

Random shocks. National or international political, social or natural events can affect the mood and attitudes of firms, governments and consumers, and thus affect aggregate demand.

Changes in government policy. In a boom, a government may become most worried by inflation and balance of payments deficits and thus pursue contractionary policies. In a recession, it may become most worried by unemployment and lack of growth and thus pursue expansionary policies. These government policies, if successful, will bring about a turning point in the cycle.

> **Pause for thought**
>
> *Why is it difficult to predict precisely when a recession will come to an end and the economy will start growing rapidly?*

Some economists argue that governments should attempt to reduce cyclical fluctuations by the use of active demand-management policies. These could be either fiscal or monetary policies, or both (see Chapter 30). A more stable economy will provide a better climate for long-term investment, which will lead to faster growth in both potential and actual output.

Aggregate supply and 'real business cycles'

New classical economists argue that the cause of cyclical fluctuations in business activity lie not on the demand side, but on the *supply* side. In a recession, the vertical short- and long-run aggregate supply curves will shift to the left (output falls) and the vertical short- and long-run Phillips curves will shift to the right (unemployment rises). The reverse happens in a boom. Since the new classical theory of cyclical fluctuations focuses on supply, it is known as **real business cycle theory** (i.e. concerned with *real* GDP).

But what causes aggregate supply to shift in the first place, and why, once there has been an initial shift, will the aggregate supply curve *go on* shifting, causing a recession or boom to continue?

The initial shift in aggregate supply could come from a structural change, such as a shift in demand from older manufacturing industries to new service industries. Because of the immobility of labour, not all those laid off in the older industries will find work in the new industries. Structural unemployment (part of equilibrium unemployment) rises and output falls. *Aggregate* demand may be the same, but because of a change in its pattern, aggregate supply shifts to the left and the Phillips curve shifts to the right.

Alternatively, the initial shift in aggregate supply could come from a change in technology. For example, a technological breakthrough in telecommunications could shift aggregate supply to the right. Or it could come from an oil price increase, shifting aggregate supply to the left.

> **definition**
>
> **Real business cycle theory**
> The new classical theory which explains cyclical fluctuations in terms of shifts in aggregate supply, rather than aggregate demand.

The persistence of effects

But why, when a shift occurs, does the effect persist? Why is there not a single rise or fall in aggregate supply? There are two main reasons. The first is that several changes may take months to complete. For example, a decline in demand for certain older industries, perhaps caused by growing competition from abroad, does not take place overnight. Likewise, a technological breakthrough does not affect all industries simultaneously.

The second reason is that these changes will affect the profitability of investment. If investment rises, this will increase firms' capacity and aggregate supply will shift to the right. If investment falls (as a result, say, of the election of a government less sympathetic to industry), aggregate supply will shift to the left. In other words, investment is causing changes in output not through its effect on aggregate *demand* (through the multiplier), but rather through its effect on aggregate *supply*.

Turning points

So far we have seen how the theory of real business cycles explains persistent rises or falls in aggregate supply. But how does it explain *turning points*? Why do recessions and booms come to an end? The most likely explanation is that, once a shock has worked its way through, aggregate supply will stop shifting. If there is then any shock in the other direction, aggregate supply will start moving back again. For example, after a period of recession, an eventual rise in business confidence will cause investment to rise and hence aggregate supply to shift back to the right. Since these 'reverse shocks' are likely to occur at irregular intervals, they can help to explain why real-world business cycles are themselves irregular.

29.5 Conclusions

Although there is some difference between economists over the precise causes of the level of business activity and just why and how much business activity is likely to fluctuate, there is nevertheless a fair measure of agreement between economists. Let us sum up what these are.

In the short run, changes in aggregate demand will have a major effect on output and employment. With the exception of extreme new classical economists, who argue that markets clear instantly and that expectations are formed rationally, all other economists would accept that the short-run aggregate supply curve is upward sloping, albeit getting steeper as potential output is approached. Similarly they would argue that the short-run Phillips curve is downward sloping. There are two major implications of this analysis.

- Reductions in aggregate demand can cause reductions in output and increases in unemployment. In other words, too little spending will cause a recession.

- An expansion of aggregate demand by the government (whether achieved by fiscal or monetary policy, or both) will help to pull an economy out of a recession. There may be considerable time lags, however, before the economy fully responds to such expansionary policies.

In the long run, changes in aggregate demand will have much less effect on output and employment and much more effect on prices. Although there is some disagreement as to whether or not the long-run aggregate supply curve is vertical, most economists would argue that it is less elastic than the short-run *AS* curve. This implies that, in order to increase a country's growth rate over the longer term, a government ought to focus on supply-side policies (i.e. policies

Key Idea 33 p548

to shift the long-run *AS* curve to the right). These policies involve measures to improve productivity though more effective incentives, improvements in the transport and communications infrastructure, increased research and development, improvements in education and training, and so on. Nevertheless, many economists still argue that changes in aggregate demand *will* have substantial effects on long-term output and employment via changes in investment and hence in potential output.

Expectations have important effects on the economy

Virtually all economists argue that expectations are crucial in determining the success of government policy on unemployment and inflation. Whatever people expect to happen, their actions will tend to make it happen.

If people believe that an expansion of money supply will merely lead to inflation (the new classical position), then it will. Firms and workers will adjust their prices and wage rates upwards. Firms will make no plans to expand output and will not take on any more labour. If, however, people believe that an expansion of demand will lead to higher output and employment (the Keynesian position), then, via the accelerator mechanism, it will.

Similarly, just how successful a deflationary policy is in curing inflation depends in large measure on people's expectations. If people believe that a deflationary policy will cause a recession, then firms will stop investing and will cut their workforce. If they believe that it will cure inflation and restore firms' competitiveness abroad, firms may increase investment.

To manage the economy successfully, therefore, the government must convince both business and consumers that its policies will work. This is as much a job of public relations as of pulling the right economic levers. It is one of the reasons for making central banks independent. If people believe that the central bank will not be swayed from its task of keeping inflation on target, either by public opinion or by political pressure, then people will come to expect low inflation and the policy will succeed.

SUMMARY

1a In the simple circular flow of income model, equilibrium national income (GDP) is where withdrawals equal injections: where $W = J$.

1b Equilibrium can be shown on a Keynesian 45° line diagram. Equilibrium is where GDP (shown by the 45° line) is equal to aggregate expenditure (E).

1c If there is an initial increase in aggregate expenditure (ΔE), which could result from an increase in injections or a reduction in withdrawals, there will be a multiplied rise in GDP. The multiplier is defined as $\Delta GDP/\Delta E$.

1d The size of the multiplier depends on the marginal propensity to consume domestically produced goods (mpc_d). The larger the mpc_d, the more will be spent each time incomes are generated round the circular flow, and thus the more will go round again as *additional* demand for domestic product. The multiplier formula is $1/1 - mpc_d$.

2a The quantity equation $MV = PY$ can be used to analyse the possible relationship between money and prices.

2b In the short run V tends to vary inversely, but unpredictably, with M. Thus the effect of a change in money supply on nominal GDP (PY) is uncertain.

2c The effect of a change in money supply on *real* GDP (Y) is less certain still. It depends on the degree of slack in the economy.

2d In the short run, the interest rate transmission mechanism between changes in money and changes in GDP is unreliable and possibly weak. The reasons are (a) an unstable and possibly elastic demand for money and (b) an unstable and possibly inelastic investment demand.

2d The exchange rate transmission mechanism is stronger but still very unpredictable.

2e In the long run, the transmission mechanisms are stronger and relatively stable. If people have an increase in money in their portfolios, they will attempt to restore portfolio balance by purchasing assets, including goods. Thus an increase in money supply is transmitted directly into an increase in aggregate demand. The interest rate and exchange rate mechanisms are also argued to be strong. The demand for money is seen to be more stable in the long run. This leads to a long-run stability in V (unless it changes as a result of other factors, such as

institutional arrangements for the handling of money).

3a If equilibrium GDP (GDP_e) is below the full-employment level of GDP (GDP_F), there will be a deflationary gap. This gap is equal to $GDP - E$ at GDP_F. This gap can be closed by expansionary fiscal or monetary policy, which will then cause a multiplied rise in GDP (up to a level of GDP_F) and will eliminate demand-deficient unemployment.

3b If equilibrium GDP exceeds the full-employment level of income, the inability of output to expand to meet this excess demand will lead to demand-pull inflation. This excess demand gives an inflationary gap, which is equal to $E - GDP$ at GDP_F. This gap can be closed by contractionary policies.

3c This simple analysis tends to imply that the AS curve is horizontal up to GDP_F and then vertical. If allowance is made for other types of inflation and unemployment, however, the AS curve will be upward sloping but getting steeper as full employment is approached and as bottlenecks increasingly occur.

3d The Phillips curve showed the apparent trade-off between inflation and unemployment for more than 100 years prior to 1958. However, after the mid-1960s, the relationship appeared to break down as both inflation and unemployment rose.

3e An explanation for this is given by the adaptive expectations hypothesis. In its simplest form the hypothesis states that the expected rate of inflation this year is what it actually was last year: $\dot{P}_t^e = \dot{P}_{t-1}$.

3f If there is excess demand in the economy, producing upward pressure on wages and prices, initially unemployment will fall. The reason is that workers and firms will believe that wage and price increases represent *real* wage and price increases. Thus workers are prepared to take jobs more readily and firms choose to produce more. But as people's expectations adapt upwards to these higher wages and prices, so ever increasing rises in nominal aggregate demand will be necessary to maintain unemployment below the equilibrium rate. Price and wage rises will accelerate: i.e. inflation will rise.

3g According to this analysis, the Phillips curve is thus vertical at the natural rate of unemployment.

SUMMARY

3h The new classical theory assumes flexible prices and wages in the short run as well as in the long run. It also assumes that people base their expectations of inflation on a rational assessment of the *current* situation. People may predict wrongly, but they are equally likely to underpredict or to overpredict. On average over the years they will predict correctly.

3i The rational expectations theory implies that not only the long-run but also the short-run *AS* and Phillips curves will be vertical. If people correctly predict the rate of inflation, they will correctly predict that any increase in *nominal* aggregate demand will simply be reflected in higher prices. Total output and employment will remain the same: at the equilibrium level.

3j Expectations can also impact upon output and employment. If business is confident that demand will expand and that order books will be healthy, then firms are likely to gear up production and take on extra labour.

3k Demand-deficient unemployment may persist because real wage rates may be sticky downwards, even into the longer term. This stickiness may be the result of efficiency real wage rates being above market-clearing real wage rates and/or outsiders not being able to influence wage bargains struck between employers and insiders. As the labour market has become more flexible, however, so this stickiness has tended to reduce.

4a Many economists, particularly those in the Keynesian tradition, explain cyclical fluctuations in the economy by examining the causes of fluctuations in the level of *demand*.

4b A major part of this explanation of the business cycle is the instability of investment. The accelerator theory explains this instability.

It relates the level of investment to *changes* in GDP and consumer demand. An initial increase in consumer demand can result in a very large percentage increase in investment; but as soon as the rise in consumer demand begins to level off, investment will fall; and even a slight fall in consumer demand can reduce investment to virtually zero.

4c The accelerator effect will be dampened by the carrying of stocks, the cautiousness of firms, forward planning by firms and the inability of producer goods industries to supply the capital equipment.

4d Other reasons for fluctuations in aggregate demand include cycles in the holding of stocks, time lags, 'bandwagon' effects, ceilings and floors to output, echo effects, swings in government policy and random shocks.

4e New classical economists argue that, with a vertical aggregate supply curve, cyclical fluctuations must arise from shifts in aggregate supply, not shifts in aggregate demand. Real business cycle theory thus focuses on aggregate supply shocks, which then persist for a period of time. Eventually their effect will peter out, and supply shocks in the other direction can lead to turning points in the cycle.

5 Despite some disagreements between economists, there is general consensus over the following: (a) in the short run, changes in aggregate demand will have an effect on output and employment; (b) in the long run, changes in aggregate demand will have a smaller or even no effect on output and employment; instead, there will be a significant effect on prices; (c) expectations play a major role in determining the outcome of government policy changes.

REVIEW QUESTIONS

1   Assume that the multiplier has a value of 3. Now assume that the government decides to increase aggregate demand in an attempt to reduce unemployment. It raises government expenditure by £100 million with no increase in taxes. Firms, anticipating a rise in their sales, increase investment by £200 million, of which £50 million consists of purchases of foreign machinery. How much will GDP rise? (Assume *ceteris paribus*.)

2   What factors could explain why some countries have a higher multiplier than others?

3   What are the implications of the relationship between the money supply (M) and the V and Y terms in the quantity equation $MV = PY$ for the effectiveness of controlling the amount of money in the economy as a means of controlling inflation?

4   In the adaptive expectations model of the Phillips curve, if the government tries to maintain unemployment below the equilibrium rate, what will determine the speed at which inflation accelerates?

5   For what reasons might the equilibrium rate of unemployment increase?

6   How can adaptive expectations of inflation result in clockwise Phillips loops? Why would these loops not be completely regular?

7   What implications would a vertical short-run aggregate supply curve have for the effectiveness of demand management policy?

8   Explain the persistence of high levels of unemployment after the 1980s recession. What policies would you advocate to reduce unemployment?

9   How can the interaction of the multiplier and accelerator explain cyclical fluctuations in GDP?

10 What is meant by 'real business cycle' theory? How can such theory account for (a) the persistence of periods of rapid or slow growth; (b) turning points in the cycle?

Additional Part J case studies on the *Economics for Business* website (www.booksites.net/sloman)

J.1   **Theories of economic growth.** An overview of classical and more modern theories of growth.

J.2   **The costs of economic growth.** Why economic growth may not be an unmixed blessing.

J.3   **Technology and unemployment.** Does technological progress destroy jobs?

J.4   **The GDP deflator.** An examination of how GDP figures are corrected to take inflation into account.

J.5   **Comparing national income statistics.** The importance of taking the purchasing power of local currencies into account.

J.6   **The UK's balance of payments deficit.** An examination of the UK's persistent trade and current account deficits.

J.7   **A high exchange rate.** This case looks at whether a high exchange rate is necessarily bad news for exporters.

J.8   **The Gold Standard.** A historical example of fixed exchange rates.

J.9   **The importance of international financial movements.** How a current account deficit can coincide with an appreciating exchange rate.

J.10   **Argentina in crisis.** An examination of the collapse of the Argentinean economy in 2001/2.

J.11   **The attributes of money.** What makes something, such as metal, paper or electronic records, suitable as money?

J.12   **Secondary marketing.** This looks at one of the ways of increasing liquidity without sacrificing profitability. It involves selling an asset to someone else before the asset matures.

J.13   **John Maynard Keynes (1883–1946).** Profile of the great economist.

J.14   **Has there been an accelerator effect since 1978?** An examination of the evidence for an accelerator effect in the UK.

J.15   **The rational expectations revolution.** A profile of two of the most famous economists of the new classical rational expectations school.

Websites relevant to Part J

Numbers and sections refer to websites listed in the Web appendix and hotlinked from this book's website at **www.booksites.net/sloman**

- For news articles relevant to Part J, see the *Economics News Articles* link from the book's website.

- For general news on macroeconomic issues, both national and international see websites in section A, and particularly A1–5, 7–9. For general news on money, banking and interest rates, see again A1–5, 7–9 and also 20–22, 25, 26, 31, 35, 36. For all of Part J, see also links to macroeconomic and financial news in A42. See also links to newspapers worldwide in A38, 39 and 43, and the news search feature in Google at A41.

- For macroeconomic data, see links in B1 or 2; also see B4 and 12. For UK data, see B3 and 34. For EU data, see G1 > *The Statistical Annex*. For US data, see *Current economic indicators* in B5 and the *Data* section of B17. For international data, see B15, 21, 24, 31, 33. For links to data sets, see B28; I14.

- For national income statistics for the UK (Appendix), see B1, *1. National Statistics* > the fourth link > *Economy* > *United Kingdom Economic Accounts* and *United Kingdom National Accounts – The Blue Book*.

- For the Human Development Index (Box 7.2) see site H17.

- For data on UK unemployment, see B1, *1. National Statistics* > the fourth link > *Labour Market* > *Labour Market Trends*. For International data on unemployment, see G1; H3 and 5.

- For international data on balance of payments and exchange rates, see *World Economic Outlook* in H4 and *OECD Economic Outlook* in B21 (also in section 6 of B1). See also the trade topic in I14.

- For details of individual countries' balance of payments, see B32.

- For UK data on balance of payments, see B1, *1. National Statistics* > the fourth link > *Economy* > *United Kingdom Balance of Payments – the Pink Book*. See also B3, 34; F2. For EU data, see G1 > *The Statistical Annex* > *Foreign trade and current balance*.

- For exchange rates, see A3; B34; F2, 6, 8.

- For discussion papers on balance of payments and exchange rates, see H4 and 7.

- Sites I7 and 11 contain links to *Balance of payments and exchange rates* in *International economics*.

- For monetary and financial data (including data for money supply and interest rates), see section F and particularly F2. Note that you can link to central banks worldwide from site F17. See also the links in B1 or 2.

- For links to sites on money and monetary policy, see the *Financial Economics* sections in I4, 7, 11, 17.

- For information on the development of ideas, see C12, 18; also see links under *Methodology and History of Economic Thought* in C14; links to economists in I4 and 17. See also sites I7 and 11 > *Economic Systems and Theories > History of Economic Thought.*

- For student resources relevant to this chapter, see sites C1–7, 9, 10, 12, 13, 19.

K Macroeconomic policy

THE FT REPORTS...

THE FINANCIAL TIMES, 25 JUNE 2003

Chancellor's plans 'could destabilise' interest rates

By CHRISTOPHER SWANN

Gordon Brown's desire to encourage long-term, fixed rate mortgages could lead to more violent swings in interest rates, the Bank of England's chief economist warned yesterday.

The chancellor has suggested reducing the prevalence of floating rate mortgages as a way of making it easier to join the euro.

Even if Britain stays outside the eurozone, Mr Brown says there is a case for promoting more fixed rate borrowing as a way of stabilising the housing market.

Giving evidence to the Treasury select committee of MPs, Charles Bean, the Bank's chief economist, suggested that this could increase instability if Britain did not sign up to the euro. 'You would certainly have to move interest rates more than you would otherwise have to do to have the same impact on demand. So in that sense, [monetary policy] would be less effective.'

Mr Bean said it would also create uncertainty as the Bank struggled to calibrate interest rate movements. . . . But Kate Barker, a member of the monetary policy committee, said that greater use of fixed rate mortgages could help smooth the housing market. Price volatility could have discouraged some from building new houses, which had restricted supply.

Another of the chancellor's policies for furthering convergence with the eurozone – adopting the European measure of inflation – was also questioned.

Stephen Nickell, an external member of the MPC, said that adopting the harmonised index of consumer prices might lead to lower interest rates. The Treasury has indicated that there would be no impact on monetary policy from the shift to HICP from RIPX.

If the apparent fall in inflation depressed wage settlements, Mr Nickell said, it could lower consumption growth. 'We would have to counteract that with monetary policy,' he said.

Sir Edward George, the outgoing Bank governor, expressed reservations about Treasury ideas to enhance the power of fiscal policy to manage economic demand if Britain entered the eurozone.

The Treasury proposed using value added tax, excise and housing taxes to fine tune demand in the economy once control of interest rates had been given to the European Central Bank. Sir Edward said this was 'logical', but warned that micro-managing the economy through taxes had 'historically not been hugely successful'.

Just as in foreign policy this new era of globalisation brings insecurities as well as opportunities, so too in economic policy insecurities and opportunities arise together and challenge us to devise modern ways of achieving our traditional economic objective: high and stable levels of growth and employment.

Gordon Brown, UK Chancellor of the Exchequer, 10 March 2003

The role of government in managing macroeconomic affairs has always been a contentious one. Sometimes government action is welcomed when, for example, the economy is languishing in recession. Yet on other occasions, the removal of government influence and interference can be equally praised.

Even when the type of intervention is agreed upon, the decision makers still have to agree on precisely what action to take. As the article opposite shows, even those who should know best cannot always be sure of the best course of action.

In this final part of the book, we consider the alternative policies open to government in its attempt to manage or influence the macroeconomy. Chapter 30 focuses on fiscal and monetary policy, which are used by government to regulate aggregate demand. We shall consider how such policies are supposed to work and how effective they are in practice. Chapter 31, by contrast, focuses on aggregate supply and considers the role of government in attempting to improve economic performance by supply-side reforms: i.e. reforms designed to increase productivity and efficiency and achieve a growth in *potential* output. Both free-market and interventionist supply-side strategies will be considered.

Finally Chapter 32 takes an international perspective. We shall see how, in a world of interdependent economies, national governments try to harmonise their policies so as to achieve international growth and stability. Unfortunately, there is frequently a conflict between the broader interests of the international community and the narrow interests of individual countries, and in these circumstances, national interests normally dictate policy.

key terms

Fiscal policy
Fiscal stance
Fine tuning
Automatic fiscal stabilisers and discretionary fiscal policy
Pure fiscal policy
Crowding out
Monetary policy
Open-market operations
Demand management
Inflation targeting
Market-orientated and interventionist supply-side policies
Regional and urban policy
Industrial policy
International business cycle
Policy co-ordination
International convergence
Economic and monetary union in Europe (EMU)
Single European currency
Currency union

CHAPTER

30 Demand-side policy

There are two major types of demand-side policy: fiscal and monetary. In each case we shall first describe how the policy operates and then examine its effectiveness. We shall also consider the more general question of whether the government and central bank ought to intervene actively to manage the level of aggregate demand, or whether they ought merely to set targets or rules for various indicators – such as money supply, inflation or government budget deficits – and then stick to them.

30.1 Fiscal policy

Fiscal policy involves the government manipulating the level of government expenditure and/or rates of tax so as to affect the level of aggregate demand. An *expansionary* fiscal policy will involve raising government expenditure (an injection into the circular flow of income) or reducing taxes (a withdrawal from the circular flow). This will increase aggregate demand and lead to a *multiplied* rise in national income. A *deflationary* (i.e. a contractionary) fiscal policy will involve cutting government expenditure and/or raising taxes.

Fiscal policy can be used to perform two main functions:

■ To prevent the occurrence of *fundamental* disequilibrium in the economy. In other words, expansionary fiscal policy could be used to prevent mass unemployment, such as that experienced in the Great Depression of the 1930s or in east and south-east Asia, Russia and Brazil in the late 1990s. Likewise deflationary fiscal policy could be used to prevent excessive inflation, such as that experienced in many countries in the early 1970s.

■ To smooth out the fluctuations in the economy associated with the business cycle. This would involve reducing government expenditure or raising taxes during the boom phase of the cycle. This would dampen down the expansion and prevent 'overheating' of the economy, with its attendant rising inflation and deteriorating balance of payments. Conversely, during the recessionary phase, as unemployment grew and output declined, the government should cut taxes or raise government expenditure in order to boost the economy. If these stabilisation policies are successful, they will amount merely to **fine tuning**. Problems of excess or deficient demand will never be allowed to get severe. Any movement of aggregate demand away from a steady growth path will be immediately 'nipped in the bud'.

definition

Fiscal policy
Policy to affect
aggregate demand
by altering
government
expenditure and/or
taxation.

Deficits and surpluses

Central government deficits and surpluses

Since an expansionary fiscal policy will involve raising government expenditure and/or lowering taxes, this will have the effect of either increasing the **budget deficit** or reducing the **budget surplus**. A budget deficit in any one year is where central government's expenditure exceeds its revenue from taxation. A budget surplus is where tax revenues exceed central government expenditure. With the exception of short periods (1969–70, 1987–90 and 1998–2001), governments in the UK, like most governments around the world, have run budget deficits.

Public-sector deficits and surpluses

Pause for thought

If government is running a budget deficit, does this mean that GDP will increase?

To get a complete view of the overall **stance of fiscal policy** – just how expansionary or contractionary it is – we would need to look at the deficit or surplus of the entire public sector: namely, central government, local government and public corporations.

If the public sector spends more than it earns (through taxes and the revenues of public corporations, etc.), the amount of this deficit is known as the **public-sector net cash requirement (PSNCR)** (previously known as the public-sector borrowing requirement (PSBR)). The reason for the name 'public-sector net cash requirement' is simple. If the public sector runs a deficit in the current year of, say, £1 billion, then it will have to borrow £1 billion this year (require 'cash') in order to finance it (see Chapter 28 for methods of government borrowing). Table 30.1 shows UK PSNCR from 1986 to 2002.

If the public sector runs a surplus (a negative figure for the PSNCR), then this will be used to reduce the accumulated debts from the past. The accumulated debts of central and local government are known as the **general government debt**. Table 30.2 shows general government deficits and debt for various countries.

definition

Fine tuning
The use of demand
management policy
(fiscal or monetary)
to smooth out
cyclical fluctuations
in the economy.

definition

Budget deficit
The excess of central
government's
spending over its tax
receipts.

definition

Budget surplus
The excess of central
government's tax
receipts over its
spending.

definition

Fiscal stance
How deflationary or
reflationary the
Budget is.

The use of fiscal policy

Automatic fiscal stabilisers

To some extent, government expenditure and taxation will have the effect of *automatically* stabilising the economy. For example, as national income rises, the amount of tax people pay automatically rises. This rise in withdrawals from the circular flow of income will help to damp down the rise in national income. This effect will be bigger if taxes are *progressive* (i.e. rise by a bigger percentage than national income). Some government expenditure will have a similar effect. For example, total government expenditure on unemployment benefits will fall,

| Table 30.1 | UK public-sector borrowing (public-sector net cash requirement, PSNCR) |

	1986	1988	1990	1992	1994	1996	1997	1998	1999	2000	2001	2002
PSNCR (+ = deficit) (£bn)	+2.6	−11.5	−1.3	+28.6	+39.4	+24.8	+11.9	−6.6	−1.3	−37.6	−2.9	+17.1
PSNCR (% of GDP)	+0.7	−2.4	−0.2	+4.7	+5.8	+3.3	+1.5	−0.8	−0.1	−4.0	−0.3	+1.6

Source: **www.statistics.gov.uk** (National Statistics): extracted from Series RURQ and YBHA

Table 30.2	General government deficits/surpluses as percent of GDP			
Country	*General government deficits (–) or surpluses (+)*		*General government debt*	
	Average 1990–95	*Average 1996–2002*	*Average 1990–95*	*Average 1996–2002*
Belgium	–6.4	–1.8	128.9	117.3
France	–4.3	–2.4	48.5	64.3
Ireland	–2.6	+2.2	84.2	52.4
Italy	–10.2	–2.7	115.4	115.5
Japan	–0.8	–5.7	68.8	108.7
Netherlands	–4.2	0.0	75.8	64.2
Sweden	–6.1	+1.2	65.3	67.8
UK	–5.3	–0.4	52.1	57.4
USA	–4.5	+0.1	72.9	66.0
Euro area	–5.1	–1.9	66.8	75.7

> **definition**
>
> **Public-sector net cash requirement (PSNCR)**
> The (annual) deficit of the public sector (central government, local government and public corporations), and thus the amount that the public sector must borrow.

if rises in national income cause a fall in unemployment. This again will have the effect of dampening the rise in national income.

Discretionary fiscal policy

If there is a fundamental disequilibrium in the economy or substantial fluctuations in national income, these automatic stabilisers will not be enough. The government may thus choose to *alter* the level of government expenditure or the rates of taxation. This is known as **discretionary fiscal policy**.

If government expenditure on goods and services (roads, health care, education, etc.) is raised, this will create a full multiplied rise in national income. The reason is that all the money gets spent and thus all of it goes to boosting aggregate demand.

> **definition**
>
> **General government debt**
> The accumulated central and local government deficits (less surpluses) over the years: i.e. the total amount owed by central and local government, both to domestic and overseas creditors.

> **definition**
>
> **Discretionary fiscal policy**
> Deliberate changes in tax rates or the level of government expenditure in order to influence the level of aggregate demand.

Cutting taxes (or increasing benefits), however, will have a smaller effect on national income than raising government expenditure on goods and services by the same amount. The reason is that cutting taxes increases people's *disposable* incomes, of which only part will be spent. Part will be withdrawn into extra saving, imports and other taxes. In other words, not all the tax cuts will be passed on round the circular flow of income as extra expenditure. Thus if one-fifth of a cut in taxes is withdrawn and only four-fifths is spent, the tax multiplier will only be four-fifths as big as the government expenditure multiplier.

> **Pause for thought**
>
> *Why will the multiplier effect of government transfer payments, such as child benefit, pensions and social security be less than the full multiplier effect from government expenditure on goods and services?*

The effectiveness of fiscal policy   30.2

How successful will fiscal policy be? Will it be able to 'fine tune' demand? Will it be able to achieve the level of GDP that the government would like it to achieve?

There are various problems with using fiscal policy to manage the economy. These can be grouped under two broad headings: problems of magnitude and problems of timing.

Discretionary fiscal policy: problems of magnitude

Before changing government expenditure or taxation, the government will need to calculate the effect of any such change on national income, employment and inflation. Predicting these effects however, is often very unreliable for a number of reasons.

Predicting the effect of changes in government expenditure

A rise in government expenditure of £x may lead to a rise in total injections (relative to withdrawals) that is smaller than £x. This will occur if the rise in government expenditure *replaces* a certain amount of private expenditure. For example, a rise in government expenditure on social services could lead to a fall in private consumer expenditure. For example, a rise in expenditure on state education may dissuade some parents from sending their children to private schools. Similarly, an improvement in the National Health Service may lead to fewer people paying for private treatment.

definition

Crowding out
Where increased public expenditure diverts money or resources away from the private sector.

Crowding out. Another reason for the total rise in injections being smaller than the rise in government expenditure is a phenomenon known as **crowding out**. If the government relies on **pure fiscal policy** – that is, if it does not finance an increase in the budget deficit by increasing the money supply – it will have to borrow the money from individuals and firms. It will thus be competing with the private sector for finance and will have to offer higher interest rates. This will force the private sector also to offer higher interest rates, which may discourage firms from investing and individuals from buying on credit. Thus government borrowing *crowds out* private borrowing. In the extreme case, the fall in consumption and investment may completely offset the rise in government expenditure, with the result that aggregate demand does not rise at all.

definition

Pure fiscal policy
Fiscal policy which does not involve any change in money supply.

Predicting the effect of changes in taxes

A rise in taxes, by reducing people's real disposable income, will reduce not only the amount they spend, but also the amount they save. The problem is that it is not easy to predict just how much people will cut down on their spending and how much on their saving. In part it will depend on whether people feel that the rise in tax is only temporary, in which case they may well cut savings in order to maintain their level of consumption, or permanent, in which case they may well reduce their consumption.

Predicting the resulting multiplied effect on national income

Even if the government *could* predict the net initial effect on injections and withdrawals, the extent to which national income will change is still hard to predict for the following reasons:

- The size of the *multiplier* may be difficult to predict, since it is difficult to predict how much of any rise in income will be withdrawn. For example, the amount of a rise in income that households save or consume will depend on their expectations about future price and income changes. The amount of a rise in income spent on imports will depend on the exchange rate, which may fluctuate considerably.

- Induced investment through the *accelerator* is also extremely difficult to predict. It may be that a relatively small fiscal stimulus will be all that is necessary to restore business confidence, and that induced investment will rise substantially. In such a case, fiscal policy can be seen as a 'pump primer'. It is used to *start* the process of recovery, and then the *continuation* of the recovery is left to the market. But for pump priming to work, businesspeople must *believe* that it will work. If they are cautious and fear that the recovery will falter, they may hold back from investing. This lack of investment will probably mean that the recovery *will* falter and that the effects of the fiscal expansion are very modest. The problem is in predicting just how the business community will react. Business confidence can change very rapidly and in ways that could not have been foreseen a few months earlier.

Random shocks

Forecasts cannot take into account the unpredictable. For that you would have to consult astrologers or fortune tellers! Unfortunately unpredictable events, such as the attack on the World Trade Center in New York in September 2001, do occur and may seriously undermine the government's fiscal policy.

> **Pause for thought**
>
> *Gives some other examples of 'random shocks' that could undermine the government's fiscal policy.*

Discretionary fiscal policy and the problem of timing

Fiscal policy can involve considerable time lags. If these are long enough, fiscal policy could even be *de*stabilising. Expansionary policies taken to cure a recession may not come into effect until the economy has *already* recovered and is experiencing a boom. Under these circumstances, expansionary policies are quite inappropriate: they simply worsen the problems of overheating. Similarly, deflationary policies taken to prevent excessive expansion may not take effect until the economy has already peaked and is plunging into recession. The deflationary policies only deepen the recession.

This problem is illustrated in Figure 30.1. Path (a) shows the course of the business cycle without government intervention. Ideally, with no time lags, the economy should be dampened in stage 2 and stimulated in stage 4. This would make the resulting course of the business cycle more like path (b), or even, if the policy were perfectly stabilising, a straight line. With the presence of time lags, however, deflationary policies taken in stage 2 may not come into effect until stage 4, and reflationary policies taken in stage 4 may not come into effect until

Figure 30.1 **Fiscal policy: stabilising or destabilising?**

BOX 30.1

Following the golden rule
Fiscal policy in a strait-jacket?

If the government persistently runs a budget deficit, the national debt will rise. If it rises faster than GDP, then it will account for a growing proportion of GDP. There is then likely to be an increasing problem of 'servicing' this debt: i.e. paying the interest on it. The government could find itself having to borrow more and more to meet the interest payments, and so the national debt could rise faster still. As the government borrows more and more, so it has to pay higher interest rates to attract finances. If it is successful in this, borrowing and hence investment by the private sector could be crowded out (see page 662).

Recognising these problems, many governments in recent years have attempted to reduce their debts.

currency, they should have sustainable deficits and debts. This was interpreted as follows: the general government deficit should be no more than 3 per cent of GDP and general government debt should be no more than 60 per cent of GDP, or should at least be falling towards that level at a satisfactory pace.

But in the mid-1990s, several of the countries which were subsequently to join the euro, had deficits and debts substantially above these levels. Getting them down proved a painful business. Government expenditure had to be cut and taxes increased. Fiscal policy, unfortunately, proved to be powerful! Unemployment rose and growth remained low.

Preparing for EMU

In signing the Maastricht Treaty in 1992, the EU countries agreed that to be eligible to join the single

The EU Stability and Growth Pact

In June 1997, at the European Council in Amsterdam, the EU countries agreed that govern-

Getting budget deficits down

ments adopting the euro should seek to balance their budgets (or even aim for a surplus) averaged over the course of the business cycle, and that deficits should not exceed 3 per cent of GDP in any one year. A country's deficit is only permitted to exceed 3 per cent if its GDP has declined by at least 2 per cent (or 0.75 per cent with special permission from the Council of Ministers). Otherwise, countries with deficits exceeding 3 per cent are required to make deposits of money with the European Central Bank. These then become fines if the excessive budget deficit is not eliminated within two years.

There are two main aims of targeting a zero budget deficit over the business cycle. The first is to allow automatic stabilisers to work without 'bumping into' the 3 per cent deficit ceiling in years when economies are slowing. The second is to allow a reduction in government debts as a proportion of GDP (assuming that GDP grows on average at around 2–3 per cent per year).

The main criticism of aiming for a zero deficit over the cycle has been that this would mean a further reduction in deficits, which by the start of the euro in 1999 were typically only just meeting the 3 per cent ceiling. In other words, meeting the zero deficit target would mean further deflationary fiscal policies: something that most political leaders in Europe felt to be inappropriate at a time when there were fears of a world recession.

Also there is the issue of whether the Pact is flexible enough. In 2002 and 2003, Germany was suffering from virtually zero growth with unemployment exceeding 11 per cent (4.7 million), a problem aggravated by the world recession. As a consequence of falling tax revenues and increased expenditure on unemployment benefits, its deficit breached the 3 per cent ceiling: it was 3.75 per cent of GDP in 2002. The German government had to make promises to rein in expenditure and raise taxes in order to escape censure by the European Commission – just at a time when the economy needed a boost to aggregate demand. Critics accused the Pact of being too restrictive and of not taking into account world economic circumstances.

Labour's golden rule

The Labour government in the UK has adopted a similar approach to that of the Stability and Growth Pact. Under its 'golden rule', the government pledges that over the economic cycle, it will borrow only to invest (e.g. in roads, hospitals and schools) and not to fund current spending (e.g. on wages, administration and benefits). Investment is exempted from the zero borrowing rule, because it contributes towards the growth of GDP. Indeed, in its 1998 'Comprehensive Spending Review', the government announced that government investment expenditure would double as a percentage of GDP. The government has also set itself the target of maintaining a stable public-sector debt/GDP ratio below 40 per cent.

To allow the golden rule to operate, government departments are set three-year spending limits and each has separate current and capital (investment) budgets.

As with the Stability and Growth Pact, the argument is that by using an averaging rule over the cycle, automatic stabilisers will be allowed to work. Deficits of receipts over current spending can occur when the economy is in recession or when growth is sluggish, helping to stimulate the economy. Surpluses can occur in boom periods, helping to dampen the economy.

But as with the Stability and Growth Pact, a major concern is whether the policy provides too much of a strait-jacket. Does it prevent the government using substantial discretionary boosts to the economy at times of serious economic slowdown? Probably, yes, but the golden rule does permit some degree of discretionary fiscal policy and, unlike the Stability and Growth Pact, does not impose a ceiling to cyclical deficits.

Question

1 *What effects will government investment expenditure have on public-sector debt (a) in the short run; (b) in the long run?*

2 *If there is a danger of global recession, should governments loosen the strait-jacket of fiscal policy targets?*

stage 2. In this case the resulting course of the business cycle will be more like path (c). Quite obviously, in these circumstances 'stabilising' fiscal policy actually makes the economy *less* stable.

There are five possible lags associated with fiscal policy.

Time lag to recognition. Since the business cycle can be irregular and forecasting unreliable, governments may be unwilling to take action until they are convinced that the problem is serious.

Time lag between recognition and action. Most significant changes in government expenditure have to be planned well in advance. The government cannot increase spending on motorways overnight or suddenly start building new hospitals.

Changes in taxes and benefits cannot be introduced overnight either. They normally have to wait to be announced in the Budget and will not be instituted until the new financial year or at some other point in the future. As Budgets normally occur annually, there could be a considerable time lag if the problems are recognised a long time before the Budget.

Time lag between action and changes taking effect. A change in tax rates may not immediately affect tax payments as some taxes are paid in arrears and new rates may take a time to apply.

Time lag between changes in government expenditure and taxation and the resulting change in national income, prices and employment. The multiplier round takes time. Accelerator effects take time. The multiplier and accelerator go on interacting. It all takes time.

Consumption may respond slowly to changes in taxation. If taxes are cut, consumers may respond initially by saving the extra money. They may only later increase consumption.

If the fluctuations in aggregate demand can be forecast, and if the lengths of the time lags are known, then all is not lost. At least the fiscal measures can be taken early and their delayed effects can be taken into account.

Side-effects of discretionary fiscal policy

The purpose of fiscal policy is to control aggregate demand. In doing so, however, it may create certain undesirable side-effects.

Cost inflation. If the economy is overheating and inflation is rising, the government may raise taxes. Although this will lower aggregate demand, a rise in expenditure taxes and corporation taxes will usually be passed on in full or in part to the consumer in higher prices. This in turn could lead to higher wage claims, as could a rise in income tax.

Welfare and distributive justice. The use of fiscal policy may conflict with various social programmes. The government may want to introduce cuts in public expenditure in order to reduce inflation. But where are the cuts to be made? Cuts will often fall on people who are relatively disadvantaged. After all, it is these people who are the most reliant on the welfare state and other public provision (such as state education).

Key
Idea

26
p402

Incentives. Both automatic stabilisers, in the form of steeply progressive income taxes, and discretionary rises in taxes could be a disincentive to effort. What is the point in working more or harder, people might say, if so much is going to be taken in taxes? It could work the other way, however: faced with higher tax bills, people may feel the need to work more in order to maintain their living standards.

Steady as you go

Given the problems of pursuing active fiscal policy, many governments today take a much more passive approach. Instead of changing the policy as the economy changes, a rule is set for the level of public finances. This rule is then applied year after year, with taxes and government expenditure being planned to meet that rule. For example, a target could be set for the PSNCR, with government expenditure and taxes being adjusted to keep the PSNCR at or within its target level. Box 30.1 looks at some examples of fiscal targets.

Monetary policy   30.3

Each month the Bank of England's Monetary Policy Committee meets to set interest rates. The event gets considerable media coverage. Pundits, for two or three days before the meeting, try to predict what the MPC will do and economists give their 'considered' opinions about what the MPC *ought* to do.

The fact is that changes in interest rates have gained a central significance in macroeconomic policy. And it is not just in the UK. Whether it is the European Central Bank setting interest rates for the eurozone countries, or the Federal Reserve Bank setting US interest rates, or any other central bank around the world choosing what the level of interest rates should be, monetary policy is seen as having a major influence on a whole range of macroeconomic indicators.

But is monetary policy simply the setting of interest rates? In reality, it involves the central bank intervening in the money market to ensure that the interest rate that has been announced is also the *equilibrium* interest rate.

The policy setting

In framing its monetary policy, the government must decide on what the goals of the policy are. Is the aim simply to control inflation, or does the government wish also to affect output and employment, or does it want to control the exchange rate?

The government must also decide where monetary policy fits into the total package of macroeconomic policies. Is it seen as the major or even sole macroeconomic policy instrument, or is it merely one of several?

A decision also has to be made about who is to carry out the policy. There are three possible approaches here.

In the first, the government both sets the policy and decides the measures necessary to achieve it. Here the government would set the interest rate, with the central bank simply influencing money markets to achieve this rate. This first approach was used in the UK before 1997.

The second approach is for the government to set the policy *targets*, but for the central bank to be given independence in deciding interest rates. This is the approach adopted in the UK today. The government has set a target rate of inflation of 2 per cent, but then the MPC is free to choose the rate of interest.

The third approach is for the central bank to be given independence not only in carrying out policy, but in setting the policy targets themselves. The ECB, within the statutory objective of maintaining price stability over the medium term, decides on (a) the target rate of inflation – currently that inflation for the eurozone should be kept below 2 per cent, and (b) the target rate of growth in money supply. It then sets interest rates to meet these targets.

Finally, there is the question of whether the government or central bank should take a long-term or short-term perspective? Should it adopt a target for money supply growth or inflation and stick to it come what may? Or should it adjust its policy as circumstances change and attempt to 'fine tune' the economy?

We will be looking primarily at *short-term* monetary policy: that is, policy used to keep to a set target for inflation or money supply growth, or policy used to smooth out fluctuations in the business cycle. It is important first, however, to take a longer-term perspective. Governments will generally want to prevent an excessive growth in the money supply over the longer term. If money supply does grow rapidly, then inflation is likely to be high.

Control of the money supply over the medium and long term

One of the major sources of monetary growth is government borrowing. If the government wishes to prevent excessive growth in the money supply over the longer term, therefore, it will have to be careful not to have an excessively high PSNCR (see page 660).

The precise effect of government borrowing on the money supply will depend on how the PSNCR is financed. If it is financed by borrowing from the Bank of England or by the sale of Treasury bills to the banking sector, the money supply will increase. If, however, it is financed by selling bills or bonds outside the banking sector or by selling bonds to the banks, the money supply will not increase (see pages 616–17).

If there is no increase in money supply, the increased demand for loans by the government will 'crowd out' lending to the private sector. To attract money the government will have to offer higher interest rates on bonds. This will force up private-sector interest rates and reduce private-sector borrowing and investment. This is known as **financial crowding out**.

If governments wish to reduce monetary growth and yet avoid financial crowding out, they must therefore reduce the level of the PSNCR.

Monetarists argue that governments should make reductions in the PSNCR (as a proportion of national income) the central part of their medium- and longer-term monetary strategy. Not only is this desirable as a means of restricting monetary growth, but if it involves cutting government expenditure (as opposed to increasing taxes), it will also increase the size of the private sector relative to the public sector: and it is the private sector that monetarists see as the main source of long-term growth in output and employment.

Short-term monetary control

Monetary policy may be off target. Alternatively, the government (or central bank) may wish to alter its monetary policy. What can it do? There are various

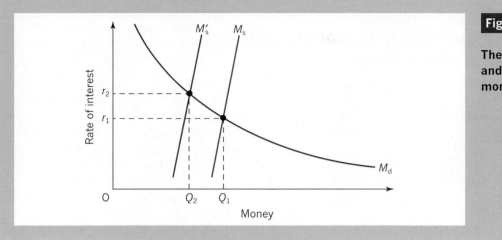

Figure 30.2

The demand for and supply of money

techniques that could be used. These can be grouped into three categories: (a) altering the money supply; (b) altering interest rates; (c) rationing credit. These are illustrated in Figure 30.2, which shows the demand for and supply of money. The equilibrium quantity of money is initially Q_1 and the equilibrium interest rate is r_1.

Assume that the central bank wants to tighten monetary policy in order to reduce inflation. It could (a) seek to shift the supply of money curve to the left: e.g. from M_s to M_s' (resulting in the equilibrium rate of interest rising from r_1 to r_2), (b) raise the interest rate directly from r_1 to r_2, and then manipulate the money supply to reduce it to Q_2, or (c) keep interest rates at r_1, but reduce money supply to Q_2 by rationing the amount of credit granted by banks and other institutions.

Techniques to control the money supply

There are four possible techniques that a central bank could use to control money supply. They have one major feature in common: they involve manipulating the liquid assets of the banking system. The aim is to influence the total money supply by affecting the amount of credit that banks can create.

Open-market operations. **Open-market operations** are the most widely used of the four techniques around the world. They involve the sale or purchase by the central bank of government securities (bonds or bills) in the open market. These sales (or purchases) are to fund additional (or reduced) government borrowing, and are best understood, therefore, in the context of an unchanged PSNCR.

If the central bank wishes to *reduce* the money supply, it sells more securities. When people buy these securities, they pay for them with cheques drawn on banks. Thus banks' balances with the central bank are reduced. If this brings bank reserves below their prudent ratio (or statutory ratio, if one is in force), banks will reduce advances. There will be a multiple contraction of credit and hence of money supply.

> **definition**
>
> **Open-market operations**
> The sale (or purchase) by the authorities of government securities in the open market in order to reduce (or increase) money supply.

> **Pause for thought**
>
> *Explain how open-market operations could be used to* increase *the money supply.*

Reduced central bank lending to the banks. The central bank in most countries is prepared to provide extra money to banks (through gilt repos, rediscounting

BOX 30.2

The daily operation of monetary policy
What goes on at Threadneedle Street?

The Bank of England does not attempt to control money supply directly. Instead it seeks to control short-term interest rates by conducting open-market operations in the gilt 'repo' and discount markets (see page 611). These operations, as we shall see, determine short-term interest rates, which will then have a knock-on effect on longer-term rates, as returns on different forms of assets must remain competitive with each other.

Let us assume that the Monetary Policy Committee of the Bank of England is worried that inflation is set to rise, perhaps because there is excessive growth in the money supply. At its monthly meeting, therefore, it decides to raise interest rates. What does the Bank of England do?

The first thing is that it will *announce* a rise in interest rates. But it must do more than this. It must back up the announcement by using open-market operations to ensure that its announced interest rate is the *equilibrium rate*. In fact, it has to conduct open market operations every day to keep interest rates at the chosen level.

How do these open-market operations work? In general, the Bank of England seeks to keep banks short of liquidity. It achieves this through its weekly sales of Treasury bills to the banks and other financial institutions (collectively known as the Bank's 'counterparties').

The counterparties thus have to borrow from the Bank of England. They do this by entering into sale and repurchase agreements (repos). This entails them selling gilts to the Bank, with an agreement that they will repurchase them from the Bank at a fixed date in the future (typically two weeks). The difference between the sale and repurchase prices will be set by the Bank of England to reflect its chosen rate of interest. By the Bank determining the repo rate in this way, there will then be a knock-on effect on other interest rates throughout the banking system.

Each morning at 9.45 the Bank of England forecasts that day's liquidity shortage. Unless the shortage is too small to necessitate action, it then provides liquidity through open market operations: i.e. through repos or the repurchasing of bills. The rate charged is that set by the MPC. At 2.30pm, the Bank revises its forecasts of the market's liquidity shortage, and if necessary undertakes a further round of open-market operations.

Then at 3.30, it publishes a final update for the day's liquidity shortage, and if necessary makes a further repo facility available, normally on an overnight basis and normally at 1 per cent above the rate set by the MPC. The rate is higher because the Bank expects its counterparties to obtain liquidity at the 9.45 and 2.30 rounds. The 3.30 round is designed to cater for any unforeseen late shortage.

Finally, at 4.20, after the market has closed, banks may apply for additional overnight liquidity through repos to allow the process of clearing to be completed. The Bank will charge them anything from the MPC's agreed repo rate to $1^{1}/_{2}$ per cent above that rate.

Although there is usually a shortage of liquidity in the banking system, on some days there may be a *surplus*. To prevent this driving market interest rates down, the Bank will invite its counterparties to bid for outright purchase of short-dated Treasury bills (i.e. ones part-way through their life) at prices set by the Bank to reflect its current (above equilibrium) interest rate: i.e. at prices lower than the market would otherwise set. At such prices, the Bank has no difficulty in selling them and hence in 'mopping up' the surplus liquidity.

Question

Assume that the Bank of England wants to reduce interest rates. Trace through the process during the day by which it achieves this.

bills or straight loans). In some countries, it is the policy of the central bank to keep its interest rate to banks *below* market rates, thereby encouraging banks to borrow (or sell back securities) whenever such facilities are available. By cutting back the amount it is willing to provide, the central bank can reduce banks' liquid assets and hence the amount of credit they can create.

In other countries, such as the UK and the eurozone countries, it is not so much the amount of money made available that is controlled, but rather the rate of interest (or discount). The higher this rate is relative to other market rates, the less will banks be willing to borrow, and the lower, therefore, will be the monetary base. Raising this rate, therefore, has the effect of reducing the money supply.

Funding. Rather than focusing on controlling the monetary base (as in the case of the above two techniques), an alternative is for the central bank to alter the overall liquidity position of the banks. An example of this approach is a change, by the central bank, in the balance of **funding** government debt. To reduce money supply the central bank issues more bonds and fewer bills. Banks' balances with the central bank will be little affected, but to the extent that banks hold fewer bills, there will be a reduction in their liquidity. Funding is thus the conversion of one type of government debt (liquid) into another (illiquid).

Variable minimum reserve ratios. In some countries (such as the USA), banks are required to hold a certain proportion of their assets in liquid form. The assets which count as liquid are known as 'reserve assets'. These include assets such as balances in the central bank, bills of exchange, certificates of deposit and money market loans. The ratio of such assets to total liabilities is known as the **minimum reserve ratio**. If the central bank raises this ratio (in other words requires the banks to hold a higher proportion of liquid assets), then banks will have to reduce the amount of credit. The money supply will fall.

Techniques to control interest rates

The approach to monetary control today in most countries is to focus directly on interest rates. Normally an interest rate change will be announced, and then open-market operations will be conducted by the central bank to ensure that the money supply is adjusted so as to make the announced interest rate the *equilibrium* one. Let us assume that the central bank decides to raise interest rates. What does it do?

In general, it will seek to keep banks short of liquidity. This will happen automatically on any day when tax payments by banks' customers exceed the money they receive from government expenditure. This excess is effectively withdrawn from banks and ends up in the government's account at the central bank. Even when this does not occur, sales of bills by the central bank will effectively keep the banking system short of liquidity.

This 'shortage' can then be used as a way of forcing through interest rate changes. Banks will obtain the necessary liquidity from the central bank through repos (see page 611) or by selling it back bills. The central bank can *choose the rate of interest to charge* (i.e. the repo rate or the bill rediscount rate). This will then have a knock-on effect on other interest rates throughout the banking system. (See Box 30.2 for more details on just how the Bank of England manipulates interest rates on a day-to-day basis.)

Techniques to ration credit

In the past, and particularly in the late 1960s, governments attempted to keep interest rates low so as not to discourage investment. This frequently meant that the demand for money exceeded the supply of money that the authorities were prepared to permit.

Faced with this excess demand, the authorities had to ration credit. Credit was rationed in two main ways. First, the Bank of England could ask banks to

definition

Funding
Where the authorities alter the balance of bills and bonds for any given level of government borrowing.

definition

Minimum reserve ratio
A minimum ratio of cash (or other specified liquid assets) to deposits (either total or selected) that the central bank requires banks to hold.

restrict their total lending to a certain amount, or to reduce lending to more risky customers or for non-essential purchases. The Bank of England had the power to order banks to obey, but in practice it always relied on persuasion. This was known as *suggestion and request* (or 'moral suasion'). Second, the authorities could restrict *hire-purchase credit*, by specifying minimum deposits or maximum repayment periods.

The use of credit rationing has been abandoned by most countries in recent years. The reason is that the open nature of world financial markets makes it very difficult for individual central banks to control credit. Banks and their customers are likely to be able to find ways of getting round the controls.

30.4 The effectiveness of monetary policy

Controlling the money supply over the medium and long term

A government committed to a sustained reduction in the growth of the money supply over a number of years will find this very difficult unless it restricts the size of the public-sector deficit. The Thatcher government in the 1980s recognised this and made reducing the public-sector deficit the central feature of its 'medium-term financial strategy'. There are serious problems, however, in attempting to reduce the deficit if it is currently high, principal among which is the difficulty in cutting government expenditure.

Cuts in government expenditure are politically unpopular. The Thatcher government as soon as it came into office met considerable opposition in Parliament, from public opinion, from local authorities and from various pressure groups, to 'cuts'. What is more, much of government expenditure is committed a long time in advance and cannot easily be cut. As a result the government may find itself forced into refusing to sanction *new* expenditure. But this will mean a decline in capital projects such as roads, housing, schools and sewers, with the net result that there is a decline in the country's infrastructure and long-term damage to the economy.

The less successful a government is in controlling the public-sector deficit, the more it will have to borrow through bond issue, to prevent money supply growing too fast. This will mean high interest rates and the problem of crowding out, and a growing burden of public-sector debt with interest on it that has to be paid from taxation, from further cuts in government expenditure, or from further borrowing.

It is for reasons such as these that in 1998 the UK Chancellor adopted his Golden Rule of fiscal policy (see Box 30.1). This is a pledge that over the course of the business cycle, the government will borrow only to invest. In other words, leaving investment aside, there is a target for the PSNCR of zero.

Similarly, under the EU Stability and Growth Pact (again, see Box 30.1), eurozone countries are required to aim for a zero government deficit over the business cycle, so that in times of economic slowdown the deficit will not exceed 3 per cent: the limit set for deficits under the Pact. A problem with this rule is that if a recession or slowdown persists, the deficit is likely to breach the 3 per cent limit (as happened in France, Germany and some other EU countries in 2003). There then may have to be deflationary cuts in expenditure or rises in taxation, just at a time when a boost to aggregate demand is called for.

Short-term monetary control

Problems with attempting to control the money supply

Targets for the growth in broad money were an important part of UK monetary policy from 1976 to 1985. Money targets were then abandoned and have not been used since. The European Central Bank targets the growth of M3 (see Box 30.3), but this is a subsidiary policy to that of setting interest rates in order to keep inflation under control. If, however, a central bank did choose to target money supply as its main monetary policy, how would the policy work?

Assume that money supply is above target and that the central bank wishes to reduce it. It would probably use open-market operations: i.e. it would sell more bonds or bills. The purchasers of the bonds or bills would draw liquidity from the banks. Banks would then supposedly be forced to cut down on the credit they create. But is it as simple as this?

The problem is that banks will normally be unwilling to cut down on loans if people want to borrow – after all, borrowing by customers earns profits for the banks. Banks can always 'top up' their liquidity by borrowing from the central bank and then carry on lending. True, they will have to pay the interest rate charged by the central bank, but they can pass on any rise in the rate to their customers.

The point is that as long as people *want* to borrow, banks and other financial institutions will normally try to find ways of meeting the demand. In other words, in the short run at least, the supply of money is to a large extent demand-determined. It is for this reason that central banks prefer to control the *demand* for money by controlling interest rates.

The effectiveness of changes in interest rates

Even though this is the current preferred method of monetary control, it is not without its difficulties. The problems centre on the nature of the demand for loans. If this demand is (a) unresponsive to interest rate changes or (b) unstable because it is significantly affected by other determinants (such as anticipated income or foreign interest rates), then it will be very difficult to control by controlling the rate of interest.

Problem of an inelastic demand for loans. If the demand for loans is inelastic (i.e. a relatively steep M_d curve in Figure 30.2), any attempt to reduce demand will involve large rises in interest rates. The problem will be compounded if the demand curve shifts to the right, due, say, to a consumer spending boom. High interest rates lead to the following problems:

- They may discourage investment and hence long-term growth.
- They add to the costs of production, to the costs of house purchase and generally to the cost of living. They are thus cost inflationary.
- They are politically unpopular, since the general public do not like paying higher interest rates on overdrafts, credit cards and mortgages.
- The necessary bond issue to restrain liquidity will commit the government to paying high rates on these bonds for the next twenty years or so.
- High interest rates encourage inflows of money from abroad. This drives up the exchange rate. A higher exchange rate makes domestically produced goods expensive relative to goods made abroad. This can be very damaging for export industries and industries competing with imports. Many firms in the UK suffered badly in the period 1999 to 2002, when higher interest rates in the UK than in the eurozone caused a high exchange rate of sterling against the euro.

Monetary policy in the eurozone
The role of the ECB

The European Central Bank (ECB) is based in Frankfurt and is charged with operating the monetary policy of those EU countries that have adopted the euro. Although it has the overall responsibility for the eurozone's monetary policy, the central banks of the individual countries, such as the Bank of France and the Bundesbank, have not been abolished. They are responsible for distributing euros and for carrying out the ECB's policy with respect to institutions in their own countries. The whole system of the ECB and the national central banks is known as the European System of Central Banks (ESCB).

In operating the monetary policy of a 'euro economy' roughly the size of the USA, and in being independent from national governments, the ECB's power is enormous. So what is the structure of this giant on the European stage, and how does it operate?

The structure of the ECB

The ECB has two major decision-making bodies: the Governing Council and the Executive Board.

■ The Governing Council consists of the members of the Executive Board and the governors of the central banks of each of the eurozone countries. The Council's role is to set the main targets of monetary policy and to oversee the success (or otherwise) of that policy.

■ The Executive Board consists of a president, a vice president and four other members. Each serves for an eight-year, non-renewable term. The Executive Board is responsible for implementing the decisions of the Governing Council and for preparing policies for the Council's consideration. Each member of the Executive Board has a responsibility for some particular aspect of monetary policy.

The ECB is one of the most independent central banks in the world. It has very little formal accountability to elected politicians. Although its president can be called before the European Parliament, the Parliament has virtually no powers to influence the ECB's actions. Also its deliberations are secret. Unlike meetings of the Bank of England's Monetary Policy Committee, the minutes of the Council meetings are not published.

The targets of monetary policy

The overall responsibility of the ECB is to achieve price stability in the eurozone. The target set at the launch of the euro in 1999 was a rate of inflation below 2 per cent. In 2003 this was changed to 'close to 2 per cent'. It is a weighted *average* rate for all 12 members, not a rate that has to be met by every member individually.

Evidence suggests that the demand for loans may indeed be quite inelastic. Especially in the short run, many firms and individuals simply cannot reduce their borrowing commitments. In fact, higher interest rates may force some people and firms to borrow more to finance the higher interest rate payments.

Problem of an unstable demand. Accurate monetary control requires the authorities to be able to predict the demand curve for money (in Figure 30.2). Only then can they set the appropriate level of interest rates. Unfortunately, the demand curve may shift unpredictably, making control very difficult. The major reason is *speculation*. For example, if people think interest rates will rise and bond prices fall, in the meantime they will demand to hold their assets in liquid form. The demand for money will rise. Alternatively, if people think exchange rates will rise, they will demand the domestic currency while it is still relatively cheap. The demand for money will rise.

It is very difficult for the authorities to predict what people's expectations will be. Speculation depends so much on world political events, rumour and 'random shocks'.

If the demand curve shifts very much, and if it is inelastic, then monetary control will be very difficult. Furthermore, the authorities will have to make

Key Idea 32 p547

The ECB also sets a target for the growth of M3, the broad measure of the money supply (see Box 28.3). The target set at the launch of the euro was $4^{1}/_{2}$ per cent. This too was still the target in 2003. The target for M3 is only an *intermediate* target, seen as a means of achieving the target rate of inflation. If the M3 target turns out to be too high or too low to achieve the target rate of inflation (perhaps because money circulates faster or slower than originally thought: see section 29.2) then the M3 target is altered. It is reviewed each year in December.

On the basis of its inflation and money supply targets, the ECB then sets the rates of interest. It sets three rates: a rate for 'refinancing operations' of the ESCB (i.e. the rate of interest charged by the ESCB for liquidity on offer to banks, largely through repos); a (higher) 'last resort' rate; and a (lower) 'deposit rate' (the rate paid to banks for depositing surplus liquidity with the ESCB). In April 2003, these rates were 2.50, 3.50 and 1.50 per cent respectively.

Interest rates are set by the Governing Council by simple majority. In the event of a tie, the president has the casting vote.

The operation of monetary policy

The ECB sets a minimum reserve ratio. It argues that this gives greater stability to the system and reduces the need for day-to-day intervention by the ECB. The ECB argues that if there were no minimum reserves, with banks free to use as much of their reserves with the ESCB as they chose, then they will do so if there is an upsurge in demand from customers. After all, the banks know that they can always *borrow* from the ESCB to meet any liquidity requirements. In such a situation, the ECB would be forced to rely much more on open-market operations to prevent excessive lending by banks to their customers, and hence excessive borrowing from the ESCB, and this would mean much greater fluctuations in interest rates.

The minimum reserve ratio is not designed to be used to make *changes* in monetary policy. In other words it is not used as a *variable* minimum reserves ratio, and for this reason is set at a low level of 2 per cent.

The main instrument for keeping the ECB's desired interest rate as the equilibrium rate is open-market operations in government bonds and other recognised assets, mainly in the form of repos. These repo operations are conducted by the national central banks, which must ensure that the repo rate does not rise above the last resort rate or below the deposit rate.

Question

What are the arguments for and against publishing the minutes of the meetings of the ECB's Governing Council and Executive Board?

frequent and sizeable adjustments to interest rates. These fluctuations can be very damaging to business confidence and may discourage long-term investment.

The net result of an inelastic and unstable demand for money is that substantial interest rate changes may be necessary to bring about the required change in aggregate demand. An example occurred in 2001, when the US Federal Reserve, seeing the economy moving rapidly into recession, had to cut interest rates several times. At the beginning of 2001, the US 'federal funds rate' was 6.5 per cent. By the end of the year it had been reduced to 1.75 per cent.

> **Pause for thought**
>
> *Assume that the central bank announces a rise in interest rates and backs this up with open-market operations. What determines the size of the resulting fall in aggregate demand?*

Using monetary policy

It is impossible to use monetary policy as a precise means of controlling aggregate demand. It is especially weak when it is pulling against the expectations of firms and consumers and when it is implemented too late. However, if the authorities operate a tight monetary policy firmly enough and long enough, they should eventually be able to reduce lending and aggregate demand. But there will inevitably be time lags and imprecision in the process.

An expansionary monetary policy is even less reliable. If the economy is in recession, no matter how low interest rates are driven, people cannot be forced to borrow if they do not wish to. Firms will not borrow to invest if they predict a continuing recession.

Despite these problems, changing interest rates can be quite effective. After all, they can be changed very rapidly. There are not the time lags of implementation that there are with fiscal policy. Indeed, since the early 1990s, most governments or central banks in OECD countries have used interest rate changes as the major means of keeping aggregate demand and inflation under control.

In the UK, the eurozone and many other countries, a target is set for the rate of inflation. As we have seen, in the UK the target is 2 per cent; in the eurozone it is 'close to' 2 per cent. If forecasts suggest that inflation is going to be above the target rate, the government or central bank raises interest rates. The advantage of this is that it sends a very clear message to people that inflation *will* be kept under control. People will therefore be more likely to adjust their expectations accordingly and keep their borrowing in check.

30.5 Attitudes towards demand management

If fiscal and monetary policies are used together, they are much more likely to be successful. For example, if there is a recession, the government may cut taxes or increase government expenditure in order to expand aggregate demand. This could lead to crowding out, however, unless the central bank simultaneously pursues an expansionary monetary policy, so that any increase in the public-sector deficit is financed by an expansion in the money supply. The central bank could go further and actively cut interest rates.

The policies reinforce each other. The expansionary monetary policy helps to ensure that increased public borrowing is not at the expense of private-sector consumption and investment. The expansionary fiscal policy helps to ensure that increased money is actually spent.

But even if fiscal and monetary policies are used together, governments and central banks will still need to decide whether to pursue an active policy of demand management at all or whether to adopt a policy of setting rules and then sticking to them. In the 1990s, as the economies of Europe and the USA seemed to be becoming more stable, so it became fashionable to set rules. These involved inflation and/or money supply targets and targets for government deficits. With the economic uncertainty of the early 2000s, however, many economists and politicians have argued that much more active fiscal and monetary policies are required. They argue for 'discretionary' policies: i.e. adjusting policies as circumstances change.

The case for rules

The case against discretionary policy centres on the problem of time lags. Both fiscal and monetary policies can involve long and variable time lags, which can make the policy at best ineffective and at worst destabilising. Taking the

Key Idea 29 p409

measures *before* the problem arises, and thus lessening the problem of lags, is no answer since forecasting tends to be unreliable.

By setting and sticking to rules, however, and then not interfering further, the government can provide a sound monetary framework in which firms are not cushioned from market forces, and are therefore encouraged to be efficient. By the government or central bank setting a clear target either for the growth of money supply, or for the rate of inflation, and then resolutely sticking to it, people's expectations of inflation will be reduced, thereby making the target easier to achieve. This sound and stable monetary environment, with no likelihood of sudden expansionary or contractionary policy, will encourage firms to take a longer-term perspective, and plan ahead. This could then lead to increased capital investment and long-term growth.

The optimum situation is for all the major countries to adhere to mutually consistent rules, so that their economies do not get out of line. This will create more stable exchange rates and provide the climate for world growth.

The case for discretion

Many economists, especially those in the Keynesian tradition, reject the argument that rules provide the environment for high and stable growth. Demand, they argue, is subject to many and sometimes violent shocks: e.g. changes in expectations, domestic political events (such as an impending election), world economic factors (such as the world economic slowdown of 2001–2003) or world political events (such as a war). The resulting shifts in injections or withdrawals cause the economy to deviate from a stable full-employment growth path.

Any change in injections or withdrawals will lead to a cumulative effect on national income via the multiplier and accelerator and via changing expectations. These effects take time and interact with each other, and so a process of expansion or contraction can last many months before a turning point is eventually reached.

Since shocks to demand occur at irregular intervals and are of different magnitudes, the economy is likely to experience cycles of irregular duration and of varying intensity.

Given that the economy is inherently unstable and is buffeted around by various shocks, Keynesians argue that the government needs actively to intervene to stabilise the economy. Otherwise, the uncertainty caused by unpredictable fluctuations will be very damaging to investment and hence to long-term economic growth (quite apart from the short-term effects of recessions on output and employment).

If demand fluctuates in the way Keynesians claim, and if the policy of having a money supply or inflation rule is adhered to, interest rates must fluctuate. But excessive fluctuations in interest rates will discourage long-term business planning and investment.

Difficulties with choice of target

Assume that the government or central bank sets an inflation target. Should it then stick to that rate, come what may? Might not an extended period of relatively low inflation warrant a lower inflation target? The government must at least have the discretion to *change* the rules, even if only occasionally.

Then there is the question of whether success in achieving the target will bring success in achieving other macroeconomic objectives, such as low unemployment

definition

Goodhart's Law
Controlling a
symptom of a
problem, or only part
of the problem, will
not cure the
problem: it will
simply mean that the
part that is being
controlled now
becomes a poor
indicator of the
problem.

and stable economic growth? The problem is that something called **Goodhart's Law** is likely to apply. The law, named after Charles Goodhart, formerly of the Bank of England, states that attempts to control an *indicator* of a problem may, as a result, make it cease to be a good indicator of the problem.

Goodhart's law. Controlling a symptom (i.e. an indicator) of a problem will not cure the problem. Instead, the indicator will merely cease to be a good indicator of the problem.

Key Idea 37

Targeting inflation may make it become a poor indicator of the state of the economy. If people believe that the central bank will be successful in achieving its inflation target, then those expectations will feed into their inflationary expectations, and not surprisingly the target will be met. But that target rate of inflation may now be consistent with both a buoyant and a depressed economy. In other words, the Phillips curve may become *horizontal*. Achieving the inflation target has not tackled the much more serious problem of creating stable economic growth and an environment which will therefore encourage long-term investment.

definition

Taylor rule
A rule adopted by a
central bank for
setting the rate of
interest. It will raise
the interest rate
if (a) inflation is
above target or
(b) economic
growth is above
the sustainable level
(or unemployment
is below the
equilibrium rate).
The rule states how
much interest rates
will be changed in
each case.

Use of a Taylor rule. For this reason, many economists have advocated the use of a **Taylor rule**,[1] rather than a simple inflation target. A Taylor rule takes *two* objectives into account – (1) inflation and (2) either the rate of economic growth or unemployment – and seeks to get the optimum degree of stability of the two. The degree of importance attached to each of the two objectives can be decided by the government or central bank. The central bank adjusts interest rates when either the rate of inflation diverges from its target or the rate of economic growth (or unemployment) diverges from its sustainable (or equilibrium) level.

Take the case where inflation is above its target level. The central bank following a Taylor rule will raise the rate of interest. It knows, however, that this will reduce economic growth. This, therefore, limits the amount that the central bank is prepared to raise the rate of interest. The more weight it attaches to stabilising inflation, the more it will raise the rate of interest. The more weight it attaches to maintaining stable economic growth, the less it will raise the rate of interest.

Thus the central bank has to trade off inflation stability against real income stability.

Key Idea 35 p568

30.6 Current demand-side policy in the UK

Fiscal policy

Since 1998, the government has set targets for government expenditure, not for just one year, but for a three-year period. Does this mean, therefore, that fiscal policy as a means of adjusting aggregate demand had been abandoned?

---

[1] Named after John Taylor, from Stanford University, who proposed that for every 1 per cent that GDP rises above sustainable GDP, real interest rates should be raised by 0.5 percentage points and for every 1 per cent that inflation rises above its target level, real interest rates should be raised by 0.5 percentage points (i.e. nominal rates should be raised by 1.5 percentage points).

In one sense, this is the case. The government is now committed to following its 'golden rule', whereby public-sector receipts should cover all current spending, averaged over the course of the business cycle (see Box 30.1). In fact, in supporting sticking to the golden rule, the Chancellor explicitly rejected Keynesian fine tuning:

> In today's deregulated, liberalised financial markets, the Keynesian fine tuning of the past, which worked in relatively sheltered, closed national economies and which tried to exploit a supposed long-term trade-off between inflation and unemployment, will simply not work.[2]

But despite this apparent rejection of short-term discretionary fiscal adjustments, there is still a role for *automatic* fiscal stabilisers: with deficits rising in a recession and falling in a boom. There is also still the possibility, within the golden rule, of financing additional *investment* by borrowing, thereby providing a stimulus to a sluggish economy.

The golden rule also permits increased government expenditure (or tax cuts) if there is a budget surplus. Thus in the 2001 Budget the Chancellor announced spending increases of 3.7 per cent per year for three years. The effect was to provide a stimulus to the economy just at a time when the world economy was slowing down. This helped to make the slowdown in UK economic growth much less severe than in many other countries.

Monetary policy

Since 1992, both Conservative and Labour governments have used monetary policy to achieve a target rate of inflation. The Conservative government chose both the target (to be within a range of 1 to 4 per cent) and also the rate of interest felt necessary to achieve that target. The interest rate, however, was chosen in consultation with the Governor of the Bank of England and was based on forecasts of the rate of inflation. The Chancellor met monthly with the Governor to discuss interest rates and the minutes of the meetings were published six weeks later, in order to give transparency to the process.

In 1997, the incoming Labour government set a target for inflation of $2^1/_2$ per cent, which remained unchanged until 2003, when it was reduced to 2 per cent.

Unlike its predecessor, however, it decided to make the Bank of England independent. Indeed, this was the first action taken by the Chancellor when the government came to power.

But why did the government give up its right to set interest rates? First, there is the political advantage of taking 'blame' away from the government if interest rates need to be raised in order to prevent inflation rising above its target. Second, an independent central bank, free to set interest rates in order to achieve a clear target, is more likely to be consistent in pursuit of this objective than a government concerned about its popularity. Then there is the question of transparency in decision making.

> If inflation is more than 1 percentage point higher or lower than the target, an open letter will be sent by the Governor to the Chancellor so that the public is fully informed as to why the divergence has occurred; the policy action being taken to deal with it; the period within which inflation is expected to

---

[2] Extract from the Chancellor's Mansion House speech, 11 June 1998.

BOX 30.4

Inflation targeting
The fashion of the age

More and more countries are turning to inflation targeting as their main macroeconomic policy. The diagram shows that in a survey by the Bank of England of 91 countries, 55 of them targeted inflation in 1998. Only nine of them targeted inflation in 1990. But why is it becoming so fashionable?

Part of the reason is the apparent failure of discretionary macroeconomic policies. Discretionary fiscal and monetary policies suffer from time lags, from being used for short-term political purposes and from failing to eliminate or even dampen the business cycle. But if discretionary policies have seemed not

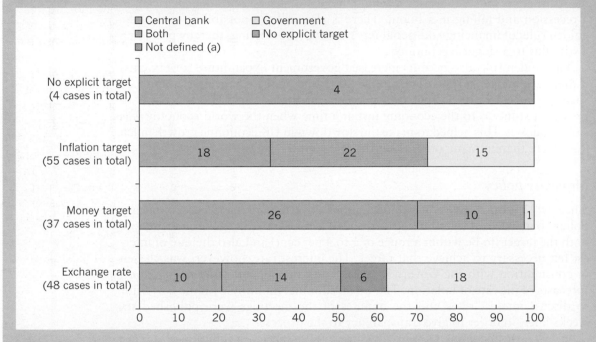

Who sets explicit targets and monitoring ranges for the exchange rate, money and inflation?

Source: *The Use of Explicit Targets for Monetary Policy: Practical Experiences of 91 Economies in the 1990s* (Bank of England, August, 1999)

return to the target; and how this approach meets the government's monetary policy objectives. Monetary policy decision-making is now among the most transparent and accountable in the world.[3]

Transparency is enhanced by the publication of the minutes of the monthly meetings of the Bank's Monetary Policy Committee (MPC) at which interest rates are set. One of the main purposes of transparency is to convince people of the seriousness with which the Bank of England will adhere to its targets. This, it is hoped, will keep people's *expectations* of inflation low: the lower expected inflation is, the lower will be the actual rate of inflation.

---

[3] *The Government's Overall Economic Strategy* (**www.hm-treasury.gov.uk/pub/html/e_info/overview/1_goes.html**).

to work, why choose an inflation target rather than a target for the money supply or the exchange rate?

Money supply targets were adopted by many countries in the 1980s, including the UK, and this policy too was largely a failure. Money supply targets proved very difficult to achieve. As we have seen, money supply depends on the amount of credit banks create and this is not easy for the authorities to control. Then, even if money supply is controlled, this does not necessarily mean that aggregate demand will be controlled: the velocity of circulation may change. Nevertheless, many countries do still target the money supply, although in most cases it is not the main target. For example, as we saw in Box 30.3, the ECB targets money supply as well as inflation. In the diagram, 31 of the 55 countries targeting inflation also targeted the money supply.

Exchange-rate targets, as we shall see in Chapter 32, may have serious disadvantages if the equilibrium exchange rate is not the one that is being targeted. The main instrument for keeping the exchange rate on target is the rate of interest. For example, if the exchange rate target were £1 = $1.50, and the exchange rate were currently £1 = $1.40, then interest rates would be raised. This would cause an inflow of money into the economy and hence push up the exchange rate. But if the rate of interest is being used to achieve an exchange rate target, it cannot be used for other purposes, such as controlling aggregate demand or inflation. Raising interest rates to achieve an exchange rate target may lead to a recession.

Inflation targets have proved relatively easy to achieve. There may be problems at first, if the actual rate of inflation is way above the target level. The high rates of interest necessary to bring inflation down, may cause a recession. But once inflation has been brought down and the objective is then simply to maintain it at the target level, most countries have been relatively successful. And the more successful they are, the more people will expect this success to be maintained, which in turn will help to ensure this success.

So, are there any problems with inflation targeting? Ironically, one of the main problems lies in its success. With worldwide inflation having fallen, and with global trade and competition helping to keep prices down, there is now less of a link between inflation and the business cycle. Booms no longer seem to generate the inflation they once did. Gearing interest-rate policy to maintaining low inflation could still see economies experiencing unsustainable booms, followed by recessions. Inflation may be controlled, but the business cycle may not be.

More details of the Bank of England study and of the relative merits of different targets are given in web case K8.

Question

Why may there be problems in targeting (a) both inflation and the money supply; (b) both inflation and the exchange rate?

With monetary policy geared to an inflation target and fiscal policy geared to following the golden rule, there seems to be virtually no scope for discretionary demand management policy. Rules appear to have replaced discretion.

When there are ever more rapid financial flows across the world that are unpredictable and uncertain, the answer is to ensure stability through establishing the right long-term policy objectives and to build credibility in the policy through well-understood procedural rules that are followed for fiscal and monetary policy.[4]

Pause for thought

Do you agree that 'ever more rapid financial flows across the world that are unpredictable and uncertain' make Keynesian discretionary fiscal (and monetary) policy less suitable? Explain.

There is, however, a new form of fine tuning: the frequent adjustment of interest rates, not to smooth out the business cycle, but to make sure that the inflation rule is adhered to.

[4] Extract from the Chancellor's Mansion House speech, 11 June 1998.

SUMMARY

1a The government's fiscal policy will determine the size of the budget deficit or surplus and the size of the PSNCR.

1b Automatic fiscal stabilisers are tax revenues that rise and benefits that fall as national income rises. They have the effect of reducing the size of the multiplier and thus reducing cyclical upswings and downswings.

1c Discretionary fiscal policy is where the government deliberately changes taxes or government expenditure in order to alter the level of aggregate demand. Changes in government expenditure on goods and services will have a full multiplier effect. Changes in taxes and benefits will have a smaller multiplier effect as some of the tax/benefit changes will merely affect other withdrawals and thus have a smaller net effect on consumption of domestic product.

2a There are problems with both automatic stabilisers and discretionary fiscal policy.

2b Automatic stabilisers take effect as soon as aggregate demand fluctuates, but they can never remove fluctuations completely. They also create disincentives and act as a drag on recovery from recession.

2c There are problems in predicting the magnitude of the effects of discretionary fiscal policy. Expansionary fiscal policy can act as a pump primer and stimulate increased private expenditure, or it can crowd out private expenditure. The extent to which it acts as a pump primer depends crucially on business confidence – something that is very difficult to predict beyond a few weeks or months. The extent of crowding out depends on monetary conditions and the government's monetary policy.

2d There are five possible time lags involved with fiscal policy: the time lag before the problem is diagnosed, the lag between diagnosis and new measures being announced, the lag between announcement and implementation, the lag while the multiplier and accelerator work themselves out, and the lag before consumption fully responds to new economic circumstances.

2e Discretionary fiscal policy can involve side-effects, such as disincentives, higher costs and adverse effects on social programmes.

2f Today many governments prefer a more passive approach towards fiscal policy. Targets are set for one or more measures of the public-sector finances, and then taxes and government expenditure are adjusted so as to keep to the target.

3a Control of the growth of the money supply over the longer term will normally involve governments attempting to restrict the size of the budget deficit.

3b In the short term, the government can use monetary policy to restrict the growth in aggregate demand in one of three ways: (a) reducing money supply directly, (b) reducing the demand for money by raising interest rates, or (c) rationing credit.

3c The money supply can be reduced directly by using open-market operations. This involves selling more government securities and thereby reducing banks' reserves when their customers pay for them from their bank accounts. Alternatively the central bank can reduce the amount it is prepared to lend to banks (other than as a last-resort measure). Or it could use funding, by increasing the sale of bonds relative to bills, thereby reducing banks' liquid assets. Finally it could operate a system of variable minimum reserve ratios. Increasing these would force banks to cut back on the amount of credit they create.

3d The current method of control involves the Bank of England's Monetary Policy Committee announcing the interest rate and then the Bank of England bringing this rate about by its operations in the discount and repo markets. It keep banks short of liquidity, and then supplies them with liquidity largely through gilt repos, at the chosen interest rate (gilt repo rate). This then has a knock-on effect on interest rates throughout the economy.

3e Credit rationing in the UK has not been used since the late 1970s.

4a It is difficult to control the growth of the money supply over the longer term without controlling the public-sector deficit. This will be difficult in a recession, when automatic fiscal stabilisers will cause a growth in government expenditure and a cut in tax revenues.

4b All forms of short-term monetary policy involve problems. The money supply is difficult to control precisely, and even if it is successfully controlled, there then arises the problem of

SUMMARY

severe fluctuations in interest rates if the demand for money fluctuates and is relatively inelastic.

4c The form of monetary policy that has been favoured in recent years is the control of interest rates. Higher interest rates, by reducing the demand for money, effectively also reduce the supply. However, with an inelastic demand for loans, interest rates may have to rise to very high levels in order to bring the required reduction in monetary growth.

4d Controlling aggregate demand through interest rates is made even more difficult by fluctuations in the demand for money. These fluctuations are made more severe by speculation against changes in interest rates, exchange rates, the rate of inflation, etc.

4e Nevertheless, controlling interest rates is a way of responding rapidly to changing forecasts, and can be an important signal to markets that inflation will be kept under control, especially when, as in the UK and the eurozone, there is a firm target for the rate of inflation.

5a The case against discretionary policy is that it involves unpredictable time lags, which can make the policy destabilising. The government may as a result overcorrect. Also the government may ignore the long-run adverse consequences of policies designed for short-run political gain.

5b The case in favour of rules is that they help to reduce inflationary expectations and thus create a stable environment for investment and growth.

5c The case against sticking to money supply or inflation rules is that they may cause severe fluctuations in interest rates and thus create a less stable economic environment for business planning. Also, given the changing economic environment in which we live, rules adopted in the past may no longer be suitable for the present. Keynesians thus argue that the government must have the discretion to change its policy as circumstances demand.

5d Achieving inflation targets is becoming increasingly easy, but unrelated to other key objectives, such as economic growth or unemployment. Some economists advocate using a Taylor rule, which involves targeting a weighted average of inflation and economic growth.

6a Since 1992, both Conservative and Labour governments in the UK have pursued a largely rules-based demand-side policy.

6b Today, fiscal policy is geared to achieving a balanced budget over the course of the business cycle. The only exception to this is borrowing for public *investment*. Monetary policy is geared to achieving a target rate of inflation of 2 per cent. The Bank of England adjusts interest rates in order to keep to this target.

REVIEW QUESTIONS

1 'The existence of a budget deficit or a budget surplus tells us very little about the stance of fiscal policy.' Explain and discuss.

2 Adam Smith remarked in *The Wealth of Nations* concerning the balancing of budgets, 'What is prudence in the conduct of every private family can scarce be folly in that of a great kingdom.' What problems might there be if the government decided to follow a balanced budget approach to its spending?

3 What factors determine the effectiveness of discretionary fiscal policy?

4 Why is it difficult to use fiscal policy to 'fine tune' the economy?

5 When the Bank of England announces that it is putting up interest rates, how will it achieve this, given that interest rates are determined by demand and supply?

6 How does the Bank of England attempt to achieve the target rate of inflation of 2 per cent? What determines its likelihood of success in meeting the target?

7 Imagine you were called in by the government to advise on whether it should adopt a policy of targeting the money supply. What advice would you give and how would you justify the advice?

8 Imagine you were called in by the government to advise on whether it should attempt to prevent cyclical fluctuations by the use of fiscal policy. What advice would you give and how would you justify the advice?

9 Is there a compromise between purely discretionary policy and adhering to strict targets?

10 Under what circumstances would adherence to an inflation target lead to (a) more stable interest rates, (b) less stable interest rates than pursuing discretionary demand management policy?

CHAPTER

31 Supply-side policy

31.1 The supply-side problem

In considering economic policy up to this point we have focused our attention upon the demand side, where unemployment and slow growth are due to a lack of aggregate demand, and inflation and a balance of payments deficit are due to excessive aggregate demand. Many of the causes of these problems lie on the supply side, however, and as such require an alternative policy approach.

Key Idea 30 p410

If successful, 'supply-side policies' will shift the aggregate supply curve to the right, thus increasing output for any given level of prices (or reducing the price level for any given level of output).

Unemployment and supply-side policies

Equilibrium unemployment – frictional, structural, etc. – is caused by various rigidities or imperfections in the market. There is a mismatching of aggregate supply and demand, and vacancies are not filled despite the existence of unemployment. Perhaps workers have the wrong qualifications, or are poorly motivated, or are living a long way away from the job, or are simply unaware of the jobs that are vacant. Generally, the problem is that labour is not sufficiently mobile, either occupationally or geographically, to respond to changes in the job market. Labour supply for particular jobs is too inelastic.

Supply-side policies aim to influence labour supply. They aim to make workers more responsive to changes in job opportunities. Alternatively, they may aim to make employers more adaptable and willing to operate within existing labour constraints.

Key Idea 8 p62

Inflation and supply-side policies

If inflation is caused by cost-push pressures, supply-side policy can help to reduce these cost pressures in two ways:

■ By reducing the power of unions and/or firms (e.g. by anti-monopoly legislation), and thereby encouraging more competition in the supply of labour and/or goods.

■ By encouraging increases in productivity through the retraining of labour, or by investment grants to firms, or by tax incentives, etc.

Growth and supply-side policies

Supply-side economics focuses on *potential* GDP. Supply-side policies aim to increase the total quantity of factors of production (e.g. policies designed to encourage the building of new factories) or they can be used to encourage greater productivity of factors of production (e.g. policies to encourage the training of labour, or incentives for people to work harder).

Supply-side policies can take various forms. They can be 'market orientated' and focus on ways of 'freeing up' the market, such as encouraging private enterprise, risk taking and competition; policies that provide incentives and reward initiative, hard work and productivity. Section 31.2 examines these *market-orientated* supply-side policies.

Alternatively they can be *interventionist* in nature and focus on means of counteracting the deficiencies of the free market. Such policies are considered in sections 31.3 and 31.4, which focus upon regional and urban, and industrial policy initiatives.

Key Idea 8 p62

31.2   Market-orientated supply-side policies

Radical market-orientated supply-side policies were first adopted in the early 1980s by the Thatcher government in the UK and the Reagan administration in the USA, but were subsequently copied by other right and centre-right governments around the world. The essence of these supply-side policies was to encourage and reward individual enterprise and initiative, and to reduce the role of government; to put more reliance on market forces and competition, and less on government intervention and regulation.

Reducing government expenditure

The desire of many governments to cut government expenditure is not just to reduce the size of the public-sector deficit and hence reduce the growth of money supply; it is also an essential ingredient of their supply-side strategy.

In most countries the size of the public sector, relative to national income, has grown substantially since the 1950s (see Table 31.1). A major aim of Conservative governments throughout the world has been to reverse this trend. The public sector is portrayed as more bureaucratic and less efficient than the private sector. What is more, it is claimed that a growing proportion of public money has been spent on administration and other 'non-productive' activities, rather than on the direct provision of goods and services.

Table 31.1 General government outlays as a percentage of GDP

	1961–70	1971–80	1981–5	1986–90	1991–5	1996–2000	2001–3
Belgium	33.7	50.6	61.5	55.3	54.1	50.9	49.7
Germany	37.0	45.3	48.2	46.0	48.2	48.6	48.6
France	38.3	42.4	51.5	50.2	53.0	54.1	53.4
Japan	–	26.8	33.2	31.5	33.2	39.1	39.9
Netherlands	39.9	49.3	59.5	55.0	53.0	47.5	47.0
Sweden	–	52.8	65.0	58.5	65.6	61.4	58.2
UK	36.5	41.2	44.6	39.8	42.3	40.0	40.8
USA	29.1	33.1	36.5	34.9	35.9	33.1	34.6

Source: Adapted from *European Economy Statistical Annex*, Spring 2003 (European Commission)

Two things are needed, it is argued: (a) a more efficient use of resources within the public sector and (b) a reduction in the size of the public sector. This would allow private investment to increase with no overall rise in aggregate demand. Thus the supply-side benefits of higher investment could be achieved without the demand-side costs of higher inflation.

In practice, governments have found it very difficult to cut their expenditure without cutting services and the provision of infrastructure.

> **Pause for thought**
>
> *Why might a recovering economy (and hence a fall in government expenditure on social security benefits) make the government feel even more concerned to make discretionary cuts in government expenditure?*

Tax cuts

Tax cuts: the effects on labour supply and employment

Cutting the marginal rate of income tax was a major objective of the Thatcher and Major governments (1979–97). In 1979 the standard rate of income tax in the UK was 33 per cent and the top rate was 83 per cent. By 1997 the standard rate was only 23 per cent (with a starting rate of just 20 per cent), and the top rate was only 40 per cent. The Blair government continued with this policy. In 2004, the standard rate was 22 per cent and the starting rate was only 10 per cent. Cuts in the marginal rate of income tax are claimed to have many beneficial effects: for example, people work longer hours; more people wish to work; people work more enthusiastically; unemployment falls; employment rises. The evidence regarding the truth of these claims, however, is less than certain.

For example, do more people wish to work? This applies largely to second income earners in a family, mainly women. A rise in after-tax wages may encourage more women to look for jobs. It may now be worth the cost in terms of transport, child minders, family disruption, etc. However, the effect of a 1 or 2 per cent cut in income tax rates is likely to be negligible. A more significant effect may be achieved by raising tax allowances: the amount of income that can be earned before taxes are paid. Part-time workers, especially, could end up paying no taxes.

Whether people will be prepared to work longer hours is also questionable. On the one hand, each hour worked will be more valuable in terms of take-home pay, and thus people may be encouraged to work more and have less leisure time (a substitution effect – see page 64). On the other hand, a cut in income tax will make people better off, and therefore they may feel less need to do overtime than before (an income effect). The evidence on these two effects suggests that they just about cancel each other out. Anyway, for many people there is no such choice in the short run. There is no chance of doing overtime or working a shorter week. In the long run, there may be some flexibility in that people can change jobs.

Despite the cuts in marginal rates of income tax, there have been significant tax *increases* elsewhere. In particular, VAT stood at only 8 per cent in 1979; in 2004 it was 17½ per cent. The marginal rate of national insurance contributions was 6½ per cent in 1979; in 2004 it was 11 per cent. The net effect was that taxes as a proportion of national income rose from 34.2 per cent in 1979 to 37 per cent in 2004.

> **Pause for thought**
>
> *If taxes as a proportion of national income have risen since 1979, does this mean that there can have been no positive incentive effects of the various tax measures taken by first the Conservative and then the Labour governments?*

Key Idea 8 p62

Key Idea 4 p27

To the extent that tax cuts do succeed in increasing take-home pay, there is a danger of 'sucking in' imports. In the UK, there is a high income elasticity of demand for imports. Extra consumer incomes may be spent on Japanese videos and hi-fi, foreign cars, holidays abroad, and so on. Tax cuts can therefore have a serious effect on the balance of trade.

Tax cuts for business and other investment incentives

A number of financial incentives can be given to encourage investment. Market-orientated policies seek to reduce the general level of taxation on profits, or to give greater tax relief to investment.

A cut in corporation tax will increase after-tax profits. This will create more money for ploughing back into investment, and the higher after-tax return on investment will encourage more investment to take place. In 1983 the main rate of corporation tax in the UK stood at 52 per cent. A series of reductions have taken place since then, and by 2004 the rate was 30 per cent for large companies and 19 per cent for small ones, with a starting rate of only 10 per cent.

Reducing the power of labour

The argument here is that if labour costs to employers are reduced, their profits will probably rise. This could encourage and enable more investment and hence economic growth. If the monopoly power of labour is reduced, then cost-push inflation will also be reduced.

The Thatcher government took a number of measures to weaken the power of labour. These included restrictions on union closed shops, restrictions on secondary picketing and enforced secret ballots on strike proposals (see page 361). It set a lead in resisting strikes in the public sector. Unlike previous Labour governments, it did not consult with union leaders over questions of economic policy. It was publicly very critical of trade union militancy and blamed the unions for many of the UK's economic ills. As a result, unions lost a lot of political standing and influence.

As labour markets have become more flexible, with increased part-time working and short-term contracts, so this has further eroded the power of labour in many sectors of the economy (see section 18.7).

Reducing welfare

New classical economists claim that a major cause of unemployment is the small difference between the welfare benefits of the unemployed and the take-home pay of the employed. This causes voluntary unemployment (i.e. frictional unemployment). People are caught in a 'poverty trap': if they take a job, they lose their benefits.

A dramatic solution to this problem would be to cut unemployment benefits. In the early 1980s the gap between take-home pay and welfare benefits to the unemployed did indeed widen. However, over the same period unemployment rose dramatically. Nevertheless, the claim that there was too little incentive for people to work was still a major part of the Thatcher government's explanation of growing unemployment.

A major problem is that, with changing requirements for labour skills, many of the redundant workers from the older industries are simply not qualified for new jobs that are created. What is more, the longer people are unemployed, the more demoralised they become. Employers would probably be prepared to pay only very low wages to such workers. To persuade these unemployed people to take low-paid jobs, the welfare benefits would have to be slashed. A 'market' solution to the problem, therefore, may be a very cruel solution. A fairer solution would be an interventionist policy: a policy of retraining labour.

Another alternative is to make the payment of unemployment benefits conditional on the recipient making a concerted effort to find a job. In the jobseeker's allowance introduced in 1996, claimants must be available for and actively seeking work and must complete a Jobseeker's Agreement, which sets out the types of work the person is willing to do and the plan to find work. Payment can be refused if the claimant refuses to accept jobs offered.

Policies to encourage competition

If the government can encourage more competition, this should have the effect of increasing national output and reducing inflation. Five major types of policy were pursued under this heading.

Privatisation. If privatisation simply involves the transfer of a natural monopoly to private hands (e.g. the water companies), the scope for increased competition is limited. However, where there is genuine scope for increased competition (e.g. in the supply of gas and electricity), privatisation can lead to increased efficiency, more consumer choice and lower prices.

Alternatively, privatisation can involve the introduction of private services into the public sector (e.g. private contractors providing cleaning services in hospitals, or refuse collection for local authorities). Private contractors may compete against each other for the franchise. This may well lower the cost of provision of these services, but the quality of provision may suffer unless closely monitored. The effects on unemployment are uncertain. Private contractors may offer lower wages and thus may use more labour. But if they are trying to supply the service at minimum cost, they are likely to employ less labour.

Deregulation. This involves the removal of monopoly rights: again, largely in the public sector. The deregulation of the bus industry in the 1980s, opening it up to private operators, is a good example of this initiative. An example in the private sector was the 'Big Bang' on the Stock Exchange in 1986. Under this the monopoly power of 'jobbers' to deal in stocks and shares on the Stock Exchange was abolished. In addition, stockbrokers now compete with each other in the commission rates they charge.

Introducing market relationships into the public sector. This is where the government tries to get different departments or elements within a particular part of the public sector to 'trade' with each other, so as to encourage competition and efficiency. The most well-known examples are within health and education.

The process often involves 'devolved budgeting'. For example, under the local management of schools scheme (LMS), schools have become self-financing. Rather than the local authority meeting the bill for teachers' salaries, the schools have to manage their own budgets. The objective is to encourage them to cut costs, thereby reducing the burden on council tax payers. However, one result is

BOX 31.1

Productivity and economic growth
The key to a better standard of living?

A country's potential output depends on the productivity of its factors of production. There are three common ways of measuring productivity. The first is output per worker. This is the most straightforward measure to calculate. All that is required is a measure of total output and employment.

The second measure is output per hour worked. This has the advantage that it is not influenced by the *number* of hours worked. So for an economy like the UK, with a very high percentage of part-time workers on the one hand, and long average hours worked by full-time employees on the other, such a measure would be more accurate in gauging worker efficiency.

The first two measures focus solely on the productivity of labour. In order to account directly for the productivity of capital we need to consider the growth in *total* factor productivity (TFP). This third measure gives output relative to the amount of factors used. Changes in total factor productivity over time provide a good indicator of technical progress.

The chart shows comparative productivity levels of four countries using the first two measures.

The importance of productivity

The faster the growth in productivity, the faster is likely to be the country's rate of economic growth. Any government seeking to raise the long-term growth rate, therefore, must find ways of stimulating productivity growth.

On what does the growth of productivity depend? There are seven main determinants:

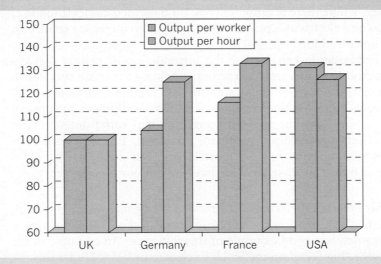

Productivity in selected countries, 2001 (UK = 100)

Source: *Budget 2003, Economic and Fiscal Strategy Report* (HM Treasury, 2003)

that schools have tended to appoint inexperienced (and hence cheaper) teachers rather than those who can bring the benefits of their years of teaching.

Perhaps the most radical example of devolved budgeting was the introduction by the Thatcher government of an 'internal market' into the national health service. General practitioners were offered the opportunity to control their own budget. The size of the budget was determined by the number of patients and by their age and health profiles. GP fundholders purchased services directly from hospitals and had to cover their drugs bill. The suppliers of treatment, the hospitals, depended for much of their income on attracting the business of GP purchasers. They were thus put in competition with other hospitals.

- Private investment in new physical capital (machinery and buildings) and in research and development (R&D).
- Public investment in education, R&D and infrastructure.
- Training and the development of labour skills.
- Innovation and the application of new technology.
- The organisation and management of factors of production.
- The rate of entry of new firms into markets: generally such firms will have higher productivity than existing firms.
- The business environment in which firms operate. Is there competition over the quality and design of products? Is there competitive pressure to reduce costs?

Question

Identify some policies a government could pursue to stimulate productivity growth through each of the above means.

But what are the mechanisms whereby productivity growth feeds through into growth of the economy?

- The capacity of the economy to grow will increase as productivity improvements extend potential output.
- Productivity improvements will drive prices downwards, stimulating demand and actual growth.
- With high returns from their investment, investors might be prepared to embark upon new projects and enterprises, stimulating yet further productivity growth and higher output.

- As labour productivity rises, so wages are likely to rise. The higher wages will lead to higher consumption, and hence, via the multiplier and accelerator, to higher output and higher investment, thereby stimulating further advances in productivity.
- In the longer term, businesses experiencing higher productivity growth would expect their lower costs, and hence enhanced competitiveness, to allow them to gain greater market share. This will encourage further investment and productivity growth.

It is clear that the prosperity of a nation rests upon its ability to improve its productivity. The more successful it is in doing this, the greater will be its rate of economic growth.

For decades the UK has invested a smaller proportion of its national income than most other industrialised nations. This has resulted in relatively low productivity growth and a comparatively low level of labour productivity. This is illustrated in the chart.

Question

In the November 1998 pre-Budget Report[1] it was stated that 'US consumers pay less than those in the UK for a significant range of products. For example, figures from the OECD show, adjusting for movements in exchange rates, British prices are higher than in the US by an average of: 56 per cent for furniture and carpets; 54 per cent for hotels and restaurants; 29 per cent for cars.' Can productivity differences explain price differences?

[1] **www.hm-treasury.gov.uk/pub/html/prebudget99/ 407603.htm, page 12**

Advocates of the internal market in the NHS argued that it created greater efficiency through competition. Critics, however, claimed that it led to growing inequalities of service between practices and between hospitals, and increased the administrative costs of the NHS.

In 2003, the Labour government introduced foundation hospitals. Foundation status would be given to hospitals which meet various quality targets. While still part of the public sector, foundation hospitals would have greater financial freedom, greater local accountability and greater ability to make their own decisions.

The Private Finance Initiative. In 1993 the government introduced its Private Finance Initiative (PFI). This became the new way in which public projects were to be financed and run. Instead of the government or local authority planning, building and then running a public project (such as a new toll bridge, a maintenance depot, a prison, a records office or a block of inner-city workshops), it merely decides in broad terms the service it requires, and then seeks tenders from the private sector for designing, building, financing and running such projects. The capital costs are borne by the private sector, but then, if the provision of the service is not self-financing, the public sector pays the private-sector firm for providing it. Thus instead of the public sector being a provider, it is merely an enabler, buying services from the private sector.

With more than 200 PFI deals signed by 2000, the UK government had already committed itself to £84 billion in revenue expenditure over the following 25 years. More immediately, some £20 billion worth of private capital was put into public services through PFI projects between 2000 and 2003. Projects include the Channel Tunnel rail link, capital investment in the London Underground, moves to modernise and privatise air traffic control and a range of health, education and transport initiatives.

The aim of these 'public-private partnerships' (PPPs) is to introduce competition (through the tendering process) and private-sector expertise into the provision of public services. It is hoped that the extra burden to the taxpayer of the private-sector profits will be more than offset by gains in efficiency. Critics, however, claim that PPPs have resulted in poorer quality of provision and that cost control has often been poor, resulting in a higher burden for the taxpayer in the long term.

Free trade and capital movements. The opening up of international trade and investment is central to a market-orientated supply-side policy. One of the first measures of the Thatcher government (in October 1979) was to remove all exchange controls, thereby permitting the free inflow and outflow of capital, both long term and short term. Most other industrialised countries also removed or relaxed exchange controls during the 1980s and early 1990s.

The Single European Act of 1987, which came into force in 1993, was another example of international liberalisation. As we saw in section 25.3, it created a 'single market' in the EU: a market without barriers to the movement of goods, services, capital and labour.

In addition to adopting supply-side measures that focus on the economy as a whole, governments might decide to target specific regions of the economy, or specific industries for policy initiatives. Such initiatives might be market based. However, they are more likely to be interventionist in nature, as our investigation of regional and industrial policy will show.

31.3 Regional and urban policy in the UK and Europe

Unemployment is not evenly distributed around the UK. Northern Ireland and parts of the north and west of England, parts of Wales and parts of Scotland have unemployment rates substantially higher than in the south-east of England.

Similarly, there are regional disparities in average incomes, rates of growth and levels of prices, as well as in health, crime, housing, etc. These disparities grew wider in the mid-1980s as the recession hit the north, with its traditional

Key Idea

26
p402

heavy industries, much harder than the south. In the recession of the early 1990s, however, it was the service sector that was hardest hit, a sector more concentrated in the south. Regional disparities therefore narrowed somewhat. Disparities are not only experienced at regional level. They are often more acutely felt in specific *areas*, especially inner cities and urban localities subject to industrial decline.

Within the Europe Union differences exist not only within individual countries, but between them. For example, in the EU some countries are much less prosperous than others. Thus, especially with the opening up of the EU in 1993 to the free movement of factors of production, capital and labour may flow to the more prosperous regions of the Union, such as Germany, France and the Benelux countries, and away from the less prosperous regions such as Portugal, Greece and southern Italy.

Causes of regional imbalance and the role of regional policy

If the market functioned perfectly, there would be no regional problem. If wages were lower and unemployment were higher in the north, people would simply move to the south. This would reduce unemployment in the north and help to fill vacancies in the south. It would drive up wage rates in the north and reduce wage rates in the south. The process would continue until regional disparities were eliminated.

The capital market would function similarly. New investment would be located in the areas offering the highest rate of return. If land and labour were cheaper in the north, capital would be attracted there. This too would help to eliminate regional disparities.

In practice, the market does not behave as just described. There are three major problems:

Labour and capital immobility. Labour may be geographically immobile. The regional pattern of industrial location may change more rapidly than the labour market can adjust to it. Thus jobs may be lost in the depressed areas more rapidly than people can migrate.

Similarly, the existing capital stock is highly immobile. Buildings and most machinery cannot be moved to where the unemployed are! *New* capital is much more mobile. But there may be insufficient new investment, especially during a recession, to halt regional decline, even if some investors are attracted into the depressed areas by low wages and cheap land.

Regional multiplier effects. The continuing shift in demand may in part be due to **regional multiplier effects**. In the prosperous regions, the new industries and the new workers attracted there create additional demand. This creates additional output and jobs and hence more migration. There is a multiplied rise in income. In the depressed regions, the decline in demand and loss of jobs causes a multiplied downward effect. Loss of jobs in manufacturing leads to less money spent in the local community; transport and other service industries lose custom. The whole region becomes more depressed.

Externalities. Labour migration imposes external costs on non-migrants. In the prosperous regions, the new arrivals compete for services with those already there. Services become overstretched; house prices rise; council house waiting lists lengthen; roads become more congested, etc. In the depressed regions,

> **definition**
>
> **Regional multiplier effects**
> When a change in injections into or withdrawals from a particular region causes a multiplied change in income in that region. The regional multiplier is given by $1/(1 - mpc_r)$, where mpc_r is the marginal propensity to consume products from the region.

services decline, or alternatively local taxes must rise for those who remain if local services are to be protected. Dereliction, depression and unemployment cause emotional stress for those who remain.

Causes of urban decay

In recent decades there has been a general movement of people from the inner areas of the big cities to the suburbs, to smaller towns and cities, and to rural areas within easy commuting distance of towns. This movement of population has been paralleled by a decline in employment in the inner cities. But with an increasing number of urban jobs being taken by people commuting into the cities, the unemployment problem for those living in these areas grew dramatically. Moreover, many of the older manufacturing industries were located in the inner cities and it was these industries that were hardest hit by the recession of the early 1980s.

The run-down nature of many inner cities causes the more mobile members of the workforce to move away. Spending in these areas has thus declined, causing a local multiplier effect. The jobs that poor people living in these areas do manage to find are often low-paid, unskilled jobs in the service sector (such as shops and the hotel and catering trade) or in petty manufacturing (like garment workshops).

Many of the newer industries prefer to locate away from the inner-city areas on sites where land is cheaper, rates are lower and there is easy access to the motorway network. At the same time, for financial reasons local authorities have found it difficult to offer inducements to firms to move into the inner cities. Nor can they afford to spend large amounts on improving the infrastructure of the blighted areas. Their council taxes are also higher, which again provides an inducement for the more mobile to move away, as well as a disincentive for new firms to move into the area.

Approaches to regional and urban policy

Market-orientated solutions

Supporters of market-based solutions argue that firms are the best judges of where they should locate. Government intervention would impede efficient decision taking by firms. It is better, they argue, to remove impediments to the market achieving regional and local balance. For example, they favour either or both of the following.

Locally negotiated wage agreements. Nationally negotiated wage rates mean that wages are not driven down in the less prosperous areas and up in the more prosperous ones. This discourages firms from locating in the less prosperous areas. At the same time, firms find it difficult to recruit labour in the more prosperous ones, where wages are not high enough to compensate for the higher cost of living there.

Reducing unemployment benefits. A general reduction in unemployment benefits and other welfare payments would encourage the unemployed in the areas of high unemployment to migrate to the more prosperous areas, or enable firms to offer lower wages in the areas of high unemployment.

The problem with these policies is that they attempt initially to widen the economic divide between workers in the different areas in order to encourage capital and labour to move. Such policies would hardly be welcomed by workers in the poorer areas!

Interventionist solutions

Interventionist policies involve encouraging firms to move. Such policies include the following.

Subsidies and tax concessions in the depressed regions. Businesses could be given general subsidies, such as grants to move, or reduced rates of corporation tax. Alternatively, grants or subsidies could be specifically targeted on increasing employment (e.g. reduced employer's national insurance contributions) or on encouraging investment (e.g. investment grants or other measures to reduce the costs of capital).

The provision of facilities in depressed regions. The government or local authorities could provide facilities such as land and buildings at concessionary, or even zero, rents to incoming firms; or spend money on improving the infrastructure of the area (roads and communications, technical colleges, etc.).

The siting of government offices in the depressed regions. The government could move some of its own departments out of the capital and locate them in areas of high unemployment.

It is important to distinguish policies that merely seek to *modify* the market by altering market signals, from policies that *replace* the market. *Regulation* replaces the market, and unless very carefully devised and monitored may lead to ill-thought-out decisions being made. *Subsidies* and *taxes* merely modify the market, leaving it to individual firms to make their final location decisions.

> **Pause for thought**
>
> 1 Think of some other 'pro-market' solutions to the regional problem.
>
> 2 Do people in the more prosperous areas benefit from pro-market solutions?

> **Pause for thought**
>
> If you were the government, how would you set about deciding the rate of subsidy to pay a firm thinking of moving to a less prosperous area?

Regional and urban policy in the UK

Regional policy

Certain areas are identified as requiring government financial assistance. These are known as **assisted areas** (AAs) and cover around 29 per cent of the UK population. They are divided into two categories. Tier 1 areas are those suffering the most acute economic problems. There are four of these areas: Cornwall, South Yorkshire, Merseyside and much of Wales. Tier 2 areas include large parts of Scotland and the north-east of England and many smaller areas affected by economic decline. The assistance comes from both the UK government (the Department of Trade and Industry) and the EU. UK government aid is in two major forms.

- *Regional selective assistance* (RSA) consists of discretionary grants given to firms for investment projects of over £500 000 and which provide skilled jobs. Grants of up to 35 per cent of investment costs are available in Tier 1 areas

> **definition**
>
> **Assisted areas**
> Areas of high unemployment qualifying for government regional selective assistance (RSA) and grants from the European Regional Development Fund (ERDF).

and up to 20 per cent in Tier 2 areas. £785 million of RSA was available in the period 2000–3. Grants are normally for at least £75 000 and amount to about £4000 per job created.

■ *Regional enterprise grants* (REGs) are a means of providing assistance to small and medium-sized firms in England employing up to 250 people in Enterprise Grant Areas (Tier 3 areas). These areas extend beyond Tiers 1 and 2, and include local authority districts with high unemployment rates and various rural development areas. £45 million of REGs was available in the period 2000–3. Separate support for small and medium-sized businesses is available in Scotland and Wales.

The largest amount of regional assistance comes from the *European Regional Development Fund* (ERDF) (see next section). The money is intended to be *additional* to any supplied by member governments. However, some countries, including the UK, have tended to use ERDF grants to *replace* domestic assistance, and have thus come into dispute with the EU.

In 1998 the government set up eight **Regional Development Agencies** (RDAs) for the different regions of England (and a ninth for London in 2000). These, along with the Scottish Parliament and Welsh Assembly, are responsible for administering economic policies for their particular parts of the UK and for developing strategies for improving local infrastructure, encouraging inward investment and promoting investment in skills and training.

> **definition**
>
> **Regional Development Agencies (RDAs)**
> Nine agencies, based in English regions, which initiate and administer regional policy within their area.

Urban policy

During the 1980s the thrust of policy shifted away from regional and towards urban policy. Several new schemes were introduced, involving the creation of various new categories of deprived area. Firms setting up in these areas were eligible for various grants or loans and were subject to fewer planning restrictions.

Currently there are five major elements of regeneration policy:

■ *Regional development agencies (RDAs).* In addition to their regional policy role, the RDAs play an important part in urban regeneration schemes. They administer the *Single Regeneration Budget (SRB)*, a fund established in 1994 to encourage a partnership between government and the private sector (the Private Finance Initiative (PFI)) and to ensure that maximum benefit is gained from European Structural Funds. The RDAs provide grants for schemes which meet various local objectives, such as increased employment, training, new businesses, better housing, crime prevention and support for ethnic minorities. Monies are allocated to partnerships drawn from local authorities, the Learning and Skills Council (LSC), and the private, community and voluntary sectors.

■ *New Deal for Communities* was established in 1998 to provide help for some of the most deprived neighbourhoods. The aim is that local people, local businesses, community and voluntary organisations, local authorities and public agencies form partnerships in each area. These partnerships draw up plans for the economic and social development of the area and submit them to the government, which then awards funds according to the plans' viability.

■ *English Partnerships*, originally the *Urban Regeneration Agency (URA)*, aims to promote the reclamation and development of derelict or contaminated land. It acts as a partner with private firms, local authorities and the voluntary sector. It provides grants, loans, guarantees and partnership investment to encourage private companies to develop and move into such areas.

- *Housing Action Trusts (HATs)* are public bodies dedicated to the regeneration of run-down housing estates in five areas of England. They repair and improve houses and improve the local environment and amenities.

- *Urban regeneration companies (URCs)*. Twelve of these companies have been set up to co-ordinate redevelopment and new investment in deprived urban areas. They work closely with local authorities, RDAs, English Partnerships and the private sector.

In addition, much of the training provided through the Learning and Skills Council and the other bodies identified in section 21.3 is focused in inner-city areas where educational attainment has been low.

Regional policy in the EU

With the signing of the Maastricht Treaty, which established the European Union in November 1993, member states agreed to work together to ensure that:

- The distribution of benefits from European unification were spread fairly.
- Economic and social development was speeded up in the less prosperous countries, so that they might play a fuller part in the EU's future development.
- Economic imbalances between countries did not distort the operation of the internal market between member states.
- Structural reforms were in place, such that the EU would be well prepared for the next century.

In pursuit of these goals, the EU currently allocates some 40 per cent of its total budget to their achievement. In 2001 the EU spent €32 billion, and over the funding period 2000–6 expects to have spent some €213 billion in total. In order to allocate these vast resources. the EU operates a series of inter-related funds, the first four of which are collectively known as the Structural Funds. These funds are used to finance projects jointly with national governments and are not intended to replace national expenditure.

The Structural Funds

The European Regional Development Fund (ERDF). This fund is managed by the Directorate-General for Regional Policy, which allocates grants for projects designed to aid development in poorer regions of the EU. In particular it focuses upon:

- Investment to create and maintain employment.
- Investment in infrastructure.
- Investments in education and health.
- Measures to enhance research and development.
- Collective measures used to support economic activity.

The European Social Fund (ESF). The ESF is managed by the Directorate-General for Employment and Social Affairs. It allocates funds to vocational training programmes, to job creation and the adaptation of worker skills to industrial change.

The Guidance section of the European Agricultural Guidance and Guarantee Fund (EAGGF). The EAGGF is managed by the Directorate-General for Agriculture and allocates funds for the development and restructuring of agriculture and rural areas in general.

The Financial Instrument for Fisheries Guidance (FIFG). The FIFG is managed by the Directorate-General for Fisheries. As with EAGGF, FIFG is concerned solely with one sector of the EU economy, namely fishing, and the problems faced by communities which rely on it.

Other funds

Cohesion Fund. This fund offers additional assistance to the four poorest nations within the EU: Greece, Portugal, Spain and Ireland. Its aim is to support the development of infrastructure projects, and enhance measures that help protect and improve the quality of the environment: for example, improving the quality of water supply and the treatment of waste.

The European Investment Bank (EIB). In addition to the Structural Funds, the EIB also offers support to the less prosperous regions within the EU (approximately two-thirds of its budget goes to such regions). However, unlike the Structural Funds, the EIB offers loans, not grants, and hence requires repayment. The EIB generally offers loans up to 50 per cent of the cost of the project, and these loans generally run for between 4 and 18 years. With only a small fee for administration, and with the EIB operating on a non-profit-making basis, interest rates changed by the EIB are low.

The allocation of Structural Funds

Given the diversity of funding alternatives, how are the resources available allocated? Support from the ERDF, ESF, EAGGF and FIFG focuses upon one or more of the following 'objectives':

Objective 1. To promote the development and structural adjustment of regions which lag behind the rest of the EU. This receives by far the largest share of the Structural Funds budget (see chart). In order to achieve objective 1 status ('Tier 1' status), a region's per capita GDP must be 75 per cent or less of the EU level for the last three years. This objective is funded by the ERDF, ESF and EAGGF.

Objective 2. To support regions adversely affected by industrial decline. In order to qualify for assistance under this objective, a region must have an unemployment rate above the EU average over the last three years. This objective is funded by the ERDF and ESF.

Objective 3. To combat long-term unemployment, and help other groups excluded from the labour market including help to those adapting to industrial change.

Other. This includes 'Community Initiatives' designed to encourage various cross-border, urban and local initiatives. It also includes help to fishing communities outside Objective 1 regions, and funding for various innovative actions to promote development.

The distribution of the structural funds between the objectives and between countries is shown in Figure 31.1.

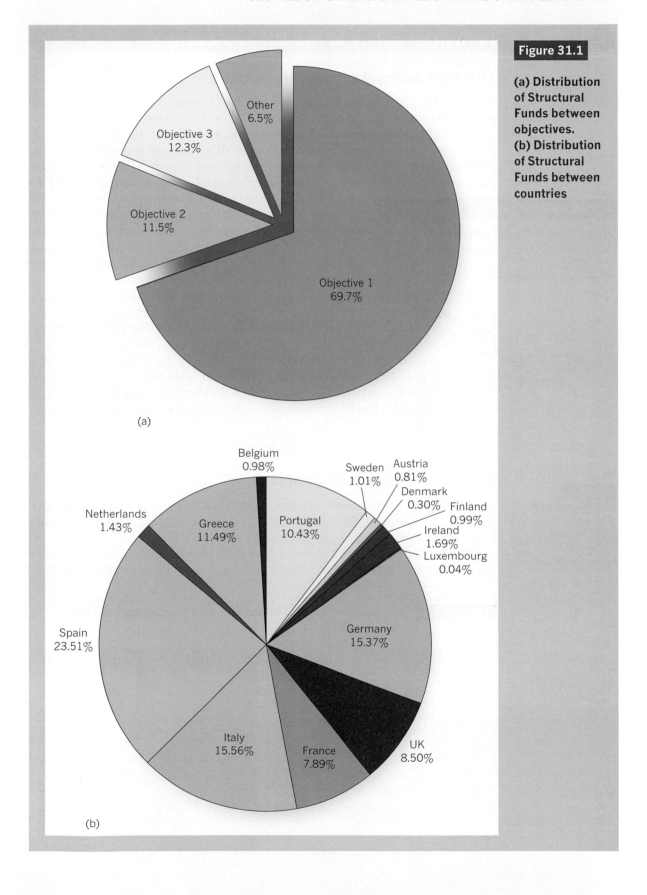

Figure 31.1

(a) Distribution of Structural Funds between objectives.
(b) Distribution of Structural Funds between countries

31.4   Industrial policy in the UK and Europe

The poor performance of UK industry

For decades, the UK has had a lower level of investment relative to national income than other industrialised countries. This is illustrated in Table 31.2.

This low level of investment has been a major reason for the UK's historically poor growth performance. It has also meant that for many industries there has emerged a widening technological gap between the UK and its major competitors such as Japan and Germany. This is reflected in the poor quality and high cost of many UK products. To some extent, however, this has been offset by the fact that wage rates in the UK have been lower than in competing countries. This has at least made the UK relatively attractive to inward investment, especially by Japanese, Korean and US companies seeking to set up production plants within the EU.

> **Pause for thought**
>
> How can the UK's low level of investment relative to national income be explained?

The poor performance of UK manufacturing firms has resulted in a growing import penetration of the UK market. Imports of manufactured products have grown more rapidly than UK manufactured exports, and since 1983 the UK has become a net importer of manufactured products.

These problems have led many economists to call for a much more active supply-side policy: one which involves government intervention, especially in the fields of education and training, research and development, and the provision of infrastructure. This has been the approach in many countries, including France, Germany and Japan.

Approaches to industrial policy

> **definition**
>
> **Industrial policies**
> Policies to encourage industrial investment and greater industrial efficiency.

Industrial policy involves the attempt to increase investment and halt or slow-down the shrinking of the industrial sector. There are two approaches to industrial policy: a demand-side approach and a supply-side one.

On the *demand side*, we have already examined (in Chapter 29) the Keynesian approach of trying to maintain a high level of activity in the economy by demand

Table 31.2   Gross fixed capital formation as a percentage of GDP: 1960–2004

Year (average)	UK	Germany[a]	Japan	EU (15)	USA
1960–7	17.7	25.2	31.0	22.8	18.1
1968–73	18.9	24.5	34.6	23.6	18.6
1974–80	19.2	21.0	31.8	22.2	19.4
1981–5	16.5	20.4	28.7	19.8	19.3
1986–90	18.9	19.9	29.8	20.1	18.3
1991–4	16.6	22.4	30.0	20.7	16.6
1995–9	16.8	20.2	27.3	19.8	18.8
2000–2004	16.4	19.3	24.1	19.7	18.7

[a] West Germany prior to 1991.
Source: *European Economy* (Commission of the European Communities)

management policy. It is based on the premise that the major determinant of investment is consumer demand.

Supply-side approaches aim to provide more incentives to invest for any given level of aggregate demand. They also attempt to improve industrial efficiency and competitiveness for any given level of investment.

The advocates of such policies highlighted a number of supply-side weaknesses of the UK economy in the 1970s: overstaffing, union restrictive practices, an outdated educational and training system insufficiently geared to industry's needs, too little research and development, misdirected research and development, and poor management that is unwilling to go out into world markets and compete aggressively. Some of these problems have eased somewhat in recent years. Others, however, such as a lack of training and too little research and development, are argued by many to have got worse.

Supply-side industrial policy can be interventionist or market orientated in nature.

Interventionist industrial policy

Research and development. The government may sponsor research and development in certain industries (e.g. aerospace) or in specific fields (e.g. microprocessors). The amount of government support in this field has been very small in the UK compared with Japan, France and the USA. What is more, the amount of support declined between the mid-1980s and the late 1990s. In 1999, however, the Labour government introduced a system of tax credits for small firms which invest in research and development. In 2002, this was extended to offer tax relief of 20 per cent of R&D expenditure by large firms.

Rationalisation. The government may encourage mergers or other forms of industrial reorganisation that would lead to greater efficiency and/or higher levels of investment. This could be done through government agencies or government departments.

Advice and persuasion. The government may engage in discussions with private firms in order to find ways to improve efficiency and innovation. It may bring firms together to exchange information so as to co-ordinate their decisions and create a climate of greater certainty. It may bring firms and unions together to try to create greater industrial harmony.

Information. The government may provide various information services to firms: technical assistance, the results of public research, information on markets, etc.

Direct provision. Improvements in infrastructure – such as a better motorway system – can be of direct benefit to industry. Alternatively, the government could provide factories or equipment to specific firms.

Training. Well-targeted training can lead to substantial improvements in labour productivity. We examined training policy in section 21.3.

Market-orientated supply-side policy

Supporters of the free market claim that interventionist industrial policy is based on a false analysis. They suggest that industry's poor investment performance is due to market rigidities, such as managerial inertia and union restrictive practices. Government intervention to support industry weakens market forces and in the long run reduces, not increases, industrial efficiency.

They argue that if the government is to help industry, it is best to reduce the tax burden on industry generally, so as to increase the return on investment and improve the operation of the market system. It is also best to resist the introduction of minimum wage rates and to reduce the power of labour through trade union reform. Finally, it is better to have open markets and open competition: for example, by having no trade barriers and no restrictions on international capital movements.

> **Pause for thought**
>
> Give some criticisms of these arguments.

Industrial policy in Japan and Europe

Japan and the Ministry of Economy Trade and Industry (METI)

Japan is now the world's largest manufacturer of steel, ships, cars and lorries, motor cycles, engines, cameras, calculators, big memory chips, televisions, video tape recorders and photocopiers. Between 1960 and 1995 investment averaged 31 per cent of GDP, industrial output grew by over 5 per cent per annum, real GDP grew by 5.7 per cent per annum and the rate of automation outpaced all Japan's economic rivals.

Part of the explanation for the rapid growth in industrial output in the 1960s and 1970s was the fact that Japan was starting from a low base and was copying and adapting technology developed in the West. But, despite a slowing down in growth after 1973 and particularly in the late 1990s, investment remains higher than in Europe and North America (see Table 30.2) and the development of new products and processes is actively encouraged by the Japanese government.

Industrial policy in Japan is guided by the Ministry of Economy, Trade and Industry (METI), formerly the Ministry of International Trade and Industry (MITI). Its role is to encourage co-operation between private companies and to help stimulate investment in new technology and product development. Using a mixture of state aid and legislative power, METI wields a considerable amount of influence. However, this power is seldom in evidence as most Japanese industry is only too willing to take advantage of the services METI can offer.

METI encourages older industries to close down or to adapt, and provides grants for this purpose. But it is for its help to the 'sunrise' industries that METI is best known. It provides subsidies and helps these industries to raise finance. It has also used tariffs and quotas to protect them from international competition while they are becoming established. It provided help in the 1950s to the steel, shipbuilding and electricity industries, and in the 1960s and 1970s to the chemical, car and electrical goods industries.

In the 1980s and 1990s, it gave substantial support to the computer industry. In 1981 it announced a ten-year project of research into 'next generation computer technology'. This encompassed twelve distinct projects covering investigations into new materials, bio-technology and semi-conductors.

BOX 31.2

A new approach to industrial policy

As with many other areas of economic policy, industrial policy throughout most of the world has undergone a radical reorientation in recent years. The government's role has shifted from one of direct intervention in the form of subsidies and protecting industry from competition, to one of focusing upon the external business environment and the conditions that influence its competitiveness.

The reasons for such a change are both philosophical and structural:

■ The 1980s saw the efficacy of government intervention questioned, and the re-emergence of the belief that, where possible, the productive potential of an economy ought to be developed by free-market forces.

■ Growing government debt, and a desire to curb public expenditure, acted as a key incentive to reduce the state's role in industrial affairs. This was argued to be one of the driving forces behind the European privatisation process in the 1980s and 1990s.

■ During the 1980s, industry became progressively more global in its outlook. As such, its investment decisions were increasingly being determined by external environmental factors, such as comparative labour costs in different countries and countries' transport and communication links. Old-style industrial policy, which focuses on the national economy in isolation and on distinct sectors within it, has become increasingly less effective and relevant in meeting the needs of national economies operating in an open trading environment, where business investment and strategy are assessed in global terms.

The new approach to industrial policy, being widely adopted by many advanced countries, is to focus on improving those factors which shape a nation's competitiveness. This involves shifting away from particular sectors to targeting what are referred to as 'framework conditions for industry'.

Such 'conditions' have been the subject of a series of recent reviews by the OECD, which found that the following initiatives are forming the basis of a new industrial competitiveness policy:

■ The promotion of investment in physical and human capital. Human capital in particular, and the existence of a sound skills base, are seen as crucial for attracting global business and ensuring long-run economic growth.

■ A reduction in non-wage employment costs, such as employers' social security and pension contributions. Many governments see these costs as too high and as a severe limitation on competitiveness and employment creation.

■ The promotion of innovation and the encouragement of greater levels of R&D.

■ Support for small and medium-sized enterprises. SMEs have received particular attention due to their crucial role in enhancing innovation, creating employment and contributing to skills development, especially in high-tech areas (see Chapter 16).

■ The improvement of infrastructure. This includes both physical transport, such as roads and railways, and information highways.

■ The protection of intellectual property by more effective use of patents and copyright. By reinforcing the law in these areas, it is hoped to encourage firms to develop new products and commit themselves to research.

These initiatives, if they are to be truly effective, are likely to require co-ordination and integration, since they represent a radical departure from established industrial policy.

Questions

1 *In what senses could these new policies be described as (a) non-interventionist; (b) interventionist?*

2 *Does globalisation, and in particular the global perspective of multinational corporations, make industrial policy in the form of selective subsidies and tax relief more or less likely?*

The focus on identifying and supporting 'winning sectors' remains a key strategic goal of METI today. With significantly increased funding to support R&D, METI has identified four 'priority fields': life sciences, information technology, environmental sciences, and nanotechnology. In addition, METI is seeking to strengthen Japan's industrial competitiveness and encourage both the creation and growth of SMEs. Although METI has not changed a great deal since its creation in 1951, it is now beginning to realise that if Japan is to remain the industrial giant it currently is, then its economy needs to change and adapt to the new global economy it now faces.

Industrial policy in the EU

The Japanese use of industrial policy to help create a vibrant and world-beating industrial sector is an approach that has been readily embraced by the European Union. During the 1960s and 1970s the EU's industrial policy amounted to little more than the use of 'protectionism' (see section 25.3), using restrictions on imports to shelter domestic producers from the rigours of global competition. Today the EU's approach is more mature and recognises that a successful industrial sector is built upon far broader foundations.

> The EU industrial policy aims at creating a knowledge-based society with enterprises operating on markets open to international competition. The policy fosters innovation, sustainable development and the removal of obstacles to change. It encourages flexibility, investment in knowledge and risk-taking as well as the spread of information and know-how.[1]

The EU's main means of creating greater industrial competitiveness is the deepening of the internal market by the removal of all barriers to trade between the member states (see section 25.3). But EU industrial policy does not end here. The White Paper on Growth, Competitiveness and Employment (1993) stressed the weaknesses of the market in providing adequate levels of research and development (R&D) and training, and the difficulties businesses might have in identifying others with whom they might work in developing new products and processes. As a result, the White Paper advocated that, in order to create a favourable environment for industry, the EU should actively promote investment, especially in the fields of training and R&D, and that it should encourage various forms of industrial co-operation. This would be achieved by setting up various bodies to support industry and by the provision of finance.

Under its Sixth Framework Programme for Research and Technological Development (FP6), the EU funds research in seven key areas: 'genomes and biotechnology for health; information society technologies; nanotechnologies and nanosciences; aeronautics and space; food safety; sustainable development; and economic and social sciences'. The overall budget for FP6 is €17.5 billion covering the four-year period 2003–2006. This represents an increase of 17 per cent over the previous programme. At the same time, research initiatives such as the European Research Co-ordination Agency (EUREKA) and the ERA-NET scheme for networking and sharing research activities have, as their primary objective, the co-ordination of R&D activities across the member states of the EU.

[1] *A Common Approach to Enhanced Competitiveness*, (DGXIII, 1998).

SUMMARY

1a Demand-side policies (fiscal and monetary) may be suitable for controlling demand-pull inflation or demand-deficient unemployment, but supply-side policies will be needed to control the other types of inflation and unemployment.

1b Supply-side policies, if successful, will shift the aggregate supply curve to the right, and possibly the Phillips curve downwards/to the left.

2a Market-orientated supply-side policies aim to increase the rate of growth of aggregate supply and reduce the rate of unemployment by encouraging private enterprise and the freer play of market forces.

2b Reducing government expenditure as a proportion of GDP is a major element of such policies.

2c Tax cuts can be used to encourage more people to take up jobs, and people to work longer hours and more enthusiastically. The effects of tax cuts will depend on how people respond to incentives.

2d Reducing the power of trade unions and a reduction in welfare benefits, especially those related to unemployment, may force workers to accept jobs at lower wages, thereby decreasing equilibrium unemployment.

2e Various policies can be introduced to increase competition. These include privatisation, deregulation, introducing market relationships into the public sector, public–private partnerships, and freer international trade and capital movements.

3a Regional and local disparities arise from a changing pattern of industrial production. With many of the older industries concentrated in certain parts of the country and especially in the inner cities, and with an acceleration in the rate of industrial change, so the gap between rich and poor areas has widened.

3b Regional disparities can in theory be corrected by the market, with capital being attracted to areas of low wages and workers being attracted to areas of high wages.

3c In practice, regional disparities persist because of capital and labour immobility and regional multiplier effects.

3d The market-orientated solution is to remove impediments to the market achieving regional balance. Policies include local, rather than national, pay bargaining and reducing unemployment benefits.

3e Interventionist solutions focus on measures to encourage firms to move to areas of high unemployment. These measures might include subsidies or tax concessions for firms which move, the provision of facilities and improved infrastructure in the depressed area, the siting of government offices in the depressed areas and the prevention of firms expanding in the prosperous ones.

3f In the UK there has been a movement away from general grants towards discretionary grants based on job creation. There are also regional grants from the EU and grants and initiatives for the regeneration of the inner cities.

3g The success of regional and urban policies has been limited by the relatively low level of government grants and by the fact that some of the money has gone to projects which would have gone ahead anyway.

3h The Maastricht Treaty committed EU states to work together to reduce regional economic imbalances. Structural Funds are designed to supplement national government funding for projects in poorer areas of the EU.

4a The UK has had a lower rate of investment than most other industrialised countries. This has contributed to a historically low rate of economic growth and a growing trade deficit in manufactures.

4b Those in favour of interventionist industrial policy point to failings of the market, such as the externalities involved in investment and training, the imperfections in the capital market and the short-term perspective of decision makers.

4c Intervention can take the form of grants, the encouragement of mergers and other forms of rationalisation, advice and persuasion, the provision of information and the direct provision of infrastructure.

4d Industrial policy in Japan is guided by the Ministry of Trade, Economy and Industry (METI). Its principal role is to encourage co-operation between private companies in new technology and product development.

4e Industrial policy in the EU is a mixture of market-orientated measures (ensuring that the internal market in goods, capital and labour is free) and interventionist measures, especially in the encouragement of research.

REVIEW QUESTIONS

1 Define *demand-side* and *supply-side* policies. Are there any ways in which such policies are incompatible?

2 Outline the main supply-side policies that have been introduced in the UK since 1979. Does the evidence suggest that they have achieved what they set out to do?

3 What types of tax cuts are likely to create the greatest (a) incentives, (b) disincentives to effort?

4 Compare the relative merits of pro-market and interventionist solutions to regional decline.

5 In what ways does the EU approach to regional and industrial policy differ from that of the UK?

6 Is the decline of older industries necessarily undesirable?

7 In what ways can interventionist industrial policy work *with* the market, rather than against it? What are the arguments for and against such policy?

32 International economic policy

32.1 International business cycles

So long as nations trade with one another, the domestic economic actions of one nation will have implications for those which trade with it. For example, if the US administration feels that the US economy is growing too fast, it might adopt various deflationary fiscal and monetary measures, such as higher tax rates or interest rates. US consumers will not only consume fewer domestically produced goods, but also reduce their consumption of imported products. Thus *foreign* producers will experience a fall in demand and, if this persists, may respond by cutting back on production and reducing the size of their labour force. This reduction in the demand for factors of production will then have effects on other firms. The process is likely to be repeated many times as the **international trade multiplier** sends ripples throughout the global economy.

> **Pause for thought**
>
> *Assume that the US economy expands. What will determine the size of the multiplier effect on other countries?*

Key Idea 36 p626

The more open an economy, the more vulnerable it will be to changes in the level of economic activity in the rest of the world. This problem will be particularly acute if a nation is heavily dependent on trade with one other nation (e.g. Canada on the USA) or region (e.g. Switzerland on the EU).

As a consequence of both trade and financial interdependences, the world economy, like the economy of any individual nation, tends to experience periodic fluctuations in economic activity – an *international* business cycle. The implication of this is that nations will tend to share common problems and concerns at the same time. At one time the most pressing problem may be world inflationary pressures; at another time it may be a world recession.

Key Idea 32 p547

In order to avoid 'beggar-my-neighbour' policies, it is better to seek *common* solutions to these common problems: i.e. solutions that are international in scope and design rather than narrowly based on national self-interest. For example, during a world recession, countries are likely to suffer from rising unemployment. An individual nation might like to stimulate aggregate demand, but be reluctant to do so if it fears that this will merely create a balance of payments problem. Indeed, faced with falling export sales as a result of the recession, it might even be persuaded to *curb* aggregate demand in order to reduce inflation and make its exports more competitive. But this will then only worsen the position for other countries. However, if other nations (which will also be experiencing higher unemployment) can be convinced to co-ordinate their policy actions, then an expansionary *international* economic policy will remove the worries of going it alone. In addition to the resulting rise in their imports, all nations will also experience rising export sales.

definition

International trade multiplier
The impact of changing levels of international demand on levels of production and output.

Even if national policies are not in the strictest sense co-ordinated, discussions between nations regarding the nature and magnitude of the problems they face help to improve the policy-making process. The sharing of information concerning their economies' performance and their intended actions enables them to assess the likely success or otherwise of their own initiatives. Would they be pursuing an incompatible policy goal? Would the cumulative actions of individual nations cause the global economy to grow too fast? With such knowledge, fluctuations in international economic activity might be more effectively regulated, if not totally removed.

Although co-operation is the ideal, in practice discord often tends to dominate international economic relations. Co-operation merely occurs in episodes, some of very short duration. Where co-operation does occur, it varies in intensity, ranging from the integration of economic strategy to the mere issuing of statements.

In the following sections we shall consider how international economic policy tends to be conducted in practice.

32.2 International harmonisation of economic policies

There is an old saying: 'If America sneezes, the rest of the world catches a cold.' Viruses of a similar nature regularly infect the world economy. A dramatic example was the 'Asian contagion' of 1997–8. As we shall see later in this section, economic crises spread rapidly around south-east and east Asia and then to Russia and then to Brazil. World leaders were seriously worried that the whole world would plunge into recession. What was needed was a co-ordinated policy response.

definition

International harmonisation of economic policies
Where countries attempt to co-ordinate their macroeconomic policies so as to achieve common goals.

What is of crucial importance is to avoid major exchange rate movements between currencies. But imbalances between the major economies of the world, such as the USA, Japan and the eurozone countries can cause huge swings in exchange rates. As we saw in Box 27.3, the dollar/euro exchange rate was $1.16 when the euro was launched in 1999. By October 2000, the euro had fallen to $0.85, only to rise back to $1.16 in March 2003. Such movements can play havoc with the profits of importers and exporters.

Changes in exchange rates that result from such imbalances are often amplified by speculation. And this problem is becoming worse. Approximately $1.5 trillion per day passes across the foreign exchange markets. The scale of such movements makes any significant speculation simply too great for individual countries to resist. And on some occasions even the concerted action of groups of countries cannot maintain exchange rate stability.

Key Idea 12 p94

Pause for thought

Referring to Table 32.1, is there any evidence that there was any greater convergence between the G7 countries in 2001 than in 1991?

The four main underlying causes of exchange rate movements are divergences in *interest rates*, *growth rates*, *inflation rates* and *current account balance of payments*. Table 32.1 shows the levels of these and other indicators for the seven major industrialised countries. As can be seen, the variations between countries have been considerable.

For many years now the leaders of these countries have met once a year (and more frequently if felt necessary) at an economic summit conference. Top of the agenda in most of these 'Group of Seven' (G7) meetings has been how to generate world economic growth without major currency fluctuations. But to achieve this it is important that there is a **harmonisation** of economic policies between

Table 32.1   **Macroeconomic indicators for the G7 countries**

	1991						
	USA	*Japan*	*Germany*	*France*	*Italy*	*UK*	*Canada*
Economic growth							
(% change in real GDP)	−0.5	3.3	5.1	1.0	1.4	−1.5	−2.1
Output gap (%)	−2.5	3.2	2.2	1.0	0.7	−1.8	−3.0
Standardised unemployment							
(%)	6.8	2.1	4.2	9.1	8.6	8.6	10.3
Inflation: GDP deflator (%)	3.6	2.9	3.5	3.0	7.6	6.7	3.0
Short-term interest rate							
(% average)	5.9	7.4	9.2	9.6	12.2	11.5	8.8
Current account							
(% of GDP)	0.1	2.0	−1.0	−0.5	−2.1	−1.8	−3.8
General government borrowing							
requirement (% of GDP)	−5.0	1.8	−2.9	−2.4	−11.7	−3.1	−8.4
General government gross debt							
(% of GDP)	71.4	64.5	38.8	40.3	116.8	44.3	82.2
Effective exchange rate							
(1995 = 100)	85.4	59.9	80.1	85.9	127.3	111.1	116.5

	2001						
	USA	*Japan*	*Germany*	*France*	*Italy*	*UK*	*Canada*
Economic growth							
(% change in real GDP)	1.2	−0.4	0.6	2.0	1.8	2.2	1.5
Output gap (%)	−0.7	−1.4	−1.4	0.5	−1.4	0.1	0.3
Standardised unemployment							
(%)	4.8	5.0	7.9	8.6	9.5	5.0	7.2
Inflation: GDP deflator (%)	2.2	−1.4	1.3	1.6	2.6	2.4	1.2
Short-term interest rate							
(% average)	3.7	0.1	4.3	4.3	4.3	5.0	4.0
Current account							
(% of GDP)	−4.1	2.2	0.1	1.8	0.3	−1.8	2.7
General government borrowing							
requirement (% of GDP)	0.5	−7.1	−2.7	−1.4	−1.5	1.0	2.4
General government gross debt							
(% of GDP)	59.5	132.8	60.3	64.8	108.7	52.5	101.6
Effective exchange rate							
(1995 = 100)	134.3	99.7	95.5	96.6	110.7	129.6	95.1

nations. In other words, it is important that all the major countries are pursuing consistent policies aiming at common international goals.

But how can policy harmonisation be achieved? As long as there are significant domestic differences between the major economies, there is likely to be conflict not harmony. For example, if one country, say the USA, is worried about the size of its budget deficit, it may be unwilling to respond to world demands for a stimulus to aggregate demand to pull the world economy out of recession. What is more, speculators, seeing differences between countries, are likely to

definition

Convergence of economies
When countries achieve similar levels of growth, inflation, budget deficits as a percentage of GDP, balance of payments, etc.

exaggerate them by their actions, causing large changes in exchange rates. The G7 countries have therefore sought to achieve greater **convergence** of their economies. However, convergence may be a goal of policy, but in practice it has proved elusive.

Because of a lack of convergence, there are serious difficulties in achieving international policy harmonisation:

■ Countries' budget deficits and national debt differ substantially as a proportion of their national income. This puts very different pressures on the interest rates necessary to service these debts.

■ Harmonising rates of monetary growth or inflation targets would involve letting interest rates fluctuate with the demand for money. Without convergence in the demand for money, interest rate fluctuations could be severe.

■ Harmonising interest rates would involve abandoning money, inflation and exchange rate targets (unless interest rate 'harmonisation' meant adjusting interest rates so as to maintain money or inflation targets or a fixed exchange rate).

■ Countries have different internal structural relationships. A lack of convergence here means that countries with higher endemic *cost* inflation would require higher interest rates and higher unemployment if international inflation rates were to be harmonised, or higher inflation if interest rates were to be harmonised.

■ Countries have different rates of productivity increase, product development, investment and market penetration. A lack of convergence here means that the growth in exports (relative to imports) will differ for any given level of inflation or growth.

■ Countries may be very unwilling to change their domestic policies to fall into line with other countries. They may prefer the other countries to fall into line with them!

If any one of the four – interest rates, growth rates, inflation rates or current account balance of payments – could be harmonised across countries, it is likely that the other three would then not be harmonised.

Total convergence and thus total harmonisation may not be possible. Nevertheless most governments favour some movement in that direction: some is better than none.

Response to the south-east Asian crisis

The need to establish greater co-operation was demonstrated by the south-east Asian crisis in 1997/8 and the shock waves it sent round the global economy (see Box 25.1 on pages 532–3). The fact that the crisis came as a total surprise to governments, international institutions, international financiers and speculators, clearly revealed the need to monitor more closely, and when necessary, regulate the world economy.

Following weeks of negotiations with the IMF and World Bank, the finance ministers and central bank governors of the G7 countries met in October 1998 to agree a package of measures designed to prevent a repeat of the 'Asian contagion' and to restore greater stability to the international financial system. The agreement included the following:

■ The provision of credit facilities, through the IMF and the World Bank, for 'well-run' economies whose currencies were victims of speculative attack. The IMF would have $90 billion for this purpose.

- The establishment of closer links between national and international regulatory bodies in order to provide more effective regulation of financial markets.
- Greater fiscal openness by governments, in order to make policy co-ordination between countries easier.

On the central issue of exchange rate regimes, however, the G7 had little to say, merely calling for 'consideration of the elements necessary for the maintenance of sustainable exchange rate regimes in emerging markets, including consistent macroeconomic policies'. But does this mean that countries would be better off with floating exchange rates, pegged exchange rates or exchange rates irrevocably fixed to some major currency, such as the dollar? On this the G7 was silent. (We considered the problems associated with various alternative exchange rate regimes in Chapter 27. We explore some possible ways forward later in this chapter.)

European economic and monetary union   32.3

European economic and monetary union (EMU) involves the complete economic and financial integration of the EU countries. It is not just a common market, but a market with a single currency, a single central bank and a single monetary policy.

The ERM

The forerunner to EMU was the exchange rate mechanism (ERM). This came into existence in March 1979 and the majority of the EU countries were members. The UK, however, chose not to join. When Greece joined the EU in 1984, it too stayed outside the ERM. Spain joined in 1989, the UK joined in 1990 and Portugal in April 1992. Then in September 1992, the UK and Italy indefinitely suspended their membership of the ERM, but Italy rejoined in November 1996 as part of its bid to join the single European currency. Austria joined in 1995, Finland in 1996 and Greece in 1998. By the time the ERM was replaced by the single currency in 1999, only Sweden and the UK were outside the ERM.

Any of the ten new members that have joined the EU in 2004 that also wish to join the euro must first be a member of an ERM version 2 for two years, with their exchange rates pegged to the euro. So too must the UK, Denmark or Sweden, if they choose to join.

Features of the ERM

Under the system, each currency was given a central exchange rate with each of the other ERM currencies in a grid. However, fluctuations were allowed from the central rate within specified bands. For most countries these bands were set at $\pm 2^{1}/_{4}$ per cent. The central rates could be adjusted from time to time by agreement, thus making the ERM an **adjustable peg** system. All the currencies floated jointly with currencies outside the ERM.

If a currency approached the upper or lower limit against *any* other ERM currency, the two countries had to intervene to maintain their currencies within the band. This could take the form of their central banks selling the stronger currency and buying the weaker one, or reducing interest rates in the case of the strong currency and raising interest rates in the case of the weak currency.

definition

Adjustable peg
A system whereby exchange rates are fixed for a period of time, but may be devalued (or revalued) if a deficit (or surplus) becomes substantial.

The ERM in practice

In a system of pegged exchange rates, countries should harmonise their policies to avoid excessive currency misalignments and hence the need for large devaluations or revaluations. There should be a convergence of their economies: they should be at a similar point on the business cycle and have similar inflation rates and interest rates.

The ERM in the 1980s. In the early 1980s, however, French and Italian inflation rates were persistently higher than German rates. This meant that there had to be several realignments (devaluations and revaluations). After 1983 realignments became less frequent, and then from 1987 to 1992 they ceased altogether. This was due to a growing convergence of members' internal policies.

By the time the UK joined the ERM in 1990, it was generally seen by its existing members as being a great success. It had created a zone of currency stability in a world of highly unstable exchange rates, and had provided the necessary environment for the establishment of a truly common market by the end of 1992.

Crisis in the ERM. Shortly after the UK joined the ERM, strains began to show. The reunification of Germany involved considerable reconstruction in the eastern part of the country. Financing this reconstruction was causing a growing budget deficit. The Bundesbank (the German central bank) thus felt obliged to maintain high interest rates in order to keep inflation in check. At the same time, the UK was experiencing a massive current account deficit (partly the result of entering the ERM at what many commentators argued was too high an exchange rate). It was thus obliged to raise interest rates in order to protect the pound, despite the fact that the economy was sliding rapidly into recession. The French franc and Italian lira were also perceived to be overvalued, and there were the first signs of worries as to whether their exchange rates within the ERM could be retained.

At the same time, the US economy was moving into recession and, as a result, US interest rates were cut. This led to a large outflow of capital from the USA. With high German interest rates, much of this capital flowed to Germany. This pushed up the value of the German mark and with it the other ERM currencies. In September 1992, things reached crisis point. First the lira was devalued. Then two days later, on 'Black Wednesday' (16 September), the UK and Italy were forced to suspend their membership of the ERM: the pound and the lira were floated. At the same time the Spanish peseta was devalued by 5 per cent.

Key Idea 12 p94

Turmoil returned in the summer of 1993. The French economy was moving into recession and there were calls for cuts in French interest rates. But this was only possible if Germany was prepared to cut its rates too, and it was not. Speculators began to sell francs and it became obvious that the existing franc/mark parity could not be maintained. In an attempt to rescue the ERM, the EU finance ministers agreed to adopt wide ±15 per cent bands. The result was that the franc and the Danish krone depreciated against the mark.

> **Pause for thought**
>
> Under what circumstances may a currency bloc like the ERM (a) help to prevent speculation; (b) aggravate the problem of speculation?

A return of calm. The old ERM appeared to be at an end. The new ±15 per cent bands hardly seemed like a 'pegged' system at all. However, the ERM did not die. Within months, the members were again managing to keep fluctuations within a very narrow range (for most of the time, within ±2¼ per cent!). The scene was being set for the abandonment of separate currencies and the adoption of a single currency: the euro.

The Maastricht Treaty and the road to the single currency

Details of the path towards EMU were finalised in the Maastricht Treaty, which was signed in February 1992. The timetable for EMU involved adoption of a single currency by 1999 at the latest.

One of the first moves was to establish a European Monetary Institute (EMI). Its role was to co-ordinate monetary policy and encourage greater co-operation between EU central banks. It also monitored the operation of the ERM and prepared the ground for the establishment of a European central bank in time for the launch of the single currency.

Before they could join the single currency, member states were obliged to achieve convergence of their economies. Each country had to meet five convergence criteria:

■ Inflation: should be no more than $1\frac{1}{2}$ per cent above the average inflation rate of the three countries in the EU with the lowest inflation.

■ Interest rates: the rate on long-term government bonds should be no more than 2 per cent above the average of the three countries with the lowest inflation.

■ Budget deficit: should be no more than 3 per cent of GDP.

■ General government debt: should be no more than 60 per cent of GDP.

■ Exchange rates: the currency should have been within the normal ERM bands for at least two years with no realignments or excessive intervention.

Before the launch of the single currency, the Council of Ministers had to decide which countries had met the convergence criteria and would thus be eligible to form a **currency union** by fixing their currencies permanently to the euro. Their national currencies would effectively disappear.

At the same time a European System of Central Banks (ESCB) would be created, consisting of a European Central Bank (ECB) and the central banks of the member states. The ECB would be independent, both from governments and from EU political institutions. It would operate the monetary policy on behalf of the countries which had adopted the single currency.

definition

Currency union
A group of countries (or regions) using a common currency.

Birth of the euro

In March 1998, the European Commission ruled that 11 of the 15 member states were eligible to proceed to EMU in January 1999. The UK and Denmark were to exercise their opt out, negotiated at Maastricht, and Sweden and Greece failed to meet one or more of the convergence criteria. (Greece joined the euro in 2001.)

All 11 countries unambiguously met the interest rate and inflation criteria, but doubts were expressed by many 'Eurosceptics' as to whether they all genuinely met the other three criteria.

■ Exchange rates. Neither Finland nor Italy had been in the ERM for 2 years (Finland had joined the ERM in October 1996 and Italy had rejoined in November 1996), and the Irish punt was revalued by 3 per cent on 16 March 1998. However, the Commission regarded these three countries as being sufficiently close to the reference value.

■ Government deficits. All 11 countries met this criterion, but some countries only managed to achieve a deficit of 3 per cent or below by taking one-off

714 CHAPTER 32 INTERNATIONAL ECONOMIC POLICY

measures, such as a special tax in Italy, and counting privatisation receipts in Germany. Yet, under the Stability and Growth Pact, eurozone countries would be required to keep their deficits within the 3 per cent limit (see Box 30.1). The concern was that countries that only just met this criterion at time of entry would find it difficult to keep within the limit in times of recession or low growth, when tax revenues were not keeping pace with government expenditure. This proved to be the case with Germany and France in 2002/3.

■ Government debt. Only four countries had debts that did not exceed 60 per cent (France, Finland, Luxembourg and the UK). However, the Maastricht Treaty allowed countries to exceed this value as long as the debt was 'sufficiently diminishing and approaching the reference value at a satisfactory pace'. Critics argued that this phrase was interpreted too loosely.

The euro came into being on 1 January 1999, but euro banknotes and coins were not introduced until 1 January 2002. In the meantime, national currencies continued to exist alongside the euro, but at irrevocably fixed rates. The old notes and coins were withdrawn a few weeks after the introduction of euro notes and coins.

How desirable is EMU?

Advantages of the single currency

Elimination of the costs of converting currencies. With separate currencies in each of the EU countries, costs were incurred each time one currency was exchanged into another, the elimination of these costs, however, was probably the least important benefit from the single currency. The European Commission estimated that the effect was to increase the GDP of the countries concerned by an average of only 0.4 per cent. The gains to countries like the UK, which have well-developed financial markets, would be even smaller.

Increased competition and efficiency. Despite the advent of the single market, large price differences remained between member states. Not only has the single currency eliminated the need to convert one currency into another (a barrier to competition), but it has brought more transparency in pricing, and has put greater downward pressure on prices in high-cost firms and countries.

Elimination of exchange-rate uncertainty (between the members). Even with a narrow-banded ERM, realignments might still have occurred from time to time if separate currencies had remained. As the events of 1992 and 1993 showed, this could cause massive speculation if it was believed that currencies were out of line. Removal of this uncertainty has helped to encourage trade between the eurozone countries. Perhaps more importantly, it has encouraged investment by firms that trade between these countries, given the greater certainty in calculating costs and revenues from such trade.

Key Idea 7 p50

Increased inward investment. Investment from the rest of the world is attracted to a eurozone of over 300 million inhabitants, where there is no fear of internal currency movements. By contrast, the UK, by not joining, has found that inward investment has been diverted away to countries within the eurozone. From 1990 to 1999, the UK's share of inward investment to the EU was nearly 40 per cent. From 1999 to 2002, it was 24 per cent.

Lower inflation and interest rates. A single monetary policy forces convergence in inflation rates (just as inflation rates are very similar between the different regions *within* a country). Provided the ECB succeeds in remaining independent from short-term political manipulation, this is likely to result in a lower average inflation rate in the eurozone countries. This, in turn, will help to convince markets that the euro will be strong relative to other currencies. The result will be lower long-term rates of interest. This, in turn, would further encourage investment in the eurozone countries, both by member states and by the rest of the world.

Opposition to EMU

Monetary union has been bitterly opposed, however, by certain groups. Many 'Eurosceptics' see within it a surrender of national political and economic sovereignty. The lack of an independent monetary and exchange rate policy is a serious problem, they argue, if an economy is at all out of harmony with the rest of the Union. For example, if countries like Italy and Spain have higher endemic rates of inflation (due, say, to greater cost-push pressures), then how are they to make their goods competitive with the rest of the Union? With separate currencies these countries could allow their currencies to depreciate. With a single currency, however, they could become depressed 'regions' of Europe, with rising unemployment and all the other regional problems of depressed regions *within* a country. This may then require significant regional policies – policies which may not be in place or, if they were, would be seen as too interventionist by the political right.

Key Idea 36 p626

> **Pause for thought**
>
> *Is greater factor mobility likely to increase or decrease the problem of cumulative causation associated with regional multipliers? (See page 693.)*

The answer given by proponents of EMU is that it is better to tackle the problem of high inflation in such countries by the disciplines of competition from other EU countries, than merely to feed that inflation by keeping separate currencies and allowing repeated devaluations, with all the uncertainty that that brings. If such countries become depressed, they argue, it is better to have a fully developed *fiscal* policy for the Union which will divert funds into investment in such regions. What is more, the high inflation countries tend to be the poorer ones with lower wage levels (albeit faster wage *increases*). With the high mobility of labour and capital that will accompany the development of the single market, resources are likely to be attracted to such countries. This could help to narrow the gap between the richer and poorer member states. The critics of EMU argue that labour is relatively immobile, given cultural and language barriers. Thus an unemployed worker in Wales could not easily move to a job in Turin or Helsinki. What the critics are arguing here is that the EU is not an **optimal currency area** (see Box 32.1).

Perhaps the most serious criticism is that the same rate of interest must apply to all eurozone countries: the 'one size fits all' criticism. The trouble is that while one country might require a lower rate of interest in order to ward off recession (such as Germany in 2003), another might require a higher one to prevent inflation. As convergence between the member economies increases, however, this problem is likely to lessen.

Another problem for members of a single currency occurs in adjusting to a shock when that shock affects members to different degrees. These are known as **asymmetric shocks**. For example, a sudden change in the price of oil would affect an oil-exporting country like the UK differently from oil importing countries. This problem is more serious, the less the factor mobility between member countries and the less the price flexibility within member countries.

> **definition**
>
> **Optimal currency area**
> The optimal size of a currency area is one that maximises the benefits from having a single currency relative to the costs. If the area were to be increased or decreased in size, the costs would rise relative to the benefits.

> **definition**
>
> **Asymmetric shocks**
> Shocks (such as an oil price increase or a recession in another part of the world) that have different-sized effects on different industries, regions or countries.

BOX 32.1

Optimal currency areas
When it pays to pay in the same currency

Imagine that each town and village used a different currency. Think how inconvenient it would be having to keep exchanging one currency into another, and how difficult it would be working out the relative value of items in different parts of the country.

Clearly there are benefits of using a common currency, not only within a country but across different countries. The benefits include greater transparency in pricing, more open competition, greater certainty for investors and the avoidance of having to pay commission when you change one currency into another. There are also the benefits from having a single monetary policy if that is delivered in a more consistent and effective way than by individual countries.

So why not have a single currency for the whole world? The problem is that the bigger a single-currency area gets, the more likely the conditions are to diverge in the different parts of the area. Some parts may have high unemployment and require reflationary policies. Others may have low unemployment and suffer from inflationary pressures. They may require deflationary policies. What is more, different members of the currency area may experience quite different shocks to their economies, whether from outside the union (e.g. a fall in the price of one of their major exports) of from inside (e.g. a prolonged strike). These 'asymmetric shocks' (see page 715) would imply that different parts of the currency area should adopt different policies. But with a common monetary policy and hence common interest rates, and with no possibility of devaluation/revaluation of the currency of individual members, the scope for separate economic policies is reduced.

The costs of asymmetric shocks (and hence the costs of a single-currency area) will be greater, the less the mobility of labour and capital, the less the flexibility of prices and wage rates, and the fewer the alternative policies there are that can be turned to (such as fiscal and regional policies).

So is the eurozone an optimal currency area? Certainly strong doubts have been raised by many economists.

- Labour is relatively immobile.
- There are structural differences between the member states.
- The transmission effects of interest rate changes are different between the member countries, given that countries have proportions of borrowing at variable interest rates and different proportions of consumer debt to GDP.
- Exports to countries outside the eurozone account for different proportions of the members' GDP, and thus their economies are affected differently by a change in the rate of exchange of the euro against other currencies.
- Wage rates are relatively inflexible.
- Under the Stability and Growth Pact (see Box 30.1), the scope for using discretionary fiscal policy is curtailed.

This does not necessarily mean, however, that the costs of having a single European currency outweigh the benefits. Also, the problems outlined above should decline over time as the single market develops. Finally, the problem of asymmetric shocks can be exaggerated. European economies are highly diversified; there are often more differences *within* economies than between them. Thus shocks are more likely to affect different industries or localities, rather than whole countries. Changing the exchange rate, if that were still possible, would hardly be an appropriate policy in these circumstances.

Question

Why is a single currency area likely to move towards becoming an optimal currency area over time?

This problem, however, should not be overstated. The divergences between economies are often the result of a lack of harmony between countries in their demand-management policies: something that is impossible in the case of monetary policy, and more difficult in the case of fiscal policy, for countries in the eurozone. Also, many of the shocks that face economies today are global and have similar (albeit not identical) effects on all countries. Adjustment to such shocks would often be better with a single co-ordinated policy, something that would be much easier with a single currency and a single central bank.

Even when shocks are uniformly felt in the member states, however, there is still the problem that policies adopted centrally will have different impacts on each country. For example, in the UK, a large proportion of borrowing is at variable interest rates. In Germany, by contrast, much is at fixed rates. Thus if the ECB were to raise interest rates, the deflationary effects would be felt disproportionately in the UK. Of course, were this balance to change – and there is some evidence that types of borrowing are becoming more uniform across the EU – this problem would diminish.

The problem for economists is that the issue of monetary union is a very emotive one. 'Europhiles' often see monetary union as a vital element in their vision of a united Europe. Many Eurosceptics, however, see EMU as a surrender of sovereignty and a threat to nationhood. In such an environment, a calm assessment of the arguments and evidence is very difficult.

Alternative policies for achieving currency stability   32.4

One important lesson of recent years is that concerted speculation has become virtually unstoppable. This was made clear by the expulsion of the UK and Italy from the ERM in 1992, the dramatic fall of the Mexican peso and rise of the yen in 1995, the collapse of various south-east Asian currencies and the Russian rouble in 1997–8, and the collapse of the Argentinean peso in 2002. In comparison with the vast amounts of short-term finance flowing across the foreign exchanges each day, the reserves of central banks seem trivial.

If there is a consensus in the markets that a currency will depreciate, there is little that central banks can do. For example, if there were a 50 per cent chance of a 10 per cent depreciation in the next week, then selling that currency now would yield an 'expected' return of just over 5 per cent for the week (i.e. 50% of 10%): equivalent to more than 5000 per cent at an annual rate!

For this reason, many commentators have argued that there are only two types of exchange rate system that can work over the long term. The first is a completely free-floating exchange rate, with no attempt by the central bank to support the exchange rate. With no intervention, there is no problem of a shortage of reserves!

The second is to share a common currency with other countries: to join a common-currency area, such as the eurozone, and let the common currency float freely. The country would give up independence in its monetary policy, but at least there would be no problem of exchange rate instability within the currency area. A similar alternative is to adopt a major currency of another country, such as the US dollar or the euro. Many smaller states have done this. For example, Kosovo has adopted the euro.

Key Idea 12 p94

Attempts by a country to peg its exchange rate is likely to have one of two unfortunate consequences. Either it will end in failure as the country succumbs to a speculative attack, or the country's monetary policy will have to be totally dedicated to maintaining the exchange rate.

So is there any way of 'beating the speculators' and pursuing a policy of greater exchange rate rigidity without establishing a single currency? Or must countries be forced to accept freely floating exchange rates, with all the uncertainty for traders that such a regime brings?

We shall examine two possible solutions. The first is to reduce international financial mobility, by putting various types of restriction on foreign exchange transactions. The second is to move to a new type of exchange rate regime which offers the benefits of a degree of rigidity without being susceptible to massive speculative attacks.

Controlling exchange transactions

Until the early 1990s, many countries retained restrictions of various kinds on financial flows. Such restrictions made it more expensive for speculators to gamble on possible exchange rate movements. It is not the case, as some commentators argue, that it is impossible to reimpose controls. Indeed Malaysia did just that in 1998 when the ringgit was under speculative attack. Many countries in the developing world still retain controls, and the last ERM countries to give them up only did so in 1991. It is true that the complexity of modern financial markets provides the speculator with more opportunity to evade controls, but they will still have the effect of dampening speculation.

Pause for thought

Before you read on, see if you can identify (a) the ways exchange transactions might be controlled; (b) the difficulties in using such policy?

In September 1998, the IMF said that controls on inward movements of capital could be a useful tool, especially for countries which were more vulnerable to speculative attack. In its 1998 annual report it argued that the Asian crisis of 1997–8 was the result not only of a weak banking system, but also of open capital accounts, allowing massive withdrawals of funds.

The aim of capital controls is not to prevent capital flows. After all, capital flows are an important source of financing investment. Also if capital moves from countries with a lower marginal productivity of capital to countries where it is higher, this will lead to an efficient allocation of world savings. The aim of capital controls must therefore be to prevent speculative flows which are based on rumour or herd instinct rather than on economic fundamentals.

Types of control

In what ways can movements of short-term capital be controlled? There are various alternatives, each one with strengths and drawbacks:

Key Idea 30 p410

Quantitative controls. Here the authorities would restrict the amount of foreign exchange dealing that could take place. Perhaps financial institutions would be allowed to exchange only a certain percentage of their assets. Developed countries and most developing countries have rejected this approach, however, since it is seen to be far too anti-market.

The exception is the use of special emergency measures to restrict capital movements in times of a currency crisis. According to Article 57 of the Treaty of Amsterdam, the EU Council of Ministers may 'adopt measures on the movement of capital to or from third countries'. Article 59 allows 'safeguard measures' to be taken if 'in exceptional circumstances, movements of capital to or from third countries cause . . . serious difficulties for the operation of economic and monetary union'. Article 60 allows member states to take 'unilateral measures against a third country with regard to capital movements and payments'.

A Tobin tax. This is named after James Tobin, who in 1978 advocated the imposition of a small tax of 0.1 to 0.5 per cent on all foreign exchange transactions, or on just capital account transactions.[1] This would discourage destabilising speculation (by making it more expensive) and would thus impose some 'friction' in the foreign exchange markets, making them less volatile.

Calls for the use of Tobin taxes have become more frequent in recent years and in November 2001, the French National Assembly became the first national legislature to incorporate into law a Tobin tax of up to 0.1 per cent. This was followed by Belgium in 2002. The EU finance ministers ordered the European Commission to undertake a feasibility study of such a tax. In late 2001, the charity War on Want declared that 13 March 2002 would be international 'Tobin tax day'. Ironically, Tobin died on 11 March 2002.

Box 32.2 assesses the potential strengths and weaknesses of a Tobin tax as a practical means of reducing exchange-rate volatility.

Non-interest-bearing deposits. Here a certain percentage of inflows of capital would have to be deposited with the central bank in a non-interest-bearing account for a set period of time. Chile in the late 1990s used such a system. It required that 30 per cent of all inflows be deposited with Chile's central bank for a year. This clearly amounted to a considerable tax (i.e. in terms of interest sacrificed) and had the effect of discouraging short-term speculative flows. The problem was that it meant that interest rates in Chile had to be higher in order to attract capital.

One objection to all these measures is that they are likely only to dampen speculation, not eliminate it. If speculators believe that currencies are badly out of equilibrium and will be forced to realign, then no taxes on capital movements or artificial controls will be sufficient to stem the flood.

There are two replies to this objection. The first is that if currencies are badly out of line then exchange rates *should* be adjusted. The second is that dampening speculation is probably the ideal. Speculation *can* play the valuable role of bringing exchange rates to their long-term equilibrium more quickly. Controls are unlikely to prevent this aspect of speculation: adjustments to economic fundamentals. If they help to lessen the wilder forms of destabilising speculation, so much the better.

Exchange-rate target zones

One type of exchange rate regime that has been much discussed in recent years is that proposed by John Williamson, of Washington's Institute for International Economics.[2] Williamson advocates a form of 'crawling peg' within broad bands. This system would involve a pegged central rate, where fluctuations around that rate would be allowed within bands (i.e. like the ERM). Unlike, the ERM, however, the central value could be adjusted frequently, but only by small amounts: hence the term 'crawling'. The system would have four major features:

■ Wide bands. For example, currencies could be allowed to fluctuate by 10 per cent of their central parity.

---

[1] J. Tobin, 'A proposal for international monetary reform', *The Eastern Economic Journal*, 4, no. 3–4, 1978, pp. 153–9.
[2] See, for example, J. Williamson and M. Miller, 'Targets and Indicators: A Blueprint for the Co-ordination of Economic Policy', *Policy Analyses in International Economics No. 22*, IIE, 1987.

BOX 32.2

The Tobin tax
A new panacea?

In the mid-1980s, the daily turnover in the world's foreign exchange markets was approximately $150 billion. By 2003, it had risen to a truly massive $1.8 trillion. But only some 5 per cent of this is used for trade in goods and services.

With the massive growth in speculative flows, it is hardly surprising that this can cause great currency instability and financial crises at times of economic uncertainty. As we saw in Box 27.3 on page 596, global financial markets have often been decisive in both triggering and intensifying economic crises. The ERM crisis in 1992, the Mexican peso crisis in 1994, the south-east Asian crisis in 1997, the Russian rouble meltdown in 1998, and the crisis in Argentina in 2001/2002, are the most significant in a long list.

The main issue is one of volatility of exchange rates. If currency markets responded to shifts in economic fundamentals, then currency volatility would not be so bad. However, it is increasingly the case that vast quantities of money flow around the global economy purely speculatively, with the herd instinct often driving speculative waves. Invariably, given the volume of speculative flows, exchange rates overshoot their natural equilibrium, intensifying the distortions created. Such currency movements are a huge destabilising force, not just for individual economies but for the global economy as a whole.

So is there anything countries can do to reduce destabilising speculation? One suggestion is the introduction of a Tobin tax.

The Tobin tax

Writing in 1978, James Tobin proposed a system for reducing exchange rate volatility without fundamentally impeding the operation of the market. This involved the imposition of an international tax of some 0.1 to 0.5 per cent payable on all spot or cash exchange rate transactions. He argued that this would make currency trading more costly and would therefore reduce the volume of destabilising short-term financial flows, which would invariably lead to greater exchange rate stability.

Tobin's original proposal suggested that the tax rate would need to be very low so as not to affect 'normal business'. Even if very low, speculators working on small margins, would be dissuaded from regular movements of money, given that the tax would need to be paid per transaction. If a tax rate of 0.2 per cent was set, speculators who moved a sum of money once a day would face a yearly tax bill of approximately 50 per cent. An investor working on a weekly movement of money would pay tax of 10 per cent per annum, and a monthly movement of currency would represent a tax of 2.4 per cent for the year. Given that 40 per cent of currency transactions have only a two-day time horizon, and 80 per cent a time horizon of fewer than seven days, such a tax would clearly operate to dampen speculative currency movements.

In addition to moderating volatility and speculation, the Tobin tax might yield other benefits. It would, in the face of globalisation, restore to the nation state an element of control over monetary policy. In the face of declining governance over international forces, this might be seen as a positive advantage of the Tobin proposals.

The tax could also generate significant revenue. Estimates range from $150–300 billion annually. Many of the world's leading pressure groups, such as War on Want, have argued that the revenue from such an international tax could be used to tackle international problems, such as world poverty and environmental degradation. The World Bank estimates that some $225 billion is needed to eliminate the world's worst forms of poverty. The revenue from a Tobin tax would, in a relatively short period of time, easily exceed this amount.

Problems with the Tobin tax

How far would a tax on currency transactions restrict speculative movements of money? The issue here concerns the rate of return investors might get from moving their money. If a currency was to devalue by as little as 3 to 4 per cent, a Tobin tax of 0.2 per cent would do little to deter a speculative transaction based upon such a potential return. Given recent devaluations of 50 per cent in Thailand and Indonesia following the 1997 crash, a 3 to 4 per cent movement in the currency appears rather modest. Raising the rate of the Tobin tax would be no solution, as it would begin to impinge upon 'normal business'.

One response to such a situation has been proposed by a German economist, Paul Bernd Spahn. He suggests that a two-tier system is used. On a day-to-day basis, a minimal tax rate, as originally envisaged by Tobin, is charged against each transaction conducted. However, during periods when exchange rates are highly unstable, a tax surcharge is levied. This would be at a far higher rate, and would only be triggered once a currency moved beyond some predetermined band of exchange rate variation.

A further problem identified with the Tobin tax concerns its administration. However, given the progressive centralisation of foreign exchange markets, both in terms of marketplaces, traders and currencies, effective administration is becoming easier. The UK, which plays a major role in traditional foreign exchange (32 per cent of the market in 1998), is well monitored already and extending such monitoring to include overseeing tax collection would not be overly problematic.

Another problem is tax avoidance. For example, the Tobin tax is a tax payable on spot exchange rate transactions. This could encourage people to deal more in futures. Foreign exchange futures are a type of 'derivative' that allow people to trade currencies in the future at a price agreed today. These would be far more difficult to monitor, since no currency is exchanged *today*, and hence more difficult to tax. One solution would be to apply a tax on a notional value of a derivative contract. However, derivatives are an important way through which businesses hedge against future risk. Taxing them might seriously erode their use to a business and damage the derivatives market as a whole, making business more risky.

Even with avoidance, however, supporters of the Tobin tax argue that it is still likely to be successful. An Oxfam report into the revenue raising potential of the Tobin tax suggests that:

> ... the main challenge for the Tobin tax idea is political. As a technical instrument, it was proposed by a renowned economist and many economists recognise its potential to help reduce volatility. The proposal is unusually clear and relatively well researched. It is also likely to be acceptable to the public since, in US political jargon, it is a tax on Wall Street, not Main Street ... Nevertheless, the idea is opposed or ignored by the leading American policy makers and by the international financial establishment.[1]

Although some countries, such as France and Belgium, have supported the introduction of a Tobin tax, most of the major economies are opposed to it. With reservations being expressed by the IMF, any concerted international action to control global financial movements will be difficult to put on the agenda, let alone put in place and administer.

Question

George Soros, multi-millionaire currency speculator, has referred to global capital markets as being like a wrecking ball rather than a pendulum, suggesting that such markets are becoming so volatile that they are damaging to all concerned, including speculators. What might lead Soros to such an observation?

---

[1] *Time for a Tobin Tax?*, Oxfam, May 1999

- Central parity set in *real* terms, at the 'fundamental equilibrium exchange rate' (FEER): i.e. a rate that is consistent with long-run balance of payments equilibrium.

- Frequent realignments. In order to stay at the FEER, the central parity would be adjusted frequently (e.g. monthly) to take account of the country's rate of inflation. If its rate of inflation were 2 per cent per annum above the trade weighted average of other countries, then the central parity would be devalued by 2 per cent per annum. Realignments would also reflect other changes in fundamentals, such as changes in the levels of protection, or major political events, such as German reunification.

- 'Soft buffers'. Governments would not be forced to intervene at the 10 per cent mark or at some specified fraction of it. In fact, from time to time the rate might be allowed to move outside the bands. The point is that the closer the rate approached the band limits, the greater would be the scale of intervention.

This system has two main advantages. First, the exchange rate would stay at roughly the equilibrium level, and therefore the likelihood of large-scale devaluation or revaluation, and with it the opportunities for large-scale speculative gains, would be small. The reason why the narrow-banded ERM broke down in 1992 and 1993 was that the central parities were *not* equilibrium rates.

Second, the wider bands would leave countries freer to follow an independent monetary policy: one that could therefore respond to domestic needs.

The main problem with the system is that it removes the pressure on high inflation countries to bring their inflation under control: after all, if inflation causes the balance of payments to deteriorate, the exchange rate can simply be allowed to crawl down. Also, if the rate of exchange has to be maintained within the zone, then monetary policy may sometimes have to be used for that purpose rather than controlling inflation.

Nevertheless, crawling bands have been used relatively successfully by various countries, such as Chile and Israel over quite long periods of time. What is more, in 1999, Germany's finance minister at the time, Oskar Lafontaine, argued that they might be appropriate for the euro relative to the dollar and yen. A world with three major currencies, each changing gently against the other two in an orderly way, has a lot to commend it.

SUMMARY

1a The more open the world economy, the more effect changes in economic conditions in one part of the world economy will have on world economic performance.

1b Changes in aggregate demand in one country will affect the amount of imports purchased and thus the amount of exports sold by other countries and hence their GDP. There is thus an international trade multiplier effect.

1c Changes in interest rates in one country will affect financial flows to and from other countries, and hence their exchange rates, interest rates and GDP.

2a Currency fluctuations can be lessened if countries harmonise their economic policies. Ideally this will involve achieving common growth rates, inflation rates, balance of payments (as a percentage of GDP) and interest rates. The attempt to harmonise one of these goals, however, may bring conflicts with one of the other goals.

SUMMARY

2b Leaders of the G7 countries meet regularly to discuss ways of harmonising their policies. Usually, however, domestic issues are more important to the leaders than international ones, and frequently they pursue policies that are not in the interests of the other countries.

3a One means of achieving greater currency stability is for a group of countries to peg their internal exchange rates and yet float jointly with the rest of the world. The exchange rate mechanism of the EU (ERM) was an example. Members' currencies were allowed to fluctuate against other member currencies within a band. The band was ±2¼ per cent for the majority of the ERM countries until 1993.

3b The need for realignments seemed to have diminished in the late 1980s as greater convergence was achieved between the members' economies. Growing strains in the system, however, in the early 1990s, led to a crisis in September 1992. The UK and Italy left the ERM. There was a further crisis in July 1993 and the bands were widened to ±15 per cent.

3c Thereafter, as convergence of the economies of ERM members increased, fluctuations decreased and remained largely within ±2¼ per cent.

3d The ERM was seen as an important first stage on the road to complete economic and monetary union (EMU) in the EU.

3f The Maastricht Treaty set out a timetable for achieving EMU. This would culminate with the creation of a currency union: a single European currency with a common monetary policy operated by an independent European Central Bank.

3g The euro was born on 1 January 1999. Twelve countries adopted it, having at least nominally met the Maastricht convergence criteria. Euro notes and coins were introduced on 1 January 2002, with the notes and coins of the old currencies withdrawn a few weeks later.

3h The advantages claimed for EMU are that it eliminates the costs of converting currencies and the uncertainties associated with possible changes in former inter-EU exchange rates. This encourages more investment, both inward and by domestic firms. What is more, a common central bank, independent from domestic governments, will provide the stable monetary environment necessary for a convergence of the EU economies and the encouragement of investment and inter-Union trade.

3i Critics claim, however, that it might make adjustment to domestic economic problems more difficult. The loss of independence in policy making is seen by such people to be a major issue, not only because of the loss of political sovereignty, but also because domestic economic concerns may be at variance with those of the Union as a whole. A single monetary policy is claimed to be inappropriate for dealing with asymmetric shocks. What is more, countries and regions at the periphery of the Union may become depressed unless there is an effective regional policy.

4a Many economists argue that, with the huge flows of short-term finance across the foreign exchanges, governments are forced to adopt one of two extreme forms of exchange rate regime: free floating or being a member of a currency union.

4b If financial flows could be constrained, however, exchange rates could be stabilised somewhat.

4c Forms of control include: quantitative controls, a tax on exchange transactions (a Tobin tax) and non-interest-bearing deposits of a certain percentage of capital inflows with the central bank. Such controls can dampen speculation, but may discourage capital flowing to where it has a higher marginal productivity.

4d An alternative means of stabilising exchange rates is to have exchange rate target zones. Here exchange rates are allowed to fluctuate within broad bands around a central parity which is adjusted to the fundamental equilibrium rate in a gradual fashion.

4e The advantage of this system is that, by keeping the exchange rate at roughly its equilibrium level, destabilising speculation is avoided, and yet there is some freedom for governments to pursue an independent monetary policy. Monetary policy, however, may still from time to time have to be used to keep the exchange rate within the bands. The system also has the drawback of removing the pressure on governments to maintain a low rate of inflation.

REVIEW QUESTIONS

1 What are the implications for a country attempting to manage its domestic economy if it is subject to an international business cycle? How might it attempt to overcome such problems?

2 What are the economic (as opposed to political) difficulties in achieving an international harmonisation of economic policies so as to avoid damaging currency fluctuations?

3 To what extent can international negotiations over economic policy be seen as a game of strategy? Are there any parallels between the behaviour of countries and the behaviour of oligopolies?

4 What are the causes of exchange-rate volatility? Have these problems become greater or lesser in the last ten years? Explain why.

5 Why did the ERM with narrow bands collapse in 1993? Could this have been avoided?

6 Did the exchange rate difficulties experienced by countries under the ERM strengthen or weaken the arguments for progressing to a single European currency?

7 By what means would a depressed country in an economic union with a single currency be able to recover? Would the market provide a satisfactory solution or would (union) government intervention be necessary, and if so. What form would the intervention take?

8 Is the eurozone likely to be an optimal currency area now? Is it more or less likely to be so over time? Explain your answer.

9 Assume that just some of the members of a common market like the EU adopt full economic and monetary union, including a common currency. What are the advantages and disadvantages to those members joining the full EMU and to those not joining?

10 Assess the difficulties in attempting to control exchange transactions. Might such a policy restrict the level of trade?

11 Would the Williamson system allow countries to follow a totally independent monetary policy?

12 If the euro were in a crawling peg system against the dollar, what implications would this have for the ECB in sticking to its inflation target of no more than 2 per cent?

Additional Part K case studies on the *Economics for Business* website (www.booksites.net/sloman)

K.1 **The national debt.** This explores the question of whether it matters if a country has a high national debt.

K.2 **Trends in public expenditure.** This case examines attempts to control public expenditure in the UK and relates them to the crowding-out debate.

K.3 **The crowding-out effect.** The circumstances in which an increase in public expenditure can replace private expenditure.

K.4 **Managing the US economy.** The use of active fiscal and monetary policy in 2001 and 2002 to stimulate the US economy.

K.5 **Central banking and monetary policy in the USA.** This case examines how the Fed conducts monetary policy.

K.6 **Goodhart's Law.** An examination of Key Idea 37.

K.7 **Should central banks be independent of government?** An examination of the arguments for and against independent central banks.

K.8 **Monetary targeting: its use around the world.** An expanded version of Box 30.4.

K.9 **Using interest rates to control both aggregate demand and the exchange rate.** A problem of one instrument and two targets.

K.10 **The USA: is it a 'new economy'?** An examination of whether US productivity increases are likely to be sustained.

K.11 **Welfare to work.** An examination of the policy of the UK Labour government whereby welfare payments are designed to encourage people into employment.

K.12 **Attempts at harmonisation.** A look at the meetings of the G7 economies where they attempt to come to agreement on means of achieving stable and sustained worldwide economic growth.

K.13 **The UK Labour government's convergence criteria for euro membership.** An examination of the five tests set by the UK government that would have to be passed before the question of euro membership would be put to the electorate in a referendum.

Websites relevant to Part K

Numbers and sections refer to websites listed in the Web appendix and hotlinked from this book's website at **www.booksites.net/sloman**

- For news articles relevant to Part K, see the *Economics News Articles* link from the book's website.

- For general news on macroeconomic policy, see websites in section A, and particularly A1–5. See also links to newspapers worldwide in A38, 39 and 43, and the news search feature in Google at A41. See also links to economics news in A42.

- For information on UK fiscal policy and government borrowing, see sites E30, 36; F2. See also sites A1–8 at Budget time. For fiscal policy in the eurozone, see *Public Finances in EMU* in H1.

- For a model of the economy (based on the Treasury model), see *The Virtual Economy* (site D1). In addition to the model, where you can devise your own Budget, there are worksheets and outlines of theories and the work of famous economists.

- Sites I7 and 11 contain links to fiscal policy: go to *Macroeconomics > Macroeconomic Policy > Taxes and Taxation*.

- For monetary policy in the UK, see F1 and E30. For monetary policy in the eurozone, see F6 and 5. For monetary policy in the USA, see F8. For monetary policy in other countries, see the respective central bank site in section F.

- For links to sites on money and monetary policy, see the *Financial Economics* sections in I4, 7, 11, 17.

- For demand-side policy in the UK, see the latest Budget Report (e.g. section on maintaining macroeconomic stability) at site E30.

- For inflation targeting in the UK and eurozone see sites F1 and 6.

- For the current approach to UK supply-side policy, see the latest Budget Report (e.g. sections on productivity and training) at site E30. See also sites E5 and 9.

- For information on training in the UK and Europe, see sites D7; E5; G5, 14.

- For support for a market-orientated approach to supply-side policy see C17 and E34.

- For European Union policies, see sites G1, 3, 6, 16, 17, 18.

- For information on international harmonisation, see sites H4 and 5.

- For student resources relevant to this chapter, see sites C1–7, 9, 10, 12, 13, 19. See also '2nd floor – economic policy' in site D1. See also the *Labour market reforms* simulation in D3.

Web appendix

All the following websites can be accessed from the home page of this book's own website (**www.booksites.net/sloman**). When you enter the site, click on the **Hotlinks** button. You will find all the following sites listed. Click on the one you want and the 'hotlink' will take you straight to it.

The sections and numbers below refer to the ones used in the web references at the end of each Part of the text. Thus, if the reference were to A21, this would refer to the Money World site.

(A) General news sources

As the title of this section implies, websites here can be used for finding material on current news issues or tapping into news archives. Most archives are offered free of charge. However, some do require you to register. As well as key UK and American sources, you will also notice some slightly different places from where you can get your news, such as the St Petersburg Times and Kyodo News (from Japan). Check out sites number 38. *My Virtual Newspaper*, 39. *Newspapers on World Wide Web*, and 43. *Guardian World News Guide* for links to newspapers across the world. Try searching for an article on a particular topic by using site number 41. *Google News Search*.

1. BBC news
2. The Economist
3. The Financial Times
4. The Guardian
5. The Independent
6. ITN
7. The Observer
8. The Telegraph
9. The Times, Sunday Times
10. The New York Times
11. Fortune
12. Time Magazine
13. The Washington Post
14. Moscow Times (English)
15. St Petersburg Times (English)
16. Straits Times
17. New Straits Times
18. The Scotsman
19. The Herald
20. Euromoney
21. Money World
22. Market News International
23. BusinessWeek online
24. Ananova
25. CNN Financial Net
26. Wall Street Journal
27. Asia related news
28. allAfrica.com
29. Greek News Sources (English)
30. Kyodo News: Japan (English)
31. RFE/RL NewsLine
32. The Australian
33. Sydney Morning Herald
34. Japan Times
35. Reuters
36. Bloomberg
37. David Smith's Economics UK.com
38. My Virtual Newspaper (links to a whole range of news sources)

39. Newspapers on World Wide Web
40. Economics in the News from Gametheory.net
41. Google News Search
42. Moreover
43. Guardian World News Guide

(B) Sources of economic and business data

Using websites to find up-to-date data is of immense value to the economist. The data sources below offer you a range of specialist and non-specialist data information. Universities have free access to the MIMAS site, which is a huge database of statistics. The last site in this set, the Treasury Pocket Data Bank, is a very useful source of key UK and world statistics, and is updated monthly. It downloads as an Excel file.

1. Economics LTSN gateway to economic data
2. Biz/ed Gateway to economic and company data
3. National Statistics
4. Data Archive (Essex)
5. Econ Links
6. Economic Resources (About)
7. Nationwide House Prices Site
8. House Web (data on housing market)
9. Incomes Data Services
10. Keynote Publications Ltd.
11. Land Registry (house prices, etc)
12. Manchester Information and Associated Services (MIMAS)
13. Global Financial Data
14. PACIFIC International trade and business reference page
15. Economagic
16. Groningen Growth and Development Centre
17. Resources for economists on the Internet
18. Joseph Rowntree Foundation
19. Social Science Information Gateway (SOSIG)
20. Slavic and East European Resources
21. OECD Statistics
22. CIA world statistics site
23. UN Millennium Country Profiles
24. World Bank statistics
25. Japan Economic Foundation
26. Ministry of International Trade and Industry (Japan)
27. Nomura Research Institute (Japan)
28. Nanyang Technological University, Singapore: Statistical Data Locators
29. Richard Tucker's Data Resources site
30. Oanda Currency Converter
31. World Economic Outlook Database (IMF)
32. Economist Country Briefings
33. OFFSTATS links to data sets
34. Treasury Pocket Data Bank (source of UK and world economic data)

(C) Sites for students and teachers of economics

The following websites offer useful ideas and resources to those who are studying or teaching economics. It is worth browsing through some just to see what is on offer. Try out the first four sites, for starters. The Internet Economist is a very helpful tutorial for economics students on using the Internet.

1. Economics Subject Centre of the UK, Learning and Teaching Support Network (LTSN)
2. Biz/ed
3. Ecedweb
4. Econ Links: student resources

5. Economics and Business Education Association
6. Tutor2U
7. Economics America
8. The Internet Economist (tutorial on using the Web)
9. Oxford School of Learning
10. Teaching resources for economists
11. Resources for University Teachers of Economics (University of Melbourne)
12. Federal Reserve Bank of San Francisco: Economics Education
13. Federal Reserve Bank of Minneapolis Economic Education
14. WebEc resources
15. BibEc papers
16. Online Opinion (Economics)
17. The Idea Channel
18. History of Economic Thought
19. Resources For Economists on the Internet (RFE)
20. Classroom Expernomics
21. VCE Economics (Economics teaching resources – Australian)
22. Paul Krugman Website
23. JokEc: economics jokes!

Economic models and simulations (D)

Economic modelling is an important aspect of economic analysis. There are a number of sites that offer access to a model for you to use, e.g. Virtual economy (where you can play being Chancellor of the Exchequer). Using such models can be a useful way of finding out how economic theory works within an environment that claims to reflect reality.

1. Virtual economy
2. Virtual factory
3. Virtual Learning Arcade
4. About.com Economics
5. Estima (statistical analysis)
6. SPSS (statistical analysis)
7. National Institute of Economic and Social Research
8. Software available on Economics LTSN site
9. RFE Software

UK government and UK organisations' sites (E)

If you want to see what a government department is up to, then look no further than the list below. Government departments' websites are an excellent source of information and data. They are particularly good at offering information on current legislation and policy initiatives.

1. Gateway site (UK Online)
2. Office of the Deputy Prime Minister
3. Central Office of Information
4. Competition Commission
5. Department for Education and Skills
6. Department for International Development
7. Department for Transport
8. Department of Health
9. Department for Work and Pensions
10. Department of Trade and Industry (DTI)
11. Environment Agency
12. UK euro information site
13. Low Pay Commission
14. Department for Environment, Food and Rural Affairs (DEFRA)
15. Office of Communications (Ofcom)
16. Office of Gas and Electricity Markets (Ofgem)
17. Official Documents OnLine

18. Office of Fair Trading (OFT)
19. Office of the Rail Regulator (ORR)
20. The Takeover Panel
21. Oftel
22. OFWAT
23. National Statistics (NS)
24. National Statistics Time Series Data
25. Strategic Rail Authority (SRA)
26. Patent Office
27. Parliament website
28. Scottish Executive
29. Scottish Environment Protection Agency
30. Treasury
31. Equal Opportunities Commission
32. Trades Union Congress (TUC)
33. Confederation of British Industry
34. Adam Smith Institute
35. Royal Institute of International Affairs
36. Institute of Fiscal Studies
37. Advertising Standards Authority

(F)   Sources of monetary and financial data

As the title suggests, here are listed useful websites for finding information on financial matters. You will see that the list comprises mainly central banks, both within Europe and further afield.

1. Bank of England
2. Bank of England Monetary and Financial Statistics
3. Banque de France
4. Bundesbank (German central bank)
5. Central Bank of Ireland
6. European Central Bank
7. Eurostat
8. US Federal Reserve Bank
9. Netherlands Central Bank
10. Bank of Japan
11. Reserve Bank of Austalia
12. Bank Negara Malaysia (English)
13. Monetary Authority of Singapore
14. National Bank of Canada
15. National Bank of Denmark (English)
16. Reserve Bank of India
17. Links to central bank websites from the Bank for International Settlements
18. The London Stock Exchange

(G)   European Union and related sources

For information on European issues, the following is a wide range of useful sites. The sites maintained by the European Union are an excellent source of information and are provided free of charge.

1. Economic and Financial Affairs: (EC DG)
2. European Central Bank
3. EU official Web site
4. Eurostat
5. Employment and Social Affairs (EC DG)
6. Site for information on the euro and EMU
7. Enterprise: (EC DG)
8. Competition: (EC DG)
9. Agriculture: (EC DG)
10. Energy and Transport: (EC DG)
11. Environment: (EC DG)
12. Regional Policy: (EC DG)
13. Taxation and Customs Union: (EC DG)
14. Education and training: (EC DG)
15. European Patent Office
16. European Commission
17. European Parliament
18. European Council

International organisations (H)

This section casts its net beyond Europe and lists the Web addresses of the main international organisations in the global economy. You will notice that some sites are run by pressure groups, such as Jubilee Research, while others represent organisations set up to manage international affairs, such as the International Monetary Fund and the United Nations.

1. Food and Agriculture Organisation
2. International Air Transport Association (IATA)
3. International Labour Organisation (ILO)
4. International Monetary Fund (IMF)
5. Organisation for Economic Co-operation and Development (OECD)
6. OPEC
7. World Bank
8. World Health Organisation
9. United Nations
10. United Nations Industrial Development Organisation
11. Friends of the Earth
12. Jubilee Research
13. Oxfam
14. Christian Aid (reports on development issues)
15. European Bank for Reconstruction and Development (EBRD)
16. World Trade Organisation (WTO)
17. United Nations Development Programme
18. UNICEF
19. EURODAD – European Network on Debt and Development
20. NAFTA
21. South American free trade areas
22. ASEAN
23. APEC

Economics search and link sites (I)

If you are having difficulty finding what you want from the list of sites above, the following sites offer links to other sites and are a very useful resource when you are looking for something a little bit more specialist. Once again, it is worth having a look at what these sites have to offer in order to judge their usefulness.

1. Gateway for UK official sites
2. Alta Plana
3. Data Archive Search
4. Inomics (search engine for economics information)
5. International Digital Electronic Access Library
6. Links to economics resources sites
7. Social Science Information Gateway (SOSIG)
8. WebEc
9. One World (link to economic development sites)
10. Economic development sites (list)
11. Biz/ed Internet catalogue
12. Web links for economists from the Economics LTSN Subject Centre
13. Yahoo's links to economic data
14. OFFSTATS links to data sets
15. UniGuide academic guide to the Internet (Economics)
16. Internet Resources for Economists
17. Google Web Directory: Economics
18. Resources for Economists on the Internet

(J) Internet search engines

The following search engines have been found to be useful.

1. Google
2. Altavista
3. Overture
4. Excite
5. Infoseek
6. Search.com
7. MSN
8. UK Plus
9. Yahoo

Key ideas

1 **The behaviour and performance of firms is affected by the business environ-ment.** The business environment includes economic, political/legal, social/cultural and technological factors.

2 **Scarcity** is the excess of human wants over what can actually be produced. Because of scarcity, various choices have to be made between alternatives.

3 The **opportunity cost** of something is what you give up to get it/do it. In other words, it is cost measured in terms of the best alternative forgone.

4 **Rational decision making involves weighing up the marginal benefit and marginal cost of any activity.** If the marginal benefit exceeds the marginal cost, it is rational to do the activity (or to do more of it). If the marginal cost exceeds the marginal benefit, it is rational not to do it (or to do less of it).

5 **The nature of institutions and organisations is likely to influence behaviour.** There are various forces influencing people's decisions in complex organisa-tions. Assumptions that an organisation will follow one simple objective (e.g. short-run profit maximisation) is thus too simplistic in many cases.

6 **The principal–agent problem.** Where people (principals), as a result of a lack of knowledge, cannot ensure that their best interests are served by their agents. Agents may take advantage of this situation to the disadvantage of the principals.

7 **Good decision making requires good information.** Where information is poor, decisions and their outcomes may be poor.

8 **People respond to incentives.** It is important, therefore, that incentives are appropriate and have the desired effect.

9 **Changes in demand or supply cause markets to adjust.** Whenever such changes occur, the resulting 'disequilibrium' will bring an automatic change in prices, thereby restoring equilibrium (i.e. a balance of demand and supply).

10 **Equilibrium is the point where conflicting interests are balanced.** Only at this point is the amount that demanders are willing to purchase the same as the amount that suppliers are willing to supply. It is a point which will be automatically reached in a free market through the operation of the price mechanism.

11 **Elasticity.** The responsiveness of one variable (e.g. demand) to a change in another (e.g. price). This concept is fundamental to understanding how mar-kets work. The more elastic variables are, the more responsive is the market to changing circumstances.

12 **People's actions are influenced by their expectations.** People respond not just to what is happening now (such as a change in price), but to what they anticipate will happen in the future.

13 **People's actions are influenced by their attitudes towards risk.** Many deci-sions are taken under conditions of risk or uncertainty. Generally, the lower

the probability of (or the more uncertain) the desired outcome of an action, the less likely will people undertake the action.

14 **The principle of diminishing marginal utility.** The more of a product a person consumes over a given period of time, the less will be the additional utility gained from one more unit.

15 **The 'bygones' principle** states that sunk (fixed) costs should be ignored when deciding whether to produce or sell more or less of a product. Only variable costs should be taken into account.

16 **Output depends on the amount of resources and how they are used.** Different amounts and combinations of inputs will lead to different amounts of output. If output is to be produced efficiently, then inputs should be combined in the optimum proportions.

17 **The law of diminishing marginal returns.** When increasing amounts of a variable factor are used with a given amount of a fixed factor, there will come a point when each extra unit of the variable factor will produce less extra output than the previous unit.

18 **Market power benefits the powerful at the expense of others.** When firms have market power over prices, they can use this to raise prices and profits above the perfectly competitive level. Other things being equal, the firm will gain at the expense of the consumer. Similarly, if consumers or workers have market power they can use this to their own benefit.

19 **Economic efficiency** is achieved when each good is produced at the minimum cost and where consumers get maximum benefit from their income.

20 **People often think and behave strategically.** How you think others will respond to your actions is likely to influence your own behaviour. Firms, for example, when considering a price or product change will often take into account the likely reactions of their rivals.

21 **Stocks and flows.** A stock is a quantity of something at a given point in time. A flow is an increase or decrease in something over a specified period of time. This is an important distinction and a common cause of confusion.

22 **The principle of discounting.** People generally prefer to have benefits today than in the future. Thus future benefits have to be reduced (discounted) to give them a present value.

23 **Efficient capital markets.** Capital markets are efficient when the prices of shares accurately reflect information about companies' current and expected future performance.

24 **Allocative efficiency in any activity is achieved where any reallocation would lead to a decline in net benefit.** It is achieved where marginal benefit equals marginal cost. Private efficiency is achieved where marginal private benefit equals marginal private cost ($MB = MC$). Social efficiency is achieved where marginal social benefit equals marginal social cost ($MSB = MSC$).

25 **Markets generally fail to achieve social efficiency.** There are various types of market failure. Market failures provide one of the major justifications for government intervention in the economy.

26 **Equity** is where income is distributed in a way that is considered to be fair or just. Note that an equitable distribution is not the same as a totally equal distribution and that different people have different views on what is equitable.

27 **Externalities are spillover costs or benefits.** Where these exist, even an otherwise perfect market will fail to achieve social efficiency.

28 **The free-rider problem**. People are often unwilling to pay for things if they can make use of things other people have bought. This problem can lead to people not purchasing things which would be to the benefit of them and other members of society to have.

29 **The problem of time lags**. Many economic actions can take a long time to take effect. This can cause problems of instability and an inability of the economy to achieve social efficiency.

30 **Government intervention may be able to rectify various failings of the market**. Government intervention in the market can be used to achieve various economic objectives which may not be best achieved by the market. Governments, however, are not perfect, and their actions may bring adverse as well as beneficial consequences.

31 **The law of comparative advantage**. Provided opportunity costs of various goods differ in two countries, both of them can gain from mutual trade if they specialise in producing (and exporting) those goods that have relatively low opportunity costs compared with the other country.

32 **Economies suffer from inherent instability**. As a result, economic growth and other macroeconomic indicators tend to fluctuate.

33 **Living standards are limited by a country's ability to produce**. Potential national output depends on the country's resources, technology and productivity.

34 **The distinction between nominal and real figures**. Nominal figures are those using current prices, interest rates, etc. Real figures are figures corrected for inflation.

35 **Societies face trade-offs between economic objectives**. For example, the goal of faster growth may conflict with that of greater equality; the goal of lower unemployment may conflict with that of lower inflation (at least in the short run). This is an example of opportunity cost: the cost of achieving more of one objective may be achieving less of another. The existence of trade-offs means that policy makers must make choices.

36 **The principle of cumulative causation**. An initial event can cause an ultimate effect which is much larger.

37 **Goodhart's law**. Controlling a symptom (i.e. an indicator) of a problem will not cure the problem. Instead, the indicator will merely cease to be a good indicator of the problem.

Index

Page numbers in blue indicate definitions